EVOLUTIONARY HISTORY
OF THE PRIMATES

EVOLUTIONARY HISTORY OF THE PRIMATES

Frederick S. Szalay

Department of Anthropology
Hunter College
City University of New York
New York, New York

Eric Delson

Department of Anthropology
Lehman College
City University of New York
Bronx, New York

 1979

ACADEMIC PRESS
A Subsidiary of Harcourt Brace Jovanovich, Publishers
New York   London   Toronto   Sydney   San Francisco

ACADEMIC PRESS, INC.
111 Fifth Avenue, New York, New York 10003

United Kingdom Edition published by
ACADEMIC PRESS, INC. (LONDON) LTD.
24/28 Oval Road, London NW1 7DX

Library of Congress Cataloging in Publication Data

Szalay, Frederick S
   Evolutionary history of the primates.

   Bibliography: p.
   1. Primates––Evolution. 2. Primates, Fossil.
3. Mammals––Evolution. I. Delson, Eric, joint
author. II. Title.
QL737.P9S92   599'.8'0438   78–20051
ISBN 0–12–680150–9

CONTENTS AND SYNOPTIC CLASSIFICATION*

Modern genera and higher taxa listed here without a page reference are not treated individually in the text but are considered under their respective families.

PREFACE

We present in this volume a documentation and analysis of the fossil record and evolutionary history of the primates. It is our hope that this effort will in some way balance the generally available literature on primate evolution, which is predominantly concerned with living species.

The training and experience we bring to the making of this book are largely those of paleobiologists, students whose main concern has been the study of fossil samples to determine their taxonomic status, phylogenetic relationships, adaptations, and ways of life—in short, a desire to understand why the bones, teeth, and other features of animals are the way they are.

The vast majority of books on primates were written by students of living species who are either ethologists, anatomists, or anthropologists. As a result, we believe many works tend to be influenced by a view that members of past radiations are "side branches," "bizarre" relict forms related to the "real" living ones, or, even worse, taxa to be judged by their varying degrees of relevance to human evolution. Although understandable as outgrowths of the interest in the evolution of our own species, such anthropocentricity and neontological bias have resulted in studies of the Primates that are neither objective nor justifiable concerning the validity of results obtained. Often, the time, effort, and excellent knowhow that go into primate studies are merely chan-

neled into inquiries as to the relevance of the species studied to hominid evolution. Zoologists and paleontologists who study primates can offer a valuable service to anthropology (a science properly concerned with the evolution of humans) by attempting to understand the evolutionary history of individual primate species in their own right. From such studies anthropology may derive lasting benefits for the study of man.

The philosophy underlying the preparation of this work has been the desire to present as much information as possible in one volume on the fossils, on primary systematic hypotheses and their tests by known facts. Anecdotes on personalities, histories of erudite debates and opinions, and many other literary (but nonscientific) sidelights that usually fill volumes on fossil primates and fossil man have been omitted.

This book does not attempt to treat the background subjects necessary for a full appreciation of the text. Therefore, some acquaintance with evolutionary biology, methods of systematics, particularly methods of phylogenetic inference, as well as basic mammalian morphology may be necessary. To partially compensate for this approach we offer a glossary in which certain technical terms that may not be within the everyday usage of all scholars are defined.

We have thus designed this book not as a completely self-sufficient work but as a synthesis of available data somewhat less formal than research papers or systematic revisions. It will be of use to the many researchers, regardless of specialty, who need a source of data and interpretations about fossil primates, as well as qualified graduate students in paleontology, primatology, zoology, and anthropology.

An arbitrary taxonomic cut-off date of January 1, 1978 was observed, so that some newer taxa are unavoidably omitted, and few 1978 or 1979 papers are included. For the purposes of zoological nomenclature, the formal date of publication of this work is December 31, 1979.

Acknowledgments

We take this opportunity to thank the numerous colleagues and students who have helped in the production of this work by allowing us to study and photograph fossil or modern specimens in their care; by providing data, casts, or photographs for publication; by reading and commenting on this work; and by assisting in the actual compilation and preparation of the manuscript. In the latter categories, we especially thank the following people. Anita Cleary, Marjorie Delson, David Doneghy, Sandra Elston, Linda Goldstein, Spencer Gustav, Lenore Khan, Alies Muskin, Alfie Rosenberger, Lisa Shorr, and Miriam Siroky have offered invaluable technical assistance during the preparation of this volume. Dr. Alfred Rosenberger read and offered substantial comment on most of the manuscript, as well as sharing with us his insights into various relationships among anthropoid primates. Drs. Peter Andrews and Meave Leakey also provided helpful comments on specific portions of this work. We thank the American Museum of Natural History for many courtesies during our long association, not the least of which being permission to reproduce the following illustrations to which the Museum holds copyright: Figures 14A,B; 18A–C; 19A, B; 23A–D, H; 24C, D; 27A–C; 30; 31A, B, D; 37; 48; 49; 56; 59; 66A–C; 77E; 90D, E, J, K; 99–111; 113–129; 135; 147C; 160D, H; 250A–O, Q–X; 259H, J; and 260A–D. Lastly and mostly we thank and dedicate this work to our wives and children.

EVOLUTIONARY HISTORY
OF THE PRIMATES

INTRODUCTION

The purpose of this book is to place on record in one volume the fossil evidence for primate evolution, primarily to facilitate the understanding of the genealogy, adaptations, dispersal, and taxonomy of the order. Throughout this book we have tried to express the view that paleontology is essentially a biological discipline, that fossils are objects not only to be collected, named, and described, but to be studied for the information they can convey about the evolution and ways of life of these vanished species. Appreciation of a functional approach to the structure of fossils is fundamental to a synthetic view of evolution, which sees evolutionary change largely as a process of adaptation, a molding of behavior, structure, and mechanical function for various biological roles through the action of natural selection. According to this view, ecological divergence and competition between animal stocks lead to behavioral, mechanical, and structural divergences. To understand evolutionary change, therefore, rather than simply to record it, we must attempt to reconstruct as best we can the ecological and behavioral factors preceding, facilitating, and precipitating structural evolution. This process, in turn, depends very largely upon interpreting the functional significance of the physical adaptations (see especially Bock and von Wahlert, 1965; Bock, 1977) preserved by the fossil record of the groups concerned.

The various activities of paleontological research are closely interdependent, yet time and human limitations make its practice multiphased and time-consuming. The discovery and collection of fossils are preceded by planning, geological reconnaissance, and resolution of problems peculiar to the particular locality. Because modern quarrying methods generally involve patient work for crews of varying sizes at any one locality for several field seasons, a relatively complete description of any taxon must await the collection of an adequate sample. The study of the fossils usually focuses on several closely related objectives. The faunistic and biostratigraphic appraisals of all species at a locality or in a faunal level are amalgams of separate studies on the sundry species from many perspectives. In studies on fossils of any one group, probably the most important and certainly the most fundamental problem is the correct delineation of the species.

This alpha taxonomy, the cornerstone of all phylogenetic and adaptational considerations as well as of supraspecific taxonomy, must solve not only problems of geographical and temporal variation in related samples from localities of known stratigraphic relationships, but also problems of variation in the study sample itself. Following alpha taxonomy of fossil species, the ultimate goal of paleobiological studies clearly must concern itself with the explanation of the known attributes of species, employing phylogenetic and adaptational analyses.

It is becoming apparent, even to the most pure taxonomist and to the most conservative descriptive paleontologists, that at least a rudimentary understanding of the functional anatomy of a species has profound effects on the phylogenetic evaluations of its morphology. Mammal teeth have long been yielding phylogenetic dividends when questions are asked about the form and mechanical function of their isolated components, of the whole tooth, or of whole dentitions. A constant evaluation of heritage components, as well as of functional aspects in any biological feature, is necessary when concentrating on the taxonomy, phyletic affinities, or mechanical and behavioral functions of one or more species. While many taxonomic studies suffer from an almost complete neglect of function, equally marred undertakings that concentrate "purely" on functional attributes of biological features also often appear. Unless the geometry of phylogeny is understood in a time-sequential framework, functional studies by themselves are unlikely to yield answers to evolutionary questions. Without a careful and continuous search for and scrutiny of the living and fossil record and the phylogeny of the group, it is difficult to discern the precarious but most important distinction between "heritage" and "habitus" features of living or extinct species.

We may briefly point to the relationship between primarily paleontological studies and more specialized undertakings on fossil specimens. The most advanced available techniques and tools that yield reasonable dividends for time and effort invested should be utilized to study all feasible biological attributes of living and extinct species to elicit functional answers. Only then will it be possible to evaluate fossil taxa to the fullest extent both phylogenetically and adaptationally in the context of their respective faunas. However, these detailed evolutionary or functional analyses of individual remains are based eventually (not only) on the presumably correct allocation of fossils to a particular taxon by the practicing paleontologist. Before cranial, dental, or postcranial elements can be allocated to the Primates, or to a particular subgroup, a great deal of primarily paleontological expertise is employed, with most variables difficult to quantify. Moreover, such studies are often based on phylogenies determined by prior investigations.

There are today a number of conflicting or only partially compatible methods of constructing hypotheses of evolutionary relationships for primates or any other group of organisms (Simpson, 1975); we ourselves are not always in full agreement (Szalay, 1977b; Delson, 1977b). A grasp of both the methodology of and the reasons for the construction of phylogenies and hypotheses of divergence is thus of prime importance for understanding any problem relating to primate biology, especially the ideas we present here. The bases of phylogenetic hypotheses are character analyses, and we may note that in this area of systematics the following levels of observation and decision, and identifiable areas of disagreement, exist (Szalay, 1977b): (1) the existence of a homology; (2) the polarity of a number of homologous states; (3) the weighting of similarities which suggest contrasting hypotheses of relationships (i.e., sorting out relative recency of shared and derived characters).

With these areas of potential disagreement in mind, the following is an attempted summary of the operations involved in character analysis and in choosing one of several competing phylogenetic schemes (Szalay, 1977b):

1. Observations are made (as an indirect result of a host of unexpressed assumptions and hypotheses), and a particular set of circumstances (a character state) is stated to be present in two or more taxa. In other words, characters are recognized and delineated. We can refer to this as data gathering.

2. If these similarities, as originally perceived, can also be recognized by others (i.e.. if they are repeatable), then it may be said that we have an empirical data base.

3. The hypothesis may now be advanced that either the similarity is the result of homology, and, more specifically, that it is the sharing of an ancient (primitive, ancestral) or less ancient (advanced, derived) character, or, if not a homology, that it is convergence. One of these hypotheses is arrived at when alternative character states are compared by an examination of both ontogenetic and adult states, as well as by mechanical analysis of the character. This pivotal phase of analysis requires the use of the biologically most sophisticated methods, techniques, and interpretive schemes. Decisions on this level profoundly affect what is commonly called "testing" of phylogenetic hypotheses.

The determination of polarity along a morphocline and, especially, the role that geochronologic age of relevant fossil taxa plays in this process are among the more hotly debated questions in modern systematics, and our own published views here differ. For obvious reasons (see Simpson, 1975), character states of a given feature are less variable at the onset of its evolutionary transformation, the ancestral condition being dominant. As time passes and adaptation proceeds, character states become progressively more variable and diversified. But can a given state be considered ancestral a priori, on the basis of its relatively great age within a group, or should age be ignored in favor of distribution patterns and outgroup comparisons? In the former view, a working hypothesis (to be rigorously screened by morphological criteria) is based on biostratigraphic evidence in order to serve as an important starting point for the establishment of polarity. On the other hand, it has been argued that, if age is held aside at this point in the analysis, there is less chance of circularity of reasoning; polarity is determined, if possible, without recourse to temporal data, which may be brought into use only when it is not otherwise possible to choose between two potential ancestral conditions. In most cases, of course, the two methods are equivalent, as morphoclines often coincide with chronoclines, but it will be seen from the text that we approach the problems involved in slightly different ways.

4. "Testing" of polarities should proceed beyond character analysis when possible, by comparing the hypothesized polarities of character clines to one another, a method referred to by Hennig (1966) as "reciprocal illumination."

5. With the known or suspected polarities of as many character clines as possible, using shared derived characters, and by weighting the phylogenetic importance of biologically different kinds of shared derived characters, a phylogenetic hypothesis is constructed (using both "sister group" and "ancestor–descendant" concepts, depending on the nature of the evidence). Into this hypothesis one attempts to place the investigated homologies in a relative time framework. When possible, attempts should be made to arrange a phylogenetic hypothesis in a time framework, using all of the available lithostratigraphic and biostratigraphic evidence. It is desirable that this phylogenetic hypothesis should postulate the least number of possible derivations for unique and functionally highly integrated features. That theory of relationships which accounts most

parsimoniously for all of the postulated polarities of the known and weighted characters is to be preferred. Should this call for parsimony not be heeded, then nothing prevents one from postulating *any* phylogenetic hypothesis, whatsoever.

When one considers all of these factors in hypothesis formulation, then one conforms most closely to the notion (Popper, 1965) of striving for hypotheses with high information content and easy testability. Contrary to some statements on the alleged untestability of ancestor–descendant hypotheses and the alleged irrelevance of functional studies, consideration of the temporal data inherent in the fossil record, along with the assessment of the biological roles of characters whose distribution is analyzed, may assure the greatest possible information content for phyletic hypotheses. Once again, our approaches to the discerning of actual ancestor–descendant relationships among known species differ somewhat, involving varying emphases on either a probabilistic analysis of multiple criteria or a parsimony-based view which also takes into account stratigraphic successions (compare Delson, 1977b, and Szalay, 1977a). Whatever the specifics, the inclusion of all possible data in a phyletic hypothesis or a scenario will certainly result in the most desirable statement about the relationships and adaptations of the taxa involved.

Classifications must obviously reflect the underlying phylogeny, but the details of this reflection again are the subject of much debate. We basically agree that related taxa should be classified together, and that taxa should be monophyletic or, when possible, holophyletic (see Glossary) and definable by a set of derived characters in common. But we both also recognize the value of patristic affinities and distinctions based on divergence. In general, such deviations from a "purely" genealogical classificatory practice will be clear from the attendant discussions.

It is our intention to employ the preceding methodology throughout the main text of this book, a systematically organized account of each primate taxon known in the fossil record. This introduction has so far laid the philosophical groundwork underlying our approach, and the following section will present the chronological framework within which all fossils can be placed.

The systematic treatment follows a standardized pattern which can be outlined here. The basic unit of discussion is the genus, long recognized as having more practical significance in paleontology than do species. For each genus and higher taxon, a complete synonymy is given, followed by the time and space distribution of each taxon and the major subtaxa included therein. The discussion then includes the diagnostic features of the group or genus, its distinctions from close relatives, phyletic position within the next higher taxon, underlying adaptations and evolutionary pattern, and major morphological distinctions within the taxon itself.

The synonymy lists each different taxonomic name (*nomen*) by which previous authors referred to the taxon involved or a major component thereof. A name in the format "*nomen* author, date" implies that the stated author coined the name and used it to refer to one or more specimens or taxa now included in the taxon under consideration, which may be termed the senior synonym. On the other hand, an entry in the format "*nomen* author, date: author, date" implies that the nomen was coined by the first author but that the second author employed that name to refer to all or part of the taxon under discussion. In some instances, the name of the first author is left out, especially if it is cited elsewhere in the same section (genus or higher taxon); the format is then "*nomen*: author, date." The term "in part" following an author implies that his concept included all or part of the taxon under consideration, as well as other taxa. The term "*nec*" in the format "*nomen* author, date, *nec* author, date" means that the first author coined a supposedly new name which in fact had previously been coined by the second author; the former name, which referred to all or part of the taxon under consideration, is a junior homonym and has no taxonomic value. A *nomen nudum* is a name that has no status in taxonomy, because it does not satisfy the criteria for availability of the International Code of Zoological Nomenclature (Stoll *et al.*, 1961), the rulebook of animal systematics. Such names, if for a genus or species, are not italicized here but may be placed in quotation marks to set them apart from available names. Quotation marks may also be used to indicate that a genus or species is not really the same as the taxon whose name is being used, but that the different form has not been formally named; an example is the Miocene cercopithecid "*Victoriapithecus*" *leakeyi*, which is probably not a species of the same genus as *Victoriapithecus macinnesi*, but *leakeyi* was originally named in the genus *Victoriapithecus* and has not yet been given a distinct generic

name. Uncertainty of reference at the genus or species level may be indicated by the use of such symbols as "?," "cf.," or "aff." The meaning of these symbols varies among authors, but, in general, a "?" placed directly in front (or behind) a generic name implies uncertainty as to whether the species involved belongs to that genus, while a queried species implies uncertain reference of specific specimens to that species. The Latin abbreviations cf. (for "*confer*," or compare) and aff. (for "*affinis*," or related) usually indicate greater or less doubts as to the correct placement of a sample of specimens in a given species. Each different name is set off in our synonymies by a period (.). A semicolon (;) is used to set off multiple usages of the same nomen and/or misspellings or lapses (lapsus). Not all usages of the same nomen are included, only those (for some genera) which referred to newly described fossil material. In the synonymies and in our choice of senior synonyms, we have been guided by the rules and recommendations of the Code; further discussion of these points may be found in a text such as Mayr (1969).

Following the synonymy is given the distribution of the taxon under discussion. The time range is listed first, by epoch or subepoch, followed by a mammal-age term when possible. Geographic range is presented by continent and region or country. For higher taxa, the next line lists included taxa of the next lowest rank employed in our classification (e.g., tribes in a subfamily or genera in a tribe). For genera, this line is only employed if subgenera are recognized, in which case the synonymy of the genus as a whole may be left out. The species known for that genus are then listed, in order of taxonomic priority after the type species; if there is more than one in the genus, they are numbered. For each species, a list of fossil localities is presented, in stratigraphic order from oldest to youngest. Each locality name is followed by a number in parentheses, which corresponds to its position in the locality list given later in this introduction. The type locality is indicated by a star (★) following its name. If the specimens from a given locality are only questionably referred to the species, then the name may be preceded by "?," (cf), or (aff.), corresponding to the synonymy entry.

The discussion sections for the genera and higher taxa obviously form the bulk of this work, representing our synthesis of all available information on the morphology, relationships, and adaptations of primate groups. The illustrations have been chosen or specially prepared to clarify the points discussed or to document our interpretations, as well as to indicate the type of fossil material available for each taxon. In describing each taxon and delineating it from relatives or other similar taxa, the characters of taxa of higher rank are generally not repeated, but are assumed, only the special features within those taxa being stressed. Thus, genus A in family B is described or compared to family C, the characters of B found in A are not discussed, but emphasis is placed on distinguishing features of A itself. Similarly, when several genera within a family, for example, are contrasted to the type genus, that type genus is not again compared to the remaining genera, but the reader is referred to the original comparison. We have tried to stress the paleobiology, or lifestyle, of the fossil forms as well as their more formal phyletic relationships, to the extent that we may be criticized for drawing too detailed conclusions from scanty remains. However, these interpretations of past dietary and locomotor adaptations offer much insight into the diversity of the varied primate radiations, and we feel that even hesitantly suggesting paleobiological roles for unique morphologies is better than treating them as inanimate objects of purely genealogical or taxonomic interest.

In a study of primate evolutionary history, it is clear that we must concentrate on fossil taxa, but their interpretation is not possible without a firm grasp of the life of extant relatives and other relevant living species. We have not tried to revise any modern genera or higher taxa with minimal fossil records, but such taxa are included in discussions and given abbreviated synonymies as a baseline for understanding our concepts of generic and higher taxon variation. Modern genera with large fossil records (e.g., some lemurids and cercopithecids) are treated in the same detail as purely extinct genera with roughly equal numbers of included species and fossil remains.

No matter how the data are utilized, a relatively firm geochronologic framework is certainly an asset to if not a prerequisite for any paleontological study. From the extensive literature on Cenozoic stratigraphy and correlations, and from our own studies and those of colleagues not yet published, we have abstracted a set of correlation charts in which all localities yielding fossil primates have been placed. Figure 1 is an overall correlation for the entire Cenozoic, on which we have aligned epochs and subepochs, "standard" European

chronostratigraphic stages, and the sequences of continent-wide mammal ages delineated for Europe, North America, and South America. A set of African land-mammal ages is given here which will be formally proposed elsewhere—each age is typified by its eponymous locality. These several sets of relative age terms are in turn placed in a chronometric framework indicated in millions of years. For the Neogene, an additional column indicates our correlation of the sequence of mammalian faunal units proposed by Mein (1975) and the sequence of northern European climatostratigraphic terms relevant to the alternating warm and cold phases of the Pleistocene.

Figures 2–5 present the approximate chronologic relationships of primate-bearing fossil localities from the Cretaceous and Paleogene, Miocene, Plio-Pleistocene (to 0.5 MY), and later Pleistocene, respectively. Tables I and II list the approximately 700 localities involved in chronological and alphabetical order, with an indication of continent and type of site: quarry, cave, or open-air surface locality. In long sequences with recognized subdivisions such as the Omo Shungura Formation or Olduvai Gorge, members or other subunits are listed separately. In Figures 2–4, age is given in millions of years before present (MYBP), oldest at the bottom, while in Figure 5, thousands of years are used (TYBP). On each chart, the spacing between lines is constant. The order of localities on a single line is generally not meaningful, as all are of comparable age, unless one number is clearly out of order, to signify its relative antiquity among its neighbors. In fact, any locality might conceivably move either up or down one line at least. Those localities placed between "⟨⟩" are even less securely dated; a group of localities within a single set of brackets is considered to be of the same age, although the precise position is uncertain. There are a few localities from which primates have been reported but not confirmed; these are placed within parentheses in the charts. When it is not possible, for reasons of space, to include all of the locality numbers on the line, the oldest and youngest are separated by hyphens, implying that all numbers between the extremes are to be included there. In several final cases, a "locality" may consist of a sequence of rock layers that have not been subdivided but that clearly span more than one or two lines on the relevant chart. Vertical lines are used to indicate the range, with the endpoints being delimited either by the locality

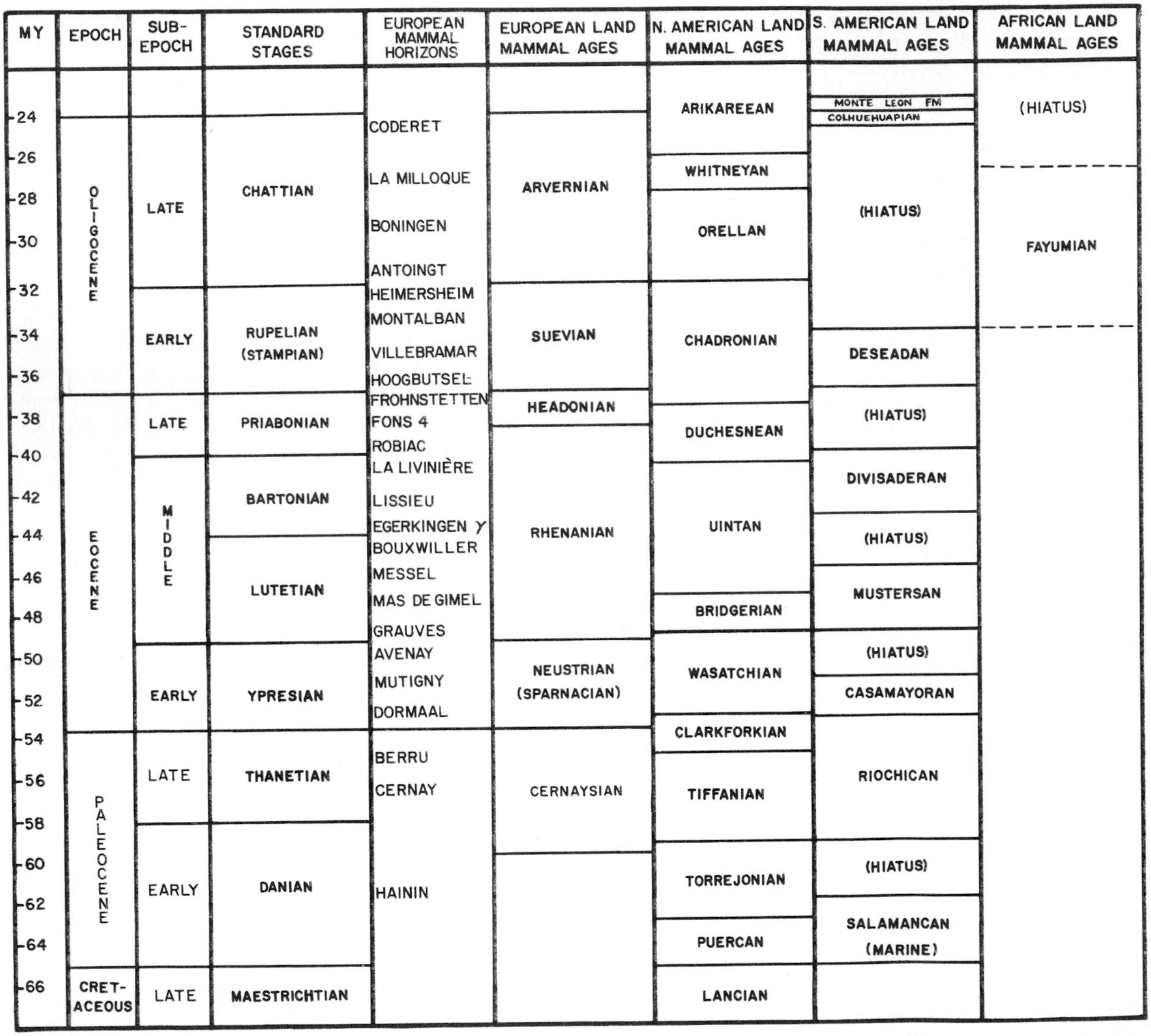

MY	EPOCH	SUB-EPOCH	STANDARD STAGES	EUROPEAN MAMMAL HORIZONS	EUROPEAN LAND MAMMAL AGES	N. AMERICAN LAND MAMMAL AGES	S. AMERICAN LAND MAMMAL AGES	AFRICAN LAND MAMMAL AGES
-24				CODERET		ARIKAREEAN	MONTE LEON FM / COLHUEHUAPIAN	(HIATUS)
-26	OLIGOCENE	LATE	CHATTIAN	LA MILLOQUE	ARVERNIAN	WHITNEYAN		
-28								
-30				BONINGEN		ORELLAN	(HIATUS)	FAYUMIAN
-32				ANTOINGT				
-34		EARLY	RUPELIAN (STAMPIAN)	HEIMERSHEIM MONTALBAN	SUEVIAN	CHADRONIAN		
-36				VILLEBRAMAR HOOGBUTSEL			DESEADAN	
-38	EOCENE	LATE	PRIABONIAN	FROHNSTETTEN FONS 4	HEADONIAN	DUCHESNEAN	(HIATUS)	
-40				ROBIAC				
-42		MIDDLE	BARTONIAN	LA LIVINIÈRE LISSIEU		UINTAN	DIVISADERAN	
-44				EGERKINGEN γ BOUXWILLER	RHENANIAN		(HIATUS)	
-46			LUTETIAN	MESSEL			MUSTERSAN	
-48				MAS DE GIMEL GRAUVES		BRIDGERIAN		
-50		EARLY	YPRESIAN	AVENAY MUTIGNY	NEUSTRIAN (SPARNACIAN)	WASATCHIAN	(HIATUS)	
-52				DORMAAL			CASAMAYORAN	
-54						CLARKFORKIAN		
-56	PALEOCENE	LATE	THANETIAN	BERRU CERNAY	CERNAYSIAN	TIFFANIAN	RIOCHICAN	
-58								
-60		EARLY	DANIAN	HAININ		TORREJONIAN	(HIATUS)	
-62								
-64						PUERCAN	SALAMANCAN (MARINE)	
-66	CRETACEOUS	LATE	MAESTRICHTIAN			LANCIAN		

Figure 1. Correlation chart of the Paleogene and Neogene epochs, subepochs, mammal ages, and Pleistocene climatic phases, with geochronology expressed in millions of years (MY). Note the changes in scale at 2 and 1 million years, respectively. (Continued on facing page.) [By A. Cleary.]

number or by horizontal lines, with the locality number at the midpoint. Special notes to each chart are given in the figure captions.

Finally, as is well known, most mammalian fossils consist of teeth, either isolated or in jaws, and most species level taxonomy is practiced on the basis of dental morphology. In order to provide a standard of terminology used in this volume, we present in Figure 6 four labeled pairs of molars (upper and lower) of four selected primates. The additional terms utilized for cercopithecids are given in Figure 159. Because most judgments about the taxonomic status and dietary

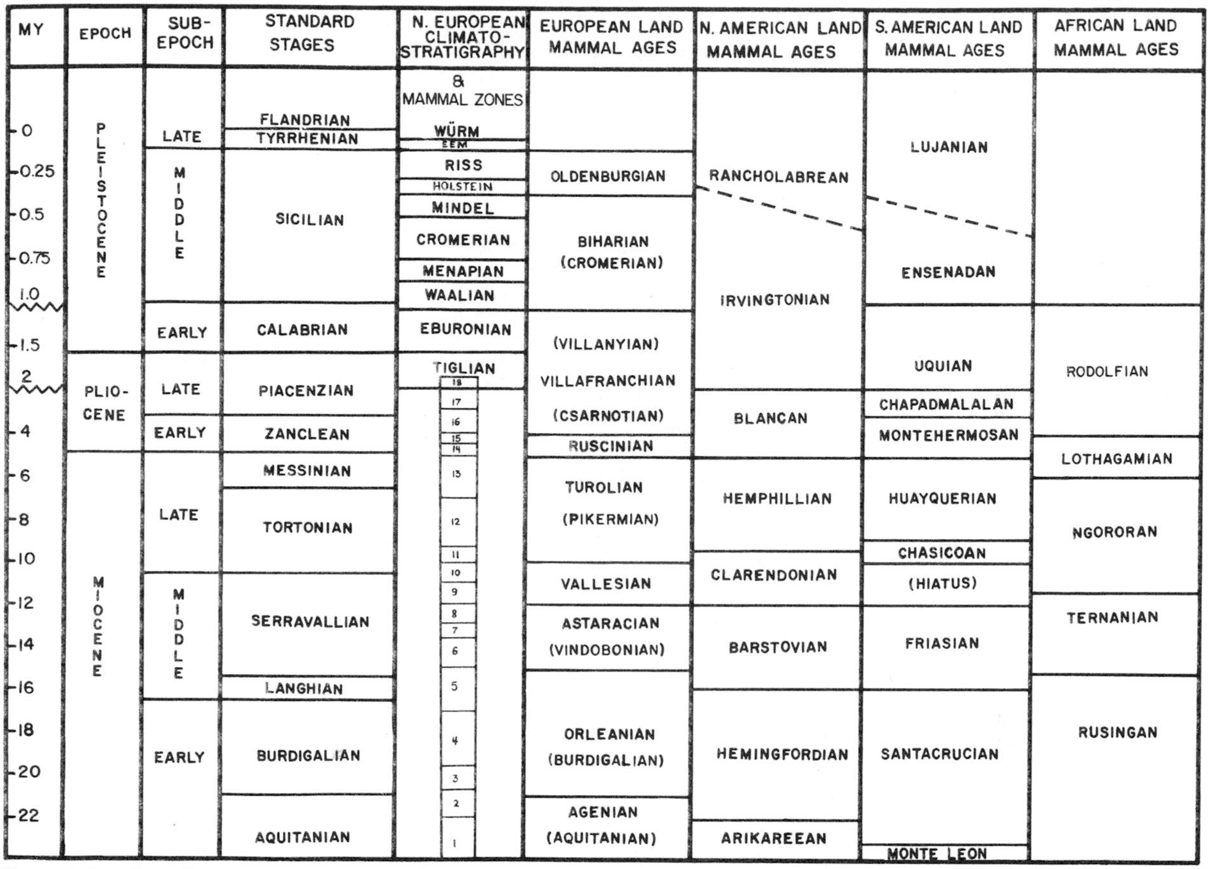

MY	EPOCH	SUB-EPOCH	STANDARD STAGES	N. EUROPEAN CLIMATO-STRATIGRAPHY & MAMMAL ZONES	EUROPEAN LAND MAMMAL AGES	N. AMERICAN LAND MAMMAL AGES	S. AMERICAN LAND MAMMAL AGES	AFRICAN LAND MAMMAL AGES
0	PLEISTOCENE	LATE	FLANDRIAN TYRRHENIAN	WÜRM EEM		RANCHOLABREAN	LUJANIAN	
0.25		MIDDLE	SICILIAN	RISS HOLSTEIN	OLDENBURGIAN			
0.5				MINDEL	BIHARIAN (CROMERIAN)		ENSENADAN	
0.75				CROMERIAN				
				MENAPIAN		IRVINGTONIAN		
1.0				WAALIAN				
1.5		EARLY	CALABRIAN	EBURONIAN	(VILLANYIAN)			
2	PLIOCENE	LATE	PIACENZIAN	TIGLIAN 18	VILLAFRANCHIAN		UQUIAN	RODOLFIAN
				17	(CSARNOTIAN)	BLANCAN	CHAPADMALALAN	
4		EARLY	ZANCLEAN	16 15 14	RUSCINIAN		MONTEHERMOSAN	
6			MESSINIAN	13	TUROLIAN	HEMPHILLIAN	HUAYQUERIAN	LOTHAGAMIAN
8	MIOCENE	LATE	TORTONIAN	12	(PIKERMIAN)			NGORORAN
10				11 10 9	VALLESIAN	CLARENDONIAN	CHASICOAN (HIATUS)	
12		MIDDLE	SERRAVALLIAN	8 7	ASTARACIAN (VINDOBONIAN)			TERNANIAN
14				6		BARSTOVIAN	FRIASIAN	
16			LANGHIAN	5				
18		EARLY	BURDIGALIAN	4	ORLEANIAN (BURDIGALIAN)	HEMINGFORDIAN	SANTACRUCIAN	RUSINGAN
20				3				
22			AQUITANIAN	2 1	AGENIAN (AQUITANIAN)	ARIKAREEAN	MONTE LEON	

Figure 1 (continued).

(and often social) behavior of fossils are based on teeth, we will review, in a nutshell, some of the more important functional and developmental notions related to cheek teeth.

An important element in the study of teeth is the movement of the mandible and lower dentition across the upper one. A consequence of these movements is the wear of teeth due to contact with food and opposing teeth. Studies by Gregory (1922), Simpson (1936), Hiiemäe and Crompton (1971), Kallen and Gans (1972), Kay and Hiiemäe (1974), Seligsohn (1977), and many others have laid a firm foundation for the analysis of wear, movement, and, subsequently, meaning of the genotypically constrained dental form for systematic studies. The summary below does not strictly apply to any one species but represents generalizations applying to most mammals.

Hiiemäe and Kay (1973) postulated a so-called "puncture-crushing" activity prior to mastication (chewing) during which the food is softened. Dental wear, described as "abrasive," is characterized by the absence of clear striation, blunting of cusps and crests, and frequent fenestration on the crowns, and is likely to result from puncture-crushing. "Attritional" or thegotic wear resulting in a flat and shiny surface with striations, on the other hand, usually occurs during the masticatory stroke. During mastication, when teeth come into occlusal contact, the stages may be subdivided into (a) the buccal phase, when the lower teeth make extreme lateral contact with the upper ones; (b) a centric occlusion at the end of the buccal phase; and (c) the lingual phase, with movement in the mesiolingual (i.e., anteromedial) direction. The attritional facets resulting from tooth on tooth contact

```
          CRETACEOUS  THROUGH  OLIGOCENE  FOSSIL  PRIMATE  LOCALITIES
AGE                                                               AGE
MYBP    AMERICAS                   EURASIA  AND  AFRICA           MYBP

24                                                                24
       384    380   382
26                                                                26

28                                                                28

30                                                                30
                              378
32                            376                                 32
       370    372             374
34                            363   364   366   368               34
                              354--362
36     340    342   344     ?294? 345   348   350   352           36
       330                    |   332   334
38                            |   314--328                        38
                              |   312
40                            |   306   308   309   310           40
       296    298   302  304  |
42                          ?294?                                 42
       292
44                                                                44

46     282                                                        46
       275    276
48     260--274                                                   48
                            250   252   253   254   256   258
50     238--248                                                   50
                            234   236   237
                            223   224   226   228   230   232
52                                                                52
       208  210  212  214  216  218   220   222
54     194  196  198  200       202   204   206                   54
       154--182                 184--192
56     124--152                                                   56
        97--122                  92    94    96
58      62---82                  86    88    90                   58
        38---60                  42
60      36                                                        60
        20---34
62      18                                                        62
        16
64      12    14                                                  64
         8    10
66                                                                66
```

Figure 2. Approximate chronologic relationships of Paleogene primate fossil localities, numbered as in Tables I and II. See text for additional notes. MYBP, million years before present.

have striations produced by enamel as well as trapped food particles, resulting in mirrorlike flat striking surfaces. As Every (1972) suggested, attritional facets might also be the result of powerful tooth on tooth movements when an organism does not eat but rather sharpens the crests and cusps of its teeth. Movement during the buccal phase, after contact of the teeth, is usually vertical from above downward, but if a well-developed lingual phase exists, as in primates and several other orders, then the mandible returning past

centric occlusion moves largely horizontally. As a broad generalization, insectivorous and carnivorous forms (with a tribosphenic and trituburcular dentition, but not in other modifications) have better developed buccal phase facets, emphasizing vertical shearing, compared to more herbivorous species, which will equally or primarily emphasize either the buccal or lingual phase facets, which may show horizontal (i.e., more transverse) rather than vertical cutting.

The angle of the matching wear facets produced on

MIOCENE FOSSIL PRIMATE LOCALITIES

AGE MYBP	EUROPE	ASIA	AFRICA	AMERICAS	AGE MYBP
5					**5**
	612 614		616		
6	608		610		**6**
	604		606		
7	600 602		598		**7**
	594	596			
8		590 592			**8**
	<580 582 584 586>	<588>			
9		<574> 576	<578>		**9**
	556 558 560 562 564 566 568 <570>	571 <572><573>			
10	(544) 546 548 550 <552>	554			**10**
	534 536 538	540	542		
11	<518 520 522 524><526> 528	530 <532>			**11**
	506 508 510 512	514	516		
12	(498) 500 (502)	504			**12**
	486 488 490	492 494 496			
13	470 472 474 476 478	480 482 484			**13**
	466 468				
14	458 460		462	<464>	**14**
	444 446 448 450 452	454 456			
15	438 442		440		**15**
	432	434 <436>			
16	428 430				**16**
	418 420 <422 423 424 425 426>		<412--416>		
17			410		**17**
		<407>	<408>		
18			404 406		**18**
			402		
19			398 400		**19**
			396		
20			394		**20**
21					**21**
22			390 392		**22**
23			388		**23**
24					**24**

Figure 3. Approximate chronologic relationships of Miocene primate fossil localities, numbered as in Tables I and II. See text for additional notes. MYBP, million years before present.

the lower and upper cheek teeth during the buccal phase (facing lingually on the upper and buccally on the lower teeth) and lingual phase (facing buccally on the upper and lingually on the lower teeth) can be measured compared to the base of the tooth. These parameters may serve as some indication of the relative importance of the mechanics of the two phases, and they predict dietary regimes (within certain limits) influenced by proportions of various parts of the dentition, the group to which the species belongs, etc.

In addition to the study of detailed mechanisms of a single species, the study of differences between species is one of the most potent generating forces of new ideas and insights. The 1960s and 1970s have been a time of uniquely sophisticated eco-ethological field studies for primates. What has come to light is a general picture that each studied species of primate has a habitual although often season-specific dietary regime which, when averaged out yearly, is a highly specific and characteristic aspect of a population, or an entire species.

Bock and von Wahlert (1965), in their powerful

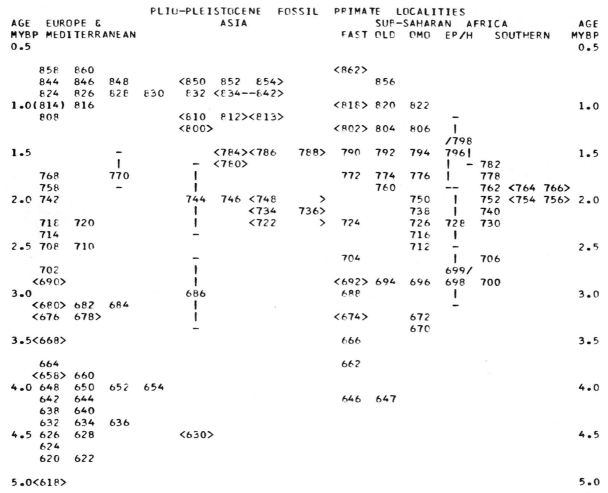

Figure 4. Approximate chronologic relationships of Pliocene and earlier Pleistocene (to 0.5 MY) primate fossil localities, numbered as in Tables I and II. Note that the group of localities 722, 734, 736, and 748 are bracketed together, fitting in one or more of the three lines indicated. Under sub-Saharan Africa, localities are ordered by column: EAST, eastern sites (some of which may overlap into other columns); OLD, Olduvai Gorge (mostly); OMO, Omo Shungura Fm.; ER/H, East Rudolf (East Turkana) and Hadar beds (note 698 and 699 are the same age); and several columns for southern sites. See text for additional notes. MYBP, million years before present.

reassessment of the meaning of evolutionary adaptation, stated the following.

Each utilized faculty (form–function complex) of a feature is controlled by a different set of selection forces and, hence, each would have a separate evolution so far as possible. Hence, it is obvious that the feature cannot be perfectly adapted to all the selection forces acting upon it, but must be a compromise between all of these selection forces. In the case of the feature having only one form, then that particular form would be a compromise so that each of its faculties satisfies as best as possible the demands of the selection force (or forces) acting upon it. A feature with one or a few utilized functions would be better adapted to each selection force as fewer faculties enter the compromise. Features that are important "functionally" would be generally less well adapted to each selection force as more faculties are involved in the compromise, and more likely at least some of these faculties and the corresponding selection forces would conflict with one another. (pp. 276–277)

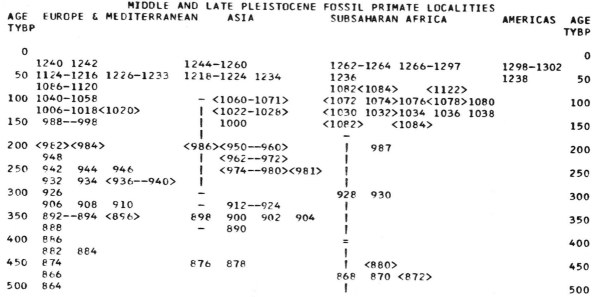

Figure 5. Approximate chronologic relationships of later Pleistocene (post 0.5 MY) primate fossil localities, numbered as in Tables I and II. Dates are thousand years before present (TYBP), rather than millions of years. Madagascar is included in sub-Saharan Africa. See text for additional notes.

Teeth of living primates studied in some detail (Seligsohn and Szalay, 1974; Rosenberger and Kinzey, 1976; Kay, 1977b; Seligsohn and Szalay, 1978; Seligsohn, 1977) appear to conform rather nicely to the above-mentioned generalizations.

It is most likely that species have specific dietetic strategies and use a basically similar masticatory cycle, employed by primates and most therians. It is now possible, in particular lineages, to view aspects of whole dentitions, but more particularly crown patterns of teeth, as specifically maximizing certain mechanical actions which in some cases may affect the relative efficiency of puncture-crushing and chewing (either buccal or lingual phases). Most evolutionary changes of teeth are the result of selective forces derived from a specific dietary regime. Thus, the recognition of the *derived* morphological–functional aspect of a dentition can be attributed to specific functional changes, and consequently the deciphering of "fossil diets" is placed on a more precise foundation, basically rooted in the recognition of convergent analogous mechanical solutions. The greatest difficulties will still rest in the explanation of the biological roles to which otherwise functionally well understood dentitions were adapted.

Selection forces, responsible for different dental morphologies from species to species, may act primarily to emphasize one or several of a spectrum of possible mechanical actions, as well as the directions in which these actions can most efficiently be performed. Thus, hypocones, for example, usually of recognizably different constructions, can evolve to perform one of a variety of functions (i.e., puncturing, crushing, cutting) with their greatest effectiveness in more derived cases limited to specific portions of the masticatory cycle. Furthermore, the mere presence of "similar" dental morphology in different species does not necessarily imply similarity in either mechanical emphasis or biological role. The pointed hypocone of the metatherian *Cercartetus*, for example, modified and used differently from that of another phalangerid, and that of the small indriid *Avahi* hold neither mechanical function nor biological role for specific diet in common (Seligsohn and Szalay, 1977).

A vast and difficult to learn spectrum of specializations exists among primates and other mammals as far as diet is concerned. It is important to remember that, although researchers are constantly tempted to draw much-needed generalizations for urgently sought-after deductive theories for the meaning of form, the

TABLE I
Fossil Primate Localities of the Late Cretaceous and Cenozoic in Approximate Chronological Sequence[a]

8	Harbicht Hill loc. (N)	120	Paskapoo locs. (N)	221	Les Salères loc. (E)
10	Bug Creek loc. (N)	122	Joe's Bone Bed loc. (Black Peaks) (N)	222	Castigaleu loc. (E)
12	Purgatory Hill loc. (N)			223	Les Badies loc. (E)
14	Garbani loc. (N)	124	Little Sand Coulee locs. (N)	224	Grauves loc. (E)
16	Wagon Road loc. (N)	126	Paint Creek loc. (N)	226	Herne Bay loc. (E)
18	Dragon loc. (N)	128	Buckman Hollow loc. (N)	228	Cuis loc. (E)
20	Silberling Q. (N)	130	Togwotee Main loc. (N)	230	Charot loc. (E)
22	Torrejon locs. (N)	132	Red Creek loc., Togwotee (N)	232	Epernay loc. (E)
24	Gidley Q. (N)	134	Susan loc., Togwotee (N)	234	Mancy loc. (E)
26	Rock Bench Q. (N)	136	Togwotee loc. 7 (N)	236	Monthelon loc. (E)
28	Swain Q. (N)	138	Togwotee loc. 18 (N)	237	Geiseltal locs. (E)
30	Circle loc. (N)	140	Verland's loc., Togwotee (N)	238	La Barge loc. (N)
31	Tongue River loc. (N)	142	Upper Sand Draw locs. (N)	240	Lost Cabin locs. (N)
32	Olive loc. (N)	144	Togwotee Lower Variegated locs. (N)	242	Cathedral Bluffs Tongue loc. (N)
34	Ekalaka loc. (N)				
36	Douglass Q. (N)	146	Plateau Valley locs. (N)	244	New Fork loc. (N)
38	Keefer Hill loc. (N)	148	Bear Creek loc. (N)	246	Huerfano VI loc. (N)
40	Scarritt loc. (N)	150	Chappo-12 loc. (N)	248	AM Q. 88, San José (N)
42	Walbeck loc. (N)	152	Clark Fork locs. (N)	249	San José beds (N)
44	Saddle loc. (N)	154	Twisty Turn Hollow loc. (N)	250	Egerkingen γ loc. (E)
46	Little Muddy Creek loc. (N)	156	Bitter Creek locs. (N)	252	Messel loc. (E)
48	Highway Blowout loc. (N)	158	Red Desert loc. (N)	253	Capella loc. (E)
50	Melville-13 loc. (N)	160	W. of Elk Mt. loc. (N)	254	Bouxwiller loc. (E)
52	Ledge loc. (N)	162	Gray Bull loc. (N)	256	Egerkingen Huppersand loc. (E)
54	Cedar Pt. loc. (N)	164	Supersite Q. (N)		
56	Battle Mt. loc. (N)	166	Dobie Butte loc. (N)	258	Lissieu loc. (E)
58	Chappo-17 loc. (N)	168	Slick Creek loc. (N)	260	Huerfano I, II, III, V locs. (N)
60	Erikson's Landing loc. (N)	170	Banjo Pocket loc. (N)	264	Powder Wash loc. (N)
62	Love Q. (N)	172	Wadi Kraus Q. (N)	265	Friars locs. (N)
64	Saddle Annex loc. (N)	174	Bone Hill loc. (N)	266	Lower Bridger locs., Black's Fork, etc. (N)
66	Twin Creek loc. (N)	176	Stonehenge Sandstone Q. (N)		
68	West End loc. (N)	178	Four Mile East Alheit Pocket loc. (N)	268	Hawk loc. (N)
70	Ray's Bone Bed loc., Black Peaks (N)			270	Fault loc. (N)
		180	Four Mile localities other than East Alheit (N)	272	Tree Road loc. (N)
72	Mason Pocket loc. (N)			274	Morrow Creek loc. (N)
74	Croc Tooth Q. (N)	182	Golden Valley locs. (N)	275	Mission Valley locs. (N)
76	Airport loc. (N)	184	Meudon loc. (E)	276	Evacuation Creek loc. (N)
78	Divide loc. (N)	185	Reims loc. (E)	278	Egerkingen α & β locs. (E)
80	Long Draw loc. (N)	186	Dormaal loc. (E)	282	Upper Bridger locs., Twin Buttes, etc. (N)
82	Malcolm's loc., Badwater area (N)	188	Pourcy loc. (E)		
		190	Mutigny loc. (E)	292	Santiago locs. (N)
86	Menat loc. (E)	191	Marne loc. (E)	294	Phosphorites of Quercy, classical locs. (E)
88	Cernay loc. (E)	192	Bumbin Nuru loc., Naran Bulak (As)		
90	Lentille loc. (E)			296	Badwater Creek locs. 5, 5a, 6 (N)
92	Berru loc. (E)	194	Milleson Draw loc. (N)		
96	Rilly loc. (E)	196	Powder River locs. (N)	298	CIT loc. 249, "Poway" (N)
97	Lower Sand Draw loc. (N)	198	Sand Coulee beds (N)	302	CIT loc. 180, Tapo Ranch, "Poway" (N)
98	Silver Coulee beds (N)	200	Almagre locs., San José (N)		
100	Princeton Q. (N)	202	Kyson loc. (E)	304	Kennedy's Hole loc., Uinta B (N)
102	Fritz Q. (N)	204	Abbey Wood loc. (E)		
104	Schaff Q. (N)	206	Avenay loc. (E)	306	Robiac loc. (E)
106	Ravenscrag UAR-1 loc. (N)	208	Lysite locs. (N)	308	Le Bretou loc. (E)
108	Titanoides loc. (N)	210	Tipton Butte loc. (N)	309	Eclépens loc. (E)
110	Middle Sand Draw loc. (N)	212	Knight Station loc. (N)	310	Grisolles loc. (E)
112	Fossil Hollow loc. (N)	214	Fossil Butte loc. (N)	312	Mormont loc. (E)
114	Bayfield loc. (N)	216	Dad loc. (N)	314	Fons 1, 2, 3, 5, 6 locs. (E)
116	Chappo-1 loc. (N)	218	Picanton loc. (E)	316	La Vergne loc. (E)
118	Dell Creek loc. (N)	220	Condé-en-Brie loc. (E)	318	Fons 4 loc. (E)

[a] Abbreviations: Af, Africa; As, Asia; E, Europe; M, Madagascar; N, North America; S, South America and Caribbean. Loc., locality; Q, quarry.

TABLE I (continued)

320	Hordle Cliff loc., Lower Headon (E)	422	Lasse loc. (E)	536	Wissberg loc. (E)
321	Memerlein loc. (E)	423	Pontigné loc. (E)	538	Seu de Urgell loc. (E)
322	Euzet loc. (E)	424	Rillé loc. (E)	540	Yassioren loc. (As)
323	Roc de Santa loc. (E)	425	Savigné loc. (E)	542	Ngorora C beds (Af)
324	Sosis loc. (E)	426	Denezé loc. (E)	544	Mollon loc. (E)
325	Prajous loc. (E)	428	Neudorf–Spalte loc. (E)	546	Grossulovo loc. (E)
326	La Bouffie loc. (E)	430	Noyant sous-le-Lude loc. (E)	548	La Tarumba I loc. (E)
327	Isle of Wight (Headon Hill) Headon beds (E)	432	Trimmelkamm loc. (E)	550	Baccinello V-1 locs. (E)
328	Les Pradigues loc. (E)	434	Paşalar loc. (As)	552	Pyrgos loc. (E)
330	CIT loc. 150, Sespe (N)	436	Taben Buluk loc. (As)	554	Haritalyangar (lower) loc. (As)
332	Yuanchu locs. 1 & 7 of Zdansky (As)	438	Göriach loc. (E)	556	Pikermi loc. (E)
334	Lushi loc. (As)	440	Maboko loc. (Af)	558	Titov Veles loc. (E)
340	Chambers Tuff loc. (N)	442	Sansan loc. (E)	560	Saloniki Classic locs. (E) (Vatiluk, Ravin X)
342	Typee Canyon loc. (N)	444	Neudorf–Sandberg loc. (E)	562	Kalimanci loc. (E)
344	Duchesne River loc. (N)	446	Elgg loc. (E)	564	Kromidovo loc. (E)
345	Pondaung loc. (As)	448	Rumikon loc. (E)	566	Gorna Susica loc. (E)
348	Aubrelong 2 loc. (E)	450	Stein am Rhein loc. (E)	568	Grebeniki loc. (E)
350	Celarie loc. (E)	452	Kreuzlingen loc. (E)	570	Taraklia loc. (E)
352	Malpérié loc. (E)	454	Çandir loc. (As)	571	Sethi Nagri locs. (As)
354	Ehrenstein locs. (E)	456	Kamlial beds (As)	572	Maragha monkey loc. (As)
356	Perrière loc. (E)	458	Przeworno 2 loc. (E)	573	Wutu loc. (As)
357	La Débruge loc. (E)	460	Klein Hadersdorf loc. (E)	574	Jabi loc. (As)
358	Gosgen loc. (E)	462	Fort Ternan loc. (E)	576	Gandakas locs. (As)
359	Headon Lignite Bed (E)	464	La Venta locs. (S)	578	Ongoliba Bone bed loc. (As)
360	Entreroches loc. (E)	466	La Grive Classic locs. (E)	580	Monte Bamboli loc. (E)
362	San Cougat loc. (E)	468	Can Mata I loc. (E)	582	Montemassi loc. (E)
363	Escamps A, B, C locs. (E)	470	St. Stefan loc. (E)	584	Casteani loc. (E)
364	Rosières 1, 2, 4 locs. (E)	472	Opole loc. (E)	586	Ribollo loc. (E)
366	Montmartre loc. (E)	474	Stätzling loc. (E)	588	Alipur loc. (As)
368	Melania Clay loc. (E)	476	Diessen am Ammersee loc. (E)	590	Hasnot (upper) loc. (As)
370	Cold Springs loc. (N)	478	Can Vila loc. (E)	592	Domeli (upper) loc. (As)
372	La Salla–Luribay loc. (S)	480	Chinji beds (As)	594	Baccinello V-2 loc. (E)
374	Yale Q. E. (Af)	482	Kanatti loc. (As)	596	Haritalyangar (upper) loc. (As)
376	Yale Q. G. (Af)	484	Hsiaolungtan loc. (As)	598	Marceau loc. (Af)
378	Yale Q. I, M. (Af)	486	St. Gaudens loc. (E)	600	Gravitelli loc. (E)
380	Gaiman loc. (S)	488	Castel de Barbera loc. (E)	602	Hatvan loc. (E)
382	Sacanana loc. (S)	490	Can Feliu II loc. (E)	604	Pestszentlörinc loc. (E)
384	Sharps beds (N)	492	Ramnagar loc. (As)	606	Lukeino beds (Af)
388	Bukwa loc. (Af)	494	Kundal Nala loc. (As)	608	Polgardi loc. (E)
390	Karungu loc. (Af)	496	Hasnot (lower) loc. (As)	610	Wadi Natrun loc. (Af)
392	Santa Cruz beds (S)	498	Kalfa loc. (E)	612	Baltavar loc. (E)
394	Koru loc. (Af)	500	Udabno loc. (E)	614	Baccinello V-3 loc. (E)
396	Songhor loc. (Af)	502	Eldar loc. (E)	616	Lothagam-1 beds (Af)
398	Gebel Zelten beds (Af)	504	Domeli (lower) loc. (As)	618	Casino loc. (E)
400	Wadi Moghara loc. (Af)	506	Rudabánya loc. (E)	620	Celleneuve locs. (E)
402	Napak I, IV, V, IX locs. (Af)	508	Mariatal loc. (E)	622	Montpellier locs. (E)
404	Moroto 2 loc. (Af)	510	Can Llobateres loc. (E)	624	Osztrámos-1 loc (E)
405	Yindirte loc. (As)	512	Can Ponsic loc. (E)	626	Serrat d'en Vacquer loc. (E)
406	Rusinga locs. (Af)	514	Hasnot (middle) loc. (As)	628	"Perpignan" locs. (E)
408	Mwfangano loc. (Af)	516	Ngorora B beds (Af)	630	Ertemte loc. (As)
410	Loperot loc. (Af)	518	Salmendingen loc. (E)	632	Ivanovce loc. (E)
412	Losidok loc. (Af)	520	Trochtelfingen loc. (E)	634	Wölfersheim loc. (E)
414	Ombo loc. (Af)	522	Melchingen loc. (E)	636	Garaet Ichkeul loc. (Af)
416	Moruarot loc. (Af)	524	Ebingen loc. (E)	638	Layna loc. (E)
418	Pontlevoy loc. (E)	526	Eppelsheim loc. (E)	640	Balaruc-2 loc. (E)
420	Manthelan loc. (E)	528	Ravin de la Pluie locs. (E)	642	Csarnota-2 loc. (E)
		530	Nagri beds, lower (As)	644	Malusteni loc. (E)
		532	Bandal loc. (As)	646	Kanapoi loc. (Af)
		534	Polinya 2 loc. (E)		

(continued)

TABLE I (continued)

647 Lothagam-3 beds (Af)	764 Coopers loc. (Af)	874 Vértesszöllös loc. (E)
648 Vialette loc. (E)	766 Minaar's Cave (Af)	876 Gongwangling loc. (As)
650 Fornace RDB loc. (E)	768 Tegelen locs. (E)	878 Jianniushan loc. (As)
652 Beresti loc. (E)	770 Montevarchi Beds (Upper	880 Kanjera loc. (Af)
654 Baraolt–Capeni beds (E)	Valdarno) (E)	882 Petralona Cave (E)
658 Gundersheim loc. (E)	772 Peninj hominid loc. (Af)	884 St. Estève Layer G (E)
660 Beremend-4 loc. (E)	774 Olduvai Lower Bed II (Af)	886 Vergranne loc. (E)
662 Ekora loc. (Af)	776 Omo Shungura Mbr. H (Af)	888 Ambrona loc. (E)
664 Hajnacka loc. (E)	778 Sterkfontein Ext. loc. (Af)	890 Choukoutien loc. 13 (As)
666 Laetolil locs. (Af)	780 Yuanmou hominid loc. (As)	892 San Vito di Leguzzano loc. (E)
668 "Odessa" loc. (E)	782 Kromdraai hominid loc. B (Af)	893 Hoxne loc. (E)
670 Omo Shungura Basal Mbr. (Af)	784 Liucheng Caves (As)	894 Montsaunès Cave (E)
672 Omo Shungura Mbr. A (Af)	786 Modjokerto Djetis beds (As)	896 "Rome" monkey loc. (E)
674 Kanam East locs. (Af)	788 Sangiran Djetis beds (As)	898 Choukoutien loc. 1 (As)
676 Budey loc. (E)	790 Chesowanja loc. (Af)	900 Choukoutien loc. 3 (As)
678 Novopetrovka loc. (E)	792 Olduvai Middle Bed II (Af)	902 Chenchiawo loc. (As)
680 Cova Bonica loc. (E)	794 Omo Shungura Mbr. J (Af)	904 Hong Kong drugstore
682 Capo Figari loc. (E)	796 Koobi Fora Upper Mbr. (Af)	"Sinanthropus officinalis"
684 Ain Jourdel loc. (Af)	798 Koobi Fora Ileret Mbr. (Af)	"loc." (As)
686 Tatrot beds (As)	800 Mien-chih monkey loc. (As)	906 Heppenloch Cave (E)
688 Chemeron hominid loc. (Af)	802 Gomboré II loc. (Af)	908 Montmaurin Niche loc. (E)
690 Mugello loc. (E)	804 Olduvai Upper Bed II (Af)	910 Littorina Cave (Af)
692 Kazinga Channel loc. (Af)	806 Omo Shungura Mbr. K (Af)	912 Choukoutien loc. 2 (As)
694 Omo Usno beds (Af)	808 Betfia-2 loc. (E)	914 Hoshangtung loc. (As)
696 Omo Shungura Mbr. B (Af)	810 Chien-shih (Jianshi) loc. (As)	916 Koloshan locs. (As)
698 Hadar beds (Af)	812 Badong primate loc. (As)	918 Hsingan Cave E (As)
699 Kubi Algi beds (Af)	813 "Hemanthropus" drugstore	920 Nishiyagi (Akashi) loc. (As)
700 Makapansgat beds (Af)	"loc." (As)	922 Tham Khuyen Cave (As)
702 Ain Brimba loc. (Af)	814 Monte Peglia loc. (E)	923 Tham Om Cave (As)
704 Kaiso Village loc. (Af)	816 Vallonet Cave (E)	924 Tham Hai Cave (As)
706 Sterkfontein Type loc. (Af)	818 Rawe beds (Af)	926 Ain Mefta loc. (Af)
708 St. Vallier loc. (E)	820 Olduvai Bed III (Af)	928 Olduvai Lower Ndutu beds
710 Kotlovina loc. (E)	822 Omo Shungura Mbr. L (Af)	(Af)
712 Omo Shungura Mbr. C (Af)	824 West Runton beds (E)	930 Swartkrans b–Mbr.2 (Af)
714 Sandalja loc. (E)	826 Gombasek loc. (E)	932 Arago (Tautavel) Cave (E)
716 Omo Shungura Mbr. D (Af)	828 Voigtstedt loc. (E)	934 Bilzingsleben loc. (E)
718 Puebla de Valverde loc. (E)	830 Hohensülzen loc. (E)	936 Thomas 1 Quarry loc. (Af)
720 Red Crag locs. (E)	832 Yenchingkou I loc. (As)	938 Thomas 3 Quarry loc. (Af)
722 Choukoutien loc. 12 (As)	834 Sangiran Trinil beds (As)	940 Salé Quarry loc. (Af)
724 Chemeron loc. JM 90/91 (Af)	836 Trinil beds (As)	942 Swanscombe loc. (E)
726 Omo Shungura Mbr. E (Af)	838 Kedung Brubus loc. (As)	944 Grays Thurrock loc. (E)
728 Koobi Fora Lower Mbr. (Af)	840 Sambungmachan loc. (As)	946 Orgnac-3 Cave (E)
730 Taung monkey loc. (Af)	842 Java mid-Pleistocene caves	948 Steinheim loc. (E)
734 Yushe "Zone III" beds (As)	(As)	950 Bijiashan loc. (As)
736 Kutitsun loc. (As)	844 'Ubeidiya beds (As)	952 Chaiyenshan loc. (As)
738 Omo Shungura Mbr. F (Af)	846 Zlaty Kun Cave C718 (E)	954 Chingshihling loc. (As)
740 Bolts Farm locs. (Af)	848 Prezletice loc. (E)	956 Feishu Cave (As)
742 Graunceanu loc. (E)	850 Bama loc. (As)	958 Heichinglungtsun loc. (As)
744 Pinjor beds (As)	852 Tahsin (Da-xing) loc. (As)	960 Hoshangpo loc. (As)
746 Kuruk beds (As)	854 Wuming loc. (As)	962 Houshan Cave (As)
748 Hsin-an loc. 54 (As)	856 Olduvai Bed IV (Af)	964 Liangfeng (Zhaicun) Cave (As)
750 Omo Shungura Mbr. G (Af)	858 Ternifine loc. (Af)	966 Shaochun Cave (As)
752 Swartkrans a–Mbr1 (Af)	860 Mauer loc. (E)	968 Shuan Cave (As)
754 Schurweburg loc. (Af)	862 Yayo (Chad) loc. (Af)	970 Tam Hang Cave (As)
756 Leba Caves (Af)	864 Mosbach-2 loc. (E)	972 Tam Pha Loi Cave (As)
758 Senèze loc. (E)	866 St. Estève Layer B (E)	974 Tanyang loc. (As)
760 Olduvai Bed I (Af)	868 Olduvai Masek beds (Af)	976 Tungtzu loc. (As)
761 Gomboré I loc. (Af)	870 Olorgesailie beds (Af)	978 Yenkouping Cave (As)
762 Kromdraai faunal loc. A (Af)	872 Lake Ndutu loc. (Af)	980 Dexingzhen (I-shan) (As)

TABLE I (continued)

981	Punung locs. (As)	1084	Sterkfontein D 16 loc. (Af)	1200	Jebel Irhoud loc. (Af)
982	Mifsud Giudice (Rabat) loc. (Af)	1086	Spy Cave (E)	1202	Haua Fteah Cave (Af)
		1088	Sipka Cave (E)	1204	Ksar-Akil loc. (As)
984	Atapuerca loc. (E)	1090	Arcy/Renne Cave (E)	1206	Ras-el-Kelb Cave (As)
986	Ngandong (Solo) beds (As)	1092	Genay loc. (E)	1208	Shukbah Cave (As)
987	Kapthurin loc. (Af)	1094	La Masque Cave (E)	1210	Shovakh (Shubbabiq) Cave (As)
988	La Rafette loc. (E)	1096	Monsempron loc. (E)	1212	Masloukh loc. (As)
990	Temara loc. (Af)	1098	Rigabe Cave (E)	1214	Geulah Cave (As)
992	Lazaret Cave (E)	1100	Soulabé Cave (E)	1216	Kebarah Cave (As)
994	Grotte du Prince Cave (E)	1102	Camerota Cave (E)	1218	Bisitun Cave (As)
996	Fontéchevade Cave (E)	1104	Monte Circeo Cave (E)	1220	Tamtama Cave (As)
998	La Chaise:Suard loc. (E)	1106	Uluzzo Cave (E)	1222	Dzhruchula Cave (As)
1000	Asych loc. (As)	1108	La Naulette Cave (E)	1224	Teshik-Tash Cave (As)
1002	Cave of Hearths (Af)	1110	St. Brelade Cave (E)	1226	Tabun Cave (As)
1004	Kanam hominid "loc." (Af)	1112	Kulna Cave (E)	1228	La Quina Cave (E)
1006	Kiik-koba loc. (E)	1114	Ochoz Cave (E)	1230	Amud Cave (As)
1008	Starosel'je loc. (E)	1116	Sala loc. (E)	1232	Velica Pecina Cave (E)
1010	Taubach loc. (E)	1118	Shanidar Cave (As)	1233	Skhul Cave (As)
1012	Sedia del Diavolo loc. (E)	1120	Kafza (=Djebel Qafzeh) Cave (As)	1234	Niah Cave basal (As)
1014	Malarnaud Cave (E)			1236	Florisbad loc. (Af)
1016	Ganovce Travertine loc. (E)	1122	Singa loc. (Af)	1238	San Diego (La Jolla) loc. (N)
1018	Cova Negra Cave (E)	1124	Angles sur l'Anglin loc. (E)	1240	Combe Capelle loc. (E)
1020	Borgio Cave (E)	1126	Arcy/Loup Cave (E)	1242	Cro-Magnon loc. (E)
1022	Hang Hum (lower) Cave (As)	1128	Arcy/Hyène Cave (E)	1244	Hsiaonanhai loc. (As)
1024	Hang Quit Cave (As)	1130	Caminero Cave (E)	1246	Lake Mungo loc. (As)
1026	Houei Hoc Cave (As)	1132	La Cave loc. (E)	1248	Choukoutien Upper Cave (As)
1027	Keo Leng Cave (As)	1134	La Chapelle Cave (E)	1250	Hsienjen loc. (As)
1028	Tung Lang Cave (As)	1136	Chateauneuf Cave (E)	1252	Shikimizu loc. (As)
1030	Gladysvale loc. (Af)	1138	Combe–Grenal loc. (E)	1254	Karnul Caves (As)
1032	Graveyard loc. (Af)	1140	La Crouzade loc. (E)	1256	Sumatran "Holocene" locs. (As)
1034	Saldanha (Hopefield) loc. (Af)	1142	La Croze del Dua loc. (E)		
1036	Omo Kibish Mbr. I (Af)	1144	La Ferrassie loc. (E)	1258	Javan "Holocene" locs. (As)
1038	Broken Hill (Kabwe) loc. (Af)	1146	Hortus Cave (E)	1260	Hang Hum (upper) Cave (As)
1040	Ehringsdorf beds (E)	1148	Marillac Cave (E)	1262	Witkrans loc. (Af)
1042	La Chaise: Bourgeois–Delaunay loc. (E)	1150	Montgaudier loc. (E)	1263	Tamar Hat loc. (Af)
		1152	Le Moustier loc. (E)	1264	"Pretoria" loc. (Af)
1044	Saccopastore loc. (E)	1154	Pech de l'Azé Cave I (E)	1265	Ambdisatra loc. (M)
1046	Zuttiyeh Cave (=Galilee loc.) (As)	1156	Petit-Puymoyen Cave (E)	1266	Ambolisatra loc. (M)
		1158	Placard Cave lower (E)	1267	Ambalisatra loc. (M)
1048	Kudaro-1 Cave (E)	1160	Putride Cave (E)	1268	Amparihingidro loc. (M)
1050	Bañolas loc. (E)	1162	Regourdou Cave (E)	1270	Ampasambazimba loc. (M)
1052	Quinzano loc. (E)	1164	Réné Simard Cave (E)	1272	Ampoza loc. (M)
1054	Montmaurin upper levels (E)	1166	Roc du Marsal Cave (E)	1273	Anavoha loc. (M)
1056	Krapina loc. (E)	1168	Vergisson Cave (E)	1274	Andrahomana Cave (M)
1058	Pofi loc. (E)	1170	Neandertal loc. (E)	1275	Ankazoabe loc. (M)
1060	Ushikawa loc. (As)	1172	Neuessing Cave I (E)	1276	Antsirabé loc. (M)
1062	Shuiyen Cave (As)	1174	Salzgitter–Lebenstedt loc. (E)	1278	Bélo-sur-Mer loc. (M)
1064	Mapa Cave (As)	1176	Wildscheuer Cave (E)	1280	Bemafandry loc. (M)
1066	Dingcun (Tingtsun) loc. (As)	1178	Devil's Tower loc. (E)	1282	Itampolo loc. (M)
1068	Ordos (Sjaraossogol) loc. (As)	1180	Forbes Quarry loc. (E)	1284	Lamboharana loc. (M)
1070	Changyang loc. (As)	1182	Subalyuk Cave (E)	1286	Lower Menarandra locs. (M)
1071	Anyang loc. (As)	1184	Archi Cave (E)	1288	Manombo loc. (M)
1072	Bodo loc. (Af)	1186	Bisceglie Cave (E)	1290	Morarano loc. (M)
1074	Afar Late Pleistocene locs. (Af)	1188	Ca'verde loc. (E)	1292	Sambaina loc. (M)
1076	Eyasi loc. (Af)	1190	Cariguela Cave (E)	1294	Taolambiby loc. (M)
1078	Kanjera hominid "loc." (Af)	1192	Lezetxiki Cave (E)	1296	Tsiravé loc. (M)
1080	Diré-Dawa (Porc-Épic) Cave (Af)	1194	St. Brais Cave II (E)	1298	Lagoa Santa Caves (S)
		1196	Ohaba-Ponor Cave (E)	1300	Long Mile Cave (S)
1082	Border Cave (Af)	1198	Rozhok loc. (E)	1302	Berna loc. (S)

TABLE II
Fossil Primate Localities of the Late Cretaceous and Cenozoic in Alphabetical Order[a]

Abbey Wood loc. (204, E)
Afar (Hadar) beds (698, Af)
Afar late Pleistocene locs. (1074, Af)
Ain Brimba loc. (702, Af)
Ain Jourdel loc. (684, Af)
Ain Mefta loc. (926, Af)
Airport loc. (76, N)
Alipur loc. (588, As)
Almagre locs., San José (200, N)
Ambalisatra loc. (1267, M)
Ambdisatra loc. (1265, M)
Ambolisatra loc. (1266, M)
Ambrona beds (888, E)
Amparihingidro loc. (1268, M)
Ampasambazimba loc. (1270, M)
Ampoza loc. (1272, M)
AM Q. 88, San José (278, N)
Amud Cave (1230, As)
Anavoha loc. (1273, M)
Andrahomana Cave (1274, M)
Angles sur l'Anglin loc. (1124, E)
Ankazoabe loc. (1275, M)
Antsirabé loc. (1276, M)
Anyang loc. (1071, As)
Arago (Tautavel) Cave (932, E)
Archi Cave (1184, E)
Arcy/Hyène Cave (1128, E)
Arcy/Loup Cave (1126, E)
Arcy/Renne Cave (1090, E)
Asych loc. (1000, As)
Atapuerca loc. (984, E)
Aubrelong 2 loc. (348, E)
Avenay loc. (206, E)
Baccinello V-1 locs. (550, E)
Baccinello V-2 loc. (594, E)
Baccinello V-3 loc. (614, E)
Badong primate loc. (812, As)
Badwater Creek locs, 5, 5a, 6 (296, N)
Baltavar loc. (612, E)
Bama loc. (850, As)
Bandal loc. (532, As)
Banjo Pocket Q. (170, N)
Bañolas loc. (1050, E)
Baraolt-Capeni beds (654, E)
Baringo (Kapthurin) loc. (987, Af)
Battle Mt. loc. (56, N)
Bayfield loc. (114, N)
Bear Creek loc. (148, N)
Bélo-sur-Mer loc. (1278, M)
Bemafandry loc. (1280, M)
Beremend-4 loc. (660, E)
Beresti loc. (652, E)
Berna loc. (1302, S)
Berru loc. (92, E)
Betfia-2 loc. (808, E)
Bijiashan loc. (950, As)
Bilzingsleben loc. (934, E)
Bisceglie Cave (1186, E)
Bisitun Cave (1218, As)
Bitter Creek locs. (156, N)
Bodo loc. (1072, Af)

Bolts Farm locs. (740, Af)
Bone Hill loc. (174, N)
Border Cave (1082, Af)
Borgio Cave (1020, E)
Bourgeois-Delaunay (La Chaise) loc. (1042, E)
Bouxwiller loc. (254, E)
Broken Hill (Kabwe) loc. (1038, Af)
Buckman Hollow loc. (128, N)
Budey loc. (676, N)
Bug Creek loc. (10, N)
Bukwa loc. (388, Af)
Bumbin Nuru loc., Naran Bulak (192, As)
Camerota Cave (1102, E)
Caminero Cave (1130, E)
Candir loc. (454, As)
Can Feliu II loc. (490, E)
Can Llobateres loc. (510, E)
Can Mata I loc. (468, E)
Can Ponsic loc. (512, E)
Can Vila loc. (478, E)
Capella loc. (253, E)
Capo Figari loc. (682, E)
Cariguela Cave (1190, E)
Casablanca (Littorina Cave) (910, Af)
Casino loc. (618, E)
Casteani loc. (584, E)
Castel de Barbera loc. (488, E)
Castigaleu loc. (222, E)
Cathedral Bluffs Tongue loc. (242, N)
Cave of Hearths (1002, Af)
Ca'verde loc. (1188, E)
Cedar Pt. loc. (54, N)
Celarie loc. (350, E)
Celleneuve locs. (620, E)
Cernay loc. (88, E)
Chaiyenshan loc. (952, As)
Chambers Tuff loc. (340, N)
Changyang loc. (1070, As)
Chappo-1 loc. (116, N)
Chappo-12 loc. (150, N)
Chappo-17 loc. (58, N)
Charot loc. (230, E)
Chateauneuf Cave (1136, E)
Chemeron hominid loc. (688, Af)
Chemeron loc. JM 90/91 (724, Af)
Chenchiawo loc. (902, As)
Chesowanja loc. (790, Af)
Chien-shih (Jianshi) loc. (810, As)
Chingshihling loc. (954, As)
Chinji beds (480, As)
Choukoutien loc. 1 (898, As)
Choukoutien loc. 2 (912, As)
Choukoutien loc. 3 (900, As)
Choukoutien loc. 12 (722, As)
Choukoutien loc. 13 (890, As)
Choukoutien Upper Cave (1248, As)
Circeo (Monte) Cave (1104, E)
Circle loc. (30, N)
CIT loc. 150, Sespe (330, N)

CIT loc. 180, Tapo Ranch, "Poway" (302, N)
CIT loc. 249, "Poway" (298, N)
Clark Fork locs. (152, N)
Cold Springs loc. (370, N)
Combe Capelle loc. (1240, E)
Combe-Grenal loc. (1138, E)
Condé-en-Brie loc. (220, E)
Coopers loc. (764, Af)
Cova Bonica loc. (680, E)
Cova Negra Cave (1018, E)
Croc Tooth Q. (74, N)
Cro-Magnon loc. (1242, E)
Cromer (West Runton) loc. (824, E)
Csarnota-2 loc. (642, E)
Cuis loc. (228, E)
Dad loc. (216, N)
Da-xing (Tahsin) loc. (852, As)
Dell Creek loc. (118, N)
Denezé loc. (426, E)
Devil's Tower loc. (1178, E)
Dexingzhen (980, As)
Djetis (Modjokerto) beds (786, As)
Djetis (Sangiran) beds (788, As)
Diessen am Ammersee loc. (476, E)
Dingcun (Tingtsun) loc. (1066, As)
Diré-Dawa (Porc-Épic) Cave (1080, Af)
Divide loc. (78, N)
Djebel Qafzeh Cave (1120, As)
Dobie Butte loc. (166, N)
Domeli (lower) loc. (504, As)
Domeli (upper) loc. (592, As)
Dormaal loc. (186, E)
Douglass Q. (36, N)
Dragon loc. (18, N)
Duchesne River locs. (344, N)
Dzhruchula Cave (1222, E)
East Rudolf (Turkana), see Koobi Fora; Kubi Algi
Ebingen loc. (524, E)
Eclépens loc. (309, E)
Egerkingen α & β locs. (278, E)
Egerkingen γ loc. (250, E)
Egerkingen Huppersand loc. (256, E)
Ehrenstein IA loc. (354, E)
Ehringsdorf beds (1040, E)
Ekalaka loc. (34, N)
Ekora loc. (662, Af)
Eldar loc. (502, E)
Elgg loc. (446, E)
Entreroches loc. (360, E)
Epernay loc. (232, E)
Eppelsheim loc. (526, E)
Erikson's Landing loc. (60, N)
Ertemte loc. (630, As)
Escamps A, B, C locs. (363, E)
Euzet loc. (322, E)
Evacuation Creek loc. (276, N)
Eyasi loc. (1076, Af)
Fault loc. (270, N)

---

[a] Abbreviations: Af, Africa; As, Asia; E, Europe; M, Madagascar; N, North America; S, South America and Caribbean. Loc., locality; Q., quarry.

TABLE II (continued)

Fayum (Yale Q. E) (374, Af)
Fayum (Yale Q. G) (376, Af)
Fayum (Yale Q. I, M) (378, Af)
Feishu Cave (956, As)
Florisbad loc. (1236, Af)
Fons 1, 2, 3, 5, 6 locs. (314, E)
Fons 4 loc. (318, E)
Fontéchevade Cave (996, E)
Forbes Quarry loc. (1180, E)
Fornace RDB loc. (650, E)
Fort Ternan loc. (462, E)
Fossil Butte loc. (214, N)
Fossil Hollow loc. (112, N)
Four Mile East Alheit Pocket loc. (178, N)
Four Mile localities other than East Alheit (180, N)
Friars locs. (265, N)
Fritz Q. (102, N)
Gaiman loc. (380, S)
Galilee (Zuttiyeh) Cave (1046, As)
Gandakas locs. (576, As)
Ganovce Travertine loc. (1016, E)
Garaet Ichkeul loc. (636, Af)
Garbani loc. (14, N)
Gebel Zelten beds (398, Af)
Geiseltal locs. (237, E)
Genay loc. (1092, E)
Geulah Cave (1214, As)
Gidley Q. (24, N)
Gladysvale loc. (1030, Af)
Golden Valley locs. (182, N)
Gombasek loc. (826, E)
Gomboré I loc. (761, Af)
Gomboré II loc. (802, Af)
Gongwangling loc. (876, As)
Göriach loc. (438, E)
Gorna Susica loc. (566, E)
Gosgen loc. (358, E)
Graunceanu loc. (742, E)
Grauves loc. (224, E)
Graveyard loc. (1032, Af)
Gravitelli loc. (600, E)
Gray Bull locs. (162, N)
Grays Thurrock loc. (944, E)
Grebeniki loc. (568, E)
Grisolles loc. (310, E)
Grossulovo loc. (546, E)
Grotte du Prince Cave (994, E)
Gundersheim loc. (658, E)
Hadar beds (698, Af)
Hajnacka loc. (664, E)
Hang Hum (lower) Cave (1022, As)
Hang Hum (upper) Cave (1260, As)
Hang Quit Cave (1024, As)
Harbicht Hill loc. (8, N)
Haritalyangar (lower) loc. (554, As)
Haritalyangar (upper) loc. (596, As)
Hasnot (lower) loc. (496, As)
Hasnot (middle) loc. (514, As)
Hasnot (upper) loc. (590, As)
Hatvan loc. (602, E)

Haua Fteah Cave (1202, Af)
Hawk loc. (268, N)
Headon Hill (Isle of Wight) (327, E)
Headon Lignite Bed (359, E)
Heichinglungtsun loc. (958, As)
"Hemanthropus" drugstore "loc." (813, As)
Heppenloch Cave (906, E)
Herne Bay loc. (226, E)
Highway Blowout loc. (48, N)
Hohensülzen loc. (830, E)
Hong Kong drugstore "Sinanthropus officinalis" "loc." (904, As)
Hopefield (Saldanha) loc. (1034, Af)
Hordle Cliff loc., Lower Headon (320, E)
Hortus Cave (1146, E)
Hoshangpo Cave (960, As)
Hoshangtung loc. (914, As)
Houei Hoc Cave (1026, As)
Houshan loc. (962, As)
Hoxne loc. (893, E)
Hsiaolungtan loc. (484, As)
Hsiaonanhai loc. (1244, As)
Hsin-an loc. 54 (748, As)
Hsingan Cave E (918, As)
Hsienjen loc. (1250, As)
Huerfano I, II, III, IV locs. (260, N)
Huerfano VI, VII locs. (246, N)
Ichkeul, Garaet (Lac) loc. (636, Af)
Ileret Mbr. (Koobi Fora) (798, Af)
Irhoud, Jebel loc. (1200, Af)
Isle of Wight (Headon Hill) (327, E)
Itampolo loc. (1282, M)
Ivanovce loc. (632, E)
Jabi loc. (574, As)
Java mid-Pleistocene caves (842, As)
Javan "Holocene" locs. (1258, As)
Jebel Irhoud loc. (1200, Af)
Jianniushan loc. (878, As)
Jian-shi (Chien-shih) loc. (810, As)
Joe's Bone Bed loc., Black Peaks (122, N)
Kabwe (Broken Hill) loc. (1038, Af)
Kafza (=Djebel Qafzeh) Cave (1120, As)
Kaiso Village loc. (704, Af)
Kalfa loc. (498, E)
Kalimanci loc. (562, E)
Kamlial beds (456, As)
Kanam East locs. (674, Af)
Kanam hominid "loc." (1004, Af)
Kanatti loc. (482, As)
Kanapoi loc. (646, Af)
Kanjera loc. (880, Af)
Kanjera hominid "loc." (1078, Af)
Kapthurin loc. (987, Af)
Karnul Caves (1254, As)
Karungu loc. (390, Af)
Kazinga Channel loc. (692, Af)
Kebarah Cave (1216, As)
Kedung Brubus loc. (838, As)

Keefer Hill loc. (38, N)
Kennedy's Hole loc., Uinta B (304, N)
Keo Leng Cave (1027, As)
Kibish Mbr. I, Omo (1036, Af)
Kiik-koba loc. (1006, E)
Klein Hadersdorf loc. (460, E)
Knight Station loc. (212, N)
Koloshan locs. (916, As)
Koobi Fora Ileret Mbr. (798, Af)
Koobi Fora Lower Mbr. (728, Af)
Koobi Fora Upper Mbr. (796, Af)
Loru loc. (394, Af)
Kotlovina loc. (710, E)
Krapina loc. (1056, E)
Kreuzlingen (452, E)
Kromdraai faunal loc. A (762, Af)
Kromdraai hominid loc. B (782, Af)
Kromidovo loc. (564, E)
Ksar-Akil loc. (1204, As)
Kubi Algi beds (699, AF)
Kudaro-1 Cave (1048, E)
Kulna Cave (1112, E)
Kundal Nala loc. (494, As)
Kuruk beds (746, As)
Kutitsun loc. (736, As)
Kyson loc. (202, E)
La Barge loc. (238, N)
La Bouffie loc. (326, E)
La Cave loc. (1132, E)
La Chaise:Bourgeois–Delaunay loc. (1042, E)
La Chaise:Suard loc. (998, E)
La Chapelle Cave (1134, E)
La Crouzade Cave (1140, E)
La Croze del Dua loc. (1142, E)
La Débruge loc. (357, E)
La Ferrassie loc. (1144, E)
La Grive Classic loc. (466, E)
La Masque Cave (1094, E)
La Naulette Cave (1108, E)
La Quina Cave (1228, E)
La Rafette loc. (988, E)
La Salla–Luribay loc. (372, S)
La Tarumba I loc. (548, E)
La Venta locs. (464, S)
La Vergne loc. (316, E)
Laetolil locs. (666, Af)
Lagoa Santa Caves (1298, S)
Lake Mungo loc. (1246, As)
Lake Ndutu loc. (872, Af)
Lamboharana loc. (1284, M)
Lantian (Chenchiawo) loc. (902, As)
Lantian (Gongwangling) loc. (876, As)
Lasse loc. (422, E)
Layna loc. (638, E)
Lazaret Cave (992, E)
Le Bretou loc. (308, E)
Le Moustier loc. (1152, E)
Leba Caves (756, Af)
Ledge loc. (52, N)
Lentille loc. (90, E)

(continued)

TABLE II (continued)

Lerida (Seu de Urgell) loc. (538, E)
Les Badies loc. (223, E)
Les Salères loc. (221, E)
Les Pradigues loc. (328, E)
Lezetxiki Cave (1192, E)
Liangfeng (Zhaicun) Cave (964, As)
Lissieu loc. (258, E)
Little Muddy Creek loc. (46, N)
Little Sand Coulee locs. (124, N)
Littorina Cave (910, Af)
Liucheng Caves (784, As)
Long Draw loc. (80, N)
Long Mile Cave (1300, S)
Loperot loc. (410, Af)
Losidok loc. (412, Af)
Lost Cabin loc. (240, N)
Lothagam-1 beds (616, Af)
Lothagam-3 beds (647, Af)
Love Q. (62, N)
Lower Bridger locs., Black Fork, etc. (266, N)
Lower Menarandra locs. (1286, M)
Lower Sand Draw loc. (97, N)
Lukeino beds (606, Af)
Lushi loc. (334, As)
Lysite locs. (208, N)
Maboko loc. (440, Af)
Makapansgat (Cave of Hearths) (1002, Af)
Makapansgat beds (700, Af)
Malarnaud Cave (1014, E)
Malcolm's loc., Badwater area (82, N)
Malpérié loc. (352, E)
Malusteni loc. (644, E)
Mancy loc. (234, E)
Manombo loc. (1288, M)
Manthelan loc. (420, E)
Mapa Cave (1064, As)
Maragha monkey loc. (572, As)
Marceau loc. (598, Af)
Mariatal loc. (508, E)
Marillac Cave (1148, E)
Marne loc. (191, E)
Mason Pocket loc. (72, N)
Masloukh loc. (1212, As)
Mauer loc. (860, E)
Melania Clay loc. (368, E)
Melchingen loc. (522, E)
Melville-13 loc. (50, N)
Memerlein loc. (321, E)
Menat loc. (86, E)
Messel, loc. (252. E)
Meudon loc. (184, E)
Middle Sand Draw loc. (110, N)
Mien-chih monkey loc. (800, As)
Mifsud Giudice (Rabat) loc. (982, Af)
Milleson Draw loc. (194, N)
Minaar's Cave (766, Af)
Mission Valley locs. (275, N)
Modjokerto Djetis beds (786, As)
Moghara, Wadi loc. (400, Af)
Mollon loc. (544, E)
Monsempron loc. (1096, E)

Monte Bamboli loc. (580, E)
Monte Circeo Cave (1104, E)
Monte Peglia loc. (814, E)
Montemassi loc. (582, E)
Montevarchi beds (Upper Valdarno) (770, E)
Monthelon loc. (236, E)
Montmartre loc. (366, E)
Montmaurin Niche loc. (908, E)
Montmaurin upper levels (1054, E)
Montpellier locs. (622, E)
Montsaunès Cave (894, E)
Morarano loc. (1290, M)
Mormont loc. (312, E)
Moroto 2 loc. (404, Af)
Morrow Creek loc. (274, N)
Moruarot loc. (416, Af)
Mosbach-2 loc. (864, E)
Mugello loc. (690, E)
Mutigny loc. (190, E)
Mwfangano loc. (408, Af)
Nagri beds, lower (530, As)
Napak I, IV, V, IX locs. (402, Af)
Natrun, Wadi loc. (610, Af)
Neandertal loc. (1170, E)
Neudorf–Sandberg loc. (444, E)
Neudorf–Spalte loc. (428, E)
Neuessing Cave I (1172, E)
New Fork loc. (244, N)
Ngandong (Solo) beds (986, As)
Ngorora B beds (516, Af)
Ngorora C beds (542, Af)
Niah Cave basal (1234, As)
Nishiyagi (Akashi) loc. (920, As)
Novopetrovka loc. (678, E)
Noyant sous-le-Lude loc. (430, E)
Ochoz Cave (1114, E)
"Odessa" loc. (668, E)
Ohaba-Ponor Cave (1196, E)
Olduvai Bed I (760, Af)
Olduvai Bed III (820, Af)
Olduvai Bed IV (856, Af)
Olduvai Lower Bed II (774, Af)
Olduvai Lower Ndutu beds (928, Af)
Olduvai Masek beds (868, Af)
Olduvai Middle Bed II (792, Af)
Olduvai Upper Bed II (804, Af)
Olive loc. (32, N)
Olorgesailie beds (870, Af)
Ombo loc. (414, Af)
Omo Kibish Mbr. I (1036, Af)
Omo Shungura Basal Mbr. (670, Af)
Omo Shungura Mbr. A (672, Af)
Omo Shungura Mbr. B (696, Af)
Omo Shungura Mbr. C (712, Af)
Omo Shungura Mbr. D (716, Af)
Omo Shungura Mbr. E (726, Af)
Omo Shungura Mbr. F (738, Af)
Omo Shungura Mbr. G (750, Af)
Omo Shungura Mbr. H (776, Af)
Omo Shungura Mbr. J (794, Af)
Omo Shungura Mbr. K (806, Af)

Omo Shungura Mbr. L (822, Af)
Omo Usno beds (694, Af)
Ongoliba Bone Bed loc. (578, As)
Opole (472, E)
Ordos (Sjaraossogol) loc. (1068, As)
Orgnac-3 Cave (946, E)
Osztrámos-1 loc. (624, E)
Paint Creek loc. (126, N)
Paşalar loc. (434, As)
Paskapoo locs. (120, N)
Pech de l'Azé Cave I (1154, E)
Peninj hominid loc. (772, Af)
"Perpignan" locs. (628, E)
Perrière loc. (356, E)
Pestszentlörinc loc. (604, E)
Petit-Puymoyen Cave (1156, E)
Petralona Cave (882, E)
Phosphorites of Quercy, classical locs. (294, E)
Picanton loc. (218, E)
Pikermi loc. (556, E)
Pinjor beds (744, As)
Placard Cave lower (1158, E)
Plateau Valley locs. (146, N)
Pofi loc. (1058, E)
Polgardi loc. (608, E)
Polinya 2 loc. (534, E)
Pondaung loc. (345, As)
Pontigné loc. (423, E)
Pontlevoy loc. (418, E)
Pourcy loc. (188, E)
"Poway" (CIT locs. 249, 180) (298, 302, N)
Powder River locs. (196, N)
Powder Wash locs. (264, N)
Prajous loc. (325, E)
"Pretoria" loc. (1264, Af)
Prezletice loc. (848, E)
Princeton Q. (100, N)
Przeworno 2 loc. (458, E)
Puebla de Valverde loc. (718, E)
Punung locs. (981, As)
Purgatory Hill loc. (12, N)
Putride Cave (1160, E)
Pyrgos loc. (552, E)
Qafzeh, Djebel Cave (1120, As)
Quinzano loc. (1052, E)
Rabat (Mifsud Giudice) loc. (982, Af)
Ramnagar locs. (492, As)
Ras-el-Kelb Cave (1206, As)
Ravenscrag UAR-1 loc. (106, N)
Rawe beds (818, Af)
Ray's Bone Bed loc., Black Peaks (70, N)
Red Crag locs. (720, E)
Red Creek loc., Togwotee (132, N)
Red Desert loc. (158, N)
Regourdou Cave (1162, E)
Reims loc. (185, E)
René Simard Cave (1164, E)
Ribollo loc. (586, E)
Rigabe Cave (1098, E)

TABLE II (continued)

Rillé loc. (424, E)
Rilly loc. (96, E)
Robiac loc. (306, E)
Roc de Santa loc. (323, E)
Roc du Marsal Cave (1166, E)
Rock Bench Q. (26, N)
"Rome" monkey loc. (896, E)
Rosières 1, 2, 4 locs. (364, E)
Rozhok loc. (1198, E)
Rudabánya loc. (506, E)
Rumikon loc. (448, E)
Rusinga locs. (406, Af)
Sacanana loc. (382, S)
Saccopastore loc. (1044, E)
Saddle loc. (44, N)
Saddle Annex loc. (64, N)
St. Brais Cave II (1194, E)
St. Brelade Cave (1110, E)
St. Estève Layer B (866, E)
St. Estève Layer G (884, E)
St. Gaudens loc. (486, E)
St. Stefan loc. (470, E)
St. Vallier loc. (708, E)
Sala loc. (1116, E)
Saldanha (Hopefield) loc. (1034, Af)
Salé Quarry loc. (940, Af)
Salmendingen loc. (518, E)
Saloniki Classic locs. (Vatiluk, Ravin
   X) (560, E)
Saloniki, Ravin de la Pluie loc. (528, E)
Salzgitter–Lebenstedt loc. (1174, E)
Sambaina loc. (1292, M)
Sambungmachan loc. (840, As)
San Cougat loc. (362, E)
San Diego (La Jolla) loc. (1238, N)
San José beds (249, N; see 200, 248)
San Vito di Leguzzano loc. (892, E)
Sandalja loc. (714, E)
Sand Coulee beds (198, N)
Sangiran Djetis beds (788, As)
Sangiran Trinil beds (834, As)
Sansan loc. (442, E)
Santa Cruz beds (392, S)
Santiago locs. (292, N)
Savigné loc. (425, E)
Scarritt loc. (40, N)
Schaff Q. (104, N)
Schurweburg loc. (754, Af)
Sedia del Diavolo (1012, E)
Senèze loc. (758, E)
Serrat d'en Vacquer loc. (626, E)
Sespe (CIT loc. 150) (330, N)
Sethi Nagri locs. (530, N)
Seu de Urgell loc. (538, E)
Shanidar Cave (1118, As)
Shaochun Cave (966, As)
Sharps beds (384, N)
Shikimizu (1252, As)
Shovakh (Shubbabiq) Cave (1210, As)
Shuan Cave (968, As)
Shuiyen Cave (1062, As)
Shukbah Cave (1208, As)

Silberling Q. (20, N)
Silver Coulee beds (98, N)
Singa loc. (1122, Af)
Sipka Cave (1088, E)
Sjaraossogol (Ordos) loc. (1068, As)
Skhul Cave (1233, As)
Slick Creek loc. (168, N)
Solo (Ngandong) beds (986, As)
Songhor loc. (396, Af)
Sosis loc. (324, E)
Soulabé Cave (1100, E)
Spy Cave (1086, E)
Starosel'je loc. (1008, E)
Stätzling loc. (474, E)
Stein am Rhein loc. (450, E)
Steinheim loc. (948, E)
Sterkfontein D16 loc. (1084, Af)
Sterkfontein Ext. loc. (778, Af)
Sterkfontein Type loc. (706, Af)
Stonehenge Sandstone Q. (176, N)
Suard, Abri (La Chaise) loc. (998, E)
Sabalyuk Cave (1182, E)
Sumatran "Holocene" locs. (1256, As)
Supersite Q. (164, N)
Susan loc., Togwotee (134, N)
Swain Q. (28, N)
Swanscombe loc. (942, E)
Swartkrans a–Mbr. 1 (752, Af)
Swartkrans b–Mbr. 2 (930, Af)
Taben Buluk loc. (436, As)
Tabun Cave (1226, As)
Tahsin (Da-xing) loc. (852, As)
Tamar Hat loc. (1263, Af)
Tam Hang Cave (970, As)
Tam Pha Loi Cave (972, As)
Tamtama Cave (1220, As)
Tan Van Caves (922, 924, As)
Tanyang loc. (974, As)
Taolambiby loc. (1294, M)
Taraklia loc. (570, E)
Tatrot beds (686, As)
Taubach loc. (1010, E)
Taung monkey los. (730, Af)
Tautavel (Arago) Cave (932, E)
Tegelen locs. (768, E)
Temara loc. (990, Af)
Ternan, Fort loc. (462, E)
Ternifine loc. (858, Af)
Teshik-Tash Cave (1224, As)
Tham Hai Cave (924, As)
Tham Khuyen Cave (922, As)
Tham Om Cave (923, As)
Thomas I Quarry loc. (936, Af)
Thomas 3 Quarry loc. (938, Af)
Tingtsun (Dingcun) loc. 100 (1066, As)
Tipton Butte loc. (210, N)
Titanoides loc. (108, N)
Titov Veles loc. (558, E)
Togwotee loc. 7 (136, N)
Togwotee loc. 18 (138, N)
Togwotee Lower Variegated locs.
   (144, N)

Togwotee Main loc. (130, N)
Tongue River loc. (31, N)
Torrejon locs. (22, N)
Tour la Reine (Pyrgos) loc. (552, E)
Tree Road loc. (272, N)
Trimmelkamm loc. (432, E)
Trinil beds (836, As)
Trochtelfingen loc. (520, E)
Tsiravé loc. (1296, M)
Tung Lang Cave (1028, As)
Tungtzu loc. (976, As)
Twin Creek loc. (66, N)
Twisty Turn Hollow loc. (154, N)
Typee Canyon loc. (342, N)
'Ubeidiya beds (844, As)
Udabno loc. (500, E)
Uluzzo Cave (1106, E)
Upper Bridger locs., Twin Buttes, etc.
   (282, N)
Upper Cave (Choukoutien) (1248, As)
Upper Sand Draw locs. (142, N)
Ushikawa loc. (1060, As)
Usno (Omo) beds (694, Af)
Valdarno, Upper (Montevarchi) beds
   (770, Af)
Vallonet Cave (816, E)
Velica Pecina Cave (1232, E)
Vergisson Cave (1168, E)
Vergranne loc. (886, E)
Verland's loc. Togwotee (140, N)
Vértesszöllös loc. (874, E)
Vialette loc. (648, E)
Voigtstedt loc. (828, E)
Wadi Kraus Q. (172, N)
Wadi Moghara loc. (400, Af)
Wadi Natrun loc. (610, Af)
Wagon Road loc. (16, N)
Walbeck loc. (42, N)
West End loc. (68, N)
W. of Elk Mt. loc. (160, N)
West Runton beds (824, E)
Wildscheuer Cave (1176, E)
Wissberg loc. (536, E)
Witkrans loc. (1262, Af)
Wölfersheim loc. (634, E)
Wuming loc. (854, As)
Wutu loc. (573, As)
Yale Fayum Q. E. (374, Af)
Yale Fayum Q. G. (376, Af)
Yale Fayum Q. I, M. (378, Af)
Yassioren loc. (540, As)
Yayo (Chad) loc. (862, Af)
Yenchingkou I loc. (832, As)
Yenkouping Cave (978, As)
Yindirte loc. (405, As)
Yuanchu locs. 1 & 7 of Zdansky (332,
   As)
Yuanmou hominid loc. (780, As)
Yüshe "Zone III" beds (734, As)
Zelten, Gebel (398. Af)
Zlaty Kun Cave C718 (846, E)
Zuttiyeh Cave (=Galilee) (1046, As)

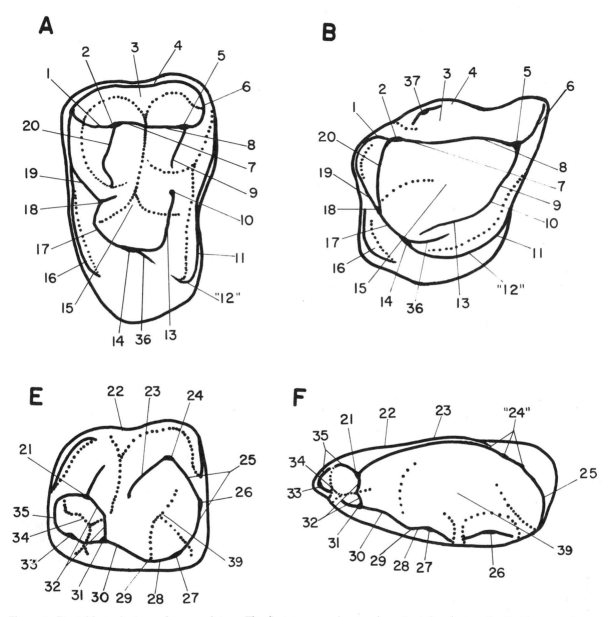

Figure 6. Dental homologies and nomenclature. The first upper molars are from the left, whereas the first lower molars are from the right, respectively. Mesial is to the left and distal is to the right. A and E represent a near primitive primate condition (*Pronothodectes matthewi*), and three additional pairs represent a few of many differently derived modifications (B and F, *Picrodus silberlingi*; C and G, *Periconodon pygmaeus*; D and H, *Homo habilis*). They are shown primarily to facilitate the recognition of homologous points or areas by the use of the same numbers. Quotation marks around some numbers are used to depict uncertainties about homologies. Numbers represented on some of the homologous teeth only (e.g., on D and H) are parts of the teeth sufficiently modified to be considered new structures. 1, preparacrista; 2, paracone; 3, stylar shelf; 4, buccal (or labial) cingulum or ectocingulum; 5, metacone; 6, postmetacrista; 7, postparacrista; 8, premetacrista; 9, hypometacrista

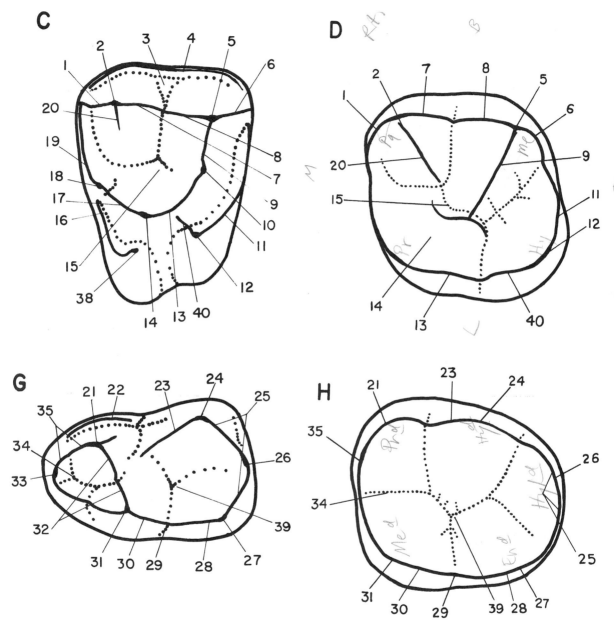

C

2 3 4 5
1 6
20
19 8
18 7
17 9
16 10
11
15
38 12
14 13 40

D

Pt B
2 7 8 5
1 6
Pa me
20 9
15 11
12
Hy
Pr
14 40
13

G

21 22 23 24
35 25
34
33 26
32 39
31 30 29 28 27

H

23
21 24
35 Pro Hy
26
34 Hypld
Med End
25
31 39 28 27
30 29

(in hominoids, often referred to as crista obliqua); 10, metaconule; 11, posthypocone crista; 12, hypocone; 13, postprotocone crista; 14, protocone; 15, trigon basin; 16, precingulum; 17, preprotocone crista; 18, paraconule; 19, preparaconule crista; 20, hypoparacrista; 21, protoconid; 22, buccal (or labial) cingulid or ectocingulid; 23, cristid obliqua; 24, hypoconid; 25, postcristid; 26, hypoconulid; 27, entoconid; 28, preentoconid cristid; 29, talonid notch; 30, postmetaconid cristid; 31, metaconid; 32, protocristid (protolophid or metalophid); 33, paraconid; 34, trigonid basin; 35, paralophid; 36, postprotocone-fold; 37, mesostyle; 38, pericone (Carabelli's cusp, when present on hominoid teeth); 39, talonid basin; 40, prehypocone crista. [By A. Cleary.]

science of dental morphology, in spite of impressive advances, has not yet reached the stage where it can adequately explain the adaptive significance of most dentitions. This is partly so because (a) the exact genetic mechanisms underlying changes in tooth morphology are not fully explained yet; (b) most often we are ignorant of the morphology preceding an adaptive shift; (c) we do not know the precise mode in which the morphology of the skull, influenced by nonmasticatory requirements, affects the chewing mechanism; and (d) we are not certain as to the exact nature and combination of several selective forces from the food substances responsible for one as opposed to another course taken by selection.

We hope that the details of form and function we attempt to present below for an entire order of mammals as diversely adapted as the primates will help colleagues in the future to study evolutionary history.

ORDER PRIMATES
Linnaeus, 1758

(= or including: Bimana, Quadrumana, other ordinal terms.)

DISTRIBUTION
Final Cretaceous to modern. Worldwide, especially tropics and subtropics.
INCLUDED TAXA
Suborders Plesiadapiformes, Strepsirhini, and Haplorhini.

Discussion

The understanding of the origins and interrelationships of the order is based largely on the fragmentary evidence of the cranium, dentition, and aspects of the postcranial skeleton. In attempting to decipher the provenance of a group, in this instance the primates, we must accomplish two separate tasks. The first task is the establishment of a roster of those characters which were probable attributes of the youngest common ancestor of that taxon. This is best approximated by the construction of a morphotype, a list of characteristics judged to be present in this common ancestor. The next procedure involves comparing the characters of this morphotype with homologous characters of other known pertinent groups, in an attempt to establish which characters are shared exclusively between the primates and some other eutherians.

No system of the hard anatomy lends itself as well to an introductory overview of primate interrelationships for our purposes in this book as does the osseous morphology of the basicranium. The associated circulatory system can be inferred with a great deal of certainty based on information obtained from living mammals. Supplemented by dental and postcranial evidence, the basicranial data suggest the following major phyletic events (Figures 7 and 8) within the order: (1) origin of the primates from a group of scandentians not unlike tupaiiforms or primitive erinaceomorph Insectivora, (2) the evolution of the Plesiadapiformes and Lemuriformes from this common primate stock, (3) the derivation of the tarsiiform primates from Paleocene lemuriforms, (4) the derivation of the Cheirogaleidae from a lemurid and subsequent origin of the lorisids from a cheirogaleid, (5) the derivation of the stem anthropoids from a tarsiiform stock. Under the appropriate higher categories we will examine these hypothesized events in detail (see also Szalay and Katz, 1973; Szalay, 1975f; Cartmill, 1975; Archibald, 1977).

Only a few characters in the basicranial region of primate skulls may be called truly primate; these are some of the diagnostic innovations of the primate ancestor in contrast to its own ancestry. In order to identify precisely this ancestry, the group of eutherians which gave rise to the primates, without the usual phraseology of referring to primitive eutherians, we must seek the taxon that shares derived eutherian characters with the primate morphotype. To determine which features are primitive or derived for the early Eutheria we also need to reconstruct, however, a eutherian morphotype for the basicranium (see Szalay, 1975f; Archibald, 1977).

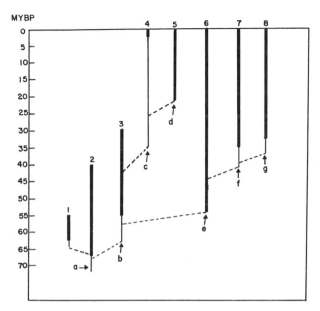

Figure 7. Phylogeny of the primates as seen in this book. The three suborders, the Plesiadapiformes (1, 2), Strepsirhini (3, 4, 5), and Haplorhini (6, 7, 8), respectively, include the following taxa: Plesiadapoidea (1), Paromomyoidea (2), Adapiformes (3), Lemuroidea (4), Lorisoidea (5), Tarsiiformes (6), Platyrrhini (7), and Catarrhini (8). Heavy lines represent known ranges of taxa, thin lines represent the estimated range of taxa defined by the origin of diagnostic characters, and broken lines show both phyletic relationships within a temporal framework and origins from ancestries specified as members of certain taxa. The arrows denote the following anagenetic events according to this book and numerous other authors listed in the text: a, petrosal bulla, reduced or lost medial carotid artery, tarsal and elbow complex adapted for habitual arboreal existence (helical movements between calcaneum and astragalus, etc.); b, bulla enclosed, ringlike ectotympanic (probably present in the ancestry of primates at "a"), postorbital bar, advanced tarsal structure with calcaneocuboid "pivot" joint and lost or very reduced peroneal process, greatly modified entocuneiform–metatarsal I joint for powerful grasping, and iliac structure with dorsolateral surface expanded; c, origin of tooth comb; d, enlargement of the ascending pharyngeal artery to become the major arterial blood transport to the circle of Willis and the subsequent reduction in size, and sometimes loss, of the promontory and stapedial arteries; e, olfactory fossa above narrowest point of interorbital septum, ossification of the annulus membrane and the subsequent formation of a tubular ectotympanic in later lineages, emphasis of the promontory artery as the major blood transport to the circle of Willis, and the transportation of a glandular moist rhinarium into a hairy nose; f, narrow tympanic at the edge of the bulla (possibly the ancestral condition present at e), great expansion of

Primitive representatives of most eutherian orders unfortunately are not well known. The complex morphological patterns offered by a smattering of skulls and petrosal bones from the early Tertiary, however, have long held the attention of students of mammalian systematics (see, for example, Kampen, 1905; Gregory, 1910, 1920; Klaauw, 1931). In a reconstruction of the hypothesized primitive eutherian ear region (Figure 9, from Szalay, 1975f) the general conformation of the bony morphology and some of the probable paths of arterial and venous circulation can be reasonably inferred (for an explanation of the abbreviations used in the figure, see Table III). Note that neither the bulla nor the shape and position of the ectotympanic are shown on this pictorial essay. Although the usual assumption is that a cartilaginous precursor of the ossified bullae of later taxa was the condition in the eutherian morphotype, this is by no means adequately demonstrated. The bullae of some primitive metatherians and various Insectivora have contributions from the basisphenoid and alisphenoid, the latter also from the petrosal, and it is very likely that a number of very ancient Cretaceous therians also had bony bullae.

Morphologists studying early eutherian or extant basicranial remains (McDowell, 1958; Van Valen, 1966; McKenna, 1966; MacIntyre, 1972; Szalay, 1972a; Bugge, 1974; etc.) generally agree with Matthew's (1909) thesis that the primitive eutherian internal carotid was originally divided into (a) a medial internal carotid artery coursing its way between the petrosal and the basioccipital and basisphenoid bones and (b) a lateral branch, the lateral internal carotid artery, which is divided into the large stapedial and the small promontory branch (MacIntyre, 1972). The evidence for the presence of this probably primitive eutherian, and perhaps also therian, character is from living as well as fossil Eutheria.

In terms of basicranial morphology and circulation, the morphotype of the Eutheria may perhaps be characterized as resembling either the "unguiculate" or "ferungulate" petrosals described by MacIntyre (1972) with the circulatory patterns shown by Butler (1956), McKenna (1963), Van Valen (1966), and Szalay

the promontory artery and loss of adult stapedial artery, "pneumatized" condition of ventral wall of bulla, petromastoid, and squamosal, and platyrrhine nose condition; g, catarrhine nose condition. [By A. Cleary.]

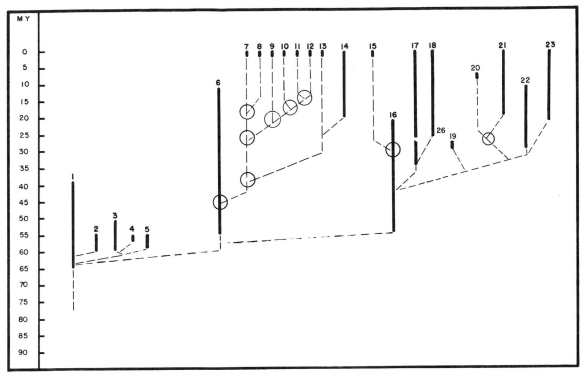

Figure 8. A hypothesis of phylogenetic relationships of the primates on the family level. Solid heavy lines represent known ranges and broken lines depict recency of relationships: 1, Paromomyidae; 2, Picrodontidae; 3, Plesiadapidae; 4, Carpolestidae; 5, Saxonellidae; 6, Adapidae; 7, Lemuridae; 8, Megaladapidae; 9, Archaeolemuridae; 10, Palaeopropithecidae; 11, Daubentoniidae; 12, Indriidae; 13, Cheirogaleidae; 14, Lorisidae; 15, Tarsiidae; 16, Omomyidae; 17, Cebidae; 18, Atelidae; 19, Parapithecidae; 20, Oreopithecidae; 21, Cercopithecidae; 22, Pliopithecidae; 23, Hominidae. Circles represent uncertainty as to even an approximate time of divergence. [By A. Cleary.]

(1969a). Most of the taxa derived from this group retain the carotid circulation of their morphotypes, a pattern here considered primitive for the Eutheria. The ancestral miacoid carnivorans have an essentially similar, primitive eutherian basicranial circulatory pattern (G. T. MacIntyre and R. H. Tedford, personal communication), although most of the "neocarnivorans" lose either the promontory or stapedial arteries while retaining the medial internal carotid.

The medial internal carotid artery has been retained in the lagomorphs (Bugge, 1967, 1974) and in the majority of hystricomorph rodents (Bugge, 1971, 1974) and can be assumed to have been present in primitive Rodentia (Wood, 1962; Guthrie, 1963; Wahlert, 1973).

With the exception of the basisphenoid, alisphenoid, and petrosal, which are utilized in the bulla construction of various insectivorans, the ectotym-panic and entotympanic are the most common components for bulla formation among eutherians. The ectotympanic is a membrane bone that ossifies from a single element and is probably a derivative of the reptilian angular bone. In contrast, the entotympanic is usually a cartilage bone, probably a neomorph among mammals. Depending on the location of the ossification, the entotympanic can be either rostral or caudal (Klaauw, 1929). Although it is often assumed that the primitive bulla cover in the eutherian morphotype was cartilaginous, we know of no conclusive evidence or detailed discussion that supports this conclusion.

We may now proceed to those known eutherians that may share derived characters with Szalay's (1975f) and Archibald's (1977) concept of the primitive primate basicranial morphology. As expected, difficulties

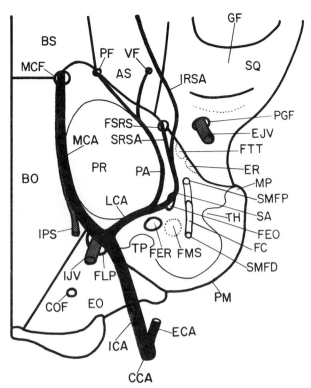

Figure 9. Schematized reconstruction of the basicranium and the associated circulatory patterns in the eutherian morphotype. For abbreviations, see Table III. [From Szalay (1975f).]

arise on all categorical levels because of uncertainty as to whether some of these character states are homologous or convergent and, if they are homologous, what their morphocline polarities are. The following list of character states, admittedly too short, may be considered primitive for the primates. However, some of these may also be features of other eutherian groups related to the primates to an unknown degree: (1) petrosal bulla; (2) partly extrabullar or intrabullar ectotympanic; (3) medial internal carotid artery lost in the ontogenetic stage beginning with cranial ossification (ontogenetic conditions prior to ossification are clearly not inferrable in fossil); (4) a rounded promontorium; (5) bony canal for the entire intrabullar carotid circulation; (6) fenestra rotunda ventrally "shielded" by the internal carotid canal.

There are not many known groups that can be meaningfully compared with this inferred ancestral primate morphology. Many students have scrutinized the tupaiid ear region for phylogenetic information. Most recently, Van Valen (1965) and McKenna (1966) have extensively commented on the tupaiid ear region and have concluded that no shared–derived characters are likely to be uniquely possessed by tupaiids and primates alone. In examining the basicranial morphology, particularly of *Ptilocercus*, we consider only the homology of the bulla, the position of the ectotympanic, and the promontory canals as noteworthy. The significance of the bulla-enclosed ectotympanic shared by tupaiids and lemuriforms is probably primitive. The differences in the construction of the bulla in tupaiids and primates may, however, not be significant. MacDowell (1958) has suggested that the primate bulla may in fact be the entotympanic of tupaiids ontogenetically fused to the petrosals. Developmental evidence for this, however, has not been published.

As noted by numerous students, the bony canal housing the promontory artery is present in diverse mammalian groups. There is a clearly recognizable distinction between the relative size of the basicranial arterial pathways in the Tupaiidae and that in known Plesiadapiformes and Lemuriformes. In *Ptilocercus* and various species of *Tupaiia*, the tube for the promontory artery is relatively very large and, as Bugge (1972) reports, the brain is largely supplied by the internal carotid, assisted by the vertebral artery. Judged by the complex qualitative information that may be gleaned from the whole basicranium, however, it appears likely that the enlargement of the tupaiid and tarsiiform promontory artery is not a homologous condition but an independently acquired one. Bony arterial canals within the bulla, however, may be shared and derived features between Scandentia (see below) and primates. In conclusion, the basicranial characters listed remain ambiguous as to Primates–Scandentia affinities. Nevertheless, postcranial evidence (Szalay, 1977c) strongly suggests that Gregory's (1910) concept of the Archonta, revived by McKenna (1975), a cohort which includes the orders Scandentia [i.e., the Tupaiidae and possibly the Mixodectidae (see Szalay. 1977c)], Primates, Dermoptera, and possibly the Chiroptera is valid.

Primitive primates share some significant similarities with the erinaceomorph morphotype. A large petrosal component is characteristic of most known erinaceomorph bullae, whether fossil or extant; in

TABLE III
Abbreviations Used on Figures for Anatomical Terms Employed for the Basicranium

ACF	anterior carotid foramen	IPSF	inferior petrous sinus foramen
AM	annulus membrane	IRSA	inferior ramus of stapedial artery
APA	ascending pharyngeal artery	JS	jugular spine
AS	alisphenoid	LCA	lateral carotid artery
B	bulla	LCAC	lateral carotid arterial canal
BO	basioccipital	MCA	medial carotid artery
BS	basisphenoid	MCAC	medial carotid artery canal
CCA	common carotid artery	MCF	medial carotid foramen
CF	carotid foramen	MP	mastoid process
CNJ	canal for nerve of Jacobson	OA	ophthalmic artery
COF	condyloid foramen	OAM	ossified annulus membrane
ECA	external carotid artery	P	petrosal
EF	eustachian foramen	PA	promontory artery
EJV	external jugular vein	PC	promontory canal
ENJ	exit for nerve of Jacobson	PF	promontory foramen (=foramen lacerum medium)
ENT	entotympanic	PGF	postglenoid foramen
EO	exoccipital	PGP	postglenoid process
ER	epitympanic recess	PM	petromastoid
ET	ectotympanic	PR	promontorium of petrosal
FC	facial canal	RI	ramus inferior
FEO	fenestra ovale	RS	ramus superior
FER	fenestra rotunda	SA	stapedial artery
FLA	foramen lacerum anterior	SBP	superior border of the petrosal
FLP	foramen lacerum posterior	SC	stapedial canal
FM	foramen magnum	SE	septum
FMS	fossa muscularis stapedius	SF	styloid fossa
FNJ	foramen for nerve of Jacobson	SMF	stylomastoid foramen
FOO	foramen ovale	SMFD	stylomastoid foramen definitivum
FSRS	foramen for superior ramus of stapedial artery	SMFP	stylomastoid foramen primitivum
FTT	fossa tensor tympani	SOAM	support for ossified annulus membrane
GF	glenoid fossa	SQ	squamosal
HS	hypotympanic sinus	SRSA	superior ramus of stapedial artery
ICA	internal carotid artery	TH	attachment for hyoid arch (tympanohyal)
IJV	internal jugular vein	TP	tympanic process
IPS	inferior petrous sinus	VF	vidian foramen

some cases the petrosal contributes up to half the entire structure (e.g., Rich and Rich, 1971). Like primates, both living and fossil erinaceids tend to be characterized by a roundly shaped promontorium. By itself, this is not a convincing special similarity as it has converged in this fashion in many groups of mammals.

We believe that the bone-enclosed arteries of the middle ear were primitive in erinaceids and probably in the erinaceomorphs, although, admittedly, the known fossils (Gawne, 1968; Rich and Rich, 1971) that may be used to test this hypothesis are not older than the Oligocene. No ear regions are known in the broadly defined group of the Adapisoricidae (Van Valen, 1967), a species of which was the likely ancestor of the Erinaceidae. The medial internal carotid artery is

not known in erinaceomorphs. The erinaceids that have their intrabullar carotid circulation enclosed in bony tubes are the Oligocene *Proterix* and the Miocene *Brachyerix* [reported by Gawne (1968) and Rich and Rich (1971), respectively] and the living genus *Paraechinus* [redescribed by Rich and Rich (1971)]. In these forms the fenestra rotunda is shielded by the carotid canal, in a fashion virtually identical to that of *Phenacolemur* and adapids. It is thus likely that primates and other archotans originated from a eutherian we now dub, *faute de mieux*, an adapisoricid insectivoran, with a basicranium not very different from that of the erinaceomorph morphotype.

It is the tarsus, and within the tarsus the calaneum and astragalus, which gives us a most useful area on the postcranium for evaluating both phylogenetic and adaptational hypotheses. The reason for this is the frequent preservation and consequent relative abundance of these elements.

Broadly significant comparisons are possible because a large number of taxa are represented by these remains. As the pes is used almost exclusively for locomotion and body support, substrate preferences, posturing, and range of movements of the articulating parts can be assessed in addition to phyletically significant information. Comparisons of plesiadapiform tarsal remains to those of representative eutherians on the one hand, and primitive lemuriform primates on the other, show that the morphology of representative plesiadapiform tarsals indicates derived similarity to tupaiids, dermopterans, and the lemuriforms but not to other eutherians.

It should suffice to say here that the diagnostic postcranial characters of *Plesiadapis* spp., and of several other known postcranial fragments belonging to hitherto dentally unidentified plesiadapiforms, suggest that these features were derived characters as far as the nonarchontan eutherian ancestry of primates is concerned.

The major outlines of primate interrelationships are summarized in two figures. Figure 7 shows the grouping of the three suborders and attempts to show the origins of those diagnostic characters by which the taxa shown are defined. Figure 8, on the other hand, while showing the same genealogical relationships, depicts the number of recognized families, their known stratigraphic range, and their approximate time of origin from the source family.

The major outlines of primate phylogeny we advocate here are not very different from the views advocated in such early and diversely based studies as those of Pocock (1918), Gregory (1920), J. P. Hill (1919), Smith (1919), Jones (1929), and Hill (1953, 1955). Our views are in agreement with most recent reviews and researchers (Goodman, 1975; Luckett, 1975, 1976; Cartmill, 1975; Hoffstetter, 1974a,b; Szalay, 1973, 1975f; Szalay and Katz, 1973). Our overview of primate phylogeny holds that an archaic primate, which would be identified as a plesiadapiform, gave rise to or shared a common ancestor with the adapiform strepsirhines, that the evolution of the Tarsiiformes has taken place from some stock of adapiform strepsirhines, and that the common ancestor of anthropoids evolved from some as yet unknown or unrecognized group of tarsiiforms.

A general disregard for developmental and nonden-

tal osteological characters has recently led to the outright rejection of highly significant neontological and fossil evidence in favor of sometimes relatively insignificant fossil data. The primate phylogeny outlined in Figures 7 and 8 has recently been rejected by Gingerich (1973a,b, 1974, 1975,a,b, 1976a), based on characters found or allegedly found in the fossil samples described or restudied by him. Gingerich's hypothesis for the phylogeny of the primates incorporates the following two major differences from the syntheses of several students of living and fossil primates. From a microsyopid stock (forms we do not consider primates at all), he would derive first the plesiadapiforms and their descendants the tarsiiforms and second the lemuriforms and their direct descendants the anthropoids. A brief reexamination of this alternate view of primate phylogeny is both necessary and instructive (see also Szalay, 1977a).

The archaic primate genus *Plesiadapis* has been known for over a century, but knowledge of the majority of the Paleocene primate radiation began with the field discoveries and descriptions of Matthew, Gidley, and Simpson in North America during the 1920s and 1930s and, more recently, through the work of D. E. Russell in Europe during the 1950s and 1960s. The hypothesis that the archaic primates gave rise directly to the Tarsiiformes was entrenched early in the paleontological literature. Simpson (1937), in his classic study of a Paleocene fauna, referred to the Eocene non-lemuriforms as "acknowledged tarsioids" and considered the majority of Paleocene primates as having tarsioid ties. In his 1940 and 1945 concept of the Anaptomorphidae he included the Paromomyinae. McKenna (1967) similarly grouped the paromomyids with the omomyids and, as recently as 1967, Russell, Louis, and Savage have espoused Simpson's 1940 and 1945 definition of the Anaptomorphidae. All of these authors, therefore, advocated a non-lemuriform origin of the Eocene tarsiiforms from some archaic primates. The view of Gingerich (1975a) that "a review of the evidence now available indicates that the affinities of *Plesiadapis* and its relatives are with early tarsier-like primates, and not with archaic lemurs" (p. 11) is therefore not a new hypothesis. Gingerich (1973a), to express this supposed relationship between the archaic primates and the Tarsiiformes, erected the suborder Plesitarsioidea and then renamed the same concept Plesitarsiiformes (Gingerich, 1975b).

The hypothesis that the Anthropoidea, the platyrrhines in particular, are derived from archaic lemuriforms is again not a novel one. It has been a tradition among paleontologists, starting with the suggestion of Leidy in 1873, continued by arguments in its favor by Wortman in 1903, and further elaborated upon by Gregory in 1920. Gingerich's (1973b) revival of this hypothesis, 50 years after Gregory's arguments, is unfortunate, particularly as he had formally proposed the suborder Anthrolemuroidea, later renamed Simiolemuriformes (Gingerich, 1975b), to express this alleged relationship.

Gingerich based his views on an analysis of dentitions and basicrania, as we have. From dental evidence (especially the incisors), he concluded that, because fossil tarsiiforms have enlarged incisors (not mentioning, however, those which do not, excepting perhaps *Teilhardina*, which, according to him, may be an adapid), the Tarsiiformes are really descendants of the Plesiadapiformes. It is highly unlikely that incisor enlargement was a unique event restricted to an alleged plesiadapiform–tarsiiform common ancestor. Examples are too numerous to even begin to list where incisor hypertrophy was independent. We believe that this assessment of the incisors in plesiadapiforms and tarsiiforms is superficial and incorrect. Gingerich (1974) states that: "Of fundamental importance is the dichotomy in incisor morphology.... Plesiadapiformes and Tarsiiformes both have enlarged, pointed procumbent incisors, whereas the earliest Lemuriformes have anthropoid-like incisors which are small, vertical, and spatulate" (p. 287). Anyone familiar with the incisors of *Ourayia* (Figure 118, p. 237), an undoubted tarsiiform, or knowing the scarcity of species with anterior dentitions must judge this view accordingly. Modest incisor enlargement is of very low phylogenetic valency in light of its ubiquitous nature in the Mammalia.

Knowledge of the incisor morphology of early Tertiary primates is a matter of record in museums and in the literature (see figures in this book). Only a small proportion of known taxa have their incisors preserved and all types of specializations occur within the tarsiiforms (see numerous figures below: *Trogolemur, Tetonius, Ekgmowechashala*, etc.) and adapids (see below: *Caenopithecus, Adapis*). The statement, therefore, that "virtually all of the early genera of primates can be identified as tarsioid or lemuroid on the basis of their anterior dentition alone" (Gingerich, 1974, p. 290) is difficult to accept.

Gingerich also failed to discuss the large number of derived characters shared between the morphotype of tarsiiforms and all known Eocene adapids. Thus, the cuboid pivot, the highly diagnostic entocuneiform-metatarsal I joint adapted for powerful grasping, the characteristically modified calcaneum, astragalus, and the ilium, to mention only a few features of the known postcranials, are characteristics which have not been adequately appreciated by him. The presence of a postorbital bar in both tarsiiforms and Eocene adapiforms, but the absence of this bar in the plesiadapiform *Palaechthon, Plesiadapis,* and microsyopids, whether or not the latter is the sister group of the primates, apparently did not influence the postulated derivation of the tarsiiforms from archaic primates.

Gingerich's second point, derivation of the anthropoids from lemurs, seems to rest on evidence he published (1973b) concerning the nature of the ectotympanic in the anthropoid *Apidium*. The assessment of this important fossil, however, lacks proper ontogenetic perspective. This developmental information can be gleaned only from samples of living primates, as shown by Hershkovitz (1974b) through his analysis of this bone in *Tarsius*. He demonstrated that the unfused anterior crus of the ectotympanic is not restricted to lemuriforms or *Apidium*, but can be found among immature *Tarsius* and even among some mature individual cebids (Figure 10). Thus, evidence is lacking from the basicranium of *Apidium* to suggest the validity of Anthrolemuroidea (see also Hoffstetter, 1974a; Cartmill 1975; Szalay, 1975f). In reaching his conclusion, Gingerich (1974, pp. 291–292) also discussed the evidence of the fetal membranes and placenta, without, however, attempting to analyze the recent strides made by the work of Luckett (1974a, 1974b). The absence of a wet glandular rhinarium in *Tarsius* and anthropoids, one of the most unique features of the haplorhines, as was carefully documented by Pocock (1918) and subsequently utilized by Hill (1953, 1955), was not considered. In this instance, a shared derived condition present without exception in all anthropoids and *Tarsius* and absent (inasmuch as having the antecedent condition, the naked rhinarium) in all strepsirhines was not even mentioned.

Thus, grave objections can be raised against Gingerich's (1974) phylogenetic hypothesis. It reflects a philosophy which would uphold the proposition that phylogeny can be understood from the fossils alone. It also shows that Gingerich practices a methodology which places greater weight on stratifi-

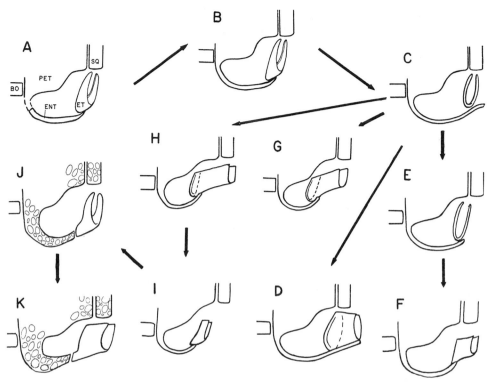

Figure 10. Ectotympanic evolution in primates. In this schema we attempt to trace derivation of various ectotympanic conditions (other aspects of basicranium are set aside for the sake of clarity) from inferred antecedent states. Note that, in this overview, primates have evolved a bony "tube" at least three times independently from a condition that can be termed primitive lemuroid. As the mechanism for the construction of this tube is extremely simple, involving only ossification of the annulus membrane, parallel evolutions are postulated for this derived condition in some plesiadapiforms, tarsiiforms, and lorisiforms. The external bony tube in the catarrhines does not involve ossification of the annulus membrane in the same manner as in three previous groups. A, hypothetical ancestor; B, intermediate between eutherian ancestor and primate morphotype; C, primate morphotype, also probably primitive condition in the Strepsirhini; D, modified lemuriform condition (e.g., *Megaladapis*) where the petrosal elongates laterally and the annulus membrane of the ectotympanic also ossifies inside the laterally expanded petrosal; E, lorisid morphotype (e.g., *Galago*), slightly more advanced than that of cheirogaleids; F, derived lorisiform condition (e.g., *Nycticebus*); G, condition shown by *Plesiadapis* (although morphology of the ectotympanic is extremely similar to that of *Rooneyia*, other aspects of basicranium strongly suggest that ectotympanic conformations are convergent); H, condition shown by *Rooneyia*, possibly representative of tarsiiform morphotype; I, advanced(?) tarsiiform condition shown by *Necrolemur*; J, platyrrhine morphotype; K, condition known among living cercopithecoids and hominoids, possibly representing catarrhine morphotype (this form of ectotympanic tube may have evolved independently from a catarrhine ancestor with a condition similar to that shown in J). For abbreviations, see Table III. See also Archibald (1977) and MacPhee (1977). [From Szalay (1975f).]

cation of fossils than on their morphology. His hypothesis ignores numerous character clines found in the fossil record and inexplicably fails to account for several unique and innovative shared and derived characters found in both the Strepsirhini and Tarsiiformes, on the one hand, and the Tarsiiformes and the Anthropoidea, on the other, by indicating an independent evolution of these features (see Szalay,

1975f,g). If, as we argue, the microsyopids are not considered primates, the derivation of the tarsiiforms from plesiadapiforms runs into several obstacles. Attempting to derive the anthropoids from strepsirhines further necessitates a large number of parallel developments of characters shared by *Tarsius* and anthropoids. On the other hand, if the microsyopids are admitted as archaic primates and if Gingerich's phylogenetic hypothesis for the evolution of the order is correct, then we have convergent and parallel evolution rampant among the primates to a degree not seen elsewhere among the vertebrates. Given the phylogeny advocated by Gingerich, the following evolutionary events occurred independently: The petrosal bulla (see Figure 9) evolved three times or microsyopids have reevolved a cartilaginous bulla; tubes for the carotid circulation evolved three times or were lost by the microsyopids; the medial internal carotid artery was lost twice, or it was reevolved by the microsyopids; the grasping big toe, characterized by the uniquely sculptured entocuneiform–metatarsal I joint, present in all known strepsirhines and haplorhines, evolved twice, or was at least partially lost in the known plesiadapiforms; a unique tarsal morphology, including a characteristic cuboid–calcaneum pivot arrangement, evolved twice; the postorbital bar evolved twice, or the archaic primates have lost this feature; the loss of a wet rhinarium occurred twice, or the strepsirhines have reevolved this ancestral therian structure from a primate ancestry which lacked it; the six uniquely shared fetal membrane and placental characters of the haplorhines evolved twice separately. It is argued by Szalay (1977a) that the occurrence of these events was highly unlikely and the phylogeny of higher taxa advocated throughout this book is suggested to be the presently still unfalsified hypothesis of genealogy and major adaptive events among the primates.

We have elsewhere (Szalay, 1975g, 1976, 1977c), and under Microchoerinae (p. 259), advanced functional arguments, which do not contradict developmental criteria (Osborn, 1973), why incisor loss usually takes place from back to front, and why premolars, opposite to this pattern, become phyletically eliminated from front to back. Ideally such a functional and developmental approach has close relevance to the determination of homologies.

Recently a large number of papers have dealt with the meaning of tooth homologies (primarily anterior teeth) among primates in particular. A number of papers, particularly Schwartz (1974, 1975) and Schwartz and Krishtalka (1977), have advocated not only a unique interpretation of primate tooth homologies but arguments based on these in support of Gingerich's "plesitarsioid"–"anthrolemuroid" model of primate phylogeny.

In essence, as we understand it, Schwartz's (1975)

view rests on the assumption that the sequence of eruption of cheek teeth is fixed and therefore the sequence of eruption in a specimen tells one the homology of these teeth, irrespective of (a) known mechanisms of tooth bud formation or repression (fide Osborn, 1973), (b) occlusal relationships to the teeth above or below, (c) relative size relationship of the antemolar cheek teeth to one another, and (d) the similarity of these relative size relationships to other species. In addition to his criteria based on replacement sequence, Schwartz (1975) accepted the tooth homologies suggested by McKenna (1975) for various groups of the Mammalia based on a mammalian morphotype with five premolars. In other words, Schwartz employed both "replacement" as well as "morphology" criteria for establishing his unique homologies. In reference to this review, it is important to note McKenna's (1975) belief that: "All tokotheres [this holophyletic group consisting of the Ferae, Insectivora, Archonta, and Ungulata] share or further modify a postcanine dental formula consisting of dP^4_1 P^2_2 P^3_3 P^4_4 dP^5_5 M^1_1 M^2_2. DP^5_5 is the tooth usually called M^1_1; the last premolar is primitively a nonmolariform P^4_4, the same tooth as the penultimate premolar in ernotheres. These homologies are fundamental" (p. 37). In addition to other arguments which pertain to the issue of ancestral eutherian tooth homologies, Szalay (1977c) has critized in detail why, in light of ontogenetic as well as paleontological data, the hypothesis of independent reduction and loss of one tooth (both deciduous and permanent) in various supraordinal groups of eutherians is a less parsimonious hypothesis than the actual loss (or predisposition for loss) of the same tooth in the common eutherian ancestor. Let us now briefly examine Schwartz's arguments for primate tooth homologies.

Schwartz (1978) has taken the dental formula of *Gypsonictops* (five premolars and three molars), using McKenna's interpretation of $P \cdot d^{1;2;3;4;5}_{1;2;3;4;5} M^{1;2;3}_{1;2;3}$, and from this base argued for the "plesitarsiod" and "anthrolemuroid" hypothesis. As pointed out and succinctly summarized by Cartmill and Kay (1978), this view by Schwartz rests on a number of assumptions and arguments:

> (1) The antepenultimate premolar in *Tarsius*, omomyids, and plesiadapoids is smaller than its neighbours, and is evidently in the process of being reduced. (2) In *Tarsius*, and perhaps in the omomyid *Absarokius*, this tooth is not replaced. By analogy with

Gypsonictops, it is interpreted as a dP3. (3) The antepenultimate premolar in "simiolemuriforms" *is* replaced; Schwartz thus regards it as homologous with the P2 of *Gypsonictops*. (4) In *Tarsius*, the second tooth in front of the supposed dP3 is also unreplaced; therefore, it is homologous with the dP1 of *Gypsonictops*. Adapids also retain this dP1, but it has been lost (like the dP3) in anthropoids and tooth-comb prosimians. (5) The most anterior tooth in *Tarsius'* maxilla, traditionally regarded as a canine, is by the foregoing analysis a P². This yields a premolar eruption sequence (P2→P5→P4) like that seen in anthropoids and strepsirhines, and provides further support for Schwartz' novel dental homologies. Similar reasoning applies to the lower teeth. (6) The anteriormost upper tooth of omomyids and plesiadapoids, traditionally regarded as an enlarged incisor, lies directly mesial to the newly-recognized dP¹; this fact and its large size prove it homologous with the canine of anthropoids and lemurs. On similar grounds, Schwartz identifies the enlarged lower front tooth of plesiadapoids and omomyids as a canine. *Tarsius* has lost this lower canine; its antemolar dental formula is thus C¹ dP⅟ P²/₅ dP³/₃ P⁴₋⅟₅.

If this account is sound, plesiadapoids and tarsioids share several synapomorphies, notably loss of all incisors and displacement of canines and premolars into the premaxilla. We reject Schwartz's account for the following reasons: 1. All the antemolar teeth of *Tarsius* are in fact permanent teeth with deciduous precursors, though the deciduous incisors and antepenultimate deciduous premolars are tiny and may be shed or resorbed before birth (Leche, 1896; Greiner, 1929). The sectioned *Tarsius bancanus* material which we examined, and on which we will report more fully elsewhere, clearly retained small deciduous precursors of the I¹; and P₂. Recognition of the adult tarsier's antepenultimate premolar as P2 implies that *Tarsius* has a typical primate premolar eruption sequence, and obviates comparisons with *Gypsonictops*. 2. Schwartz's dental homologies imply that "plesitarsioids" differ from other mammals in having a lower canine which occludes *behind* the upper one. We regard this as unlikely. 3. If Schwartz is right, the premaxillary teeth of *Tarsius* are premolars and canines. Schwartz apparently takes this to mean that the premaxillary–maxillary suture has shifted backward relative to the dental lamina of the upper jaw. But the upper dental lamina is not a unitary structure. Its formation is induced by neural-crest cells migrating into the frontonasal eminence (the ancient front end of the vertebrate head) and the maxillary process (derived from the first branchial arch), whose fusion to form a single "upper jaw" (and hence a single dental lamina) is developmentally and phylogenetically secondary. When this fusion fails to occur in fetal mammals, both sets of incisors develop anyway in the isolated premaxilla suspended from the nasal septum. This shows that the premaxillary part of the dental

lamina is induced by neural-crest cells which enter the frontonasal process before it fuses with the maxillary process. However, a tooth which develops in one bone may secondarily migrate into the other. In rodents, for instance, the upper incisor's root lies in the maxilla, and so it might be identified as a canine, as *Daubentonia's* upper incisor has been on similar grounds (Tattersall and Schwartz, 1974). But when premaxilla and maxilla fail to fuse in rodents (and presumably in *Daubentonia* too), the upper incisor root grows backward from its original premaxillary locus into the nasal septum, taking the only caudad pathway available (Reed and Snell, 1931). To claim, in the face of this, that the upper incisors of rodents are really canines could only mean that the lamina-inducing cells which migrate into the frontonasal processes of rodents are in some sense homologous with cells which migrate into the maxillary processes of other mammals. Whether or not we would still want to call the resulting teeth homologous is a matter of definition. Yet some such ambiguous and untestable assertion is the only sense we can place on Schwartz's claim that tarsiers lack upper incisors, since published studies of dental ontogeny in *Tarsius* appear to rule out the possibility that the premaxillary teeth of the adult form originally in the maxilla and migrate forward secondarily. We conclude that Schwartz's novel dental homologies are either empirically false or untestable, depending on how we interpret them. (pp. 208–209)

We concur with this refutation of Schwartz's view of tooth homologies.

It should be noted here that the content of the order Primates advocated in this book was recently disputed by Cartmill (1972, 1974b) and Martin (1972). These authors contend that the archaic primates should be excluded from the order. This view has been briefly examined by Szalay, Tattersall, and Decker (1975) and Szalay (1975c) and it is briefly reviewed here.

The arguments for delineation of the order Primates do not differ from those suggested to be part of a philosophical system that unites, e.g., all cetaceans or all bats. The rare, but crucial, postcranial evidence (Szalay and Decker, 1974; Szalay, Tattersall, and Decker, 1975) indicates that the common ancestors of all primates (the Plesiadapiformes included) had acquired adaptations related to habitual arboreal existence from a terrestrial ancestry and that this adaptational complex is the basis of all further elaborations in this milieu. One may argue then that all subsequent adaptations have been added to this broad complex. In fact, these characters of the postcranial anatomy of early primates, in addition to such "markers" of the cranium as a petrosal bulla, are the shared derived features delimiting the primates from their ancestors and contemporaries.

Cartmill (1972, 1974b) nevertheless advocates a new diagnosis of the order. He suggests (Cartmill, 1972, p. 121) that primates should be delineated at the precise point where, he believes, "the ancestral primate adaptation involved nocturnal, visually directed predation on insects in the terminal branches of the lower strata of tropical forests" arguing further that "a monophyletic and adaptively meaningful order Primates may be delimited by taking the petrosal bulla, complete postorbital bar and divergent hallux or pollex as ordinally diagnostic."

We have no quarrel with Cartmill's statement that some of the characteristic traits of living primates cannot be explained simply as adaptations to arboreal life. Features of any group are somewhat specific because of their unique transformation of specific inherited features for their own purposes. The only character, however, which is common to the skull of "real primates" (*sensu* Cartmill), the orbital ring and its loose relation to orbital convergence, is so pervasive in so many different mammals that it appears unlikely that its adaptive significance is anything but similar from group to group. No one would dispute that the adaptive modifications of the skulls of, e.g., *Varecia*, *Megaladapis*, *Palaeopropithecus*, *Ateles*, *Daubentonia*, *Pongo*, and *Hylobates* are quite divergent, and that furthermore these modifications have some vague patristic similarity to the last common ancestor of these taxa. This ancestor might very well have been a small, visual, nocturnal predator. All these and other primate taxa, however, bear the stamp of various modes of ancestral primate arboreal adaptations on the postcranium!

Excluding the arboreal Plesiadapiformes from the Primates (*fide* Cartmill, 1972, or Martin, 1972), however, when in fact we know that the arboreal adaptations of the order have been well established before the last common ancestor of the Strepsirhini and Haplorhini (*contra* Kay and Cartmill, 1977, see especially under *Palaechthon*), would seem to be a violation of a practice which takes into account the broadest adaptive significance of shared derived characters in a monophyletic grouping of lineages. Most primate radiations are known to have been primarily arboreal and show extremely varied feeding adaptations and catholic dietary preferences from one species to another. In addition, whole radiations are known to be

primarily phytophagous. The delineation of the order Primates in an arboreal milieu, but based on the alleged adaptations for visual–manual predation of the last common strepsirhine–haplorhine ancestor, as Cartmill (1972, 1974b) suggests, therefore seems unsound. Were this practice to be followed widely we would be left with the Paleocene primates (many probably having been visual predators) sharing a host of derived characters with other primates but either considered as a group in limbo or allocated to another, adaptively dissimilar, group of the Eutheria.

The causal explanation for the evolution of orbital convergence for the ancestor of strepsirhines and haplorhines runs into some difficulties when taxa other than those Cartmill (1974b) has examined are scrutinized. It is a fact that the most convergent orbits among the Malagasy strepsirhines, found on the large and long-snouted *Palaeopropithecus*, are not the result of an allometric factor. The even larger, closely related *Archaeoindris* does not show the former's extreme of orbital convergence. Admittedly, fossil taxa are difficult to assess in terms of their feeding adaptations, but that *Palaeopropithecus*, a large, forearm-dominated locomotor, was likely a facultative herbivore seems extremely likely from its entire feeding mechanism. At least in this instance, the predation hypothesis correlates negatively with increased orbital convergence.

It follows from Cartmill's views that evolution of the complete postorbital bar and the divergent hallux or pollex may be causally related to visually directed predation. It is not our aim to dispute Cartmill's hypothesis on the adaptations of the common ancestry of the Strepsirhini and Haplorhini. Cartmill's assertion, however, that the grasping feet and postorbital bar of living primates may be causally related is not supported by examination of other Mammalia. In *Vandeleuria oleracea*, the long-tailed climbing mouse, for example (Maser and Maser, 1973), toe opposability (that of V) is well developed but the animal apparently prefers nuts and cereals as its main diet staple. A host of arboreal marsupials, and very likely the marsupicarnivoran morphotype, although probably possessing grasping feet, did not develop a postorbital bar. On the other hand, tupaiids, herpestine viverrids, suids, camels, hippos, cervids, bovids, giraffids, numerous other ungulates, and even a sirenian, *Manatus senegalensis*, have complete postorbital bars but no grasping feet. As far as we know, a petrosal covered auditory bulla is unique to *all* primates, *in combination* with a lost medial carotid artery and a complex of derived postcranial characters attesting to grasping arboreal adaptations. This complex might have been derived from an arboreal insectivore or frugivore (the differences in feeding regimes are minor in these two categories), but a plesiadapiform with a full dentition [see Clemens' (1974) account of the lower jaw of *Purgatorius*] probably did not possess a postorbital bar. Research on feeding adaptations by Hladik *et al.* (1971) points out that frugivores, as well as folivores (the former more than the latter), take a large percentage of insects. Because insects contain protein and lipids, but leaves as a rule have only protein and carbohydrates and fruits have largely carbohydrates, insectivory is a necessary occupation for most arboreal mammals.

A host of plesiadapiform genera were probably insectivorous (e.g., *Navajovius, Palenochtha, Palaechthon, Saxonella*); we have no knowledge, however, as to the nature of their orbits or the opposability of the pollex or hallux. What are we to do in the future if we discover that, e.g., two sister lineages of the Paromomyidae differ from one another in that one possesses an incipient postorbital bar (as does *Palaechthon*) and perhaps some other shared characters with a strepsirhine–haplorhine morphotype? Are we then to include this ancestral twig and leave out,

along with other paromomyids, the picrodontids, plesiadapids, and carpolestids? This might suit the needs of primatologists and anthropologists whose primary concern is with man and primates alone (in increasing importance proportional to their manlike qualities) and who may regard all other considerations having to do with biological balance as secondary. But it is doubtful that systematic research on the Mammalia has much to gain from the exclusion of the Plesiadapiformes from the Primates. To retain this archaic group in the order, however, will undoubtedly continue to enrich the biological and historical perspective of primatologists about the living members of the Primates.

We note here that throughout the book we employ the vernacular term euprimates to indicate with a common name the monophyly, and therefore evolutionary unity, of the Strepsirhini and Haplorhini, in contrast to the Plesiadapiformes. We do not recognize a formal *nomen* as this would require the acceptance of an additional rank between order and suborder, a practice we shun. Our usage of euprimates is analogous to other such vernacular concepts with a precise phylogenetic meaning as the anthropoids and the eucatarrhines among the Haplorhini.

SUBORDER PLESIADAPIFORMES
Simons and Tattersall in Simons, 1972

(= or including: ?Suborder Plesiadapoidea: Romer, 1966. Microsyopoidea: Van Valen, 1969, in part. Infraorder Plesiadapiformes Simons and Tattersall in Simons, 1972. Paromomyiformes Szalay, 1973. Plesitarsioidea Gingerich, 1973a, in part. Plesitarsiiformes Gingerich, 1975b, in part. Plesiadapiformes: Gingerich, 1976a, in part.)

DISTRIBUTION
   Late Cretaceous to late Eocene (Maestrichtian to Uintan and Thanetian to Neustrian). North America and Europe.
INCLUDED TAXA
   Superfamilies Paromomyoidea and Plesiadapoidea.

Discussion

Taxa included in the Plesiadapiformes (Figure 11) are known from the latest Cretaceous to the late Eocene of western North America and from the middle Paleocene to early Eocene of western Europe. The report by Sudre (1975) that the Eocene African *Azibius* is a plesiadapiform primate is not considered likely. We have extensively compared the cast of *Azibius*, generously supplied by Dr. Sudre, to a range of representative taxa and found no similarities between the African taxon and other primates which may be thought of as homologously shared and derived.

Formal superfamilial grouping of the archaic primates, other than their allocation to either the Tarsiiformes or Lemuriformes, was indicated by Romer (1966) but first discussed by Van Valen (1969). He united the Microsyopidae, Plesiadapidae, Car-

polestidae, Paromomyidae, and Picrodontidae in the Microsyopoidea and grouped the superfamily in the "Prosimii." Simons (1972) has later referred to the Paromomyidae, Picrodontidae, Plesiadapidae, and Carpolestidae as "infraorder Plesiadapiformes—Simons and Tattersall" in the summary classification of his book. No paper by Simons, or by Simons and Tattersall, was ever published in which this taxon was either defined or diagnosed. Shortly afterward Szalay (1973) published a diagnosis and a discussion of a higher taxon then called suborder Paromomyiformes which contained the same four families. The name Plesiadapiformes has priority over Paromomyiformes, and although rules of the International Code of Zoological Nomenclature do not require it, we follow the overall spirit of the rules in using Plesiadapiformes.

As noted above in the discussion of the order, Gingerich (1974) used the infraorder Plesiadapiformes as part of the suborder he named the Plesitarsoidea, and later Plesitarsiiformes. The concept used by Gingerich under the name Plesiadapiformes is, however, identical to that of Van Valen's (1969) Microsyopoidea, and the microsyopids are represented as the ancestral primate group. In fact, the Microsyopidae itself is shown to give rise to the Tarsiiformes in Gingerich's (1974) phylogenetic scheme.

The families Paromomyidae, Picrodontidae, Plesiadapidae, Saxonellidae, and Carpolestidae (Figure 8) make up the Plesiadapiformes (Paromomyiformes) as

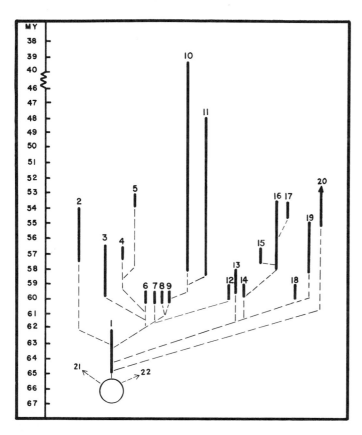

Figure 11. Known stratigraphic range (solid lines) and suggested phylogenetic relationships (broken lines) of taxa of the Plesiadapiformes. 1, *Purgatorius*; 2, *Navajovius* and *Berruvius*; 3, *Picrodus* and *Zanycteris*; 4, *Micromomys*; 5, *Tinimomys*; 6, *Palenochtha*; 7, *Palaechthon*; 8, *Paromomys maturus*; 9, *Paromomys depressidens*; 10, *Ignacius*; 11, *Phenacolemur*; 12, *Plesiolestes*; 13, *Saxonella*; 14, *Pronothodectes*; 15, *Chiromyoides*; 16, *Plesiadapis* 17 *Platychoerops*; 18, *Elphidotarsius*; 19, *Carpodaptes* (including *Carpolestes*); 20, segment of stratigraphic range of Adapidae; 21, unknown lineage to Scandentia; 22, unknown lineage to Dermoptera. [By A. Cleary.]

defined by Szalay (1973). The first are grouped here in the superfamily Paromomyoidea and the latter two in the superfamily Plesiadapoidea.

We will briefly review here the important basicranial evidence for this suborder. Basicrania for taxa of the Plesiadapiformes are very few; only two genera, *Phenacolemur* and *Plesiadapis*, are known. *Plesiadapis* has received detailed treatment by D. E. Russell (1964), Saban (1963), Szalay (1975f) and Gingerich (1976a). A new specimen of *Plesiadapis tricuspidens* (Gingerich, 1976a) clarifies previously unknown aspects of the genus. *Phenacolemur* has also been described (Szalay, 1972a) and has been reviewed by Cartmill (1975) and Szalay (1975f, 1976).

A review of the evidence (Figure 12) from *Phenacolemur* and *Plesiadapis* by Szalay (1976) shows that the entry of the carotid into the bulla was posterior and the promontory artery was relatively insignificant as, apparently, in all primitive Eutheria. A bony canal was probably present, at least for the portion of the

internal carotid inside the bulla prior to the branching off of the stapedial. In *Phenacolemur* the canal appears to be continuous, but in *Plesiadapis tricuspidens* it runs only a short distance. The fenestra rotunda appears to be obstructed in *Phenacolemur* when viewed ventrally. The ventrally shielded fenestra rotunda is a conspicuous feature not only of *Phenacolemur* but also of strepsirhines, and it may be that this was also a diagnostic character of the primate morphotype. There is no appreciable petromastoid enlargement in either *Plesiadapis* or *Phenacolemur*, and in both genera the ectotympanic is partly extrabullar, although, significantly, to different degrees. This bone, although not simply ringlike in either genus, suggests a probably ringlike ancestral condition. In both genera the auditory tube is formed by the ectotympanic and probably the ossified annulus membrane.

How can the differences in the conformation of the ectotympanics be explained in these two plesiadapiforms, and which of these conditions is most likely to be primitive? As noted, the middle ear morphology of the two genera differ inasmuch as *Plesiadapis* has a large number of septae and in general a more inflated bulla. *Phenacolemur*, on the other hand, has only a longitudinal septum which houses the lateral carotid artery and its craniad continuation, the promontory artery. The great inflation of the bulla in *Plesiadapis* may supply the clue to the developmental events

which led to the condition of the ectotympanic displayed by the genus. We may postulate an ancestral condition in which the ectotympanic was ringlike and intrabullar (as in tupaiids or Lemuriformes) and view the development in *Plesiadapis* as the result of the lateral displacement of the petrosal during the general hypertrophy of the bulla itself. As in many other mammalian lineages, selection for

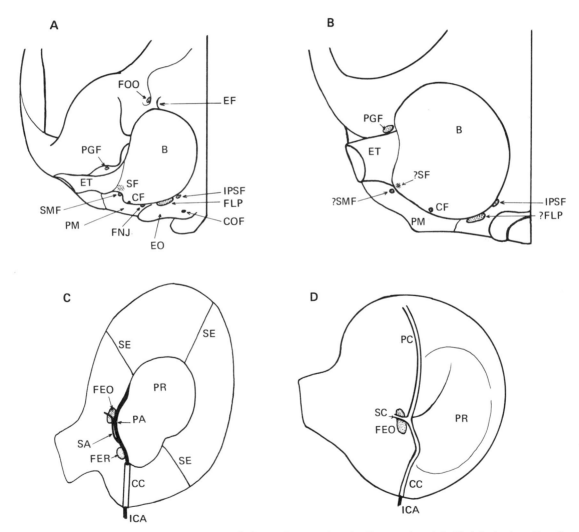

Figure 12. Simplified schema of the basicranial morphology in known Plesiadapiformes. A and C, *Plesiadapis tricuspidens* (late Paleocene); B and D, *Phenacolemur jepseni* (early Eocene). Above, basicranium intact; below, the bulla and ectotympanic removed to show carotid circulation. *Plesiadapsis* probably had a complete promontory canal. For abbreviations, see Table III. [From Szalay (1975f).]

increase in auditory sensitivity would have been accomplished by an increase in middle ear cavity volume. An extension of the middle ear cavity laterally, below the ear drum, would surround the medial end of the auditory meatus by the tympanic cavity and thus make a large portion of the ectotympanic (true ectotympanic plus the ossified annulus membrane) intrabullar. Such a mechanism is in fact known in developing lemuriforms and it is shown schematically by Cartmill (1975).

Phenacolemur, unlike *Plesiadapis,* apparently has only a tiny portion of its ectotympanic within the tympanic cavity, and this is largely the crista tympani supporting the tympanic membrane. This condition, as that of *Plesiadapis,* could be even more derived from a ringlike condition, or may just possibly be the primitive primate condition. The possibility is very strong, however, that the extrabullar condition of *Phenacolemur* had been derived along pathways *analogous* to those of *Tarsius* from an ancestor with an ectotympanic enclosed by the middle ear cavity.

Characters which may be decipherable in terms of the group's adaptations come from the postcranial morphology. The single, most important, and earliest broad adaptation of the primates, which served as background for all subsequent radiation, appears to have been related to a change from a terrestrial to arboreal substrate preference (Szalay and Decker, 1974). This is particularly significant when we realize that, among the known eutherian mammals of the Paleocene, the primates were among the first to colonize an arboreal milieu. It is more than likely that the arboreal environment was the habitat of the first major archontan radiation while the terrestrial arctocyonians (=condylarths in part) were the first eutherians in the large-scale successful exploitation of the terrestrial herbivorous opportunities. The small herbivorous arctocyonians were replaced by rodents while some evolved into the dominant herbivorous orders of the Tertiary (Van Valen, 1966). Contrary to what has been stated in the past, the Plesiadapiformes, at least in North America, were probably replaced by strepsirhine and haplorhine primates as well as by arboreal rodents.

To characterize the ancestral plesiadapiform (i.e., by definition, the ancestral primate) is difficult for several reasons. We are uncertain as to the exact group of the non-primate eutherians, which were the source of the earliest primate, and know even less of their mode of life. We are equally unsure of many of the specific adaptations of the fossil plesiadapiforms as we have no living representatives to supply us with the necessary clues. However, we may note that, cranially, the major difference of the first primate from its nearest relatives appears to lie in the tube-enclosed carotid circulation within the petrosal-derived bulla, and, judged from the proportions of the cranium in *Plesiadapis,* the brain was perhaps relatively larger than in contemporary eutherians (Jerison, 1973; but see Radinsky, 1977). Preliminary studies of archontan relationships and adaptations strongly suggest that the classical view, which depicts the earliest primate as arboreal, is not far off the mark. They were probably *Ptilocercus*-like animals as far as their substrate preference and locomoter habits were concerned. This view is unlike the suggestion of Jenkins (1974), who envisages the earliest primate as both terrestrial and arboreal. It can be added, however, that some features of the pes, particularly the pronounced groove for the tendon of the flexor digitorum fibularis on the calcaneum, suggest a grasping ability by the toes in plesiadapiforms that has not evolved in tupaiids.

The dentition of the primate ancestor was very likely extremely similar to the ancient *Purgatorius unio.* The teeth are discussed and illustrated under the genus (p. 41), so it will suffice to point out here the close similarity of this taxon to primitive condylarths and erinaceomorphs.

As noted under the discussion of the order (p. 28) several workers (Gingerich, 1974, 1976a; Bown and Rose, 1976) consider the Microsyopidae as part of the Plesiadapiformes. The Microsyopidae was reviewed by Szalay (1969a) and was subsequently restudied in the light of its relevance to the plesiadapiforms (Szalay, 1972a, 1976, and 1977a). Microsyopid relationships to primates, in our opinion, have merely been postulated on dental ground, but no corroborative evidence other than similarities, which are likely to be convergent, has been generated by anyone. For example, Bown and Gingerich (1973) made detailed comparisons between *Plesiolestes problematicus* and the early Eocene microsyopid *Cynodontomys latidens;* these comparisons revealed to them that these forms were very closely related, which made them consider microsyopids as primates. This has received general endorsement from Simons (1976c), Radinsky (1977), and

Dashzeveg and McKenna (1977). Both the comparison and the interpretation of the similarities they report have been disputed previously by Szalay (1975f, 1976, 1977a).

First, the microsyopid taxon used by Bown and Gingerich for comparison is not the oldest and most primitive of known phena, but *Cynodontomys latidens,* a middle Wasatchian form, is preceded by two more primitive and older taxa, *C. wilsoni* and *C. augustidens* (for illustration of all of these see Szalay, 1969a,b). As *C. latidens* is almost certainly the descendant of the more primitive early Wasatchian forms, the proper comparison of *Plesiolestes problematicus* is with *C. wilsoni* and *C. augustidens.* This has not been carried out because, we suspect, the similarity between the premolars of these species with *Plesiolestes* is not particularly striking, and the molars themselves further show that the primitive microsyopid dentitions is only superficially, and not in a special way, similar to some Paleocene primates. But even if we compare *Cynodontomys latidens* to *Plesiolestes* it can be quickly grasped that the similarities are convergent. The trigonids of the P₄'s of the taxa compared by Bown and Gingerich, although both molariform inasmuch as they have the all three cusps, are very distinctive. In *Cynodontomys latidens* they have robust, large conical cusps, whereas in *Plesiolestes problematicus* they are small, and the protoconid still dominated the trigonid. When we examine the early Wasatchian *Cynodontomys* sample, it becomes apparent that the P₄ trigonid of *C. latidens* evolved from that condition and its resemblance, a poor one at that, to *Plesiolestes* is convergent. The

Uintasoricinae, sister group of the microsyopines, have premolariform P₄ like early Wasatchian *Cynodontomys.*

When we compare the molars (for dental homologies and nomenclature used throughout this book, see Figure 6) of the taxa chosen by Bown and Gingerich (1973), we find that the significant diagnostic feature of microsyopids, the twinned entoconid–hypoconulid, is not present in *Plesiolestes.* This character is present in mixodectids and also in tupaiids, so both mixodectids and possibly microsyopids may be archontans along with a number of genera often referred to the Erinaceomorpha. Hypocone construction is entirely different in microsyopids from that seen in *Plesiolestes,* or in any other *bona fide* paromomyid. Unlike the condition in these primates, the microsyopid hypocone is an independent cusp on the distal cingulum and not the ill-defined portion of the postcingulum leading to the protocone. The latter condition is almost certainly primitive for the Primates. With all these groups, before referral to the Archonta can be made with any degree of certitude, evidence other than teeth must also be considered. To sum up, the dental evidence marshaled by Bown and Gingerich (1973) for microsyopid–early primate affinities is not any stronger than that which could be used to argue for hyopsodontid–primate or dichobunid artiodactyl–adapid affinities. The basicranial evidence, on the other hand, is opposed to a close link between microsyopids and plesiadapiform (or later) primates.

SUPERFAMILY PAROMOMYOIDEA
Simpson, 1940

DISTRIBUTION

Late Cretaceous to late Eocene (Maestrichtian to Uintan and Thanetian to Neustrian). Western North America and western Europe.

INCLUDED TAXA

Families Paromomyidae and Picrodontidae.

DISCUSSION

It appears that this superfamily, by contrast to the Plesiadapoidea, is a less firmly established group. It represents a conglomeration of taxa united within the Paromomyidae which are not unequivocally most recently related to one another. This group has validity primarily in contrast to the Plesiadapoidea.

Family Paromomyidae
Simpson, 1940

(= or including: Anaptomorphidae: Simpson, 1937, in part. Paromomyinae Simpson, 1940. Phenacolemuridae Simpson, 1955. Anaptomorphidés: Russell, 1964, in part. Purgatoriinae Van Valen and Sloan, 1965; Microsyopidae: Szalay, 1969a, in part: Bown and Rose, 1976, in part.)

DISTRIBUTION
Latest Cretaceous to late Eocene (Maestrichtian to Uintan and Thanetian to Neustrian). Western North America and Western Europe.
INCLUDED TAXA
Tribes Purgatoriini, Paromomyini, Micromomyini, and Navajoviini.

DISCUSSION

Paromomyids are the most ancient of the known families of primates. These archaic forms were predominantly tiny (mouse-sized) to small mammals, with only a few species of *Phenacolemur* attaining sizes slightly above a common rat. Aside from the specializations of the incisors and the reduction in the numbers of incisors and premolars in later genera, the common ancestor of the family was probably one of the most primitive forms of the order as far as the lower jaw morphology and cheek tooth structure are concerned, and almost certainly so in its postcranial remains.

The subdivision of the Paromomyidae at the subfamily level is a very difficult task. Family groups of tribal ranking, as in the Adapidae or Cercopithecidae, are easily recognized, but their further grouping is as yet rather arbitrary. As biologically meaningful diagnoses cannot be attributed to either the Purgatoriinae or the Paromomyinae (subfamilies of past classifications), the use of these categories is abandoned for the Paromomyidae. Instead, four tribes, the Purgatoriini, Paromomyini, Micromomyini, and Navajoviini, are employed to order the genera of the family. Each of these taxa is believed to be monophyletic, and it is reasonably certain that the Paromomyini originated from a purgatoriin. Thus far there is only dental evidence that the Paromomyidae is a monophyletic taxon. That it is a paraphyletic grouping of archaic primates cannot be ruled out.

Bown and Rose (1976), following Gingerich (1974, 1976a), have recently included *Palaechthon*, *Plesiolestes*, *Torrejonia*, and *Palenochtha* in the Microsyopinae within the Microsyopidae; the genera *Navajovius* and *Berruvius* in the Uintasoricinae; and the Micromomyini in the Microsyopidae *incertae sedis*. The dental evidence bearing on the allocation of the genera to the Microsyopidae previously considered paromomyids may be reviewed below. There is nothing in the arguments offered by these authors that would indicate a greater degree of relationships of *Palaechthon*, *Plesiolestes*, and *Palenochtha* to microsyopids than to *bona fide* paromomyids, as brought out in the comparisons of Simpson (1955). By virtue of the special molar similarity of *Micromomys* to *Palenochtha*, the allocation of the Micromomyini to the Microsyopidae appears groundless. Szalay (1969a), who suggested that *Navajovius* may be an early microsyopid, later (1975c) changed his view to suggest that the known molar morphology of the most primitive early Eocene microsyopids, both microsyopines and uintasoricines, bears no special similarity to any of the known archaic primates. There is a distinctly more significant similarity of the primitive paromomyid taxa in general to such suspected archontans as *Tupaiodon*, *Messelina*, *Litolestes*, and others than to primitive microsyopids.

Bown and Rose (1976) stated that: "The present evidence, in the absence of well preserved basicrania of Paleocene insectivores, microsyopids, and paromomyids, is equivocal; it remains possible that microsyopids are not primates in spite of strong dental evidence" (p. 133). The evidence, similarities vaguely alluded to by Bown and Rose (1976) and by Gingerich (1974, 1975b), is not any more striking than that observed between some Eocene primates and artiodactyls.

Furthermore, this view of Bown and Rose (1976) and that of Gingerich (1974, 1976a) take no recognition of the practice of morphotype reconstruction, which should consider all available evidence. The *sui generis* features of the primate morphotype basicranium are entirely absent from the excellent skull of *Cynodontomys latidens*, which instead has its own specializations (Szalay, 1969a).

Tribe Purgatoriini
Van Valen and Sloan, 1965

(= or including: Purgatoriinae Van Valen and Sloan, 1965.)

DISTRIBUTION
Latest Cretaceous and early Paleocene (Maestrichtian to Puercan). Western North America.
INCLUDED TAXON
Purgatorius.

DISCUSSION

Without question the known dental remains of this group are the most primitive ones known among the paromomyids and other primates. In light of the known ancestral complex of characters, this tribe is tentatively separated from the diverse Paromomyini.

As Savage, Russell, and Waters (1977) succinctly state: "*Purgatorius* is the earliest and the best available standard with which to compare later primates. *Purgatorius* is thus our *model of primitiveness*, our *primordial primate*, but we do not wish to imply or claim that *Purgatorius* is the phyletic ancestor of all early Eocene primates" (p. 160). We concur with this carefully worded and straightforward statement.

PURGATORIUS Van Valen and Sloan, 1965

DISTRIBUTION
Latest Cretaceous to early Paleocene (Maestrichtian to Puercan). Rocky Mt. region.
KNOWN SPECIES
1. *Purgatorius unio* Van Valen and Sloan, 1965, type species
LOCALITIES: Purgatory Hill★ (12); Garbani loc. (14).
2. *Purgatorius ceratops* Van Valen and Sloan, 1965
LOCALITIES: Harbicht Hill★ (8).

DISCUSSION

Purgatorius is known only from dental remains (Figure 13). Of the two species, only the early Paleocene *P. unio* is known relatively well. The only specimen of *P. ceratops* is the name-bearing holotype from the late Cretaceous, a right lower molar. Both species were probably the size of a small rat, the length of each of the lower molars being about 2 mm. *Purgatorius unio* appears more advanced in having a relatively wider lower molar talonid than *P. ceratops*. Because of the relative abundance of material all further discussion of the genus is based on *P. unio* (for illustrations see also Szalay, 1969a; Clemens, 1974).

As *Purgatorius* is the earliest and dentally the most primitive known primate, its morphology is of particular importance. The genus is unique in the Paromomyidae in having three incisors, a relatively large canine, and retaining $P_{\overline{1}}$ (Clemens, 1974; Savage, Russell, and Waters, 1977). The known lower premolars are premolariform–semimolariform with a tall and pointed protoconid, but the talonid area is wide and has a small talonid basin. The allocated fourth upper premolar has a long cutting postparacrista. The known, relatively narrow $P_{\overline{4}}$ has a very small paraconid, but lacks a metaconid, and its basined talonid has two cusps.

The lower and upper molars show a mixture of characters that appear to be intermediate between an ancestral stock of archontans or erinaceomorph insectivorans and the other Tertiary primates. Although the lower molar trigonids are relatively taller than those of any other primates (the prismatic teeth of the lorisine *Arctocebus* are secondarily high crowned), the paraconid is not as bulbous as the metaconid in *Purgatorius*. In fact it is very similar to the same structure in the archontan or erinaceomorph *Leptacodon*, more so, for example, than the paracristids of either *Palaechthon*, *Palenochtha*, *Teilhardina*, or *Chlororhysis*. This particular type of paraconid, although not of cingular origin (Savage *et al.*, 1977), is clearly correlated with the enlarged hypocone. In spite of the relatively smaller paraconid than metaconid a cutting edge is very prominent on the paracristid. As in other primitive primates, however, the trigonid is characteristically inclined mesially. There is a weak cingulum which extends around the mesial and buccal sides of the trigonid.

The talonids are relatively wide but slightly narrower than the trigonids. The talonid cusps are not bulbous as they are, for example, in the early Oligocene *Parapithecus* or *Apidium*. The hypoconulid

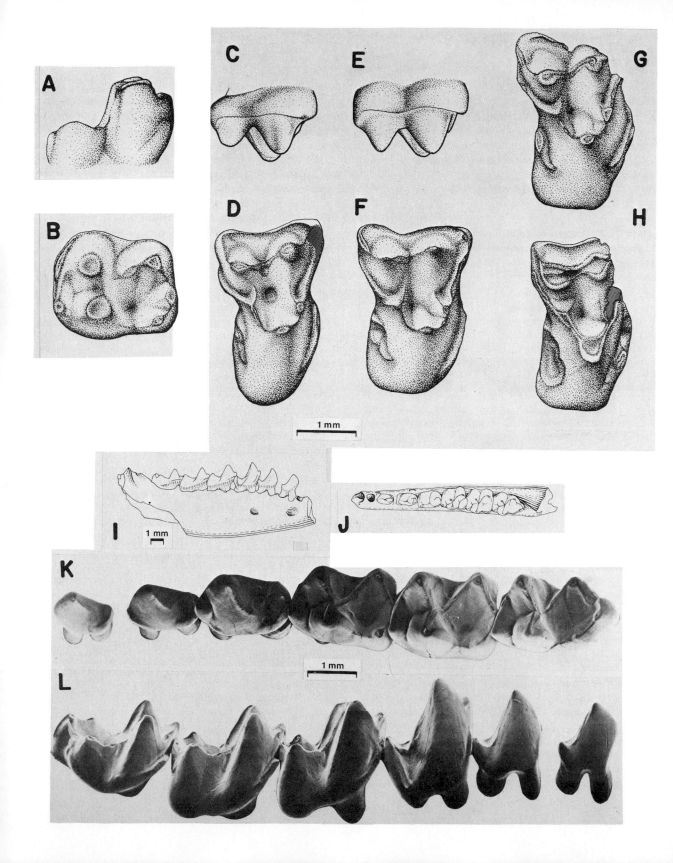

is distinct, but small, approximately halfway between the entoconid and hypoconid, and it is reduced from a primitively larger eutherian hypoconulid.

Among known primitive primates the relatively very wide upper molars have the most extensive remnant of the stylar shelf of a more primitive eutherian ancestry with a tribosphenic upper molar crown. As in other primitive eutherians the paracone is distinctly larger than the metacone. The crest going mesially from the paracone ends at the base of this cusp, whereas the postmetacrista runs to the buccal border and has a distinct metastyle. The paracone and metacone maintain a V-shaped cutting edge between them as in primitive archontans and erinaceomorph insectivorans, but they have enlarged the distolingual area of the protocone into a hypocone as in many early Tertiary primates and, of course, as in other Tertiary mammals. The paraconule and metaconule are distinct, the former higher, with sharp crests which are basally not as broad as those of later paromomyids. The disposition of the protocone displays the most clearly primate feature of the upper molars. It is skewed slightly mesiobuccally and its apex is more mesiobuccal on the crown than in any late Cretaceous or Paleocene non-primate. The pre- and postcingula on the upper molars are distinct but they do not connect lingually around the protocone.

The dental formula of *Purgatorius* is I$\frac{2 \cdot 3}{1 \cdot 2 \cdot 3}$; C$\frac{1}{1}$; P$\frac{2 \cdot 3 \cdot 4}{1 \cdot 2 \cdot 3 \cdot 4}$; M$\frac{2 \cdot 3}{1 \cdot 2 \cdot 3}$.

In *Purgatorius*, the characteristic, mesiolingually tilted trigonid and mesiobuccally skewed protocone, and the consequently mesially shifted preprotocrista, are probably the results of the earliest selective forces known to have shaped a diagnostically primate molar morphology and function. This modification occurred as the previously primarily cutting function of the prevallum (mesial cutting edges of the upper molar) and the postvallid (distal cutting edge of the lower molar trigonid) were transformed into somewhat lower, blunter ridges. The change in morphology was probably related to a changing function from primarily slicing fibrous animal tissues into crushing and grinding certain amounts of softer plant foods. The hypocone, which is usually (but not always) associated with lingual phase cutting and herbivorous adaptation (at least at its inception), the rather extensive apical wear on the top of the molar cusps, and the lack of comparable wear on the cutting edge would indicate an insectivorous–frugivorous diet. However, this is clearly only a very tenuous hypothesis. *Purgatorius*, then, like many living aboreal primates that can be called insectivorous, consumed a fair amount of fruits, unlike a putative terrestrial pre-primate insectivore similar in its diet to a living soricoid, for example.

Tribe Paromomyini
Simpson, 1940

(= or including: Phenacolemuridae Simpson, 1955, in part. Microsyopidae: Bown and Rose, 1976, in part.)

DISTRIBUTION
   Middle Paleocene to late Eocene (Torrejonian to Uintan). Western North America.
INCLUDED TAXA
   Subtribes Palaechthonina and Paromomyina.

DISCUSSION

The genera included in this taxon share certain broad adaptive similarities which justify this classification. Moderate to great enlargement of the incisors, loss of at least the first lower premolar, reduction of the canine size, and the loss of the protocone on P^3 are the complex of confirmed or inferred derived features which serve to unite these genera.

Removal of all but *Paromomys* into the Microsyopinae by Bown and Rose (1976) and by Bown and Gingerich (1973) appears groundless to us. What they refer to as similarity of these genera to early Eocene microsyopids (see p. 39) is what appears to be convergent similarity in contrast to what can be recognized as special similarity between *Paromomys* and the remaining paromomyins. The basis of the phylogenetic ties of these genera advocated here is supported by Kay and Cartmill (1977).

Figure 13. *Purgatorius*. Late Cretaceous (A and B) and early Paleocene (C–L), western North America. *Purgatorius ceratops* (A and B) and *Purgatorius unio* (C–L). Right lower molar: A, buccal view; B, occlusal view. Left upper molars: C and E, buccal views; D, F, G, and H, occlusal views. Right mandible fragment with alveoli for C, P$_T$, and teeth P$_2$–M$_3$: I, lateral view; J, occlusal view. Right P$_2$–M$_3$: K, occlusal view; L, buccal view. Scales represent 1 mm. [A–H by A. Cleary; I–L from W. A. Clemens, *Science* **184**. Copyright 1974 by the American Association for the Advancement of Science.]

SUBTRIBE PALAECHTHONINA
Szalay, 1972b, new rank

(= or including: Palaechthonini Szalay, 1972b.)

DISTRIBUTION
Middle to late Paleocene (Torrejonian to Tiffanian). Western North America.
INCLUDED TAXA
Palaechthon, Plesiolestes, and *Palenochtha.*

DISCUSSION

Similarity between *Palaechthon* and *Plesiolestes* is very great. Whatever the most recent affinity of these genera may be, they are united here because of the great overall, probably special, resemblance. The somewhat more specialized *Palenochtha* is possibly the ancestor of the poorly known *Micromomys*, yet until upper molars of the latter are known this hypothesis cannot be considered sufficiently probable.

PALAECHTHON Gidley, 1923

(= or including: *Talpohenach* Kay and Cartmill, 1977.)

DISTRIBUTION
Middle Paleocene (Torrejonian). Rocky Mt. region.
KNOWN SPECIES
1. *Palaechthon alticuspis* Gidley, 1923, type species
LOCALITIES: Silberling Q.⋆ (20), Gidley Q. (24), Rock Bench Q. (26), Swain Q. (28).
2. *Palaechthon woodi* Gazin, 1971
LOCALITIES: Keefer Hill Shotgun⋆ (38).
3. *Palaechthon nacimienti* Wilson and Szalay, 1972
LOCALITIES: Torrejon⋆ (22).
4. *Palaechthon torrejonius* (Kay and Cartmill, 1977)
(=*Talpohenach torrejonius* Kay and Cartmill, 1977)
LOCALITIES: Torrejon⋆ (22).

DISCUSSION

Palaechthon is a somewhat varied genus, known by four species. *Palaechthon alticuspis* and *P. nacimienti* were about the size of a small Norway rat; the length of the jaws is between 12 and 14 mm. The type species is known by numerous specimens (Simpson, 1937, 1955), whereas the other two species are less well sampled.

The earliest skull (Figures 14 and 15) of a paromomyid primate is that of *Palaechthon nacimienti*. The badly crushed specimen has been recently studied by Wilson and Szalay (1972) and Kay and Cartmill (1974, 1977). Figure 15 indicates the extent to which the skull is preserved. There are traces of ossified bullae, but their relative size is difficult to estimate as that whole area is poorly preserved.

The sizes of the facial and neural components of the skull are about equal. One suspects that this is the result of a slight foreshortening of the preorbital rostrum. It is likely that in the primitive primate condition of the facial skull is slightly longer than the neurocranium proper.

The supraorbital shelf is prominent and an area of breakage indicates the presence of a superior postorbital process. It is unlikely, however, that a postorbital bar was present. The orbits, in general, were relatively small, located relatively forward over the dentition. Anterior displacement of the orbits could be related to the considerable expansion of the anterior temporalis. A notable feature on the rostrum is the relatively large infraorbital foramen, suggesting ample blood supply and well-developed innervation to the vibrissae and to the rhinarium. This is very likely to be an ancestral character, present in the skulls of *Ignacius* and *Plesiadapis* also.

There are a sufficient number of bony crests preserved on the skull and mandibular fragments of *P. nacimienti* so that a reasonable assessment of the chewing muscles can be made. As noted in conjunction with the orbits, the anterior temporalis muscle originates well forward, approximately above the last upper molar. The linea obliqua of the mandible for the insertion of the temporalis muscle is not any more robust than that in most early Tertiary primates. In its development this crest is of average strength.

Contrary to the suggestion of Kay and Cartmill (1974), the principal axis of the temporalis fibers is judged not to have been nearly vertical with respect to the occlusal plane. Further assessment of the alignment of this axis is impossible without the back part of the skull, which is missing at present. The superficial masseter takes its origin on the usual place, the ventral surface of the zygoma and the orbital floor, somewhat

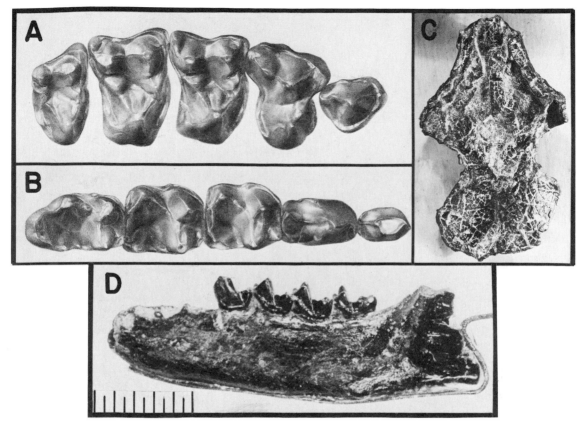

Figure 14.   (A,B,D) *Palaechthon*. Middle Paleocene, western North America. *Palachthon alticuspis*. Right P$\underline{2}$M$\underline{3}$: A, occlusal view. Left P$\overline{3}$–M$\overline{3}$: B, occlusal view. Left mandible fragment with P$\overline{4}$–M$\overline{3}$: D, lateral view. Subdivisions on scale, applicable to D, represent 0.5 mm. C, *Palaechthon nacimienti*. Crushed skull with rostrum and back missing (see Figure 15 for reconstruction): C, dorsal view. [A and B from Simpson (1955).]

forward, however, but not as forward as in *Plesiadapis*. The medial and lateral pterygoid laminae are widely divergent, as recognized by Kay and Cartmill (1974), and the enclosed large pterygoid fossa suggests a relatively large medial pterygoid muscle.

As *Palenochtha*, species of *Palaechthon* also have tall trigonids, but the paraconid is very small, probably (but not certainly) an advanced condition. The fourth lower premolar is rather simple, having only a small manifestation of the paraconid and metaconid and only a poorly developed talonid. The double-rooted fourth upper premolar has a large metacone, but the third premolar almost completely lacks a protocone, being a single-rooted tooth. In *P. nacimienti* the canines are slightly larger than either the second pre-

molar (the first premolar is lost) or the second incisor (the third incisor is lost).

The specimen described by Wilson and Szalay (1972) and tentatively assigned to *Palaechthon nacimienti*, and subsequently raised to the level of a new species and a new genus by Kay and Cartmill (1977), is included in the genus as a valid species. Although it can be delineated from *Palaechthon nacimienti* and *P. alticuspis*, its overall morphology does not, at present, warrant recognition of generic distinction. The single specimen by which *P. torrejonius* is represented may be, we believe, merely an unusual member of *P. nacimienti*. Until a better sample from the type locality of *P. torrejonius* is collected, this cannot be ruled out. Given such doubts of specific distinction the generic

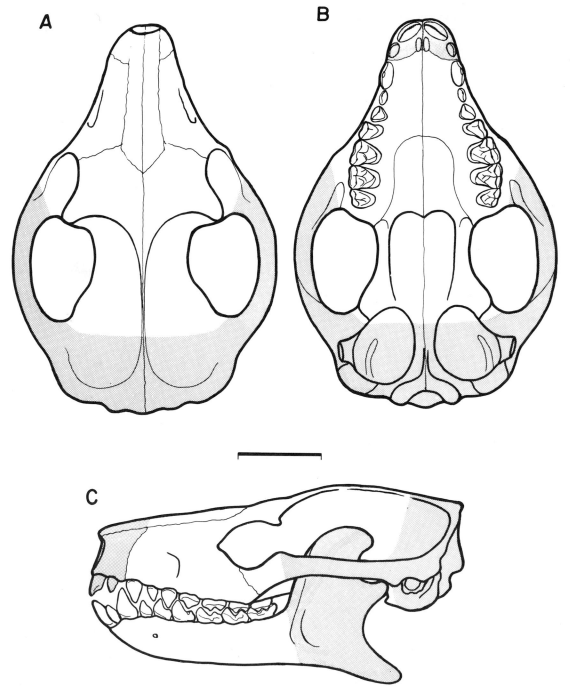

Figure 15. *Palaechthon nacimienti*. Middle Paleocene, western North America. Skull and mandible reconstructed from crushed and broken specimens: A, dorsal view; B, ventral view; C, lateral view. Scale represents 1 cm. [By A. Cleary.]

rank given to the specimen by Kay and Cartmill cannot be accepted. As the species stand at present, *P. torrejonius* differs primarily from *P. nacimienti* in its slightly more squared molars and its P³ being slightly more elongated than that of the generotype.

As Kay and Cartmill (1977) state: "Were it not for the P³ protocone and the somewhat better developed stylar shelf on the molars of *Talpohenach*, the genus *Palaechthon* could be stretched to include this taxon. Certainly the two are very closely related" (p. 46). The small protocone and differences in stylar shelf development on a single specimen for a taxon with a sample of one are not a significant morphological difference that usually warrants generic distinction.

The dental formula of *Palaechthon* is I$\frac{2}{1\cdot2}$; C$\frac{1}{1}$; P$\frac{2\cdot3\cdot4}{2\cdot3\cdot4}$; M$\frac{1\cdot2\cdot3}{1\cdot2\cdot3}$.

Judged primarily from dentition, this genus appears to have been quite omnivorous. The reduced canines but somewhat enlarged incisors perhaps suggest manipulation of fruits, rather than using canines to stab insects. Kay and Cartmill's (1977) analysis of the adaptations of *Palaechthon* and early Tertiary primates cannot be supported by us and this issue is in fact separately treated in detail (Szalay, in press). But, more specifically, the adaptational appraisal of *Palaechthon* and *Plesiolestes* by Kay and Cartmill utilized the allegedly analogous similarity of the anterior dentition of the European hedgehog and the Paleocene primates. Comparisons of the anterior dentition of *Plesiolestes* (the best-preserved nearly complete plesiadapiform dentition), various tupaiids (*Ptilocercus, Tupaia, Lyonogale*), *Erinaceus* and *Schoinobates* (a gliding marsupial phalanger) quickly reveals that hedgehogs (*contra* Kay and Cartmill, 1977) are neither morphologically nor mechanically similar in their anterior dentition to *Plesiolestes*. Although the upper anterior dentition of the species compared in their study of *Plesiolestes* was not analyzed by Kay and Cartmill, it is obvious that paromomyids and *Erinaceus* have distinctive incisivation areas. *Erinaceus* has widely separated, pointed incisors, quite in contrast to known paromomyids (e.g., *Palaechthon*), which have either rounded or multicusped incisors in close contact. The enlarged lower incisors of *Erinaceus* present two distinct apical points as the two teeth are separated by a diastema resulting, in effect, in two caniniform anterior teeth which happen to be incisors. In sharp contrast, *Plesiolestes*, tupaiids, and *Schoinobates* have a broad-surfaced scoop constructed by the close juxtaposition of the mesial surface of the enlarged incisors.

The anterior dentition of *Erinaceus* and *Plesiolestes* is crudely convergent morphologically [only from the lateral view, at that, of the somewhat simplified drawings shown by Kay and Cartmill (1977)], but the mechanics of the incisors are very distinctive. As there is no mechanical convergence beyond relative enlargements, it appears to be inappropriate to use the roles performed by the hedgehog anterior dentition as a model for the biological roles performed by *Plesiolestes*.

The hypothesis of Kay and Cartmill (1977) that the relatively large infraorbital foramen area to skull length of *Palaechthon* is evidence for the terrestrial habits of this genus has been tested and can be falsified by using the Tupaiidae and other relevant groups as test cases (Szalay, in press). For instance, *Ptilocerus lowii*, the most arboreal of the tree shrews, has a relatively larger infraorbital foramen area to skull length than the most terrestrial members of that group which have a similar skull size.

PLESIOLESTES Jepsen, 1930b

(= or including: *Torrejonia* Gazin, 1968.)

DISTRIBUTION

Middle and late Paleocene (Torrejonian and Tiffanian). Rocky Mt. region.

KNOWN SPECIES

1. *Plesiolestes problematicus* Jepsen, 1930b, type species
LOCALITIES: Rock Bench Q.⋆ (26); Tongue River (31).

2. *Plesiolestes wilsoni* (Gazin, 1968)
(= *Torrejonia wilsoni* Gazin, 1968.)
LOCALITIES: Torrejon⋆ (22).

3. *Plesiolestes sirokyi* Szalay, 1973
LOCALITIES: Saddle⋆ (44).

DISCUSSION

The genus is known only by dental and mandibular remains (Figure 16). As in *Palaechthon*, the third premolar lacks the lingual root. The upper molars are rather transverse with well-developed conules and the

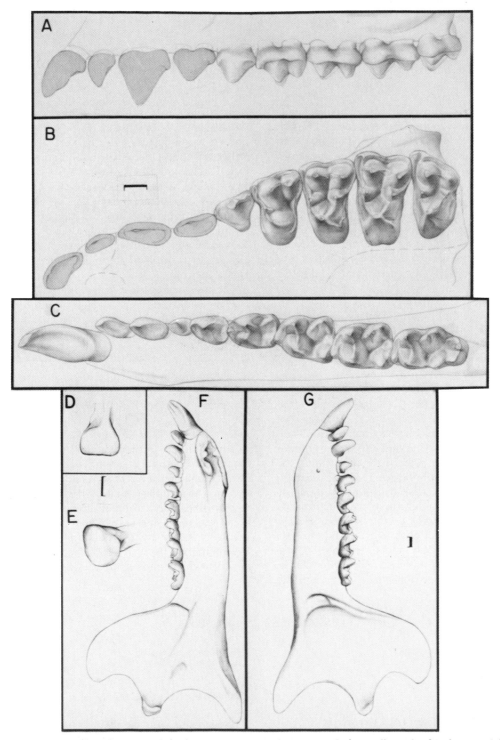

Figure 16. *Plesiolestes problematicus*. Late Paleocene, western North America. Left maxilla with P^3–M^3, with I^{1-2}, C, and P^2 reconstructed: A, buccal view; B, occlusal view. Right mandible with $I_{\overline{1}}$–$M_{\overline{3}}$: C, occlusal view. Articular condyle: D, dorsal view; E, posterior view. Left mandible with $I_{\overline{1}}$–$M_{\overline{3}}$: F, medial view; G, lateral view. Scales represent 1 mm. [From Szalay (1973).]

third lower molar is specialized in having an unusually long talonid, relatively longer than in *Palaechthon*. The dental formula appears to be the same as that for *Palaechthon*.

The major diagnostic difference of *P. sirokyi* from the generotype lies in its approximately 50% larger size and in lacking a paraconid and metaconid on $P_{\overline{4}}$. The latter distinction also applies to *P. wilsoni* when compared to *P. problematicus*. *P. sirokyi* further slightly differs from *P. problematicus* in its hypocone construction. The distal cingulum, which usually connects to the apex of the protocone in the generotype, connects lower in *P. sirokyi*. Some authors (Bown and Gingerich, 1973; Kay and Cartmill, 1977) hold that the difference in *P. wilsoni* (namely, its premolariform $P_{\overline{4}}$) from *P. problematicus* are sufficiently significant to maintain the generic separation of "*Torrejonia*" (based on "*T.*" *wilsoni*) from *Plesiolestes*. In light of the close special similarity between the species allocated to *Palaechthon*, *Plesiolestes*, and *Paromomys*, we consider it unnecessary splitting to recognize either *Torrejonia* Gazin, 1968, or *Talpohenach* Kay and Cartmill, 1977.

Whatever the phylogenetic relationship of the various samples allocated by us to the three recognized genera, the known morphological diversity is not great enough to recognize two additional groups of generic rank.

Unlike Bown and Gingerich (1973), we cannot ascertain any significant shared and derived similarity between *Plesiolestes* and primitive microsyopids and, therefore, as noted above, consider the origin of that family from either *Plesiolestes* or other paromomyids unlikely.

The mandible of *Plesiolestes* is well known, and Figure 16 shows the morphology of the unexpanded angle and the minimally transverse mandibular condyle. The symphysis was clearly unfused and probably mobile during mastication. The dentition of all three known species, in particular the low crowned molars, the enlarged third molars, and the anterior dentition, suggests a primarily phytophagous, probably frugivorous, feeding preference. The discussion on adaptations under *Palaechthon* (p. 47) is also closely pertinent to *Plesiolestes*.

PALENOCHTHA Simpson, 1937

(= or including: *Palaechthon*: Gidley, 1923, in part.)

DISTRIBUTION
  Middle Paleocene (Torrejonian). Rocky Mt. region.
KNOWN SPECIES
  Palenochtha minor (Gidley, 1923), type species
  (=*Palaechthon minor* Gidley, 1923.)
  LOCALITIES: Gidley Q.⋆ (24); Swain Q. (28).

DISCUSSION

This genus, known by partial dentitions and jaws of a single species (Figure 17), was a tiny, mouse-sized form. Its diagnostic features are the reduced dentition, large incisors, relatively high trigonids, heavy buccal cingulid, and presence of a large paraconid. The presence of a relatively larger and more distinct paraconid renders this form distinctive from purgatoriins and paromomyins.

Premolar morphology of this genus cannot be considered to reflect a primitive primate condition because the reduction of the premolars, combined with

jaw shortening, caused changes in the relative position of the last premolars within the dentition and consequently altered the primitive posterior premolar morphology.

The lower and upper molars are probably advanced compared to *Purgatorius*, and sharpness of the cusps is probably related to the apparently extreme insectivorous adaptations of this tiny form. The protocones are skewed anteriorly and the apex of the cusp is relatively buccal (Szalay, 1968b).

The dental formula is $I^{1\cdot2}_{1\cdot2}$; C^1_1; $P^{3\cdot4}_{3\cdot4}$; $M^{1\cdot2\cdot3}_{1\cdot2\cdot3}$.

Palenochtha is quite an advanced early primate with respect to its anterior dentition. It has already lost its first two premolars, its most anterior incisor is quite enlarged, and its canine is a rather small tooth.

The mandible is perhaps primitive for the family in being relatively shallow, having a long, narrow mandibular angle, a small elipsoidal articular surface on the condyle, and a large coronoid process.

It is very likely that this form was primarily insectivorous.

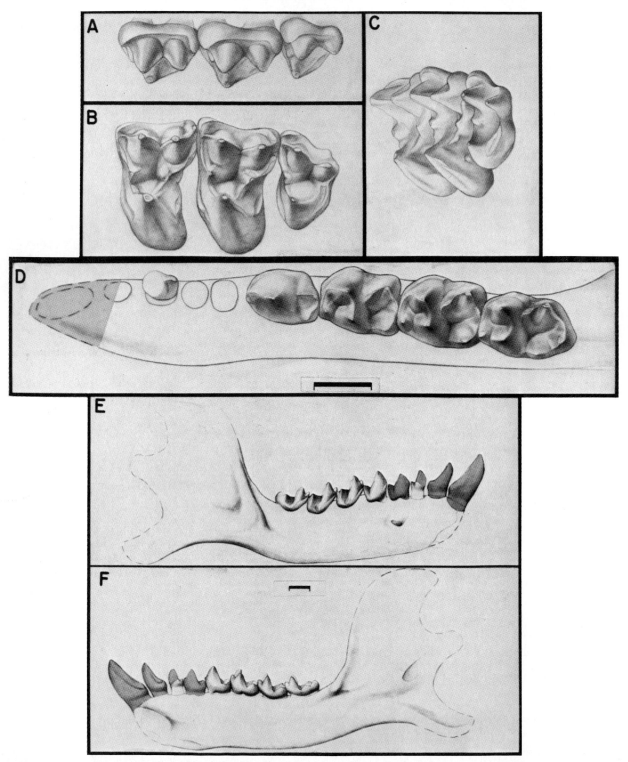

Figure 17. *Palenochtha minor.* Middle Paleocene, western North America. Left M¹–M³. A, buccal view; B, occlusal view; C, occlusodistal view. Right mandible with C₁, P₄, M₁–M₃. D, occlusal view; E, lateral view; F, medial view. Broken lines and stippling represent reconstruction. Scales represent 1 mm. [By A. Cleary.]

SUBTRIBE PAROMOMYINA
Simpson, 1940

(= or including: Plesiadapidae: Matthew and Granger, 1921, in part.
Paromomyidae Simpson, 1940, in part. Phenacolemuridae Simpson,
1955, in part. Microsyopidae: Bown and Rose, 1976, in part.
Phenacolemurini: Schwartz and Krishtalka, 1977.)

DISTRIBUTION
   Middle Paleocene to late Eocene (Torrejonian to Uintan). Western
North America.
INCLUDED TAXA
   Paromomys, Ignacius, and *Phenacolemur.*

DISCUSSION

The most diagnostic feature for this taxon is the mesiodistal constriction of the trigonids. The trigonids functionally become distal crests of the greatly enlarged talonid basin of the teeth preceding them. This is perhaps the mechanical explanation for the reduction of the paracristid in these genera. Coupled with the molar morphology, *Ignacius* and *Phenacolemur* are further characterized by the extreme enlargement of the medial incisor and the loss of lateral incisors and canines, which make these taxa, at least dentally, very distinctive primates.

PAROMOMYS Gidley, 1923

DISTRIBUTION
   Middle Paleocene (Torrejonian). Rocky Mt. region.
KNOWN SPECIES
   1. *Paromomys maturus* Gidley, 1923, type species
LOCALITIES: Siberling Q. (20); Gidley Q.⋆ (24); Swain Q. (28).
   2. *Paromomys depressidens* Gidley, 1923
LOCALITIES: Gidley Q.⋆ (24); Swain Q. (28).

DISCUSSION

The dental and mandibular remains, the only parts known of these animals (Figure 18), indicate that the two species appear to differ mainly in size; the jaw of the larger *P. maturus* was about the size of that of the lemurid *Lepilemur leucopus* while the jaw of the smaller species was roughly the size of that of the cheirogaleid *Phaner furcifer.* Bown and Rose (1976) have noted that *P. depressidens* is more similar to *Ignacius* in its dental morphology than to *P. maturus:* "The markedly oblique attitude of the postparacone and premetacone cristae of the upper molars in *Ignacius* is foreshadowed

in *P. depressidens* but absent in *P. maturus*" (p. 112). It appears, then, that there is a consensus on the closely knit special similarity of the genera united under the Paromomyina.

The molars in *Paromomys* become more squared off than those of the Palaechthonina. The hypocone, essentially a bulging cingulum without the formation of a cusp, becomes highly conspicuous on the upper molars. Correlated with this is the mesiodistal narrowing of the trigonids. Both the upper and lower molars, which are low crowned, are heavily crenulated and the elongation of the third molar talonid is pronounced. The anteriormost incisor is moderately enlarged (Simpson, 1937, 1955; Szalay, 1968b).

The dental formula of *Paromomys* is $I\frac{1\cdot2}{1\cdot2}$; C; $P\frac{2\cdot3\cdot4}{2\cdot3\cdot4}$; $M\frac{1\cdot2\cdot3}{1\cdot2\cdot3}$.

Paromomys is suspected to have been derived from a species near the common ancestry of *Palaechthon* and *Plesiolestes.* The total balance of derived characters of this genus suggests a primarily frugivorous diet.

IGNACIUS Matthew and Granger, 1921

(= or including: Matthew, 1915: Simpson, 1935a; *Phenacolemur;*
Robinson, 1968. Gazin, 1971.)

DISTRIBUTION
   Late Paleocene (Tiffanian), to late Eocene (Uintan). Rocky Mt.
region.
KNOWN SPECIES
   1. *Ignacius frugivorous* Matthew and Granger, 1921, type species
(=*Phenacolemur* sp. Jepsen, 1934. *Phenacolemur frugivorous:* Simpson,
1935a.)
LOCALITIES: Scarrit Q. (40); Mason Pocket⋆ (72); Joe's Bone Bed, Black
Peaks (122).

   2. *Ignacius fremontensis* (Gazin, 1971)
(=*Phenacolemur fremontensis* Gazin, 1971. *Ignacius fremontensis:* Bown
and Rose, 1976.)
LOCALITIES: Keefer Hill, Shotgun⋆ (38).
   3. *Ignacius graybullianus* Bown and Rose, 1976
LOCALITIES: Gray Bull⋆ (162).
   4. *Ignacius mcgrewi* (Robinson, 1968)
(=*Phenocolemur mcgrewi* Robinson, 1968. *Ignacius mcgrewi:* Bown and
Rose, 1976.)
LOCALITIES: Badwater Creek⋆ (296).

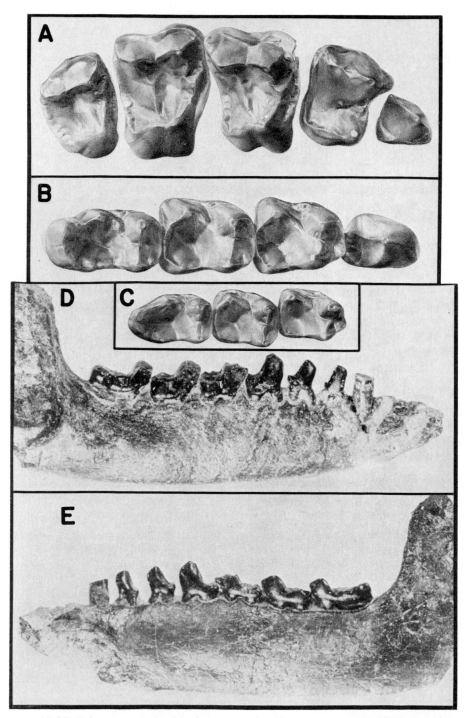

Figure 18. *Paromomys.* Middle Paleocene, western North America. *Paromomys maturus.* Right P$^{\underline{3}}$–P$^{\underline{4}}$, M$^{\underline{1}}$–M$^{\underline{3}}$: A, occlusal view. Left P$_{\overline{4}}$, M$_{\overline{1}}$–M$_{\overline{3}}$: B, occlusal view. Right mandible with C, P$_{\overline{2}}$–P$_{\overline{4}}$, M$_{\overline{1}}$–M$_{\overline{3}}$: D, lateral view; E, medial view. *Paromomys depressidens.* Left M$_{\overline{1}}$–M$_{\overline{3}}$: C, occlusal view. [A–C from Simpson (1955).]

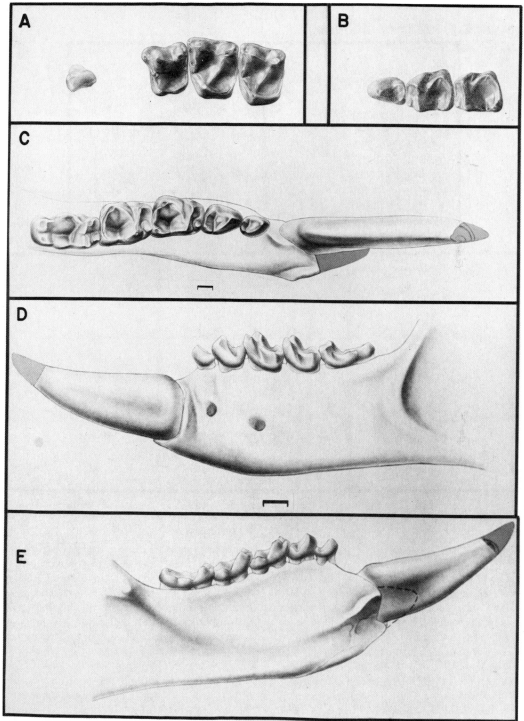

Figure 19. *Ignacius.* Late Paleocene, western North America. *Ignacius frugivorous.* Left P$^{\underline{2}}$ and P$^{\underline{4}}$–M$^{\underline{2}}$: A, occlusal view. Right P$_{\overline{4}}$–M$_{\overline{2}}$: B, occlusal view. *Ignacius fremontensis.* Left mandible fragment with dentition (I and P$_{\overline{3}}$–M$_{\overline{3}}$): C, occlusal view; D, lateral view; E, medial view. Scales represent 1 mm. [A and B from Simpson (1955); C–E by A. Cleary.]

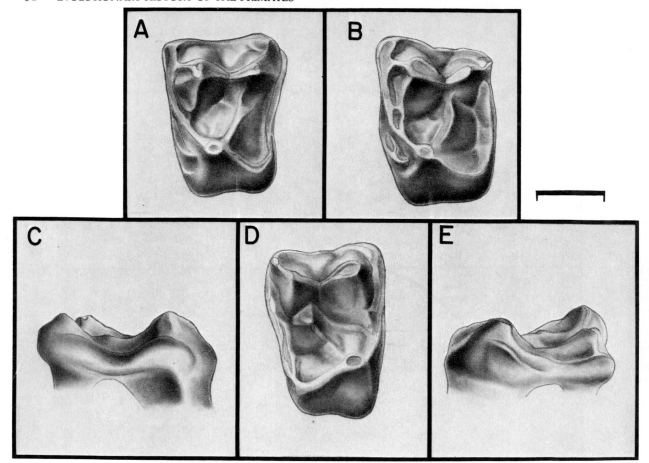

Figure 20. *Ignacius fremontensis.* Late Paleocene, western North America. Upper molars: A, left M¹; B, left M²; C,D, and E, right M¹ in distal (C), occlusal (D), and mesial (E) views. Scale represents 1 mm. [By A. Cleary.]

DISCUSSION

Although a probable derivative of *Paromomys depressidens*, this genus shows a number of clearly recognizable and strongly diagnostic characters distinguishing its species both from *Paromomys*, its putative ancestor, and from *Phenacolemur*, its own probable descendant. The molars of *Ignacius* are somewhat less squared than those of *Phenacolemur*, thus retaining more primitive proportions. The upper and lower molar basins of *Ignacius* (Figures 19 and 20) appear to be shallower and the upper molars somewhat lower crowned than those of *Phenacolemur*. The basins formed by the distal cingulum and the postprotocrista are distinctly larger than those in *Paromomys*, being in fact, one of the most clearly

diagnostic aspects of the upper molars. Both this feature and the transverse upper molars, however, are less advanced in *Ignacius* than in *Phenacolemur*. Unlike the premolar dentition of *Phenacolemur*, the fourth lower premolar of *Ignacius* is usually less tall than the first lower molar, and a diminutive third premolar is primitively present. The enlarged lower incisor of *Ignacius* (e.g., *I. fremontensis*) is very distinct from that of *Phenacolemur praecox* or *P. pagei* (Szalay, in preparation). In *Ignacius* this tooth is buccolingually constricted and very deep at its base and throughout the basal two-thirds of its crown. It also lacks the distobuccal cutting edge characteristic of *Phenacolemur*. The most recent students of the genus were Bown and Rose (1976).

The recently reported and well-illustrated skull

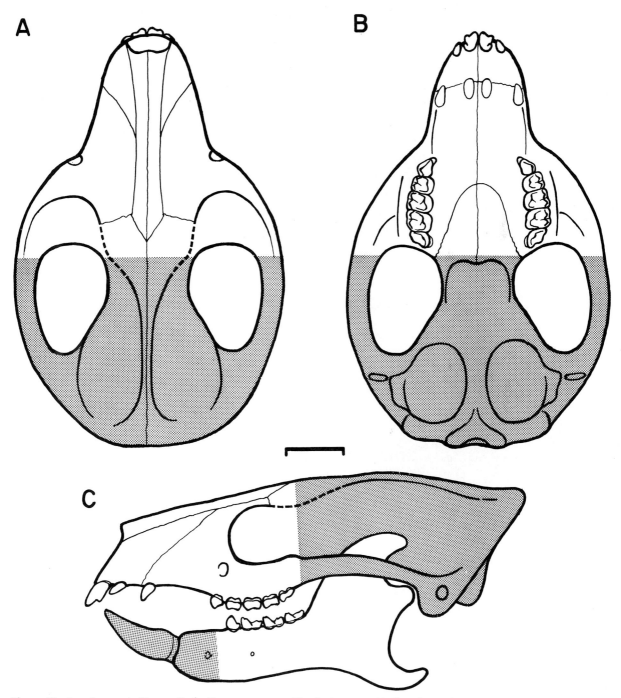

Figure 21. *Ignacius graybullianus.* Early Eocene, western North America. Skull and mandible reconstructed from broken specimens: A, dorsal view; B, ventral view; C, lateral view. Stippling indicates reconstruction. Scale represents 1 cm. [By A. Cleary.]

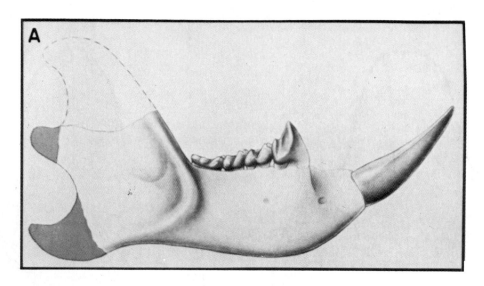

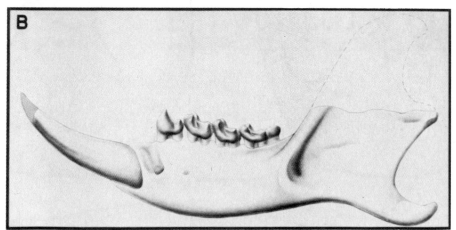

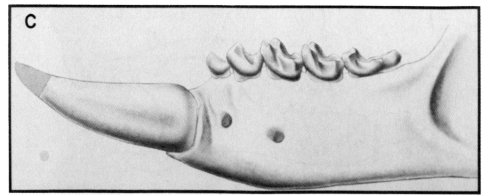

Figure 22. Comparison of lateral views of some paromomyinan mandibles: C, *Ignacius fremontensis*; B, cf. *Ignacius frugivorous*; A, *Phenacolemur pagei*. The structural sequence represented is increasingly derived from C to A. [By A. Cleary.]

fragment of *Ignacius graybullianus* (in Rose and Gingerich, 1976) allows some important comparative observations to be made about the growing number of early Tertiary primate crania. The skull fragment is that of the largest and perhaps most specialized species of the genus, although the inadequately known late Eocene *I. mcgrewi* may have been more derived. The most interesting features of the poorly preserved facial skull are the extremely long diastema between the canine and $P^{\underline{3}}$ and the moderate gap between the canine and I^2. In addition to the large premaxilla, another difference of *Ignacius* from the known skull fragments of *Palaechthon* is the sharp posterolateral turn of the root of the zygoma. It is impossible to tell whether or not a postorbital process of the frontal was present. The specimen is well enough preserved, however, to show that the orbits themselves were remarkably deep. Our reconstruction (Figure 21) differs from that given by Rose and Gingerich (1976), emphasizing some of the details noted above. The angle of the mandible (Figure 22) is very primitive in its proportions, being less expanded than those of *Phenacolemur* or *Plesiadapis*, for example.

The dental formula of *Ignacius* is $I\frac{2}{1,2}$; $C\frac{1}{1}$; $P^{2,3,4}_{2,3,4}$; $M\frac{1,2,3}{1,2,3}$.

It is difficult to offer a meaningful assessment of the feeding preferences in any of the species of *Ignacius*, except that they were likely to have been phytophagous forms specialized either for some fruits or, as the elongated incisor suggests, for a diet with a fair portion of insects and grubs taken, along with fruits.

Ignacius frugivorous and *I. fremontensis* appear in the Torrejonian, thus being the earliest members of the genus. According to Gazin (1971), *Ignacius fremontensis* has a much smaller $P_{\overline{4}}$ than *I. frugivorous*. Although a size difference between the molars is cited, no adequate case is made for this distinction. *Ignacius graybullianus* is cited by Bown and Rose (1976) as being the largest species of *Ignacius*, with a "P^4 and upper molars more squared posterolingually than in *I. frugivorous*; buccal outline of P^4 not emarginate as in the latter species. Postparacone and premetacone cristae more obliquely oriented than in *I. frugivorous*." The late Eocene *Ignacius mcgrewi* is a small, poorly known form. According to Bown and Rose (1976), this species shares the more oblique orientation of the postparacone and postmetacone cristae with *Ignacius graybullianus* compared to *I. frugivorous* or *I. fremontensis*.

PHENACOLEMUR Matthew, 1915

DISTRIBUTION

Late Paleocene to middle Eocene (Tiffanian to early Bridgerian), Rocky Mt. region; early Eocene (Neustrian), Paris Basin.

KNOWN SPECIES

1. *Phenacolemur praecox* Matthew, 1915, type species
(=*P. praecox praecox* Simpson, 1955.)
LOCALITIES: Gray Bull⋆ (162); Four Mile (178, 180); Powder River (196); Sand Coulee (198).

2. *Phenacolemur citatus* Matthew, 1915
(=*P. praecox citatus* Simpson, 1955.)
LOCALITIES: Gray Bull⋆ (162); Lysite (208).

3. *Phenacolemur pagei* Jepsen, 1930a
LOCALITIES: Silver Coulee⋆ (98).

4. *Phenacolemur jepseni* Simpson, 1955
(=*P. jepseni simpsoni* Robinson, 1966.)
LOCALITIES: Lysite (208); Huerfano (246); AM Quarry 88, San José⋆ (248).

5. *Phenacolemur simonsi* Bown and Rose, 1976
LOCALITIES: Gray Bull⋆ (162); Supersite Q. (164); Slick Creek (168); Wadi Kraus Q. (172); Powder River (196).

6. *Phenacolemur fuscus* Russell, Louis and Savage, 1967
LOCALITIES: Mutigny⋆ (190).

7. *Phenacolemur lapparenti* Russell, Louis and Savage, 1967
LOCALITIES: Avenay⋆ (206).

DISCUSSION

The diagnosis under *Ignacius* suffices to delineate *Phenacolemur* from the former genus, its closest ally. In addition to being one of the dentally most highly specialized genera of paromomyids, *Phenacolemur* is one of the more abundant and diversified taxa of the family (Simpson, 1955; Bown and Rose, 1976). One of its key adaptations appears to be the characteristically enlarged pair of lower incisors (Figures 22 and 23), but, contrary to repeated statements, these teeth are not rodentlike. These incisors are procumbent and not very broad at their base. They do not have a beveled edge and they are very rarely found heavily worn. Along with probably pronglike upper incisors, they appear to have been used for grasping or killing and manipulating food objects rather than for gnawing. These rather long incisors also lack the characteristic rodent attribute of permanent growth.

Unlike in *Ignacius*, the enlarged $P_{\overline{4}}$ of *Phenacolemur* is

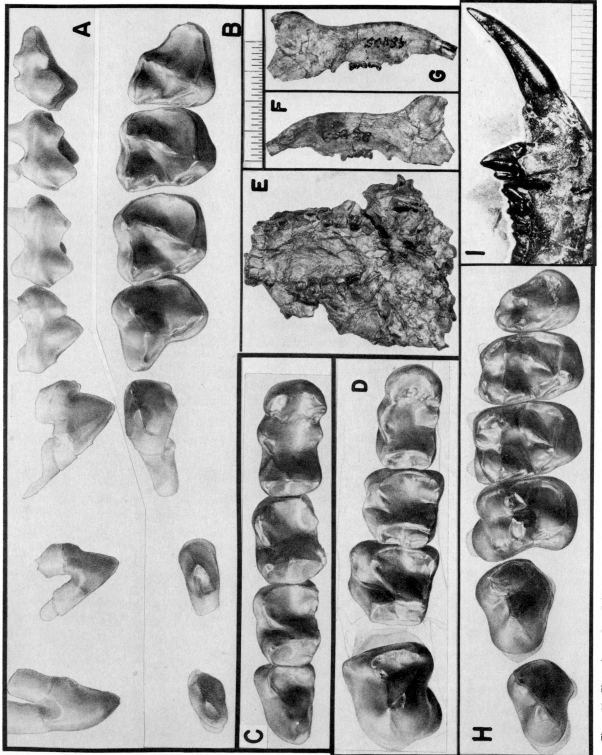

Figure 23. *Phenacolemur.* Late Paleocene to early Eocene, western North America. *Phenacolemur jepseni*, early Eocene. Left C, P²–P⁴, and M¹–M³. A, buccal view: B, occlusal view. Right P₄, M₁–M₃; C, occlusal view. Crushed skull: E, ventral view. Left mandible with broken I₁ and M₁–₃: F, medial view; G, lateral view. *Phenacolemur pagei*, late Paleocene. Right P₄, M₁–M₃: D, occlusal view. Left P²–M³: H, occlusal view. Right mandible (shown partially) with I₁ and P₄–M₃: I, lateral view. Subdivisions on scales (pertinent to F, G, and I) represent 0.5 mm. [A–D, and H from Simpson (1955).]

a conspicuous specialization of this geı.us (Figure 23). In addition to the extreme reduction of the lower antemolar dentition between the first incisor and the fourth premolar, the molars are also considerably specialized, at least as compared to other paromomyids. In general, the cheek teeth are robust (Figure 24), particularly the protocones, and there is a tendency for the major cusps to become partly incorporated into the crests leading to them. The conules lose their distinctness and the hypocones spread out so that, in effect, the most advanced species of the genus had nearly square upper molars. The extreme enlargement of the hypocone on M^3, compared to the size of hypocones on M^1 and M^2, is also a distinctive characteristic. Coupled with these dental adaptations is a relatively short, expanded mandibular angle.

A crushed skull of *Phenacolemur jepseni* (Figure 23) gives evidence that the cranium was low and broad and that the postpalatal length was probably shorter than the palatal (Simpson, 1955; Szalay, 1972a). There was a sagittal crest and the slightly concave palate was unusually broad. The basicranial structure unmistakably shows a bulla formed from the petrosal, and a broad, platelike ectotympanic, probably derived from a ringlike condition, is in contact with the lateral edge of the bulla (Szalay, 1976). Phylogenetically significant details of the basicranium are discussed above under the order.

A detailed treatment of the included species can be found in Simpson (1955) and Bown and Rose (1976). Of the North American species, the oldest, *P. pagei*, is well known from jaws and palates. By Tiffanian time the hypertrophied $P_{\overline{4}}$ is already established and this character seems to unite a *P. pagei–P. praecox–P. citatus* complex. As recognized by Bown and Rose (1976), in contrast to the latter clade, the diminutive *P. simonsi* can be grouped with *P. jepseni* and *P. fuscus*, these taxa being characterized by a less hypertrophied $P_{\overline{4}}$. The fourth premolar is unknown in *P. lapparenti*, the second European species from the Paris Basin. *Phenacolemur praecox* is perhaps the largest species of the genus, although it is only slightly larger than *P. citatus* in the dimensions of $P_{\overline{4}}$.

The dental formula is $I_{\overline{1}}^{\cdot 2}$; $C_{\overline{1}}^{1}$; $P_{\overline{4}}^{2,3,4}$; $M_{\overline{1},\overline{2},\overline{3}}^{1,2,3}$.

The broad-based enlarged fourth premolars (Figure 24) may have been implemental in cracking and crushing function. Hence, only as a guesstimate, the primary feeding preferences of *Phenacolemur* spp. were

some specialized form of phytophagy rather than zoophagy. A large proportion of insects, however, was likely part of the diet.

Tribe Micromomyini
Szalay, 1974b

(= or including Microsyopidae, *incertae sedis*: Bown and Rose, 1976.)

DISTRIBUTION
  Middle Paleocene to early Eocene (Torrejonian to Wasatchian). Western North America.
INCLUDED TAXA
  Micromomys and *Tinimomys*.

Discussion

The two included genera differ from the purgatorins, and paromomyins other than *Phenacolemur*, in having distinctly enlarged fourth premolars, and from *Phenacolemur* in having enlarged the fourth premolar independently and in a divergent manner. There is little doubt that the extreme enlargement of the central incisors and the enlargement of $P_{\overline{4}}$ are independent from these attributes of all other paromomyids. These genera enlarged their fourth premolars somewhat convergently with those of *Phenacolemur*, but, unlike the latter which emphasized a broad-based cone, micromomyins developed a trenchant paracristid. The molar morphology of this tribe is strikingly distinctive from those of paromomyinans, attesting to the independent derivation of both the latter and micromomyins from a more primitive palaechthoninan paromomyid ancestry.

If we consider the extremely small size and the lost premolars as derived features shared between *Palenochtha* and micromomyins, then the latter may have originated from the former, or a form near it. These two features listed, however, have very low phylogenetic valency as they are common and therefore they may have evolved independently. Another suggestion of affinity among these three genera may be the well-developed cuspate paraconid, but it is uncertain whether this is a primitive or derived feature among Plesiadapiformes.

Statements by Bown and Rose (1976) and Gingerich (1976a) that micromomyins are microsyopids are not substantiated by any convincing shared and derived characters. In fact, known cheek teeth of microsyopids

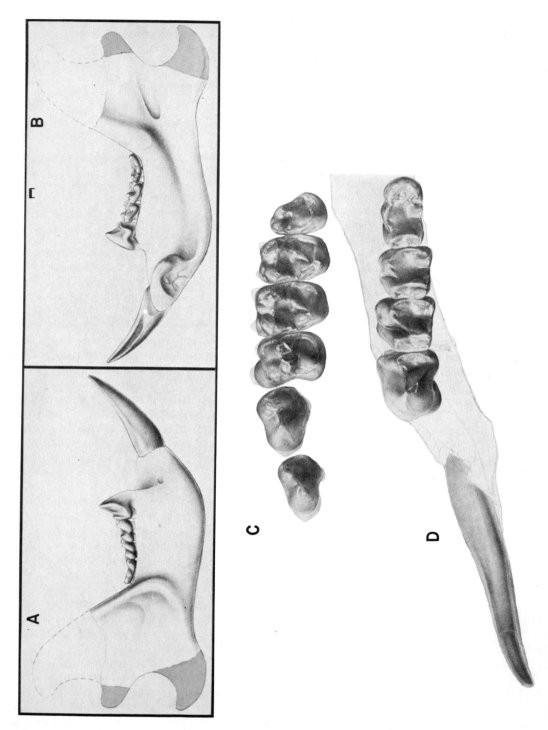

Figure 24. *Phenacolemur pagei.* Late Paleocene, western North America. Right mandible with I, and P$_4$–M$_3$: A, lateral view; B, medial view. Left P^2–M^3: C, occlusal view. Right I$_1$, P$_4$–M$_3$: D, occlusal view. Broken lines and stippling represent reconstruction. Scale represents 1 mm. [A and B by A. Cleary; C and D from Simpson (1955).]

and micromomyins are clearly divergent in their morphology. The only potentially derived character shared between these groups is the enlarged incisor, a feature which cannot be corroborated by the cheek dentition to be a homologous condition (see pertinent discussions on pp. 39–40).

MICROMOMYS Szalay, 1973

DISTRIBUTION
Late Paleocene (Tiffanian). Rocky Mt. region.
KNOWN SPECIES
Micromomys silvercouleei Szalay, 1973, type species
LOCALITIES: Silver Coulee⋆ (98).

DISCUSSION

This is a very distinctive although poorly known tiny genus that is both highly specialized and, in some respects of its molar morphology, perhaps primitive. It differs from other paromomyids in having a combination of a very tall fourth lower premolar and a molar construction with tall, sharp-crested trigonids and a relatively broad talonid (Figure 25).

Micromomys, as well as *Tinimomys*, represent unusually adapted primates which, convergently to some species of *Phenacolemur*, have evolved a large $P_{\overline{4}}$. The morphology of the molars clearly shows that the $P_{\overline{4}}$ enlargement was entirely independent from that of *Phenacolemur (sensu stricto)*.

The dental formula of *Micromomys*, known from the type specimen only, appears to be the same as that of *Palenochtha minor*, in having two incisors, the canine retained, and two premolars and three molars.

The teeth anterior to the enlarged $P_{\overline{4}}$ are not known but an approximate picture can be gained as to their size relationship. The anterior incisor was enlarged, distinctly more than the one posterior to it. The canine was not large, yet probably slightly larger than the incisor in front of it. $P_{\overline{3}}$ was double rooted, the anterior root being particularly constricted mesiodistally.

The enormously enlarged $P_{\overline{4}}$ has sweeping cutting edges on its mesial and distal borders and also a small, but distinct, talonid. Judged from the distinct, deep hypoflexid on the $P_{\overline{4}}$, the hitherto unknown P^4 probably had a deep, bladelike paracone which fitted into the hypoflexid and sheared against the distobuccal edge of the protoconid and cristid obliqua. The probable complex of this little plesiadapiform is not unlike that of *Uintanius*, a middle Eocene omomyid. It is likely that *Micromomys* was insectivorous.

It may be noted that both the jaw and known teeth of this tiny primate are smaller than those of the smallest living primate *Microcebus murinus*. It is in fact the smallest known primate. *Micromomys silvercouleei* is even smaller than *Palenochtha minor*.

TINIMOMYS Szalay, 1974b

DISTRIBUTION
Early Eocene (Wasatchian). Rocky Mt. region.
KNOWN SPECIES
Tinimomys graybulliensis Szalay, 1974b, type species
LOCALITIES: Gray Bull (162); Slick Creek (163); Supersite (164); Dobie Butte (166); Bone Hill⋆ (174).

DISCUSSION

Tinimomys differs from all other known primates in its combination of having a semimolariform fourth upper premolar, and in having the preand postcingula strongly confluent lingually on the known upper teeth (Figure 26). It obviously differs from *Purgatorius*, *Palenochtha*, *Palaechthon*, and *Plesiolestes* in having the strong lingual cingulum and from such more advanced paromomyids as *Paromomys* and *Phenacolemur* and from omomyids in lacking the protocone fold on the distolingual slope of upper molars. It can be clearly differentiated from known carpolestids in the lack of proliferation of the buccal cusps and conules on the fourth upper premolar and in the presence of a strong lingual cingulum. The referred specimens of this genus (Szalay, 1974b; Bown and Rose, 1976) show a $P_{\overline{4}}$ smaller than and of slightly different conformation from that of *Micromomys*.

Judging from the size of its teeth, *Tinimomys*, as *Micromomys*, was distinctly smaller than the smallest living primates, the Malagasy cheirogaleid *Microcebus*.

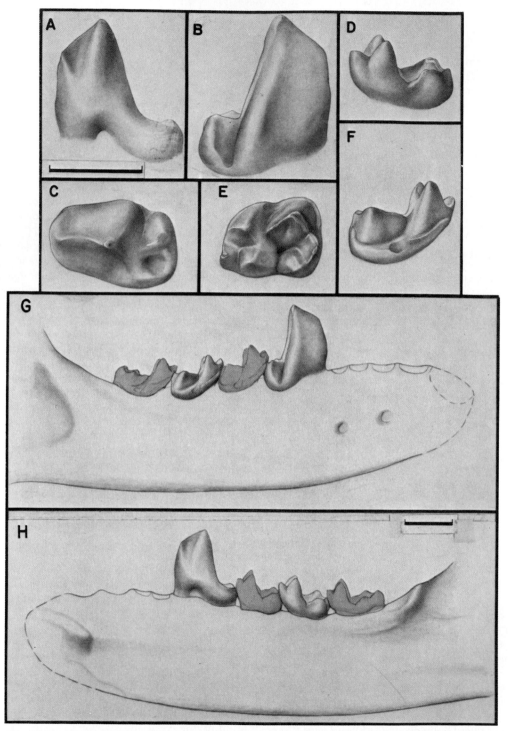

Figure 25. *Micromomys silvercouleei.* Late Paleocene, western North America. Right $P_{\overline{4}}$: A, lingual view; B, buccal view; C, occlusal view. Right $M_{\overline{3}}$: D, lingual view; E, occlusal view; F, buccal view. Right mandible fragment with $P_{\overline{4}}$ and $M_{\overline{2}}$, with $M_{\overline{1}}$ and $M_{\overline{3}}$ reconstructed: G, lateral view; H, medial view. Scales represent 1 mm. [From Szalay (1973).]

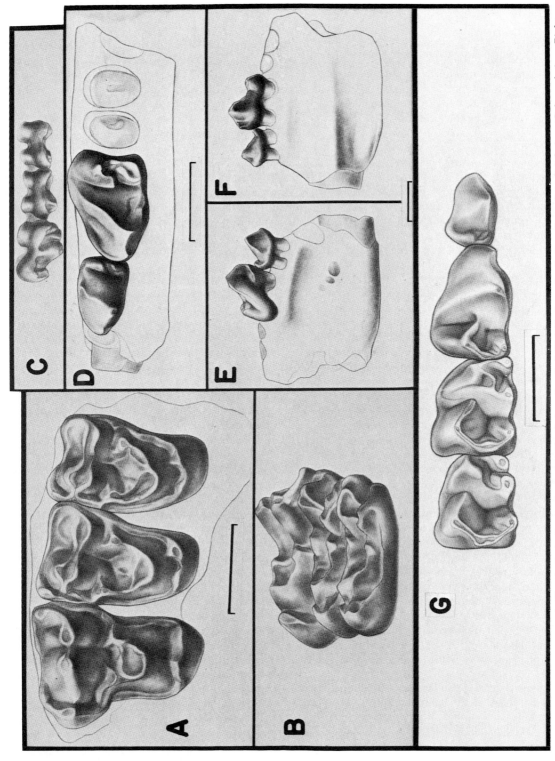

Figure 26. *Tinimomys graybulliensis*. Early Eocene, western North America. Left P⁴–M². A, occlusal view; C, buccal view. Right mandible with P₃–P₄: D, occlusodistal view; B, occlusodistal view; E, lateral view; F, medial view. Left P₄–M₂: G, occlusal view. Scales represent 1 mm. [A–F from Szalay (1974b); G by A. Cleary.]

There is little doubt that *Tinimomys* is a plesiadapiform primate (Szalay, 1974b; Bown and Rose, 1976). The construction of the fourth premolar, the low cusps, the complete absence of the preparacrista, and the short postmetacrista with an incipient metastyle are features of most of the primitive early Tertiary primates.

Establishing family ties of the genus, based on the name-bearing upper molars, however, is a difficult task. Coupled with the scarcity of specimens is the peculiar morphology of the enlarged fourth premolars and, more important, the enlarged lower incisor of the referred specimen, suggesting paromomyid ties. The P^4 of *Tinimomys* is more similar to that of the primitive *Palaechthon* than to that of any other known early Tertiary genus. The cusps are low and bulbous, the preparacrista is completely reduced, and the stylar shelf is almost completely absent. *Palaechthon* shares the following features with *Tinimomys:* The buccal half of P^4 is wide, a strong parastyle is present, the paracone and metacone are connate, and the P^4 is buccally longer than the following molar. *Palaechthon* has an incipient paraconule on the P^4, a feature of minor importance which may have been present on the fourth premolar of *Tinomomys*.

One might argue that the lingual part of the upper molars of this genus poses serious difficulty to an unquestionable allocation of *Tinimomys* to the Paromomyidae. *Purgatorius, Palaechthon, Palenochtha, Paromomys, Phenacolemur,* carpolestids, primitive anaptomorphines, and plesiadapids have a distinct continuity (of varying strength) between the apices of the hypocone (usually ill-defined) and protocone. These same primates, with the occasional exception of *Pronothodectes,* have pre- and postcingula that are not connected around the lingual border of the teeth. *Tinimomys* has neither a connection between the apices of the hypocone and protocone nor is the lingual connection of the pre- and postcingula absent. Although in some omomyids, such as *Omomys,* the connection between the hypocone and protocone is lacking and the pre- and postcingula are connected, affinities of *Tinimomys* with omomyids are not advocated.

The upper fourth premolar of the Paleocene plesidapid *Pronothodectes* is semimolariform, as is that of *Tinimomys* and *Palaechthon.* In *Pronothodectes,* however, the parastyle is small and the paraconule is exceptionally large on P^4. This tooth is also shorter anteroposteriorly than the molar following it. There is no known evidence for *Tinimomys* that indicates carpolestid affinities. The characteristic tendency for the proliferation of the buccal cusps and conules on the P^4 of known carpolestids is not present in this genus.

The enigmatic primate *Navajovius* (here tentatively considered a paromomyid) has a P^4 that could be called semimolariform, although the metacone is completely incorporated into a long crest (the centrocrista and the postmetacrista) that runs from the apex of the paracone to the distobuccal corner of the tooth. Although the hypocone is not connected to the apex of the protocone in *Navajovius,* the postcingulum sharply ends with the hypocone without any traces of connection to the precingulum around the lingual border of the molars.

The originally referred specimen (Figure 26) from the type locality holds the key to the affinity of this genus. It is a right lower jaw fragment with P_{3-4}, the broken root of a greatly enlarged incisor, and an alveolus between the latter and P_3. Szalay (1974b) judged this specimen to have been conspecific with the holotype, basing this view on the degree and kind of enlargement of the P_4, occlusal factors, as well as on the appropriateness of the size of this specimen. The P_4 is enlarged in a manner distinctive from that seen in *Phenacolemur praecox* or *P. pagei.* Unlike that of *Phenacolemur,* but strikingly similar to that of *Micromomys,* the P_4 has a very distinctive paracristid and a lingually discernible paraconid aligned exactly mesial to the protoconid. This tooth is clearly less tall, however, in *Tinimomys.* This genus, in spite of the fact that it has a somewhat less derived P_4 than the Paleocene form, has an apparently more derived dental formula in having one less tooth between the P_4 and the enlarged incisor. Both *Tinimomys* and *Micromomys* have greatly enlarged incisors.

The close affinity between *Micromomys* and *Tinimomys* appears to be reasonably certain. The two genera occupy a phenetically distinct position in respect to other Paromomyidae, as expressed by the tribal distinction accorded to them.

There are three major factors to be considered in assessing the form–function of the remains of this species: (1) the extreme small size and (2) the enlarged fourth premolar are characters of the holotype, but (3) the enlarged incisor is a feature of the referred specimen.

The very small size of this taxon would suggest

some form of insectivory, yet the construction of the premolars suggests a possibly phytophagous diet involving some sort of concentrated energy source such as gums, resins, or seeds. These teeth, although the cusp apices are relatively high, are enlarged primarily at their base and in the protocone and protoconid. Large surface areas of the molars are also made up by the well-developed cingula and hypocone. The enlarged incisor of the referred specimen is probably primitive for both *Micromomys* and perhaps for *Palenochtha* and several other paromomyids also.

It is not likely, therefore, that the large size of the anterior teeth alone may be a uniquely derived feature of *Tinimomys*, and consequently it is not very useful in assessing adaptations of this genus. If the particular crown morphologies of the various large-incisored paromomyids were to become known, the differences, of course, would become valuable in assessing their feeding mechanism.

Tribe Navajoviini, new

(= or including: Anaptomorphidae: Simpson, 1937, in part. Microsyopidae: Szalay, 1969a, in part. Uintasoricinae: Bown and Rose, 1976, in part.)

DISTRIBUTION
   Late Paleocene to early Eocene (Tiffanian to Wasatchian), Rocky Mt. region; early Eocene (Neustrian). Western Europe.

INCLUDED TAXA
Navajovius and *Berruvius*.

DISCUSSION

This group, based on *Navajovius*, differs from all other known paromomyids in having an $M_{\overline{3}}$ shorter and generally smaller than $M_{\overline{2}}$ and in lacking the extensive lingual slope of the protocone on the upper molars. Highly characteristic of *Navajovius* (but not known in *Berruvius*) is the construction of the postcanine teeth anterior to P^4. The buccal half of the P^4 is elongated and trenchant, and P^3 and C^1 are bladelike and completely lack a protocone. This is unlike in any omomyid, all of which, where known, retain the primitive condition of P^3 in having a distinct protocone, usually subequal to the paracone. There are no derived features shared between navajoviins and primitive adapids or omomyids. An eventual recognition of more recent affinities of these forms with some other archontans, perhaps tupaiids, or erinaceomorph Insectivora, rather than with the morphotype of the paromomyids, is a possibility. As voiced elsewhere (Szalay, 1972b), there is no evidence that would uphold the suggestion (Szalay, 1969a) that *Navajovius* and microsyopids are particularly closely related.

NAVAJOVIUS Matthew and Granger, 1921

DISTRIBUTION
   Late Paleocene to early Eocene (Tiffanian to Wasatchian). Rocky Mt. region.
KNOWN SPECIES
   1. *Navajovius kohlhaasae* Matthew and Granger, 1921, type species
LOCALITIES: Mason Pocket⋆ (72); Joe's Bone Bed, Black Peaks (122).
   2. *Navajovius mckennai* Szalay, 1969a
(=*Navajovius? mckennai* Szalay, 1969a.)
LOCALITIES: AM Quarry 88, San José⋆ (248).

DISCUSSION

The type species, represented by upper and lower dentitions (Figure 27), was a very small animal. It has long been controversial, having been referred to the Omomyidae (incl. Anaptomorphidae), Paromomyidae, and the Microsyopidae, and is clearly a difficult genus to evaluate. The molars show probably primitive features, possibly even more primitive than those present in the earliest form one would call a primate. The antemolar dentition appears to be specialized for shearing in a fashion that is *sui generis* and perhaps also indicative of some unknown relationships.

As in paromomyids, but as in numerous other small mammals also, the incisors, at least the first pair, are enlarged. Unlike in most other paromomyids, the last lower molar is slightly shorter, with relatively less surface than the preceding molars. The paraconids are only slightly smaller than the metaconids.

The mandible is relatively shallow and the mandibular angle is short and slender. There are no recognized unusual adaptations on the known mandibular specimens.

The dental formula is probably $I_{\frac{1+2}{1+2}}$; $C_{\frac{1}{1}}$; $P_{\frac{3+4}{3+4}}$; $M_{\frac{1+2+3}{1+2+3}}$.

Navajovius was likely to have been highly zoophagous, probably some form of specialized insectivore.

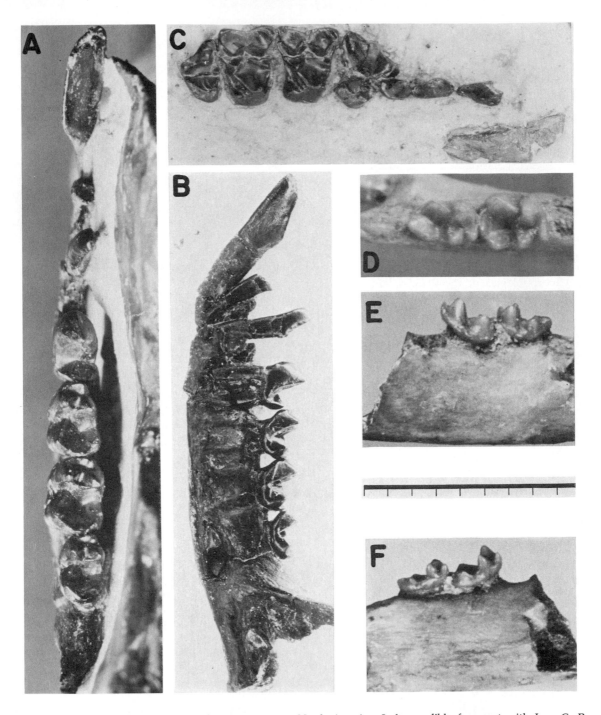

Figure 27. *Navajovius kohlhaasae.* Late Paleocene, western North America. Left mandible fragment with I$_{\overline{1-2}}$, C, P$_{\overline{3-4}}$, M$_{\overline{1}}$–M$_{\overline{3}}$: A, occlusal view; B, lateral view. Upper dentition, I (or canine lying on its side), P^{1} or C, P^{2}–P^{4}, M^{1}–M^{3}: C, occlusal view. *Berruvius lasseroni.* Late Paleocene, France. Left mandible fragment with M$_{\overline{2}}$–M$_{\overline{3}}$: D, occlusal view; E, buccal view; F, lingual view. Subdivisions on scale represent 0.5 mm. [A–C from Szalay (1969a); D–F from Russell (1964), courtesy of D. E. Russell.]

BERRUVIUS Russell, 1964

(= or including: *Navajovius*: Szalay, 1972b.)

DISTRIBUTION
    Late Paleocene to early Eocene (Cernaysian to Neustrian). Paris Basin.
KNOWN SPECIES
    Berruvius lasseroni Russell, 1964, type species
    (=*Navajovius lasseroni*: Szalay, 1972b.)
    LOCALITIES: Berru★ (92); Mutigny (190); Marne (191).

DISCUSSION

The type sample (Figure 27) from Mouras Quarry of Berru is known by two teeth, and consequently the diagnosis of this taxon is very inadequate. The genus is similar to *Navajovius* and it was in the past considered as possibly congeneric with the North American genus (Szalay, 1972b). Although there are similarities between the species (see also Russell *et al.*, 1967), particularly the small M₃, *Berruvius* is here considered to be valid.

At present no other characters can be recognized on the few known specimens, which would suggest broader affinities other than those discussed under the Navajoviini (p. 65).

Judged by the extreme small size and similarities to *Navajovius*, *Berruvius* was also very likely insectivorous.

Family Picrodontidae
Simpson, 1937

(= or including: Picrodontini: Schwartz and Krishtalka, 1977.)

DISTRIBUTION
    Middle to late Paleocene (Torrejonian to Tiffanian). Western North America.
INCLUDED TAXA
    Picrodus and *Zanycteris*.

DISCUSSION

The ordinal affinities of the dentally very advanced tiny picrodontids of the North American Paleocene have long been a problem for students of early Tertiary mammals. The highly altered molar morphology of picrodontids caused earlier workers, like Matthew and Simpson, to suspect rather vague relationships with either insectivorans, bats, or primates. The steadily accumulating evidence from new specimens and new studies, however, indicates with a sufficiently high degree of probability that picrodontids are paromomyid primate derivatives (Szalay, 1968b). Picrodontids are known only from two species each of monotypic genera, *Picrodus* and *Zanycteris*, *P. silberlingi* occurring in both middle and late Paleocene sediments, and *Z. paleocenus* in late Paleocene deposits only.

The major changes during the evolution of the picrodontids from a more primitive tribosphenic ancestry seem to be largely restricted to the cheek teeth among the known anatomical features.

As in paromomyids such as *Palaechthon*, *Palenochtha*, or *Paromomys*, the mandible of *Picrodus* is shortened and moderately deep. The masseteric fossa is extensive, and, although a complete coronoid process is not known, it was probably large, indicating that both the ectental and orthal components of the masticatory stroke were important. As in paromomyids, the angle of the mandible in *Picrodus* is long and relatively narrow, primitive in its proportions, and very similar to those of early Tertiary Insectivora. The articular condyle is small and rounded, not suggestive of any particular specialization restricting masticating actions of the mandible. If anything, this structure shows a considerable freedom of movement at the jaw articulation.

The only known cranium of a picrodontid is the type specimen of *Zanycteris paleocenus*, a partial, crushed skull which consists mainly of the palatal portion. The muzzle was relatively narrow compared to the expanded posterior half of the palate. The root of the zygoma is above the first and second molars, and the relative dimensions of this structure do not suggest any particular specialization. The skull reveals a potential wealth of information yet, at the same time, poses many tantalizing unanswered questions. Judged from the occlusal relationships of the anterior teeth, there were two incisors anterior to the large, buccolingually constricted canine (Szalay, 1972b). Posterior to the long diastema behind the canine, there were three double-rooted premolars, probably the second, third, and fourth. Judged from the alveoli, these teeth were elongated, and P^4, usually the molarlike of the upper premolars, had no lingual alveolus and hence presumably no protocone, or at least not a prominent one.

In general, in both genera there is a great reduction in the height of the cusps of the upper molars, and the conules are eliminated. The extensive enlargement of the metacone on the first upper molar results in the disproportionate emphasis on the posterobuccal components of the ancestral upper molar, resulting in the distorted, unusual appearance of the picrodontid M^1.

In the lower molars the trigonids are drastically reduced, whereas the talonid, particularly on the first molar, is greatly enlarged. The hypoconid is obliterated, and as a result of the posterobuccal extension of the talonid, the entoconid and hypoconulid are anterolingually displaced. For further discussions on the homologies of the topography of picrondontid molars, Szalay (1968b, 1972b) and Figure 6 should be consulted.

The enlarged lower medial incisor is not noticeably different from those of the more primitive paromo-

myins. Its apical half (i.e., the edge of the elongated tooth) is narrower than the basal part, so in effect this enlarged tooth is knifelike with a long edge on it. The homologies of the three anterior lower teeth—the two incisors and the small, premolariform canine—are judged to be the same as those of known paromomyids (other than *Phenacolemur*), carpolestids, and *Pronothodectes*.

The enamel of the basined parts of both upper and lower molars is unusually papillated, thus greatly increasing the total available surface for occlusal contact. It appears that the unorthodox flattening and spreading of the upper molars and the elongation of the buccal and posterior crests of the lower molars are the result of selection for crushing and shredding plant materials, which were not very abrasive. Flattening and elongating of the molars is probably significantly coupled with the transversely strongly constricted premolars. The combined effect of the transversely narrow upper canine and premolars might have served as a very effective slicing device against the lower premolars, canine, and enlarged incisor. The low crowned teeth of picrodontids could not have withstood abrasive attrition for even the very short life span of mammals their size. Their peculiar, phyllostomatid batlike dental adaptation might have been the result of selection for juicy fruit, tree exudate, or a nectar-feeding diet.

PICRODUS Douglass, 1908

(= or including: *Megopterna* Douglass, 1908.)

DISTRIBUTION
   Middle and early late Paleocene (Torrejonian and early Tiffanian). Rocky Mt. region.
KNOWN SPECIES
   Picrodus silberlingi Douglass, 1908, type species
   (=*Megopterna minuta* Douglass, 1908.)
   LOCALITIES: Silberling Q.★ (20); Gidley Q. (24); Swain Q. (28); Saddle (44); Keefer Hill (38).

DISCUSSION

   This genus is represented by one species, a very small primate about the size of *Palenochtha minor*. *Picrodus* is reasonably well known from upper and lower dentitions (Figures 28 and 29); no crania or

postcranial elements are known. The peculiar, highly derived dental morphology of *Picrodus* is discussed under the treatment of the family. By contrast to the derived molars, however, the mandible is not altered from what might be considered a primitive paromomyin condition.

   The differences of this genus from *Zanycteris*, the only other member of the family, lie in the following characters: The parastylar area is more reduced, the stylar shelf is more pronounced, the mesial crest of the metacone is relatively longer than the distal crest of the paracone, the paracone is more reduced, and the postprotocrista does not join the apex of the protocone.

   The dental formula of *Picrodus* is $I\frac{1,2}{1,2}$; $C\frac{1}{1}$; $P\frac{2,3,4}{3,4}$; $M\frac{1,2,3}{1,2,3}$.

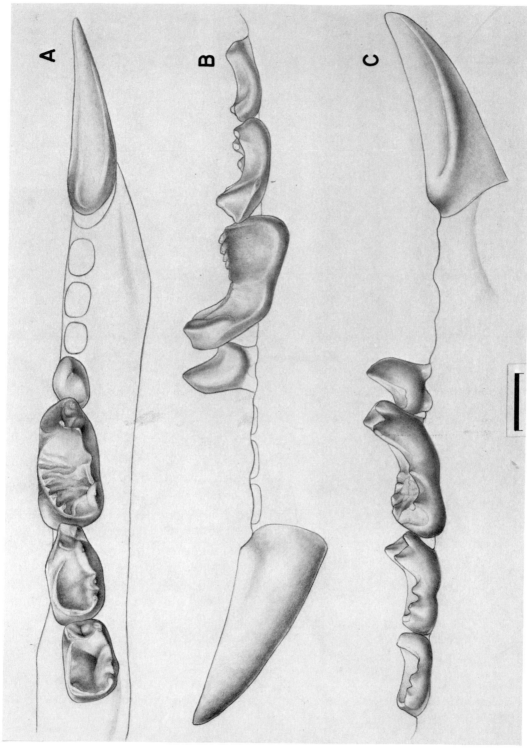

Figure 28. *Picrodus silberlingi*. Middle Paleocene, western North America. Left mandible with I_1, P_4, M_1–M_3: A, occlusal view; B, buccal view; C, lingual view. Scale represents 1 mm. [By A. Cleary.]

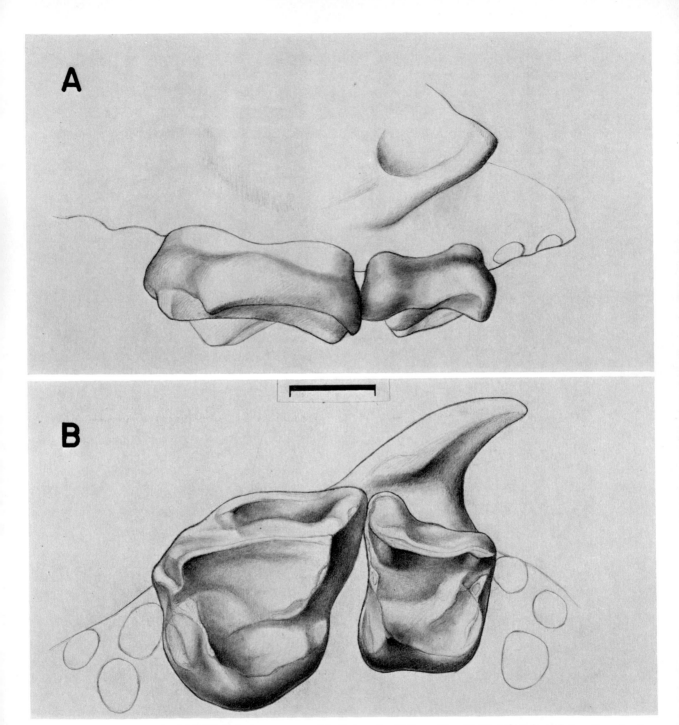

Figure 29. *Picrodus silberlingi.* Middle Paleocene, western North America. Left maxilla with M¹–M²: A, buccal view; B, occlusal view. Scale represents 1 mm. [By A. Cleary.]

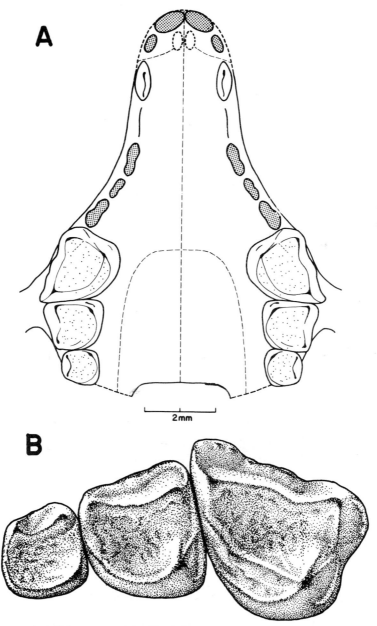

Figure 30. *Zanycteris paleocenus.* Late Paleocene, western North America. Reconstructed palate: A, occlusal view. Right M$^{1-3}$: B, occlusal view. [From Szalay (1968b).]

ZANYCTERIS Matthew, 1917a

(= or including: *Palaeonycteris* Weber and Abel, 1928.)

DISTRIBUTION
   Late Paleocene (Tiffanian). Rocky Mt. region.

KNOWN SPECIES
   Zanycteris paleocenus Matthew, 1917a, type species
(=*Palaeonycteris paleocenica* Weber and Abel, 1928.)
LOCALITIES: Mason Pocket★ (72); Joe's Bone Bed, Black Peaks (122).

DISCUSSION

The first reported specimen of the only known species of this genus is a crushed skull (see Szalay, 1968b), but no elements of the lower jaw or lower dentition are known. Additional teeth were reported by Scheibout (1974).

The badly distorted skull has a posteriorly wide palate, probably an enlarged medial incisor in front of a smaller one, a canine, three premolars, and three molars (Figure 30). The diagnostic differences of the teeth from those of *Picrodus* are listed under the latter, and the skull is discussed under the family.

The dental formula of *Zanycteris* is probably I⅟₂; C⅟₁; P²⁄₂,³⁄₃,⁴⁄₄; M¹⁄₁,²⁄₂,³⁄₃.

SUPERFAMILY PLESIADAPOIDEA
Trouessart, 1897

(= or including: Microsyopoidea: Van Valen, 1969, in part.)

DISTRIBUTION
   Early Paleocene to early Eocene (Puercan to Clarkforkian and Thanetian to early Neustrian). Western North America and Western Europe.
INCLUDED TAXA
   Families Plesiadapidae, Saxonellidae, and Carpolestidae.

DISCUSSION

There are three family–group taxa united under the Plesiadapoidea, as they probably shared a common ancestor after their separation from paromomyoids. The evidence, however, is still inadequate to recognize the recency of relationships within this monophyletic superfamily. Judged from the morphology of the most primitive members of the Plesiadapidae (*Pronothodectes*) and of the Carpolestidae (*Elphidotarsius*) the plesiadapoid common ancestor was a form with two incisors, a canine, three premolars, and three molars. No particular specialization of the premolars can be deduced for this morphotype, although the central incisors were probably slightly enlarged and the canines reduced. The molars were probably similar to those in *Pronothodectes*, *Elphidotarsius*, and *Saxonella*, with mesiodistally slightly constricted trigonids, broad talonids, and the upper molars with a protocone apex more central than the more mesial paromomyoid condition.

Family Plesiadapidae
Trouessart, 1897

(= or including: Platychoeropidae Lydekker, 1887. Apatemyidae: Matthew, 1915, in part. Chiromyidae: Teilhard de Chardin, 1922. "Tillarvernidae" Piton, 1940.)

DISTRIBUTION
   Early Paleocene to late Paleocene (Puercan through Clarkforkian) and late Paleocene to early Eocene (Thanetian to early Neustrian). Western North America and western Europe.
INCLUDED TAXA
   Plesiadapis, *Pronothodectes*, *Platychoerops*, and *Chiromyoides*.

DISCUSSION

This family is undoubtedly the most successful of Paleocene primates. The group, recently revised by Gingerich (1976a), is usually identified by its extreme incisor specializations, an adaptive complex probably at least in part independently attained from those of the *Ignacius–Phenacolemur* group.

An undescribed plesiadapid is known by isolated premolar and molar teeth from North American early Paleocene beds (Puercan of Purgatory Hill). It cannot be determined whether this taxon had any of the more striking incisor specializations displayed by later members of the family, but it may have had the full primate complement of teeth displayed by *Purgatorius*.

Not considering the undescribed form, the morphotype condition for the published plesiadapids is almost certainly embodied in the morphology of the middle Paleocene *Pronothodectes matthewi*. This form, not because of its relative age, but due to its known morphology, is a perfect choice as a structural ancestor of *Plesiadapis*. The age of *Pronothodectes*, of course, corroborates this hypothesis.

PRONOTHODECTES Gidley, 1923

DISTRIBUTION

Middle Paleocene (Torrejonian). Rocky Mt. region.

KNOWN SPECIES

1. *Pronothodectes matthewi* Gidley, 1923, type species

LOCALITIES: Gidley Quarry★ (24); Tongue River (31); Saddle (44).

2. *Pronothodectes jepi* Gingerich, 1975b

LOCALITIES: Rock Bench Q.★ (26).

DISCUSSION

Pronothodectes, known by teeth, maxilla, and jaw fragments (Figure 31), is diagnosed largely by its primitive characteristics when contrasted to other plesiadapids. Unlike *Plesiadapis*, which has only one lower incisor, the enlarged one, a small lower canine, I$_{\bar{2}}$, as well as an additional premolar below is retained by *Pronothodectes*.

The dental formula is I$\frac{2}{2}$; C$\frac{1}{1}$; P$\frac{2,3,4}{2,3,4}$; M$\frac{1,2,3}{1,2,3}$.

The shortening of premolars and the expansion of the third lower molar, so characteristic of other plesiadapids, are easily recognizable. It appears reasonable to hypothesize, as noted under the family discussion, that one of the species of *Pronothodectes* was ancestral to *Plesiadapis*.

The two species of *Pronothodectes* were approximately in the size range of the living *Lepilemur leucopus*. Although the deep-jawed middle Paleocene *Pronothodectes* retains an additional small incisor and a small canine, its enlarged, procumbent medial incisors are already robust with massive roots, indicating the establishment of a *Plesiadapis*-like habitus, at least as far as incisor structure and function are concerned.

PLESIADAPIS Gervais, 1877

[= or including: (*Tricuspidens*) Lemoine, 1887. *Sciurus:* Launay, 1908. *Nothodectes* Matthew, 1915. *Tetonius:* Gidley, 1923. *Sciuroides:* Piton, 1940. *Menatotherium* Piton, 1940. *Pronothodectes:* Gazin, 1956a, in part. (*Ancepsoides*) D. E. Russell, 1964. *Nannodectes* Gingerich, 1974.]

DISTRIBUTION

Late Paleocene to early Eocene (Tiffanian to Clarkforkian, and Thanetian to earliest Neustrian). Rocky Mt. region and western Europe.

KNOWN SPECIES

1. *Plesiadapis tricuspidens* Gervais, 1877, type species

(=*Plesiadapis gervaisi* Lemoine, 1887. *Plesiadapis rhemensis* Rütmeyer, 1891. *Plesiadapis remensis:* Stehlin, 1916. *Plesiadapis trouessarti* Schlosser, 1921, in part.)

LOCALITIES: Cernay (88); Lentille (90); Berru (92); Rilly★ (96).

2. *Plesiadapis intermedius* Gazin, 1971

(=*Pronothodectes* cf. *matthewi:* Gazin, 1956a. *Pronothodectes* cf. *simpsoni:* Gazin, 1956a. Cf. *Pronothodectes matthewi:* Gazin, 1969. *Nannodectes intermedius* Gingerich, 1974. *Nannodectes gazini* Gingerich, 1974.)

LOCALITIES: Douglass Q. (36); Keefer Hill★ (38); Saddle (44); Little Muddy Creek (46).

3. *Plesiadapis simpsoni* (Gazin, 1956a)

(=*Pronothodectes simpsoni* Gazin, 1956a. *Plesiadapis jepseni:* Gazin, 1956a, in part. *Nannodectes simpsoni:* Gingerich, 1974.)

LOCALITIES: Ledge★ (52); West End (68).

4. *Plesiadapis gidleyi* (Matthew, 1917b)

(=*Nothodectes gidleyi* Matthew, 1917b. *Plesiadapis tricuspidens:* Teilhard, 1922, in part. *Plesiadapis gidleyi:* Simpson, 1928. *Nannodectes gidleyi:* Gingerich, 1974.)

LOCALITIES: Mason Pocket★ (72); Joe's Bone Bed, Black Peaks (122).

5. *Plesiadapis fodinatus* Jepsen, 1930b

(=*Plesiadapis rubeyi* Gazin, 1942. *Plesiadapis farisi* Dorr, 1952. *Plesiadapis* cf. *fodinatus:* Gazin, 1956a. *Plesiadapis* cf. *jepseni:* Gazin, 1956a.)

LOCALITIES: Princeton Q.★ (100); Schaff Q. (104); Ravenscrag UAR-1 (106); Titanoides (108); Fossil Hollow (112); Chappo-I (116); Dell Creek (118).

6. *Plesiadapis dubius* (Matthew, 1915)

(=*Nothodectes dubius* Matthew, 1915. ?*Plesiadapis* sp. indet.: Simpson, 1928. *Plesiadapis* cf. *fodinatus:* Van Houten, 1945. *Plesiadapis? pearcei* Gazin, 1956c.)

LOCALITIES: Paint Creek (126); Variegated (144); Plateau Valley (146); Bear Creek, Togwotee Lower (148); Chappo-12 (150); Clark Fork★ (152).

7. *Plesiadapis anceps* Simpson, 1936

(=*Plesiadapis jepseni* Gazin, 1956a. *Plesiadapis praecursor* Gingerich, 1974.)

LOCALITIES: Tongue River (31); Douglas Q. (36); Keefer Hill (38); Scarritt Q.★ (40); Saddle (44); Highway Blowout (48).

8. *Plesiadapis rex* (Gidley, 1923)

[=*Tetonius rex* Gidley, 1923. *Nothodectes* cf. *gidleyi:* Simpson, 1927.

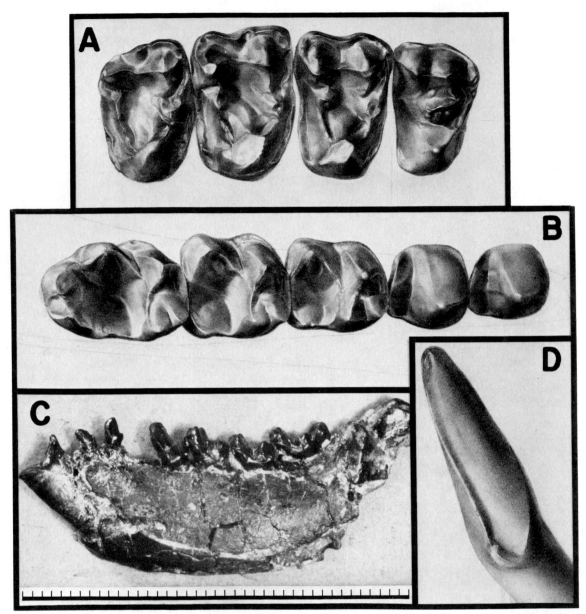

Figure 31. *Pronothodectes matthewi.* Middle Paleocene, western North America. Right P^4, M^1–M^3: A, occlusal view. Left P$_3$–P$_4$, M$_1$–M$_3$: B, occlusal view. Left mandible fragment with broken I$_1$–I$_2$, C, P$_4$, M$_1$–M$_3$: C, lateral view (subdivisions on scale represent 0.5 mm). Left I$_1$: D, occlusal view. [A,B,D from Simpson (1955).]

Plesiadapis rex: Simpson, 1937. *Plesiadapis jepseni:* Gazin, 1956a, in part. *Plesiadapis* cf. *fodinatus:* Gazin, 1956a. *Plesiadapis gidleyi:* Dorr, 1958. *Plesiadapis rubeyi:* Gazin (in Oriel), 1962b, in part. *Plesiadapis paskapooensis* Russell, 1964. *Plesiadapis* sp. McKenna (in Love), 1973.]
LOCALITIES: Melville 13★ (50); Ledge (52); Cedar Point (54); Battle Mt. (56); Chappo-17 (58); Erikson's Landing (60); Love Q. (62); Twin Creek (66); West End (68).

9. *Plesiadapis churchilli* Gingerich, 1974
(=*Plesiadapis farisi:* Krishtalka *et al.,* 1975.)
LOCALITIES: Croc Tooth (74); Airport (76); Long Draw★ (80); Malcolm's, Badwater area (82); Lower Sand Draw (97).

10. *Plesiadapis simonsi* Gingerich, 1974
LOCALITIES: Sand Draw, middle level★ (110).

11. *Plesiadapis cookei* Jepsen, 1930b

(=*Plesiadapis* cf. *cookei*: Gazin, 1942. *Plesiadapis cookei*: Gazin 1956c, in part.)

LOCALITIES: Little Sand Coulee Area★ (124); Paint Creek (126); Red Creek, Togwotee (132); Susan, Togwotee (134); Togwotee, 7 and 18 (136, 138); Verland's, Togwotee (140).

12. *Plesiadapis insignis* (Piton, 1940)

(=*Sciurus feignouxi*: Launay, 1908. *Sciuroides* sp. Piton, 1940. *Menatotherium insigne* Piton, 1940. *Plesiadapis insignis*: D. E. Russell, 1967.)

LOCALITIES: Menat★ (86).

13. *Plesiadapis walbeckensis* D. E. Russell, 1964

(=*Plesiadapis tricuspidens*: Weigelt, 1939, in part.)

LOCALITIES: Walbeck★ (42).

14. *Plesiadapis remensis* Lemoine, 1887

(=*Plesiadapis tricuspidens*: Teilhard, 1922, in part. *Plesiadapis* sp. indet., Teilhard, 1927. Primate *incertae sedis*, Cooper, 1932. *Plesiadapis* cf. *tricuspidens* Russell, Louis, and Savage, 1967.)

LOCALITIES: Cernay★ (88); Lentille (90); Berru (92).

15. *Plesiadapis russelli* Gingerich, 1974

(=''Renard'' and ''Civette?'' Orbigny, 1836, *Plesiadapis* sp. Stehlin, 1916. *Plesiadapis* inc. sp. Teilhard, 1922. *Plesiadapis* aff. *daubrei*: Teilhard 1922. *Platychoerops daubrei*: Russell, Louis and Savage, 1967, in part.)

LOCALITIES: Meudon★ (184).

DISCUSSION

Plesiadapis is one of the best known early Tertiary primates in that an incomplete and complete skull (Figures 32 and 33) and the large part of the skeleton (Figures 34–36) are known. *Plesiadapis* differs from *Pronothodectes* in lacking an $I_{\overline{2}}$ in all of the species allocated to it, although it preserves two upper incisors. The lower canine is retained in the North American *P. intermedius* and *P. simpsoni* but not in *P. gidleyi* and the European species of *Plesiadapis*.

Gingerich (1974) has erected the genus ''Nannodectes,'' in which he has included ''N.'' *intermedius*, ''N.'' *gazini*,'' ''N.'' *simpsoni*, and ''N.'' *gidleyi* (Figure 37). According to this author the sequence of these species represents an evolving lineage which separated from *Plesiadapis*. The diagnostic characters of ''*Nannodectes*'' are shared derived characters of this taxon with *Plesiadapis*, although, according to Gingerich, their derivation is independent on stratigraphic and geographic grounds. The validity of this genus would depend on distinctions in adaptations and on the strength of the phylogenetic hypothesis presented by Gingerich. The latter is, unfortunately, based primarily on the stratigraphic method of lineage construction and minor fluctuations in size rather than both stratigraphy and on morphological criteria of convincing strength. These species, whether or not an actual lineage, fall within the morphological character complex distinguishing *Plesiadapis* from *Pronothodectes*. Differences from *Chiromyoides* and *Platychoerops* are noted below under these genera.

The dental formula for the genus is $I_1^{1,2}$; $C_{\overline{1}}^{0-1}$; $P_{(\overline{2}),\overline{3},\overline{4}}^{2,3,4}$; $M_{\overline{1},\overline{2},\overline{3}}^{1,2,3}$.

The following distinguishing features of the species of *Plesiadapis* follow largely Gingerich (1976a), who was the last reviser of the genus.

Plesiadapis intermedius differs from *Pronothodectes* in lacking $I_{\overline{2}}$ and from the contemporary and sympatric *Plesiadapis anceps* in being smaller and having narrower teeth. *Plesiadapis simpsoni* is larger than *P. intermedius* but, like it, retains the lower canine; it is smaller than *P. gidleyi*. *Plesiadapis gidleyi* also differs from *P. intermedius* and *P. simpsoni* in having a cristid obliqua on the lower premolars and a mesostyle on the upper molars. *Plesiadapis anceps* retains $P_{\overline{2}}$ and lacks mesostyles on the upper molars, in contrast to *P. gidleyi* and *P. rex*. *Plesiadapis anceps*, unlike *P. rex*, lacks centroconules on I^1 and has a more rounded heel on $M_{\overline{3}}$. *Plesiadapis rex* is diagnosed as having a distinct centroconule on I^1 and in generally possessing mesostyles on M^{2-3}, and a squared, fissured heal on $M_{\overline{3}}$. *Plesiadapis rex* retains $P_{\overline{2}}$ in 50% of known specimens, has a well-developed diastema between $I_{\overline{1}}$ and $P_{\overline{3}}$, and has well-developed mesostyles on the upper molars. This species differs from *P. fodinatus* and *P. dubius* in being larger and with a more squared entoconid corner on $M_{\overline{1-2}}$. *Plesiadapis fodinatus* retains $P_{\overline{2}}$, has curved and crested entoconids, and has strong mesostyles on all upper molars. *Plesiadapis fodinatus* is very similar to, but is larger than, *P. dubius*, but smaller than *P. simpsoni* and *P. cookei*. *Plesiadapis dubius* consistently lacks $P_{\overline{2}}$ and has slightly more angular cusps and crests on its molars than *P. fodinatus*. The highly crenulated enamel of *P. dubius* differentiates it from earlier *Plesiadapis*. *Plesiadapis insignis*, represented by a complete crushed specimen in a slab, but not by good jaws, which would facilitate comparison, cannot be adequately diagnosed from *P. anceps*. It represents, however, the smallest of the European *Plesiadapis*, and it retains $P_{\overline{2}}$.

Plesiadapis walbeckensis is larger than *P. insignis*, but it is smaller than the remaining European *Plesiadapis*. *Plesiadapis walbeckensis* differs from the similar-sized *P. anceps* and *P. rex* in lacking $P_{\overline{2}}$ in some specimens. The European species also has a wider incisor and more crenulated enamel on the occlusal surface of the $M_{\overline{3}}$ hypoconulid than *P. anceps* and differs from *P. rex* in lacking I^1 centroconules and in general having a more

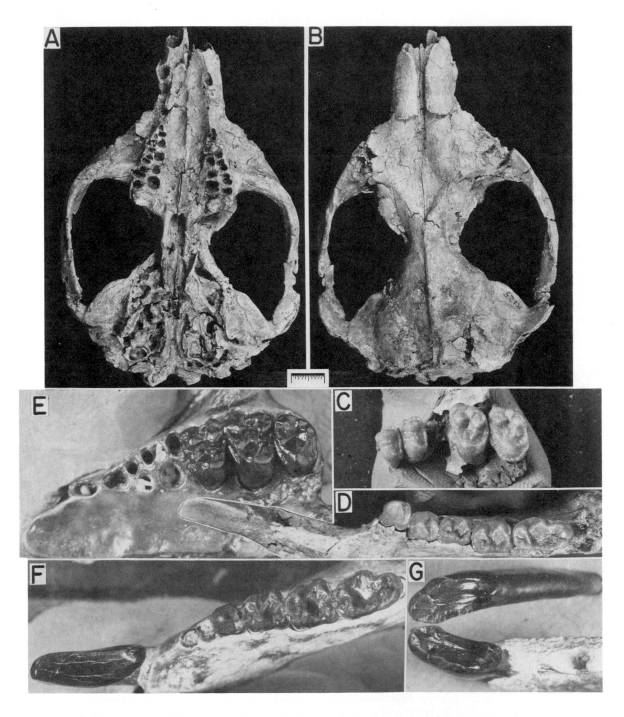

Figure 32. *Plesiadapis tricuspidens.* Late Paleocene, western Europe. Skull: A, ventral view; B, dorsal view. Left P$^{3-4}$ and M$^{2-3}$: C, occlusal view. Right mandible with I$_{\overline{1}}$ and P$_{\overline{3}}$–M$_{\overline{3}}$: D, occlusal view. Left maxilla fragment with M$^{1-3}$: E, occlusal view. Left mandible with I$_{\overline{1}}$ and P$_{\overline{4}}$–M$_{\overline{3}}$: F, occlusal view. Left and right I^{1}: G, occlusodistal view. Subdivisions on scale, applicable to A and B, represent 0.5 mm. [From Russell (1964), courtesy of D. E. Russell.]

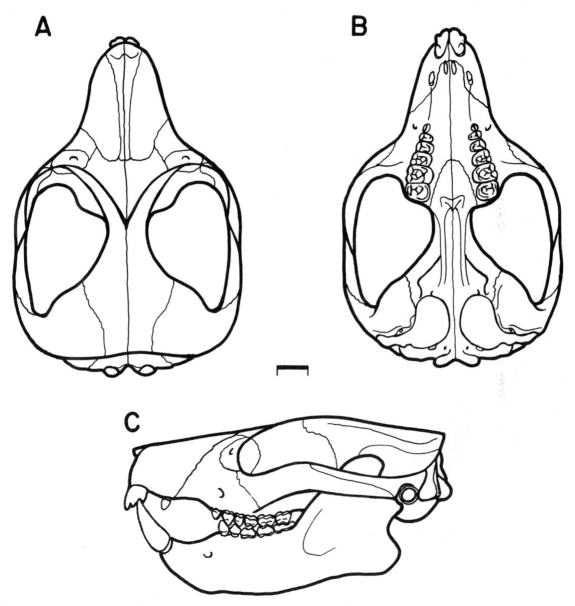

Figure 33. *Plesiadapis tricuspidens.* Late Paleocene, western Europe. Skull and mandible: A, dorsal view; B, ventral view; C, lateral view. Scale represents 1 cm. [By A. Cleary.]

rounded unfissured heel on M$\overline{3}$. *Plesiadapis remensis* is larger than *P. insignis* and *P. walbeckensis* and generally lacks P$\overline{2}$. It is smaller than *P. tricuspidens* and *P. russelli*. It is smaller than *P. simonsi* and differs from *P. churchilli* in consistently showing curved entoconid crests on M$\overline{1-2}$, and in having more crenulated enamel on the occlusal surfaces and lacking P$\overline{2}$. *Plesiadapis tricuspidens* is larger than *P. remensis*, *P. insignis*, and *P. walbeckensis*. It differs from *P. simonsi* in having a deeper mandible and relatively narrower cheek teeth. It is smaller

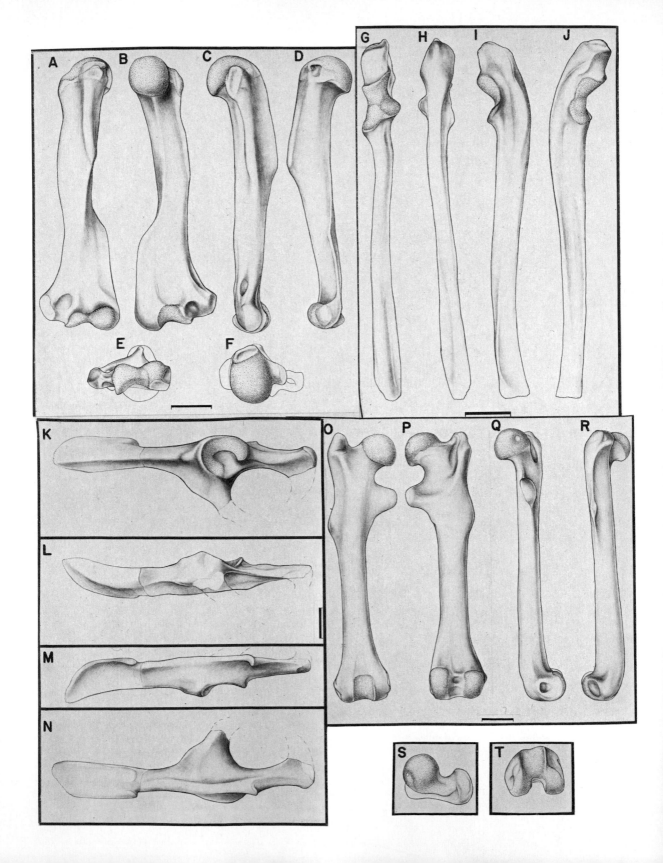

than *P. russelli* and *P. cookei,* and unlike the latter two species it has a distinct centroconule on I^1 and a distinct paraconule on P^4. *Plesiadapis russelli* is judged to be intermediate between *P. tricuspidens* and *Platchoerops daubrei* in morphology by Gingerich (1976a). It is larger than *P. tricuspidens,* lacks the *Plesiadapis*-type paraconules on P^{3-4}, lacks the centroconule crest, and has a much smaller laterocone on I^1. It differs from *Platychoerops daubrei* in having a small laterocone on I^1 and in having less molarized premolars with the paraconule usually seen on molars only incipiently present on P^4. *Plesiadapis russelli* differs from *P. cookei* in having a more reduced laterocone on I^1, an incipient paraconule on P^4, and in the consistent presence of a distal cingulid on $M_{\overline{3}}$.

As "*Nannodectes gazini*" Gingerich, 1974, is not significantly distinguishable from *Plesiadapis intermedius* Gazin, 1971, so "*Plesiadapis praecursor*" Gingerich, 1974, is equally undiagnosable from *Plesiadapis anceps* Simpson, 1936 [compare measurements of cheek teeth of *Plesiadapis* in Gingerich (1976a)].

All the evidence appears to point to the fact that two species of *Plesiadapis* were ancestral to *Chiromyoides* and *Platychoerops.* In Gingerich (1974, p. 188), the newly named "*Ples. praecursor*" gives rise to *Ples. anceps,* whereas (p. 198), *Ples. insignis* gives rise to *Ples. anceps.* The discussion and the two separate phylogenetic trees given for plesiadapids, one for those from North America and one for those from Europe, imply a rigid enforcement of the notion that the most parsimonious phylogenetic hypothesis is one that first satisfies local stratigraphic superpositions regardless of morphological evidence. We do not espouse this point of view (see Szalay, 1977a,b; Delson, 1977b). In addition, much of our disagreement with Gingerich's (1974, 1976a) hypothesis rests on (*a*) the recognition of different samples as of specific rank and (*b*) the utilization of shared and derived characters along with stratigraphic evidence in inferring descent.

As the cranial and postcranial remains of *Plesiadapis* represent rare specimens for early Tertiary primates, which are known largely by teeth, the following sa-

lient characters of their morphology are highlighted. In spite of the enlargement of the most anterior incisors, this genus is much less of an atypical archaic primate than the aye-aye is a bizarre lemur. With the exception of the enlargement of the incisors (*the* most common evolutionary trend, i.e., an independent unilinear character transformation, among the primates), *Plesiadapis* gives us a remarkable insight into levels of morphological organization of the archaic primates. Although clearly many of the features are *sui generis* for the genus, they are nevertheless also quite revealing of the more primitive common ancestry with all other known primates.

The cranial morphology of *Plesiadapis* is best known from D. E. Russell's (1964) studies of the skull of *Plesiadapis tricuspidens* from France. The figures (Figures 32 and 33) show the outlines of the skull and some of the sutural contacts of the cranial bones. The broad, flat, phalanger-like skull of *Plesiadapis tricuspidens* lacked a postorbital bar, and, judged from the estimated ratio of the neural cavity to the size of the skull and known postcranial remains, the brain was relatively larger than contemporary non-primates such as the similar-sized arctocyonids (Jerison, 1973; but see Radinsky, 1977).

As the accompanying illustrations show, the postcranial osteology of *Plesiadapis tricuspidens* is reasonably well known (Figures 34–36). These bones clearly take on a greater significance than they would if the plesiadapiforms were better known postcranially. It must be remembered that *P. triscuspidens* is a large and relatively late plesiadapiform. Much of our assessment as to the nature of adaptations in the archaic level of organization of primates is derived from remains of this species in addition to *P. gidleyi* and a number of additional, unassociated humeral and ulnar ends, pelvic fragments, and various astragali and calcanea assignable to Paleocene North American plesiadapiforms (Szalay and Drawhorn, in press).

The postcranial morphology of this genus, originally described by Simpson (1935a), has been recently reassessed by Szalay and Decker (1974) and Szalay *et al.* (1975). It shows without question that non-

Figure 34. *Plesiadapis tricuspidens.* Late Paleocene, western Europe. Left humerus: A, anterior view; B, posterior view; C, medial view; D, lateral view; E, distal view; F, proximal view. Right ulna: G, anterior view; H, posterior view; I, medial view; J, lateral view. Left innominate: K, lateral view; L, ventral view; M, dorsal view; N, medial view. Right femur: O, anterior view; P, posterior view; Q, medial view; R, lateral view; S, dorsal view; T, distal view. Scales represent 1 cm. [From Szalay *et al.* (1975).]

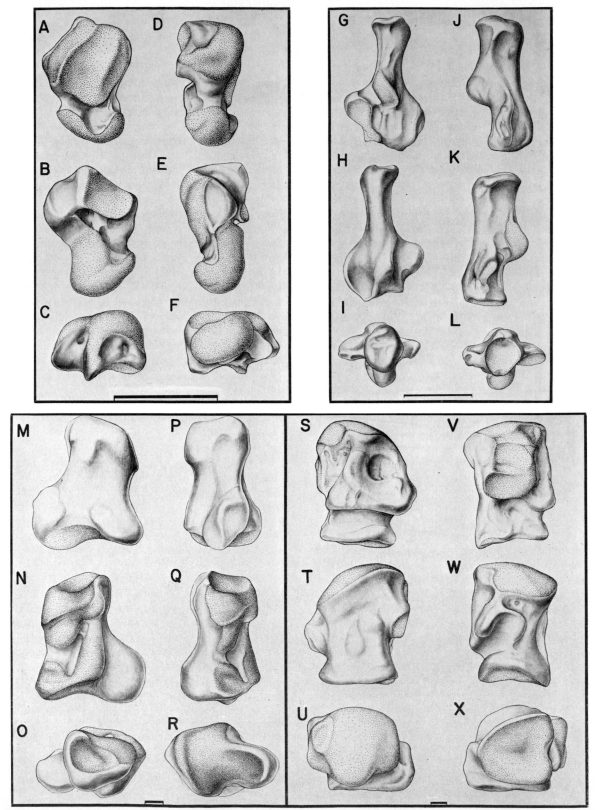

Figure 35. *Plesiadapis tricuspidens.* Late Paleocene, western Europe. Right astragalus, A–F; left calcaneum, G–L; left entocuneiform, M–R; right cuboid, S–X. Scales represent 1 mm. [From Szalay *et al.* (1975).]

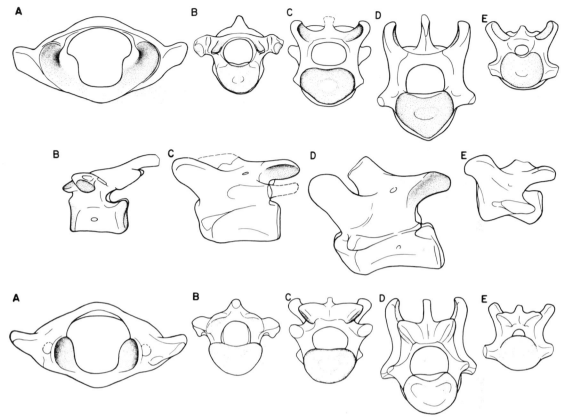

Figure 36. *Plesiadapis gidleyi.* Late Paleocene, western North America. Representative vertebrae: A, atlas; B, cervical; C, thoracic; D, lumbar; E, caudal. Proximal (top), lateral (middle), and distal (bottom) views are shown. [From Szalay *et al.* (1975).]

plesiadapiform primates have close affinities with this suborder and that the plesiadapiform characters of the postcranium are mechanical solutions to climbing, arboreal posturing, and arboreal locomotion. This conclusion is independent of the amount of relative degree of arboreality of various species of *Plesiadapis*. We note here that the sacrum, well preserved in *P. gidleyi*, is astonishingly similar to that of the gray squirrel, *Sciurus carolinensis*. Although *Plesiadapis* lacks the robust dorsal spines of the latter on the second and third sacrals, the similarity is either a convergent or a primitive condition, significant, differently, either way.

The humerus is the best represented bone of the forelimb, both in *P. tricuspidens* and in *P. walbeckensis*. As discussed by Szalay *et al.* (1975), the shaft is robust with a strong sigmoid curvature in lateral view,

although there is some variation among species (e.g., this curvature is somewhat less marked in *P. tricuspidens* than in *P. gidleyi* or *P. walbeckensis*). The head is subhemispherical, facing mostly backward. The deltopectoral crest is thin, prominent, gradually narrowing distally, and possibly more robust in *P. tricuspidens* and *P. walbeckensis* than in *P. gidleyi*. The greater tuberosity is weak and pitted laterally for infraspinatus insertion, and the lesser tuberosity is strongly developed and pronounced medially and slightly superiorly. The bicipital groove is shallower in *P. tricuspidens* than in *P. gidleyi*. The teres tuberosity is oblong, rounded, and pronounced in *P. gidleyi* but less well developed in the other species. The medial epicondyle faces directly medially and it is pronounced, a condition probably more primitive for eutherians than for most strepsirhines. The capitulum

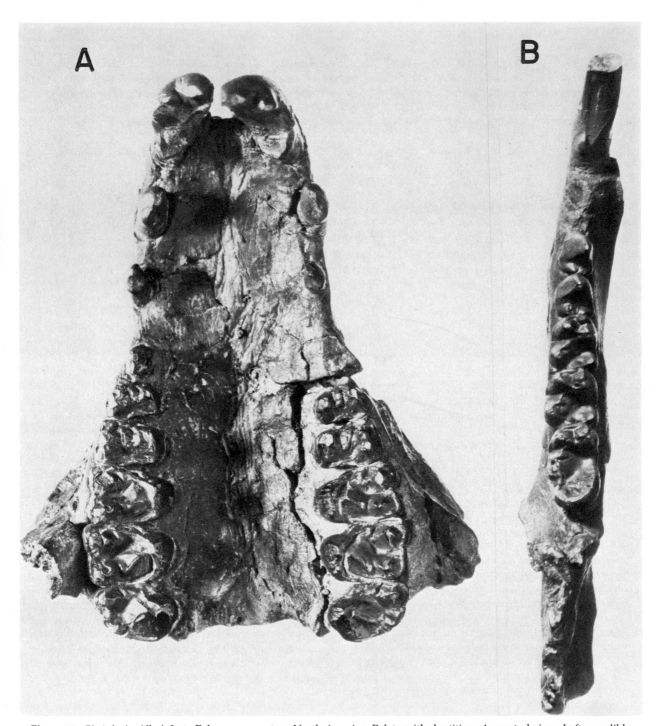

Figure 37. *Plesiadapis gidleyi.* Late Paleocene, western North America. Palate with dentition: A, ventral view. Left mandible with dentition, $P_{\overline{2}}$ missing due to breakage: B, occlusal view.

is spheroidal to subspheroidal and faces slightly superiorly, and the supracapitular depression is deep. The trochlea is not broader than the capitulum and there is no distinct ridge separating the two. It is also very narrow or constricted at its junction with the capitulum but expands laterally. The lateral epicondyle is weakly developed. The distolateral crest ("brachioradialis flange") is large and flared slightly backward. The olecranon fossa is present as a small shallow depression. A deep pit of small diameter is present on the posterior surface of the medial epicondyle adjacent to the trochlea; it is probably for the medial ligament (due to poor preservation of the bone it is difficult to see in either distal humerus of *P. gidleyi*). The entepicondylar foramen is large and opens mediosuperiorly.

One of the major differences between the humeri of *Plesiadapis* on the one hand and strepsirhines, tarsiiforms, and many New World monkeys on the other is the absence of a semicylindrical shape to the trochlea on the former plus a ridge demarcating it from the capitular area; they are all similar in having a more or less ball-shaped capitulum. Reviewing the characters of the living insectivorans, Cretaceous leptictimorphs, the Tertiary carnivorans, and the extant squirrels, it is clear that the primitive eutherian capitulum is more spindle-shaped, as in the late Cretaceous leptictimorphs, artocyonids, and early Tertiary creodonts. For example, the degree of curvature in a coronal plane is less than in a parasagittal plane, whereas in *Plesiadapis*, as in later primates, the two are subequal. However, the form of the trochlea, although variable, is unlike the semicylindrical form of strepsirhines and many other primates. We maintain that the nearly ball-shaped capitulum of *Plesiadapis* is the primitive state of a shared homologous specialization with other primates, whereas the trochlea represents either the primitive primate or *sui generis Plesiadapis* morphology. Incidentally, the conformation of the trochlea in *Plesiadapis* is more similar to those of arctocyonids than to those of Cretaceous and Paleocene leptictimorphs.

The shaft of the ulna is robust, with distinct anteroposterior sigmoid curvature. In cross section, it is lunate at its midpoint because of a strong excavation laterally in the area of origin of the *abductor pollicis longus*. The olecranon process is large and moderately long; its posterior margin is strongly inclined forward, and its superior and posterolateral aspects are rugose

for the triceps insertion. Medially the olecranon process is compressed by the proximal portion of the large groove accommodating the *flexor carpi ulnaris*. The trochlear notch is not particularly deep; inferiorly the notch slopes steeply down, and laterally it is not well differentiated from the radial facet.

According to Simpson's (1935a, pp. 15–16) assessment, the ulna, particularly the proximal half, strongly resembles the homologous region in *Notharctus*. In particular, two characters show this resemblance: the relative shallowness of the trochlear notch and the slight forward curvature of the proximal end. However, distally the shaft may change direction and curve posteriorly in *Plesiadapis*, a configuration exhibited by many insectivorans and other eutherians and probably primitive for the Eutheria. It is more continuously bowed in *Notharctus* and lemuroids. The radial facet is very slightly shaped as the homologous region of this facet in *Notharctus* and lemuroids. Although the olecranon process is by no means small, it is distinctly relatively smaller than in leptictimorphs and arctocyonids known to us and at least approaches the strepsirhine condition.

The robust shaft of the radius is bowed laterally (not anteriorly) and possesses a sharply defined interosseous border. The head is tilted to face somewhat anteriorly and laterally. The articular surface of the head is suboval in profile and is quite well excavated in a subspheroidal fashion corresponding to the capitular shape. In addition, a small eminence on the lateral margin of this capitular depression, articulating with the anterior aspect of the capitulum and so characteristic of the primitive eutherian conformation, is, as in lemuriforms and other primates, absent in *Plesiadapis*. The ulnar facet is slightly oval, extensive, and quite sharply curved. Detail has been obliterated in the area of *pronator quadratus* insertion, but this was apparently quite extensive. The outline of the carpal articular surface is pear-shaped, slightly convex, and tilted to face slightly medially and anteriorly. The styloid process is small and rounded; distally, on the posterior aspect, there is a strongly marked groove for the carpal extensor tendons. The neck, although short, is well defined and the bicipital tuberosity, as in other primates, is well developed. The nature of the articular surface of the head and the head in general are clearly more similar to strepsirhines than to other early Tertiary Eutheria, and this similarity is probably a homologous derived condition.

Only a few elements of the carpus and cheiridia are known in *P. tricuspidens*. These bones have not been analyzed as yet. Note should be made here of the basally robust and strongly curved claws found in Cernay, which probably belong to *Plesiadapis*. These very strongly suggest a well-founded claw climbing, scansorial habit.

The pelvis is well known in *Plesiadapis gidleyi, P. tricuspidens,* and *P. walbeckensis*. In general, the morphological conformation of the innominate is not unlike that of the inferred primitive eutherian condition. As in squirrels, but unlike in known adapids or omomyids, the obturator foramen is characteristically elongated. In all three known species of *Plesiadapis* in which the pelvis is available, the iliac spine, just cranial to the acetabulum, is a blunt tuberosity. The ilium has a primitive eutherian triangular cross section. Three faces may be distinguished; an inner or medial face, a dorsolateral face, and a ventrolateral face. The dorsolateral face is somewhat broader than the ventrolateral one, more so cranially; the former is even more greatly expanded in modern primates, as found independently in many other mammalian groups. The tupaiid pelvis appears to be specialized, perhaps independently from an archontan stock in a direction similar to that of modern primates. Among living species of this family, the dorsolateral surface is enlarged at the expense of the ventrolateral one.

Plesiadapis shows at least one character of the acetabulum which sets this genus, and probably all other plesiadapiforms, apart from the primitive eutherian morphology displayed by arctocyonids, Paleocene Insectivora from Walbeck, and, for example, *Sciurus carolinensis*. The relatively greater diameter of the acetabulum in the primate is striking when compared to these and to the other primitive eutherians.

Three major areas of the lunate facet, corresponding to the regions of the innominate (pubis, ilium, ischium), may often be distinguished. These areas may be connected to one another by a constricted area of the facet or separated by a nonarticular gap. These junctures often roughly approximate the lines of fusion in the innominate. In shape and relative dimensions of the lunate facet the few specimens of *Plesiadapis gidleyi* and *Plesiadapis tricuspidens* are essentially similar. The length of the ischial region is more than half that of the entire facet and is of nearly uniform diameter; it narrows very slightly and

gradually from the posterior corner forward to the ilio–ischiac constriction. Thus, in this region, the breadth of the constriction is not much less than that of the posterior corner. The ilio–ischiac constriction is marked in one specimen of *Plesiadapis gidleyi*. The maximum breadth of the iliac region (at the level of the iliac spine) is somewhat greater than that of the posterior corner; the ratios of the former to the latter are 1.1 and 1.2 in two specimens of *Plesiadapis gidleyi*. As is exhibited by the one almost complete facet in a specimen of *Plesiadapis gidleyi* and partially in *Plesiadapis tricuspidens*, the iliac region narrows into the short pubic region of the facet without any obvious discontinuity.

The only major difference between the lunate facets of *Notharctus* and *Hemiacodon* on the one hand and *Plesiadapis* (based on two specimens of *P. gidleyi*) on the other is an enlargement of the iliac region. The ratio of the diameter of this region to that of the posterior corner is approximately 1.50 and more (1.7) in *Notharctus* and 1.50 in *Hemiacodon*, as compared to the lower values for *Plesiadapis* given above. *Plesiadapis* exhibits more nearly primitive proportions in this respect. The ischial region tapers somewhat more craniad in *Hemiacodon*, giving a teardrop appearance to this region.

The femur is best known in *Plesiadapis tricuspidens*. The shaft is straight, robust, and short relative to the large proximal moiety. Suboval in cross section at its midpoint, it is, however, flattened on its posterior surface. The head is subspherical and faces medially and superiorly. The fovea for the *ligamentum teres* is fairly distinct and lies slightly inferior and posterior to the center of the articular surface of the head. The neck is short and robust, but moderately well defined, and with the head forms an approximately angle of 120° with the shaft (less than in *Notharctus* and *Hemiacodon*). The greater trochanter is robust and subequal in height to the head. As in *Notharctus*, a roughened area for muscular attachments on the trochanter is disposed on its lateral aspect and elongated in the direction of the shaft axis, whereas this area is tilted to face more superiorly and is elongated anteroposteriorly in *Hemiacodon*. The trochanteric fossa is long and quite deeply excavated, more so in *Plesiadapis* than in *Hemiacodon* and *Notharctus* (being relatively nearly one and a half times as long as in *Hemiacodon*). The groove between the head and the trochanter is deep in *Plesiadapis* (giving a constricted appearance to the neck), but is shallower in *Notharctus,* and shallower still in *Hemiacodon.* The lesser trochanter is large and projects medially to a distance subequal to that of the femoral head. It is smaller in *Notharctus* and *Hemiacodon,* where it is also directed more posteriorly as well as medially. *Plesiadapis tricuspidens,* like *Notharctus* and *Hemiacodon,* differs from *P. gidleyi* in the absence of an excavated depression on the anterior surface. The third trochanter is laterally projecting; it is long in its vertical dimension, but is also fairly rounded in profile. The intertrochanteric crest is faintly distinguishable throughout its course from greater to lesser trochanter in *P. gidleyi,* less so in *P. tricuspidens,* and is certainly discontinuous in *Hemiacodon* and *Notharctus.* The third trochanter is immediately below the level of the lesser trochanter in *Plesiadapis,* whereas it is at the level of the lesser trochanter in *Notharctus* and is slightly above the mean level of the lesser trochanter in *Hemiacodon.*

In distal view the proportions of the femoral end contrast with those in *Hemiacodon* or *Notharctus.* These latter two genera exhibit relatively high distal ends (ratios of height to breadth: *Hemiacodon,* 1.29; *Notharctus,* two specimens, 1.25 and 1.21) compared to *Plesiadapis* (*P. gidleyi,* 1.01; *P. tricuspidens,* two specimens, 0.88 and 0.83). Much of this discrepancy in height is precondylar; the base of the patellar groove does not extend beyond the anterior level of the shaft as in *Notharctus* and *Hemiacodon.* The patellar groove is much more shallow than in the other two. Its medial and lateral ridges are only weakly developed, whereas *Notharctus* and *Hemiacodon* exhibits pronounced rounded lateral crests. This, in part, accounts for the greater lateral height in *Notharctus* and *Hemiacodon,* whereas the opposite is true of *Plesiadapis.* Lorisines and galagines provide a similar contrast in most of the above characters, although the patellar groove is not as broad and shallow in *Plesiadapis* as in lorisines. Medial and lateral epicondylar surfaces are strongly pitted for the collateral ligaments of the knee in *Plesiadapis.*

The tibia and fibula are known in *P. tricuspidens,* but both are too badly crushed to be of much value. However, the proximal and distal ends of the tibia are preserved in *P. gidleyi* but offer no distinctive characters worth noting here.

Two tarsals of the foot of *Plesiadapis,* the astragalus and calcaneum, have been discussed in some detail by Szalay and Decker (1974) and Szalay *et al.* (1975). Only these two elements of the tarsus can be allocated with

certainty to *Plesiadapis,* although a cuboid, a mesocuneiform, and several entocuneiforms known also probably belong to *P. tricuspidens.* The comparative value of the tarsals other than the astragalus and the calcaneum depends on how well known these are in early Tertiary eutherians. These elements, therefore, because of their very rare associations with dental taxa, are of limited value.

In spite of the superficially primitive eutherian nature of plesiadapiform tarsals, there are a number of derived characters on these bones which we confidently consider specializations shared with strepsirhines and other primates. These primitive primate (but advanced eutherian) characters are (1) a pronounced groove for the *flexor fibularis* tendon on the plantar side of the calcaneum; (2) an astraglar head broad both medially and laterally and oriented slightly dorsoventrally; (3) an enlarged facet for the plantar calcaneonavicular ligament bridging the gap between the sustentacular and navicular facets; (4) a tibial trochlea of astragalus longer than wide, the upper ankle articulation showing a trochlear radius disparately larger laterally than medially, and the axis of the tibial shaft forming an acute angle laterally with the transverse plane of its articulation with the trochlea; (5) a helical-shaped posterior astragalocalcaneal articulation.

Mechanical interpretations of the postcranium compel us, as they did Szalay, Tattersall and Decker (1975), to hypothesize arboreal biological roles for these features. The elbow joint clearly did not permit full extension of the antebrachium. The olecranon fossa is too shallow and the shaft of the ulna is bent forward. However, the deeply excavated supracapitular fossa and the anterosuperior orientation of the capitulum indicate that considerable flexion was possible; therefore, the forelimb was habitually held in a somewhat flexed position. In addition, the olecranon process is bent forward to give considerable leverage to the triceps only in flexed positions. These appear to be similar to conditions seen in living lemuriforms and are even possibly primitive for eutherians. As stated before, the spheroidal articulation in *Plesiadapis* had been modified from a primitive eutherian state in which the articulation was more ovoid or spindle-shaped. This modification has the effect of centering the axis of rotation through the articulation of the antebrachium. The plesiadapiforms share this specialization with all known primates. The forelimb, including manus, was then capable of achieving dimensions of mobility comparable to those discussed for the foot below. The origins of these characters are interpreted as adaptations to adjust the limbs to variably oriented substrates (that is, to the branch environment of an arboreal habitat) more precarious and geometrically different from those for which primitive Eutheria were adapted. These adaptations fulfilled, then, the same role they do for many living primates.

Due to incongruence of corresponding articular facets, the area of contact at any given moment may be smaller than the area of overlap. However, an increase in the size of the hip articulation in *Plesiadapis* probably relates to an increase in the area of contact, thereby reducing the stresses of larger forces transmitted here compared to contemporary comparably sized Eutheria. The relatively large size of the hip articulation in *Plesiadapis* probably constitutes an apparent difference of significant functional consequence from primitive and contemporary Eutheria of comparable size.

Since all known specimens are largely devoid of muscular rugosities, it is difficult to assess muscular dispositions along the femur of *P. tricuspidens*. Nevertheless, some suggestions can be made from the size and dispositions of the major bony features. The uniformly strong development of almost all features of the proximal end of the femur suggests a very powerful hindlimb. A capacity for strong retraction of the upper hindlimb is indicated by an extensive area for the insertion of the *gluteus minimus* and *medius* on the anterolateral portion of the greater trochanter and by the great enlargement of the third trochanter, which served as the site of insertion of *gluteus maximus*.

The discrepancy in proportions of the distal femoral end of *Plesiadapis* can be noted when compared, for example, to *Hemiacodon*, *Notharctus*, and living lemuriforms. This end in *Plesiadapis* is less pronounced anteriorly than in the other primates. Also, the tibial tuberosity in *P. gidleyi* is less pronounced than in *Notharctus* or Malagasy lemuriforms. These characters affect the moment arm of the *quadriceps femoris*, which passes via the patella and *ligamentum patella* over the knee to the tibial tuberosity, increasing it in the non-plesiadapiforms. These primates also exhibit high patellar cresting, especially laterally, in order to maintain the alignment of the patella. A similar contact occurs between the closely related galagines and

lorisines, the former showing the leverage for knee extensors that the latter do not. We are not professing that *Plesiadapis* was necessarily a slow climber, or even arboreal on the basis of this character, but simply that it did not emphasize certain characters of the knee apparently arising as leaping specializations in some primates. In fact, the knee of *Plesiadapis* does not appear to be modified to the extreme of lorisines.

The majority of the characters of the known parts of the tarsus both in *Plesiadapis* spp. and in several other plesiadapiforms are consistently related to free mobility of the foot, permitting its inversion and eversion to adjust [as emphatically stated by Szalay and Decker (1974)] to arboreal branch substrates as, for example, in lemuriforms and other primates. The tarsus distal to the astragalocalcaneal pair may tilt superiorly and inferiorly, mobility being facilitated largely by the calcaneocuboid articulation. Associated with these motions via the astragalonavicular articulation are the rotations between astragalus and calcaneus analogous to radioulnar rotations on sets of anterior and posterior gliding articulations. The associated tilt of the distal tarsus and astragalocalcaneal rotation permit the inversion and eversion of the foot. Since the navicular slides medially on the astragalar head during inversion, the pronounced medial development of the navicular facet on the astragalar head and its slight dorsomedial orientation favor the reception of stresses in inverted orientations of the foot. As indicated by its enlarged facet on the astragalus, the plantar calcaneonavicular ligaments also play an increased role in medially buttressing this articulation. Tilting of the distal tarsus approximates and draws distant during inversion and eversion, respectively, the navicular and calcaneal aspect of the lower ankle joint. This would ordinarily crowd the astragalus and force separation of the lower ankle joint or, barring this, inhibit inversion and eversion to any great degree. This problem is resolved by the helical configuration of the posterior astragalocalcanear articulation, which permits helical motion. Thus provided is the rotation necessary to invert and evert the foot and pitch to adjust astragalocalcaneonavicular relationships. Therefore, extreme orientations of the pes may be achieved while articular surfaces remain coadapted to receive stresses in these positions. The calcaneal plantar groove for the flexor fibularis tendon can be explained as a feature designed to maintain the alignment of the tendon and, therefore, efficiency on its attachments in the various positions realized by inter-tarsal adaptations.

The characters of the upper ankle joint are associated with an axis of rotation that is not very perpendicular to the lateral or fibular side of the trochlea. These developments have been associated in the Primates with the mobility of the fibula and its capacity to resist inversion and eversion strains in various positions of flexion and extension of the ankle joint (Barnett and Napier, 1953).

A complete assessment of the genus from the point of view of either locomotor or feeding adaptations is not possible as yet. Although the teeth are better known than the skeleton, we cannot characterize the whole genus by any one particular type of feeding adaptation, as clearly there must have been both feeding and locomotor differences between the numerous species. The best estimate is to imagine the various species of *Plesiadapis* to have occupied niches similar to the various subtropical members of the family Sciuridae and the Australian marsupial phalangeroids.

CHIROMYOIDES Stehlin, 1916

(= or including: *Plesiadapis*: Teilhard, 1922, in part. *Nothodectes*: Gidley, 1923, in part.)

DISTRIBUTION
   Late Paleocene and early Eocene (Tiffanian to Clarkforkian and earliest Wasatchian and Thanetian). Rocky Mt. region and Texas, and Paris Basin.
KNOWN SPECIES
   1. *Chiromyoides campanicus* Stehlin, 1916, type series
(=*Plesiadapis campanicus:* Teilhard 1922, in part.)
LOCALITIES: Cernay★ (88); Berru (92).
   2. *Chiromyoides caesor* Gingerich, 1973a
LOCALITIES: Mason Pocket (72); Crock Tooth Q.★ (74).
   3. *Chiromyoides minor* Gingerich, 1974
(=*Plesiadapis gidleyi:* Schiebout, 1974, in part.)
LOCALITIES: Chappo-17★ (58); Ray's Bone bed (70).
   4. *Chiromyoides potior* Gingerich, 1974
(=*Nothodectes gidleyi:* Matthew, 1917b, in part. *Plesiadapis gidleyi:* Simpson, 1937, in part. *Chiromyoides caesor:* Schiebout, 1974.)
LOCALITIES: Mason Pocket★ (72); Joe's Bone bed, Black Peaks (122); Little Sand Coulee (124); Bear Creek (148).
   5. *Chiromyoides major* Gingerich, 1974
LOCALITIES: Paint Creek★ (126); Upper Sand Draw (142).

DISCUSSION

The differences of *Chiromyoides* from *Plesiadapis*, its probable ancestor, are in a complex of features that reflect a feeding mechanism more heavily stressed during some phase of food procurement, although not necessarily mastication, than those of any other plesiadapids. The mandible and muzzle are shortened, the horizontal ramus is considerably deepened, and the mandibular angle is very much expanded, showing the great increase and nearly vertical orientation of the internal pterygoid and superficial masseter muscles (Figure 38). The robust incisors well reflect these differences. The crown height compared with

the length of the root is relatively less and the mesiodistal diameters of the crowns are relatively greater than in upper incisors of *Plesiadapis*.

The dental formula is $I_{\frac{1}{1}}^{\cdot 2}; C_{\frac{1}{1}}^{1}; P_{\frac{3}{3},\frac{4}{4}}^{2,\frac{3}{3},\frac{4}{4}}; M_{\frac{1}{1},\frac{2}{2},\frac{3}{3}}^{1,\frac{2}{2},\frac{3}{3}}$.

Gingerich (1973a, 1974, 1975b) has described four new species of *Chiromyoides*, all based on differences in incisor structure and size. Incisor variation, unfortunately, is not analyzed or known in any samples of *Chiromyoides*. Not one sample of the adequately known *C. campanicus* offers an opportunity to evaluate the extent of size and morphological variation in the upper incisors. A description of these species, therefore, is essentially equivalent, for the time being, to the extension of the range of *Chiromyoides* to several localities in North America, but cannot as yet supply a meaningful diagnosis to any of these species. Although listed here, the validity of these species cannot be tested.

Origins of the genus, although suspected to be from species that would be allocated to *Plesiadapis*, are not yet known. *Chiromyoides* was relatively short-faced and the distance between the incisor and P_3 was also short. In spite of its relatively conservative plesiadapid molar morphology, the generally great robustness of the feeding mechanism suggests a mode of life considerably different from those of species of *Plesiadapis*. The skull length of *C. campanicus* is estimated to have been 7–8 cm.

In any attempt to speculate on its mode of life, the short-faced *Chiromyoides*, with a transverse cutting edge on the robust incisors, invites analogy with the jaws and teeth of *Daubentonia* (see especially Cartmill, 1974c) and the marsupials *Dactylonyx trivirgata* and *Dactylopsila palpator*. These forms use their robust

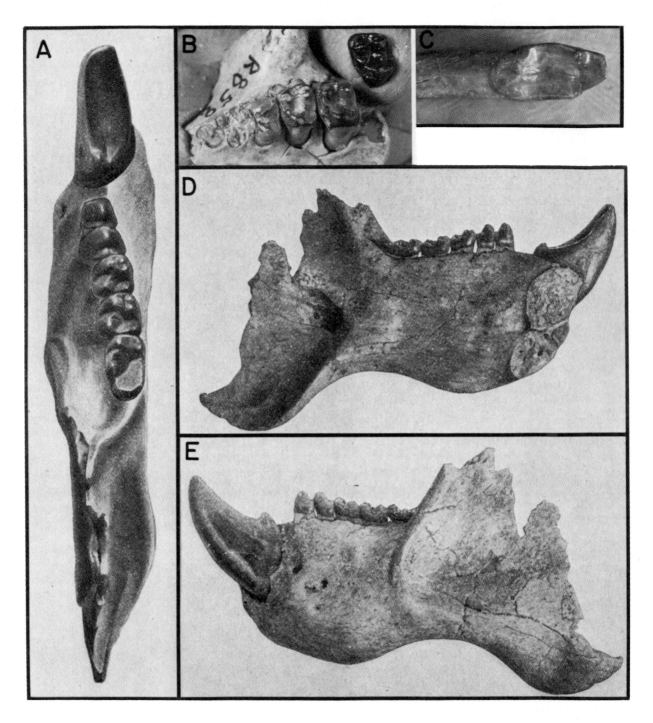

Figure 38. *Chiromyoides campanicus.* Late Paleocene, western Europe. Right mandible with $I_{\overline{1}}$, $P_{\overline{3}}$–$P_{\overline{4}}$, $M_{\overline{1}}$–$M_{\overline{3}}$: A, occlusal view; D, medial view; E, lateral view. Left maxilla with $P^{\underline{4}}$–$M^{\underline{2}}$ and isolated $M^{\underline{2}}$: B, occlusal view. Right $I^{\underline{1}}$: C, occlusal view. [A,D,E From Stehlin (1916); B and C from Russell (1964), courtesy of D. E. Russell.]

incisors to gnaw into the cambium and woody tissues of trees bearing larvae of wood-boring insects. Gingerich (1974) has proposed seed-eating as a dietary model for the explanation of *Chiromyoides*. This view, we believe, is partly based on the assumption that plesiadapids were terrestrial, as asserted by Gingerich. It is difficult to account for the extreme robustness of the incisors by seed-eating. A *Daubentonia*-like mode of life, however, would explain this only known, major derived character of*Chiromyoides* in contrast to *Plesiadapis*.

PLATYCHOEROPS Charlesworth, 1854

[= or including: *Miolophus* Owen, 1865. *Plesiadapis:* Lemoine, 1880, in part. *Plesiadapis (Subunicuspidens)* Lemoine, 1887. *Platychaerops:* Hill, 1953, in part.]

DISTRIBUTION
   Early Eocene (Neustrian and early Rhenanian). Western Europe.
KNOWN SPECIES
   1. *Platychoerops richardsonii* Charlesworth, 1854, type species
(=*Miolophus planiceps* Owen, 1865. *Plesiadapis daubrei*: Teilhard, 1922, in part. *Platychaerops richardsonii*: Hill, 1953, in part).
Localities: Grauves (224); Herne Bay★ (226).
   2. *Platychoerops? richardsonii*: Gingerich, 1976a
(=*Plesiadapis daubrei*: Teilhard, 1922, in part. *Platychoerops daubrei*: Russell, Louis and Savage, 1967, in part.)
Localities: Grauves (224); Herne Bay★ (226).
   3. *Platychoerops daubrei* (Lemoine, 1880)
(=*Plesiadapis daubrei* Lemoine, 1880. *Plesiadapis daubrei*: Teilhard, 1922, in part. *Platychoerops daubrei*: Simpson, 1929. *Platychoerops richardsonii*: Hill, 1953, in part.)
Localities: Reims★ (185); Dormaal (186); Pourcy (188); Mutigny (190); Avenay (206); Condé-en-Brie (220).

Discussion

The differences of *Platychoerops* from *Plesiadapis*, its ancestor, appear to be in its possession of two- rather than three- cusped incisors, slightly more molarized premolars, well-developed molar mesostyles, and, in general, its rugose, crenulated enamel (Gingerich, 1976a). *Platychoerops* also has a system of very broad cingulae on the upper molars (Figure 39).

According to the studies of Gingerich (1976a), the following features distinguish the two described species as well as a third sample, which is referred to as *Platychoerops? richardsonii* by Gingerich (1976a). *Platychoerops daubrei* is significantly smaller than *P. richardsonii*. The former differs from *P.? richardsonii* in the possession of a fissure in the lingual crest of the $M_{\overline{3}}$ talonid, in the absence of a crest connecting the protoconid and paraconid, and in its smaller size. *Platychoerops richardsonii* is known only by a palate (Figure 39) and isolated teeth, and diagnosis therefore from *P. daubrei* is difficult. Differences may lie in the possibly larger size of *P. richardsonii* and in having slightly more crenulated enamel. The sample referred to *P.? richardsonii* by Gingerich (1976a) represents a form larger than *P. daubrei*, and it also differs from the latter as stated above. Because lower teeth are not known for *Platychoerops richardsonii*, the Grauves sample of *P.? richardsonii* cannot be adequately compared to it, although the teeth do appear to be of the same general size.

Platychoerops spp. were larger animals than species of *Plesiadapis*. Their large, crenulated upper molars broadly surrounded by cingulae strongly suggest a folivorous, perhaps to some degree frugivorous, dietary regime. Reduction of the cusps on the upper incisors may support this view.

Family Saxonellidae
Russell, 1964

(= or including Saxonellinés Russell, 1964)

DISTRIBUTION
   Late Paleocene (Thanetian). Germany.
INCLUDED TAXA
   Saxonella.

Discussion

Originally *Saxonella* was allocated to the Carpolestidae by D. E. Russell (1964), but subsequently Van Valen (1969) favored closer relationships to

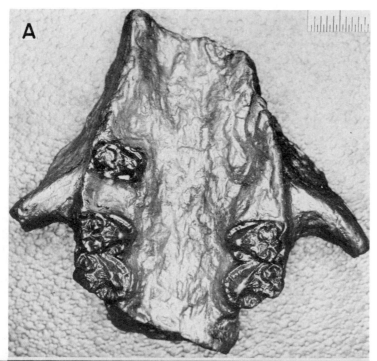

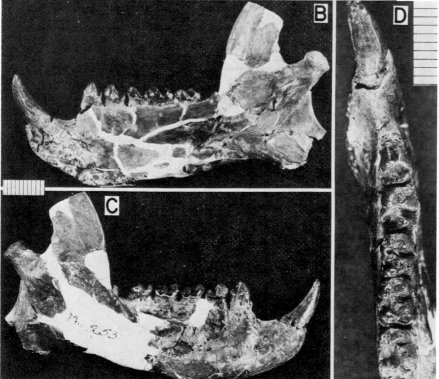

Figure 39. *Platychoerops.* Early Eocene, western Europe. *Platychoerops richardsonii.* Partial palate with right P⁴, and M²⁻³, and left M²⁻³: A, ventral view. *Platychoerops daubrei.* Right mandible with I, and P₃–M₃: B, medial view; C, lateral view; D, occlusal view. Scales represent 1 cm (on A) and 0.5 cm (on C and D), and their subdivisions represent 0.5 mm. [Courtesy of T. Olson.]

plesiadapids. In his recent review of the Carpolestidae, Rose (1975) has suggested that: "The morphology of *Saxonella* points to affinities with both carpolestids and plesiadapids, but its specializations are comparable in magnitude, although different from, those of either family. Accordingly, *Saxonella* should be separated from both at the family level, as the Saxonellidae, but grouped with them in the superfamily Plesiadapoidea" (p. 51). We concur with Rose's view.

Although we agree with having the Saxonellidae as a family, and classify it within the Plesiadapoidea alongside the Plesiadapidae and Carpolestidae, it is nevertheless clear that the more recent affinities of *Saxonella* are with the plesiadapids (see discussion under genus).

SAXONELLA Russell, 1964

DISTRIBUTION
   Late Paleocene (Thanetian). Germany.
KNOWN SPECIES
   Saxonella crepaturae, Russell, 1964
LOCALITIES: Walbeck⋆ (42).

DISCUSSION

Saxonella is distinct from other plesiadapoids by virtue of its unique specialization of the third lower premolar. Coupled with the plagiaulacoid $P_{\overline{3}}$, the genus possesses a simple, premolariform $P_{\overline{4}}$ and an enlarged, long incisor (Figure 40).

The dental formula of *Saxonella* is $I_{\overline{1}}^{.2}$; $C_{\overline{1}}^{1}$; $P_{\overline{3},\overline{4}}^{2.3.4}$; $M_{\overline{1},\overline{2},\overline{3}}^{.2.3}$.

As discussed under the family, the closest affinities, judged from the morphology of the molars, appear to be with plesiadapids and carpolestids. The lack of specialization in the fourth premolars indicates that the ancestry of *Saxonella* is best referred to as a plesiadapid rather than a carpolestid.

The type mandible of *Saxonella* (see Russell, 1964) is one of the best preserved Paleocene primate lower jaws (Figure 40). The coronoid process, the angle, and the articular condyle are intact. The horizontal ramus is short and deep and the coronoid process is high and relatively wide anteroposteriorly. The angle is somewhat reduced in length and it is not particularly deep. It appears, judging from the deep masseteric fossa and the trenchant $P_{\overline{3}}$, that the orthal and ectental (side to side) components of the bite were more important than the propalinal component. The fully plesiadapid-like mitten-shaped upper incisors of *Saxonella* are relatively wider transversely than those of plesiadapids and the pronglike cusps are more separated from each other on a horizontal plane. This may reflect a more efficient grasping, anchoring, husking ability than that of the known homologous plesiadapid teeth.

The distal half of a right humerus (Figure 41) of a plesiadapiform primate from Walbeck is almost certainly that of *Saxonella*. Its unique adaptations, which are being evaluated (Szalay and Dagosto, in preparation), should eventually shed more light on the way of life of the genus.

Family Carpolestidae
Simpson, 1935b

DISTRIBUTION
   Middle to earliest Eocene (Torrejonian to Wasatchian). Rocky Mt. region.
INCLUDED TAXA
   Carpodaptes (including *Carpolestes*) and *Elphidotarsius*.

DISCUSSION

This is a relatively small family of primates, ranging in size from mice to rats, and is characterized by one set of key adaptations, the plagiaulacoid modification of their lower fourth premolars, and by their coadapted peculiar third and fourth upper molars (Figures 42–44). The bladelike specialization of either the upper or lower premolars is of course not unique among the Mammalia, but of the primates only the carpolestids and saxonellids developed this type of lower tooth adaptation. As noted under the Saxonellidae, in that family the third lower premolar is hyper-

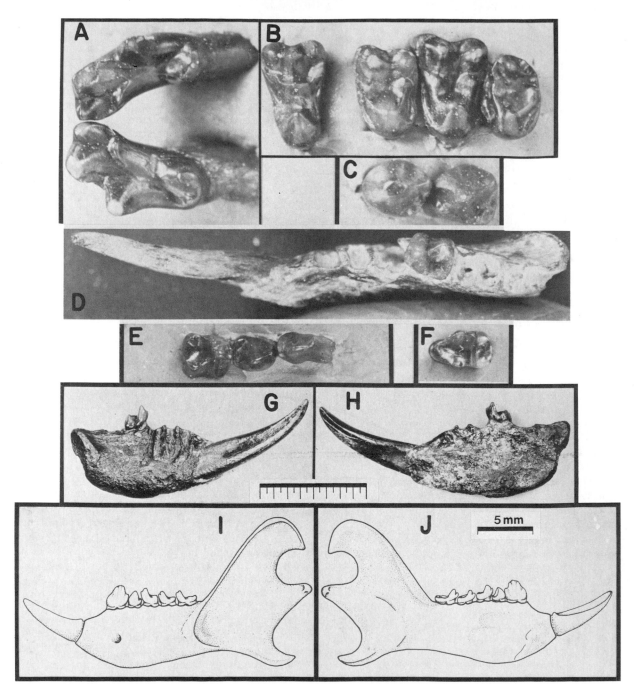

Figure 40. *Saxonella crepaturae.* Late Paleocene, western Europe. First pair of enlarged upper incisors: A, occlusal view. $P^{\underline{3}}$, $M^{\underline{1}}$–$M^{\underline{3}}$: B, occlusal view. C–$P^{\underline{2}}$: C, occlusal view. Right mandible fragment with I_T and M_T: D, occlusal view. Right $P_{\overline{3}}$–M_T: E, occlusal view. Left $M_{\overline{3}}$: F, occlusal view. Right mandible fragment with I_T and M_T: G, lateral view; H, medial view. Subdivisions on the scale between G and H represent 0.5mm. Reconstructed left mandible with I_T, $P_{\overline{3}}$–$P_{\overline{4}}$, M_T–$M_{\overline{3}}$: I, lateral view; J, medial view. Scale for I and J represents 5mm. [A–F from Russell (1964), courtesy of D. E. Russell, I. and J. from Szalay (1972b).]

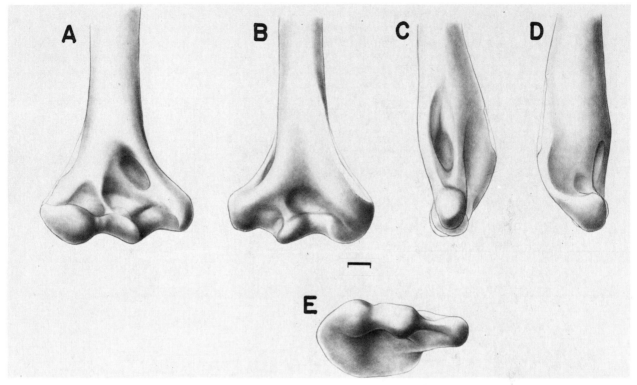

Figure 41. *Saxonella crepaturae?* Late Paleocene, western Europe. Right humerus, distal half: A, anterior view; B, posterior view; C, medial view; D, lateral view; E, distal view. Scale represents 1 mm. [By A. Cleary.]

trophied, attesting to the independent development of plagiaulacoidy. Along with the development of the trenchant $P_{\overline{4}}$, carpolestids are also diagnosed by the polycuspate $P^{\underline{3-4}}$, at least in *Carpodaptes*. These specializations are discussed in detail under the two recognized genera.

The carpolestid antemolar dentition is relatively similar among the species for which this area is known. The medial incisor is enlarged and medially inclined, whereas the lateral incisor is considerably reduced. The canine, although judged to be present, is small, and so is $P_{\overline{2}}$, which is tiny with a nodular crown in *Carpodaptes*. $P_{\overline{3}}$ is small in *Elphidotarsius* and it is even more reduced in *Carpodaptes*. The plagiaulacoid, enlarged $P_{\overline{4}}$ is a polycuspate tranchant blade. In *Carpodaptes* the trigonid of $M_{\overline{1}}$ is longer mesiodistally than in $M_{\overline{2}}$, and this portion of the tooth forms an effective posterior extension of the $P_{\overline{4}}$ blade. The upper anterior dentition is poorly known, although almost certainly there were four additional teeth anterior to $P^{\underline{3}}$. Of

these, two were incisors, the small canine, and a small, single-rooted $P^{\underline{2}}$. In *Carpodaptes*, $P^{\underline{3}}$ and P^4 have rows of several cusps parallel to each other.

The second and third molars of carpolestids, particularly of the most primitive genus of the family, *Elphidotarsius*, bear an overall similarity to the plesiadapid *Pronothodectes*. This resemblance, although possibly a primitive primate similarity, is more likely specially shared between primitive plesiadapids and carpolestids and is probably derived from a common ancestry. This is the basis for postulating close plesiadapid–carpolestid ties and for including the Carpolestidae in the Plesiadapoidae.

Reasons for the inclusion of *Carpolestes* in *Carpodaptes* are given in the discussion under *Carpodaptes* (p. 98).

The genealogy of the known species of the family is not clear-cut, although the origins of *Carpodaptes* from some species of *Elphidotarsius* is as well documented as one can expect for a group known exclusively from

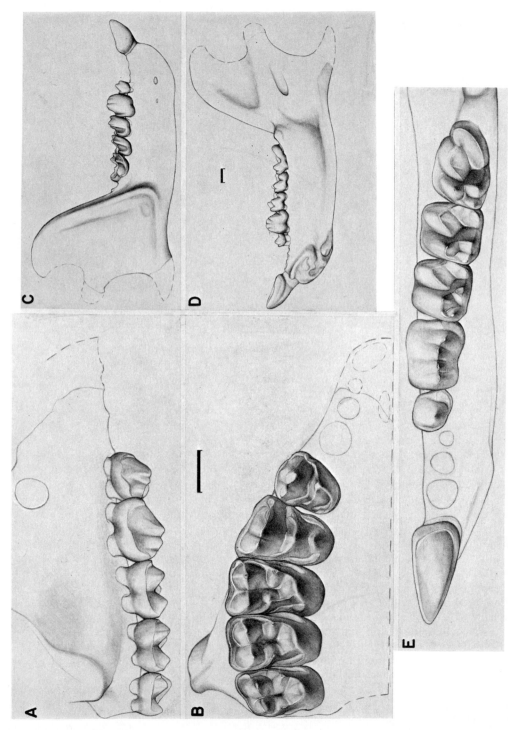

Figure 42. *Elphidotarsius florencae.* Middle Paleocene, western North America. Right maxilla with P³–P⁴, M¹–M³: A, lateral view; B, occlusal view. Right mandible with I₁, P₃–P₄, M₁–M₃: C, lateral view; D, medial view; E, occlusal view. Scales represent 1 mm. [By A. Cleary.]

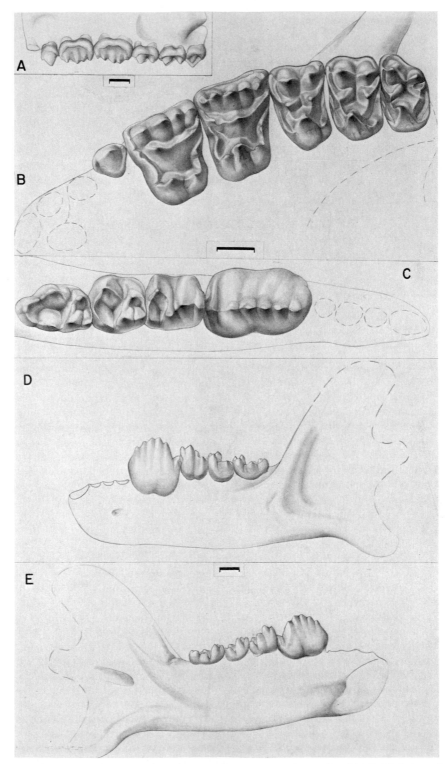

Figure 43. *Carpodaptes hazelae.* Late Paleocene, western North America. Left maxilla with P$^{\underline{2}}$–M$^{\underline{3}}$: A, buccal view; B, occlusal view. Left mandible with P$_{\overline{4}}$–M$_{\overline{3}}$: C, occlusal view; D, lateral view; E, medial view. Scales represent 1 mm. [By A. Cleary.]

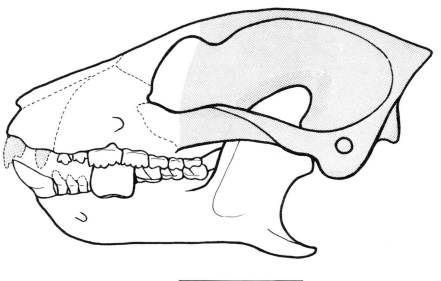

Figure 44. *Carpodaptes dubius.* Late Paleocene, western North America. Reconstructed skull and mandible, mandibular angle based on *Carpodaptes hazelae.* Stippling represents reconstruction. Sutures are indicated by broken lines. Scale represents 1 cm. [By A. Cleary, modified from Rose (1975).]

dental samples. This uncertainty of exact phylogenetic relationships between the various species samples is well expressed by Rose (1975, Figure 40). The lack of shared derived features between the similar dental phena hampers a reliable construction of phylogeny, even though general conclusions on the generic level may be substantiated. A similar skepticism is a must in the rigorous evaluation of the various samples of the other abundant Paleocene primate groups, as in the genus *Plesiadapis* (but see Gingerich, 1976a).

Simpson (1933) has examined the adaptive significance of plagiaulacoid dentitions in the Mamalia with a greater thoroughness and detail than anyone before or since, but could only conclude that it is an adaptive complex that has evolved to deal with a diet of coarse vegetation. He drew attention to the fact that, although superficially similar, plagiaulacoid teeth (the term is an allusion to the dentition of the primitive suborder of multituberculates, the Plagiaulacoidea) among multituberculates, several independently evolved lineages of metatherians, and primates are rather divergent in morphology and probably also in function. The recent occlusal analysis of carpolestid teeth by Rose (1975) concluded that most shearing and grinding was accomplished by the molars, whereas the $P_{\overline{4}}, P^{\underline{3-4}}$ complex was primarily used to saw and tear some unspecified foods of a more or less omnivorous dietary regime. As stated by Szalay (1972b), it appears that the carpolestids represent taxa adapted to

an unknown vegetable diet of high fiber content. The detailed convergence (at least of the lower premolars) between distantly related mammals such as multituberculates of the Mesozoic and early Cenozoic, caenolestoid marsupials of the early and later Tertiary (abderitine caenolestids, polydolopids), and the late Tertiary phalengeroid marsupials (phalengerids and macropodids) is probably due to adaptations to similar vegetable diet. Unfortunately, although there are several extant species of marsupials with plagiaulacoid-type premolars, no detailed study of the morphology, ecology, and diet of these forms has been undertaken to elucidate the possible roles associated with this type of dentition. As noted, the plagiaulacoid premolars, at least in small- to medium-sized mammals, probably evolved in response to a diet that contained a large percentage of tough fibers. Perhaps this food was roots, bark, or fruits with a tough fibrous coat. This hypothesis, however, is largely unsubstantiated.

It is suspected that the carpolestid premolar–molar dentition functioned differently from that of other known therians with a plagiaulacoid dentition. This may be concluded from the combined upper and lower cheek tooth morphology and the wear facets on the teeth. In living mammals such as the macropodid *Hypsiprymnodon* or the phalangerid *Burramys*, the plagiaulacoid lower premolars occlude against trenchant upper premolars, and this arrangement is true of most fossil caenolestoids. Unlike other plagiaulacoid therians, however, carpolestids utilized their cheek teeth in a different manner. The cutting edge of the lower dentition is supplied primarily by the bladelike hypsodont $P_{\overline{4}}$, whose cutting edge is supplemented by the peculiar trigonid elongation of the first molar in more advanced carpolestids. It appears that, once lateral excursion of the mandible has occurred (the "preparatory stroke"), the apical edge of $P_{\overline{4}}$ contacted the upper cheek teeth, commencing medial excursion of the active mandible ("power and/or shearing stroke"). As $P_{\overline{4}}$ moved across the occlusal surface of $P^{\underline{3}}$ and $P^{\underline{4}}$, moving slightly upward, mesially and lingually, the cutting edge of its blade worked against the filelike, studded surface of the third and fourth upper premolars. This arrangement explains why the carpolestid blade is so much higher crowned than the upper premolars. The relatively narrow occlusal surface of $P_{\overline{4}}$ (compared with the large occlusal surface of the combined third and fourth upper premolars) is worn at a much more rapid rate, but the speed of wear

is compensated by the great height of its crown. Thus, the hypsodont carpolestid blade is a compromise solution for a device that is both trenchant and long-lasting in occlusion with the flat upper premolars with unusually large surface area.

A significant feature of the poorly known cranial morphology [see Rose's (1975) thorough treatment of what is known], represented by a fragmentary facial skull of *Carpodaptes dubius,* is a large infraorbital foramen. It is located above and slightly after the posterior root of $P^{\underline{3}}$. The roots of the zygoma are robust. Rose (1975) has described a small ("emissary") foramen anterolateral in each maxilla slightly outside the orbital margin. Palatal fenestra were noted by Jepsen (1930b), but additional specimens at hand did not clarify the nature of these (Rose, 1975). A reconstruction, based on *C. dubius* specimens and in part based on the tentative reconstruction of Rose (1975), is presented in Figure 44.

ELPHIDOTARSIUS Gidley, 1923

DISTRIBUTION
    Middle Paleocene (Torrejonian). Rocky Mt. region.
KNOWN SPECIES
    1. *Elphidotarsius florencae* Gidley, 1923, type species
(=*Elphidotarsius* sp. cf. *E. florencae:* Rose, 1975.)
LOCALITIES: Gidley Q.★ (24); Rock Bench Q. (26); Tongue River (31).
    2. *Elphidotarsius shotgunensis* Gazin, 1971
LOCALITIES: Keefer Hill★ (38).

DISCUSSION

The two species included in *Elphidotarsius* are the oldest and smallest, as well as the most primitive, members of the family. The $P_{\overline{4}}$ is enlarged, larger than $M_{\overline{1}}$, but bears only four small apical cusps, and the primitively large protoconid is still discernable (Figure 42). $P^{\underline{3-4}}$, however, are only slightly different from the morphology seen in the plesiadapid *Pronothodectes.*

There are only two buccal cusps on both $P^{\underline{3}}$ and $P^{\underline{4}}$, in contrast to those of *Carpodaptes,* where there are five buccal cusps.

Elphidotarsius florencae is smaller and more primitive than *E. shotgunensis.* $P_{\overline{4}}$ and $M_{\overline{1}}$ are shorter mesiodistally but broader buccolingually in the type species. The trigonid elongation of $M_{\overline{1}}$ is less advanced in *E. florencae* than in *E. shotgunensis.*

The dental formula is $I\frac{2}{2}$; $C\frac{1}{1}$; $P\frac{2,3,4}{2,3,4}$; $M\frac{1,2,3}{1,2,3}$.

As noted under the family discussion, *Elphidotarsius* is not very different from *Pronothodectes* except for the morphology of the fourth lower premolar. There is no disagreement among students of carpolestids that *Elphidotarsius* gave rise to the ancestral species of *Carpodaptes.*

The adaptations of carpolestids are treated under the family discussion.

CARPODAPTES Matthew and Granger, 1921

(= or including: *Carpolestes* Simpson, 1928. *Litotherium* Simpson, 1929.)

DISTRIBUTION
    Late middle Paleocene to earliest Eocene (late Torrejonian to earliest Wasatchian). Rocky Mt. region.
KNOWN SPECIES
    1. *Carpodaptes aulacodon* Matthew and Granger, 1921, type species

LOCALITIES: Mason Pocket★ (72).
    2. *Carpodaptes hazelae* Simpson, 1936
LOCALITIES: Scarritt Q.★ (40); Cedar Pt. (54); Ravenscrag UAR-1 (106).
    3. *Carpodaptes hobackensis* Dorr, 1952
(=*Carpolestes cygneus* Russell, 1967. *Carpodaptes cygnaeus:* Rose, 1975.)
LOCALITIES: Ravenscrag UAR-1 (106); Dell Creek★ (118); Paskapoo (120).

4. *Carpodaptes jepseni* Rose, 1975
LOCALITIES: Divide★ (78).
5. *Carpodaptes nigridens* (Simpson, 1928), new combination
(=*Carpolestes nigridens* Simpson, 1928. *Litotherium complicatum* Simpson, 1929. *Carpolestes aquilae* Simpson, 1929.)
LOCALITIES: Paint Creek (126); Bear Creek★ (148); Clark Fork (152).
6. *Carpodaptes dubius* (Jepsen, 1930b), new combination
(=*Carpolestes dubius* Jepsen, 1930b.)
LOCALITIES: Princeton Q.★ (100; Fritz Q. (102); Schaff Q. (104).

DISCUSSION

Carpodaptes differs from *Elphidotarsius* in having lost $P_{\overline{2}}$, and in having increased the cuspules on $P_{\overline{4}}$ and $P^{\underline{3-4}}$ (Figure 43). Cuspules on the $P_{\overline{4}}$ blade number five to nine and the number of buccal cuspules on $P^{\underline{3-4}}$ is five on each. The $M_{\overline{1}}$ trigonid cusps are mesiodistally aligned, forming an extension to $P_{\overline{4}}$. In general, the $P_{\overline{4}}$ blade is enlarged far beyond the condition in *Elphidotarsius*, and $P^{\underline{3-4}}$ are transformed into relatively very large, polycuspidate surfaces.

The dental formula is $I\frac{1\cdot 2}{1\cdot 2}$; $C\frac{1}{1}$; $P\frac{2\cdot 3\cdot 4}{2\cdot 3\cdot 4}$; $M\frac{1\cdot 2\cdot 3}{1\cdot 2\cdot 3}$.

In his excellent review of the family, Rose (1975) continued to use the generic concept *Carpolestes* to accommodate the two latest Paleocene carpolestids "*C.*" *nigridens* and "*C.*" *dubius*. In 1928, when Simpson (pp. 7–10) described "*Carpolestes*" *nigridens*, the generotype of "*Carpolestes*," he gave no adequate diagnosis, primarily because sample variations were not well known and there were no characters of generic magnitude. Rose (1975), while studying the large samples of the five species (only four are accepted here) allocated to *Carpodaptes* and the two relegated to "*Carpolestes*," found that the number of apical cusps on the $P_{\overline{4}}$ is five to seven in *Carpodaptes* (see figures in Rose), whereas in *Carpolestes* the number ranges from eight to nine. $P^{\underline{3-4}}$, however, in all non-*Elphidotarsius* species, bear the identical number of buccal and lingual cusps. In general, it is clear that a post-*Elphidotarsius* adaptive complex changed only in a very minor way. Rose (1975, p. 63) admits a closer resemblance between samples of *Carpodaptes* and *Carpolestes* than between any of these and any of those of *Elphidotarsius*. Whatever differences exist between *Carpodaptes* and "*Carpolestes*," the morphological and size gaps were closed by the description of *Carpodaptes jepseni* Rose, 1975. For biological reasons, *Carpodaptes* is considered to include "*Carpolestes*," as suggested by Szalay (1972b). Morphological criteria for the separation of "*Carpolestes*" are inadequate and stratigraphic

considerations alone for the maintenance of "*Carpolestes*" are then unacceptable.

According to Rose (1975), the last reviser of the family, the following features diagnose the various species. In *Carpodaptes aulacodon* $P_{\overline{4}}$ bears five ill-defined apical cusps, followed by a low and distinct distal heel. $P_{\overline{4}}$ in this species is longer than in *C. hazelae*, *C. hobackensis*, or *C. cygneus*, but shorter than in *C. jepseni*, *C. nigridens*, and *C. dubius*. *Carpodaptes hobackensis* is smaller than other *Carpodaptes*. Following Rose (1975), the "$P_{\overline{4}}$ [is] lower and more gently rounded in lateral profile than in other species of *Carpodaptes*, except *C. cygneus*; crest S-shaped in occlusal view due to deep posterointernal excavation of tooth, bearing 5 small but distinct apical cusps and a talonid cusp; talonid not so clearly separated from main blade as in *C. hazelae* or *C. aulacodon*" (p. 30). No adequate characters differentiate *C. hobackensis* from the subsequently described "*C. cygneus*." Due to the nature of serration on the carpolestid $P_{\overline{4}}$'s, it is not always possible to give exact and comparable counts of the cusps present.

Carpodaptes jepseni is about the size of *C. nigridens* and *C. dubius* and it bridges the gap previously maintained between *Carpodaptes* and "*Carpolestes*." As noted above, no discernible novel adaptations characterize the samples of "*Carpolestes*" beyond the mechanical solutions already well established in *Carpodaptes*. Rose (1975) characterized *Carpodaptes jepseni* as having "$P_{\overline{4}}$ very high crowned, bearing six well-developed apical cusps followed by lower, separate talonid heel; last apical cusp lower but better developed than those anterior to it, as in *C. cygneus*; talonid lower than trigonid of $M_{\overline{1}}$, and distinctly separated from main blade as in *C. hazelae* and *C. aulacodon*; lateral profile close to that of *C. aulacodon* approaching a more pointed form than other species. Paraconid on $M_{\overline{1}}$ only slightly subordinate to protoconid. Molars longer and broader than in other species" (p. 33). *Carpodaptes nigridens* and *C. dubius* differ from other *Carpodaptes* in having eight or nine closely spaced and variably patterned apical cusps on $P_{\overline{4}}$. $P^{\underline{3}}$–$P^{\underline{4}}$ cuspules develop as in other species of *Carpodaptes* but the teeth are relatively longer. The mandible is slightly deeper in *C. nigridens* and *C. dubius* than in the other species of the genus. *Carpodaptes nigridens* can be differentiated from *C. dubius* in that its $P^{\underline{3}}$ has five buccal cusps with a prominent buccomesial "spur," whereas in the later species the most mesial buccal cusp, and therefore the "spur," is much less developed.

SUBORDER STREPSIRHINI
E. Geoffroy, 1812

(= or including: Heteronychae Gray, 1821, in part. Mesodonta Cope, 1876, in part. Lemuriformes Gregory, 1915b, in part. Lorisiformes Gregory, 1915b, in part. Anthrolemuroidea Gingerich, 1973b, in part. Simiolemuriformes Gingerich, 1975b, in part. Lemuriformes of various authors.)

DISTRIBUTION
Early Eocene to modern. North America, Europe, Asia, Africa, Madagascar, and the Comoro Islands.

INCLUDED TAXA
Infraorders Adapiformes and Lemuriformes.

DISCUSSION

The concept of Strepsirhini espoused here includes the living tooth-combed primates, the Lemuriformes, and the mainly early Tertiary primates grouped under the Adapiformes. The "lemur–loris" group, the Lemuriformes, is easy enough to diagnose based on derived characteristics, because they possess the unique tooth comb. Even those subfossil groups that modify their anterior dentition leave clear signs of the ancestral tooth comb arrangement (e.g., Palaeopropithecidae). Many derived primate characters, however, which are present in known adapids are also present in the tarsiiforms and the tooth-combed strepsirhines. Thus, the postorbital bar and various postcranial features are difficult to use in the delineation of the Adapiformes. It is perhaps best to define the ancestral strepsirhine assemblage, the Adapiformes, as a group whose common ancestor was different from the putative antecedent plesiadapiforms in its advanced characters such as an enlarged stapedial ar-

tery, a postorbital bar, grasping hallux and pollex (possibly also present in the earliest plesiadapiform), and a number of osteological characters of the postcranium such as the flat blade of the ilium and the distinct separation by a ridge of the capitular and trochlear facets of the distal end of the humerus. Most of the adapiforms, as the plesiadapiforms, however, are only known by molar characters, which are discussed in detail under the various taxa.

Already the known early members of the Strepsirhini represent the "lemur" level of organization, an awkward concept in light of the great variety known among the living strepsirhines. Nevertheless, this characterization serves as a vehicle to depict an ancestral level of organization in which minor changes in cranial anatomy are accompanied by the establishment of grasp-leaping arboreal adaptations in the postcranial anatomy rivaling those of any other modern non-strepsirhine primate. Thus, the breakthrough from plesiadapiforms to strepsirhines was likely to have been by a species with superior grasp-leaping arboreal adaptations, necessitated by a particular feeding regime. This first strepsirhine, the first adapiform, or the first "lemur" acquired the diagnostic characters suggested above.

We will now briefly review the salient features of the basicranial evidence in the Strepsirhini (Figures 45 and 46). Morphology of this region will greatly aid in assessing both the nature of relationships between strepsirhines and other primates as well as the phylogeny within this suborder. In addition to the

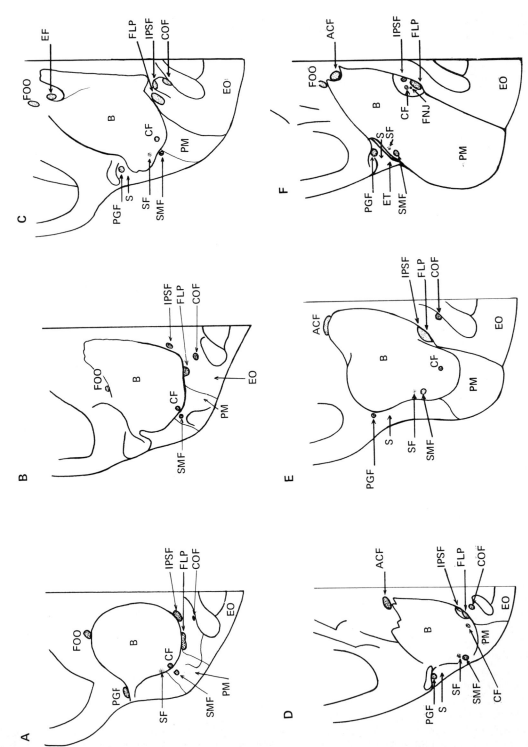

Figure 45. Simplified schema of intact basicranial morphology of some representative Strepsirhini. A, *Pronycticebus* (?late Eocene); B, *Adapis parisiensis* (middle–late Eocene); C, *Lemur* sp. (modern); D, *Microcebus* sp. (modern); E, *Komba* sp. (early Miocene); F, *Galago crassicaudatus* (modern). A–C represent the relatively primitive strepsirhine condition, whereas D–F represent the progressively more advanced lorisoids. For abbreviations, see Table III. [From Szalay (1975f).]

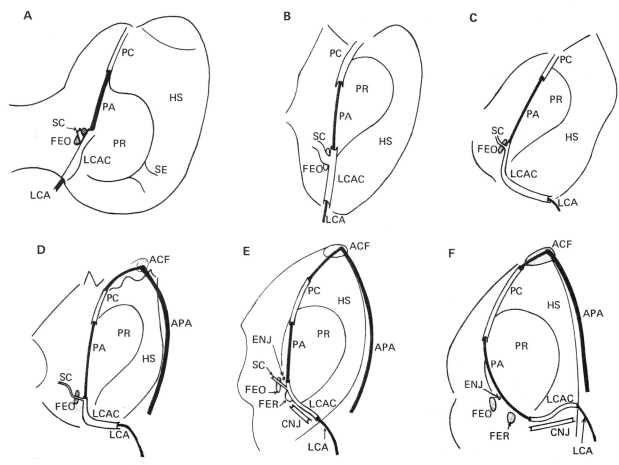

Figure 46. Simplified schema of middle-ear morphology and associated carotid circulation in (A) *Adapis parisiensis* (middle–late Eocene); (B) *Lemur* sp. (modern); (C) *Lepilemur* sp. (modern); (D) *Microcebus* sp. (modern); (E) hypothetical condition based on the external morphology of *Komba* sp. (early Miocene); and (F) *Galago crassicaudatus* (modern). The bulla and ectotympanic are removed to show the carotid circulation. As in Figure 45, the various conditions depicted in A–F approximate the polarity of a morphocline for the character complex shown. For abbreviations, see Table III. [From Szalay (1975f).]

wealth of extant and subfossil species, fossil strepsirhines are reasonably well known basicranially. Skulls or skull fragments of *Pelycodus, Notharctus, Smilodectes, Adapis, Leptadapis, Mahgarita,* and *Pronycticebus* give a fair idea of the diversity of this region. The two Miocene crania of lorisids, those of *Komba* and *Mioeuoticus,* suggest both a degree of anagenetic advance and at least an upper limit for the time of origin of lorisid skull morphologies.

It is likely that much of the evidence, especially of the ectotympanic, that we consider primitive strepsirhine in both adapiforms and later lemuriforms is largely a primitive retention from some unknown plesiadapiform, but one that was unlike *Plesiadapis* or *Phenacolemur.*

The relative size of the blood vessels in fossil forms will be of some importance in our discussion. The only measure of the relative importance of blood transport in arteries of fossils is the relative size of the bony canals that housed them. Gregory's (1920) assertion about the differences in the relative sizes of the promontory and stapedial arteries in primitive strepsirhines and haplorhines can be confirmed on new and, in the case of adapids, more primitive fossil material. Diameters of the lateral internal carotid and the promontory and stapedial canals have been drawn (Szalay, 1975f) from a petrosal of *Pelycodus* sp. from the early Eocene and a skull of *Necrolemur antiquus*. The relative diameters show that the size of the promontory artery is by no means insignificant in *Pelycodus*, but in this primitive notharctine the stapedial artery appears to have been the larger vessel immediately after the separation of the lateral internal carotid artery into the two former ones. This is the condition overwhelmingly established for *Adapis*, *Leptadapis*, *Notharctus* (but see Gingerich, 1973b), *Smilodectes*, *Mahgarita*, and the extant Lemuridae (*sensu stricto*), Indriidae, and Daubentoniidae. As stated by Gregory (1920), *Necrolemur* and *Tetonius* clearly show the greater emphasis of the promontory as opposed to the stapedial canals and therefore presumably of the arteries also. Thus, the recognition of the early dichotomy between strepsirhine and haplorhine intrabullar circulation appears justified.

The diversified basicranial morphology of the strepsirhines does not contradict the hypothesis of relationships suggested by Szalay and Katz (1973), namely, that some lemurids gave rise to the cheirogaleids, one of which, in turn, was the ancestor of the lorisid radiation.

For purposes of our discussion, three major basicranial categories may be recognized among the strepsirhines. The adapids, most lemurids, most indriids, and daubentoniids share basic similarities, which can be described as those of a primitive strepsirhine pattern. The Cheirogaleidae, the second group, are uniform in some of their distinctive characters. Similarly, the lorisids, the third group, are closely knit in sharing a number of clearly derived character states.

A review of strepsirhine basicrania indicates that the character states shared by the known Adapidae and, to some degree, by the Lemuridae and Indriidae represent relatively unmodified versions of the primitive pattern for strepsirhines, although not necessarily for the order. Whenever we choose to determine polarity for any of the several characters found in two or more conditions, it is invariably the adapid–lemurid pattern that appears to be primitive, and the lorisid one derived. The cheirogaleids show an intermediate condition in some features, although they possess some primitive and some derived character states like those found in the lorisids. The most conspicuous advanced feature of the latter two families is the presence of an enlarged ascending pharyngeal artery (Szalay and Katz, 1973; Cartmill, 1975) and an anterior carotid foramen in all forms here called lorisoids.

The following basicranial characters mirror the significant differences among the strepsirhines: (1) place of entry of the carotid and ascending pharyngeal arteries into the bulla; (2) absence or presence of an anterior carotid foramen and enlarged ascending paryngeal artery; (3) relative size, or presence or absence, of the stapedial canal and artery; (4) relative size of the promontory canal and artery; (5) relative size of the petromastoid; and (6) relative size and position of the ectotympanic in relation to the petrosal.

Neither the details of the morphology nor some of the problems of function and homology surrounding the basicranium can be discussed in great length here. Lamberton's (1940) and Saban's (1956, 1963, 1975) contributions give excellent details of strepsirhine basicranial morphology, and Szalay and Katz (1973), Cartmill (1975), and Szalay (1975f) recently discussed some issues of homology and morphocline polarity as they relate to strepsirhine phylogeny. The pertinent evidence and the interpretation of the homologies of vessels and openings in the basicrania are shown in Figures 45 and 46, and interpretations of the morphocline polarities are briefly stated below.

The basicranial evidence is compelling in that it points to some well-understood morphocline polarities. As this is one of the better known and most uniquely diagnostic morphological complexes of strepsirhines, inasmuch as it clearly differentiates the major groups, it can be given much weight in deciding their phylogenetic as well as anagenetic relationships. We may conclude, therefore, that the most ancient and ancestral strepsirhines were animals that can be characterized in terms of the known morphology of the adapids. Apart from the relatively larger brain and a tooth comb, the most recent common ancestor of the Lemuridae and Indriidae was either the most recent common ancestor of all the known tooth-combed strepsirhines or was, at least, more like a lemurid than a cheirogaleid or lorisid. The Cheirogaleidae were derived from a lemuroid, a form not unlike *Lepilemur*. The derived characters shared by cheirogaleids and lorisids, and the clear evidence of the entire skeleton favoring the primitiveness of the cheirogaleids compared with the lorisids, indicate that a strepsirhine species of cheirogaleid affinity and of a similar level of organization was the ancestor of lorisids. The

Lorisoidea, then, including both the Cheirogaleidae and Lorisidae, are derived descendants of much more primitive *bona fide* lemuroids, and most of the characters shared by all lorisoids are advanced features not only among primates but also within the tooth-combed strepsirhines (for a different interpretation, see Martin, 1972).

There is no reason to doubt that the tooth comb is homologous in all the lemuriforms. The term tooth comb has recently been replaced by Martin (1972) with the concept of "tooth scraper," and he has stated that, although most living species of strepsirhines use their tooth combs for grooming, this is a secondary function. Using the field observations made on cheirogaleids and galagines, some of which gather plant exudates with the aid of the "tooth scraper," and on *Propithecus verreauxi,* which pries bark, Martin argued that gum and resin scraping were the original function of the tooth comb. This view was also recently espoused by Gingerich (1975d).

The understanding of the anterior dentition of the Lemuriformes is of special importance for the evolution of this group. As some differences exist between Martin's and Gingerich's methods of phylogenetic and morphological anlysis and conclusions and those of Szalay (1976) and Szalay and Seligsohn (1977), we will briefly present the arguments advanced by the latter authors. Since a functional analysis of the morphological entities that Martin (1972) sought to explain was not presented, one is forced to conclude that Martin (1972) was heavily influenced by his conviction that the cheirogaleids and lorisids are the most primitive among living strepsirhines. This phylogenetic inference has apparently molded his view that the use of the tooth comb in the ancestral lemuriform (present sense) mode of life was more like that in galagos and cheirogaleids than in the more diurnal, larger, more gregarious taxa of lemurids.

The pivotal argument, however, to explain the origins of the tooth comb for sap eating and bark prying should be based on an analysis of the most highly adapted sap eaters *Phaner* and *Allocebus* (Petter, Schilling, and Pariente, 1971), in contrast to their closest relatives *Cheirogaleus* and *Microcebus,* and to living lemuroids (except *Daubentonia*) such as *Propithecus,* which utilizes the comb as a wedge. Among Malagasy strepsirhines it is *Phaner* that excessively enlarges the central upper incisors in a manner opposite to those

found in other forms, displays robust and dorsoventrally depened canines, adds another caniniform tooth, the second premolar, to the upper dental battery, minimizes the flexion of the crowns of the tooth comb on their roots, and clearly extremely reduces the relative postcaniniform surface area of the cheek teeth. From a mechanical point of view, it appears that these seemingly derived conditions came about to serve as tools that can best withstand the great axially directed compressive stresses and parasagitally directed bending moments incurred during piercing, nipping, and tearing of bark, and they mirror the decreased necessity of the cheek teeth for trituration of a food that is usually very soft. The African *Euoticus* shows the same adaptations of the anterior dentition as does *Phaner* and tends to contrast similarly with *Galago* and *Galagoides.*

The reduced number of teeth that make up the tooth comb of *Propithecus verreauxi* or of the other indriids is a derived condition, as everyone will agree. This condition of a four-toothed as compared to a six-toothed "comb" appears to be correlated with a greater robusticity of the individual teeth of the "comb," which are relatively wider buccolingually and shorter mesiodistally. In fact, the four-toothed "comb" of the indriids is usually relatively wider and presents more apical cutting edges than the six-toothed comb of the lemurids. One might also point to the archaeolemurids and palaeopropithecids, which "redevelop," from a tooth-combed ancestry, relatively short and apically wide "incisors" (and canines). Consistent with the need of the tooth "comb" in *Propithecus* to withstand the relatively large axially directed compressive forces and parasagitally directed bending moments generated during extensive bark-prising activities are the dorsoventrally deepened canines and incisors and linearly aligned tooth crowns and roots.

A specific comparison between the most gumivorous lemuriform such as *Phaner furcifer,* the frugivorous-folivorous *Lemur fulvus,* and the folivore *Propithecus verrauxi* is instructive because the tooth combs differ from each other as outlined above and discussed below. In *Lemur,* where it is primarily used for combing, an apical ridge on the distal slope of the incisors and the spaces between the teeth are nearly parallel. The apical edge of the tooth comb is zig-zagged, each tooth having an apex, resulting in a **V**-shaped tip on the teeth. By contrast, the sap scraper *Phaner,* which, as noted above, possesses a derived anterior dentition compared to lemuroids and other cheirogaleids, has a considerably constricted tooth comb. The most significant modification in *Phaner*, however, in contrast to the other lemuriforms, is the apical edge of the teeth of the tooth comb. Rather than wedge-shaped, these teeth have transversely nearly straight edges, and thus all six teeth form a nearly continuous cutting edge. In *Propithecus*, the reduced number of teeth in the "comb" is positively correlated with the great robusticity of the component teeth.

We may now ask the question whether or not it may be advantageous to evolve a dental tool whose primary function is to have a transverse cutting edge at its apical extremity by elongating the incisors, thus making them more prone to damage from bending moments, and laying the transformed canine parallel to them, creating five long interdental spaces where food compaction must be a considerable liability. The daubentoniids, archaeolemurids, and palaeopropithecids have done away with a tooth comb to develop robust and, at least in the case of the last two families, broader and less tall teeth with extensive apical edges. Numerous primates feed on gums, yet the modifications of various New World and Old World anthropoids do not even approximate anything like a tooth comb.

The curious fact that the canine joins the incisor area and takes up the derived form of the incisors is significant in two respects. First, it is probably not selection for a long mesial cutting edge that prompted this event. Increasing the cutting edge of the anterior teeth by adding another pointed, narrow tooth to that area of the dentition creates a discontinuous edge which probably has neither the cutting ability of a continuous one nor the strength or penetrating ability of a single, pointed, and basally robust tooth (see *Daubentonia*, for example). Second, the canine joining the incisors in the front results in a significant feature, the creation of an additional, long, narrow interdental space on each side. The same clearly applies for the modifications of the whole tooth comb; the six front teeth have five narrow, evenly distributed spaces in between them in the primitive lemuriform tooth comb. Unlike incisors among most primates, the apical extremities of the anterior teeth are not any nearer to one another than the basal portions.

The nature and morphology of the dental crowns and interdental spaces of the tooth comb may reflect on the differential severity of the problems relating to tooth-comb sanitation in specialized sap-feeders and non–sap-feeders. In a sap-feeder like *Phaner*, for example, the tooth comb is transversely "compressed," resulting in the reduction of the interdental spaces. Furthermore, the morphology of the incisors is relatively more simplified, resulting in smoother tooth surfaces and interdental areas. While this situation is certainly consistent with efficient sap ingestion, it also may reflect selection pressures to ensure a minimum of food entrapment along the crown surfaces and interdental spaces and may facilitate the cleaning action of the sublingua.

Since most non–sap-feeding strepsirhines do, however, emphasize long, continuous interdental spaces in their tooth combs, we may postulate that this condition was the ancestral one. Assuming this, and also assuming that most food material is probably more chemically reactive than (keratinized) hair or desquamated skin epithelium, it seems more likely that the ancestral condition would have been selected for as a fur-grooming device. It would appear that the primitive lemuriform tooth comb, had it served a primarily sap-procuring biological role, would have been more prone to food entrapment and tooth decay in the interdental regions.

With the foregoing in mind we must conclude (Szalay, 1976; Szalay and Seligsohn, 1977) that the primitive lemuriform tooth comb was primarily adapted for the efficient maintenance of optimally long, parallel, narrow spaces rather than resistance of stresses incurred by the apices of the teeth in cutting or scraping. The biological role that would explain this ancestral morphology appears to be fur combing, originally attributed to this specialization, during which forces are not excessive and are distributed more or less evenly on the long and narrow occlusal surfaces of the anterior teeth. A self-evident but important fact should be added here: Among the living primates it is the strepsirhines who possess a tooth comb, and these primates are also the ones which use it as a comb for the explicit purpose of grooming. Aside from the mechanical function of the tooth comb, the suggestion from mere correlation is very strong that this derived anterior dental structure, along with additional modifications of the tongue in the form of the sublingua (Jones, 1929), is the direct result of selection to fulfill the biological role of fur cleansing.

Infraorder Adapiformes, new

DISTRIBUTION

Early Eocene to late Miocene (Wasatchian and Neustrian to Uintan and Headonian, respectively, and ?Vallesian in Asia). North America, Europe, and Asia.

INCLUDED TAXA

Family Adapidae.

Discussion

As noted under the Strepsirhini, the tooth-combed strepsirhines are most likely monophyletic and therefore, in this respect, are separate from known adapiforms. Although there is no doubt in our minds that the lemuroid ancestor which acquired the characteristic tooth comb could be considered a derived adapid, the absence of this derived character complex serves as a convenient and instructive line of demarcation between the ancestral strepsirhine radiation and the numerous fossil and surviving forms of the holophyletic tooth-combed Lemuriformes. The discussions under the Strepsirhini and Lemuriformes are closely relevant to this infraorder.

The known adapiform taxa are relatively numerous in the fossil record, yet this diversity almost certainly only represents the tip of an iceberg, a mere glimpse of what must have been an extremely varied and long-lasting adaptive radiation in the Holarctic of the Paleocene and Eocene, and probably well into the Miocene. The tooth comb, a character complex that ties lemuriforms into a monophyletic, as well as holophyletic, taxon, is not present in any of the known adapiforms. See under Adapidae for morphological details.

Family Adapidae
Trouessart, 1879

(= or including: Pachylemuridae: Zittel, 1892, in part.)

DISTRIBUTION

Same as for infraorder.

INCLUDED TAXA

Subfamilies Notharctinae and Adapinae.

Discussion

The majority of the primates recognized as adapids are Eocene in age. They are known largely by dentitions but several genera (*Pronycticebus, Adapis, Leptadapis, Mahgarita, Notharctus,* and *Smilodectes*) are also known by skulls. Postcranial remains are reasonably well known for the Notharctinae but the Adapinae are still poorly represented.

The subdivision of the Adapidae is a very difficult undertaking, primarily because the phylogeny is not adequately understood (see Figure 47). For the present, it seems appropriate to continue a separation

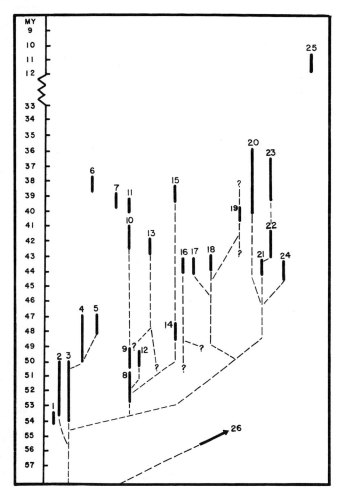

Figure 47. Known stratigraphic ranges (solid lines) and suggested phylogenetic relationships (broken lines) of the Adapidae. 1, *Donrussellia*; 2, *Copelemur*; 3, *Pelycodus*; 4, *Notharctus*; 5, *Smilodectes*; 6, *Lushius*; 7, *Amphipithecus*; 8, *Protoadapis curvicuspidens*; 9, *Protoadapis filholi*; 10, *Protoadapis brachyrhynchus*; 11, *Protoadapis ulmensis*; 12, *Agerinia*; 13, *Pronycticebus*; 14, *Europolemur*; 15, *Mahgarita*; 16, *Microadapis*; 17, *Periconodon*; 18, *Anchomomys*; 19, *Huerzeleris*; 20, *Adapis parisiensis*; 21, *Leptadapis priscus*; 22, *Leptadapis rütimeyeri*; 23, *Leptadapis magnus*; 24, *Caenopithecus*; 25, *Indraloris*; 26, segment of the stratigraphic range of the Omomyidae. [By A. Cleary.]

of the genera into the Notharctinae and Adapinae. Judged from the remains of *Pelycodus*, the oldest notharctines, this genus might represent the most primitive dental morphology within the Adapidae. The third molars are unreduced, and $M_{\overline{3}}$ in particular has an elongated heel. The hypocone is undeveloped and only a well-formed protocone fold bulges on the distolingual part of the tooth. The conules are pronounced on the upper molars. The paraconids are well developed and the trigonids become progressively more mesiodistally constricted from $M_{\overline{1}}$ to $M_{\overline{3}}$. All the premolars are present and they can be characterized as premolariform. The canines appear to be distinctly caniniform and larger than the teeth mesial and distal

to them. The incisors are not well known in *Pelycodus*, but in other adapids, e.g., *Notharctus* and *Smilodectes*, they are rather low crowned and small.

The Adapidae contains species both very small (e.g., *Anchomomys*, *Huerzeleris*) and cat sized (e.g., *Notharctus*, *Leptadapis*). There is no question in our minds that members of this family were extensively arboreal.

The importance of significant, hence valid, distinctions between species samples cannot be sufficiently emphasized, particularly in light of the recent proliferation of new species described among the adapids (Gingerich and Simons, 1977; Gingerich, 1977a). In most of these instances, even when the author(s) states that one sample is indistinguishable from another, the phrase "of significant size difference" is constantly used to justify new taxa. The statement is usually not accompanied by the relevant *comparative* statistics, and the Student *t* test or other supporting evidence is not presented, we suspect, because they cannot be generated.

The phylogeny of the Adapidae presented by Gingerich (1977a) is, as far as we can judge, completely "stratophenetic." This author does not attempt a character analysis of the available dental evidence, but, in our view, incorrectly utilizes stratigraphic and arbitrarily chosen mensurational parameters. The most sensitive available mirror of the extinct genotypes, therefore, the morphology, is virtually ignored. Thus, *Cercamonius,* morphologically indistinguishable from *Protoadapis,* is considered valid by Gingerich (1977a), and *Huerzeleris,* morphologically easily distinguishable from the phenetically closest taxa, is regarded as invalid, because (Ginerich, 1977a), as stated by this author, "given present knowledge of phylogenetic relationships, their recognition obscures rather than clarifies the unified nature of the adapid radiation" (p. 61). He adds that "however, it is necessary to retain *Caenopithecus,* . . . *Pronycticebus,* . . . and *Cercamonius* as monotypic genera because of their distinctive specializations" (Gingerich, 1975c). We find these taxonomic views internally inconsistent.

The Notharctinae (as well as the Adapinae) have been recently somewhat oversplit on the species level by Gingerich and Simons (1977). The Notharctinae, not counting the poorly known Asiatic taxa tenatively referred to it, represents a relatively minor, although numerically abundant, adaptive radiation. The *Pelycodus–Notharctus* clade can easily be characterized by size increase and accompanying hypocone and mesostyle development, whereas *Smilodectes* is merely a short-faced *Notharctus*-like genus. The significant aspect of this group as it relates to other primates lies in the morphology of *Pelycodus.* This early Eocene genus, when one considers all the available morphology of the Omomyidae and Adapinae, suggests that the morphotype conditions of the grasp-leaping higher primates, the euprimates (Strepsirhini and Haplorhini), might have been *Pelycodus*-like.

Gingerich (1977b) has recently made an interesting comparison between *Azibus trerki* described by Sudre (1975) from the Eocene of North Africa and *Anchomomys gaillardi,* the tiny Eocene adapid. The

only meaningfully comparable teeth are $M_{\overline{2}}$, as $M_{\overline{1}}$ of *Azibius* is both damaged and considerably derived, noticeably influenced by the plagiaulacoid $P_{\overline{4}}$. We grant a similarity in the squared preprotocristid and reduced paraconid to *Anchomomys,* and to other primates, but also to various archontans, apatemyid insectivorans, and a number of marsupial groups. So, as noted before, we are even doubtful as to the primate affinities of *Azibius,* although it may well have been an early African representative of the order. Until a taxon can be reasonably regarded to have certain highly corroborated ties with material that can be meaningfully tested by comparisons, we cannot endorse the type of paleogeographical scenario outlined by Gingerich. We particularly oppose the use of such highly tenuous scenarios as "supporting" arguments for, e.g., the origins of anthropoids from adapids.

Gingerich (1977b) has also deftly and, in our opinion, significantly compared and pointed out the great similarity between the $M_{\overline{2}}$ of the Asiatic Eocene *Hoanghonius* and that of *Oligopithecus.* Our difference of opinion (see under *Hoanghonius*) lies in the interpretation of the ties of the Asian primate. We see no evidence for its categorically stated adapid ties. For each feature in which *Hoanghonius* resembles adapids it also resembles omomyids. This is a small wonder as the two families share a host of primitive cranial, molar, and postcranial traits, attesting to their common ancestry after their separation from the Plesiadapiformes (Szalay, 1975f,g; 1977a). As discussed under the genus, we consider *Hoanghonius* a tarsiiform. However, if *Hoanghonius* proves to be an adapid, then adapid ties for the African *Oligopithecus* becomes an available hypothesis (see pp. 269 and 271).

Of great significance is the confirmation based on excellent series of jaws and maxillae with teeth (unpublished as yet), that *Indraloris* of the northern Indian Miocene is an adapid. The conformation of the molars, the fused symphysis, the large canines and small incisors make it clear that this primate is not a lemuriform (present sense), but rather an adapid. Another undescribed Miocene genus, collected by Dr. Chopra, and the likelihood of *Amphipithecus* and *Pondaungia* having adapid affinities (but see our differences of opinion on the latter taxon, pp. 145 and 517) make it clear that Asia, in addition to the presence of tarsiiforms (*Altanius*), was the theater of an extensive adapiform radiation during the early and mid Tertiary.

SUBFAMILY NOTHARCTINAE
Trouessart, 1879

(= or including: Notharctidae Trouessart, 1879.)

DISTRIBUTION
Early to middle Eocene (Wasatchian to Bridgerian), and early Eocene (Neustrian). Western North America, western Europe, and possibly eastern Asia (see above).

INCLUDED TAXA
Pelycodus, *Notharctus*, *Smilodectes*, and *Copelemur*.

DISCUSSION

This subfamily is perhaps best distinguished from the adapines as the slightly more primitive group. Whether or not the genus *Pelycodus* is a representative of the primitive adapid morphology, as outlined in the discussion under the Adapidae, it appears certain that the *Pelycodus*–*Notharctus*–*Smilodectes*–*Copelemur* group represents a monophyletic grouping within the Adapidae.

There are a number of reasons why a form like *Pelycodus*, clearly the most primitive among the notharctines, is considered to be representative of the ancestral adapid morphology. Through well-sampled stages, as early as 1920, Gregory has clearly demonstrated that transformation sequences from advanced middle Eocene species can be traced back to the earliest Eocene samples of *Pelycodus*. The genus is equally ancient in Europe, and the older (and contemporaneous) *Protoadapis* suggests that much of the European adapid radiation stems from a *Pelycodus*-like taxon. In addition to this hypothesis gleaned from a combined analysis of morphology and the biostratigraphic record, the analysis of the Omomyidae (see below) suggests an ancestor for that family not unlike a diminutive *Pelycodus*-like form. It is important to remember that we use the concept of this genus in a broad structural sense, especially as it relates to the cheek teeth.

PELYCODUS Cope, 1875

(= or including: *Prototomus*: Cope, 1874. *Tomitherium*: Cope, 1877, in part. *Notharctus*: Osborn, 1902, in part. *Protoadapis*: Cooper, 1932. *Cantius* Simons, 1962b.)

DISTRIBUTION
Early Eocene (Wasatchian and Neustrian). Rocky Mt. region, Paris, and London Basins.

KNOWN SPECIES
1. *Pelycodus jarrovii* (Cope, 1874), type species
(=*Prototomus jarrovii* Cope, 1874. *Pelycodus jarrovii*: Cope, 1875. *Tomitherium jarrovii*: Cope, 1877. *Notharctus venticolis* Osborn, 1902. *Notharctus nunienus* Robinson, 1966, in part. "*Notharctus*" *venticolus*: Gingerich, 1976c.)
LOCALITIES: Lost Cabin (240); San José★ (249).
2. *Pelycodus ralstoni* Matthew, 1915
(=*Pelycodus mckennai* Gingerich and Simons, 1977.)
LOCALITIES: Lower Gray Bull (162); Four Mile (178, 180); Powder River (196); Sand Coulee★ (198).
3. *Pelycodus trigonodus* Matthew, 1915
(=*Pelycodus frugivorous*: Osborn, 1902. *Pelycodus jarrovii*: Matthew, 1915, in part. *Pelycodus* cf. *ralstoni*: Jepsen, 1963. *Notharctus nunienus*: Guthrie, 1971, in part.)
LOCALITIES: Upper Gray Bull★ (162).
4. *Pelycodus frugivorous* Cope, 1875
(=*Tomitherium frugivorous*: Cope, 1877. *Pelycodus nunienum*: Cope, 1881. *Notharctus nunienus*: Osborn, 1902; *Pelycodus nuniensis*: Loomis, 1906, lapsus. *Pelycodus jarrovii*: Matthew, 1915, in part. *Notharctus limosus* Gazin, 1952. *Pelycodus* cf. *jarrovii*: Kelley and Wood, 1954. *Notharctus nunienus*: Robinson, 1966, in part. "*Notharctus*" *nunienus*: Gingerich, 1976. *Pelycodus abditus* Gingerich and Simons, 1977.)

LOCALITIES: Almagre, San José (200); La Barge (238); Lost Cabin (240); New Fork★ (244); Huerfano (246).
5. *Pelycodus eppsi* (Cooper, 1932)
(=*Protoadapis eppsi* Cooper, 1932. *Cantius eppsi*: Simons, 1962b. *Pelycodus savagei* Gingerich, 1977.)
LOCALITIES: Dormaal (186); Pourcy (188); Mutigny (190); Abbey Wood★ (204); Avenay (206); Grauves (244).

DISCUSSION

Pelycodus is the earliest adapid and it is one of the more common early Eocene mammals in North America. It is dentally (Figure 48) the most abundant among primates of that time period.

Pelycodus is best distinguished from *Notharctus* by the lack of symphyseal fusion of the mandibular rami. As noted by Gingerich and Simons (1977), the development of mesostyle and the establishment of the robust hypocone in *Notharctus* were very gradual, and these features are also present in *Pelycodus*. Thus, co-ossification of the mandibular halves marks the arbitrary beginnings of *Notharctus* but at least provides a stratigraphic boundary between *Pelycodus* and *Notharctus*. This feature renders *Pelycodus* early Eocene, whereas *Notharctus* is middle Eocene (Gingerich and Simons, 1977). The artificiality of this separa-

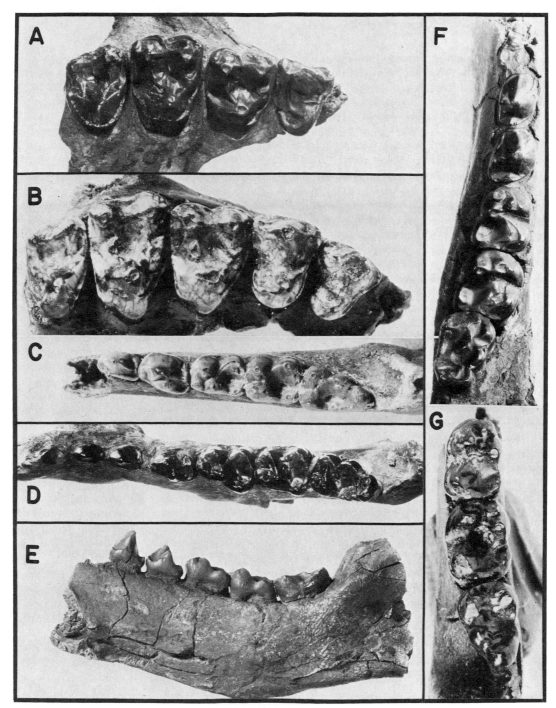

Figure 48. *Pelycodus.* Early Eocene, North America and Europe. *Pelycodus trigonodus,* western North America. Right maxilla with P^4–M^3: A, occlusal view. Right mandible fragment with $P_{\overline{2}}$–$M_{\overline{3}}$: D, occlusal view. *Pelycodus eppsi,* western Europe. Right maxilla with P^3–M^3: B, occlusal view. Right mandible fragment with $P_{\overline{3}}$–$M_{\overline{3}}$: C, occlusal view. *Pelycodus jarrovii,* western North America. Right mandible fragment with $P_{\overline{3}}$–$M_{\overline{3}}$: E, lateral view; F, occlusal view. Left mandible fragment with $M_{\overline{1-3}}$: G, occlusal view.

tion is striking, however, for anyone studying the late early Eocene and early middle Eocene samples of notharctines. In a previous paper, Gingerich (1976c) suggested that *Pelycodus* ranges back into Clarkforkian deposits. This view was altered by Gingerich and Simons (1977) stating that the specimen responsible for this range extension was almost certainly derived from overlying Wasatchian deposits.

Aside from these few gnathal and dental characters, there appears to be little in the known cranial fragments and scattered, fragmentary postcranial remains that would justify the separation of *Pelycodus* from *Notharctus*. With the possible exception of some species of *Protoadapis*, *Pelycodus* is distinguished from adapines by its incipiently developed hypocone, a protocone fold, which arises from the distal slope of the protocone. We suspect that this upper molar morphology is primitive for the Adapidae. The talonid of the last molar is elongated, and, in general, the molars are low, with bulbous, sometimes crenulated, cusps. The third and fourth premolars, however, are not molariform.

The following diagnostic distinctions may be recognized for the species considered valid by us. *Pelycodus ralstoni*, the oldest North American form, is the smallest of the North American species of the genus. This species generally lacks a hypocone even in its most rudimentary form, and only occasionally has a small mesostyle. The small-toothed European *P. eppsi* seems to differ very little from *P. ralstoni*. We question the significance of the absence of an incipient hypocone on the basal cingulum of *P. ralstoni*

(Gingerich and Simons, 1977) in contrast to *P. eppsi*. At any rate, the two earliest Eocene samples of *Pelycodus* are extremely close to one another and they might have been conspecific in spite of the enormous distance between them. *Pelycodus trigonodus* is larger than *P. ralstoni* or *P. eppsi* and has small to medium-sized mesostyles. This species generally lacks well-developed hypocones. *Pelycodus frugivorous* is intermediate in hypocone and mesostyle development and in size between *P. trigonodus* and *P. jarrovii*.

Most known samples of *Pelycodus*, as demonstrated by Gregory (1920) and as further documented by Gingerich and Simons (1977), form a nearly uninterrupted sequence from the early Wasatchian *P. ralstoni* to the middle and late Wasatchian *P. trigonodus* to the late Wasatchian *P. frugivorous* and *P. jarrovii*.

The jaws are relatively deep, but, as the angle on the mandible is not particularly enlarged in *Notharctus*, it was unlikely to have been so in *Pelycodus*.

The dental formula is $I\frac{2}{2}$; $C\frac{1}{1}$; $P\frac{1.2.3.4}{1.2.3.4}$; $M\frac{1.2.3}{1.2.3}$.

The last detailed treatment of European *Pelycodus* is by Russell, Louis and Savage (1967). Although these authors clearly established the very close similarity of "*Cantius*" *eppsi* to other *Pelycodus*, they have not firmly rejected the use of the generic designation "*Cantius*." A consensus now exists, however, that "*Cantius*" is a synonym of *Pelycodus*.

The tooth morphology and prevalence of apical wear suggest some emphasis on puncture-crushing type of chewing. Species of *Pelycodus* were probably frugivorous and insectivorous, but not likely folivorous.

NOTHARCTUS Leidy, 1870

(= or including: *Limnotherium* Marsh, 1871. *Hipposyus* Leidy, 1872b. *Tomitherium* Cope, 1872b. *Thinolestes* Marsh, 1872a. *Telmatolestes* Marsh, 1872a. *Prosinopa* Trouessart, 1897.)

DISTRIBUTION
Late early Eocene to middle Eocene (late Wasatchian to Bridgerian). Rocky Mt. region.
KNOWN SPECIES
1. *Notharctus tenebrosus* Leidy, 1870, type species
(=*Limnotherium tyrannus* Marsh, 1871. *Hipposyus formosus* Leidy, 1872b. *Tomitherium rostratum* Cope, 1872b. *Thinolestes anceps* Marsh, 1872a. *Limnotherium affine* Marsh, 1872a. *Notharctus osborni* Granger and Gregory, 1917.)
LOCALITIES: Lower Bridger (266); Upper Bridger★ (282).
2. *Notharctus pugnax* Granger and Gregory, 1917
(=*Notharctus tenebrosus?*: Robinson, 1957.)

LOCALITIES: Lower Bridger★ (266).
3. *Notharctus robustior* Leidy, 1872c
(=*Telmatolestes crassus* Marsh, 1872a)
LOCALITIES: Upper Bridger★ (282).

DISCUSSION

Notharctus (Figures 49–52), here accepted as a Bridgerian (middle Eocene) genus, is undoubtedly a descendant of late Wasatchian *Pelycodus* (Gregory, 1920). The species suggested to have given rise to *Notharctus* is probably *Pelycodus jarrovii*, the late Wasatchian form from New Mexico (Gingerich and Simons, 1977). Unfortunately, *P. jarrovii* is very poorly

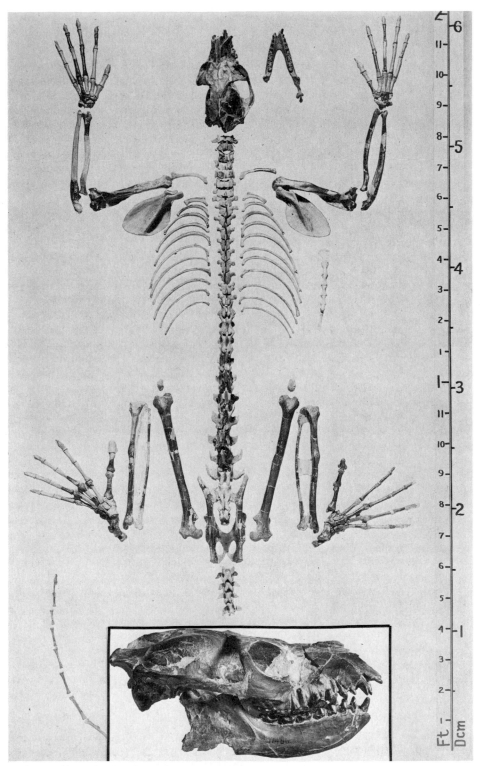

Figure 49. *Notharctus tenebrosus.* Middle Eocene, western North America. Dorsal view of articulated skeleton and lateral view of the skull and mandible. [From Gregory (1920).]

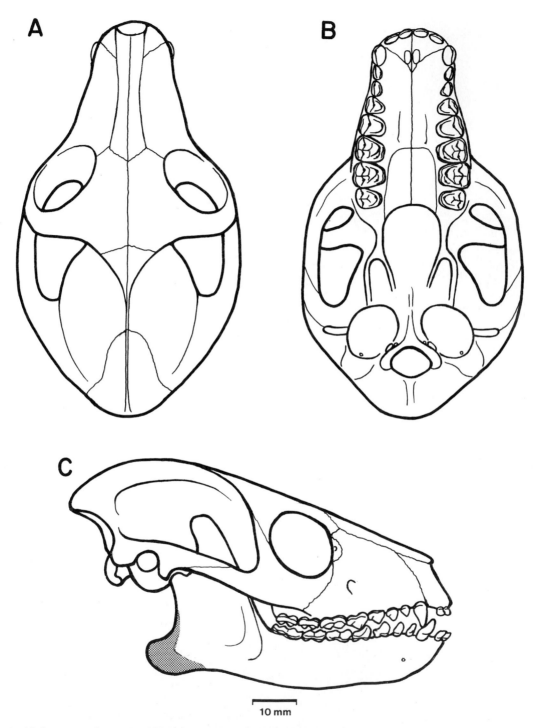

Figure 50. *Notharctus tenebrosus*. Middle Eocene, western North America. Skull and mandible reconstructed from crushed specimens: A, dorsal view; B, ventral view; C, lateral view. Stippling indicates reconstruction. [By A. Cleary.]

10 mm

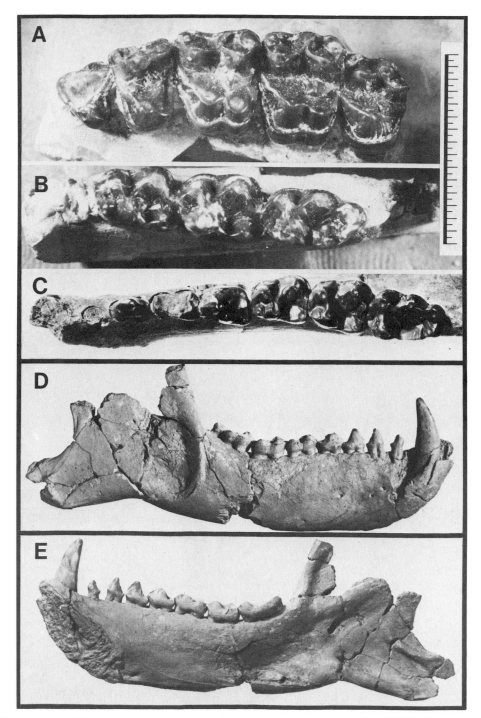

Figure 51. *Notharctus.* Middle Eocene, western North America. *Notharctus robustior,* left P³–M³: A, occlusal view. Right mandible fragment with M₁–M₃: B, occlusal view. *Notharctus nunienus,* right mandible fragment with P₂–M₃ and roots of C and P₁: C, occlusal view. *Notharctus venticolus,* nearly complete right mandible with C–M₃: D, lateral view; E, medial view. Subdivisions on scale for A and B represent 0.5 mm. [C,D,E from Gregory (1920).]

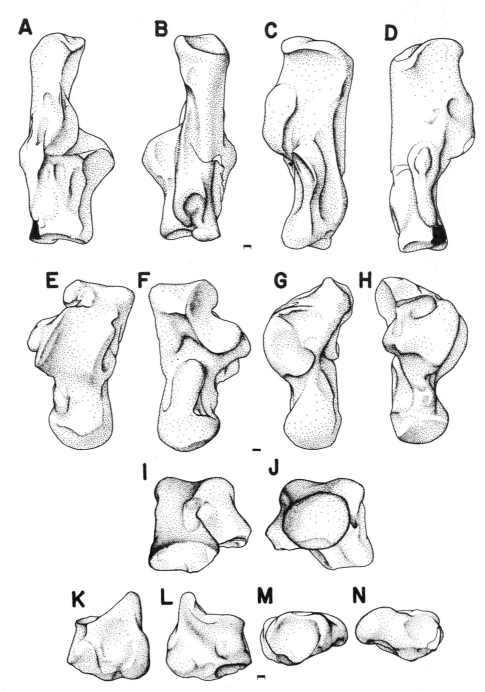

Figure 52. *Notharctus* sp. Middle Eocene, western North America. Right calcaneum (A–D), right astragalus (E–J): A and E, dorsal view; B and F, plantar view; C and G, medial view; D and H, lateral view; I, proximal view; J, distal view. Right navicular: K, dorsal view: L, plantar view; M, proximal view; N, distal view. Scales represent 1 mm. [By A. Cleary.]

known. The upper molar morphology, however, has the unmistakable stamp of well-developed hypocones and mesostyles so characteristic of *Notharctus* and *Smilodectes*.

Notharctus differs from *Pelycodus* primarily in having a fused mandibular symphysis and more advanced molars. The hypocone is well developed and cuspate, and specimens have a distinct mesostyle. The differences from *Smilodectes* are noted under that genus. The dental formula of *Notharctus* is the same as for *Pelycodus*.

The species of *Notharctus* are rather uniform in morphology. The late Wasatchian *Pelycodus jarrovii* is similar in every known dental detail to the later but significantly larger *Notharctus robustior*. *Notharctus tenebrosus* and *N. robustior* both share the characteristically strong, cuspate hypocone and strong cingulae surrounding the teeth and a well-developed mesostyle. The large samples of both *Pelycodus* and *Notharctus*, particularly the Bridger collection made by Dr. R. M. West, will undoubtedly yield answers as to the extent of diversification of the notharctines, the number of lineages, and the most suitable taxonomic framework in which the various samples of this very successful group should be arranged.

Notharctus is the best known of the adapids (see Gregory, 1920; Gazin, 1958; Decker and Szalay, 1974). What is astonishing about the postcranial morphology of this genus is its close resemblance to some of the living lemuriforms, such as *Lemur* and *Propithecus*. The postcranial morphology of *Notharctus*, along with the known cranial evidence, has been monographed by Gregory (1920), and further studies on the crania have been carried out by Gazin (1958). The cranial and mandibular morphology of *Notharctus* is known adequately in *Notharctus osborni* (Figure 50). In virtually every respect, features of *Notharctus* appear to be more primitive than those in adapines with known skulls. The basicranial region in particular is illustrated and described in detail under Strepsirhini.

In *Notharctus* the braincase is small with pronounced sagittal and nuchal crests, features shared with known adapines. The face is long, nearly in line with the braincase in both *Notharctus* and known adapines. The orbits are relatively less convergent than in the lemuriforms. The marked postorbital constriction, contrary to the view of Radinsky (1977), strongly indicates that the relative size of the brain was smaller in *Notharctus* and *Smilodectes* as well as in adapines than

in comparably sized living or subfossil lemuriforms. The lacrimal foramen is slightly behind the anterior crest of the orbit and the malar is nearly or in contact with the lacrimal. The occiput is narrow and pointed posterodorsally. The petromastoid bears a prominent tuberosity which is more or less cancellous and it is excluded from the brain cavity by the petrosal proper. The external pterygoid plate in *Notharctus* and in adapids in general is connected with the anterolateral process of the bulla, the entoglenoid process of the squamosal above the eustachian foramen. The postglenoid foramen is, as in primitive mammals, prominent in both *Notharctus* and other adapines. It should be noted here that Gazin (1958, pp. 33-42) has made valuable and extensive comparisons between excellent cranial material of *Notharctus* and *Smilodectes*, which was then newly recovered, and compared these in detail to European *Adapis* and *Leptadapis*. His reference to "*Adapis*" should be read to include *Leptadapis*.

As was noted by Gregory (1920), the known skeletal morphology of *Notharctus*, and for that matter also the remains of *Pelycodus*, is essentially similar to that of *Lemur*, *Lepilemur*, and *Propithecus*. Gregory's monograph laid down the grounds for this widely accepted view. Since 1920, however, much new skeletal, particularly postcranial, material has been discovered for *Notharctus*, *Smilodectes*, *Pelycodus*, various European adapids, and some plesiadapiforms. A major restudy of all of the early Tertiary postcranial morphology from a more modern perspective employing more mechanical analysis in addition to comparative anatomy is needed. Information pertinent to the skeletal morphology of *Notharctus* has been published, in addition to Gregory's study, in Simpson (1935a, 1940), Cartmill (1972), Szalay and Decker (1974), Decker and Szalay (1974), and Szalay, Tattersall, and Decker (1975). The discussion under *Plesiadapis*, various lemuriforms, and the tarsiiforms is relevant.

Of the scapula, clavicle, humerus, radius, and ulna, Gregory (1920) has concluded that: "All these considerations are in harmony with other evidence to the effect that in *Notharctus* the forearm was habitually partly supinated, as a part of the limb-grasping series of adaptations." Supporting this view is both Gregory's assessment of the pes and a more detailed restudy by Decker and Szalay (1974) of the evolutionary morphology of the pes in known Adapidae. The structure and mechanical function of the adapid pedal complex, but most particularly that of *Notharctus*, have been examined in some detail recently by Decker and Szalay (1974). A significantly consistent character of both adapiforms and lemuriforms is the form of the posterior trochlear shelf as well as the presence of a shelflike projection of the astragalar body (Figure 52) for the fibular malleolus, largely absent in plesiadapiforms. These developments are probably associated with the flexibility of the foot and the power exerted at the upper ankle joint during plantarflexion.

The adapids as well as younger lemuriforms possess a pivot type of calcaneocuboid joint, increasing the total potential for rotations in the middle of the tarsus along the long axis of the pes. This represents an advance in comparison to the condition in late Cretaceous eutherians and in the majority of plesiadapiform primates, some of which, however, may possess an incipient pivot. The pivot type of calcaneocuboid joint, developed first in marsupials, is also a structural innovation in the primates, although it is modified in various living terrestrial forms and in *Archaeolemur*, as well as in some arboreal specialists such as *Tarsius*.

Adapis, Leptadapis, and notharctines differ from the younger lemuriforms in the presence of some probably primitive primate characters such as a peroneal tubercle and a high, narrow lateral side to the trochlea. Changes in the peroneal tubercle are assessed as correlates of changing directions of the forces required by the calcaneocuboid and lower ankle joints of the peroneal muscles resulting from elongation of the tarsus, as well as changes in the nature of the calcaneocuboid joint. In one specialization (which, however, may be primitive for strepsirhines), the extent of the posterior trochlear shelf of the astragalus, *Notharctus* is better developed than later lemuriforms, including the presence of a larger posterior fibular facet, suggesting a remarkable force during plantar flexion that required well-developed muscles. Compared to living lemuriforms (except *Daubentonia*), the construction of the tarsus of *Notharctus* is less efficiently rigid in the middle and in the cuneiform complex.

The dentition of *Notharctus* indicates a primarily herbivorous feeding-habit. The mesostyle might be indicative of folivory, although the bulbous cusps are more suggestive of frugivory. The various species differing in size probably also differed in their diets.

One cannot argue without the necessary detailed study, which is not yet available (Szalay and Dagosto, in preparation), whether or not *Notharctus* and *Smilodectes* were vertical clingers and leapers. It seems certain, however, that these fossil taxa were limber and agile arborealists, grasp-leapers, capable of long leaps, probably occasionally practicing leaping and vertical grasp clinging, and generally rapid locomotion among the larger branches of the forest canopy.

SMILODECTES Wortman, 1903

(= or including: *Hyopsodus:* Marsh, 1871, in part. *?Microsyops:* Leidy, 1872, in part. *Aphanolemur* Granger and Gregory, 1917. *Pelycodus:* Granger and Gregory, 1917, in part. *Notharctus:* Gregory, 1920, in part.)

DISTRIBUTION
Middle Eocene (Bridgerian). Rocky Mt. region.
KNOWN SPECIES
Smilodectes gracilis (Marsh, 1871), type species
(=*Hyopsodus gracilis* Marsh, 1871. *?Microsyops gracilis* Leidy, 1872. *Smilodectes gracilis* Wortman, 1903. *Aphanolemur gibbosus* Granger and Gregory, 1917. *Notharctus matthewi* Granger and Gregory, 1917. *Pelycodus relictus* Granger and Gregory, 1917. *Notharctus gracilis:* Gregory, 1920.)
LOCALITIES: Grizzly Buttes★ (266); Black's Fork (266); Morrow Creek (274); Evacuation Creek (276); Twin Buttes (282).

DISCUSSION

Smilodectes contrasts with *Notharctus* primarily in its smaller size, relatively short muzzle, and various cranial details (Figure 53) noted under *Notharctus*. The anterior margin of the orbits is as far forward as the mesial border of M^1, whereas in *Notharctus* the orbit extends only to the limit delineated by the mesial border of M^2. In *Smilodectes* the braincase is relatively shorter, and the occiput, posteriorly inclined in *Notharctus*, is more vertical. The sagittal crest is shorter and the zygoma are deeper than either of these features in *Notharctus*. Compared to the latter genus, both the upper and lower canines are relatively shorter and smaller and mandibular symphyseal fusion appears to be absent. Postcranially, *Smilodectes* is the best known but most poorly studied of adapid genera; outstanding skeletal materials await description. As a general remark, however, we can state that the known postcranial elements of *Smilodectes* do not appear to differ greatly from the well-studied remains of *Notharctus* spp.

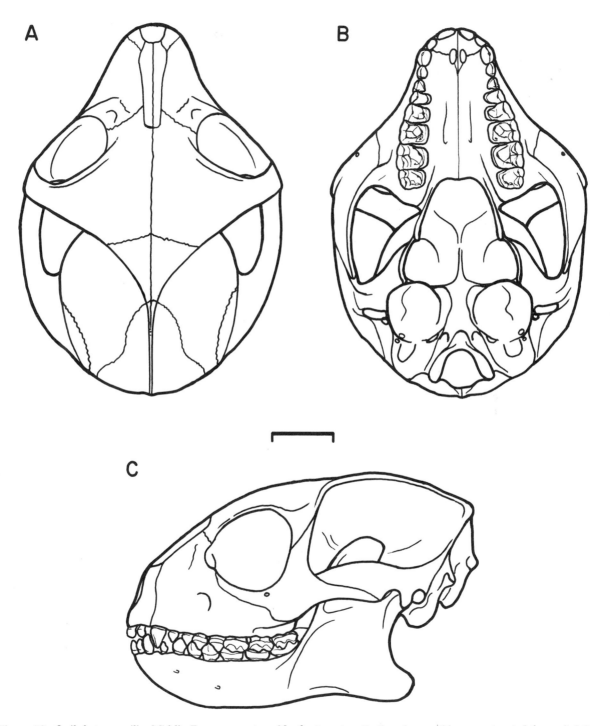

Figure 53. *Smilodectes gracilis.* Middle Eocene, western North America. Skull and mandible reconstructed from slightly deformed specimens: A, dorsal view; B, ventral view: C, lateral view. Scale represents 1 cm. [By A. Cleary.]

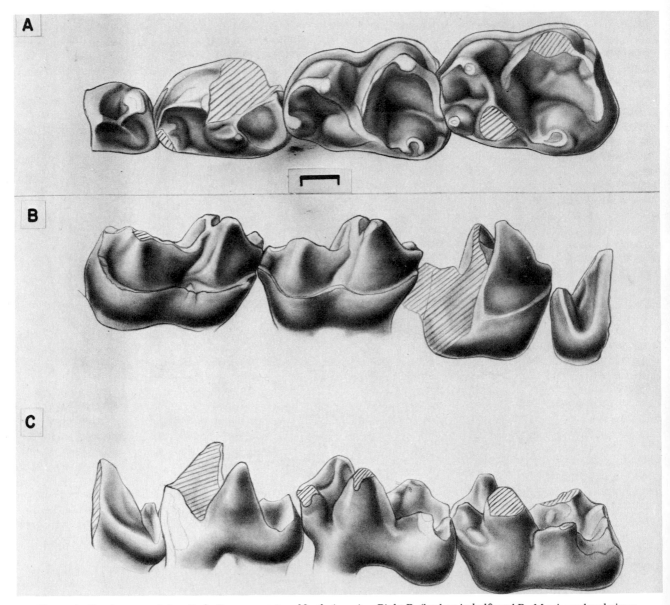

Figure 54. *Copelemur praetutus*. Early Eocene, western North America. Right P$\overline{3}$ (broken in half) and P$\overline{4}$–M$\overline{2}$: A, occlusal view; B, buccal view; C, lingual view. Hatched area depicts reconstruction. Scale represents 1 mm. [By A. Cleary.]

The dental formula is the same as in *Pelycodus* and *Notharctus*. Like the latter, this genus may have evolved evolved from *Pelycodus jarrovii*.

The continuous wear on the molar crests of the known dentitions suggests emphasis on the buccal phase of mastication. The molar morphology of *Smilodectes*, as that of *Notharctus*, probably performed extensive mesiolingual shear. The genus, as some of the species of *Notharctus*, was probably folivorous.

COPELEMUR Gingerich and Simons, 1977

(= or including: *Tomitherium*: Cope, 1877 in part. *Pelycodus*: Cope, 1881 in part. *Pelycodus?*: Gazin, 1962a. *Notharctus* Guthrie, 1971, in part.)

DISTRIBUTION
Early Eocene (Wasatchian). Rocky Mt. region.
KNOWN SPECIES
1. *Copelemur tutus* (Cope, 1877), type species
(=*Tomitherium tutus* Cope, 1877. *Pelycodus tutus*: Cope, 1881 in part. *Pelycodus? tutus* Gazin, 1962a.)
LOCALITIES: San José★ (249).
2. *Copelemur praetutus* (Gazin, 1962a)
(=*Pelycodus? praetutus* Gazin, 1962a.)
LOCALITIES: Bitter Creek★ (156).
3. *Copelemur feretutus* Gingerich and Simons, 1977
(=*Pelycodus frugivorous* Matthew, 1915 in part. *Notharctus nunienus* Guthrie, 1971 in part.)
LOCALITIES: Lysite★ (208).
4. *Copelemur consortutus* Gingerich and Simons, 1977
(=*Pelycodus frugivorous*: Matthew, 1915 in part. *Notharctus nunienus*: Guthrie, 1971, in part.)
LOCALITIES: Lost Cabin★ (240); San José beds (249).

DISCUSSION

The genus *Copelemur* (Figure 54) was recently erected by Gingerich and Simons (1977). The taxon is made up of small samples of *C. praetutus*, *C. feretutus*, *C. consortutus*, and *C. tutus*, in decreasing age.

Gingerich and Simons (1977) diagnosed the genus *Copelemur* as different from *Pelycodus* in having a more open talonid, a more distinct notch between the entoconid and hypoconulid; this notch is usually lacking in *Pelycodus*. We believe that *Copelemur* indeed does represent a distinct clade extending back to the base of the Eocene.

The choice of the type specimen for the type species, *Copelemur tutus*, is unfortunate. The type is designated as "Unnumbered right mandible with $P_{\overline{3-4}}$ and $M_{\overline{1}}$, now lost, from the Wasatchian of New Mexico." In addition to *C. tutus*, Gingerich and Simons (1977) assigned to *Copelemur C. praetutus* (Gazin, 1962a) *C. feretutus* Gingerich and Simons, 1977, and *C. consortutus* Gingerich and Simons, 1977. *Copelemur feretutus* is said to be significantly larger than *C. praetutus* and *C. consortutus* and significantly smaller than *C. tutus*. It is said to differ from *C. praetutus* in "having relatively broader molars with the paraconid more closely approximated to the metaconid on $M_{\overline{1}}$ and $M_{\overline{2}}$. Differs from *C. consortutus* and *C. tutus* in having less well developed hypocones and

mesostyles on the upper molars" (Gingerich and Simons, 1977, p. 268). *Copelemur consortutus* is differentiated from *C. feretutus* and *C. tutus* as being smaller. The authors state that it "differs from *C. feretutus* in tending to have larger mesostyles in the upper molars. Differs from *C. tutus* in retaining more distinct paraconids on $M_{\overline{1}}$ and $M_{\overline{2}}$. Differs from *C. praetutus* in having relatively broader lower molars, with the paraconids on $M_{\overline{1}}$ and $M_{\overline{2}}$ more closely approximated to the metaconids" (Gingerich and Simons, 1977, p. 270). Gingerich and Simons (1977) remarked that the upper molars of *C. feretutus* and *C. consortutus* are virtually the same as those of *Pelycodus trigonodus*.

This interesting genus, clearly different from *Pelycodus*, although still poorly known, shows telling differences as to the mechanical functions involved in the dentition. Unlike those of *Pelycodus*, the cusps on the known lower teeth of *Copelemur* are relatively taller and more acute. This is particularly apparent on the fourth premolars, which have a tall and distinct metaconid. The generically diagnostic features of this clade suggest their evolution from a *Pelycodus* species toward a diet that involved more piercing by the teeth than in the common Wasatchian *Pelycodus*. As suggested by the rarity of these specimens, in addition to the characteristic morphology of the teeth, species of *Copelemur* may have had a diet not unlike the living *Arctocebus*, which specializes on a caterpillar diet.

SUBFAMILY ADAPINAE
Trouessart, 1879

(=Adapidae Trouessart, 1879)

DISTRIBUTION
Early Eocene to late Miocene (Neustrian to Headonian, Vintan, and ?Vallesian in Asia). Western North America and Eurasia.
INCLUDED TAXA
Tribes Protoadapini, Microadapini, Anchomomyini, Adapini, and Indralorisini.

DISCUSSION

The Adapinae are not a well understood group. Although they contain both primitive (e.g. *Protoadapis*) and advanced (e.g. *Caenopithecus*) genera, it is clear that the phylogenetic diversity of this Holarctic group is a long time away from being well understood. It appears that eastern North America (see the western North American *Mahgarita*), southern and eastern Europe, and Asia were probably fully occupied by various adapids during the Eocene. The known genera are arranged into five monophyletic tribes, and the suggested relationships are shown in Figure 47.

Assessment of the ancestral morphotype of this subfamily is difficult. Most species are known by teeth although the skulls of *Mahgarita*, *Pronycticebus*, *Adapis*, and *Leptadapis* and the poorly preserved crushed cranium of *Europolemur* suggest that as in the notharctines, the full dentition, elongated muzzle, complete postorbital bar, and a *Mahgarita*-like ear region were probably to be found in the *Pelycodus* or *Protoadapis*-like ancestor.

Both the alpha taxonomy and the hypothesis of relationships of the known samples of Adapinae have been somewhat simplified by the recent study of Gingerich (1977a). In describing the new species *Pelycodus savagei*, *Protoadapis russelli*, *Protoadapis louisi*, *Protoadapis weigelti*, and *Periconodon lemoinei*, the samples are merely noted to differ "significantly" in size. No attempt is made to delineate these proposed taxa from other samples of *Pelycodus*, *Protoadapis*, or *Periconodon*. The remaining new species described by Gingerich (1977a) are equally impossible to test, based on the information he supplied. In describing *Adapis sudrei* and *Adapis stirtoni*, and by allocating *Adapis laharpei*, *Adapis ruetimeyeri*, *Adapis magnus*, and *Adapis sciureus* to *Adapis*, he has in effect forfeited all pretense that morphological analysis has relevance to a stratophenetic approach. Stratophenetics appears to have influenced the views of this author so that he has named mere samples of already well-delineated species as distinct, on one hand, and he generically lumps morphologically divergent, allegedly time-

sequential samples to connect morphologically unacceptable "lineages." There is no attempt, at least in that paper, to test his "stratophenetic lineages" with any seriously relevant character analysis of morphology. The phylogenetic hypothesis of the Adapinae (with *Mahgarita stevensi*, *Protoadapis filholi*, and *Huerzeleris quercyi* omitted) presented by Gingerich (1977a) is unacceptable to us. His "*Protoadapis*-group" and "*Adapis*-group" appear to be questionable when the dental morphology of all adapid samples is taken into account.

Tribe Protoadapini, new

DISTRIBUTION
   Eocene (Neustrian to Headonian, and Uintan). Europe and North America.
INCLUDED TAXA
   Protoadapis, *Europolemur*, *Mahgarita*, *Pronycticebus*, and *Agerinia*.

DISCUSSION

Protoadapin adapids differ from other groups of the subfamily in having the following ancestral combination of characters. The postprotocone fold (*Nannopithex* fold) is not present on upper molars; the $M_{\overline{3}}$ talonid lacks a lingually expanded lobe of the hypoconid and is wider than its trigonid. These conditions are unlike those in ancestral notharctines which have a wider $M_{\overline{3}}$ trigonid than talonid and a lingually expanded hypoconid. Molar paraconids are usually not cuspate and the paracristid in taxa other than *Protoadapis* does not extend as far lingually as in *Pelycodus*. It appears that a $P_{\overline{3}}$ subequal in height to $P_{\overline{4}}$ or even slightly taller than $P_{\overline{4}}$ was a feature in the morphotype of this group. This character alone, therefore, cannot be used to effectively diagnose any of the genera within this tribe.

PROTOADAPIS Lemoine, 1878

(= or including: *Protadapis*: Stehlin, 1912, lapsus. *Adapis*: Filhol, 1883, in part; Stehlin, 1912, in part. *Cercamonius* Gingerich, 1975c.)

DISTRIBUTION
   Early to late Eocene (Neustrian to Headonian). Western Europe.
KNOWN SPECIES
   1. *Protoadapis curvicuspidens* Lemoine, 1878, type species
[=*Protoadapis recticuspidens* (Lemoine, 1878).]
LOCALITIES: Grauves (224); Cuis (228); Epernay (232); Mancy (234);

Monthelon (236) (type locality uncertain, in the teredine sands of the region of the listed localities).
   2. *Protoadapis filholi* Gingerich, 1977
   (=*Adapis angustidens* Filhol, 1888, nec Filhol, 1883. *Protoadapis angustidens*: Teilhard, 1922, in part. *Protoadapis weigelti* Gingerich, 1977. *Protoadapis russelli* Gingerich, 1977a. *Protoadapis louisi* Gingerich, 1977.)
   LOCALITIES: Geiseltal (292); Phosphorites of Quercy★ (294).
   3. *Protoadapis brachyrhynchus* Stehlin, 1912

[=*Protoadapis brevirostris* Stehlin, 1916. *Cercamonius brachyrhynchus:* Gingerich, 1975c.]

LOCALITIES: Prajous★ (325).

   4. *Protoadapis ulmensis* (Schmidt-Kittler, 1971)

(=*Adapis ulmensis* Schmidt-Kittler, 1971. "*Protoadapis*" *ulmensis:* Gingerich, 1977a.)

LOCALITIES: Ehrenstein I A★ (354).

DISCUSSION

This long-ranging genus shows a large number of primitive protoadapin features such as the presence of a large canine, a P_3 which is usually higher than P_4 (the latter premolariform but with a metaconid), and small or indistinct hypoconulids on the molars. The very similar lower molars of *Protoadapis* and *Pronycticebus* can be differentiated on the basis of the strength and development of protoconids and metaconids. The more inflated cusps in *Protoadapis* (Figure 55) are separated by a narrow, V-shaped trigonid notch, whereas in *Pronycticebus* the space between the metaconid and protoconid is greater and U-shaped due to the less bulbous character of the cusps. In this respect, *Protoadapis* is more similar to *Pelycodus* than the latter is to *Pronycticebus* and *Agerinia*. Judged from all the available morphology, the degree of relationship between *Protoadapis*, *Pronycticebus*, and *Agerinia* is more recent than between any of these and *Pelycodus*. *Protoadapis* seems to differ from *Europolemur* in still retaining a metaconule and in having less well-developed hypocones.

Gingerich (1977a) erected the following new species of *Protoadapis*: *P. russelli*, *P. louisi*, and *P. weigelti*. He renamed *P. angustidensis* to *P. filholi* due to the preoccupation of the former name by a subspecific homonym. As the photographs of the lateral views of the type of *Protoadapis weigelti* in Gingerich (1977a) show, it is not significantly larger than *P. angustidens* on the same photograph. The additional distinction given by Gingerich (1977a) is that "it appears to difer from *Protoadapis filholi* and other species of *Protoadapis* in having the protoconid and paraconid more closely approximated" (p. 66). As we know the type specimen, it is clear to us that the two preserved molars do not permit this seemingly qualitative statement. These two molars in the mandible are the entire hypodigm.

Gingerich (1977a), when describing *Protoadapis russelli* and *P. louisi*, each based on isolated teeth, only showed the type M_1 specimens on one photograph. Not only did he fail to distinguish between the two minimum samples (both from Avenay), but he did not even mention the possible relationships (size or morphology) to the earliest, previously recognized *Protoadapis*, *P. curvicuspidens*, the type species. As noted before, *P. filholi* (i.e., *P. angustidens*) is not shown on his numerical and stratophenetic phylogenetic tree (Gingerich, 1977a, p. 77).

Until proven otherwise, *Protoadapis russelli*, *Protoadapis louisi*, and *Protoadapis weigelti* described by Gingerich (1977a) are considered tentatively to be *Protoadapis filholi*. In light of the limits of other species samples, the size ranges [of log($L \times W$) of M_1] cited for these samples by Gingerich (1977a) are not significantly different from *Protoadapis curvicuspidens*. A future revision may permit the distinction of *P.* "*recticuspidens*" from the type species, and this new concept of *P.* "*recticuspidens*" may eventually include the species proposed by Gingerich.

Gingerich (1975c) has also recently erected the genus "*Cercamonius*," based on *Protoadapis brachyrhynchus* (Figure 55). After restudy of the unique type specimen, "*Cercamonius*" is considered as an undoubted synonym of *Protoadapis*. In his diagnosis of "*Cercamonius*," Gingerich (1975c) used the larger size of P_3 compared to P_4 as a generic distinction, in addition to the lack of P_1 in *Protoadapis brachyrhynchus*. Gingerich failed to realize that the type species, *P. curvicuspidens*, has P_1 variably present or absent (Russell *et al.*, 1967) and that a larger P_3 than P_4 is a characteristic of *Pronycticebus*, *Protoadapis*, and *Europolemur*—an ancestral feature of all protoadapins.

The dental formula of *Protoadapis* is $I\frac{1,2}{1,2}$; $C\frac{1}{1}$; $P\frac{1,2,3,4}{1,2,3,4}$; $M\frac{1,2,3}{1,2,3}$.

Protoadapis may have given rise to *Pronycticebus* as well as to *Europolemur*. The species of this genus are relatively easily distinguishable from one another. *Protoadapis filholi* and *P. brachyrhynchus* are the largest and were probably the most phytophagous; judging by their robust teeth and thick mandible they lived on a coarse diet. *Protoadapis curvicuspidens* was not necessarily any less herbivorous, although its teeth suggest a diet of softer consistency than that of the late Eocene or early Oligocene *P. filholi* and *P. brachyrhynchus*. *Protoadapis ulmensis* is similar in size to *P. filholi*, but the molars described appear to be, in general, more bunodont in the former.

This genus is badly in need of a careful restudy and documentation.

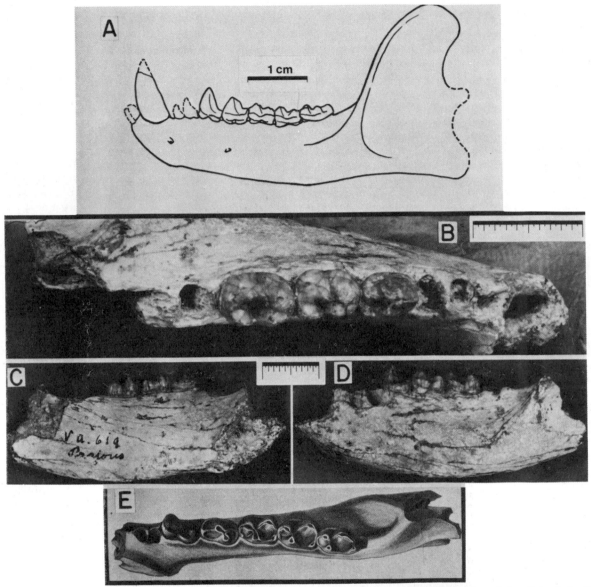

Figure 55. *Protoadapis.* Eocene, Europe. *Protoadapis curvicuspidens.* Left mandible with C and $P_{\overline{3}}$–$M_{\overline{3}}$ and alveoli for $I_{\overline{1}}$, $I_{\overline{2}}$, $P_{\overline{1}}$, and $P_{\overline{2}}$: A, lateral view. Right mandible fragment with $P_{\overline{3}}$–$M_{\overline{3}}$ and alveoli for $P_{\overline{1}}$ and $P_{\overline{2}}$: E, occlusal view. *Protoadapis brachyrhynchus.* Left mandible fragment with $P_{\overline{4}}$–$M_{\overline{2}}$: B, occlusal view; C, medial view; D, lateral view. Subdivisions on scales represent 0.5 mm. [A by A. Cleary; E. from Stehlin (1916).]

AGERINIA Crusafont-Pairo and Golpe-Posse, 1973

(= or including: *Agerina* Crusafont-Pairo, 1967, *nec* Leach, 1814. *Periconodon:* Gingerich, 1977a, in part.)

DISTRIBUTION
  Late early Eocene (early Rhenanian), Spain.

KNOWN SPECIES
  Agerinia roselli (Crusafont-Pairo, 1967), type species
  (=*Agerina roselli* Crusafont-Pairo, 1967. *Agerinia roselli:* Crusafont-

Pairo and Golpe-Posse, 1973. *Periconodon roselli:* Gingerich, 1977a.)
LOCALITIES: Condé-en-Brie (220); Castigaleu∗ (222); Grauves (224).

DISCUSSION

Agerinia is known only by teeth (Figure 56). It differs from all known species of *Protoadapis* in having $P_{\overline{3}}$ and $P_{\overline{4}}$ subequal in height and in lacking a distinct, anteroposteriorly oriented cristid obliqua on the $P_{\overline{4}}$ talonid. Unlike the trigonids of *Protoadapis* or *Pronycticebus*, those of *Agerinia* are sealed off lingually by the union of the metaconid mesially and the paracristid distally. Although the paracristid is very low in *Agerinia*, this crest invariably extends lingually almost to the limits of the metaconid, whereas in *Pronycticebus* the paracristid extends only midway on $M_{\overline{1}}$ and slightly more lingually on $M_{\overline{2}}$ and $M_{\overline{3}}$. Differences between *Agerinia* and *Adapis* and *Leptadapis* are most noticeable in the complete absence of a metastylid on the lower molars of the former genus. *Agerinia* differs from *Caenopithecus* in having a larger metaconid on $P_{\overline{4}}$ and in lacking a metastylid and any trace of an entoconid. Talonid cusps of *Agerinia* are generally less bulbous than those of *Caenopithecus*. *Agerinia* differs from *Pelycodus* in lacking the distinct, cuspate paraconid on $M_{\overline{1}}$ and in the generally less bulbous nature of the talonid cusps. The discussion under *Protoadapis* is pertinent to the treatment of this genus

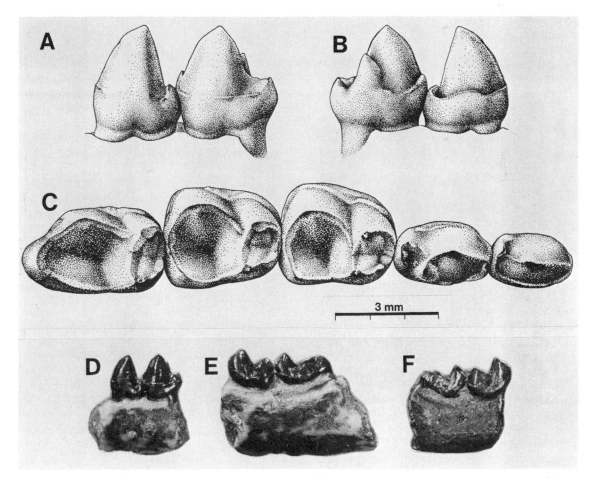

Figure 56. *Agerinia roselli.* Middle Eocene, western Europe. Left $P_{\overline{3-4}}$: A and D, buccal views; B, lingual view. Left $P_{\overline{3}}$–$M_{\overline{3}}$: C, occlusal view. Left and right mandible fragments with $M_{\overline{2-3}}$: E and F, lateral views, respectively. [From Szalay (1971).]

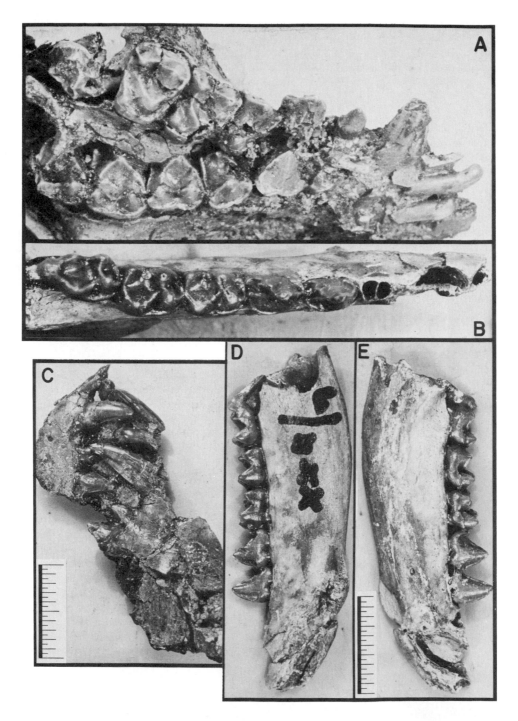

Figure 57. *Europolemur klatti.* Middle Eocene, western Europe. Partial dentition of crushed skull: A, occlusal view. Right mandible fragment with $P_{\overline{3}}$–$M_{\overline{3}}$ and alveoli for $I_{\overline{1}}$, $I_{\overline{2}}$, C, $P_{\overline{1}}$, and $P_{\overline{2}}$: B, occlusal view; D, medial view; E, lateral view. Crushed anterior segment of skull and mandible: C, lateral view. Subdivisions on scales represent 0.5 mm.

(see also Szalay, 1971; Gingerich, 1977a). The recently published M^1 of *A. roselli* (Gingerich, 1976) shows the presence of a *Nannopithex* fold distinguishing this species from *Periconodon pygmaeus*.

The origin of *Agerinia* from a species of *Protoadapis* is a likely possibility. Until larger samples of both lower and upper teeth of this genus become better known, a precise recognition of its ties cannot be meaningfully hypothesized.

The dental formula of *Agerinia* cannot be determined.

The relatively low crowned, blunt cusped, and crested lower teeth and the fairly robust mandible suggest either omnivory or frugivory, rather than primarily insectivory, as the postulated dietary regime for this genus.

EUROPOLEMUR Weigelt, 1933

(= or including: *Megatarsius* Weigelt, 1933.)

DISTRIBUTION
Middle Eocene (Rhenanian), German Democratic Republic.
KNOWN SPECIES
Europolemur klatti Weigelt, 1933, type species
(=*Megatarsius abeli* Weigelt, 1933. *Protoadapis klatti:* Simons, 1962. *Periconodon lemoinei* Gingerich, 1977a.)
LOCALITIES: Grauves (224); Geiseltal Unterkohle; Leonhardt Coal Mine★ (280).

DISCUSSION

This middle Eocene adapid, well known from several jaws and a crushed skull (Figure 57), differs from *Protoadapis* in a number of significant characters. The hypoconulid is well defined on $M_{\overline{1-2}}$, and, unlike *Protoadapis curvicuspidens*, the type species of *Protoadapis*, *Europolemur* as a rule lacks a metaconule. The crests are sharp on the unworn molar teeth of

Europolemur, and the upper molars have well defined cingula and hypocones, except $M^{\underline{3}}$, which lacks a hypocone. Characteristically, the mesial and distal cingula of the upper molars are lingually continuous.

Among protoadapins, *Europolemur* is the only genus in which the upper incisors are known. These are relatively small, low crowned, and spatulate. The canines are moderately large and sharp crested, and $P_{\overline{1}}$, when present, is very small, as in most other adapids which retain it. The $P_{\overline{3}}$, as in the whole tribe, is slightly taller than $P_{\overline{4}}$ with trenchant anterior and posterior crests. The discussion under *Mahgarita* and *Protoadapis* are closely relevant to this genus.

The dental formula was $I\frac{1\cdot2}{1\cdot2}$; $C\frac{1}{1}$; $P\frac{1\cdot2\cdot3\cdot4}{1\cdot2\cdot3\cdot4}$; $M\frac{1\cdot2\cdot3}{1\cdot2\cdot3}$.

The total known morphology of the dentition of *Europolemur* suggests an animal that was frugivorous–insectivorous.

MAHGARITA Wilson and Szalay, 1976

(= or including: *Margarita* Wilson and Szalay, 1976, nec Leach, 1814.)

DISTRIBUTION
Late Eocene (Uintan), Texas.
KNOWN SPECIES
Mahgarita stevensi Wilson and Szalay, 1976, type species
(=*Margarita stevensi* Wilson and Szalay, 1976.)
LOCALITIES: Typee Canyon★ (342).

DISCUSSION

Mahgarita (Figure 58) differs from other known Adapidae in the following combination of characters. Unlike in *Protoadapis* or *Europolemur*, $P_{\overline{1}}$ is lost and $P_{\overline{2}}$ is extremely reduced. Unlike on the generitype of *Pro-*

toadapis, *P. curvicuspidens*, the metaconules are absent as distinct cusps as opposed to the presence of an essentially uninterrupted ridge of the postprotocone crista, and the postmetaconule crista leads directly buccally rather than distobuccally; the hypocone is tall, sharp, with a distinct apex, and the precingula and postcingula are broadly continuous. *Mahgarita* differs from *Europolemur klatti*, possibly its nearest relative, in having one less premolar and a considerably reduced $P\frac{2}{2}$. The protocone on $P^{\underline{3}}$ is greatly reduced, unlike the more primitive condition in *Europolemur* and other adapids. The reduced $P^{\underline{3}}$ protocone is still distinct, unlike the condition in *Pericono-*

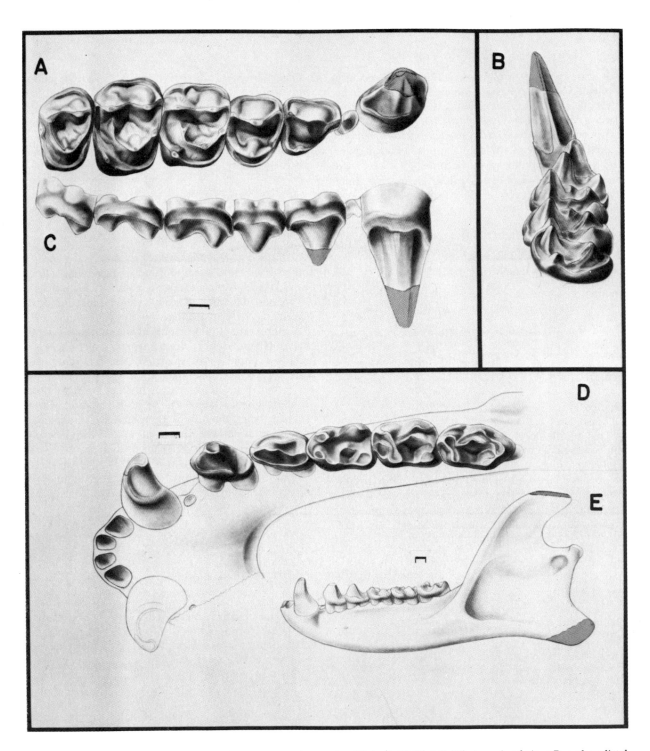

Figure 58. *Mahgarita stevensi*. Late Eocene, Western North America. Right C, P$^{\underline{2}}$–P$^{\underline{4}}$, M$^{\underline{1}}$–M$^{\underline{3}}$: A, occlusal view; B, occlusodistal view; C, buccal view. Mandible with both alveoli for I$_{\overline{1}}$–I$_{\overline{2}}$, C, alveolus for P$_{\overline{2}}$, P$_{\overline{3}}$–P$_{\overline{4}}$, M$_{\overline{1}}$–M$_{\overline{3}}$, and left C: D, occlusal view. Left mandible: E, lateral view. Scales represent 1 mm. [From Wilson and Szalay (1976).]

don, which only has a cingulum lingually surrounding the paracone.

The dental formula is $I\frac{1\text{-}2}{2}$; $C\frac{1}{1}$; $P\frac{2,3,4}{2,3,4}$; $M\frac{1,2,3}{1,2,3}$.

As cranial material is scarce in fossil primates and because the skull of *Mahgarita* is considerably crushed, the dental characters better reflect the genealogy of this genus. The postprotocone fold (*Nannopithex* fold) and the twinned M_3 paraconid and metaconid, both of which may be primitive adapid characteristics, also found in the primitive notharctine *Pelycodus*, are lacking in *Mahgarita.* The enlarged, bulbous hypocones of *Notharctus* and *Smilodectes,* and in general the dental specializations of these advanced notharctines, are distinctive from the Texas adapid. The presence of a metastylid and the heavily molarized P^4_4 in *Adapis* and *Leptadapis,* the almost complete loss of the protocone on the P^3_4, and the spatulate incisiform anterior dentition in *Adapis* preclude *Mahgarita* from being closely related to either of these genera.

Although the dentition of *Mahgarita* shows such advanced features as the loss of P^1_4, the extreme reduction of P^2_4, and the reduction of the protocone of P^3_4, it seems to share a number of significant similarities with *Europolemur klatti* from the middle Eocene. One suspects that some of these similarities of the molars are shared derived features of a common ancestry and thus signify the closest affinities of these taxa. The presence of continuous cingula surrounding the upper molars, at least lingually, could be a primitive retention, but the sharpness of these crests and the acuteness of the angle between the two slopes suggest that the similarities are derived. The hypocones are tall and sharp, with a distinct apex. The metaconules are poorly defined. Unlike *Protoadapis curvicuspidens,* the faintly distinct postmetaconule crista is not directed distobuccally, but rather it is continuous with the postprotocone crista, which is buccally oriented on the buccal half of the tooth.

The morphology of the canines of *Mahgarita* and that of the canines *Europolemur* are extremely similar, although it is difficult to decide whether or not this is merely an ancestral adapid condition or a shared derived homology.

The middle ear cavity is known in detail (Wilson and Szalay, 1976, Figures 7 and 8). The long continuous bony canal which traverses the ventral surface of the promontorium is relatively thick. There are no details of any apparent significance in which the basicranial morphology differs from such well-known adapid basicrania as those of *Adapis, Leptadapis,* or *Notharctus.* Although the ectotympanic is not preserved, it seems very likely that it was similar to those of other adapids, ringlike, and inferiorly unattached except to the annulus membrane. The entry of the interior carotid artery was on the posterolateral surface of the bulla, as it is in the inferred primitive condition of the Strepsirhini. The petromastoid is well exposed but its inflation is minimal, if any.

The two halves of the lower jaw of *Mahgarita* are thoroughly synostosed. Although this is a derived condition, it is by no means unique or uncommon either in the Adapidae or in other groups of mammals, and therefore its possession among adapids is not necessarily indicative of a shared derived condition. Judged from the unfused condition in *Pelycodus, Microadapis,* and *Protoadapis,* it is most likely that fusion of the lower jaws occurred at least twice, independently among notharctines and adapines. Synostosis of the mandibular symphysis is also a common evolutionary trend among the tooth-combed strepsirhines.

Only the alveoli of the lower incisors are known, and from these the same number is inferred for the upper incisors. These alveoli show that the circumferences of the roots of the lower lateral incisors were somewhat larger than those of the central ones. From this we may infer that the lateral incisors had somewhat larger crowns than the central ones.

Sufficient detail for skull and teeth is known for this genus so that a functional appraisal is possible. The skull of *Mahgarita* is approximately in the upper size range of skulls of the living *Lepilemur leucopus.* As it is dorsoventrally crushed, an assessment of its general proportions must proceed with appropriate caution. In spite of the crushing it is clear that the skull possessed postorbital rings and petrosal bullae. It is also evident that the occipital height of the skull, perhaps in some ways indicative of relative brain size, was very low. The skull has a foramen magnum which is considerably more posteriorly directed than those of *Lepilemur* and *Hapalemur.* We judge this to be an expression of a relatively less encephalized brain (see Biegert, 1963, in particular) in *Mahgarita* than in *Lepilemur,* to which it is similar in skull, tooth, and perhaps body size. The infraorbital foramen of *Mahgarita* is sizable and has a vertically elongated opening.

Without postcranial elements, the substrate preference of *Mahgarita* cannot be reliably assessed. In light of the evidence from known postcranials, adapids were arboreal, and presumably so was *Mahgarita*.

The canines are tall and sharply pointed, the lower canines curving slightly distally and laterally. Notable on the mesiolingual base of the lower canine is a well-developed cingulid which runs apically and mesially toward the tip of the cusp. The upper canine is long, with sharp edges running apically on the distal and mesial surfaces. Less pronounced but discernible ridges range from the encircling basal cingulum on both the lingual and buccal surfaces of this tooth. The paracristid of the tall $P_{\overline{3}}$ was in occlusal contact with the distal edge of the upper canine. The result of this interaction is a greatly sharpened edge on the upper canine. Reduction of $P_{\overline{4}}^2$ may be the result of selection for $P_{\overline{3}}$ honing of the upper canine. The most notable functional aspect of the buccal halves of the two premolars is that $P^{\underline{3}}$ is distinctly deeper than $P^{\underline{4}}$. The paracones consist of sharp mesial and distal cutting edges.

Although the molars are rectangular in outline and a large hypocone is present, it is unlikely that this form was primarily either frugivorous or folivorous. The very deep and sharp $P^{\underline{3}}$, the sharp canines, and the sharp cusped protocone all suggest cutting and piercing functions primarily along a more vertical plane. The angles between components of the ectoloph on a vertical plane are more acute than, for example, the homologous angles in *Lepilemur*.

Crest morphology, the sharpness of the cusps, including the hypocone, and the specialization of $P_{\overline{4}}^2$ suggest a primarily insectivorous primate. It should be pointed out, however, that the dental morphology and interpreted function suggest this role and not the size of either the teeth or the skull. *Lepilemur*, with a similar skull, is a facultative folivore, albeit with a dentition that testifies to that feeding regime.

PRONYCTICEBUS Grandidier, 1904

DISTRIBUTION
  Late Eocene (Headonian), France.
KNOWN SPECIES
  Pronycticebus gaudryi Grandidier, 1904, type species
LOCALITIES: Memerlein∗ (321).

DISCUSSION

Pronycticebus is known by the type specimen only, a relatively well-preserved skull and a horizontal ramus, both containing teeth (Figure 59). As the figure shows, *Pronycticebus*, with a *Hapalemur griseus*-sized skull, was a relatively short-faced adapid, yet all of its teeth and a sizable canine are retained. The postorbital bar is not preserved, although it was clearly present (Simons, 1962b; Szalay, 1971). The relative size of the brain case in comparison to the face was distinctly smaller than those of comparably sized skulls of extant strepsirhines. The ectotympanic was inside the bulla proper and there is no significant petromastoid inflation. The basicranium is very similar to that which one may infer to be the primitive adapid condition.

The dentition combines an interesting mixture of characters probably advanced for Eocene adapids. In addition to the generally primitive proportions of the four conventionally recognized regions of the dentition, the upper molars are relatively transverse, more so than in either *Pelycodus* or *Protoadapis*, and have a small but well-defined protocone without appreciable traces of a protocone fold. Unlike the canines of the lemurines, for example, those of *Pronycticebus* are roundly based and suggest the presence of a conical, robust structure with an emphasis on the apex rather than on the distal crest. The known premolars are relatively higher than the molars and have sharp apices. The last molars are exceptionally enlarged. The diagnostic differences between *Pronycticebus* and some other adapines are listed under *Agerinia*; the discussions under *Protoadapis*, *Mahgarita*, and *Agerinia* are closely pertinent to the treatment of this genus.

The dental formula was probably $I_{\overline{1,2}}^{1,2}$; $C_{\overline{1}}^1$; $P_{\overline{1,2,3,4}}^{2,3,4}$; $M_{\overline{1,2,3}}^{1,2,3}$.

The morphology of the sharp cusps and particularly the narrowly based crests, the almost complete lack of crenulations, and the well-developed piercing premolars and canine suggest a dentition with a primarily orthally directed function. Both the morphology and the inferred function point to probably an insectivorous–carnivorous mode of life.

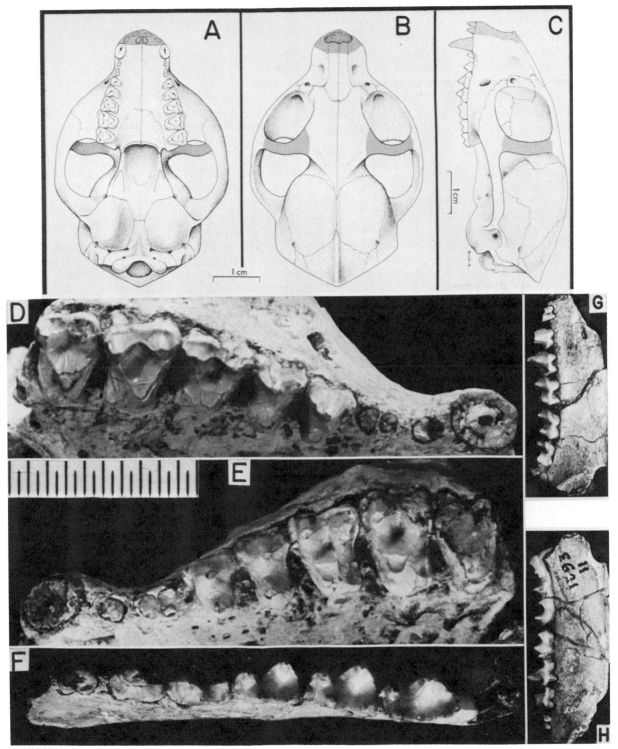

Figure 59. *Pronycticebus guadryi.* Late Eocene, western Europe. Skull: A, ventral view; B, dorsal view; C, lateral view. Dentition of skull, P³–M³, and alveoli with roots of C, P¹, and P². D, occlusal view of right side; E, occlusal view of left side. Right mandible fragment with P₃–M₃ and roots of P₂: F, occlusal view; G, lateral view; H, medial view. [From Szalay (1971).]

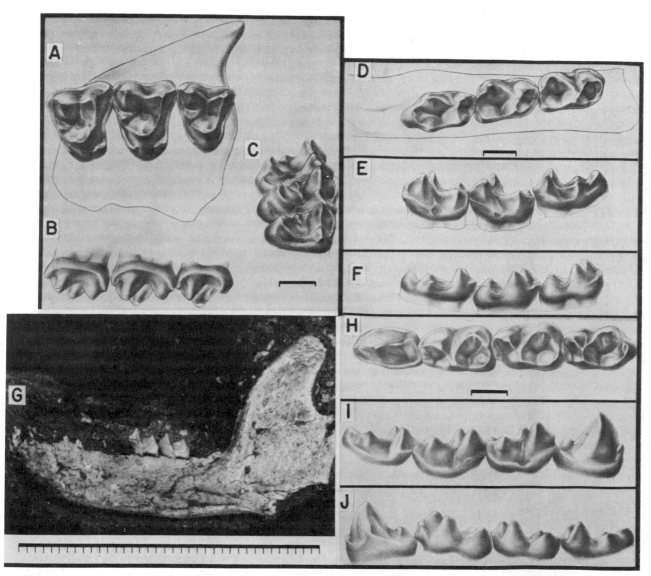

Figure 60. *Anchomomys gaillardi.* Middle Eocene, western Europe. Left M$^{1-3}$: A, occlusal view; B, buccal view; C, occlusodistal view. Left M$_{1-3}$: D, occlusal view; E, buccal view; F, lingual view. Right P$_4$–M$_3$: H, occlusal view; I, buccal view; J, lingual view. Scales represent 1 mm. Left mandible with M$_{1-2}$: G, lateral view. Subdivisions on scale represent 0.5 mm. [From Szalay 1974a).]

Tribe Anchomomyini, new

DISTRIBUTION
  Middle Eocene (Rhenanian). Western Europe.
INCLUDED TAXA
  Anchomomys, Huerzeleris, and *Periconodon.*

DISCUSSION

The species united in this tribe are unique among the Adapinae both morphologically and in their inferred adaptations. *Anchomomys, Periconodon* and

Huerzeleris are small and very likely insectivorous forms, whereas the two larger-sized tribes, the Protoadapini and Adapini, represent, with the exception of *Pronycticebus*, medium-sized insectivores–frugivores and medium-sized to larger folivores, respectively. The distinction of the Anchomomyini from the Microadapini is discussed under *Anchomomys*.

ANCHOMOMYS Stehlin, 1916

DISTRIBUTION
   Middle Eocene (Rhenanian). Western Europe.
KNOWN SPECIES
   Anchomomys gaillardi Stehlin, 1916, type species
(=*Anchomomys pygmaeus:* Szalay, 1974a, in part. *Anchomomys stehlini* Gingerich, 1977.)
LOCALITIES: Lissieu loc.⋆ (258); Egerkingen γ loc. (250).

DISCUSSION

Anchomomys is distinguished from *Huerzeleris* in lacking the conspicuous development of the buccal half of the upper molars, that is, in retaining the more primitive proportions of the paracone and the metacone to the protocone (Figure 60). *Anchomomys* differs from *Microadapis* in having generally less robust molars, relatively much smaller hypocones, and in lacking a distinct metaconule. The entoconid of *Anchomomys* lower molars is more distolingual to the hypoconid than that of *Microadapis*. The talonid notch of the former is more V-shaped, whereas that of the latter has a configuration closer to a U. *Anchomomys* can be delineated from *Periconodon* in lacking the well-developed pericone of the latter and in having $M_{\overline{3}}$ hypoconulid more buccally placed. The genus, as diagnosed here, displays a remarkable combination of characters. In the molar dimensions, the tiny size of the species of *Anchomomys* is not equaled among the Adapidae.

Szalay (1974a), largely guided by his view that the type specimen of "*Anchomomys*" *pygmaeus* was distinct from *A. gaillardi*, attempted to find diagnostic features between the lower dentitions from Egerkingen γ and from the type locality at Lissieu. There appear to be no significant size or morphological factors which would warrant the specific recognition of the Egerkingen γ samples. The type of "*A.*" *pygmaeus,* an upper molar, is damaged, as correctly pointed out by Gingerich (1977a), and reexamination shows it to be conspecific with *Periconodon* "*helveticus*" (see under *Periconodon*).

The recently described specimens, previously allocated by Szalay (1974a) to "*A.*" *pygmaeus* because of a confusion of labels indicating provenance, and the newly named *Anchomomys* "*stehlini*" by Gingerich (1977a) cannot be diagnosed as different from the stratigraphically, slightly younger type species, *A. gaillardi*. There are no significant size differences (contra Szalay, 1974a; Gingerich, 1977a) between the two small samples. Any claim of difference is contrary to Figure 6 of Gingerich (1977a), which shows the $M_{\overline{2}}$ of the type of *A.* "*stehlini*" falling into the estimated normal range, based on the narrow range displayed by the few *A. gaillardi* specimens.

The most anterior tooth known is $P_{\overline{3}}$, although alveoli are preserved for all the other teeth. Unless $P_{\overline{2}}$ was a very unusually elongated, double-rooted tooth, the dental formula for this genus is $I\frac{2}{2}$; $C\frac{1}{1}$; $P\frac{2,3,4}{1,2,3,4}$; $\frac{3}{3}$. *Anchomomys* was a tiny insectivore.

HUERZELERIS Szalay, 1974a

(= or including: *Anchomomys:* Stehlin, 1916, in part. *Anchomomys?:* Gingerich, 1977a, in part.)

DISTRIBUTION
   Middle or late Eocene (Rhenanian). Western Europe.
KNOWN SPECIES
   Huerzeleris quercyi (Stehlin, 1916), type species
(=*Anchomomys quercyi* Stehlin, 1916. *Anchomomys? quercyi:* Gingerich, 1977a.)
LOCALITIES: Phosphorites of Quercy⋆ (294).

DISCUSSION

This genus is known by a single specimen (Figure 61) and therefore its appraisal is necessarily incomplete. The most clearly diagnostic character of *Huerzeleris*, when compared to such related adapids as *Anchomomys*, *Microadapis*, or *Periconodon*, lies in the combination of its relatively slightly enlarged upper

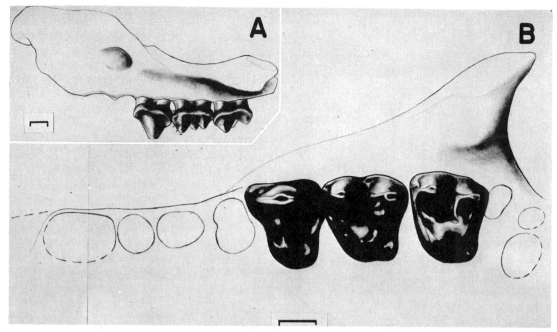

Figure 61. *Huerzeleris quercyi.* Late(?) Eocene, western Europe. Left maxilla fragment with P^4–M^2: A lateral view; B, occlusal view. Broken lines depict reconstruction. Scales represent 1 mm. [From Szalay (1974a).]

molars in a mesiodistal direction, relatively increased size of the paracone and metacone, and relatively small hypocone. The paraconule, well developed in *Anchomomys*, is almost completely reduced in *Huerzeleris.*

The dental formula cannot be determined accurately.

One would suggest the closest affinity of *Huerzeleris* to be with *Anchomomys*, but the lower dentition is necessary to test this hypothesis further. The sharp, but broadly based cusps of the tiny *Huerzeleris*, resting on transversely narrow molars, suggest insectivory and possibly feeding on tree exudates.

PERICONODON Stehlin, 1916

(= or including: *Caenopithecus:* Rütimeyer, 1890, in part. *Pelycodus:* Rütimeyer, 1891. *Anchomomys:* Stehlin, 1916, in part. *Anchomomys:* Szalay, 1974a, in part.)

DISTRIBUTION
Early middle Eocene (Rhenanian). Western Europe.
KNOWN SPECIES
Periconodon pygmaeus (Rütimeyer, 1890), type species
(=*Caenopithecus pygmaeus* Rütimeyer, 1890. *Caenopithecus(?) pygmaeus* Rütimeyer, 1891. *Pelycodus helveticus* Rütimeyer, 1891. *Periconodon helveticus* Stehlin, 1916. *Anchomomys pygmaeus:* Stehlin, 1916. *Anchomomys pygmaeus:* Szalay, 1974a, in part. *Periconodon pygmaeus:* Gingerich, 1977a. *Periconodon huerzeleri* Gingerich, 1977a.)
LOCALITIES: Egerkingen Huppersand★ (256); Bouxwiller (254).

DISCUSSION

Periconodon (Figure 62) has for some time been considered an omomyid (Simons, 1962b), and it was recently excluded from the Adapidae by Gingerich (1975a, Figure 1). In 1977, however, Gingerich correctly synonymized the type species of the genus with "*Anchomomys*" *pygmaeus*, correcting Szalay (1974a), who mistakenly recognized the two as separate taxa. The gestalt of *Periconodon* clearly aligns this genus with the middle Eocene European adapids (Szalay, 1974a). From these it differs primarily in having a well-developed hypocone, a conspicuous pericone, and a P$\underline{3}$ with a reduced protocone. The characters are, incidentally, extremely similar, although probably convergently so, to species of *Lemur (sensu stricto)*. The crest between the metacone and protocone bears a faint metaconule. The P$\overline{4}$ is premolariform, lacking a metaconid, and the lower molars have greatly reduced paracristids.

Relationships of *Periconodon* are with the Anchomomyini, but exact phylogenetic ties, despite Gingerich's (1977a,b) phylogenetic tree, cannot be ascertained or even meaningfully hypothesized.

The species *Periconodon lemoinei* described by Gingerich (1977a) is based on isolated teeth from Grauves. Gingerich states that it "differs from contemporary species of *Protoadapis* in being significantly smaller, and in lacking or having a much reduced paraconid on M$\overline{1}$" (p. 67). No morphological evidence of any sort is presented, and therefore we cannot judge its validity. We tentatively synonymize it with *Agerinia roselli*. Another species, *Periconodon huerzeleri*, was described by Gingerich (1977a) based on specimens which to us clearly represent lower teeth of *P. pygmaeus* and not a new taxon. The overwhelming use

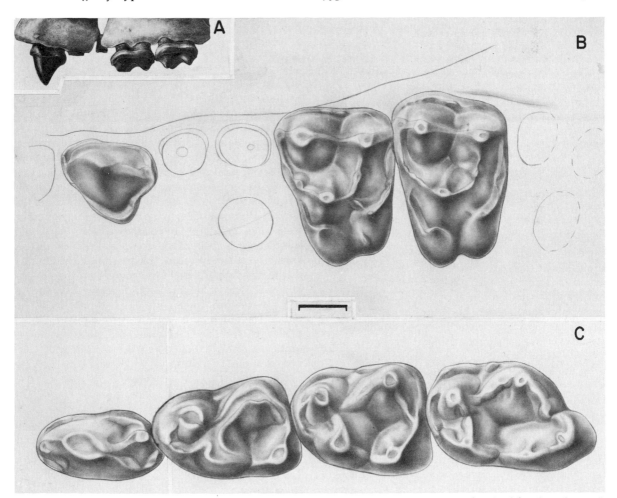

Figure 62. *Periconodon pygmaeus*. Middle Eocene, western Europe. Left maxilla fragment with P$\underline{3}$ and M$\underline{1-2}$: A lateral view; B, occlusal view. Right P$\overline{4}$–M$\overline{3}$: C, occlusal view. Scale represents 1 mm. [By A. Cleary.]

of stratophenetics in the description of new taxa by Gingerich (e.g., 1977a) necessitates the especially careful appraisal of the morphology of his proposed taxa, as often no morphological evidence is marshaled for the new nomina.

The dental formula of this genus cannot be determined.

The small size and the tall, acute cusps on P^2 coupled with the known molars suggest that this form was primarily insectivorous.

Tribe Microadapini, new

DISTRIBUTION
  Middle Eocene (Rhenanian). Western Europe.

INCLUDED TAXA
  Microadapis.

Discussion

These primates, known only by the type genus, are unique among adapids in having a combination of well-developed conules and a hypertrophied hypocone. The cusps are robustly based and quite rectangular in outline. The lack of a metastylid and the otherwise advanced nature of the molars indicate that the specializations of this group evolved independently from those seen in the Adapini.

MICROADAPIS Szalay, 1974a

(= or including: *Adapis:* Stehlin, 1916, in part.)

DISTRIBUTION
  Early middle Eocene (Rhenanian). Switzerland.
KNOWN SPECIES
  Microadapis sciureus (Stehlin, 1916), type species
  (= *Adapis sciureus* Stehlin, 1916.)
  LOCALITIES: Egerkingen γ* (250).

Discussion

Microadapis is clearly distinguishable from both *Adapis* and *Leptadapis* in having well-developed paraconules and metaconules, a less distally placed entoconid, an unfused, medially less-developed symphysis, and semimolariform as opposed to molariform fourth premolars (Figure 63). It further differs from *Adapis* in having a large, well-developed canine, quite dissimilar to the incisiform canine of *Adapis*. Unlike *Leptadapis*, *Microadapis* has a well-developed entoconid on $M_{\overline{3}}$ and lower incisors clearly relatively larger than those of the former. The differences of *Microadapis* from *Anchomomys* and *Huerzeleris* are noted under these genera.

The dental formula is $I\frac{2}{3}$; $C\frac{1}{1}$; $P\frac{1,2,3,4}{1,2,3,4}$; $M\frac{1,2,3}{1,2,3}$.

The description and analysis of this genus by Szalay (1974a) necessitated the reinterpretation of the morphology of *Adapis* and *Leptadapis*, as well as of *Caenopithecus*. As the diagnostic characters of *Microadapis* indicate, *Adapis* and *Leptadapis* differ very significantly not only from this small genus but also from each other.

The most impressive morphological characters of the known *Microadapis* feeding apparatus lie in the combination of its low crowned teeth, semimolariform fourth premolars, a relatively large canine, molars with broad based cusps, an upper molar with a very well-developed hypocone, and an unfused symphysis. As far as we know, the most derived combination of characters of *Microadapis* lies in the nature of the crown pattern, namely, in the broad based cusps of the teeth and the large hypocone–reduced paraconid combination. Lack of other specialized characters known would only permit the general conclusion that this form was perhaps more frugivorous than insectivorous. The relatively well-developed canine, a primitive feature, has an extensive cingulid, as do the premolars and molars, which may help corroborate this hypothesis. The cingulids could, however, represent a character not *sui generis* for *Microadapis*.

Tribe Adapini
Trouessart, 1879

DISTRIBUTION
  Middle Eocene to early Oligocene (Rhenanian to Headonian). Western Europe.
INCLUDED TAXA
  Subtribes Adapina and Caenopithecina.

Discussion

The Adapini appear to be a radiation of medium- to large-sized primate herbivores of the Eocene. From a

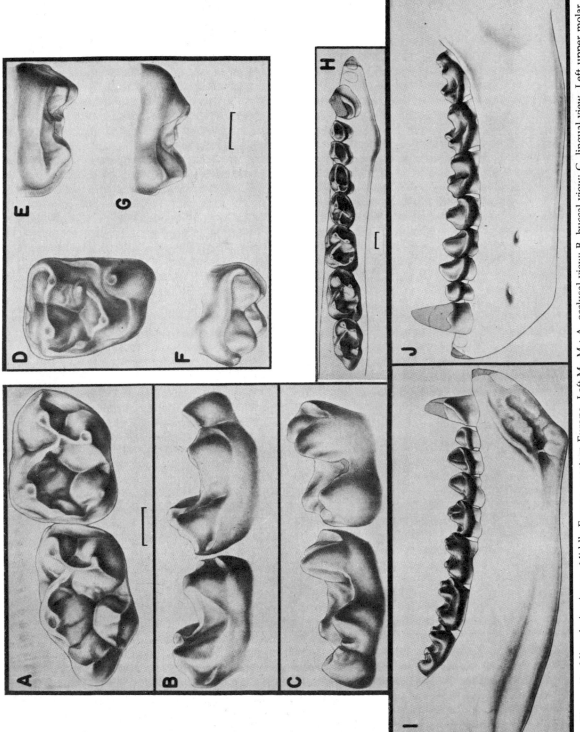

Figure 63. *Microadapis sciureus.* Middle Eocene, western Europe. Left M₂–M₃: A, occlusal view; B, buccal view; C, lingual view. Left upper molar, probably M¹: D, occlusal view; E, mesial view; F, buccal view; G, distal view. Left mandible with alveoli of I₁–I₂, C, P₁–P₄, M₁–M₃: H, occlusal view; I, medial view; J, lateral view. Scales represent 1 mm. [From Szalay (1974a).]

common ancestry, they share a distinctive metastylid and upper molars with a well-developed hypocone. The distinctions between the Adapina and Caenopithecina are discussed under the respective subtribes.

SUBTRIBE ADAPINA
Trouessart, 1879

DISTRIBUTION
    Same as for tribe.
INCLUDED TAXA
    Leptadapis and *Adapis*.

DISCUSSION

This group of primates within the Adapini possesses relatively conservative features when compared with the closely related *Caenopithecus*. The full dental formula of adapids is retained and a mesostyle is lacking.

The association of *Leptadapis* and *Adapis* has been usually very close, and most past systematists have treated them as members of one genus. Restudy (Szalay, 1974a, and in preparation) of the various dental and cranial samples, as well as a study of new postcranial remains, leaves no doubt as to the distinction between these groups, particularly in the anterior dentition and postcranial morphology. The derived cropping dentition of *Adapis* sharply contrasts with the robust grooved canines and incisiform incisors of *Leptadapis* (see under *Leptadapis*). Some of the postcranial differences are noted under *Adapis*. Gingerich (1977a,b) continued the use of the concept of *Adapis* that included both of these taxa and postulated the evolution of *Adapis parisiensis* from *Leptadapis magnus*, naming an allegedly intermediate sample as "*Adapis stintoni*." In defining the species, Gingerich's (1977a) sole criterion to distinguish it from the generotypes of *Adapis* and *Leptadapis* was as follows: "*Adapis stintoni* differs from *Ad. magnus* in being significantly smaller" (p. 72). This diagnosis clearly implies that, except for size differences, the morphological distinctions between *Adapis* and *Leptadapis* are not important.

LEPTADAPIS Gervais, 1876

(= or including: *Adapis*: Filhol, 1874 and others, in part. *Dichobune*: Rütimeyer, 1891, in part. *?Arisella* Crusafont-Pairo, 1967.)

DISTRIBUTION
    Middle to late Eocene (Rhenanian to Headonian). Western Europe.
KNOWN SPECIES
    1. *Leptadapis magnus* (Filhol, 1874), type species
    [= *Adapis magnus* Filhol, 1874. *Leptadapis magnus*: Gervais, 1876. *Adapis stintoni* Gingerich, 1977a, in part.]
    LOCALITIES: Phosphorites of Quercy★ (294); Fons 1 and 6 (314); Fons 4 (318); Euzet (322); Ehrenstein IA (354).
    2. *Leptadapis ruetimeyeri* (Stehlin, 1912)
    (= *Adapis duvernoyi*: Rütimeyer, 1888. *A. parisiensis*: Rütimeyer, 1891, in part. *Dichobune mülleri*: Rütimeyer, 1891. *Adapis (Leptadapis) rütimeyeri* Stehlin, 1912.)
    LOCALITIES: Egerkingen α★ (278).
    3. *Leptadapis priscus* (Stehlin, 1916) new combination
    (= *Adapis priscus* Stehlin, 1916.)
    LOCALITIES: Egerkingen α★ (278).
    4. *Leptadapis capellae* (Crusafont-Pairo, 1967) new combination
    (= *?Arisella capellae* Crusafont-Pairo, 1967.)
    LOCALITIES: Capella★ (253).

DISCUSSION

The distinction of *Leptadapis* (Figures 64 and 65) from *Adapis* is clear in several important characters, especially of the anterior dentition (Szalay, 1974a).

Unlike the canines of *Adapis*, *A. parisiensis*, those of *Leptadapis* are strong and well developed, probably representing the primitive condition. The round based upper canines have a series of apically converging, deep grooves in the tooth surface. In sharp contrast to the continuous apical edge of the canine–incisor row of *Adapis* in which the incisors are particularly prominent, the area remaining between the canine and the alveoli for the incisors in *Leptadapis* is all but eliminated. As noted under *Adapis*, the strikingly different morphologies of the anterior dentition, coupled with their concomitant mechanical functions, are distinct in the two genera and consequently their adaptations must have been commensurately divergent. The first premolar of *Leptadapis*, unlike the condition in *Adapis*, is considerably reduced in size, perhaps to facilitate the function of the large canines. *Leptadapis* preserves a relatively large protocone on P^3, whereas in *Adapis* this cusp is considerably reduced.

The dentition of *Leptadapis ruetimeyeri* Stehlin, 1912, has been reexamined (Szalay, 1974a) and Stehlin's original allocation to *Leptadapis* is corroborated. Slightly smaller than *L. magnus*, *L. ruetimeyeri* is unquestionably more similar to the generitype of *Lep-*

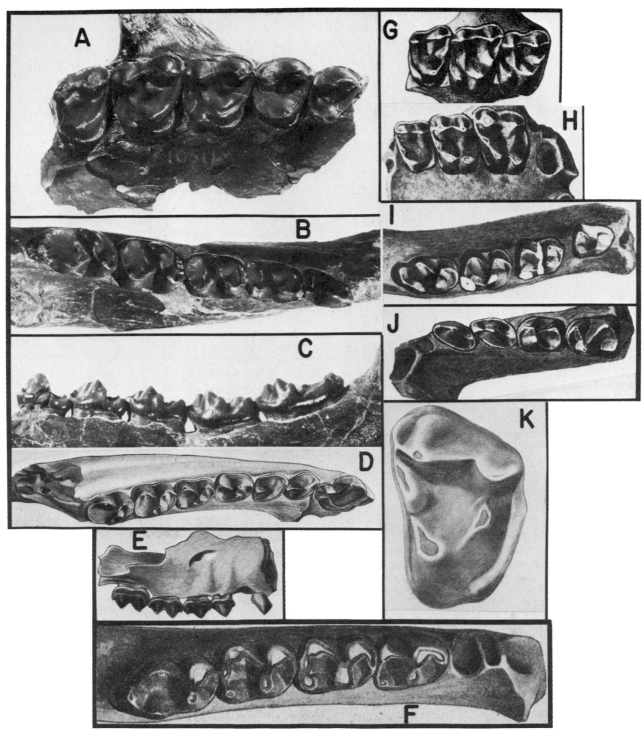

Figure 64. *Leptadapis*. Late Eocene, western Europe. *Leptadapis magnus*. Right maxilla fragment with P^3–M^3: A, occlusal view. Right mandible fragment with P_3–M_3: B, occlusal view; C, medial view. Left mandible with C–M_3: D, occlusal view. Left maxilla fragment with P^1, P^3–M^2: E, lateral view. *Leptadapis ruetimeyeri*. Right M^{1-3}: G, occlusal view. Left P^4–M^2: H, occlusal view. Left P_4–M_3: I, occlusal view. Right P_2–M_1: J, occlusal view. *Leptadapis priscus*. Left mandible fragment with P_4–M_3: F, occlusal view. *Leptadapis? capellae*. Left M^3: K, occlusal view. [D–J from Stehlin, 1916; K from Crusafont-Pairo (1967).]

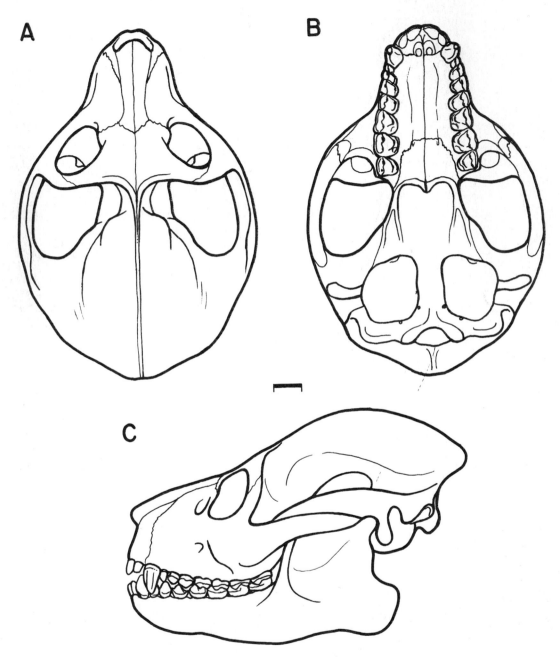

Figure 65. *Leptadapis magnus.* Late Eocene, western Europe. Skull and mandible: A, dorsal view; B, ventral view; C, lateral view. Scale represents 1 cm. [By A. Cleary.]

tadapis than to that of *Adapis*. *Leptadapis ruetimeyeri* shares with *L. magnus* relatively large and conical hypocones. On the lower molars the metastylids of *L. magnus* are pronounced but on *L. ruetimeyeri* there is only a barest hint of this structure.

The dental formula in *Leptadapis* was $I^{1,2}_{2}$; C^{1}_{1}; $P^{1,2,3,4}_{1,2,3,4}$; $M^{1,2,3}_{1,2,3}$.

The skull of the genus (Stehlin, 1912) is well known, and the discussion under *Notharctus*, for comparisons, is closely relevant. Judged from the large sagittal crest and zygoma (see Figure 65), the temporalis and masse-

ter muscle masses were extensive. There is little doubt that *Leptadapis magnus* and *Leptadapis ruetimeyeri* were phytophagous, probably folivorous.

The massive humerus of *Leptadapis* has an extremely well-developed brachioradialis crest, not unlike the condition in many marsupials or in *Plesiadapis* or *Notharctus*. The primitive strepsirhine, as well as lemuriform, condition of the astragalus in *Leptadapis* is noted under *Adapis*. The latter has a more derived astragalar body, distinguishing it from *Leptadapis*.

ADAPIS Cuvier, 1821

(= or including: *Aphelotherium* Gervais, 1859. *Lophiotherium:* Pictet and Humbert, 1869, in part. *Palaeolemur* Delfortrie, 1873.)

DISTRIBUTION
Eocene to early Oligocene (Rhenanian to Headonian). Western Europe.
KNOWN SPECIES
Adapis parisiensis Cuvier, 1821, type species
(=*Aphelotherium duvernoyi* Gervais, 1859. *Lophiotherium laharpei* Pictet and Humbert, 1869. *Palaeolemur betillei* Delfortrie, 1873. *Adapis sudrei* Gingerich, 1977a. *Adapis stintoni* Gingerich, 1977a, in part.)
LOCALITIES: Phosphorites of Quercy★ (294); Robiac (306); Headon Lignite (359); Escamps A, B, C (363); Rosières 1, 2, 4 (364).

DISCUSSION

The genus, as defined here, includes only one morphological species, a vast collection of specimens roughly covering the size of *Galago crassicaudatus*. A detailed study of all of the specimens, however, may result in the recognition of more than one species. *Adapis*, along with *Notharctus* and *Leptadapis*, is the best known Eocene adapid as far as cranial morphology is concerned (see Figures 66 and 67). The skulls are characterized by the dominance of the facial portion over the braincase, quite in contrast to proportions displayed by even the long-snouted modern lemuriforms. As noted under the discussion of the strepsirhines, the basicranium is typically lemuriform. Much of the discussion on cranial anatomy under *Notharctus* is closely relevant to *Adapis*. Differences from *Anchomomys* and *Microadapis* are listed under these genera.

Adapis presents a number of specializations which indicate that this genus should not include *Leptadapis*

magnus (Szalay, 1974a). The canines are reduced in size, forming part of an anterior dentition which is modified as a cropping mechanism. In *Leptadapis*, however, the lower canine is caniniform. In *Adapis* the long mesial cutting edge of the canine is developed to form a continuous blade with the cutting edges of the mesiodistally flattened incisor.

The brachioradialis crest of the humerus in *Adapis* is quite small, approaching the reduced condition seen in most of the platyrrhine humeri. The astragalus, as the humerus, is distinctive in *Adapis* (Figure 66) when contrasted to that of *Leptadapis* (Decker and Szalay, 1974). The former appears to have lost the primitive strepsirhine condition of the tibial trochlea on the body of the astragalus, which is extended out and elongated onto a distal platform in such adapids as *Pelycodus*, *Notharctus*, and *Leptadapis* and in the majority of the subfossil and modern lemuriforms.

The species *Adapis sudrei* recently described by Gingerich (1977a) is not adequately delineated by its author from *Adapis parisiensis*. Usage of such characters as the "slightly more molarized premolars, especially P³" and the lack of symphyseal fusion of the few known specimens do not take into account variation in the large samples of *A. parisiensis*. Specimens of young *A. parisiensis* individuals sometimes display lack of ossification at the symphysis and P³ molarization is variable enough to include the condition of that tooth in the type specimen of *A. sudrei*. Another species, *A. stintoni*, described by Gingerich (1977a), is allegedly significantly larger than *A. parisiensis*. The tests for this significance are not shown. Until clearly established otherwise, we will consider both *A. sudrei* and *A. stintoni* as synonyms of *Adapis parisiensis*.

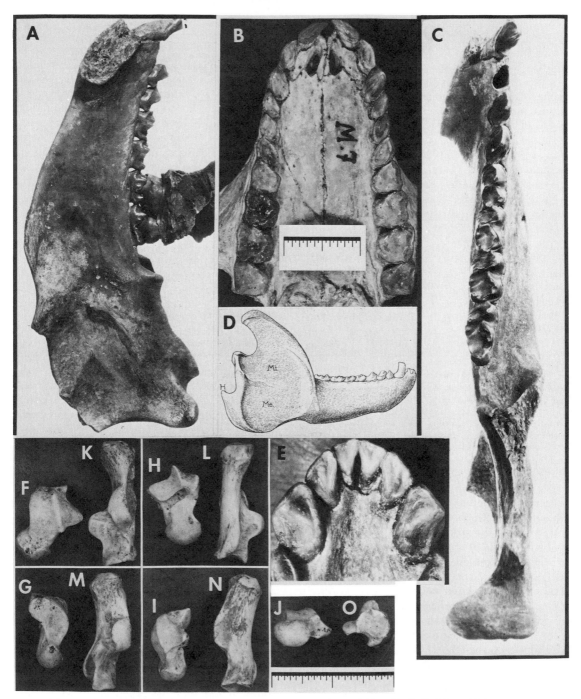

Figure 66. *Adapis parisiensis.* Middle–late Eocene, western Europe. Left mandible with C, P$\overline{2}$–M$\overline{3}$ and left maxilla with M$^{\underline{2}}$–M$^{\underline{3}}$: A, medial view. Palate with complete right dentition: B, occlusal view. Right mandible with C, alveolus for P$\overline{1}$, P$\overline{2}$–P$\overline{4}$, M$\overline{1}$–M$\overline{3}$: C, occlusal view. Right mandible with C, P$\overline{1}$–M$\overline{3}$: D, lateral view. Anterior lower dentition with left and right I$\overline{1}$–I$\overline{2}$, C: E, occlusal view. Left astragalus: F, dorsal view; G, medial view; H, ventral view; I, lateral view; J, distal view. Left calcaneum: K, dorsal view; L, ventral view; M, medial view; N, lateral view; O, distal view. Subdivisions on scales are 0.5 mm. [D from Stehlin (1916).]

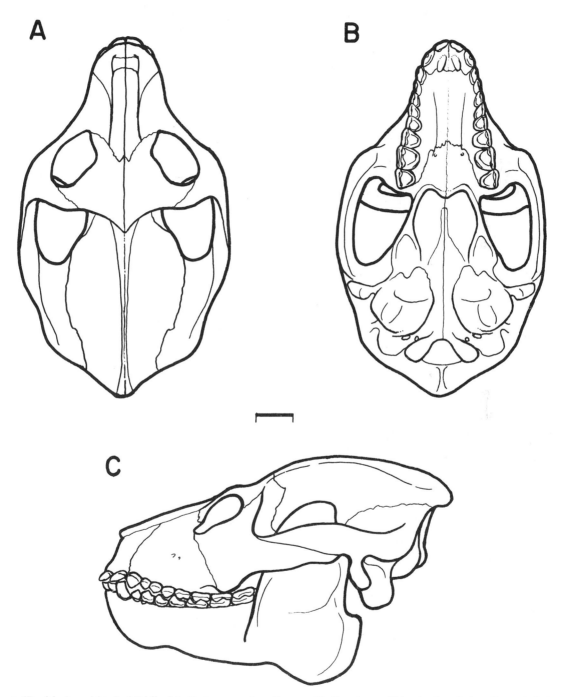

Figure 67. *Adapis parisiensis.* Middle–late Eocene, western Europe. Skull and mandible: A, dorsal view; B, ventral view; C, lateral view. Scale represents 1 cm. [By A. Cleary.]

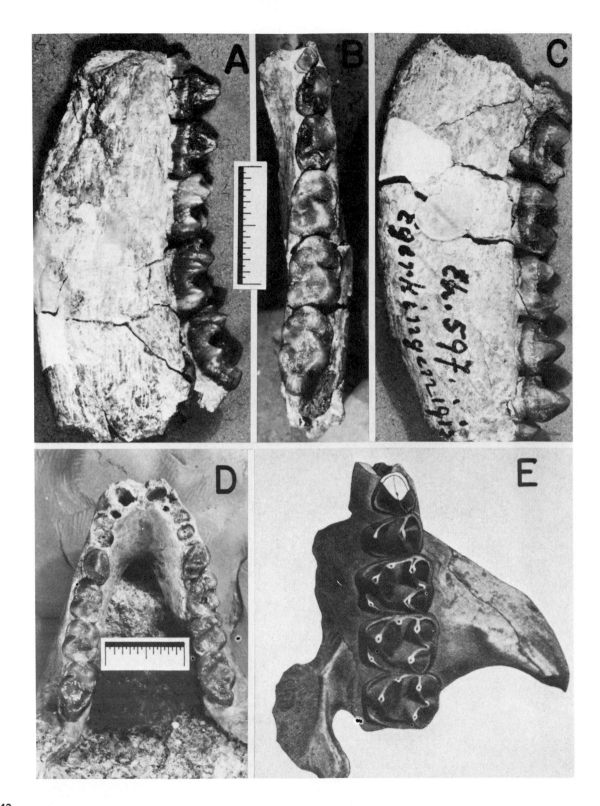

The dental formula of *Adapis* was $I\frac{1,2}{1,2}$; $C\frac{1}{1}$; $P\frac{1,2,3,4}{1,2,3,4}$; $M\frac{1,2,3}{1,2,3}$.

Aspects of the dentition of *Adapis* have been recently reviewed by Gingerich (1975d), who suggested that the genus was the ancestor of the tooth-combed lemuriforms. His arguments are based on the allegedly homologous similarity of the anterior dentition of *Adapis* and tooth-combed forms. As pointed out by Szalay and Seligsohn (1977), the inferred mechanical function in tooth-combed strepsirhines is divergent rather than convergent with those of *Adapis*. Nevertheless some adapine was likely the ancestor of the tooth-combed lemuriforms.

SUBTRIBE CAENOPITHECINA, NEW

DISTRIBUTION
 Middle Eocene (Rhenanian). Western Europe.

INCLUDED TAXA
 Caenopithecus.

DISCUSSION

Caenopithecus represents a notable departure from the common adapin ancestry, sharply distinct from the adapinans. The loss of a pair of incisors and $P_{\overline{1}}$, and the reduction of $P_{\overline{2}}$, along with the mesially projecting canines, the well-developed molar mesostyles, and the premolariform $P\frac{4}{}$ represent the major known distinctions from the Adapina. In spite of these differences, judged from the trigonid morphology and the metastylid, the Caenopithecina are probably more recently related to the Adapina than to any other group of Adapidae.

CAENOPITHECUS Rütimeyer, 1862

DISTRIBUTION
 Middle Eocene (Rhenanian). Western Europe.
KNOWN SPECIES
 Caenopithecus lemuroides Rütimeyer, 1862, type species
LOCALITIES: Egerkingen γ★ (250); Bouxwiller (254); Egerkingen Huppersand (256).

DISCUSSION

Caenopithecus lemuroides (Figure 68) is an animal with a jaw in the approximate size range of *Propithecus verreauxi*. This form is unique in possessing the following combination of characters (Szalay, 1974a). The mandibular symphysis is fused and it appears that the snout was somewhat shortened. The first lower premolar and one of the two adapid incisors are lost and the second premolar is considerably reduced in size. The fourth premolars are distinctly premolariform and the molars have mesostyles and metastylids, above and below, respectively. The upper cingula are well developed and a distinctly cuspate hypocone along with a strong paraconule are present. The metaconules, at least on the known specimens, have

disappeared. The most conspicuous difference from *Leptadapis*, the genus which *Caenopithecus* resembles most closely among the adapids, is the possession of the mesostyle and the premolariform, as opposed to molariform, fourth premolars.

The dental formula was probably $I\frac{1,2}{}$; $C\frac{1}{1}$; $P\frac{2,3,4}{2,3,4}$; $M\frac{1,2,3}{1,2,3}$.

The mesially directed canine alveoli suggest an adaptation not unlike that in indriids, particularly in *Propithecus*. Perhaps *Caenopithercus* used its canines as indriids use their robust and modified tooth comb for prying up bark. This suggestion might not be too farfetched when one considers that the molar teeth of this genus have well-developed mesostyles and hypocones and, in general, a gestalt of molar characteristics found in the folivorous indriids.

Tribe Indralorisini, new

DISTRIBUTION
 Late Miocene (?Vallesian). Northern India.
INCLUDED TAXA
 Indraloris.

Figure 68. *Caenopithecus lemuroides.* Middle Eocene, western Europe. Right mandible with $P_{\overline{2}}$–$M_{\overline{3}}$: A, medial view; B, occlusal view; C, lateral view. Mandible with alveoli for C, $P_{\overline{2}}$–$P_{\overline{3}}$, with left $P_{\overline{4}}$–$M_{\overline{3}}$ and right $P_{\overline{4}}$–$M_{\overline{3}}$: D, occlusal view. Left maxilla with $P\frac{3}{}$–$M\frac{3}{}$: E, occlusal view. Subdivisions on scales represent 0.5 mm. [E from Stehlin (1916).]

DISCUSSION

The large, as yet undescribed samples of *Indraloris* leave no doubt of the existence of an endemic, subhimalayan group of adapid primates. These forms may be characterized as relatively large, similar in size to the Adapini, with a unique talonid construction displaying a closely twinned entoconid and hypoconulid, and with a trigonid mesiodistally constricted. Clearly, *Indraloris* only hints at this Asian adapid diversity. Considering the indralorisins, *Amphipithecus*, *Lushius*, and probably *Pondaungia*, however, the variety of Asian strepsirhines must have been remarkably extensive.

INDRALORIS Lewis, 1933

(= or including: *Sivanasua:* Pilgrim, 1932, in part.)

DISTRIBUTION
    Same as for tribe.
KNOWN SPECIES
    Indraloris himalayensis (Pilgrim, 1932), type species, new combination
(= *Sivanasua himalayensis* Pilgrim, 1932. *Indraloris lulli* Lewis, 1933.)
LOCALITIES: Nagri beds★ (530).

DISCUSSION

Although Indian collections of fossil primates contain a great wealth of new specimens discovered during the past decade, among them new fossils of *Indraloris*, these have not as yet been described. Courtesy of Dr. Chopra, we had the opportunity to

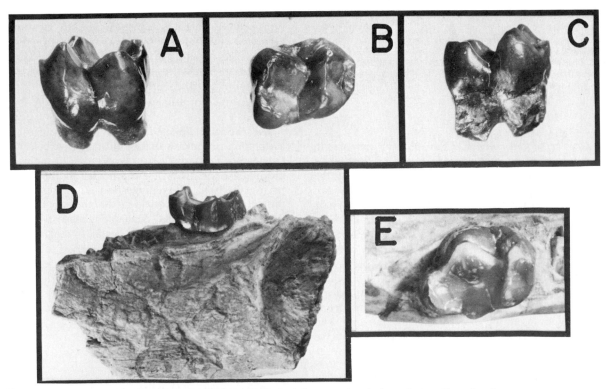

Figure 69. *Indraloris lulli.* Late Miocene, northern India. Left lower molar: A, buccal view; B, occlusal view; C, lingual view. Left mandible fragment with M₃: D, lateral view; E, occlusal view. [From Tattersall (1968), POSTILLA (Peabody Mus. Nat. Hist., Yale Univ.) No. 123, 1968, Figs. 1, 2b.]

examine briefly a substantial sample of *Indraloris,* soon to be published by him. Until this sample is described in detail, our characterization is necessarily limited. The upper molars lack a hypocone, and from the few worn molars available to us it is impossible to determine whether a protocone fold was present. The lower molars are characterized by a closely twinned entoconid and hypoconulid and a mesiodistally constricted trigonid with lophodont crests rather than clearly sculptered cusps. The fourth premolars are molarized. Upper and lower canines are large and interlocking. The symphysis is solidly fused and judged from the alveoli the incisors were small like in most other adapids. The lack of any modification which would hint similarity to a tooth comb, of course, precludes any affinity (on these grounds) to lemuriforms. The only presently available figures of *Indraloris* (Figure 69) are of two isolated molars, illustrated by Tattersall (1968), who also suggested the synonymy we accept here.

Based on incomplete examinations and some of the wear exhibited on the studied sample, *Indraloris* was a folivore.

Family Adapidae, *incertae sedis*

AMPHIPITHECUS Colbert, 1937

DISTRIBUTION
   Late Eocene, Burma.
KNOWN SPECIES
   Amphipithecus mogaungensis Colber, 1937, type species
LOCALITIES: Pondaung⋆ (345).

DISCUSSION

Most students who studied the scanty remains (Figure 70) of *Amphipithecus* (e.g., Colbert, 1937, 1938; Simons, 1963b, 1965, 1971; Simons and Pilbeam, 1965; Van Valen, 1969) did not seriously doubt the originally suggested affinities of this genus and allocated it to the Anthropoidea, more precisely to the catarrhines. This was questioned by Szalay (1970, 1972c), and the suggestion was made that *Amphipithecus* was possibly a strepsirhine. Further comparisons have not changed our views as suggested by Szalay (1970, pp. 355–357).

One of the diagnostic characters of the early Oligocene catarrhines (see under the respective taxa) is the shape of the $M_{\overline{1-2}}$ talonid, more particularly the distinct, large, cuspate, and nearly centrally placed hypoconulid and its relationship to the clearly delineated hypoconid and entoconid. The distolingual corner of the talonid is rounded in such a way that both the entoconid and hypoconulid partake equally in rounding out the contour, although these two cusps are distinct and well separated. A glance at *Parapithecus, Apidium,* and *Propliopithecus* (including *Aeqyptopithecus*) confirms the ubiquitous presence of this feature, particularly when contrasted with other groups of primates. Because most Paleocene and Eocene primates lack this character, and because it appears in the Oligocene primates from the Fayum, it may be assumed that it was present in the ancestors of parapithecids, hominoids, and other catarrhines. Furthermore, it seems reasonable that it was acquired by these unknown ancestors after their separation from known groups of early Tertiary primates. There are indications that a transversely narrow talonid is prevalent among Fayum primates, particularly on the second lower molar, with the notable exception of *Oligopithecus.* Except for a narrow ledge, the area of the trigonid anterior to the protoconid and metaconid lacks a distinct paraconid in both the parapithecids and the other Fayum catarrhines.

There is no indication that the hypoconulid on the relatively well-preserved first lower molar of *Amphipithecus* was placed like the hypoconulid in the Fayum catarrhines. Although the moderately worn entoconid is chipped off, it seems that the crest connecting the entoconid and the hypoconid was continuous except for the interruption by a tiny hypoconulid immediately distolingual to the hypoconid. From the inferred position of the hypoconulid (the cusp is slightly nicked on the specimen), it is clear that the hypoconulid was indistinct and was closer to the hypoconid than to the entoconid. The talonid of *Amphipithecus* is different from the Fayum primates; it

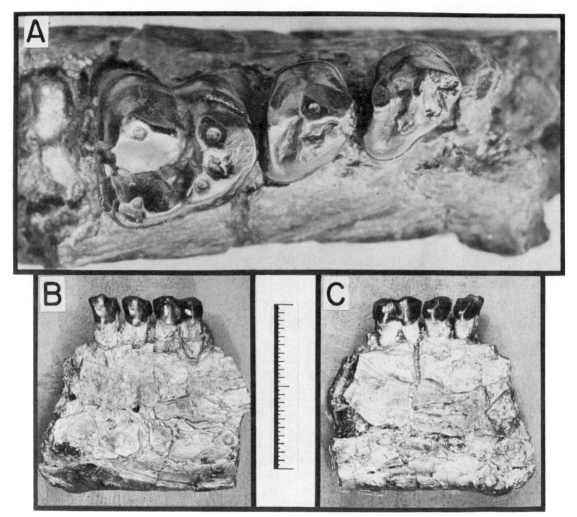

Figure 70. *Amphipithecus mogaungensis*. Later Eocene, southern Asia. Mandible fragment with P$_{\overline{3}}$–M$_{\overline{1}}$: A, occlusal view; B, lateral view; C, medial view. Subdivisions on scale represent 0.5 mm.

is even more distinct from the talonids of the latter than those of omomyids are from the talonids of adapids or, for example, the talonids of tarsiids, plesiadapids, and lorisids are from the talonids of either of the former families. On the anterior surface of the first molar of *Amphipithecus*, there is a tiny pit which suggests the presence of a cuspate paraconid. The prescence of a paraconid in such a position is more characteristic of adapiforms and omomyids than of known cercopithecoids or hominoids. Taking the scanty evidence of the molars into account, it is

therefore unlikely that *Amphipithecus* had close ties with the ancestors of Fayum catarrhines.

The construction of the talonid on P$_{\overline{3}}$ and P$_{\overline{4}}$ of *Parapithecus, Apidium,* and *Propliopithecus* is similar, in a much simplified form, to the molar talonids. Distal to the more prominent protoconid and metaconid there is at least one and sometimes two or more distinctly bulbous talonid cusps on these premolars. In *Amphipithecus*, the fourth and third premolars are mesiobuccally skewed like those of the Fayum genera, but the features of the rudimentary

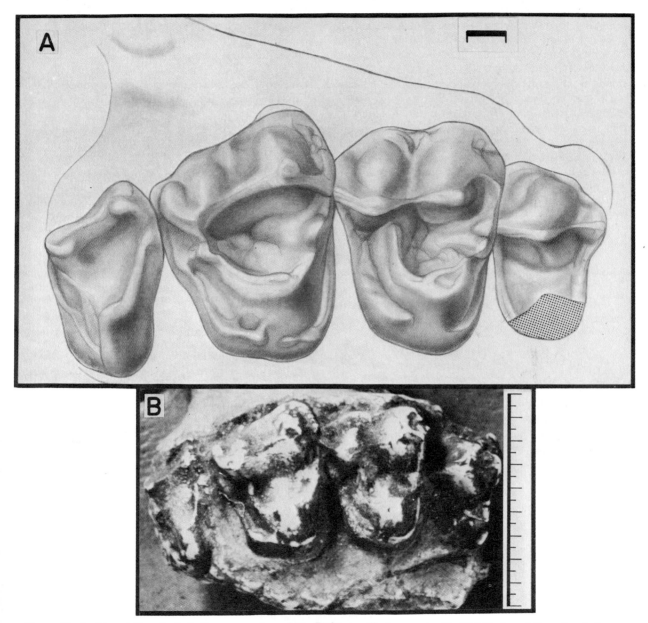

Figure 71. *Lushius qinlinensis*. Late Eocene, eastern Asia. Right maxilla fragment with P^4–M^3: A and B, occlusal views. Stippling depicts reconstruction. Drawn scale represents 1 mm. The subdivisions on the photographed scale are 0.5 mm. [A by A. Cleary.]

talonids show a construction unlike the Fayum primates. Only one cusp, presumably the hypoconid, is slightly accentuated, and a crest extends lingually to delineate the extent of the talonid basin. In spite of some convergent similarities, the premolars of *Amphipithecus* and those of the Fayum early catarrhines are dissimilar.

The combined evidence from the three cheek teeth (particularly the characters of the M_T talonid and the premolars) and from the symphyseal area seems to indicate that *Amphipithecus* may be an advanced early Tertiary primate. On the other hand, omomyid ties cannot be ruled out. On the basis of molar construction, the Burmese primate does not seem far removed from a notharctine, or some other, unknown, primitive adapid, and a comparison of the symphysis of

Amphipithecus with those of numerous specimens of *Pelycodus* and *Notharctus* does not contradict this. It must be remembered, however, that primitive dental features of omomyids cannot be shown to be significantly different from those of adapids. *Amphipithecus mogaungensis* was a relatively short-faced, heavy-jawed species, and these adaptations undoubtedly transformed the crown and root pattern of the more anterior elements of the dentition and profoundly modified the construction and alignment of the symphysis. We consider the features of the molar to be primitive, whereas the morphology of the premolars and the mandible is somewhat more advanced. The similarity of the premolars of *Amphipithecus* to the Fayum catarrhines is probably the result of convergence rather than common inheritance.

LUSHIUS Chow, 1961

DISTRIBUTION
  Late Eocene. China.
KNOWN SPECIES
  Lushius qinlinensis Chow, 1961, type species
LOCALITIES: Lushi★ (334).

DISCUSSION

This approximately cat-sized primate is known only from a maxilla fragment with P^4–M^3 (Figure 71). The known upper teeth are characterized by a very well-developed continuous crest, the ectoloph, on the buccal side. As far as we can judge, there was a small hypocone on the cingulum. The author of this taxon reports that the thickening of the enamel is observable in the area where the mesostyle is usually located, and the enamel is wrinkled. P^4 is relatively small compared

to the molars, being premolariform with a paracone and a relatively smaller protocone. M^3 of *Lushius* is diagnostically constricted mesiodistally, resulting in a morphology similar to that of some anaptomorphine $M^{3'}$s.

This genus could be either adapid or omomyid. It is classified within the Adapidae because of a suggestion of primitive adapid morphology. Phylogenetically it may well have been a sister lineage of one of the acknowledged anaptomorphines.

Adaptationally, the meager evidence points to emphasis of buccal phase transverse cutting by the cheek teeth, a mechanical solution often associated with leaf-eating, or at least with some form of herbivory not emphasizing soft fruits.

Infraorder Lemuriformes
Gregory, 1915b

(= or including: Lemuroidea and Lorisoidea of numerous authors. Lorisiformes Gregory, 1915. Indriiformes Tattersall and Schwartz, 1974.)

DISTRIBUTION
  Early Miocene to modern. Africa, Madagascar, Asia.
INCLUDED TAXA
  Superfamilies Lemuroidea, Indrioidea, and Lorisoidea.

DISCUSSION

There is difficulty in expressing the diversity of the strepsirhine primates in a balanced manner using the various Linnean hierarchies. Traditionally, the adapids were classified in the same superfamily as the lemurids because, in terms of total known morphological divergence, the differences between them were not very great. On the other hand, although great differences have evolved among the Malagasy primates, the custom to include all the non-lorisoids in one superfamily has long persisted and all have usually been accommodated in either of two families, the Lemuridae and Indriidae. We departed only slightly from these practices in order to emphasize phylogenetic as well as patristic aspects of lemuriform evolution.

Their distinctive character complex, the tooth comb made up of both incisors and incisiform canines, is a uniquely derived character, not just among the Primates but among the Mammalia as well. It serves as a diagnostic character delineating the monophyletic category Lemuriformes (Figures 72 and 73) and identifies a morphological stage, with specific adaptive modifications, that is ancestral to subsequent lemuriforms. The recent views of Szalay (1976) and Szalay and Seligsohn (1977) on the origins of the tooth comb are relevant (see discussion under Strepsirhini). An important detailed analytical study by Seligsohn (1977) deals with molar adaptations of the lemuriform strepsirhines.

SUPERFAMILY LEMUROIDEA
Gray, 1821

(= or including: Lemuriformes Gregory, 1915b, in part.)

DISTRIBUTION
  Modern (living and subfossil). Madagascar and the Comoro Islands.

INCLUDED TAXA
  Families Lemuridae and Megaladapidae.

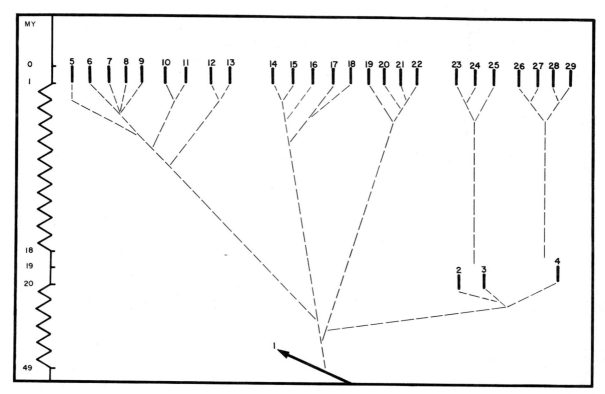

Figure 72. Known stratigraphic ranges (solid lines) and suggested phylogenetic relationships (broken lines) of taxa of the tooth-combed Lemuriformes. 1, Segment of the stratigraphic range of the Adapidae; 2, *Komba*; 3, *Progalago*; 4, *Mioeuoticus*; 5, *Daubentonia*; 6, *Indri*; 7, *Propithecus*; 8, *Mesopropithecus*; 9, *Avahi*; 10, *Palaeopropithecus*; 11, *Archaeoindris*; 12, *Archaeolemur*; 13, *Hadropithecus*; 14, *Lemur*; 15, *Varecia*; 16, *Hapalemur*; 17, *Lepilemur*; 18, *Megaladapis*; 19, *Microcebus*; 20, *Cheirogaleus*; 21, *Allocebus*; 22, *Phaner*; 23, *Euoticus*; 24, *Galagoides*; 25, *Galago*; 26, *Loris*; 27, *Nycticebus*; 28, *Perodicticus*; 29, *Arctocebus*. [By A. Cleary.]

DISCUSSION

In addition to excluding the Adapidae from the Lemuroidea and raising these Paleogene primates to infraordinal level within the Strepsirhini, we exclude the Cheirogaleidae from the Lemuroidea and include it within the Lorisoidea, as suggested by Szalay (1975f). The rationale for this action is explained more fully in the discussion under the Lorisoidea. Lemuroids, as defined here, would represent both the stem group and a specific radiation of the tooth-combed strepsirhines, which retained the original six teeth of the tooth comb and have not drastically modified their basicranial morphology from a stage represented by known adapids such as *Notharctus*, *Smilodectes*, *Adapis*, and *Mahgarita*.

It appears that the first colonizers of the island of Madagascar were lemurid-like animals. The date and direction of this colonization are unknown to us. If the lemuriforms reached Madagascar from Africa, then it is likely that this event occurred prior to the colonization by or the radiation of the known catarrhines. Whether the colonization was from East Africa (Martin, 1972) or from Asia via the Arabian peninsula (or a nearby region) it could have been as early as the Paleocene.

Schwartz (1975) has noted that "the *Lepilemur–Megaladapis* sister groups may be part of a larger group with *Hapalemur* and the adapids" (p. 62). Gingerich (1977b) has also recently stated that "the resemblances shared by *Adapis* with living genera like *Hapalemur* and *Lepilemur* can all be explained away as retained primitive characteristics or convergent specialization if one wishes, but the fact remains that *Adapis*,

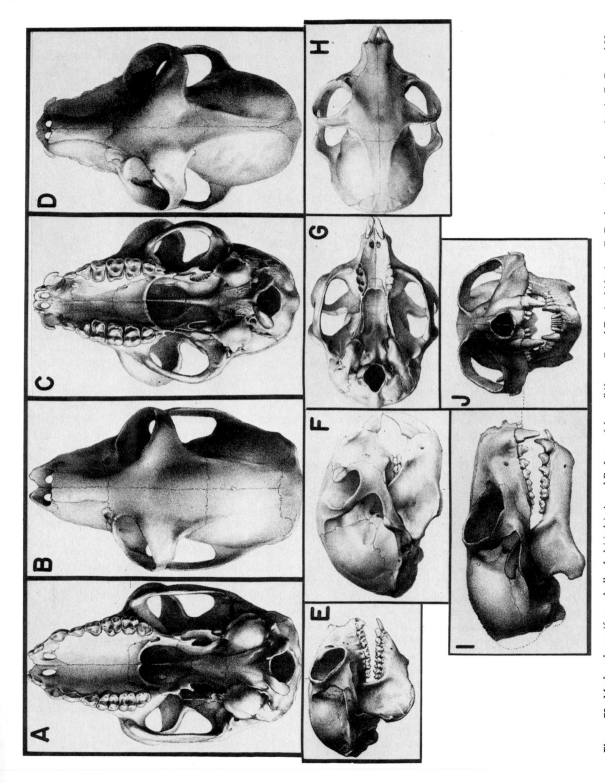

Figure 73. Modern lemuriform skulls. *Indri indri:* A and B; *Lemur fulvus albifrons:* C and D; *Avahi laniger:* E; *Daubentonia madagascariensis:* F, G, and H; *Galago crasicaudatus:* I and J. Ventral views: A, C, and G. Dorsal views: B, D, and H. Lateral views: E, F, and H. Frontal view: J. [From de Blainville (1839).]

Hapalemur, and *Lepilemur* are remarkably similar in spite of a gap in the fossil record of some 35 my" (p. 176). This view, as well as others which would regard, for example, the similarity of *Lepilemur*, *Hapalemur*, and *Megaladapis* to adapids to be more special and derived than the tooth comb shared by lemurids and other lemuriforms, and would therefore imply independent evolution from adapiforms, is not accepted by us. These hypotheses, in our view, are remarkably unparsimonious. For no convincing reason, they postulate some dental similarities (which can be adequately explained as primitive retentions) as derived, at the expense of having to evolve a unique character complex like the tooth comb more than once.

Family Lemuridae
Gray, 1821

(= or including: Lemurinae Mivart, 1864. Lepilemurina Gray, 1870. Nesopithecidae Major, 1893.)

DISTRIBUTION
   Modern (living and subfossil). Madagascar and the Comoro Islands.

INCLUDED TAXA
   Lemur, *Varecia*, *Lepilemur*, and *Hapalemur*.

DISCUSSION

The Lemuridae (*sensu stricto*) is largely defined by the combination of its primitive lemuroid characters and its advanced character states. Many of these, however, are shared with other Malagasy strepsirhines.

The characteristic lower tooth combs set lemurids, as well as other living and subfossil strepsirhines, apart from any of the known adapids. This morphological complex is clearly a key character combination, but in other respects the lemurids, and for that matter the indriids, are not very different postcranially and cranially from the better known adapids such as *Notharctus*, *Smilodectes*, *Adapis*, and *Leptadapis*. On the other hand, there was clearly an increase in the relative size of the brain from adapids to the common ancestor of the Lemuriformes, as this may be judged from the proportions of the skull and the relative height of the occiput in comparison to the length of the skull. Unlike most of the known adapids, lemurids show a slight inflation of the petromastoid and perhaps a slight reduction in the relative size of the promontory artery.

The living representatives of the lemurids appear to be the remnants of a herbivorous radiation of the original colonizers of Madagascar. Lemurid diets encompass stem feeding (*Hapalemur*), leaf eating (*Lepilemur*), and frugivory–folivory (*Lemur*). *Varecia* is suspected to feed on hard nuts or seed pods. Lemurids living today are largely arboreal, although *Lemur catta* troops spend considerable periods of time on the ground. As noted under *Varecia*, it appears that the known, large fossil species of this genus was terrestrial.

Lepilemur mustelinus, as *Hapalemur*, is found in all forested areas of Madagascar. It is a nocturnal, solitary form, specializing on coarse leaves. *Hapalemur* are crepuscular animals and are found all around Madagascar in forested areas, except for the dry southwestern region. Some groups are restricted to the reed beds of Lake Aloatra. Although other leaves and some fruits are eaten, bamboo appears to be the preferred food, particularly the stems of the leaves. *Lemur* is clearly the most successful genus of lemurids on Madagascar, and all areas with some tree cover are occupied by one of the species of this group. Species of *Lemur* are gregarious, primarily arboreal forms, with the exception of *Lemur catta*, which regularly spends time on the ground. The species are diurnal or crepuscular and feed primarily on fruits, leaves, and flowers. *Lemur catta* prefers fruits and gums primarily, whereas *Lemur fulvus* has its preferences reversed. The diet of *Lemur mongoz* is unknown. *Varecia variegatus*, a highly arboreal, gregarious species, is confined to the northeast of Madagascar. This species is very poorly known. Its diet is supposed to be hard seed pods or nuts (R. Sussman, personal communication; Seligsohn and Szalay, 1974).

To reconstruct a morphological morphotype for the Lemuridae is a rather difficult task because the group contains morphologically varied taxa. Dentally (but not postcranially) it appears that among the forms included *Lepilemur* approaches most closely what may be called ancestral morphology. Seligsohn (1977) notes that: "The ancestral lemurine may have possessed an upper second molar similar to that of *Lepilemur*, and a lower second molar most similar to that of *Megaladapis*. The ancestral lemurine M^2 would probably have differed, however, from that of *Lepilemur* in possessing a more inflated ectoloph, and a mesio-distally narrower protocone, while the ancestral $M_{\overline{2}}$ would have differed from that of *Megaladapis* in lacking a metaconulid, and perhaps demonstrating a long, continuous but low relief entocristid" (p. 89).

The dental apparatus of the living lemurids has recently been subjected to some scrutiny in order to attempt an explanation of morphology in terms of mechanical functions and biological role (Seligsohn and Szalay, 1974; Seligsohn and Szalay, 1977). Seligsohn (1977) has summarized some of the key morphological and mechanical features of lemurid molars as follows.

The M^2 and M^3 of *Lemur fulvus* and *Lemur macaco* differ from those of *Lemur catta* in possessing more inflated cusps of lower relief and acuity, while their protocones and hypoconids, respectively, are mesio-distally very broad, with very extensive, planar incision surfaces. The trigon and talonid basins are far more shallow and mesio-distally oriented.

These features indicate a greatly reduced functional emphasis on point penetration, and greater emphases on "horizontal" point-cutting and efficient crushing and grinding....

The second molars of *Lemur catta* differ from those of other congeneric species in respectively demonstrating more acute cusps and relatively deep and smoothly concave trigon and talonid basins which are fully confined by relatively high relief and greatly narrowed, crests. The protocone and hypoconid are less wide mesio-distally. The $M_{\overline{2}}$ is particularly distinc-

tive in emphasizing relatively great relief in the protocristid, postcristid and entoconid.

These features would appear to indicate relatively greater functional emphases on point penetration, "punching" and "vertical" point cutting. (pp. 91–92)

The genera listed below are known by living species. Some are also represented in the fossil record. Of the lemurids only *Varecia* is treated in detail because this genus is represented by an unusual fossil species. The fossil species of *Lemur* and *Hapalemur*, however, are not significantly different in their known morphology from living members of these genera. Although ecoethologically these fossil species may have been distinctive, their morphological details are equivocal in this regard.

Lemur Linnaeus, 1758

(= or including: *Prosimia* Brisson, 1762. *Procebus* Storr, 1780. *Catta* Link, 1806. *Maki* Muirhead, 1819. *Mococo* Trouessart, 1878.)

1. *Lemur catta* Linnaeus, 1758, type species
2. *Lemur macaco* Linnaeus, 1766
3. *Lemur mongoz* Linnaeus, 1766
4. *Lemur fulvus* (E. Geoffroy, 1812)

Hapalemur I. Geoffroy, 1851

(= or including: *Myoxicebus* Lesson, 1840. *Prolemur* Gray, 1871. *Prohapalemur* Lamberton, 1936b.)

1. *Hapalemur griseus* (E. Geoffroy, 1796), type species
2. *Hapalemur simus* (Gray, 1871)

Lepilemur I. Geoffroy, 1851

(= or including: *Galeocebus* Wagner, 1855. *Lepidolemur* Peters, 1874. *Mixocebus* Peters, 1874.)

Lepilemur mustelinus I. Geoffroy, 1851, type species
(= *Lepilemur ruficaudatus* A. Grandidier, 1867.)

VARECIA Gray, 1863

(= or including: *Lemur*: Filhol, 1895, *Pachylemur* Lamberton, 1948, and others in part.)

DISTRIBUTION

Modern (living and subfossil). Madagascar.

KNOWN SPECIES

1. *Varecia variegatus* (Kerr, 1792), type species, living
2. *Varecia insignis* (Filhol, 1895)

(= *Lemur jullyi* Standing, 1905. *Lemur majori* Standing, 1908. *Pachylemur jullyi*: Lamberton, 1948.)

LOCALITIES: Ambolisatra (1266); Ampasambazimba (1270); Ampoza (1272); Anavoha (1273); Andrahomana Cave (1274); Taolambiby (1294).

DISCUSSION

Both species of this genus can be easily delineated from other lemurids based on postcranial and craniodental evidence (Figures 74–76). *Varecia* spp. are distinct from their probably most recent relatives, *Lemur* spp., in having more acute cusps, a less extensive protocone rotated mesially and lacking a well-developed postprotocone crista and thus opening the trigon basin distally, and a continuous broad upper

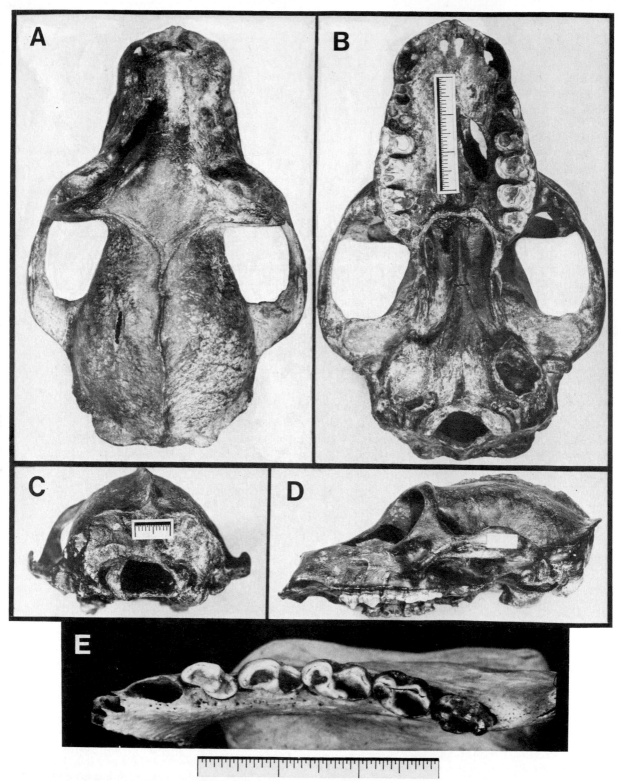

Figure 74. *Varecia insignis.* Modern (subfossil) Madagascar. Skull: A, dorsal view; B, ventral view; C, posterior view; D, lateral view. Right mandible fragment with $P_{\overline{3}}$–$M_{\overline{3}}$: E, occlusal view. Scale on B is 3 cm and on C and D 1 cm. Subdivisions on scale for E represent 0.5 mm.

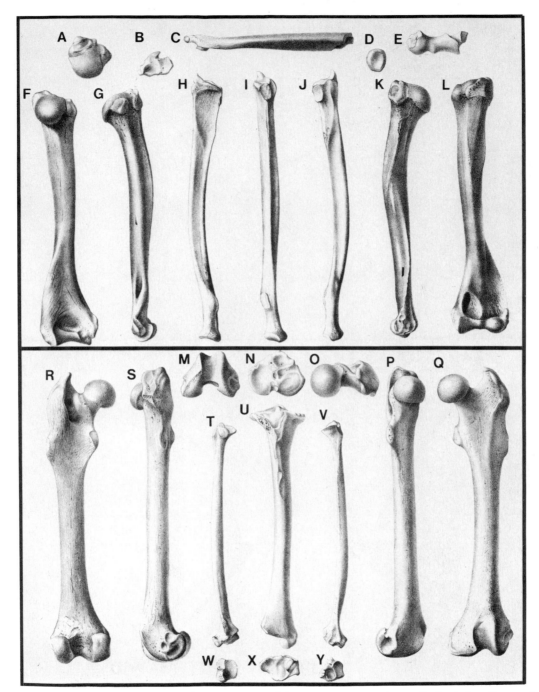

Figure 75. *Varecia insignis.* Modern (subfossil) Madagascar. Left humerus: A, proximal view; E, distal view; F, posterior view; G, medial view; K, lateral view; L, anterior view. Left radius: B, distal view; H, medial view; I, posterior view; J, lateral view; D, proximal view. Broken right ulna: C, lateral view. Left femur: R, posterior view; S, lateral view; M, distal view; O, proximal view; P, medial view; Q, anterior view. Right tibia: N, proximal view; U, anterior view; X, distal view. Right fibula: T, anterior view; V, posterior view; W, distal view; Y, proximal view. [From Grandidier (1905).]

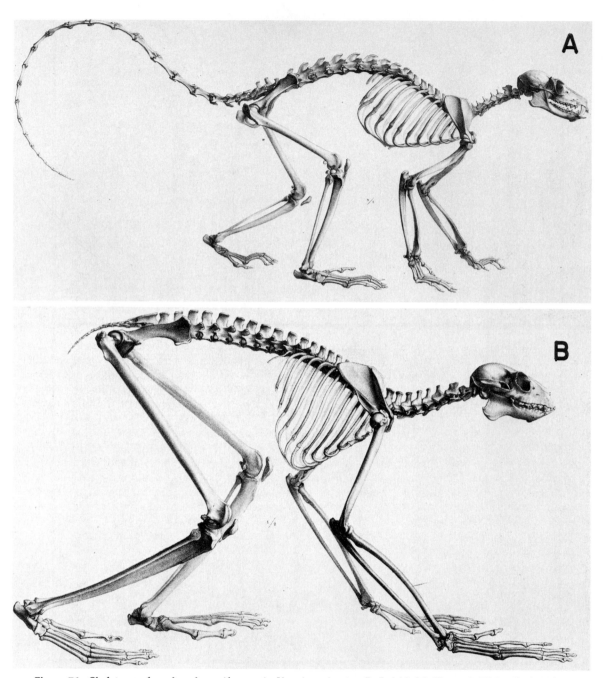

Figure 76. Skeletons of modern lemuriforms: A, *Varecia variegatus*; B, *Indri indri*. [From de Blainville (1839).]

cingulum on the upper molars. The lower molars have a spoutlike exit between the entoconid and the buccal portion of the talonid (for additional characters see Seligsohn and Szalay, 1974; Seligsohn, 1977).

The only recognized subfossil species, *V. insignis*, well represented by both cranial and postcranial remains, was larger than the living species and its postcranial remains were more robust. This form also differed in its limb proportions in that the fore-and hindlimbs were more equal in size than in the arboreal extant *V. variegatus*. The sum total of evidence suggested to one of the most recent students of this genus, Walker (1967), that *Varecia insignis* was to some degree terrestrial, unlike the high canopy-dwelling extant *V. variegatus*, the ruffed lemur. Recently, however, Walker (1974a) has become skeptical of this interpretation and has suggested that subfossils were merely more robust and less agile. In spite of the unreduced, powerful hallux, it was suggested by Decker and Szalay (1974) that this form may have been a frequent ground visitor, as advocated by Walker (1967). This view is based on limb proportions and robusticity, as well as on the relative shallowness of the calcaneocuboid joint.

The dental formula of the fossil species is the same as that of most other lemurids, namely, $I\frac{2}{1,2}$; $C\frac{1}{1}$; $P\frac{2,3,4}{2,3,4}$; $M\frac{1,2,3}{1,2,3}$. *Varecia insignis* was some sort of herbivore, feeding on coarse or tough plant materials.

Family Megaladapidae
Flower and Lydekker, 1891

(= or including: Megaladapinae Flower and Lydekker, 1891. Megaladapidae: Major, 1893.)

DISTRIBUTION
   Modern (subfossil). Madagascar.
INCLUDED TAXA
   Megaladapis.

DISCUSSION

This group is recognized on the basis of its extreme divergence from its closest relatives, the lemurids, and, more specifically, *Lepilemur*. Not only did cranial form and function change very appreciably, but, with the possible exception of palaeopropithecids, the postcranial skeleton of *Megaladapis* is probably the most derived among the Lemuriformes. As far as we know, the adaptive radiation of this group was modest, but, in light of the missing fossil record on Madagascar, this cannot be a meaningful statement.

In addition to such primitive lemuriform characters as the complete lower tooth comb and the bulla enclosed ectotympanic, megaladapids share only a few derived craniodental characters with lemurids, in particular with *Lepilemur* (Tattersall and Schwartz, 1974). *Lepilemur* and megaladapids share a derived condition of the dentary–squamosal joint: in addition to the transverse articular surface of the mandible, a vertical articular area is present medially in both (Tattersall and Schwartz, 1974). The stapedial artery is reduced in *Lepilemur* (Szalay and Katz, 1973), and it appears to be similarly small in *Megaladapis* (Lamberton, 1941; Tattersall and Schwartz, 1975). The remaining morphological characters of the cranium and postcranium, however, are rather unique to megaladapids, not shared with *Lepilemur*, and they are discussed under the genus.

MEGALADAPIS Major, 1894

(= or including: *Peloriadapis* Grandidier, 1899; *Palaeolemur* Lorenz, 1900; *Mesoadapis* Lorenz, 1900; *Megalindris* Standing, 1908.)

DISTRIBUTION
   Modern (subfossil). Madagascar.
KNOWN SPECIES
   1. *Megaladapis madagascariensis* Major, 1894, type species
LOCALITIES: Ambdisatra (1265); Ambolisatra⋆ (1266); Ampoza (1272); Anavoha (1273); Andrahomana Cave (1274); Monombo (1288).

   2. *Megaladapis edwardsi* (G. Grandidier, 1899)
(= *Peloriadapis insignis* Grandidier, 1899; *Megaladapis insignis* Major, 1900; *Palaeolemur destructus* Lorenz, 1900; *Mesoadapis destructus* Lorenz, 1900; *Megaladapis brachycephalus* Lorenz, 1900; *Megaladapis dubius* Lorenz, 1900)
LOCALITIES: Ambolisatra⋆ (1266); Ampoza (1272); Anavoha (1273); Andrahomana Cave (1274); Monombo (1288).

   3. *Megaladapis grandidieri* Standing, 1903
(= *Megalindris gallienii* Standing, 1908.)
LOCALITIES: Ampasambazimba⋆ (1270).

DISCUSSION

Megaladapis (Figures 77 and 78) differs from all other lemuriforms in its unique cranial construction and skeletal morphology. The skull is elongated and the facial skeleton is retroflexed relative to the plane of the cranial base. These features are accompanied by occipital condyles oriented perpendicular to the cranial base and a backward-facing foramen magnum. The auditory bulla is flat and extends out laterally to form a bony auditory meatus, inside which the ectotympanic also extends outward, largely by the ossification of the annulus membrane [but see the important arguments made by MacPhee (1977)]. The auditory meatus, however, is not formed by the ectotympanic but is made up by the petrosal. Although very similar to *Lepilemur* in its cheek teeth, *Megaladapis* differs in having a more inflated ectoloph, lacking an entocristid, and having a metaconulid and a mesiodistally narrower hypoconulid.

The three species differ largely in their absolute size and in the relative size of the cheek teeth from one species to another (Standing, 1908; Lamberton, 1934). The largest was *Megaladapis edwardsi*, with a distribution common in the south and southwest, whereas the smallest, *M. madagascarensis*, had a similar distribution. The intermediate sized *M. grandidieri* has been found only in the central parts of Madagascar (Lamberton, 1941). As noted by Tattersall (1973), the extremely large skulls of *Megaladapis* have given rise to exaggerated views of body size for species of the genus. In fact, the carefully described and sorted (Lamberton, 1956) postcranial skeletal material suggests that the largest animals were in the size range of a 100- to 120-pound dog.

The dental formula of *Megaladapis* was $I\frac{deciduous}{1,2}$; $C\frac{1}{1}$; $P\frac{2,3,4}{2,3,4}$; $M\frac{1,2,3}{1,2,3}$.

As facial elongation in *Megaladapis* is probably related to feeding, so the great elongation of the neurocranium also appears to be related to masticatory requirements (Tattersall, 1973, 1975). The posterior temporalis muscle was enormously enlarged and displaced posteriorly, as the well-developed posterior sagittal and nuchal crests indicate. The anterior temporalis muscle, however, was somewhat reduced. The posterior displacement of the temporalis and the consequent elongation of the neurocranium explain the great development of the frontal sinuses which serve as compensatory space between the facial and neural moieties of the cranium. The relatively small brain (compared to the size of the skull and to other lemuroids) is therefore an artifact produced by the relatively large body size and the relatively large skulls of these animals brought about by the unique masticatory requirements. The deflated nature of the auditory bulla in *Megaladapis*, as in palaeopropithecids, is probably also related to the relatively large size of the skull (Tattersall, 1973), but in what functional manner, aside from allometric factors, is not yet understood.

The postcranial morphology displayed by *Megaladapis* is perhaps one of the most unique among the primates. The convergent similarity of some aspects of the *Megaladapis* skeleton to that of *Phascolarctos*, the koala, is revealing (Walker, 1967). The general differences from the koala lie primarily in the construction of hands and feet; those of *Megaladapis* have long cheiridia and were undoubtedly powerful graspers. From what is known of the individual tarsals, however, the foot does not appear to be typically lemuroid, as it is more modified than those of any of the other known strepsirhines.

The feeding mechanism and preferences of *Megaladapis* spp. appear to be reasonably well understood. The cranial morphology suggests a browsing habit. The loss of permanent upper incisors (as in *Lepilemur*), presumably replaced by a pad, and the long, downwardly curved nasals that overlap the nasal aperture suggest a mobile snout and point to an efficient cropping apparatus. The frontal and nasal bones are thick and highly vascularized on the skull, hinting that thick skin covered these areas. The emphasis on cheek teeth with extremely elongated talonids and mesiodistally running prominent crests strongly suggests folivory, as in *Lepilemur*, rather than fruit-eating habits.

Separate analyses of the feeding and locomotor mechanisms can sometimes be dovetailed to match a fossil form with a living animal analogue. The nocturnal and solitary koala is a habitual leaf-eater, and the habitual posturing of this marsupial is similar to some vertically clinging lemuriforms. This is likely to have been the case for megaladapids, as suggested by Walker (1967a) and Tattersall (1973). Terming the locomotion of the koala (or *Megaladapis*) "vertical clinging and leaping," however, would be an exaggeration of the fact that the living marsupial most often sits on inclined branches or in the forks between them; its occasional leaping is cautious and awkward.

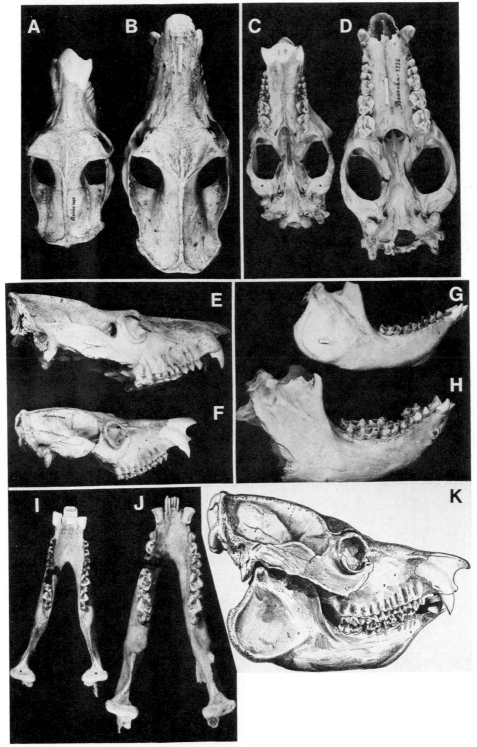

Figure 77. *Megaladapis madagascariensis* (A, C, F, G, I, and K) and *M. edwardsi* (B, D, E, H, and J). Modern (subfossil), Madagascar. Skulls: A and B, dorsal views; C and D, ventral views; E, F, and K, lateral views. Mandibles: G and H, lateral views; I and J, occlusal views. K, lateral view. Scales on B, D, and E represent 3 cm and on G and I 1 cm. [K courtesy of I. Tattersall.]

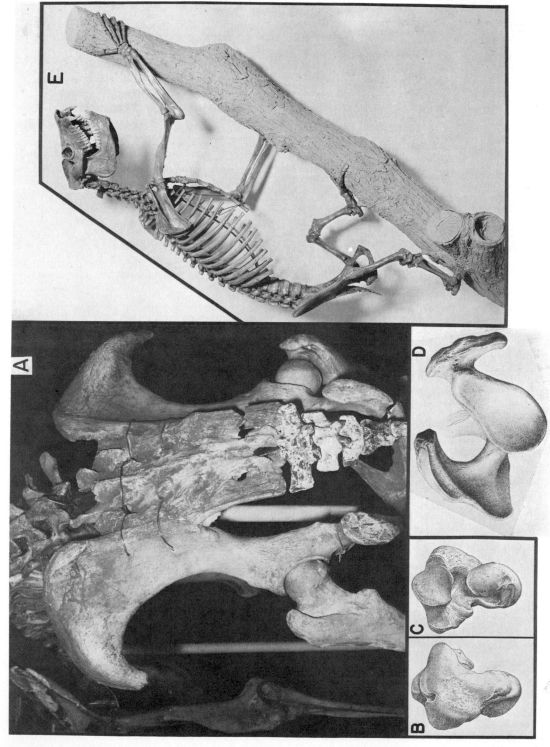

Figure 78. *Megaladapis.* Modern subfossil Madagascar. Pelvic, sacra, and caudal vertebrae, and proximal ends of left femur: A, posterolateral view. Right astragalus: B, dorsal view; C, plantar view. Scapula: D, anteroventral view. Mounted skeleton (E) is largely based on casts of various specimens of *Megaladapis* spp. in the American Museum of Natural History.

Similarly, *Megaladapis* spp. were likely to have been powerful climbers, restive "sitters," and slow moving, occasional cautious jumpers. The construction of the skeleton and the large heads seem to preclude any of the acrobatics associated with the locomotion of the few extant leapers and vertical grasp clingers.

SUPERFAMILY INDRIOIDEA
Burnett, 1828

(= or including: Lemuriformes Gregory, 1915b, in part. Indriiformes Tattersall and Schwartz, 1974.)

DISTRIBUTION
   Modern (living and subfossil). Madagascar.
INCLUDED TAXA
   Families Indriidae, Daubentoniidae, Palaeopropithecidae, and Archaeolemuridae.

DISCUSSION

The studies by Gregory (1920), Lamberton (1939), and, more recently, Tattersall (1973, 1975) and Tattersall and Schwartz (1974, 1975) leave little doubt that the four families included in this superfamily are monophyletic. It is very likely that the ancestor of this group had only four instead of six teeth in the tooth comb and the upper molars had a well-developed hypocone, not unlike the one found in the indriids. According to Tattersall and Schwartz (1974):

[The morphotype of the indrioids] possessed a relatively globular braincase, with a short facial skeleton tucked somewhat beneath it. The orbits were widely separated and fairly well frontated; in the medial orbital wall the frontal was in broad contact with the maxilla. This latter bone was robust and relatively deep. The corpus of the mandible was deep and laterally narrow; the unfused symphysis was long and oblique, with a well-marked genial fossa, and the gonial angle was expanded and well rounded-out. A large digastric was present, reflecting itself in an excavated attachment area on the medial aspect of the horizontal ramus, and in the presence of a salient paroccipital process. The considerably raised condyle possessed an extended, transversely convex articular surface, and reposed in a deep glenoid fossa. The nasal area was high and relatively broad. An inflated bulla was present; the tympanic ring and carotid circulation were as in the indriines. (p. 164)

Although the Indrioidea represent a heterogeneous assemblage of taxa, the anterior dentition of the indriids and the cheek dentition of *Palaeopropithecus*, respectively, may be representative of the dental morphotype for the superfamily.

Given the phylogeny shown in Figure 72, in which *Daubentonia* is shown to share a more recent ancestor with the indriids (*sensu stricto*) than either of these with any other group, classification of the *Archaeolemur–Hadropithecus* and the *Palaeopropithecus–Archaeoindris* groups within the Indriidae is not tenable unless we also classify *Daubentonia* as a subfamily of the Indriidae. Only in this way could we preserve a strict monophyly of this family category. We prefer Daubentoniidae to be maintained here as a family because its habitus and its phenetic divergence from the ancestral indriids are remarkable. It seems important, particularly in such cases, that the already phylogenetically oriented classifications should be tempered by considerations of economy in not using too many names and by adaptational considerations, as difficult as these judgments and decisions may be to make. Moreover, in spite of the greater cranial and postcranial divergence of the palaeopropithecids from the living indriids, it appears that these two groups are more recently related to one another than either is to the Archaeolemuridae.

Family Indriidae
Burnett, 1828

(= or including: Indridae Burnett, 2828. Indrisina I. Geoffroy, 1851. Indrisidae Alston, 1878.)

DISTRIBUTION
   Modern (living and subfossil). Madagascar.

INCLUDED TAXA
   Indri, Propithecus, Avahi, and *Mesopropithecus.*

DISCUSSION

The following living species are known:

Indri E. Geoffroy and Cuvier, 1795
(= or including: *Indris* Cuvier, 1800. *Indrium* Rafinesque, 1815. *Sylvanus* Oken, 1816. *Pithelemur* Lesson, 1840.)
  Indri indri (Gmelin, 1788), type species

Propithecus Bennet, 1832
(= or including: *Macromerus* A. Smith, 1833.)
  1. *Propithecus diadema* Bennet, 1832, type species
  2. *Propithecus verreauxi* A. Grandidier, 1867

Avahi Jourdan, 1834
(= or including: *Lichanotus* Illiger, 1811. *Microrhynchus* Jourdan, 1834. *Habrocebus* Wagner, 1840. *Semnocebus* Lesson, 1840. *Iropocus* Gloger, 1841.)
  Avahi laniger (Gmelin, 1788) type species

The living and subfossil Indriidae are distinguished mainly by the loss of P$\frac{2}{2}$ and the reduction of one pair of teeth from the tooth comb. Thus, the latter, consisting of only two pairs of teeth, is made up by one pair of incisors and the canines. All known indriids have large hypocones on the upper molars, a feature not well developed in lemurids. The morphotype indriid cheek teeth probably closely resembled *Palaeopropithecus*. The face and mandible are usually foreshortened and the mandibular angle is expanded.

Indriids can be distinguished from archaeolemurids in having fewer premolars and in retaining the primitive indrioid incisor–canine morphology. The short and robust anterior teeth of palaeopropithecids, like those of archaeolemurids, are derived when compared to indriids. Whether or not the long snouted diagnostic condition of palaeopropithecids is an advanced (as implied by Tattersall and Schwartz, 1974) or a primitive trait is difficult to determine. All the living indriids are folivorous leapers and vertical grasp clingers. The same probably applies also to *Mesopropithecus*.

The cheek tooth adaptations of the Indriidae appear to have been derived from a structural condition represented by the molar teeth of *Palaeopropithecus ingens*. Seligsohn (1977) has noted that:

The subfossil *Palaeopropithecus*, *Propithecus verreauxi*, *Avahi laniger*, and *Indri indri* form a graded series with molar features associated with crosslophing least evident in *Palaeopropithecus*, and most evident in *Indri*. The transverse alignment and differential relief of the buccal and lingual cusps, the parity in size of the mesial and distal moieties of the molars, the development of crosslophs and the obliteration of the primitive basins, and the shift in the termination of the protocristid from the apex of the metaconid to the centroflexid, are all least evident in *Palaeopropithecus*, somewhat more evident in *Propithecus*, still more demonstrated in *Avahi*, and most greatly demonstrated in *Indri*. These trends in molar features suggest that the functional capacities to both extensively point cut and pleat food are greatest in *Indri*, less in *Avahi* and *Propithecus*, and least by far in *Palaeopropithecus*. (p. 95)

MESOPROPITHECUS Standing, 1905

(= or including: *Neopropithecus* Lamberton, 1936b.)

DISTRIBUTION
  Modern (subfossil). Madagascar.
KNOWN SPECIES
  1. *Mesopropithecus pithecoides* Standing, 1905, type species
LOCALITIES: Ampasambazimba★ (1270).
  2. *Mesopropithecus globiceps* (Lamberton, 1936b)
(=*Neopropithecus globiceps* Lamberton, 1936b; *Neopropithecus platyfrons* Lamberton, 1936b; *Mesopropithecus*: Tattersall, 1971.)
LOCALITIES: Ankazoabo (1275); Bělo-sur-Mer (1278); Lower Menarandra (1286); Tsiravé★ (1296).

DISCUSSION

The two known species are extremely similar to living indriids (Figure 79). Tattersall's (1971) generic separation of *Mesopropithecus* from *Propithecus* is followed here mainly on the basis of postcranial characters (Walker, 1967a). The skulls are approximately in the size range of those of *Indri*, although the cranial proportions are more similar to *Propithecus*. The recognized cranial differences from the latter genus are the slightly smaller and more convergent orbits, more pronounced postorbital constriction, steeper facial angle, great frequency of confluent temporal lines or sagittal crest, distinct nuchal ridge confluent with posterior root of zygoma, robust postorbital bar, more robust mandible, and slightly larger anterior dentition.

The dental formula is the same as in other indriids: I$\frac{2}{2}$; C$\frac{1}{1}$; P$\frac{3}{3}$$\frac{4}{4}$; M$\frac{1}{1}$$\frac{2}{2}$$\frac{3}{3}$.

The bones allocated to this genus in Walker's 1967 studies are distinct from those of other indriids. The short humerus bears a large greater tuberosity, a low

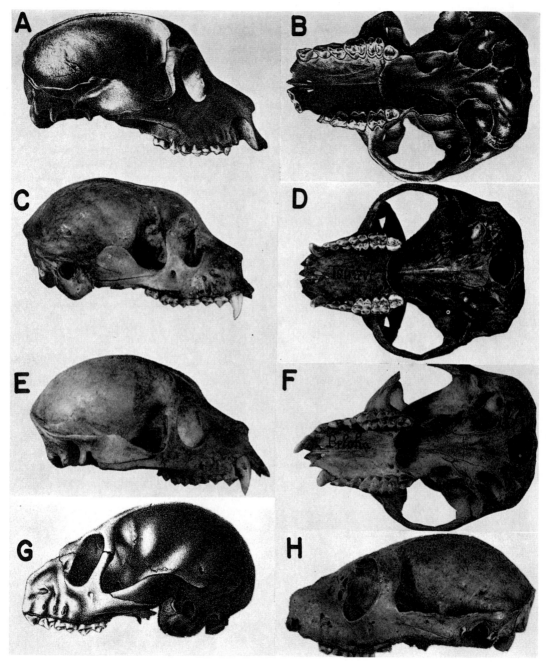

Figure 79. *Mesopropithecus*. Modern subfossils, Madagascar. *Mesopropithecus pithecoides*. Skulls: A and G, lateral views; B, ventral view. *Mesopropithecus globiceps*. Skulls: E, C, and H, lateral views; D and F, ventral views. [From Tattersall (1971).]

deltopectoral crest, a wide brachialis flange, a very large medial epicondyle, and a narrow trochlear surface. The neck of the femur is short and bears a globular head; it also displays a short greater trochanter, a constricted digital fossa, a wide patellar groove, a widely divided *linea aspera,* and an anteroposteriorly flattened shaft. The allocated tibia has expanded extremities, a slightly bowed shaft, and a short, robust malleolus (Walker, 1967a). Providing that the postcranial remains are correctly referred, the combination of these features shows *Mesopropithecus* to have been postcranially quite distinct from other known indriids.

Like the extant indriids, the species of *Mesopropithe-*

pithecus were also probably herbivorous, more specifically folivorous, as inferred from a basically indriid dental apparatus (Seligsohn, 1977). According to Walker (1967a), the postcranial elements allocated to the two known species of *Mesopropithecus* seem to resemble those of *Megaladapis.* Thus, these animals might have been slower, more deliberate, and less saltatorial in their locomotor habits than the acrobatic living indriids. The crural index given by Walker (1967a) for *Mesopropithecus pithecoides* is 98.3, and for *M. globiceps* it is 84.9. As noted by Walker, these indexes fall within the range of living quadrupeds and vertical clingers and leapers.

Family Daubentoniidae
Gray, 1863

(= or including: Cheiromydae Gray, 1821. Daubentoniadae Gray, 1863. Daubentoniidae Gray, 1870. Daubentonioidea Gill, 1872.)

DISTRIBUTION
  Modern (living and subfossil). Madagascar.
INCLUDED TAXA
  Daubentonia.

DISCUSSION

See under *Daubentonia.*

DAUBENTONIA E. Geoffroy, 1795

(= or including: *Scolecophagus* E. Geoffroy, 1795. *Aye-aye* Lacépède, 1799. *Cheiromys* Cuvier, 1800. *Psilodactylus* Oken, 1816. *Myspithecus:* Blainville, 1839. *Myslemur* Blainville, 1846.)

DISTRIBUTION
  Modern (living and subfossil). Madagascar.
KNOWN SPECIES
  1. *Daubentonia madagascariensis* (Gmelin, 1788) type species
  2. *Daubentonia robusta* Lamberton, 1934
LOCALITIES: Tsiravé★ (1296).

DISCUSSION

Daubentonia is known widely because of the convergent specialization of its anterior dentition to those of rodents. Only one living species exists and there is virtually no fossil record for this group except for the large subfossil species of *Daubentonia* represented by postcranials alone, recovered from the Tsiravé locality. The molars of *Daubentonia,* unlike those of indriids, are nearly featureless and flat. These molars are not equipped to point cut but only to crush and grind.

The distinct behavioral and anatomical specializations of *Daubentonia* (Figure 73) are well known and have been recently described in detail by Petter and Petter-Rousseaux (1967). Although *Daubentonia* is clearly highly modified in its cranial and forelimb anatomy, its hindlimb is typically lemuroid in construction. As proposed by Gregory (1915b) and Tattersall and Schwartz (1975), the closest relationships of daubentoniids most likely lie with early indriids (*sensu stricto*). Loss of the tooth comb, acquisition of perpetually growing, gnawing incisors with thick enamel on their mesial borders, correspondingly modified cranial structure and external brain morphology, and a specialized manus are features fully justifying family separation.

The long recognized, highly specialized adaptations of *Daubentonia* can be related to its habit of gnawing open crevices on tree trunks in search of insects. Once found, wood-boring insects are squashed with the long middle finger of the hand. In addition, the aye-

aye is very adept at gnawing open coconuts to get at the nutritious pulp inside. As speculated by Martin (1972), the ancestral shift to *Daubentonia* might have involved a form which had a diet of tree exudates such as sap, and insects living in crevices, which subsequently shifted its specialization to the gnawing–insectivorous habitus. In addition to the aye-aye, the Paleogene eutherian apatemyids and the nocturnal metatherian phalangers *Dactylonax* and *Dactylopsila* have evolved similar adaptations (Cartmill, 1974c). Among living marsupials, feeding habits similar to those of *Daubentonia* corroborate hypotheses of causal relationship between biological roles and the cranial morphology in the genus.

The dental formula is I_1^1; C_0^0; P_0^1; $M_{\frac{1,2,3}{?}}$.

The fossil species has bones approximately 30–50% longer than those of the living form, but the morphological details are virtually identical. The minor differences in details of the known postcranium of *D. robusta* from the living aye-aye were recorded in detail by Lamberton (1934) and subsequently by Walker (1967a). As noted by Walker (1967a): "In his comparison between the proportions of *D. robusta* and *D. madagascariensis* Lamberton found the extinct species to be 17–55% longer and 50–110% more robust than the modern species. The length of the forelimb was 37% more and the length of the hindlimb 19% more than in the modern species."

Family Archaeolemuridae
Major, 1896

(= or including: Nesopithecidae Major 1896. Archaeolemurinae Grandidier, 1905. Hadropithecinae Abel, 1931.)

DISTRIBUTION
  Modern (subfossil). Madagascar.
INCLUDED TAXA
  Archaeolemur and *Hadropithecus*.

DISCUSSION

Archaeolemurids differ from indriids in having retained the original three premolars of the indrioid ancestor. Unlike that of indriids, the ancestral archaeolemurid tooth comb is modified to form robust cutting teeth that function together with the enlarged upper incisors. The cheek teeth of archaeolemurids are mesiodistally more compressed than those of indriids. Archeolemurids have prominent crosslophs which are less sharp than those of indriids. The symphysis, as in palaeopropithecids, but unlike in indriids, is strongly ankylosed and has distinct superior and inferior transverse tori.

The dental formula in both genera is $I_1^{1,2}$; C_1^1; $P_{2,3,4}^{2,3,4}$; $M_{1,2,3}^{1,2,3}$.

The modest archaeolemurid radiation may be characterized by adaptations primarily suited to semiterrestrial modes of life. The archaeolemurids had a neural and peripheral sensory organization not advanced beyond those of living indriids (Tattersall, 1973). Their brain casts show a typically lemuriform pattern in the areas responsible for the organization of the visual, olfactory, and auditory systems. It appears likely that such typically strepsirhine external features of the olfactory apparatus as labial vibrissae, the naked rhinarium, and a naked philtrum were present. Furthermore, it is unlikely that their retina was other than afoveate, a condition characterizing the eyes of living lemuriforms. The cranial differences of archaeolemurids from other indrioids can be explained primarily by the mechanical functions of the feeding mechanisms, both the dentition and the musculature. Amply documented postcranial elements studied by Lamberton (1938) and Walker (1967a) leave little doubt that both genera were semiterrestrial, although adapted to different locomotor behaviors.

ARCHAEOLEMUR Filhol, 1895

(= or including: *Lophiolemur* Filhol, 1895. *Dinolemur* Filhol, 1895, in part. *Nesopithecus* Major, 1896. *Globilemur* Major, 1897. *Bradylemur* Grandidier, 1899. *Protoindris* Lorenz, 1900.)
DISTRIBUTION
  Modern (subfossil). Madagascar.

KNOWN SPECIES
  1. *Archaeolemur majori* Filhol, 1895, type species
  (= *Nesopithecus australis* Major, 1896. *Protoindris globiceps* Lorenz, 1900. *Bradylemur robustus* Grandidier, 1899. *B. bastardi* Grandidier, 1900.)

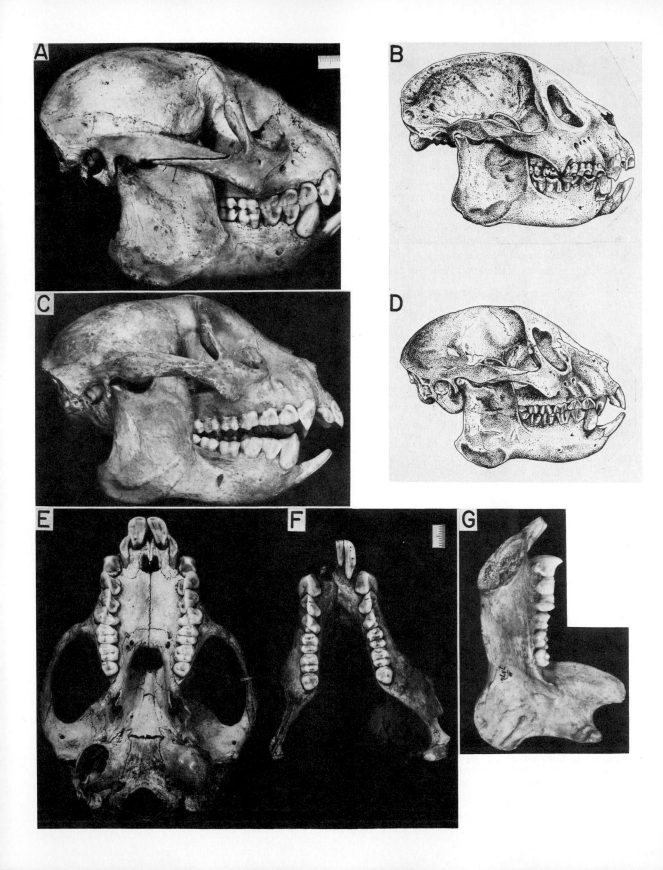

LOCALITIES: Ampoza (1272); Andrahomana Cave (1274); Bélo-sur-Mer★ (1278); Bemafandry (1280); Lamboharana (1284); Lower Menarandra (1286); Manombo (1288); Taolambiby (1294); Tsiravé (1296).

2. *Archaeolemur edwardsi* (Filhol, 1895)
(= *Lophiolemur edwardsi* Filhol, 1895. *Nesopithecus roberti* Major, 1896. *A. platyrrhinus* Standing, 1908.)
LOCALITIES: Amparihingidro (1268); Ampasambazimba (1270); Antsirabe (1276); Bélo-sur-Mer★ (1278); Morarano (1290); Sambaina (1292).

DISCUSSION

Diagnostic differences of *Archaeolemur* (Figures 80 and 81) from *Hadropithecus*, its closest relative, are noted under the latter genus. In almost all respects *Archaeolemur* represents the primitive condition from which *Hadropithecus* evolved.

The two similar-sized species of *Archaeolemur* have bladelike, buccolingually compressed premolars that form a prominent mesiodistally aligned cutting tool, followed by bilophodont molars. Along with the robust lower incisors, the uppers are also greatly enlarged and spatulate. The most important cranial differences from indriids reside largely in the masticatory system of both this genus and *Hadropithecus*. It appears that an early species of *Archaeolemur* was ancestral to *Hadropithecus*, because most of the distinguishing characters of the former genus are present in a more derived condition in *Hadropithecus*.

The studies of Standing (1908), Lamberton (1933, 1937, 1938), Walker (1967a, 1974a), Jolly (1970c), and Tattersall (1973) show that *Archaeolemur* and cercopithecine monkeys have converged in some aspects of their cheek dentitions. The bilophodont nature of the molars, the cutting edge created by the premolars and upper canine, and the enlarged incisors suggest a feeding mechanism well developed for cropping, or, more likely, for husking and pulping some unknown vegetation. The bilophodonty of *Archaeolemur* is distinctly more similar to that of cercopithecines than to that of the colobines. The blunter, cercopithecine-like cheek teeth of these lemuriforms along with the hypertrophied incisors therefore suggest frugivory, or at least a mixed diet not unlike that of various mangabeys, macaques, and baboons.

Lamberton's (1933, 1937, 1938) pioneering and astute works, and some recent studies of the mechanical functions of *Archaeolemur*'s postcranium (Walker, 1967a, 1974a; Decker and Szalay, 1974) indicate a host of characters associated with terrestrial mammals. Nevertheless, the grasping foot of this genus cautions against the conclusion that these species were exclusively terrestrial. The scapula, unlike those of most cursorial terrestrial quadrupeds, is rounded, shaped like an equilateral triangle, and shows signs of relatively large infraspinatus and supraspinatus muscles. On the humerus, the large greater tuberosity is rugose and surpasses the height of the head. Like the previous character, the small brachialis flange is also characteristic of terrestrial monkeys (Jolly, 1965), as is the poorly developed, backwardly and medially directed medial epicondyle. The elbow joint is similar to those of terrestrial quadrupeds. There is a poorly rounded humeral capitulum and poorly differentiated trochlear and capitular surfaces. The olecranon fossa is wide and pronounced. The olecranon process of the ulna is directed posteromedially and the well-excavated radial notch is depressed. The radius is only slightly curved and strongly built with a relatively poorly defined neck. The elbow joint and the forearm reflect adaptations to stability and the efficient transmission of largely compressive forces. The robust femur shows strong bowing of the shaft, a large greater trochanter, and a shallow patellar groove. All of these features are also found in terrestrial monkeys (Jolly, 1965; Walker, 1967a, 1974a).

The foot is reasonably well known. The whole pes is broader (relative to its length) than those of lemurids and indriids, and the calcaneum is exceptionally robust. The differential enlargement of the facets suggests a foot less habitually inverted in *Archaeolemur* than in indriids, for example; this feature is a likely correlate of habitual, although not exclusive, existence on a terrestrial substrate (Decker and Szalay, 1974).

HADROPITHECUS Lorenz, 1899

DISTRIBUTION
Modern (subfossil). Madagascar.
(= or including *Pithecodon* Lorenz, 1900)

KNOWN SPECIES
Hadropithecus stenognathus Lorenz, 1899, type species

Figure 80. *Archaeolemur.* Modern subfossils, Madagascar. *Archaeolemur edwardsi.* Cranium and mandible: A and B, lateral views; E and F, occlusal views of dentition. *Archaeolemur majori.* Cranium and mandible: C and D, lateral views; G, lingual view of mandible with complete dentition. [B and D courtesy of I. Tattersall.]

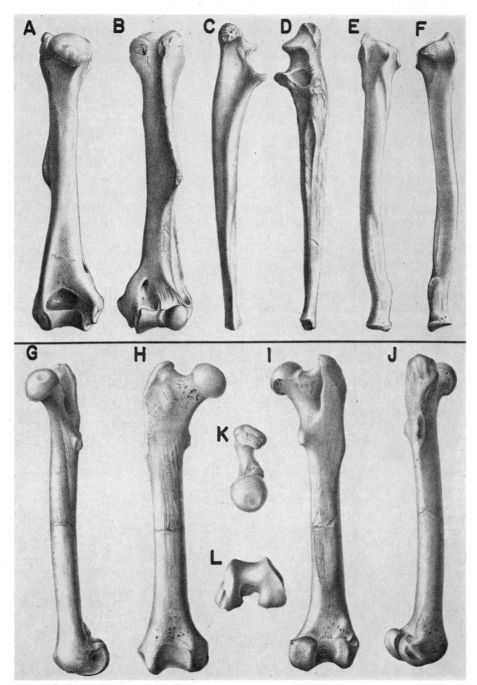

Figure 81. *Archaeolemur* sp. Modern subfossil, Madagascar. Left humerus: A, posterior view; B, anterior view. Left ulna: C, medial view; D, lateral view. Left radius: E, medial view; F, lateral view. Right femur: G, medial view; H, anterior view; I, posterior view; J, lateral view; K, dorsal view; L, distal view. [From Grandidier (1905).]

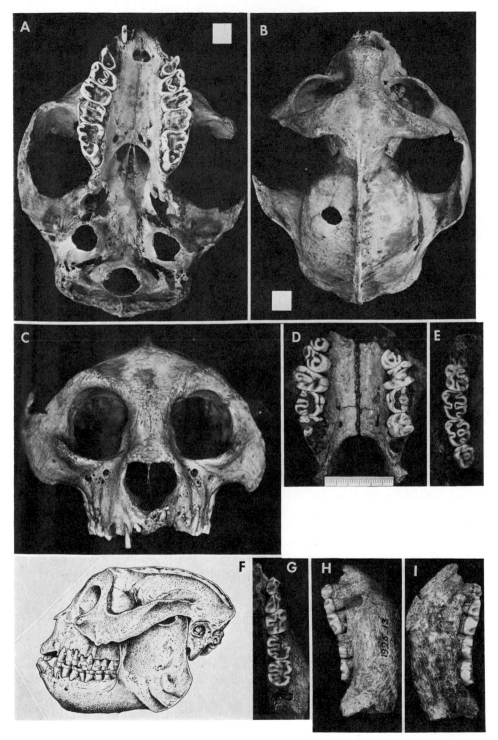

Figure 82. *Hadropithecus stenognathus.* Modern subfossil, Madagascar. Skull: A, ventral view; B, dorsal view; C, frontal view. Palate with right P²–M² and left P³–M²: D, occlusal view. Right mandible fragment with P₄–M₃: E, occlusal view. Reconstructed skull and mandible: F, lateral view. Right mandible fragment with P₂–M₂: G, occlusal view; H, lateral view; I, medial view. Scales on A and B represent 1 cm and that on D 3 cm. [F courtesy of I. Tattersall.]

(= *Pithecodon sikorae* Lorenz, 1900. *Hadropithecus globiceps* Lorenz, 1900. *H. platyfrons* Lamberton, 1936b.)
LOCALITIES: Ampasambazimba (1270); Ampoza (1272); Andrahomana Cave⋆ (1274); Bélo-sur-Mer (1278); Tsiravé (1296).

DISCUSSION

The only known species is similar in cranial size to *Archaeolemur edwardsi* but has a deeper and shorter face. Compared to the postulated ancestral condition similar to *Archaeolemur*, the incisors, the canines, and the caniniform $P_{\overline{2}}$ (anterior dentition) are reduced, whereas the $P_{\overline{4}}^{4}$ and the molars are enlarged. The row of premolar crests found in *Archaeolemur* becomes molarized in *Hadropithecus* (Figure 82). By losing their bladelike function, these teeth acquire additional transversely aligned cutting edges. The low relief bilophodont condition of the molars of the *Archaeolemur* ancestor is further elaborated into additional crests, strongly reminiscent of the shift that has occurred from *Papio*-like teeth to those of *Theropithecus*.

The molars of *Hadropithecus* differ from those of *Archaeolemur* in having sharper crests, mesiodistally more compressed crosslophs, and continuous, robust cingula which surround the molars. Unlike in *Archaeolemur*, in which point-cutting is reduced, wear on *Hadropithecus* molars generates long curved as well as horizontal cutting edges which point-cut extensively (Seligsohn, 1977).

The masticatory system of *Hadropithecus*, like that of the living gelada (see below, under *Theropithecus*), has probably also evolved to masticate the tough and gritty fare of grass rhizomes, seeds, and blades, along with other ground living plants and perhaps also some insects (Jolly, 1970a,c). The convergence of the two genera is remarkable and thus the correlations between the morphology of the feeding mechanism and habitus of the surviving gelada permit a likely partial reconstruction of the dietary ecology of *Hadropithecus*. The drastically reduced incisors and the correspondingly increased cutting edges of the cheek teeth suggest that the incisal preparation required of the foods eaten was minimal. Yet, the wear and tear on cheek teeth caused by this diet was considerable, suggesting a great deal of grit responsible for the heavily worn condition. Like geladas, *Hadropithecus* also possessed a robust mandible and deep maxilla as a mechanical response and solution to a forceful masticatory apparatus and only indirectly to the specific diet postulated. The hypothesized close analogy of the feeding mechanisms of *Hadropithecus* and *Theropithecus* to that of early hominines by Jolly (1970a) is restricted to the hypertrophy of bones and muscles resulting from heavy stressing, but the analogy is absent when the dentition is taken into consideration. The parallel dental adaptations of *Hadropithecus* and *Theropithecus*, therefore, are clear and undoubted, yet any mechanically and biologically significant similarities between these dentitions and those of the postulated hominine morphotype [as suggested by Jolly (1970a) and subsequently endorsed by Tattersall in his 1973 study of *Hadropithecus*] are lacking (see Szalay, 1975e). The dental similarity of *Hadropithecus* to *Theropithecus* strongly suggests a terrestrial lemuriform grazer.

Hadropithecus is not as well known postcranially as *Archaeolemur*. The preserved specimens of this genus are not unlike those of *Archaeolemur* except that they are more slender. This perhaps indicates a form more cursorial than *Archaeolemur*, or even the living *Theropithecus* for that matter. Walker (1967a) made the suggestion that *Hadropithecus* may have been as thoroughly committed to the ground as the patas monkey and that perhaps it was as fast a runner as the living cercopithecine.

Family Palaeopropithecidae
Tattersall, 1973

DISTRIBUTION
  Modern (subfossil). Madagascar.
INCLUDED TAXA
  Palaeopropithecus and *Archaeoindris*.

DISCUSSION

The major differences between this family and the Archaeolemuridae and Indriidae lie in the absolutely larger size of the included genera (a very poor diagnostic feature), the construction of the cranium and postcranium, and the characteristically very long, fused, and nearly horizontal mandibular symphyses. The petrosal is elongated to form an auditory tube (Lamberton, 1941; Saban, 1963), similar to the condition independently evolved by *Megaladapis*. The ectotympanic itself may be elongated inside the petrosal shell, but it is important to note the difference from such groups as tarsiiforms and extant cercopithecids and pongids, which have a tubular ectotympanic outside the petrosal bone. Other distinguishing characteristics of the palaeopropithecids are the upturned and swollen superior portions of the premaxillary bones and the enormously expanded mandibular angles.

The lower incisors and canines of palaeopropithecids lack the narrow-crowned morphology of the corresponding teeth of indriids. They are rather more robust, wider, and more separated from one another. The cheek teeth are characterized by well-developed crests aligned largely mesiodistally. There is little progress toward crosslophing when compared, for example, with a form like *Avahi*.

The dental formula of the known palaeopropithecids is $I_1^{1,2}$; C_1^1; $P_{3,4}^{3,4}$; $M_{1,2,3}^{1,2,3}$.

Although postcranial anatomy is not adequately known, it is evident that the group is very derived when compared, for example, with indriids or daubentoniids, the postcranially most primitive representatives of the indrioids.

PALAEOPROPITHECUS G. Grandidier, 1899

(= or including *Bradytherium* Grandidier, 1901.)
DISTRIBUTION
   Modern (subfossil). Madagascar.
KNOWN SPECIES
(= *Palaeopropithecus maximus* Standing, 1904. *P. raybaudii*, Standing, 1904. *Bradytherium madagascariense* Grandidier, 1901.)
LOCALITIES: Ambalisatra (1267); Amparihingidro (1268); Ampasambazimba (1270); Ampoza (1272); Bélo-sur-Mer★ (1278); Lower Menarandra (1286); Manombo (1288); Morarano (1290); Taolambiby (1294).

DISCUSSION

Palaeopropithecus (Figures 83 and 84) differs from *Archaeoindris*, and also other indrioids, in having the plane of the facial skull, compared to that of the neurocranium, considerably dorsally rotated at the approximate point of the *sella turcica*. This reversed kyphosis, a retroflexion of the facial skull relative to the cranial base, is similar to the condition displayed by the platyrrhine *Alouatta*. Although the angle of the mandible is enlarged in *Archaeoindris*, this condition is further exaggerated in *Palaeopropithecus*.

The primitive indriid-like dentition of *Palaeopropithecus*, coupled with the enlarged incisors which, as noted under the family discussion, no longer form the primitive tooth comb, suggests some form of browsing diet. Whether the staple consisted mainly of fruits or leaves, and what kinds of each, is difficult even to guess. The prominence of the incisors, however, a derived character in both this genus and *Archaeoindris*,

suggests that, following separation from some indriid, the shift to the palaeopropithecid ancestry involved modifications primarily related to the anterior rather than the cheek dentition. As enlarged incisors often imply specialization in cropping and extensive food preparation, this group probably was more frugivorous than, for example, species of *Megaladapis* or the extant indriids. Skull morphology of *Palaeopropithecus* has been treated in detail by Standing (1908) and Lamberton (1934).

Walker (1967a, 1974a), who has studied in detail the known postcranial anatomy of *Palaeopropithecus* (monographed by Lamberton, 1945), suggests that the morphological characteristics of the skeleton may be explained by a locomotor behavior very similar to that of orangutans. The intermembral index (147) is like those of hylobatids and *Pongo*, and the brachial index (95) is closer to the latter than to the former. The crural index (101) exceeds that of *Pongo*.

The glenoid of the scapula in *Palaeopropithecus* faces cranially; along with other features, and taking into account inferred muscular insertions, this suggests a thorax which was habitually suspended. The medial torsion of the head of the humerus is essentially similar to that of hylobatids and *Ateles* (Walker, 1974a), and the low greater and lesser tuberosities suggest a mobile shoulder joint. A strong ridge separates the ball-like capitulum and the well-defined trochlea. The

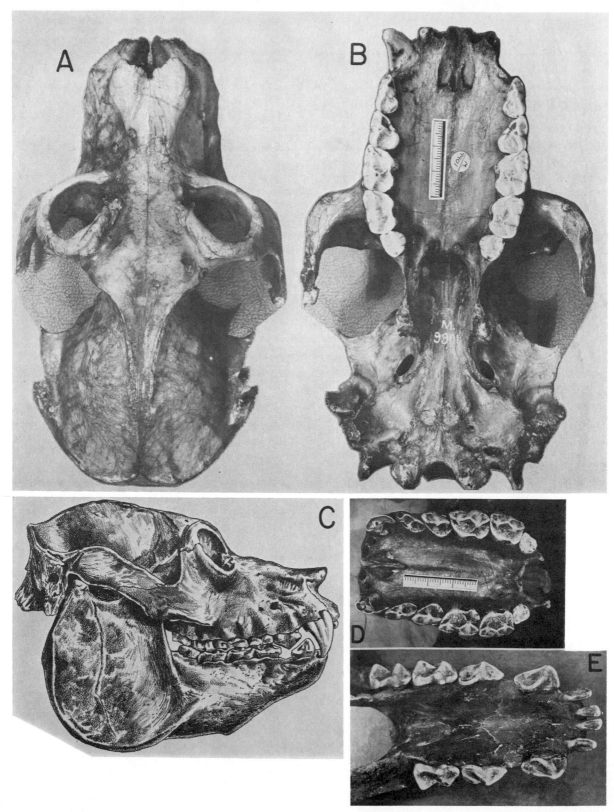

172

ulnar olecranon is strikingly short and the coronoid process is curved backward as in living hylobatids. The long-shafted ulna is convex posteriorly, and the styloid process is well defined with a neck, a condition unlike that of hominoids. The radius has a relatively long neck, a laterally bowed shaft, a well-developed interosseous membrane crest, and an anteriorly tilted carpal surface (Walker, 1974a).

The hand, known only by the 2–5 cheiridia, resembles a long and thin hook (Walker, 1974a). The distal articular surfaces of the long, curved metacarpals and phalanges are grooved, and the grooves for the flexor tendons are strongly developed.

The hindlimb is perhaps even more curious and extremely modified than the forelimb. The pelvis has a long ilium with an anteriorly curving iliac crest and an anterolaterally facing superior iliac spine. The concave ventral iliac surface forms a basin. The ischium is relatively short and the pubis is wide and flat. The sacrum is made up of six fused vertebrae, a record number for lemuriforms. The femur is very sloth-like, yet resembles that of *Pongo* in that the shaft is flattened anteroposteriorly, the neck angulation is high, the greater trochanter is small, and the shallow patellar groove is wide. According to Walker (1974a), there appears to be a premium placed on hip joint mobility rather than stability, and emphasis on adduction rather than extension of the thigh. The tibia and fibula are thin and long and lack malleoli, the latter feature suggesting considerable ankle joint mobility. The foot, known only from phalanges and metatarsals, is hook-like, with well-developed flexors.

There is little doubt that *Palaeopropithecus* was a completely arboreal mammal. Some interpretations in the literature suggest that this form was a brachiator or a slow climber. It seems more likely that this animal was perhaps a sloth-like species, a "four-handed" climber and "hanger" in its locomotor mode, but probably less habitually suspended from all four limbs than sloths.

ARCHAEOINDRIS Standing, 1908

(= or including: *Lemuridotherium* Standing, 1910.)

DISTRIBUTION
  Modern (subfossil). Madagascar.
KNOWN SPECIES
  Archaeoindris fontoynonti Standing, 1908, type species
  (=*Lemuridotherium madagascariensis* Standing, 1910.)
  LOCALITIES: Ampasambazimba★ (1270).

DISCUSSION

Compared to *Palaeopropithecus*, the rare (known by a skull and mandible) and larger *Archaeoindris* (Figure 85) has a slightly less derived indrioid cranial morphology than the former genus to which it is closely related. As in the postulated ancestral indrioids, the face is shorter and the orbits less dorsally oriented than in *Palaeopropithecus*. The teeth are very similar to *Palaeopropithecus*, and the dental formula is the same as in the latter.

Walker (1967), who last studied the meager postcranial remains of *Archaeoindris*, suggests that morphologically the immature bones (femur, tibia, fibula) allocated by Lamberton (1934) to *Archaeoindris* are very similar to those of *Megaladapis*. Humeri and an available ulna are fragmentary and hence poorly known. There is a convergent similarity between the bones (and probably also the locomotor mode) of *Archaeoindris* and *Megaladapis*. Given a generally similar ancestry for both (an indriid for the former and a lemurid for the latter), this convergence is not unexpected for large, tree-dwelling herbivores. Furthermore, if we accept the poor postcranial evidence at face value, *Archaeoindris* is not only cranially but also postcranially more primitive than *Palaeopropithecus*.

Archaeoindris was probably a folivore.

Figure 83. *Paleopropithecus ingens*. Modern (subfossil), Madagascar. Skull: A, dorsal view; B, ventral view. Reconstructed skull and mandible: C, lateral view. Palate with C–M^3: D, occlusal view. Mandible showing posterior limit of symphysis extending back to M_2: E, dorsal view. Subdivisions on scales represent 0.5 mm. [C courtesy of I. Tattersall.]

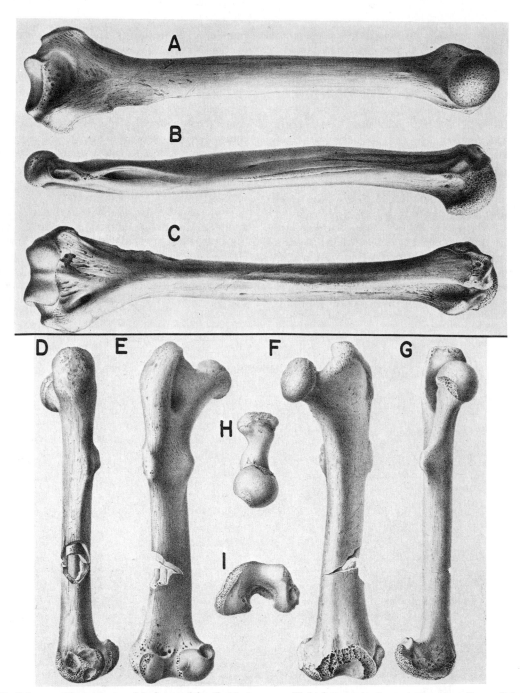

Figure 84. *Palaeopropithecus ingens.* Modern subfossil, Madagascar. Right humerus: A, posterior view; B, medial view; C, anterior view. Left femur: D, lateral view; E, posterior view; F, anterior view; G, medial view; H, dorsal view; I, distal view. [From Grandidier (1905).]

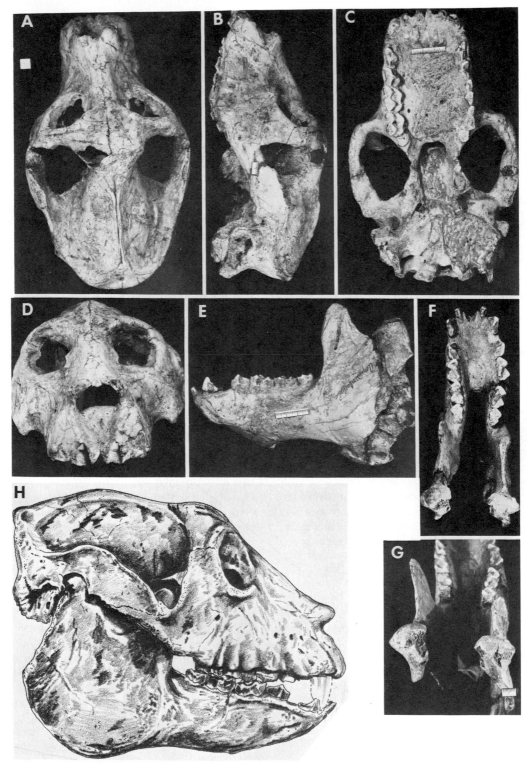

Figure 85. *Archaeoindris fontoynonti.* Modern subfossil, Madagascar. Skull with right P^3–M^3 and left P^2–M^4. A, dorsal view; B, lateral view; C, ventral view; D, frontal view. Right side of mandible showing C, P$_{\overline{2}}$, and P$_{\overline{4}}$–M$_{\overline{3}}$: E, lateral view; F, occlusal view. Distal view of articular condyles of mandible showing right C, P$_{\overline{2}}$, and P$_{\overline{4}}$–M$_{\overline{3}}$: G. Reconstructed skull and mandible: H, lateral view. Scales on mandible (E) and palate (C) represent 3 cm. Scales on B and G represent 1 cm. [H courtesy of I. Tattersall.]

SUPERFAMILY LORISOIDEA
Gray, 1821

(= or including: Loridae Gray, 1821, in part. Nycticebidae Nicholson 1870, in part. Lorisiformes Gregory, 1915b, in part; Lemuroidea of past authors in part; Lorisoidea: Szalay, 1975f.)

DISTRIBUTION
  Early Miocene (Rusingan) to modern. Africa and Asia.
INCLUDED TAXA
  Families Cheirogaleidae and Lorisidae.

DISCUSSION

It appears very probable that the source of the common ancestor of galagines, lorisines, and the Miocene lorisids was a taxon that, if known, would be unquestionably allocated on patristic grounds to the Cheirogaleidae (Szalay and Katz, 1973; Szalay, 1975f). Because this latter group of primates has a number of derived character states that are present or have further evolved in the lorisids, we consider it important to classify the Cheirogaleidae within the Lorisoidea. Although there is general agreement with the phylogeny advocated by Szalay and Katz (1973) and Szalay (1975f), acceptance of this schema of classification is still not unanimous (Cartmill, 1975). Because the most diagnostic of the distinguishing character states of the lorisids are also present in the Cheirogaleidae, a meaningful definition of lorisoids cannot exclude them. The enlarged ascending pharyngeal artery and the anterior carotid foramen are distinct specializations shared only by the taxa allocated to the Lorisoidea. This superfamily is then monophyletic, containing the ancestral group of this taxon which diverged from lemuroid lemuriforms. The heuristic merit of this classification lies in uniting the primitive (Cheirogaleidae) and advanced (Lorisidae) groups which not only represent and contain various levels of derived organizations but are each monophyletic taxa. In addition to the morphological characters, there are some shared derived aspects of their way of life (nocturnal insectivory) which are likely due to derivation from the lorisoid ancestor.

The ancestral lorisoid probably possessed an ear region not unlike that found in cheirogaleids. This form probably had an enlarged ascending pharyngeal artery and an anterior carotid foramen, as well as a promontory artery which was relatively larger than the greatly reduced stapedial artery. This relationship merely reflects the reduced role of the stapedial, rather than the increase in size of the promontory artery. The carotid entered the bulla posteriomedially.

The dental morphology of lorisoids suggests that one of the most characteristic features of this group, aside from a complete tooth comb inherited from a lemurid ancestry, is the hypocone of the first and second upper molars. As in *Microcebus* and the lorisids, this cusp is usually tear-shaped and quite distolingual on the tooth. *Phaner*, *Allocebus*, and *Cheirogaleus* represent the primitive cheirogaleid molar morphology, which evolved as a response to the highly gumivorous diet pursued by the cheirogaleid ancestry. The dental formula is $I\frac{2}{2}$; $C\frac{1}{1}$; $P\frac{2,3,4}{2,3,4}$; $M\frac{1,2,3}{1,2,3}$.

Family Cheirogaleidae
Gray, 1872

(= or including: Microcebina Gray, 1870. Cheirogaleina, Gray 1872. Cheirogaleinae Gregory, 1915b.)

DISTRIBUTION
  Modern (living and subfossil). Madagascar.
INCLUDED TAXA
  Cheirogaleus, *Microcebus*, *Phaner*, and *Allocebus*.

DISCUSSION

As noted under the Lorisoidea, the family was transferred by Szalay (1975f) from the Lemuroidea to the Lorisoidea, for reasons that are rooted in their phylogenetic relationships and their overall morphology as well as in their mode of life.

All of the cheirogaleids, as all the known lorisids, are small, nocturnal primates which are to a marked degree insectivorous as well as often gum and resin feeders. Whether or not this mode of life was attained from largely diurnal, more herbivorous lemurids is difficult to corroborate, but it seems likely. Judged from the morphocline polarities of a number of characters which strongly suggest a lemurid→cheirogaleid→lorisid derivation sequence, insectivory and resin feeding are probably the derived mode of life among the tooth-combed strepsirhines (see discussion under Strepsirhini, pp. 102–104).

There are no known fossil cheirogaleid taxa, with the exception of some subfossil representatives of living forms. The following living genera and species are known:

Cheirogaleus E. Geoffroy, 1812

(= or including: *Myspithecus* F. Cuvier, 1833. *Cebugale* Lesson, 1840. *Myscebus* Lesson, 1840. *Myocebus* Wagner, 1841. *Myslemur* Blainville, 1846. *Opolemur* Gray, 1872. *Chirogale*: Major, 1894.)

1. *Cheirogaleus major* E. Geoffroy, 1812, type species
2. *Cheirogaleus medius* E. Geoffroy, 1812

Phaner Gray, 1870

(= or including: *Lemur*: Blainville, 1839. *Cheirogaleus*: I. Geoffroy, 1850.)

Phaner furcifer, 1839, type species

Allocebus Petter-Rousseaux and Petter, 1967

(= or including: *Chirogaleus*: Gunther, 1875. *Chirogale*: Major, 1894.)

Allocebus trichotis (Gunther, 1875) type species

Microcebus E. Geoffroy, 1828

(= or including: *Scartes* Swainson, 1835. *Gliscebus* Lesson, 1840. *Mirza* Gray, 1870. *Azema* Gray, 1870. *Muirlemur* Gray, 1870.)

1. *Microcebus murinus* (Miller, 1777), type species
2. *Microcebus coquereli* (A. Grandidier, 1866)

Microcebus is found throughout Madagascar in all sorts of habitats including scrub, brush, woodland, and forests. The nocturnal mouse lemurs are insectivorous and to some degree frugivorous. *Cheirogaleus*

has a similar distribution; its two species occupy the eastern (*C. major*) and western (*C. medius*) part of the island. *Phaner* is distributed on the northern and western parts of Madagascar. The diverse morphology within the Cheirogaleidae makes assessment of a morphotype difficult. Dentally perhaps *Cheirogaleus* comes closest to a reconstructed common ancestor. (Seligsohn, 1977).

According to Seligsohn (1977), the molars of *Cheirogaleus major* "greatly differ from those of *Phaner*, and especially from those of *Microcebus* in demonstrating greater mesio-distal width, very blunt, squat cusps of exceedingly low relief, crests of minimal length, salience and sharpness, and basins which are virtually undefined. These features all suggest greatly reduced functional emphases on point penetration and point-cutting, and instead suggest capabilities limited almost totally to crushing and grinding" (p. 92).

Molars of *Microcebus murinus* differ from those of *Cheirogaleus* "in demonstrating great mesio-distal constriction, more conical cusps of relatively great relief and acuity, respective trigon and talonid basins of great depth, concavity and mesio-distal confinement, and relatively long, salient, sharp-edged crests. These features suggest much greater functional emphases on point penetration and 'vertical' point cutting" (Seligsohn, 1977, p. 93).

Furthermore, this author notes that the molars of *Phaner furcifer* "differ from those of *Microcebus* in being mesio-distally slightly wider, with slightly reduced cusp relief and acuity. Molars also demonstrate a great reduction in relative size. The functional capabilities of the M^2 and $M_{\overline{2}}$ of *Phaner* are similar to, but somewhat more reduced than, those of *Microcebus*" (Seligsohn, 1977, p. 93).

Family Lorisidae
Gray, 1821

(= or including: Loridae Gray, 1821. Nycticebinae Mivart, 1864. Nycticebidae Nicholson, 1870. Lorisidae Gregory, 1915b. Galagidae of authors.)

DISTRIBUTION
  Early Miocene (Rusingan) to modern. Africa and southern Asia.
INCLUDED TAXA
  Subfamilies Galaginae and Lorisinae.

DISCUSSION

This group of lorisoids differs from the closely related cheirogaleids primarily in having the ectotympanic usually outside the bulla proper in the form of either a ring (e.g., *Galago*) or a bony plate (e.g., *Nycticebus*) and, as in *Allocebus* (see Cartmill, 1975) but

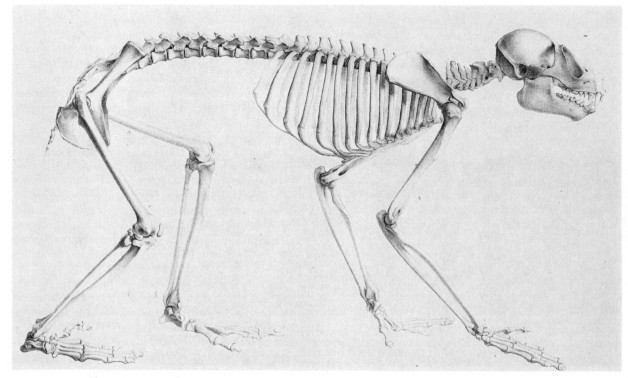

Figure 86. *Nycticebus coucang.* Modern, southeast Asia. Skeleton. [From de Blainville (1839).]

not in other cheirogaleids, having a distinctly inflated petromastoid broadly continuous with the auditory bulla proper. The middle ear cavity is subdivided by numerous septae, and the sinus in the petromastoid is probably continuous with the medial sinus of the middle ear cavity.

The fossil record of this family (see Figures 86–92) is restricted to the early Miocene of eastern Africa. The remains consist of two skulls, numerous dentitions, and some fragmentary, but well-preserved, postcranial specimens (Figures 87–90). The Miocene African occurrence of the lorisids clearly represents only a minimum date for the distinctness of the lorisids and their presence at this time obviously does not rule out their Asiatic existence.

Walker (1974b), in his recent study of the Miocene lorisids, suggested a number of distinguishing features in cranial construction which appear to differentiate the two subfamilies. These are discussed under the respective taxa.

Of the living galagines, *Euoticus* is distributed in the forest belt along the Niger in Guinea and also in Zaire.

Galago senegalensis is found in savannahs and scrub throughout the Sudan and most of East Africa. *Galago crassicaudatus* is pan East African, in savannah and scrub country, whereas *G. alleni* is confined to the forests of Gabon and parts of the Cameroons. *Galagoides* is found in the rain forest belt from Senegal, through Fernando Po into the eastern Rift Valley.

Of the living lorisines, *Arctocebus*, the angwantibo or golden potto, is found in thick forests of West Africa. It is an unusual dietary specialist inasmuch as it feeds on noxious caterpillars. *Perodicticus*, the potto, is essentially equatorial in its distribution in Africa. *Loris*, the slender loris, is found in some forests of southern India and the island of Ceylon. *Nycticebus*, the slow loris, occurs in the forests of Burma and Vietnam and on some islands of Indonesia, such as Borneo, Java, Banka and Natuna.

The Galaginae is dentally fairly homogeneous and perhaps *Galago alleni* reflects the morphotype condition for the dentition. Of the more varied Lorisinae, *Nycticebus* appears to be closest to an ancestral dental condition (Seligsohn, 1977).

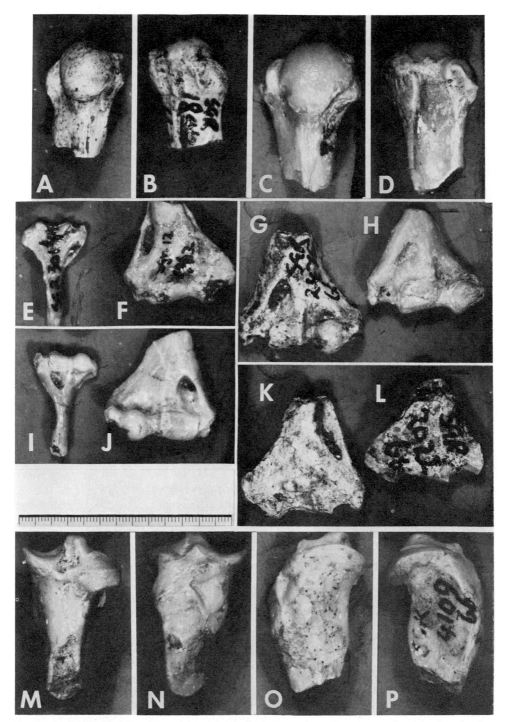

Figure 87. Postcranial fragments of early Miocene lorisids from East Africa. Fragments of proximal ends of humeri: A–D. Fragments of proximal ends of humeri: E–L. Fragments of proximal end of tibia: M–P. Subdivisions on scale represent 0.5 mm.

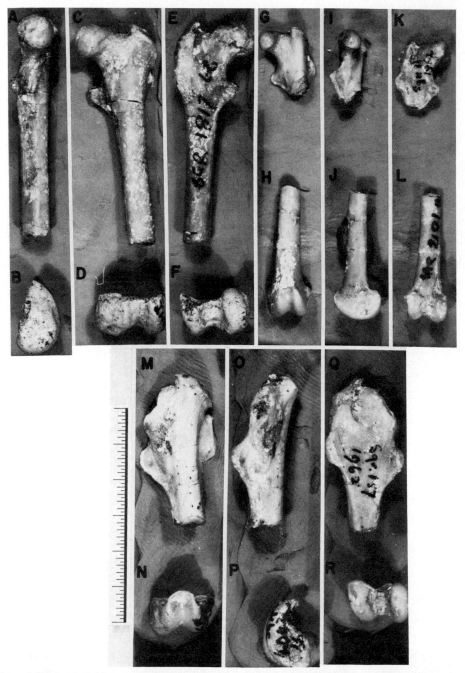

Figure 88. African Miocene lorisid postcranial remains. Left proximal and distal femur fragment (A–F). Left proximal and distal femur fragment (G–L). Right proximal and distal femur fragment (M–R). Subdivisions on scale represent 0.5 mm.

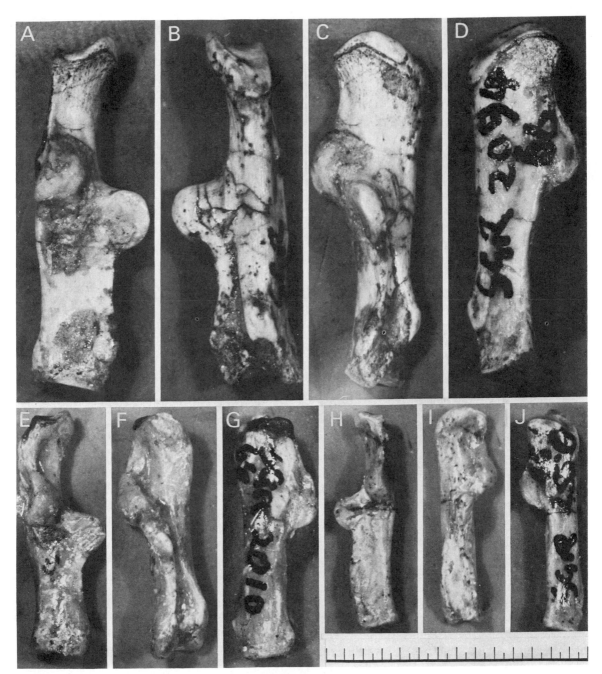

Figure 89. African Miocene lorisid calcanea. Right calcaneum: A, dorsal view; B, ventral view; C, medial view; D, lateral view. Right calcaneum: E, dorsal view; F, medial view; G, lateral view. Left calcaneum: H, dorsal view; I, medial view; J, dorsal view. Subdivisions on scale represent 0.5 mm.

A landmark on the eco-ethology of five West African lorisoid species was recently published by Charles-Dominique (1977). It is also the most complete and best general source on the ecology and behavior of nocturnal primates.

SUBFAMILY GALAGINAE
Gray, 1825

(= or including: Galagonina Gray, 1825. Galaginae Mivart, 1864. Galaginidae Alston, 1878.)

DISTRIBUTION
Early Miocene (Rusingan), early Pleistocene (late Rodolfian) to modern. Africa.
INCLUDED TAXA
Galago, Galagoides, Euoticus, Progalago, and *Komba.*

DISCUSSION

The following living genera and species are known:

Galago E. Geoffroy, 1796

(= or including: *Chirosciurus* Cuvier and Geoffroy, 1795, nomen nudum. *Macropus:* Fischer, 1811. *Otolicnus* Illiger, 1811. *Otolemur* Coquerel, 1859. *Callotus* Gray, 1863.)

1. *Galago senegalensis* E. Geoffroy, 1796, type species
   FOSSIL LOCALITIES: Olduvai Bed I (760)
2. *Galago crassicaudatus* E. Geoffroy, 1812
3. *Galago alleni* Waterhouse, 1837

Galagoides A. Smith, 1833

(= or including: *Mioxicebus:* Lesson, 1840. *Otolicnus:* Temminick, 1853. *Hemigalago* Dahlbom, 1857.)

Galagoides demidovii (Fischer, 1806), type species

Euoticus Gray, 1863

(= or including: *Otogale* Gray, 1863.)

Euoticus elegantulus (Le Conte, 1857), type species

The living galagine primates are best characterized by the striking specializations of some aspects of their postcranial anatomy. These quickly running, often leaping animals have greatly elongated calcanea and naviculars, and in general their hindlegs are elongated. Their tails are long and the lumbar parapophyses are elongated. The femur has a small third trochanter, in contrast to the lorisines in which this process seems

to be most reduced. The spines of the twelfth and thirteenth dorsal vertebrae are directed forward, unlike those of lorisines, which are directed backward.

Galagine cranial morphology may be characterized (Walker, 1974b) by light construction, weak temporal lines, fairly laterally directed orbits, slender postorbital process and zygomatic arch, and strongly inflated bullae and petromastoid. The zygomatic branch of the squamosal is entirely in front of the external auditory meatus and, unlike in lorisines, the posterior nares are usually behind the second and not the third upper molar.

The galagines, in contrast to the cheirogaleids and lorisines, appear to be less diverse dentally. According to Seligsohn (1977), the morphotype condition for the subfamily is most closely approximated by the cheek teeth of *Galago alleni.* In spite of the rough resemblances of the cheek teeth among galagines, there are instructive, morphological, and mechanical differences. Seligsohn (1977) notes that:

> [The molars of *Galago crassicaudatus,*] when compared to those of *G. senegalensis,* demonstrate greatly reduced cusp relief and acuity, greatly rounded crest edges, greatly reduced basin depth, concavity, and confinement, and greater mesio-distal width.
> These features appear to suggest that point penetration and "vertical" point-cutting are greatly de-emphasized functions, while low penetrative, incusive functions are emphasized.... The ... molars of *G. senegalensis,* by contrast, demonstrate great mesio-distal constriction, conical cusps of very great relief and acuity, basins of great depth, concavity and mesio-distal confinement, and a marked emphasis on transversely oriented, sharp-edged crests which demonstrate greater relief.
> These features suggest that efficient point penetration and "vertical" point-cutting are very strongly emphasized functions. (p. 93)

Seligsohn (1977) further observes that the molars of *Galagoides demidovii* "are very similar to those of *G. senegalensis,* both morphologically and functionally, except, most notably, for the fact that the molars of the former species demonstrate crests of somewhat greater sharpness and angularity" (p. 94). On the other hand (Seligsohn, 1977), the molars of *Euoticus elegantulus* "are similar to those of *G. demidovii,* but differ from those of the latter in being more mesiodistally elongated. They also demonstrate cusps of slightly lower relief and acuity, basins of somewhat less depth and concavity, and crests of less transverse orientation. The molars also demonstrate a great reduction in relative size. These features suggest the

somewhat reduced functional emphases on point penetration and 'vertical' point-cutting" (p. 94).

PROGALAGO MacInnes, 1943

DISTRIBUTION
Early Miocene (Rusingan). East Africa.
KNOWN SPECIES
1. *Progalago dorae* MacInnes, 1943, type species
LOCALITIES: Songhor★ (396); Napak (402).
2. *Progalago songhorensis* Simpson, 1967
LOCALITIES: Songhor★ (396); Rusinga (406).

DISCUSSION

The two known species of this genus (Figure 90) are approximately in the size range of the extant *Galago crassicaudatus*. One of the distinctive characters is the posteriorly deepening mandible, reaching its greatest depth under M3. In contrast to *Progalago*, for example, posterior deepening of the mandible does not occur in *Komba*. Molars are low crowned with equally high trigonids and talonids, and the trigonids are greatly constricted mesiodistally. Of the two species, *P. dorae* is the larger and has slightly shorter molar trigonids and more expanded talonids. As in *Komba*, the elliptically shaped symphyseal surfaces are not fused, and all known specimens possess a well-developed inferior symphyseal tubercle for the insertion of the

anterior belly of the digastric muscle. The dentitions of *Progalago* are, in general, more bunodont than those of *Komba*. Mental foramina on known mandibles of this genus are single.

The upper molars of *Progalago* are very similar to those of *Galago*, but differ from the latter in having less distinct hypocones and transversely less wide teeth. The fourth upper premolar of *Progalago*, like that of *Komba*, is not very molariform. The third molars in the fossils *Progalago* and *Komba*, unlike those of modern species of this subfamily, are not as reduced.

The dental formula appears to have been the same as in living lorisids. The last major study of the genus is by Simpson (1967).

Progalago spp. were animals with greatly enlarged internal pterygoid and superficial masseter muscles. These enlarged muscles, coupled with a relatively bunodont dentition characterized by enlarged talonids, suggest emphasis on either puncturing or crushing or more likely on the buccal phase of the masticatory cycle. These forms were unlikely to have been purely insectivorous; they were more likely to have been frugivorous and insectivorous.

KOMBA Simpson, 1967

(= or including: *Progalago*: Le Gros Clark and Thomas, 1952, in part.)

DISTRIBUTION
Early Miocene. East Africa.
KNOWN SPECIES
1. *Komba robustus* (Le Gros Clark and Thomas, 1952), type species
(=*Progalago robustus* Le Gros Clark and Thomas, 1952.)
LOCALITIES: Koru (394); Songhor★ (396); Napak (402); Rusinga (406); Mwfangano (408).
2. *Komba minor* (Le Gros Clark and Thomas, 1952)
(=*Progalago minor* Le Gros Clark and Thomas, 1952.)
LOCALITIES: Songhor★ (396); Napak (402); Moroto 2 (404); Rusinga (406).

DISCUSSION

As noted under *Progalago*, the genus to which *Komba* (Figure 91) in many ways appears to be most similar, these are lorisids with a generally similar dentition to the extant genera. *Komba* differs from *Progalago* in having molars with sharper cusps. P4 has a talonid relatively narrower than that of *Progalago*, and in general the trigonids are larger and the molar trigonids are higher than the talonids. Unlike in *Progalago*, the mandible does not progressively

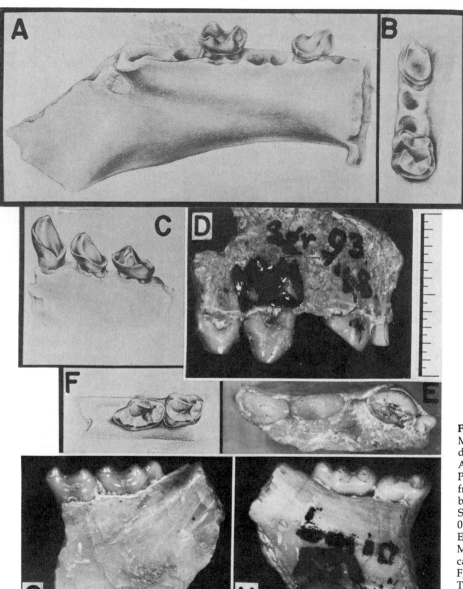

Figure 90. *Progalago dorae.* Early Miocene, East Africa. Left mandible fragment with $P_{\overline{4}}$ and $M_{\overline{2}}$: A, lingual view; B, occlusal view. $P_{\overline{2}}$–$P_{\overline{4}}$: C, lingual view. Maxilla fragment with I^2, C, P^2–P^3: D, buccal view; E, occlusal view. Subdivisions on scale represent 0.5 mm. *Progalago songhorensis.* Early Miocene, East Africa. Left $M_{\overline{2}}$–$M_{\overline{3}}$: F, occlusal view; G, buccal view; H, lingual view. [A–C, F, G from Le Gros Clark and Thomas (1952) by permission of the Trustees of the British Museum (Natural History).]

deepen posteriorly; it is shallow under $M_{\overline{3}}$. The dental formula is the same as in the other lorisids.

Komba robustus is much larger than *K. minor.* The latter, unlike the former, has buccal cingulids on the lower molars. As Simpson (1967) noted, the differences between the two species are morphologically very distinct, and furthermore the generic separation of *Komba* from *Progalago* seems well founded. In contrast to *Progalago,* species of *Komba* appear to have been primarily insectivorous.

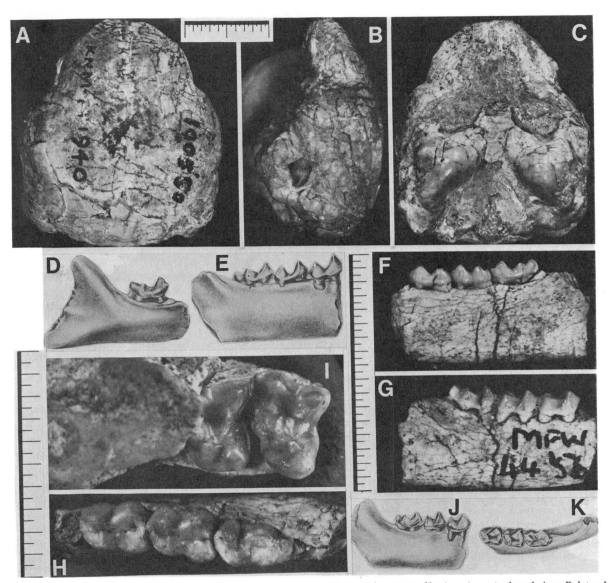

Figure 91. *Komba robustus.* Early Miocene, East Africa. Endocast with skull fragment of basicranium: A, dorsal view; B, lateral view; C, ventral view. Right $M_{\overline{3}}$ in jaw fragment: D, lateral view. Right $M_{\overline{1-3}}$ in jaw fragment: E, lateral view. Left M^{1-2} in maxilla fragment: I, occlusal view. Right $M_{\overline{1-3}}$ in jaw fragment: F, medial view; G, lateral view; H, occlusal view. *Komba minor.* Early Miocene, East Africa. Right $M_{\overline{1-3}}$ in jaw fragment: J, lateral view; K, occlusal view. Subdivisions on scales represent 0.5 mm. [D, E, J, K from Le Gros Clark and Thomas (1952) by permission of the Trustees of the British Museum (Natural History).]

SUBFAMILY LORISINAE
Gray, 1821

DISTRIBUTION
Early Miocene (Rusingan) to modern. Africa and southeast Asia.
INCLUDED TAXA
Loris, Nycticebus, Arctocebus, Perodicticus, and *Mioeuoticus.*

DISCUSSION

The following living genera and species are known:

Loris E. Geoffroy, 1796
(= or including: *Tardigradus* Boddaert, 1784. *Lori* Lacépède, 1799.
Stenops Illiger, 1811. *Loridium* Rafinesque, 1840.)
   Loris tardigradus (Linnaeus, 1758), type species

Nycticebus E. Geoffroy, 1812
(= or including: *Bradycebus* Gervais, 1836. *Stenops:* Van der Hoeven,
1834. *Bradylemur* Blainville, 1839.)
   Nycticebus coucang (Boddaert, 1784), type species

Arctocebus Gray, 1863
   Arctocebus calabarensis (Smith, 1860), type species

Perodicticus Bennet, 1831
(= or including: *Potto* Lesson, 1840.)
   Perodicticus potto (E. Geoffroy, 1812), type species

The living lorisine primates (see Figure 86, for
example), as the galagines, are quite specialized in
their postcranial anatomy. These slow, deliberate
climbers and stealthy stalkers of prey have powerful
grasping extremities. Their tails are very short and the
lumbar parapophyses are shortened.

Lorisine cranial morphology may be characterized
(Walker, 1974b) by strong construction, raised and
distinct temporal ridges, a wide occiput, forwardly
directed (convergent) orbits, a wide postorbital process, a stout zygomatic arch, and moderately inflated
bullae and petromastoids. The zygomatic branch of
the squamosal is continuous with the external auditory meatus. An equally characteristic feature is the
opening of the posterior nares usually behind the last
upper molar.

A recent study by Cartmill and Milton (1977) has
revealed a number of interesting adaptations in the
wrist joint of lorisines. These authors note that in
lorisines "the tip of the ulna is reduced to the
dimensions of a styloid process, a new and more

proximal ulnar head is developed, and the pisiform is
displaced distally away from its primitive contact with
the ulna. In some *Nycticebus,* intra-articular tissues
separate the ulna from the triquetrum. These traits are
not seen in other quadrupedal primates, but they are
characteristic of extant hominoids. Among hominoids, these features have been interpreted as
adaptations to arm-swinging locomotion. Since
hominoid-like features of the wrist joint are found in
lorisines, but not in New World monkeys that practice
arm-swinging locomotion, these features may have
been evolved in both lorisines and large hominoids to
enhance wrist mobility for cautious arboreal locomotion involving little or no leaping" (p. 249). We might
add that the common selectional force in the two
groups appears to be the need to both hang and freely
rotate the wrist in a range of positions under branches.
These adaptations in the lorisines clearly postdate the
galagine–lorisine separation.

In contrast to the Galaginae, dental morphology in
the Lorisinae is somewhat more diversified due to
some extreme dietary specializations (see especially
Charles-Dominique, 1977). As Seligsohn (1977) notes,
the intergeneric variability renders morphotype
reconstruction difficult, although he suggests that the
dentition of *Nycticebus* perhaps most closely approximates the ancestral condition. The molars of
Nycticebus "are very similar to those of *Perodicticus,* but
differ from those of the latter in demonstrating
somewhat greater cusp and crest relief, and basin
depth. These features perhaps suggest that the molars
of *Nycticebus* somewhat more efficiently perform point
penetration and 'vertical' point-cutting than do those
of *Perodicticus*" (Seligsohn, 1977, p. 95). The molars of
the other Asiatic genus, *Loris* "are basically similar to
those of *Arctocebus,* both morphologically and functionally, but differ from those of the latter in
demonstrating somewhat less cusp relief and acuity,
and somewhat more cusp and crest inflation"
(Seligsohn, 1977, p. 94).

The African genera *Perodicticus* and *Arctocebus* were
compared to each other along similar lines. The molars
of *Perodicticus* "strongly contrast with those of
Arctocebus and *Loris* in demonstrating blunt very low
relief and greatly inflated cusps, as well as very shallow basins, which are very weakly concave and very
poorly confined. Crests are shortened and blunt, and
do not rigidly adhere to a transverse orientation.
Molars also demonstrate moderately reduced relative

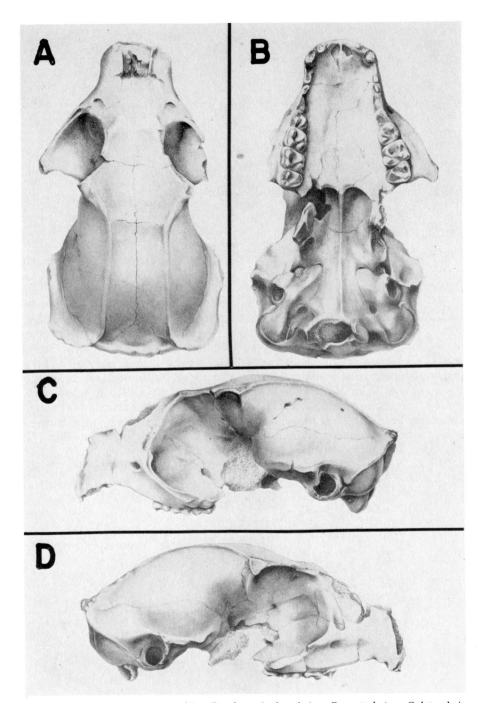

Figure 92. *Mioeuoticus* sp. Early Miocene, East Africa. Cranium: A, dorsal view; B, ventral view; C, lateral view of left side; D, lateral view of right side. [From Le Gros Clark (1956) by permission of the Trustees of the British Museum (Natural History).]

size. These features indicate a great reduction in the functional efficiency of point penetration and 'vertical' point-cutting, and suggest instead emphases on incisive functions" (Seligsohn, 1977, p. 94).

The molars of *Arctocebus* "contrast with those of all other lorisines in demonstrating greatly compressed (i.e., narrow) crests. The molars of this species also exceed those of all other lorisines (including *Loris*) in cusp relief and acuity. Compared to the molars of *Perodicticus* and *Nycticebus*, those of *Arctocebus* demonstrate very conical cusps as well as crests of great length, salience and sharpness which emphasize a transverse orientation. Basins are very deep, greatly concave and mesio-distally greatly confined. These features suggest very strong functional emphases on efficient point penetration and 'vertical' point-cutting" (Seligsohn, 1977, p. 94).

MIOEUOTICUS Leakey, 1962

DISTRIBUTION
Early Miocene (Rusingan). East Africa.
KNOWN SPECIES
1. *Mioeuoticus bishopi* Leakey, 1962, type species
LOCALITIES: Napak⋆ (402).
2. *Mioeuticus* n. sp: Walker, 1974b
LOCALITIES: Rusinga (406).

DISCUSSION

As expected from the morphology of the upper molars, the referred lower dentition of *Mioeuoticus* has broad talonids. The upper teeth of *Mioeuoticus* differ from those of *Progalago* and *Komba* in having well-developed cingula and being nearly square in their outline. Unlike what has been suggested by Walker (1974b), we find the adaptive resemblance of the upper teeth to those of *Perodicticus* much more striking than to those of the highly derived lorisine dentition of *Arctocebus*. The dental formula is the same as in the other lorisids.

The well-known cranium (Figure 92), described by Le Gros Clark (1956) and allocated to this genus by Walker (1974b), has a number of characters reminiscent of the extant lorisines. The strongly constructed skull is only slightly flexed basicranially, has upwardly directed orbits, strong temporal ridges, and moderately inflated bullae. The wide internal nares, as in living lorisines, open posterior to $M^{\underline{3}}$.

The morphological adaptations of *Mioeuoticus* appear to be very similar to those of *Perodicticus*. It is therefore suggested that this form, as the living potto, fed primarily on tough, ripe fruits, but also on a substantial amount of Hymenoptera, Coleoptera, gastropods, and caterpillars.

SUBORDER HAPLORHINI
Pocock, 1918

(= or including: Anthropoidea Mivart, 1864. Paleopithecini Wortman, 1904. Anthrolemuroidea Gingerich, 1973a, in part. Plesitarsioidea Gingerich 1973a, in part. Plesitarsiiformes Gingerich, 1975b, in part. Simiolemuriformes Gingerich, 1975b, in part. Simiiformes Hoffstetter, 1974a.)

DISTRIBUTION

Early Eocene to modern (Wasatchian and Neustrian to Chadronian and Headonian, respectively; Fayumian and Deseadan to modern). North America, Europe, Asia, South America, and Africa.

INCLUDED TAXA

Infraorders Tarsiiformes, Platyrrhini, and Catarrhini.

DISCUSSION

The concept of Haplorhini espoused here is that advocated in detail by Pocock (1918) and especially by Jones (1929). It embraces the Tarsiiformes (the Tertiary representatives included), the Platyrrhini, and the Catarrhini. The suborder makes its appearance in the form of tarsiiforms in the early Eocene of North America, Europe, and Asia. The tarsiiform abundance, as far as we know it, was at its peak during the Eocene in North America and Europe, and probably also in Asia (see *Altanius* and *Hoanghonius*).

The haplorhine infraorders characteristic of South America and the Old World make their appearance in the early Oligocene, but their earlier evolution, for example, in the late Eocene, is not unlikely. Although the origins and radiation of the three higher taxa included in the Haplorhini are discussed below, under the respective taxa, it is appropriate here to pose some questions regarding the origins of the suborder.

Although we continue to use the vernacular "anthropoid" to refer collectively to the platyrrhine and catarrhine primates, we do not formally recognize a taxon Anthropoidea. The reason for this is based on our attempt to maintain the number of ranks in the linean system at a manageable level. Similarly, we employ no formal taxon which includes the Strepsirhini and Haplorhini. Since these have been collectively referred to as modern primates, perhaps the vernacular euprimates is a satisfactory term expressing this phylogenetic communality.

When comparing the three infraorders, and attempting to construct a morphotype for each, one cannot escape the conclusion that the tarsiiform morphotype has by far the more primitive character states. This strongly suggests that it was a tarsiiform which gave rise to the anthropoids. The most compelling areas of evidence for this hypothesis so far are the basicranium of living and fossil forms (Szalay, 1975f; discussed in some detail below), the external nose, presence of the olfactory lobe above the greatest constriction of interorbital septum, the development of fetal membranes (Luckett, 1975), and the various lines of biochemical evidence (Goodman, 1975).

The enlargement of the promontory artery entering the bulla medially and the extrabullar position of the ectotympanic appear to have characterized the haplorhine ancestor (see Figure 93), and, judged from the living forms, one may reasonably conjecture that the wet rhinarium of living strepsirhines, the primitive therian condition, was transformed into the hairy nose present in *Tarsius*. The primitive rhinarium of strepsirhines, the hairy nose of *Tarsius*, and the platyrrhine and catarrhine noses in fact clearly constitute a morphocline with a well-definable polarity (in the sequence listed), and no doubt this is phylogenetically very significant. The first haplorhine, or the first tarsiiform, is perhaps best characterized as a species which evolved a number of cranial and reproductive characters which set it apart from adapids. The change involved a transformation of the rhinarium (for somewhat obscure adaptive reasons), a suspected increase in relative brain size (based on the criterion of relative proportions of cranial morphology), and a probably correlated increase in the relative size of the promontory artery which carries oxygen-rich blood to the brain. These diagnostic features of the ancestral haplorhine are primarily cranial, although possibly subtle, as yet unknown, postcranial modifications accompanied the ancestral adaptive complex.

As in previous suborders, the ear regions are a great aid in understanding the evolution of haplorhines. It was Gregory (1915b) who recognized the significance of the basicranium of the early Eocene omomyid *Tetonius* and stated that "the basicranial region, as a whole, is remarkably similar to that of *Tarsius*" (pp. 430–431). Further study of the specimen (Szalay, 1975f, 1976) confirmed Gregory's suggestion that the septum on the cochlea housed the promontory artery. This condition is identical to that of *Necrolemur* (Stehlin, 1916; Simons and Russell, 1960). It is equally clear that virtually all other preserved details of the middle ear cavity in *Tetonius* match those of *Necrolemur*. Tarsiiform basicrania containing various amounts of information are known for *Rooneyia* (Figure 94), *Tetonius* (an incompletely preserved specimen, see Figure 108), *Necrolemur* (Figure 95), and, of course, *Tarsius* (Figure 96). This sample is far from adequate and it appears sufficient only to allow assessment for a few characters which may diagnose the tarsiiform morphotype.

When we view the middle ear cavity of the known tarsiiforms and compare them to specimens of adapids such as *Notharctus tenebrosus, Smilodectes gracilis, Adapis parisiensis, Leptadapis magnus*, or *Mahgarita stevensi*, it becomes evident that a series of morphological stages, at least in a number of characters, are represented when we arrange these along a morphocline. One shared and derived character, the enlargement of the promontory branch of the internal carotid artery, ties all known tarsiiform basicrania together. Differences exist in the degree of the inflation of the petromastoid and the area of enlargement of the middle ear cavity proper, as well as in the degree to which the ectotympanic is within the bulla. The differences among *Rooneyia, Necrolemur,* and *Tarsius* supply crucial clues for the construction of hypotheses which may help to explain the interrelationships within Tarsiiformes. The features loosely identified as petromastoid inflation and differential hypertrophy of the middle ear cavity in tarsiiforms are probably not isolated phenomena, although some appear to vary independently from one another. If we examine the tarsiiform morphocline of the ectotympanic we see three distinct conditions known so far (see Figure 93). The condition described for *Rooneyia* is one with the ectotympanic well inside the bulla. On the ectotympanic of *Necrolemur,* the bone has a distinct edge near the lateral wall of the bulla; there are also two struts below the ossified annulus membrane (probably homologous to those in *Rooneyia*). In *Tarsius* the ectotympanic is closely fused with the lateral wall. In all three genera there is an extension of both the ossified annulus membrane and the ossified component of the tissues which made up the external auditory canal lateral to the edge of the bullae.

The polarity of the three ectotympanic conditions is probably approximated in a *Rooneyia→Necrolemur→ Tarsius* sequence. The interpretation is based on the position of the ectotympanic in the putative ancestral group for the tarsiiforms, the Adapidae. The thickened lower rim of the intrabullar ectotympanic of *Rooneyia* corresponds to the homologous portion of the ectotympanic ring in adapids and most toothcombed lemuroids. The ossified lateral segment of the ectotympanic is in the position where the annulus membrane is usually found in these strepsirhines (but see MacPhee, 1977). If this condition in *Rooneyia* is considered to be more primitive than in other tarsiiforms, then it is easy to establish that both *Necrolemur* and *Tarsius* represent differentially derived conditions for the tarsiiforms. Another hypothesis of polarity for the ectotympanic differences may be argued on the basis of the extreme medial incursion of the ectotympanic of *Rooneyia*. This

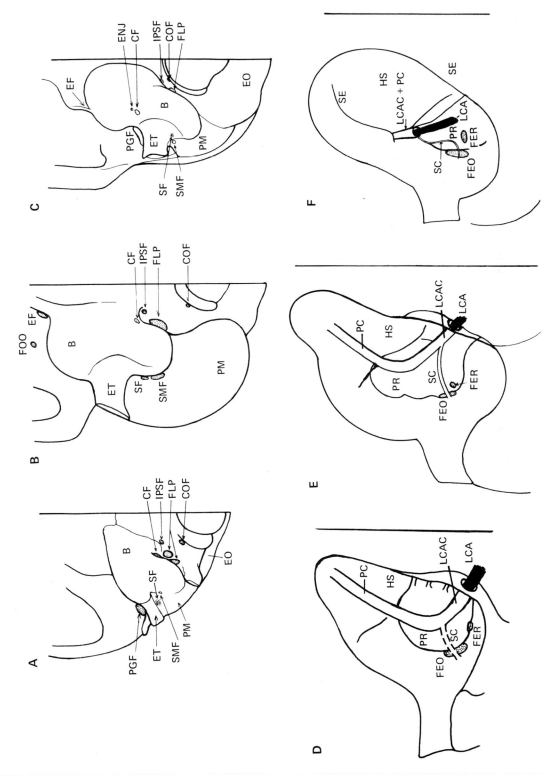

Figure 93. Simplified schema of some aspects of basicranial morphology in a few known tarsiiform Haplorhini. (A and D) *Rooneyia viejaensis* (late Eocene); (B and E) *Necrolemur antiquus* (Middle Eocene); (C and F) *Tarsius* sp. (Modern). Above, basicrania intact; below, the bulla and ectotympanic are removed to show carotid circulation. Broken lines represent reconstruction. For abbreviations, see Table III. [From Szalay (1975f).]

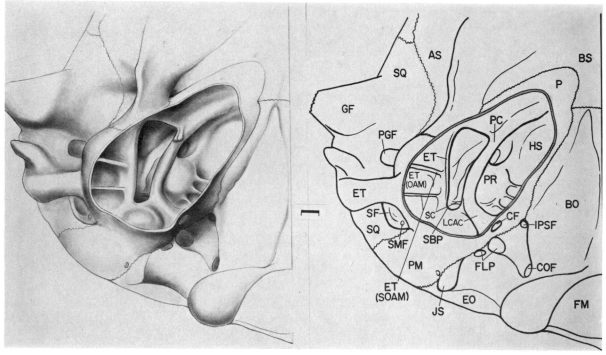

Figure 94. Basicranial morphology of *Rooneyia viejaensis* with only the ventral floor of the bulla removed. Ventral and slightly medial view. Identification of structures is shown on the right. For abbreviations, see Table III. Scale represents 1 mm. [From Szalay (1976).]

condition in *Rooneyia* may be as derived a condition as the extreme lateral position of this bone in *Tarsius*, and thus *Necrolemur* would represent the more nearly ancestral position for the ectotympanic. The position of the "intrabullar" ectotympanic is undoubtedly modified by the selectional demands of middle ear size and the subsequent minor differences in the way the middle ear cavity is expanded below the annulus membrane. Until the mechanical function of these features in respect to middle ear function in general is understood, however, it will be very difficult to understand the polarity of this morphocline. One may argue that as *Rooneyia* neither enlarged the hypotympanic sinus nor inflated the petromastoid, it expanded its middle ear cavity well below and lateral to the "ectotympanic-ossified annulus membrane" floor of the auditory meatus.

As mentioned elsewhere (Szalay, 1975f, 1976), notable differences exist between *Necrolemur* (and other microchoerine omomyids) and *Tarsius* in the basicranium construction. *Necrolemur* differs from *Tarsius*

in having an enormously enlarged petromastoid, a condition which *Tarsius* completely lacks. *Tarsius* differs from *Necrolemur* in the enlargement of the hypotympanic sinus and in having the carotid enter the bulla ventrally and ascending vertically to the circle of Willis. The characters in which these taxa differ from each other are derived tarsiiform characters. Lack of shared and derived tarsiiform characters (beyond those which unite tarsiiforms) between microchoerines and *Tarsius* fail to corroborate the hypothesis (Simons, 1961b) that special relationships exist between these taxa beyond the conclusion that they are all tarsiiforms.

Rather than only viewing the three tarsiiforms as representing three phylogenetic stages and thus as an aid in gaining a picture of the phylogeny of this structure, we may study the remaining characteristic morphologies of the middle ear cavities in order to supply a partial adaptational explanation for the ectotympanic conformation. The middle ear cavities of all three tarsiiforms are exceptionally enlarged, yet in a divergent manner, suggesting independent evolution. As selection independently favored an increased relative size of the middle ear cavity, perhaps for increased auditory sensitivity, divergent pathways were emphasized, probably as a result of slightly different base (heritage) morphologies available for these taxa. *Rooneyia* extended the tympanic cavity below and lateral to the ectotympanic, and *Necrolemur* enormously inflated the petromastoid, whereas *Tarsius* hypertrophied the hypotympanic sinus.

The point of medial or ventral entry of the carotid into the bulla is coupled with the enlargement of the promontory artery in known tarsiiforms. The medial entry of the internal carotid is a primitive condition for the tarsiiforms and haplorhines, but it is derived when compared with the primitive strepsirhine and primate conditions. The path of the lateral internal carotid

artery in *Tarsius* is clearly a more advanced version of what is seen in *Rooneyia, Necrolemur,* and *Tetonius*. In all these forms the promontory artery is relatively very large and relatively much more important than in any known strepsirhines. The comparative dimensions of the promontory and stapedial arteries in strepsirhine and tarsiiform fossils have already been noted above.

The known omomyid basicrania, when integrated with postcranial evidence, suggest that the major characters which may be considered derived, having diverged after their origin from a primitive ancestral condition that can best be called adapid, were (a) increase in the relative size of the promontory artery compared with the stapedial artery; (b) medial shift in the entry of the carotid artery into the bulla; and (c) an increasingly extrabullar position of the ectotympanic, particularly as epitomized in *Tarsius*, derived from an

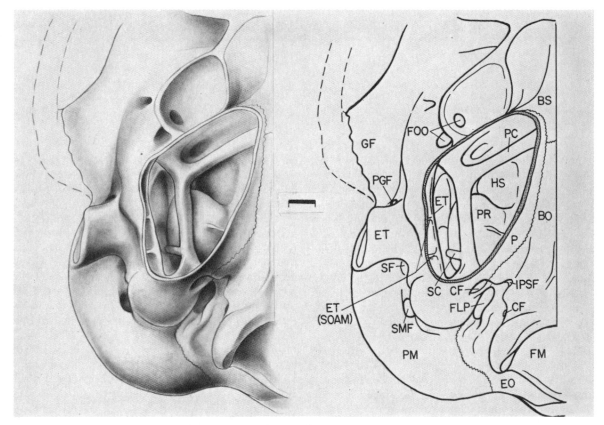

Figure 95. Basicranial morphology of *Necrolemur antiquus* with only the ventral floor of the bulla removed. Ventromedial view. Identification of structures is shown on the right. For abbreviations, see Table III. Scale represents 1 mm. [From Szalay (1976).]

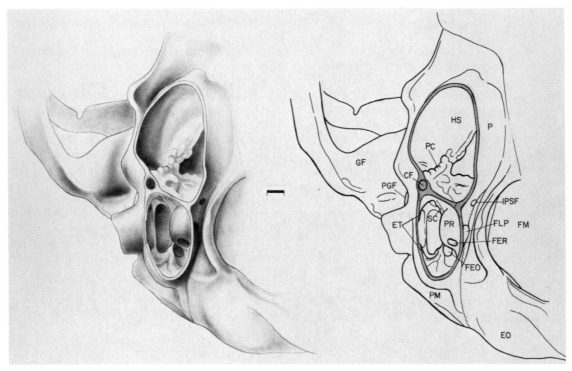

Figure 96. Basicranial morphology of *Tarsius syrichha,* with only ventral floor of the bulla removed. Ventromedial view. Identification of structures is shown on the right. For abbreviations, see Table III. Scale represents 1 mm. [From Szalay (1976).]

intrabullar ectotympanic ring, through the ossification of the annulus membrane; and (*d*) possibly slightly more enhanced adaptations for jumping.

Minor but significant gaps exist between either the tarsiiform morphotype or any of the known tarsiiforms and what can be judged the more primitive basicrania of known anthropoids. Considering the tarsiiform evidence, the most primitive living anthropoid basicranial morphology appears to be possessed by the cebids, forms relatively conservative among themselves in this respect.

The suggestion has been made recently by Cartmill and Kay (1978) that *Tarsius* is the closest known tarsiiform relative of anthropoids. The ventral entry of the internal carotid into the bulla of *Tarsius* is, when assessed at first, a similarity, and is seemingly a derived character shared between the Tarsiidae and some of the anthropoids. However, when one takes into account the existing morphocline in the basicranial morphology of the platyrrhines and catarrhines (Figure 97), we believe that the similarity can be explained as convergence rather than homologous synapomorphy. As far as the semantics of the statement is concerned, *Tarsius* and catarrhines do share a similarly placed ventral entry of the internal carotid into the bulla. When we examine the anthropoid basicranial morphocline, however, and compare it with the basicranium of *Tarsius,* it becomes apparent that platyrrhines and catarrhines share, among a host of other details of the basicranium, a unique pattern in having the canal for the internal carotid (LCAC & PC on Figure 97) traverse the promontorium ventrally. Furthermore, this pattern is unaffected by a postulated polarity for the entry of the carotid from medially, as seen in platyrrhines, to the advanced condition ventrally, as seen in catarrhines. In other words, it is apparent that ventral entry of the internal carotid in catarrhines was derived from a medially entering condition displayed by platyrrhines and not from a *Tarsius*–catarrhine or *Tarsius*–anthropoid common ancestor which shared ventral entry.

A right petrosal and squamosal of the early

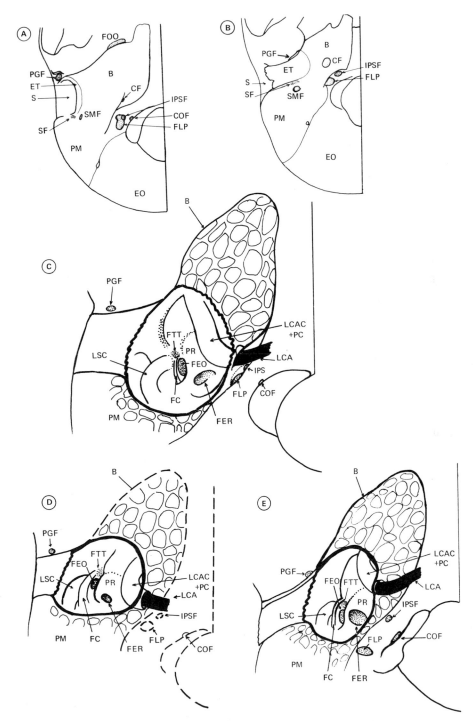

Figure 97. Simplified schema of some aspects of basicranial morphology in a few representative genera of anthropoid Haplorhini: A and C, *Saimiri* sp. (Modern); B and E, *Cercopithecus* sp. (Modern); D, *Apidium* sp. (Oligocene). Above, basicrania intact; below, the bulla and ectotympanic are removed and the internal architecture of the pneumatized regions is schematically shown. Heavy line around middle ear cavity shows where bone is cut to expose the morphology inside. Broken lines represent reconstruction. For abbreviations, see Table III. [From Szalay (1975f).]

Oligocene catarrhine *Apidium*, described by Gingerich (1973b), have been used as a vehicle to advocate special strepsirhine–anthropoid ties. Gingerich's (1973) statement that *"Apidium* provides positive evidence that anthropoid primates evolved directly from a lemuroid ancestor" (p. 335) has been a challenge to the concept of haplorhine holophyly. We believe that it has been amply refuted by Hoffstetter (1974a), Hershkovitz (1974b), and Szalay (1975f). It is important, however, to cite here Gingerich's arguments for the validity of the "Simiolemuriformes" (i.e., a strepsirhine–anthropoid group), as they are not misrepresentative of procedures of phylogenetic analysis sometimes encountered among students of fossils. Gingerich (1973b) essentially argued as follows (quoted from Szalay, 1975f, p. 113):

1. Characters of soft anatomy are not known from fossils and therefore it is nearly impossible to tell whether suggested haplorhine similarities are synapomorphies, merely primate symplesiomorphies, or independently acquired characters; hence soft anatomical features bearing on haplorhine monophyly can be dismissed.
2. Only osteological characters should be used to test the validity of the Haplorhini.
3. There is no evidence for any derived osteological features shared by *Tarsius* and anthropoids which can be shown to be the result of common inheritance.
4. Postorbital closure in *Tarsius* is different from anthropoids; the promontory arteries of primitive lemuroids are not as relatively small as has been reported, hence the diagnostic differences between the carotid circulation of living lemuroids and *Tarsius* were not as yet established by the medial Eocene.
5. Presence of a free ctotympanic in tupaiids proves that the primitive primate condition of the bone was as seen in lemuroids.
6. Because *Necrolemur* and *Rooneyia* are widely separated geographically and morphologically, a tubular ectotympanic was an early acquisition of tarsiiforms.
7. Early catarrhines and platyrrhines lack a tubular ectotympanic; hence anthropoids were derived from primates more primitive than any known tarsioids.
8. *"Apidium* provides positive evidence that anthropoid primates evolved directly from a lemuroid ancestor" (Gingerich, 1973, p. 335).
9. Because *Pelycodus* and close relatives can be found during the early Eocene in both North America and Europe, the distribution pattern of anthropoids does not require rafting hypotheses.

These arguments and the general approach were answered by Szalay (1975f, pp. 114–115), and his views are still representative of our current hypotheses and arguments.

Both *Apidium* and *"Aegyptopithecus,"* unlike later cercopithecoids and hominoids, have a platyrrhine-like ring rather than a tube. This type of ringlike ectotympanic may have been primitive for the anthropoids, and, as argued by Szalay (1975f), this configuration may have been present in *bona fide*, unknown tarsiiforms. Lorisids show the fully differentiated features of their family, inherited from a cheirogaleid which diverged from a lemuroid ancestry, yet they display a variety of conformations of the ectotympanic (contrast *Galago* versus *Nycticebus*, for example). This character, as noted, is apparently quite independent from major alterations in the circulatory pattern or the degree of petromastoid inflation. The ectotympanic morphology alone cannot supply significant evidence for anthropoid origins from any group.

The evidence from the petrosal of *Apidium* is important for both genealogical and anagenetic assessment of anthropoid ·origins. An anthropoid specialization, contrasted to those of other primates, is the extreme enlargement of the promontory artery. This vessel plunges into the petrosal quite medially and appears, in its probably primitive form, both in *Apidium* and some platyrrhines and catarrhines as a raised surface on the medial side of the promontorium. Another character that is a homologous shared derived feature between *Apidium*, platyrrhines, and catarrhines is the pneumatized nature of both the petrosal and squamosal. This feature could link an anthropoid morphotype with a group of early tarsiiforms that had an enlarged petromastoid and an ectotympanic ring outside the bulla proper. Furthermore, the sinus-filled bullar portion of anthropoids (Figure 97) corresponds to the area in tarsiiforms (but not *Tarsius*) that usually has a large hypotympanic sinus.

In conclusion, the medial entry of the internal carotid into the bulla, the enlargement of the promontory artery, and the auditory tube composed of an intrabullar ectotympanic and an ossified annulus membrane of the tarsiiform morphotype are judged to be derived from adapids. The anthropoid basicranial morphotype, typified by most living platyrrhines and also the fossil *Apidium*, is most easily derivable from a hypothetical tarsiiform with an enlarged promontory artery, enlarged hypotympanic sinus, and a greatly inflated petromastoid, but with no lateral extension of the auditory tube.

Finally, a unique cranial feature is shared between tarsiiforms and anthropoids. In contrast to adapids and other strepsirhines which have their greatest interorbital constriction above the olfactory lobes, haplorhines diagnostically have their olfactory lobes above the narrowest partition of the orbits. This feature dramatically contrasts the fossil tarsiiform crania, along with their incipient postorbital partitions, with adapid skulls.

Infraorder Tarsiiformes
Gregory, 1915b

(= or including: Heteronychae Gray, 1821, in part. Paleopithecini Wortman, 1903. Anaptomorphidae: Simpson, 1937, in part. Plesitarsioidea Gingerich, 1973a, in part. Plesitarsiiformes Gingerich, 1975b, in part; Tarsioidea of various authors; Lemuroidea of various authors, in part.)

DISTRIBUTION
  Early Eocene to modern (Wasatchian to Arikareean, Neustrian to Headonian). North America, Europe, and Asia.
INCLUDED TAXA
  Families Omomyidae and Tarsiidae.

DISCUSSION

The populations of southeast Asian *Tarsius* are the only living representatives of this group of primates that once flourished in spectacular variety and abundance (see Figure 98). The heyday of the tarsiiforms, as far as we know, was the Eocene. They were clearly differentiated from an adapid ancestry somewhere in the Paleocene and survived into the Miocene in North America, into the Oligocene in Europe, and today are represented merely as a relic by *Tarsius*. Unlike their contemporaries, the adapids, which produced species as large as *Leptadapis magnus*, or the several species of *Pelycodus* or *Notharctus*, no known tarsiiform was larger than a South American capuchin or uakari. What the known tarsiiforms lacked in size, however, they apparently made up in the diversity of their known structural adaptations. This is particularly true of the dentition, so far their best known aspect. Their feeding strategies were probably highly diversified,

and, one may suspect, this was also true of the locomotor habits of the various species, although, admittedly, the postcranial morphology is not as well known as their dental adaptations.

In spite of the limited size range of the tarsiiforms, their striking morphological diversity is expressed by the subdivision of the infraorder into two families and by the further partitioning of the Omomyidae into four subfamilies and several tribes and subtribes. It appears that most small primate niches in North America were occupied by the omomyids, whereas in Europe (and possibly in Asia) the adapids are found both in the large bodied as well as the smaller bodied niches, the latter, of course being shared with the omomyid microchoerines. Although the majority of the omomyids were in the size range covered by callitrichines, [judged by the estimated length of tooth row in both living and fossil samples (see Szalay, 1976, Fig. 177)], *Necrolemur, Hemiacodon, Ekgmowechashala, Rooneyia, Macrotarsius,* and *Ourayia* reached the size estimated to be equivalent to the owl monkey or some of the smaller pithecines. It is interesting to note that in North America this "burst of growth" largely coincides with the disappearance, at least in the Rocky Mountain region, of the notharctines.

The phylogenetic ties of the Omomyidae have long been in doubt and in a confusing state. Views on the relationships of the Omomyidae Trouessart, 1879 (including the Anaptomorphidae Cope, 1883, and Microchoeridae Lydekker, 1887) have fluctuated,

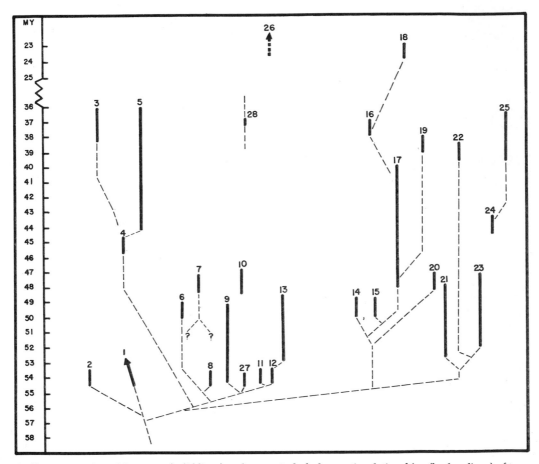

Figure 98. Known stratigraphic ranges (solid lines) and suggested phylogenetic relationships (broken lines) of taxa, primarily of the Tarsiiformes. 1, segment of the stratigraphic range of the Adapidae; 2, *Donrussellia*, a possible adapiform; 3, *Pseudoloris*; 4, *Nannopithex*; 5, *Necrolemur* and *Microchoerus*; 6, *Chlororhysis*; 7, *Anaptomorphus*; 8, *Teilhardina*; 9, *Anemorhysis*; 10, *Trogolemur*; 11, *Mckennamorphus*; 12, *Tetonius*; 13, *Absarokius*; 14, *Loveina*; 15, *Shoshonius*; 16, *Rooneyia*; 17, *Washakius*; 18, *Ekgmowechashala*; 19, *Dyseolemur*; 20, *Hemiacodon*; 21, *Uintanius*; 22, *Chumashius*; 23, *Omomys*; 24, *Ourayia*; 25, *Macrotarsius*; 26, unspecified source of origin for *Tarsius*; 27, *Altanius*; 28, *Hoanghonius*. [By A. Cleary.]

although the creation of these family concepts indicated that the group was early recognized as distinct from the Adapidae. Szalay (1976) has reviewed in detail the rising and ebbing debate over the affinities of the various taxa within the Omomyidae. It appears certain that disagreement will long continue as many of these genera are poorly known.

Early in this century Wortman (1903–1904) asserted the closer ties of *Tarsius* and allies to the platyrrhines and catarrhines than to lemuroids. He used the suborder Anthropoidea (a concept originally intended,

however, for platyrrhines and catarrhines only) for the three groups. Within the tarsioid primates, which he referred to as Paleopithecini, he recognized the Tarsiidae and the Anaptomorphidae. He divided the Anaptomorphidae into the Omomyinae and Anaptomorphinae and he included *Microchoerus* and *Necrolemur* in the latter. Years later, the Tarsiiformes, erected by Gregory (1915b), included two families, the Microchoeridae and the Tarsiidae. The latter encompassed both the Anaptomorphinae and Omomyinae of Wortman. Subsequently, Gregory (1920) again indicated his allocation of the Anaptomorphidae when he referred to skulls of *Tetonius* and *Necrolemur* as those of tarsiiforms.

Simpson (1937) referred to the Eocene non-lemuroids as "acknowledged tarsioids" and considered the Paleocene genera, now grouped under the Paromomyidae, as having tarsioid ties. In years to come he carried this suggestion further (see below) by including the Paromomyinae in the Anaptomorphidae. However, in his 1940 study of the skeletal remains of *Hemiacodon*, Simpson came to doubt the clear-cut differentiation of tarsioid–lemuroid traits in Eocene primates, saying little about the phylogeny per se of these groups. Through his study of *Hemiacodon*, Simpson essentially cast the most serious doubt on the validity of a tarsiiform–adapiform dichotomy, an agnostic view which he espoused again, with even greater persuasiveness, in his 1955 work on the Phenacolemuridae. Simpson's 1940 and 1945 concept of the Anaptomorphidae included the Omomyinae, Paromomyinae, Anaptomorphinae, Necrolemurinae, and Pseudolorisinae.

Simpson's studies were not the only ones which cast a shadow of doubt on the exact phyletic relationships of the ancient tarsiiform omomyids. In 1946 and 1948 Hürzeler published works on the cranial morphology of *Necrolemur*, emphasizing the taxonomic characters of the ear region. His assessment of the facts compelled him to suggest that anatomical characters allied *Necrolemur* and relatives with the strepsirhines rather than with the living *Tarsius*. Undoubtedly, Simpson (1955) was influenced by Hürzeler, whose work rekindled doubts voiced in his 1940 studies. In 1955, Simpson considered the "Anaptomorphidae" not a natural family and noted the following.

> There is no convincing evidence that any early primate is more "tarsioid" than "lemuroid" in natural affinities. The mooted "tarsioid" characters are some features of the cheek dentition, characters for the most part merely primitive for prosimians now known (as in the genera just named) to be of possible association with "lemuroid" skulls; enlargement of the orbits (e.g., in *Tetonius*), which does not reach the *Tarsius* extreme or resemble it in detailed anatomy and which has certainly occurred independently in many primates, especially those that became nocturnal; and in a few cases elongation of the tarsus, which again is not demonstrably like *Tarsius* in extent or detail, which also occurs among "lemuroids" (or, notably, Lorisiformes, and also among nominal insectivores),

and which in some instances at least (e.g., *Hemiacodon*) is different from the truly tarsioid trend and quite surely independent. (p. 438)

Thus, in this rather radical departure from the early, turn of the century views on the Eocene primates, Simpson, with the full weight of his authority, again cast serious doubt on the previously suggested probabilities on "prosimian" relationships. However, Hürzeler's assertion that the ectotympanic is free in the bulla in *Necrolemur*, contrary to Stehlin (1916), who demonstrated it to be fused to the rim of the bulla, was reinterpreted by Simons and Russell (1960) and Simons (1961b), who have suggested that Stehlin's studies on basicranial morphology were correct.

In Szalay's studies of the Plesiadapiformes, strepsirhines, and tarsiiforms during the years 1968–1973, the hypotheses of tarsiiform relationships advocated below (Szalay, 1975f,g, 1976) were formulated. Figure 98 presents the most plausible phylogeny from Szalay (1975g) for the known species. Almost all of the evidence for the Omomyidae is dental, and therefore most phylogenetic decisions concerning species of the family were based on the hypothesized polarity of the morphology of teeth.

It is difficult to determine what the most primitive omomyid, adapid, or plesiadapiform molar morphology was like. The inferred primitive conditions of both omomyid and adapid molars were probably very similar to one another. Morphotypes of both these groups appear to be somewhat more advanced than that of an inferred primitive plesiadapiform, and certainly more advanced in molar morphology than *Purgatorius*. It appears certain, however, that the morphotypes of the euprimates had an $I_{1,2}^{1,2}$; C_1^1; $P_{1,2,3,4}^{1,2,3,4}$; $M_{1,2,3}^{1,2,3}$ dental formula. In addition to these general remarks, we cannot state with any degree of certainty whether the omomyid or adapid morphotypes are more primitive or derived dentally.

The most complete skeletal remain of any omomyid is still the fragmentary skeleton of *Hemiacodon gracilis* (Figures 99 and 100), although a fair variety of other omomyids are also known by tarsal and elbow material (Szalay, 1975g, 1976, and in preparation). Simpson (1940, pp. 195–197) emphasized that the skeletal remains of *Hemiacodon* were close to his morphological concept of the Lemuroidea. The latter, judged from his comparisons, included such phenetically, temporally,

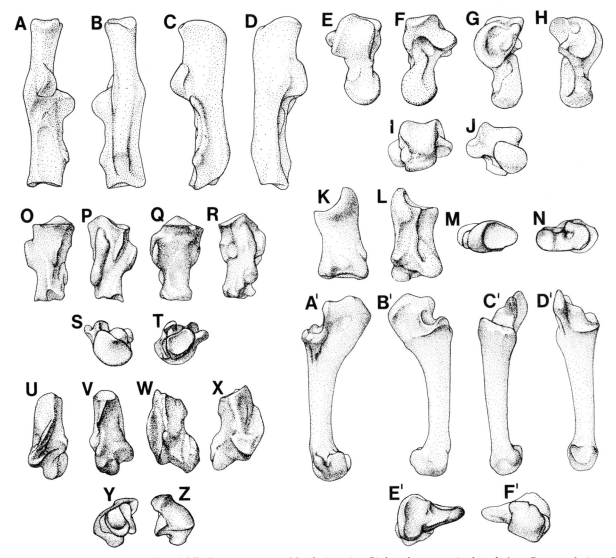

Figure 99. *Hemiacodon gracilis.* Middle Eocene, western North America. Right calcaneum: A, dorsal view; B, ventral view; C, medial view; D, lateral view. Right astragalus: E, dorsal view; F, ventral view; G, medial view; H, lateral view; I, proximal view; J, distal view. Right navicular: K, dorsal view; L, ventral view; M, proximal view; N, distal view. Right cuboid: O, dorsal view; P, ventral view; Q, lateral view; R, medial view; S, proximal view; T, distal view. Right entocuneiform: U, ventral view; V, dorsal view; W, lateral view; X, medial view; Y, proximal view; Z, distal view. First right metatarsal: A', ventral view; B', dorsal view; C', lateral view; D', medial view; E', proximal view; F', distal view. Scales represent 1 mm. [From Szalay (1976).]

and phyletically widely separated forms as *Notharctus, Lemur* and *Galago;* the last genus was to typify the long footed lemuroids. He also suggested the possibility, improbable to him, "either (1) that *Hemiacodon* and its allies are true and fully differentiated tarsioids resembling the lemuroids only by convergence or in pre- or proto-primate characters, or (2) that they are lemuroids convergent toward the tarsioids in some respects" (Simpson, 1940, p. 197).

Simpson (p. 195) correctly indicated that calcanea of *Hemiacodon* and *Teilhardina* are similar and, although stated differently, he concluded that the similarities

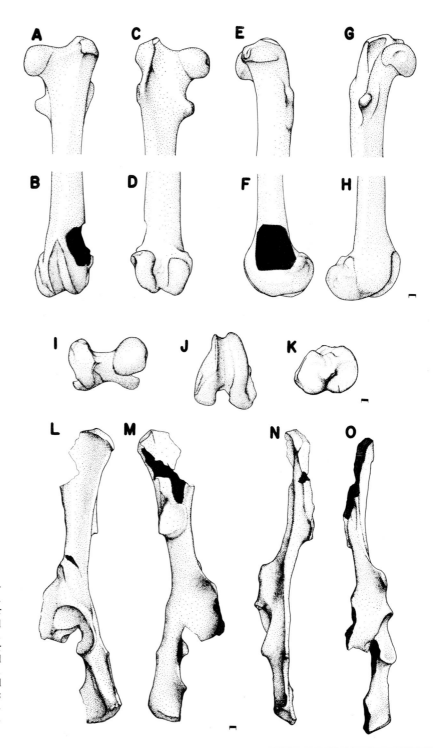

Figure 100. *Hemiacodon gracilis.* Middle Eocene, western North America. Proximal end of left femur: A, anterior view; C, posterior view; E, lateral view; G, medial view; I, dorsal view. Distal end of left femur: B, anterior view; D, posterior view; F, lateral view; H, medial view; J, distal view. Proximal end of tibia: K, proximal view; Left innominate: L, lateral view; M, medial view; N, dorsal view; O, ventral view. Scales represent 1 mm. [From Szalay (1976).]

indicated close relationships. As Simpson (1940) pointed out, the poor illustrations of the postcranials, mistakenly allocated to *Pseudoloris* by Weigelt (1933), show "considerable resemblance to *Hemiacodon* in the hindlimb" (p. 196). It might be added that, in light of the complex of similarities which tie microchoerines to omomyids and which are clearly derived primate features, there is no reason to suspect that calcaneal elongations in *Nannopithex* and *Necrolemur* are not equally shared primitive omomyid characters.

Several broadly based studies on the evolutionary morphology of early Tertiary primate skeletal remains have been recently published (Szalay and Decker, 1974; Decker and Szalay, 1974; Szalay *et al.*, 1975; Szalay, 1976). Although work is still underway, some selected parts of the postcranial anatomy offer some additional information for omomyid phylogeny. Several different kinds of small primate calcanea and astragali are known from various Eocene localities (Szalay, 1976). Many of these tarsals are almost certainly from omomyids, although allocation to genera is uncertain. Probabilities of referral to dentally described taxa vary from locality to locality. Thus, calcanea and an astragalus from Dormaal, Belgium, are almost certainly those of *Teilhardina belgica*. Nonadapid and non-plesiadapiform calcanea and astragali from the Four-Mile localities of Colorado are likely to be remains of one of the two species of *Tetonius* present there (Figure 101) and a genus of omomyids, recently collected by D. E. Savage and associates, is known by tarsals from the early Eocene Bitter Creek localities. Several types of omomyid calcanea, which are not those of *Hemiacodon*, are also known from Bridger beds.

Calcaneal elongation appears to characterize as phyletically distant genera of omomyids as *Hemiacodon*, *Teilhardina*, *?Tetonius*, the Bitter Creek and Bridger omomyids (with generically uncertain allocation), *Necrolemur*, and *Nannopithex*. Until proven to the contrary, it appears reasonable to assume that calcaneal elongation shown by these taxa is an ancestral omomyid character. This feature, if validly inferred as primitive for the omomyids, separates the family from any known plesiadapiform or the primitive condition inferred for adapids.

Comparison of omomyid tarsals with adapids reveals that relative elongation of the moment arm is as advanced in *Hemiacodon* and others as it is in some cheirogaleids or galagines. Combined characters of any of these taxa, when compared to one another, therefore, indicate that this feature was independently attained by lorisoid cheirogaleids and lorisids on the one hand and the omomyids on the other.

The relevance of the African Miocene lorisoid calcanea (see Figure 88) recently reported by Walker (1970) must be noted at this point. In discussing these bones, Walker noted that "the shape of the fossil calcanea, apart from the lesser distal elongation, compares closely with those of modern galagos even to the extent of having a joint surface showing the presence of an anterior calcaneonavicular synovial joint as described by Hall-Crags (1965)" (p. 253). The presence of a well-developed and distally displaced calcaneonavicular joint, as in galagos, cannot be ascertained, and no other shared derived similarities between the calcanea of living galagos and the fossils can be found. Any one of them, on the other hand, could represent the calcaneum of a common ancestor and may even be the actual common ancestor of lorises and galagos, were it not for the cranial specializations attained by lorisids by this time. Rather than sharing special similarities with galagos, the Miocene calcanea are primitive lorisoid and astonishingly similar to those of such cheirogaleids as *Cheirogaleus* and *Phaner*. Similarity between the Miocene lorisid calcanea and those of known omomyids, excluding that of *Necrolemur*, is great. One suspects, however, that this similarity is partly due to both having aspects of primitive morphology, that of a strepsirhine ancestor, and to independent acquisition, that is, the distal elongation of the calcaneum.

The upper ankle joint, as shown by the body of the astragalus and, at least as indicated by *Necrolemur* and *Nannopithex*, the distally fused tibia and fibula, was significantly different in omomyids compared to adapids and plesiadapiforms. Many lemuriforms retain at least the dorsal astragalar foramen leading into the astragalar canal. However, no known omomyid astragali show traces of this canal.

The body of the astragalus of *Teilhardina* shows a posterior extension which might be considered homologous to the posterior trochlear shelf of adapids described in Decker and Szalay (1974). As this feature is best developed in *Teilhardina*, but not as large in *Hemiacodon* or in *?Tetonius*, its moderate expression in the European omomyid might reflect a feature retained from an ancestral adapid condition (see Figures 102 and 103). This posterior trochlear shelf, suggested

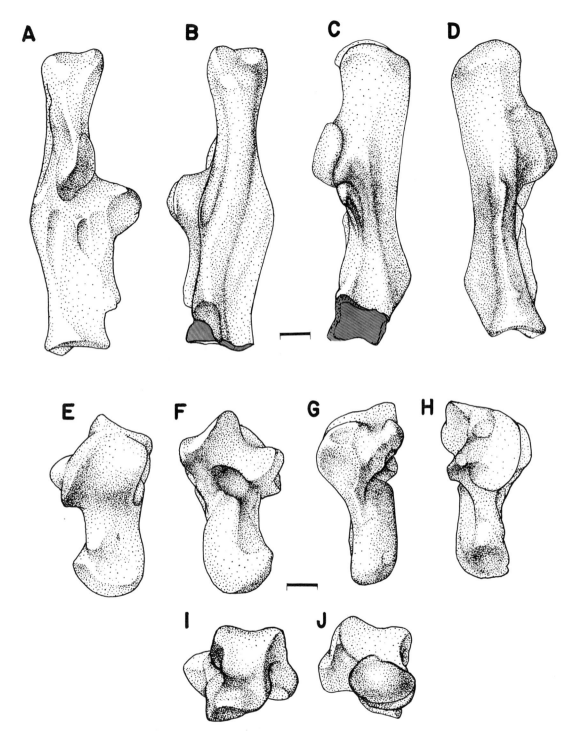

Figure 101. Anaptomorphine. Early Eocene, western North America. Right calcaneum: A, dorsal view; B, ventral view; C, medial view; D, lateral view. Right astragalus: E, dorsal view; F, ventral view; G, medial view; H, lateral view; I, proximal view; J, distal view. Scales represent 1 mm. [From Szalay (1976).]

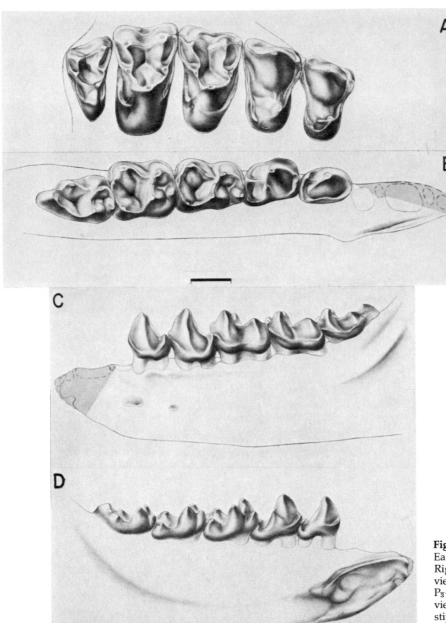

Figure 102. *Teilhardina belgica.* Early Eocene, western Europe. Right upper P^3–M^3. A, occlusal view. Left horizontal ramus with $P_{\overline{3}}$–$M_{\overline{3}}$: B, occlusal view; C, lateral view; D, medial view. Uniform stippling and broken lines indicate reconstruction. Scales represent 1 mm. [From Szalay (1976).]

as a character of the adapid morphotype as it is widely present in most subsequent strepsirhine taxa, was probably also present in the ancestor of the Omomyidae.

In summarizing the tarsal evidence, it appears that a few of the character states known for omomyid calcanea and astragali appear to be derived ones when compared to their homologues in the adapid morphotype, yet these bones in the tarsiiforms were similar to the primitive adapid condition. Such fea-

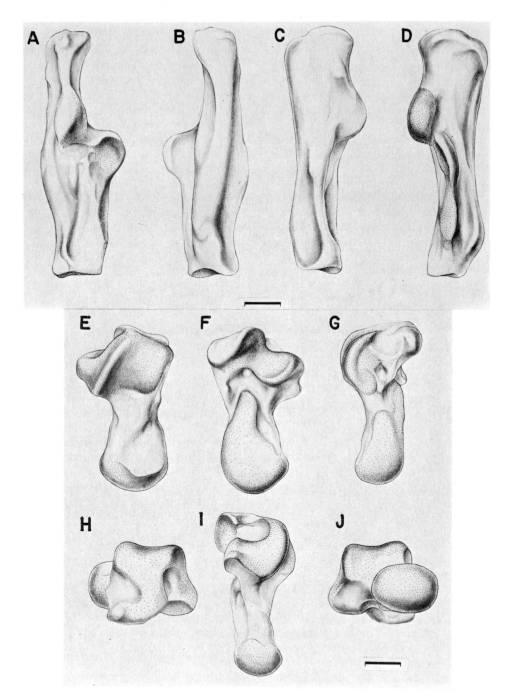

Figure 103. *Teilhardina belgica.* Early Eocene, western Europe. Right calcaneum: A, dorsal view; B, ventral view; C, medial view; D, lateral view. Right astragalus: E, dorsal view; F, ventral view; G, medial view; H, proximal view; I, ventral view; J, distal view. Scales represent 1 mm. [From Szalay (1976).]

tures as the helical (screw-type) lower ankle joint are primitive for the whole order (Szalay and Decker, 1974) and for euprimates.

There are a number of cranial features which appear to be shared by the known crania and well-preserved maxilla fragments of the Eocene–Oligocene fossil tarsiiforms and the extant *Tarsius*. The repeated occurrence of these characters suggests that the tarsiiform morphotype possessed such a suite of features. In general, compared to most primitive adapids, there is a reduction in the snout, an increased convergence and enlargement of the orbits, and a consequent reduction in the width of the interorbital septum. The convergence of the tooth row anteriorly has been listed as another primitive tarsiiform feature by Simons (1961b), but it is likely that this is a primitive primate feature inherited from a non-primate eutherian with a similar condition. Fusion of the frontals in the midline may or may not have been present in the ancestral tarsiiform. Aspects of the basicranium were discussed under the Haplorhini.

A recent review by Szalay and Dagosto (in preparation) of Paleogene primate humeri revealed that the distal end of these bones in omomyids is remarkably similar to humeri of primitive anthropoids. The elongated trochlea of euprimates in known omomyids, Fayum anthropoids, and a number of platyrrhines curves distally on the medial side. The functional significance of this character is not entirely clear, but it is possible that this similarity shared among omomyids and primitive anthropoids is a derived one.

Family Omomyidae
Trouessart, 1879

(= or including: Omomynae Trouessart, 1879. Anaptomorphidae Cope, 1883. Hyopsidae: Schlosser, 1887, in part. Omomyinae: Wortman, 1904. Tarsiidae: Gregory, 1915b, in part. Tetoniidae Abel, 1931. Omomyidae: Gazin, 1958. Teilhardinidae Quinet, 1964.)

DISTRIBUTION
  Early Eocene to late Oligocene (Wasatchian to Arikareean, and Neustrian to Suevian). Western North America and western Europe.
INCLUDED TAXA
  Subfamilies Anaptomorphinae, Omomyinae, Ekgmowechashalinae, and Microchoerinae.

Discussion

This family differs from known Tarsiidae in having generally slightly reduced canines (but see several genera as exceptions) and incisors enlarged or reduced to varying degrees. Although dentally some genera show either more primitive or derived characters than the known tarsiids, omomyids known by basicrania differ from the former in having a less enlarged promontory artery and lacking the extremely enlarged hypotympanic sinus of *Tarsius*. The postcranial remains shown by the known bones of *Hemiacodon* are distinctly more primitive than those of *Tarsius*.

Omomyidae appear to differ from the Plesiadapiformes primarily in the relatively greater enlargement of the brain and of the promontory artery, and in the modification of much of the known postcranium, most of these features being shared with the Adapidae.

There are some consistent differences between the anterior dentitions of omomyids and paromomyids. The primitive condition in omomyids is the presence of a distinct protocone on P^3 as on P^4, i.e., a transversely wide tooth. This condition is matched in both the plesiadapid–carpolestid groups and in adapids, suggesting the omomyid condition to be primitive and the paromomyid one, in which P^3 is without a well-defined protocone, to be a derived feature among primates.

The external ectotympanic, varying degrees of petromastoid inflation, the entrance of the internal carotid on the medial side of the bulla, and the specializations of the tarsus together distinguish the omomyids from known adapids.

The dental morphotype of the Omomyidae (and therefore also of the Haplorhini) may be characterized as having had two pairs of small incisors (like in *Teilhardina*), moderate-sized canines (like in *Chumashius*, *Teilhardina*, and *Chlororhysis*), four premolars (like in *Teilhardina*), and molars with modest hypocones and progressively more mesiodistally constricted trigonids (as in *Loveina*, *Anemorhysis tenuiculus*, or *Teilhardina belgica*). The last molar was unlikely to have been reduced to the proportions found in *Teilhardina*.

SUBFAMILY ANAPTOMORPHINAE
Cope, 1883

(= or including: Anaptomorphidae Cope, 1883. Tetoniidae Abel, 1931. Anaptomorphinae: Simpson, 1940, in part. Teilhardinidae Quinet, 1964.)

DISTRIBUTION
Early to middle Eocene (Wasatchian to Bridgerian, and Neustrian). Western North America and western Europe.
INCLUDED TAXA
Tribes Anaptomorphini and Trogolemurini.

DISCUSSION

The Anaptomorphinae are much less diverse, or numerous, than the Omomyinae. They represent the earliest known species of the family, and the dental morphotype visualized for the subfamily suggests them to be dentally perhaps somewhat more primitive than the Omomyinae. Taxa in this subfamily appear to be characterized by the presence of a protocone-fold (sometimes referred to in the literature as *Nannopithex*-fold) and a type of hypocone which is an indistinct elevation on the distal slope of the protocone, although this also appears in the Microchoerinae and occasionally, probably as a primitive character, in the Omomyinae. Along with this type of hypocone construction anaptomorphines are usually also characterized by low and relatively bulbous trigonid cusps and relatively shallow talonids.

It seems clear that the *Tetonius–Absarokius* group, *Anemorhysis* spp., and particularly *Trogolemur* had a distinctly enlarged medial incisor. A clear absence of this condition in *Anaptomorphus*, then, as a result either of reduction of the enlarged state or as a retention of the primitive one, would argue against singling out the Anaptomorphinae as a natural group adaptively distinct on the family level. Incisor enlargement cannot be used as a diagnostic feature of this probably monophyletic subfamily.

Tribe Anaptomorphini
Cope, 1883

(= or including: Anaptomorphidae Cope, 1883, in part. Anaptomorphini: Szalay, 1976.)

DISTRIBUTION
Same as for subfamily.
INCLUDED TAXA
Subtribes Teilhardinina, Anaptomorphina, and Tetoniina.

DISCUSSION

These are anaptomorphines that lack a combination of the following characters: extremely enlarged medial incisor which extends under the molars, extremely reduced or lost canines, and an M_3 relatively much longer than the more anterior molars. The lack of these extreme specializations separates the Anaptomorphini from the Trogolemurini.

SUBTRIBE TEILHARDININA
Quinet, 1964

(= or including: Teilhardinidae Quinet, 1964. Teilhardinina: Szalay, 1976.)

DISTRIBUTION
Early Eocene (Wasatchian and Neustrian). Western Europe and western North America.
INCLUDED TAXA
Teilhardina and *Chlororhysis.*

DISCUSSION

These are primitive anaptomorphins with low, premolariform fourth premolars, unreduced second lower premolars, not very reduced canines, and unenlarged incisors. The two included genera are perhaps dentally the most primitive representatives of the Anaptomorphinae or perhaps of the family Omomyidae.

It is possible that, once the phylogeny of the Omomyidae is better understood, teilhardininans may be found to be more recently related to omomyines than to the remaining Anaptomorphinae. For the present, however, it is believed (Szalay, 1976) that the reduced M_3^3 in *Teihardina* is a shared derived feature with undoubted anaptomorphines.

TEILHARDINA Simpson, 1940

(= or including: *Omomys:* Teilhard de Chardin, 1927, in part. *Protomomys* Teilhard de Chardin, 1927, suppressed name.)

DISTRIBUTION
Early Eocene (Neustrian). Paris Basin.
KNOWN SPECIES
Teilhardina belgica (Teilhard de Chardin, 1927), type species
(=*Omomys belgicus* Teilhard de Chardin, 1927.)
LOCALITIES: Dormaal⋆ (186).

DISCUSSION

These are anaptomorphines that differ from other members of the subfamily in having the largest number of teeth known in the group, although $P_{\overline{1}}$ appears to be all but lost from the small, laterally crowded alveolus. Unlike the small canine of *Tetonius, Anaptomorphus, Anemorhysis,* or *Chlororhysis, Teilhardina* retained an apparently primitive large canine.

The dental formula is $I\frac{2}{2}$; $C\frac{1}{1}$; $P\frac{2,3,4}{1,2,3,4}$; $M\frac{2,3}{1,2,3}$.

Based on the total available morphology of this genus (Figures 102 and 103), there seems to be little doubt that it is a close relative of the other Eocene omomyids, as stated or implied by Teilhard de Chardin (1927) and Simpson (1940), and not an adapid as suggested by Gingerich (1976). The species *Teilhardina ?gallica* Russell, Louis, and Savage, 1967, was recognized as a new genus, *Donrussellia* Szalay, 1976. It is treated under the Omomyidae *incertae sedis*, although its affinities may well be more recent with primitive adapids, as noted by Szalay (1976).

Whether *Teilhardina* should be placed within the Anaptomorphinae or the Omomyinae is a difficult point to decide. It has been traditionally placed with omomyines (formerly Omomyidae *sensu stricto*), and until 1976 (Szalay, 1976) no one had offered serious arguments against it being an omomyine. A detailed comparison of specimens of *Teilhardina belgica* with both early Eocene anaptomorphines and *Omomys* and *Loveina,* however, indicates a more recent affinity of the European genus with forms like *Chlororhysis, Anemorhysis,* and *Tetonius.*

Unlike *Omomys,* but like *Anemorhysis* and *Tetonius,* the upper molars of *Teilhardina* bear a distinct protocone-fold, admittedly a primitive character. The $M^{\underline{3}}$ of *Teilhardina,* however, like those of the anaptomorphines compared, is very reduced and mesiodistally constricted, a derived character state. $M^{\underline{3}}$ of both *Loveina* (admittedly a referred specimen of the latter)

and *Omomys* are large and not constricted mesiodistally. Szalay (1976) judged the base of the trigonid cusps of *Teilhardina* to be considerably inflated as in anaptomorphines, although not to the degree seen in either *Anemorhysis* or *Tetonius.* In *Omomys* or *Chumashius* there is virtually no basal inflation of the trigonid cusps. Although perhaps not significant, as in *Tetonius,* but unlike in *Omomys,* the hypoconulid in *Teilhardina* is closer to the hypoconid than to the entoconid. The $P_{\overline{4}}$ of *Teilhardina* is semimolariform, i.e., with a distinct metaconid and paraconid, as apparently is the primitive condition in the early Eocene omomyid subfamilies, but like in *Anemorhysis,* for example, without having the paracristid as elongated as in *Omomys.*

Bown (1976) has named and described as *"Teilhardina americana"* a sample from early Wasatchian beds of Wyoming. The form, based on an excellent lower jaw, is not *Teilhardina* but may be *Anemorhysis,* possibly *Anemorhysis tenuiculus.* *"Teilhardina americana"* has not been distinguished from *Anemorhysis tenuiculus* when described. In our opinion it cannot be.

The dental morphology (Figure 102) strongly suggests a more anaptomorphine than omomyine character complex for *Teilhardina.* It is also apparent that the unreduced canines and incisors which were not enlarged were very probably the primitive condition for the Eocene subfamilies of the Omomyidae and for the family also.

This genus is undoubtedly one of the most important ones among early Tertiary primates because it is one of the most primitive of known primates in retaining $P_{\overline{1}}$ and a relatively primitive primate molar morphology, while, on the other hand, its primitive dentition is coupled with advanced euprimate postcranial morphology, as this is judged from the astragalus and calcaneum. Whether it is ancestral to the anthropoids as Quinet (1966) stated is an unlikely but moot point at present. The nature of calcaneal advancement of the genus would argue against that hypothesis.

Adaptational assessment of *Teilhardina* is very difficult largely because it is in many ways a very primitive omomyid. Nonetheless, the third molars show signs of slight reduction from a relatively larger ancestral condition. The lower canine was large and a vestigial $P_{\overline{1}}$ was present. Judged from the alveoli, the lingual slope of the protocone is very extensive, probably an ancestral primate character, but perhaps a secondary acquisition of this feature by *Teilhardina*.

The jaw presents an interesting morphology rarely seen in other omomyids. The unfused symphysis was nearly horizontal, forming a low angle with the inferior border of the horizontal ramus, and, in general, the mandible anterior to $P_{\overline{3}}$ is very shallow. This is in particular contrast to the relatively great depth of the mandible under $M_{\overline{2}}$ and $M_{\overline{3}}$. Based on these features *Teilhardina belgica* is judged to have been insectivorous.

CHLORORHYSIS Gazin, 1958

DISTRIBUTION

Late early Eocene (late Wasatchian). Rocky Mt. region.

KNOWN SPECIES

Chlororhysis knightensis Gazin, 1958, type species

LOCALITIES: Milleson Draw⋆ (194); upper Wasatch beds.

DISCUSSION

Very faint or absent cingulids along with a small metaconid on the $P_{\overline{4}}$ appear to set this group aside from *Anemorhysis* and *Teilhardina*, the taxa most similar to *Chlororhysis* within the Anaptomorphinae. The two incisors were not as large as those of either *Anemorhysis* or *Tetonius* and the canine is relatively larger than in either of the latter. Molar characters, because of uncertainty of association, are not used in this diagnosis.

The type specimen of the only known species (Figure 104) shows this taxon to be dentally possibly one of the most primitive omomyids in North America (Szalay, 1976). Unfortunately, the only firm basis for the belief that *Chlororhysis knightensis* is an anaptomorphine rather than an omomyine is a referred specimen. The base of the trigonid cusps of that specimen is distinctly bulbous, which combined with the relatively shallow talonid basins of *Chlororhysis* compared, for example, to *Loveina*, of similar age and size, and the anaptomorphine $M_{\overline{3}}$ as in *Anemorhysis* and *Tetonius* strongly suggest anaptomorphine rather than omomyine ties.

There are some differences between the $P_{\overline{4}}$ construction of *Chlororhysis* and *Loveina*. The most outstanding one is the slightly more molarized character of the $P_{\overline{3-4}}$ of *Loveina* compared to *Chlororhysis*, but these characters alone might not be sufficient for generic separation of the two species. If the referred specimen is *Chlororhysis knightensis*, however, then the molar differences noted clearly warrant generic separation of *Chlororhysis* from *Loveina*.

The known lower molars, part of a referred specimen, show that the construction of the trigonids in this genus is similar to the condition displayed by *Anemorhysis* spp., *Tetonius* spp., and *Absarokius* spp., that is, having the bulbous based, somewhat crowded cusps, perhaps the primitive anaptomorphine complex of characters. This is unlike the less inflated trigonid cusp morphology of omomyines, such as displayed, for example, in *Chumashius*, *Omomys*, or *Uintanius*.

The dental formula is $I_{\overline{1}\cdot\overline{2}}^{1\cdot2}$; $C_{\overline{1}}^{1}$; $P_{\overline{2}\cdot\overline{3}\cdot\overline{4}}^{2\cdot3\cdot4}$; $M_{\overline{1}\cdot\overline{2}\cdot\overline{3}}^{1\cdot2\cdot3}$.

The symphysis on the holotype of the type species is not as horizontal as, for example, that of *Teilhardina*. In addition to the inferior transverse torus a bony shelf above the former indicates that transverse forces were perhaps habitually incurred. The symphysis was clearly unfused and mobile.

The incisors inferred from the position and size of the alveoli were moderate, not enlarged like those of *Tetonius homunculus*, *Anemorhysis* spp., or *Absarokius* spp. Both the paraconids and the metaconids are low and a lingual cingulid passes between these cusps on $P_{\overline{3}}$ and $P_{\overline{4}}$. Lingual cingulids are prominent on both $P_{\overline{2}}$ and the canine. The latter, a premolariform rather than a caniniform tooth, is mesially elongated with a fairly long cutting edge (paracristid). The apex of the canine is not appreciably pointed.

There are two features of the canine, providing the homology of the tooth is correct, which are suggestive of the dental adaptations of *Chlororhysis*. The canine is a small tooth and not very pointed and piercing. The well-developed lingual cingulum as well as the crown morphology make this tooth part of the premolar series rather than a tooth with canine functions. Much of what may be said of the adaptations of the antemolar teeth would depend on the assessment of the incisors of the species. Although, judged from the alveoli, two incisors were present and neither was very enlarged, lack of actual teeth prevent any further judgment. Yet, the absence of very enlarged incisors

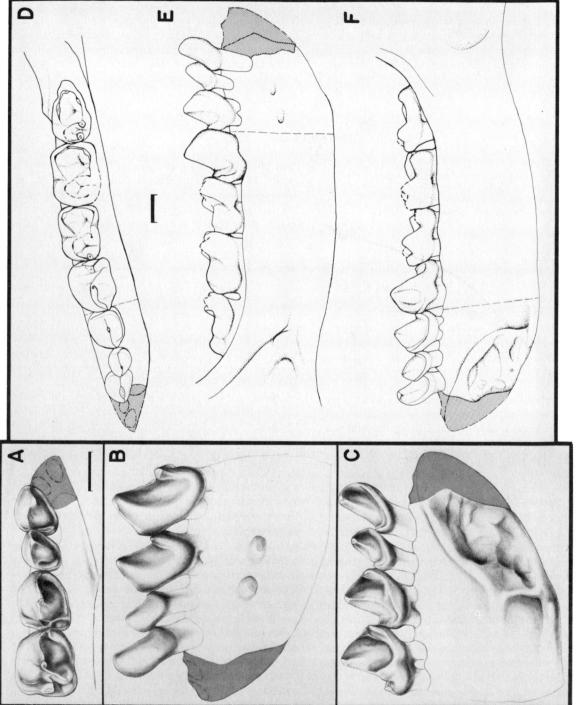

Figure 104. *Chlororhysis knightensis.* Late early Eocene, western North America. Left mandible fragment with reconstructed alveoli for I_1 and I_2, and C–P_4: A, occlusal view; B, lateral view; C, medial view. Reconstructed right mandible with C–M_3, and alveoli for I_1 and I_2: D, occlusal view; E, lateral view; F, medial view. Scales represent 1 mm. [From Szalay (1976).]

and the short crowned, premolariform canine are poor mechanical equipment for food procurement which might involve habitual piercing of live prey. This is not necessarily a statement that *Chlororhysis knightensis* was not habitually insectivorous. It is a tentative interpretation of the meager evidence that the mechanical requirements usually associated with habitual prey catching and killing do not appear to be present.

SUBTRIBE ANAPTOMORPHINA
Cope, 1883

(= or including: Anaptomorphidae Cope, 1883, restricted. Anaptomorphina: Szalay, 1976.)

DISTRIBUTION
Middle Eocene (Bridgerian). Rocky Mt. region.
INCLUDED TAXA
Anaptomorphus.

DISCUSSION

These are considerably distinct anaptomorphines with relatively large molars, a small anterior dentition, and short, U-shaped jaws. The most significant diagnostic difference of the Anaptomorphina from the other subtribes of the Anaptomorphini is the probably derived nature of the anterior dentition. Unlike the enlarged first incisor in the Tetoniina or the primitively large canine of *Teilhardina,* the Anaptomorphina show a lack of incisor hypertrophy and a reduction of the canines. This is distinctly specialized from the other groups, based largely on its lack of size distinction and on its inferred lack of major morphological distinction between the incisors and canines.

ANAPTOMORPHUS Cope, 1872

(= or including: *Euryacodon:* Wortman, 1903.)

DISTRIBUTION
Middle Eocene (Bridgerian). Rocky Mt. region.
KNOWN SPECIES
1. *Anaptomorphus aemulus* Cope, 1872, type species
(=*Euryacodon lepidus:* Wortman, 1903. *Anaptomorphus wortmani* Gazin, 1958.)
LOCALITIES: Lower Bridger★ (266).
2. *Anaptomorphus westi* Szalay, 1976
LOCALITIES: Hawk★ (268); Fault (270); Tree Road (272); Upper Bridger (282).

DISCUSSION

These anaptomorphines (Figure 105) differ from *Tetonius* and *Absarokius* in having the $P_{\overline{4}}$ approximately the same height as the first lower molar. They differ from *Anemorhysis* and *Chlororhysis* in lacking a metaconid on $P_{\overline{4}}$ and from anaptomorphines other than *Chlororhysis* and *Teilhardina* in having relatively small lower incisors and canines.

The dental formula is $I^{1\cdot 2}_{1\cdot 2}$; C^1_1; $P^{3\cdot 4}_{3\cdot 4}$; $M^{1\cdot 2\cdot 3}_{1\cdot 2\cdot 3}$.

Recent works dealing with *Anaptomorphus* are those of Gazin (1958), West (1973), and Szalay (1976). Both species of *Anaptomorphus* appear to be very similar in their molar morphology to *Tetonius homunculus* or *Anemorhysis tenuiculus,* and derivation from a species similar to these, or one of these forms, with a $P_{\overline{2}}$ and smaller $P_{\overline{4}}$ is likely.

As expected from the lower molars the upper ones are similar both to *Tetonius homunculus* and to *Absarokius* spp. The last molar, as in the latter, is considerably reduced and M^2 is strikingly larger than M^1. As in the other anaptomorphines cited, the lingual slope of the protocone is long and gently sloping. The relief is low on the molars, and the crest originating from the protocone and oriented distally, making up essentially the cutting edge of the hypocone, is extensive. In general, the molars are slightly less wide transversely than those of *Tetonius homunculus,* but quite similar in proportions to those of *Absarokius* spp. As far as is known, the two valid species of *Anaptomorphus* differ in size only, *A. westi* being about 30% larger than the type species.

Anaptomorphus combines primitive molar and premolar (at least the fourth premolar, which is the only one known) morphology with a reduced dentition that appears to have been arranged in a nearly U-shaped manner (Szalay, 1976). Alveoli of the teeth anterior to $P_{\overline{4}}$ show that the roots were buccolingually wide and mesiodistally constricted. The dimensions of the alveoli indicate that stresses to the mandible were transversely directed. The unusually extensive inferior transverse torus also lends support to this hypothesis. Emphasis in this genus is on the cheek teeth, particularly the first and second molars; the molars are low crowned and the protocone crest is very well de-

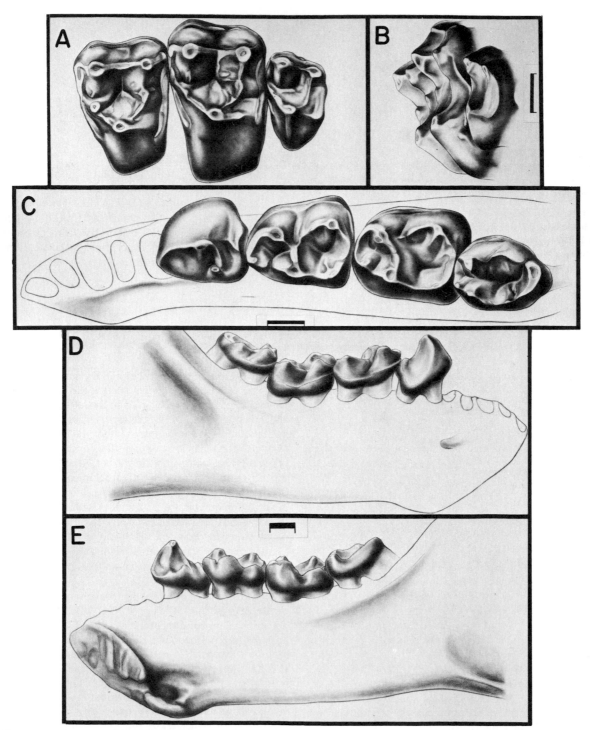

Figure 105. *Anaptomorphus westi.* Middle Eocene, western North America. Left M$^{1-3}$: A, occlusal view; B, occlusodistal view. Right mandible with P$_{4}$–M$_{3}$: C, occlusal view; D, lateral view; E, medial view. Scales represent 1 mm. [From Szalay (1976).]

veloped. The dentition suggests that this small form was a frugivore and only marginally insectivorous.

SUBTRIBE TETONIINA
Abel, 1931

(= or including: Tetoniidae Abel, 1931, restricted. Tetoniina: Szalay, 1976.)

DISTRIBUTION
Early Eocene (Wasatchian). Western North America and Mongolia.
INCLUDED TAXA
Tetonius, Anemorhysis, Absarokius, Altanius, and *Mckennamorphus.*

DISCUSSION

The forms included are anaptomorphines with an enlarged first incisor, relatively small canines, and reduced third molars, which appear to share a more recent common ancestor with each other than with any other omomyid. Other than the character complex cited, no additional features help to diagnose this subtribe.

There is little doubt concerning the close, probably ancestor–descendant, relationship of *Tetonius* and *Absarokius.* Similarly, the evolution of *Mckennamorphus* from a form like *Tetonius homunculus,* via a *T. ambiguus*-like stage, seems convincing. The exact phylogeny of *Anemorhysis,* however, is much less firmly understood than the other taxa included in this subtribe. That genus ranges through the Wasatchian, occurs at several localities, and does not share the characteristic $P_{\overline{4}}$ of the *Tetonius–Absarokius* clade.

The Asiatic *Altanius* is equally problematic. Its large $M_{\overline{3}}$ and molar proportions in general are reminiscent of *Trogolemur,* yet it lacks the specialized long rooted incisor of the latter and shares the enlarged $P_{\overline{4}}$ of *Tetonius.*

TETONIUS Matthew, 1915

(= or including: *Anaptomorphus:* Cope, 1882. *Paratetonius* Seton, 1940. ?*Tetonoides:* Robinson, 1967, in part. *Pseudotetonius* Bown, 1974.)

DISTRIBUTION
Early Eocene (Wasatchian). Rocky Mt. region.
KNOWN SPECIES
1. *Tetonius homunculus* (Cope, 1882), type species
(=*Anaptomorphus homunculus* Cope, 1882. *Paratetonius steini* Seton, 1940. ?*Tetonoides* sp.: Robinson, 1967.)
LOCALITIES: Gray Bull⋆ (162); Four-Mile (178, 180); Powder River (196).
2. *Tetonius ambiguus* (Matthew, 1915)
(=*Pseudotetonius ambiguus:* Bown, 1974.)
LOCALITIES: Gray Bull⋆ (162).
3. *Tetonius* sp.
(=cf. *Anemorphysis minutus:* McKenna, 1960, in part. *Anemorhysis musculus:* Guthrie 1967. *Tetonius musculus:* Delson, 1971b, in part.)
LOCALITIES: Four Mile, East Alheit Pocket (178).

DISCUSSION

Tetonius spp. (Figure 106) have premolariform fourth premolars which lack distinct paraconids and metaconids, or they have minimal development of these; the lower fourth premolar is higher crowned than any of the other premolars or molars. They are distinct from *Anemorhysis* in having taller and more robust $P_{\overline{4}}$ and less well-developed molar cingulids. The major difference of this genus from *Absarokius* lies in the relatively lower and less robust $P_{\overline{4}}$. *Tetonius* appears to be the ancestral genus from which *Absarokius* evolved. The differences from *Mckennamorphus* and *Altanius* are listed under these taxa.

The dental formula is $I_{\overline{1}\cdot\overline{2}}^{1\cdot2}$; $C_{\overline{1}}^{1}$; $P_{(\overline{2}),\overline{3},\overline{4}}^{(2),3,4}$; $M_{\overline{1}\cdot\overline{2}\cdot\overline{3}}^{1\cdot2\cdot3}$.

Tetonius is one of the few omomyids which is known also by a skull (Figures 107 and 108). The small skull, barely 3 cm long when complete, lacks most of the occiput and premaxilla (see Szalay, 1976) and is badly crushed. Nevertheless, it clearly shows that the relatively large-brained (Radinsky, 1967) small tarsiiform was large eyed and relatively short faced. As in *Rooneyia* and *Tarsius* it has a double infraorbital foramen. In spite of its large eyes (and because of the crushing of the specimen accurate measurements are impossible) judgments on whether it was diurnal or nocturnal cannot be meaningfully made. The relatively large brain and the small size of this species are both factors which may influence the relative size of the eyes.

Recent workers dealing with this genus were Kelley and Wood (1954), Morris (1954), McKenna (1960), Robinson (1967), Bown (1974), and Szalay (1976). The dentition shows a combination of features which is so far unique in the family. On all specimens known the tooth rows are tightly packed. No diastemata appear

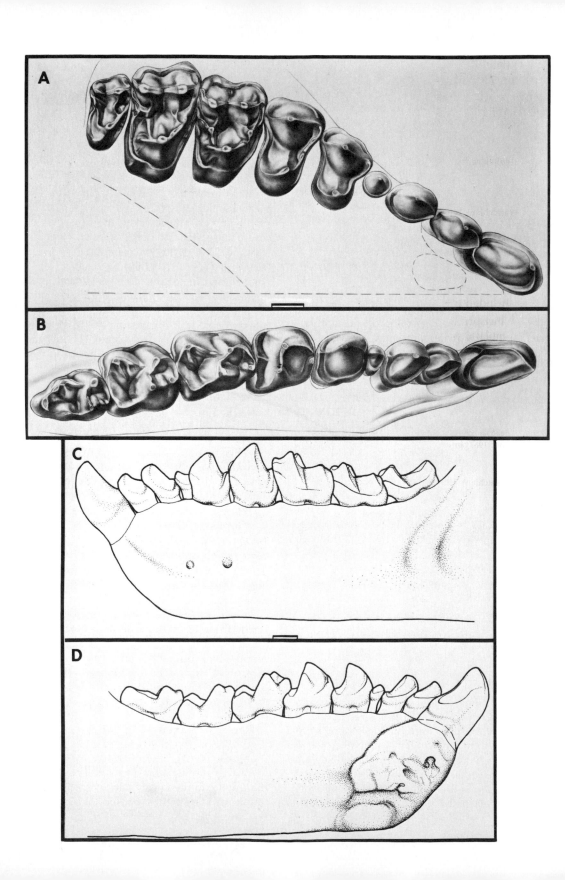

and the teeth overlap and crowd one another. The medial lower incisors are enlarged and bear low crowns and heavy cingulids, and, when the two are viewed together, it is apparent that they formed a robust device, each with a long cutting edge running from the apex to the distal extremity of the crown. It is unlikely that this pair of teeth was used as an awl-like tool. Their long apical edge suggests fruit procuring, peeling, or any activity involving extensive incisal handling.

The upper central pair of incisors, isolated teeth referred to the genus by Szalay (1976), are long, mesiodistally broad, yet buccolingually constricted, with prominent mesiodistal cutting edges. They are basally wide in all directions and have a distinct lingual cingulum. What was judged to be I^2 has a distal, vertically oriented, sharp cutting edge, with a small, basal, distally oriented prominence.

The enlarged lower tooth has a robust root and, in terms of relative size and surface area, it is the most important element of the antemolar dentition, along with the equally relatively prominent $P_{\overline{4}}$. In effect, these two teeth appear to be the most distinctive elements of the dentition of this genus. Both the incisors and the canine are characterized by being transversely broad, probably a derived condition for the anaptomorphines. Both $P_{\overline{3}}$ and $P_{\overline{4}}$ have a distolingually enlarged talonid.

The most distinctive character of the lower molars is the basal inflation of the trigonid cusps and the shallowness of the talonid basin. Except on $M_{\overline{1}}$, the paraconid is closely twinned with the metaconid, and the paracristid extends more mesially than the paraconid, forming a low, but apparently important, cingulid. $M_{\overline{3}}$ is reduced, although the relatively longer talonid of this tooth suggests derivation from an ancestry in which $M_{\overline{3}}$ was relatively larger and longer than those of the molars anterior to it.

M^1 is distinctly less transverse than M^2, and M^3 is much smaller than M^1. The molar hypocone is an anomalous thickening of the postcingulum. In addition to the hypocone there is a well-developed protocone fold. Lingual fusion of the pre- and postcingula occurs in many specimens.

The molar roots of *Tetonius homunculus* are of some interest. Because a very large number of isolated teeth are known, the root structure can be studied in detail. The most significant feature appears to be the extent of roots under the crowns. The lingual root of the upper molars is particularly massive and its tip (i.e., the part farthest from the crown) is flared out and very broad. Both mesially and distally the root extends buccally, whereas in between them a deep furrow can usually be found, the extensions substantially adding perhaps to the surface area of the root. The centrally facing surfaces of both buccal roots of the upper molars also have a broad furrow, and, similarly, the roots of the lower molars are broadly furrowed on the sides facing the transverse midline of the tooth. It appears that the furrows are the result of increase in root size. Comparisons with isolated molars of *Omomys carteri*, for example, clearly show differences in both root construction and some aspects of crown morphology (Szalay, 1976). The trigon and talonid basins of *Omomys carteri* are significantly and consistently deeper than those of *Tetonius homunculus*. There seems to be a causal correlation between the basin morphology and the extent and shape of root structure. The deeper basins and the consequently higher crests surrounding them suggest more extensive, orthal cutting in *Omomys*. On the other hand, the surprisingly shallow basins of *Tetonius homunculus* and the lower and relatively thicker based crests hint that masticatory movements were relatively more mesiolingual than those in *Omomys carteri*. The more robust root patterns of *Tetonius homunculus* appear to reflect that in this species buttressing was better developed to resist the more transversely directed forces than those in *Omomys carteri*.

The two halves of the mandible are relatively uncurved anteriorly. The lower jaw was more or less V-shaped, and the symphysis was almost certainly unfused. The symphysis is relatively very large, however, with a superior and inferior transverse torus and, as in most other omomyids, a distinct canal associated with some of the tongue muscles. No known specimen preserves the ascending ramus.

Enlarged incisors of the particular kind described,

Figure 106. *Tetonius homunculus.* Early Eocene, western North America. Right maxilla with composite I^1–I^2, C, and P^2–M^3: A, occlusal view. Left mandible with $I_{\overline{1}}$–$I_{\overline{2}}$, C, and $P_{\overline{2}}$–$M_{\overline{3}}$: B, occlusal view; C, lateral view; D, medial view. Scales represent 1 mm. [From Szalay (1976).]

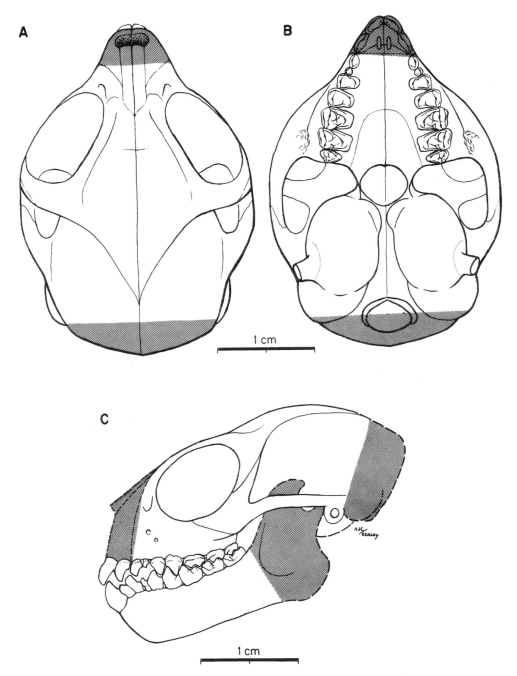

Figure 107. *Tetonius homunculus.* Early Eocene, western North America. Reconstructed skull and mandible: A, dorsal view; B, ventral view; C, Lateral view. [From Szalay (1976).]

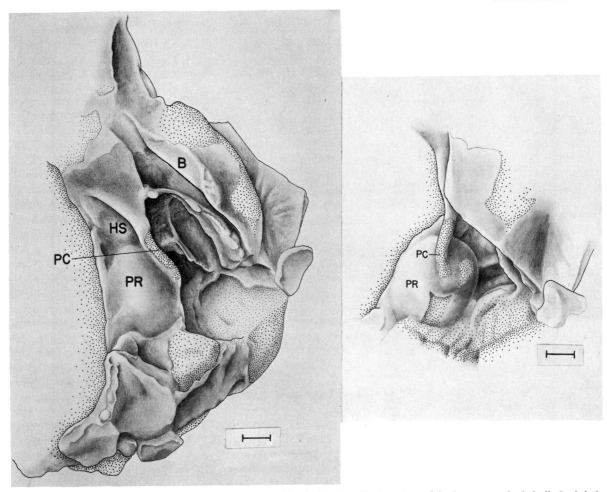

Figure 108. *Tetonius homunculus.* Early Eocene, western North America. Basicranium of the known crushed skull. On left the view is ventral, whereas on the right only the middle ear cavity is shown in ventrolateral view. Scales represent 1 mm. Stippling represents exposed matrix on the fossil. For abbreviations, see Table III. [From Szalay (1976).]

slightly enlarged fourth premolars, and slightly reduced M_3^3 suggest reduction of molar function in favor of incisor and premolar use. Enlarged incisors and reduced molar teeth are usually associated with highly omnivorous, partly frugivorous taxa (*Pan, Pithecia,*

Chiropotes, and *Cacajao*), and, short of a detailed analysis of occlusion and wear, this also might be the best interim hypothesis for the diet of *Tetonius homunculus.*

ABSAROKIUS Matthew, 1915

(= or including: *Anaptomorphus:* Loomis, 1906, in part.)

DISTRIBUTION

Early to early middle Eocene (Wasatchian to early Bridgerian). Rocky Mt. region.

KNOWN SPECIES

1. *Absarokius abotti* (Loomis, 1906), type species (=*Anaptomorphus abotti,* Loomis, 1906.)
LOCALITIES: Lysite★ (208).

2. *Absarokius noctivagus* Matthew, 1915

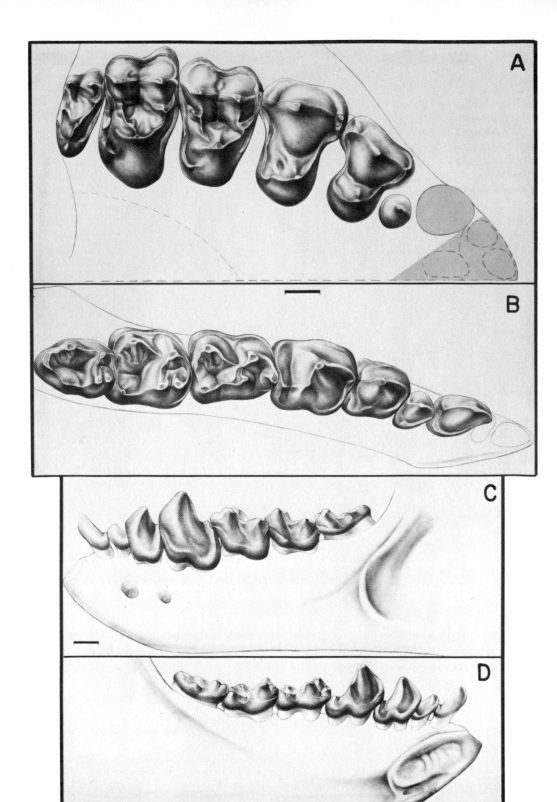

(=*Absarokius noctivagus nocerai* Robinson, 1966.)
LOCALITIES: Lost Cabin⋆ (240); La Barge (238); Huerfano (260).
  3. *Absarokius witteri* Morris, 1954
LOCALITIES: Cathedral Bluffs Tongue⋆ (242).

DISCUSSION

Absarokius spp. (Figures 109 and 110) differ from other genera of the subfamily chiefly in the enlargement of the third and fourth premolars. Although there is also a slight enlargement of $P\frac{4}{}$ in *Tetonius*, this condition is considerably surpassed in *Absarokius*. The central, enlarged lower incisors appear to be relatively smaller than those of *Tetonius*, but, because of great overall similarity and the fact that *Tetonius homunculus* had two incisors, a canine, and three premolars, the *Tetonius homunculus–A. abotti–A. noctivagus* lineage appears probable. The moderately enlarged $P\overline{4}$ and the relatively large $P\overline{3}$ of *T. homunculus*, however, may be enough of a difference from the species of *Absarokius* to maintain the generic distinction. The morphology of the molar teeth of *Absarokius* spp. is quite similar to that of *Tetonius homunculus*, the generic differences between the species being largely restricted to the third and fourth premolars.

The dental formula of *Absarokius* spp. are as follows:

A. abotti: $I\frac{1\cdot2}{}$; $C\frac{1}{}$; $P\frac{2\cdot3\cdot4}{}$; $M\frac{1\cdot2\cdot3}{}$.
A. noctivagus and *A. witteri*: $I\frac{1\cdot2}{}$; $C\frac{1}{}$; $P^{2\cdot3\cdot4}$; $M\frac{1\cdot2\cdot3}{}$.

The differences between the three known species of *Absarokius* are again restricted to the increase in the size of $P\overline{4}$, slight reduction of $P\overline{3}$, and the loss of $P\overline{2}$. There is, in addition, an unclear trend toward size increase and some minor morphological differences in the molars.

A striking feature of the symphyseal area of the preserved *Absarokius* mandibles, possibly a generic character, is the broad, wedge-shaped opening between the superior and inferior transverse tori of the symphysis.

As shown by the morphology, selection affected the $P\frac{2}{2}$–$P\frac{4}{4}$ complex more than the molar dentition. The alveolar evidence indicates that the first incisor was reduced in *A. noctivagus* compared to *A. abotti*.

Absarokius is one of those unusual genera known by three chronologically successive samples (Kelley and Wood, 1954; Morris, 1954; Robinson, 1966), two of which may be in an ancestor–descendant relationship to one another (Szalay, 1976). The following facts appear obvious from the detailed treatment of the individual species by Szalay (1976): The mandible has become more robust and shorter, and the $P\overline{2}$ was lost from *A. abotti* to *A. noctivagus*; the third and fourth premolars have become progressively both transversely and mesiodistally more robust but have not become more molarized, the change being largely the result of the increased robusticity of the paracones and protoconids; the first incisor is apparently somewhat more reduced in the more advanced *A. noctivagus*; the symphysis is progressively more vertical in the younger species; and perhaps both the upper and lower dental arcades have become more U-shaped from *A. abotti* to *A. noctivagus*.

All these derived characters indicate a deemphasis of the anterior dentition and the obvious emphasis shifted to the premolars. The robusticity of the latter compels one to conclude that the large forces incurred resulted in the correlated mechanical solution of relative tooth size increases. It appears that this described shift might represent the change associated with specializations of a frugivore to certain hard fruits, or nuts, and these specializations are not likely to be derived adaptations either for folivory or insectivory.

ANEMORHYSIS Gazin, 1958

(= or including: *Tetonius*: Matthew, 1915. *Paratetonius?*: Gazin, 1952. *Uintalacus* Gazin, 1958. *Tetoioides* Gazin, 1962. *Teilhardina*: Bown, 1976.)

DISTRIBUTION
  Early Eocene (Wasatchian). Rocky Mt. region.

KNOWN SPECIES
  1. *Anemorhysis sublettensis* (Gazin, 1952), type species
(=*Paratetonius ?sublettensis* Gazin, 1952.)
LOCALITIES: La Barge⋆ (238).
  2. *Anemorhysis musculus* (Matthew, 1915)
[=*Tetonius musculus* (Matthew, 1915). *Paratetonius musculus*

Figure 109. *Absarokius abotti.* Early Eocene, western North America. Right maxilla with P^2–P^4, M^1–M^3: A, occlusal view. Left mandible with C, $P\overline{2}$–$M\overline{3}$: B, occlusal view; C, lateral view; D, medial view. Scales represent 1 mm. [From Szalay (1976).]

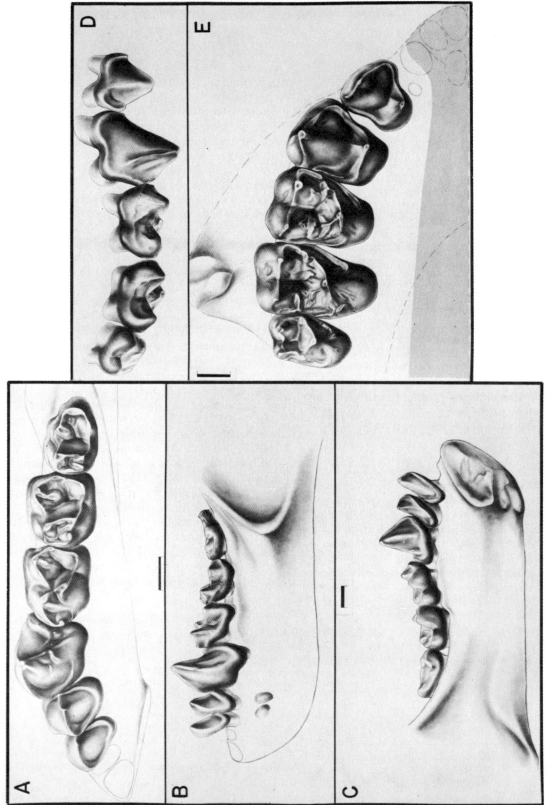

Figure 110. *Absarokius noctivagus.* Late early Eocene, western North America. Right corpus with C and P₃–M₃: A, occlusal view; B, lateral view; C, medial view. Right palate with P²–M²: D, buccal view of teeth; E, occlusal view. Stippling and broken lines indicate reconstructions. Scales represent 1 mm. [From Szalay (1976).]

(Matthew, 1915). *Anemorhysis muscula* (Matthew, 1915).]
LOCALITIES: Lysite★ (208).

3. *Anemorhysis tenuiculus* (Jepsen, 1930a)

(=*Tetonius tenuiculus* Jepsen, 1930a. *Paratetonius ?tenuiculus:* Gazin, 1952. *Tetonoides pearcei* Gazin, 1962. *Tetonoides tenuiculus:* Gazin, 1962. *Teilhardina americana* Bown, 1976.)
LOCALITIES: Gray Bull★ (162); Golden Valley (182); La Barge (238).

4. *Anemorhysis* sp.

(=*Uintalacus nettingi* Gazin, 1958.)
LOCALITIES: Powder Wash★ (264).

DISCUSSION

Anemorhysis spp. are small primates with fourth lower premolars which are semimolariform to premolariform and have distinct paraconids and metaconids lower or subequal to the height of the molars. Buccal cingulids of lower molars are distinct, more often better developed than those of *Tetonius*. Differences of *A. tenuiculus* from *A. sublettensis* and *A. musculus* appear to lie primarily in the proportions of the antemolar dentition (Szalay, 1976). *Anemorhysis tenuiculus* (Figure 111) has a relatively large $P_{\overline{2}}$, whereas in the latter, younger species, $P_{\overline{2}}$ is rudimentary or absent. Numerous samples described under various names (see synonymy list) have been recently restudied and allocated to this genus by Szalay (1976). The poorly known *Anemorhysis* sp., based on "*Uintalacus nettingi*," is discussed in detail by Szalay (1976). It may represent a specimen of *A. sublettensis*.

The dental formulas of *Anemorhysis* spp. are as follows:

A. tenuiculus and *A. musculus:* $I\frac{1\cdot2}{1\cdot2}$; $C\frac{1}{1}$; $P\frac{2\cdot3\cdot4}{2\cdot3\cdot4}$; $M\frac{1\cdot2\cdot3}{1\cdot2\cdot3}$.
A. sublettensis: $I\frac{1\cdot2}{1\cdot2}$; $C\frac{1}{1}$; $P^?\frac{3\cdot4}{3\cdot4}$; $M\frac{1\cdot2\cdot3}{1\cdot2\cdot3}$.

No single published sample is large enough to allow a meaningful assessment of the upper and lower dentition of any of the species allocated to *Anemorhysis*. A new genus from the Wasatchian Bitter Creek, however, recently collected by D. E. Savage, B. Waters, and H. Hutchison is a form close to *Anemorhysis*, and it is known from a large sample.

Unlike *Chlororhysis* and *Tetonius*, which have only a rudimentary metaconid on $P_{\overline{4}}$, the earliest known *Anemorhysis*, *A. tenuiculus*, has a large metaconid on $P_{\overline{4}}$ and thus also a protocristid running transversely on this tooth.

The heavy cingulids, the slightly molarized $P_{\overline{4}}$, and the gradually reduced antemolar dentition along with the increasing premolarization of $P_{\overline{4}}$ are enigmatic. Judged from the alveoli, the central lower incisor was enlarged (Szalay, 1976). The molars are well suited for mesiolingual cutting, but this should be corroborated from the mandible and the temporomandibular joint, a task which must be delayed due to lack of appropriate specimens. The overall robust β-thegosed molars (Every, 1972) might reflect a more phytophagous than zoophagous diet. On the other hand, if the enlarged incisors, once they become known, will show pointed, gracile cusps, features associated with prey catching, perhaps a primarily insectivorous way of life will then become a more suitable explanation for the total dental morphology of *Anemorhysis*.

ALTANIUS Dashzeveg and McKenna, 1977

DISTRIBUTION
Early Eocene. Mongolian People's Republic.
KNOWN SPECIES
Altanius orlovi Dashzeveg and McKenna, 1977, type species
LOCALITIES: Bumbin Nuru, Naran Bulak Fm.★ (192).

DISCUSSION

This recently discovered tiny primate (smaller than *Microcebus murinus*) represents the oldest undoubted Asiatic fossil tarsiiform. As its authors noted, *Altanius* resembles the tetoniinan anaptomorphines more closely than any other group of tarsiiforms. In particular, the resemblance is to *Anemorhysis* and, to some degree, *Tetonius*. *Altanius* is known from a single specimen (see Figure 112), a right lower jaw fragment with $P_{\overline{4}}$-$M_{\overline{3}}$. Given this limited information, the major known significant morphological difference from other tetoniinans lies in the combination of a mesiodistally very narrow $M_{\overline{1}}$ talonid and an unusually large $M_{\overline{3}}$ talonid compared to those of the first and second molars. The diagnosis given by the authors (Dashzeveg and McKenna, 1977) of this genus—"heel of $P_{\overline{4}}$ reduced but $P_{\overline{4}}$ metaconid present; $M_{\overline{1}}$ trigonid open, with unreduced, conical paraconid: $M_{\overline{3}}$ with large, lingually placed paraconid, expanded talonid; molars lacking mesoconids. Jaw deep" (p. 127)—also characterizes *Trogolemur* and, with the exception of the state of the $M_{\overline{3}}$ talonid, *Teilhardina* and *Anemorhysis*. The diagnosis is a good characterization of the morphotype of the Anaptomor-

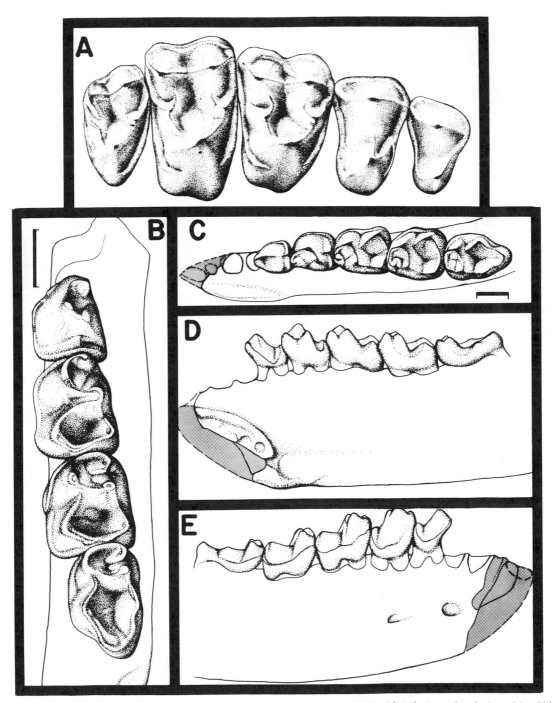

Figure 111. *Anemorhysis tenuiculus*. Early Eocene, western North America. Right P^3–M^3: A, occlusal view. Mandible with P_4–M_3: B, occlusal view. Right mandible with P_3–M_3 and alveoli of anterior dentition: C, occlusal view; D, medial view; E, lateral view. Stippling and broken lines represent reconstruction. Scales represent 1 mm. [From Szalay (1976).]

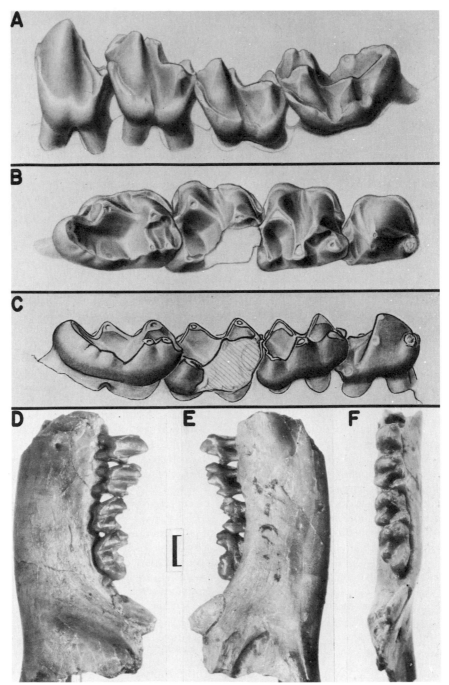

Figure 112. *Altanius orlovi.* Early Eocene, eastern Asia. Left mandibular fragment with $P_{\overline{4}}$–$M_{\overline{3}}$: A and D, lateral views; B and F, occlusal view; C and E, medial views. Hatching represents broken area. Scale, applicable to D, E, and F, represents 1 mm. [From Dashzeveg and McKenna (1977), courtesy of M. C. McKenna.]

phinae, which probably did have a relatively larger $M_{\overline{3}}$ than that of most anaptomorphines known.

Dashzeveg and McKenna (1977) draw attention to various differences from microsyopines (including, according to them, *Plesiolestes*), *Purgatorius*, *Palenochtha*, paromomyids and *Saxonella*, *Elphidotarsius*, *Omomys*, *Hoanghonius*, *Tarsius*, *Teilhardina*, *Tetonius*, "*Pseudotetonius*," *Anemorhysis*, *Micromomys*, and *Tinimomys*. These differences, cited by them from the taxa listed, however, are not unique to *Altanius* and, therefore, they do not throw any light on the significant characters of the genus and therefore the possible degree of relationships of the taxa compared to *Altanius*.

Significantly, the most striking aspect of *Altanius* (and other anaptomorphines), the progressively more mesiodistally constricted trigonids, is not likely to be a derived omomyid character. *Pelycodus*, the most primitive known notharctine, has trigonid construction identical to that of *Altanius* and other anaptomorphines. In fact, the relatively large $M_{\overline{3}}$ is a character of *Pelycodus*. In contrast to the statement of Dashzeveg and McKenna (1977) that "Anaptomorphine omomyids are . . . synapomorphous with *Altanius* in the shared-derived acquisition of a high, incipiently blade-like $P_{\overline{4}}$" (p. 130) stands the fact that $P_{\overline{4}}$ in *Pelycodus* is premolariform, tall, and shortheeled as in *Altanius*. It is not unlikely that this combination represents a condition near the omomyid morphotype. Although Dashzeveg and McKenna (1977) do not point out these fundamental similarities of not only *Altanius* but of other anaptomorphines to the earliest known *Pelycodus*, they do, however, allude to some nebulous ties with carpolestids and note that "Carpolestid molars are somewhat exodaenodont, a presumably derived condition shared with the anaptomorphines" (p. 130).

In light of the clearly shared derived molar features of carpolestids with plesiadapids, the autapomorphous nature of carpolestids, and the unquestioned shared derived condition of known aspects of the skeleton between omomyids and adapids, these similarities may have adaptational meaning but have relatively little phylogenetic significance.

Rather than relegating *Altanius* to limbo or to the Adapidae, there is one suggestion that the genus is an anaptomorphine from the character of $P_{\overline{4}}$, which is rather short mesiodistally. This tooth suggests crowding anteriorly as in *Anemorhysis* or *Tetonius*. Given the tiny size and the overall patristic similarity of *Altanius* to the small anaptomorphines, the most reasonable hypothesis is that it is one of them. It must be stated that this conclusion is not unequivocally supported by any other undisputed shared and derived characters with anaptomorphines alone, but rather by an overall patristic similarity.

In considering the adaptations of *Altanius*, its tiny size is a significant factor. Dashzeveg and McKenna (1977) noted that "such a small animal probably lived in a warm climate in which food was rather constantly available, probably in the form of insects and other small invertebrates rather than primarily fruit or gums" (p. 121). It should be added that in warm climates with a perennial food supply insects abound largely because fruits and tree exudates are present. Many animals, including primates, are competitors of insects and vice versa for fruits and tree resins. The evolution of the smallest living primates, the cheirogaleids and the callitrichines, is suspected to be the direct result of evolutionary specialization for a gumivore–insectivore diet (see under these groups). The specialization required when such shifts take place often involves dental adaptations associated with scraping with the dentition and size reduction. As the anterior dentition is not known in *Altanius*, this may be a moot point. Nevertheless, the common specialization of the enlarged anterior dentition of many omomyids, particularly of the tetoniinan and trogolemurin anaptomorphines, suggests at least partial specialization for gumivory.

MCKENNAMORPHUS Szalay, 1976

(= or including: *Trogolemur:* McKenna, 1960.)

DISTRIBUTION
  Early Eocene (Wasatchian). Rocky Mt. region.
KNOWN SPECIES
  Mckennamorphus despairensis Szalay, 1976, type species
LOCALITIES: Four Mile, Despair Q.★ (180).

DISCUSSION

Mckennamorphus, based on a single specimen (Figure 113), differs from the contemporary and sympatric *Tetonius* in having almost 100% more robust enlarged lower incisor. The premolars (only $P_{\overline{3}}$ is known), the

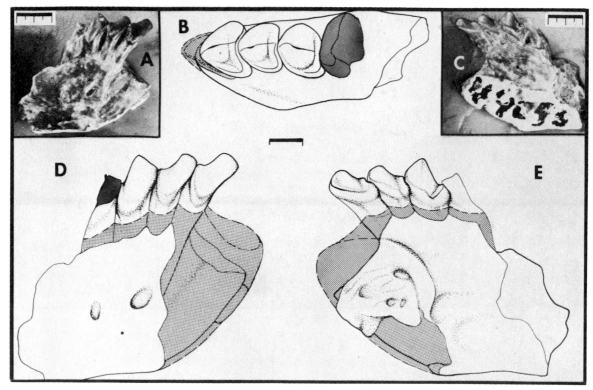

Figure 113. *Mckennamorphus despairensis.* Early Eocene, western North America. Right mandible fragment with root of I, I$_{\overline{2}}$, C, P$_{\overline{3}}$, and fragment of P$_{\overline{4}}$: A and D, lateral views; B, occlusal view; C and E, medial views. Scale in the middle represents 1 mm. Subdivisions on the scales on the photographs represent 0.5 mm. [From Szalay (1976).]

canine, and the small second incisor have crowns with a relatively greater occlusal surface area than the homologous teeth in undoubted *Tetonius,* except possibly in *Tetonius ambiguus* (Matthew, 1915), which has recently been named "*Pseudotetonius ambiguus*" by Bown (1974). *Mckennamorphus* differs from known *Trogolemur* in having the antemolar dentition much more tightly packed and consequently having an antemolar crown pattern relatively mesiodistally shorter and buccolingually wider than in *Trogolemur.*

This is a poorly known, and therefore problematical, genus although its generic distinctness from the sympatric *Tetonius* is clear (McKenna, 1960). From the symphyseal morphology and the little that is known of its cheek teeth it is certainly an omomyid primate and very likely an anaptomorphine related to *Tetonius.* Although the greatly enlarged incisor might suggest generic affinities with *Trogolemur* (McKenna, 1960), the crown morphology of the antemolar teeth tends to preclude this and the differences, noted above, indi-

cate a clear generic distinction from *Trogolemur* or any other known omomyid.

The dental formula is probably I$_{\overline{1,2}}^{1,2}$; C$_{\overline{1}}^{1}$; P$_{\overline{3,4}}^{2,3,4}$; M$_{\overline{1,2,3(?)}}^{1,2,3(?)}$.

There are two highly significant features which are easily discernible even on the fragmentary type specimen. The anterior incisor, I$_{\overline{1}}$, was nearly vertically implanted (unlike its horizontally placed homologue in *Trogolemur*) and was clearly the dominant feature of the mandible. The crown was probably enormous and, judged from the teeth posterior to it, had a mesiodistally running cutting edge, perhaps not unlike that of *Tetonius.* Thus I$_{\overline{2}}$, C, and P$_{\overline{3}}$ distal to the root of I$_{\overline{1}}$ are fairly uniform in shape; they are characterized by having closely packed crowns each more wide than long. Their great relative width and nearly continuous cutting edges show these to be highly functional and not "reduced" teeth.

The large incisors are clearly a selective response to the great stresses incurred by this tooth. This indicates

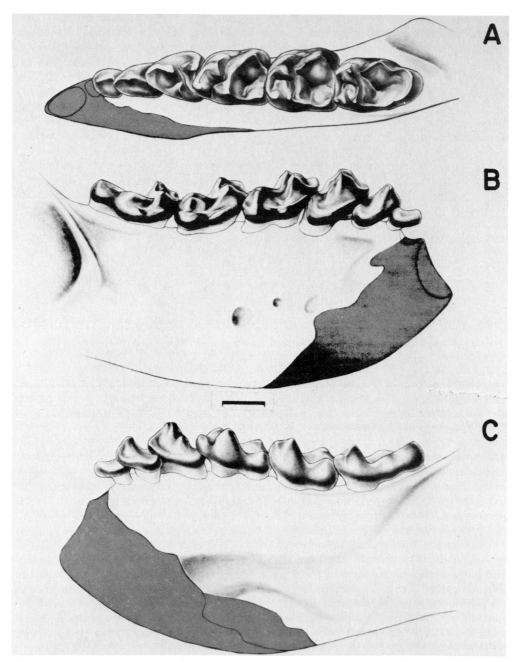

Figure 114. *Trogolemur myodes.* Middle Eocene, western North America. Right horizontal ramus with C, and $P_{\overline{3}}$–$M_{\overline{3}}$: A, occlusal view; B, lateral view; C, medial view. Uniform stippling indicates reconstruction. The scale represents 1 mm. [From Szalay (1976).]

a specialized activity probably related to food procurement. To speculate on the nature of the mechanics of this activity is difficult, however, as only the crown of this tooth would permit the formulation of any hypothesis. Judged by the teeth with crowns one suspects that a mesiodistally oriented rather than a transverse edge dominated this tooth. It was then probably unlike the rodent-like transverse cutting edges of the enlarged incisors of the plesiadapid *Chiromyoides* or the lemuriform *Daubentonia*. Thus, perhaps the enlarged teeth of *Mckennamorphus* are not adaptations for gnawing wood, like those of *Daubentonia*, but rather for manipulation of a particular kind(s) of hard fruits or seed pods. The broad crowns of the antemolar teeth also suggest an active preparatory and perhaps even some masticatory function by these teeth.

The symphysis is sufficiently preserved to deserve comment. The dorsal part, best referred to as the superior transverse torus, is more of a semicircle than a shelf and it is anteroposteriorly the widest part of the symphysis. The extent of the symphysis clearly reflects unusually great stresses, a hypothesis well in harmony with the presence of the enlarged incisor. The very large superior transverse torus perhaps reflects buttressing as a result of contralateral muscle input (?temporalis) into the function of the enlarged ipsilateral incisor.

This specialized genus is not likely to be primarily either insectivorous or folivorous, but rather should be considered to have been frugivorous and omnivorous.

Tribe Trogolemurini
Szalay, 1976

DISTRIBUTION
  Middle Eocene (Bridgerian). Western North America.
INCLUDED TAXA
  Trogolemur.

DISCUSSION

These anaptomorphines differ from all other taxa of the subfamily in having an extremely reduced canine (? or $P_{\overline{2}}$) and relatively very long third molars. The first pair of incisors is greatly enlarged, extending under the molars, unlike in *Mckennamorphus* or in any other anaptomorphines in which the enlarged incisors are more vertically placed and extended only under the anterior premolars.

Trogolemurins are the most distinctive and in many ways morphologically the most derived among anaptomorphines (Figure 114). This is taxonomically expressed by the tribal rank. The most significant characters which support the anaptomorphine ties of this group are the shallowness of the talonid basins and the basal inflation of trigonid cusps.

The molar proportions of *Altanius* are suggestive of a possible tie between *Trogolemur* and *Altanius* or close relatives. As noted under the Tetoniina, *Trogolemur* does not share the enlarged condition of $P_{\overline{4}}$ with *Altanius*. The large $M_{\overline{3}}$ shared by the two genera might have been independently derived.

TROGOLEMUR Matthew, 1909

DISTRIBUTION
  Middle to late Eocene (Bridgerian to Uintan). Rocky Mt. region.
KNOWN SPECIES
  1. *Trogolemur myodes* Matthew, 1909, type species
LOCALITIES: Upper Bridger★ (282).
  2. *Trogolemur* sp.: Robinson, 1968
LOCALITIES: Badwater Creek, 5a★ (296).

DISCUSSION

The salient features of *Trogolemur* are noted under the tribal discussion. The major changes from a *Chlororhysis-, Anemorhysis-,* or *Altanius*-like ancestry involved an increase in the relative size of the root of $I_{\overline{1}}$, the loss of $P_{\overline{2}}$, the loss of the anterior roots of $P_{\overline{3}}$ and $P_{\overline{4}}$,

and a slight increase in the relative size of $M_{\overline{3}}$ compared to $M_{\overline{1}-\overline{2}}$. This latter trait might be an ancestral character retained in *Trogolemur*.

The dental formula is $I_{\frac{1\cdot2}{1\cdot2}}$; $C_{\frac{1}{1}}$; $P^{2\cdot\frac{3}{3}\cdot\frac{4}{4}}$; $M_{\frac{1\cdot2\cdot3}{1\cdot2\cdot3}}$.

Trogolemur is poorly known (Figure 114), yet the known hypodigm gives an adequate idea at least of the highly characteristic lower dentition and part of the mandible. The anterior incisor is very enlarged and extends as far back as the talonid of $M_{\overline{3}}$. The tooth behind it, presumably an $I_{\overline{2}}$, was very small by comparison and its crown was tucked under the third tooth of the jaw, probably the canine. This tooth was greatly overlapped by $P_{\overline{3}}$, this in turn by $P_{\overline{4}}$, and the latter by $M_{\overline{1}}$. The premolars, like the molars, are low crowned with an elongated paracristid and a metaconid on $P_{\overline{4}}$. The molar row is relatively very long and the crowns are broad and extensive. Molar trigonids are relatively wide and long mesiodistally and the paraconids and metaconids are not as closely twinned as either in *Tetonius* or *Anaptomorphus*.

The symphysis on the holotype (Figure 114), although most of it is broken, is the best one known and is very long and extensive. It lies nearly parallel with the inferior edge of the mandible as, for example, in *Anemorhysis*. The anterior half of the mandible is very robust, clearly to accommodate the enlarged incisors. Three mental foramina, one quite large, are present under $P_{\overline{4}}$ and $M_{\overline{1}}$. This latter might be of some significance for the physiology of the teeth, probably of the incisor. Continuous growth for the enlarged incisor is a possibility.

Trogolemur myodes was an extremely tiny mammal, with a skull probably barely exceeding 2 cm in length. This small size renders interpretations of the known morphology an additionally difficult task because the feeding habits of the smaller living mammals are much more poorly known than of the larger species. *Microcebus* is the only living primate in the size range of *Trogolemur* and its dental proportions suggest little adaptational similarity to those of this anaptomorphine.

A few general remarks, however, can be made of the available evidence. The open $M_{\overline{1}}$ trigonids and talonids of the molars and the crowns of the antemolar teeth appear to have maximized the cutting edges. Judged from the conformation of the cheek teeth the large incisor was probably also a long-edged cutting tooth, but at any rate a tooth on which considerable stresses were incurred. The large $M_{\overline{3}}$ talonid, relatively the largest among known omomyids, was of obvious significance for food processing in *Trogolemur*. A large $M_{\overline{3}}$ talonid has come to be associated with extremes of some form of phytopagous rather than zoophagous diet. Thus, it is possible that the combination of very large incisor, well-developed cutting edges on the cheek teeth, and a relatively large $M_{\overline{3}}$ talonid might reflect a diet in which food procurement and mastication were primarily dependent on prolonged incisor use and efficient slicing by the cheek teeth. Without more evidence from specimens, comparative occlusal studies are not possible. Some specialized form of frugivory coupled with gum, resin, grub, and insect eating should suffice as a preliminary hypothesis for the diet of *Trogolemur* (Szalay, 1976).

SUBFAMILY OMOMYINAE
Trouessart, 1879

(= or including: Omomynae Trouessart, 1879. Omomyinae: Wortman, 1904. Omomyidae: Gazin, 1958. Mytoniinae Robinson, 1968.)

DISTRIBUTION
Early Eocene to early Oligocene (Wasatchian to Chadronian). Western North America.
INCLUDED TAXA
Tribes Omomyini, Washakiini, Uintaniini, Utahiini, and Rooneyiini.

DISCUSSION

The Omomyinae are the most diversified and longest lasting subfamily of the Omomyidae and in many features they appear to be unquestionably quite primitive. Mastoid inflation was, as far as it can be assessed, well developed in the anaptomorphine *Tetonius* and extremely developed in the microchoerine *Necrolemur*, but it is barely advanced in the only known complete cranium of an omomyine, that of *Rooneyia*. At least in several members of the subfamily the trigonid crests are rather high and the cusps are not broadly based like those of anaptomorphines. Along with the generally low crowned molars, uninflated trigon cusps, and relatively tall trigonid crests, the talonid basins of the early representatives tend to be deep. In omomyines, unlike in anaptomorphines, $M_{\overline{3}}$ tends to be mesiodistally longer than $M_{\overline{2}}$ and the $M_{\overline{3}}$ talonid somewhat more transverse than those of anaptomorphines.

The omomyines, as understood by Szalay (1976), make their first appearance in *Omomys minutus* during the medial Wasatchian (Lysitean), whereas the last known taxon of this category (*Macrotarsius montanus*) is early Oligocene (Chadronian) in age. As noted under the family discussion, omomyines are the most varied of the subfamilies of the Omomyidae, requiring the tribal subdivisions utilized to express this diversity. These tribes represent a dentally highly diversified radiation of primates. Although all are very likely derived from a common omomyine ancestry, their interrelationships (see Figure 98) are poorly understood. This is largely due to the fact that we know them mostly by a few teeth and rarely by complete dentitions. Furthermore, because they are highly diversified they share relatively few, not well understood, character states beyond primitive omomyine features. To give a detailed account of what may represent dentally the primitive omomyine condition, however, is probably not possible with any degree of confidence. The most notable omomyine dental trait may be the relatively open nature of the trigonids in contrast to the primitive anaptomorphine condition.

Molar morphology of the ancestral microchoerine was likely to have been similar to the teeth of *Nannopithex raabi,* and therefore not significantly different from the postulated primitive omomyine condition. The clade Microchoerinae, however, can be easily delineated from known omomyines by pointing out the incisor specializations of the European tarsiiforms (see under Microchoerinae).

Although very likely omomyine derived, the Ekgmowechashalinae is maintained as a distinct subfamily. Among living mammals, primates or bats, for example, dental adaptations as distinctive as those of the North American Miocene omomyid are often given at least subfamily recognition.

Tribe Omomyini
Trouessart, 1879

(= or including: Mytoniinae Robinson, 1968. Omomyini: Szalay, 1976.)

DISTRIBUTION
Early Eocene to early Oligocene (Wasatchian to Chadronian). Western North America.
INCLUDED TAXA
Subtribes Omomyina and Mytoniina.

Discussion

Omomyins are characterized by the probably derived absence of a protocone-fold, three premolars, and moderately enlarged first incisors. The taxa included in this tribe appear to be monophyletic. These two groups may be viewed as representative of two minor levels of dental organization, in which the more primitive group is more ancient and the ancestor of the younger and more derived one. Late Eocene–early Oligocene mytoniinans are most likely derived from some early middle Eocene omomyinans.

SUBTRIBE OMOMYINA
Trouessart, 1879

(= or including: Omomyina: Szalay, 1976.)

DISTRIBUTION
Early to late Eocene (Wasatchian to Duchesnian). Western North America.
INCLUDED TAXA
Omomys and *Chumashius.*

Discussion

These taxa are omomyins with a usually continuous lingual cingulum on the upper molars and, when known, with a moderately piercing anterior dentition. The similarity between the dentitions (particularly the cheek teeth) of taxa of this group and the callitrichines could be significant. The dentition of *Chumashius,* for example, is an ideal structural ancestor for that of a platyrrhine morphotype with a somewhat *Branisella-* or callitrichine-like molar dentition.

OMOMYS Leidy, 1869

(= or including: *Euryacodon* Marsh, 1872a. *Palaeacodon* Marsh, 1872a. *Notharctus:* Loomis, 1906, in part. *Washakius:* Simpson, 1959, in part.)

DISTRIBUTION
Early to middle Eocene (Wasatchian to Bridgerian). Rocky Mt. region.
KNOWN SPECIES
1. *Omomys carteri* Leidy, 1869, type species
(=*Hemiacodon nanus* Marsh, 1872a. *Hemiacodon pucillus* Marsh, 1872a.

Euryacodon lepidus Marsh, 1872a. *Palaeacodon vagus* Marsh, 1872a. *Washakius insignis:* Simpson, 1959.)
LOCALITIES: Powder Wash (264); Lower Bridger B★ (266).
2. *Omomys lloydi* Gazin, 1958
LOCALITIES: Powder Wash★ (264).
3. *Omomys minutus* (Loomis, 1906)
(=*Notharctus minutus* Loomis, 1906. ?*Anemorhysis minutus:* McKenna, 1960, in part.)
LOCALITIES: Lysite★ (208).

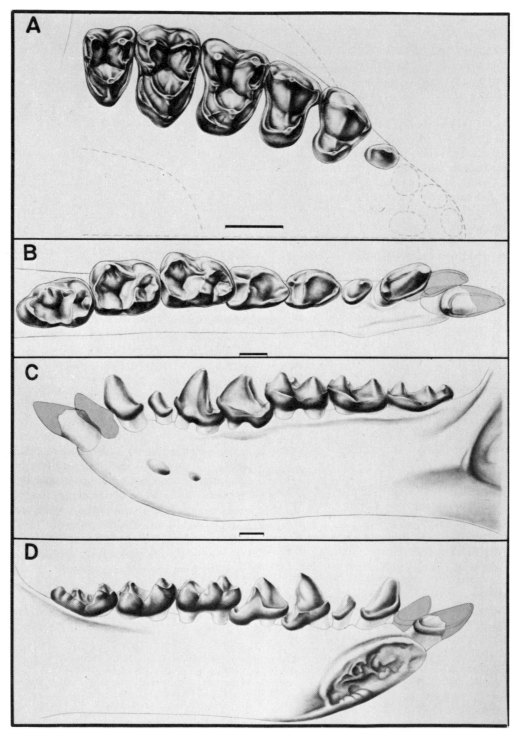

Figure 115. *Omomys carteri.* Middle Eocene, western North America. Right palate with P^2–M^3. A, occlusal view. Left horizontal ramus with I$_{\overline{1-2}}$, C, and P$_{\overline{2}}$–M$_{\overline{3}}$: B, occlusal view; C, lateral view; D, medial view. Stippling and broken lines indicate reconstruction. Scales represent 1 mm. [From Szalay (1976).]

Discussion

Omomys (Figure 115) differs from most omomyines, except *Chumashius* and *Dyseolemur*, in having lingually continuous cingula on the upper molars. It differs from *Chumashius* in having relatively taller third and fourth premolars. Although pericones occur in other omomyines in addition to *Omomys*, this genus is very distinct in having large, pointed pericones on the mesiolingual portion of the broad lingual cingulum as well as an equally distinct true hypocone distolingually. The lack of any trace of protocone-fold is possibly a specialization of *Omomys* that separates this genus from most other omomyines, except *Chumashius*. The

most recent students of the genus have been Gazin (1958) and Szalay (1976).

The dental morphology of most Eocene tarsiiforms has often been compared with *Omomys*, as there is a tacit assumption in the works of most students that the dental morphology of *Omomys* is primitive both for the family and for the infraorder. The original description of *Teilhardina belgica* illustrates this point as that dentally primitive European species was held to be a species of *Omomys* and then later an omomyid, *sensu stricto*. Comparisons of *Omomys carteri* with paromomyids and anaptomorphine omomyids such as *Teilhardina*, *Anemorhysis*, and *Tetonius* reveal that the molar morphology of *Omomys* is different from the

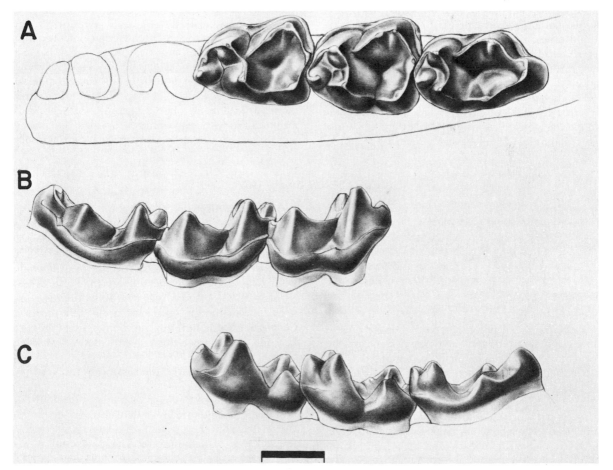

Figure 116. *Omomys minutus.* Early Eocene, western North America. Right mandible with M$_{\overline{1}}$–M$_{\overline{3}}$. A, occlusal view; B, buccal view; C, lingual view. Scale represents 1 mm. [From Szalay (1976).]

above genera in lacking the extensive slope distolingual to the apex of the protocone, and the protocone-fold. Instead, unlike the anaptomorphines cited, the hypocone function is performed by a hypocone formed on the postcingulum itself. The distinctive pericone is an advanced feature and the true hypocone on the postcingulum is very probably also a derived character (Szalay, 1976).

The canines are considerably reduced in size and the incisors are moderately enlarged. The third premolars have rather robust and tall paracones and protoconids, respectively, an adaptation difficult to understand. It is an area of the tooth row which may have performed a role of piercing or puncturing in conjunction with the relatively small canines.

Perhaps another unusual feature of the known parts of this genus is the relatively long mandible. The second premolar is small, yet it is not packed in between the adjacent teeth. As far as one can tell of the meager sample of this region it has diastemata mesial and distal to it.

Omomys minutus (Figure 116) is smaller than either *O. carteri* or *O. lloydi*. Due to lack of an adequate sample the percentage of the size differences is not very meaningful. The mandible is distinctly shallower and more slender than those in *O. carteri* or *O. lloydi*. This small species is very close to *Omomys lloydi* in size and there appear to be some morphological differences on the type which may warrant doubting the generic assignment to *Omomys*. It should be pointed out, however, that generic separation of *Omomys minutus* based on known material is not warranted. The teeth of *Omomys lloydi* and *Omomys minutus* are not of greatly different size, those of *Omomys lloydi* being slightly larger. The mandible of *Omomys minutus*, however, is distinctly shallower than that of specimens of *Omomys lloydi*. There is also a strong hint of relatively higher trigonid cusps in *Omomys minutus* and a more lingual paraconid, especially on $M_{\overline{2}}$, than in either *O. carteri* or *O. lloydi*. These noted differences, on the other hand, should not be taken as necessarily diagnostic differences of generic rank. Better samples of this species might strengthen the allocation to *Omomys* even more.

As noted under *Tetonius*, the dental evidence suggests a somewhat more orthal movement in occlusion than in *Tetonius* and perhaps this is indicative of a more vertical shear, often associated with zoophagy rather than with phytophagy. Species of *Omomys* were probably primarily insectivorous–carnivorous.

CHUMASHIUS Stock, 1933

DISTRIBUTION
    Late Eocene (Duchesnean). California.
KNOWN SPECIES
    Chumashius balchi Stock, 1933, type species
LOCALITIES: CIT 150, Sespe★ (330).

DISCUSSION

Chumashius is an omomyine with relatively large canines and small incisors, low crowned molars, no apparent hypocone but lingually continuous pre- and postcingula, and an M^3 distinctly less wide than M^2. The genus differs from *Omomys* in lacking the distinct pericone and hypocone of the latter, in having relatively less tall third and fourth premolars, and, judged by the size of the alveoli, in having a relatively larger canine.

Chumashius (Figure 117) is very similar to *Omomys* (Stock, 1933; Gazin, 1958; Russell *et al.*, 1967; Szalay, 1976), and this similarity appears to be a derived gestalt which these two genera share from a common ancestor. Yet, *Omomys* shows a number of more derived character states beyond such shared derived features as the heavy cingulum and the lack of protocone-fold. Therefore, derivation of *Chumashius* from *Omomys* is much less likely than the reverse (Szalay, 1976). *Omomys* was probably derived from a species which might be meaningfully referred to as *Chumashius*, although this ancestral species probably had relatively larger third molars than *Chumashius balchi*.

The dental formula of *Chumashius* is $I_{\overline{1},\overline{2}}^{\underline{2}}$; $C_{\overline{1}}^{\underline{1}}$; $P_{\overline{2},\overline{3},\overline{4}}^{\underline{2},\underline{3},\underline{4}}$; $M_{\overline{1},\overline{2},\overline{3}}^{\underline{1},\underline{2},\underline{3}}$.

The trigonids of *Chumashius* are long mesiodistally and the paraconids are low, but distinct on $M_{\overline{1}}$ and $M_{\overline{2}}$. Correlated with the presence of distinct paraconids is the absence of a hypocone. The paraconid is well developed on $P_{\overline{4}}$ with a long paracristid, and $P_{\overline{3}}$ and $P_{\overline{4}}$ are long mesiodistally. The teeth are flat, with relatively smooth enamel and the cingula are very well

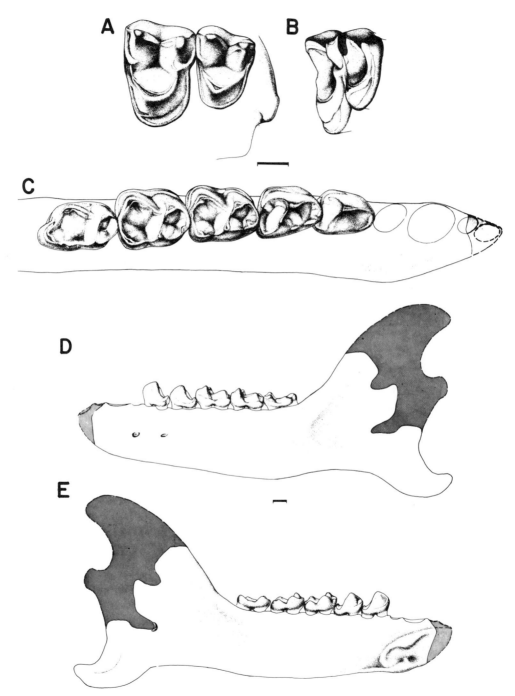

Figure 117. *Chumashius balchi.* Late Eocene, western North America. Left M²⁻³: A, occlusal view; B, occlusodistal view. Left mandible with P₃–P₄, M₁–M₃: C, occlusal view; D, lateral view; E, medial view. Scales represent 1 mm. [From Szalay (1976).]

developed. The canines were not small or reduced but of fair size, and the incisors were not relatively large.

The long, shallow, straight (i.e., uncurved at the symphyseal region) horizontal ramus indicates no excessive transverse stressing of the mandible. The angle is not enlarged and therefore the specialization to increase the force generated by the internal pterygoids was not developed. Similarly, the shallow masseteric fossa signals the relative unimportance of the masseteric musculature. One can determine little from the dental mechanism of the known sample of this genus. The teeth, particularly the upper ones, show a very great similarity to those of callitrichines. Whether this is a synapomorphy or convergence does not detract from the suggestion that the dentition appears perhaps better suited for an insectivorous and perhaps gumivorous rather than a more herbivorous diet.

SUBTRIBE MYTONIINA
Robinson 1968

DISTRIBUTION
    Late Eocene to early Oligocene (Uintan to Chadronian). Western North America.
INCLUDED TAXA
    Macrotarsius and Ourayia.

DISCUSSION

These forms are omomyins with rugose, robust, transversely narrowed upper molars. Anterior incisors, when known, are spatulate and rounded on their apex, and canines are relatively small.

The genera included in this subtribe are the largest among the Omomyinae. This is perhaps of some significance in regard to their general adaptations because known omomyids, as a rule, are small Callithrix- and Tarsius-sized animals. The dental adaptations, along with the hint of correlated size increase, indicate perhaps enhanced adaptations to some form of phytophagy.

OURAYIA Gazin, 1958

(= or including: Microsyops: Osborn, 1895. Mytonius Robinson, 1968. Hemiacodon: Robinson, 1968.)

DISTRIBUTION
    Middle Eocene (Uintan). Rocky Mt. region.
KNOWN SPECIES
    Ourayia uintensis (Osborn, 1895), type species
[=Microsyops uintensis Osborn, 1895. ?"Microsyops" uintensis Osborn, 1902. Omomys uintensis Wortman, 1904. Ourayia uintensis: Gazin, 1958. Hemiacodon jepseni Robinson, 1968. Mytonius hopsoni Robinson, 1968.]
LOCALITIES: Kennedy's Hole, Uinta B★ (304).

DISCUSSION

Ourayia is a mytoniinan with furrowed enamel, nearly squared molars, small hypocones and smaller pericones, and moderately large, spoon-shaped incisors. It differs from both Omomys and Chumashius in lacking the extensive lingual cingula, in having crenulated enamel on the cheek teeth, and in possessing relatively smaller third and fourth premolars. Differences from Hemiacodon are the distinctly less-modified talonid, the relatively smaller hypocone, and the relatively smaller third and fourth premolars. Ourayia (Figure 118) differs from Macrotarsius in having, judged from the alveoli, relatively larger canines and incisors and in having a symphysis both less extensive and more horizontally inclined. Ourayia lacks the derived cutting edges between the metaconid and entoconid, so characteristic of Macrotarsius (Szalay, 1976).

The dental formula is $I\frac{2}{2}$; $C\frac{1}{1}$; $P\frac{2,3,4}{2,3,4}$; $M\frac{1,2,3}{1,2,3}$.

The derivation of Ourayia from Hemiacodon is highly unlikely and the ancestry of Ourayia should rather be sought near Omomys. The large, cuspate hypocone and the unusual conformation of the large and relatively very broad talonid basin of Hemiacodon are derived features not possessed by Ourayia. Absence of a protocone-fold is a specialization shared with Omomys and Chumashius, but the crenulated enamel of the crown surface is not necessarily a homologously shared derived character with Hemiacodon. In light of the differences of the molar patterns it is likely that this latter feature is a specialization acquired independently from Hemiacodon. The derivation of Ourayia

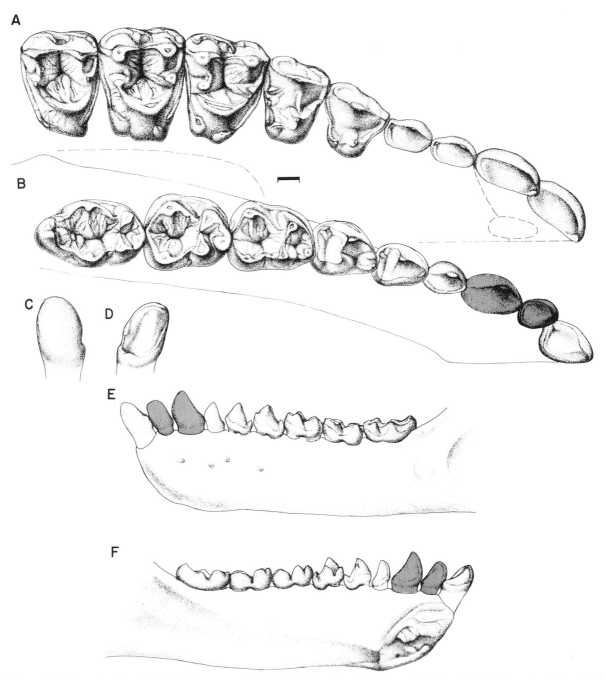

Figure 118. *Ourayia uintensis.* Middle Eocene, western North America. Right upper dentition, I^1–M^3. A, occlusal view. Left corpus with dentition, I$_1$–M$_3$; B, occlusal view; C, buccal view of left I$_1$; D, lingual view of left I$_1$; E, lateral view; F, medial view. Scale represents 1 mm. Uniform stippling and broken lines represent reconstruction. [From Szalay (1976).]

from *Omomys* or a genus near it is more probable than its origin from *Hemiacodon* (Szalay, 1976).

This genus is one of those few omomyids for which we have nearly the entire dentition preserved. By and large the dentition is a molar- and incisor-dominated one inasmuch as the fourth and third premolars are distinctly smaller than the molars, and the canine, at least the upper one, appears reduced. The cheek teeth in general are characterized by crenulated enamel and particularly extensive buccal cingula on $P^{\underline{3}}$–$M^{\underline{3}}$. Incipient metastylids are present on the upper molars which have mesiodistally broad protocones but lack a protocone-fold. Very small hypocones and tiny pericones are present on the first two upper molars. The lower molars have greatly expanded talonids, fairly tight talonid notches, and an extensive hypoconulid lobe on the third molar. Although the trigonids are mesiodistally wide, they are low and in general the cheek teeth are low crowned.

As far as one can judge, the teeth formed a continuous, tightly packed battery that extended across the midline of the skull. The low, but mesiodistally extensive, crowns of the lower central incisor have a broad distal base from which the spoon-shaped continuous apical crest of this tooth emanates. The somewhat flat but apically rounded upper incisors are mesiodistally extensive. The two pairs of lower incisors and the lower canines apparently worked against the individually relatively larger first and second pairs of incisors, an arrangement one encounters in *Callicebus*, for example. The known mandibles are relatively robust, the symphysis is probably unfused, and the arrangement of the lower tooth row is in a somewhat long limbed **U**, rather than **V**-shaped.

The combined evidence suggests that *Ourayia uintensis* was primarily phytophagous, probably mainly frugivorous–omnivorous, with of course a probably significant portion of its diet coming from insect prey. The conformation of the molars, the small size of the canines, and the morphology of the incisors suggest, however, no specializations for insectivory but rather for frugivory.

MACROTARSIUS Clark, 1941

DISTRIBUTION
   Middle Eocene to early Oligocene (Uintan to Chadronian). Rocky Mt. region.
KNOWN SPECIES
   1. *Macrotarsius montanus* Clark, 1941, type species
LOCALITIES: Cold Springs★ (370).
   2. *Macrotarsius siegerti* Robinson, 1968
LOCALITIES: Badwater Creek★ (296).

DISCUSSION

Macrotarsius is a genus with relatively large molars, small premolars, and very small canines. Known materials of *Macrotarsius* differ from all other genera of omomyines in having the talonid notch elevated to a widely open, shallow **V**-shaped crest between the metaconid and entoconid and in having small cuspules, analogues of the metastylid of *Shoshonius* and *Washakius*, on a crest running basally and distally from the apical half of the metaconid (Szalay, 1976).

The most recent students of the genus have been Robinson (1968) and Szalay (1976). *Macrotarsius* (Figure 119) is clearly more derived in its known morphology than *Ourayia*. Perhaps because of a geographical proximity, a near temporal sequence, and a convenient categorization of *Ourayia* in several features as more primitive and *Macrotarsius* as more derived, one may tentatively suggest some form of *Ourayia* as being ancestral to *Macrotarsius*. There are no clear-cut shared derived features to back this derivation, although the squared molars of the two genera might well represent such a shared derived condition.

The dental formula is $I\frac{1\cdot2}{1\cdot2}$; $C\frac{1}{1}$; $P\frac{2\cdot3\cdot4}{2\cdot3\cdot4}$; $M\frac{1\cdot2\cdot3}{1\cdot2\cdot3}$.

Szalay (1976) could ascertain no taxon specific differences other than size between the holotype of *M. montanus* and the sample of *M. siegerti*. Thus, all remarks on the lower dentition pertain equally to both samples.

Macrotarsius has an abundance of cheek tooth crests with relatively narrow bases. The trigonids are **V**-shaped, dominated by relatively straight crests with very little apical relief. The external wall of the cristid obliqua, like that of the buccal portion of the postcristid, is hollowed out. Genus-specific crests run between the paraconid and metaconid and between the latter and the entoconid. Buccal cingula are prominent and the anterior cingulids on the lower molars are particularly pronounced. The long ectolophs and extensive protocone crests are accompanied by well-

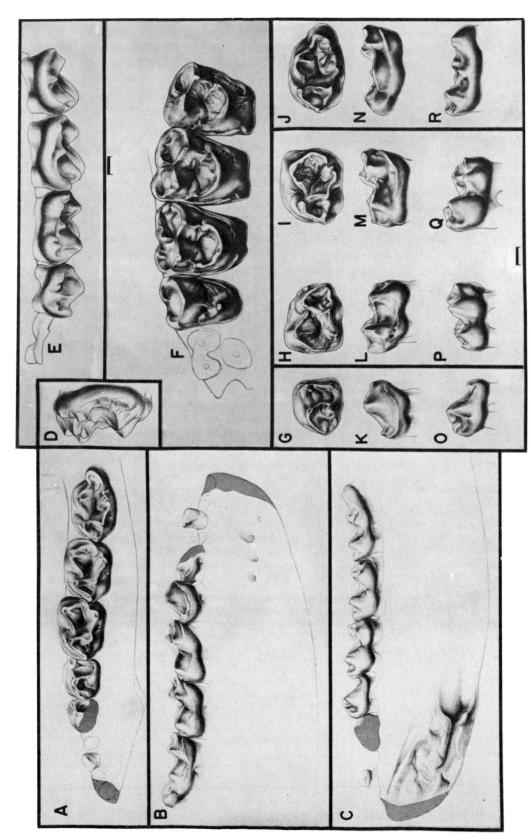

Figure 119. *Macrotarsius montanus*. Early Oligocene, western North America. Right mandible with C, and P₃–M₃: A, occlusal view; B, lateral view; C, medial view. Stippling and broken lines indicate reconstruction. *Macrotarsius siegerti*. Middle Eocene, Rocky Mt. region. Left maxilla fragment with P⁴–M³: D, distal view; E, buccal view; F, occlusal view. Right P₄ (G,K, and O), left M₁ (H, L, and P), right M₂ (I,M, and Q), and right M₃ (J,N, and R): G,H,I, and J, occlusal views; K,L,M. and N, buccal views; O,P,Q, and R, lingual views. Scales represent 1 mm. [From Szalay (1976).]

developed mesostyles, although the conules are not especially large. The canine is relatively small and, judged from the incisor alveoli, the dentition anterior to it was not particularly enlarged. The extensive crests on the large molars, virtually lacking rounded, bulbous cusps, and the unenlarged anterior teeth suggest folivory, rather than insectivory, frugivory, or omnivory, as a dietetic specialization. This inference is considerably strengthened by the convergent similarity between both the molar gestalt and the derived molar features of *Macrotarsius* and the atelid *Alouatta,* a confirmed folivore.

Tribe Washakiini
Szalay, 1976

DISTRIBUTION
Early to middle Eocene (Wasatchian to Uintan). Western North America.

INCLUDED TAXA
Washakius, Loveina, Shoshonius, Dyseolemur, and *?Hemiacodon.*

DISCUSSION

These are omomyines with both a protocone-fold and a moderately developed hypocone (except in *Loveina* and *Shoshonius*). Extreme widening of the talonids appears to be a primitive trait in the group. Although this feature reaches an extreme in *Hemiacodon* and the upper molars of that genus appear to be very similar to those of *Loveina,* allocation of the former to this tribe is not at all certain.

As noted below, the metastylid is believed to be a shared derived character between *Shoshonius* and *Washakius.*

LOVEINA Simpson, 1940

(= or including: *Tetonius:* Seton, 1940.)

DISTRIBUTION
Late early Eocene (late Wasatchian). Rocky Mt. region.
KNOWN SPECIES
Loveina zephyri Simpson, 1940, type species
(= *Tetonius barbeyi* Seton, 1940.)
LOCALITIES: Lost Cabin⋆ (240); Huerfano (248).

DISCUSSION

Loveina is a washakiin with a protocone-fold, moderate canines, and small incisors. It differs from its closest relatives, *Shoshonius* and *Washakius* (Simpson, 1940; Gazin, 1958), in lacking a metastylid. Unlike *Washakius, Loveina* (Figure 120) lacks the double metaconule and the cuspate, distinct hypocone and small pericone. Unlike *Shoshonius* it lacks a mesostyle. On the slope mesiolingual to the metacone there is a unique, tiny cuspule and on the homolgous area of the upper teeth of *Shoshonius* one, two, or three similar wrinkles might be found. Sharing this feature, but not

the metastylid and mesostyle, with *Shoshonius* indicates speciation prior to the acquisition of the latter characters. The metastylid found in both *Shoshonius* and *Washakius* suggests separation of the ancestral species of these genera after *Loveina* became phyletically distinct from the common *Shoshonius–Washakius* stock (Szalay, 1976).

Loveina is an important omomyid; in its molar and premolar morphology it is perhaps one of the most primitive of the known taxa of the subfamily, and the anterior dentition, judged by the alveoli, does not appear to be particularly advanced either.

The dental formula is $I\frac{1.2}{1.2}$; $C\frac{1}{1}$; $P\frac{2.3.4}{2.3.4}$; $M\frac{1.2.3}{1.2.3}$.

The unique combination of adaptations of *Loveina* lies in the relatively small canines, small incisors, crenulated teeth, relatively very broad talonids, squared off first and second upper molars which do not have a hypocone, and the presence of distinguishable superior and inferior transverse tori.

The small size and all the molar features suggest a probably frugivorous–insectivorous adaptation.

SHOSHONIUS Granger, 1910

DISTRIBUTION
Late early Eocene (late Wasatchian). Rocky Mt. region.

KNOWN SPECIES
Shoshonius cooperi Granger, 1910, type species
LOCALITIES: Lost Cabin⋆ (240); Huerfano (248).

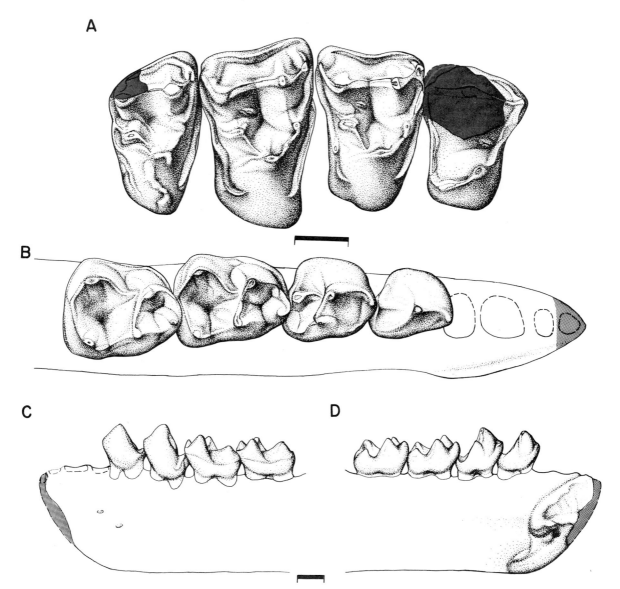

Figure 120. *Loveina zephyri.* Early Eocene, western North America. Right P⁴–M³. A, occlusal view. Partial left mandible with P₃–M₂, and alveoli for I₁, I₂, C, and P₂: B, occlusal view; C, lateral view; D, medial view. Scales represent 1 mm. Uniform stippling and broken lines represent reconstruction. [From Szalay (1976).]

DISCUSSION

This rare species is an omomyid with protocone-fold, mesostyle, and metastylid. *Shoshonius* (Figure 121) differs from *Loveina* in the latter specializations and from *Washakius* in having the well-developed mesostyle and metacone on P³ and P⁴ and in lacking a cuspate hypocone.

The similarities between *Loveina* and *Shoshonius* have been discussed above, under the former genus. Evaluation of the resemblances suggests derivation of *Shoshonius* from an ancestor very much like *Loveina zephyri.*

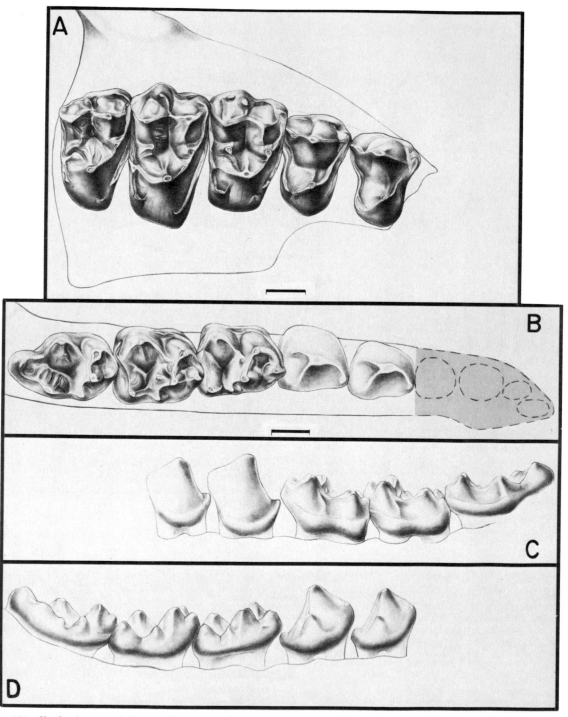

Figure 121. *Shoshonius cooperi.* Late early Eocene, western North America. Right maxilla with P³–M³: A, occlusal view. Left lower teeth, P₃–M₃: B, occlusal view; C, buccal view; D, lingual view. Stippling and broken lines represent reconstruction. Scales represent 1 mm. [From Szalay (1976).]

When *Shoshonius* is compared with *Washakius* it appears convincing that, on the basis of the total character of the molars, the molar metastylids are homologous. Judged from the cheek teeth, both *Shoshonius* and *Washakius* have somewhat divergent specializations. Unlike the apparently *de novo* hypocone off the distolingual corner of the molars of *Washakius*, *Shoshonius* has only the well-developed, probably primitive, omomyid protocone-fold. The $M_{\overline{2}}$ and $M_{\overline{3}}$ trigonids of *Shoshonius* are usually mesiodistally long and the paraconids and metaconids are well separated, whereas in *Washakius* the trigonid is more constricted (Szalay, 1976). The dental formula was probably similar to that of *Washakius*.

This is a dentally poorly known genus; we know nothing, for example, of the teeth anterior to $P_{\overline{3}}$ (Guthrie, 1971). In addition to crenulated enamel, *Shoshonius* has a metastylid, broad talonids, very extensive buccal cingula coupled with robust mesostyles, and metacones on the third and fourth upper premolars.

Evidence on the anterior dentition is needed before a reliable assessment may be made of its feeding adaptations. Yet the combination of characters, particularly the derived character states, suggests some phytophagous specializations.

WASHAKIUS Leidy, 1873

(= or including: *Hemiacodon*: Wortman, 1904, in part. *Yumanius* Stock, 1938. *Shoshonius*?:Simpson, 1959.)

DISTRIBUTION

Middle Eocene (Bridgerian to Uintan). Rocky Mt. region and California.

KNOWN SPECIES

1. *Washakius insignis* Leidy, 1873, type species
(=*Hemiacodon pygmaeus* Wortman, 1904; *Shoshonius? laurae* Simpson, 1959.)
LOCALITIES: Lower Bridger★ (266); Morrow Creek (274).

2. *Washakius woodringi* (Stock, 1938)
(=*Yumanius woodringi* Stock, 1938.)
LOCALITIES: CIT 249, Poway★ (298).

DISCUSSION

Washakius spp. are omomyids which differ from other genera in having a combination of metastylid, double metaconule, and distinct, cuspate hypocone broadly based on the distal cingulum. *Washakius* (Figure 122) differs from *Shoshonius*, probably its most recent relative, in having robust parastyles on the third and fourth premolars and in lacking the latter's small metacone (?metastyle) on these teeth.

Relatively little or no controversy exists as to the closest relationships of this genus within the Omomyidae (Simpson, 1940; Gazin, 1958; Russell *et al.*, 1967; Szalay, 1976). Comparisons have been made with *Shoshonius*, *Omomys*, and *Hemiacodon*, and its close tie to *Loveina* has been accepted. As stated under the generic discussions of *Loveina* and *Shoshonius*, these two taxa are probably the most recently related and also the most closely similar to *Washakius*.

The dental formula was $I\frac{1\cdot2}{1\cdot2}$; $C\frac{1}{1}$; $P\frac{2\cdot3\cdot4}{2\cdot3\cdot4}$; $M\frac{1\cdot2\cdot3}{1\cdot2\cdot3}$.

Washakius woodringi differs from the type species in having more pointed cusps and a well-developed protocone-fold. There is a distinct possibility that *W. woodringi* shares a more recent ancestor with *Dyseolemur pacificus* than with *W. insignis* (Szalay, 1976). Were this confirmed in the future by better samples of the California taxa, it might necessitate, if not inclusion of *Dyseolemur* in *Washakius*, referral of Stock's species to *Dyseolemur*. As much as we suspect this genealogy to be correct, nothing is gained at present by transferring "*Yumanius woodringi*" from *Washakius* to *Dyseolemur*, as the mere two teeth of *W. woodringi* can be argued to show close ties with either.

The major specializations of *Washakius* lie in the presence of metastylids, greatly elongated $M_{\overline{3}}$ talonid, large conules on the upper molars, an additional metaconule, well-developed hypocones, cingula, and cingulids, and robust parastyles on the two known upper premolars, $P^{\underline{3}}$ and P^4. The lower $P_{\overline{3}}$ and canine and the alveoli of P^2 and the upper canine show transversely widened teeth, clearly a derived omomyid character. In stark contrast to this emphasis, the incisors were surely of lesser importance than in most omomyids. Interestingly, among the molars of many specimens of *Washakius insignis* a large number are relatively well worn, and some show the extreme conditions of attrition.

The combined evidence of the dentition and the somewhat enlarged angle of the mandible indicate that *Washakius insignis* was probably a herbivore, and

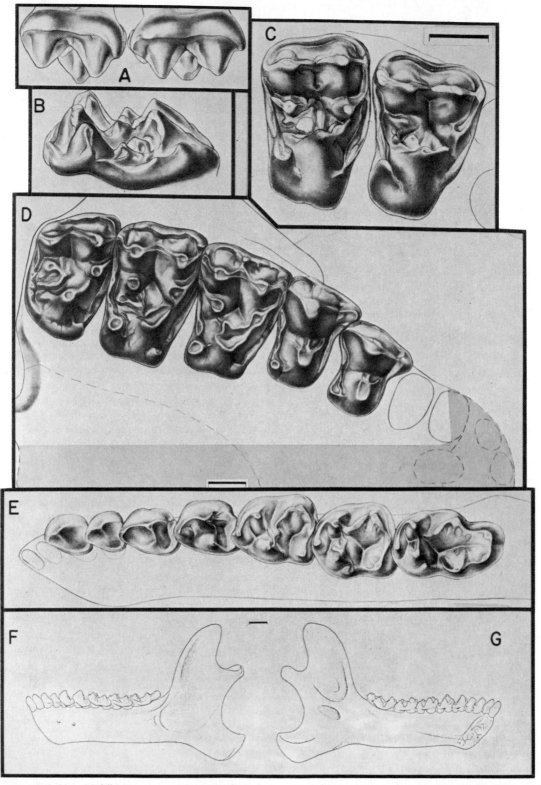

Figure 122. *Washakius*. Middle Eocene, western North America. *Washakius woodringi*. Late Eocene. Right M$^{1-2}$: A, buccal view; B, distal view; C, occlusal view. *Washakius insignis*. Middle Eocene. Right palatal fragment with P^3–M^3: D, occlusal view. Right mandible with C–M$_3$: E, occlusal view. Left mandible: F, lateral view; G, medial view. Scales represent 1 cm. [From Szalay (1976).]

in particular a specialized folivore (Szalay, 1976). The little we know of *Washakius woodringi,* however, does not necessarily reflect adaptations to folivory. Although the primitive(?) features of this species clearly reflect an ancestry like *Washakius insignis,* the high, pointed cusps of this taxon suggest adaptations to a more insectivorous diet.

DYSEOLEMUR Stock, 1934

DISTRIBUTION
  Middle Eocene (Uintan). California.
KNOWN SPECIES
  Dyseolemur pacificus Stock, 1934, type species
LOCALITIES: CIT loc. 180, Tapo Ranch⋆ (302).

DISCUSSION

Dyseolemur differs from all other omomyids, except *Shoshonius, Washakius,* and *Ekgmowechashala,* in the possession of a metastylid. It differs from *Shoshonius* in the absence of the mesostyle and in having a well-developed cingular area distolingually which can be defined as the hypocone. *Dyseolemur* (Figure 123) differs from *Washakius* in the apparent absence of the "second" metaconule and particularly in having the paraconid removed to the extreme mesiobuccal corner of the lower tooth. In addition, the $M_{\overline{3}}$ tends to be relatively smaller than that in *Washakius. Dyseolemur* appears to be linked with both *Shoshonius* and *Washakius* (Stock, 1934; Gazin, 1958; Russell *et al.,* 1967; Szalay, 1976) in possessing a metastylid, but the special resemblances are with *Washakius.* The hypocone of the postcingulum is well developed in both *Dyseolemur* and *Washakius.* Both these genera lack the mesostyle shown by *Shoshonius.* The talonid notch of *Dyseolemur* is shaped in a manner identical to that of *Washakius,* a feature whereby $M_{\overline{1}}$ and $M_{\overline{2}}$ of both may be distinguished from *Shoshonius* (Szalay, 1976).

The trigonid structure of *Dyseolemur* shows specializations beyond those of *Washakius.* The paraconid is in an extreme mesiobuccal position and consequently the paracristid is relatively shorter than that of *Washakius.* Judged by the morphology of $M_{\overline{3}}$ it appears that this relatively shorter tooth of *Dyseolemur* was reduced from a relative size similar to that shown by *Washakius.*

The lower molars of *Dyseolemur* and *Shoshonius* are distinctive. In contrast to the latter, which have the primitively long paracristids, those of *Dyseolemur* are very short and do not extend as far lingually as in *Shoshonius.*

The dental formula is $I\frac{?}{2}; C\frac{1}{1}; P\frac{2\cdot3\cdot4}{2\cdot3\cdot4}; M\frac{1\cdot2\cdot3}{1\cdot2\cdot3}.$

Perhaps the somewhat more bunodont cusps (a rather subjective appraisal) of *Dyseolemur* along with relatively larger protocone crest and the greater enlargement of the lingual third of the postcingulum as a hypocone represent the major morphological differences from *Washakius.* The mechanical functions of these characters may have been related to increasing crushing and/or transverse shear. Whatever the differences of *Dyseolemur* from *Washakius* may be, the gestalt of known dental characters suggests a herbivore, very likely a frugivore.

HEMIACODON Marsh, 1872a

(= or including: *Omomys:* Osborn, 1902.)

DISTRIBUTION
  Middle Eocene (Bridgerian). Rocky Mt. region.
KNOWN SPECIES
  Hemiacodon gracilis Marsh, 1872a, type species
  (=*Omomys gracilis:* Osborn, 1902).
LOCALITIES: Upper Bridger⋆ (282).

DISCUSSION

Hemiacodon (Figure 124) has very heavily folded enamel, a fourth lower premolar subequal in height to the first lower molar, heavy cingulids on the lower molars, unusually wide talonids on the first and second lower molars, well-developed conules on the upper molars, and a distinct distal protocone-fold. A combination of the heavily crenulated enamel, large conules, and talonids relatively much wider than trigonids (all derived features) distinguishes *Hemiacodon* from other omomyines, *Ourayia* and *Macrotarsius* included. The hypoconulid is distinct in *Hemiacodon,* unlike in *Ourayia,* and it is somewhat nearer to the entoconid than to the hypoconid.

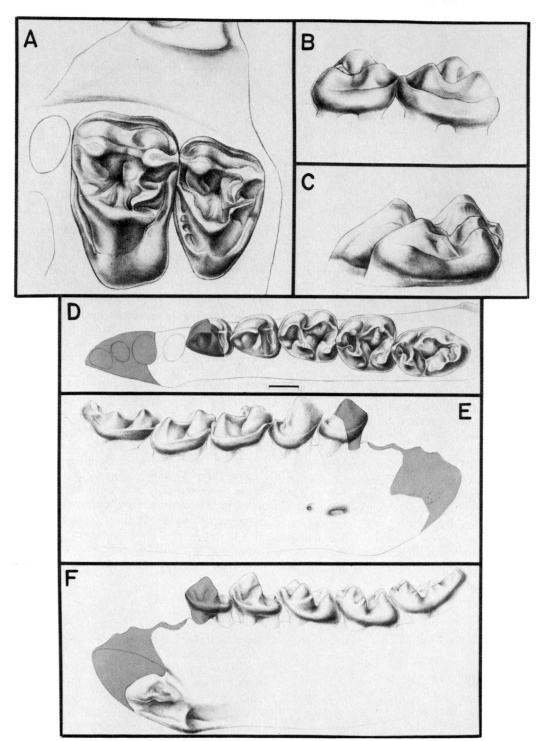

Figure 123. *Dyseolemur pacificus.* Middle Eocene, western North America. Left M²–M³ in maxilla fragment: A, occlusal view; B, buccal view, crowns facing upward; C, occlusodistal view. Right horizontal ramus with P₃–M₃: D, occlusal view; E, lateral view; F, medial view. Stippling indicates reconstruction. Scale, pertinent to lower jaw (D–F), represents 1 mm. [From Szalay (1976).]

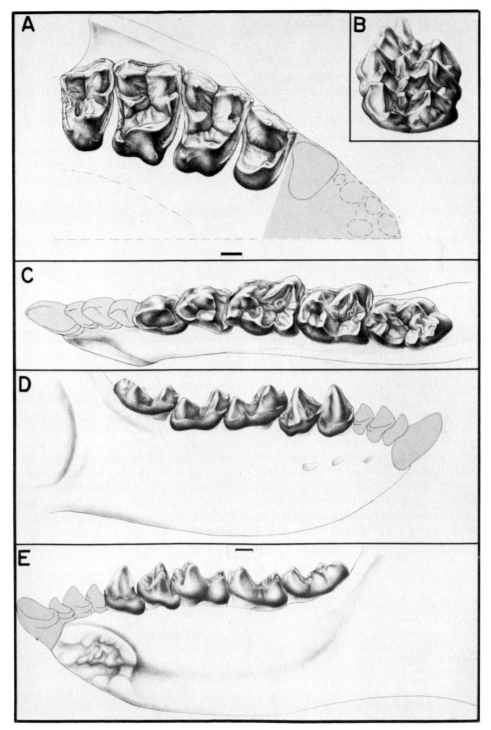

Figure 124. *Hemiacodon gracilis.* Middle Eocene, western North America. Right maxilla with P^4–M^3: A, occlusal view; B, occlusodistal view. Right mandible with P_3–M_3 (I_{1-2}, C, and P_2 are reconstructed): C, occlusal view; D, lateral view; E, medial view. Scales represent 1 mm. [From Szalay (1976).]

The known dental morphology is distinct from any of the other omomyines, particularly omomyins, and the most recent affinities appear to be possibly with *Loveina* (Szalay, 1976).

The dental formula is $I\frac{1\cdot2}{1\cdot2}$; $C\frac{1}{1}$; $P\frac{2\cdot3\cdot4}{2\cdot3\cdot4}$; $M\frac{1\cdot2\cdot3}{1\cdot2\cdot3}$.

Judged from the cranial and postcranial remains, *H. gracilis* was the size of *Tarsius spectrum* or slightly larger. The known material shows a number of highly derived character states which are very suggestive of mechanical adaptation for processing large amounts of vegetable foods. The hypocone is well developed, the conules are exceptionally large and rounded, the talonids are relatively very broad, cingula and cingulids are very well developed, and the enamel is heavily crenulated on all known specimens. The lower anterior dentition appears to be tightly packed and the incisors very robust. The jaw tends to be deep and robust, and the symphysis, although not synostosed, shows very extensive rugosity on older specimens. This suggests symphyseal rigidity during mastication. The listed adaptations point to an increase in mechanical efficiency to deal with a rather tough frugivorous diet.

The known fragmentary skeleton of *Hemiacodon* is discussed under *Plesiadapis* and the Tarsiiformes in conjunction with the few other published omomyid postcranial remains. The most notable aspects of the specimen are (1) euprimate characteristics shared with known skeletons of adapids, in contrast to the features seen in plesiadapiforms; (2) an unusually well-developed keel-shaped process on the first metatarsal; (3) articular surface of the acetabulum indicative of habitual vertical posturing and probably also vertical clinging and leaping locomotion. Unlike in adapids (and other strepsirhines) and platyrrhines, the last features suggest a specialization perhaps not necessarily shared by other omomyids. Elbow remains, particularly the distal end of the humerus, are not preserved for *Hemiacodon*. The elbow is proving to be a highly sensitive indicator of vertical posturing or climbing and/or of leaping in a vertical position (Szalay and Dagosto, in preparation).

Tribe Uintaniini
Szalay, 1976

DISTRIBUTION
    Early to middle Eocene (Wasatchian to Bridgerian). Western North America.
INCLUDED TAXA
    Uintanius.

DISCUSSION

These animals are unique omomyines with greatly enlarged third and fourth premolars, which are clearly convergent, however, to a somewhat similar specialization of the anaptomorphine *Absarokius*. In order to express the striking specializations of this genus within the confines of the Omomyinae, and to balance the taxonomy within the whole family, the tribe Uintaniini was established by Szalay (1976). This tribe taxonomically emphasizes the convergence of *Uintanius* to the paromomyid Micromomyini and the tetoniinan anaptomorphine *Absarokius* among early Tertiary primates.

UINTANIUS Matthew, 1915

(= or including: *Omomys*: Wortman, 1904, in part. ?*Loveina*: Simpson, 1940. *Huerfanius* Robinson, 1966.)

DISTRIBUTION
    Early to middle Eocene (Wasatchian to Bridgerian). Rocky Mt. region and New Mexico.
KNOWN SPECIES
    1. *Uintanius ameghini* (Wortman, 1904), type species
(=*Omomys ameghini* Wortman, 1904. *Uintanius turriculorum* Matthew, 1915. *Huerfanius rutherfurdi* Robinson, 1966.)
LOCALITIES: Lower Bridger★ (266); Huerfano II and III (260).
    2. *Uintanius vespertinus* (Matthew, 1915)
(=?*Omomys vespertinus* Matthew, 1915. ?*Loveina vespertina*: Simpson, 1940. *Uintanius vespertinus*: Szalay, 1976.)
LOCALITIES: Gray Bull★ (162); Almagre (200).

DISCUSSION

Uintanius (Figure 125) differs from all other taxa of the subfamily in having greatly enlarged paracones and protoconids on the third and fourth premolars of the generotype. The latter's M_T paraconid is characteristically more mesial than in other omomyines. The presence of the protocone-fold distinguishes the upper molars of *Uintanius* from those of *Chumashius* and *Omomys*.

Uintanius is more similar to *Loveina*, *Omomys*, and *Chumashius* than to any of the Anaptomorphinae. The

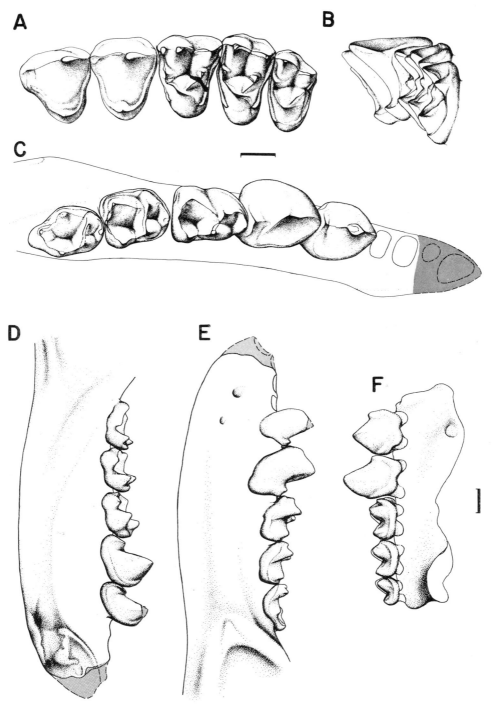

Figure 125. *Uintanius ameghini.* Middle Eocene, western North America. Left P³–M³: A, occlusal view; B, occlusodistal view. Left mandible with P₃–M₃: C, occlusal view; D, medial view; E, lateral view. Left maxilla with P³–M³: F, lateral view. Scales represent 1 mm. [From Szalay (1976).]

trigonid cusps lack the inflated base characteristic of the latter group, and the last molars are not much smaller than the more anterior ones. The morphology of the $M_{\overline{3}}$ talonid is very similar to that found in the omomyines cited. It is possible that all of the noted similarities to omomyines represent primitive omomyid characters and, genealogically, *Uintanius* has more recently shared a common ancestor with some unknown anaptomorphine. This is doubted, however, and furthermore the derived character states of the third and fourth premolars are not homologous with those of *Absarokius*, which is the previously implied base for considering *Uintanius* an anaptomorphine (Simons, 1963; Robinson, 1966; McKenna, 1967; Russell *et al.*, 1967). Modifications of the premolars in the two genera are almost certainly convergent (Szalay, 1976).

The dental formula is $I\frac{1\cdot2}{1\cdot2}$; $C\frac{1}{1}$; $P\frac{2\cdot3\cdot4}{2\cdot3\cdot4}$; $M\frac{1\cdot2\cdot3}{1\cdot2\cdot3}$.

The assessment of adaptations refers to the type species *U. ameghini*, although most of the characters of the latter are present at least in an incipient form in *U. vespertinus*. Obviously the most derived adaptations of *Uintanius* lie in the great vertical and mesiodistal enlargement of the paracones and protoconids of the third and fourth premolars. The relatively transverse upper molars are not very broad lingually, a protocone-fold is well developed, but a true hypocone is absent. Neither upper nor lower last molars are reduced. The trigonids are relatively large and that of $M_{\overline{1}}$ is derived in that it is mesiodistally stretched out, clearly adding to the extensive cutting edges of the premolars running in that direction.

Among the modern forms, particularly *Phaner*, and to some degree *Euoticus* and *Perodicticus*, there is excessive enlargement of one premolar behind a very large upper canine and the large caniniform $P_{\overline{2}}$. In *Phaner*, this has been correlated with gum and resin feeding habits (Petter *et al.*, 1971) inasmuch as these teeth, along with the hypertrophied tooth comb and upper incisors, are used to scrape bark to get at these nutrients. In *Uintanius* the enlarged teeth are probably too far back in the mouth for a similar biological role.

It is very difficult to judge the specialized adaptations in the tiny *Uintanius*. Because the emphasis is not on the canine or the incisors but on the posterior premolars, one may suggest at first that food preparation (i.e., mastication in a broad sense) rather than procurement, grasping, or killing was the likely selective factor. The adaptations, however, greatly accentuated shear in a limited area on the tooth row, namely, the buccal side of the premolars. This might signify specializations for a particular type of plant material which required either tearing off as the material was placed in the mouth or opening and slashing of succulent fruits or seed pods, which necessitated the generation of great force for penetration but no particular need to continually triturate. It is equally possible, however, that the premolar specialization might be a compromise for some specialized frugivory as well as insectivory.

Tribe Utahiini
Szalay, 1976

DISTRIBUTION

Early to middle Eocene (Wasatchian to Uintan). Western North America.
INCLUDED TAXA
Utahia and *Stockia*.

DISCUSSION

These are omomyines with a derived, constricted trigonid construction and concomitant enlargement of the talonid.

This is one of the most poorly known tribes of the family. The trigonid construction is highly diagnostic and is very similar to the constricted trigonids of most platyrrhines with well-developed hypocones. This character state is perhaps tied to an adaptation in which the talonid function is much more important than that associated with the mechanics of the trigonid.

UTAHIA Gazin, 1958

(= or including: *Omomys*: Gazin, 1962.)

DISTRIBUTION
Early to middle Eocene (late Wasatchian to early Bridgerian). Rocky Mt. region.

KNOWN SPECIES
Utahia kayi Gazin, 1958, type species
(=*Omomys sheai* Gazin, 1962.)
LOCALITIES: Powder Wash★ (264).

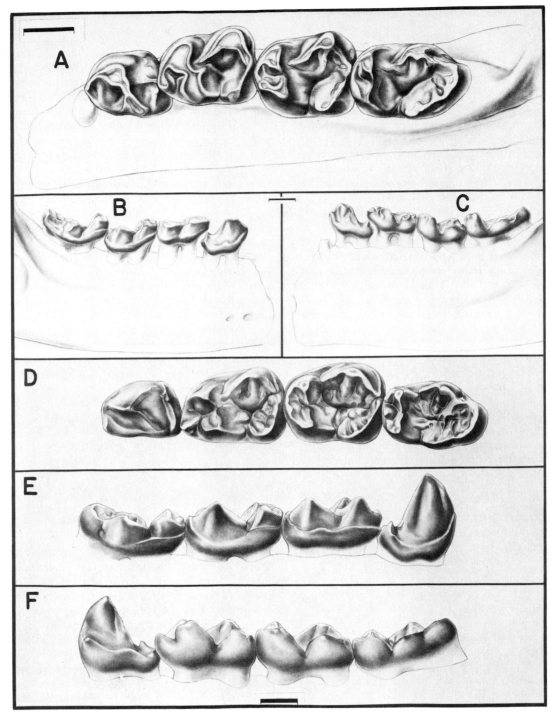

Figure 126. *Utahia kayi.* Late early Eocene, western North America. Right horizontal ramus with $P_{\overline{4}}$–$M_{\overline{3}}$: A, occlusal view; B, lateral view; C, medial view. *Stockia powayensis.* Middle Eocene, western North America. Right $P_{\overline{4}}$–$M_{\overline{3}}$: D, occlusal view; E, buccal view; F, lingual view. Scales represent 1 mm. [From Szalay (1976).]

Discussion

Utahia (Figure 126) has a relatively large $M_{\overline{3}}$ and mesiodistally constricted trigonids on $M_{\overline{2}}$ and $M_{\overline{3}}$. It differs from *Stockia* in having a relatively smaller $P_{\overline{4}}$, higher trigonids, much less crenulated enamel, and a talonid notch which is V to U-shaped and basally rounded; it differs from both *Shoshonius* and *Washakius* in lacking a metastylid on the lower molars (Szalay, 1976). The dental formula cannot be determined from the known material.

Szalay (1976) could not find shared advanced similarities of this genus with *Hemiacodon*, as suggested by Gazin (1958), and both *Utahia* and *Washakius* have distinct, derived features of their own. *Utahia*, like *Stockia*, has strongly constricted trigonids on $M_{\overline{2}}$ and $M_{\overline{3}}$, a character unlike the more ancestral omomyine condition shown by *Washakius*. The latter has the derived lower molar metastylids not present in *Utahia*. It appears, then, that *Utahia* is most closely related to *Stockia* among the known omomyids. Comparisons of *Utahia* and *Stockia* are hindered by the fact that the only good specimen of the former genus is the holotype with considerably worn teeth, whereas the *Stockia* material consists largely of unworn teeth. The specific distinction of the two samples does not appear to be in question as, in spite of the differences in wear, the diagnostic features seem to be relatively clear-cut. One should, however, question the value of slightly higher trigonids and lack of crenulations along with some apparent differences in the shape of the talonid notch of *Utahia* as sufficiently different attributes to warrant separation of *Stockia* on the generic level. In light of the lack of information on the anterior dentition and upper teeth and the existing differences between the lower teeth of the two samples, we suggest the maintenance of separate generic ranking, as did Szalay (1976), for the time being.

The sample is very limited and consequently any comments on adaptations are of a very tentative nature. The most striking character of *Utahia*, as well as *Stockia*, lies in the very open $M_{\overline{1}}$ trigonid on the one hand and the mesiodistally constricted and lingually closed $M_{\overline{2-3}}$ trigonids on the other. Correlated with this are the relatively large talonids of the last two molars. The only mandible fragment known, with well-worn teeth, is not particularly thick mediolaterally. Unusually heavy stressing in a transverse direction, therefore, appears to have been unlikely as a habitual mode of mastication. The reduction of the trigonids suggests reduction in the components usually involved in shear when the mandible is moved in an orthal direction.

The meager evidence perhaps suggests frugivorous–insectivorous adaptation, although a knowledge of the anterior dentition might considerably alter this hypothesis.

STOCKIA Gazin, 1958

DISTRIBUTION
  Middle Eocene (Uintan). California.
KNOWN SPECIES
  Stockia powayensis Gazin, 1958, type species
LOCALITIES: CIT loc. 249, Poway★ (298).

Discussion

Stockia (Figure 126) has crenulated enamel, mesiodistally constricted trigonids on the last two molars, and a relatively long last molar. It is clearly separable from *Hemiacodon* in having a relatively taller $P_{\overline{4}}$, a relatively less wide talonid, and a paraconid on both $M_{\overline{2}}$ and $M_{\overline{3}}$ that is close and directly mesial to the trigonid notch. *Stockia* differs from *Utahia* in having a relatively taller $P_{\overline{4}}$, more crenulated enamel, a more lingually placed paraconid on $P_{\overline{4}}$, and a talonid notch which is very narrow and constricted basally. As far as can be judged, this is a taxon distinct on the generic level from other known omomyines, including *Utahia*, although it probably shared a more recent common ancestor with the latter than with any other genus known (Szalay, 1976). The dental formula cannot be determined from the known material.

The $P_{\overline{4}}$ is tall and distinctly higher than any of the molars. There is a small, lingually turned paracristid–paraconid on that premolar and a broad distal shelf. The most characteristic features of the molars are their crenulated enamel and the buccally open trigonid of $M_{\overline{1}}$ in contrast to the mesiodistal constriction of the last two teeth as in *Utahia*. This trigonid reduction is extreme, particularly in contrast with the long and wide talonids. The talonid notches of the molars are narrow, as are both the distal base of the metaconid and the mesial portion of the entocristid. The known mandible fragments are very thin mediolaterally and relatively deep, indicating, as in *Utahia*, a relative absence of unusually forceful mediolateral stressing by the masticatory muscles.

The crenulations on the molars perhaps indicate an adaptation to increase the surface area of the talonids. It is in this respect that the crenulations represent additional sharp edges which facilitated division of the food.

The tall $P_{\overline{4}}$ and the somewhat unusual low crowned molars might have evolved as a response for a

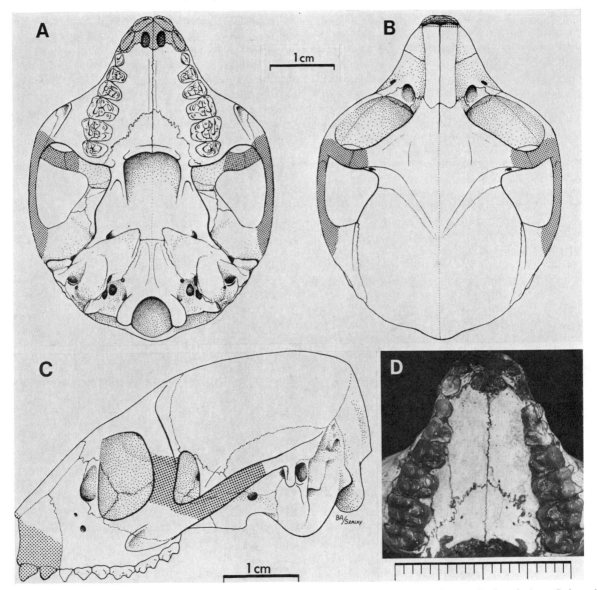

Figure 127. *Rooneyia viejaensis*. Early Oligocene, western North America. Skull: A, ventral view; B, dorsal view; C, lateral view. Uniform stippling represents reconstruction. Palate with left and right $P^{\underline{2}}$–$M^{\underline{3}}$: D, occlusal view. Subdivisions on scale represent 0.5 mm. [From Szalay (1976).]

frugivorous, perhaps even nectarivorous, type of diet (Szalay, 1976). None of these characters, in the combination they appear in *Stockia*, suggests exclusive adaptations for either insectivory or folivory.

Tribe Rooneyiini
Szalay, 1976

DISTRIBUTION
  Early Oligocene (Chadronian). Western North America.
INCLUDED TAXA
  Rooneyia.

DISCUSSION

Rooneyia (Figures 127 and 128) represents omomyids with compact, low crowned, robust molars. These teeth have cuspate, exceptionally developed conules and a hypocone on the postcingulum which is almost equal in size to the protocone. In addition to these characters distinguishing them from all other omomyids, rooneyiinins have two premolars and a small canine. Unlike known skulls of anaptomorphines and microchoerines, the petromastoid is not inflated.

Dental comparisons of *Rooneyia* with the genera *Callicebus* and *Aotus* are interesting, although at the outset it must be clearly stated that the presence of two premolars in the former and three in the latter precludes any ancestor–descendant relationship. Furthermore, the partly bulla-enclosed and elongated ectotympanic, lack of orbital funnels, and the less encephalized brain of *Rooneyia* are in direct contrast

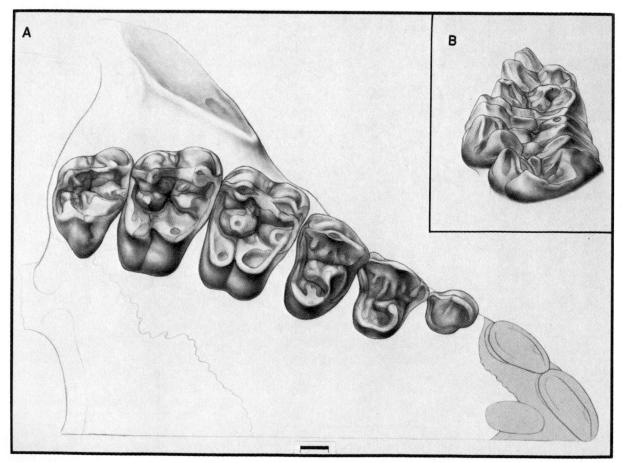

Figure 128. *Rooneyia viejaensis*. Early Oligocene, western North America. Right palate with C–M$_{\overline{3}}$: A, occlusal view; B, occlusodistal view. Stippling indicates reconstruction. Scale represents 1 mm. [From Szalay (1976).]

with the different character states of these features in platyrrhines. Yet the Chadronian primate, with the exception of its more reduced antemolar dentition, is in general more primitive than the platyrrhine morphotype.

The development of the hypocone in *Aotus* and *Callicebus* is similar to that of *Rooneyia*, although the former two lack the well-developed conules of the latter and have advanced, less transverse molar pro-

portions. The premolars of *Rooneyia* and the extant genera noted are quite similar, and this probably stems from their relatively great mesiodistal length.

On dental characters alone tribal separation of *Rooneyia* from other omomyids is warranted. Recognizing the rooneyiins, in addition to the other tribes, allows a taxonomic expression of the strikingly greater diversity of the Omomyinae compared to the Anaptomorphinae.

ROONEYIA Wilson, 1966

DISTRIBUTION
   Early Oligocene (early Chadronian). Texas.
KNOWN SPECIES
   Rooneyia viejaensis Wilson, 1966, type species
LOCALITIES: Chambers Tuff★ (340).

DISCUSSION

Rooneyia is the only known genus in this tribe, known only by a uniquely preserved cranium lacking the premaxilla. The most compelling dental argument for its omomyid affinities is the reduced condition of the canine, which is unfortunately not a unique gestalt character of any one of the dental complexes found in the group. Unlike other primates, except known plesiadapiforms, the known omomyid genera exhibit a widespread condition of canine reduction. Although there are exceptions to this among primitive members of the family (e.g., *Chumashius*, *Teilhardina*, and *Chlororhysis* to some degree), most of the reduced canines are perhaps expressions of an inherited condition rather than numerous, parallel, or convergent adaptations (Szalay, 1976).

The dental formula is probably $I\frac{1.2}{1.2}$; $C\frac{1}{1}$; $P\frac{3.4}{3.4}$; $M\frac{1.2.3}{1.2.3}$.

The size of the canine and the non-lemuriform character of the basicranium represent a combination that indicates an omomyid stamp more than any other family level ties. Unlike the extreme inflation of the mastoid in *Tetonius*, an anaptomorphine, and *Necrolemur*, a microchoerine, the moderate mastoid inflation of *Rooneyia* suggests a non-anaptomorphine and, perhaps by default, an omomyine derivation. The relatively large M^3 and a hypocone development reminiscent of *Washakius* appear to confirm the subfamily ties of *Rooneyia*.

The assessment that *Rooneyia* is a Texan catarrhine

by Simons (1968) may be explained, perhaps, by the convergent similarity of the upper molars to those of *Apidium*. In both genera the cusps are bulbous, the conules are large, and the hypocone is enlarged. The mesial and distal cusps (paracone, paraconule, protocone versus metacone, metaconule, hypocone) are aligned in two rows more or less parallel to one another. This structurally "pre-cercopithecoid" arrangement of the molar relief is similar in *Rooneyia* to that of the parapithecid *Apidium* and probably to the more derived *Parapithecus*. Unlike the premolars of the Fayum parapithecids, however, those of *Rooneyia* have one less premolar and a relatively smaller canine.

The extent of the dental arch and the approximate size and estimated area of the individual molars in *Rooneyia viejaensis* are about the same as those of *Aotus trivirgatus*. The relative sizes of the orbits and the brain, however, are strikingly smaller in *Rooneyia*. Judged from the position of the foramen magnum, the skull of the Texas primate is only very slightly kyphosed, much less than in callitrichines (e.g., *Callithrix jacchus*) with a comparable endocranial volume.

A large flange of the frontal descends behind the orbits. Judged from the postorbital constriction of the skull, part of the major mass of the temporalis muscle extended slightly anteriorly above the orbits. In the case of *Rooneyia*, the postorbital partition, perhaps the homologue of that part of the postorbital funnel in *Tarsius*, platyrrhines, and catarrhines, appears to be the bony wall which kept the muscle from intruding into the orbit. Possibly this partition is the initial adaptation responsible for the role of protecting the eyeballs and associated structures from the contraction of the temporalis.

The relative size of the orbits of *Rooneyia* is difficult

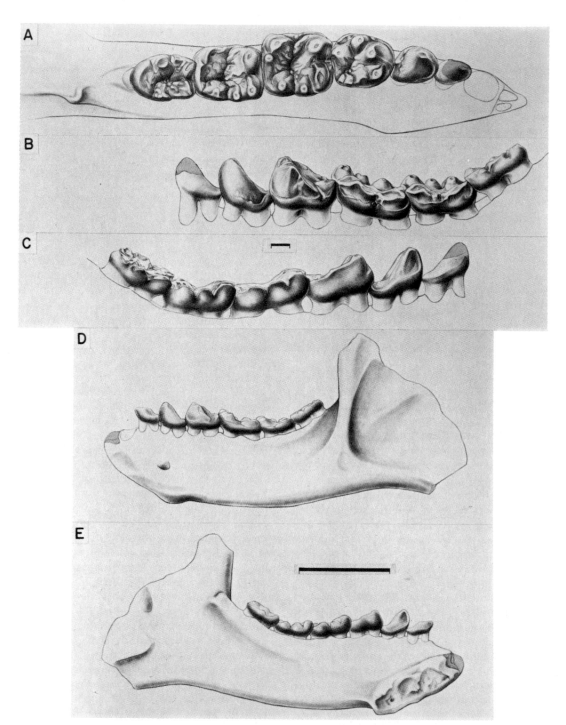

Figure 129. *Ekgmowechashala philotau*. Early Miocene, western North America. Partial left mandible with $P_{\overline{2}}$–$M_{\overline{3}}$ and alveoli for $I_{\overline{1}}$, $I_{\overline{2}}$, and C: A, occlusal view; B, buccal view; C, lingual view; D, lateral view; E, medial view. Scales represent 1 mm (above) and 1 cm (below). Stippling and broken lines represent reconstruction. [From Szalay (1976).]

to assess. If one were to plot the length of the skull against the diameter of the orbits, as Walker (1967b) did for the Malagasy lemurs, and plot it on this author's graph, *Rooneyia* would fall, as suggested by Simons (1972), with the nocturnal forms. Yet *Rooneyia*'s orbits are not relatively very large and it is not unlikely that its orbit to skull length proportions are perhaps primitive features from a relatively much larger eyed ancestry.

Unlike in other known omomyids, the tooth rows appear to be more widely separated in *Rooneyia*. The known teeth show a combination of characters not seen in any primarily insectivorous or carnivorous primate. The cusps are rounded, not very pointed, and the crests are broadly based, not high. The cusps and cuspules are greatly expanded and swollen so they touch one another at their base. *Rooneyia* was probably primarily frugivorous (Szalay, 1976).

SUBFAMILY EKGMOWECHASHALINAE
Szalay, 1976

DISTRIBUTION
  Early Miocene (early Arikareean). Western North America.
INCLUDED TAXA
  Ekgmowechashala.

DISCUSSION

The Ekgmowechashalinae, represented by one species, differs from other omomyids in having an unambiguous $M_{\overline{1}}>M_{\overline{2}}>M_{\overline{3}}$ size relationship, peculiarly flattened molars, a large molarized fourth premolar, and large, closely twinned entoconids and metastylids. Unlike other omomyids, except some microchoerines, the molar paraconids are completely reduced and the paracristid is indistinguishable from the precingulid. The degree of reduction of the two incisors, coupled with a relatively much larger canine, is unique within the Omomyidae. The mandibular symphysis of the type genus, in lacking any trace of distinguishable inferior or superior transverse tori, is significantly different from the symphysis of any other known omomyid.

The Ekgmowechashalinae is very distinct from members of the Anaptomorphinae, Omomyinae, and Microchoerinae, and the differences displayed by the type genus warrant recognition of the subfamily rank. The morphology of *Ekgmowechashala* (Figure 129) was recently discussed in detail by Szalay (1976).

EKGMOWECHASHALA Macdonald, 1963

DISTRIBUTION
  Early Miocene (early Arikareean). South Dakota.
KNOWN SPECIES
  Ekgmowechashala philotau Macdonald, 1963, type species
LOCALITIES: Sharps beds★ (384).

DISCUSSION

As its somewhat uncommon name would suggest, *Ekgmowechashala* (i.e., "little cat man" in Sioux) is surely one of the most unusual fossil primates. Although we suspect it to be omomyine derived, from a form like *Rooneyia*, its closer affinities within the Omomyidae are impossible to ascertain as most of its features are quite unique.

The dental formula is $I\frac{2}{1,2}$; $C\frac{1}{1}$; $P\frac{2,3,4}{2,3,4}$; $M\frac{1,2,3}{1,2,3}$.

The known morphology of the dentition is unlike others known among the primates. The first molar is the largest tooth and those following it diminish in size. The talonid portion of $P_{\overline{4}}$ is enlarged, whereas the trigonid area holds a subequal protoconid and metaconid. The size difference of $P_{\overline{3}}$ compared to $P_{\overline{4}}$ is relatively abrupt, the former being distinctly smaller and premolariform. $P_{\overline{2}}$ is similar to but slightly smaller than $P_{\overline{3}}$ and both are double-rooted. The canine, judged from its alveolus, was larger than $P_{\overline{2}}$ and roundly based. The alveoli show the two incisors to have been very small and the roots constricted, not unlike the roots of some of the lemurid tooth combs, although a functional parallel is not suggested.

The cheek teeth, in general, are very low crowned, buccally and mesially bordered by cingula, and the occlusal surfaces are etched by a delicate dendritic system of grooves. The hypoconid occupies the distobuccal corner of rather square-shaped first and second molars, and the entoconid and a robust metastylid are closely twinned on the middle of the lingual border. The result of the twinning is a lingual profile of two notches and three cusps for each tooth.

The paraconids are completely lost, the functional unit on the trigonid of the molars being the vague ridge formed by the protoconid and the wedge-shaped metaconid.

The coronoid process was apparently very high and there are indications on the best-preserved specimen that the mandibular angle was quite expanded. The moderately deep mandible is unusually thin transversely, indicating a minimum of requirements to withstand transversely directed forces. The mandibular symphysis, well displayed on some specimens, is a most unusual one among the omomyids. It was certainly not synostosed and has the outline of a very flat ellipse. There is no sign of a superior transverse torus and the usual pocket on the ventral part of the symphysis for the genioglossus and geniohyoid muscle is missing. The diagnostic insertions appear to have been slightly behind the inferior border of the symphysis.

The low crowned, but broad, cheek teeth, along with the mandible structure, suggest a diet which was neither hard nor poor in nutrients so that it did not require large daily portions. The cuspate, crenulated, low-relief molars and the molarized fourth premolar suggest adaptations for crushing materials that were not very fibrous and, hence, probably reflect specializations for frugivory. The dentition of *Ekgmowechashala*, at least the cheek teeth, is convergent to that of *Bassaricyon*, the cuataquil or olingo, an arboreal procyonid reported to be frugivorous (Szalay, 1976).

SUBFAMILY MICROCHOERINAE
Lydekker, 1887

(= or including: Microchoeridae Lydekker, 1887. Necrolemurinae Simpson, 1940. Pseudolorisinae Simpson, 1940.)

DISTRIBUTION
  Middle Eocene to early Oligocene (Rhenanian to Headonian). Western Europe.
INCLUDING TAXA
  Microchoerus, Nannopithex, Necrolemur, and *Pseudoloris.*

DISCUSSION

All of the tarsiiforms included in this subfamily are European. Their diagnostic feature is primarily the conformation of the homologous enlarged upper and lower first incisors. Unlike in tarsiids, for example, or in some omomyids in which the anterior dentition is known (e.g., *Ourayia*), the first pair of upper incisors of microchoerines are slightly separated from one another, and the lateral upper incisors are placed directly behind the medial pair. In the ear region, unlike in the tarsiid bulla in which the hypotympanic sinus is greatly enlarged anteromedially, the known microchoerines have a greatly inflated petromastoid.

As far as known, the diagnostic characters of the Microchoerinae, separating them from other omomyids, are not clearly definable, although there is no doubt that they represent a monophyletic category. Known similarities to the Anaptomorphinae are numerous, and it may be that microchoerines are most recently related to the former stock among the Omomyidae. Among the recognized microchoerines the molars and third and fourth premolars of *Nannopithex raabi* appear to be the most primitive, judged from their similarity to primitive omomyine and anaptomorphine omomyids. Although the molars of *Nannopithex* show primitive omomyid features (which are also primitive euprimate traits), there is no doubt that *Nannopithex* also represents primitive microchoerine characters. The increasingly buccal paraconid on a progressively shorter paracristid from $M_{\overline{1-3}}$, moderately squared upper molars with a continuous cingulum running from the mesial side to the distal one, and unreduced third molars coupled with enlarged first incisors characterize the microchoerine morphotype. Both the stratigraphic position and the distinctive, yet primitive, dental morphology of *Nannopithex* eminently qualify it as an ancestor for this limited (as far as known) European omomyid radiation.

Whether the European tarsiiform genera *Nannopithex, Necrolemur, Microchoerus,* and *Pseudoloris* are recognized as being sufficiently divergent to represent an independent family or only a subfamily of the Omomyidae is a problem which should largely depend on the homologies of the antemolar dentition. It was suggested by Szalay (1976) that, providing the homologies and the general conformation of these teeth can be shown to be the same as in some omomyid taxa, and that the basicranium of *Necrolemur* can be reconciled with those of other omomyids such as *Tetonius* and *Rooneyia* rather than *Tarsius,* the Microchoerinae should be placed within the Omomyidae.

The most important first step in deciphering the homologies of the anterior teeth should be the establishment of the premaxillary–maxillary suture. Of the nine upper teeth, the distal six are certainly P^2–M^3, the most anterior is I^1, and therefore the second and third teeth are in question as to their homologies. Simons (1961b), who has attempted to solve the antemolar homologies of microchoerines, has extensively discussed some aspects of this problem, but he bypassed the crucial issue by stating that "the upper dental formulae of all species of both groups (i.e. of microchoerines and *Tarsius*) are apparently the same (2.1.3.3) as are the sizes of the teeth relative to each other" (p. 58). This reflects the acceptance of the premaxillary–maxillary suture as originally shown for *Necrolemur antiquus* by Stehlin (1916) and by Simons and Russell (1960). Repeated examinations by Szalay of all *Necrolemur antiquus* skulls in European and North American collections failed to confirm the suture mesial to the seventh tooth from the back or distal to the second one from the front. One specimen may be interpreted in such a way that a suture might have passed between the first and second upper teeth. Fusion apparently occurred between the premaxillary and maxillary bones at a very early stage in ontogeny and this question is still unsettled. Szalay (1975g, 1976) found no unequivocal evidence which would either support or contradict Stehlin's original designation.

Simons (1961b) has further argued that the enlarged microchoerine lower tooth is a canine. His evidence consisted of two specimens of *Microchoerus* in the British Museum which, according to him, show small alveoli anterior to the enlarged procumbent tooth. He cites additional specimens of the same taxon in the Paris collections. Szalay's (1975g, 1976) interpretation of these openings on specimens which are usually broken differs from his. He considers the openings as parts of the abundant nutrient canals on *Microchoerus* mandibles. This genus, for adaptive reasons obscure at present, had a great number of nutrient vessels entering and leaving the anterior part of the mandible. This condition is particularly well documented by the numerous, irregularly placed mental foramina on the side of the jaw.

A strict application of upper and lower tooth occlusal relationships cannot be applied to microchoerine dentitions. There are nine teeth above and eight below, although the second lower tooth is so small that it takes no part in occlusion, and, therefore, the number of operational lower teeth is better considered as seven. In order to analyze microchoerine tooth homologies and mechanical function, two important selective factors must be postulated. First, there was selection either for a reduced face, including both the upper and lower jaws, or for reduction of the length of the lower jaw. Second, there was clearly selection for enlargement of the pair of anterior teeth both above and below. We will assume that phylogenetic enlargement of both upper and lower anteriormost teeth occurred simultaneously as their mechanical function and biological role are closely tied together. Thus, as the upper enlarged tooth is not a canine, it is probable that the enlarged lower tooth is the incisor originally occluding with the enlarged upper one. As this incisive function appears to have been of extreme importance, judged by the size of these teeth in all microchoerines, disturbance of the role of this area by phyletically losing the lower incisor and replacing it with the lower canine was unlikely. Selection for maintaining occlusion of a lower canine with an upper one was unlikely to have been of greater importance than the maintenance of the adaptively important occlusion by the incisors. If this was the case, then it is probable that, following the enlargment of the anterior teeth, tooth reduction occurred distal to them. Clearly, the same number of teeth were not lost above and below. Thus, tooth reduction, a response to either mandibular shortening or disproportionate enlargement of the anterior teeth, occurred in a manner to fill the available space on the mandible with the phylogenetically and ontogenetically most developed teeth at the time of eruption.

Which of the upper teeth is most likely to be the canine? Lacking evidence from the suture we cannot decide whether the second or third tooth from the front is the canine. In either case, in our view, the homology of the enlarged anterior teeth does not influence the decision about the upper canine. The two teeth posterior to the enlarged lower incisors are either $P_{\overline{1}}$ and $P_{\overline{2}}$ as suggested by Simons or an incisor and a canine as the dental formulas in either *Omomys* or *Tetonius* are interpreted by Szalay (1976), and others. If the second upper tooth is the canine, then the derived enlargement of the P^1 could be considered a major distinction of microchoerines from all other known tarsiiforms. Therefore, their separation from the omomyids as a family, the Microchoeridae, could perhaps be supported. This alternative is not accepted here; instead the upper teeth are interpreted as I^1, I^2, C, P^2–M^3, while the lowers are $I_{\overline{1}}$, $I_{\overline{2}}$, C, $P_{\overline{3}}$–$M_{\overline{3}}$.

Attention has been paid to the alleged similarities between dentitions of the late Eocene (Quercy) *Pseudoloris* and those of *Tarsius* (see in particular

Teilhard de Chardin, 1916–1921; Simons, 1961b). Simons (1972) in particular has recently placed great emphasis on this resemblance and, as noted, he allocated the Microchoerinae to the Tarsiidae. Szalay (1975g, 1976), however, found that some of the alleged similarities are not similarities at all, whereas others are convergent. The most important difference between the two genera, previously alleged to be a similarity, is the manner of arrangement and occlusal function of the anterior dentition. These, in turn, strongly suggest (and this is borne out by the cheek tooth morphology) that the premolars and molars are similar due to convergence rather than as a result of deriving their conformation from a common ancestor.

The dentition of *Tarsius* and its inferred functional features are so unique that a brief account clarifies some important points as they relate to microchoerines. Articulating skulls with their mandibles show that a distinct incisive stroke is present. During this incisive bite the mesial edges of the lower canines shear against the greatly enlarged central upper incisors and the small lateral pair of incisors (Szalay, 1976, Figures 153 and 154). The cutting edges of the two pairs of upper incisors are almost exactly transverse to the long axis of the skull. The molar crests are high and movement of the lower jaw appears to be mostly orthal with a very minimal mesiolingual component. The mandibular fossa is very unusual among primates. Anteroposteriorly long and transversely narrow, it is a trough which permits extensive propalinal but very little transverse movement. This is also reflected by the articular condyle, which is long anteroposteriorly but very narrow transversely. The arrangement of the anterior dentition of *Pseudoloris*, however, is exactly like that of other microchoerines. Unlike the antecanine teeth of *Tarsius*, those of *Pseudoloris* are lined up mesiodistally. In addition to this pronounced difference, the reduced microchoerine lower canine is not the major lower piercing tooth; this role is assumed by the enlarged incisor. Selection for the performance of the same functions and probably biological roles, piercing and cutting, by the antecanine dentitions of *Pseudoloris* and *Tarsius* has resulted in highly divergent relative sizes, morphology, and manner of mechanical function, dictated by the morphology of their respective ancestry.

Although the morphology of the postcanine teeth of *Pseudoloris* is similar to that of *Tarsius*, several clues suggest that the similarities are not shared derived character states. A close examination of the molars and premolars reveals that the most important shared similarities between the two genera are the acuity of the cusps and the relatively high crests; there are no other significant similarities beyond these. *Pseudoloris* has a well-defined hypocone, suggesting an ancestry not unlike *Nannopithex*.

Until proof is available as to the exact homologies of the upper teeth distal to the enlarged incisor, the Microchoerinae are best considered a subfamily of the Omomyidae, but not of the Tarsiidae. As noted under the Haplorhini, microchoerines do not share some of the characteristic specializations of the tarsiid ear region. Short of a probably shared early tarsiiform specialization of the tarsus and possibly the crus (not as advanced, however, as seen in *Tarsius*), they do not appear to share advanced traits exclusively with the Tarsiidae, or display antecedent, more primitive, characters to diagnostic tarsiid features.

NANNOPITHEX Stehlin, 1916

(= or including: *Necrolemur:* Chantre and Gaillard, 1897. *Pseudoloris:* Weigelt, 1933).

DISTRIBUTION
 Middle Eocene (Rhenanian). France, Germany.
KNOWN SPECIES
 1. *Nannopithex filholi* (Chantre and Gaillard, 1897), type species
(= *Necrolemur filholi* Chantre and Gaillard, 1897. *Nannopithex pollicaris* Stehlin, 1916.)
LOCALITIES: Bouxwiller (254); Egerkingen Huppersand★ (256); Lissieu (258).
 2. *Nannopithex raabi* (Heller, 1930)

(= *Necrolemur raabi* Heller, 1930. *Pseudoloris abderhaldini* Weigelt, 1933.)
LOCALITIES: Geiseltal★ (237).

DISCUSSION

Nannopithex (Figure 130) apparently represents the most primitive known evolutionary stage of the microhoerines (Simpson, 1940). Although the first pair of lower incisors are considerably enlarged, the molars

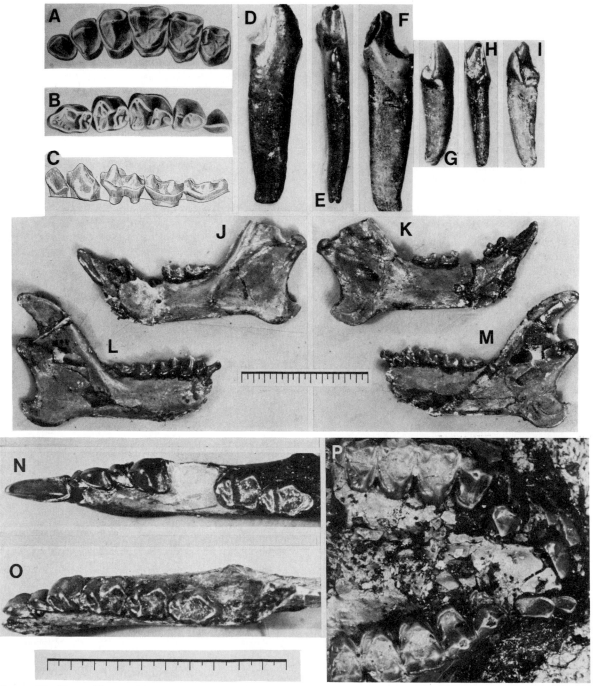

Figure 130. *Nannopithex.* Middle Eocene, western Europe. *Nannopithex pollicaris.* Left P^2–M^3. A, occlusal view. Left P$_{\overline{3}}$–M$_{\overline{3}}$: B, occlusal view; C, buccal view. *Nannopithex raabi.* Right central upper incisor (I^1): D, mesial view; E, occlusodistal view; F, distal view. Right lateral incisor (I^2): G, mesial view; H, occlusodistal view; I, distal view. Left mandible with I$_{\overline{1-2}}$, C, P$_{\overline{3}}$, and M$_{\overline{2}}$–M$_{\overline{3}}$: J, lateral view; K, medial view. Right mandible with C–M$_{\overline{3}}$: L, lateral view; M, medial view. Right mandible with I$_{\overline{1}}$–P$_{\overline{4}}$, M$_{\overline{2}}$–M$_{\overline{3}}$: N, occlusal view. Right mandible with C–M$_{\overline{3}}$: O, occlusal view. Palate with left I^2, C, P^3–M^3 and right C, P^3–M^3: P, occlusal view. Subdivisions on scales represent 0.5 mm. [A–C from Hürzeler (1948).]

261

are reminiscent of primitive tarsiiforms and adapids in general without any striking specializations except for some crenulations. There is a protocone-fold (originally called the *Nannopithex*-fold) and an incipient hypocone, unlike that, for example, on the molars of *Pseudoloris*. Unlike the typically anaptomorphin greatly reduced M^3_3 of *Teilhardina* or *Tetonius*, the last molars of *Nannopithex* are unreduced. *Nannopithex* is very likely ancestral to *Necrolemur*, but the exact origins of *Nannopithex* itself (and of the subfamily) are obscure.

The dental formula of *Nannopithex* and those of other microchoerines have been discussed by Simons (1961b) and Szalay (1976) and also above under the Microchoerinae. According to the interpretation of Szalay, the formula is tentatively given as $I^{1\cdot2}_{1\cdot2}$; C^1_1; $P^{2\cdot3\cdot4}_{2\cdot3\cdot4}$; $M^{1\cdot2\cdot3}_{1\cdot2\cdot3}$.

Several excellently preserved mandibles and a nearly complete (but, unfortunately, crushed) cranium of *N. raabi* are known (see Szalay, 1975g). The eyes were large, like those of *Tetonius* and *Necrolemur*, and there seem to be indications that the petromastoid was inflated like in these latter genera. *Nannopithex* preserves a mandibular construction that is considerably primitive inasmuch as the coronoid process is high and the mandibular angle, although relatively large, protrudes posteriorly. The deemphasis of canine function in favor of incisor enlargement apparently had relatively little effect on the realignment of the muscles and consequently on the construction of the mandible.

Weigelt (1933) figured a hindlimb associated with the cranial material of *N. raabi*. Unfortunately, despite Professor Matthes's efforts in Halle to locate the specimens for study during 1970, these important bones could not be found.

The enlarged orbits and incisors of *Nannopithex* suggest nocturnal insectivory.

NECROLEMUR Filhol, 1873

DISTRIBUTION

Middle to late Eocene (Rhenanian to early Headonian). France.

KNOWN SPECIES

1. *Necrolemur antiquus* Filhol, 1873, type species

LOCALITIES: Phosphorites of Quercy★ (294); La Vergne (316); La Bouffie (326); Les Pradigues (328); Mormont (312); Aubrelong 2 (348); Ehrenstein I (A) (354).

2. *Necrolemur zitteli* Schlosser, 1887

LOCALITIES: Phosphorites of Quercy★ (294); Robiac (306); Grisolles (310); Le Bretou (308).

DISCUSSION

The outstanding differences between *Necrolemur* and *Nannopithex*, its very plausible ancestor, lie in the former having evolved slightly more squared molars, more pronounced crenulations, and the somewhat shortened and expanded mandibular angle. Squaring of the upper molars is a direct result of the relative increase in the size of the hypocone. The skull of this genus is very well known (Figures 131 and 132) and most of the pertinent morphology is detailed under the discussion of the higher categories Microchoerinae, Omomyidae, and Tarsiiformes. The orbits were large and the petromastoid was exceptionally inflated. A number of studies, beginning with those of Stehlin (1916) and continuing with those of Hürzeler (1946, 1948), Simons and Russell (1960), Simons (1961b),

Szalay (1975g, 1976), and Szalay and Wilson (1976), have firmly established the details of the skull morphology, particularly of the ear region in this genus. It appears that claims by Simons (1961b) that *Necrolemur* and other microchoerines are specially related to *Tarsius* within the Tarsiiformes may have been based on primitive tarsiiform characters rather than on special, derived tarsiid characters. The discussions under the Tarsiiformes and Microchoerinae are therefore pertinent.

The dental formula, as discussed under the Microchoerinae, can be tentatively given as $I^{1\cdot2}_{1\cdot2}$; C^1_1; $P^{2\cdot3\cdot4}_{2\cdot3\cdot4}$; $M^{1\cdot2\cdot3}_{1\cdot2\cdot3}$.

The large-eyed *Necrolemur* has a mandibular morphology which is distinctly derived when compared to *Nannopithex*. The primitive hook-like appearance of the mandibular angle of *Nannopithex* is transformed into a short and dorsoventrally broadened structure. Compared to *Nannopithex*, the enlarged incisors of *Necrolemur* are widened and shortened. The molars, as noted, are squared by the phyletic development of the hypocone. Added to this complex of features are the crenulated, low crowned molars. The combination of these derived characters very strongly suggests a highly frugivorous, rather than insectivorous, group of primates.

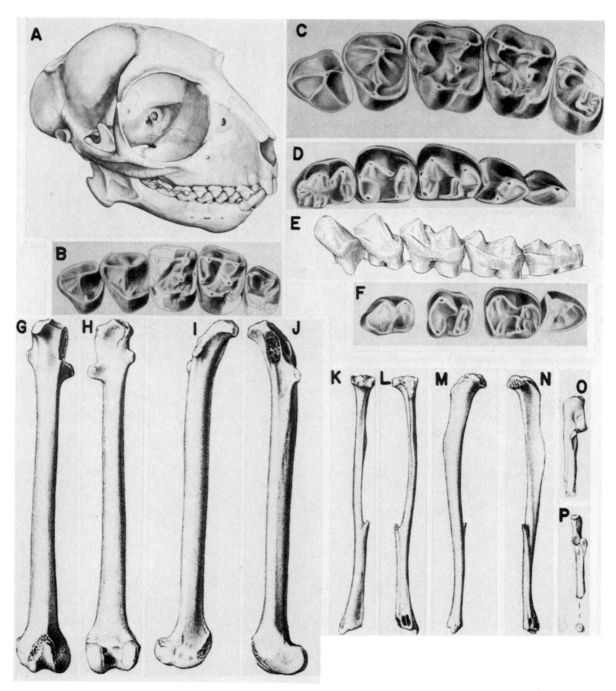

Figure 131. *Necrolemur.* Middle Eocene, western Europe. *Necrolemur antiquus:* A, skull and mandible. Left P$^{\underline{3}}$–M$^{\underline{3}}$: C, occlusal view. Left cheek teeth P$_{\overline{3}}$–M$_{\overline{3}}$: D, occlusal view; E, buccal view. *Necrolemur* cf. *zitteli.* Right P$^{\underline{3}}$–M$^{\underline{3}}$: B, occlusal view. Left P$_{\overline{4}}$–M$_{\overline{3}}$: F, occlusal view. *Necrolemur* sp. Right femur: G, anterior view; H, posterior view; I, lateral view; J, medial view. Right tibio-fibula: K, posterior view; L, anterior view; M, medial view; N, lateral view. Right calcaneum: O, medial view; P, dorsal view. [A from Simons and Russell (1960); B–F from Hürzeler (1948).]

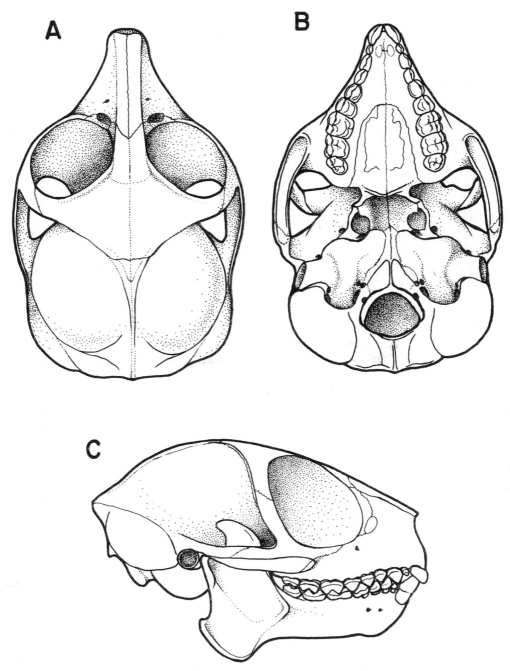

Figure 132. *Necrolemur antiquus.* Late Eocene, western Europe. Reconstructed skull: A, dorsal view; B, ventral view; C, lateral view. [By A. Cleary.]

MICROCHOERUS Wood, 1846

(= or including: *Necrolemur*: Filhol, 1880, in part. *Microchaerus* Forbes, 1894, lapsus?)

DISTRIBUTION

Late Eocene to early Oligocene (Headonian). England, France, Germany.

KNOWN SPECIES

1. *Microchoerus erinaceus* Wood, 1846, type species

[= *Necrolemur edwardsi* Filhol, 1880. *Microchoerus edwardsi* (Filhol, 1880).]

LOCALITIES: Phosphorites of Quercy (294); Grisolles (310); Fons 1–6 (314); Hordle Cliff★ (320); Euzet (322); Sosis (324); Isle of Wight (327); Malpérié (352); Ehrenstein I (A) (354); Perrière (356); La Débruge (357); Gosgen (358).

2. *Microchoerus ornatus* Stehlin, 1916

LOCALITIES: Mormont★ (312); Entreroches (360); San Cugat (362).

DISCUSSION

Microchoerus (Figure 133) differs from the phenetically closest and probably also most recently related genus, *Necrolemur*, primarily in the heavily crenulated morphology of its cheek teeth. It also contrasts with its probable ancestor, an early species of *Necrolemur*, in its great proliferation of cusps and cutting edges. The crowns of the cheek teeth are low and wide and the incisors are also broad and much less attenuated than, for example, those of *Nannopithex*. The most recent treatments of the species of *Microchoerus* were by Schmidt-Kittler (1971) and Louis and Sudre (1975).

The dental formula is the same as that of *Necrolemur*.

The great total length of mesiodistally aligned new cutting edges on the cheek teeth and the squared off shape of these teeth are the strongest hints that *Microchoerus* was primarily herbivorous. Whether the staple diet of the included species was more fruit than leaf is difficult to decide. In light of the predominance of sharp edges and their continuous maintenance throughout various wear stages in the ontogeny of *Microchoerus*, one suspects the genus to have been primarily folivorous [see in particular Seligsohn and Szalay (1977b) for a discussion of wear in some living folivores].

PSEUDOLORIS Stehlin, 1916

(= or including: *Necrolemur*: Filhol, 1889–1890. *Pivetonia* Crusafont-Pairo, 1967.)

DISTRIBUTION

Late Eocene (Rhenanian). France, Spain.

KNOWN SPECIES

1. *Pseudoloris parvulus* (Filhol, 1889–1890), type species

(= *Necrolemur parvulus* Filhol, 1889–1890. *Pseudoloris parvulus*: Stehlin, 1916. *Pseudoloris reguanti* Crusafont-Pairo, 1967.)

LOCALITIES: Phosphorites of Quercy★ (294); Euzet (322); Sosis (324); San Cugat (362).

2. *Pseudoloris isabenae* (Crusafont-Pairo, 1967), new combination

(= *Pivetonia isabenae* Crusafont-Pairo, 1967.)

LOCALITIES: Capella★ (253).

DISCUSSION

Pseudoloris, first carefully discussed and illustrated by Teilhard de Chardin (1916–1921), has long been cited as an undoubted tarsiid (Simons, 1972). Several excellently preserved palates and facial skulls are known and the dentition is well known (Teilhard de Chardin, 1916–1921; Simons, 1961b; Szalay, 1976). *Pseudoloris* (Figure 134) differs from other microchoerines in having acute cusped and sharp-crested cheek teeth. The conformation of the anterior dentition leaves little doubt that *Pseudoloris* is especially similar to both *Necrolemur* and *Microchoerus* and that the antemolar dentitions of these taxa are homologous. The basicranial morphology which would be crucial in the phylogenetic assessment of *Pseudoloris* is unknown. Unquestionably there are similarities in both the large orbits and short muzzle, and in aspects of the dentition of *Pseudoloris* and *Tarsius*. However, scrutiny of the dentitions, detailed under the discussion of the Microchoerinae, strongly suggests that the striking dental similarities between *Pseudoloris* and *Tarsius* are convergent.

The strong dental convergence of the dentition, in spite of the fact that the homologies of the piercing teeth differ, is compelling to suggest a mode of life for *Pseudoloris* very similar to *Tarsius*.

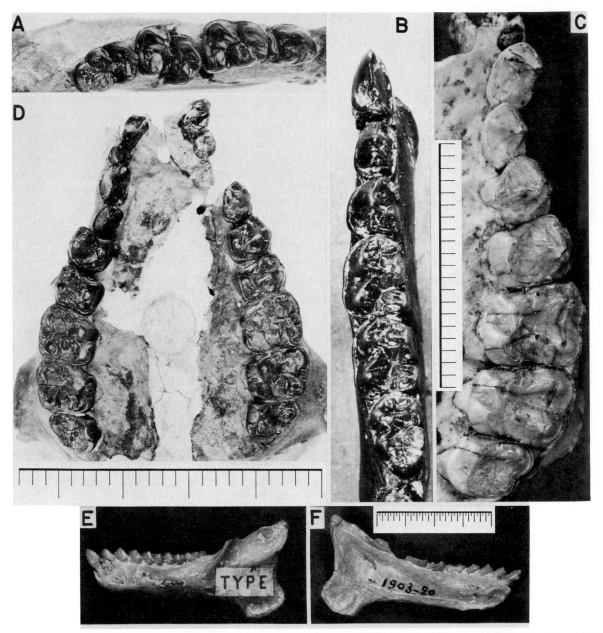

Figure 133. *Microchoerus edwardsi.* Late Eocene, western Europe. Left mandible with $P_{\overline{4}}$–$M_{\overline{3}}$: A, occlusal view. Left mandible with C, $P_{\overline{3}}$–$P_{\overline{4}}$, $M_{\overline{1}}$–$M_{\overline{3}}$: B, occlusal view. Left maxilla with C, $P^{\underline{3}}$–$P^{\underline{4}}$, $M^{\underline{1}}$–$M^{\underline{3}}$: C, occlusal view. Palate with left $I^{\underline{1}}$–$I^{\underline{2}}$, $P^{\underline{3}}$–$P^{\underline{4}}$, $M^{\underline{1}}$–$M^{\underline{3}}$ and right $I^{\underline{1}}$–$I^{\underline{2}}$, C, $P^{\underline{2}}$–$P^{\underline{4}}$, $M^{\underline{1}}$–$M^{\underline{3}}$: D, occlusal view. Left mandible with $I_{\overline{1}}$–$I_{\overline{2}}$, C, $P_{\overline{3}}$–$P_{\overline{4}}$, $M_{\overline{1}}$–$M_{\overline{3}}$: E, lateral view; F, medial view. Scale divisions on C and D are in millimeters. Subdivisions on scale in F represent 0.5 mm.

266

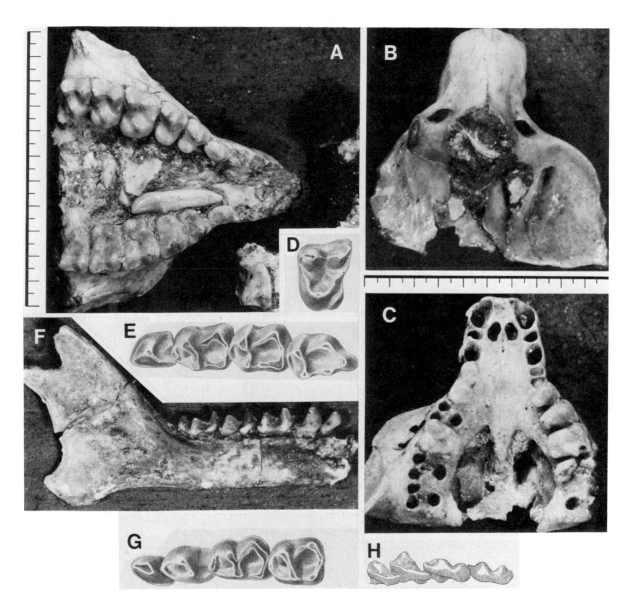

Figure 134. *Pseudoloris.* Late Eocene, western Europe. *Pseudoloris parvulus.* Palate with right P²–M³ and left P²–M³, and isolated anterior tooth: A, occlusal view. Skull fragment: B, dorsal view; C, occlusal view. Left M¹: D, occlusal view. Right P₄–M₃: E, occlusal view. Right mandible with P₃–M₃: F, lateral view. *Pseudoloris isabenae.* Right P₃–M₂: G, occlusal view; H, lingual view. Subdivisions on scales represent 0.5 mm. [D, E, G, H from Crusafont-Pairo (1967).]

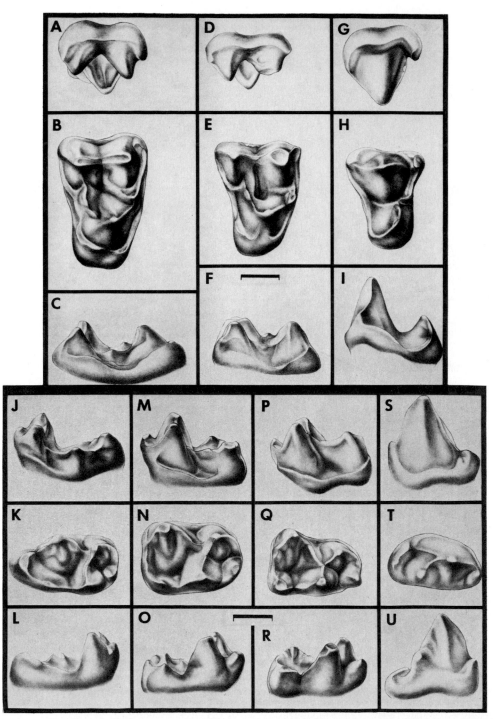

Figure 135. *Donrussellia gallica.* Early Eocene, western Europe. Upper teeth. From left to right: M², M¹, and P⁴. From top to third row down: buccal, occlusal, and distal views. Lower teeth. From left to right: $M_{\bar{3}}$, $M_{\bar{2}}$, $M_{\bar{1}}$, and $P_{\bar{4}}$. From fourth to sixth row down: buccal, occlusal, and lingual views. Scales represent 1 mm. [From Szalay (1976).]

Family Omomyidae,
incertae sedis

DONRUSSELLIA Szalay, 1976

(= or including: *Teilhardina?*: Russell, Louis, and Savage, 1967. *Teilhardina (Donrussellia)*: Savage, Russell, and Waters, 1977.)

DISTRIBUTION
  Early Eocene (Neustrian). France.
KNOWN SPECIES
  Donrussellia gallica (Russell, Louis, and Savage, 1967), type species [=*Teilhardina? gallica* Russell, Louis, and Savage, 1967. *Teilhardina (Donrusellia) gallica*: Savage, Russell, and Waters, 1977.]
  LOCALITIES: Avenay★ (206).

DISCUSSION

Donrussellia, known from teeth (Figure 135), differs from an acknowledged primitive omomyid such as *Teilhardina*, for example, in the following features: The P_4 is transversely less wide; the basal part of the trigonid cusps, particularly the metaconids, is less inflated; the third molars are relatively larger; the upper premolars (either P^3 or P^4) are relatively longer mesiodistally than either P^3 or P^4 of *Teilhardina*; the molars are less transverse; the metaconule on known molars is not clearly defined, being part of the post-protocrista; the M_3 talonids, unlike those of *Teilhardina*, are not reduced.

The remarkable aspect of this genus lies in what we suspect to be its "intermediate," that is, nearly equally similar, nature between an adapid like *Protoadapis* and the omomyid morphotype. Studying the known evidence one finds it difficult to decide, based both on overall similarity and on sharing of a variety of subtle specializations, whether this taxon is more recently related to *Teilhardina* or other omomyids, on the one hand, or to the common ancestors of *Pronycticebus*, *Anchomomys*, *Protoadapis*, and *Pelycodus*, on the other. Because the real possibility exists that *Donrussellia* does share a more recent common ancestor with the omomyids than with adapids and because it does in fact represent the most primitive known dental morphology if we consider it of the Omomyidae, the new genus is placed in the Omomyidae, following Szalay, (1976), with a query. Recovery of anterior teeth and postcranials in association with cheek teeth will undoubtedly shed further light on the affinities of this genus. We do not agree with the otherwise cogent analysis of Savage *et al.* (1977) that *Donrussellia* should be included with *Teilhardina* as a subgenus.

Donrussellia has low crowned, slightly squared molars with low conules combined with relatively high-cusped premolars. The best guess about the relatively poor sample is that it was of an omnivorous animal subsisting both on some fruits and insects. There are no outstanding specializations in the known material which would warrant postulation of any particular type of herbivory.

HOANGHONIUS Zdansky, 1930

DISTRIBUTION
  Middle or late Eocene. Northern China.
KNOWN SPECIES
  Hoanghonius stehlini Zdansky, 1930, type species
  LOCALITIES: Yuanchu 1 and 7 (Zdansky)★ (332).

DISCUSSION

This is a poorly known genus (Figure 136) with some unresolved problems concerning its family affinites. Judged by the type specimen, a lower jaw, one may tentatively consider this genus to be an omomyid. This view is reinforced by the maxilla fragment published by Woo and Chow (1957). The lower jaws published in that paper, however, are artiodactyl (Gingerich, 1976; Delson, 1977a). The large lingual cingulum and the pericone on the upper molar clearly do not relate *Hoanghonius* in any special degree to *Periconodon* (or any other adapid), as suggested by Gingerich (1976), as this structure is fairly common among primates and could have easily evolved convergently.

In dealing with *Hoanghonius*, mention must be made of the striking similarity between the M_2 (the only

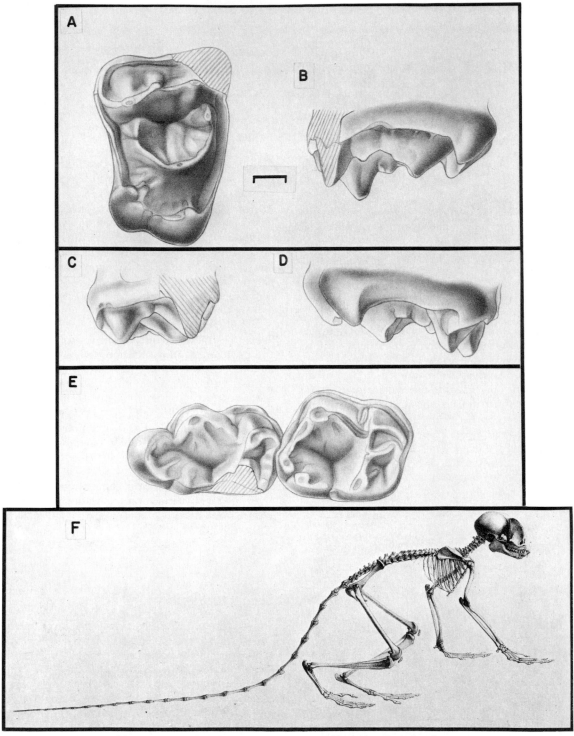

Figure 136. *Hoanghonius stehlini*. Middle or late Eocene, eastern Asia. Right molar: A, occlusal view; B, mesial view; C, buccal view; D, distal view. Left M$_{\overline{2-3}}$: E, occlusal view. Hatched area depicts reconstruction. Scale represents 1 mm. *Tarsius* sp. Modern, Southeast Asia. F, Skeleton. [A–E by A. Cleary; F, from de Blainville (1839).]

homologous unit known in both samples) of this taxon and that of the oldest Fayum primate, *Oligopithecus* (see comparison by Gingerich, 1977b). Judged from the similarity of talonid construction in *Oligopithecus* and the later Fayum primates, it is possible that the former is also a catarrhine. It is for this reason that the similarity of *Hoanghonius* to *Oligopithecus* takes on some significance.

The original sample of *Hoanghonius* described by Zdansky (1930) consists of a right upper molar, probably M^2, and a left mandible fragment with $M_{\overline{2-3}}$. This material has been recently reexamined by Gingerich (1977b), who concluded that *Hoanghonius* is an adapid. The material from Stockholm is known to us from excellent casts, whereas the more recently discovered material (Woo and Chow, 1957) is known to us only from inadequate casts. Consequently our observations pertain only to the material in Stockholm.

The characteristically twinned and distolingually displaced entoconid–hypoconulid configuration as well as the reduced paracristid closely appressed to the metacristid are significant derived features shared between the $M_{\overline{2}}$ of *Hoanghonius* and *Oligopithecus*. Let us, for the time being, assume that these two taxa are special relatives. What group, then, would *Hoanghonius* and *Oligopithecus* suggest as their source of origin? Contrary to Gingerich's view, there is no character or combination of characters which would mandate adapid ties for *Hoanghonius*. The known molars of *Hoanghonius*, in fact, share some of the diagnostic characters of *Macrotarsius*. Furthermore,

the construction of $P_{\overline{4}}$ and $P_{\overline{3}}$ of *Oligopithecus* is extremely similar to those features of omomyine omomyids. Nevertheless, the possible adapid ties of *Hoanghonius*, and also *Oligopithecus*, cannot be dismissed. Were they to be corroborated by better samples of these forms, then *Oligopithecus* should clearly be taken out of the Catarrhini. As our discussion under *Oligopithecus* suggests, there are no unequivocal traits which link this genus with the younger Fayum primates. Detailed comparisons of dental morphology among *Hoanghonius*, *Oligopithecus*, and *Indraloris* might prove revealing.

Whether or not similarities between *Hoanghonius* and *Oligopithecus* (unknown from upper teeth) go beyond the confines of $M_{\overline{2}}$ is yet to be seen. The little we know about the morphology of *Hoanghonius* suggests that this intriguing form may have had its closest phylogenetic ties with omomyine Omomyidae.

The following characters give some indication of the adaptational significance of the dentition. The cingulum is strongly developed in the only known specimens of upper dentition. Judged by the prevalence of broadly based cusps as opposed to dominance of crests, as in *Lushius*, for example, orthal movements, crushing, and puncturing appear to have dominated the masticatory cycle. In terms of diet, the best guess we can make at present is that *Hoanghonius* was not extremely specialized for frugivory or folivory. Some type of specific omnivorous regime of fruits, shoots, and predominantly insects must suffice as an initial explanatory hypothesis.

Family Tarsiidae
Gray, 1825

(= or including: Tarsina Gray, 1825. Tarsidae Burnett, 1828. Tarsiidae Gill, 1872.)

DISTRIBUTION
  Modern. Southeast Asia.
INCLUDED TAXA
  Tarsius.

TARSIUS Storr, 1780

(= or including: *Macrotarsus* Link, 1795. *Rabienus* Gray, 1821, *Cephelophachus* Swainson, 1835, *Hypsicebus* Lesson, 1840.)

DISTRIBUTION
  Modern. The Phillipines, western Malaysia, eastern Celebes.

KNOWN SPECIES*
  1. *Tarsius syrichta* (Linnaeus, 1758), type species
  2. *Tarsius spectrum* (Pallas, 1778)
  3. *Tarsius bancanus* (Horsfield, 1821)

---

*The three commonly recognized species may very well be regarded as a considerably polytypic species or superspecies.

DISCUSSION

It has often been stated that the living *Tarsius* is a representative of a once diversified Holarctic radiation of tarsiiforms—in many but not in all ways. In a number of unique character complexes *Tarsius* is a testimony to its own complex adaptational history and it would be a mistake to use this form in an unanalytical manner as the model for understanding all tarsiiforms. Specializations abound in the cranial and postcranial anatomy of *Tarsius* which probably reflect several diachronous adaptations rather than one single specialization (Todd Olson, personal communication). An eco-ethological study of *Tarsius* was recently published by Fogden (1974), and this work should greatly facilitate future analyses of the morphology of tarsiers.

The most important cranial modifications of *Tarsius* (Figure 136), long recognized by various authors, are as follows: (*a*) reduction of the rostrum, (*b*) reduction of the interorbital distance as a result of the great enlargement of the eyes, (*c*) partial posterior closure of the orbit from the temporal fossa by the incomplete partition formed by the frontal, jugal, and alisphenoid bones, (*d*) very short zygomatic arch, (*e*) very small temporal fossa, (*f*) pronounced basicranial flexion, (*g*) downward orientation of foramen magnum, (*h*) fusion of the lateral pterygoid lamina to the bulla, (*i*) great enlargement of the hypotympanic sinus, and (*j*) a carotid canal entering vertically upward into the bulla and basicranium. The question is unsettled as to how many of these features are the direct result of the greatly enlarged eyes of *Tarsius*, its considerably encephalized brain, or locomotor behavior. The dental mechanics of *Tarsius* are treated under the Microchoerinae, where the genus is compared to *Pseudoloris*.

Tarsiers are insectivorous–carnivorous, nocturnal, and not gregarious. They are confined to certain islands of the Indonesian and Philippine Archipelagos. These are Sumatra, Bangka, Belitung (=Billiton), Karimata, South Natuna Islands, Borneo, Celebes, Great Sanghi Island, Samar, Leyte, Bohol, and Mindanao. Although tarsiers in many ways are reminiscent of some of the strepsirhines, Hill (1972), the eminent anatomist who has championed their true affinities, characterizes them as follows.

> On the whole, tarsiers give the impression of prosimian status recalling galagos in their soft woolly pel-

age, grotesquely large eyes, expanded membranous ears and elongated hind limbs, adapted for saltatory locomotion in an arboreal environment. They are, however, at once set apart by the absence of a naked rhinarium, for their shortened muzzles are characterized by the presence of completely rounded nostrils widely separated by an internarial septum covered by normal, hairy skin, which also surrounds the somewhat outwardly directed nostrils up to their margins—This narial condition is brought about developmentally by the complete fusion of the mesial and lateral nasal process forming, in addition to the broad internarial septum, a median part of the upper lip or philtrum in place of the median cleft lip of the lorisoids and lemurs. Coincident with this, the upper lip is freed, being no longer tethered to the gum rendering it mobile and hence available for expression of emotions. (pp. 156–157)

An equally striking aspect of *Tarsius* is its locomotor pattern, and therefore we will briefly characterize the postcranial morphology (Figure 136). Hill (1972) notes that "the tail of the tarsier is unique among Primates; its closest resemblance is to that of *Ptilocercus*, but the resemblance is superficial only. It is very long and slender and the major part of its length is virtually naked; the base, however, is hairy and there is a terminal sparse tuft varying with the species. The organ is adapted to the peculiar resting pose of the animal on a twig and to affording a purchase in leaping from the resting position to a new situation. In fact, like the tail of the kangaroo or a jerboa, it serves as the third limb of a tripod" (pp. 157–158). It would be unreasonable to presume, however, that all postcranial features of *Tarsius* are the direct result of vertical clinging and leaping from that position. It would appear a better explanation that the postulated, all pervasive influence of grasp leaping left its initial marks, as in strepsirhines and other tarsiiforms, and the subsequent specializations of vertical posturing and leaping superimposed on that heritage contributed to the morphological uniqueness of the *Tarsius* skeleton. In contrast to the powerful hindlimbs, the forelimbs are short, and relatively weak. The long recognized specializations of the calcaneum and navicular, inasmuch as they are tremendously elongated, are not unlike those found in other saltatorial mammals. The loss of the pivotal cuboid–calcaneal articulation is probably a direct outcome of the tarsifulcrumating specialization of *Tarsius* (Szalay, 1976). The great relative size of the big toe can be related to the animal's needs for a powerful grasp, not only during vertical rest, but also during takeoff and landing, both of which are implemented through the foot.

It appears that one of the most unique characteristics of the entire postcranium is the ability of the hindlimb to perform extremes of flexion and extension. It has been pointed out by Hall-Craggs (1964) that elongation of the hindlimb, in particular that of the noted tarsal bones, results in a very long arc of movement. The result is that the body is propelled by this lever system for a relatively longer period of time than by a less elongated hindlimb. The straight-shafted femur has a rather cylindrical head, and the crus is made up primarily by the long tibia to which the fibula is fused. The knee joint is greatly elongated anteroposteriorly. Grand and Lorenz (1968) pointed out the specializations of the pelvis; the acetabulum is deep to receive the cylindrical femoral head and the ilium is long and narrow, whereas the ischium is reduced in size. Hall-Craggs (1964) convincingly showed, in detail, how the joint specializations of the tarsier's hindlimb and flexor and extensor functions of the musculature, emphasized at the expense of the adductor and abductor roles, have come to restrict movement to the saggital plane during saltation.

As Hill (1972) notes, "Further adaptations affect the hands and feet, both of which are virtually naked; terminal pads of fingers and toes are expanded into round, flattened discs which function both as tactile pads and, by enlarging the area of contact, serve to increase stability, preventing slipping of the grip. Nails are small and scale-like, except on the index and middle toes of the foot, both of which (instead of only the index as in lemurs and lorisoids) are provided with upstanding conical claws for use in combing the fur. In the digital formula of the hand, the middle finger is longest, not the fourth (cf. lemuroids)" (p. 159).

Infraorder Platyrrhini
E. Geoffroy, 1812

(= or including: Quadrumana, Illiger 1811, in part. Platyrrhina Hemprich, 1820. Platyonychae Gray, 1821, in part. Gampstonychae Gray, 1821. Simiae Burmeister, 1854. Simiadae Jardine, 1866. Platyrrhinae Weidenreich, 1943, lapsus.)

DISTRIBUTION
  Early Oligocene (Deseadan) to Modern. South and Central America.
INCLUDED TAXA
  Families Cebidae and Atelidae

Discussion

The study of platyrrhine phylogeny has been plagued not only by the lack of an adequate fossil record, but also by the absence of relatively balanced phylogenetic analyses of the living species. As with the study of other groups, platyrrhine relationships (Figure 137) have been debated in terms of whether or not the ancestor of the whole group or various lower category taxa were either marmosets or cebids, or more like one living representative as opposed to another. Contrary to this approach are a few encouraging studies which are beginning to concern themselves with the reconstruction of sweeps of ancestral character states, taking one character after another and utilizing as stringent a character analysis as the available data permit (cf. Rosenberger, 1977). The picture thus gained of inferred common ancestors on a given level is decidedly more testable and data oriented than the often fruitless debates emanating from a purely phenetic or "classificatory," rather than a phylogenetic, point of view.

Platyrrhines make up about 35% of all living primate species. Short of having terrestrial representatives, they are very diversified in their feeding and locomotor strategies, exploiting the subtropical and tropical forests of Central and South America. Platyrrhines range from southern Mexico into Colombia, Venezuela, the Guianas, Brazil, northeastern Argentina, Paraguay, Bolivia, part of Peru in the Amazonian drainage system, and Ecuador east of the Andes as well as on the west coast south of the equator. Although in the past platyrrhines were found in Jamaica and Hispaniola, their presence in Trinidad (*Cebus albifrons* and *Alouatta seniculus*) appears to be the result of human introduction. Altitudinally, they range from sea level to up to 3000 m in the Andes of Colombia.

As the subsequent account indicates, the extent of our knowledge of platyrrhine history is meager. The fossil record is more tantalizing than informative as yet. This record begins in lower Oligocene sediments of the Bolivian Andes (*Branisella*) and briefly continues in the late Oligocene to early Miocene of Southern Argentina and the middle Miocene of Central Colombia. It terminates with the subrecent localities of Jamaica and Hispaniola.

The uniform presence of the platyrrhine nose in South American primates (Pocock, 1918) is still a strong diagnostic character. Nevertheless, this probably nearly primitive haplorhine or anthropoid charac-

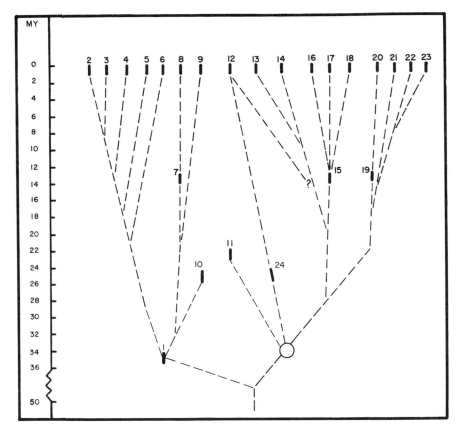

Figure 137. Known stratigraphic ranges (solid lines) and suggested phylogenetic relationships (broken lines) of the Platyrrhini. 1, *Branisella*; 2, *Callithrix*; 3, *Cebuella*; 4, *Leontopithecus*; 5, *Saguinus*; 6, *Callimico*; 7, *Neosaimiri*; 8, *Saimiri*; 9, *Cebus*; 10, *Dolichocebus*; 11, *Homunculus*; 12, *Aotus*; 13, *Xenothrix*; 14, *Callicebus*; 15, *Cebupithecia*; 16, *Cacajao*; 17, *Chiropotes*; 18, *Pithecia*; 19, *Stirtonia*; 20, *Alouatta*; 21, *Lagothrix*; 22, *Brachyteles*; 23, *Ateles*; 24, *Tremacebus*. [By A. Cleary.]

ter must be supplemented if we are to make a case for platyrrhine monophyly. Added to the broad internarium (Hofer, 1976), which may represent a derived character state relative to the condition seen in *Tarsius*, are such undoubtedly primitive anthropoid features as three premolars and a relatively larger and externally more elaborate cerebrum than that seen in tarsiiforms. Another feature which may well be a genuinely platyrrhine character is a unique sutural pattern of the pterion region (Ashley-Montague, 1933). The pattern, a zygomatic contact with the parietal, precluding a frontal–alisphenoid suture, was considered a platyrrhine specialization by Le Gros Clark (1959) and recently argued by Rosenberger (1977). In addition, Rosenberger (1977; cf. Gazin, 1958) notes that this pattern of sutures "may also be indicative of historically independent phases of postorbital closure in platyrrhines and catarrhines" (see, however, the discussion under *Tremacebus*). According to Rosenberger (1977), "A second, perhaps related, characteristic of

the platyrrhine pterion region is the presence of one or more foramina at or near the zygomaticoparietal suture, the zygomaticoparietal foramen (see Anthony, 1946b: 'lateral orbital fissure' of Hershkovitz, 1974a). This foramen is not present in *Tarsius* or strepsirhines and may thus also be a uniquely derived character indicative of the ceboids' monophyletic origin" (p. 463).

There is little doubt that many other characters of both soft and hard anatomy (Figures 138–140) have bearing on platyrrhine monophyly at various levels. The literature (see Hill, 1957, 1960, 1962) abounds in examples of character clines, although few have been critically evaluated for polarity. For instance, as discussed in detail below, the tegulae (collective term referring to the claws and nails of platyrrhines) present two distinct character states, with the clawlike form of all callitrichines (present concept) very likely representing the derived condition (but see Cartmill, 1974a). There are, however, no similar, securely established derived character states which would unite the traditional concept of the Cebidae.

As noted below, the molar morphology of the platyrrhine morphotype is nearly perfectly represented, based on an analysis of the molars in living taxa by Rosenberger (1977), by the Oligocene fossil genus *Branisella*. Ciochon and Corrucini (1975) have strongly argued, based on morphometrics of femora,

that the callitrichine (or at least the callitrichine-like) femora and other osteological elements represent the primitive platyrrhine condition. It appears to us, however, that the size factor of the elements analyzed has influenced the results provided by their analysis.

The close ties between *Alouatta* (and *Stirtonia*) and the other Atelini seem certain (contra the views of Ciochon and Corrucini, 1975), and *Cebus* appears to

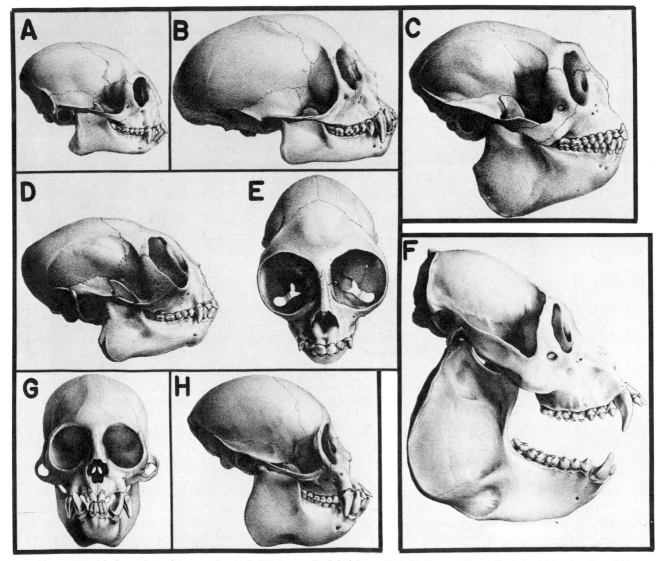

Figure 138. Modern platyrrhine crania. A, *Callithrix* sp.; B, *Saimiri* sp.; C, *Callicebus* sp.; D and E, *Aotus trivirgatus*; G and H, *Cacajao* sp. F, *Alouatta* sp. [From de Blainville (1839).]

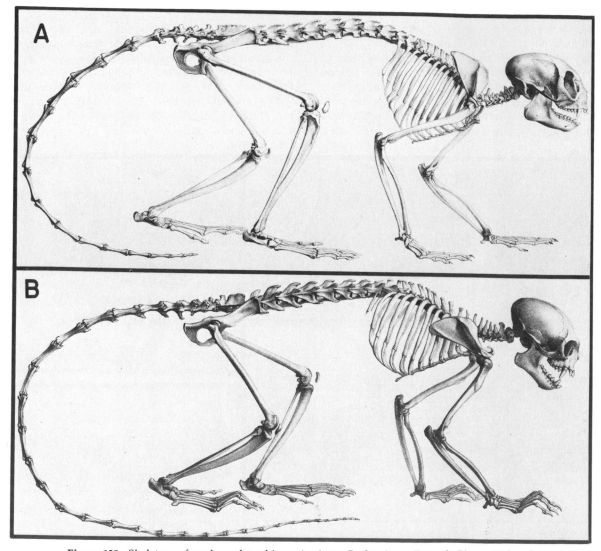

Figure 139. Skeletons of modern platyrrhines. A, *Aotus*; B, *Saguinus*. [From de Blainville (1839).]

be the closest living relative of the squirrel monkeys and *Neosaimiri* [see Rosenberger (1977) and his arguments detailed below]. The group most recently related to *Callicebus* (Rosenberger, in preparation) is perhaps *Cebupithecia* and the remaining pitheciines, the extant genera *Pithecia*, *Cacajao*, and *Chiropotes*. Although *Aotus* and *Saimiri* share a number of features with other platyrrhines, perhaps primitive features, their more recent ties are probably with pitheciines and *Cebus*, respectively. As discussed below, the relationships of *Xenothrix* are enigmatic. *Tremacebus* may

be the nearest known relative of the owl monkey, and *Dolichocebus* was closely related to the ancestry of *Saimiri*.

Although the doubts expressed in Figure 137 are real, a valuable attempt at reconstructing a platyrrhine morphotype morphology has been carried out by Rosenberger (1977). He found that the most likely primitive character states of the molars in the modern platyrrhines are to be found in *Callimico* and *Saimiri*. It follows that the small but distinct hypocones of *Callimico* and *Saimiri* represent the primitive condi-

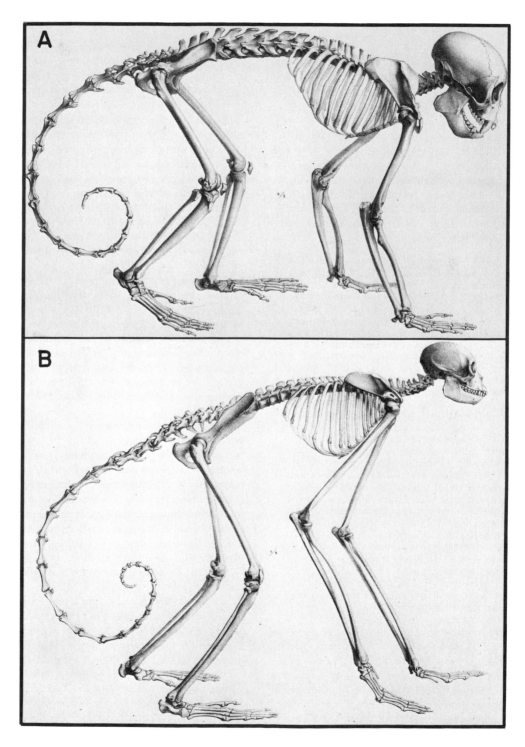

Figure 140. Skeletons of modern platyrrhines. A, *Chiropotes*; B, *Ateles* [From de Blainville (1839).]

tion. The most ancient known probable platyrrhine, *Branisella*, is a positive test corroborating the "small-hypoconed molar" hypothesis for ancestral platyrrhines and probably also for atelids and cebids (present concepts).

Students in the past alternatively considered either atelids and cebines or marmosets and tamarins as the more faithful representatives of the ancestral platyrrhines. Recently Ciochon and Corruccini (1975) reviewed the history of vacillations in platyrrhine phylogenetic research and noted the following (using the nomenclature which recognized a marmoset-non-marmoset dichotomy).

> Differences of opinion over the phylogenetic relationships of the families Callithricidae and Cebidae have persisted through this century. These fall into two basic schools of thought. The first school regards the callithricids as a specialized offshoot of a primitive platyrrhine stock morphologically similar to *Aotus* or *Callicebus*. The family is viewed as dwarfed ceboids which suffered retrogressive modifications in their dentition and locomotor apparatus. This position is most eloquently presented by Gregory (1920) though its foundations can be seen in the works of Weber (1904), Bolk (1916), Pocock (1917, 1920, 1925) and it is most recently discussed by Hill (1957, 1959) and Hoffstetter (1969). The second school regards the callithricids as the most primitive of all Platyrrhini. Here the family is viewed as extant representatives of a side branch of the basal stock which gave rise to the early Tertiary ceboid adaptive radiation. Hershkovitz (1969, 1970a,b, 1972, in press) is the most recent proponent of this school though its foundations lie in writings of Geoffroy-Saint Hilaire (1841) and Forbes (1896). Other more recent authorities who support this position are Elliot (1913), Elliot-Smith (1924), Wood-Jones (1929), Le Gros Clark (1934, 1959), Stirton (1951), and Piveteau (1957). Hershkovitz (1970a, p. 3) summarizes this view when he states that "marmosets... are the smallest and most primitive of living monkeys. They comprise an old, isolated stem which could not have been derived from or have given rise to any known platyrrhine group." (p. 210)

Based on their study of platyrrhine femoral morphometrics Ciochon and Corruccini (1975) support the second school of thought. We maintain, however, as noted in our discussion above, that in a number of characters (the tegulae, the molar pattern, grasping ability of the hallux) it appears certain that the marmosets display primarily derived character states.

Ciochon and Corruccini (1975) generally produced phenetic data supportive of the groupings of living genera proposed by Simpson (1945) and others. As shown elsewhere, however, we are not persuaded by the marmoset-like plot of the femur of *Cebupithecia*. The derived dental features of this taxon undoubtedly tie it to pitheciins.

The traditionally accepted view of platyrrhine relationships, implicit in the commonly used classifications (e.g., Simpson, 1945; Hershkovitz, 1977; Napier, 1976), envisions a major dichotomy between the marmosets and tamarins (ranked as Callitrichidae) and the remaining platyrrhines (ranked as the Cebidae). In the following discussions, the platyrrhines are treated within the framework of a classification which has been derived from a phylogenetic hypothesis proposed and documented by Rosenberger (1977, and in preparation). The previously accepted family divisions within the platyrrhines were not abandoned lightly. Only after careful evaluation of Rosenberger's hypothesis were we compelled to express, with Rosenberger's aid, the new theory of relationships based exclusively on morphological characters. The phylogenetic hypothesis accepted here is incompatible and in direct opposition to two of the most recently generated immunological trees (Baba *et al.*, 1975; Cronin and Sarich, 1975).

The classification followed here satisfies, we believe, a number of requirements which we consider to be of overriding importance. It maintains the taxonomic integrity of a distinct and derived group of platyrrhines, the marmosets. The concept Callitrichinae serves the same communicatory purpose as did the Callitrichidae. Inclusion of the Cebinae and the Callitrichinae in the same family expresses the phyletic unity of these two groups in contrast to the remaining platyrrhines, grouped together under the Atelidae. Within the Atelidae strong cases may be made for two distinctly monophyletic groups, the Atelinae and Pitheciinae. Further monophyletic groupings within the subfamilies are expressed by usage of tribes.

We consider it a special attribute of this classification that neither were new categories created nor was it necessary to coin new names for the new taxonomic concepts. The names used below in the discussions (in which taxonomic concepts are linked with various authors) are the taxonomic concepts of the classifications presented here.

The taxonomy of the extant platyrrhine species has recently been reviewed in detail by P. Napier (1976) and Hershkovitz (1977).

Family Cebidae
Bonaparte, 1831

(= or including: Cebina Bonaparte, 1831, in part. Cebidae Swainson, 1835, in part. Callitrichidae Thomas, 1903. Callimiconidae Thomas, 1903. Saimirinae Miller, 1924. Branisellidae Hershkovitz, 1977. See all other concepts under Callitrichinae.)

DISTRIBUTION
   Early Oligocene (Deseadan) to modern. Central and South America.
INCLUDED TAXA
   Subfamilies Cebinae, Branisellinae, and Callitrichinae.

DISCUSSION

As noted before, we espouse Rosenberger's (in preparation) hypothesis which states that the cebines (present concept) and marmosets are specially related to each other. This hypothesis, which is currently being further developed by Rosenberger, rests on a number of similarities which are believed to be conditions evolved after the split of the platyrrhine common ancestral species into the parent stocks of cebids and atelids. Marmosets (clawed platyrrhines) and cebines share a very gracile zygomatic arch as well as an open glenoid fossa. These features, along with the still less clearly understood similarities of the posterior border of the palate and the masticatory musculature, and a typically reduced or absent M¾, suggest a unique pattern shared by marmosets, squirrel monkeys, and capuchins. In addition to this significant character complex, enlarged canines, canine–premolar honing also appears to be a shared derived character complex of this group. The generally small canines of atelids like *Aotus* and *Callicebus* are perhaps indicative of the platyrrhine ancestral condition.

The affinities of *Dolichocebus* are very difficult to assess due largely to the crushed nature of the skull and the edentulous state of the specimen. Following Rosenberger, however, we tentatively include this genus within the Cebinae. In addition to *Dolichocebus*, *Branisella* is the only other fossil cebid believed to be known. The following living genera and species of cebids are recognized here.

Family Cebidae Bonaparte, 1831
   Subfamily Cebinae Bonaparte, 1831
   (= or including: Crysotrichinae Cabrera, 1900.)
      Saimiri Voigt, 1831

(= or including: *Chrysothrix* Kamp, 1835. *Pithesciurus* Lesson, 1840).
      1. *Saimiri sciureus* (Linnaeus, 1758), type species
      2. *Saimiri oerstedii* (Reinhardt, 1872)
   Cebus Erxleben, 1777
   (= or including: *Pseudocebus* Reichenbach, 1862. *Calyptrocebus* Reichenbach, 1862. *Otocebus* Reichenbach, 1862. *Eucebus* Reichenbach, 1862.)
      1. *Cebus capucinus* (Linnaeus, 1758), type species
      2. *Cebus albifrons* (Humboldt, 1811)
      3. *Cebus nigrivittatus* (Wagner, 1847b)
      4. *Cebus apella* (Linnaeus, 1758)
   Subfamily Callitrichinae Thomas, 1903
   Tribe Callitrichini Thomas, 1903
   Callithrix Erxleben, 1777
   (= or including: *Hapale* Illiger, 1811. *Sylvanus* Rafinesque, 1815. *Arctopithecus* Virey, 1819. *Ouistitis* Burnett, 1826. *Midas*: E. Geoffroy, 1828. *Liocephalus* Wagner, 1840. *Mico* Lesson, 1840. *Micoella* Gray, 1870.)
      1. *Callithrix jacchus* (Linnaeus, 1758), type species
      2. *Callithrix argentata* (Linnaeus, 1766)
      3. *Callithrix humeralifer* (E. Geoffroy, 1812)
   Cebuella Gray, 1866
      1. *Cebuella pygmaea* (Spix, 1823)
   Saguinus Hoffmannsegg, 1807
   (= or including: *Marikina* Lesson, 1840. *Oedipomidas* Reichenbach, 1862. *Tamarin* Gray, 1870. *Hapanella* Gray, 1870. *Seniocebus* Gray, 1870. *Tamarinus* Trouessart, 1899.)
      1. *Saguinus midas* (Linnaeus, 1758) type species
      2. *Saguinus mystax* (Spix, 1823)
      3. *Saguinus labiatus* (E. Geoffroy, 1812)
      4. *Saguinus oedipus* (Linnaeus, 1758)
      5. *Saguinus fuscicollis* (Spix, 1823)
      6. *Saguinus inustus* (Schwarz, 1951)
      7. *Saguinus imperator* (Goeldi, 1907)
      8. *Saguinus bicolor* (Spix, 1823)
      9. *Saguinus nigricollis* (Spix, 1823)
      10. *Saguinus leucopus* (Gunther, 1876)
      11. *Saguinus graellsi* (Jiménez de la Espada, 1870)
   Leontopithecus Lesson, 1840
   (= or including: *Midas* E. Geoffroy, 1812. *Leontocebus* Wagner, 1840. *Marikina*: Reichenbach, 1862. *Leontideus* Cabrera, 1956.)

   1. *Leontopithecus rosalia* (Linnaeus, 1766)
Tribe Callimiconini Thomas, 1913
   Callimico Ribiero, 1911
   1. *Callimico goeldi* (Thomas, 1904)

SUBFAMILY CEBINAE
Bonaparte, 1831

(= or including: Cebina Bonaparte, 1831, in part. Crysotrichinae Cabrera, 1900. Saimirinae Miller, 1924.)

DISTRIBUTION
Late Oligocene (Colhuehuapian) to modern. Central and South America.
INCLUDED TAXA
   Cebus, Saimiri, Neosaimiri, and *Dolichocebus.*

DISCUSSION

Capuchins (*Cebus*) are highly polytypic (subsequently species distinctions are unclear) and omnivorous, and live in variably sized polygamous troops of 20 to 30. As noted elsewhere, they are characterized by a quasi-prehensile, but completely hairy, tail. *Saimiri,* the gregarious small squirrel monkeys, are perhaps more marmoset-like than any other noncallitrchine. *Saimiri* spp. inhabit dense forests bordering riverbeds and subsist on a diet of flowers, fruit, nuts, and insects.

Elliot (1913) and others, because of the near prehensility of the tail in *Cebus,* grouped this genus with the fully prehensile-tailed atelines. The tails of capuchins, however, lack the distinct terminal hairless undersurface and the associated nerve supply characterizing the Atelinae (present sense). Capuchins have been also grouped as part of the climber group by Erikson (1963), and not as part of the brachiator group, which consists of the atelin atelids and is characterized by conspicuously divergent limb proportions.

The suggestion has been made by Hill (1960) and more recently by Rosenberger (1977) that, as detailed in Hill (1960, 1962), special relationships may exist between *Saimiri* and *Cebus.* This siter group relationship is based upon some specialization of the visual cortex (Le Gros Clark, 1959), relative narrowness of the interorbital distance, and very distinct, relative enlargement of the upper premolars. Rosenberger further postulated that the maxillary molar morphology of *Cebus* is derived from a *Saimiri*-like stage. If we are to accept these features as homologously shared and derived, then we would be forced to postulate the acquisition of a nearly prehensile tail in *Cebus* as convergent or at least parallel with the Ateline. We believe that Rosenberger's development of this hypothesis is a sound one, and that the semiprehensility of *Cebus* is distinct and independent from the ateline atelids.

As noted under the discussion of *Neosaimiri,* the similarities of the fossil genus to *Saimiri* are so compelling that no serious doubt exists about their close, probably ancestor–descendant relationship.

An interesting addition to the *Saimiri* group is the recently described *Saimiri bernensis* Rimoli, 1977, from subfossil deposits of Hispaniola. This relative of living squirrel monkeys, known only from a maxilla fragment with P⁴–M², probably represents a distinct genus from *Saimiri.* This fossil, along with *Xenothrix,* confirms the previous existence of a Central American–Caribbean diversity of platyrrhines.

SAIMIRI Voigt, 1831

(= or including: *Chrysothrix* Kamp, 1835. *Pithesciurus* Lesson, 1840.)

DISTRIBUTION
Modern (living and subfossil). South America and Hispaniola.
KNOWN SPECIES
   1. *Saimiri sciureus* (Linnaeus, 1758), type species
   2. *Saimiri oerstedii* (Reinhardt, 1872)
   3. *Saimiri? bernensis* Rimoli, 1977
LOCALITIES: Berna⋆ (1302).

DISCUSSION

One of the more interesting recent discoveries of a platyrrhine fossil primate is that of a maxillary fragment with P⁴–M² from the Dominican Republic. Rimoli (1977) described the specimen as a species of *Saimiri,* and there is no doubt that it is distinct from all known samples of squirrel monkeys. It may in fact turn out to represent a species generically distinct from *Saimiri.* Rimoli published a radiometric date of

3850 ± 135 years with the specimen, which makes that sample the oldest of Antillean primates.

Saimiri? bernensis is larger than extant *Saimiri* and it also differs in tooth proportions and occlusal morphology. A. Rosenberger (personal communication)

believes that the tibia published by Miller (1929) from Semana Bay (160 km northwest of Cueva Berna) is in the same size range as the fossil named by Rimoli (1977).

NEOSAIMIRI Stirton, 1951

DISTRIBUTION
  Middle Miocene (Friasian). Colombia.
KNOWN SPECIES
  Neosaimiri fieldsi Stirton, 1951, type species
LOCALITIES: La Venta★ (464).

DISCUSSION

This genus is undoubtedly a close relative, the postulated ancestor, of the living squirrel monkeys. The talonids of *Neosaimiri* (Figure 141) are slightly more

elongated than those of *Saimiri,* retaining the primitive cebid condition. In spite of the differences emphasized in the literature (Stirton, 1951) the mandibular construction of *Neosaimiri* is similar in all its important aspects to that of *Saimiri* (Hershkovitz, 1970a).

The significantly close derived similarity and near identical size of *Saimiri* and *Neosaimiri* suggest a habitus for the fossil species very much like that of its closest living relatives, which are frugivorous and insectivorous.

DOLICHOCEBUS Kraglievich, 1951

DISTRIBUTION
  Late Oligocene (Colhuehuapian). Argentina.
KNOWN SPECIES
  Dolichocebus gaimanensis Kraglievich, 1951
LOCALITIES: Gaiman★ (380).

DISCUSSION

We recognize *Dolichocebus,* designated by Kraglievich (1951) as distinct from *Homunculus,* on the authority of A. Rosenberger (in press). The only known specimen is a skull that is badly crushed, but apparently very dolichocephalic (Figure 142). This is difficult to appreciate because the skull is crushed laterally, which would at first account for its long and attenuated shape. The orbits were unlike those of *Tremacebus* or *Aotus;* i.e., they were not enlarged. According to Hershkovitz (1974), the orbitotemporal partition was almost nearly complete, "nasal bones narrow as in *Saimiri,* muzzle narrower than in *Tremacebus,* frontal contour convex, angle formed at intersection of posterior occipital plane and Frankfort plane about 60°, foramen magnum directed more nearly backward than downward; root to root, inclusive, of zygomatic arch actually and relatively shorter than in smaller *Tremacebus;* palatal arch low with compara-

tively slight curvature; dental arcade markedly convergent anteriorly and distinctly V-shaped; incomplete posterior border extending beyond plane of M^2, molars unusually wide, as in *Homunculus;* M^3 absent, but large size of M^2 and alveolar-like texture of truncated mineralized bone behind indicate normal occurrence of third molar in living *Dolichocebus*" (pp. 9–10).

Rosenberger's (in press) discovery of an interorbital fenestra in *Dolichocebus* places this genus as the sister-taxon of *Saimiri,* the only living platyrrhine to present this feature (consistently in adults). This further implies great antiquity not only for the *Saimiri* lineage, but also for the Cebinae and Callitrichinae. Moreover, it refutes Hershkovitz's (1974) union of *Homunculus* and *Dolichocebus* in a family of their own, the Homunculidae. Rosenberger and Szalay (in preparation) are currently describing and analyzing the significance of the ear region of *Dolichocebus* and the evidence of its affinities to cebines.

Dolichocebus was in the pitheciine size range, and its unenlarged orbits suggest it was most likely diurnal. Because the skull lacks teeth, any hypothesis as to the dietary regime of the species is likely to remain untestable.

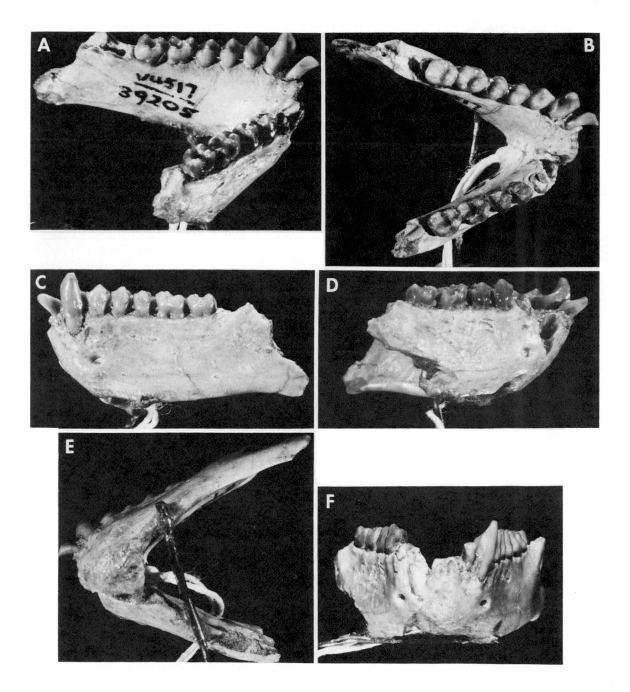

Figure 141. *Neosaimiri fieldsi*. Middle Miocene, northwestern South America. Mandible with right $P_{\overline{3}}$–$M_{\overline{2}}$ and left $I_{\overline{2}}$, C, $P_{\overline{2}}$–$M_{\overline{2}}$: A, occlusolingual (for left side) and occlusobuccal (for right side) views; B, occlusal view; C, lateral view of left side; D, lateral view of right side; E, ventral view; F, anterior view. [From Hershkovitz (1970a), courtesy of P. Hershkovitz.]

284

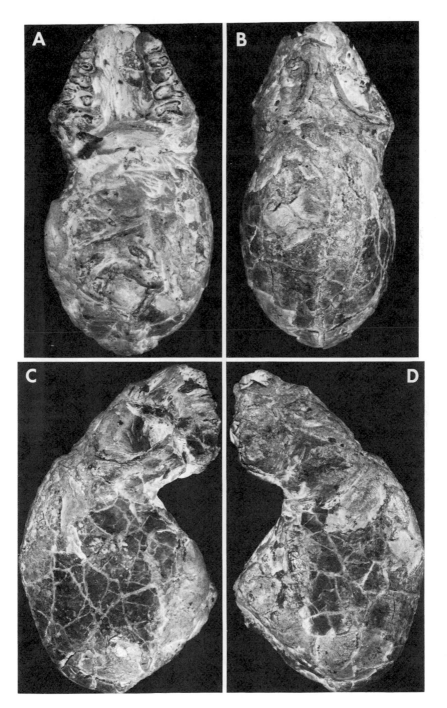

Figure 142. *Dolichocebus gaimanensis.* Late Oligocene, southern South America. Crushed skull: A, ventral view; B, dorsal view; C, right lateral view; D, left lateral view. [From Hershkovitz (1970a), courtesy of P. Hershkovitz.]

SUBFAMILY BRANISELLINAE
Hershkovitz, 1977

(= or including: Branisellidae Hershkovitz, 1977.)

DISTRIBUTION
Early Oligocene (Deseadan). Bolivia.

DISCUSSION

See discussion under the genus.

INCLUDED TAXA
Branisella.

BRANISELLA Hoffstetter, 1969

DISTRIBUTION
Early Oligocene (Deseadan). Bolivia.
KNOWN SPECIES
Branisella boliviana Hoffstetter, 1969, type species
LOCALITIES: La Salla-Luribay⋆ (372).

DISCUSSION

The most ancient of South American primates, from the La Salla-Luribay Tertiary basin of Bolivia, is significant inasmuch as it is the oldest of the platyrrhines as well as quite primitive in its known dental characters (Figure 143). The only described specimen (Hoffstetter, 1969) suggests a dental formula of $I\frac{1 \cdot 2}{1 \cdot 2}$; $C\frac{1}{1}$; $P\frac{2 \cdot 3 \cdot 4}{2 \cdot 3 \cdot 4}$; $M\frac{1 \cdot 2 \cdot 3}{1 \cdot 2 \cdot 3}$. *Branisella* differs from known omomyids in the combination of lacking a buccal cingulum and a paraconule, at least on M^2. The P^2 was a single-rooted, small tooth, as may be inferred from the preserved root. Whether the tooth was caniniform or premolariform is difficult to judge. The root, however, shows a distinctly greater transverse, buccolingual (rather than mesiodistal) dimension. Later platyrrhines are usually characterized by the presence of a protocone on P^2, and, in general, a morphology not unlike that of P^3. That this was the condition in the last common ancestor of all living platyrrhines is indicated by the presence of this type of P^2 in both families. In omomyids we find a whole range of conditions. In *Tetonius*, *Omomys*, or *Ourayia*, for example, the P^2 is single-rooted, mesiodistally elongated, lacks a protocone, and could be described as caniniform. On the other hand, in *Washakius*, and probably in other taxa as well, the single root was much more transverse than long, and the crown probably had a protocone on the lingual cingulum. In *Branisella*, P^3, like P^2, is only known by its robust, transversely very wide root, but there is no doubt that its crown morphology was like that of P^4. This latter tooth carries a tall paracone and a somewhat lower protocone; a broad cingulum surrounds the tooth lingually.

The molars are quite transverse (a primitive condition) and carry a hypocone originating from the cingulum (as in *Washakius*, but not *Tetonius*, for example). The protocone is a robust cusp, and in general the molar dentition suggests a premium on crushing rather than slicing. As noted, the paraconule is absent from M^2 (M^1 is too worn to tell). The metaconule is pronounced on M^1 but rather faint on M^2. M^3, judged by the alveoli, was smaller than M^2.

An undescribed specimen (Figure 143) from the Princeton University Deseadan collections warrants mention here as it is probably the second known specimen of this important primate. PU6510 is a left lower jaw fragment with $M_{\overline{2}}$ intact, although badly worn, and the clearly discernible alveoli for $P_{\overline{3}}$, $P_{\overline{4}}$, $M_{\overline{1}}$, and $M_{\overline{3}}$. The wear on $M_{\overline{2}}$ appears to be of the same exact type displayed on the type specimen. $M_{\overline{3}}$, judged from the shape of the roots, was short, constricted on the talonid, and probably quite similar in outline (but not necessarily in details of the crown) to such other anthropoids as "*Aeolopithecus*" and *Parapithecus*. The mandible fragment shows a pronounced curvature at the level of $P_{\overline{2}}$, suggesting a distinctly U-shaped mandibular symphysis.

As Hoffstetter (1969) stated, *Branisella* is a short-faced primate. Its affinities, suggested primarily by the condition of the P^2 root, the base of the zygoma, and the geography, are probably with the platyrrhines, and for that matter with the very base of the radiation. Close overall dental similarity to *Saimiri*, and *Cebus* suggests to us that *Branisella's* closest ties are with the Cebidae. Had this taxon been found in the Eocene of North America, however, many competent workers probably would not hesitate in referring it to the Omomyidae.

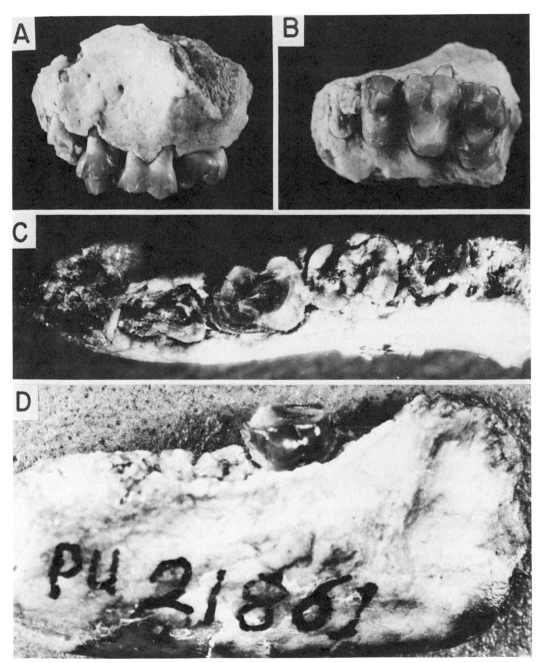

Figure 143. *Branisella boliviana.* Early Oligocene, western South America. Left maxilla with P^3–M^2: A, lateral view; B, occlusal view. Left mandible fragment with M_T: C, occlusal view; D, lateral view. [A and B courtesy of R. Hoffstetter.]

SUBFAMILY CALLITRICHINAE
Thomas, 1903

(= or including: Arctopitheci E. Geoffroy, 1812. Callitricidae Gray, 1821. Gampstonychae Gray, 1821. Harpaladae Gray, 1821. Hapalidae Gray, 1821. Platyonychae Gray, 1821. Trichuri Spix, 1823. Callitricina Gray, 1825. Harpalina Gray, 1825. Sariguidae Gray, 1825. Ouistidae Burnett, 1828. Ouistitidae Burnett, 1828. Titidae Burnett, 1828. Hapalina Bonaparte, 1838. Hapalidae Wagner, 1840. Hapalineae Lesson, 1840. Arctopithecina Gravenhorst, 1843. Jacchina Gray, 1849. Arctopithecae Dahlbom, 1856. Mididae Gill, 1872. Arctopithecini Huxley, 1872. Hapalini Winge, 1895. Callitrichidae Thomas, 1903. Leontocebinae Hill, 1959.)

DISTRIBUTION
   Modern. South America.
INCLUDED TAXA
   Tribes Callitrichini and Callimiconini.

DISCUSSION

The marmosets are among the smallest of living primates. We recognize five genera, *Callithrix*, *Cebuella*, *Saguinus*, *Leontopithecus*, and *Callimico*. They span the size range exhibited by tree squirrels, to which they are not dissimilar in some aspects of their ecology. Unlike their close relatives the cebines, the marmosets lead a squirrel-like life, running up and down tree trunks, supporting their weight on the tips of long and sharp clawlike tegulae. Their claws are in sharp contrast to the long bilaterally compressed nails found in cebines and other platyrrhines.

Marmosets tend to be insectivorous and gumivorous. The dietary specialization, such as that of *Cebuella*, a sap feeder (Kinzey *et al.*, 1975), and *Leontopithecus*, a grub feeder in the fashion of the aye-aye or the phalanger *Dactylopsila*, points to marmoset origins from a niche where claw climbing was selected for rather than the grasp leaping or the grasp climbing type of ancestral locomotion. The transformation of nails into long, recurved clawlike tegulae on all but the hallucial terminal phalanges is supported by various arguments (see Szalay, 1975g; Rosenberger, 1977). It has been shown by both Le Gros Clark (1936) and Thorndike (1968) that both the nails and claws of platyrrhines, referred to collectively as tegulae, have the same epidermal backing, with reduced terminal matrix and deep stratum. In fact both Weber (1928) and Le Gros Clark (1936) used this criterion to distinguish them from other claws such as the falculae of tupaiids and from catarrhine nails, ungulae, in which these components are lost. Cartmill's (1974a)

recent argument, therefore, that the callitrichine claw is the primitive platyrrhine condition is, in our view, untenable, the histology alone being insufficient to decide polarity in the morphocline of platyrrhine tegulae. Pocock (1917) astutely argued that the reduced hallux and the narrow hands and feet suggest marmoset tegulae to be derived. Among the relevant facts perhaps the reduced but still grasping big toe with a nail is one of the most important sources of information which can be parsimoniously explained only if we consider the marmoset extremities derived. The joint morphology between metatarsal I and the entocuneiform leaves little doubt that, in spite of the drastically decreased range of mobility, the joint was derived from a condition with a much greater range of mobility, as for example, the ones displayed by *Saimiri* or *Aotus*.

An additional important argument was put forward by Rosenberger (1977), who noted the following.

(1) According to Le Gros Clark, in considering the functional significance of falcula histology, "The deep stratum is the mechanically important part . . . on it depends the maintenance of a sharp and strong point" (1959: 173). If the last common ceboid or haplorhine ancestor depended on sharp recurved falculae for efficient postural and locomotor functions, it then would be difficult to explain why selection favored the reduction of (a) the mechanically advantageous deep stratum and (b) important anatomical features of the primitive but well developed flexor and extensor mechanism (Le Gros Clark, 1936). (2) Evolution of relatively flattened nails is possibly related to the elaboration and increased tactile efficiency of apical pads (Le Gros Clark, 1936; Preuschoft, 1970). Significantly, apical pads are well developed in *Callithrix*, *Saguinus*, *Leontopithecus* (Le Gros Clark, 1936; Thorndike, 1968) and probably other callitrichids. They lie ventral to the body of the terminal phalanx rather than beneath the distal interphalangeal joint as in tupaiids. The association of long, recurved tegulae and well developed terminal pads is somewhat difficult to reconcile, for the pads' position distal to the interphalangeal fulcrum suggests it does not play an important sensory role during claw-clinging. In fact, in *Saguinus* it often does not contact the substrate while the tegulae are embedded (Sonek, 1969). Moreover, assuming clawlike tegulae to have been present before the origination of living callitrichids creates additional difficulties in explaining selection for elaborate pads since they are decidedly inferior to claws in the arboreal locomotion of small primates. (p. 464)

Callitrichines, then, may be viewed as representing a radiation taking its origin in an ancestral species which evolved clawlike tegulae from the nail-like ones found in other platyrrhines, possibly in order to pursue a gum-resin and/or insect diet on broad branches and tree trunks. Claw climbing on tree trunks and large branches where sap and, consequently, insects abound would be far more efficient than continuing the grasping climb of the ancestors. As Gregory (1951) noted of marmosets, "it is difficult to conceive that their clawed feet are not in specialized association with the great reduction in body size and with the assumption of clinging habits" (pp. 469–470).

An important case has been made by Rosenberger (1977) for special relationships between *Cebuella* and *Callithrix*. He argues as follows.

> Derived characteristics of the anterior dentition and mandibular morphology suggest that marmosets, *Cebuella* and *Callithrix*, are descendants of a common ancestor not shared with other living ceboids. The ceboid mandibular dental arcade morphocline, described and discussed by Hershkovitz (1970) and Kinzey (1974), depicts an array having three poles: posteriorly divergent and narrowed anteriorly (V-shaped), divergent but rounded anteriorly (U-shaped), and parallel sided (U-shaped). By analogy with living strepsirhines and Tertiary primates, these authors assert that the V-shaped jaw is the ancestral ceboid condition. Distribution of arcade shape within platyrrhines and examination of functionally interrelated aspects of the anterior teeth and mandible strongly indicate the contrary, that the V-shaped jaw is derived. This condition, seen only in *Cebuella* and *Callithrix*, is presumably related to the *en echelon* spacing of the incisor and canine teeth (see Hershkovitz, 1970); the medial incisors are set anterior to the lateral

and the lateral anterior to the canine. The incisors themselves, however, differ radically from those of other anthropoids, and the probable ancestral anthropoid condition, in lacking spatulate, blade-like crowns and in being greatly enlarged buccolingually. In part, this may explain the transversely narrow symphyseal region. The buccolingual diameter of the canine is also markedly greater than the mesiodistal (Table 1) and differs from the typically ovoid-roundish cross-section seen in other anthropoids. Further, *Cebuella* and *Callithrix* have long been characterized as the "short tusked" callithricids, as the difference in cervical–apical heights of canine *versus* incisors is not marked. Contrary to the implications of the colloquialism, the "short tusked" condition will probably prove to be a function of a novel relative increase in incisor crown height, not a decrease in canine size.

> I suggest that these characters of the anterior teeth and jaws of marmosets, and probably others in the masticatory appartus still to be elaborated, are critical parts of a derived adaptive complex which is related to gouging and scraping holes in bark in pursuit of exudates. The small body size of *Cebuella,* and the vertical positional behaviors seen in both marmoset genera (Moynihan, 1975; Kinzey, Rosenberger and Ramirez, 1975; Coimbra-Filho and Mittermeier, in press) are related adaptations and strongly indicates that relatively *tiny* body size is not the ancestral condition among callithricids or ceboids. (pp. 465–466)

Rosenberger's (1978) more recent demonstration of a rodent-like loss of lingual enamel and greatly thickened buccal enamel on lower incisors of *Callithrix* and *Cebuella* reinforces the interpretations of the marmoset (as opposed to tamarin) dentition as derived and perhaps originally especially adapted to gumivory (exudativory).

Family Atelidae
Gray, 1825

(= or including Atelina Gray, 1825. Lagotrichina Gray, 1870. Lagothrichinae Cabrera, 1900.)

DISTRIBUTION

Late Oligocene (Colhuehuapian) to modern. Central and South America.

INCLUDED TAXA

Subfamilies Atelinae, Pitheciinae, and Aotinae.

DISCUSSION

The Atelidae is the more varied (see Figure 137) of the two platyrrhine families. The dental formula of all atelids (except *Xenothrix*) as well as of the cebine cebids is $I\frac{1\cdot2}{1\cdot2}$; $C\frac{1}{1}$; $P\frac{2\cdot3\cdot4}{2\cdot3\cdot4}$; $M\frac{1\cdot2\cdot3}{1\cdot2\cdot3}$. In contrast to callitrichines, as discussed above, the tegulae of cebines and atelids are nail-like though compressed. The hallux is capable of a firm grasp, but the pollex is not opposable. Unlike the much decorated, tufted ears of the marmosets, cebine and atelid pinnae are usually naked (but see *Saimiri*). As a rule, a single young is born in these animals and carried on the back of the mother.

Following Rosenberger (personal communication) the features listed below may have characterized the atelid common ancestor: posteriorly deepened mandibular corpus; moderate to large hypocones; probably reduced paracone; nonreduced $M_{\overline{3}}^{3}$; robust zygomatic arch and pterygoid complex; and relatively deep glenoid fossa. Of these, the first two are definitely derived within the platyrrhines.

The following living genera and species of atelids are recognized here.

Family Atelidae Gray, 1825
  Subfamily Atelinae Gray, 1825
    Tribe Atelini Gray, 1825
      Ateles E. Geoffroy, 1806
        (= or including: *Sapajou* Lacépède, 1799. *Paniscus* Rafinesque, 1815. *Montaneia* Ameghino, 1911. *Ameranthropoides* Montandon, 1929.)
        1. *Ateles paniscus* (Linnaeus, 1758), type species
        2. *Ateles belzebuth* E. Geoffroy, 1806
        3. *Ateles geoffroyi* (Kuhl, 1820)
        4. *Ateles fusciceps* (Gray, 1866)
      Lagothrix E. Geoffroy, 1812
        (= or including: *Gastrimargus* Spix, 1823. *Oreonax* Thomas, 1927.)
        1. *Lagothrix lagotricha* (Humboldt, 1812), type species
        2. *Lagothrix flavicauda* (Humboldt, 1812)
      Brachyteles Spix, 1823
        (= or including: *Eriodes* I. Geoffroy, 1829.)
        1. *Brachytles arachnoides* (E. Geoffroy, 1806), type species
    Tribe Alouattini Elliot, 1904
      Alouatta Lacépède, 1799
        (= or including: *Mycetes* Illiger, 1811. *Stentor* E. Geoffroy, in Humboldt, 1811.)
        1. *Alouatta belzebul* (Linnaeus, 1766), type species
        2. *Alouatta seniculus* (Linnaeus, 1766)
        3. *Alouatta caraya* (Humboldt, 1811)
        4. *Alouatta fusca* (E. Geoffroy, 1812)
        5. *Alouatta villosa* (Gray, 1845)
        6. *Alouatta palliata* (Gray, 1849)
  Subfamily Pitheciinae Mivart, 1865
    Tribe Pitheciini Mivart, 1865
      Subtribe Callicebina Pocock, 1925
      Callicebus Thomas, 1903
        1. *Callicebus personatus* (E. Geoffroy, 1812), type species
        2. *Callicebus moloch* (Hoffmannsegg, 1807)
        3. *Callicebus torquatus* (Hoffmannsegg, 1807)

      Subtribe Pitheciina Mivart, 1865
      Pithecia Desmarest, 1820
        (= or including: *Yarkea* Lesson, 1840.)
        1. *Pithecia pithecia* (Linnaeus, 1766), type species
        2. *Pithecia monachus* (E. Geoffroy, 1812)
      Chiropotes Lesson, 1840
        1. *Chiropotes satanas* (Hoffmannsegg, 1807), type species
        2. *Chiropotes albinasus* (I. Geoffroy and Deville, 1848)
      Cacajao Lesson, 1840
        (= or including: *Brachyurus* Spix, 1823, in part.)
        1. *Cacajao melanocephalus* (Humboldt, 1811), type species
        2. *Cacajao calvus* (I. Geoffroy, 1847)
        3. *Cacajao rubicundus* (I. Geoffroy and Deville, 1848)
    Tribe Homunculini Ameghino, 1891
      Aotus Illiger, 1811
        (= or including: *Nocthora* E. Cuvier, 1812, in part. *Nyctipithecus* Spix, 1823. *Glisebus*: Lesson, in part, 1840.)
        1. *Aotus trivirgatus* (Humboldt, 1811). type species

SUBFAMILY ATELINAE
Gray, 1825

(= or including: Atelina Gray, 1825. Mycetinae Gray, 1825. Alouattinae Trouessart, 1897. Atelinae: Miller, 1924. Stirtoniinae Hershkovitz, 1970a.)

DISTRIBUTION
  Middle Miocene (Friasian) to modern. Central and South America.
INCLUDED TAXA
  Tribes Alouattini and Atelini.

Discussion

Supporting the similarities of dental morphology between *Alouatta* and *Brachyteles,* and the presence of equally prehensile tails in *Alouatta* and Atelini, are the studies of biochemical affinities between these taxa by Cronin and Sarich (1975). Also, the close similarity in femoral morphometrics between *Alouatta* and *Lagothrix* is emphasized by Ciochon and Corruccini (1975).

The most significant evidence of monophyly appears to be the prehensile tail with its glabrous distal underside covering one-third of its length (Biegert, 1963) and its pronounced innervation through the enlarged aperture of the sacral canal (Ankel, 1972).

The naked tactile pad of the tail is supplied with papillary ridges similar to those found on fingertips. Rosenberger (1977) suggests that the proportions of the limbs and vertebral column, shown by Erikson (1963) to be characteristic of this group, are probably a shared derived constellation of characters.

Tribe Alouattini
Trouessart, 1897

(= or including: Alouattinae Trouessart, 1897, in part. Stirtoniinae Hershkovitz, 1970a, in part.)

DISTRIBUTION
  Middle Miocene (Friasian) to modern. Central and South America.
INCLUDED TAXA
  Alouatta and *Stirtonia*.

DISCUSSION

  The living howler monkeys are among the largest platyrrhines. Males of some species have evolved a greatly inflated hyoid bone containing an air sac derived from the larynx (Hill, 1962). The mandible is greatly expanded for masticatory reasons and the braincase had not rolled up as one would expect in an anthropoid primate (Biegert, 1963). For a long time, this lack of kyphosis was interpreted as primitive cranial morphology in contrast to the other platyrrhines. It seems more likely that the fore and aft braincase alignment is an effect of the adaptation to increased development of the masseter complex in an extremely folivorous group. Howlers are vegetarians, with special gut adaptations such as an enlarged stomach and large intestines to cope with a primarily leafy diet.

STIRTONIA Hershkovitz, 1970a

(= or including: *Homunculus:* Stirton, 1951, in part.)

DISTRIBUTION
  Middle Miocene (Friasian). Colombia.
KNOWN SPECIES
  Stirtonia tatacoensis (Stirton, 1951)
  (=*Homunculus tatacoensis* Stirton, 1951)
LOCALITIES: La Venta★ (464).

DISCUSSION

  This genus is larger than the Patagonian *Homunculus*. Its most firmly established dental difference from *Homunculus* is in the arrangement of its incisors. Although only the alveoli are known in *Stirtonia* it can be assessed that, while in *Homunculus* the incisors curve considerably mesially, in *Stirtonia* (Figure 144) they are squeezed directly between the erectly implanted canines. On the lower molars the trigonids are elevated and the talonids are distinctly wider than the trigonids. The second molar is longer than the first, and the third molar, judged by the alveoli, was apparently smaller than the preceding molars.

  This large fossil platyrrhine, within the size range of *Alouatta* spp., does not possess a single well-defined character that can clearly differentiate it on the tribal level from living species of *Alouatta*. In fact,

Hershkovitz in his description of the genus *Stirtonia* could cite no adequate qualitative features which would significantly set apart the Miocene form from its undoubted living relatives, the howlers. Pending complete review of the evidence by Rosenberger, we tentatively maintain its original ranking. To call the mandible of either the Miocene *Stirtonia* or the modern *Alouatta* V-shaped is deceptive, as the symphyseal front is quite rounded and the tooth rows are only slightly divergent. Granting subfamily distinction to this undoubted alouattin would not only continue to upset the taxonomic balance of platyrrhine genera, recently worsened by an inflation of family–group taxa (Hershkovitz, 1974, 1977), but would also obscure the clear phylogenetic, as well as patristic, ties of this Miocene primate to its probable descendants, the living howlers.

Tribe Atelini
Gray, 1825

(= or including: Atelina Gray, 1825. Atelinae Miller, 1924.)

DISTRIBUTION
  Modern. Central and South America.
INCLUDED TAXA
  Ateles, *Brachyteles*, and *Lagothrix*.

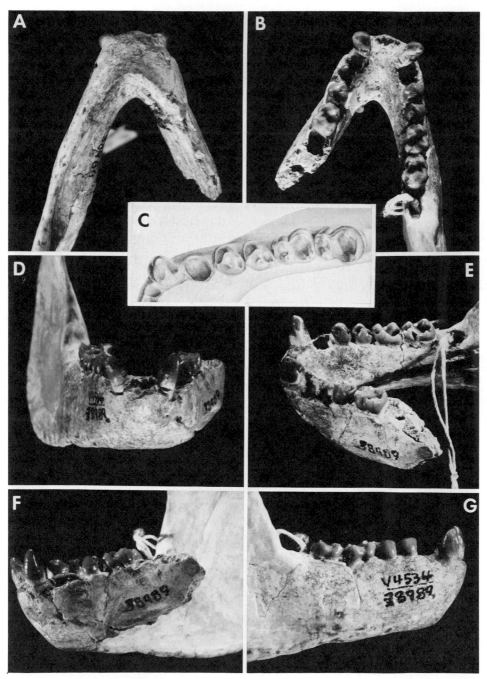

Figure 144. *Stirtonia tatacoensis.* Middle Miocene, northwestern South America. Juvenile mandible with C and $P_{\overline{3}}$–$M_{\overline{2}}$: A, inferior view; B, C, and E, occlusal views; D, anterior view; F and G, right and left lateral views. [A, B, and D through G from Hershkovitz (1970a), courtesy of P. Hershkovitz; (from Stirton (1951).]

DISCUSSION

The spider monkeys, wooly spiders, and wooly monkeys, like *Alouatta*, possess a highly prehensile tail, which is used in suspensory postures and locomotion as well as a tactile, investigating organ (see especially Erikson, 1963). They lack the cranial specialization of *Alouatta*, but *Ateles* and *Brachyteles* have developed highly derived hands either lacking a pollex or retaining it merely as a vestige. The hooklike hands are used in a special kind of brachiation aided by the tail. The Atelini are largely frugivorous, although the poorly known wooly spider, *Brachyteles arachnoides*, has not been sufficiently studied.

A. Rosenberger (personal communication) believes that *Brachyteles* and *Ateles* represent a monophyletic group characterized by a $2n$ chromosome number of 34, unique among platyrrhines, and by a reduced or absent pollex. This theory of relationships is depicted in Figure 137.

The fossil *Montaneia anthropomorpha* described by Ameghino (1911) from Cuba is a fragmentary specimen referable to *Ateles* cf. *A. fusca* (Miller, 1916; Williams and Koopman, 1952).

Subfamily Pitheciinae
Mivart, 1865

DISTRIBUTION
   Middle Miocene (Friasian) to modern. South America.
INCLUDED TAXA
   Tribes Pitheciini, Xenothrichini, and Homunculini.

DISCUSSION

A special relationship, based on convincingly argued shared and derived characters found in *Callicebus* and pitheciins, has recently been hypothesized by A. Rosenberger (personal communication). These features include the rather unique attenuated and narrow incisors long known in pitheciins but also found in *Callicebus*. Pitheciins, except for *Callicebus*, also have uniquely enlarged canines. This is an important combination of characters and we doubt that it has evolved twice independently.

Based on the shared, and very likely derived, mandibular morphology of *Xenothrix* with *Callicebus*, we classify the unique Jamaican primate within the Pitheciinae.

Tribe Pitheciini
Mivart, 1865

(= or including: Pitheciidae: Ludwig, 1883. Callicebinae Pocock, 1925.)

DISTRIBUTION
   Middle Miocene (Friasian) to modern. South America.
INCLUDED TAXA
   Subtribes Callicebina and Pitheciina.

DISCUSSION

The sakiwinkis or sakis (*Pithecia*), bearded sakis (*Chiropotes*), and ouakaris (*Cacajao*) are frugivorous and omnivorous, and *Pithecia* are known to eat small animals. All three pitheciinans are characterized by exceptionally broad external noses and, along with *Cebupithecia*, form a monophyletic group which may be recognized as the subtribe Pitheciina, along with the subtribe Callicebina.

The grouping of the pitheciins has support from many different lines of evidence going back to Mivart (1865). Dental and cranial morphology, as well as their myology (Bodini, 1972), and the transferrin/albumin studies of Cronin and Sarich (1975) point to a monophyly of the group. The dental morphology of the Miocene *Cebupithecia* is unequivocal in tying the genus to the living pitheciins, apart from *Callicebus*.

The pitheciinan dentition characteristically entails the following features: narrow, procumbent upper and lower incisors; robust, long canines with a round base; and cheek teeth with enlarged hypocones and greatly reduced relief. Rosenberger (1977) suggested that this pattern may have been derived from an ancestral condition near to *Aotus* or *Callicebus*, but recently he (personal communication) has specified a common ancestor for *Callicebus* and the "Pitheciinae" of most authors.

CEBUPITHECIA Stirton and Savage, 1951

DISTRIBUTION
   Middle Miocene (Friasian). Colombia.

KNOWN SPECIES
   Cebupithecia sarmientoi Stirton and Savage, 1951, type species
   LOCALITIES: La Venta⋆ (464).

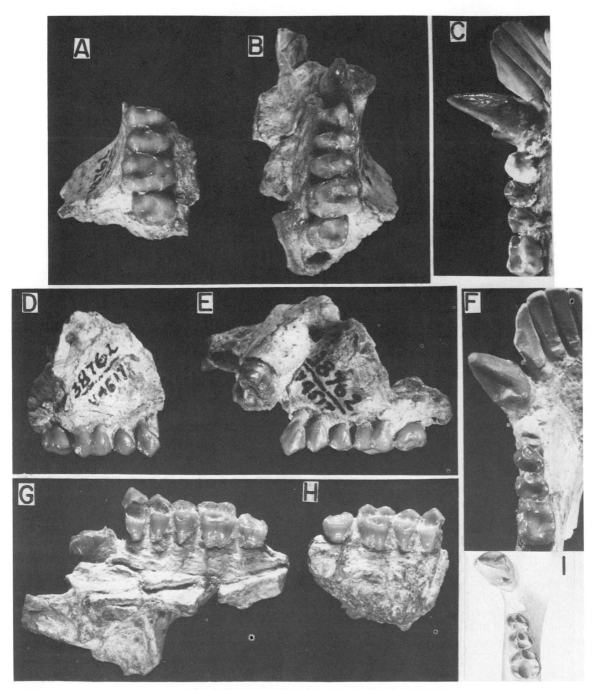

Figure 145. *Cebupithecia sarmientoi.* Middle Miocene, northwestern South America. Right P³–M²: A, occlusal view; D, buccal view; H, lingual view. Left canine root, P²–M²: B, occlusal view; E, buccal view; G, lingual view. Left restored I$_{\overline{1}}$–I$_{\overline{2}}$, C, restored P$_{\overline{2}}$, P$_{\overline{3}}$–M$_{\overline{1}}$: C, occlusolingual view; I and F, occlusal views. [From Hershkovitz (1970a), courtesy of P. Hershkovitz.]

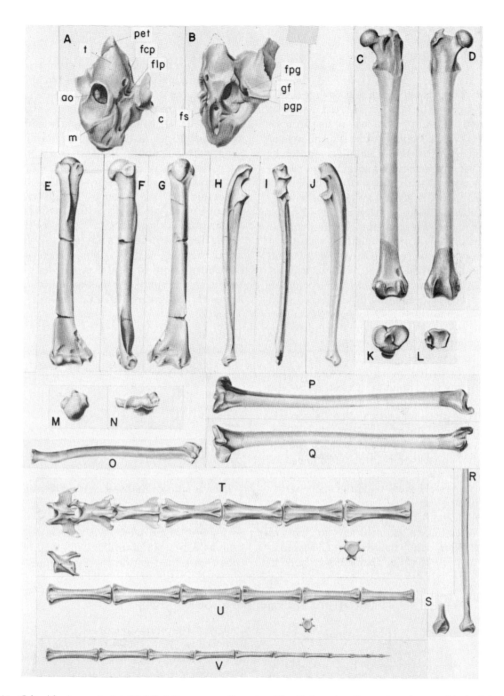

Figure 146. *Cebupithecia sarmientoi*. Middle Miocene, northwestern South America. Ear regions (petrosals): A, right side; B, left side. Right femur: C, posterior view; D, anterior view. Right humerus: E, anterior view; F, lateral view; G, posterior view; M, proximal view; N, distal view. Left ulna: H, medial view; I, anterior view; J, lateral view. Left radius: O, medial view. Left tibia: K, proximal view; L, distal view; P, anterior view; Q, posterior view. Left fibula, proximal segment: R, medial view. Right fibula, distal segment: S, medial view. Caudal vertebrae: T, U, and V. [From Stirton (1951).]

DISCUSSION

The original diagnosis by Stirton and Savage (1951) states that the incisors are large and procumbent and the tip of the root of the upper canine is at the border of the orbit, in front of the lacrimal foramen. The base of the upper canine is encircled by a cingulum; the lower canine, as in other pithecines, is triangular in outline, with a conspicuous distal cusp and a faint buccal cingulid. The large M_T is slightly longer than wide.

The robust upper canines, as well as the diastema between canines and incisors, identify *Cebupithecia* (Figures 145 and 146) as morphologically (but not necessarily temporally) very likely near the common ancestor of the living pitheciinans, *Pithecia*, *Cacajao*, and *Chiropotes*. The following combination of known dental features characterizes this fossil genus, with most of these characters also present in other pitheciins. The canines are robust and round-based, the small premolars are crowded, and the first molar is distinctly larger than either P_4^4 or M_2^2. The enamel, unlike that of the living pitheciinans, is smooth, unwrinkled. A lingual cingulum is present on the upper molars. It is significant that most, and perhaps all, of the dental features which delineate *Cebupithecia* from extant pitheciins are probably primitive pitheciinan characters. There is no question, for example, that the ancestral pitheciinan had robust canines and somewhat procumbent incisors. Furthermore, once this condition was established, regardless of whether or not subsequent species had smooth or wrinkled enamel, the pitheciinan adaptive complex was clearly defined. This conclusion is contrary to that of Hershkovitz (1970a), who stated that *Cebupithecia* lacked the distinctive pithecinan characters ascribed to it. As we usually place no great emphasis on dendritic molar wrinkling alone (as testified by the retention of non-*Pongo* apes within the Ponginae), exclusion of *Cebupithecia* from the Pitheciina on the basis of its smooth enamel would be unwarranted hair-splitting of a species-specific character for purposes of supra-generic classification. The last common ancestor of living pitheciinans probably had the wrinkled enamel condition and approximately equal-sized molars. Despite this fact, exclusion of *Cebupithecia* from that subtribe is not advisable as the fossil genus has the other strongly diagnostic hallmarks of the group.

The living pitheciinans are primarily fruit and, to a lesser degree, insect eaters. The similarities of *Cebupithecia* both in dental proportions and particularly in anterior dental specializations strongly suggest a primarily frugivorous feeding regime.

Tribe Xenotrichini
Hershkovitz, 1970a

(= or including: Xenothricidae Hershkovitz, 1970a.)

DISTRIBUTION
    Subfossil. Jamaica.?
INCLUDED TAXA
    Xenothrix.

DISCUSSION

This unique primate, recently thoroughly reevaluated by Rosenberger (1977), is still a phylogenetic enigma. Based on the morphology of its mandible and its few preserved teeth, we believe it to be derived from an ancestor not unlike *Callicebus*. Therefore, the tribe is classified within the Pitheciinae.

XENOTHRIX Williams and Koopman, 1952

DISTRIBUTION
    Subfossil. Jamaica.
KNOWN SPECIES
    Xenothrix mcgregori Williams and Koopman, 1952, type species
LOCALITIES: Long Mile Cave* (1300).

DISCUSSION

The only known specimen of this unusual primate, well described by the authors of this genus, is characterized by the unmistakable dental formula of two molars, three premolars, one canine, and two incisors, resembling, in this respect, the marmosets. The two known molars, $M_{\overline{1-2}}$, are low crowned with low and bunodont cusps. The enlarged, wide-based cusps have, in effect, virtually obliterated both the trigonid and talonid basins. Specific to *Xenothrix* are the mesoconids between the protoconids and hypoconids, and the metastylid, that is, topographically, a cusp located distal to the metaconid and mesial to the entoconid (Figure 147). The antemolar dentition

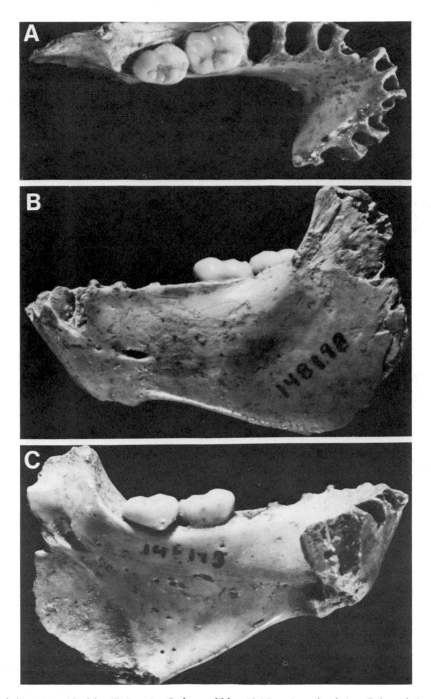

Figure 147. *Xenothrix mogregori* (subfossil), Jamaica. Left mandible with $M_{\overline{1-2}}$: A, occlusal view; B, lateral view; C, medial view.

may be judged only from the alveoli. The three single-rooted premolars were mesiodistally compressed, as in most atelids and cebines, and, like *Callicebus* but unlike *Cebus*, *Pithecia*, or *Cacajao*, for example, the size progressively increases from $P_{\overline{2}}$–$P_{\overline{4}}$. The canine was small, perhaps being that of a female (although not necessarily, as some *Aotus* and *Callicebus* lack marked sexual dimorphism in this respect), and $I_{\overline{1}}$ was apparently larger than $I_{\overline{2}}$. These teeth were slightly procumbent, but not nearly as enlarged as those of pitheciins. The symphysis slopes obliquely as in marmosets, unlike the more vertical condition displayed in living atelids and cebines. There is enough of the posterior part of the mandible remaining to show that the angle was considerably expanded as in *Callicebus*, *Alouatta*, or *Brachyteles*.

The phylogenetic affinities of *Xenothrix* are very difficult to assess and they remain obscure, as reflected in the works of Williams and Koopman (1952), Hershkovitz (1970a), and Rosenberger (1977). It is not especially near *Alouatta* or the Atelini, but, beyond that, matters of judgment become largely arbitrary as there are no satisfactorily established shared derived characters between *Xenothrix* and other atelids. The dental formula could easily have been attained independently from marmosets and the expanded angle may be a very common response to certain mechanical requirements of the chewing musculature. The sloping symphysis may well be a direct correlate of a shortened mandible, or it may have served some specific buttressing function in chewing. To sum up, the most likely affinity of *Xenothrix* is with some unknown stock near *Callicebus* or the ancestry of the pitheciins.

The cusp morphology of the molars suggests mainly crushing functions, whereas the parallel alignment of metaconid–metastylid–entoconid and paraconid–mesoconid–hypoconid suggests cutting. The known material suggests a frugivorous feeding regime.

Tribe Homunculini
Ameghino, 1894

(= or including: Nyctipithecinae Mivart, 1865, not available. Homunculidae Ameghino, 1894. Aotinae Poche, 1908. Tremacebinae Hershkovitz, 1974.)

DISTRIBUTION
Late Oligocene (Colhuehuapian) to modern. South America.
INCLUDED TAXA
Aotus, *Homunculus*, and *Tremacebus*.

DISCUSSION

This tribe is used to unite a small collection of relatively primitive atelids. We consider our procedure of using shared patristic features for low level grouping preferable to the designation of family rank taxa for relatively poorly understood animals (Hershkovitz, 1970, 1974) or to the practice of uniting taxa on poorly tested or understood characters which may not be shared and derived.

The extant *Aotus* and the fossils *Homunculus* and *Tremacebus* have been placed together chiefly because we consider them to be the most primitive representatives of the Atelidae, with some derived characters of their own and without known special ties to any other living atelids. This should not be interpreted, however, to mean that they are clearly more recently related to one another than to other atelids. We take the course of uniting this horizontal category only because their ties cannot as yet be satisfactorily established.

The living douroucoulis, or owl, or night monkeys (*Aotus*) are the sole living representatives of this group and they are also the only nocturnal anthropoids. These large-eyed forms (with pure rod retinas) spend the day sleeping in tree hollows and travel during the night in small family bands, eating fruits and insects and occasionally catching small birds and bats. Social behavior in night monkeys has recently been reviewed by Moynihan (1976) and Wright (1978).

HOMUNCULUS Ameghino, 1891

(= or including: ?*Anthropops* Ameghino, 1891.)

DISTRIBUTION
Early Miocene (Santacrucian). Argentina.
KNOWN SPECIES
Homunculus patagonicus Ameghino, 1891, type species

(=*Homunculus ameghini* Bluntschli, 1931. ? =*Anthropops perfectus* Ameghino, 1891.)
LOCALITIES: Santa Cruz beds⋆ (392).

DISCUSSION

Specimens referred to this genus have been described and discussed by Ameghino (1891b, 1893, 1902, 1906, 1907), Bluntschli (1931), Rusconi (1935a,b), Stirton and Savage (1951), and Hershkovitz, (1970, 1974). The only known remains are a nearly complete mandible, a partial face, and a femur.

The lower dentition and the mandible (Figure 148) have been studied by Hershkovitz (1970a). The teeth are badly worn and the mandible has been characterized as "U-shaped" and "marmoset-like." The premolars are unique. The roots of several upper teeth are known from the type skull fragment of *H. patagonicus*, but unfortunately little or nothing can be assessed even of the most rudimentary aspects of the molar morphology.

This poorly defined Miocene taxon shows some similarities in its mandibular form to *Aotus* (A. Rosenberger, personal communication), but the possibility exists that this may merely represent ancestral atelid similarities. A. Rosenberger (personal communication) suggests that in its craniofacial morphology *Homunculus* is not unlike the reconstructed primitive pitheciin pattern.

There is nothing in the known morphology of the various samples of *Homunculus* and *Tremacebus* that would suggest too great a divergence of a form such as *Aotus* from a *Homunculus*-like ancestry, or the divergence of these two taxa from a common ancestor quite similar to both. Until details of the genealogy are more decipherable, this similarity is best expressed by keeping *Homunculus* and *Tremacebus* associated with *Aotus* in the same tribe.

Ciochon and Corruccini (1975) have recently reassessed the femoral morphology in *Homunculus*. They considered it to be morphologically callitrichine-like and perhaps primitive in this respect. As noted above, their analysis seems to have been strongly influenced by size.

TREMACEBUS Hershkovitz, 1974a

(= or including: *Homunculus*: Rusconi, 1933, in part.)

DISTRIBUTION
    Late Oligocene (Colheuhuapian). Argentina.
KNOWN SPECIES
    Tremacebus harringtoni (Rusconi, 1933)
(= or including: *Homunculus harringtoni*, Rusconi, 1933.)
LOCALITIES: Sacanana★ (382)

DISCUSSION

When Hershkovitz (1974a) redescribed the genus *Tremacebus*, a skull damaged and lacking a mandible (Figure 149), he made comparisons with *Homunculus, Aotus, Callicebus,* and *Saimiri.* The genus is still known only by the badly damaged holotype with a relatively large orbitotemporal fenestra and laterally expanded orbits (Hershkovitz, 1974a).

Hershkovitz (1974a) characterized *Tremacebus* as having a "*Callicebus* size skull, with short face, braincase steeply vaulted, posterior occipital plate and foramen magnum directed more nearly backward than downward, orbits oriented fronto-laterally, interorbital region wide, muzzle broad, zygomatic arch relatively long, dental arch more nearly U- than V-shaped, occlusal surface of dental row moderately curved" (p. 1).

In spite of the great wealth of descriptive details (many due to crushing) noted and the comparisons made by that author, the closest patristic similarity of *Tremacebus* appears to be with *Aotus.* Aside from the likely synapomorphy of the enlarged orbits, much of this similarity may represent atelid, or perhaps even platyrrhine, ancestral similarities. Hershkovitz's work on *Tremacebus* lacks an approach that might have allowed him to make phylogenetic sense of the various character complexes which are closely interrelated.

It appears to us that *Tremacebus* played an important role in the hypothesis put forward by Hershkovitz (1974a) that a large orbital fissure (the opening between the orbits and the temporal fossae) was primitive in platyrrhines, as shown in *Tremacebus* or *Aotus.* We believe, however, and A. Rosenberger (personal communication) concurs, that the unusual size of the orbital fissures in these taxa is correlated with their equally unique enlargement of the orbits. If orbital enlargement is a result of nocturnality, and if nocturnality is a derived anthropoid mode of life, as we believe it is, then the size of the orbital fissure is secondarily large, causally tied to orbital expansion.

The upper molars of *Tremacebus harringtoni* are inadequately known; available teeth are perhaps more similar to those of *Callicebus* or the pitheciin

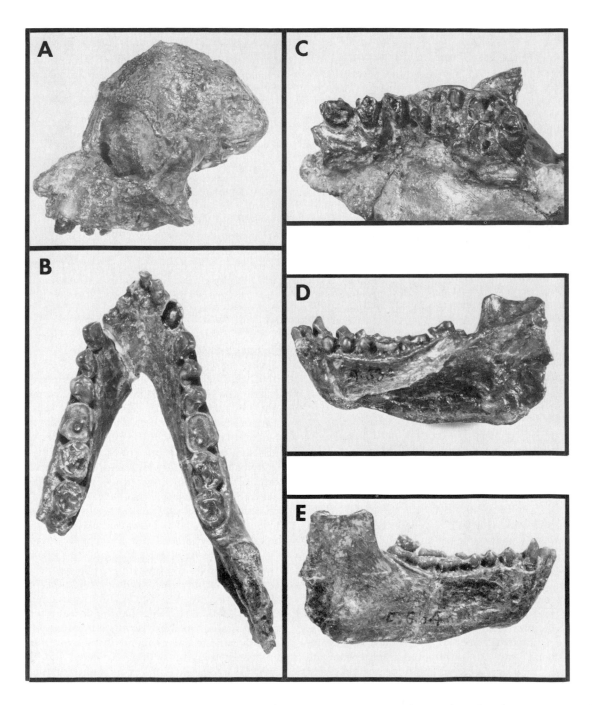

Figure 148. *Homunculus patagonicus*. Early Miocene, southern South America. A, left side of crushed facial skull, lateral view; C, ventral view with broken dentition. Mandible with right $I_{\overline{1}}$–$I_{\overline{2}}$, C, $P_{\overline{2}}$–$P_{\overline{4}}$, $M_{\overline{1}}$–$M_{\overline{3}}$ and left $P_{\overline{2}}$–$P_{\overline{4}}$, $M_{\overline{1}}$–$M_{\overline{3}}$: B, occlusal view; D, lateral view of left side; E, lateral view of right side. [From Hershkovitz (1970a), courtesy of P. Hershkovitz.]

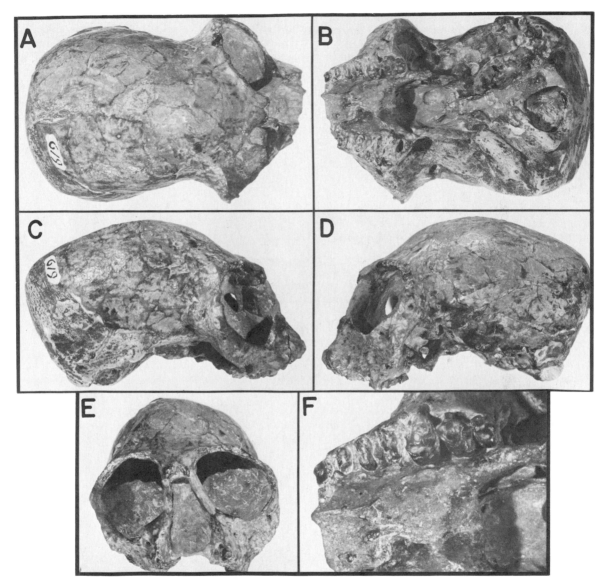

Figure 149. *Tremacebus harringtoni.* Late Oligocene, southern South America. Cranium: A, dorsal view; B, ventral view; C, lateral view of right side; D, lateral view of left side; E, frontal view. Maxilla with left M^1–M^3: F, occlusal view. [From Hershkovitz (1970a), courtesy of P. Hershkovitz.]

morphotype than to *Saimiri* (Hershkovitz, 1974a), with heavy lingual cingula, a robust protocone, and a well-defined hypocone independent from the cingulum itself. The first upper molar displays a small but unmistakable pericone and, as a consequence, the mesiolingual border of the tooth is more lingual than the distolingual portion adjacent to the hypocone. The third molar is considerably reduced compared to the second, and its hypocone is diminutive.

The conformation of the hypocone is perhaps of some significance inasmuch as it appears distinct from the cingulum immediately adjacent to it. The conditions fulfill the definition of a pseudohypocone, although whether the origin was similar to that in the *Pelycodus–Notharctus* lineage, for example, cannot be ascertained. In the latter genera the "hypocone" had its origin from a "pseudohypocone," budding off from the side of the protocone and eventually phyletically becoming part of the cingulum in *Notharctus* rather than remaining on the side of a protocone, as in *Pelycodus*.

The suggestion that *Tremacebus* was nocturnal has been put forward by Rusconi (1935a,b). Hershkovitz's (1974a) assessment that "the callitrichid-like skull, complex quadritubercular molars, and well defined cranial ridges point to an arboreal animal preponderantly herbivorous, possibly with a preference for leaves" (p. 18) is only partly endorsed. The teeth certainly suggest herbivory, but the arboreality of the animal is only assumed because as far as we know platyrrhines have had no terrestrial lineages.

Infraorder Catarrhini
E. Geoffroy, 1812

(= or including: Catarrhina Hemprich, 1820. Eucatarrhini Delson, 1977b. Paracatarrhini Delson, 1977b.)

DISTRIBUTION
?Late Eocene–early Oligocene; mid-Oligocene to modern. Old World tropics into temperate zones (worldwide in "domestication").
INCLUDED TAXA
Superfamilies Parapithecoidea, Hominoidea, and Cercopithecoidea.

DISCUSSION

The catarrhines are the Old World branch of the anthropoids or higher primates. There have been several successive radiations, of which two are still flourishing: the hominines and the cercopithecids. The group probably arose in Africa, with an eventual ancestry in Europe or, possibly, depending on the relationships of taxa such as *Pondaungia*, in Asia. Analyses of ancestral morphology for and relationships within the Catarrhini have been provided recently by Delson and Andrews (1975) and Kay (1977a), especially.

As far as can now be determined, the ancestral catarrhine morphotype would probably have been characterized by a dental formula of $I_{1,2}^{1,2}$, C_1^1, $P_{2,3,4}^{2,3,4}$, $M_{1,2,3}^{1,2,3}$; small incisors relative to molar size, generally narrow and high-crowned, with a conical or caniniform I^2 and wide I^1; canines the tallest teeth, occluding with if not honing on each other, I^2 and P_2; a mesial sulcus was probably but not surely present on the crown of C^1; of the lower premolars, P_2 was probably small and simple, P_3 perhaps slightly larger in area, both with only one major cusp and little fovea development; P_4 may have been largest in area, with well-developed, subequal protoconid and metaconid, probably with its long axis in line with those of the molars; the upper premolars were rather simple, buccolingually broad bicuspid oval teeth, the paracone slightly taller than the protocone, with a slight lingual cingulum; height probably decreased posteriorly, although P^3 may have been largest in area; the lower molars would have had five major cusps, with a sixth, the paraconid, occurring variably, especially on M_1 (and usually on dP_{3-4}); trigonid length was moderate, and a small distal fovea would have been present lingual to the midline hypoconulid (also small, except perhaps on M_3); molar length increased distad; buccal cingulum was present and distinct; upper molars would have presented four main cusps and probably two moderate conules, the paraconule linked by crests to both paracone and protocone, as in tarsiiforms, the metaconule linked at least to the protocone; the teeth were probably broad subrectangles, with distinct lingual and little or no buccal cingulum; the mesial fovea was small, but delineated by crests from the paraconule; the lingual cusps were placed slightly distal to their buccal neighbors. In terms of molar occlusion (Kay, 1977a), facets 7n, 10n, and 8 had essentially replaced facets 7 and 10, with 10n being rather small and anterior to the hypocone on uppers; facet X was present behind the trigonid on lower molars. The mandibular corpus was probably moderately deep, of relatively constant depth under the cheek teeth, and the symphysis fused early in life.

Given the uncertainties involved in discussions of morphoclines in the catarrhine skull, reconstruction of a morphotype is much more difficult. The interorbital region was surely broad, and the postorbital bar was well developed, but closure may not yet have been complete (perhaps roughly comparable to *Tarsius?*), using *Apidium* as a model. Estimates of relative facial, nasal, or neurocranial length and of choanal shape are not yet feasible. The external auditory meatus was presumably annular, much as in living platyrrhines. Postcranial information is, if possible, even more questionable, but, once again, the characteristics described below for *Apidium* may be tentatively interpreted as ancestral for the infraorder.

As argued strongly by Delson (1977b, 1975c; Delson and Andrews, 1975), the major split within the catarrhines lies between the Parapithecidae and other taxa. Superficially, the parapithecids [especially *Parapithecus* (see Figure 150)] appear more conservative, but, in fact, the morphotype for this group would have presented numerous derived conditions. Thus, the $P_{\overline{2}}$ would have been the tallest premolar, although probably not larger in area than $P_{\overline{3}}$; the $P_{\overline{4}}$ metaconid would have been reduced (conceivably the ancestral condition for all catarrhines); a bulbous conule would have been present on upper premolars; on lower molars, the buccal cingulum would have been somewhat reduced, and a "waisted" shape developed; on the uppers, the conules would have increased in size, the paraconule especially becoming isolated from other cusps as its connecting crests were deemphasized, and, concomitantly, the mesial fovea would have become shorter mesiodistally but wider; the corpus may have become shallower, especially mesial. Further discussion of this pattern and differences between the two genera are presented under the family, below.

On the other hand, a smaller number of changes from the postulated ancestral catarrhine morphotype would have characterized the inferred latest common ancestor of the Pliopithecidae, Hominidae, Cercopithecidae, and Oreopithecidae. These would have included the following: loss of $P_{\overline{2}}$ and development of true honing function of $C^{\underline{1}}$ on $P_{\overline{3}}$, which became larger and buccolingually compressed, with a mesiobuccal flange; the canines also probably became more compressed, taller, and more clearly sexually dimorphic in

size and perhaps form; on the upper molars, a crista obliqua developed, as the homologue of the tarsiiform "*Nannopithex*-fold" crest and a mesiolingual crest from the metacone met at the metaconule; perhaps linked to this change, facet 10n, buccal to the hypocone, increased somewhat in area; the paraconule retained its basic position, but may have dissociated somewhat from the paracone. Although there are still uncertainties due to the rather long face seen in *Propliopithecus zeuxis*, the latest common ancestor of living catarrhines, if not the ancestral eucatarrhine, probably had a relatively wide and short face, with short and broad nasal bones, possibly low and wide choanae, the lacrimal fossa partly bounded by the maxilla, ethmoid participating in the orbit wall, nearly complete closure of the lateral orbital wall and brain showing a size increase over that of tarsiiforms, at least, with sulcal pattern perhaps as in hylobatines (see Delson and Andrews, 1975). At least at this stage, if not earlier, ischial callosities may have been present and separated by a patch of haired skin, while the diploid chromosome number may have been 44.

This pattern was essentially preserved in the Pliopithecidae, while numerous additional alterations characterized the morphotypes of the other three families, as described for each below. One branch of the morphocline is approximated by the transformation from *Propliopithecus* to *Sivapithecus* (Figure 150, C and D).

On the basis of these differences between the morphotypes of the Parapithecidae and other catarrhines, Delson (1977b) proposed to recognize formally two monophyletic groups at a rank below that of infraorder, employing McKenna's (1975) category parvorder. The Paracatarrhini was based on the Parapithecidae, especially *Parapithecus*, while the Eucatarrhini, based eventually on *Homo*, included the Hominidae, Pliopithecidae, and Cercopithecidae. Oreopithecidae was there ranked as parvorder *incertae sedis*, but it is now seen more likely to be a cercopithecoid (see also Figure 151). Here, we have decided not to recognize taxa of parvorder rank, instead accepting three superfamilies within the catarrhines. The terms "paracatarrhine" and, especially, "eucatarrhine," are used at intervals in the vernacular sense in discussions of relationships among catarrhine higher taxa. A hypothesis of relationships among taxa of genus–group rank, including but not based upon stratigraphic range data, is presented in Figure 151,

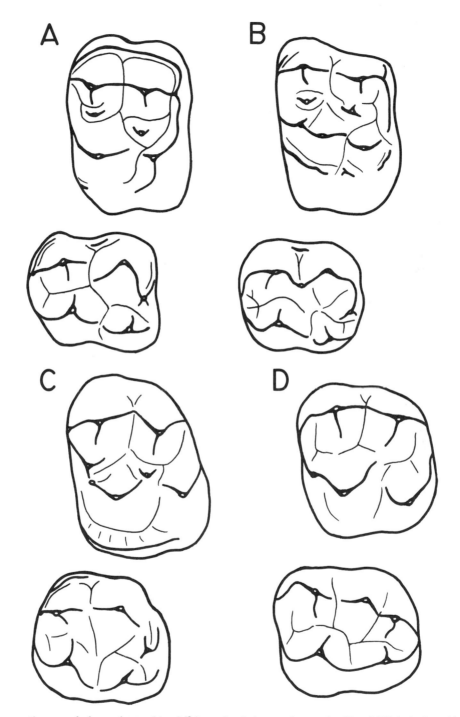

Figure 150. Comparative morphology of catarrhine M²⁄₃ in occlusal view, redrawn after Kay (1977a): A, *Parapithecus grangeri*, mid-Oligocene, Africa; B, *Apidium moustafai*, mid-Oligocene, Africa; C, *Propliopithecus zeuxis*, mid-Oligocene, Africa; D, *Sivapithecus sivalensis*, middle Miocene, Asia. Note that the transformations A to B and C to D approximately correspond to morphoclines in the Parapithecoidea and Hominoidea, respectively, while a form somewhat intermediate between A and C might correspond to an ancestral catarrhine. [By A. Cleary.]

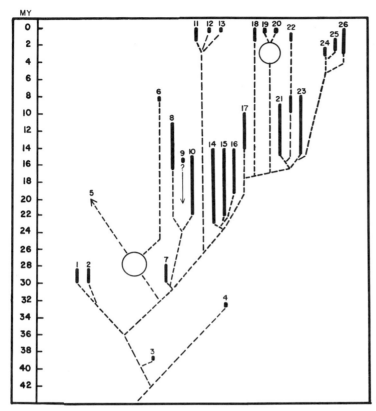

Figure 151. Known stratigraphic range (solid lines) and suggested phylogenetic relationships (broken lines) of the Catarrhini. 1, *Apidium*; 2, *Parapithecus*; 3, *Pondaungia*; 4, *Oligopithecus*; 5, Cercopithecidae (see Figure 162); 6, *Oreopithecus*; 7, *Propliopithecus*; 8, *Pliopithecus*; 9, "Kansupithecus"; 10, *Dendropithecus*; 11, *H. (Hylobates)*; 12, *Hylobates (Nomascus)*; 13, *Hylobates (Symphalangus)*; 14, *Dryopithecus (Limnopithecus)*; 15, *Dryopithecus (Proconsul)*; 16, *Dryopithecus (Raŋgwapithecus)*; 17, *D. (Dryopithecus)*; 18, *Pongo*; 19, *Pan (Gorilla)*; 20, *P. (Pan)*; 21, *Sivapithecus*; 22, *Gigantopithecus*; 23, *Ramapithecus*; 24, *A. (Australopithecus)*; 25, *A. (Paranthropus)*; 26, *Homo*. [By A. Cleary.]

the cercopithecids having been displayed separately in Figure 162 for reasons of space.

The major implications of this diagram, as discussed in more detail under the relevant taxa below, are that, among eucatarrhines, four families (pliopithecids and hominids, cercopithecids and oreopithecids) can be dichotomously linked with some certainty; that pliopithecids are essentially an early, conservative "radiation" of hominoids; and that two outlying very early ?catarrhine genera are now known. Only the last of these points need be considered further here. *Pondaungia* is known from a few badly weathered jaw fragments which are phenetically similar to some pliopithecids, but on which the essential catarrhine wear facets cannot be discerned due to damage. One of us (Szalay) believes, however, that the scanty remains of *Pondaungia* show close patristic similarity to notharctines in features which might be considered primitive euprimate morphology. It seems therefore inadvisable to consider this genus a *bona fide* anthropoid. Even less securely grouped with the catar-

rhines is *Oligopithecus*, of which the well-preserved unique holotype presents no advanced wear facets or a distal fovea on the lower molars, suggesting that the hypocone was poorly developed; the loss of $P_{\overline{2}}$ and development of apparent C' honing on $P_{\overline{3}}$ may have evolved convergently with those patterns in eucatarrhines, with which the genus is more commonly grouped (compare, e.g., Simons, 1972, with Kay, 1977a, and Delson, 1977b).

Relationships of the Catarrhini as a unit are discussed further under Haplorhini (p. 196). Despite various suggestions about transatlantic migrations it now seems unlikely that there was any genetic contact between the predecessors of the Old and New World anthropoids after the early late Eocene. Presumably, an anthropoid-grade catarrhine ancestor entered Africa from Eurasia by late Eocene or early Oligocene to give rise to the last common ancestor of parapithecoids and other catarrhines, an animal which would have conformed to the morphotype delineated above. If *Pondaungia* is indeed a catarrhine (but see our disagreement above), its presence in Asia on the northeastern side of Tethys might be explained by independent dispersal from Europe at the protocatarrhine grade, later dispersal of catarrhines from Africa, or most probably by assuming that early catarrhines entered Africa from eastern Asia (eventually from western North America).

Within the catarrhines, there appear to have been a number of sequentially replacing radiations. The parapithecids were clearly the dominant group in the Fayum region, but it is not certain that this would have been the case elsewhere in the as yet unknown African Oligocene; the eucatarrhines appear to have radiated rapidly at this time. The conservative pliopithecids were rare in the Fayum and remain at least taxonomically restricted in the African early Miocene, where a fair number of *Dryopithecus* species (Hominidae, Ponginae) are known. These forest-dwellers exited Africa via an apparently forested corridor to the northeast by the middle Miocene, when *Dryopithecus* and *Pliopithecus* species were known mostly to the

southwest of European Paratethys, while *Ramapithecus* and *Sivapithecus* occurred to the east and north, continuing across Asia, in more open habitats. Cercopithecids are very rare in the African early and middle Miocene, although representatives of four or five species occur sparsely, but they became a dominant element of Old World primate faunas by the late Miocene, as far as can be observed; *Oreopithecus*, a distinctive cercopithecoid, also flourished at this time. Hominoids seem to have been outcompeted in most habitats, both forested and more open, from later Miocene into Pleistocene times, only a few genera maintaining isolated footholds in Asia. In Africa, *Pan* species appear to have avoided competition through size increase and niche specialization, while the hominine lineage(s) developed bipedality and eventually culture in mainly savannah and gallery-forest biomes. By the early Pleistocene, *Homo erectus* was able to depart Africa and eventually spread widely throughout the Old World and give rise to the only truly successful living hominoid.

SUPERFAMILY PARAPITHECOIDEA
Schlosser, 1911

(= or including: Parapithecidae Schlosser, 1911. Parapithecoidea: Kälin, 1961. Paracatarrhini Delson, 1977b.)

DISTRIBUTION
    Oligocene (later Fayumian). Egypt.
INCLUDED TAXA
    Family Parapithecidae.

Family Parapithecidae
Schlosser, 1911

(= or including: Parapithecinae: Simons, 1970.)

DISTRIBUTION
    Oligocene (later Fayumian). Egypt.
INCLUDED TAXA
    Parapithecus and *Apidium*.

DISCUSSION

The Parapithecidae comprises a group of small, early catarrhines which have conservatively retained three premolars but developed a number of apparently derived trends or conditions that separate them

from other catarrhines, contemporaneous and later. The main derived conditions uniting *Parapithecus* and *Apidium* species are the following: $P_{\overline{2}}$ (and P^2?) probably the tallest premolar; upper premolars with well-developed paraconule; upper molars with large and isolated bulbous conules (i.e., not linked by crests to the main cusps) and short and wide mesial fovea; lower molars waisted (constricted between trigonid and talonid) and with somewhat reduced buccal cingulum; mandible shallowing slightly mesiad. In addition, known parapithecids or their morphotype presented such probably ancestral features as a dental formula of $I\frac{2}{1\cdot2}$, $C\frac{1}{1}$, $P\frac{2\cdot3\cdot4}{2\cdot3\cdot4}$, $M\frac{1\cdot2\cdot3}{1\cdot2\cdot3}$; robust canines; upper premolars buccolingually wide with paracone taller than protocone; upper molars buccolingually wide with lingual cingulum (perhaps buccal as well) and well-developed hypocone; lower $P_{\overline{3-4}}$ with small metaconid, especially on $P_{\overline{3}}$; lower molars with: moderate length trigonid, lingually placed posterior fovea, midline distal hypoconulid, paraconid possibly present variably, and length probably increasing distad. Wear facets X, 7n, 8, and 10n (Kay, 1977a) were presumably present in the ancestral parapithecid as well. Cranial and postcranial characters are only known in *Apidium*, but main features probably included fused frontals with a complete postorbital ring and partial closure, probably unfused annular tympanic and "*Cebus*-like" limb and tarsal elements. The most important features among those listed are of course the derived states, especially relative premolar size, upper cheek tooth conules, and perhaps lower molar waisting. The latter is found elsewhere among anthropoids only in Cercopithecidae and Oreopithecidae, neither of which shares other derived states with ancestral Parapithecidae, suggesting convergence in this character state. Premolar conules are unique among Primates, and the large molar conules may be a meristic expression of the same morphogenetic "field" effect. The presence of three premolars is, of course, an ancestral retention, but the relatively large size of $P\frac{2}{2}$ is probably significant and derived.

As originally defined by Schlosser, the family was designed for the reception only of *Parapithecus*, then known from a single damaged mandible. With the recovery of additional specimens of both *Apidium* and *Parapithecus*, Simons (1967c et seq.) argued for the inclusion of both genera in a single family–group taxon, which he further considered to have cercopithecid affinities. In different papers (see review in Delson, 1975c), Simons ranked the taxon as a subfamily of Cercopithecidae or a family of Cercopithecoidea, a view which has been widely accepted (e.g., Le Gros Clark, 1971; Szalay, 1975d). Delson (1975c; Delson and Andrews, 1975) has argued against this interpretation, based on the lack of clearly demonstrable shared derived similarities between the parapithecid and cercopithecid morphotypes. Most recently, Kay (1977a) suggested that, while *Parapithecus* might be close to the ancestors of Old World monkeys as Simons had suggested, the phyletic affinities of *Apidium* were with

"*Aegyptopithecus*" and later catarrhines, based especially on the shared presence of a protoconule (his "cusp a") on the upper molars (Figure 150). Consideration of Kay's drawings and analyses as well as original specimens and illustrations leads to the rejection of this hypothesis also, however. Instead, as Delson (1977b) has argued, the parapithecids are best interpreted as representing the known members of an ancient catarrhine radiation. Here we recognize three superfamilies of the Catarrhini, also employing the terms paracatarrhine (for parapithecids) and eucatarrhine (for hominoids plus cercopithecoids) in the vernacular.

Considering Kay's suggestion first, his main argument rested on the identification of both a paraconule and a protoconule ("cusp a") in specimens of *Apidium moustafai* and "*Aegyptopithecus*" (*Propliopithecus zeuxis*). As noted under *Propliopithecus* below, however, other specimens of *P. zeuxis* have only a single cuspule in the region between paracone and protocone, and it may be surmised that the paraconule was twinned in the individual whose skull we possess; in that individual and in isolated teeth, crests connect the small paraconule(s) to both main mesial cusps. In *Apidium*, on the other hand, a large and bulbous topographic protoconule is present mesiobuccal to the protocone and mesial to the paraconule. Crests are faint if present at all, unlike their sharp condition in *Propliopithecus* (see Figures 150, 154, 223, and 224). The two configurations are distinctly different and probably not fully homologous, at least with respect to the protoconule. The relative position of these conules was mentioned in Kay's (1977a) text, but not in his Figure 12 or the list of character states under discussion. Moreover, *Apidium* differs from *Propliopithecus* species and other eucatarrhines in the additional characters noted above for the family, further supporting Kay's alternative but less preferred hypothesis of parapithecid unity.

As to Simons' views on the parapithecid–cercopithecid relationship, these depend essentially on the anthropoid grade of the former and on minor similarities of *Parapithecus* to selected cercopithecids. These resemblances are outweighed by the several derived features and trends exhibited by *Parapithecus*, as dealt with in greater detail under the genus. The most reasonable interpretation remains that of ecological–functional convergence, rather than phyletic relationship or ancestry, between the two taxa. In grade terms, parapithecids are primitive anthropoids, but they are phyletically far from all eucatarrhines.

The possibility has also been voiced (e.g., Hoffstetter, 1972) that some parapithecid or other early catarrhine reached South America via waif dispersal from Africa across a narrower late Eocene Atlantic to give rise to platyrrhines. Although this is an intriguing hypothesis, especially given the simplistic equality in premolar number, a special relationship between parapithecids and platyrrhines is not supported by details of morphology and is rejected by the derived characters which militated against links to Old World monkeys above. Moreover, Simons (1976c) has suggested that a small primate would probably die of thirst on such a lengthy raft voyage.

Parapithecids are by far the most common primates and are among the most common mammals in the Fayum deposits, and their demise by the end of the Oligocene is not yet fully explicable. In part, it was perhaps their success which led Simons to seek potential descendants. It is most probable that the late Oligocene saw the rise of relatives or descendants of *Propliopithecus* ancestral in turn to *Dryopithecus* species of the Miocene, and these forms outcompeted the parapithecids through either enhanced locomotor ability or dietary adaptation. Further data on the nature of parapithecid diversity and their replacement will only become available when additional African (later) Oligocene deposits are discovered, as the Fayum clearly represents a short-lived window on only one small corner of African mammalian evolution.

PARAPITHECUS Schlosser, 1910

DISTRIBUTION

Mid-Oligocene (later Fayumian). Fayum depression, Egypt.

KNOWN SPECIES

1. *Parapithecus fraasi* Schlosser, 1910, type species

LOCALITIES: "Fayum," horizon uncertain, probably middle faunal level★ (376).

2. *Parapithecus grangeri* Simons, 1972 (1974b)

LOCALITIES: Yale Fayum Quarry I★ (378).

DISCUSSION

Parapithecus is similar in size to the smallest modern cercopithecid (*C. talapoin*) and partly convergent to Old World monkeys in molar adaptation. In the lower molars, the buccal cingulum is much reduced, the crown is slightly waisted, a small paraconid is present (variably?), a moderate-sized hypoconulid is placed distomedially, the anterior fovea is rather long, the posterior fovea is placed lingually, the oblique cristid and lateral postcristid diverge, and the several advanced catarrhine wear facets (X, 7n, 8, 10n) are present (Figures 150A and 152). The three molars are subequal in size, with $M_{\overline{3}}$ always shorter and narrower than $M_{\overline{2}}$, and than $M_{\overline{1}}$ when present, but with $M_{\overline{1}}$ sometimes larger than $M_{\overline{2}}$ (Simons, 1974b). The $dP_{\overline{4}}$ is like a narrow $M_{\overline{1}}$, but with a stronger paraconid; the only known $dP_{\overline{3}}$ is too damaged to preserve much morphology (Figure 152A).* There are three premolars, of which $P_{\overline{4}}$ is the largest and most complex (with a variable-sized metaconid, always smaller than the protoconid), $P_{\overline{3}}$ smaller and with a very small metaconid, and $P_{\overline{2}}$ probably the tallest and simplest, being nearly unicuspid (but rarely preserved); all three have small talonids, with some lingual cingulum (Figures 152 and 153A). The canine (in *P. fraasi*) is tall and somewhat incisiform, about the height of $P_{\overline{2}}$ but more gracile and with less cingulum. The incisors are poorly known, only two of four lowers being present in *P. fraasi* (Figure 153A). There seem to be some small differences between the two, and it is not certain if they are both centrals, as suggested by Simons (1967c). Only a few isolated anterior elements are known for *P. grangeri* (Figure 152E). The mandibular corpus

---

*Cachel (1975) noted that *Parapithecus* differed from cercopithecids in that the deciduous premolars are not "progressive" toward bilophodonty. This is not meaningful, as all catarrhine deciduous premolars are basically similar to permanent molars. In cercopithecids, dP_4^4 is nearly indistinguishable from M_1^1, while dP_3^3 is slightly different mesially, especially the lower, which occludes with a canine. But they do not "foreshadow" the molar pattern, or vice versa—both classes are bilophodont rather equally. The known deciduous dentition of *Parapithecus* is as expected given its permanent teeth.

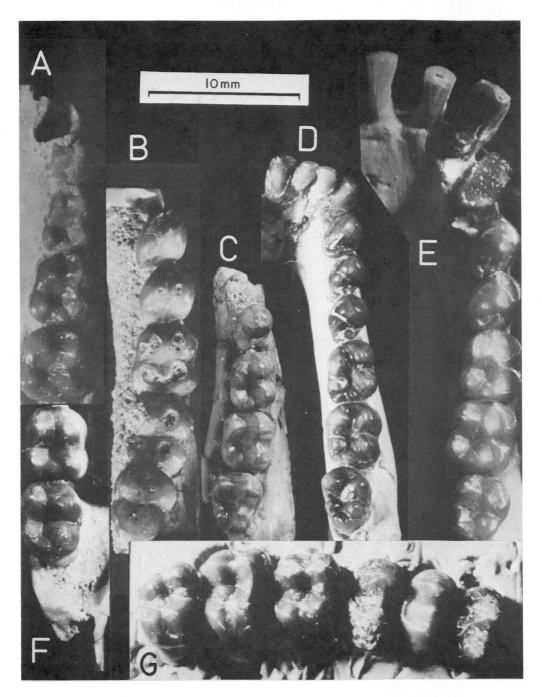

Figure 152. *Parapithecus.* Middle Oligocene, Africa. Dentitions in occlusal view. *P. grangeri:* A, juvenile right corpus with dP$_{\overline{3}}$–M$_{\overline{2}}$; B, right P$_{\overline{3}}$–M$_{\overline{3}}$ (photographically reversed); C, right corpus with P$_{\overline{4}}$–M$_{\overline{3}}$ (reduced to size of D); E, right corpus with P$_{\overline{3}}$–M$_{\overline{3}}$, also unassociated left I$_{\overline{1?}}$, right I$_{\overline{2}}$, C$_{\overline{1}}$ and P$_{\overline{2}}$; F, right corpus with M$_{\overline{2-3}}$; G, unassociated upper cheek teeth referred to *P. grangeri*, possibly right P$^{\underline{2}}$–M$^{\underline{3}}$. *P. fraasi:* D, part of mandible with left C$_{\overline{1}}$, I$_{\overline{7}}$, right I$_{\overline{7}}$, C$_{\overline{1}}$–M$_{\overline{3}}$ (photographically reversed). [C courtesy of and © E. L. Simons.]

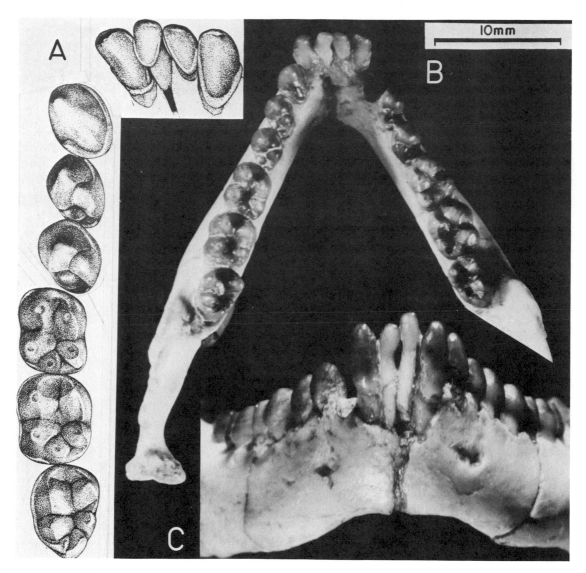

Figure 153. *Parapithecus fraasi.* Middle Oligocene, Africa. Mandible with left I$_{\overline{7}}$, C$_{\overline{1}}$–M$_{\overline{3}}$, right I$_{\overline{7}}$, C$_{\overline{1}}$, P$_{\overline{3}}$–M$_{\overline{3}}$: A, drawing of left teeth and right I$_{\overline{7}}$–C$_{\overline{1}}$, occlusal view, not precisely aligned; B, occlusal view; C, anterior view. The scale is for B. [A from Kälin (1961).]

deepens somewhat distally; the ramus is incompletely known (Figure 154). The upper molars are squarish, with the two lingual cusps set nearly transversely to their buccal counterparts (Kay, 1977a), large but isolated conules partly incorporated into functional lophs, a short and wide mesial fovea, and a reduced lingual, but variable buccal cingulum (Figures 150A

and 152G). The upper premolars are transversely wide with a strong conule and very tall paracone. This description is based on isolated maxillary cheek teeth allocated to *P. grangeri* by analogy with those of *Apidium*.

Parapithecus shares with *Apidium* retention of P$_{\overline{2}}^{2}$, presence of large bulbous isolated conules on upper

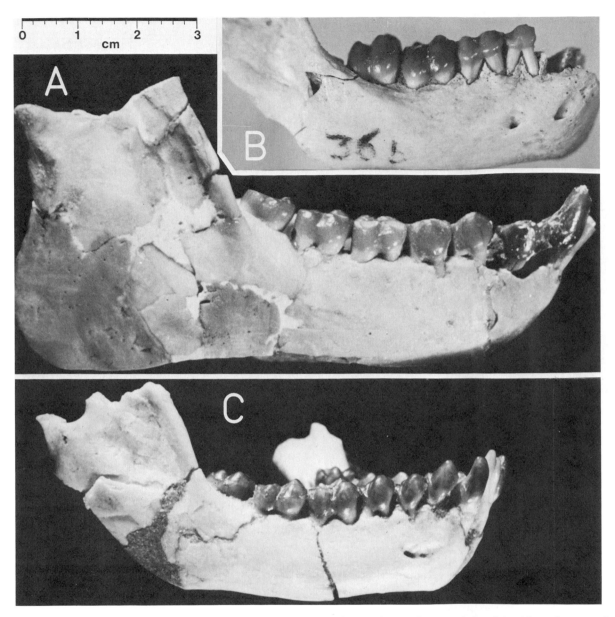

Figure 154. *Parapithecus.* Middle Oligocene, Africa. Mandibles in right lateral view. *P. grangeri:* A, adult with partly restored ramus, P$_{\overline{3}}$–M$_{\overline{3}}$, unassociated I$_{\overline{2}}$–P$_{\overline{2}}$; B, juvenile with dP$_{\overline{3}}$–M$_{\overline{2}}$. *P. fraasi:* C, young adult with I$_{\overline{7}}$, C$_{\overline{1}}$–M$_{\overline{3}}$ (photographically reversed).

cheek teeth, moderate lower molar waisting and cingulum reduction, lower premolar form and mesially shallowing mandibular corpus. It differs from *Apidium* in the shorter $M_{\overline{3}}$; relatively larger canine and premolars (especially $P^{\underline{2}}$); reduction of lingual and presence of buccal cingulum on upper molars; lack of centroconid, protoconule. and pericone; smaller paraconule; taller premolar paracone; presence of paraconid at least sometimes; and greater transversality of upper molar cusps. From non-parapithecids *Parapithecus* differs in its enlarged $P^{\underline{2}}$, small $P_{\overline{4}}$ metaconid, large isolated bulbous conules, placement of upper molar cusps and lower molar waisting (shared with cercopithecoids), resembling contemporaneous catarrhines only in the presence of a distomedial hypoconulid and the basic molar wear facets.

The relationships of *Parapithecus* have been in question and under discussion since its original description (see under the family). The unique holotype of *P. fraasi* (Figure 153) was well illustrated, described, and partly interpreted by Kälin (1961), who epitomized the widespread uncertainty about the homology of the known anterior teeth: Were the three teeth mesial to $P_{\overline{3}}$ two incisors and a canine or one incisor, a canine, and a $P_{\overline{2}}$? It was not until new specimens of *Parapithecus* and especially of *Apidium* were recovered that Simons (1967c) was able to demonstrate that the type of *P. fraasi* was defective, two incisors (as well as the right $P_{\overline{2}}$) having been lost before Schlosser studied it. This situation becomes clear as soon as one is aware of the possibility: Kälin's radiographs and a simple anterior photograph (Figure 153C) indicate that the symphysis is asymmetrically incomplete, not merely unfused in the midline. Simons (1969b) first applied the new name *P. grangeri* to the more recently collected material without any indication of distinctions; these were briefly noted in 1972, thereby formally validating the name [despite Simons' (1974b) arguments to the contrary]. The two species of *Parapithecus* differ (Figure 152) in that *P. grangeri* is 10–25% larger (measurements in Simons, 1974b), and its $M_{\overline{3}}$ is relatively smaller, $P_{\overline{3-4}}$ metaconids are larger, the cusps are slightly less bulbous on the molars (and premolar protoconids?), and the mandibular corpus deepens distally (rather than more nearly of constant depth). No additional specimens of *P. fraasi* are definitely known, but some may occur in Quarry G. As yet, no cranial or postcranial specimens from the Fayum have been allocated to *Parapithecus*: some are too large and

have been identified as *Propliopithecus zeuxis*, while the majority from Quarry I were assigned to *Apidium* on the basis of homogeneity of morphology and *Apidium*'s greater dental representation in the assemblage (Conroy, 1976a).

Simons, in a series of papers between 1967 and 1974 (see summary in Delson, 1975c), has presented and argued the case for a special, phyletic relationship between *Parapithecus* and the Cercopithecidae. Delson suggested that this argument was based mainly on the anthropoid grade reached by *Parapithecus* and some dental similarities to *Cercopithecus talapoin*, which Simons (1969b, p. 323) considered as "possibly most primitive" among Old World monkeys. To the contrary, *C. talapoin* is a probably derived member of a strongly derived cercopithecid group and thus is not a useful standard of comparison. When *Parapithecus* is compared with the cercopithecid ancestral morphotype (see p. 321 and in Delson, 1975c), the main similarities are the ancestral catarrhine states of high-crowned molars, distal hypoconulids, and moderately deep mandible (found in most Fayum species), among others. While the derived conditions of lower molar waisting and upper molar transverse cusp placement also may be shared (though less developed in parapithecids), they could easily be convergent, as is probably the approach to lophodonty in upper teeth of *Parapithecus* through incorporation of conules (Figure 152G). Major differences between *Parapithecus* and hyothetical ancestral cercopithecids include reduced lower molar buccal cingulum without development of flare, the presence of a strong upper molar buccal (but weak lingual) cingulum, short $M_{\overline{3}}$, small to moderate $P_{\overline{4}}$ metaconid, and especially enlarged $P^{\underline{2}}$ which might have been involved in canine honing or sectorialism. As Delson (1975c) argued, such a distinctive adaption would be unlikely to have been lost in descendants, especially as the ancestral condition probably involved small $P^{\underline{2}}$. Kay (1977a) has recently championed Simons' hypothesis from a cladistic viewpoint based especially on an analysis of molar occlusion facets. However, he has considered fewer characters and interpreted, observed, or weighted some differently than do we. In brief, to derive an ancestral Old World monkey dentition from those of a *Parapithecus*-like form would require: loss of $P^{\underline{2}}$ (which had become larger even than in *Apidium*, representing the presumed ancestral condition, and which may have been involved in C′ occlusion); enlargement of $P_{\overline{4}}$

metaconids beyond the level seen in *P. grangeri* (in turn larger than in *P. fraasi,* whose condition may have been ancestral for the genus); enlargement of $M_{\overline{3}}$ back to the ancestral condition; loss of upper molar cingulum and development of molar flare by a means other than incorporation of lower buccal and upper lingual cingulum (already reduced in *P. grangeri* without flare); and elimination of conules which had previously enlarged from the ancestral condition. This calls not only for several convergent developments in the ancestors of monkeys and apes ($P^{\underline{2}}$ loss, $P_{\overline{3}}/C^1$ honing development, $P_{\overline{4}}$ metaconid increase, not to mention mandibular shape and a tubular external auditory meatus of apparently identical form and homology) but also for reversal of several trends obvious in the evolution of *Parapithecus* from a common catarrhine ancestor (without arguing which species of the genus is more derived). Kay (1977a) attempted to circumvent part of this argument by suggesting that an early parapithecid (he considered *Apidium* unrelated) might have developed upper molar cusp repositioning, lower molar waisting, enlargement of the anterior fovea, and cingulum reduction before reducing $M_{\overline{3}}$ and greatly enlarging conules, thus being less derived

compared to a cercopithecid morphotype. Even if the last two of those features are put aside as more derived than in an ancestral monkey, several of the above criteria remain, especially if *Apidium* is considered a parapithecid, as it is here. To go back to a still earlier parapithecid ancestor would mean merely an ancestral catarrhine, which of course would have been ancestral to both *Parapithecus* and cercopithecids, without implying a special relationship between them.

In sum, total evaluation of early catarrhine morphology and morphotypes suggests that *Parapithecus* was not particularly closely linked to Old World monkeys, but was related to *Apidium*. The several ways in which *Parapithecus* dentally resembles cercopithecids may be regarded as evidence of a similar adaptation, as suggested by Delson (1975c): perhaps another parallel catarrhine approach to folivory. A similar pattern of upper molar semi-lophodonty through incorporation of conules is seen in *Cebus* (Rosenberger and Kinzey, 1976), which also presents some transversality of upper molar cusps. On the other hand, *Cebus* has more bulbous cusps (as in *P. fraasi?*) and is omnivorous, eating few leaves.

APIDIUM Osborn, 1908

(= or including: ?*Oligopithecus* Simons, 1962a, in part.)

DISTRIBUTION
  Mid-Oligocene (later Fayumian). Fayum depression, Egypt.
KNOWN SPECIES
  1. *Apidium phiomense* Osborn, 1908, type species
(= *Apidium phiomensis* Osborn, 1908. ?*Oligopithecus* Simons, 1962a, in part.)
LOCALITIES: Yale Fayum quarries I and M and surface★ (378).
  2. *Apidium moustafai* Simons, 1962a
LOCALITIES: Yale Fayum Quarry G★ (376).

DISCUSSION

Apidium is the smallest known catarrhine, comparable in size to *Callicebus* among anthropoids. It is the most common small mammal in the upper and middle Fayum horizons, well represented by almost all dental elements, some unassociated postcranials, and rare cranial fragments (Figure 155). A nearly complete mandible unquestionably demonstrates the same dental formula as in *Parapithecus,* additionally documented in other specimens of both species (Figures

156 and 157). In the lower dentition, the molars increase in length posteriorly, are slightly waisted, have reduced cingulum, no flare, distomedial hypoconulid, no paraconid, well-developed centroconid (mesoconid), moderate length trigonid, and standard catarrhine wear facets (X, 7n, and 10n of Kay, 1977a) (Figure 150B). The three premolars increase in height but decrease in caliber and complexity mesiad, with metaconid low on $P_{\overline{4}}$, faint on $P_{\overline{3}}$, and absent on $P_{\overline{2}}$; talonids are quite small. The canine is tall and simple, much like $P_{\overline{2}}$, with lingual cingulum surrounding nearly half the crown base. The incisors are slightly procumbent (Figure 156E); the centrals are simple and would seem to have been narrower than the laterals, judging from the alveoli. Variation in tooth size suggests sexual dimorphism in both species. Deciduous teeth are not published, but their replacement sequence is $M_{\overline{1}}$ (?$I_{\overline{1}}$, $I_{\overline{2}}$), $M_{\overline{2}}$, $P_{\overline{2}}$, $M_{\overline{3}}$, $P_{\overline{4}}$, $P_{\overline{3}}$, $C_{\overline{1}}$; the mandibular symphysis fuses early (preadult?). The mandibular corpus is of moderate depth, shallowing slightly mesially (Figure 156, E and F); a ramus has

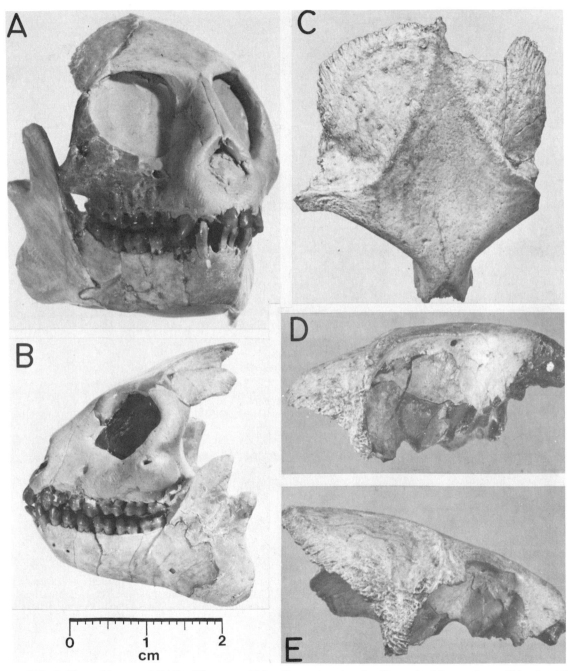

Figure 155. *Apidium phiomense.* Middle Oligocene, Africa. Reconstruction (by Simons) of face and mandible: A, oblique frontal view; B, left lateral view. Referred isolated frontal bone (used in reconstruction): C, dorsal view; D, oblique right lateral–frontal view; E, right lateral view. The scale is for B; C–E are at twice that scale. [A,B courtesy of and © E. L. Simons; C–E coutesy of C. Tarka.]

315

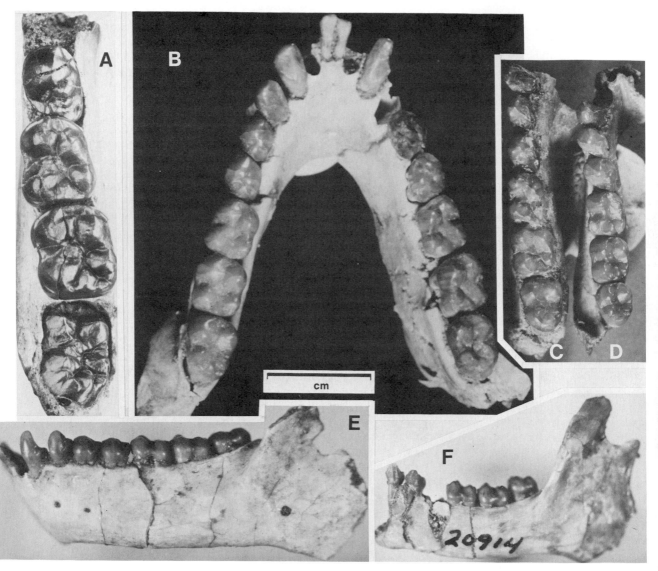

Figure 156. *Apidium phiomense.* Middle Oligocene, Africa. Juvenile left corpus with $P_{\overline{4}}$–$M_{\overline{3}}$, (erupting): A, occlusal view. Mandible with left $I_{\overline{1}}$, $C_{\overline{1}}$–$M_{\overline{3}}$, right $I_{\overline{1}}$, $C_{\overline{1}}$, $P_{\overline{3}}$–$M_{\overline{3}}$: B, occlusal view; E, left lateral view. *Apidium moustafai.* Middle Oligocene, Africa. ?Male left corpus with $P_{\overline{2}}$–$M_{\overline{3}}$: C, occlusal view. ?Female left corpus with $P_{\overline{2}}$–$M_{\overline{3}}$, alveoli for $I_{\overline{1}}$–$C_{\overline{1}}$ and right $I_{\overline{1-2}}$: D, occlusal view. Left corpus and ramus with $P_{\overline{2-3}}$, $M_{\overline{1-3}}$: F, left lateral view. The scale is for B–D; E and F are at ⅔ scale; A is at 3/2 scale. [A courtesy of C. Tarka.]

been reconstructed by Simons (Figure 155B). In the upper dentition (Figure 157), the molars decrease in size posteriorly, with M^1 only slightly larger than M^2, which is much larger than M^3; the metacone is variably reduced on M^2 and nearly nonexistent on M^3. The upper molars are transversely wide, with hypo-

cone lingual to the large protocone, large bulbous isolated paraconule and metaconule, small "protoconule" on the "preprotocrista," short and wide mesial fovea, moderate lingual cingulum, usually with a pericone lingual to the protocone, but no buccal cingulum. At least in *A. phiomense*, there may sometimes be additional extra cusps, and several of the mesial cusps blur and fuse with wear. The three upper premolars are also wide, decrease in size mesiad, and have some lingual cingulum and especially a large bulbous paraconule; the canine is robust, but not very tall. The face of *Apidium* is relatively short (Figure 155, A and B), and the postorbital ring is complete and thick, but orbital closure was probably incomplete (less than *Tarsius?*) (Figure 155, D and E); a sagittal crest may have been present. A partial endocast is known, but Radinsky (1974) could extract little information from it. Gingerich (1973b) described the morphology of two specimens identified as the auditory region of *Apidium*; there has been doubt as to his identifications and interpretations, as discussed in detail under Haplorhini. Isolated postcranial elements allocated to *Apidium* are similar to *Cebus* or *Saimiri* in size, form, and function (Figure 158).

Comparisons between *Apidium* and *Parapithecus* are noted under *Parapithecus*. *Apidium* differs from Fayum and later non-parapithecids in the greatly enlarged and isolated paraconule on upper cheek teeth, the presence of a protoconule partly linked to the protocone but not to the paraconule, small $P_{\overline{4}}$ metaconid, retention of $P^{2}_{\overline{2}}$, lower molar waisting (resembles *Oreopithecus* and cercopithecids), and the presence of a centroconid (resembles *Oreopithecus*).

Apidium phiomense was first described by Osborn (1908) from a fragmentary juvenile mandible (Figure 156A) and, as a result, uncertainty about its affinities persisted until new and more complete remains were recovered by Simons in the early 1960s. Now, over 20 partial dentitions of *A. moustafai* (Simons, 1968) and about 60 partial jaws and teeth of *A. phiomense* as well as three frontals, an ear region, and nearly 100 postcranial specimens (Simons, 1974b; Conroy *et al.*, 1975) are known. Detailed descriptions, however, are rare, although some data are given by Simons (1972) and Kay (1977a), with measurements of some *A. moustafai* in Simons (1962a). Most authors (e.g., Simons, 1972; Delson, 1975c; Szalay, 1975d) have agreed to the close relationships of *Parapithecus* and *Apidium*, but Kay

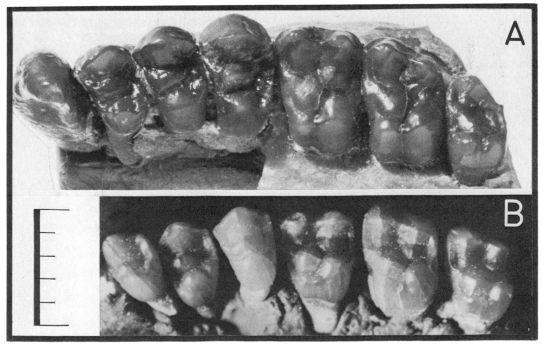

Figure 157. *Apidium.* Middle Oligocene, Africa. Maxillae in occlusal view. A, *A. phiomense,* left C^{1}–$M^{3}_{.}$ moderate wear; B, *A. moustafai,* left unassociated P^{2}–M^{3}(?), slight wear (photographically reversed). Scale divisions are in millimeters. [A courtesy of E. L. Simons.]

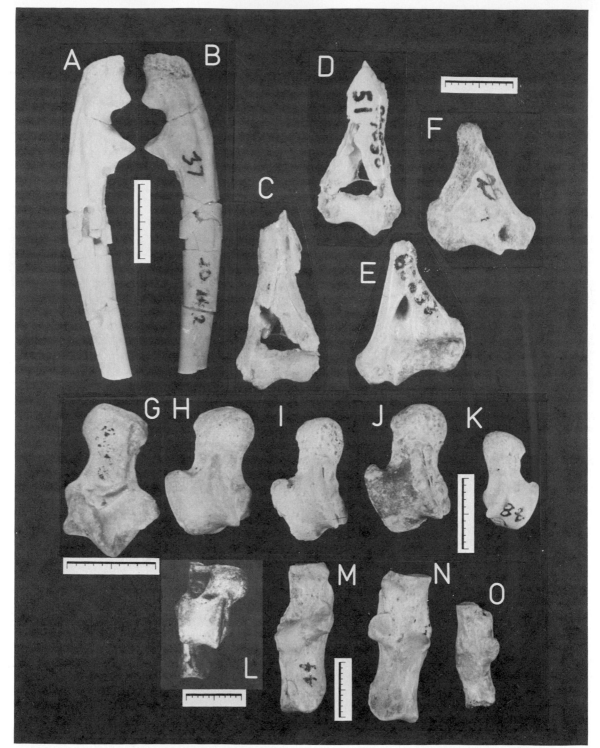

Figure 158. *Apidium phiomense*. Middle Oligocene, Africa. Proximal portion of right ulna: A, lateral view: B, medial view. Distal portions of two left humeri: C and E, anterior views; D and F, posterior views. Left astragali: H, I, and J, dorsal views; G, plantar view of H. Right astragalus: K, dorsal view. Left calcanei: M and N, dorsal views. Right calcaneus: O, dorsal view. Left ?associated astragalus and calcaneus (same as I and M): L, dorsal view. The divisions of the scales associated with each group of views are in millimeters. [From Conroy (1976a), courtesy of G. Conroy.]

(1977a) has challenged this view, suggesting that *Apidium*, instead, shared a more common ancestor with *Propliopithecus* and later catarrhines. This interpretation is not accepted here, as discussed under the family, above.

Oreopithecus has also been considered a potential phyletic relative of *Apidium* (Gregory, 1922; Simons, 1960, 1972; Delson and Andrews, 1975; Kay, 1977a), but this relationship is now considered unlikely because of the many uniquely derived dental character states of both genera. The centroconid is placed and occludes differently in each (see *Oreopithecus*), and molar waisting, although superficially similar, may well have evolved in parallel (or convergently) in parapithecids and cercopithecoids.

The dental morphology of *Apidium* is summarized above in some detail. The two species differ in size by about 10–15%, although no series of measurements has yet been presented to demonstrate this distinction statistically, and there is moderate variation within the taxa. Kay (1977a) has remarked that little morphological difference is found between the two, and in his original description Simons (1962a) only indicated less buccal cingulum and fewer accessory cusps in the *A. moustafai* cheek teeth. This can also be seen in Figure 156, as can a possible tendency toward reduction of $M_{\overline{3}}$; in the upper teeth, the metacone is less reduced in M^{2-3} and the protocone possibly less enlarged in *A. moustafai* (Figure 157). It is probable that more complete evidence would indeed confirm the distinctness of the two forms, especially as no other relatively well-studied primate or rodent species occurs in both middle and upper Fayum horizons (see also Wood, 1968).

Simons (1959) described an isolated frontal bone from (probably) the upper Fayum "zone" which demonstrated postorbital closure and early fusion of the metopic suture (Figure 155,C–E). This specimen was questionably allocated to *Apidium* at first and then (Simons, 1962a, 1963a) questionably to *Oligopithecus,* but with the recovery of a similar frontal associated with *Apidium* teeth its identity was confirmed. Gingerich (1973) described the ear region of the associated specimen, but there has been controversy over its interpretation (see under Haplorhini); however, there is at least agreement on the generally conservative anthropoid nature of the *Apidium* auditory region. The endocast of the original frontal was most recently reviewed by Radinsky (1974), who found no clearly indicated sulci (nor would any have

been expected in such a small anthropoid) and considered the olfactory bulbs perhaps slightly larger than in other anthropoids, including "*Aegyptopithecus,*" compared to body size estimates.

The isolated postcranial elements from the Fayum have been treated in detail by Conroy (1976a), who allocated all but the largest to *Apidium* spp. based on approximate size and the relative frequency of that genus in the relevant quarries. The humerus has an entepicondylar foramen, moderate brachialis flange, large and medially projecting medial epicondyle with deep epitrochlear fossa, and a faint ridge separating the trochlea and capitulum distally (Figure 158, C–F). Comparative anatomical and morphometric analyses indicated the greatest similarity to quadrupedal climbers like *Cebus* and *Saimiri*. Two partial ulnae of *A. phiomense* are known, of a size compatible with the humeri. A proximal fragment (Figure 158, A and B) is strongly convex dorsally, with a shallow radial articular facet and a small olecranon, as in arboreal quadrupeds; a distal end presents a distally projecting styloid process and is similar to those of Old and New World monkeys, rather than apes. Astragali and calcanei are also known (Figure 158, G–O), one of the latter from Quarry G presumably representing *A. moustafai*; other than in size, it is identical to the rest. One other Fayum astragalus has been described by Szalay (1975d) which appears to represent *Propliopithecus*. The astragali and calcanei reveal retention of the ancestral primate helical or "screwlike" joint surface between them. One astragalus and one calcaneum were found to articulate well enough to be considered possibly as representing a single individual (Figure 158L), which morphometrically resembled *Saimiri* and *Cebus*. In all, the Fayum postcranials so far analyzed were most similar to those of quadrupedal platyrrhines, rather than to any catarrhines, probably as a result of conservative anthropoid retentions.

The overall adaptations of *Apidium* would seem to have been most closely analogous to living cebines. The bunodont, highly polycuspidate cheek teeth suggest comparison to *Cebus* (Rosenberger and Kinzey, 1976), an omnivore, even more than do those of *Parapithecus*. The parallel resemblances in the postcranium are closer still. As the most common Fayum small mammal, *Apidium* would appear to have made its living running and leaping among the branches of the floodplain and riverine gallery forests, predominantly eating fruit and insects.

SUPERFAMILY CERCOPITHECOIDEA
Gray, 1821

(= or including: Cercopithecidae Gray, 1821. Menocerca Haeckel, 1866. Cynomorpha Huxley, 1872. Cercopithecoidea: Simpson, 1931. Hominidae: Hürzeler, 1958, in part.)

DISTRIBUTION
Early Miocene (Rusingan) to modern. Old World (see under families).

INCLUDED TAXA
Families Cercopithecidae and Oreopithecidae.

DISCUSSION

In essentially all recent treatments, the cercopithecoids comprise only the living Old World monkeys and their close relatives, sometimes including the Parapithecidae (see above). As most authors accept only a single family for the monkeys (although some employ two or more, see below), the superfamily category is left out by numerous workers as superfluous. A reassessment of the relationships of *Oreopithecus*, spurred especially by suggestions of A. Rosenberger (personal communications), has confirmed previous suggestions (Szalay, 1975d) that this genus is likely to be the sister-taxon of the Cercopithecidae, and thus it is included in the superfamily as a monotypic family. Discussions of the structure of *O. bambolii* are given under the genus, while comparisons are presented mostly in the family discussion, so that the present section will concentrate on shared cercopithecoid morphology.

Compared to the (eu)catarrhine morphotype described above (p. 304), the ancestral cercopithecoid presented increased relief and reduced cingulum on all cheek teeth. Molariform teeth would have been rather elongate, especially the uppers, with occluding teeth relatively similar in overall construction (although not as much so as in cercopithecids). In lower molariform teeth, the trigonid basin was enlarged distally, while, on $dP_{\overline{4}}$–$M_{\overline{2}}$ at least, the hypoconulid may have been slightly reduced and the distolingual corner expanded somewhat to produce a larger distal fovea; on $M_{\overline{3}}$, the hypoconulid was part of a large distal lobe. Superficially, the $dP_{\overline{4}}$ of *Oreopithecus* (Hürzeler, 1958) appears to be the closest known analogue to molar form in an ancestral cercopithecoid, presenting the six tribosphenic cusps but lacking a centroconid.

There is no direct evidence for early cercopithecoid as opposed to eucatarrhine cranial morphology, but the wide and relatively short face of colobines and *Oreopithecus* surely implies an approach to this condition. In many features, the postcranium was presumably conservative, except that the astragalo–calcaneal joint had lost its helical component in favor of a less screw-like rotational movement. This implies at least some degree of terrestriality involved in the ancestral cercopithecoid adaptation (Szalay, 1975d). The major distinctions in forelimb joint architecture between cercopithecids and *Oreopithecus* militate against any shared alterations from the ancestral catarrhine conditions.

It is not yet possible to be definite about the dietary adaptations of ancestral cercopithecoids, especially as only representatives of relatively derived conditions within the group are known. Increased relief of cheek teeth produced longer marginal shearing crests which usually signal folivory in primates, but the concurrent trend toward terrestrial life is unexpected for a habitual leaf-eater. Perhaps it instead reflects a broadening of diet toward omnivory, coupled with expansion into a range of habitats and substrates, which eventually blossomed into the immense range of niches occupied by Plio-Pleistocene cercopithecoids.

The overall picture of cercopithecoid evolution might thus have begun with a reduction of cingulum (perhaps in the manner seen or foreshadowed in "*Moeripithecus*") coupled with increase of crown relief. Increased behavioral venturing toward the ground might then have led to selection for altering the lower ankle joint, permitting further flexibility of locomotion. Increase of lower molar trigonid length and hypoconulid reduction, elongation of upper molars (and premolars), and some approach to the "mirror-image" condition of upper and lower molar resemblance appear to have also occurred at this time. Circumstantial evidence (especially that relevant to the hominoid radiation) suggests that cercopithecoids diverged from the more numerous early hominoids (i.e., protopliopithecids) around the time of *Oligopithecus*, estimated at some 32–33 MY (see Figure 151). By the end of the Oligocene, perhaps 26–27 MY ago, it appears likely that the *Oreopithecus* lineage diverged from that leading to Cercopithecidae, which first occurs by 20 MY. The evolutionary histories of these two groups are discussed in detail under the respective families, below.

Family Cercopithecidae
Gray, 1821

(= or including: Cynopithecina I. Geoffroy, 1843. Lasiopygidae Elliot, 1913; Victoriapithecinae von Koenigswald, 1969.)

DISTRIBUTION
   Early Miocene (Rusingan) to modern. Old World excluding deserts, north to southern England, Germany, southern central Asia, northern India, central China, Korea, Japan.
INCLUDED TAXA
   Subfamilies Cercopithecinae and Colobinae.

Discussion

The Old World monkeys are among the most successful of all primates, certainly of Neogene groups, with 11 still living and 13 known extinct genera and well over 100 species. As is common today, they are grouped in a single family, included in a superfamily with Oreopithecidae to distinguish this sister group from the two recognized families of Hominoidea (apes or anthropomorphs). The Old World monkeys retain a widespread distribution, having retreated only from Europe, which they occupied during the Pleistocene. They are quite varied in ecological, ethological, and locomotor adaptations, although their cranial and especially dental morphology is relatively stereotyped.

The special features of each subtaxon are listed below, but the shared characters of the family as a whole are given here. Most typical is the dentition, generally termed bilophodont, wherein the molariform teeth consist of an asymmetrically high ("hypsodont") crown with four marginal cusps linked by transverse ridges or loph(id)s and three foveas separated by the two ridges. Upper teeth are generally mirror images of their lower serial homologues, with buccal and lingual features reversed. The crowns widen or flare outward laterally from the cusp apexes to the cervix, especially on the lingual surface of uppers and buccally on lowers. The lower third molar generally adds a hypoconulid on the distal shelf; a paraconid is present on $dP_{\overline{3}}$ mesial to the trigonid and usually is linked to the protoconid by a paralophid.

The $dP^{\underline{3}}$ has more rounded corners than other uppers, as well as a mesiobuccal extension in most cases. Two sets of nomenclature for the topographical features of cercopithecid molars are presented in Figure 159, taken from Delson (1975a, the source for much of this summary) and from Kay (1977a). More complete drawings of the tooth rows of representatives of the four main dental "types" are given under their respective subtaxa. Cercopithecid premolars are less easily characterized morphologically and are more homogeneous among taxa. The $P_{\overline{4}}$ consists of a small trigonid with subequal metaconid and protoconid, molariform protolophid, and large talonid; $P_{\overline{3}}$ is unicuspid, with a (sexually dimorphic) sloping mesial flange for honing C' and a distal fossa. Upper premolars are rather D-shaped, the buccal face being straight, with a single loph joining a high paracone with a lower (but variably developed) protocone. On $P^{\underline{3}}$ there is a mesiobuccal prolongation of enamel into a flange similar to that of $P_{\overline{3}}$, which may be considered an "overflow" effect from a $C/P_{\overline{3}}$ morphogenetic sharpening field (also seen in some $P_{\overline{4}}$). Cercopithecid canines are almost always sexually dimorphic and relatively large. In males especially, upper canines are marked by a deep compressed sulcus or cleft on the mesial face which continues past the cervix onto the root, distinguishing these from hominoid canines where the sulcus always ends at or apical to the cervix.

These features, common to almost all known cercopithecids, living and fossil, may be considered as part of the group's ancestral morphotype. Other characters are more variable, with different states in the several subtaxa, as described below. In terms of probable ancestral conditions, however, one can add the following: relatively small incisors, with $I^{\underline{2}}$ conical and $I^{\underline{1}}$ possibly trapezoidal; molars with long but shallow trigonids, moderate flare, low rounded cusps, shallow notches, and mesial loph(id) wider than distal; and subequally long $M^{\underline{2}}$ and $M^{\underline{3}}$. Several of these features were inherited unchanged from the common catarrhine ancestor of hominoids and cercopithecoids.

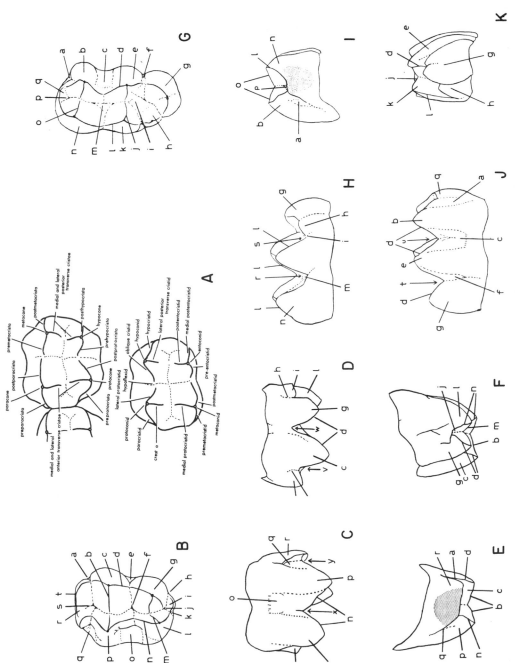

Figure 159. Nomenclature of cercopithecid molariform teeth. After Kay (1977a), illustrated on left M² (above) and right M₂ (below) of *Macaca*, mesial to right: A, occlusal view. After Delson (1975a, also 1973); Jolly (1972), illustrated on left M³ (B–F) and right M₃ (G–K) of *Theropithecus*: B, occlusal view; C, lingual view; D, buccal view; E, mesial view, stippling indicates contact area with M²; F, distal view: a, mesial buccal cleft; b, paraloph; c, paracone; d, buccal margin; e, median buccal cleft; f, trigon basin; g, metacone; h, distal buccal cleft; i, distal shelf; j, distal fovea (talon basin); k, distal lingual cleft; l, hypocone; m, metaloph; n, lingual margin; o, median lingual cleft; p, protocone; q, mesial lingual cleft; r, mesial shelf; s, mesial fovea; t, mesial margin; u, distal buccal notch; v, mesial buccal notch; w, median buccal notch; x, median lingual notch; y, mesial lingual notch. G, occlusal view; H, lingual view; I, mesial view, stippling indicates contact area with M₂; J, buccal view; K, distal view: a, mesial buccal cleft; b, protoconid; c, median buccal cleft; d, buccal margin; e, hypoconid; f, distal buccal cleft; g, hypoconulid; h, 6th cusp (tuberculum sextum); i, distal fovea; j, hypolophid; k, entoconid; l, lingual margin; m, talonid basin; n, metaconid; o, protolophid; p, trigonid basin (mesial fovea); q, mesial shelf; r, median lingual notch; s, distal lingual notch; t, distal buccal notch; u, median buccal notch. In all views, elevated features (crests, ridges, outlines) are represented by solid lines, while depressed features (grooves, clefts) are indicated by broken lines. See also Figure 6.

Others are interpreted as derived conditions in the earliest monkeys and would thus not be expected in an early catarrhine (ancestor or morphotype—see above). These include the extension of the upper canine sulcus past the cervix; the loss of dP$\overline{4}$–M$\overline{3}$ hypoconulids and concomitant(?) development of new ridges to form the loph(id)s; and lateral molar flare. Delson (1975a,c) has suggested that the latter feature is a result of the incorporation of catarrhine cingulum (also found most commonly on the buccal face of lowers and lingually on uppers) into the side walls of the tooth while increasing both height and width for greater effective tooth life. Kay (1977a, 1978) has commented extensively on the function of loph(id)s as intercusp guides rather than actual shearing devices, although nonetheless related to an increased dietary concentration on fibrous, leafy foods which probably was a major factor in the differentiation of Old World monkeys from more primitive early catarrhines.

Cranial morphology of cercopithecids is less easily characterized, as most features are either ancestral for catarrhines in general or variable within the family. More extended discussions and descriptions are found especially in Verheyen (1962), Vogel (1966), and Delson (1973). Among the more important variable characters are interorbital and facial width, nasal or facial length and facial height, construction of the lacrimal fossa, proportions of the internal choanae, development and placement of a sagittal crest (of more functional than phyletic importance), vault height, and the depth and shape of the mandibular corpus. The distribution of states of these features will be discussed by subtaxon, but as a cercopithecid morphotype, Delson (1975a) and Delson and Andrews (1975) have proposed the following: a relatively wide interorbital pillar, and face in general, linked to short nasal bones and only moderately deep and projecting face; the lacrimal fossa partly formed by the maxilla, with the ethmoid participating in the orbit wall; probably a relatively low vault; perhaps a mandible of moderately great and constant depth between M$\overline{3}$ and P$\overline{4}$ at least, with a nearly upright ramus. Most of these characters are those postulated also for an early catarrhine and found in modern colobines, although some persist in cercopithecines (see Figure 160). As discussed above, it has not yet been possible to interpret or predict the variability of choanal shape among catarrhines unambiguously.

Radinsky (1974) and especially Falk (1976) have discussed the external anatomy of the cercopithecid brain, locating a number of variable structures and postulating several ancestral conditions. The latter are basically as described below for colobines, which both workers considered conservative in retaining, among other features, a relatively small occipital lobe which is not expanded rostrally to obliterate the paroccipital sulcus. For more details, see under the subfamilies. All cercopithecids differ from hominids in having a concave arcuate sulcus whose limbs surround the sulcus rectus, rather than a frontal sulcus medial to the latter. The ancestral condition is not clear. At least some ceboids share the arcuate sulcus, suggesting it to be conservative retention, although Le Gros Clark (1971) thought the similarities between New and Old World monkeys were convergent.

A summary of postcranial morphology for the Old World monkeys is even more difficult. Many characters are closely tied to habitus rather than heritage adaptations, with states occurring convergently in distantly related taxa with similar positional behavior patterns. Few features vary within the group in a manner paralleling dental and cranial morphoclines, while those that are common to all cercopithecids are often ancestral retentions from an earlier condition. Thus, in general, cercopithecids are typified by the presence of an external tail, numerous lumbar but few sacral vertebrae, and a laterally compressed thorax, all of which are also found in platyrrhines, being those which contrast the "monkey" with the "ape" grade (along with relative encephalization and size) (see Figure 161). As a probable consequence of thorax shape (see Andrews and Groves, 1975), the humeral head faces dorsally, the scapula is placed dorsolaterally and the clavicle is short. The ulna has a long olecranon process proximally, while distally it articulates with the wrist via the styloid process. The pelvis is narrow, with an elongate ilium. In the ankle, the astragalo–calcaneal joint is of the rotational, and not the primitive primate helical, type [in most modern forms and the morphotype reconstruction (see Szalay, 1975d)]. Biegert and Maurer (1972; also Andrews and Groves, 1975) have shown that there are allometric trends relating arm and leg length to body (trunk) size in catarrhines, and all cercopithecids appear to conform to these relationships. Thus, the relatively long forelimbs in some large (fossil) species are in great part due to absolutely large body sizes and are not necessarily related to terrestriality. On the other hand,

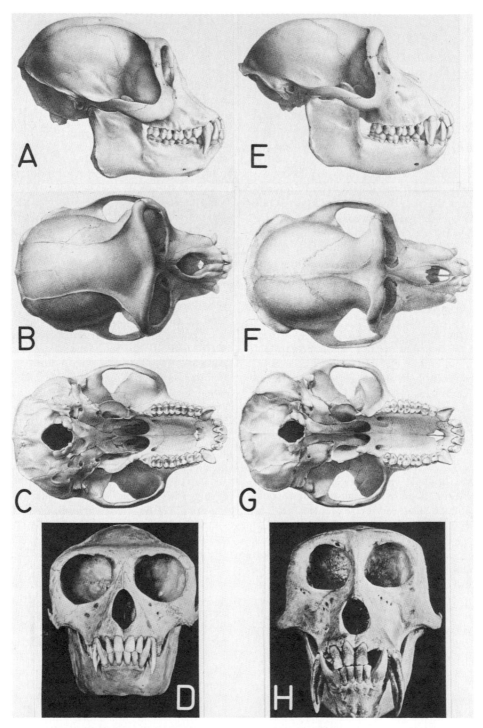

Figure 160. Morphology of cercopithecid crania. *Pygathrix nemaeus*, modern. A, right lateral view; B, dorsal view; C, basal view; D, frontal view. *Macaca* sp., modern. E, right lateral view; F, dorsal view; G, basal view; H, frontal view. [A–C, E–G from de Blainville (1839); D, H from Elliot (1913).]

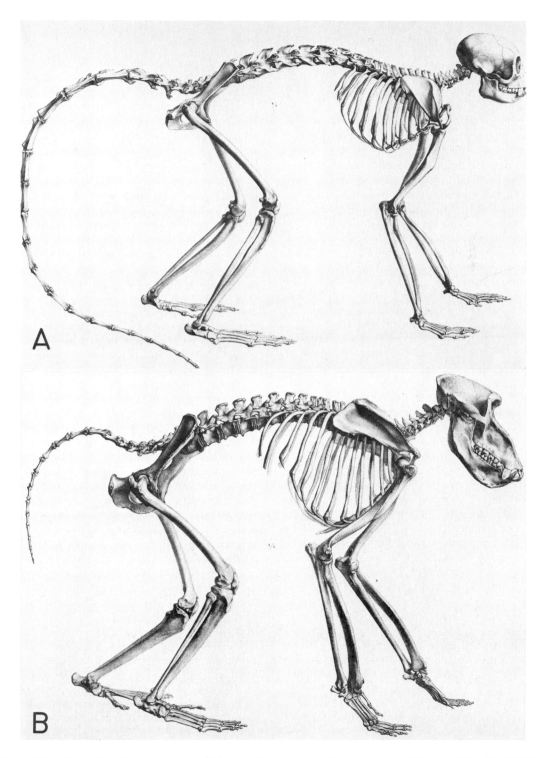

Figure 161. Cercopithecid skeletons in right lateral view. A, *Cercopithecus*; B, *Papio*. [From de Blainville (1839).]

relative length of the digits, scapular shape, and construction of the elbow joint (as shown by Jolly, 1967) are all closely tied to locomotor adaptations and are good predictors of habitus.

Although not available in the fossil record, several soft-tissue characters are important in typifying cercopithecids and their subgroups. All Old World monkeys develop ischial callosities, which appear early in the prenatal period (see Pocock, 1925b; Hill, 1966–1974); the ancestral condition, with callosities discontinuous across the midline, was probably a retention from an earlier catarrhine stage. The specialized digestive tract of colobines and the buccal pouches of cercopithecines are novelties which appeared after these taxa diverged in the Miocene. Diploid chromosome number is also variable within the family (see under subtaxa), but Delson (1975a) has suggested that $2n = 44$ may have been ancestral for cercopithecids (and catarrhines in general).

The origin of Old World monkeys, as the origin of any group, involves a double question: From whom and for what adaptive reason did they arise? The first part is discussed under Catarrhini above, with the conclusion that forms like *Propliopithecus* may be nearer cercopithecid ancestry than *Parapithecus*, although no ancestral species or genus has yet been identified. On the other hand, the selective pressures underlying this origin, whatever its source, have been discussed by Napier (1970) and Delson (1975a), among others. It is clear that the most characteristic feature of cercopithecids is their dentition, which in turn reflects at least their ancestral dietary adaptations. Napier (1970) suggested, and Delson (1975a) accepted, that if the ancestors of monkeys inhabited forested regions subject to seasonal climatic fluctuations, it might have been highly adaptive for them to have developed the ability to ingest leaves during those times of the year when fruit might have been scarce. This type of adaptation, although required during only a relatively short span of an animal's total lifetime, may nonetheless have been of such major selective advantage that it canalized future evolutionary change. Thus, perhaps in more marginal habitats of the late Oligocene(?), one or more lines which began to concentrate on folivory to a greater extent than their ancestors might have been more successful than contemporary "dental apes." Cercopithecines, whose cheek teeth have been suggested to conform more closely to the ancestral pattern than those of colobines, are generally eclectic

feeders (although some are more restricted), lending support to the idea that low-cusped lophodont teeth permitted early cercopithecids to ingest enough leaves to supplement a basically frugivorous diet. R. Kay (1977b; personal communication) has suggested that a more terrestrial way of life might have engendered similar, but stronger, selective pressures on diet and thus dentition, noting that modern arboreal apes may be strongly folivorous without lophodonty. However, such apes also are moderate to large in body size, thus facilitating folivory in a different manner. Some increase in terrestriality compared to contemporaneous hominoids is reasonable for early monkeys, but further analysis of living anthropoid cheiridia and major appendicular joints is necessary to permit postulation of ancestral conditions and biomechanical interpretation of their adaptations. Known fossils do indicate that by the middle Miocene at least some line(s) of cercopithecids were probably semiterrestrial, while other(s) may have been much more arboreal. Further details of phylogeny are presented under subfamilies and tribes below, but an overall indication of genus–group genealogy and ranges is given in Figure 162.

The earliest known cercopithecids, all of later early and earlier middle Miocene age, have not yet been subjected to sufficiently rigorous study to accurately determine their phyletic affinities. Two genera are recognized here, although at least one and perhaps two or three more may eventually be distinguished. Previous studies generally did not compare known specimens with a cercopithecid ancestral morphotype, so that it was not possible to determine which features presented by the fossils were merely retentions of ancestral conditions as opposed to derived states indicating special phyletic relationship or uniqueness.

As yet, no known Oligocene fossils are referable to the Cercopithecidae, although some Old World monkey-like features are seen in some Fayum and Pondaung species. Furthermore, none of the earliest Miocene African localities has yet yielded any plausibly cercopithecid remains, the oldest such fossils being younger than about 19 MY old; on the other hand, primates are rare in the oldest Neogene sites, and future collections might reveal early cercopithecids. The single oldest known specimen is the tooth from Napak V referred below to *Victoriapithecus* sp. and first described by Pilbeam and Walker (1968). In that paper, this tooth was recognized as cercopithecine in morphology, while a frontal fragment from

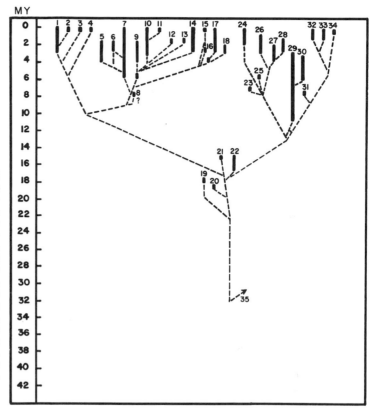

Figure 162. Known stratigraphic range (solid lines) and suggested phylogenetic relationships (broken lines) of Cercopithecidae. 1, *Cercopithecus*; 2, *C. (Miopithecus)*; 3, *Erythrocebus*; 4, *Allenopithecus*; 5, *Paradolichopithecus*; 6, *Procynocephalus*; 7, *Macaca*; 8, cf. *Macaca* sp., Marceau; 9, *Parapapio*; 10, *Papio (Chaeropithecus)*; 11, *Papio (Papio)*; 12, *Dinopithecus*; 13, *Gorgopithecus*; 14, *Cercocebus*; 15, *T. (Theropithecus)*; 16, early *Theropithecus*, Lothagam, Ain Jourdel; 17, *Theropithecus (Simopithecus)*; 18 "*Theropithecus brumpti*"; 19, *Prohylobates*; 20, *Victoriapithecus* sp., Napak; 21, "*Victoriapithecus*" *leakeyi*; 22, *Victoriapithecus macinnesi*; 23, ?*Colobus flandrini*; 24, *Colobus*; 25, *Libypithecus*; 26, *Cercopithecoides*; 27, *Paracolobus*; 28, Colobinae, new genus; 29, *Mesopithecus*; 30, *Dolichopithecus*; 31, ?*Presbytis sivalensis*; 32, *Presbytis*; 33, *Pygathrix*; 34, *Nasalis*; 35, to Hominoidea. [By. A. Cleary.]

Napak IX was thought to be colobine-like. It was thus suggested that the two subfamilies had diverged by 19 MY ago or before. Delson (1975a), however, showed that these morphologies were to be expected in an ancestral cercopithecid, thus shedding no light on phyletic divergence dates. Moreover, it would now appear, following Radinsky (1974), that the frontal might be from a small hominoid, probably *Dryopithecus* cf. *legetet*, which is known from Napak in quantity (Fleagle, 1975). The best evidence for cercopithecid subfamilial divergence is that from Maboko, where two species coexisted, one relatively conservative (cercopithecine-like) and the other dentally derived (colobine-like). These forms are considered below as *Victoriapithecus* species, even though the former may require a new genus when fully studied. More fragmentary remains from North Africa are placed in two species of *Prohylobates*, which is in some ways more conservative than *Victoriapithecus*, but is uniquely derived as well. These two genera are here grouped *incertae sedis* because they share a common "level of organization," although in the future, *Victoriapithecus* species might be allocated to modern subfamilies, while *Prohylobates* might be placed in its own subfamily.

SUBFAMILY CERCOPITHECINAE
Gray, 1821

(= or including: Cynocephalina Gray, 1825. Macacidae Owen, 1843. Cynopithecinae Mivart, 1843. Cercopithecinae: Blanford, 1888. Cercopithecidae: Hill, 1966 and others.)

DISTRIBUTION
   Late Miocene (late Turolian) to modern. Old World, see under family above.
INCLUDED TAXA
   Tribes Cercopithecini and Papionini.

DISCUSSION

   The cercopithecines are the more numerous and widely distributed subfamily of Old World monkeys, generally derived in cranial, anterior dental, and post-cranial character states. Their most typical feature is one of soft anatomy, the cheek pouches, which Murray (1975) has interpreted to reflect a "fundamental niche" of arboreal and semi-terrestrial forest feeding. This is most interesting in view of earlier speculations that the pouches were of special value on the ground, whereas Murray has shown that, in fact, terrestrial African cercopithecines have reduced pouches. Today, the subfamily includes members of all locomotor types, from high-canopy species which almost never descend to the ground through semi-arboreal and semi-terrestrial forms to several genera which hardly ever climb trees. It has been widely thought that some terrestrial adaptation was at the root of the group's origin, and Murray's work confirms this, but may reduce the degree of terrestriality to be expected in the ancestral cercopithecine.

Considering the main body systems which are preserved in fossils, the dentition of the Cercopithecinae includes three main morphological variants: those of guenons, geladas, and "typical" papionins (baboons, mangabeys, and macaques). The only character states common to all of these, and thus to the group's morphotype, are large trigonids on lower molars (ancestral); shallow notches and generally low relief on cheek teeth (ancestral, but not in *Theropithecus*); and somewhat enlarged upper incisors, especially I^2 (compare the macaque teeth of Figure 165).

In the cranium, cercopithecines are characterized by a relatively elongate face with long, narrow nasal bones, linked with a narrow interorbital pillar and generally narrow but very high face, in the zygoma especially. As part of the facial lengthening, in addition to the nasal elongation, the lacrimal bone expands anteriorly out of the orbital cavity and envelops the lacrimal fossa, the vomer expands to form part of the medial orbit wall, and the ethmoid seems to expand anteriorly in the midline but then is covered by the frontal (see Trevor Jones, 1972). In most cercopithecines, the choanae are high and narrow, the mandibular ramus is back-tilted (but more upright in shorter-faced species), the corpus is somewhat shallow, deepening mesially, and the mandibular symphysis is pierced by the median mental foramen [which is rare in other catarrhines (Vogel, 1968)]. The skull of a conservative cercopithecine (a macaque) is illustrated in Figure 160, E–H.

Brain morphology typical of cercopithecines reflects rostral expansion of the occipital lobe and general increase of visual and association cortex, perhaps as a consequence of more complex social behavior and vocalization (Falk, 1976). Compared to colobines, this morphology is derived and can be characterized by: relatively sinuous sulcus rectus, diverging from the orbital margin; fronto-orbital sulcus frequently present; Sylvian and superior temporal sulci converging, not parallel; lunate and intraparietal sulci relatively straight, never linked by the paroccipital sulcus which is totally lacking; and occipito-temporal sulcus frequently present, but superior branch of the lateral calcarine sulcus infrequently so.

In the postcranial skeleton, several common features are due to the early development of terrestriality. The long bones are commonly rather robust and straight-shafted, the cheiridia and their digits are short, at least compared to the colobines, although the most arboreal cercopithecines are in many ways more similar phenetically to colobines than to baboons (see Figure 161, compare A and B). The lower ankle joint has almost completely lost the helical pattern of early catarrhines. In the elbow joint, cercopithecines typically have moderate-sized supra-radial and supra-ulnar fossae on the humerus, with the former usually smaller and less deeply excavated. The humeral articular surface is somewhat narrow transversely, and the radial articular surface on the ulna is usually doubled, with rough, nonarticular bone in between. Again, these features are contrasted with opposing states in Colobinae, but no morphocline polarities have been satisfactorily determined. Two other soft-anatomical characters can be mentioned: There is no sign of the colobine specialization of the digestive tract, that of cercopithecines being similar to the hominoid condition; the diploid chromosome number is variable, but patterns do appear at the tribe level. Delson and Andrews (1975) and Delson (1973) provided more detailed references.

The origin of the subfamily is certainly linked to its cheek pouches, as discussed above. If, however, the ancestral cercopithecid was partly terrestrial, and the first cercopithecines not much more so, this adaptation would not seem to be as important as previously thought (e.g., Napier, 1970; Delson, 1975a). The dentition of the subfamily is relatively conservative, so much so that early fossils cannot be assigned to the Cercopithecinae on the basis of cheek tooth form. For example, Pilbeam and Walker (1968) postulated the divergence of the two subfamilies early in the early Miocene because of the occurrence at Napak of a cercopithecine-like upper molar and a possibly colobine-like frontal bone, both merely ancestral conditions. These characters are potentially expected in a single species of early monkey. The major adaptation of the subfamily, then, would appear to be the facial elongation, leading to a reorganization of bony relationships in the orbit and mid-face. The selective pressures for such enlargement might reflect the advantages of larger jaws and teeth, for masticating tougher foods requiring longer processing, especially with the anterior dentition. This, in turn, might again suggest increased terrestriality of such animals.

Tribe Cercopithecini
Gray, 1821

(= or including: Cercopithecinae: Hill, 1966. Cercopithecini: Jolly, 1966 and others.)

DISTRIBUTION
Late Pliocene (Rodolfian) to modern. Africa south of the Sahara.
INCLUDED TAXA
Cercopithecus, Erythrocebus, and *Allenopithecus.*

DISCUSSION

This tribe is the least well represented by fossil remains, only some dozen specimens of *C. (Cercopithecus)* sp. having been reported. Although most species are arboreal, *Erythrocebus* is among the most terrestrial of all cercopithecids, and *Cercopithecus* species include one semiterrestrial and some semiarboreal forms. Most are omnivorous, as common for cercopithecines, but again some *Cercopithecus* spp. are partly to highly folivorous (especially *C. lhoesti,* fide Kay, 1978).

Dentally, the most important cercopithecin derived feature is the loss of $M_{\overline{3}}$ hypoconulids. This is a state found at low frequency among many cercopithecid species, even typically in a few species, but constantly among all Cercopithecini. Each $M_{\overline{3}}$ is much like its preceding $M_{\overline{2}}$, but with a smaller distal fovea. In conjunction, the upper third molar is reduced distally even more than usual. Another common feature is the relative elongation of the cheek teeth, in part related to a rather low degree of lateral flare, especially in the large *Erythrocebus* (whose teeth have been used to typify the tribe in Figure 163). On the other hand, the dentition of *Allenopithecus* is quite distinctive in that lateral flare is about as great as in the most extreme papionin, *Cercocebus* (see under the genus, below).

The lower incisors appear to retain the normal amount of lingual enamel, and accessory cuspules are rare to nonexistent. More detailed discussions can be found in Delson (1973), Lampel (1963), and Ockerse (1959).

In cranial morphology, cercopithecins generally conform to the pattern described for the subfamily. The choanae are low and wide in some species of *Cercopithecus,* however, and the face may be somewhat less elongate (perhaps due to generally small absolute size). Verheyen (1962) gives excellent descriptions of the cranium of the genera and many species, considering that, in some ways, *Allenopithecus* is most conservative. The postcranium of Cercopithecini does not appear to present any unique character states, the long bones varying greatly in robusticity, curvature, and joint morphology; the tail is always long. The skeleton of *C. (M.) talapoin* is illustrated in Figure 161A.

There is also a fair amount of interspecific variation in soft anatomy within the tribe. *Cercopithecus (Miopithecus)* is characterized by a high degree of female sexual swelling, while *Allenopithecus* has less and the other taxa none at all. The ischial callosities are distinct on either side, being separated by a patch of haired skin, the condition which Pocock (1925b) considered ancestral. Diploid chromosome number shows the most interesting pattern, with *Allenopithecus* at 48, *Erythrocebus* and *C. (Miopithecus)* at 54, and other species modally at 60, 66, and 72. This separation by units of 6 is even more suggestive in light of the universal diploid number of 42 in Papionini. As first discussed by Delson (1975a), there may have been a series of sectional duplications, such that 6 metacentric chromosomes divided into 12, with more acrocentrics found at higher diploid numbers. Such mass duplications might have enhanced rapid speciation, either early in cercopithecin history (as suggested by Delson) or more recently, as implied by Murray's (1975) ideas of niche separation in *Cercopithecus.* Once the relationships among species of this genus are better understood, it may be possible to test these two alternatives: If widely differing species have similar diploid numbers, the increases probably were late; but if each number "level" contains related species, one of which is perhaps linked to higher-numbered groups, a sequential pattern might be substantiated.

In terms of a scenario for evolution of the tribe, no early fossil evidence exists, and none can be firmly expected, in view of the joint problems of forest soil's poor preservation qualities and the factor of small size

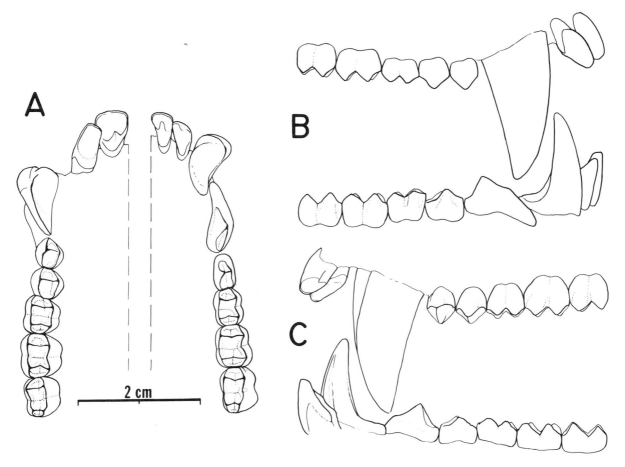

Figure 163. Dental morphology of Cercopithecini. *Erythrocebus patas;* male, modern. A, occlusal view, right upper tooth-row on left, right lower tooth-row on right; B, buccal view; C, lingual view. [By B. Akerbergs.]

hampering visual recovery. Nonetheless, it may be suggested that, roughly 10 MY ago (early late Miocene), one or more small(?) cercopithecines entered the high canopy forest to compete with colobines. *Allenopithecus* may be the most distinctive (or conservative) form, sharing both dental flare and sex-

ual swelling with papionins, but perhaps convergently. The relationships of *Erythrocebus* are unclear, although it has been suggested as specially linked with the semiterrestrial *C. aethiops*, which might tie in with its apparently still increasing range (Hill, 1966).

CERCOPITHECUS Linnaeus, 1758

INCLUDED SUBGENERA
   Cercopithecus (Cercopithecus) and *C. (Miopithecus).*

CERCOPITHECUS (CERCOPITHECUS) Linnaeus, 1758

(= or including: *Cercopithecus* Brunnich, 1772, *nec* Linnaeus; *Cercopithecus* Erxleben, 1777, *nec* Linnaeus; *Cercocephalus* Temminck,

1853, lapsus. *Lasiopyga* Illiger, 1811. "*Monichus*" Oken, 1816, work rejected. *Cebus* Rafinesque, 1815, *nec* Erxleben, 1777. *Callithrix* Reichenbach, 1862, *nec* Erxleben, 1777. *Petaurista* Reichenbach, 1862, *nec* Link, 1795. *Diademia* Reichenbach, 1862. *Mona* Reichenbach, 1862. *Chlorocebus* Gray, 1870. *Cynocebus* Gray, 1870. *Diana* Trouessart, 1878, *nec* Risso, 1826. *Rhinostictus* Trouessart, 1897, *Otopithecus* Trouessart,

1897. *Pogonocebus* Trouessart, 1897. *Allochrocebus* Elliot, 1913. *Insignicebus* Elliot, 1913. *Melanocebus* Elliot, 1913. *Neocebus* Elliot, 1913. *Neopithecus* Elliot, 1913, *nec* Abel, 1902, lapsus for *Neocebus*. *Rhinostigma* Elliot, 1913.

DISTRIBUTION

Late Pliocene (Rodolfian) to modern. Fossil in Ethiopia and Kenya; living throughout sub-Saharan Africa.

KNOWN SPECIES

Cercopithecus diana (Linnaeus, 1758), type species, and numerous living forms whose classification remains obscure.

FOSSIL LOCALITIES of *Cercopithecus* spp.: Kanam East (674); Kubi Algi (699); Omo Group Usno (694), Shungura mbrs. B (696), G (750), J (794), Koobi Fora upper mbr. (796); Afar Late Pleistocene (1074).

CERCOPITHECUS (MIOPITHECUS) I. Geoffroy, 1842

(= or including: *Miopithecus* I. Geoffroy, 1842; *Meiopithecus* Reichenbach, 1862, lapsus; *Myiopithecus* Wallace, 1876, lapsus.)

DISTRIBUTION

Modern only, western central Africa.

KNOWN SPECIES

Cercopithecus (M.) talapoin Schreber, 1774, subgeneric type

DISCUSSION

Cercopithecus, the most widespread and abundant genus of African monkeys, is here divided into two subgenera. In the nominate subgenus 12 to 21 species are recognized, depending upon the reviewer, and arranged in numerous subgenera, superspecies, or species-groups (compare Hill, 1966; Kuhn, 1967; Thorington and Groves, 1970). No further attempt at grouping is made here. *Cercopithecus (Cercopithecus)* is the most generalized of the Cercopithecini in morphology, although the numerous sympatric species testify to its ethological specializations. Most species are arboreal frugivores, although some come to the ground at times, and others concentrate on leaf-eating. *Cercopithecus aethiops* is the most anatomically distinct, being adapted to a more commonly terrestrial existence, which is reflected in its skeleton. All species are of small size, with skull and dentition of

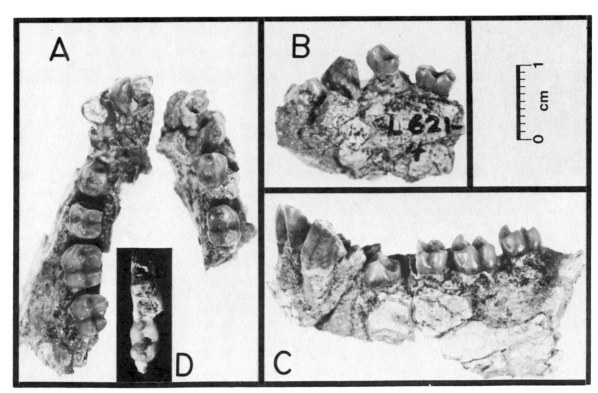

Figure 164. *Cercopithecus* spp. Pliocene, Africa, Partial ?male mandible with left $I_{\overline{1}}$–$C_{\overline{1}}$, $P_{\overline{4}}$–$M_{\overline{3}}$, right $P_{\overline{3}}$–$M_{\overline{1}}$: A, occlusal view; B, right lingual view; C, left lateral view. Juvenile right corpus fragment with erupting $dP_{\overline{4}}$: D, occlusal view. The scale is for A–C; D is at 1.5 times scale. [A–C with permission from G. G. Eck, *Journal of Human Evolution 6*, 1977. Copyright by Academic Press Inc. (London) Ltd.]

a rather stereotyped form, rendering identification of fragmentary fossils essentially impossible. The talapoin, C. *(Miopithecus)*, is the smallest species of *Cercopithecus*, indeed of all Cercopithecidae. Verheyen (1962) has shown rather clearly that it is essentially identical to "typical" *Cercopithecus* in cranial morphology, its small size resulting in a somewhat neotenous appearance comparable to the juvenile stages of larger species. It is here ranked as a subgenus on the basis of soft-anatomical and behavioral distinctions, including the presence of female sexual skin and female position in the large troop. No fossils are known, nor are any expected, given its habitat in swampy forest regions.

Fossil material referable to *Cercopithecus** is extremely rare, having been reported only in the past few years from two regions. The most complete specimen is a partial mandible (Figure 164, A–C) from the middle levels at Omo, described by Eck and Howell (1972). Despite extensive metrical and some morphological comparison, they were unable to allocate the specimen to any living species, attesting to the uniformity of morphology noted above. Other Omo specimens include only a partial mandible with one tooth and five isolated teeth from several localities (Eck, 1976). At East Rudolf, M. Leakey (1976) has reported two different taxa cf. *Cercopithecus*, neither of which is thought to be conspecific with the Omo species. A very small species is known from a mandible with $M_{\overline{2}\text{-}\overline{3}}$ in the oldest, Kubi Algi horizon, while a younger tooth and partial femur suggested C. *aethiops* to Leakey, but further comparison is needed to support this view and distinction from the Omo sample. A juvenile mandible with erupting $dP_{\overline{4}}$ (Figure 164D) from Kanam East was collected by L. Leakey in 1935 but has remained undescribed; it appears to represent a very small species of *Cercopithecus*, potentially that known from contemporaneous Kubi Algi deposits. C. Jolly (personal communication) has identified numerous remains from as yet uncertainly dated upper levels in the Afar region.

ERYTHROCEBUS Trouessart, 1897

DISTRIBUTION
Modern, central Africa, Mauretania to northern Tanzania.

KNOWN SPECIES
Erythrocebus patas (Schreber, 1775), type species

ALLENOPITHECUS Lang, 1923

DISTRIBUTION
Modern, eastern Congo basin of central Africa.

KNOWN SPECIES
Allenopithecus nigroviridis (Pocock, 1907), type species

DISCUSSION

These two monotypic genera are clearly related to *Cercopithecus*, but are more distinctive than the talapoin. *Erythrocebus* is a medium-sized form, the largest of the Cercopithecini, which inhabits the open savannahs south of (and perhaps into) the Sahara, but does not penetrate farther south as do baboons and vervets (C. *aethiops*). Its postcranial skeleton reflects this terrestrial adaptation in joint structure, digit shortening and limb elongation. Cranially and dentally, it is similar to Cercopithecus except that the teeth may be slightly elongate (Delson, 1973). *Allenopithecus* is little known, either in the wild or in museums, and cranially demonstrates no special characters, so that it is often included within the genus *Cercopithecus*. Yet its dentition, as first discussed by Lang (1923), is quite distinctive. Although the third lower molar lacks a hypoconulid, and the lower incisors appear to bear lingual enamel, the cheek teeth present a high degree of flare, giving them almost the appearance of a *Cercocebus*, as opposed to the rather straight-sided teeth of other cercopithecins. This development might be a convergence on papionins, but could well represent synapomorphy or conservative retention. An ectostylid is also present on (some?) lower molars at the base of the median buccal notch.

Tribe Papionini
Burnett, 1828

(= or including: Papionidae Burnett, 1828, restricted. Cercocebini Jolly, 1966, in part. Papionini: Kuhn, 1967. Cynopithecinae: Hill, 1970).

---

*For the species termed "*Cercopithecus*" *asnoti*, see under *Presbytis*.

DISTRIBUTION

Late Miocene (late Turolian, Lothagamian) to modern. Old World, see under family.

INCLUDED TAXA

Subtribes Papionina, Macacina and Theropithecina.

DISCUSSION

Of the two cercopithecine tribes, Papionini is by far the more successful and widely distributed, as well as the one with a good fossil record, including more extinct genera (5) than living ones (4). The division of the subfamily into tribes was first suggested in a modern sense by Jolly (1966), who separated out a *Theropithecus* group (mistakenly including a number of genera more closely linked to *Papio*). However, overlooking the rules of nomenclature, he based the name on *Cercocebus*. Kuhn (1967) made the division as accepted here for the first time. A number of students (e.g., Thorington and Groves, 1970) have not considered the distinction between the two cercopithecine subtaxa "important" enough to name, while others (especially Hill, 1970, 1974; also Maier, 1970) both ignore the rules and, in our view, overrank all higher taxa.

The majority of living papionins are eclectic omnivores, mostly terrestrial and semiterrestrial, but some macaques and most mangabeys are strongly arboreal and frugivorous. A number of cranial and dental features appear to characterize the whole group and may be included in an ancestral morphotype, although there is some variation among taxa even in these. The cheek teeth of most papionins (except *Theropithecus*) are rather conservative, remaining essentially unchanged from the early cercopithecid form. Thus, there is a hypoconulid on $M_{\overline{3}}$ (except in rare cases), the trigonid basin is relatively long, and tooth relief (notch depth) is low (Delson, 1973, 1975a). Flare tends to be increased, especially in *Cercocebus*, but also in the other genera. Accessory cuspules are common in the lingual notches of lower molars, and the $M_{\overline{3}}$ often has a large sixth cusp (tuberculum sextum) between hypoconulid and entoconid (see the illustration of macaque teeth, typical for this tribe, in Figure 165). Such accessory cuspules are also common in the buccal notches of uppers, but a fifth, distal cusp is rare on $M^{\underline{3}}$, which instead may be reduced distally. In distal view, the tooth margin is symmetrical, unlike the situation in colobines. If the mesial and distal widths are compared on individual teeth, the former is greater for $dP^{\underline{3}}$–$M^{\underline{3}}$, as in all cercopithecids; on the lowers,

however, the distal width is generally greater for $dP_{\overline{3}}$–$M_{\overline{1}}$, but not on $M_{\overline{2-3}}$. This pattern is considered ancestral for the tribe, and perhaps for the subfamily, but the cercopithecid morphotype includes $M_{\overline{3}}$ mesial width less than distal (as in colobines and hominoids). In two papionin species studied by Delson (1973)—*M. sylvanus* and *C. torquatus*—the mesial width was greater on $M_{\overline{1}}$ but less on $M_{\overline{2}}$, suggesting independent derivation from the postulated ancestral condition. Of the premolars, $P_{\overline{3}}$ is elongate with a rather large distal fovea, while $P_{\overline{4}}$ is wide, with an inflated rather than flangelike mesiobuccal region, and the metaconid is always greater than or equal to the protoconid in both height and width.

The anterior dentition of papionins is more distinctive, especially characterized by the apparent (nearly?) complete lack of enamel on the lingual surfaces of the lower incisors, effectively producing a self-sharpening, nearly rodent-like chisel edge on these teeth. This point was first discussed by Noble (1969) and examined further (without histological work) by Delson (1973), who found no indication of lingual enamel on newly erupted teeth in museum specimens of all papionin genera, although both colobines and cercopithecins have a normal enamel sheath. The upper incisors of papionins are strongly enlarged, with both high and wide (long) crowns, the I^2 often inclined apically and mesially so that it contacts the incisal edge of I^1, although their roots are far separated.

In the cranium, papionins are similar to ancestral cercopithecines, but the face is even more elongated. This may be due at least partly to the greater overall size of the animals, which also leads to a rearward inclination of the mandibular ramus and perhaps a lower neurocranial vault. As Jolly (1970b) has discussed, the relative size and placement of the sagittal crest and temporal musculature, as well as ramus position (see also Vogel, 1962), are linked to the feeding mechanism, a posteriorly placed crest and inclined ramus correlating with large and powerfully used incisors. The terrestrial habitus of many papionins is reflected in their postcranial morphology, as indicated above for the subfamily, but, again, the more arboreal macaques and mangabeys are often quite morphologically different from baboons. In terms of soft anatomy, cheek pouches are present, as for the subfamily; ischial callosities are often contiguous or confluent across the midline; female sexual swelling is pronounced in almost all species (except some small macaques, presumably a secondary reduction on be-

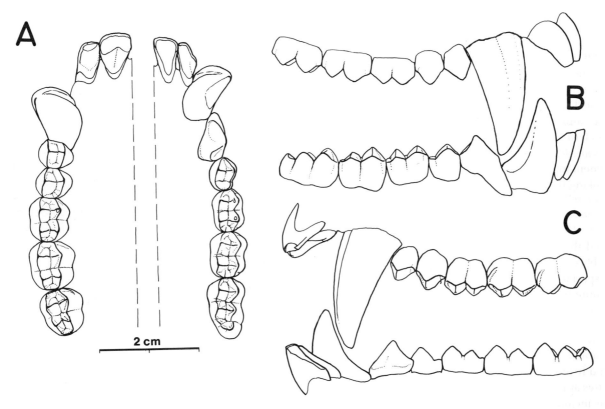

Figure 165. Dental morphology of "typical" Papionini. *Macaca thibetana;* modern, male. A, occlusal view, right upper tooth-row on left, right lower tooth-row on right; B, buccal view; C, lingual view. [By B. Akerbergs.]

havioral grounds?); and the diploid chromosome number is a constant 42.

A combination of morphological and zoogeographical data has led to the suggestion of division of the tribe into three subtaxa whose cladistic relationships cannot yet be fully ascertained. A similar view, although expressed at higher rank, has been taken by Maier (1970) and, with some alterations, by Hill (1970, 1974), while Jolly (1966) originally separated only *Theropithecus* from other papionins but later suggested a possible closer linking of the African forms among themselves. The character states which support this treatment are presented under the subtribes below, but they include the dental and cranial autapomorphies of *Theropithecus*, the shape of the muzzle, development of maxillary and mandibular fossae, molar flare, and paleogeography.

As suggested by Delson (1973, 1975b), a scenario for

the differentiation and dispersal of the group might begin with the separation of cercopithecins from papionins roughly 10 MY ago (see Figure 162). After that time, one or more species of moderate-sized papionins may have spread over much of Africa, especially in the woodland–savannah intergrades, with increasing use of the terrestrial habitat. At least one of these species would have reduced lingual enamel on lower incisors and perhaps developed female catamenial swelling and approximated callosities, as well as the dental traits noted above as ancestral for the tribe. The facial skull probably would have been of macaque-like form, with sloping dorsal profile and small lateral fossae, if any. During the earlier late Miocene, it may have been possible for such semi-terrestrial animals to cross the proto-Sahara with little difficulty, although there is evidence of its presence at that time. The populations at Marceau (Algeria) and

Ongoliba (Zaire) might represent such ancestral papionins (see under *Macaca*).

But, by the end of the Miocene, some drying of the peri-Mediterranean lands had occurred, as reflected in fossil mammal assemblages. On top of this, the Mediterranean basin itself became desiccated during the later Messinian (ca. 6 MY ago), from tectonic causes (Hsü *et al.*, 1977), which in turn probably led to increased aridity on land. At this time, the Sahara may well have become a harsh barrier to migration between south–central and northern Africa, cutting off gene flow between populations of early papionins. A northern group, ancestors of the macaques, were able to depart Africa at this time, probably by an eastern or perhaps a western (Gibraltar) route, to enter and spread across Eurasia. In the south, the more conservative early papionins, perhaps much like known *Parapapio* in cranial shape, occupied a number of habitats, both forest and fringing parkland, eventually radiating into the several known genera. Following Jolly (1970b, 1972), the original niche of *Theropithecus* may have been edaphic grasslands, into which their ancestors moved in the early Pliocene (or late Miocene) and from which they spread into drier savannah, only to be replaced in turn by *Papio* (*Chaeropithecus*).

The development of highly terrestrial forms would thus seem to be a common parallelism within the Papionini, occurring at least in *Theropithecus*, *Papio*, *Procynocephalus*, and *Paradolichopithecus*, to a lesser degree in some *Cercocebus* and *Macaca* species, and perhaps in the large extinct *Dinopithecus* and *Gorgopithecus* as well. Although the common ancestor of these forms is postulated to have been only semi-terrestrial, that adaptation perhaps canalized morphogenetic patterns in its descendants, so that a high degree of terrestrial, cursorial locomotion was attained through continuation of this early trend.

SUBTRIBE PAPIONINA
Burnett, 1828 (new rank)

(= or including: Papionidae Burnett, 1828 restricted. Papionini Maier, 1970.)

DISTRIBUTION
Late Miocene(?) (early Lothagamian) to modern. Sub-Saharan Africa, fossil in eastern and southern Africa only.
INCLUDED TAXA
Papio, *Cercocebus*, *Parapapio*, *Dinopithecus*, and *Gorgopithecus*.

DISCUSSION

The papioninans are the typical large monkeys of Africa today, including baboons, mangabeys, and mandrills. Only two genera remain extant, each with two subgenera, and a total of seven living species as recognized here. Three extinct genera (two monotypic and inconclusively distinct) plus extinct and still living species of the modern genera bring the fossil species total above a dozen. This total is quite high, compared to, say, the Macacina, and reflects preservation and intensity of collecting due to association with early man, as well as occupation of diverse biotopes. There are few clear-cut characters which link this group together, other than simple geographic proximity and a well-developed trend toward facial elongation. This is most evident, as expected, in the larger forms, most of which also tend to be terrestrial. Another probably shared derived character is the variable development of deep maxillary and mandibular fossae, rare in macaques but also seen in some *Theropithecus* species. There is also a trend to development of a steep anteorbital drop, making the facial profile rather concave. This feature may have developed independently in the several genera which show it, but as *Dinopithecus* and *Gorgopithecus* are so poorly known, and as *Cercocebus* only shows it in an intermediate state, no decision is yet possible. It is probable that *Theropithecus* may also have developed this feature in parallel with *Papio*, in part due to attainment of large size. The ancestral condition is interpreted to be that found in *Parapapio*, which is comparable in this and other characters to *Macaca*. In fact, clear distinction between these two conservative genera is quite difficult at present, reflecting their retention of many cranio-dental traits from the last common papionin ancestor of late Miocene age (see Papionini).

A tentative reconstruction of the history of Papionina is also difficult, as so little is known about the two large "genera" or about the locomotor adaptations of *Parapapio*. The latter genus may well have been semi-terrestrial, like macaques, inhabiting wide reaches of Africa in varying habitats by the end of the Miocene. It may be that the smaller species of *Papio* was the first to develop, but this may only reflect the long preoccupation of paleontologists with Cope's Law of size increase over time. This small form and a larger *Papio*, here ranked as a subspecies of the living *P. hamadryas*, occur at Sterkfontein, perhaps 2.5 MY ago. In earlier deposits, such as Makapan and Laetolil (and probably Hadar and East Rudolf), only *Parapapio* is found, often alongside abundant *Theropithecus*. By the early Pleistocene, *Papio* is the common or only papioninan in most localities, but *Dinopithecus* and *Gorgopithecus* also occur, as does *Theropithecus*, espe-cially in eastern Africa. There is as yet no evidence for the origin of mandrills, *P. (Papio)*, i.e., no fossils demonstrating any of their morphological peculiari-ties. *Cercocebus* has also been recognized in both continental regions recently, but without any clear indication of the history of that genus.

PAPIO Müller, 1773*

DISTRIBUTION

Late Pliocene (Rodolfian) to modern. Fossil in South Africa, Tan-zania to Ethiopia; living in sub-Saharan Africa, southwestern coastal Arabia.

INCLUDED SUBGENERA

Papio (Papio) and *P. (Chaeropithecus)*.

PAPIO (PAPIO) Müller, 1773

(= or including: *Simia (Papio)* Müller, 1773. *Cynocephalus* E. Geoffroy and G. Cuvier, 1795, *nec* Boddaert, 1768: Desmarest, 1820. *Paphio* Gray, 1821, lapsus. *Mandrillus* Ritgen, 1824; *Mandrill* Berthold, 1827, lapsus?. *Simia (Mandril)* Voigt, 1831. *Mormon* Wagner, 1839; Lesson, 1840; *nec* Illiger, 1811. *Sphinx* Gray, 1843, *nec* Linnaeus, 1758. *Drill* Reichenbach, 1862. *Chaeropithecus* Gray, 1870, *nec* Gervais, 1839. *Maimon* Trouessart, 1904, *nec* Wagner, 1839.)

DISTRIBUTION

Modern. Central West African rain forest, Nigeria to Congo, Fernando Po.

KNOWN SPECIES

1. *Papio (P.) sphinx* (Linnaeus, 1758) type species
2. *Papio (P.) leucophaeus* (Cuvier, 1807)

PAPIO (CHAEROPITHECUS) Gervais, 1839

(= or including: *Papio* Erxleben, 1777, *nec* Müller, 1773. *Cercopithecus* Erxleben, 1777, in part. *Cynocephalus* E. Geoffroy and G. Cuvier, 1795, *nec* Boddaert, 1768. *Simia (Chaeropithecus)* Gervais, 1839; Senechal, 1839. *Choeropithecus* Reichenbach, 1862. *Hamadryas* Lesson, 1840, *nec* Hübner, 1806. *Cercopithecus* Linnaeus, 1758: Peters, 1853, in part. *Choiropithecus* Reichenbach, 1862. *Comopithecus* Allen, 1925. *Dinopithecus* Broom, 1937: Broom, 1940, in part. *Papio (Chaeropithecus)*: Ellerman, Morrison-Scott and Heyman, 1953. *Parapapio* Jones, 1937: Freedman, 1957, in part.)

DISTRIBUTION

Late Pliocene (Rodolfian) to modern. Fossil in South Africa, Tan-zania to Ethiopia; modern in sub-Saharan Africa, except western rain forest and desert, and southwestern coastal Arabia.

KNOWN SPECIES

3. *Papio (C.) hamadryas* (Linnaeus, 1758) subgeneric type species (with subspecies):

a. *Papio (C.) h. hamadryas* (Linnaeus, 1758)

b. *Papio (C.) h. cynocephalus* (Linnaeus, 1766)
c. *Papio (C.) h. ursinus* (Kerr, 1792)
(=*Papio spelaeus* Broom, 1936b; *P. ursinus spelaeus* Freedman, 1976.)
LOCALITIES: Swartkrans b (930); Witkrans (1262); "Pretoria" (1264).
d. *Papio (C.) h. papio* (Desmarest, 1820)
e. *Papio (C.) h. anubis* (Lesson, 1827)
f. *Papio (C.) h. kindae* Lönnberg, 1919; new combination
g. *Papio (C.) h. robinsoni* Freedman, 1957; new combination
(=*Dinopithecus ingens* Broom, 1937: Broom, 1940, in part. *Parapapio* sp.: Robinson, 1952. *Papio robinsoni* Freedman, 1957. *Parapapio whitei* Broom, 1940: Freedman, 1957, 1976, in part.)
LOCALITIES: Sterkfontein (706); Bolts Farm (740); Swartkrans a★ (752); Schurweberg (754); Kromdraai A (762); Cooper's (764); Kromdraai B (782); Gladysvale (1030); Sterkfontein Dump 16 (1084).
4. *Papio (C.)* cf. *hamadryas* sspp.
(=*Papio* sp: Remane, 1925; Eck, 1976. *Papio* sp. nov.: M. Leakey and R. Leakey, 1976, in part.)
LOCALITIES: Omo Group, Usno (694), Shungura mbrs. A–G, J, K (672), (696), (712), (716), (726), (738), (750), (794), (806); Olduvai Gorge; ?Bed I (760), ?Bed II (792), horizon uncertain [?Bed IV (856).]
5. *Papio (C.) izodi* Gear, 1926
(= *Papio izodi* Gear, 1926. *Papio africanus* Broom, 1934, in part. *Parapapio izodi*: Broom, 1940. *Parapapio angusticeps* Broom, 1940. *Papio angus-ticeps*: Freedman, 1957. *Parapapio antiquus* Haughton, 1925: Freedman, 1957, in part. *Papio wellsi* Freedman, 1961a. *Parapapio whitei*: Freed-man, 1965, in part. *Papio* sp.: Eisenhart, 1975.)
LOCALITIES: Sterkfontein (706); Taung★ (730); Kromdraai A (762); Cooper's (764); Minaar's Cave (766); Kromdraai B (782).
6. *Papio (C.) baringensis* R. Leakey, 1969
LOCALITIES: JM 90/91★, Chemeron Fm. (724).

DISCUSSION

Papio is a medium to large cercopithecine with an extended muzzle, steep anteorbital drop, usually deep facial (mandibular and maxillary) fossae, and strong sexual dimorphism in cranial (and sometimes dental) size and shape. If a sagittal crest occurs on the skull roof, it is placed rather posteriorly, well behind bregma, and is usually highest at inion and confluent with a nuchal crest. The postcranium presents numer-ous specializations indicative of adaptation to terres-trial life (Figure 161), although limb bone robusticity is variable. In modern forms, external characters such as tail length and carriage, facial and hair coloration, and size vary widely as well. *Papio (Papio)*, the more ar-

---

*Delson and Napier (1976) have petitioned the ICZN to rule on the correct generic names for mandrills and baboons, essentially determining to which of these the name *Papio* belongs. Pending a ruling, current usage (of Delson, 1975a, and others) is retained here.

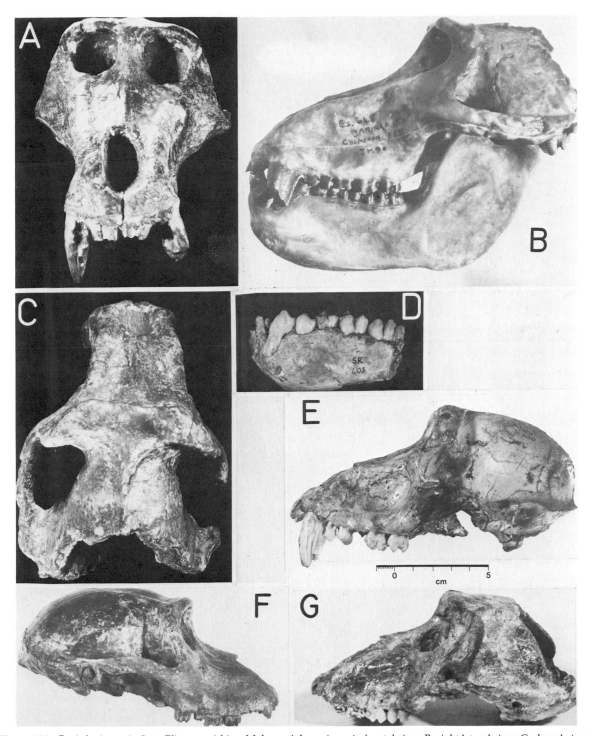

Figure 166. *Papio baringensis*. Late Pliocene, Africa. Male partial cranium: A, frontal view; B, right lateral view; C, dorsal view. *Papio hamadryas robinsoni*. Late Pliocene, Africa. Male left corpus with $C_{\bar{1}}$–$M_{\bar{3}}$: D, lateral view. *Papio izodi*. Late Pliocene, Africa. Male cranium (*P. "angusticeps"*): E, left lateral view. Female cranium (*P. "wellsi"*): F, right lateral view. Male cranium: G, left lateral view. The scale refers to all parts. [E from Freedman (1957), courtesy of L. Freedman.]

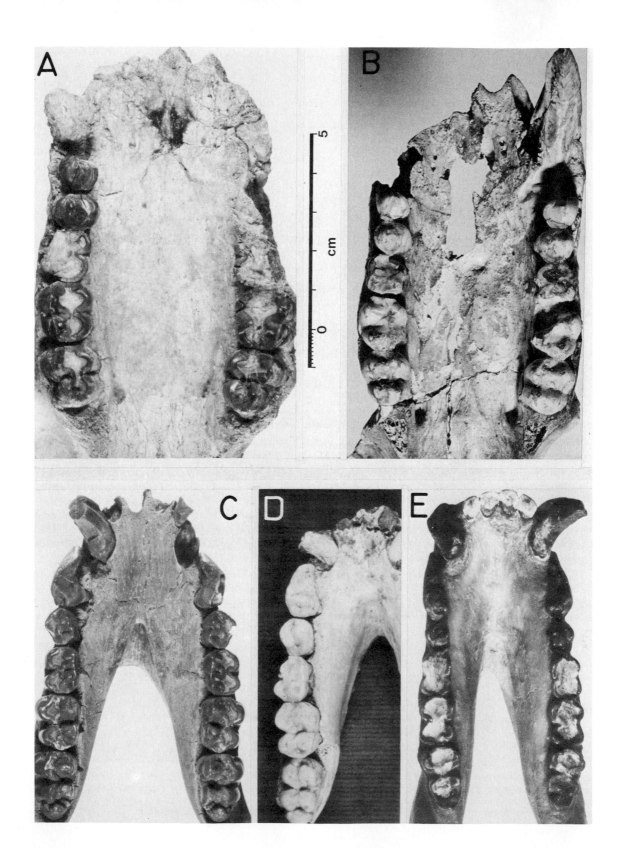

boreal form, is restricted to western rain forests, often has strong facial coloration, as well as a short tail, somewhat lower crowned teeth, more frequent sagittal cresting, ridged male muzzle, and distinctive typical social organization. As yet, there is no fossil record of these two species.

Typical or "savannah" baboons are fairly well represented in the fossil record, but the taxonomy of both living and extinct forms is unstable. Only one modern species is recognized here, although recent studies have accepted up to five, with numerous subspecies. Part of the problem is that earlier authors essentially named multiple subspecies or even species based on isolated populations or individuals, without considering intergradation. Jolly (1965, 1966) discussed some of these problems and suggested that the majority of typical forms were part of a single species which demonstrated a number of clinal trends linking the numerous populations spread across Africa. Only *P. hamadryas* was held apart, due to its distinctive social organization, ecology, and external morphology. More recently, however, Nagel (1973) demonstrated a zone of hybridization and genetic interchange at the boundary between *P. "cynocephalus" anubis* and *P. hamadryas* in Ethiopia, and these populations appear to be conspecific as well (see Jolly and Brett, 1973).

Two size groups of *Papio* baboons occurred in eastern and southern Africa during the late Pliocene and early Pleistocene. The large southern form was described as *Papio robinsoni* in most detail by Freedman (1957, also 1965) from Swartkrans (Figure 166D), Kromdraai, and Bolts Farm. Freedman and Brain (1972) reported additional specimens from Kromdraai B, and Eisenhart (1974) showed convincingly that some "*Parapapio whitei*" from Sterkfontein were in reality *P. robinsoni*. In his original discussion, Freedman (1957) compared fossils only with "*P. ursinus*," finding such minor differences as the flatter muzzle dorsum, maxillary ridges raised higher than nasal bones, and, in a single male specimen preserving this region, partial overlapping of the nasals by the maxillae at their upper end, near nasion. Minor differences in size and dental proportion were also cited, but overall similarity to modern *Papio* stressed. As com-

pared to *P. baringensis* below, the incisors of *P. h. robinsoni* are large, and other features of the skull and dentition (Figure 167, B and D) appear to be no more different from any living subspecies than they are from each other.

Other large forms of *Papio* are known in East Africa, but they are rarer than might be expected, given the wide distribution of the genus today. Jolly (1972) has explained this by suggesting that early *Papio* was more of a forest or forest-fringe dweller, while the moist open grasslands were inhabited by early *Theropithecus* (q.v.), who eventually were replaced by the more eclectic, opportunistic *Papio*. A juvenile cranium from Olduvai (Remane, 1925) compares well to modern specimens of similar dental age, but its exact provenance is unknown; other fragmentary Olduvai jaws from Beds I and II are probably *Papio* but require further analysis. Eck (1977) has reported several fragmentary remains from the Omo sequence (Figure 167, A and C) and new specimens were reconstructed while this work was in press. These share the lack of facial fossae and flat male muzzle, as in *Dinopithecus* (q.v.), where they are best referred, although the remaining cranial morphology preserved is not clearly distinct from *P. hamadryas*. On the other hand, an associated mandible and skull (broken behind bregma) (Figure 166, A–C) from the Chemeron Fm. was named *P. baringensis* by R. Leakey (1969). M. and R. Leakey (1976) have described another fragmentary specimen and stressed the distinctions of *P. baringensis* from *P. hamadryas*: small, nonprotruding incisors (Figure 167E), extremely marked postorbital constriction (Figure 166C) with anteriorly situated junction of temporal lines, and infraorbital region differing in more anteriorly placed maxillary fossa, zygomatic bone with wide orbital process and smooth connection with the maxilla, and robust zygomatic arch. The small incisors are perhaps conservative, as the Leakeys indicate, although those of both *Parapapio* and *Macaca* are not so small; the postorbital narrowing is probably derived rather than ancestral. A more complete neurocranium might demonstrate a functional complex involving smaller incisors, larger molars, differently placed temporal musculature, robust zygoma-

---

Figure 167. *Papio.* Pliocene, Africa. Dentitions in occlusal view. ?*Papio* sp., Omo: A, male palate with right C^1–M^3, left M^{1-3}; C, male mandible with right P_3–M_3, left C_1–M_3. *P. hamadryas robinsoni*: B, male palate with left C^1–M^3, right P^3–M^3; D, portion of male mandible with left C_1–M_3, part right C_1. *P. baringensis*: E, male mandible with complete dentition. [A and C with permission from G. G. Eck, *Journal of Human Evolution*, 6, 1977. Copyright by Academic Press Inc. (London) Ltd.]

tic arch, and strong postorbital constriction, all results of masticatory adaptations in some ways paralleling those of *Theropithecus*. A phyletic relationship to the latter genus is not suggested here and is not likely, but functional convergence is a possibility (as in *Libypithecus* also, perhaps).

At present, there are no crania from East Africa which might be regarded as small forms of *Papio*, but three full species have been named in South Africa. *Papio izodi* and *Papio wellsi* were based on damaged female skulls from Taung, but more complete specimens (Figure 166, F and G) show them to be variants of a single taxon. A closely similar juvenile cranium was recognized at Sterkfontein by Eisenhart (1974). *Papio izodi* differs from the similarly sized living *P. hamadryas kindae* in having relatively larger teeth and orbits, especially. More similar to the modern form are apparently younger fossils termed *Papio angusticeps* (Figure 166E), which vary somewhat among known samples. The presence of these small specimens alongside larger *P. h. robinsoni* suggests them to be specifically distinct from *P. hamadryas*. Considering the total known variation, it appears reasonable to refer them to *Papio izodi*, as previously suggested tentatively by Wells (1971) and Delson (1973, 1974a, 1975a). *Papio izodi* is thus the only small species recognized from the South African caves, and it may be the case that some *Parapapio* specimens, especially those reported from Taung, Kromdraai, and perhaps Swartkrans, should be referred here also (see also under *Cercocebus*).

The pattern of evolution within *Papio* has rarely been considered, as few authors (except Freedman, 1957) had sufficient material to attempt an analysis. Freedman, advocating a different systematic arrangement from that presented herein, started with the premise that Taung was oldest and that *P. izodi*

was somehow close to *Parapapio antiquus*, a point doubted here. He did not know of the presence of early *Papio* of both sizes at Sterkfontein, however. At present, it seems that Sterkfontein is the oldest locality in Africa containing undoubted *Papio*, and both large and small species occur there. At earlier sites (Makapan, Laetolil, early Omo, and Hadar), only *Parapapio* and *Theropithecus* occur, suggesting that *Papio* may have originated after 3.0 MY. Associated (or otherwise allocated) postcranial elements of small *Papio* and *Parapapio*, as well as detailed cranial comparisons among *Papio* species, may eventually indicate more clearly the morphoclines involved here, and thus the origin of *Papio*'s adaptation to terrestrial life and its probably concomitant high degree of dimorphism. The small *Papio* may have been an early version, so to speak, but this is not documented in the fossil record. Moreover, it is about the same size as the smallest living race (*P. h. kindae*), often thought secondarily small. It might, in fact, be hard to argue for full species status for *P. izodi* in the absence of postcranial material, except that it is sympatric with *P. h. robinsoni* at four localities at least. Perhaps a small *Papio* arose to fill or overlap the' niche occupied by *Parapapio jonesi*, while *Parapapio whitei* was replaced by early *P. hamadryas*. Then at Taung, *Parapapio broomi* was locally replaced by *P. antiquus*, although it occurred at the roughly contemporaneous Bolts Farm alongside *P. h. robinsoni*. Finally, at the apparently youngest sites, Kromdraai and Swartkrans, only *Papio* (and often a "giant" relative) occurs. It must have been during the middle Pleistocene that the smaller version finally gave way completely, perhaps in competition with the larger *P. hamadryas* and/or *Cercopithecus aethiops*. Alternatively, it may merely have represented an arid-country variety (like *P. h. kindae*).

CERCOCEBUS E. Geoffroy, 1812

(= or including: *Aethiops* Martin, 1841 type species uncertain; *Leptocebus* Trouessart, 1904, type species uncertain; *Cercopithecoides* Mollet, 1947: Broom and Hughes, 1949, in part. *Parapapio* Jones, 1937: Freedman, 1957, in part.)

DISTRIBUTION

Late Pliocene to early Pleistocene (Rodolfian), modern. Fossil in South Africa, Kenya and possibly Tanzania and Ethiopia; living in central Africa.

INCLUDED SUBGENERA

Cercocebus (*Cercocebus*) and *C.* (*Lophocebus*)

CERCOCEBUS (CERCOCEBUS) E. Geoffroy, 1812

KNOWN SPECIES
1. *Cercocebus torquatus* Kerr 1792, type species
2. *Cercocebus galeritus* Peters, 1879

CERCOCEBUS (LOPHOCEBUS) Palmer, 1903

(= or including: *Semnocebus* Gray, 1870, *nec* Lesson, 1840. *Cercolophocebus* Matschie, 1914.)

KNOWN SPECIES
3. *Cercocebus* (*L.*) *albigena* (Gray, 1850), subgeneric type
4. *Cercocebus* (*L.*) *aterrimus* (Oudemans, 1890)

KNOWN FOSSILS

Cercocebus spp. indeterminate.

(= or including: *Cercopithecoides williamsi* Mollett, 1947: Broom and Hughes, 1949, in part. *Parapapio jonesi* Broom, 1940: Freedman, 1957, etc., in part. *Cercocebus* sp.: Delson, 1975a, 1973; Eisenhart, 1975, 1974; M. Leakey, 1976; M. and R. Leakey, 1976. Papionini indet. sp. A: Eck, 1976, 1977.)

LOCALITIES: Kanam East (674); Omo Group, Usno (694), Shungura members B, C (696), (712); Makapansgat (700); East Rudolf, Koobi Fora Fm., Lower, Upper and Ileret mbrs. (728), (796), (798); Swartkrans a (752); Olduvai Upper Bed II (804).

DISCUSSION

The mangabeys represent a group of small to moderate-sized species now generally arranged in two species-groups. The *torquatus*-group is more terrestrial in behavior and more outwardly similar to *Papio*, but recent biomolecular studies (Cronin and Sarich, 1976; Hewett-Emmett, Cook and Barnicot, 1976) indicate strong differences from "savannah" baboons at least. On the other hand, the *albigena*-group is almost wholly arboreal, cranially more distinctive and unlike *Papio*, but supposedly biochemically closer to *P. hamadryas* than to *C. torquatus*. Morphologically, the two species-groups are broadly similar in size, outward appearance (long tails, whitish eyelids and hair pattern), and deeply excavated suborbital maxillary fossae. In other features, their similarities are mainly those of all Papionini, especially some shared with *Papio*, but there is some serious question as to their continued union in a single genus. For the present, the long outmoded genus *Lophocebus* is resuscitated at subgeneric level, but further studies (C. P. Groves, personal communication) may indicate full generic separation more suitable.

The main distinctions between *C. (Cercocebus)* and *C. (Lophocebus)* which may be of use in paleontology relate to the facial fossae and the dental wear pattern. While females of the two groups appear nearly indistinguishable, males of *C. (Cercocebus)* present less extremely excavated maxillary fossae than those of *C. (Lophocebus)*, although the feature is variable. The facial profile in both subgenera is almost as smoothly concave as in *Parapapio*, not as steeply dropping anteorbitally as in *Papio*. The face may be longer and the inclination greater in *C. (Cercocebus)*, while the frontal rises higher in *C. (Lophocebus)* and inion is placed quite high. The nasal bones of *C. (Lophocebus)* are relatively concave, rather than straight, and the malar foramen is large, not minute as in *C. (Cercocebus)*. Finally, the face

is narrower than the braincase in *C. (Lophocebus)*, the reverse in the nominate subgenus.

Dentally, *C. (Lophocebus)* presents a wear pattern as in other typical Papionini, with the lower molar buccal cusps planing down faster than the lingual ones. In *C. torquatus* and *C. galeritus*, however, the molars wear to a flatter surface, with lingual cusps wearing as rapidly as buccal ones on lower molars. This suggests a more frugivorous diet, with teeth adapted to crushing, not slicing, but morphometric analysis of unworn second molars by Kay (1978) revealed the opposite: In *C. (Cercocebus)*, the teeth plotted out closer to colobines and other folivorous forms than in *C. albigena*. In yet a third character, relative size of the teeth as compared to skull size appears to be greater in *C. (Cercocebus)*, a situation which Kay found to hold for cercopithecines versus colobines generally. Moreover, all *Cercocebus* teeth tend to have a high degree of lateral flare, that is, they widen strongly from cusp apexes toward the cervix, providing extra wear surface when heavily worn; this is especially true of *C. (Cercocebus)*. Finally, the incisors are larger relative to molar size in *C. (Lophocebus)*, which Hylander (1975) has shown also to be correlated with greater relative frugivory (using body mass as the comparison and finding the same contrast between *C. albigena* and *C. torquatus*). Possibly as a correlate, the maxillary diastema is longer compared to palate length in *C. (Lophocebus)*. In sum, it would appear that a mosaic pattern is present in the teeth of the two taxa, bringing them to nearly equal degrees of dietary adaptation. *Cercocebus (Cercocebus)* teeth flare more, are larger relative to body size, and wear flatter, but the individual teeth are more "folivorous" in form and the incisors smaller, the opposite being true of *C. (Lophocebus)*. Until more actual dietary information is available, no further interpretive comments are reasonable. As yet, no detailed study has been made of postcranial differences between the two subgenera.

The identification of fossil material of *Cercocebus* has been a relatively recent occurrence. Specimens are still quite rare and mostly fragmentary, the only partial skull being that from Makapan (Figure 168, A–C), first described by Maier (1971a) as *Parapapio jonesi* and later recognized as more likely to be *Cercocebus* sp. by Eisenhart (1974, 1975), who also assigned to the same taxon four other specimens identified as *P. jonesi* by Freedman (1957, 1961). Unfortunately, the facial area of this juvenile female cranium is lacking, so the full

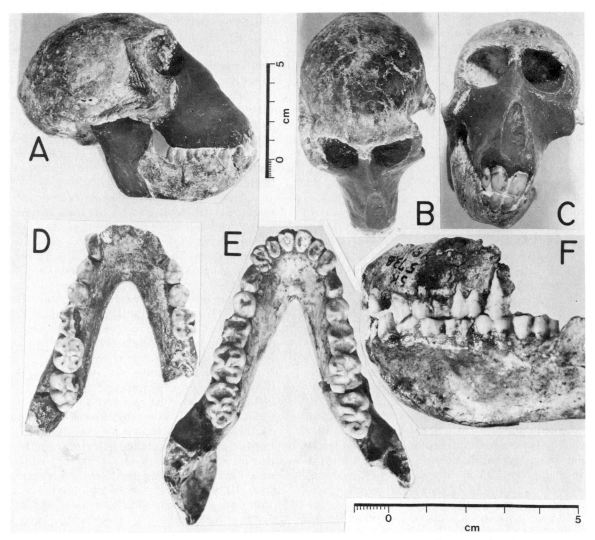

Figure 168. Cf. *Cercocebus* sp. Pliocene, South Africa. Presumably associated reconstructed juvenile female cranium and mandible: A, right lateral view; B, dorsal view; C, frontal view; Female mandible with damaged left $C_{\overline{1}}$–$M_{\overline{3}}$, right $P_{\overline{3}}$–$M_{\overline{3}}$: D, occlusal view. Female mandible with complete dentition: E, occlusal view; F, left lateral view in occlusion with associated partial maxilla with left I^1–M^2 (broken). A–D, E–F may be separate species. Upper scale pertains to A–C; lower scale to D–F.

extent of any facial fossae is not discernible, and the wear pattern is obscured on this and other specimens by both damage and age factors—too young to show the pattern or too old to retain it. Nonetheless, the weak supraorbital tori, deep ophryonic groove, shape of the zygomatic region, and low position of the greatest bi-temporal breadth all indicate assignment to *Cercocebus* rather than to *Parapapio* for the cranium,

and the other similarly sized Makapan specimens fit the dental pattern as far as can be observed (Figure 168D). Several jaws from Swartkrans (Figure 168, E and F) and Kromdraai were also assigned to *P. jonesi* by Freedman (1957), but Eisenhart (1974) suggested them to be distinct in tooth wear and presence of fossae. They might be either small *Papio* or *Cercocebus*; the latter, however, now seems more likely on size and wear grounds. Eisenhart has further suggested that these specimens are morphologically closer to the *C. (Cercocebus)* group than to *C. (Lophocebus)* in both cranial and dental characters.

In East Africa, specimens are more numerous but less complete; most have recently been reviewed by M. and R. Leakey (1976). The only named species of *Cercocebus* in the fossil record is *C. ado* Hopwood (1936), based on a damaged female mandible from Laetolil. This specimen and others from the region are treated here under *Parapapio*, for the somewhat inadequate reasons given there. M. and R. Leakey (1976)

have reported a collection from East Rudolf in which relative incisor size is large compared to molars, and the teeth themselves are large for living members of the genus but comparable to fossils from South Africa. Mandibular fossae are present on some mandibles, while one well-preserved maxilla shows a deep fossa, although damage prevents determination of the presence of an overhanging infraorbital bar. Reference to *Cercocebus* is probably correct, and Eisenhart (1974) has even suggested closer affinity to *C. (Lophocebus)*, on the basis of similar dental wear patterns.

PARAPAPIO Jones, 1937

(= or including: *Papio* "Erxleben, 1777": Haughton, 1925; Gear, 1926, in part; M. and R. Leakey, 1976, in part. *Cercocebus* E. Geoffroy, 1812: Hopwood, 1936. *Papio (Simopithecus)* (Andrews, 1916): Dietrich, 1942. *Brachygnathopithecus* Kitching, 1952, in part. *Papio (Parapapio)*: Delson, 1975a. Papionini gen. et. sp. indet. B: M. and R. Leakey, 1976.)

DISTRIBUTION

?Late Miocene to early Pleistocene, especially late Pliocene (Lothagamian to Rodolfian). South Africa, ?Angola, Kenya, Ethiopia, ?Tanzania.

KNOWN SPECIES

1. *Parapapio broomi* Jones, 1937, type species
(=*Parapapio makapani* Broom and Hughes, 1949. *Brachygnathopithecus peppercorni* Kitching, 1952, in part. *P. whitei*: Freedman, 1965, in part. *P. jonesi*: Maier, 1971a, in part.)
LOCALITIES: Makapan (700); Sterkfontein★ (706); Bolts Farm (740).

2. *Parapapio jonesi* Broom, 1940
LOCALITIES: Makapan (700); Sterkfontein★ (706); ?Taung (730); ?Swartkrans a (752); ?Kromdraai A (762); cf.: Hadar (698), Kubi Algi (699).

3. *Parapapio whitei* Broom, 1940
[=*P. broomi*: Freedman, 1957, 1961b, 1965, in part; Maier, 1971a, in part. (?)*Parapapio* sp.: Arambourg and Mouta, 1954; Antunes, 1962, 1965; Minkoff, 1972.]
LOCALITIES: Makapan (700); Sterkfontein★ (706); ?Leba (756).

4. *Parapapio antiquus* (Haugton, 1925)
(=*Papio antiquus* Haughton, 1925; Gear, 1958. *Papio africanus* Gear, 1926. *Parapapio africanus*: Broom, 1940. *Parapapio antiquus*: Freedman, 1957.)
LOCALITIES: Taung★ (730).

5. ?*Parapapio ado* (Hopwood, 1936), new combination
[=*Cercocebus ado* Hopwood, 1936. *Papio (Simopithecus) serengetensis* Dietrich, 1942, in part. *Parapapio jonesi*: Patterson, 1968. Papionini genus et species indet. (B): M. and R. Leakey, 1976.]
LOCALITIES: Kanapoi (646); Ekora (662); Laetolil★ (666).

6. ?*Parapapio* spp. indet.
[= Papionini gen. et sp. indet. (B): Eck, 1976; M. Leakey, 1976. Papionini genus et species indet. (A): M. and R. Leakey, 1976. Cf. *Papio* sp. nov.: M. and R. Leakey, 1976, in part. Cf. *Papio* sp. indet.: M. and R. Leakey, 1976.]

LOCALITIES: Lothagam-1 (616); East Rudolf, Kubi Algi (699), Koobi Fora Fm. lower mb. (728); Omo Group Usno (694), Shungura mbrs. B (696), C (712), E (726), F (738), G (750), H (776); Olduvai Bed I (760).

DISCUSSION

Parapapio is a medium to large papionin known only in the South and East African fossil record. Its dentition is typical of the group, except that sexual dimorphism in cheek-tooth size appears low. No associated or otherwise identified postcranial remains have yet been described, but some are now known at Hadar. Its main distinction from the other well-known African papionins (*Cercocebus* and *Papio*) lies in its facial shape and proportions. Most important, as clearly stated by Freedman (1957), is the rather straight profile of the muzzle dorsum from nasion to rhinion and beyond, to nasospinale, rather than the relatively steep anteorbital drop found in *Papio* and, to a lesser degree, in *Cercocebus*. While *Papio* thus has a deeply concave facial outline in lateral view, that of *Parapapio* is nearly linear, sometimes with a break at rhinion (see Figures 169 and 170). Eisenhart (1974) further summarized additional characteristics as follows: "Glabella and the supraorbital tori are not pronounced, and no ophryonic groove exists behind the superciliary arches. The maxillary ridges are weak in development, and the suborbital fossae are poorly excavated. The muzzle is wide and extended," and sexual dimorphism in the cranium is limited to size, not shape. In the mandible, also, as far as can be told from poor associations, fossae are weakly excavated, although in the largest individuals there is more hollowing.

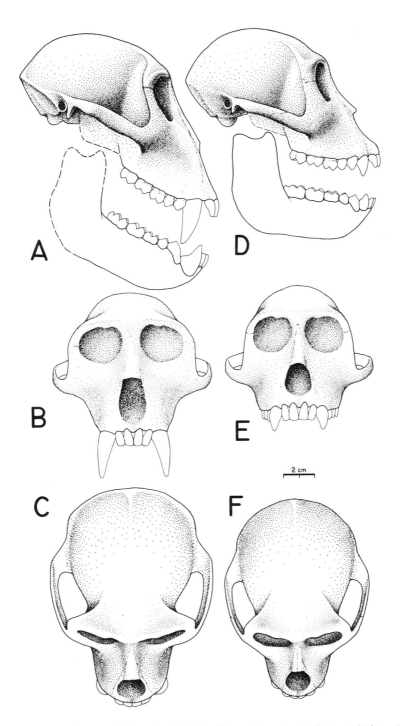

Figure 169. *Parapapio broomi*. Late Pliocene, Africa. Crania in Frankfurt orientation. Male: A, right lateral view; B, frontal view; C, dorsal view. Female: D, right lateral view; E, frontal view; F, dorsal view. [By B. Akerbergs.]

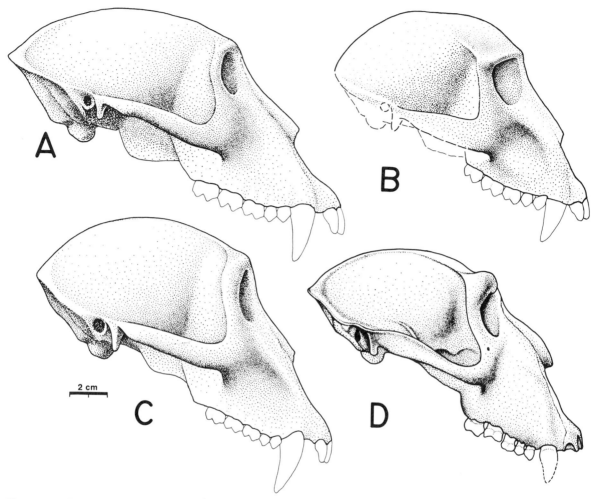

Figure 170. *Parapapio.* Late Pliocene, Africa. Male crania in Frankfurt orientation, right lateral views. A, *P. whitei*; B, *P. antiquus*; C, *P. jonesi* or *P. broomi*; D, *P.* cf. *jonesi*, Hadar. [A–C by B. Akerbergs; D by A. Cleary.]

There has always been a problem about the reality of the distinctions of *Parapapio* from *Papio* and among the species assigned to this genus. Delson (1975a, 1973) ranked the group as a subgenus of *Papio*, but it now seems craniologically more distinct than mandrills, *P. (Papio)*, so that full generic rank is reinstated. M. and R. Leakey (1976) have gone further, suggesting simple variation and full synonymy. It may well be that the description and interpretation of postcranial elements either directly associated with *Parapapio* remains or allocated to *Parapapio* by other paleontological methods will in part solve this problem, at least if these

bones are not typical of the intense terrestrial adaptations of *Papio* spp.

As to individual species, three were originally distinguished at Sterkfontein by Broom (1940) on the basis of molar size. With the recovery of much additional material, Freedman (1957) hesitantly followed the same system, defining his "species" so that Broom's types remained with the size group originally intended. Other workers questioned the validity of these species, but Freedman and Stenhouse (1972) and Freedman (1976) attempted to demonstrate statistically that they were at least a reasonable way of dividing the observed variability at Sterkfontein (and Makapansgat). Eisenhart (1974) produced histograms of several molar measurements at the two sites, revealing a lack of any clear pattern, trimodal or otherwise; instead, there is nearly continuous variation in metric characters. He went on to suggest that only comparative study of cranial morphology would solve the problem and proposed some distinctive criteria for differentiating the species he recognized. More recently, Freedman (1976) has allocated some specimens to different species, especially enlarging *P. broomi*, but four species can still be roughly distinguished.

Parapapio broomi, the type species (Figure 169), has a large skull, but moderate-sized cheek teeth, as well as a short and broad palate, straight nasal profile, and large, deep-set orbits with weak supraorbital tori. The holotype is a damaged male from Sterkfontein, but another good skull appears similar (Figure 169, A–C), while larger specimens from high in the Makapan sequence present longer muzzles but no larger teeth. *Parapapio whitei* from Sterkfontein includes the type female mandible (Figure 171C) and a few dental remains (Figure 171E), but many specimens have now been reallocated to *Papio h. robinsoni*. On the other hand, several new skulls from Makapan (Maier, 1971a; Freedman, 1976; e.g., Figures 170A and 171, B and D) would appear to match the holotype in its large tooth size. These skulls are only a bit larger than those of *P. broomi*, and share its rather elongate M^1 and M^3, but they also are more elongate overall, with a high sagittal crest at inion, deep palate, high and relatively short muzzle (in some individuals), defined maxillary ridges, slight interorbital nasal drop, small orbits, possibly a weak ophryonic groove in some individuals, and weak supraorbital tori. In the caves near Leba, Angola, several workers have recovered some fragmentary juvenile specimens whose teeth are large and whose facial profile suggests *Parapapio*, so they are here tentatively identified as *P. whitei*. The smallest Sterkfontein species is *P. jonesi*, with a damaged female cranium (almost the only skull) as holotype. Some of the small-toothed larger skulls from Makapan (Figure 170C) identified as *P. jonesi* by Eisenhart (1974) and Maier (1971a) have now been transferred to *P. broomi*, but other Makapan material may still be questionably referred to *P. jonesi*, although Eisenhart considered the Makapan population distinctive in having a rather stout, high muzzle and small teeth (Figure 171, A and J).

At Taung, the dominant cercopithecid is a different *Parapapio* species, *P. antiquus*. Only recently have moderately well-preserved skulls become available (Figure 170B) and some of its distinctions clarified. Maier (1971b) showed that the distal reduction of M^3 noted by Freedman (1957, 1965) reflects a general increase in the length of a "P^4–M^2" field, compared to the similarly sized *P. broomi* (compare Figure 171, G and H), which may in turn indicate a forward shift of the area of heaviest chewing. The temporal lines do not meet to form a crest but incline laterally, suggesting a more rearward placement of the main muscle mass, as expected if the chewing focus shifted forward. In addition, the maxillary ridges are prominent, the fossae more deeply excavated, and the nasals raised well above the muzzle dorsum. The female skull is close in size to that of *P. broomi*, but the one well-preserved male (Figure 170B) is significantly smaller than male *P. broomi* (compare Figure 169A), reflecting a lesser emphasis on cranial sexual dimorphism.

Other, even less complete materials assigned to *Parapapio* spp. have been reported from East Africa. M. and R. Leakey (1976) have described a partial skull with very large teeth from Olduvai which appears most similar to *Parapapio*, but, not recognizing a separate genus, they have called it *Papio*. Smaller-sized fossils occur at East Rudolf and Omo. More interesting are the unpublished remains from the Hadar region of Afar, Ethiopia, which include a good male skull (Figure 170D), a female dentition in a crushed face, further dental remains, and some possibly associated postcranials. While the skull is generally similar to Makapan *Parapapio* (*P.* cf. *jonesi*), its nasal bones are even more raised and uniquely curved convexly, and there are some special features of the basicranial region. The same taxon may occur low in the East Rudolf sequence. The oldest sub-Saharan African papionin is a partial mandible from Lothagam-1, of possibly latest Miocene age. It has recently been described by M. and R. Leakey (1976), who did not name it or assign it to a genus, but it is most probably *Parapapio*, in the broad sense of this term.

Nomenclatural as well as taxonomic problems arise when dealing with the several collections of fragmentary dentitions recovered from Laetolil region of Tanzania. Originally, a partial female mandible was reported by Hopwood (1936) and named *Cercocebus ado*. Later, Dietrich (1942) reported additional primates as *Papio (Simopithecus) serengetensis*; the term

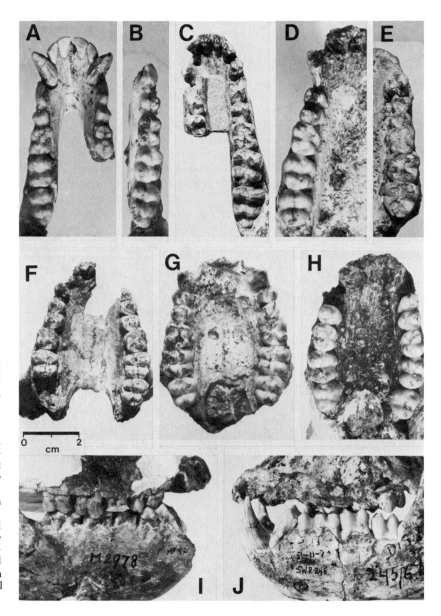

Figure 171. *Parapapio.* Pliocene, South Africa. Dentitions. *P. jonesi.* Nearly adult male mandible with left $I_{\overline{1}}$–$M_{\overline{3}}$, right $I_{\overline{1}}$–$M_{\overline{1}}$: A, occlusal view; J, left lateral view in occlusion with associated maxilla with erupting $M^{\underline{3}}$. Female palate with right $I^{\underline{1}}$, $C^{\underline{1}}$–$M^{\underline{2}}$, left $C^{\underline{1}}$–$M^{\underline{3}}$: F, occlusal view. *P. whitei.* Male right corpus with $P_{\overline{3}}$–$M_{\overline{3}}$: B, occlusal view. Partial palate of same male, with right $I^{\underline{1}}$–$M^{\underline{3}}$: D, occlusal view. Female mandible with left $I_{\overline{1}}$–$P_{\overline{4}}$, right $I_{\overline{1}}$–$M_{\overline{3}}$: C, occlusal view. Female left maxilla with $C^{\underline{1}}$–$M^{\underline{3}}$: E, occlusal view. *P. broomi.* Female palate with left and right $C^{\underline{1}}$–$M^{\underline{3}}$: G, occlusal view. Male right corpus and maxilla in occlusion, with $P^{\underline{3}}$–$M^{\underline{3}}$: I, right lateral view. *P. antiquus.* Female palate with right $P^{\underline{4}}$–$M^{\underline{3}}$, left $P^{\underline{3}}$–$M^{\underline{3}}$: H, occlusal view.

"*Simopithecus*" was used *sensu* Remane (1925) to indicate merely a fossil form of *Papio*, Dietrich not having understood the relationship of typical *Simopithecus* to *Theropithecus* (see below). This collection included several specimens of a medium-sized colobine here referred to ?*Paracolobus*, as well as two dozen jaws and teeth of a papionin which does not display either facial fossae or clear sexual dimorphism. If the variable sample from Laetolil, including "*C. ado*," indeed represents a single species, it seems best to allocate it tentatively to *Parapapio*, rather than to *Cercocebus* (as did M. and R. Leakey, 1976) or *Papio*. The partial mandible from Kanapoi (*P. jonesi* for Patterson, 1968) and tooth from Ekora (M. and R.

Leakey, 1976) are also tentatively allocated to *?Parapapio ado*.

The relationships of *Parapapio* have been discussed in most detail by Freedman (1957), Maier (1971b), and Eisenhart (1974), each coming to slightly different conclusions. It was clear to all from the apparent ancestral retentions of facial form, shared with *Macaca*, that *Parapapio* was probably little changed from the common ancestor of all (sub-Saharan at least) papionins. As Eisenhart noted, it is most likely that *Cercocebus* (as interpreted here) and *Papio* are about equally close to *Parapapio*, rather than the last two being especially related to one another. Eisenhart indicated that the cranial outline of *Parapapio* is not so distinct from *Cercocebus*, in fact being somewhat more similar than either is to larger *Papio*, but the small *Papio* species may close this morphological gap. On the basis of its relative conservatism, *Parapapio* may be considered as the ancestral or "archetypal" African papionin. Thus, rather than leaving them completely indeterminate, the several specimens noted above are tentatively allocated to this genus.

Within *Parapapio*, relationships of the several species are not clear, and a major systematic revision is long overdue. Freedman (1957 et seq.) has not really discussed this matter specifically, but it has been covered by Maier (1971b, especially) and Eisenhart (1974). Due in part to its wide distribution, Maier suggested that *P. jonesi* might be the most conservative species, but this is now seen to be based on several probable misidentifications. *Parapapio broomi* and *P. whitei* were considered closely related, while *P. antiquus* was the most derived, possibly even close to some *Papio*. On the other hand, Eisenhart, while realizing that there had been insufficient analysis to determine morphoclines clearly, agreed that the larger species were similar, but thought that *P. broomi* might represent the most ancestral morphology. The placement of East African species within this framework is obviously not feasible without more knowledge of their skulls, but certain similarities of the Hadar and Makapansgat small *Parapapio* are intriguing. In addition, the paleobiology of *Parapapio* cannot be interpreted without securely allocated postcranial remains. The small size but relatively well-developed muzzles of known skulls suggests *Macaca*-like, mixed arboreal and terrestrial adaptations, but that is based as much on a subjective view of papionin history as it is on fossil evidence. A study of relative incisor shape and molar proportion (see Kay, 1978) might resolve some of these questions.

DINOPITHECUS Broom, 1937

(= or including: *Papio*: Maier, 1971b, in part.)

DISTRIBUTION

Late Pliocene (later Rodolfian). South Africa, Angola; ?Ethiopia.
KNOWN SPECIES
Dinopithecus ingens Broom, 1937
LOCALITIES: (aff.) Omo Shungura Fm. mbs D–G (716, 726, 738, 750); Swartkrans a (752); Schurweberg★ (754); Leba (756).

DISCUSSION

Dinopithecus is one of the largest cercopithecids known, being exceeded in general size only by the largest *Theropithecus* and perhaps some modern mandrills. The cranium and dentition (Figures 172 and 173) as known are essentially similar to those of *Papio* (*Chaeropithecus*), although the maxillary and mandibular fossae are only slightly excavated, with the muzzle flattened dorsally; it is possible that *D. ingens* does not merit generic distinction. The skull is robust, with strong nuchal crests in both sexes and an indication of a low sagittal crest from inion to bregma in some males. There appears to be strong sexual dimorphism in cheek-tooth size. No postcranial elements are securely identified as *D. ingens*.

This genus, as with *Gorgopithecus* and some of the fossil colobines, is essentially known from a single sample, in this case from Swartkrans. Of the skull, one nearly complete but damaged female is known (Figure 172, A and C), and Freedman (1957) has discussed but not illustrated a partial male and other females. A juvenile female(?) skull with I^1 and M^1 in place gives some idea of the growth pattern in the species (Figure 172, B, D, and E). The only adequate interpretation of *Dinopithecus* is that given by Freedman (1957). Skull and tooth forms are nearly identical to those of "savannah" baboons, the greater robusticity of *Dinopithecus* perhaps relating to its larger size. Freed-

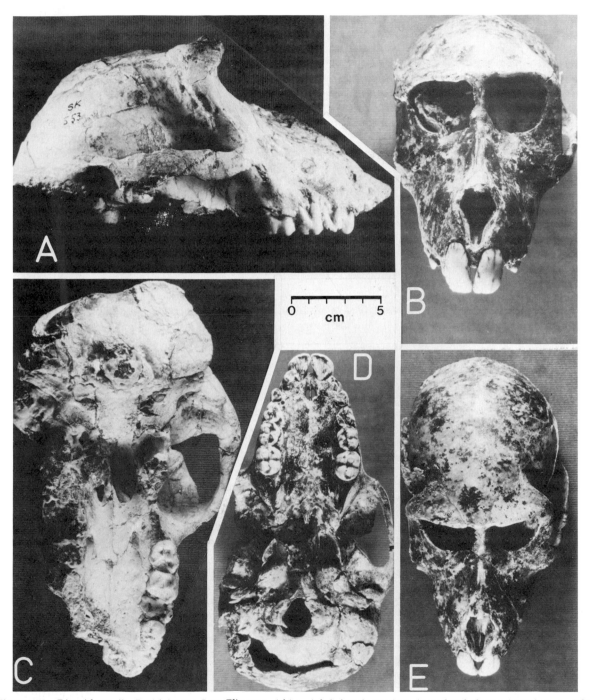

Figure 172. *Dinopithecus* (?=*Papio*) *ingens*. Late Pliocene, Africa. Adult female cranium, in occlusal plane orientation: A, right lateral view; C, basal view. Juvenile cranium, in occlusal plane orientation; B, frontal view; D, basal view; E, dorsal view. [Courtesy of and © R. L. Ciochon.]

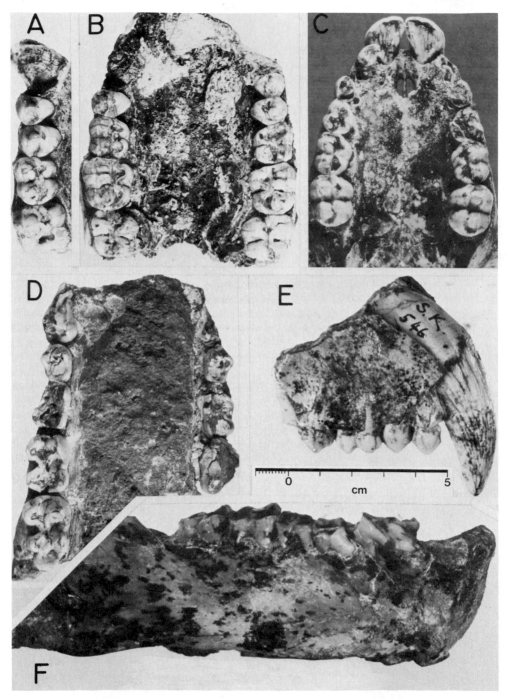

Figure 173. *Dinopithecus* (?=*Papio*) *ingens*. Late Pliocene, Africa. Subadult male right maxilla with erupting C^1, P^3–M^2 (broken): A, occlusal view; E, buccal view. ?Female palate with right P^4–M^3, left P^3–M^3: B, occlusal view. Palate of juvenile with right I^1, dI^2–M^1, left I^1, dC^1–M^1: C, occlusal view. Male mandible with left P$_3$–M$_3$, damaged right P$_4$–M$_2$: D, occlusal view. Male mandible with right P$_3$–M$_3$ visible: F, right lateral view. [A,B,D–F from Freedman (1957), courtesy of L. Freedman; C, courtesy of and © R. L. Ciochon.]

man (1957, also 1976) suggested dental similarities to *Simopithecus*, but he seems to have been more impressed by size than by the typical papionin morphology actually present in *Dinopithecus*. The presence of large incisors (Figure 173C) is another similarity to *Papio*, but the lack of maxillary and mandibular fossae suggests some differences, perhaps in the orientation of the cheek pouches or distribution of chewing stress. Freedman reported great sexual dimorphism in the cheek teeth as well as the more usual dimorphism in the canine–premolar complex. In part, however, this dimorphism was estimated from a few well-sexed specimens by sexing others on the basis of tooth size only; at least some of the dimorphism could be artificial.

As mentioned above, there are no known postcranial elements which may be confidently allocated to *Dinopithecus*. Freedman (1957) mentioned a large partial pelvis and femur from Sterkfontein, where Eisenhart (1974) has recently identified the large *Papio hamadryas robinsoni*, to which taxon the bones most likely belonged.

Jolly (1967) suggested that some postcranial elements from Olduvai Bed II might represent *Dinopithecus* and suggested a semiterrestrial, mandrill-like habitus, but M. and R. Leakey (1973a) have briefly mentioned these specimens as being associated with dentitions of *Theropithecus*. Freedman also indicated dental specimens of the size of *D. ingens* from Sterkfontein and Kromdraai—at least one of the Sterkfontein jaws is now identified as *P. h. robinsoni*, while the Kromdraai teeth are probably large *Gorgopithecus major* (q.v.). On the other hand, several important but unpublished specimens from Leba, Angola, do appear referable to *Dinopithecus*, and this may also hold for large specimens from Omo (see *Papio*).

It is thus not yet possible to attempt an interpretation of the adaptations of *Dinopithecus ingens* from the direct fossil evidence. However, all known Cercopithecidae of similar size are highly terrestrial animals, and the relatively open-country nature of the Swartkrans bovid assemblage (Vrba, 1975) supports analogy of this animal with large *Papio (Chaeropithecus)* species. On the other hand, it occurs alongside the similarly sized *Theropithecus "danieli"* at Swartkrans, and this interpretation would suggest some competition between the two forms. Such competition is not out of the question, of course, especially as *Theropithecus* does not occur again in South Africa until the latest middle Pleistocene of Hopefield.

In sum, there is little evidence at present to merit recognition of *Dinopithecus* as a genus distinct from *Papio*, as also indicated by Maier (1971b). Until a planned revision is completed, however, it would be unwise to hurriedly synonymize the taxon with *Papio*, only to find later that it does indeed present adaptational differences. It is therefore retained as generically independent, as is *Gorgopithecus*, but with uncertainty.

GORGOPITHECUS, Broom and Robinson, 1949a

[= or including: *Parapapio* Jones, 1937: Broom, 1940, 1946, in part. *Simopithecus* Andrews, 1916: Oakley, 1954, Hopwood and Hollyfield, 1954, in part. *Papio:* Maier, 1971b, in part. *Dinopithecus (Gorgopithecus):* Delson, 1975a.]

DISTRIBUTION
Late Pliocene (later Rodolfian). Central South Africa.
KNOWN SPECIES
Gorgopithecus major (Broom, 1940), type species.
(=*Parapapio major* Broom, 1940. *Simopithecus major:* Hopwood and Hollyfield, 1954.)
LOCALITIES: Kromdraai A★ (762).

DISCUSSION

Gorgopithecus is a large cercopithecine known only by a few specimens from a single locality. Although often referred to as a "giant baboon," it is in fact well within the size range of the largest living "savannah baboons" and mandrills, both dentally and cranially. Only one badly damaged male cranium is known (Figure 174) and one female maxilla (Figure 175, B and F), so that diagnostic features are difficult to discern clearly. Broom and Robinson (1949) and Freedman (1957) have not made clear the skull's distortion and especially the "reconstruction" of much of the facial region and vault in plaster (Delson, 1975a). It is not possible to tell if this plaster was merely inserted to approximate Broom's idea of how the skull should have looked, or whether it was modeled after some indications in the original matrix, now removed. In addition, the base of the skull has never been freed

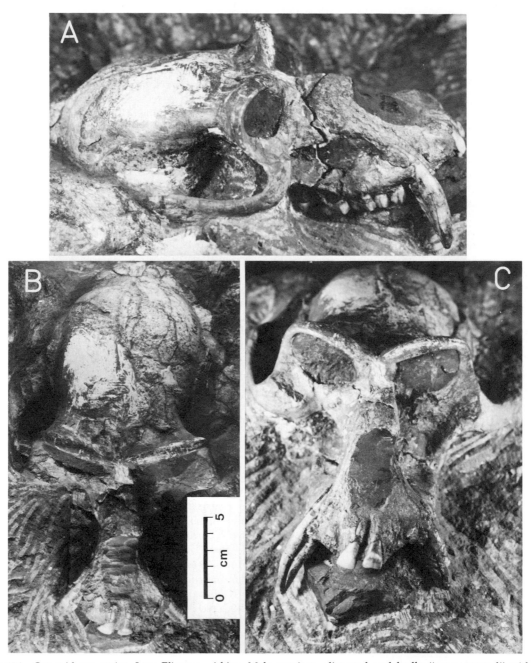

Figure 174. *Gorgopithecus major*. Late Pliocene, Africa, Male cranium, distorted and badly "reconstructed" with plaster (especially frontal bone): A, right lateral view; B, dorsal view; C, frontal view. [Courtesy of and © R. L. Ciochon.]

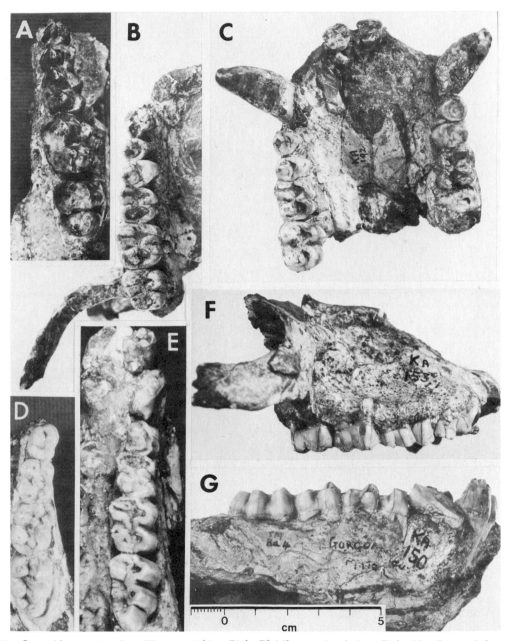

Figure 175. *Gorgopithecus major.* Late Pliocene, Africa. Right P$^{\underline{3}}$–M$^{\underline{3}}$: A, occlusal view. Right C^1–M$^{\underline{3}}$ in undeformed female maxilla: B, occlusal view; F, lateral view. Partial palate of male skull (see Figure 174) with left and right I^1, C^1–M$^{\underline{2}}$ (left M$^{\underline{2}}$ damaged): C, occlusal view. Right P$_{\overline{4}}$–M$_{\overline{3}}$: D, occlusal view. Right C$_{\overline{1}}$–M$_{\overline{3}}$ in male mandible: E, occlusal view; G, lateral view. [A,D,E courtesy of and © R. L. Ciochon; B,C,F,G from Freedman (1957), courtesy of L. Freedman.]

from the enclosing matrix; only the maxillary region was removed along breaks. According to Freedman (1957), the major distinctions of this taxon are that there is little sexual dimorphism, the muzzle is short and high, maxillary fossae are deep while mandibular fossae are weak, and the zygoma is nearly vertical. Dentally, there is no special feature except, again, for low dimorphism (despite Freedman's suggestion of similarity to *Simopithecus*).

Considering each of these characters briefly, the question of sexual dimorphism does appear to be diagnostic, although it may not warrant generic separation, a view which led Delson (1975a) to suggest that this taxon be ranked as a subgenus of the slightly larger *Dinopithecus*. At present, we retreat from this stand until a more complete study of the skulls can be undertaken. In the similarly sized, large living baboons, sexual dimorphism in cranial dimensions averages between 20 and 40% (i.e., M/F = ca. 1.2–1.4). In *G. major* only a few percent separate the sexes in comparable measures, even though one of these, muzzle length, is highly dimorphic in *Papio*. Similarly, dental dimorphism in *Papio* averages 15%, while the teeth of the single known male and female maxillae of *G. major* are subequal, with the presumed female in some cases being even larger (probably not due to wear). These values are of course based only on single specimens, but they do suggest a significantly lesser overall pattern of sexual dimorphism in the fossil species. On the other hand, the distinctive shape of the muzzle in both sexes of *Gorgopithecus* may be related to its lack of dimorphism. The maxilla is short and narrow, but quite high, sloping steeply up to a narrow peak formed by rather short nasal bones. The nasal orifice is large, extending nearly half the length of the short muzzle. The zygoma is upright rather than backwardly tilted as in *Papio*, while the large and deep maxillary fossa extends back beneath the orbit, as in the smaller but not larger modern African cercopithecines. In combination with this deep excavation, the apparent shallowness of the mandibular fossa is unexpected.

The remainder of the face in *Gorgopithecus* has been described as being very broad, with wide oval orbits and strong supraorbital ridges. This wide interorbital region led Verheyen (1962) to place *Gorgopithecus* with colobines on the basis of a facial index, although he realized this was a misclassification. Unfortunately, this region is almost completely plaster "reconstruc-

tion," the bone alongside being badly warped. The undeformed skull would more likely have had a narrow interorbital nasal pillar, rounder orbits, and robust but less protruding tori than shown in Figure 174. The weak temporal lines converge toward bregma but they do not fuse into a low crest until slightly anterior to inion where they meet a moderately developed nuchal crest. This suggests relatively weak chewing musculature, as a stronger sagittal crest is common in the larger male cercopithecines, including many smaller than *Gorgopithecus*. The incisors are large, although Freedman (1957) erroneously allocated the unworn specimens to *Dinopithecus*; those in adult tooth rows, of course, are rather worn. Except for canines and $P_{\overline{3}}$, the few sexed teeth demonstrate no dimorphism. Overall, *Gorgopithecus* appears to be more distinct from *Papio* than is *Dinopithecus*.

Until more is known about its cranial morphology, the most interesting features of *Gorgopithecus* are its size and the fauna with which it is associated. Two faunal assemblages are known from Kromdraai: (1) the hominid-bearing deposits (B) with the colobine *Cercopithecoides* and two baboons, the large *Papio h. robinsoni* and small *P.* cf. *izodi* (=*P.* "*angusticeps*'); and (2) the "faunal site," Kromdraai A, without *Australopithecus* or *Cercopithecoides*, but with *Gorgopithecus* and a rare small cercopithecine (*Parapapio* or *Cercocebus*), as well as the two *Papio* species. Kromdraai A is the only major site in South Africa lacking *Cercopithecoides*, and the absence of *Theropithecus* [found at the nearby (in time and space) Swartkrans a locality] may also be important. The frequency of bovid occurrence at Kromdraai A led Vrba (1975) to suggest a relatively open environment with tree cover intermediate between Swartkrans a and Kromdraai B, sites where *Australopithecus robustus* is known. No clear pattern emerges from this analysis, and other than a simplistic reference to typical "savannah" baboons, complicated by the apparent lack of sexual dimorphism, no further assessment of the habits of *Gorgopithecus* can be made without further cranial and, especially, postcranial specimens.

SUBTRIBE MACACINA
Owen, 1843

(= or including: Macacidae Owen, 1843, restricted. Cercocebini Jolly, 1966; Hill, 1974, restricted. Macacini: Maier, 1970. Macacina: Delson, 1975a.)

DISTRIBUTION

Late Miocene (late Turolian) to modern. Northern Africa, Eurasia south of: southern England, Germany, Romania, Central Asia, northern India, central China, Japan.

INCLUDED TAXA

Macaca, Procynocephalus, and *Paradolichopithecus.*

Discussion

The Macacina is probably the most conservative of the papionin subtribes, most species retaining the ancestral morphology of teeth, skull, and other structures which characterized the last common ancestor of all papionins. The teeth are quite uniform, although some metrical variation of proportions occurs (Kay, 1977b; Hylander, 1975), linked with dietary differences. Some of the Celebesian macaques are the most distinctive cranially (Fooden, 1969), in some ways closely resembling *Parapapio broomi* and other species of that genus. The gently sloping dorsal curve of the muzzle in lateral view and the typical lack of maxillary and mandibular fossae are further similarities to *Parapapio,* considered the most conservative, in its turn, of the Papionina.

The living macaques are placed in a single genus without subgenera by Fooden (1976), and the two fossil genera are so similar in cranial proportions that they are placed here also. It is, of course, possible that they (or even the subgroups of *Macaca*) are the result of additional invasions of Eurasia by conservative Afri-

can papionins, but there is no evidence for this hypothesis. Much of Fooden's work on subdividing macaque species into natural groups is based on the penis and baculum, hardly ever preserved in the fossil record, so it is unlikely that the extinct forms will be aligned with living ones by this means. Unfortunately, skulls of Eurasian fossil papionins are also notably rare, only a few populations being even moderately represented. On the other hand, studies of past climate and geography (see Delson, 1975b) suggest that the ancestors of macaques and relatives were genetically isolated from sub-Saharan papionins by a Saharan barrier (see under Papionini, above), which implies a monophyletic origin of the group.

Evolution within the Macacina is still quite unclear, especially as it is not yet possible to be certain that *Procynocephalus* and *Paradolichopithecus* are not a single genus (or even lineage). In outline, once early macaques had entered Eurasia, they first spread along the northern shore of the Mediterranean and probably slowly eastward, although they do not appear in Asia until late in the Pliocene. The large and terrestrial European *Paradolichopithecus* may have developed *in situ,* especially as it is known as early as 4 MY ago. But whether that lineage gave rise to Asian *Procynocephalus* or if the latter developed independently in Asia is still an open question. The possible pattern of dispersal within *Macaca* is discussed under that genus, below.

MACACA Lacépède, 1799

(= or including: *Macaco* Oken, 1817; *Macacus* Desmarest, 1820; lapsi. *Simia* Linnaeus, 1758, in part, suppressed. *Pithecus* E. Geoffroy, 1812, suppressed; *Pithes* Burnett, 1828, lapsus? *Inuus* E. Geoffroy, 1812; *Innuus* Berthold, 1827, lapsus. "*Sylvanus*" Oken, 1816, work rejected, *nec* Latreille, 1807. *Silenus* Goldfuss, 1820. *Cynocephalus* Gray, 1821, *nec* Boddaert, 1768. *Magotus* Ritgen, 1824. *Magus* Lesson, 1827. *Rhesus* Lesson, 1830. *Cynopithecus* I. Geoffroy, 1836; *Cygnopithecus* Rensch, 1936, lapsus. *Maimon* Wagner, 1839. *Ouanderou* Lesson, 1840. *Salmacis* Gloger, 1841, *nec* Zetterstedt, 1840. *Pithex* Hodgson, 1841, lapsus for *Pithecus*? *Lyssodes* Gistel, 1848. *Semnopithecus* Desmarest, 1822: Beyrich, 1861, in part. *Vetulus* Reichenbach, 1862. *Cynamolgus* Reichenbach, 1862; *Cynomolgus* Trouessart, 1904, lapsus? *Zati* Reichenbach, 1862. *Nemestrinus* Reichenbach, 1862, *nec* Latreille, 1802. *Gymnopyga* Gray, 1866b. *Aulaxinuus* Cocchi, 1872; *Aulaxinus* Lydekker, 1889; *Auxalinus* Bernsen, 1930; lapsi. *Mesopithecus* Wagner, 1839: Trouessart, 1878, in part. *Opthalmomegas* Dehaut, 1910: Dehaut, 1914, in part. *Papio* "Erxleben, 1777": Stromer, 1920. *Szechuanopithecus* Young and Liu, 1950. *Cynomacaca* Khajuria, 1953; *Cynomaca* Walker *et al.,* 1964, lapsus. *Dolichopithecus* Déperet, 1889: Kretzoi, 1962, in part;

Dolicopithecus: Michaux, 1969a, in part, lapsus. "*Anomalopithecus*" Arambourg, 1970. *Libypithecus* Stromer, 1913: Hill, 1970, in part.)

DISTRIBUTION

Late Miocene (late Turolian) to modern. Circum-Mediterranean (North Africa, Levant, Europe to 50+°N) and southern Asia (India through north central China and eastern Indonesia).

KNOWN SPECIES

MACACA SYLVANUS species group

1. *Macaca sylvanus* (Linnaeus, 1758), type species
   a. *Macaca sylvanus sylvanus* (Linnaeus, 1758)
[= *Simia sylvanus* Linnaeus, 1758. *Simia inuus* Linnaeus, 1766. *Inuus ecaudatus* E. Geoffroy, 1812. *Macacus trarensis* Pomel, 1892. *Macacus proinuus* Pomel, 1896. *Pithecus gesilla* Blainville, 1839: Flamand, 1902 (nomen originally a lapsus for *P. gorilla* in illustration of *G. gorilla*).]
LOCALITIES: Ain Mefta (926); Tamar Hat (1263); Neolithic to modern in Maghreb★.
   b. *Macaca sylvanus* cf. *sylvanus*

[=*Macaca* (sp.): Arambourg and Coque, 1959. "Anomalopithecus bicuspidatus" Arambourg, 1970.]
LOCALITIES: Ichkeul (636); Ain Brimba (702).

    c. *Macaca sylvanus pliocena* Owen, 1846
[=*Macacus pliocenus* Owen, 1846; *M. pliocaenus:* Major, 1872; *M. pliocenicus:* Bernsen, 1930; lapsi. *Semnopithecus? pliocenus:* Beyrich, 1861. *Inuus suevicus* Hedinger, 1891. *Macacus tolosanus* Harlé, 1892. *Innuus (Aulaxinuus) florentinus* (Cocchi, 1872): Portis, 1916, in part, and others. *Inuus ecaudatus fossilis* Theis, 1926. *Macaca sylvana suevica:* Adam, 1959; *M. s. suecia:* Janossy, 1969, lapsus. *Dolichopithecus arvernensis* Déperet, 1929: M.-F. and E. Bonifay, 1963, in part. Cf. *Semnopithecus:* M.-F. and E. Bonifay, 1969. *Macaca mulatta* (Zimmerman, 1780): Maier, 1970, in part. *Macaca florentina:* Franzen, 1973, in part. *Macaca* sp., or equivalent: Hinton, 1908; Kormos, 1914b, Kahlke, 1961; Vereschagin, 1959; Vlcek, 1961; de Lumley *et al.*, 1963; Bartolomei, 1965; Thenius, 1965; etc.]
LOCALITIES: Betfia-2 (808); ?Monte Peglia (814); Vallonet (816); West Runton (824); Gombasek (826); Voigtstedt (828); Hohensülzen (830); 'Ubeidiya (844); Zlaty Kun (846); Mosbach-2 (864); St.-Estève layers B (866) and G (884); Ambrona (888); San Vito di Leguzzano (892); Hoxne (893); Montsaunès (894); "Rome" (896); Heppenloch (906); Grays Thurrock★ (944); Orgnac-3 (946); Borgio (1020); Kudaro-1 (1048).

    d. *Macaca sylvanus prisca* Gervais, 1859
[=*Macacus priscus* Gervais, 1859. *Semnopithecus monspessulanus* Gervais, 1849; Gervais, 1867, in part. *Macacus monspessulanus:* Déperet, 1887, in part. *?Mesopithecus monspessulanus:* Trouessart, 1878, in part. *Macacus florentinus* (Cocchi, 1872): ?Major, 1879; ?Heller, 1936; Kormos, 1937; Kretzoi, 1956; Hürzeler, 1967, in part. *Macacus praeinuus* Kormos, 1914. cf. *Dolichopithecus* sp. indet: Kretzoi, 1962; *Dolicopithecus ruscinensis* Déperet, 1889: Michaux, 1969a, in part. *?Macaca* sp.: Delson, 1971.]
LOCALITIES: Montpellier★ (623); Csarnota-2 (642); Fornace RDB (650); ?Gundersheim (658); Beremend-4 (660); ?Cova Bonica (680).

    e. *Macaca sylvanus florentina* (Cocchi, 1872)
(=*Macacus priscus* Gervais, 1859: Major, 1872, in part. *Aulaxinuus florentinus* Cocchi, 1872. *Macacus florentinus:* Major, 1875. Macacus ausonius Major, 1875, nomen nudum. Florentine macaque: Kurten, 1968. *Macaca* sp.: Crusafont, 1965; Heintz, Delson and Crusafont, 1972.)
LOCALITIES: ?Mugello (690); ?St.-Vallier (708); ?Sandalja (714); ?Puebla de Valverde (718); Senèze (758); Tegelen (768); Montevarchi Group, Upper Valdarno★ (770).

    f. *Macaca ?sylvanus majori* Azzaroli, 1946
(=*Opthalmomegas lamarmorae* Dehaut, 1910: Dehaut, 1914, in part. *Macacus* sp.: Major, 1914; Schlosser, 1924; Schaub, 1943. *Macacus majori* Azzaroli, 1946; Comaschi Caria, 1968.)
LOCALITIES: Capo Figari★ (682).

    2. *Macaca libyca* (Stromer, 1920)
(=Semnopithecine: Stromer, 1913; 1920, in part. *Aulaxinuus libycus* Stromer, 1920. *Papio* sp. indet.: Stromer, 1920. *Libypithecus markgrafi* Stromer, 1913: Hill, 1970, in part. *Macaca libyca:* Simons, 1970.)
LOCALITIES: Wadi Natrun★ (610).

    3. *?Macaca* sp. nov.
(= or including: *Macaca flandrini* Arambourg, 1959, in part. ?Cf. *Macaca* c.q. *Mesopithecus:* Hooijer, 1963, 1970. *?Macaca* sp.: Delson, 1975a.)
LOCALITIES: ?Ongoliba (578); Marceau (598).

MACACA SILENUS species group

    4. *Macaca silenus* (Linnaeus, 1758)
    5. *Macaca nemestrina* (Linnaeus, 1766)

(=*?Inuus nemestrinus* "mut." *saradana* Deninger, 1910.)
FOSSIL LOCALITIES: ?Middle Pleistocene caves, eastern Java (842); late Pleistocene and "Holocene" caves in Borneo, Malaysia and Sumatra (1256).

    6. *Macaca nigra* (Desmarest, 1822)
    7. *Macaca maura* (Schinz, 1825)
    8. *Macaca ochreata* (Ogilby, 1841)
    9. *Macaca nigrescens* (Temminck, 1849)
    10. *Macaca tonkeana* (Meyer, 1899)
    11. *Macaca hecki* (Matschie, 1901)
    12. *Macaca brunnescens* (Matschie, 1901)

MACACA FASCICULARIS species group

    13. *Macaca fascicularis* (Raffles, 1821–1822)
FOSSIL LOCALITIES: ?Middle Pleistocene caves, eastern Java (842); late Pleistocene and "Holocene" caves in Borneo, Sumatra (1256), Java (1258).

    14. *Macaca mulatta* (Zimmerman, 1780)
    15. *Macaca cyclopis* (Swinhoe, 1863)
    16. *Macaca fuscata* (Blyth, 1875)
FOSSIL LOCALITIES: ?Late middle and late Pleistocene and "Holocene" of Japan, especially Shikimizu (1252).

MACACA SINICA species group

    17. *Macaca sinica* (Linnaeus, 1771)
    18. *Macaca radiata* (E. Geoffroy, 1812)
    19. *Macaca assamensis* (McClelland in Horsfield, 1870)
    20. *Macaca thibetana* (Milne Edwards, 1870)
    21. *(?)Macaca anderssoni* Schlosser, 1924
[=*Macacus anderssoni* Schlosser, 1924. *Macacus robustus* Young, 1934. *Szechuanopithecus yangtzensis* Young and Liu, 1950. *Macaca speciosa subfossilis* Jouffroy, 1959. *Macaca* (or *Macacus*) sp.: numerous authors, see Delson, 1977a.]
LOCALITIES: ?Liucheng (784); Mien-chih★ (800); Bama (850); ?Wuming (854); Gongwangling (876); Jianniushan (878); Choukoutien localities 13 (890), 1 (898), 3 (900), 2 (912), ?Koloshan (916); ?Tung Lang (1028).
    22. *Macaca arctoides* (I. Geoffroy, 1831)

Species group uncertain

    23. *?Macaca palaeindica* (Lydekker, 1884)
(=*Semnopithecus palaeindicus* Lydekker, 1884. *Presbytis palaeindicus:* Pilgrim, 1915.)
LOCALITIES: Tatrot Beds★ (686).
    24. *Macaca* sp.
(= *Macaca* sp. or *M. robusta* of various authors)
LOCALITIES: Tham Khuyen (922); Tham Om (923); Tam Hai (924); Chaiyenshan (952); Chingshihling (954); Heichinglungtsun (958); Hoshangpo (960); Houshan (962); Liangfeng (964); Shuan (968); Tam Hang (970); Tam Pha Loi (972); Tanyang (974); Tungtzu (976); Yenkouping (978); Punung (981); Hang Hum lower (1022); Keo Leng (1027); Hsienjen (1250).
    25. *?Macaca* sp.
LOCALITIES: Wutu (573).

DISCUSSION

Macaca is an essentially conservative papionin (macacinan) inhabiting Eurasia and northern Africa. There is an extreme range of external and internal variation in morphology and size among the living species, which are allocated to species groups here on the basis of male (and female) reproductive-system characters, mostly after Fooden (1975, 1976). There is as yet no clear correlation between these apparently synapomorphic complexes and craniodental morphology, rendering allocation of fossil forms even more doubtful than usual. Additional external characters, such as tail length, vary in parallel within species groups, but Fooden (1975) has argued that, in general, long tails are conservative, shorter tails (and large body size) being adaptations to more northern climates attained convergently in each group.

In terms of skeletal characters which would be of use in identifying fossils, macaques are small to medium-sized cercopithecids, with skulls retaining what is here considered the ancestral papionin facial pattern: The muzzle is moderately developed, and the facial profile is smooth and linear or slightly concave, without a steep anteorbital drop, but much as in *Parapapio* species (Figures 160, E–H, and 176). Variation between species is great in such superstructural features as sagittal and nuchal crests, supraorbital tori, and zygomatic arch size; maxillary and mandibular fossae are rare, but may be variably present in some species. The dentition presents no constant peculiarities (Figures 165, 177, and 178), molar flare being moderate, accessory cuspules rather rare, and loss of M_3 hypoconulids occurring only in some individuals of small species. The species vary widely in degree of terrestriality, and thus the cursorial adaptations of their limb bones are equally nonuniform in distribution. To some degree, the placement of all the living (and thus fossil) species in a single genus *Macaca* is more a matter of zoogeographical distribution than shared derived characters, but it does appear likely that the group is holophyletic. On the other hand, until more is known about the origin and relationships of the large Eurasian genera *Paradolichopithecus* and *Procynocephalus*, which are here also placed in the Macacina, paraphyly is not ruled out.

No clear hypothesis of relationships among the living species has yet been formulated, although Fooden (1975) has suggested that the *silenus–sylvanus* group is closer to the *fascicularis* group than to either of the others. On the other hand, these groups would appear to be conservative in their reproductive organs, characters which Fooden uses to relate them, suggesting that their similarity may only be symplesiomor-

phic. Given the derived nature of penial morphology in the *sinica* group and especially in *M. arctoides* and the short tail of the latter, it seems reasonable to suggest that *M. arctoides* may have evolved from a short-tailed form of the *sinica* group, perhaps the common ancestor of *M. assamensis* and *M. thibetana* before these species differentiated (see also Fooden, 1976). Delson (in press a) has advocated formally placing *M. sylvanus* in its own species-group, mainly on paleozoogeographical grounds, while including *M. arctoides* in the *sinica* group, and these suggestions are followed here.

The earliest fossils which may pertain to this genus are from north (and central) Africa. Arambourg (1959) described as *Macaca flandrini* a collection of some 50 teeth from Marceau, Algeria. Delson (1973, 1975a) showed that the type and some other specimens were colobine (see ?*C. flandrini*), while the remaining 40 or so teeth were indeed macaque-like (Figures 177C and 178 I–K), and probably of late Miocene age. A fair range of size is present, especially in M_3 (Figure 178I), suggesting the possible presence of two taxa of similar morphology. These teeth include representatives of almost all adult elements and are comparable to those of macaque species, but taxonomic allocation is based more on geography than on morphology; if the collection were found in East Africa, it might be termed ?*Parapapio*. In fact, the single M_3 (of probably similar age) from Ongoliba, Zaire, which Hooijer (1963, 1970) described as "Cf. *Mesopithecus* c.q. *Macaca*," is nearly identical to those from Marceau. It may be that these specimens represent one or more taxa of papionins which occurred across Africa before the speciation events which led to the differentiation of the three subtribes. Cranial elements might aid in solving this problem, but not until more complete comparative studies have been made of such well-known genera as *Parapapio*, *Macaca*, and *Papio*.

Only slightly younger is a collection of jaw fragments and teeth (Figures 177G and 178, F and H) from Wadi Natrun, Egypt, which occurs alongside *Libypithecus markgrafi*. Stromer's (1920) species *Macaca libyca* is recognized here on mainly geographic grounds, again. Mandibles do not indicate the presence of fossae, but this is an ancestral feature also retained in *Parapapio*. The taxon involved is probably distinct from contemporary papionins known at Lothagam, Kenya, on the basis of tooth morphology, but generic allocation is still nearly indeterminate. According to the dispersal hypotheses outlined above, the species

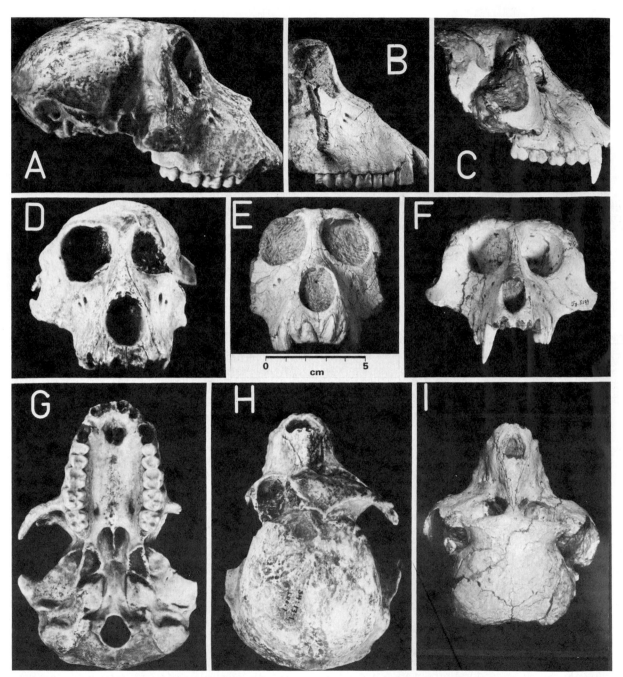

Figure 176. *Macaca*. Pleistocene, Eurasia. Crania in occlusal plane orientation. *Macaca ?anderssoni (Macaca ''robusta'')*. Middle Pleistocene, Asia (Choukoutien).   A, right lateral view; D, frontal view; G, occlusal view; H, dorsal view. *Macaca anderssoni*. Early Pleistocene, Asia. B, right lateral view; E, frontal view. *Macaca majori*. Late Pliocene, Europe. C, right lateral view; F, frontal view; I, dorsal view. All skulls male.

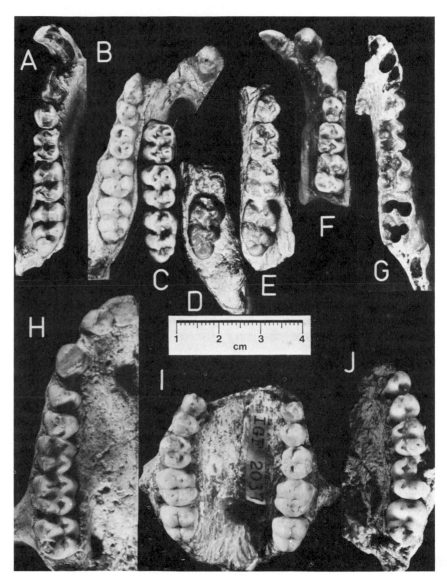

Figure 177. *Macaca.* Miocene–Pleistocene, Eurasia and Africa. Dentitions in occlusal view. *M. sypvanus florentina;* late Pliocene, Europe: A, male left corpus with $C_{\overline{1}}$–$M_{\overline{3}}$. *M. ?sylvanus majori;* late Pleistocene, Europe: B, male mandible with left $P_{\overline{3}}$–$M_{\overline{3}}$, damaged symphysis, and right $C_{\overline{1}}$; I, palate with right and left $P^{\underline{3}}$–$M^{\underline{3}}$. *?Macaca* sp. nov.; late Miocene, Africa: C, isolated but possibly associated left $M_{\overline{1-3}}$ (photographically reversed). *M. palaeindica;* Pliocene, Asia: D, right corpus with $M_{\overline{3}}$: E, right corpus with $P_{\overline{4}}$–$M_{\overline{3}}$. *M. sylvanus prisca;* early Pliocene, Europe: F, male right corpus with realigned $I_{\overline{2}}$–$M_{\overline{2}}$. *M. libyca;* late Miocene, Africa: G, female right corpus with $P_{\overline{3}}$–$M_{\overline{2}}$. *M. anderssoni;* late Pliocene–middle Pleistocene, Asia: H, right side of palate from male skull with $I^{\underline{1}}$–$M^{\underline{3}}$. *M. sylvanus pliocena;* middle Pleistocene, Europe: J, left maxilla with $P^{\underline{3}}$–$M^{\underline{3}}$.

might represent the "stage" when macaques were first expanding into Eurasia, probably via northeast Africa.

Plio-Pleistocene fossil macaques of the circum-Mediterranean region have been assigned to about a dozen nominally distinct species, none of which is clearly or significantly distinguishable from the living northwest African *M. sylvanus*, and, pending a more complete revision, all are referred to subspecies of this taxon, defined in part by biochronology. *Macaca sylvanus prisca* is somewhat smaller than the living form (Figures 177F and 178L) and represents the first macaque known from Europe, probably the oldest cercopithecine outside Africa. Its range is Pliocene, from earliest Ruscinian to early Villafranchian, in relatively wooded environments where it is often as-

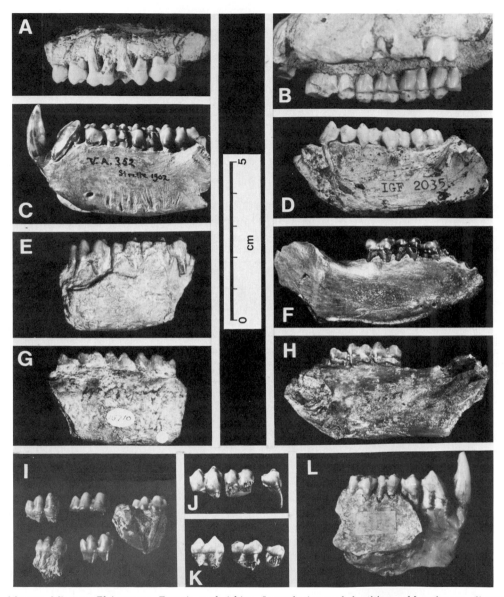

Figure 178. *Macaca.* Miocene–Pleistocene, Eurasia and Africa. Lateral views of dentitions. *M. sylvanus pliocena;* middle Pleistocene, Europe: A, buccal view maxilla with left P^3–M^3. *Macaca anderssoni;* early Pleistocene, Asia: B, lingual view maxillary dentition of right side, slightly oblique, with left incisors and M^3 visible. *Macaca sylvanus florentina;* Plio-Pleistocene, Europe: C, male left mandible with C_1–M_3, buccal view. *Macaca ?sylvanus majori;* late Pliocene, Europe: D, male left mandible with P_3–M_3, buccal view. *Macaca palaeindica;* late Pliocene, Asia. Partial mandible with right P_4–M_3: E, buccal view; G, lingual view. *Macaca libyca;* late Miocene, Africa. Right corpus female mandible with P_4–M_2: F, buccal view; H, lingual view. ?*Macaca* sp. nov; late Miocene, Africa. Five right lower third molars, note size variation: I, buccal view. Isolated but possibly associated P_4, M_1, and M_2: J, right teeth, buccal view; K, left teeth, lingual view. *Macaca sylvanus prisca;* Pliocene, Europe. Male mandible with right C_1–M_2: L, buccal view.

sociated with *Dolichopithecus ruscinensis* and *Mesopithecus monspessulanus* and perhaps also with *Paradolichopithecus* sp. Rare specimens of similar age are known in northwest Africa, a humerus at Ichkeul and two isolated molars from Ain Brimba. The latter teeth were erroneously associated with machairodont premolars by Arambourg (1970), who gave them the name "Anomalopithecus bicuspidatus," a nomen nudum because it lacked a type designation. These specimens may be referred to *M. s. sylvanus* on solely geographical (and size) grounds.

European macaques of late Pliocene and early Pleistocene age (middle through final Villafranchian) are known from seven "fields" or localities and may be termed *M. s. florentina*. The type mandible, (Figure 177A), from the "Upper Valdarno," is still the most complete specimen and presents deep mandibular fossae, but other male specimens from this and other sites do not (Figure 178C), reflecting the low taxonomic weight of this character. Other more fragmentary remains are known from as far north as the Netherlands and eastward into Yugoslavia, all of similar size and morphology to the living variety. Also basically similar in size are the middle Pleistocene Mediterranean macaques, which do tend to have somewhat wider, more robust teeth, however. The oldest name applied to any fossil macaque is associated with an isolated upper molar from Grays Thurrock, England, which is probably of post-Hoxnian (early "Riss") age and fits within this sample. Thus, *M. s. pliocena* includes specimens from at least 22 localities, almost all fragmentary and often single jaws or teeth (Figures 177J and 178A). Most appear to be associated with a temperate faunal assemblage, suggesting southward migration during glacial intervals, although whether macaques remained only in southern European refugia or departed Europe altogether during glacial maxima is unknown. The range of *M. s. pliocena* is quite extensive, from Spain to southern England to the Caucasus and Israel, and it is often found in human occupation sites, where it was presumably a rare food item. Vlcek (1961) reported some partial limb bones from Zlaty Kun, Czechoslovakia, which he thought pertained to both macaque (associated with a warmer, forest fauna) and baboon (with more open-country species), but it is more likely than sexual dimorphism in a single robust macaque species (matched by *M. s. sylvanus*) was involved. No definite occurrences of macaques are known from

localities of Eemian age, suggesting that the later "Riss" glacial advances were too extreme for them (Borgio, Italy, and Kudaro-1, Russian Caucasus, are possible exceptions, but their ages are uncertain). Some dental remains of Late Paleolithic and later age are known in northwest Africa, and Pomel (1892, 1896) named two species from the same set of fragmentary limb bones recovered at Ain Mefta, in the Traras region of Algeria, whose age may be somewhat older (see Jaeger, 1975a); all are referred to *M. s. sylvanus* at present. *Macaca* sp. was also reported in Amud Cave, Israel, from a Middle Paleolithic layer by Takai (1970), but, from his illustration, it appears that the tooth involved is not primate.

One final European form is the supposedly "dwarf" macaque, termed *M. majori* by Azzaroli (1946). This taxon is known from a large collection of teeth, jaws, partial skulls, and bones (Figures 176, C, F, and I; 177, B and I; 178D; and 179, A–C) from the Capo Figari breccia on the northern tip of Sardinia. *Macaca majori* has been considered to be of "Holocene" age, but recent study of the associated faunal assemblage suggests a late Pliocene date instead. Preliminary comparisons suggest dental size differences from modern *M. sylvanus* on the order of only 5–10%, probably too low to qualify as a true dwarf (compared to later Pleistocene insular dwarf mammals). The cheek teeth appear rather more inflated or "puffy" than in other forms here assigned to *M. sylvanus*, however, and more detailed study of the crania and joints is required to determine if this form can be allocated full species status, as appears likely.

By comparison to Europe, the fossil record of macaque (or of any monkeys) in Asia is quite restricted. Several species have been named, but few specimens are complete enough to permit comparison with modern skulls, and these have never been fully studied. The oldest remains comprise two partial mandibles (Figures 177, D and E, and 178, E and G) from Tatrot-equivalent(?) levels in northern India which were originally described in 1837. Lydekker (1884) later considered them to be colobine, but, as indicated by Delson (1973, 1975a), the teeth are of cercopithecine morphology, although the corpus in the type specimen is deep and thin. Once again, employing the modern genus as a "form-genus," these jaws may be termed *?Macaca palaeindica*, although generic allocation remains insecure. This taxon might well represent the earliest macaques in Asia,

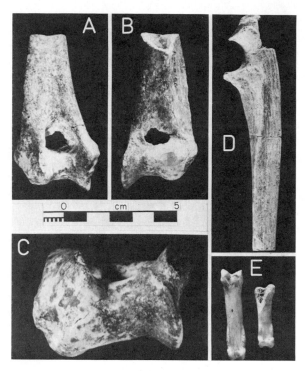

Figure 179. *Macaca majori.* Late Pliocene, Europe. Left humerus: A, posterior view; B, anterior view; C, distal view. *Macaca sylvanus florentina.* Plio-Pleistocene, Europe, Left ulna: D, lateral view. *Macaca sylvanus* cf. *prisca.* Pliocene, Europe. Phalanges: E, plantar view.

spreading outward from a probable Afghanistan–Pakistan–southern India entry point; it is little different in size or morphology from the Pleistocene forms known in China and Vietnam (see below). Older specimens have previously been referred to *Macaca*, but they are here identified as *?Presbytis* (q.v.). One other possibly ancient Asian cercopithecine is a partial mandible from Wutu, Kansu province, China, which has not yet been described. This local fauna was stated to be of "early Pliocene" (here late Miocene) age, but without publication of the fossils no decision is yet possible (see Delson, 1977a).

Remains attributed to various modern species have been reported from middle and later Pliocene localities throughout Asia, but few are of more than local importance. Hooijer (1962) suggested that dental remains from the middle Pleistocene caves of Java (Trinil equivalent) may be *M. fascicularis*, but Fooden (1975) showed that they also might represent *M. nemestrina*,

with no clear choice yet possible. Various ?late middle or late Pleistocene macaque fossils from Japan have been reported, many cited by Iwamoto (1975), who described a nearly complete skull of rather late date. He argued that this cranium differed somewhat from modern *M. fuscata* in the way Chinese Pleistocene forms might, but it is doubtful that there is a phyletic relationship here, as suggested by Iwamoto, given the following interpretation of the Chinese material.

By far the most interesting Asian fossil macaques are those from the Chinese Plio-Pleistocene. Schlosser (1924) first described the male facial fragment of *M. anderssoni* (Figures 176, B and E; 177H; and 178B) as of "Pontian" (later Miocene) age, but it would now appear to date near the Plio-Pleistocene boundary. Young (1934) named *M. robusta* for a collection of jaws, teeth, and some bones from Choukoutien which he thought to be smaller than *M. anderssoni* and slightly different in facial morphology. Additional fragmentary remains from numerous other Chinese Pleistocene localities have been referred to this species, although most were not more than included in a faunal list. Finally, Jouffroy (1959) briefly described a skull from Tung-Lang, North Vietnam (?early late Pleistocene age), as *M. speciosa subfossilis*, making closest comparisons with *M. arctoides* and *M. thibetana* (*M. s. speciosa* and *M. s. thibetana* to her).

In 1936, Pei mentioned the find of a nearly complete skull of *M. robusta* from Choukoutien, but this was never described. A cast of what must be this skull was located in the American Museum of Natural History and serves to tie together the three named fossil forms (Figure 176, A, D, G, and H). Preliminary comparisons indicate that there are few constant differences between the crania of male *M. thibetana* and *M. arctoides*, with the fossil (probably male, though lacking canines) falling within the range thus obtained. It also compares well with Jouffroy's figures and descriptions (including the globular neurocranium which she thought separated *M. thibetana* from *M. arctoides*) and does not differ greatly from the somewhat older *M. anderssoni* holotype. At present, the most reasonable course appears to be synonymizing the several taxa as a single species inhabiting southern and central China and perhaps Indochina from the late Pliocene into the middle Pleistocene. Such a species might conceivably represent the hypothetical common ancestor of *M. thibetana*, *M. assamensis*, and *M. arctoides* (see Delson, in press a, for more detail on Asian macaque deployment). Today, *M. mulatta* [according to Fooden (1976), related to *M. fuscata* of Japan and *M. cyclopis* of Taiwan] inhabits southeastern China, with a population near Choukoutien which was possibly introduced in historical times. It would be of some interest to determine if any of the later middle Pleistocene specimens especially were referable to *M. mulatta* rather than to *M. anderssoni* or its potential relatives (both *M. arctoides* and *M. thibetana* also occur in southern and western China).

The range of dietary and locomotor adaptation in living macaque species is so great that no simple characterizations can be made. The genus is the most adaptable non-human primate, ranging today from rain forest to rocky gorges, high elevations, and snow-covered plains, although it does not seem to have expanded its range into Pleistocene periglacial zones.

PROCYNOCEPHALUS Schlosser, 1924

(= or including: *Semnopithecus* Desmarest, 1822: von Meyer, 1848, in part. *Cynocephalus* E. Geoffroy and Cuvier, 1795 *nec* Boddaert, 1768: Falconer, 1884, in part. *Papio* Erxleben, 1777: Pilgrim, 1910, in part. ?*Macaca* Lacépède, 1799: Jolly, 1967, in part.)

DISTRIBUTION

Late Pliocene (?middle and late Villafranchian; Pinjor). East–central China, northern India.

KNOWN SPECIES

1. *Procynocephalus wimani* Schlosser, 1924, type species

[=*Cynocephalus* cf. *wimani*: Teilhard, 1938. ?*Cynocephalus* (or ?*Macacus*) sp.: Teilhard, 1938.]

LOCALITIES: Choukoutien loc. 12 (722); Yüshe (734); Kutitsun (736); Hsin-an loc. 54★ (748).

2. *Procynocephalus subhimalayanus* (von Meyer, 1848)

[=large Quadrumana: Baker and Durand, 1836. *Semnopithecus subhimalayanus* von Meyer, 1848. *Cynocephalus subhimalayanus*: Lydekker, 1884. *Cynocephalus* sp.: Lydekker, 1884. *Cynocephalus falconeri* Lydekker, 1886. *Papio subhimalayanus*: Pilgrim, 1910. *Papio falconeri*: Pilgrim, 1910. *Macaca* cf. *anderssoni* Schlosser, 1924: Jolly, 1967. cf. *Procynocephalus subhimalayanus*: Jolly, 1967. "*Cynocephalus*" *subhimalaynus*: Simons, 1970, lapsus. *Procynocephalus pinjorii* Verma, 1969.]

LOCALITIES: Pinjor "beds," near Dehra Dun★ (744), and near Bunga (744).

DISCUSSION

Procynocephalus is a large-sized macaque-like cercopithecine with adaptations to terrestrial (cursorial) habits in the postcranium. The female muzzle is relatively short and smoothly rounded anteriorly and passes upward toward nasion in a smooth curve, not abruptly as in *Papio*. The mandible and maxilla are nearly featureless laterally, with little or no development of a fossa. An unpublished male specimen is said to show similar features (Teilhard, 1938). On the distal humerus, the medial epicondyle is bent posteriorly, while the ulnar olecranon is well developed if only slightly retroflexed.

The dentition is typically papionin, with large anterior teeth and a rather high degree of lateral molar flare. The known remains suggest an adaptation basically similar to that of the living "savannah" baboons: terrestrial foraging for roots, fruit, and grasses in an open-plains environment. This appears consistent with the only moderately-well-known faunal assemblage associated with this primate, that from loc. 12 of Choukoutien. Despite the large number of references, *Procynocephalus* is known from very few specimens, of which one (or more) of the best was never published and now appears lost. The two species are not well distinguished other than by mandibular robusticity and geographic separation, but they are retained here as distinct pending complete revision, which must also consider the relationships of this genus and *Paradolichopithecus*.

The type specimen from China includes a nearly complete mandible and partial upper dentition of a young female (Figures 180, A and D, and 181, B, E, and H), found or bought in several pieces but probably of a single individual. The teeth are comparable in size and form to those of large living baboons, much larger than any macaque, and the maxilla is not complete enough to clearly indicate a baboon or a macaque type of dorsal outline. This led to referral of those species to baboons under various names over the years. Fragmentary dental specimens were reported from Kutitsun (Young and Pei, 1933) and from Choukoutien loc. 12 (Teilhard, 1938). The latter fossils, however, were associated with a number of postcranial elements, which Teilhard considered as two related species; Jolly (1967) more reasonably suggested that the size difference reflected sexual dimorphism in a large single species. As Jolly further indicated, the male(?) ulna

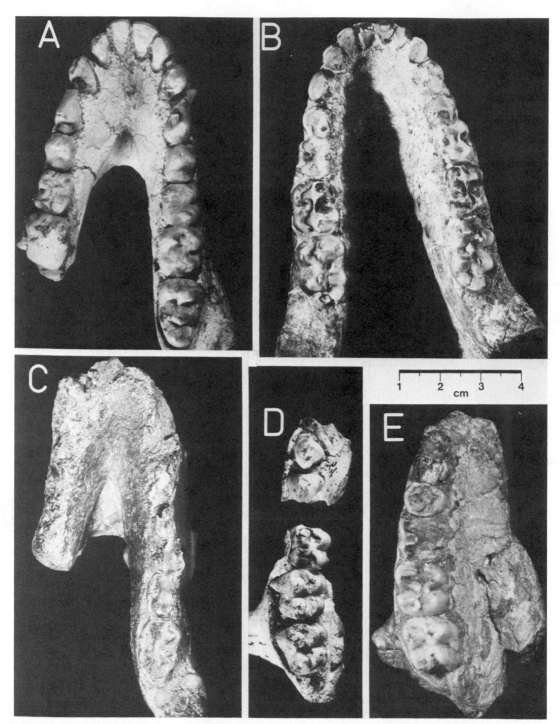

Figure 180. *Procynocephalus.* Late Pliocene, Asia. Dentitions in occlusal view. *P. wimani:* A, female mandible lacking left $M_{\overline{3}}$; D, parts of right female maxilla with $C^{\underline{1}}$–$P^{\underline{3}}$, $M^{\underline{1-3}}$, ?associated with mandible. *P. subhimalayanus:* B, female mandible with complete but damaged dentition; C, referred ?male mandible with damaged right $P_{\overline{4}}$–$M_{\overline{3}}$; E, female right maxilla with $C^{\underline{1}}$–$M^{\underline{3}}$.

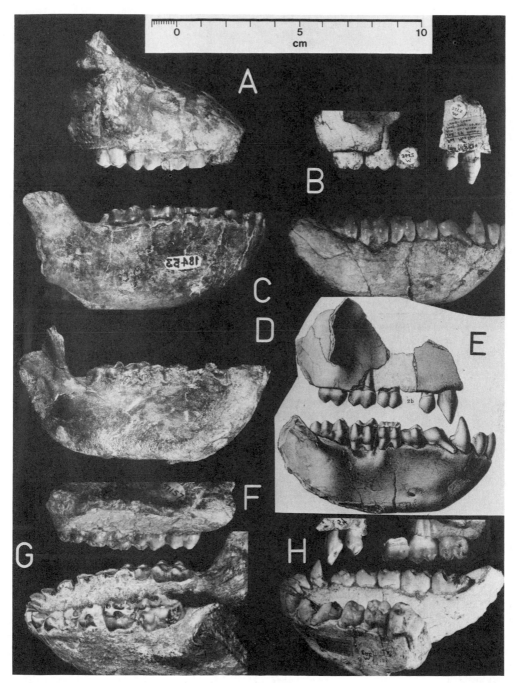

Figure 181. *Procynocephalus subhimalayanus.* Late Pliocene, Asia. Female maxilla with right C^1–M^3: A, lateral view; F, lingual view. Female mandible with complete dentition: C, right lateral view (photographically reversed); G, oblique right lingual (and left buccal) view. Referred ?male mandible with damaged right P_3–M_3: D, right lateral view. *Procynocephalus wimani.* Late Pliocene, Asia. Female mandible lacking only left M_3 and ?associated right C^1–P^3 and M^{1-3} in maxillary fragments: B, right lateral view; E, partial reconstruction of same; H, right lingual view (oblique of mandible, with left buccal showing also). [E from Schlosser (1924).]

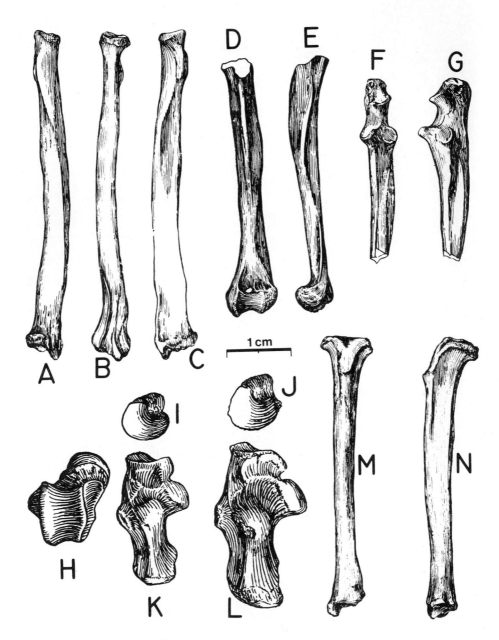

Figure 182. *Procynocephalus wimani.* Late Pliocene, Asia. Left ?male radius: A, anterior view; B, lateral view; C, posterior view. Left ?female humerus lacking proximal end: D, anterior view; E, lateral view. Left ?male ulna: F, anterior view; G, lateral view. Left ?female astragalus: H, dorsal view. Left ?female calcaneus: I, distal view; K, plantar view. Left ?male calcaneus: J, distal view; L, plantar view. Left ?female tibia: M, anterior view; N, lateral view. [From Teilhard (1938).]

and female(?) humerus figured by Teilhard (Figure 182, D–G) are similar in shape to those of terrestrial cercopithecines, demonstrating distinction of this species from *Macaca*. Unfortunately, neither the Kutitsun nor Choukoutien specimens could be located during a recent trip to Peking, and the same is true for upper and lower jaws from Yüshe, mentioned by Teilhard (1938).

Even fewer remains are known from India, namely, two mandibles and a maxilla from sediments of supposedly Pinjor-equivalent age. It is of minor interest to note that the maxilla (Figures 180E and 181, A and F) which is now the type of *Procynocephalus subhimalayanus* was the first fossil monkey to have been published (Baker and Durand, 1836) and the first fossil recognized as being primate. The mandible named "*C.*" *falconeri*, which was found soon afterward, is of an old male with the few remaining cheek teeth strongly worn and reduced in length (Figures 180C and 180D). It is somewhat smaller, with shorter teeth than the maxilla, which is female, and thus it has long been thought that two species had to have been represented. However, the dentition is similar in size to that of *P. wimani*, and if wear and mesial drift are considered, it is possible that one is dealing with two members of a single species, perhaps with a male smaller than average in size. This conclusion is reinforced by the recent discovery by Verma (1969) of a female mandible (Figures 180B and 181, C and G), which conforms well to the maxilla. The "*falconeri*" mandible is larger than any known macaque, including *M. anderssoni* to which Jolly (1967) referred it, and is deep

and robust like the female, but unlike *P. wimani*. The most parsimonious course, taken here, is to consider all three Indian specimens as *P. subhimalayanus*.

The two species seem to differ slightly in size and especially in mandibular robusticity (see Figure 181), although with so few specimens no clear idea of variation can be formulated. They share large size and lack fossae on the mandible and maxilla. More important, the Indian maxilla is damaged dorsally, but seems clearly enough to have had the macaque type of profile, rather than the steep drop found in baboons. Both this character and the unhollowed maxilla or mandible are probably ancestral but suggest derivation from the Eurasian cercopithecines rather than secondary invasion by *Papio*-related forms, which might have been inferred to some extent from the "terrestrial" joint proportions.

A very similar form in Europe, *Paradolichopithecus*, is now better known both cranially and postcranially. Jolly (1967) suggested possibly, and Simons (1970) stated more definitely, that these two genera might be synonymous because they share those features which are used here to distinguish *Procynocephalus*. On the other hand, it is almost as simple to argue on grounds of similar dental morphology that *Procynocephalus* is congeneric with *Dinopithecus* or *Gorgopithecus*, as its cranial shape is so little known. It appears that the maxilla drops more steeply anteorbitally in *Procynocephalus* than in *Paradolichopithecus*, and until a full study is completed, both genera, as well as both species of *Procynocephalus*, are recognized here.

PARADOLICHOPITHECUS Necrasov, Samson, and Radulesco, 1961

(= or including: *Dolichopithecus* Déperet, 1889: Déperet, 1929 and many others. ?*Procynocephalus* Schlosser, 1924: Simons, 1970. "*Dolichopithecus*": Delson, 1974b. *Paradolichopithecus* "genero nuevo": Aguirre and Soto, 1975, lapsus.)

DISTRIBUTION

Pliocene (early through late Villafranchian). Northeastern Spain, south–central France, southern Romania; ?Tadzhikistan, Soviet Central Asia.

KNOWN SPECIES

1. *Paradolichopithecus arvernensis* (Déperet, 1929), type species
(=*Dolichopithecus arvernensis* Déperet, 1929. *Paradolichopithecus geticus* Necrasov, Samson, and Radulesco, 1961. ?*Procynocephalus arvernensis*: Simons, 1970. "*Dolichopithecus*" *arvernensis*: Delson, 1974b. *Paradolichopithecus arvernensis*: Delson, 1975a. *Dolichopithecus gallicus* Necrasov: Macarovici, 1975, lapsus.)
LOCALITIES: Graunceanu (742); Senèze* (758).

2. *Paradolichopithecus sp.*
(=*Dolichopithecus ruscinensis* Déperet, 1889: Simionescu, 1930, in part. *Dolichopithecus arvernensis*: Schaub, 1943, in part. Large cercopithecine cf. *Papio*: Delson, 1971; Aguirre and Soto, 1975. "*Dolichopithecus*" cf. *arvernensis*: Delson, 1974b. cf. *Paradolichopithecus* sp.: Delson, 1975a. *Paradolichopithecus* sp.: Delson and Plopsor, 1975. Monkey: Trofimov and Reshetov, 1975.)
LOCALITIES: Malusteni (644); Vialette (648); Cova Bonica (680); Puebla de Valverde (718); ?Kuruk (746).

DISCUSSION

Paradolichopithecus is a second large terrestrial Eurasian monkey which resembles macaques cranially and baboons postcranially. The form of the skull is now

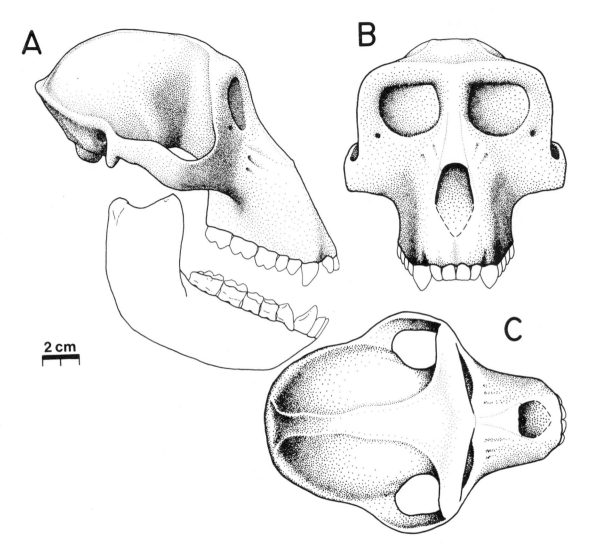

Figure 183. *Paradolichopithecus arvernensis.* Late Pliocene, Europe. Reconstruction of female cranium, in Frankfurt orientation: A, right lateral view; B, frontal view; C, dorsal view. [By. B. Akerbergs.]

known in both males and females, which are essentially similar in shape but larger in size than the largest known macaques. Sexual dimorphism is slight in the cranium, especially with respect to overall size (see below). Both maxilla and mandible are unhollowed by fossae, which would be pronounced in baboons of similar size. The muzzle in a female (Figure 183) descends from glabella in a smooth, hollow curve to rhinion, which projects slightly; the lower face then descends more steeply and in a somewhat convex manner to prosthion. In an undescribed male face, the essential pattern is similar, although the lower face especially is deeper. The lateral flanks of the muzzle are rather deeply grooved below the orbits for vessels exiting the infraorbital foramina. The temporal lines do not meet in the one complete female, but in another they form a low sagittal crest from bregma to lambda, which joins a relatively strong nuchal crest. The neurocranium is somewhat more globular in the female and more elongate in the male. The brain (Radinsky, 1974) is typically cercopithecine. The mandible is of moderate and constant depth; the ramus is somewhat back-tilted (Figure 185). The dentition (Figure 184) is papionin, with large front teeth and moderate molar flare. Postcranial remains (Figure 186) reveal a marked adaptation to terrestrial locomotion: The humerus is robust, with the medial epicondyle well retroflexed; the ulnar olecranon is large and somewhat tilted posteriorly; partial femora are robust; and some phalanges are rather stout. All of these features are seen in terrestrial baboons and other similarly adapted monkeys.

While the female skull is larger than those of the largest living female baboons, the male is smaller than its modern counterpart; moreover, the fossil teeth are not sexually dimorphic. This indicates much less difference between the sexes in cranial dimensions than would be expected in large cercopithecids, recalling *Gorgopithecus* of southern Africa, which is quite similar in known dimensions but apparently distinctive in cranial form. *Paradolichopithecus* is also similar to southern African *Dinopithecus* in the lack of mandibular or maxillary fossae, but the latter has a *Papio*-like muzzle. Neither African genus yet possesses securely allocated postcranial elements. The greatest similarities of the European genus, however, are with east Asian *Procynocephalus*, from which distinction is difficult. Unfortunately, *Procynocephalus* (q.v.) lacks well-preserved facial or cranial parts, rendering direct comparison problematical. Jolly (1967) and especially Simons (1970) suggested synonymizing these two genera, but we refrain from this step here until a complete review of known specimens has been accomplished. The two well-known populations of *Paradolichopithecus* are now considered to represent a single species, while the somewhat older and smaller, more fragmentary remains are not specifically assigned, nor are the essentially unpublished but extensive fossils from the Soviet Union. As with its Asian counterpart, the best estimate of the adaptations of *Paradolichopithecus* involves terrestrial, eclectic feeding in an open habitat, often associated with macaque or *Dolichopithecus*.

Delson and Plopsor (1975) summarized the taxonomic history of this taxon, including its frequent confusion with the colobine *Dolichopithecus*. In brief, Déperet (1929) first described the nearly complete skull and mandible (Figures 183; 184, C and D; and 185, A and B) of an old female from Senèze, considering that it was a later stage in a lineage including his Ruscinian species *D. ruscinensis*; in fact, Déperet linked the two more by size-related characters than by distinctive morphology. As the younger skull was much more complete than those of the earlier "congener," it was the one usually illustrated as an example of the genus (e.g., Piveteau, 1957), which caused problems for reviewers such as Verheyen (1962) and eventually led some (e.g., Vogel, 1966; Jolly, 1967) to suggest removal of *Dolichopithecus* from the Colobinae. A partial face of a large monkey, including the jaws (Figure 184E), was one of the first fossils to be recovered from the Romanian site of Graunceanu, and Necrasov *et al.* (1961) described this as a new form similar to Déperet's. They argued that it was probably colobine, but with some cercopithecine dental features, as well as the unique character of possessing a double notch (for blood vessels) at the superointernal corner of each orbit; this double notch is, in fact, a single notch, typical of larger cercopithecines, especially, next to the broken region where the medial orbit margin turns down along the nasal bones. In preserved regions, this and other Romanian specimens cannot be distinguished from the Senèze holotype, which is still the only specimen of this taxon recovered from that highly fossiliferous locality despite intensive collecting over many years.

The Graunceanu sample, however, now includes a reasonable number of specimens on which to base an idea of population variability: parts of eight crania or mandibles (three subadult) and several postcranial elements (Figures 184, A and F; 185, C–F; and 186). Considering the range of size variation in the teeth of these Graunceanu individuals, the Senèze specimen would be impossible to distinguish from them statistically, as might also be the older specimens (Figure 184, B and G).

All of the latter are somewhat smaller as well as geologically older than the Senèze and Graunceanu populations, but otherwise they are not sufficiently well known to be distinguishable. It is most interesting that such a high percentage of juveniles is represented among known *Paradolichopithecus* specimens, nearly half having died before the third molars erupted. By comparison, of several hundred *Mesopithecus pentelici* jaws from Pikermi, only 4 were subadult, as were perhaps 5 of 30 or more partial tooth rows of *D.*

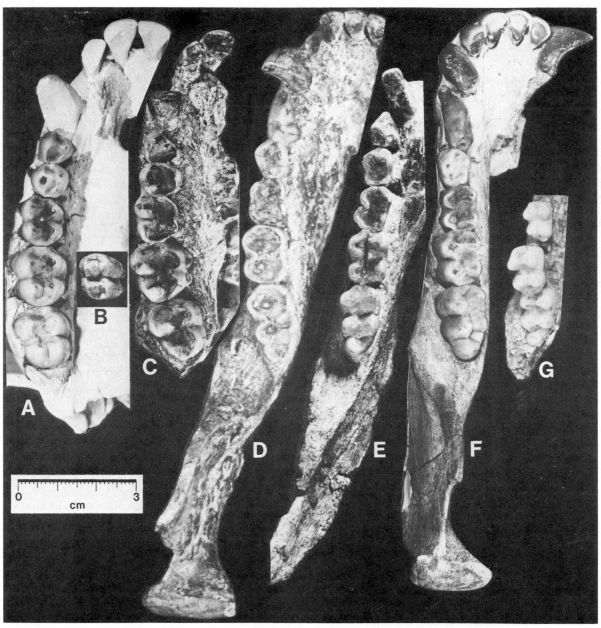

Figure 184. *Paradolichopithecus.* Pliocene, Europe. Occlusal view. *P. arvernensis:* A, male right maxilla with P^3–M^3 and right I^1–C^1 and left I^1 (casts of unassociated teeth); F, portion of mandible of same individual, with left I_1–M_3, right I_1–C_1; C, right maxilla and premaxilla of female with all teeth; D, part mandible of same female with left I_1, C_1–M_3, right I_{1-2}; E, left corpus of female with C_1–M_3. *Paradolichopithecus* sp.: B, isolated right $M^{2?}$; G, left M_{1-3} from juvenile male mandible.

370

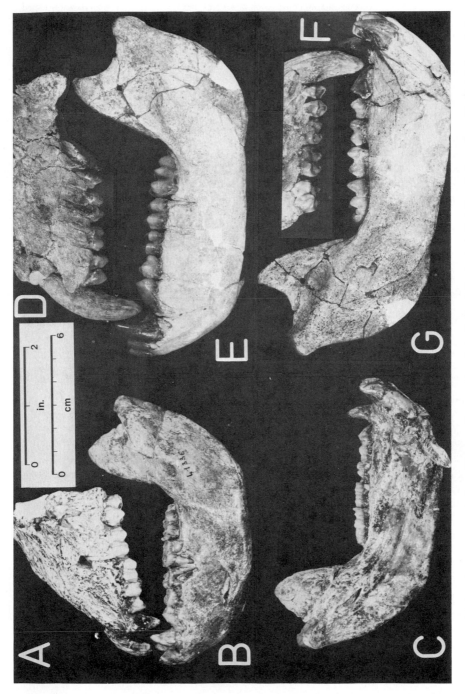

Figure 185. *Paradolichopithecus arvernensis.* Late Pliocene, Europe. Female individual (Senèze). A. Left lateral view of mandible; C, internal view, left mandible. Male (Graunceanu, specimens not associated). D, lateral view of left maxilla; E, lateral view of left mandible; F, lingual view, left C₁–M₃; G, internal view of left mandible with L M₃–R C₁.

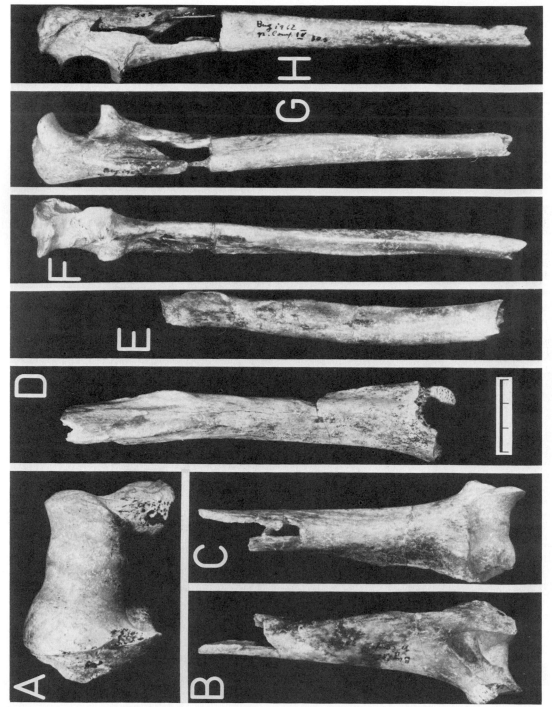

Figure 186. *Paradolichopithecus arvernensis.* Late Pliocene, Europe. Right humerus: A, distal view; B, posterior view; C, anterior view. Left humerus lacking epiphyses: D, anterior view. Right radius lacking head: E, anterior view. Right ulna: F, anterior view; G, lateral view; H, medial view. Each scale division equals 1 cm.

ruscinensis from Perpignan; only *Macaca majori* from Capo Figari has a similar proportion of juveniles among the sample, perhaps indicating some taphonomical similarity.

SUBTRIBE THEROPITHECINA
Jolly, 1966

(= or including: Theropithecini Jolly, 1966.)

DISTRIBUTION
  Pliocene (late Lothagamian) to modern. Africa (see under genus).
INCLUDED TAXA
  Theropithecus I. Geoffroy, 1843.

DISCUSSION

The erection or retention of a monotypic higher taxon always demands some justification. Vram (1922) was the first to suggest a family–group taxon solely for *Theropithecus*, although he indicated a subfamily, without actually naming it. Jolly (1966) included in his tribe [set off from the Cercopithecini and Cercocebini (=Macacina plus Papionina of this arrangement)] not only *Theropithecus* and *Simopithecus* but also *Dinopithecus* and *Gorgopithecus*, which have since proved to be more closely related to *Papio*. The distinctiveness of *Theropithecus* rests especially in its dentition and in the complex of cranial and some postcranial features (see under the genus) related to its dietary habits. The genus presents some features which ally it with the Eurasian macaques (dispersed nature of the female sexual skin, especially) and other features which are more like *Papio*: ancestrally deep facial fossae, steep anteorbital drop, moderate to high molar flare, protein homologies, and karyology, as well as those features reflecting size and terrestrial adaptation which are most likely parallel developments. The dental and cranial allomorphic trends described by Jolly (1972) are opposed to those seen in *Papio*, in terms of anterior

tooth size, mandibular shape and ramus height, and temporal musculature development.

The question, then, is whether *Theropithecus* is a relatively recent offshoot of the Papionina, especially close to *Papio* as suggested by some molecular (and morphological) studies, or an ancient lineage which merits recognition at suprageneric rank. From both morphology and historical zoogeography, it appears that macaque ancestry was distinct from that of sub-Saharan papionins at least by the time of divergence of *Theropithecus*, which yields an upper limit for the latter of some 6 MY. On the other hand, dental remains attributable to *Theropithecus* sp. are known in eastern Africa as early as 4 MY ago and in northern Africa by perhaps 3.5 MY ago. By 3 MY, *Theropithecus* populations are common and diverse between South Africa and Ethiopia. If these fossils are indeed closely related to the living *T. gelada*, as now appears indisputable, the molecular results demand that lineages leading to the mandrills and the two mangabey groups had already differentiated, in addition to the separation of *Theropithecus* from *Papio* (*Chaeropithecus*) and its diversification, in a time period of less than 3 MY. Moreover, during that time period, there is no definite indication in the known fossil record of any *Papio* species, the common papioninan being the conservative *Parapapio*. Thus, it may well be that the morphological features shared by *Theropithecus* and *Papio* are more dependent on increased size than on recent common ancestry, although this explanation cannot clearly be used to account for the several molecular similarities. These molecular similarities require further study and perhaps functional analysis, but at present they seem to be outweighed by the above evidence. In sum, given also the large number of autapomorphic states characterizing *Theropithecus*, it appears most reasonable to postulate an environmentally controlled allopatric division of late Miocene Papionini into three sections (see under the tribe) and to rank these equally as subtribes.

THEROPITHECUS I. Geoffroy, 1843

(Synonymy listed under subgenera.)

DISTRIBUTION
  Mid-Pliocene (late Lothagamian) to modern. Algeria, eastern Africa from northern Ethiopia to the Cape of Good Hope.

INCLUDED SUBGENERA
  Theropithecus (*Theropithecus*), *T.* (*Simopithecus*), and unnamed, new subgenus.

THEROPITHECUS (THEROPITHECUS) I. Geoffroy, 1843

(= or including: *Macacus:* Rüppell, 1835. *Gelada* Gray, 1843.*
Theropythecus Vram, 1922, lapsus? *Papio:* Buettner-Janusch, 1966.)

DISTRIBUTION

Modern. Central Ethiopian plateau.

KNOWN SPECIES

1. *Theropithecus (T.) gelada* (Rüppell, 1835), type species
(= *Macacus gelada* Rüppell, 1835. *Gelada rueppelli* Gray, 1843.
Theropithecus senex Pucheran, 1857. *Theropithecus nedjo* Reichenbach,
1863. *Theropithecus gelada obscurus* Heuglin, 1863; *Macacus obscurus:*
Schlegel, 1876.)

THEROPITHECUS (SIMOPITHECUS) Andrews, 1916

(= or including: *Simopithecus* Andrews, 1916. *Papio* Erxleben, 1777:
Broom and Jensen, 1946; Mollett, 1947; Kitching *et al.*, 1948; Broom
and Robinson, 1949; Dart, 1949; Hopwood and Hollyfield, 1954, all in
part. *Dinopithecus* Broom, 1937: Broom and Hughes, 1949, in part.
Gorgopithecus Broom and Robinson, 1949a: Kitching, 1953, in part.
Brachygnathopithecus Kitching, 1952, in part.)

DISTRIBUTION

Late Pliocene (Rodolfian) to late middle or late Pleistocene. Algeria,
eastern Africa from northern Ethiopia to the Cape of Good Hope.

KNOWN SPECIES AND SUBSPECIES

2. *Theropithecus (S.) oswaldi* (Andrews, 1916), subgeneric type
(synonymy and localities under subspecies)
   a. *Theropithecus (S.) oswaldi oswaldi* (Andrews, 1916)
[=*Simopithecus oswaldi* Andrews, 1916. *Simopithecus oswaldi oswaldi:*
Leakey and Whitworth, 1958. *Theropithecus (S.) o. oswaldi:* Jolly, 1972.]
LOCALITIES: Kanjera★ (880).
   b. *Theropithecus (S.) oswaldi leakeyi* (Hopwood, 1934)
[= *Simopithecus leakeyi* Hopwood, 1934. *Simopithecus oswaldi "oldu-
vaiensis"* Leakey and Whitworth, 1958, nomen nudum, no type designated. *Simopithecus oswaldi leakeyi:* Leakey, 1965. ?*Theropithecus (S.)
darti danieli* (Freedman, 1957): Jolly, 1972, in part. *Theropithecus (S.) o.
leakeyi:* Jolly, 1972.]
LOCALITIES: Olduvai Gorge, ?Bed I (760), ?lower Bed II (774), upper
Bed II (804), Bed III (820), Bed IV★ (856).
   c. *Theropithecus (S.) oswaldi danieli* (Freedman, 1957), new combination.
[=*Simopithecus* sp.: Robinson, 1952. *Simopithecus danieli* Freedman,
1957. *Simopithecus oswaldi danieli:* Singer, 1962. *Theropithecus (S.) darti
danieli:* Jolly, 1972. *Simopithecus darti danieli:* Freedman, 1976.]
LOCALITIES: Swartkrans a★ (752).
   d. *Theropithecus (S.) oswaldi jonathoni* (Leakey and Whitworth,
1958), new combination
[=*Simopithecus jonathoni* Leakey and Whitworth, 1958. *Theropithecus
(S.) oswaldi leakeyi:* Jolly, 1972, in part.]
LOCALITIES: Olduvai Gorge, lower Ndutu Beds★ (928).
   e. *Theropithecus (S.) oswaldi mariae* Jolly, 1972

---

*There has long been a question as to which generic name
for the gelada was published earlier in 1843. Through the
courtesy of librarians in the London and Paris museums of
natural history, we have been informed that Gray's work
appeared in late May or early June, whereas Geoffroy's work
probably was published as a separate fascicle at the end of
1842 or quite early in 1843. Thus, Geoffroy's name has
priority, confirming common usage.

(= *Simopithecus oswaldi mariae* L. Leakey and Whitworth, 1958, *nomen
nudum,* no type; M. Leakey and R. Leakey, 1973a.)
LOCALITIES: Olorgesailie★ (870).
   f. *Theropithecus (S.) oswaldi hopefieldensis* (Singer, 1962)
[=*Simopithecus oswaldi hopefieldensis* Singer, 1962. *Theropithecus (S.)
oswaldi* cf. *leakeyi:* Jolly, 1972; *Simopithecus darti hopefieldensis:* Freed-
man, 1976.]
LOCALITIES: Gladysvale (1030); Hopefield★ (1034).
   g. *Theropithecus (S.) aff. oswaldi* subsp. indet. A
[= *Simopithecus* cf. *major:* Cooke, 1963, *nomen nudum. Theropithecus
(Simopithecus) aff. oswaldi* subsp.: Delson, 1975a.]
LOCALITIES: Ternifine (858).
   h. *Theropithecus (S.) aff. oswaldi* subsp. indet B
(=*Theropithecus oswaldi:* Eck, 1976; M. Leakey, 1976.)
LOCALITIES: Omo Group, Shungura members ?E (726) and F, G, H, J,
and L (738), 750), (776), (794), and (822); East Rudolf, Koobi Fora Fm.,
Lower (728), Upper (796), and Ileret (798) members; ?Afar region
earlier Pleistocene.
   i. *Theropithecus (S.) aff. oswaldi*
(=*Simopithecus* sp.: Hopwood, 1939. *Simopithecus oswaldi:* Cooke and
Coryndon, 1970.)
LOCALITIES: Kaiso Village (704).

3. *Theropithecus (Simopithecus) darti* (Broom and Jensen, 1946)
[=*Papio darti* Broom and Jensen, 1946. *Dinopithecus* sp.: Broom and
Hughes, 1949, in part. *Brachyganthopithecus peppercorni* Kitching, 1952,
in part. *Gorgopithecus wellsi* Kitching, 1953. *Gorgopithecus darti:* Kitch-
ing, 1953. *Simopithecus darti:* Freedman, 1957. *Simopithecus oswaldi
darti:* Singer, 1962. *Theropithecus (S.) darti darti:* Jolly, 1972.
Simopithecus darti darti: Freedman, 1976.]
LOCALITIES: Makapan★ (700); ?aff: Hadar (698); East Rudolf Koobi
Fora lower mbr. (728).

THEROPITHECUS, new and unnamed subgenus

(=*Dinopithecus* Broom, 1937: Arambourg, 1947, in part. *Simopithecus*
Andrews, 1916: Freedman, 1957. *Theropithecus:* Jolly, 1972, in part.)

DISTRIBUTION

Later Pliocene (mid Rodolfian). Lake Turkana basin: southern
Ethiopia and northern Kenya.

KNOWN SPECIES

4. *Theropithecus brumpti* (Arambourg, 1947)
[=*Dinopithecus brumpti* Arambourg, 1947. *Simopithecus oswaldi:*
Leakey and Whitworth, 1958, in part. *Theropithecus* (cf. *darti*): Jolly,
1972. *Theropithecus brumpti:* Eck, 1976; M. Leakey, 1976.]
LOCALITIES: Omo Group, Usno Fm. (694), Shungura Fm. members
A–G and ?H, (672), (696), (712), (716), (726), (738), (750), and ?(776);
East Rudolf, Kubi Algi (699).

THEROPITHECUS, subgenus indeterminate

KNOWN SPECIES

5. *Theropithecus* spp. indet.
(=*Cynocephalus atlanticus* Thomas, 1884. *Papio atlanticus:* Romer, 1928.
Simopithecus sp.: Patterson *et al.*, 1970. *Theropithecus* sp.: Delson,
1974b. *Theropithecus "atlanticus":* Delson, 1975a.)
LOCALITIES: Lothagam-3 (647); Ain Jourdel (684).

DISCUSSION

Theropithecus species are large, terrestrial baboon-
like monkeys whose fossils dominate the primate

faunas of the African Plio-Pleistocene. As will be seen from the immense list of synonymy, they have been intensively studied, especially by Jolly (1972), but there is still disagreement about the classification and relationships of the numerous sampled populations. This arrangement is a modification of Jolly's, based in part on additional material discussed below.

The basic adaptations of *Theropithecus*, as interpreted by Jolly (1972, also 1967, 1970b) and Maier (1972a especially), are related to its terrestrial life, diet, and feeding posture. The interaction of these three aspects of its biology can be observed in the living *T. (T.) gelada,* but in fact Jolly (1965) suggested some of these factors for the fossil forms before the first accurate reports of behavior had been published (by Crook, 1966). The common features linking the diverse members of the genus include a distinctive molar pattern, which somewhat converged on colobine-like crown relief from a typical papionin ancestry; reduction of the anterior dentition, proportionately smaller in larger forms; retention of an upright mandibular ramus (higher in larger forms) and a deep and short face; sagittal crest placed anteriorly (if present); elongate forelimb, especially humerus; expanded and back-tilted olecranon process of the ulna, combined with small and retroflected medial epicondyle of the humerus (see Figure 191); and short, stout phalanges, reduced hallux, but long and mobile pollex (in the living gelada, unknown in fossils). In terms of soft anatomy, *T. (T.) gelada* has accessory sitting pads, a pair of fat-filled cushions ventral to the typically papionin ischial callosities, and a pectoral area of naked skin, which in females develops a catamenial swelling; in addition, they share typical papionin cheek pouches [although Murray (1975) reports these to be quite small] and a diploid chromosome number of 42.

The dental (and some cranial) specializations are most distinctive and are the major reason for the decision to rank *Theropithecus* as subtribally separate from other papionins. The cheek teeth have especially high crowns with greatly increased relief, with foveae deeply excavated and notches deeply incised, nearly to the cervix; the trigonid is somewhat foreshortened, as in colobines, but still deep; and the cusps are somewhat columnar in form, as a result of their separation from one another by the deep basins. The lower molar mesial buccal cleft is flattened at its base into a "pocket" instead of blending smoothly onto the buccal face; the lophids and trigonid basin are angled

mesiolingually, oblique to the long axis of the lower molars; and, on $M_{\overline{2}}$ (and some $M_{\overline{1}}$), there is a large distal accessory cuspule, which projects backward toward the succeeding tooth. The appearance of a longitudinal crest is produced by the position of the buccal margin (lingual in uppers) nearly on the midline at the notch bases, so that the margin itself, especially when somewhat worn, seems to be a loph(id) (see Freedman's 1957 descriptions). Combined with a delayed eruption pattern of the posterior cheek teeth, the high relief and molar complexity produce a distinctive wear pattern which prolongs the functional life of the tooth-row and is eminently adapted to the mastication of grass blades, seeds, and rhizomes, which make up the bulk of the gelada diet. Moreover, with wear, the teeth become mesiodistally crowded and shortened. The anterior dentition demonstrates a trend to reduction which differs among the known species: Incisors are typically smaller than usual for papionins, while the canines are also reduced in larger forms, especially *T. (S.) oswaldi.* Most of these features (but not canine reduction) can be observed in the illustration of *T. (T.) gelada*'s dentition (Figure 187), as well as in the photographs of fossil teeth (Figures 189 and 190). Similar patterns of dentition are seen, among other primates, in the lemuriform *Hadropithecus* (see Figure 81) and, among other mammals, in proboscideans, some suids, and especially kangaroos (Macropodidae), all of which share some of the gelada's grazing habits.

Cranial morphology is more variable among the several subgenera of *Theropithecus* (see Figures 188 and 189), but shared derived characters include the upright mandibular ramus, deep posterior maxilla, short and generally convex premaxilla with vertical incisors, relatively steep anteorbital drop and hollowed maxillary profile, narrow postorbital constriction, vertical zygoma, anteriorly placed temporal musculature (and sagittal crest, if present), unraised nasal bones, and divided temporomandibular articular surface. Most of these, other than perhaps the last two, can be interpreted again as part of a functional complex adapted to prolonged chewing, with a concentration on the distal elements, perhaps ontogenetically canalized by continuation of growth in the posterior maxilla, coupled with delayed eruption of distal teeth and early cessation of premaxillary expansion.

The described postcranial characters include a number of adaptations to an exclusively terrestrial existence (in the elbow, foot, and shoulder) coupled

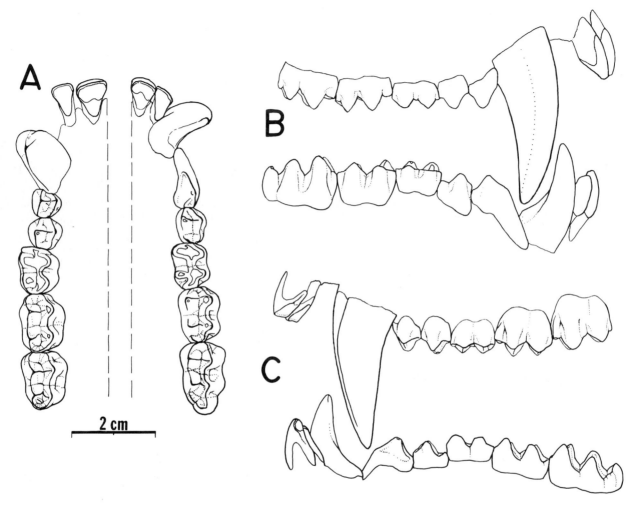

Figure 187. Dental morphology of Theropithecina. *Theropithecus gelada;* modern, male, Africa. A, right upper tooth-row on left, right lower tooth-row on right, occlusal view; B, buccal view; C, lingual view. [By B. Akerbergs.]

with those which reflect the feeding posture seen at least in *T. (T.) gelada.* This species sits in groups in open grasslands, gathering food by hand, especially plucking items with the long and mobile thumb, then transferring them directly to the mouth, where the incisors do minimal work before the cheek teeth take over. Jolly (1972) has considered that the long forelimb is a part of this complex, but in view of the allometric relationships reported by Biegert and Maurer (1972), this feature may reflect only large size, although perhaps the relatively long humerus (compared to radius or femur) is in fact an aspect of "hand-grazing."

This point is important, for no pollicial digits are known in the fossil record which can substantiate Jolly's view (based solely on forelimb elongation) that *T. (Simopithecus)* had a similar diet and ecology to *T. (Theropithecus).* Further analysis of the allometry involved may require some changes in this model, which is accepted here in the interim. Given this interpretive foundation and Jolly's (1972) demonstration that the most common occurrences of *Theropithecus* fossils are in waterside, especially seasonally flooded habitats, it appears reasonable that the origin of the group reflects an occupation of this type of

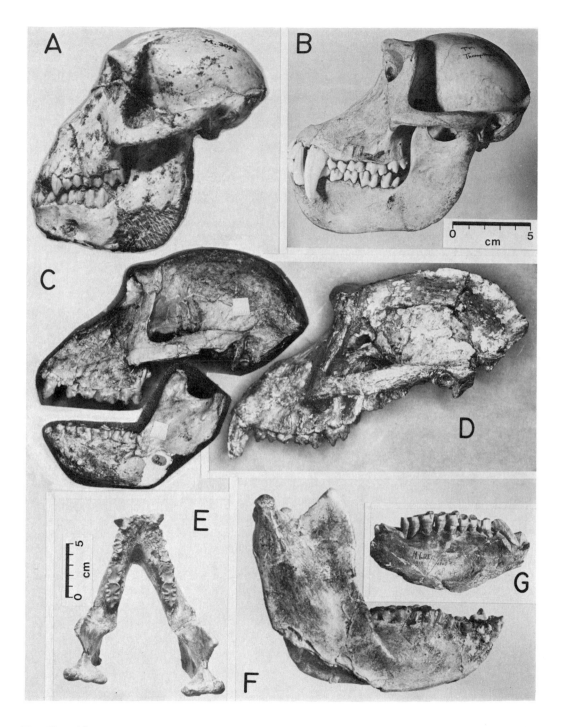

Figure 188. *Theropithecus (T.) gelada,* modern. Nearly adult male skull and mandible: B, left lateral view. *Theropithecus (Simopithecus) darti.* Subadult female skull and mandible: A, left lateral view. Male mandible with right P₃-M₃: G, right lateral view. *T. (S.) oswaldi oswaldi.* Female mandible and unassociated female skull: C, left lateral view. Male skull: D, left lateral view. *T. (S.) oswaldi jonathoni.* Male mandible with damaged right and left C̄ₜ-M̄₃: E, occlusal view; F, right lateral view. The scale on B is for all but E (own scale).

377

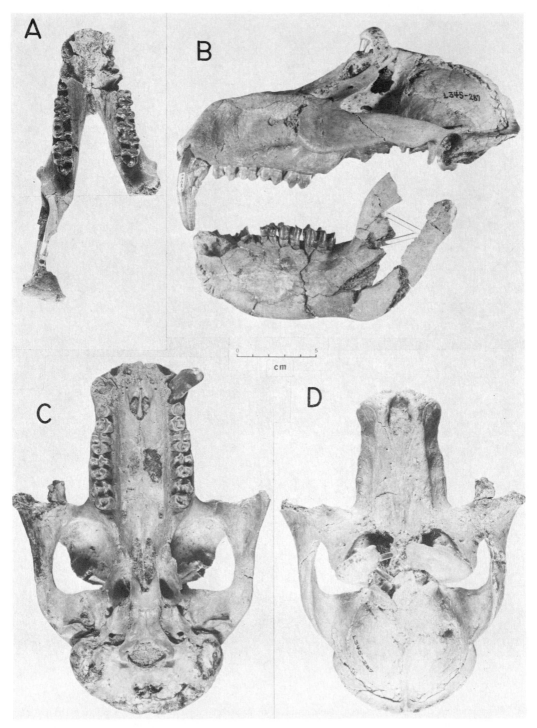

Figure 189. *Theropithecus brumpti*. Pliocene, Africa. Unassociated male cranium and mandible. A, mandible in occlusal view; B, left lateral view; C, basal view; D, dorsal view. [With permission from G. G. Eck, *Journal of Human Evolution*, 6, 1977. Copyright by Academic Press Inc. (London) Ltd.]

biome, with only the living species restricted to a relict distribution in drier grasslands.

The main characters and evolutionary relationships of the several subgenera can be briefly reviewed, based on the above framework. *Theropithecus (Theropithecus)* includes only the single living species, which is morphologically conservative in a number of craniodental features, as well as being the smallest recognized species, at the smaller end of the modern *Papio* range. The ancestral retentions of this subgenus include somewhat lower crowned and less complex molars, hollowed internal symphyseal profile, mesially deepening mandibular corpus, deep maxillary and mandibular fossae, and low anterior muzzle (all more as in typical Papionini, especially Papionina); see Figure 188B. The small size of *T. (T.) gelada* may account in part for the relatively less reduced incisors and quite little reduced canine–$P_{\overline{3}}$ complex, following Jolly's allomorphic hypothesis. Jolly (1972) has further suggested that the upright ramus of the gelada and some but not all fossil forms may have been developed convergently, but it seems more likely to have been at least partly retained from a small, ancestral papionin. The autapomorphic characters of the subgenus *T. (Theropithecus)* include a narrow nasal aperture (suggested to be an adaptation to breathing the cold and dry air of the high plateau), an evenly concave facial profile (related to the very low anterior maxilla), paired tubercles on the inferior border of the anterior nasal opening, and hemispherical premaxilla (both related to a lip-raising facial display?). Jolly (1972) and Maier (1972b) argued for an early separation of the gelada line from the other subgenera, perhaps around 3.5 MY ago, based on the distribution of known fossils. The lineage may have remained in northern Ethiopia throughout its existence, but this hypothesis cannot be disproved without finding fossils elsewhere which pertain to it.

The taxon *Simopithecus* has always been recognized as having close relationships with modern *Theropithecus*, but authors have interpreted it variably as (1) representing all fossil "baboons" (Remane, 1924; Dietrich, 1942); (2) being distinct from both *Theropithecus* and *Papio*, if somewhat closer to the former (Leakey and Whitworth, 1958); (3) being a distinct genus, but nonetheless having special phyletic links to *Theropithecus* (Freedman, 1957, 1976; Maier, 1970, 1972a,b; M. and R. Leakey, 1973a); or (4) being best ranked as a subgenus of *Theropithecus* (Jolly, 1970b).

With the recognition of the existence of at least one other well-defined group of *Theropithecus*-like fossils here (see below), it seems most useful to accept subgeneric rank for each, with the possibility that more detailed analysis of the better fossils being recovered may lead to one or more subgenera being raised in rank to full generic status within the subtribe.

The diagnostic features of *T. (Simopithecus)* are manifested as a series of generally concordant morphoclines, rather than as constant "key characters." These "trends" include reduction (shallowing) of maxillary and mandibular fossae; shallowing of symphysis and reduction of planum excavation; constancy of mandibular corpus depth (rather than deepening mesially); increasing complexity of cheek tooth crowns; extreme reduction of incisors, especially in larger forms; similar reduction of male (and female) canine–$P_{\overline{3}}$ complex in large forms; delaying of third molar eruption; and perhaps increasing robusticity of body build (see Figures 190 and 191). Many of these features may be canalized allometrically by increasing body size. In addition, the ancestral shape of the premaxilla and nasal aperture is retained from typical papionins. The major differences between the two recognized species would appear to be that *T. (S.) oswaldi* had progressed farther along the morphoclines indicated above than had *T. (S.) darti*. Thus, in the former, the fossae are quite shallow or absent, the female muzzle is lower anteriorly, the male mandible is of constant corpus depth, the upper surface of the symphysis is rather flat, and the incisors and male canines and $P_{\overline{3}}$ are quite small, although there is some variation in these characters and especially in size among the subspecies (compare crania and mandibles of the two species in Figure 188, A, C, and D). The morphocline placements of most, but by no means all, populations agree with predictions based on stratigraphy: The Kanjera specimens, for example, are much more "primitive" (small in size with ancestral morphology of some features) than would be expected from their apparently late date. Further material may indicate that only one lineage is indeed being sampled (Jolly, 1972), in which case a single species might be the best way to recognize this situation taxonomically.

Theropithecus darti has been described only from Makapan (Figures 188, A and G, and 190G), but numerous specimens from East Africa appear best referred to this species, especially on the basis of large incisors. Maier (1972b) contested Jolly's (1970b) view

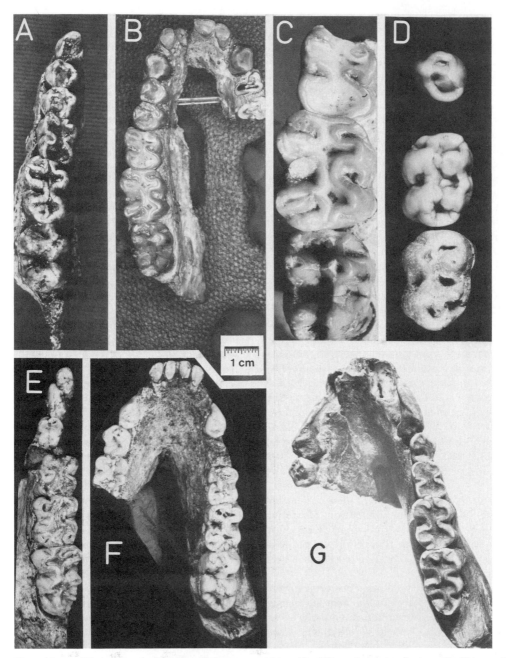

Figure 190. *Theropithecus (Simopithecus)*. Pliocene–Pleistocene, Africa. Dentitions in occlusal view. *T. (S.) oswaldi danieli:* A, female right maxilla with C^1–M^3; E, female left corpus with $C_{\overline{1}}$–$M_{\overline{3}}$; F, female mandible with left $I_{\overline{1-2}}$, $P_{\overline{3}}$–$M_{\overline{1}}$, right $I_{\overline{1-2}}$, $P_{\overline{3}}$, $M_{\overline{1-3}}$. *T (S.) oswaldi oswaldi:* B, female partial palate with right I^2–M^3, left I^1–C^1; C, enlargement of same right M^{1-3}. *T. (S.) aff. oswaldi* subsp. indet. A: D, isolated and unassociated left P^4, M^{2-3}, less wear than C. *T. (S.) darti:* G, male mandible with left $P_{\overline{3-4}}$, right $P_{\overline{3}}$–$M_{\overline{3}}$. [A courtesy of and © R. L. Ciochon.]

380

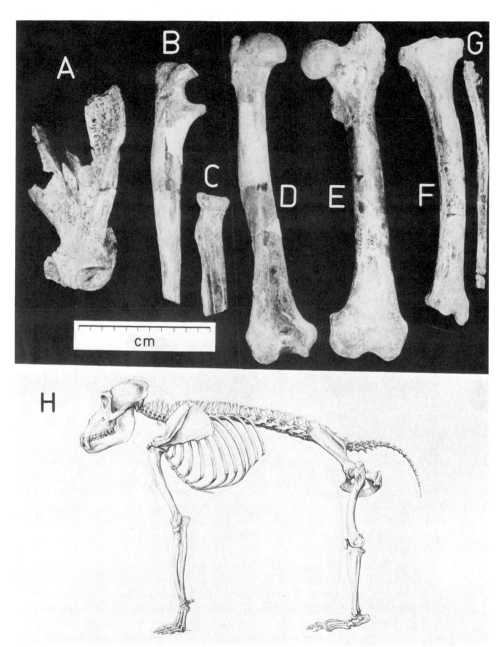

Figure 191. *Theropithecus (Simopithecus) oswaldi leakeyi* Early Pleistocene, Africa. Associated partial skeleton of male. A, right scapula, dorsal view; B, right ulna, lateral view; C, right radius, anterior view; D, right humerus, posterior view; E, right femur, anterior view; F, right tibia, anterior view; G, partial right fibula, anterior view. H, reconstruction of complete skeleton; note cranium and anterior dentition too *Papio*-like. [H by J. M. Matternes, courtesy of and © National Geographic Society.]

that incisor reduction was under way in Makapan *T. (S.) darti,* but his own descriptions indicate that it had indeed begun, as compared to the ancestral papionin. Although both Jolly (1972) and Freedman (1976) grouped the Swartkrans population with *T. darti,* "*S. danieli*" is morphologically more like *T. oswaldi,* sharing mainly geographical occurrence with *T. darti.*

All of the Olduvai *Theropithecus* specimens were ranked as *S. oswaldi leakeyi* by M. and R. Leakey (1973a), but specimens from Bed I and lower Bed II are only tentatively referred to this taxon (see also Jolly, 1972), pending further knowledge of the anterior dentition. The single specimen of "*S. jonathoni*" (Figure 188, E and F) was originally considered female, but Jolly (1972) and, especially, M. and R. Leakey (1973a) have argued that it could well be a male which had reduced its $P_{\overline{3}}$ mesial flange almost completely because of an inferred lateral placement of the upper canine, removing it from $P_{\overline{3}}$ occlusion. This apparent continuation of the typical *T. (S.) oswaldi* trend leads to the present interpretation of this specimen as representing a subspecies thereof. It is worth noting further that Hay (1976) indicated that this specimen derives from the lower Ndutu Beds, higher in the Olduvai sequence than had been previously thought. *Theropithecus oswaldi* was extensively hunted by Acheulean peoples at Olorgesailie and probably at Olduvai, and Jolly (1972) has suggested that an early late Pleistocene increase in human population, which centered on the lakeside habitats preferred by *Theropithecus,* brought both increased predation and disturbance of the local ecology, thus leading to the extinction of this subgenus and the reduction of the genus to its relict state.

Eck (1976, 1977) has now been able to show that two forms of *Theropithecus* occur in the Omo sequence, and M. Leakey (1976) reports the same two at East Rudolf but in different proportions; in both areas, *Theropithecus* is the dominant element in the primate fauna. Eck tentatively employed Arambourg's (1947) name *brumpti* (originally based only on a few teeth) for the cranially distinctive species occurring alongside *T. (S.)* cf. *oswaldi.* The new form would appear to merit at least subgeneric status, on the basis of the large, flaring zygomatics and deeply excavated maxillary and mandibular fossae on both males (Figure 189) and females, as well as large posteriorly placed sagittal crest and large anterior dentition, in males at least. Apart from the autapomorphy involved in the zygomatic development, this group may be more simi-

lar to *T. (Theropithecus)* than to *T. (Simopithecus)* in muzzle shape, fossa development, and, most important, the possible presence of prenasal tubercles (Jolly, personal communication).

The Lothagam-3 specimen has never been illustrated, but it is clearly typical of *Theropithecus,* confirming the presence of the genus at least as early as 4 MY ago. An unworn lower (first?) molar from Ain Jourdel, Algeria, was long thought to be a typical papionin, but in fact has *Theropithecus* morphology, although it is slightly elongate and lacks a flattened base to its median lingual notch.

SUBFAMILY COLOBINAE
Blyth, 1875

(= or including: Presbytina Gray, 1825. Semnopthiecidae Owen, 1843. Colobidae Blyth, 1875. Colobinae Elliot, 1913.)

DISTRIBUTION
  Late Miocene (Turolian, Ngororan) to modern. Old World; as for the family, except Asia, northern limits Iran, northern India, and southern China.,
INCLUDED TAXA
  Subtribes Colobina and Semnopithecina.

DISCUSSION

Today, the colobines, or leaf-eating Old World monkeys, are in general a more arboreal and geographically restricted group than the cercopithecines, but the fossil record shows that this was not always the case, and adds greatly to an understanding of their true diversity. Once again, their predominant typifying character is one of soft tissues, namely, the great expansion of the digestive tract involved in the processing of large quantities of foliage (see Kuhn, 1964; Bauchop and Martucci, 1968). Unfortunately, no detailed comparative study across the whole subfamily has been made of these organs, comparable to Murray's (1975) review of cercopithecine cheek pouches, but Kuhn's work did not indicate any major differences in form or function among those species studied, both African and Asian. Thus, the "fundamental niche" of the colobines would appear to have been a concentration on leaves and other immature tree parts in the middle and upper canopy, perhaps especially the terminal branches, a habitat now occupied by many living colobines.

In composing the ancestral morphotype of the Colobinae (Delson, 1975a), one finds that the anterior dentition, skull, and perhaps postcranium are relatively conservative, while the cheek teeth, mandible, and soft parts are derived, by comparison to the ancestral cercopithecids. The small incisors, especially the conical I^2, of colobines are thus retentions, although the shape of the lower incisor crowns [e.g., lateral "prong" on $I_{\overline{2}}$ (Delson, 1973)] may be derived. The molariform teeth and premolars are characterized by an increase in crown relief, such that the lower molar lingual notches are extremely deep, reaching almost to the cervix (see Figure 192, illustrating *Nasalis*). This is less true of upper cheek teeth, but their relief does seem to be greater than in cercopithecines, and they are further distinguished by an asymmetrical curve of the distal margin of the teeth. The trigonid basin is mesiodistally shortened on the lower molariform teeth, accessory cuspules are very rare, and the mesial width is less than the distal, except on $M_{\overline{3}}$ (but also there in some African colobines). The $M_{\overline{3}}$ hypoconulid is usually lacking only in rare specimens, especially in smaller species (e.g., *Mesopithecus*), but is almost always missing or reduced in *P. (Presbytis)*. The distal fovea behind the $dP_{\overline{3}}$ hypolophid may be reduced or lost entirely, and the mesial lingual notch is shallower than expected. The upper third molar seldom is reduced distally, but instead may present a fifth, midline cusp. Also on upper teeth, the median lingual cleft often continues to the cervix, while the median buccal notch is not extremely deep. In the premolars, the colobine P^3 is somewhat broad, with a small distal fovea, while the $P_{\overline{4}}$ mesiobuccal region is more flangelike than in cercopithecines and the tooth may be angled with respect to the molar row; the $P_{\overline{4}}$ metaconid is less tall and wide than the protoconid or subequal to it. Both the $P_{\overline{4}}$ metaconid and the P^3 protocone may be reduced, especially in *Colobus* species.

In the cranium, colobines share many features with gibbons, as discussed by Vogel (1966). The face is short, while the neurocranium is often globular and sometimes relatively high. As a consequence of the former, the orbits are widely spaced, the nasal bones and face in general are wide and not high, the lacrimal bone is within the orbit, its fossa extending onto the maxilla, and the ethmoid is a component of the medial orbital wall. Choanal shape is quite variable, with high and narrow, low and wide, and intermediate high and wide patterns occurring, often in species of quite

similar sizes and facial projections. The mandibular corpus is generally deep, often with a bulge under $M_{\overline{3}}$ and an enlarged angle; the body is of constant depth or may shallow mesially; and the ramus is typically subvertical. A median mental foramen occurs only in one modern species, *Colobus verus*, but also in some African fossils. In those colobines with elongated muzzles, especially *Nasalis* and *Dolichopithecus*, the nasals may narrow and elongate and the ramus may tilt back somewhat, in response to functional and morphogenetic demands.

The external brain morphology of colobines appears to be broadly conservative, reflecting less expansion of the occipital, visual, and related areas than in cercopithecines, but possibly with slightly more area linked to limb control (Falk, 1976). The main sulcal characteristics include rectus relatively straight, not diverging from the orbital margin; fronto-orbital sulcus infrequently present; superior temporal and Sylvian sulci subparallel, not converging markedly; lunate and intraparietal sulci arched or dorsorostrally convex, with paroccipital sulcus commonly (but not always) linking the two; and superior branch of the lateral calcarine sulcus present, but occipitotemporal lacking in lateral view.

Colobine long bones are generally gracile, only slightly muscle-marked, reflecting these animals' slender bodies. The foot and all digits are elongate, enabling the animals to better grasp an arboreal substrate, while the lower ankle joint has secondarily redeveloped helical movement. The tail is long, but the thumb is typically reduced, most in the African species and least in early fossils, suggesting that the trend began early in the subfamily's history. The supraradial fossa on the distal humerus is both deeper and larger in area than the ulnar, and the articular surface is wide; the radial articulation on the ulna is shallow and usually single, indicating a less tightly bound joint. Once again, however, the standard caveats about terrestrial colobines resembling cercopithecines still hold.

In terms of soft tissues, the Colobinae have a specialized gut, as discussed above, but no cheek pouches. Their ischial callosities are generally widely separated, and a female sexual swelling occurs only in some *Colobus* subgenera (Kuhn, 1972). The diploid chromosome number is generally 44, but *Nasalis* has 48. This similarity to typical gibbons has led to the suggestion that 44 is the ancestral catarrhine number.

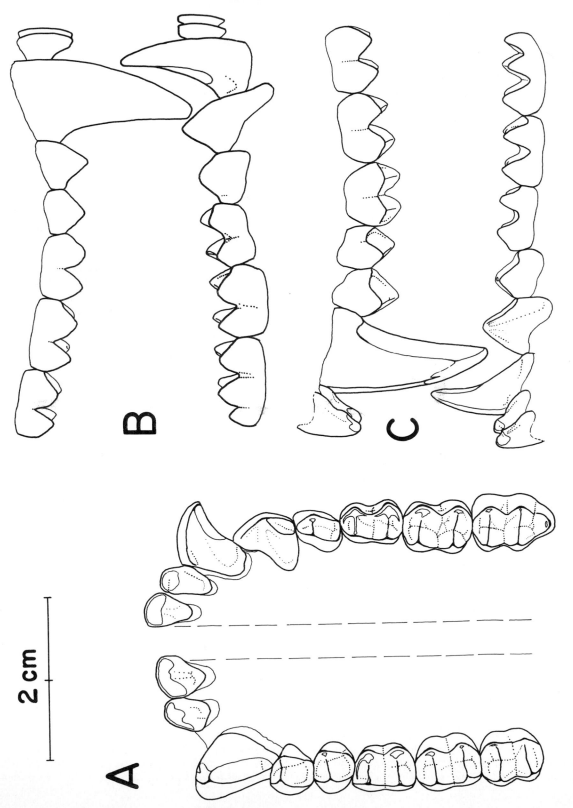

Figure 192. Dental morphology of Colobinae. *Nasalis larvatus*; modern male, Asia. A, right upper tooth-row on left, right lower tooth-row on right; B, buccal view; C, lingual view. [By B. Akerbergs.]

2 cm

From the preceding passages, the characters of the colobine morphotype can be separated from those few states which only occur in isolated members of the subfamily. This morphotype is seen to be quite distinct from that of the cercopithecines, and it would appear that, in the earlier Miocene, ancestors of the two taxa began to diverge strongly along different adaptational pathways, the cercopithecines remaining eclectic feeders but coming more frequently to the ground. The colobines, however, stayed in (or entered) the higher branches, reducing their thumb to permit more efficient climbing and leaping and developing dental and digestive specializations to permit the ingestion of large quantities of leaf matter, thus exploiting to the limit a food source which was at the center of the original cercopithecid differentiation. The earliest known colobine-like fossil, *Victoriapithecus macinnesi* of the middle Miocene (see below), had already shortened its lower molar trigonids but had not yet increased its crown relief, and it is not certain if that is the order in which the mosaic progressed in actual colobine ancestors. The next oldest relevant fossil, *Mesopithecus*, is fully colobine in all known features, including a somewhat reduced pollex. Given the importance of digestive as well as dental adaptations to leaf-eating, it may be suggested that the two went hand in hand (or tooth in gut) and thus that *Mesopithecus* and other early colobines already had a fully developed colobine stomach and intestines.

As with the Papionini, the Colobinae appear to fall into three main subgroups, which are about as diverse and different from each other as are the papionin subtribes. Therefore, the tribal category is avoided in this classification of colobines and the division made into subtribes instead, in order to indicate their rough equivalence with cercopithecine subtribes and not tribes. A scenario of colobine history might see the ancestral members of the taxon appearing late in the middle Miocene, as African arboreal leaf-eaters, but with some cranial features more as in the smaller Asian forms. At least one semi–terrestrially adapted group appears to have made the crossing out of Africa, following *Pliopithecus* and *Dryopithecus* into Eurasia by way of a steadily less-forested pathway. *Mesopithecus* and its probable descendant *Dolichopithecus* entered southern Europe, where they followed a trend to increasing terrestrial life in savannah and then woodland. The earliest Asian colobines are here termed *?Presbytis*, with this taxon used as a "form–genus," but

so far they are almost impossible to separate from *Mesopithecus* either, as the latter's distinctions are postcranial. The living Asian genera (*Presbytis*, *Pygathrix*, and *Nasalis*) appear to be linked by a small number of morphological features, as well as by geography, with the former two perhaps closer than the latter; together, they may be termed the Semnopithecina. There is limited evidence that the European genera are specially related to this subtribe, but without further supportive data they are ranked here as subtribe *incertae sedis*. The African radiation of colobines, both living and extinct, appears to have been essentially arboreal. Even the larger Colobina, such as *Paracolobus*, have long phalanges, indicative of grasping and thus a tree-climbing habitus. It was suggested by Delson (1973, 1975a) that, when the hands of any of these genera are recovered, they will reveal an extensive reduction of the thumb.

SUBTRIBE COLOBINA
Blyth, 1875

(= or including: Colobidae Blyth, 1875, restricted. Colobina: Delson, 1975a).

DISTRIBUTION
Late Miocene (?Ngororan, late Turolian) to modern. Africa: Algeria, Egypt, central and eastern Africa (Liberia to Tanzania and Ethiopia), South Africa, Angola.

INCLUDED TAXA
Colobus, *Libypithecus*, *Cercopithecoides*, and *Paracolobus*.

DISCUSSION

Based on preliminary studies (Delson, 1973), all African colobines appear to share a complex of character states which link them into a phyletic unit, recognized here as a subtribe. There do not appear to be any unifying shared derived characters common to *all* members of the Colobina, but links among them include the following: C. (*Colobus*), *Cercopithecoides*, and some *Paracolobus* (and ?*C. flandrini*?) all display lower third molars in which the distal lophid is wider than the mesial, a feature unique in the Cercopithecidae; P^3 protocone reduction is also common; and cranial morphology of *Paracolobus* and *Cercopithecoides* also appears similar, although the former has a wider face (as in *Pygathrix*) and the latter is more like *Colobus*. On the other hand, R. Leakey (1969) and M. and R. Leakey (1973b) indicate that *Paracolobus* is in mandibular morphology more like some *Colobus* than is *Cercopithecoides*. A new genus and other undescribed material similar to *Paracolobus* is discussed under that genus. The cranium of *Libypithecus* is most similar to that of *Colobus badius*, and its dentition also is like that of some African colobines. It may eventually prove

possible to link certain fossils to living forms, which may in turn lead to generic division of modern *Colobus*. The oldest known African (or perhaps any) colobine to date is an undescribed very small mandible from Ngorora, member B (516) (Pickford, in preparation).

COLOBUS Illiger, 1811

(= or including numerous taxa listed under subgenera.)

DISTRIBUTION
Late Miocene (late Turolian) through modern. North Africa; central and eastern Africa.

COLOBUS (COLOBUS) Illiger, 1811

(= or including: *Colobolus* Gray, 1821, lapsus. *Guereza* Gray, 1870. *Stachycolobus* Rochebrune, 1887. *Pterycolobus* Rochebrune, 1887; *Pterygocolobus* Trouessart, 1897, lapsus?)

DISTRIBUTION
Modern. Central Africa, Liberia to Ethiopia and Tanzania; ?later Pleistocene, Sudan.
KNOWN SPECIES
1. *Colobus (C.) polykomos* (Zimmerman, 1780), type species
2. *Colobus (C.) guereza* Rüppell, 1835

C. (PROCOLOBUS) Rochebrune, 1887

(= or including: *Lophocolobus* Pousargues, 1895.)

DISTRIBUTION
Modern. Western central Africa, Ghana to Guinea.
KNOWN SPECIES
3. *Colobus (Procolobus) verus* Van Beneden, 1838

COLOBUS (PILIOCOLOBUS) Rochebrune, 1887

(= or including: *Tropicolobus* Rochebrune, 1887.)

DISTRIBUTION
Modern. Central Africa, Guinea and Senegal discontinuously to Zanzibar.
KNOWN SPECIES
4. *Colobus (Piliocolobus) badius* (Kerr, 1792)

?COLOBUS subgenus indeterminate

(= or including: *Macaca* Lacépède: Arambourg, 1959, in part.)
KNOWN SPECIES
5. *?Colobus flandrini* (Arambourg, 1959)
(=*Macaca flandrini* Arambourg, 1959, in part. *?Colobus flandrini*: Delson, 1975a.)
LOCALITIES: Marceau★ (598).
6. *Colobus* spp. indet.
LOCALITIES: ?Lothagam-3 (647); ?Laetolil (666); Kanam East (674); Omo Group, Shungura members J (or K) (794), L (822); Koobi Fora, Ileret mb (798); Kapthurin (987); Afar late Pleistocene (1074).

DISCUSSION

Colobus is a common modern genus, the only living African member of the Colobinae. It is best divided into three subgenera distinguished on the basis of cranial, pelage, and behavioral criteria. Four or five living species may be recognized, most with numerous subspecies, all smaller than any fossil African colobine genus except for the new Ngorora specimen, which compares to *C. verus*, and some overlap of the largest *Colobus* with *Libypithecus*. The most complete discussion of cranial morphology was by Verheyen (1962), while Struhsaker (1975) compared behavioral patterns in the genus. External characters were reviewed by Rahm (1970) and Kuhn (1972) and the dentition by Leutenegger (1971, 1976).

Most fossil specimens in the smaller size range of colobines have been identified as *Colobus* for want of evidence to the contrary. Simons (1967a) reported a nearly complete skull attributed to *Colobus guereza* from undifferentiated (but probably late) Pleistocene deposits near Wadi Medani, central Sudan, but this is the only cranial fragment yet described. Small samples, often of isolated teeth or partial tooth-rows (Figure 193, A and H–J), have been described from several Pliocene and earlier Pleistocene East African localities, all of which may best be termed *Colobus* sp. indet. until cranial material has been recovered or dental characters found which unequivocally differentiate known species. It is important in this regard that observers have reported different frequencies of character-state variations in samples drawn from the same species, suggesting that diagnostic dental characters may be rare and not suitable for assignment of individual specimens (cf. Hornbeck and Swindler, 1967; Delson, 1973; Swindler and Orlosky, 1973).

Among the 50 or so late Miocene fossil monkey specimens described by Arambourg (1959) from Mar-

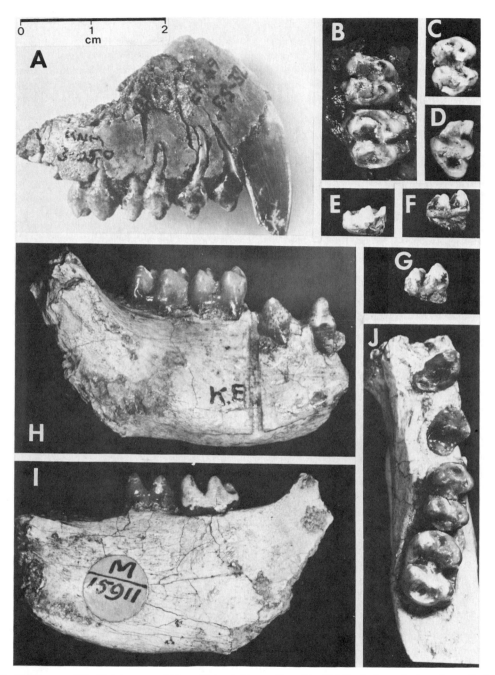

Figure 193. *Colobus* sp. Plio-Pleistocene, Africa. Male right maxilla with C^1–M^2: A, buccal view. Juvenile ?female right mandible with M$_{\overline{1-2}}$, erupting P$_{\overline{3-4}}$: H, buccal view; I, lingual view; J, occlusal view. ?*Colobus flandrini*. Late Miocene, Africa. Right maxilla with M$^{\underline{1-2}}$: B, occlusal view. Right isolated M$_{\overline{2?}}$: C, occlusal view; E, lingual view (photographically reversed); G, buccal view. Left partial isolated M$_{\overline{3}}$: D, occlusal view (photographically reversed); E, lingual view. The scale is for A and H–J. B–G are at approximately 10% smaller scale. [A courtesy of M. G. Leakey and © Trustees National Museums of Kenya.]

ceau, 8 are colobine, while the remainder are cercopithecines as he originally considered (Delson, 1973). Unfortunately, the type maxillary fragment of *Macaca flandrini* is colobine, necessitating the transfer of this species to a different genus; *Colobus* is used in this case as a "form–genus" for African colobines

pending more accurate identification. The teeth (Figure 193, B–G) are similar to those of *Cercopithecoides williamsi* in size, form, and relative width (of upper molars), but they are not referred to that genus in order to emphasize their uncertain allocation.

LIBYPITHECUS Stromer, 1913

DISTRIBUTION
  Late Miocene (late Turolian). Northern Egypt.
KNOWN SPECIES
  Libypithecus markgrafi Stromer, 1913, type species
  (= or including: Semnopithecine: Stromer, 1920, in part.)
  LOCALITIES: Wadi Natrun★ (610).

DISCUSSION

Libypithecus is known from a single, nearly complete male skull and a referred, worn, isolated lower molar. It is a colobine of medium size, with a projecting facial region (facial angle, ≈50°) and a prominent sagittal crest, at least in males. The interorbital breadth is somewhat low for colobines, as is usual in longer-faced forms, and the choanae are possibly high and relatively narrow (although damaged in the only skull); the supraorbital torus is not strongly developed. The upper dentition is typically colobine, with molars increasing in size posteriorly and incisors relatively small. The braincase is elongate and somewhat low, with sagittal and nuchal crests increasing in height toward inion. This suggests posterior placement of the main temporal muscle mass and a back-tilted ramus with small gonion on the as yet unknown mandible.

The type skull is among the best-preserved single specimens of a pre-Pleistocene primate, but unfortunately its unique nature makes the study of normal variation impossible. The skull is nearly undeformed, but the majority of the basicranium and part of the midface are lacking or crushed, as are portions of the vault. The dentition is essentially complete, although ante-mortem trauma led to the breakage of the right canine crown and thrusting of the right incisors around and mesial to the left incisors (Figure 194D). This damage occurred significantly before death, as the incisors and $P^{\underline{3}}$'s show differing wear patterns and degrees, while the alveolar area between the right $P^{\underline{3}}$ and the mesially forced canine root is roughened,

perhaps representing a healed fracture. The individual was just barely adult at death: The canines and $M^{\underline{3}}$'s are fully erupted and in wear, and all the sutures appear closed. The worn protocones of $P^{\underline{3}}$ are small, as in some species of *Colobus* and other African colobines. There is a fifth cusp on both $M^{\underline{3}}$'s, distobuccal to the metacone, which adds to making it the largest in the series. The only other specimen from Wadi Natrun which may be referred to *Libypithecus* is an isolated, heavily worn lower molariform tooth, probably an $M_{\overline{1}}$ (Figure 195, H–J). In size, the known teeth of *L. markgrafi* are nearly indistinguishable from those of the roughly contemporaneous *Mesopithecus* species, except that $M^{\underline{3}}$ is larger in the Egyptian fossil and its $P^{\underline{3}}$ protocone is reduced.

The distinguishing features of *Libypithecus* are those of its skull. The most striking of these is the very strong sagittal crest, beginning near bregma (the actual landmark is obscured) with the fusion of the temporal lines, then rising rapidly as the braincase roof falls away. At inion, flaring nuchal crests meet the sagittal crest at its maximum height. The ventral surface of the nuchal crest is roughened by attachments for a large neck musculature, and the shape of the sagittal crest further suggests a posterior placement of the main mass of the temporalis. The large size of this muscle is also indicated by the expanded temporal root of the zygomatic process, suggesting a rather wide arch and capacious temporal fossa.

The basicranium is extensively broken away, but this has permitted study of the endocranium by means of a cast. Radinsky (1974) has interpreted the brain as that of a modern-type colobine, with a few minor variations. The upper and lower portions of the facial skeleton are nearly complete, but the midface region is damaged so that interpretation of facial hafting is problematic. The bases of the relatively small orbits have been broken away, and the maxilla is attached to

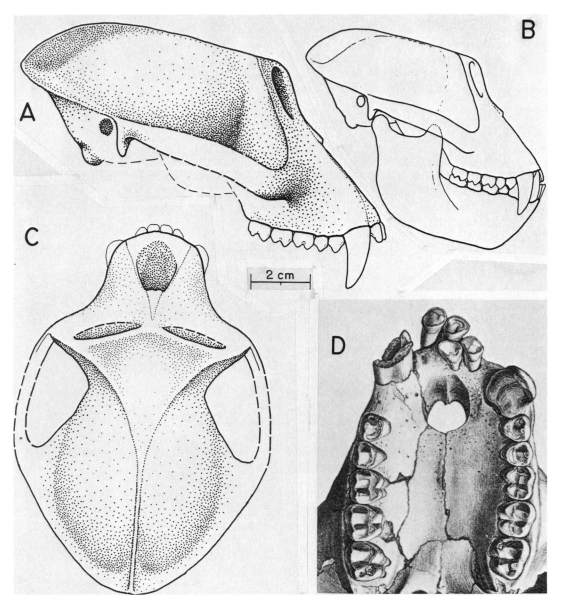

Figure 194. *Libypithecus markgrafi*. Late Miocene, Africa. Male cranium, restored: A, right lateral view; B, same with hypothetical mandible in occlusion; C, dorsal view (Frankfurt orientation); D, palate with complete dentition (note damage to right C^1 and offset of right incisors). The scale is for A and C; B is one-third smaller, while D is twice as large as the scale. [A–C by B. Akerbergs; D from Stromer (1913).]

the frontal at only two points of contact as currently restored (Figure 195). Considering the resulting steep profile of the nasal region (see also Jolly, 1967) and the space required for the sphenoid complex, Delson (1973) suggested that a better reconstruction would

rotate the lower face down and back toward basion. A more complete pictorial restoration has now been produced (Figure 194), in which the alveolar plane is more steeply angled with respect to the Frankfurt plane than in the specimen as now preserved. Other important

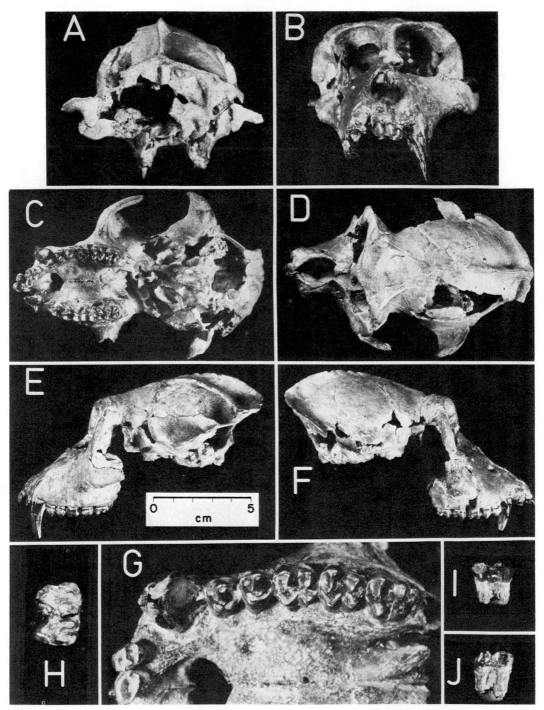

Figure 195. *Libypithecus markgrafi*. Late Miocene, Africa. Male cranium in Frankfurt orientation (but see Figure 194A for reconstructed orientation): A, occipital view; B, frontal view; C, basal view; D, dorsal view; E, left lateral view; F, right lateral view; G, occlusal view of left I^1–M^3. Isolated referred left $M_{\overline{1-3}}$: H, occlusal view; I, buccal view; J, lingual view. The scale is for A–F; G–J are three times as large.

facial features include colobine position of the lacrymal fossa, partly bounded by the maxilla; narrow interorbital region, typical in longer-faced colobines, and long nasal bones; and anterior root of zygomatic process arising above the paraloph of M^2, farther mesiad than in really long-faced cercopithecids.

The phylogenetic relationships of *Libypithecus* have long been in doubt, as the original specimen was seldom studied by its interpreters. Its long face led several workers to consider it a cercopithecine without much comment, but the evidence of the teeth and, more equivocally, that of the brain (the colobine pattern is ancestral) and perhaps even of the neurocranial form (see below) combine to demonstrate colobine affinity. Jolly (1967) has discussed several different possible relationships and similarities, of which the most likely seems the proposed likeness of skull and sagittal crest form to the red colobus, *C. badius*. The fossil has a higher crest, but other features are close, and the mandible of the living form of similar size may be carefully used as a model for *Libypithecus*, as reconstructed here. Although the teeth of *Libypithecus* are nearly identical to those of *Mesopithecus pentelici*, there is such a great difference in skull form that, without postcranial evidence, there seems to be no indication of a special relationship. It is entirely feasible that *M. monspessulanus* might be closer to the Egyptian form than to *M. pentelici*, but the lack of concrete data substantiating such a hypothesis, along with zoogeographical and rare postcranial morphological considerations, suggests uniting the two European forms closely. *Dolichopithecus ruscinensis* was also considered possibly congeneric with *Libypithecus* by Jolly (1967) on the basis of temporal line form in males, but the one male skull of the former (see Figure 210B) is so badly deformed that no significant comparison can be made. The distinctive locomotor adaptations of *Dolichopithecus* require similar postcranial fossil remains to support any serious suggestion of close relationship; there is no question of species identity in this case, given the great differences in absolute size.

In relation to the habitus of *Libypithecus*, there appears to be an interesting anomaly in craniodental proportions and relationships. As has been shown, the skull indicates a far posterior placement of temporal musculature, which Jolly (1970) and others have correlated with more anterior emphasis of chewing force and a rather inclined mandibular ramus and line of muscle action. On this basis, the reconstructed ramus shown in Figure 194B is back-tilted more than in *C. badius*. But *Libypithecus* also presents very large M^3, suggesting that heavy chewing went on distally, as in *Theropithecus* species with anteriorly placed sagittal crest height and nearly vertical ramus. In addition, the incisors of *Libypithecus* are small, not relatively large as in mandrills with a similar crest pattern. The reconciliation of these apparently opposing adaptations is not yet clear, but was obviously functionally important in the fossil genus. A difference in diet from similar-sized *Colobus badius* is to be expected, but the direction of such a change cannot yet be estimated confidently, although Simons and Delson (1978) tentatively considered small-object feeding, taking into account the associated open-country fauna.

Overall, *Libypithecus* is best considered as one of several lineages of African colobines, perhaps closer to at least some *Colobus* species than to the *Paracolobus–Cercopithecoides* group. Given that almost all members of the Colobina are arboreal, it would not be expected that *Libypithecus markgrafi* was strongly adapted to terrestrial life. On the other hand, some terrestriality might be suggested (Simons and Delson, 1978) if the small-object feeding hypothesis proved correct.

CERCOPITHECOIDES Mollett, 1947

(= or including: *Parapapio* Jones, 1937: Broom, 1940; Broom and Robinson, 1950; Freedman, 1957, in part. *Brachygnathopithecus* Kitching, 1952, in part.)

DISTRIBUTION

Late Pliocene (Rodolfian) through middle Pleistocene. Southern and Eastern Africa: South Africa, Angola, Kenya, Ethiopia.
KNOWN SPECIES

1. *Cercopithecoides williamsi* Mollett, 1947, type species
(=*Parapapio jonesi* Broom, 1940, in part. *Parapapio coronatus* Broom and Robinson, 1950. *Brachygnathopithecus peppercorni* Kitching, 1952, in part. *Cercopithecoides molletti* Freedman, 1957.)

LOCALITIES: Makapansgat★ (700); Sterkfontein (706); (aff.) East Rudolf Koobi Fora Fm., Lower (728) and Upper (796) Mbs.; Bolts Farm (740); Swartkrans a (752); Leba (756); Cooper's (764); Sterkfontein extension and dumps (778); Kromdraai B (782); ?Swartkrans b (930); Graveyard (1032).

2. *Cercopithecoides* sp. nov.: M. Leakey and R. Leakey, 1973b (to be named by M. Leakey, in press).

LOCALITIES: East Rudolf Koobi Fora Fm., Lower mb. (728).

3. *?Cercopithecoides* sp(p).
(=Cf. Colobinae: M. Leakey and R. Leakey, 1973; Eisenhart, 1974.)
LOCALITIES: Makapansgat (700); Olduvai Gorge, ?Upper Bed II (804?) and ?Bed III (820).

DISCUSSION

Cercopithecoides is a medium to large-sized colobine monkey characterized by a somewhat long and narrow face (especially in males), short premaxilla (squared across the front), deep ophryonic groove, and strong sexual dimorphism in cranial and facial shape. The South African *C. williamsi* is best known and serves as the basis for the description. In males, the skull is basically long and narrow (Figures 196 and 197) and the braincase is ovoid with inion at or below the level of nasion (in Frankfurt orientation). The temporal lines do not meet, but fade out behind bregma, so that there is no sagittal crest, and the nuchal musculature is also relatively weakly developed. The orbits are widely spaced, but not extremely so. The mandibular corpus is somewhat shallow, but of constant depth, and there is no bulging of gonion; the ramus is slightly back-tilted. At least in some mandibles, there is a median mental canal. In females (Figure 196, B and D), the face is much shorter, and the braincase appears foreshortened to an extreme degree. Both known female skulls are damaged (Figure 197, C and F), but the vault appears to have been subspherical, short and high, the ophryonic groove especially deep, inion low, and the temporal lines converging nearly to meet before fading out near lambda. The teeth of the two sexes show no clear dimorphism, except, of course, in the canine–$P_{\overline{3}}$ complex. The dentition is typically colobine, and of African affinity, with reduced $P^{\underline{3}}$ protocone, wide $M_{\overline{3}}$ hypolophid, and sometimes reduced $P_{\overline{4}}$ metaconid (Figure 198). The second upper molar is very large and especially broad across the paraloph. Postcranial materials have not yet been clearly allocated to *Cercopithecoides williamsi*. The genus is distinguished from most other colobines because of its large size and lack of gonial expansion, as well as the only moderately wide face for its length. Facial width and lack of cranial superstructures differentiate it from *Libypithecus* and the *Colobus badius* group. Dental and some facial characters appear to ally it most closely with *Paracolobus* (Delson, 1973).

The major samples of *Cercopithecoides williamsi* are from Makapansgat, Sterkfontein, and Bolts Farm, with fewer or less complete specimens from other localities. Several nearly complete male crania and faces are known (Figure 197), but only two females, both damaged posteriorly. All of the better preserved South African material may be considered as the single species *C. williamsi*, but the male face from the lower "grey breccia" at Makapan (Figure 197, E and H) is broader and in other ways different from the upper "pink breccia" skulls (see Maier, 1971a). Freedman (1957) erected the species *C. molletti* for somewhat larger dental material from Swartkrans, but later synonymized it with *C. williamsi* on the basis of increased knowledge of variability in that species. *Cercopithecoides* is the longest-ranging form in South Africa, occurring from the earliest sites probably into the middle Pleistocene (a distinction now difficult to make in southern Africa) and lacking only at the Kromdraai B ("faunal") site. This absence is surprising, as Kromdraai B appears to be chronologically intermediate among the other sites on the basis of cercopithecines, but it also lacks *Australopithecus*.

In East Africa, Leakey and Leakey (1973b) have recovered specimens which they referred to *Cercopithecoides*, including a reasonably complete female cranium and male mandible (Figure 197, D and I). This skull is larger than those in South Africa and more elongate, and its referral to a distinct species of this genus appears reasonable. More fragmentary and rarer material from East Rudolf (M. Leakey, 1976 and personal communication) may indicate the presence of a form close to *C. williamsi* as well. Associated postcranial elements suggest terrestrial adaptations for this form. A partial braincase, associated with teeth of nearly cercopithecine form, probably documents a possibly different large species of *Cercopithecoides* from the upper horizons of Bed II (or higher) at Olduvai Gorge, Tanzania (M. Leakey and R. Leakey, 1973b). Finally, several large isolated teeth from Makapan (e.g., Figure 198, F and I), identified as colobine by Eisenhart (1974), might also represent this genus.

The lack of many definitely identified postcranial remains renders assessment of the life-style of *Cercopithecoides* difficult. This lack is due to the dissociation of skeletal material in the South African breccias, mixing bones of several species of generally similar size. Nonetheless, some conclusions can be drawn from known craniognathic elements. The gracile mandible and zygoma and the faint, widely separated

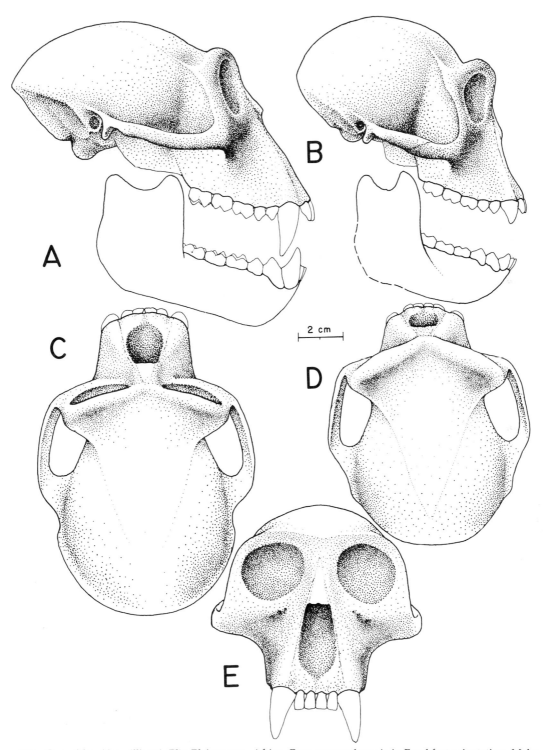

Figure 196. *Cercopithecoides williamsi.* Plio-Pleistocene, Africa. Reconstructed crania in Frankfurt orientation. Male: A, right lateral view; C, dorsal view; E, frontal view. Female: B, right lateral view; D, dorsal view. [By B. Akerbergs.]

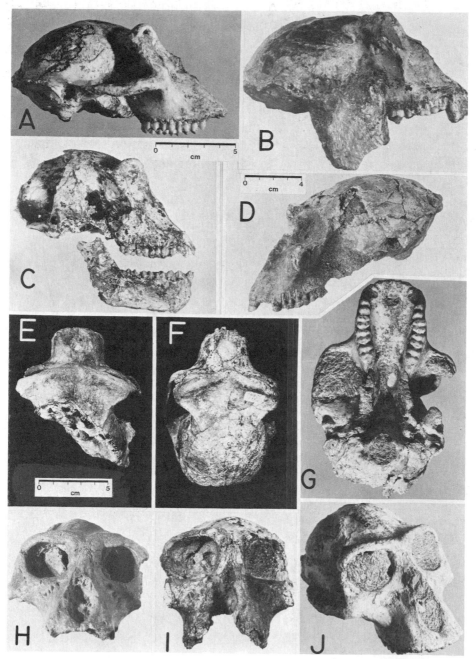

Figure 197. *Cercopithecoides williamsi.* Plio-Pleistocene, Africa. Male crania in occlusal plane orientation: A, right lateral view; B, right lateral view; E, dorsal view; G, basal view; H, frontal view; J, right fronto-lateral oblique view. Female crania in occlusal plane orientation: C, right lateral view; F, dorsal view. *Cercopithecoides* sp. nov. Plio-Pleistocene, Africa. Female cranium in Frankfurt orientation: D, left lateral view; I, frontal view. The scale between A and C pertains to A, B, C, G, H, and J. There are separate centimeter scales for D and E–F. [D, I courtesy of M. G. Leakey and © Trustees of National Museums of Kenya.]

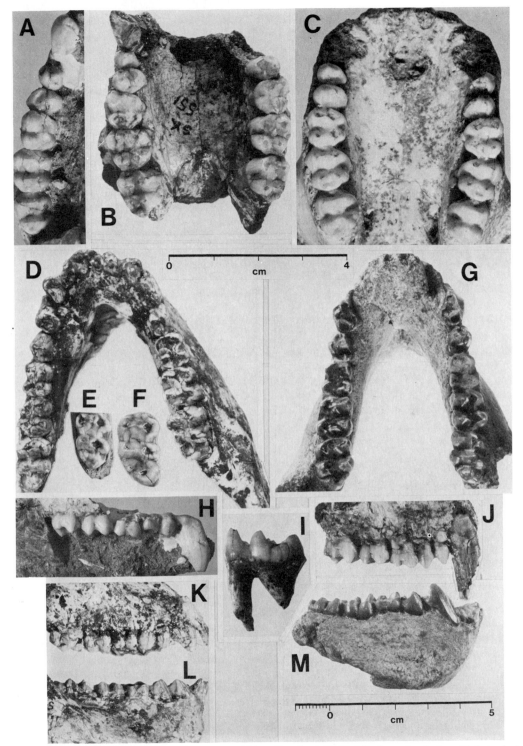

Figure 198. *Cercopithecoides williamsi.* Plio-Pleistocene, Africa. Female right C^1–M^3: A, occlusal view; H, buccal view. Male palate with right C^1–M^3, left P^4–M^3: B, occlusal view; J, right buccal view. Male palate with right and left P^3–M^3: C, occlusal view. Female mandible with complete but worn dentition: D, occlusal view; L, right buccal view; K, right buccal view of upper teeth of same individual. Unwarped male mandible with right and left P_3–M_3 and anterior alveoli: G, occlusal view; M, right buccal view. Isolated right M_3 (for comparison to F): E, occlusal view. *?Cercopithecoides* sp. Late Pliocene, Africa. Isolated right M_3: F, occlusal view; I, lingual view. The upper scale is for A–G, I; the lower is for H, J–M.

temporal lines indicate only slight development of the chewing musculature, but heavy tooth wear is common. This pattern is unmatched in living colobines, but suggestive of a diet poor in tough and fibrous material requiring heavy slicing; perhaps soft but gritty items (causing rapid tooth wear but requiring little mastication) were a more important part of the diet than in most colobines. The overall size of *Cercopithecoides* suggests some degree of terrestriality, as does the constant death association with both large and smaller baboons and hominids, often in a landscape suggested to be relatively open (Vrba, 1976). The few East African postcrania seem to confirm these suggestions.

PARACOLOBUS R. Leakey, 1969

DISTRIBUTION
Pliocene (Rodolfian). East Africa (Kenya, southern Ethiopia).
KNOWN SPECIES
1. *Paracolobus chemeroni* R. Leakey, 1969, type species
LOCALITIES: Chemeron Fm., loc. JM 90/91★ (724).

2. Cf. *Paracolobus* sp.
[=Colobinae, gen. et sp. indet. (C): Eck, 1976, 1977.]
LOCALITIES: Omo Group, Shungura Fm., Mbs. C–G (712), (716), (726), (738), (750); East Rudolf Koobi Fora Fm., lower mb. (728).

Other East African Fossil Colobines, as yet unnamed

1. Colobinae gen. et sp. nov.: M. Leakey and R. Leakey, 1973b; Eck, 1976. To be named by M. Leakey, in press.
LOCALITIES: Hadar (700); Omo Group, Usno Fm. (694), Shungura Fm., Mbs. Basal–H (670), (672), (696), (712), (716), (726), (738), (750), (776); East Rudolf Koobi Fora Fm., lower mb. (728).
2. Colobinae, gen. et sp. indet., larger
[=*Papio (Simopithecus) serengetensis* Dietrich, 1942, in part.]

LOCALITIES: Laetolil (666).
3. Colobinae, gen. et sp. indet., smaller
[=Colobinae, gen. et sp. indet. (A): Eck, 1976.]
LOCALITIES: Hadar (700); Omo Group, Shungura Fm., Mbs. B (696), C (712).

DISCUSSION

Paracolobus is a colobine of large size, with a relatively short and broad face and broad interorbital region. The muzzle is somewhat flattened dorsally, the postorbital constriction is well-marked, the choanae are wide and somewhat high, and the temporal lines are strong, converging toward bregma in the holotype male skull (Figure 199 A, F, and G). The palate is wide, high-vaulted, and somewhat long. The teeth (Figures 200B and 201A) are clearly colobine, with deep lingual notches on the lowers and $M_{\overline{3}}$ hypolophid wider than protolophid, as seen only in some African members of the subfamily (*Cercopithecoides* and some *Colobus* spp.). The incisors are small, the I^2 is conical, the protocone is reduced on $P^{\underline{3}}$ as in some African colobines, but the $P_{\overline{4}}$ metaconid appears moderately well developed and the tooth itself is narrow. The mandibular corpus deepens posteriorly to a large gonion, while the ramus is nearly vertical and strongly muscle-marked. The long bones (Figure 202, A–H) are robust, especially for a colobine, the femur being among the stoutest known in the family. The forelimb is about as long as the hindlimb, with a humerus nearly the length of the femur; the estimated radial length is also subequal to that of the humerus. The elbow joint suggests terrestriality in its rather strong trochlear flange and posteriorly bent medial epicondyle on the humerus, although the ulnar olecranon angulation and radial notch depth are less than in the most terrestrial colobines. However, phalanges (Figure 202M) are rather long, indicating a long and prehensile foot, typical of arboreal colobines; the manus and thus the relative thumb length are unknown. *Paracolobus* is distinguished from its apparent relative *Cercopithecoides* by a wider face, as well as by greater size—as noted, postcranial elements are almost unknown in the latter. The combination of facial shape and postcranial morphology sets it apart from all other colobines, although the dental pattern is essentially African.

Most knowledge of *Paracolobus* is due to the nearly complete holotype individual from the Chemeron. This male specimen was found fully articulated, lacking only the rear of the braincase, the hands and distal forearm, and other minor elements, but it has not yet been fully described or analyzed. The overall impression obtained is of a large, mainly arboreal animal which was able to travel on the ground at times,

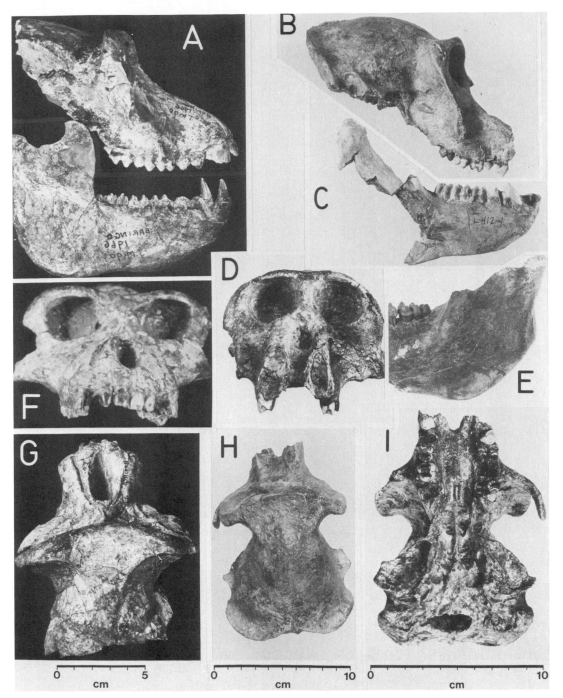

Figure 199. *Paracolobus chemeroni*. Late Pliocene, Africa. Male skull and mandible in occlusal plane orientation: A, right lateral view (photographically reversed); F, frontal view; G, dorsal view. Cf. *Paracolobus* sp. Late Pliocene, Africa. Portion of left mandibular corpus: E, lateral view. Colobinae, gen. et sp. nov. Plio-Pleistocene, Africa. Male cranium in Frankfurt orientation: B, right lateral view; D, frontal view; H, dorsal view; I, basal view. Male mandible: C, right lateral view. The scale under G is for A, E, F, and G. The scale under H is for B, C, D, and H. The scale under I is for I only. [B–D, H, I courtesy of M. G. Leakey and © Trustees National Museums of Kenya; E with permission from G. G. Eck, *Journal of Human Evolution, 6*, 1977, copyright by Academic Press Inc. (London) Ltd.]

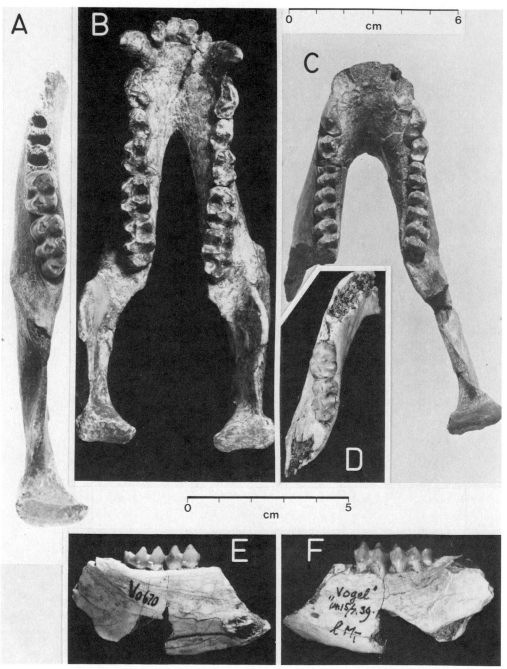

Figure 200. East African Pliocene large colobine dentitions. ?*Paracolobus* sp., partial left mandible with $M_{\overline{2-3}}$: A, occlusal view. *Paracolobus chemeroni,* male mandible with complete dentition: B, occlusal view. Colobinae, gen. et. sp. nov., partial male mandible with right and left $P_{\overline{3}}$–$M_{\overline{3}}$ ($M_{\overline{3}}$ hypoconulids broken): C, occlusal view. Genus and species indeterminate, Laetolil, female mandible with left $M_{\overline{2-3}}$: D, occlusal view; E, lingual view; F, buccal view. The scale to right of B is for B only; the other scale is for A, C–F. [A with permission from G. G. Eck, *Journal of Human Evolution, 6,* 1977. Copyright by Academic Press Inc. (London) Ltd. C courtesy of M. G. Leakey and © Trustees National Museums of Kenya.]

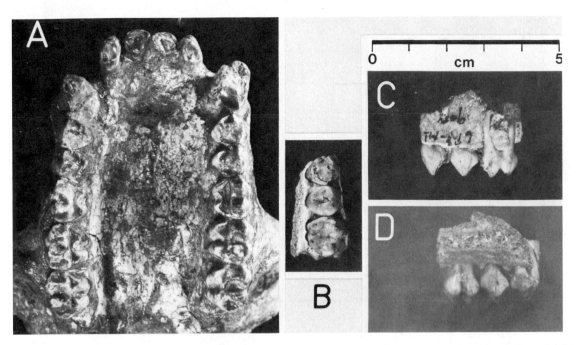

Figure 201. *Paracolobus chemeroni.* Late Pliocene, Africa. Male maxilla with complete dentition: A, occlusal view. Colobine genus and species indeterminate, Laetolil, Pliocene. Partial ?male left maxilla with P³–M¹: B, occlusal view; C, buccal view; D, lingual view.

perhaps somewhat similar to *Nasalis larvatus*, although larger. The femur appears to have been shortened, compared to the typical allometric relation in catarrhines.

Eck (especially 1977) has reported a few fragmentary colobine specimens even larger than *P. chemeroni* from the middle range of the Omo (members C–G), as "Colobine sp. C." He has compared the extreme gonial development of one partial mandible (Figures 199E and 200A) to that seen in *Mesopithecus,* but other large colobines have similar, if not such pronounced, mandibular angles, and allometry may be responsible. A maxilla from Koobi Fora is comparable in size and morphologically close to *P. chemeroni,* suggesting the referral of all these specimens to *Paracolobus,* possibly as a distinct species.

More interesting is another large colobine (to be named by M. Leakey, in press), of which a male skull and unassociated mandible from Omo were described by M. Leakey and R. Leakey (1973b) and which is also known from East Rudolf (Leakey, 1976). The size and form of the teeth are comparable to those of *P. cheme-* roni, but Leakey and Leakey (1973b) have considered that cranial and mandibular morphology distinguishes these fossils from that genus. The skull is rather low, with a moderately long muzzle, strong nuchal crests, and a rather angulated occiput (Figure 199, B, D, H, and I). Unfortunately, the lack of the nasal bones and premaxillary area results in an effective distortion of the midface in this specimen, which renders comparison with the *P. chemeroni* face difficult. The teeth of the new taxon (Figure 200C) are higher-crowned, but relatively smaller than those of *Paracolobus,* leading to a shorter and perhaps narrower palate; the orbits are also smaller and perhaps less widely spaced. The braincase broadens toward the rear, developing large nuchal flanges and a steeply angled basioccipital region. This area is broken away in the Chemeron specimen, but may have been similar. The mandible (Figure 199C) has a deep corpus, deepening distally, but the gonial region is not expanded inferiorly in the single referred specimen presenting it; the ramus is both long and tall; a median mental canal is typically present. Postcranial elements

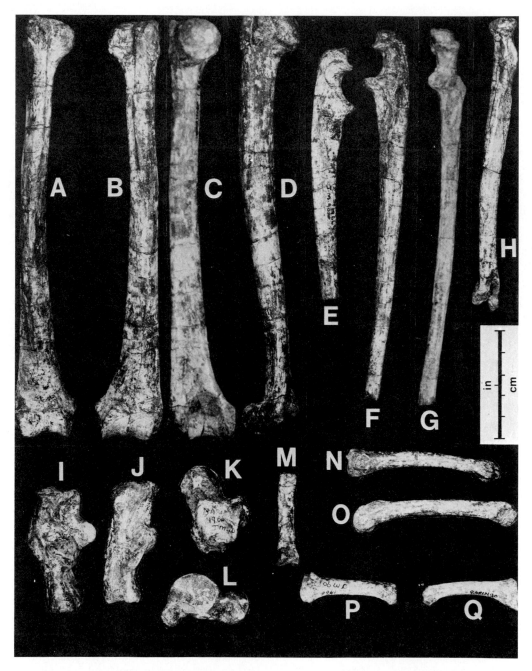

Figure 202. *Paracolobus chemeroni.* Late Pliocene, Africa. Male postcranial elements. Right humerus: A, anterior view. Left humerus: B, anterior view; C, posterior view; D, lateral view. Right ulna: E, lateral view. Left ulna: F, lateral view; G, anterior view. Left radius: H, anterior view. Left calcaneum: I, dorsal view; J, plantar view. Right astragalus: K, dorsal view; L, lateral view. Middle pedal phalanx: M, plantar view. Damaged metatarsals: N and O, lateral views. Left hallucial metatarsal (I): P, plantar view; Q, lateral view. The scale at H is for A–H, the divisions are in inches and centimeters; I–Q are at twice scale.

associated with a jaw referred to this species are distinct from those of *P. chemeroni* and more like those of modern colobines. This new form has been treated here, rather than separately, as it has not yet been formally described, but specimens were examined through the courtesy of M. Leakey, and it does appear to be a taxon distinct from both *Paracolobus* and *Cercopithecoides* at generic rank.

Two other groups of specimens cannot be so easily assessed, especially as the characters differentiating the three diagnosed genera are mainly cranial. Among the specimens which Dietrich (1942) described as *Papio serengetensis*, from Laetolil, are a number of teeth (e.g., Figure 201, B–D) and a partial ?female mandible (Figure 200, D–F) of a colobine comparable in size to several later East African species. When these and additional specimens collected more recently are fully described, it may be possible to allocate them generically. Other specimens, smaller than these but larger than most *Colobus*, are known from several sites, especially at Hadar, which has yielded a partial skull with associated skeletal elements. The greatest similarities of this taxon appear to lie with *Paracolobus*. The variety of Pliocene colobines in eastern Africa is quite intriguing, perhaps comparable (and ecologically equivalent) to the diversity of smaller papionins (*Parapapio* and *?Cercocebus*) in southern sites.

SUBTRIBE SEMNOPITHECINA
Owen, 1843

[= or including: Presbytina Gray, 1825, restricted and deprived of priority (Delson, 1976). Semnopithecidae Owen, 1843, restricted.]

DISTRIBUTION
Late Miocene (or early Pliocene), Pleistocene to modern. Southern Asia: Pakistan to southern China to Indonesia.
INCLUDED TAXA
Presbytis, Pygathrix, and *Nasalis.*

DISCUSSION

As for the African colobines, the Asian forms appear to comprise a natural group delimited by some shared (but not clearly derived) characters, as well as mere geographic proximity. In this case, there being no clear evidence for a closer relationship of any genus with an African one, it is more parsimonious to group them together, rather than postulate multiple invasions of Asia. Fossils are quite rare, most representing modern species in or near their current ranges, with only one small collection of ?late Miocene teeth indicating the presence of pre-Pleistocene Asian colobines. Of the living genera, *Presbytis* and *Pygathrix* appear to be linked by cranial morphology, although these may in part be ancestral retentions: rounded skull, short face, wide upper face and orbits (extreme in *Pygathrix*), and mandible which deepens distally. These genera also exhibit a substantial bulging of the inferior border of the mandibular corpus under $M_{\overline{3}}$. *Nasalis* is clearly more distinct because of its facial elongation, but the morphologically intermediate *N. (Simias)* is similar in skull form to some *Presbytis*. In addition, Groves (1970) has indicated that *Nasalis* and *Pygathrix* species share high intermembral indexes among the Colobinae. Groves thought this reflected persistence of an ancestral condition, but considering Biegert and Maurer's (1972) work on allometry of limb length, it may simply reflect the large size of these two genera. It is interesting to note that *Nasalis* shares relatively constant mandibular corpus depth with *Colobus*, but, as this pattern may be ancestral, it probably does not indicate phyletic relationship. The similarity of *Mesopithecus* to some *Presbytis* in cranial shape suggests that all the Eurasian species might be grouped together, but, as noted above, the evidence for this is too slight as yet.

PRESBYTIS Eschscholtz, 1821

(= or including numerous synonyms listed below.)

DISTRIBUTION
?Late Miocene; middle Pleistocene to modern. Pakistan through Malaysia and Indonesia.
INCLUDED SUBGENERA
Presbytis (Presbytis), P. (Semnopithecus), P. (Trachypithecus), and *P. (Kasi).*

PRESBYTIS (PRESBYTIS) Eschscholtz, 1821

(= or including: *Presbytes* Gray, 1843, lapsus?. *Lophopithecus* Trouessart, 1878. *Corypithecus* Trouessart, 1879.)

DISTRIBUTION
Middle Pleistocene to modern. Southeast Asia, Malaysia and Indonesia.

KNOWN SPECIES

Presbytis (Presbytis) aygula (Linnaeus, 1758), type species, and numerous others not recently revised

LOCALITIES OF FOSSIL *P. (Presbytis)*: Middle Pleistocene of Java (842); Niah (1234); Sumatran "Holocene" (1256).

PRESBYTIS (SEMNOPITHECUS) Desmarest, 1822

(= or including: *Entellus* Gray, 1870.)

DISTRIBUTION

Late Pleistocene to modern. India, Ceylon.

KNOWN SPECIES

Presbytis (Semnopithecus) entellus (Dufresne, 1797)

LOCALITIES: Karnul caves (1254).

PRESBYTIS (TRACHYPITHECUS) Reichenbach, 1862

DISTRIBUTION

?Early Pleistocene to modern. South and southeast Asia, Burma to Indonesia.

KNOWN SPECIES

Presbytis (Trachypithecus) cristatus (Raffles, 1821), type species, and several others not recently revised

FOSSIL LOCALITIES OF *P. (Trachypithecus)*: ?Early or middle (842) Pleistocene of Java; ?Tham Khuyen (922); ?Tham Hai (924); ?Keo Leng (1027); ?Hang Hum lower (1022); Niah (1234); "Holocene" of Sumatra (1256); "Holocene" of Java (1258).

PRESBYTIS (KASI) Reichenbach, 1862

(= or including: *Presbytis* Reichenbach, 1862, *nec* Eschscholtz. *Presbypithecus* Trouessart, 1879.)

DISTRIBUTION

Modern. Ceylon, southern India.

KNOWN SPECIES

Presbytis (Kasi) senex (Erxleben, 1777), type species

Presbytis (Kasi) johnii (Fischer, 1829)

?PRESBYTIS subgenus indeterminate

DISTRIBUTION

Late Miocene. Pakistan.

KNOWN SPECIES

?Presbytis sivalensis (Lydekker, 1878)

(=*Macacus sivalensis* Lydekker, 1878. *Cercopithecus asnoti* Pilgrim, 1910. *Semnopithecus asnoti:* Pilgrim, 1915; *Semnopithecus hasnoti:*

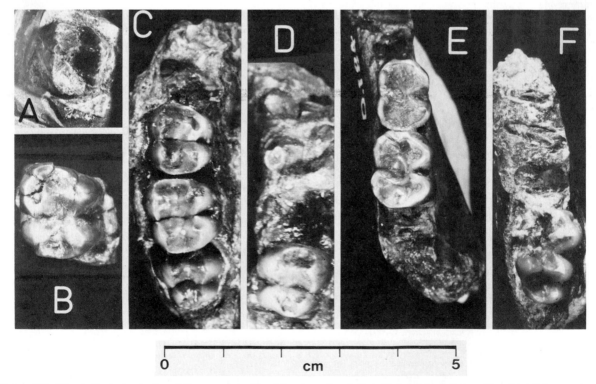

Figure 203. *?Presbytis sivalensis*. Late Miocene, Asia. Dentition in occlusal view. C, juvenile right maxilla with M^{1-2}, erupting M^3; D, left maxilla with M^3; E, right corpus fragment with M_{1-2}; F, right corpus fragment with damaged M_3 (photographically reversed). Cf. *?P. sivalensis*: A, unerupted right P^4 crown; B, isolated right $M^{2?}$.

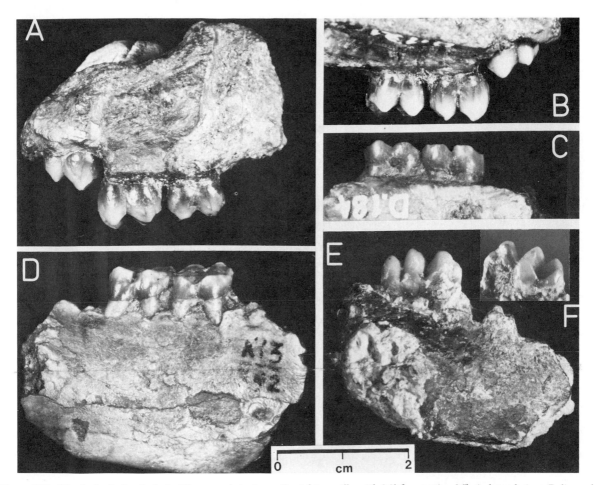

Figure 204. *?Presbytis sivalensis.* Late Miocene, Asia. Juvenile right maxilla with M^{1-2}, erupting M^3: A, lateral view; B, lingual view of teeth. Right corpus fragment with M_{1-2}: C, lingual view of teeth; D, lateral view. Right corpus fragment with damaged M_3 (photographically reversed): E, lateral view; F, oblique lingual view of teeth.

Matthew, 1929, lapsus. *Macacus?* cf. *sivalensis:* Pilgrim, 1915. *Presbytis? asnoti:* Remane, 1965; Simons, 1970. *?Presbytis sivalensis:* Delson, 1975a.)
LOCALITIES: Hasnot-upper★ (590); ?Domeli-upper (592).

DISCUSSION

Presbytis is the most common and widespread colobine in Asia, with numerous species extending across its total range. It is often divided into four subgenera, based on cranial and pelage characters (the latter especially of newborns), but the distinctions and allocations of individual species are less clear-cut than for *Colobus,* and there have been few detailed modern studies. The species demonstrate a broad range of character states, especially in such features as size, arboreality, and morphology, but all share a simple external nose and moderate facial width (both ancestral states), as opposed to the derived conditions found in *Nasalis* and *Pygathrix.* Pocock (1934), Washburn (1944), and Hooijer (1962) have discussed the subgeneric distinctions.

As with *Colobus,* a number of Pleistocene localities have yielded more or less fragmentary remains of small colobines which can be identified as *Presbytis* species, often of the same taxon now inhabiting the same region. Many of these are late Pleistocene, but a number of localities in central Java, discussed by Hooijer (1962), have also yielded *Presbytis* and are listed as being of middle Pleistocene age. Of these, some may be as old as the Djetis faunal "zone," which is probably more accurately considered early Pleistocene, but no distinctions are made by Hooijer. No other Plio-Pleistocene specimens of *Presbytis* have been reported from southern Asia, except the two termed "*Semnopithecus palaeindicus*" (Lydekker, 1884), which are in fact a cercopithecine referred to *?Macaca* (Delson, 1975a).

A small series of partial jaws and isolated teeth (Figures 203 and 204) from Pakistan appears to represent the oldest occurrence of a cercopithecid in Asia. Individual specimens of this group have previously been allocated to three different genera, but Simons (1970) demonstrated that at least those previously termed *asnoti* were certainly of a small colobine. The

remainder of the Hasnot fossils are essentially identical to those, indicating the presence of a small colobine in Pakistan at the same time that *Mesopithecus pentelici* was common in southern Europe. A single tooth from near Domeli (Figure 203B) is slightly different, being larger in size but possibly within the expected range of variation; it might represent a second, probably colobine taxon. An unerupted P^4 (Figure 203A), apparently removed from the now-missing (1975) holotype maxilla of "*C. asnoti*," also seems large compared to the molars. Unfortunately, with only partial dental remains, it is not possible to link this species with any known genus or separate it from living species of similar size. For the present, it may be retained as a distinct species, allocated to *Presbytis* as a "form-genus" for Asian colobines. It could almost as easily be included in *Mesopithecus*, but this would imply a zoogeographical relationship which is completely unfounded on present evidence.

PYGATHRIX E. Geoffroy, 1812

INCLUDED SUBGENERA
Pygathrix (Pygathrix) and *P. (Rhinopithecus)*

PYGATHRIX (PYGATHRIX) E. Geoffroy, 1812

(= or including: *Daunus* Gray, 1821. *Lasiopyga* Reichenbach, 1862; *nec* Illiger, 1811.)

DISTRIBUTION
Modern. Vietnam and Laos.
KNOWN SPECIES
1. *Pygathrix (Pygathrix) nemaeus* (Linnaeus, 1771), type species

PYGATHRIX (RHINOPITHECUS) Milne-Edwards, 1872

(=*Presbytiscus* Pocock, 1924. *Macaca* Lacépède: Young, 1932, in part. *Pygathrix (Rhinopithecus)*: Groves, 1970.)

DISTRIBUTION
Early Pleistocene through modern. Southwestern China.
KNOWN SPECIES
2. *Pygathrix (Rhinopithecus) roxellanae* (Milne-Edwards, 1870), subgeneric type species

3. *Pygathrix (Rhinopithecus) brelichi* (Thomas, 1903)
[=*R. tingianus* Matthew and Granger, 1923. *R. roxellanae tingianus*: Colbert and Hooijer, 1953. *P. (R.) brelichi tingianus*: Groves, 1970.]
LOCALITIES: Yenchingkou I (832).
4. *Pygathrix (Rhinopithecus) avunculus* (Dollmann, 1912)
5. *Pygathrix (Rhinopithecus)* species
(=*Macaca* sp.: Young, 1932; Bien and Chia, 1938.)
LOCALITIES: Liucheng (784); Hoshangtung (914); Tungtzu (976).

DISCUSSION

As recognized by Groves (1970), these two previously disparate genera are linked by a number of derived characters, including the extremely broad face (see Figure 160). A partial skull and several partial tooth rows from Yenchingkou I and various isolated dental remains from other Chinese sites confirm its presence well back into the Pleistocene (Delson, 1977a).

NASALIS E. Geoffroy, 1812

INCLUDED SUBGENERA
Nasalis (Nasalis) and *N. (Simias)*

NASALIS (NASALIS) E. Geoffroy, 1812

(= or including: *Hanno* Gray, 1821. *Rhinolazon* Gloger, 1841. *Rhynchopithecus* Dahlbohm, 1856.)

DISTRIBUTION
Modern. Borneo.
KNOWN SPECIES
1. *Nasalis (N.) larvatus* (Wurmbach, 1787), type species

NASALIS (SIMIAS) Miller, 1903

[= or including: *Simias* Miller, 1903. *Nasalis* Geoffroy, 1812: Groves, 1970. *N. (Simias):* Delson, 1975a.]

DISTRIBUTION
Modern. Mentawi Islands, Indonesia.
KNOWN SPECIES
2. *Nasalis (S.) concolor* (Miller, 1903)

SUBFAMILY COLOBINAE, *incertae sedis*

MESOPITHECUS Wagner, 1839

(= or including: *Semnopithecus* Desmarest, 1822: Gervais, 1849, etc. *Macaca* Lacépède, 1799: Depéret, 1887, etc. *Anthropodus* Lapouge, 1894. *Presbytis* Eschscholtz, 1821: Simons, 1970, etc.)

DISTRIBUTION
Late Miocene through late Pliocene (late Vallesian through middle or ?late Villafranchian). Southern and central Europe (between 40° and 50° N and 0°–30° E) plus southeastern England and Iran.

KNOWN SPECIES
1. *Mesopithecus pentelici* Wagner, 1839,* type species
[=*Mesopithecus pentelicus* Wagner, 1839. *Mesopithecus major* Roth and Wagner, 1854. *Semnopithecus (Mesopithecus) pentelicus:* Wagner, 1857. *Mesopithecus pentelici* Wagner, 1839: Gaudry, 1862. *Mesopithecus* n. sp.: Gremyatskii, 1957. "*Mesopithecus orientalis* Kittl": Vereschchagin, 1957, lapsus. *(Mesopithecus)* "ukrainicus" Gremyatskii, 1961, nomen nudum. Cercopithecide *(?Mesopithecus):* Lorenz, 1968.]
LOCALITIES: Wissberg (536); ?Grossulovo (546); Pikermi★ (556); Titov Veles (558); Saloniki (560); Kalimanci (562); Kromidovo (564); Gorna Susica (566); Grebeniki (568); ?Taraklia (570); Maragha (572); Hatvan (602); ?Polgardi (608); ?Baccinello "V3" (614).
2. *Mesopithecus monspessulanus* (Gervais, 1849)
(=*Semnopithecus monspessulanus* Gervais, 1849. *Mesopithecus monspessulanus:* Trouessart, 1879. *Mesopithecus pentelici* Wagner, 1839: Petho, 1884. *Macacus monspessulanus:* Depéret, 1887. *Semnopithecus* cf. *monspessulanus:* Ristori, 1890. *Anthropodus rouvillei* Lapouge, 1894. *Macacus florentinus* Cocchi, 1872: Simionescu, 1922, in part; *M(acaca). florieni:* Haas, 1966, lapsus. *Macacus?:* Mottl, 1939; *Macaca:* Tobien, 1952. cf. Colobinae sp.: Vlcek, in Fejfar, 1964. Primate?: Michaux, 1966. cf. *Semnopithecus monspessulanus:* Savage and Curtis, 1970. *?Mesopithecus monspessulanus:* Delson, 1974b.)
LOCALITIES: Gravitelli (600); Baltavar (612); Casino (618); Celleneuve (620); Montpellier★ (622); Perpignan (628); Ivanovce (632); Wölfersheim (634); Malusteni (644); Fornace RDB (650); Baraolt-Capeni (654); Hajnacka (664); Red Crag (720).

---

*Gaudry's incorrect 1862 emendation of Wagner's spelling has been accepted by all succeeding authors and is followed here.

DISCUSSION

The dentition of *Nasalis larvatus* is employed to illustrate the dental pattern of Colobinae in Figure 192. This species has the most elongated face of any living (or perhaps fossil) colobine, but *N. concolor* represents a structurally intermediate link to *Presbytis*, while sharing various derived features with *N. larvatus*.

DISCUSSION

Mesopithecus species are colobine monkeys of small to medium size, with a rather short, upright face (Figure 205; facial angle circa 55°–60° in most specimens). There is pronounced sexual dimorphism in the skull, postcranial skeleton, and canine/premolar complex. The skull and teeth (Figures 205–207) are typically colobine in almost all features. The nasal bones are slightly long for colobines of similar size, resulting in a somewhat low position of rhinion, nearly level with the base of the orbit (in males; females have somewhat lower orbits). The choanae are neither high and narrow nor low and wide, but intermediate, as in *Pygathrix* and *Presbytis entellus*. The presence of a sagittal crest in males is uncertain or variable; if present, it was probably low and far posterior on the vault (see reconstruction in Figure 205 C and F). The mandibular angle is moderately enlarged and the corpus depth relatively constant between $M_{\overline{3}}$ and $P_{\overline{4}}$. The long bones are relatively robust, at least in *M. pentelici*, more similar to those of macaques than to colobines of similar size (see Figure 208). The elbow joint is suggestive of a terrestrial habitus: The humeral medial epicondyle is reflected posteriorly, while the trochlea is more developed than in most colobines; the ulnar olecranon process is moderately retroflexed (angle approximately 30°–35°) and the shaft is not anteriorly concave as in typical colobines. The phalanges are also stouter than is usual in members of the subfamily, but the thumb is long by comparison to other digits, although reduced slightly from the ancestral cercopithecid condition. The tarsus, on the other hand, is

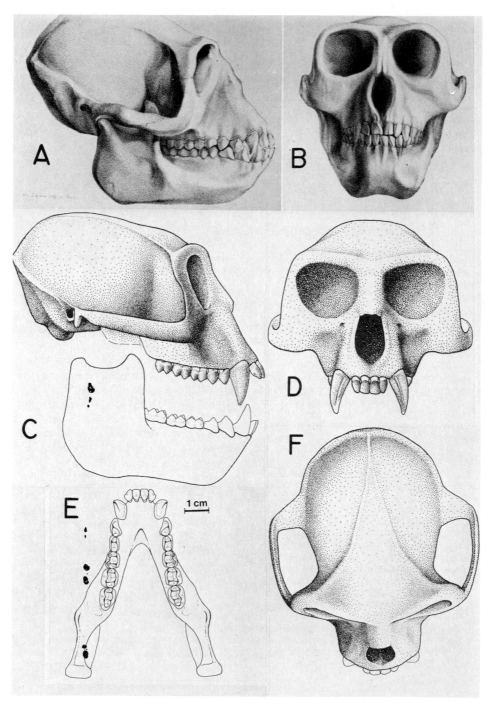

Figure 205. *Mesopithecus pentelici.* Late Miocene, Eurasia. Reconstructed female skull and mandible: A, right lateral view; B, frontal view. Reconstructed male skull and mandible: C, right lateral view; D, frontal view; E, mandible in occlusal view; F, dorsal view. Scale is 1 cm. [A, B from Beyrich (1861); C–F by B. Akerbergs.]

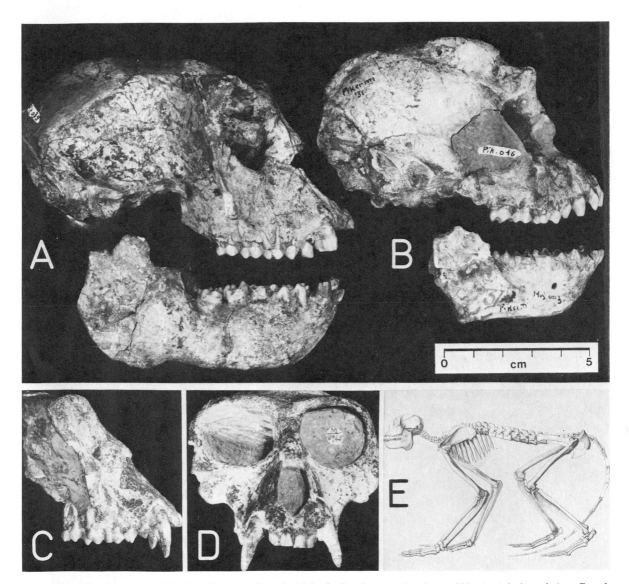

Figure 206. *Mesopithecus pentelici*. Late Miocene, Eurasia. Male skull and unassociated mandible: A, right lateral view. Female skull and unassociated mandible: B, right lateral view. Male undistorted face: C, right lateral view; D, frontal view. Restoration of composite female skeleton: E, left lateral view. [E from Gaudry (1862).]

short and typically colobine. More detailed description and measurements are presented by Delson (1973).

Mesopithecus is known essentially from the large sample of *M. pentelici* collected at Pikermi since the 1830's. Many male and female skulls (Figure 206) are represented in the collections of numerous museums,

and all teeth (except anterior deciduous ones) are known (Figure 207). Most elements of the postcranial skeleton are also represented (Figure 208), and Gaudry (1862), the first major student of the genus, was able to restore a female skeleton from unassociated elements (Figure 206E). The two species differ

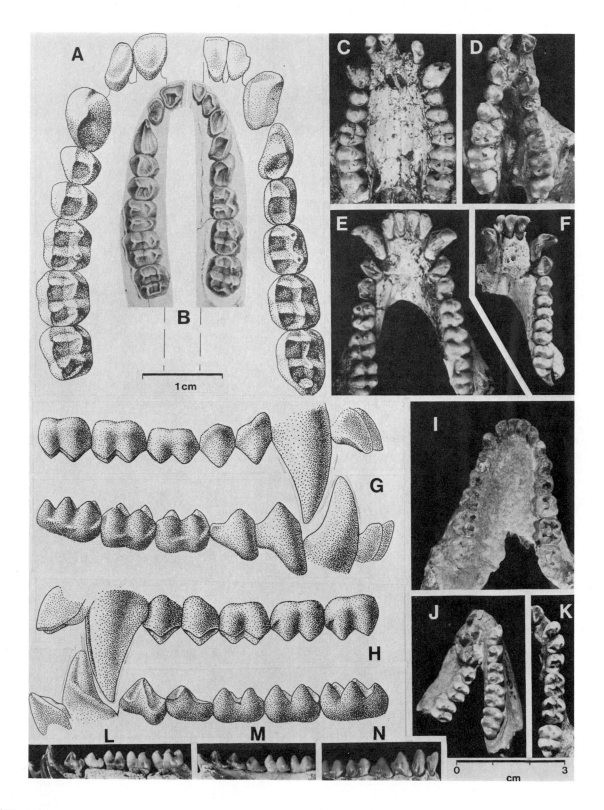

only slightly in known parts, and taxonomy of the younger form has long been a problem. It is represented by mandibles (Figure 207, F, J, and K), some loose upper teeth, and a few partial limb bones (Figure 208 A and C), generally suggesting slightly smaller overall size, slightly narrower lower molars, and a somewhat less terrestrially adapted elbow joint (and probably postcranium as a whole). Moreover, there is little or no temporal overlap between the species, although the isolated specimens near the Turolian/ Ruscinian boundary do not readily lend themselves to positive identification. *Mesopithecus monspessulanus* was previously only questionably allocated to the genus *Mesopithecus*, but several new postcranial elements have since become available which indicate that sufficient similarity exists between the two species to consider them congeneric.

The rather large number of specimens known of *M. pentelici* permits the recognition of the usual amount of individual variation seen in modern monkeys (Delson, 1973). There does not seem to be any major distinction between specimens from Pikermi and those from the less numerous collections of other sites. One minor point is that the upper molar accessory cuspules present on about one-third of Pikermi individuals ($N = 30$) are missing in other samples. At least one individual of each species congenitally lacked the $M_{\overline{3}}$ hypoconulid unilaterally, a condition seen variably in modern small colobines as well. The $P^{\underline{3}}$ protocone is strong, approaching the paracone in height, while the $P_{\overline{4}}$ metaconid is slightly smaller than the metaconid in most cases, but nearly lacking in one Pikermi specimen, almost to the point seen in some *Colobus* species. These features and those noted for the mandible compare most closely with those found in modern *Nasalis* species, but the taxonomic value of such variations is uncertain. The endocast of *Mesopithecus pentelici* has been described as essentially modern colobine in form, but this pattern is probably ancestral for the family (Radinsky, 1974). The cranium as a whole is most similar to those

of similar-sized *Presbytis* species, rather than the larger (and more derived) *Colobus* and especially *Nasalis*. Zoogeographic arguments suggest a closer relationship to the Asian colobines, unless there were two colobine migrations out of Africa, but the only shared characters are ancestral ones. In its cranium and dentition, *Mesopithecus* reveals mostly ancestral colobine features and, given · its spatiotemporal position, could well be representative of early members of the subfamily.

Rather more interesting from a paleobiological standpoint is the postcranium, which combines a few colobine heritage features with a habitus more terrestrial than any living colobine. In the former category are the deeper supraradial fossa on the distal humerus, shallow radial notch on the ulna, short tarsus, and moderately long pedal phalanges. In modern colobines, these are part of a functional–behavioral complex involving climbing, running, grasping, and leaping in an arboreal environment. In *Mesopithecus pentelici*, however, the other features of this complex are absent. The thumb is longer than in any extant colobine, but shorter than in any cercopithecine (compared to the length of the middle finger bones). This reflects retention in *Mesopithecus pentelici* of an ancestral pattern just beginning to be altered and possibly indicative of an independent thumb reduction in Asian and African colobines (greatest in the latter). The long bones are rather robust, most like the larger macaques, rather than the gracile modern colobines and the intermediate terrestrial cercopithecines, in turn suggesting a rather heavily built body. Sexual dimorphism is marked, with about a 10% difference in linear dimensions. Length comparisons between catarrhine long bones reflect overall size as well as locomotor pattern, but the further similarity of *Mesopithecus* to macaques in these ratios can also be noted. Comparing unassociated long bones of female *M. pentelici* with a sample of other cercopithecids reveals that female modern colobines of similar size have quite different indexes, both among

Figure 207. *Mesopithecus pentelici.* Late Miocene, Eurasia. Male dentition: A, occlusal view, upper right tooth-row on left, lower right tooth-row on right; G, buccal view; H, lingual view. Female dentition: B, occlusal view. Male maxilla lacking only left $I^{\underline{1}}$: C, occlusal view. Crushed female maxilla lacking left $I^{\underline{2}}$ and $P^{\underline{3}}$: D, occlusal view. Male mandible with complete dentition: E, occlusal view. Female mandible, unwarped, complete dentition: I, occlusal view. Female right $I_{\overline{1}}$, $C_{\overline{1}}$–$M_{\overline{3}}$: K, occlusal view. Juvenile female right $I_{\overline{2}}$–$M_{\overline{2}}$: M, lingual view; N, buccal view. *Mesopithecus monspessulanus.* Pliocene, Europe. Male mandible with left $I_{\overline{1}}$–$C_{\overline{1}}$, right $I_{\overline{1}}$, $C_{\overline{1}}$–$M_{\overline{3}}$: F, occlusal view; L, lingual view. Female mandible, crushed, with left $C_{\overline{1}}$–$M_{\overline{2}}$, right $P_{\overline{3}}$–$M_{\overline{3}}$: J, occlusal view. The scale below A and B is for A, G, and H; B is at ⅔ that scale. The scale below J is for C–F and I–N. [A, G, H by B. Akerbergs; B from Beyrich (1861).]

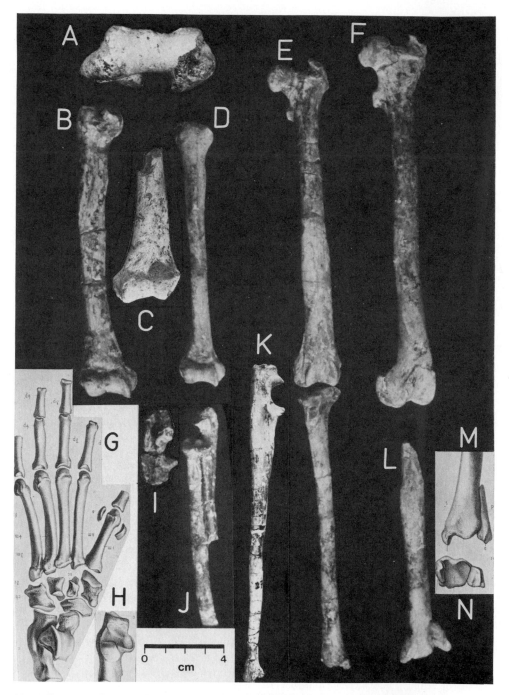

Figure 208. *Mesopithecus pentelici.* Late Miocene, Eurasia. Male right humerus, slightly distorted: B, anterior view. Female right humerus: D, anterior view. Female left femur and tibia: E, anterior view. Male left femur, slightly distorted: F, anterior view. Associated partial left foot, ?male: G, dorsal view; H, calcaneum alone, dorsal view. Male right ulna, proximal end: I, lateral view. Linked female left ulna (to right) and radius: J, anterior view. Female left ulna: K, lateral view. Male left tibia (distal two-thirds) and attached distal fibula: L, anterior view; M, drawing of same; N, distal view. *M. monspessulanus.* Pliocene, Europe. Left humerus, distal third: A, distal view; C, anterior view. The scale is for B–N; A is at twice scale. [G, H, M, N from Gaudry (1862).]

themselves and from *Mesopithecus*. Macaques (such as *M. sylvanus*) make the closest approach to the fossil's pattern of values.

Morphological features of the elbow joint confirm these similarities. The distal humerus presents a larger trochlear flange and a more posteromedially reflected medial epicondyle than any living colobine save the most robust *Presbytis entellus*, while the ulnar olecranon is moderately developed and the shaft straight. Jolly (1967) has interpreted these characters as indicating terrestrial adaptation when most pronounced—in *Mesopithecus*, the mosaic pattern corresponds best, again, with that in semiterrestrial macaques. In the same vein, the few available phalanges from Pikermi are rather stout, as in baboons and some macaques. In each of these features, the rare and fragmentary specimens of *M. monspessulanus* are more like those of modern colobines, suggesting greater arboreality.

Overall, it would appear that *Mesopithecus* (at least *M. pentelici*) was a colobine which had begun to converge toward a more terrestrial, macaque-like way of life. The most terrestrial living colobine is *Presbytis entellus*, which lives semi-terrestrially in areas of high population density and/or adverse environmental conditions. Although most skeletons of *P. entellus* are typically colobine and "arboreal-looking," the most robust ones approach the pattern seen in macaques and *Mesopithecus*. The fossil species was probably at least as terrestrial as the langur, and its overall behavior pattern might be predicted as similar.

This interpretation agrees well with evidence about the paleoenvironment at Pikermi and contemporary sites. The earlier Turolian in southern Europe appears to have been characterized by an increase of open-country "steppe/savannah" mammals and a grassland flora with moderately developed evergreen forest (see Delson, 1975b). Watercourses may have been intermittent, and, in fact, the Pikermi deposits may be the result of floods after seasonal drought. Many bones are intact except for diagenetic deformations, but few associations among elements remain. It may thus be supposed that *M. pentelici* lived in troops in gallery forest and savannah fringe, spending a good part of the day feeding terrestrially or moving between arboreal feeding sites. On the other hand, the younger species inhabited a more wooded and well-watered environment and appears to have been adapted to a more arboreal habitus, perhaps under the influence of competition from contemporary *Dolichopithecus ruscinensis* (see Delson, 1973, 1975a).

DOLICHOPITHECUS Dépéret, 1889

(= or including: *Semnopithecus* Desmarest, 1822: Dépéret, 1886, in part. *Macaca* Lacépède, 1799: Dépéret, 1886, in part; and others. ?"*Adelopithecus*" Gremyatskii, 1961.)

DISTRIBUTION

Pliocene (and latest Miocene?) (?late Turolian through early Villafranchian). Southern and central-eastern Europe.

KNOWN SPECIES

Dolichopithecus ruscinensis Dépéret, 1889, type species
(=*Semnopithecus monspessulanus* Gervais, 1849: Dépéret, 1886. *Macacus priscus* Gervais, 1859: Dépéret, 1886. *Macacus monspessulanus*: Dépéret, 1887. *Macacus florentinus* Cocchi 1872: Athanasiu, 1912. *Macaca*: Mottl, 1939; Tobien, 1952. *Dolichopithecus* cf. *arvernensis* Dépéret, 1929: Kretzoi, 1954; Crusafont and Golpe, 1969.)

LOCALITIES: Pestszentlörinc (604); Serrat d'en Vacquer★ (626); "Perpignan" (628); Wölfersheim (634); Layna (638); Balaruc-2 (640); Malusteni (644); Beresti (652); Baraolt-Capeni (654); ?"Odessa" (668); Budey (676); Novopetrovka (678); Kotlovina (710).

DISCUSSION

Dolichopithecus is distinguished from all other known colobines by its extreme adaptations to terrestrial life and from known cercopithecines postcranially in the mosaic pattern of this adaptation. It is a colobine of moderately large size, with dentition typical for the subfamily (Figure 211). The face is rather long [facial angle about 45°–50° in females (Figure 209), less—i.e., more protruding—in damaged males], and, as usual in such cases, the interorbital distance is low for colobines. There is pronounced sexual dimorphism in postcranial elements, in the canine–$P_{\overline{3}}$ complex, and apparently in the skull. The choanae seem rather narrow, and a sagittal crest may have been present in males. The mandibular angle is enlarged but not extreme, while the corpus depth is constant between $M_{\overline{3}}$ and $P_{\overline{4}}$. The long bones are robust; the humerus is apparently relatively long, with large trochlea and backwardly reflected medial epicondyle; the ulnar shaft may be slightly concave anteriorly, the olecranon rather large. The phalanges are stouter than in other colobines, as in terrestrial cercopithecines; relative lengths of pollex and hallux are unknown.

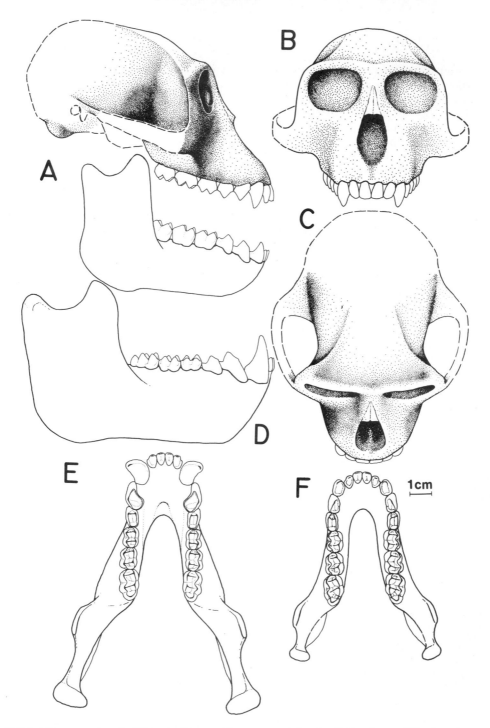

Figure 209. *Dolichopithecus ruscinensis.* Pliocene, Europe. Reconstructed female skull and mandible: A, right lateral view; B, frontal view; C, dorsal view; F, mandibular occlusal view. Reconstructed male mandible: D, right lateral view; E, occlusal view. [By B. Akerbergs.]

Dolichopithecus differs from the closely related *Mesopithecus* in its more extreme terrestrial adaptations, limb proportions, and in size; from *Libypithecus* in size, proportions of the upper cheek teeth, and probably skull form, although comparable parts are not available; from *Cercopithecoides* and especially *Paracolobus* in much narrower interorbital pillar and face and stouter phalanges. Additional description and measurements are provided by Delson (1973).

Like *Mesopithecus pentelici*, *Dolichopithecus ruscinensis* is mostly known from the large sample at its type locality. This includes a partial crushed male face (Figure 210, B, G, and K), two less damaged female crania (Figure 210, A, E, J, D, and F), numerous mandibles of both sexes (Figure 210, H, I, L, and M), isolated teeth and a selection of mostly partial long bones, and some tarsal elements and phalanges (Figure 212), most of which can be sexed. Specimens from the other localities consist mostly of isolated teeth and some mandibular fragments, but the best known ulna is a nearly complete specimen from Pestszentlőrinc, Hungary, the oldest locality yielding the genus (Figure 212A).

The teeth of *Dolichopithecus* (Figure 211) are rather standard for a Eurasian colobine of its size. Among minor points of interest, the $P_{\overline{4}}$ is relatively narrow, the metaconid is nearly as high as the protoconid, and there is a moderately developed mesial flange, especially in males. All $M_{\overline{3}}$'s lack sixth cusps and the mesial lophids are wider than the distal ones on $M_{\overline{3}}$, but almost never on $M_{\overline{2}}$. The $P^{\underline{3}}$ has a well-developed protocone and mesial flange.

Considering the reconstructed female cranium (Figure 209), the nasal bones are relatively long for a colobine (as expected given the long face), and they widen greatly from nasion to rhinion; as part of the same complex, the interorbital pillar is slightly narrow, although the face is rather wide. The supraorbital torus is lightly built, but the face is deep, especially in the malar region. The choanae are damaged, but appear to have been narrow. The temporal lines are strong on the frontal, but do not appear to have converged to a crest. They may have been nearly parallel or turned laterally near bregma. Dépéret (1890) figured the male skull with an apparent sagittal crest, but this is not visible on the actual specimen as preserved—a crest may have existed, but this possibility is less likely given its absence in most other known large colobines. Most female mandibles are badly crushed, but, from several good male specimens, it appears that the corpus depth was constant, gonion only slightly enlarged, angle between symphysis and base about 120°, that of the ramus about 100°, and the notch between condyle and coronoid shallow, suggesting an anterior placement of the temporalis.

In its known postcranial elements, *Dolichopithecus* presents a combination of colobine hallmarks and adaptations to a highly terrestrial life-style. The bones of the forelimb show few muscle markings, the supraradial fossa on the humerus is deep, and the radial notch on the ulna is shallow and single, all common features in colobines. But, even more clearly than in *Mesopithecus*, these traits are overlain by convergences toward a "baboon-like" locomotor pattern. The humeral medial epicondyle is reflected far backward, and the trochlear flange is strongly developed to form a tightly locking elbow joint with the ulna, whose olecranon process is large and slightly back-tilted. The ulnar shaft is not complete in any specimen, but it appears straight, although it narrows from the radial articulation distad, giving the impression of some anterior concavity. There is a bimodality of size in long bones and tarsal elements, the smaller measuring some 85% of the larger. This is probably due to sex dimorphism, the differences being close to those seen in *Mesopithecus*, more than in most colobines and similar to macaques. Robusticity of the male humerus and femur is also great, again as in macaques and *Mesopithecus*. Several phalanges of *D. ruscinensis* are quite robust, in the range of mandrills, macaques, and *Mesopithecus*.

One feature of possible significance relates to the proportions of the limbs in *D. ruscinensis*. The length of the male femur and radius can be well estimated from complete or nearly complete fossils. Tibial length can be estimated from a complete fibula combined with a tibial head. Unfortunately, the most complete humerus lacks a head and is crushed proximally, and Delson (1973) was unable to find any obtainable measurement which correlated closely with total length. But, from examination of the specimen and comparison with modern samples, a narrow range and probable length estimate was reached, essentially equal to femoral length. This value is surprising, as no living cercopithecid has so long a humerus, but a shorter value would yield similarly extreme values for robusticity. The relative proportions of the four limbs compare most closely with modern baboons (*Papio*

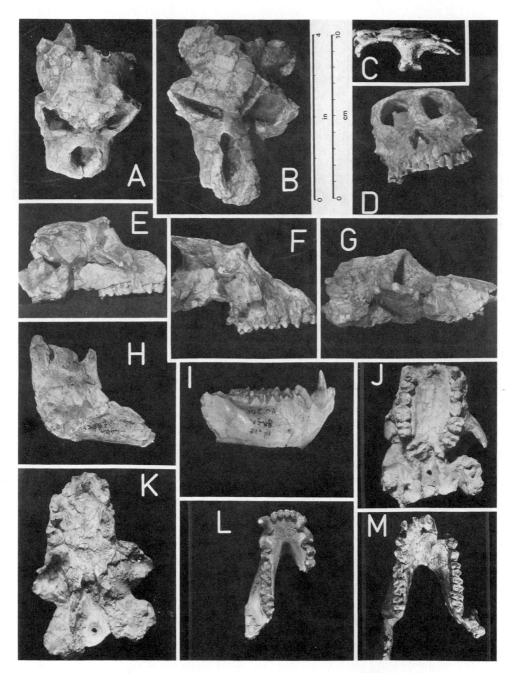

Figure 210. *Dolichopithecus ruscinensis.* Pliocene, Europe. Female cranium: A, dorsal view; E, right lateral view; J, occlusal view. Crushed male cranium: B, dorsal view; G, right lateral view; K, occlusal view. Female cranium: D, frontal view; F, right lateral view. ?Female frontal bone: C, frontal view. ?Male mandibular ramus: H, right lateral view. Male mandibular corpus lacking only right molars: I, right lateral view (photographically reversed); L, occlusal view. Female mandible lacking left C_T and I_T, right I_T–C_T displaced: M, occlusal view. Scale divisions are in inches and centimeters.

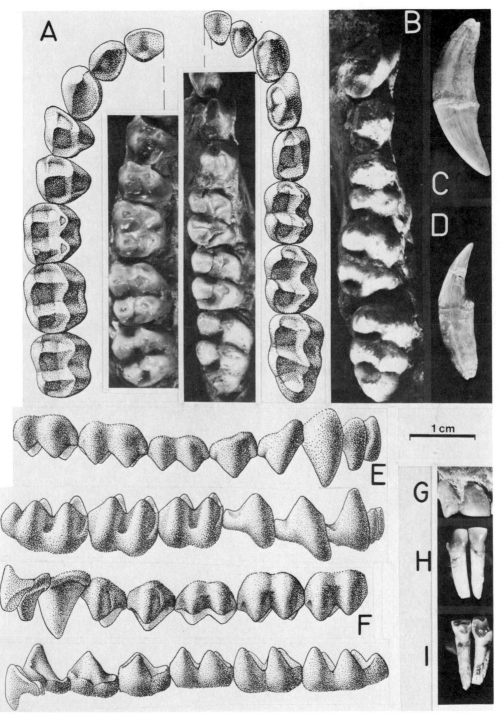

Figure 211. *Dolichopithecus ruscinensis.* Pliocene, Europe. Right female dentition: A, occlusal view, upper to left, drawing and photographs (photographs lacking I¹–C); E, buccal view; F, lingual view. Male right $P_{\overline{3}}$–$M_{\overline{3}}$ (photographically reversed): B, occlusal. Left male C¹: C, buccal view. Left male C,: D, buccal view. Right I¹⁻²: G, labial view. Right I$_{\overline{1-2}}$: H, labial view; I, lingual view. Scale refers to A, B, E, and F; C and D are ½ that scale; G. H, and I are ¾ that scale. [A, E, F by B. Akerbergs.]

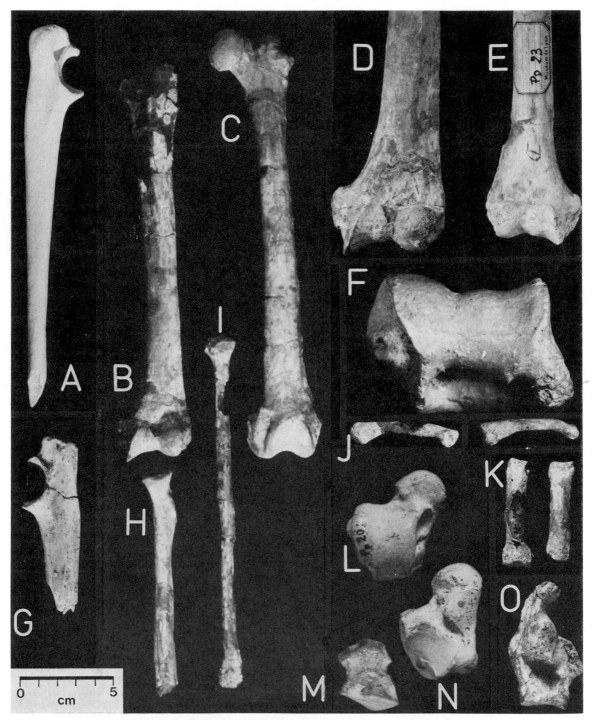

Figure 212. *Dolichopithecus ruscinensis.* Pliocene, Europe. ?Male left ulna: A, medial view. ?Male left humerus: B, anterior view; D, anterior view, distal articular surface. ?Male left femur: C, anterior view. ?Female right humerus: E, anterior view, distal articular surface; F, distal view. ?Female right ulna: G, medial view. ?Male right radius: H, anterior view. ?Male left fibula: I, anterior view. Phalanges, proximal (to left) and middle: J, lateral; K, dorsal. ?Male astragalus: L, right, dorsal view; N, left, plantar view. ?Male left cuboid: M, dorsal view. ?Male right calcaneum: O, dorsal view. The scale is for A, B, C, G, H, and I; D and E are at 1.5× that scale; J–O are at 2× that scale; F is at 3× that scale.

and *Theropithecus*), but differ from these in longer humerus compared both to femur and to radius. *Theropithecus (Simopithecus) oswaldi* specimens from several Middle Pleistocene sites described by Jolly (1972), however, approach more closely the pattern found in *Dolichopithecus*, although they also present extreme terrestrial adaptations in the elbow and phalanges. Jolly considered that their long humerus (and generally long forelimb) was an adaptation to level-surface walking, as opposed to the speed-oriented longer forearm in modern forms. Biegert and Maurer (1972) have discussed an allometric relationship of relative limb length and body size, with forelimb lengthening faster than hindlimb as trunk size increases, but a preliminary comparison suggests that the relationships seen in *Dolichopithecus* are more extreme than would be expected from its size alone.

The phyletic relationships of *D. ruscinensis* are clearly with the colobines, despite some prior confusion. Within the subfamily, there is little or no similarity to African genera or to the smaller Asian *Presbytis* and (broad-faced) *Pygathrix*. The cranial resemblance to *Nasalis* (and less so to *Libypithecus*) is related to facial lengthening, but whether it was achieved convergently or inherited from a common source is unknown. A phyletic link with *Nasalis* is conceivable but not strongly indicated. More meaningful are the derived postcranial features shared with *Mesopithecus*: robust limbs and phalanges, tightly locking elbow, and marked sexual dimorphism, all more extreme in *Dolichopithecus* than in *M. pentelici*. The evidence as presented (Delson, 1973, 1975a) permits and in no way denies a hypothesis of an *in situ* European trend toward greater terrestriality and facial lengthening in a colobine lineage represented by these two species. There are no derived characters of *Mesopithecus* which

are not seen (and almost always in a more derived condition) in *Dolichopithecus*. It must be accepted that the two taxa shared a common ancestor. Moreover, consideration of temporal, geographical, and environmental evidence allows a more detailed scenario to be proposed.

Late Miocene *M. pentelici* was adapted to semiterrestrial life in an open-country environment. To the north and east of its range, however, forest or parkland remained dominant, while the south became drier at the end of the Miocene. The oldest known specimen of *Dolichopithecus*, the Pestszentlörinc ulna, with all typical features developed, comes from this northeastern area at the close of the Miocene. The early Pliocene saw a renewal of humid forests in southern Europe as well as the spread of *Dolichopithecus*, suggesting that this genus evolved from a marginal population of *M. pentelici* adapting to forest-floor life. Its competition with *Mesopithecus* in the new environment may in turn have induced the more arboreal nature of *M. monspessulanus* via character displacement. In this interpretation, *M. pentelici* is seen as the actual ancestor of both Pliocene species. *Dolichopithecus ruscinensis* is accorded distinct generic rank because of its extreme locomotor adaptations by comparison with both smaller species. The habitus of *Dolichopithecus* is best seen as a convergence to mandrills, foraging on the forest floor, and at times ascending into the trees. Its postcranial anatomy is a mosaic comparable to that seen in the most terrestrial macaques rather than in baboons, but combined with a relative humeral length exceeded only in the most terrestrial extinct cercopithecine. On the other hand, it retained a typical colobine dentition, with no increase in incisor area or other adaptation to increased frugivory.

Family Cercopithecidae, *incertae sedis*

PROHYLOBATES Fourtau, 1918

(= or including: *Dryopithecus* Lartet, 1856: Fourtau, 1918, in part; and others. *Pliopithecus* Gervais, 1849: Abel, 1931, in part; and others.)

DISTRIBUTION
Early Miocene. Egypt, Libya.

KNOWN SPECIES
1. *Prohylobates tandyi* Fourtau, 1918, type species
(=?*Dryopithecus mogharensis* Fourtau, 1918. *Pliopithecus tandyi*: Abel, 1931.)

LOCALITIES: Wadi Moghara★ (400).
   2. *Prohylobates simonsi* Delson, in press b
LOCALITIES: Jebel Zelten★ (398).

DISCUSSION

Prohylobates is a small to medium-sized cercopithe-cid with incompletely developed bilophodonty of the lower cheek teeth, $M_{\overline{3}}$ of varied length, perhaps a small median hypoconulid on $M_{\overline{2}}$, and relatively deep mandibular corpus. Each species is known by only one to three mandibles from its type locality. Fourtau (1918, reprinted with minor changes in 1920) described three partial mandibles from Moghara, of which the less complete pair were placed in a species tentatively allocated to *Dryopithecus*. Fourtau considered the single specimen of *P. tandyi* as somehow related to gibbons, including *Pliopithecus*. Remane (1924) re-viewed the material briefly on the basis of Fourtau's poor illustrations, suggesting a possible relationship between *Prohylobates* and the Oligocene *Prop-liopithecus* from the nearby Fayum deposits, and perhaps the same ancestry for *?D. mogharensis* as well. Simons (1969a) thought that this proposed relation-ship was based more on geographical proximity than on morphological similarity, a point which will be contested below. In the interim, few authors consid-ered these fossils. Abel (1931) and others, for example, placed *P. tandyi* in *Pliopithecus* without comment. Le Gros Clark and Leakey (1950) did recognize the cer-copithecid nature of the *P. tandyi* teeth, but proceeded no further. In 1965, Simons and Pilbeam and, inde-pendently, Remane realized the correct affinity of the Moghara material, the former authors including *?D. mogharensis* in the same taxon. Finally, Simons (1969a) described these fossils in detail and compared them to other catarrhines. One jaw from Jebel Zelten was recognized and described as a distinct species by Del-son (in press b).

Of the three Moghara specimens, only the type (Figure 213, B and D) is sufficiently well preserved to permit much morphology to be recognized. Simons (1969a) indicated that the referred specimen of "*D. mogharensis*" had been damaged in casting at Cairo in 1936, only a $P_{\overline{4}}$ remaining, but he did offer a drawing of the teeth (Figure 213A) based on that remnant, casts, and Fourtau's photograph. The type of "*D. mogharensis*" is nearly edentulous, the molar crowns being eroded and broken, although it does provide

some idea of the corpus shape. From it, Simons reconstructed a ramus orientation, which cannot be accepted without serious question. The type mandible is damaged inferiorly, but the alveolar border extends to the midline or slightly beyond. The incisor sockets are broken away, but at least parts of the canine and $P_{\overline{3}}$ alveoli remain, as do the strongly worn crowns of $P_{\overline{4}}$–$M_{\overline{3}}$, the latter lacking its lingual half. No details of cusp placement can be seen on $M_{\overline{1}}$ or on $P_{\overline{4}}$, but the latter tooth appears to have had a short trigonid and a somewhat bulging, rather than flanged, mesiobuccal corner. Simons indicated that the tooth is rotated slightly buccally, oblique to the molar axis, a feature which he thought was also present only in *Victoria-pithecus* but which in fact occurs frequently among colobines as well. As Simons further indicated, there were probably two roots to $P_{\overline{3}}$, but the extent of this tooth is impossible to judge because of damage to the alveolar border.

The distinctive molar morphology of *Prohylobates* is thus identifiable only on the worn last two molars of the type specimen of *P. tandyi* (on which $M_{\overline{3}}$ is dam-aged lingually) and the unique jaw of *P. simonsi* (Fig-ure 213, C, E, and F). In both, the pattern is less completely bilophodont than in any other cer-copithecid. It is interesting to note that Fourtau's de-scription essentially leads to the same conclusion, although he did not see the parallel himself. Lophids are poorly developed, but the relatively heavy wear obscures their original delineation. A low and nearly linear structure links the hypoconid and metaconid on unbroken teeth; this is probably part of the worn protoconid median slope, rather than a true cristid obliqua. The trigonids are short, but this is probably another artifact of wear: They are no longer in cer-copithecines with similar attrition. The tooth crowns are relatively high, as in cercopithecids, but the relief is low—the lingual notches are shallow and the cusps little raised above the basins (Figure 213E). The $M_{\overline{2}}$'s and apparently also the $M_{\overline{1}}$'s are nearly square, with the mesial width slightly greater than the distal, as in some derived cercopithecines (convergently?). The molars all have deep median buccal clefts, as in later cercopithecids, but there are also cingular bulges (not shelves, however).

Two major features of morphology separate the two species. In *Prohylobates tandyi*, the third molar of the type was only fractionally longer than $M_{\overline{2}}$, and it may even have been shorter in the more damaged

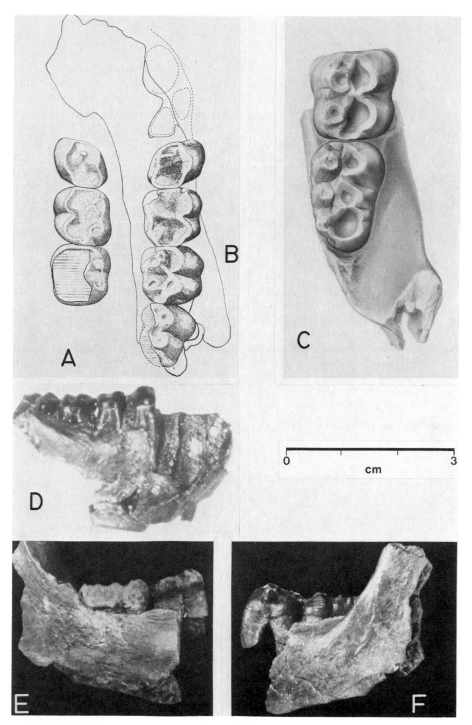

Figure 213. *Prohylobates.* Early Miocene, North Africa. *P. tandyi.* Restored left $P_{\overline{4}}$–$M_{\overline{2}}$: A, occlusal view. Damaged right mandibular corpus with anterior alveoli and $P_{\overline{4}}$–$M_{\overline{2}}$, broken $M_{\overline{3}}$: B, occlusal view; D, lateral view. *P. simonsi,* partial left corpus with $M_{\overline{2-3}}$: C, occlusal view (reversed); E, lingual view; F, buccal view. The scale is for D–F; A–C are at 1.5× that scale. [A, B from Simons (1969a); C by C. Tarka.]

specimen ("*?D. mogharensis*"); in the Zelten jaw, however, M$\overline{3}$ is significantly longer than M$\overline{2}$, the postulated ancestral catarrhine condition. A similar pattern of variation is seen among the species of *Propliopithecus*. Moreover, on the M$\overline{2}$ of *P. tandyi*, Simons (1969a) discerned a small circular dentine exposure distally, which he considered as evidence of a true hypoconulid; no such feature is seen on *P. simonsi*. On the other hand, a similar situation occurs variably in *Theropithecus* (q.v.), in which a small distal cuspule, not a true cusp or center of enamel growth, may add to the complexity of surface detail. Finally, the Zelten specimen is over 1.5 times as large as the Moghara specimens, supporting its specific distinction. Similarly, the corpus is rather more robust, at least thicker, suggesting heavier chewing stresses (it is broken just under the roots). As Simons (1969a) suggested, the corpus of *Prohylobates* is somewhat deep compared to dental size, in the range of smaller colobines such as *Mesopithecus* or *Presbytis* and slightly deeper than the type of *Victoriapithecus macinnesi*. The basic adaptation was probably frugivory, but the robust jaws might suggest some heavier chewing, perhaps facultative folivory, which agrees well with hypotheses as to the original niche of the Cercopithecidae.

Relationships of *Prohylobates* are still uncertain. Without additional, less worn material, it is premature to allocate it to, or even suggest resemblances with, a modern cercopithecid subfamily. In terms of the suite of characters shared by the two species, *Prohylobates* is morphologically the most conservative known cercopithecid; if Simons was right, retention of a hypoconulid would support this. On the other hand, this conservatism may not be all-pervasive. It is conceivable, but not likely, that unworn trigonids might be short, which would indicate either a link to colobines or strong distinction; the latter might also be true if a short M$\overline{3}$ were ancestral for the genus. In sum, the two species were not referable to any other known genus, which permits clear recognition of *Prohylobates* as distinct, but it must be ranked *incertae sedis* within the family. *Victoriapithecus* is similarly ranked, but it shares no derived feature with *Prohylobates*, instead being more "advanced" in its possession of complete molar lophids. The conservative nature of *Prohylobates* also might have been responsible for Remane's (1924) having linked it to the more conservative *Propliopithecus*, which is probably the *known* genus morphologically closest to the ancestral cercopithecoid.

VICTORIAPITHECUS von Koenigswald, 1969

(= or including: *Mesopithecus* Wagner, 1839: MacInnes, 1943, in part. *Prohylobates* Fourtau, 1918: Romer, 1966, in part.*)

DISTRIBUTION
  Early to middle Miocene. Kenya, Uganda.
KNOWN SPECIES
  1. *Victoriapithecus macinnesi* von Koenigswald, 1969, type species (=*Mesopithecus* sp.: MacInnes, 1943, in part. *V. leakeyi* von Koenigswald, 1969, in part.)
LOCALITIES: Loperot (410); Ombo (414); Maboko★ (440).
  2. *Victoriapithecus* sp. indet.
LOCALITIES: Napak V (402).
  3. "*Victoriapithecus*" *leakeyi* von Koenigswald, 1969 (=*V. macinnesi* von Koenigswald, 1969, in part.)
LOCALITIES: ?Ombo (414); Maboko★ (440).

---

*The name *Victoriapithecus* was first published by Romer (1966, p. 382) as a synonym of *Prohylobates* in a generic listing *cum* classification of vertebrates. This must have been based on a prepublication communication from von Koenigswald, but no authorship is given in the list. The name is considered to date from von Koenigswald, 1969.

DISCUSSION

Victoriapithecus species are small cercopithecids of modern type which retain a number of ancestral features but have well-developed loph(id)s, shallow lingual notches on lower cheek teeth, and long M$\overline{3}$ compared to M$\overline{2}$. The two named species are probably not referable to a single genus or even subfamily, but they are treated together here for the sake of convenience, pending complete revision. Originally, von Koenigswald (1969) recognized two species, distinguished by size differences. As has been indicated elsewhere (Delson, 1975a, 1973), several of the specimens he illustrated and discussed are not monkey but anthropomorph, while a morphological dichotomy among all known Maboko specimens appears to cut across a wide size variation.

Victoriapithecus macinnesi, the type species, has squarish lower cheek teeth (Figure 214, A, B, and D)

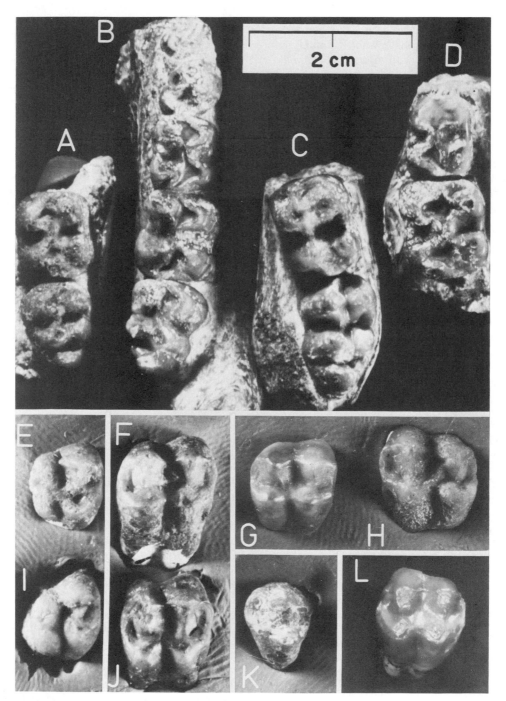

Figure 214. *Victoriapithecus*. Middle Miocene, Africa. Teeth in occlusal view. *V. macinnesi:* A, left corpus with $M_{\overline{2-3}}$; B, right corpus with $P_{\overline{4}}$–$M_{\overline{3}}$; D, left corpus with $M_{\overline{1-2}}$; E and I, referred right $M^{\underline{3}}$; F and J, referred right $M^{2?}$; K, tentatively referred right $P^{\underline{4}}$. *"V." leakeyi:* C, left corpus with $M_{\overline{2-3}}$; G, right $M^{1?}$; H, left $M^{2?}$. *Victoriapithecus* sp. Early Miocene, Africa: L, left damaged $M^{\underline{1or2}}$.

421

which combine ancestrally shallow notches and bulging cingulum remnants with apparently derived colobine-like short trigonids, thus conforming to a prediction of the possible mosaic pattern for an ancestral colobine. Upper molars are uncertainly referred, but appear to be basically of ancestral, cercopithecine-like form, with moderately high flare and symmetrical distal margins. Mandibular corpus depth is moderate, but within the range for small colobines (and perhaps small cercopithecines). Several possibly relevant postcranial elements (Figure 216, D and J–L) suggest an arboreal, colobine-like habitus, with medially projecting medial epicondyle on the humerus and elongate phalanges.

Six partial mandibles with teeth are apparently referable to this species. Although they present a rather great range in size, the morphology of the specimens is fairly constant, as can be seen from Figure 214. Only the type mandible preserves any corpus morphology (Figure 215, A and C): It seems of moderate and rather constant depth, although it is a bit deeper under $P_{\overline{4}}$ than under $M_{\overline{3}}$, as in most cercopithecines. The ramus is broken away, but there is the suggestion of deepening toward gonion and a rather upright anterior border. The $P_{\overline{4}}$ of the type is set oblique to the tooth-row, as in *Prohylobates* and some colobines.

Although most of the lower molars (in mandibles or isolated) are worn, they do appear to share a square outline, low relief, and short trigonids. Lateral flare is low, but there is some bulging or even cingulum on the buccal surface, especially on the Loperot and larger Maboko teeth, suggesting a previously greater cingular development, as seen also in *Prohylobates*. The teeth are apparently fully bilophodont, which sets them clearly apart from the latter genus, and the $M_{\overline{3}}$'s are slightly longer than $M_{\overline{2}}$ (ca. 107%) in the two jaws which preserve them. The size range is not out of place for a single population, althought the variability may be slightly high. Distal width is greater than mesial on all $M_{\overline{1}}$, while mesial width is the larger in three $M_{\overline{2}}$'s and both $M_{\overline{3}}$'s. Isolated lower third molars are difficult to allocate between the two recognized morphs, because both size and wear are varied and there is little to serve as a standard; further associations are required for more definitive identification. All upper teeth (e.g., Figure 214, E, F, and I–K) are isolated and again difficult to allocate because wear obscures the details, but several appear to occlude with the lower jaws. The uppers are squarish, with low cusps, but apparently

less cingulum-like bulging than in the Napak tooth (Figure 214L), which may be termed *Victoriapithecus* sp. None shows a crista obliqua.

The holotype of von Koenigswald's second species, *"Victoriapithecus" leakeyi*, is an upper $M^{\underline{2}2}$, unworn but with an eroded surface, which is distinctive in presenting a crista obliqua which links the metacone and protocone (Figure 214H). A paraloph is well formed, but there is no connection between metacone and hypocone. It is probable that this represents a conservative retention from an ancestral condition, from which state the buccal part of the crista obliqua joined a new ridge from the hypocone to form a metaloph. The three basins appear long, but the mesial width is slightly greater than the length, in turn rather larger than the distal width. Of greatest importance is the inferred congruent occlusion between this tooth and a referred lower jaw, which suggests they represent a single taxon, separate from *V. macinnesi*. Only one other molar shows a crista obliqua (although weakly due to heavier wear than the type), and this tooth may also be tentatively assigned here as an $M^{\underline{1}2}$ (Figure 214G).

The referred mandible, with $M_{\overline{2-3}}$, is highly diagnostic (Figures 214C and 215, B and D). Although its low occlusal relief and molar width are similarities to the type of *V. macinnesi*, the teeth of *"V." leakeyi* are relatively much longer (thus narrower) and the trigonids are especially well developed. Elongate molars with long trigonids are typical of cercopithecines and are considered to represent the ancestral cercopithecid condition, so that this specimen is conservative. The central fovea or talonid basin is also quite long, however, which may be distinctive. Compared to $M_{\overline{2}}$, the third molar is long (about 127%). The ramus of this jaw is broken away, but its origin suggests possible greater inclination than in the *V. macinnesi* type. Few isolated lowers can be associated with this jaw, partly because of wear differences, but a broken $M_{\overline{2?}}$ from Ombo may pertain, as also may one or more $M_{\overline{3}}$'s. *"Victoriapithecus" leakeyi* is thus seen as a dentally more conservative, somewhat cercopithecine-like species, with narrow teeth, long $M_{\overline{3}}$, and retained crista obliqua on upper molars ($M^{\underline{3}}$ uncertain).

The Maboko collection also includes a number of isolated anterior teeth and postcranial elements, as well as new specimens as yet undescribed. The teeth include one upper and one lower second(?) incisor, both somewhat colobine-like in form and thus per-

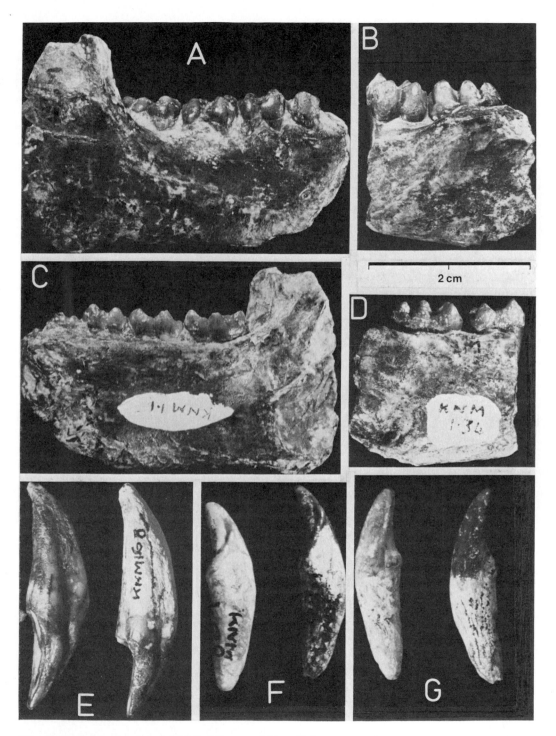

Figure 215. *Victoriapithecus macinnesi*. Middle Miocene, Africa. Right corpus with $P_{\overline{4}}$–$M_{\overline{3}}$: A, lateral view; C, lingual view. *"Victoriapithecus" leakeyi*. Middle Miocene, Africa. Left corpus with $M_{\overline{2-3}}$: B, lateral view; D, lingual view. Cf. *Victoriapithecus* sp.: E, two left C^1 in lingual view—note continuous sulcus; F, two left $C_{\overline{1}}$ in disto-lingual view; G, same, mesio-buccal view.

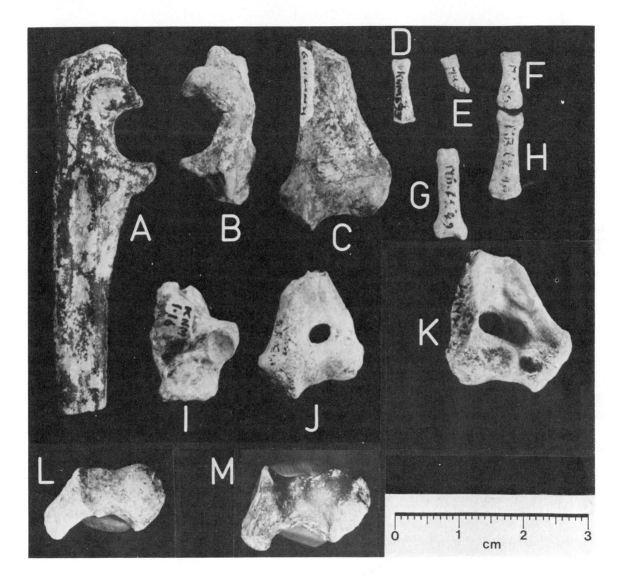

Figure 216. Cf. *Victoriapithecus* sp. Middle Miocene, Africa. Right ulna, proximal third: A, lateral view. Left ulna, proximal end: B, lateral view. Left humerus, distal end: C, anterior view; M, distal view. Intermediate phalanges: D, E (broken), F, and H, dorsal view. Proximal phalanx: G, dorsal view. Left calcaneus: I, dorsal view. Left humerus, distal end: J, anterior view; K, posterior view; L, distal view.

haps of ancestral morphology. At least 6 upper and 16 lower canines are present as well. All are of male type, that is, all have a tall crown compared to root length, and, in the uppers, the mesial sulcus continues from the crown onto the root (Figure 215E). However, the apparently cercopithecid lower canines (Figure 215, F and G) are nearly indistinguishable from those associated at other sites with molars of *Dendropithecus macinnesi*. Thus, it is not yet possible to allocate these teeth among the two sexes of two species recognized in the collection on the basis of molars.

Eleven postcranial elements are also among the

original group of specimens. These include two proximal ulnae and two distal humeral fragments. The two ulnae (Figure 216, A and B) could easily be of opposite sides of the same individual, although this is not *necessarily* true. As first indicated by von Koenigswald (1969), who discussed only the more complete ulna, the morphology is similar to that seen in semiterrestrial cercopithecids. It is quite similar to *M. pentelici* and to some *Cercocebus* species, as well as to *C. aethiops*, but the shaft is straighter and the olecranon is back-tilted as much as in some larger Papionini. In addition, the radial notch or facet is divided and rather deep. This suggests functional comparisons with semiterrestrial cercopithecines and the most terrestrial colobines. The larger humeral fragment (Figure 216, C and M) is slightly too small to fit the ulnae, but it could well be from a smaller individual of the same species. It demonstrates similar adaptations in the rather retroflected medial epicondyle and moderate trochlear flange; some matrix still obscures the supra-articular and olecranon fossae. The smaller humerus (Figure 216, J–L), however, has a long and rather medially directed medial epicondyle, perhaps a shorter trochlear flange, and apparently a colobine-type supra-articular fossa construction. A proximal and two middle phalanges (Figure 216, F–H) are rather stout, as in baboons or even geladas, and would seem to represent a taxon at least as terrestrially adapted as *Cercopithecus aethiops*. A third middle phalanx (Figure 216D) is more slender, which could indicate the presence of a more arboreal species with elongated, grasping cheiridia. Given the range in size of *V. macinnesi* teeth, it is questionable to which dental

taxon each set of bones might pertain. Delson (1975a, 1973) suggested that the larger and more terrestrially adapted bones went with the teeth of "*V.*" *leakeyi* on the basis of size, but this partly ignored the larger *V. macinnesi* teeth. This view does seem most likely because of the apparent relationships of the two taxa from dental morphology, even though it involves some circular reasoning. It may be retained as a very tentative working hypothesis, pending actual associations.

Taken together, the totality of the Maboko (and referred) evidence suggests the sympatric occurrence of two small cercopithecid taxa in the middle Miocene. One of these, *Victoriapithecus macinnesi*, was probably arboreal and may have been part of a lineage which developed colobine dental traits, thus potentially near the ancestry of the subfamily. With more and better dental evidence, this relationship could be more clearly substantiated, but a later member of this lineage with deep lingual lower molar notches is really required to document the appearance of full-fledged colobines. The second species, "*Victoriapithecus*" *leakeyi*, appears to be a larger form with more conservative cercopithecine-like (ancestral) cheek teeth, retaining a crista obliqua on (some) upper molars, but with an elbow joint and phalanges suggesting terrestrial, or at least cursorial, life. Facial elements (and perhaps anterior dentition) would be the most useful in further assessing the possible relationships of this species to later Cercopithecinae. At present it is reasonable to suggest that the subfamilies had indeed become distinct by early in the middle Miocene.

Family Oreopithecidae
Schwalbe, 1915

DISTRIBUTION
  Late Miocene (Turolian). Europe.
INCLUDED TAXA
  Oreopithecus.

Discussion

From the time of its first description, the distinctiveness of *Oreopithecus* has been recognized, although its affinities have been in doubt. Four major alternative

interpretations of these phyletic links have been presented over the years, viewing *Oreopithecus* as a relative of cercopithecids, of hominids (especially hominines), of *Apidium* or as a distinctive form (sometimes as a "transition" between other groups). Each of these views will be briefly assessed here, based on the detailed description found under the genus, beginning with the first and oldest interpretation, which we now espouse. Despite the several derived characters which *Oreopithecus* shares with cercopithecids, however, it differs in a number of unique features which suffice to distinguish it at family rank from all other catarrhines (see below). It may also be noted here that *Mabokopithecus,* described by von Koenigswald (1969) as an oreopithecid, is known from a single damaged tooth which is probably not primate.

According to Hürzeler (1948, 1958), Gervais (1872) and especially Schlosser (1887) detected a number of resemblances to the cercopithecids in the lower teeth of the type specimen of *O. bambolii.* This view was taken up by numerous later authors, few of whom examined any original specimens, and was the most common interpretation until the 1950s, when Hürzeler dismissed it, essentially out of hand. In this he was followed by Delson and Andrews (1975), although Szalay (1975d) suggested that the shared derived loss of helical movement in the lower ankle joint was strong evidence for this phyletic linkage. Our current reassessment of the dental evidence has brought out a number of apparently shared derived features which support Szalay and, indirectly, the early workers. These synapomorphies include moderate to great cheek-tooth crown relief, elongate upper (and lower) molariform teeth, approach to overall similarity in shape of occluding upper and lower molars (dP_4^4–M_2^3), reduction in cingulum with remnants similarly placed (e.g., upper mesial lingual cleft, lower mesial buccal cleft) and crowns flaring smoothly, not with cingular shelving; lowers with relatively large trigonid basins, reduced hypoconulid (dP_4–M_2) and distal fovea, some degree of transverse cresting between pairs of cusps set nearly at corners of a square talonid basin, pinched in or "waisted" buccally and lingually, dP_4 (especially) with smoothly convex lingual surface and protoconid subequal to or larger than metaconid on P_4; upper molars with lingual cusps only slightly (if at all) distal to buccal pair, relatively long mesial fovea and large talon and at least partial connection of metacone to both hypocone and protocone.

On the other hand, it is clear now, as it was to Hürzeler and earlier authors, that *Oreopithecus* does not share cercopithecid bilophodonty (not even to the extent seen in *Prohylobates*), nor does it partake of such cercopithecid derived features as mesial sulcus of male C^1 continuing onto the root, nearly complete loss of upper cheek-tooth cingulum, and eventual loss of crista obliqua. Moreover, *Oreopithecus* has a number of unique derived features which further set it apart: large projecting lingual cusp (cingulum to some

authors) on I^1, distinct molar conules, bicuspid P_3, relatively low crowned canines, presence of a centroconid on lower molars, strongly reduced ulnar olecranon process, and somewhat elongate forelimb (and hindlimb). Thus, although *Oreopithecus* is certainly not a cercopithecid, its most recent relative was apparently the common ancestor of Cercopithecinae, Colobinae, and the fossil cercopithecoids of unknown affinity. The best way to express this relationship, and to account for the overall distinctions of *Oreopithecus bambolii*, is to recognize Schwalbe's family Oreopithecidae within the Cercopithecoidea. It is interesting to note that Robinson (1956, p. 164n) observed some of the morphological features discussed above and came to a similar conclusion about the phyletic position of *Oreopithecus*, but never returned to this comment.

It remains to at least partially counter the arguments of those who have proposed that *Oreopithecus* is related to either *Apidium* or hominines. The suggestion of the first phyletic linkage dates from Gregory (1922) and Simons (1960), who depended only on the juvenile type mandible of *Apidium phiomense* and little besides the type mandible of *Oreopithecus*. These authors listed as common features the presence of a lower molar centroconid, elongate M_3, polycuspidation, reduced paraconid on M_1 (lacking on M_{2-3}), and a presumed relationship of both to cercopithecids. Delson and Andrews (1975) further noted that both forms have bicuspid P_3 and upper molar conules, but were not convinced of the homologous nature of these features or of phyletic relationship of the genera. Kay (1977a) noted molar "waisting" in common among *Oreopithecus,* cercopithecids, and *Apidium,* but ignored the possibility of the relationship discussed above after setting *Parapithecus* and cercopithecids apart from all other catarrhines. Kay considered derivation of *Oreopithecus* from *Propliopithecus* (as interpreted here) slightly more likely than from *Apidium*, based on a weighted cladistic approach. Of all these features, the most telling are the shared presence of lower molar "waisting" and centroconid in *Apidium* and *Oreopithecus*, really as two aspects of a single complex. When considered in detail, however (see p. 430), the centroconid is placed farther buccally in *Apidium,* its crest-to-cusp linkages are different, and its occlusal contacts are quite distinct; moreover, the impression of "waisting" in *Apidium* is due entirely to the turning-in of the buccal margin at the centroconid, with no lingual component. *Oreopithecus*, furthermore, lacks any of the derived characters of the Parapithecidae (q.v.), such as premolar conules, large and bulbous molar conules, and ?enlarged retained P$_{\overline{2}}$. It thus appears that no derived characters other than those most likely to be convergently developed (e.g., bicuspid P$_{\overline{3}}$) are shared by the two genera, and there is no reason to continue to consider a special phyletic relationship between them.

A rather similar situation holds for the purported links to hominines proposed by Hürzeler (e.g., 1958, 1960, 1968). He based this view on such shared features as relatively small canine without diastemata, bicuspid P$_{\overline{3}}$, and a number of features associated with a short face (steep symphysis, vertical incisors, length proportions of the teeth, relatively high mental foramina in a deep jaw), combined with the generally hominid nature of the trunk and forelimb. In fact, the small canine may also be in part due to a short face, and there does appear to be evidence of C^1 honing on

P$_{\overline{3}}$, despite Hürzeler's contrary finding. The P$_{\overline{3}}$ is bicuspid, but it still presents a clear mesial flange and the metaconid could easily develop independently in different lineages. The shoulder is not known in *Oreopithecus* and the wrist is not well studied, so that it is unclear if any derived hominid features are present, but the ulna is about equally hominid-like in *Palaeopropithecus*, which also was a presumed arm-swinger/hanger. Far from being a potential hominine, there is little but retained ancestral catarrhine features to suggest placing *Oreopithecus* among the hominoids. Nor, given the phyletically close relationship to cercopithecids detailed above, is there any further need for the equivocal stance of such authors as Delson (1977b), who placed the genus *incertae sedis* within the infraorder. Only further fossils will tell whether the Oreopithecidae were represented throughout their history by a single lineage or if (and where) they underwent an adaptive radiation, however brief it may have been.

OREOPITHECUS Gervais, 1872

DISTRIBUTION
   Late Miocene (Turolian). Italy; ?Russia.
KNOWN SPECIES
   Oreopithecus bambolii Gervais, 1872, type species
LOCALITIES: Baccinello V1 (550); Monte Bamboli⋆ (580); Montemassi (582); Casteani (584); Ribollo (586); ?Baccinello V2 (594); ?Kalfa (498); ?Eldar (502); ?Taraklia (570).

DISCUSSION

Oreopithecus bambolii is a medium-sized primate known from a group of mostly lignitiferous localities in a small region of Grossetto province northern Italy. It has been variably reported from southwestern Russia, but no specimens have been illustrated, and those found early in this century appear to have been lost. *Oreopithecus* combines relatively conservative cranial morphology and generally hominoid-like postcranials (but nonhelical astragalocalcaneal joint) with uniquely derived cheek-tooth structure, bicuspid P$_{\overline{3}}$, low crowned canines, and large I^1 with projecting lingual cusp (see Delson and Andrews, 1975), a mosaic that sets it off from close (intrafamilial) ties with other catarrhines.

The dentition (Figures 217 and 218) has been most thoroughly discussed by Hürzeler (1949, 1958) and by

Butler and Mills (1959). Both pairs of incisors are implanted vertically; the lowers are not well known, but appear small and subequal in size. The I^2 is conservatively conical, but I^1 is large, with a unique, strong projecting lingual cusp. The canines are sexually dimorphic with robust but not very high crowns, and they do not strongly interlock. The uppers were said by Hürzeler to wear down from the tip rather than honing heavily on P$_{\overline{3}}$, but at least one large "male" specimen does present a sharp distal edge indicative of honing action. The larger C^1 teeth also have a hominoid-like mesial sulcus on the crown which does not continue past the cervix. The lower canines apparently honed somewhat on the uppers, but not on I^2 which shows no facet. The lower premolars are bicuspid and subequally large, with subequal protoconid and metaconid (the latter sometimes smaller on P$_{\overline{4}}$). On P$_{\overline{3}}$, there is more of a mesial flange and the distobuccal corner is reduced. The upper premolars are also subequal in size, oval, but rather longer relative to width than in pliopithecids; they present a large paracone, lower protocone, sometimes a small metacone, but never a trace of a conule, although a low crest may connect the two main cusps. A rather strong lingual cingulum may continue around the protocone or may

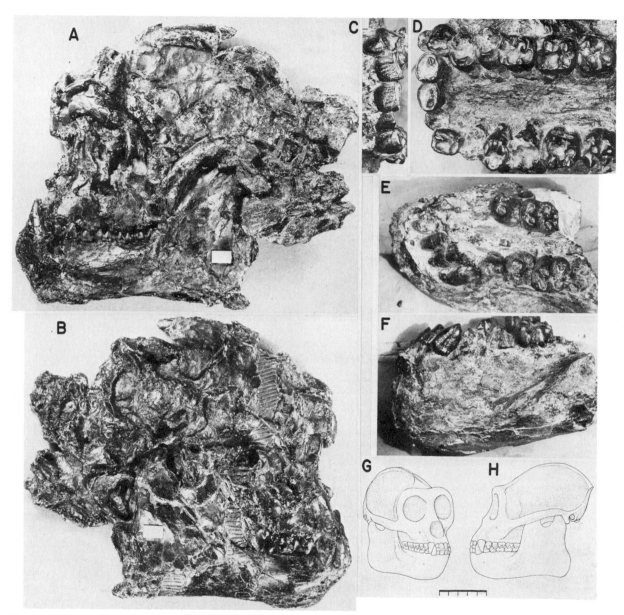

Figure 217. *Oreopithecus bambolii.* Late Miocene, Europe. Crushed male skull and cervical vertebrae: A, left lateral view, B, right lateral view. Reconstruction of same skull: G, oblique right antero-lateral view; H, left lateral view. ?Female palate with complete dentition: C, buccal view of incisors and canines; D, occlusal view. Crushed anterior portion of male mandible with left $I_{\overline{1}}$–$M_{\overline{1}}$, right $P_{\overline{4}}$–$M_{\overline{1}}$: E, oblique occlusal view; F, left lateral view. The white scale on ramus in A and B is 1 cm; scale divisions under G and H are in centimeters; C–F are at about 2× the scale of A and B. [A, B, G, H from F. Szalay and A. Berzi, *Science, 180,* copyright 1973 by the American Association for the Advancement of Science.]

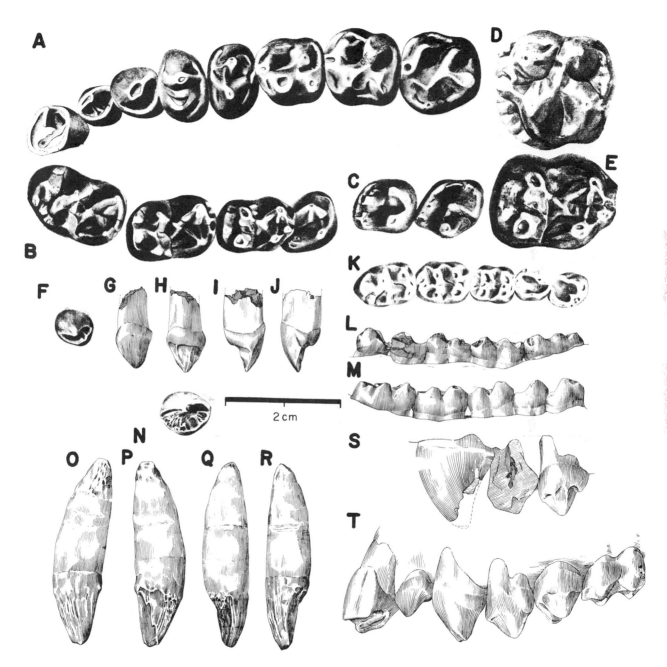

Figure 218. *Oreopithecus bambolii.* Late Miocene, Europe. Left I^1–M^3: A, occlusal view. Left P$_{\overline{4}}$–M$_{\overline{3}}$: B, occlusal view. Left P$_{\overline{3-4}}$: C, occlusal view. Left M^2: D, occlusal view. Left M$_T$: E, occlusal view. Left upper female canine: F, occlusal view; G, buccal view; H, lingual view; I, mesial view; J, distal view. Left P$_{\overline{3}}$–M$_{\overline{3}}$: K, occlusal view; L, buccal view; M, lingual view. Left upper male canine: N, occlusal view; O, buccal view; P, lingual view; Q, mesial view; R, distal view. Left male C^1–P^4: S, buccal view. Left female I^1–M^1: T, buccal view. The scale is for F–R; A–C, S, and T are at 1.5× that scale; D and E are at 2.5× that scale. [A–C, S, T from Hürzeler (1949b); D–R from Hürzeler (1958).]

be interrupted at its base. All of the cheek teeth are quite high crowned, with moderate to rather high relief (tall cusps and deep notches); the molariform teeth are elongate, and the opposing uppers and lowers approach the cercopithecid condition of being mirror images of one another.

The lower molars are relatively narrow, with the four standard catarrhine cusps well developed and situated nearly at the corners of a square. A centroconid (or mesoconid) occurs on the cristid obliqua, midway between the hypoconid and metaconid; a crest from the protoconid may also reach the centroconid or may fall just short. The centroconid is lacking on the single known $dP_{\overline{4}}$, perhaps related to the enlarged metaconid. A paraconid is present typically on $M_{\overline{1}}$ (and the $dP_{\overline{4}}$), rarely on $M_{\overline{2}}$ and never on even unworn $M_{\overline{3}}$; it is lingual to the midline and may be connected by a crest to the metaconid, but a mesial crest from the protoconid does not appear to reach it. A hypoconulid is present on all lower molariform teeth; on $dP_{\overline{4}}$–$M_{\overline{2}}$, it is small and situated on the midline, but expanded on $M_{\overline{3}}$ as part of a large heel, which may also contain a sixth cusp lingually. Lingual to the hypoconulid on $dP_{\overline{4}}$–$M_{\overline{2}}$ is a moderately distinct distal fovea, absent or reduced on $M_{\overline{3}}$; the trigonid basin is large and long in $dP_{\overline{4}}$ and $M_{\overline{3}}$, but apparently shorter in $M_{\overline{1-2}}$, perhaps as a result of wear. The trigonid is bounded distally by a low and often incomplete crest between protoconid and metaconid, especially on $M_{\overline{1-2}}$, while an even less distinct crest may appear between the hypoconid and entoconid; when worn, this latter bears a striking resemblance to that on a cercopithecid tooth, as does the worn $M_{\overline{3}}$ in general. By comparison, the $M_{\overline{3}}$ of *Oreopithecus* bears little overall resemblance to that of pliopithecids [and *D. (Proconsul)*], which are rather triangular, or to that of later hominids, which are quite similar to their preceding $M_{\overline{1-2}}$. The crowns of all the lower molars in *Oreopithecus* are strongly "waisted," in that the buccal margin is pinched in toward the centroconid, while the median lingual notch is deep and slightly flattened at its base. "Waisting" also occurs in cercopithecids and in *Apidium*, but, in the latter, the centroconid is a small cusp on the buccal margin linked to both protoconid and hypoconid (and probably not homologous with that in *Oreopithecus*), while "waisting" is less pronounced. Cingulum is lacking entirely on the lingual faces of the lower cheek teeth of *Oreopithecus* and is rare buccally, but small

clefts, much as in cercopithecids, may represent cingular remnants on the mesial face of the protoconid and the distal slope of the hypoconid.

The four main upper molar cusps are rather acute, the lingual ones only slightly distal to the buccal pair. A large metaconule lies on the crista obliqua and may be connected to the hypocone by a crest which forms a deep median lingual cleft; a small but distinct paraconule forms the lingual corner of a narrow and short mesial fovea which is bounded distally by a small accessory cuspule. The trigon basin is deep but restricted in area, only slightly larger than the talon (which is reduced on $M^{\underline{3}}$). Cingulum is present on both the lingual and buccal faces: Lingually, it occurs strongly at the mesiolingual corner (where cercopithecids have a strong cleft) and weaker between the protocone and hypocone, although these areas may nearly join around the protocone in some $M^{\underline{3}}$; buccally, cingulum is patchy at both corners and at the base of the large paracone. The dP^4 is strongly molarized and elongate, although the conules and buccal cingulum are indistinct, while $dP^{\underline{3}}$ is more nearly premolariform, with two main cusps, a small metacone barely distinct from the paracone and linked to the protocone by a crista obliqua, and a variably present small hypocone on the distolingual cingulum.

Butler and Mills (1959) have discussed occlusion in *Oreopithecus*, finding some differences from Cercopithecidae and an overall similarity to patterns seen in various Hominidae (the ancestral eucatarrhine pattern). Two points are of special interest, however. The centroconid appears to have contacted the accessory cusp lingual to the paracone, as the lingual part of the cristid obliqua sheared past the protocone–paraconule crest; in *Apidium*, the centroconid occluded between the paracone and paraconule. Although not discussed by Butler and Mills specifically, their Figure 8 shows that lingual phase wear facets in *Oreopithecus* are not as extensive on cusp slopes as in several hominids figured. This may in part be due to differences in individual age and degree of wear, but it may also reflect the great height of *Oreopithecus* cusps above the intercusp notches, resulting in less extensive wear at comparable tooth ages.

Although Hürzeler (1960, 1968) considered the crushed partial cranium of *Oreopithecus* (Figure 217, A and B) to have resembled that of man, Szalay and Berzi (1973) demonstrated that this was based on misinterpretations of morphology, offering a more

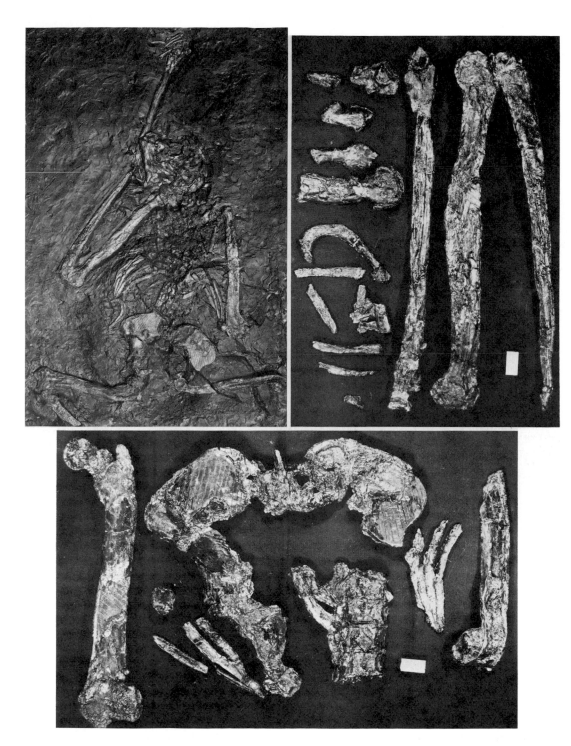

Figure 219. *Oreopithecus bambolii.* Late Miocene, Europe. Crushed 1958 skeleton before preparation (upper left). Various prepared elements of the hand and arm, and some ribs (upper right), and pelvis, femur, lumbar vertebrae, and ribs (below). The two scales represent 1 cm each.

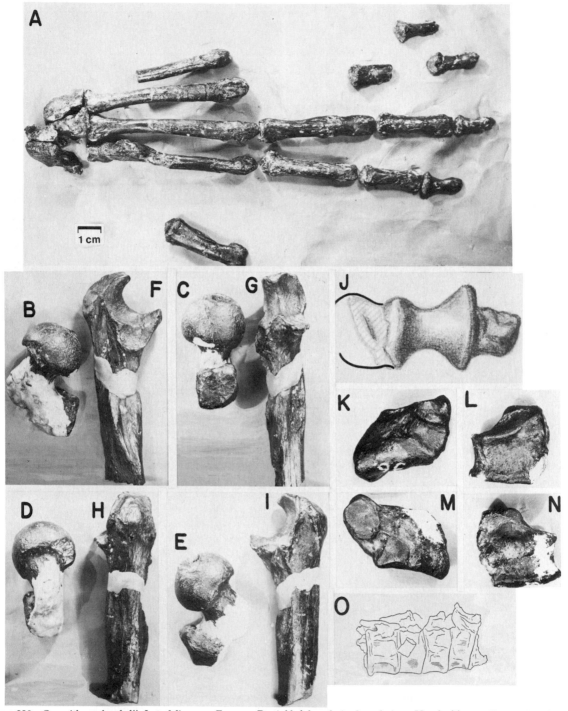

Figure 220. *Oreopithecus bambolii.* Late Miocene, Europe. Partial left hand: A, dorsal view. Head of femur: B, anterior view; C, dorsal view: D, lateral view; E, posterior view. Right ulna: F, lateral view; G, anterior view; H, posterior view; I, medial view. Distal end of right humerus: J. Right eutocuneiform: K, medial view; M, lateral view; Right cuboid: L, dorsal view; N, ventral view. Crushed lumbar vertebrae: O, lateral view. The scale on A is for A–I. [J modified from W. Straus, in *Classification and Human Evolution*, edited by S. L. Washburn, Viking Fund Publications in Anthropology, No. 37. Copyright 1963 by the Wenner-Gren Foundation for Anthropological Research, New York. O from Hürzeler (1968).]

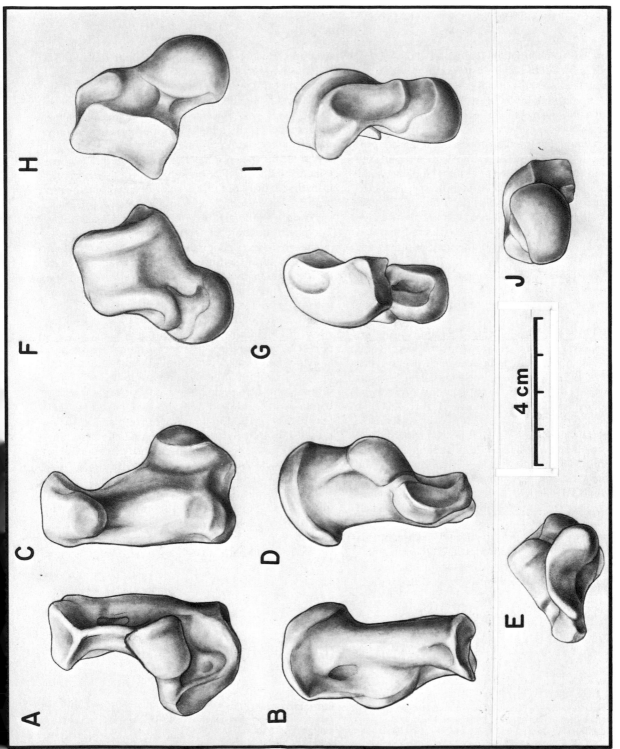

Figure 221. *Oreopithecus bambolii.* Late Miocene, Europe. Left calcaneus (A–E) and astragalus (F–J): A and F, dorsal views; C and H, plantar views; B and G, lateral views; D and I, medial views; E and J, distal views. [By A. Cleary.]

monkey-like reconstruction (Figure 217, G and H). The face is broad and slightly projecting, with wide interorbital area, short nasals, sloping snout, and strong supracanine eminences; the supraorbital tori are strong and the zygomatic arches slightly bowed; a low but distinct sagittal crest meets a low nuchal crest at a high inion, giving a flat appearance to the occiput. Hürzeler reported a large auditory meatus on one fragment—it is crushed on the skull. The robust mandible has a smoothly rounded symphysis, deep corpus, expanded gonion, and vertical ramus (see also Hürzeler, 1968). Szalay and Berzi estimated the endocranial volume at about 200 cm³, compared to much higher values (400 ± 125 cm³) suggested by Straus and Schön (1960).

The postcranium of *Oreopithecus* shows a number of similarities to that of hominids, but many of these may be convergences; one nearly complete but crushed skeleton (Figure 219) has been partly described by Straus (1963). Both forelimb and hindlimb are apparently quite elongated compared to trunk length, and the intermembral index is high as well (Delson and Andrews, 1975), which may relate to large size and/or to increased use of the arm in support and locomotion. The number of lumbar vertebrae (Figure 220O) is reduced and that of sacrals is increased by comparison to ancestral catarrhines. There is a strong ventral keel on the vertebrae for ligamentous attachment, as in cercopithecids and platyrrhines, thus probably the ancestral condition. The ulnar olecranon (Figure 220, F–I) is reduced in length, as in modern hominids (and also *Paleopropithecus*, for example), the sigmoid notch is shallow, with a median ridge, the radial facet is also shallow, and the shaft is robust; the distal humerus is thin but transversely broad (Figure 220J), with a median keel and medially projecting medial epicondyle. The hand as reconstructed here (Figure 220A) is elongate and gracile. Straus (1963) thought that the astragalus was "mobile" and like that of cercopithecids, while the calcaneus reminded him more of apes (Figure 221); Szalay (1975d) noted that the joint between these bones was derived among primates in being rotational rather than helical, as found elsewhere only in cercopithecids and (differently) in *Homo*. Riesenfeld (1975) found that the metatarsals of *Oreopithecus* retained the ancestral primate pattern of size decrease from first to fifth, but that they were quite robust, as in terrestrial hominids (which are also large primates, suggesting a relationship with body weight as well as locomotor substrate preference).

The phyletic relationships of *Oreopithecus bambolii* have been discussed under the family (above), with the conclusion that its most recent relative was the common ancestor of all Cercopithecidae. In terms of paleobiology, the high crowned cuspidate and cristodont cheek teeth and generally relatively small incisors of *Oreopithecus* suggest folivory, which is supported by its presence in a forest faunal association and lignitic coal-swamp deposits. The long hand and mobile elbow joint indicate climbing ability, while the several similarities (here judged convergences) to hominids in trunk and limb proportions suggest extensive use of the forelimb for support and perhaps propulsion, that is, arm-swinging and climbing. The nonhelical ankle joint and the robust metatarsals are found elsewhere only in terrestrial catarrhines, but great use of the ground is doubtful for *Oreopithecus*. Although these features were presumably inherited from a semiterrestrial cercopithecoid ancestor, it is uncertain at present why they were retained in *O. bambolii*, since some colobines, for example, redeveloped a semihelical ankle joint after reemphasizing arboreality.

SUPERFAMILY HOMINOIDEA
Gray, 1825

(= or including: Hominidae Gray, 1825. Anthropomorpha Huxley, 1872. Hominoidea: Simpson, 1931. Pongoidea Elliot, 1913: Kälin, 1961. Dryopithecidae Gregory and Hellman, 1939: Pilbeam, in Pilbeam *et al.*, 1977. Ramapithecidae Simonetta, 1957: Pilbeam, in Pilbeam *et al.*, 1977.)

DISTRIBUTION
Middle Oligocene to modern. Old World.
INCLUDED TAXA
Families Hominidae and Pliopithecidae.

DISCUSSION

The Hominoidea of this classification is a probably holophyletic group, but one of very mixed affinities. It includes all catarrhines not placed in the Parapithecidae, Cercopithecidae, Oreopithecidae, or incertae sedis. Its main component is the Hominidae (used here in a wider sense than usually), a monophyletic group including the modern anthropomorphs and their closest extinct relatives (dryopiths in the broadest sense). The second included family, however, includes three genera of Oligo-Miocene age which are essentially conservative catarrhines, linked together mainly because of shared primitive retentions.

For this reason, it is difficult to characterize a morphotype for the hominoids, at least beyond that delineated above for the common non-parapithecid ancestor. The pliopithecids, especially *Pliopithecus* and *Propliopithecus*, appear to have diverged little from the common hominoid ancestor, or in fact from the ancestral eucatarrhine, and their inferred common ancestor cannot be distinguished from the latter at present. As discussed under Pliopithecidae below (and in Delson and Andrews, 1975; Delson, 1977b), it is not even certain that the known pliopithecids are the closest relatives of Hominidae. Given the essentially conservative nature of pliopithecid morphology and the detailed homology of the tubular external auditory meatus in Cercopithecidae and Hominidae, it is quite possible (if slightly less likely) that the two modern families shared a common ancestry after the known pliopithecids differentiated. Therefore, the decision has been made here to follow Delson (1977b) and widespread usage in retaining the Hominoidea as usually construed, thus interpreting the pliopithecids as an early radiation paralleling the hominids in approaching the "ape" grade. Further detailed study of the crania of *Pliopithecus* and *Propliopithecus* ("*Aegyptopithecus*") is required to determine the morphocline polarity involved in their differences (see under pliopithecids, below).

On the other hand, the Hominidae are characterized below by a number of derived characters of the teeth (e.g., reduced canine honing, cheek-tooth elongation, buccal shifting of hypoconulid, and increase of distal fovea size), skull (tubular auditory meatus), and especially postcranial skeleton (reorientation of the forelimb, thorax, and pelvis, among others). These features are shared by all living hominids and apparently by the later Miocene forms as well, but they do not all occur in *Dryopithecus* species. The latter are placed in Hominidae mainly on dental grounds, but their postcranium appears to have a few derived characters beyond the pliopithecid grade, which may imply some convergent developments in hylobatines and pongines (and hominines).

The hominoids appear to have been mainly a forest-dwelling, frugivorous group for most of their existence, although both folivory and adaptations to open-country life arose several times. The earliest genera to depart Africa, *Pliopithecus* and *Dryopithecus*, were both probably forest animals which entered southern Europe and spread westward. About the same time (early middle Miocene), ancestral sugrivapithecins (e.g., *Sivapithecus*) may have moved eastward into Eurasian mixed woodland, developing into what Simons (1976a) has termed "ground apes," and then spreading both farther east and westward, mostly southeast of the Paratethys sea. Only in a few places do the two Eurasian radiations come into contact (e.g., *Pliopithecus* with *Sivapithecus* at Neudorf-Sandberg and Rudabánya). The pliopithecids and *Dryopithecus* appear to have become extinct by the early late Miocene, after which time the "ground apes" also reduced in number, perhaps as a result of growing competition with cercopithecids, leaving only the ancestors of modern apes in their refuges and the early hominines on the forest fringe to continue the hominoid pattern.

Family Pliopithecidae
Zapfe, 1961a

(= or including: Pliopithecinae Zapfe, 1961a. Propliopithecidae Straus, 1961. Pliopithecidae: Remane, 1965. Propliopithecinae: Delson and Andrews, 1975.)

DISTRIBUTION

Middle Oligocene to late Miocene (Fayumian to Ternanian; Orleanian to Vallesian). Egypt, Kenya, Europe; ?China.

INCLUDED TAXA

Propliopithecus, Pliopithecus, Dendropithecus, and(?) "Kansupithecus."

DISCUSSION

Pliopithecus and *Propliopithecus* (including *Aegyptopithecus*) are clearly among the most conservative catarrhine genera, and, as will be argued below, *Dendropithecus* appears to be closely linked at least to the former. Unfortunately, the small set of features shared by these genera are all either patristic or ancestral characters, which set them off from more modern catarrhines but do not conclusively link them to one another. However, given the strong similarity to Hominidae in the dentition and the complete lack of special relationship to Cercopithecidae, these forms may be considered as primitive Hominoidea, and, until their ties are more clear, they are grouped as a distinct family. Remane (1965) was the first to give *Pliopithecus* separate family status, rather than placing it with *Hylobates*, while Groves (1972, 1974) included the other genera as well. Groves further considered the Pliopithecidae to include the common ancestors of Cercopithecidae and Hominidae, a point which will be considered below.

The family Pliopithecidae can be characterized by the combination of platyrrhine-like (ancestral catarrhine) postcranium and ear region, wide but ape-like teeth with strong canine honing, and variable cranial proportions (in the very small known sample). More specifically, the known genera share narrow incisors; rather tall canines; upper canines with deep mesial sulcus ending at the cervix, honing on bilaterally compressed, often tall $P_{\overline{3}}$; transversely broad cheek teeth; upper premolars with little lingual cingulum, the paracone quite tall; four-cusped upper molars with moderate to faint conules and strong lingual cingulum, M^2 being largest, with the third molar slightly larger than the first but often with reduced hypocone; and five-cusped lower molars of variable relative length, with some buccal cingulum and often rather centrally placed hypoconulids, especially on anterior elements. There is no development of an auditory tube in *Propliopithecus,* but it appears to be short and incomplete in *Pliopithecus.* The long bones, where known, are generally gracile and most comparable to those of ateline ceboids (more robust in *Propliopithecus*), with long ulnar olecranon, wide distal humerus (sometimes with entepicondylar foramen), and possibly a femoral third trochanter, as well as a tail of at least moderate length. A prehallux is retained in *Propliopithecus,* but not in *Pliopithecus.* Limb proportions are those of an ancestral catarrhine. Further details are given under the respective genera.

The dental formula of $I\frac{2}{2}$, $C\frac{1}{1}$, $P\frac{3\cdot4}{3\cdot4}$, $M\frac{2\cdot3}{1\cdot2\cdot3}$ and the lack of enlarged isolated conules distinguish the pliopithecids from parapithecids, while molar morphology separates them from *Oreopithecus,* cercopithecids, or ceboids and allies them with hominids. The anterior dentition, being conservative, is similar to that of cercopithecids, and known cranial morphology could be acceptable in an ancestral Old World monkey, but there is no indication of even "incipient" bilophodonty or increased crown relief. The postcranium is similar to that of cercopithecids as opposed to modern apes and in fact is closest in certain features to that of some ceboids (see Corruccini *et al.,* 1976; Ciochon and Corruccini, 1977). As compared to hominids (*sensu lato*), pliopithecids share the basic molar cusp pattern which was probably ancestral for all eucatarrhines, but differ in having smaller incisors and wider molars, less buccal placement of hypoconulids, more cingulum, and especially strong canine honing development (all features found more commonly in *Dryopithecus* than in later hominids, except *Hylobates*). The postcranium is even less like that of apes with no apparent adaptations for increased shoulder or wrist mobility, no thoracic broadening, and no alteration of vertebral number or limb proportions from a catarrhine morphotype condition.

The relationships of the three pliopithecid genera to later forms have been widely debated. *Propliopithecus haeckeli* has been considered an ancestor of gibbons, by way of *Pliopithecus* (e.g., Gregory, 1922), a possible human ancestor [e.g., by Kurtén (1972), who misinterpreted its small, probably female canine] and a possible relative of cercopithecids (by Delson, 1975c). *Propliopithecus zeuxis* is regarded by Simons (e.g., 1965, 1974a) and many others as the ancestor of *Dryopithecus* and most later hominids. *Pliopithecus* is generally considered the ancestor of *Hylobates* (e.g., Hürzeler, 1954; Frisch, 1973), although this view is losing ground: More often now *Dendropithecus* is offered as a likely (if not *the*) ancestral gibbon (e.g., Simons and Fleagle, 1973; Andrews and Groves, 1975). Even the fragmentary *?Propliopithecus chirobates* was proposed as a gibbon forerunner (Simons, 1965, 1972). On the other hand, Ferembach (1958), Remane (1965), Groves (1972, 1974), Delson and Andrews (1975), and Ciochon and Corruccini (1977) have withdrawn from these views to see pliopithecids as a group of conservative early catarrhines which persisted into the Miocene alongside more modern forms like *Dryopithecus*. Given this interpretation, the question is then whether pliopithecids are to be grouped with Hominidae on patristic grounds or considered a third, independent, eucatarrhine (super)family, possibly ancestral to both hominids and cercopithecoids.

This situation is further complicated by consideration of the pliopithecid cranium, which has not been discussed above: Only two examples are known, one as yet incompletely published, and they differ strongly from one another. The cranium of *Pliopithecus* is as hypothesized for the common ancestor of cercopithecoids and hominids, rather like those of gibbons or colobines. On the other hand, the skull of *Propliopithecus zeuxis* is much longer, lower, and snoutier, although also wide interorbitally. This condition might be derived, but it is more likely to be conservative, perhaps a retention from a "primitive" eucatarrhine or even proto-catarrhine, with allometric size increase.

Two alternative interpretations of the evidence are reasonable. In the first, which we prefer tentatively, pliopithecids are viewed as the sister-taxon of Hominidae, their divergence postdating the cercopithecoid–hominoid split. The strong dental similarities between pliopithecids and hominids are thus not only ancestral retentions but may involve some shared derived conditions. Moreover, the apparent trend to increased use of the forelimb in support postures or locomotion links the two families. Cranial shape in *Propliopithecus zeuxis*, if not autapomorphic, would then be conservative of that in ancestral eucatarrhines, while that in *Pliopithecus* would better typify early pliopithecids (or hominoids in general). On the other hand, *Pliopithecus* is independently derived in its projecting orbital rims and in the loss of the prehallux, retained in *Propliopithecus*, *Dryopithecus*, and *Hylo-*

bates. This interpretation requires the acceptance of some parallelism in the development of the eucatarrhine auditory tube, which appears more similar (if not identical) in construction between cercopithecids and hominids than between any other primate families with such a tube. In the same way as gibbons might have reduced the olecranon process, however (see below), it is possible that the auditory tube had begun development by the time of the cercopithecoid–hominoid split and then proceeded in both groups by means of canalized morphogenesis. This is especially likely given that the *P. zeuxis* cranium was very conservative and that the condition in *Pliopithecus* adults corresponded to that in juvenile modern catarrhines.

On the other hand, proponents of an alternative view might see pliopithecids, especially *Propliopithecus*, as the sister-taxon of all other eucatarrhines, potentially but not necessarily including their common ancestor (much as suggested by Groves, 1972, 1974). In this view, the skull of *Propliopithecus zeuxis* would represent a condition antecedent to the morphotype postulated by Delson and Andrews (1975), and the auditory tube would have been fully developed in the as yet unknown common ancestor of hominids and cercopithecoids. Pliopithecids would then be merely similar in shared ancestral retentions to hominids, or convergent to them. Accurately reflecting this phylogenetic hypothesis in a "purely" cladistic classification would require either recognizing one superfamily for Pliopithecidae and another for Hominidae, Cercopithecidae, and Oreopithecidae or just accepting four families without higher grouping.

At present, we consider that this second hypothesis is possible but less likely, and thus we include the Pliopithecidae in Hominoidea. This reflects not only their apparent phyletic links but also their patristic affinities, and it preserves some historical continuity. More intensive study of original material is required to solve this major problem in catarrhine phylogeny. It is further possible that such a study would reveal closer phyletic ties between specific pliopithecid genera and later catarrhines.

PROPLIOPITHECUS Schlosser, 1910

(= or including: *Moeripithecus* Schlosser, 1910. *Pliopithecus* Gervais, 1849: Simonetta, 1957, in part. *Aegyptopithecus* Simons, 1965. *Aeolopithecus* Simons, 1965.)

DISTRIBUTION
Middle Oligocene (later Fayumian). Fayum Depression, Egypt.

KNOWN SPECIES

1. *Propliopithecus haeckeli* Schlosser, 1910, type species
[=*Pliopithecus (Propliopithecus) haeckeli*: Simonetta, 1957.]
LOCALITIES: Fayum, level uncertain (middle zone?)⋆ and Yale Fayum Quarry G (376).

2. *Propliopithecus markgrafi* (Schlosser, 1910)
(=*Moeripithecus markgrafi* Schlosser, 1910. *Propliopithecus markgrafi*: Simons and Pilbeam, 1972.)
LOCALITIES: Fayum, level uncertain (middle zone?)⋆ (376).

3. *Propliopithecus zeuxis* (Simons, 1965), new combination
(=*Aegyptopithecus zeuxis* Simons, 1965.)
LOCALITIES: Yale Fayum Quarries I⋆ and M (378).

4. *?Propliopithecus chirobates* (Simons, 1965), new combination
(=*Aeolopithecus chirobates* Simons, 1965.)
LOCALITIES: Yale Fayum Quarry I⋆ (378).

DISCUSSION

Propliopithecus species are relatively small to medium-sized early catarrhines characterized especially by bulbous-cusped, bunodont molars, variable relative length of $M_{\overline{3}}$ (perhaps within as well as between species), midline hypoconulid, lingual position of distal fovea on lower molars, pronounced sexual dimorphism and sectorial-honing C–$P_{\overline{3}}$ complex, relatively deep mandibular corpus, and nearly upright ramus. Cingulum development varies among species on both lower and upper molars, but upper cheek teeth (where known) are transversely broad, with clear lingual cingulum; upper canines have a mesial sulcus on the crown only. The following are known only from one specimen of each element (all identified as *P. zeuxis*): cranium low and elongate, with a projecting muzzle but relatively wide interorbital pillar, somewhat as in *Leptadapis*, orbits with complete ring and nearly complete closure, moderately strong postorbital constriction, low sagittal crest, annular tympanic meatus; brain with somewhat reduced olfactory bulbs compared to lemuriforms, a clear central sulcus but no frontal sulci; ulna robust, slightly concave anteriorly, with long olecranon and somewhat deep trochlear notch, low coronoid process, and small radial notch, overall pattern like *Alouatta* or (although more robust) *Pliopithecus*; hallux metatarsal with facet for large prehallux sesamoid, as in atelids.

Four genera have been named to receive the 30 or so specimens of pre-1978 Fayum "modern-type catarrhines," but the reality of their taxonomic separation has not previously been seriously questioned. Simons (1967c *et seq.*) did indicate that *Moeripithecus markgrafi* was probably congeneric with *P. haeckeli* and later suggested that *A. zeuxis* might have been a later stage

of the same lineage (Simons and Pilbeam, 1972; Simons and Fleagle, 1973). In his original description and diagnosis of *Aegyptopithecus* and *Aeolopithecus*, Simons (1965) considered size of major importance in separating these two genera from each other and from *Propliopithecus* (i.e., *P. haeckeli*), also including the large canine and more strongly heteromorphic premolars of the new genera and considerations of relative $M_{\overline{3}}$ length. In fact, these features, and some of the others also cited, are either greatly variable, related to sexual dimorphism, or of the kind which characterize and distinguish species of a single genus; no character brought forward by Simons or any other author appears compatible with features differentiating widely recognized genera or even subgenera of catarrhine primates. Andrews (personal communication, 1974) suggested the lack of significant (generic) distinction among the known specimens. Generic identity is accepted here and documented by Delson *et al.* (in preparation).

By far the majority of specimens attributed to *Propliopithecus* belong to *P. zeuxis*, mostly on the basis of size, but many are not fully described, rendering questions of variability difficult to evaluate. The most important material of *P. zeuxis* includes the type and several other mandibles and isolated teeth (Figure 224), a nearly complete skull (Figures 222 and 223; incisors hypothetical), as well as a partial ulna (Figure 223), metatarsal, and proximal phalanx. *Propliopithecus haeckeli* is based on a single mandible (Figure 224, E and F), broken near the symphysis and lacking the right incisors and the left teeth and corpus anterior to $P_{\overline{3}}$; many of the distinguishing features of this specimen's anterior dentition reflect its probably female sex (Delson, 1975c). *Propliopithecus markgrafi* was recognized to be a juvenile *Propliopithecus* by Simons (1967c) as early as 1965; the type is a fragment of mandible with $M_{\overline{1-2}}$ (Figure 224H). Additional specimens of both these nominal species have been reported but not published from Quarry G, in the middle of the Fayum sequence, and it is presumed that the types also came from this horizon, if not the Lower Fossil Wood Zone. Of *?P. chirobates*, there is known only the holotype mandible (Figure 226), lacking the incisors, the rami, and much of the corpus, and with tooth crown surfaces worn and eroded (nearly featureless).

Simons (1965a, 1974a) has argued that, in the lower dentition, *P. zeuxis* differs from *P. haeckeli* in having more inflated molar cusps, located less laterally on the

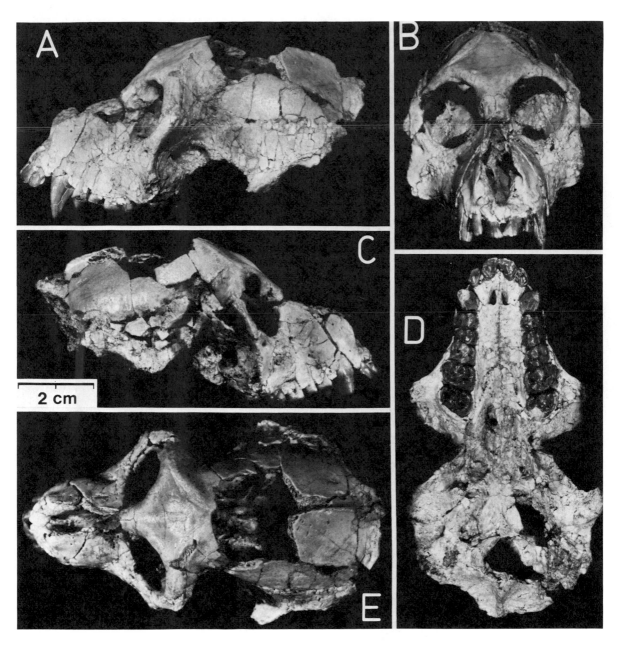

Figure 222. *Propliopithecus zeuxis.* Middle Oligocene, Africa. Male cranium in occlusal plane orientation: A, left lateral view; B, frontal view; C, right lateral view; D, basal view; E, dorsal view. [Courtesy of E. L. Simons.]

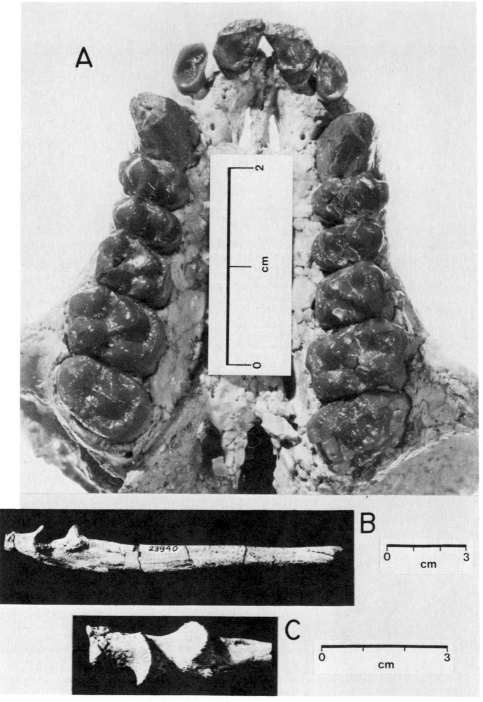

Figure 223. *Propliopithecus zeuxis.* Middle Oligocene, Africa. Palate from male skull, with left and right C^1–M^3; incisors hypothetical: A, occlusal view. Right ulna lacking proximal tip and distal end: B, lateral view; C, anterior view. [A courtesy of E. L. Simons; B, C from Conroy (1976a), courtesy of G. Conroy.]

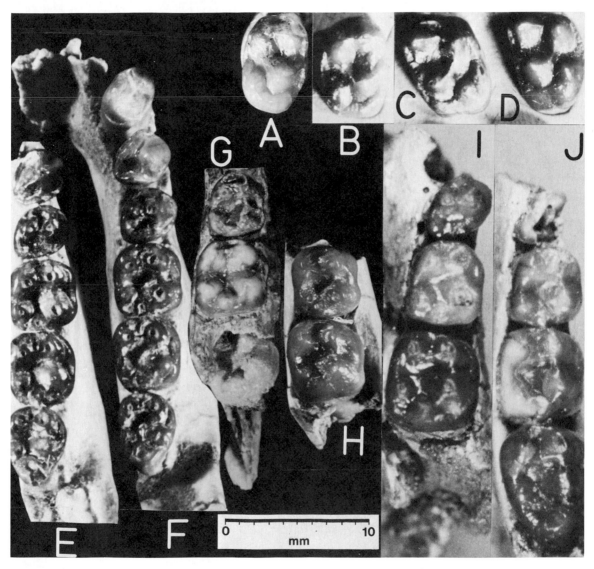

Figure 224. *Propliopithecus*. Middle Oligocene, Africa. Dentitions in occlusal view. *P. haeckeli:* A, referred right $M^{1\,or\,2}$; E, right corpus with $P_{\overline{3}}$–$M_{\overline{3}}$ of female (photographically reversed); F, right corpus with $C_{\overline{1}}$–$M_{\overline{3}}$ and incisor alveoli of same female; G, referred juvenile right corpus with $dP_{\overline{4}}$, $M_{\overline{1}}$, and erupting $M_{\overline{2}}$. *P. zeuxis:* B, right $M^{1\,or\,2}$; C, left $M^{1\,or\,2}$; D, left $M^{1\,or\,2}$ (compare B–D with A); I, right corpus with $P_{\overline{4}}$–$M_{\overline{2}}$; J, right $M_{\overline{1}\text{-}\overline{3}}$ (photographically reversed). *P. markgrafi:* H, juvenile right corpus with $M_{\overline{1}\text{-}\overline{2}}$. Scale divisions are in millimeters. [A courtesy of and © J. G. Fleagle.]

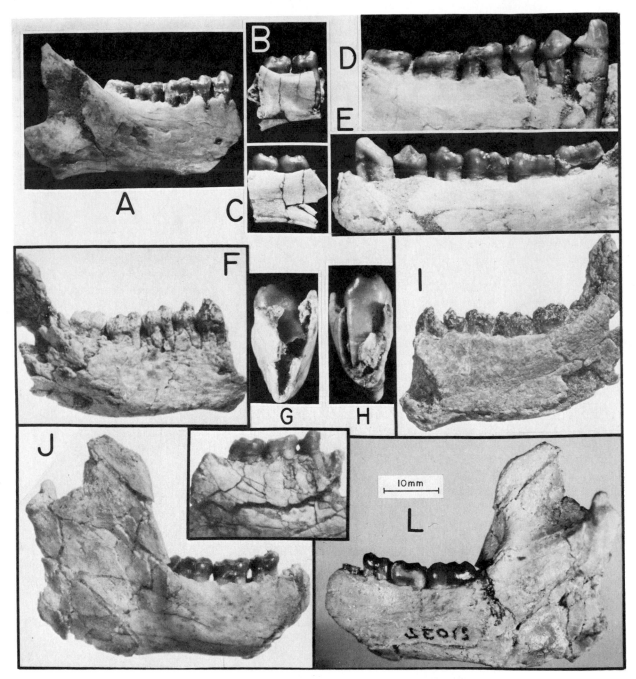

Figure 225. Mandibles of *Propliopithecus* species. Middle Oligocene, Africa. *P. haeckeli*, female. Right corpus with $P_{\overline{3}}$–$M_{\overline{3}}$ (photographically reversed): A, buccal view. Right $C_{\overline{1}}$–$M_{\overline{3}}$: D, buccal view; E, lingual view. *P. markgrafi*, juvenile with right $M_{\overline{1-2}}$: B, buccal view; C, lingual view; G, distal view—note open posterior $M_{\overline{2}}$ root; H, mesial view—note flare near cervix. *P. ?zeuxis*, male right corpus with $P_{\overline{3}}$–$M_{\overline{3}}$ (photographically reversed): F, buccal view; I, lingual view. *P. zeuxis*. Right $P_{\overline{4}}$–$M_{\overline{2}}$ (photographically reversed): K, buccal view. Right ramus and part corpus with $M_{\overline{1-3}}$: J, buccal view; L, lingual view. The scale on L is for all except D, E, G, and H, which are $\frac{3}{5}$ that scale. [F, I–K courtesy of E. L. Simons.]

442

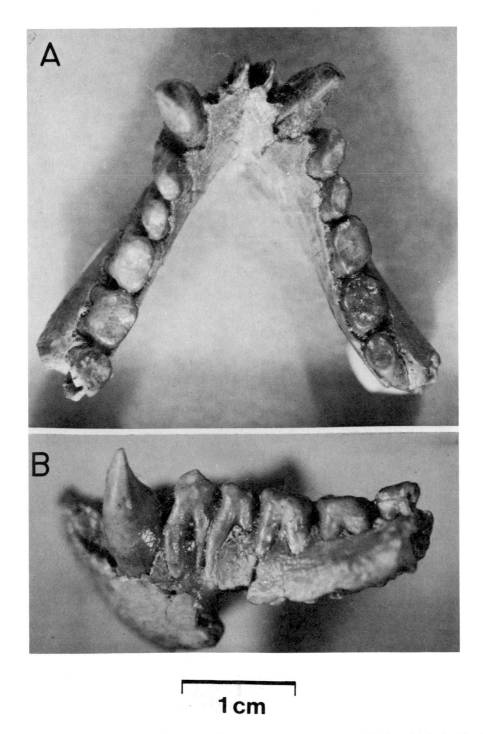

Figure 226. ?*Propliopithecus chirobates*. Middle Oligocene, Africa. Male mandible with eroded left and right $C_{\overline{1}}$–$M_{\overline{3}}$: A, occlusal view; B, left lateral view.

crown and with $M_{\bar{2}}$ and especially $M_{\bar{3}}$ relatively larger and more elongate compared to $M_{\bar{1}}$. The first two features are not consistent, but the molars are certainly more elongate (and larger compared to $M_{\bar{1}}$) in *P. zeuxis* than in either of Schlosser's types (Figure 224), as well as being much larger. *?Propliopithecus chirobates* resembles *P. zeuxis* in apparent tooth shape, but resembles *P. haeckeli* in the similarity of $M_{\bar{1}}$ and $M_{\bar{2}}$ size; cusp pattern can almost be made out on $M_{\bar{2}}$, where it appears to resemble the other species. The relative length of $M_{\bar{3}}$ was considered an important character in separating the three "genera," but, in fact, $M_{\bar{3}}$ is known only in four cases: In *P. haeckeli*, it is slightly longer and narrower than $M_{\bar{2}}$; the same appears true of an incompletely published specimen of *P. zeuxis* (Figure 225, F and I), while, in a more commonly illustrated *P. zeuxis* mandible, $M_{\bar{3}}$ is wider and much longer, being rather triangular in shape (Figure 224J); finally, in *?P. chirobates*, $M_{\bar{3}}$ is significantly shorter and narrower than $M_{\bar{2}}$ or $M_{\bar{1}}$. As Szalay (1976) has indicated, the relative length of teeth may vary within even local populations of a single species, so that the observed variation in $M_{\bar{3}}$ of *P. zeuxis* is not exceptional and is certainly not a character indicating generic separation of the species involved. Buccal cingulum is clearly developed in *P. haeckeli* and *P. zeuxis*, but lacking in *P. markgrafi,* which also presents a moderate amount of basal flare, as otherwise seen only in cercopithecids. Delson (1975c) suggested that this might be a result of the incorporation of ancestrally present cingulum into the crown, providing a model for (and perhaps a shared derived character with) Old World monkeys. This is the main distinction between *P. markgrafi* and *P. haeckeli*, which are only minimally different in size. The trigonid may be somewhat shorter in these taxa than in *P. zeuxis*.

The $P_{\bar{4}}$ in *P. zeuxis* and *P. haeckeli* are nearly identical, with two subequal cusps and some buccal cingulum. The $P_{\bar{3}}$ is a unicuspid, narrow tooth in the three species for which it is known, but more extremely so in the presumed males of *P. zeuxis* and *P. chirobates*; in the apparently female *P. haeckeli* type, it is broader, with strong lingual cingulum and less honing facet. Similarly, the low and robust canine of *P. haeckeli* contrasts with the compressed, tall and sharp canine of *?P. chirobates* (and isolated referred specimens of *P. zeuxis*) in the manner typical of catarrhine sexual dimorphism.

Parts of the mandibular corpus and ramus are known in several specimens of *P. zeuxis* and the type of *P. haeckeli* (Figure 225). The corpus appears to be of rather constant depth between $M_{\bar{3}}$ and $P_{\bar{4}}$, perhaps deepening slightly more anteriorly, although no specimen preserves this region clearly. The depth is moderate, compared to tooth length or height, but there is some variation among Quarry I specimens, possibly correlated with sex. The ramus is almost complete in one *P. zeuxis*, and other *Propliopithecus* specimens confirm the pattern observed: nearly upright, rising steeply or vertically just behind $M_{\bar{3}}$, relatively long anteroposteriorly, condyle well above tooth-row and coronoid rather higher still, gonial region large but not projecting inferiorly or posteriorly. Simons (1965, 1972) has differentiated *P. zeuxis* from *P. haeckeli* on the former's longer ramus compared to corpus depth at $M_{\bar{3}}$. In part this difference may be size related, but it may also be due to a concavity of the corpus below $M_{\bar{3}}$ in *P. zeuxis* and the incompleteness of the *P. haeckeli* ramus. In several specimens, the $M_{\bar{3}}$ is set slightly oblique to the occlusal plane of the other teeth, its distal end turned upward, possibly reflecting age or a curve of Spee. The *?P. chirobates* specimen does not preserve the base of the corpus or any of the ramus, so that the statement that its corpus shallows distally or is shallow (e.g., Simons, 1965 *et seq.*) is hard to verify.

The upper dentition of *Propliopithecus* has previously been described only in *P. zeuxis*, but Dr. J. Fleagle has recently recovered an isolated upper molar referred to *P. haeckeli*; he will be describing it, but has kindly permitted its illustration here (Figure 224A). Before the recovery of the cranium of *P. zeuxis*, isolated teeth allocated to that species were illustrated and briefly discussed by Simons (1967b); these are somewhat smaller than those in the skull, but they are probably still referable to *P. zeuxis* as understood here (Figure 224, B–D).

In the dentition of the *P. zeuxis* cranium (Figure 223A), the first and second molars are constructed similarly, with the four main cusps bulbous and about equal in size; M^3 is broader than M^1 but presents only two major cusps. The lingual cingulum is strong and beaded. On M^2 especially, the protocone is slightly distal to the paracone, with a small metaconule on the crista obliqua and a paraconule on the preprotocrista; there is a tiny second swelling mesiobuccal to the paraconule, beyond which two crests separate to surround the small mesial fovea, the distal one ending almost at the paracone apex. This second "conule" was identified as the paraconule by Kay (1977a; see Figure 150C, p. 305), who termed the large cuspule "cusp a," homologizing it with the "protoconule" of *Apidium*, although its crest linkages are completely different. As the second cuspule does not occur clearly on M¹ of the skull or on the several isolated teeth, it may be merely an individual variation.

The upper premolars are transversely broad ovals, with two main cusps, the paracone larger and taller than the protocone. The P³ is larger and perhaps taller than P⁴, which may have a slight lingual cingulum (also seen on an isolated tooth from Quarry G). The canine is tall and bladelike (still incompletely erupted in the skull).

The cranium of *P. zeuxis* has not yet been described in any detail, but a number of features either have been mentioned (e.g., Simons, 1972) or are clear from photographs (Figure 222) and casts. The face is long and low, quite large compared to the braincase. In some ways, it is reminiscent of *Leptadapis*, perhaps because of their similar size; no omomyid skull of similar dimensions is known, however, so comparisons are incomplete. The orbits are large and fully frontated, almost completely closed off from the temporal fossa as in other comparably sized anthropoids. The interorbital pillar is wide, but the nasal bones are quite long and the premaxilla is extremely so. On the neurocranium, the supraorbital tori are weak, the postorbital constriction is strong for an anthropoid, but only moderate compared to *Leptadapis* (more as in the smaller *Rooneyia*), and there is a low, mostly posterior sagittal crest, joined to a strong nuchal plate. Basally, the choanae are tall and narrow, while there is no tubular extension of the tympanic into an external auditory meatus, merely a ringlike aperture set back somewhat medially from the temporal wall, with a partial "archway" formed by a roofing of the temporal, but without the "pronglike" ventral elements seen in *Pliopithecus* (q.v.). Radinsky (1973, 1974) has analyzed the endocast, finding a pattern intermediate between advanced "prosimians" and primitive anthropoids. There is relatively more visual cortex anterior to the central sulcus, itself rare in prosimians, while the olfactory bulbs appear to have been small. On the other hand, despite its moderately large size (about 27 cm³), the endocast presents a relatively little-expanded frontal lobe with no clear sulci, thus being less derived than brains of modern anthropoids.

Three postcranial elements have been described for *P. zeuxis:* an ulna, a metatarsal I, and a proximal phalanx, while isolated caudal vertebrae have been reported (Simons, 1972). The proximal two-thirds of a right ulna (Figure 223, B and C) was recovered from Quarry M, site of the *P. zeuxis* skull; like the other specimens, it is allocated on the basis of size and anthropoid morphology. The bone is most similar to that of *Alouatta*, or to *Pliopithecus*, although it is more robust (Fleagle *et al.,* 1975). The olecranon process is long, with no retroflexion of the type found in terrestrial quadrupeds. A slight anterior concavity facilitated radial movement around the ulna and suggests strong digital flexors, as in arboreal climbers; the small radial notch confirms joint flexibility. The sigmoid notch is long, with a broad articular surface without keeling. Conroy (1976a) has inferred from its structure that the corresponding humerus would have lacked keels lateral to the olecranon fossa, projecting trochlear flange, or confluence of trochlea and capitulum, as are sometimes found in terrestrial cercopithecids. Preuschoft (1975) suggested adaptation to stresses of quadrupedal walking and climbing with the forearm pronated, as well as the possible use of a lowered, crouched position without great energy expenditure. The metatarsal of the great toe also lacks its distal third, but its proximal end preserves a facet for a prehallux bone (Conroy, 1976b), as found only in most platyrrhines and *Hylobates* among modern anthropoids. The bone's longitudinal curvature suggests strong flexor tendons, while the form of the proximal joint surface with the medial cuneiform indicates adaptation for opposability. The proximal phalanx is long and slender, with moderate longitudinal curvature and a tilted distal joint surface, as in climbers, combined with a dorsally inclined proximal joint surface and proximally deepening height, as in more terrestrial forms (Preuschoft, 1975). In sum, *P. zeuxis* at least may have been an agile climber and branch-runner, with grasping feet (and presumably hands), but perhaps also capable of palmigrade terrestrial locomotion, as in some larger atelids; analogies seem closest with *Alouatta* or perhaps *Ateles*, but certainly without the prehensile tail.

The dental and cranial adaptations of *Propliopithecus* also compare favorably with those of ateline platyrrhines, the gnathic musculature being well developed but not exaggerated, while the large incisors and relatively bulbous cheek-tooth cusps with little cresting suggest a frugivorous diet. This would also fit well with the more folivorous–omnivorous pattern suggested above for its Fayum contemporaries, the parapithecids.

Major distinctions of *Propliopithecus* from *Pliopithecus* are listed under the latter. Moreover, at least in the *P. zeuxis* cranium, M^1 is much smaller than M^2, a relationship not seen in *Pliopithecus* spp. *Dendropithecus macinnesi* is not yet known from cranial remains, but its postcranium is even more gracile than that of *Pliopithecus*. Its ulna is therefore less similar to that of *Propliopithecus zeuxis*, but again conforms broadly in preserved morphology; no other comparable bones are known. The C^1 of *Dendropithecus* has a second mesial groove and may not be as tall as in *P. zeuxis* (or *?P. chirobates*). The P_4 is more elongated and P^4 is only slightly smaller than P^3, if at all, while M_3 is only slightly larger and little longer than M_1 in *Dendropithecus*. The upper cheek teeth of *Dendropithecus* are about as broad as those of *Propliopithecus*, but the cusps are somewhat closer to the margins of the teeth, lacking the heavy lingual cingulum or the sloping buccal walls of the buccal cusps; the conules are indistinct, and, while the hypocone is variably absent on M^3, the metacone is present but slightly reduced. On the lower molars, the trigonids are small in both genera, but they are narrower than the talonids in *Propliopithecus*, and the hypoconulid is shifted buccally in all three molars of *Dendropithecus*, increasingly so distad.

As Simons has often argued, *Propliopithecus* species share many features with *Dryopithecus*, but almost all are clearly ancestral retentions rather than shared derived conditions indicative of phyletic linkage. Cranial proportions of *P. zeuxis* and *D. (P.) africanus* are clearly distinct, the latter much more derived in the direction of later apes and also possessing a tubular auditory meatus. Conservatively, ulnar morphology is broadly similar, and the medial cuneiform and metatarsal I of *D. africanus* apparently retained a prehallux facet (Lewis, 1972). Andrews (1973) has noted closest similarities between *P. zeuxis* and *D. macinnesi* in the upper molars, but with *D. (L.) legetet* and perhaps *D. (Proconsul)* in the lowers, although no definite shared derived states can be identified. In almost all of their known features, *Propliopithecus* species retain states which may be considered ancestral for most eucatarrhines, rendering placement of the genus difficult in a cladistic sense. It is further difficult to determine as yet if some possibly derived conditions, such as the elongation of the face and nasals, and the high choanae, are in fact merely retentions of the (ancestral) morphology present in the common ancestor of all catarrhines and thus not inferrable from a study of only known (late) catarrhines. Such a situation would only imply that *Propliopithecus* was at or near the ancestry of both monkeys and apes, an admittedly untestable hypothesis which cannot yet be clearly controverted.

PLIOPITHECUS Gervais, 1849

(= or including: *Pithecus* G. Cuvier and E. Geoffroy, 1795: de Blainville, 1839. *Protopithecus* Lartet, 1851 *nec* Lund, 1841. *Hylobates* Illiger, 1811: Rütimeyer, 1867. *Pliopithecus (Epipliopithecus)* Zapfe and Hürzeler, 1957. *Pliopithecus (Plesiopliopithecus)* Zapfe, 1961a. *Pliopithecus (Anapithecus)* Kretzoi, 1975. *Crouzelia* Ginsburg, 1975.]

DISTRIBUTION

Early middle to early late Miocene (late Orleanian to Vallesian). Southern and Central Europe.

KNOWN SPECIES

1. *Pliopithecus antiquus* (de Blainville, 1839), type species
[=*Pithecus antiquus* de Blainville, 1839. *Pithecus fossilis europaeus* de Blainville, 1839. *Pliopithecus antiquus*: Gervais, 1849. *Protopithecus antiquus*: Lartet, 1851. *Pliopithecus platyodon* Biederman, 1863. *Hylobates antiquus*: Rütimeyer, 1867. *Pliopithecus antiquus* (race) *chantrei* Déperet, 1887. *P. (liopithecus) goeriachensis* Sera, 1917. *Pliopithecus* cf. *antiquus*: Hürzeler, 1954. *Pliopithecus* sp.: Hürzeler, 1954. *Pliopithecus antiquus* var. *auscitanensis* Bergounioux and Crouzel, 1964 (unavailable: provisional and only variety), 1965 (also unavailable: variety).

Crouzelia auscitanensis "(Bergounioux and Crouzel, 1965)" Ginsburg, 1975 (1974, *nomen nudum*). *Pliopithecus* cf. *platyodon*: Ginsburg, 1975.]
LOCALITIES: Göriach (438); Sansan⋆ (442); Neudorf-Sandberg (444); Elgg (446); Rümikon (448); Stein am Rhein (450); Kreuzlingen (452); Przeworno 2 (458); La Grive (466); Opole (472); Stätzling (474); Diessen am Ammersee (476).

2. *Pliopithecus piveteaui* Hürzeler, 1954
(=*Pliopithecus antiquus*: Gervais, 1876, in part; Mayet et Lecointre, 1909, in part; Simonetta, 1957, in part. *Pliopithecus antiquus* var. *piveteaui*: Bergounioux and Crouzel, 1965.)
LOCALITIES: Pontlevoy (418); Manthelan⋆ (420); Lasse (422); Pontigné (423); Rillé (424); Savigné (425); Denèzé (426); Noyant Sous-le-Lude (430)

3. *Pliopithecus vindobonensis* Zapfe and Hürzeler, 1957
[=*Pliopithecus antiquus*: Zapfe, 1949, 1952, in part. *Pliopithecus (Epipliopithecus) vindobonensis* Zapfe and Hürzeler, 1957; Zapfe, 1961a. *Pliopithecus vindobonensis*: Ginsburg, 1975.]
LOCALITIES: Neudorf-Spalte⋆ (428).

4. *Pliopithecus lockeri* Zapfe, 1961a
[=*Pliopithecus (Plesiopliopithecus) lockeri* Zapfe, 1961a. *Pliopithecus lockeri:* Ginsburg, 1975.]
LOCALITIES: Trimmelkamm★ (432).
   5. *?Pliopithecus hernyaki* Kretzoi, 1975
[=*Pliopithecus (Anapithecus) hernyaki* Kretzoi, 1975 (1974 *nomen nudum*).]
LOCALITIES: Rudabánya★ (506).
   6. *Pliopithecus* [sp.]: Crusafont, 1976
LOCALITIES: Castel de Barbera (488); Can Feliu II (490).

DISCUSSION

Pliopithecus is a gibbon-sized, relatively archaic catarrhine known from a number of European populations, most of which have been given species or even subgenus rank on minimal criteria. The most complete remains are those of three individuals of *P. vindobonensis* on which the discussion is primarily based. The facial region (Figure 227) is like that of gibbons, thus quite conservative, with short muzzle, wide interorbital pillar and upper face, short and broad nasals, moderate maxillary sinus, and relatively deep zygoma. The orbits are large and round, almost certainly with complete closure (although damaged), and the rims are slightly protruding, with a strong supraorbital torus, as in *Hylobates*. The temporal lines are strong, but do not appear to have formed more than a short, low sagittal crest, even in the more robust individuals (Figure 227D). The auditory tube (Figure 228) is intermediate in morphology between that of *Propliopithecus* (and platyrrhines) and that of modern catarrhines: In two adults a short tube is roofed superiorly by the temporal, but bounded inferiorly only by two narrow prongs of bone which probably supported cartilage in life. This pattern is essentially that found in juvenile living catarrhines. The mandible (Figures 227 and 230) is moderately gracile, although much more robust than that of *Hylobates*. The corpus is slightly shallow, deepening mesially; the symphysis is quite vertical, with variably developed superior and/or inferior tori; and the ramus is vertical, long and high, all features quite unlike the mandible of *Hylobates* (see Zapfe, 1961a).

Dentally (Figures 229 and 230), *Pliopithecus* is reminiscent of gibbons, but more similar in detail to *Propliopithecus* and *Dendropithecus* as well as to *Dryopithecus*. The incisors are low and quite narrow, the $I_{\overline{2}}$ with a small distal prong, as in colobines, the $I_{\overline{1}}$ simple, while I^2 is conical and $I^{\underline{1}}$ broader, with moderate lingual cingulum. The canines are very tall and sharp, uppers strongly dimorphic in height and shape, lowers apparently less so. $P_{\overline{3}}$ is elongate, compressed, and moderately tall; $P_{\overline{4}}$ is morphologically a quite variable tooth, but essentially slightly elongate, with a weak buccal cingulum. $P^{\underline{3}}$ is larger than P^4, and its paracone is relatively larger, especially buccally; in both premolars, the paracone is taller than the protocone. Both upper and lower molars present extensive occlusal wrinkling. The uppers have a large trigon, small mesial fovea, and moderate to large distal fovea; the buccal face slopes outward from the cusp apexes to the cervix, giving the crown a restricted appearance; the protocone is the largest cusp, although the buccal cusps are taller. The hypocone is well developed on $M^{\underline{1-2}}$, placed lingual to the protocone, on the cingular shelf, and linked to the crista obliqua by a short crest (homologous to the postmetaconule crista, although that cuspule is lacking); on $M^{\underline{3}}$, the hypocone is generally not present. The lower molars are rather narrow, but $M_{\overline{3}}$ is only slightly longer than the preceding teeth. A weak to moderate buccal cingulum is always found, but cusp positions vary among the known populations: Generally the hypoconulid is median or slightly buccal on $M_{\overline{1}}$, more buccal distad, and the distal fovea correspondingly larger; no paraconid is ever present; the mesial width is less than the distal on $M_{\overline{1-2}}$, but greater on most $M_{\overline{3}}$; the trigonid basin is distinct to large, and the ectoflexid is well developed (pliopithecine triangle of some authors). Detailed descriptions of the dentition of *Pliopithecus* are given by Hürzeler (1954) and Zapfe (1961a).

Nearly all regions of the skeleton are represented in at least one of the three known individuals of *P. vindobonensis*, described in detail by Zapfe (1961a) and summarized by Zapfe (1958) and by Simons and Fleagle (1973). Despite numerous supposed relationships to gibbons, few anatomical features correspond to those of apes, as recently summarized by Andrews and Groves (1975), the closest modern analogy being the ateline platyrrhines. The preserved (acromial) part of the scapula (Figure 231N) and the rather short, robust, and curved clavicle both resemble *Lagothrix* and relatives. The humerus (Figure 231, A and O–R) is straight-shafted and shorter than the femur; its head displays a large degree of medial torsion perhaps suggesting some modern-ape–like truncal broadening; its distal articulation is very wide, with an enlarged medial epicondyle and a wide trochlea, and an

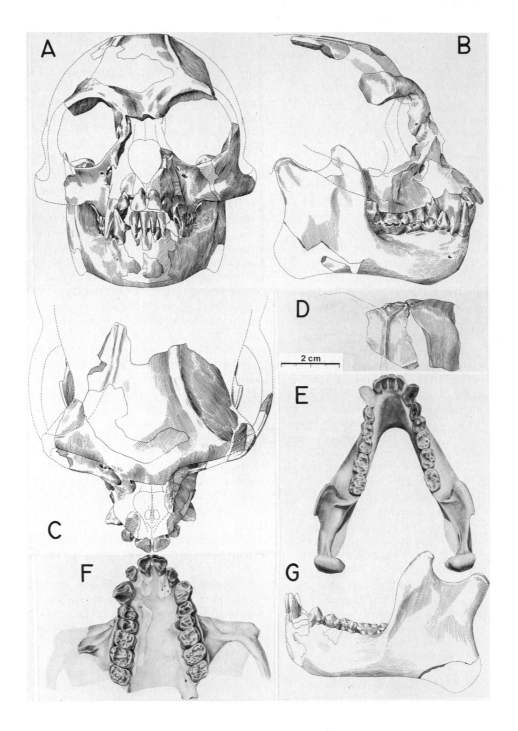

Figure 227. *Pliopithecus vindobonensis.* Middle Miocene, Europe. Restored male face and mandible: A, frontal view; B, right lateral view; C, dorsal view; F, palate, occlusal view; E, mandible, occlusal view; G, mandible, left lateral view. Portion of left (and right) parietal bones of different individual, showing low sagittal and nuchal crests: D, dorsal view. [From Zapfe (1961a).]

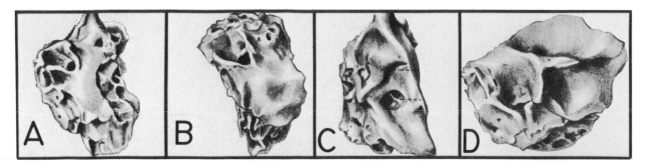

Figure 228. *Pliopithecus vindobonensis.* Middle Miocene, Europe. Portion of left temporal bone: A, basal view (external auditory meatus opens toward upper left of figure). Portion of left temporal bone of different individual: B, basal view (as in A); C, endocranial view. Portion of right temporal bone of same individual: D, lateral view (left to right, external auditory meatus, postglenoid process, glenoid fossa). All are 1.5× natural size. [From Zapfe (1961a).]

entepicondylar foramen is retained, all characters reminiscent of some atelids and prosimians. The ulna (Figure 231, B and F–M) is gracile and convex anteriorly; the sigmoid notch is broad, the radial facet is small and laterally oriented, the olecranon process is elongate, and the styloid is prominent (suggesting the lack of any meniscus development in the wrist articulation). The radial shaft is rounded and gracile, the neck is long, and the head is small and rounded. The manual digits (Figure 231AA) are of moderate length, as in ateline ceboids, not greatly elongated or shortened. Various vertebrae and fragments are known; of these, the lumbars have accessory processes as in some monkeys and prosimians, but their centra are said by Ankel (in Simons and Fleagle, 1973) to be hominoid-like. Ankel (1965, *loc. cit.*) also suggested, contrary to Zapfe (1961a), that *Pliopithecus* had a tail of moderate length, perhaps in the process of reduction (based on the sacral canal and its similarity to that of *Cacajao*); the sacrum itself contained only three elements. The femur (Figure 231D) is gracile, with no clear muscle markings, but somewhat more robust than that of a gibbon of equal length; judged from the proximal end, the hip joint was quite mobile, without special adaptation to either leaping or quadrupedal running (Simons and Fleagle, 1973). The broad distal condyles may also indicate mobility at the knee; again, similarities are to ateline ceboids, and possibly *Hylobates*, but not to cercopithecids. The ankle joint appears to be adapted for dorsiflexion, but without great lateral mobility; the astragalocalcaneal articulation was of the ancestral primate, helical, pattern. The foot (Figure 231BB) is moderately long, with proportions as

in some ceboids and *Hylobates;* there is no facet for a prehallux on the hallucial metatarsal. Compared to estimated trunk length, the proportions of the limbs (Figure 231CC) are as expected in a typical catarrhine, not elongated as in *Hylobates* (Biegert and Mauer, 1972).

As indicated under the family Pliopithecidae above, *Pliopithecus* is grouped in this taxon with *Dendropithecus* and *Propliopithecus* more on the basis of grade characteristics (retained catarrhine symplesiomorphies or patristic affinities) than on clear shared derived states. From *Dendropithecus,* it is distinguished by its lack of a second mesial sulcus on C', less molar cresting and cingulum, longer M^{1-3} and $M_{\overline{3}}$, $P^{\underline{3}}$ usually larger than $P^{\underline{4}}$, slightly lower incisors and broader $P_{\overline{4}}$, less elongate long bones (especially humerus: humero–femoral index of 85 versus 90), and presence of humeral entepicondylar foramen. *Pliopithecus* differs from *Propliopithecus* in its shorter and wider face, projecting orbital rims, more "modern" auditory meatus, shallower mandibular corpus, lower and narrower incisors, more elongate $P_{\overline{4}}$, somewhat less cheek-tooth cingulum, and lack of prehallux. Most other taxa may be clearly distinguished from *Pliopithecus* by their respective familial characteristics, but *Hylobates* requires further comment because of the long history of purported relationship between the two genera.

Much of this was based essentially on small size and shared ancestral catarrhine features of the teeth, including the honing $C^{\underline{1}}$–$P_{\overline{3}}$ complex and simple cusp pattern (see, e.g., Frisch, 1973, and above); cranial similarities are limited to the somewhat protruding

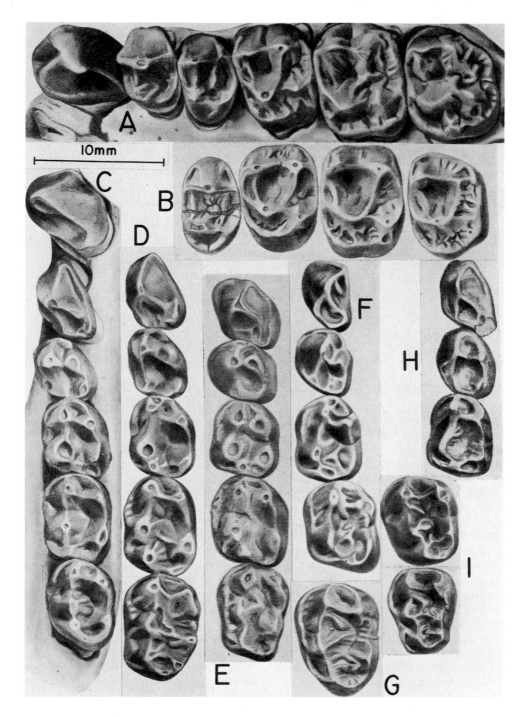

Figure 229. *Pliopithecus.* Middle Miocene, Europe. Dentitions in occlusal view. *P. vindobonensis:* A, left C¹–M³ of male; C, left male C$_{\overline{1}}$–M$_{\overline{3}}$; D, left male P$_{\overline{3}}$–M$_{\overline{3}}$. *P. antiquus:* B, left P⁴–M³ (mirror image of right); E, left P$_{\overline{3}}$–M$_{\overline{3}}$ of male; F, left P$_{\overline{3}}$–M$_{\overline{2}}$; G, left M$_{\overline{3}}$. *P. lockeri:* H, left P$_{\overline{3}}$–M$_{\overline{1}}$ of ?male. *P. piveteaui:* I, left M$_{\overline{2}}$ and erupting M$_{\overline{3}}$ from mandible (mirror image of right). [A, C, D, H from Zapfe (1961a); B, E–G, I from Hürzeler (1954).]

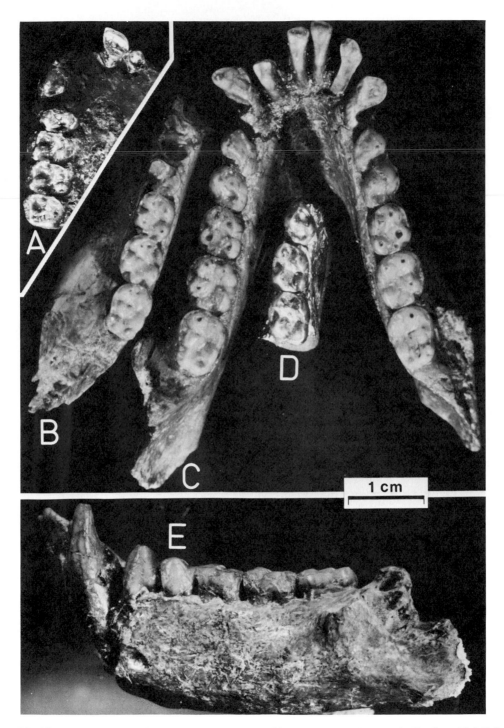

Figure 230. *Pliopithecus antiquus.* Middle Miocene, Europe. Part of female palate with right C^1, P^4–M^3, and left I^{1-2}: A, occlusal view. Partial left corpus with P_4–M_3: B, occlusal view. ?Male mandible with complete dentition: C, occlusal view; E, left lateral view. Partial left corpus with dP_{3-4} and M_1: D, occlusal view.

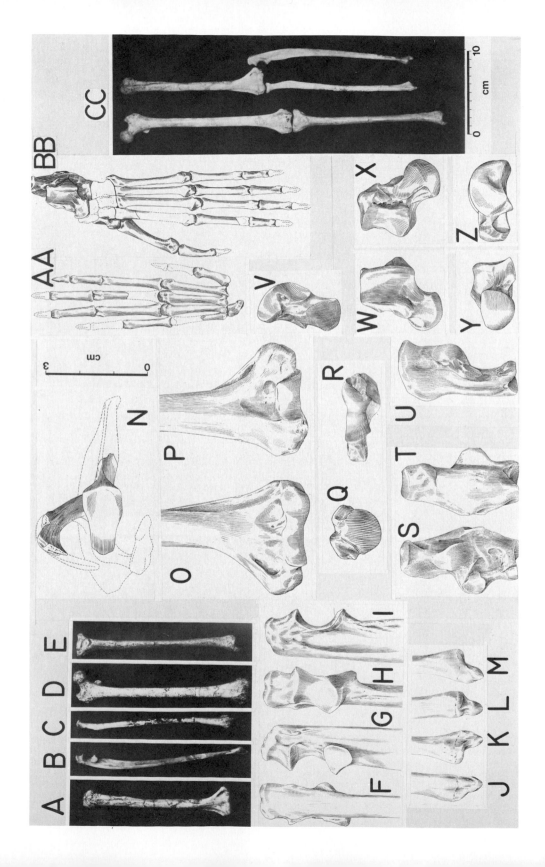

circum-orbital rims and shallow mandible, in which *Pliopithecus* perhaps converges on *Hylobates*, while the only postcranial resemblance is the gracile shape of long bones without muscle scars, probably an allometric effect of small size, not heritage. *Pliopithecus* specifically differs from *Hylobates* in having smaller and more caniniform lateral upper incisors; spatulate upper central incisors with somewhat more extensive cutting edges; apparently sexually dimorphic (upper) canines and lowers often with a distal tubercle; and broad rather than square or elongate upper molars. The trigonid basin (anterior fovea) is more prominent in *Pliopithecus* than in living *Hylobates*, and all molars, unlike those of *Hylobates*, have characteristically heavily wrinkled enamel and well-developed external cingulae, with the occasional appearance of lingual cingulids also. There are thus no taxa with whom *Pliopithecus* shares unique derived features, the closest relationship perhaps being with *Dendropithecus* (Delson and Andrews, 1975; Andrews and Groves, 1975).

Taxonomy within the genus is still chaotic, with several widely recognized species and subgenera and even a recent newly erected genus. The meaningful differences among these nominal taxa are few, and some researchers have suggested that only one species need be recognized for all the middle Miocene specimens (e.g., Andrews, 1973). Pending a serious revision of the known material by a single researcher, several species have been retained here on the basis of the minor differences listed below, which are roughly comparable to those found in polytypic early Tertiary genera with comparable sample sizes; following Ginsburg (1975), subgenera have been suppressed as superfluous. The comparisons are essentially based on the lower dentition (Figures 229 and 230), as several upper teeth are known in only two species. Cranial remains are restricted to *P. vindobonensis*, while only a few fragments of postcranium are known for *P. antiquus*: A proximal humeral fragment from La Grive is identical in size and shape to those from Neudorf, as far as can be determined.

The type specimen of *Pliopithecus antiquus* (Figures 230, C and E, and 231E) is from Sansan, as are three other partial mandibles. Hürzeler (1954) suggested that one of these (Figure 230B) represented a distinct unnamed species based on its small size, but later authors have rejected this view. Bergounioux and Crouzel (1964, 1965) termed another Sansan mandible with three teeth (Figure 230D) *P. antiquus* var. *auscitanensis*. Ginsburg (1975) has suggested that this jaw represents a new genus, *Crouzelia*, differing from sympatric *P. antiquus* in several dental features. These depend on the determination of tooth homologies, which seem to have been misinterpreted both by Ginsburg and by Bergounioux and Crouzel: As the most distal tooth shows the heaviest wear, they considered it to be $M_{\overline{2}}$, preceded by $P_{\overline{4}}$-$M_{\overline{1}}$. The features which set "*Crouzelia*" off from *Pliopithecus* are the short and high $P_{\overline{4}}$ with a short and narrow talonid, but a large trigonid, and the long $M_{\overline{1-2}}$ with hypoconulid indistinct on $M_{\overline{1}}$, clearer and on the midline on $M_{\overline{2}}$. Hürzeler (1954) has illustrated and described deciduous teeth of *P. antiquus* from Göriach which correspond in exactly these features to those of "*Crouzelia*," if the latter are interpreted as $dP_{\overline{3}}$-$M_{\overline{1}}$. Not only would this interpretation remove the need to recognize a distinct genus or species at Sansan sympatric with *P. antiquus*, but the tooth sizes fit as well, leaving only the slightly anomalous heavy wear on $M_{\overline{1}}$ incompletely explained. Numerous other, mostly fragmentary, remains allocated to *Pliopithecus antiquus* have been described from eleven other localities by Hürzeler (1954) and by Kowalski and Zapfe (1974); the largest sample is from Göriach, Austria, with closely similar age and morphology (Figure 229G) to Sansan. The nominal taxa *P. platyodon* and *P. antiquus chantrei* (from Elgg and La Grive, respectively) appear to be merely synonyms of the generic type.

Figure 231. *Pliopithecus vindobonensis*. Middle Miocene, Europe. Right humerus: A, anterior view. Right ulna: B, lateral view. Right radius: C, medial view. Right femur: D, anterior view. Left tibia: E, anterior view. Note relative length of elements. Left ulna (reversed from right). Proximal end: F, posterior view; G, lateral view; H, anterior view; I, medial view. Distal end: J, posterior view; K, lateral view; L, anterior view; M, medial view. Left scapula (reversed from right): N, view into glenoid articulation. Left humerus (reversed from right): O, distal end, anterior view; P, posterior view; Q, proximal view; R, distal view. Right calcaneus: S, dorsal view; T, plantar view; U, medial view. Left astragalus: V, medial view (distal end down); W, dorsal view; X, plantar view; Y, distal view; Z, lateral view. Left hand, restored: AA, dorsal view. Left foot, restored: BB, dorsal view. Hindlimb (to left) and forelimb, arranged in approximate anatomical position to demonstrate relative limb length: CC. The scale to the right of N is for E–P and S–Z; Q and R are ¾ this scale; AA and BB are ½ this scale. [F–BB from Zapfe (1961a).]

Ginsburg (1975) has also redescribed and illustrated most of the French early middle Miocene specimens, which he placed in *Pliopithecus piveteaui,* following Hürzeler (1954). This taxon is represented by the type mandible with M_{2-3} (Figure 229I) and 10 isolated teeth (P_4–M_3, P^4, and M^3). The teeth differ from those of *P. antiquus* in slightly smaller size, reduced buccal cingulum, and distally narrow M_3; the type M_3 (unerupted) is shorter than its M_2, but Frisch (1973) has suggested that this may be due to a large M_2, rather than true M_3 reduction. This group is perhaps the least distinct from *P. antiquus,* of which it might represent a temporal variant.

Pliopithecus vindobonensis was also distinguished by minor dental differences from *P. antiquus,* such as a groove in the lingual cingulum on I^1, possibly more extensive lingual cingulum on upper molars and slightly longer P_3, wider M_3 talonid, and more buccal placement of the hypoconulid on M_{2-3} (Figure 229, A, C, and D) (Zapfe, 1961a). The single specimen from Trimmelkamm (Figure 229H) described by Zapfe (1961a,b) as *P. (Plesiopliopithecus) lockeri* is perhaps somewhat more distinctive in its elongate teeth, P_4 trigonid closed mesially and M_1 broader distally. By comparison, the P^4 trigonid opens mesially in both *P. antiquus* and *P. vindobonensis* and apparently also in *P. piveteaui; P. antiquus* also has much broader premolars with less heteromorphy and more separation of the M_1 cusps. In measurements, *P. lockeri* is most comparable to *P. vindobonensis,* which shows a good deal of variation among the three individuals. In addition to the illustrated cheek teeth, the specimen preserves two lower incisors and a cast of a large canine.

More recently, Crusafont (1975) has reported over a dozen specimens of *Pliopithecus* from two Spanish localities, but without illustration, measurements, or an attempt at description or allocation, although he suggested possible affinity to *P. lockeri.* Kretzoi (1975) described a subadult mandible (dP_4, P_4–M_3) from the early Vallesian of Rudabánya, Hungary, as *P. (Anapithecus) hernyaki,* characterized by large size, rounded P_4, and large distal fovea. The published photograph does not permit clear allocation to *Pliopithecus* rather

than *Dryopithecus,* but the size is comparable to *D. brancoi,* known from several sites of comparable age and area, and also associated with larger apes. However, the presence of apparently sexually dimorphic canines (Kretzoi, 1975) suggests *Pliopithecus* rather than *Dryopithecus,* and the specimen is here tentatively recognized as a distinct species of *Pliopithecus.*

The adaptations of *Pliopithecus* are moderately well understood, given its representation by skeletal as well as a variety of dental specimens. Dentally, the emphasis is on the ridges of the broad molars with their deeply folded enamel surface; the edges and cingulae are the active elements, while basins, especially the talonid, are more restricted. Combined with this, the extended tooth-row, narrow incisors, anterior origin of masseter, and large temporalis contrast strongly with the frugivorous adaptations of *Hylobates.* The combination of increased cutting and shredding by cheek teeth with reduced incisor preparation suggests an adaptation to folivory, which may have permitted noncompetitive sympatry with larger hominids.

The postcranial morphology of *Pliopithecus* has been considered by some (e.g., Tuttle, 1972; Simons, 1972) as essentially "preadaptive" for the true brachiation characteristic of *Hylobates,* but this view is oversimplified and does not imply phyletic relationship. As discussed above and in greater detail by Ciochon and Corruccini (1977), Corruccini *et al.* (1976), and references therein, the skeleton of *Pliopithecus vindobonensis* is structurally most similar to that of atelines save for the lack of a prehensile tail. Thus, it would have been an agile, active arborealist, engaging in some suspensory postures as well as running, climbing, and leaping. Zapfe (1958) has suggested that *Pliopithecus* might have been partly terrestrial, assuming that it entered the Neudorf fissures while still alive. This is most unlikely, morphologically, ethologically, and taphonomically; instead the carcasses of arboreal *Pliopithecus* individuals were likely to have been washed into the fissure openings.

DENDROPITHECUS Andrews and Simons, 1977

[= or including: *Xenopithecus* Hopwood, 1933a: Hopwood, 1933b, in part; MacInnes, 1943, in part. *Limnopithecus* Hopwood, 1933a: MacInnes, 1943; Le Gros Clark and Leakey, 1950, and later authors, in part. *Proconsul* Hopwood, 1933a: Le Gros Clark and Leakey, 1951, Le Gros Clark, 1952, in part. *Pliopithecus* (Gervais, 1849) (*Propliopithecus*) Schlosser, 1910: Simonetta, 1957, in part. *Pliopithecus (Limnopithecus):*

Simons, 1965. *Aegyptopithecus* Simons, 1965: Andrews, 1970, in part. *"Limnopithecus":* Andrews, 1974a. *Dendropithecus* "Andrews, Pilbeam, and Simons, 1976": Delson and Andrews, 1975, intentionally as nomen nudum in advance of formal publication.]

DISTRIBUTION
Early to early middle Miocene (Rusingan to Ternanian). Kenya.
KNOWN SPECIES
Dendropithecus macinnesi (Le Gros Clark and Leakey, 1950), type species
[= *Xenopithecus koruensis* Hopwood, 1933a: Hopwood, 1933b, MacInnes, 1943, in part. *Limnopithecus macinnesi* Le Gros Clark and Leakey, 1950, 1951. *Limnopithecus legetet* Hopwood, 1933a: MacInnes, 1943, Le Gros Clark and Leakey, 1951, in part. *Proconsul africanus* Hopwood, 1933a: Le Gros Clark and Leakey, 1951, Le Gros Clark, 1952, in part. *Pliopithecus (Propliopithecus) macinnesi:* Simonetta, 1957. *Aegyptopithecus* sp.: Andrews, 1970. *"Limnopithecus" macinnesi:* Andrews, 1974. *Dendropithecus macinnesi:* Delson and Andrews, 1975.]
LOCALITIES: Karungu (390); Koru (394); Songhor (396); Rusinga⋆ (406); Mfwangano (408); Maboko (440).

DISCUSSION

Dendropithecus macinnesi is a small catarrhine comparable in dental size to the siamang (*Hylobates syndactylus*); several limb elements are known, but no cranial region other than the dentition (Figures 232 and 233). The incisors are high crowned and narrow (mesiodistally); canines show marked sexual dimorphism, moderately tall in both sexes, the male C^1 having two mesial sulci on the crown (Figure 233B); the $P_{\overline{3}}$ is strongly "sectorial" or honing in both sexes, quite narrow and elongated, as is $P_{\overline{4}}$; the upper premolars are quite broad and of subequal size, but the $P^{\underline{3}}$ paracone is very tall. The lower molar cusps are placed around the margin of the crown, surrounding large basins and connected by clear ridges or crests; the metaconid–protoconid and entoconid–hypoconulid ridges are strongest, with the hypoconulid and hypoconid weakly joined and no connection between entoconid and metaconid; the buccal cingulum is weak, $M_{\overline{3}}$ only slightly longer than $M_{\overline{2}}$, not much elongated, and the hypoconulid is nearly median on $M_{\overline{1}}$, more buccal on $M_{\overline{2}}$, and nearly in line with the other buccal cusps on $M_{\overline{3}}$. The upper molars have a weak hypocone (usually lacking on $M^{\underline{3}}$), well-defined trigon, and indistinct or no paraconule. The mandibular corpus and symphysis are robust, the corpus being of moderate and even height; the superior transverse torus is well developed, and an inferior torus is also often present, and equally projecting; the ramus is unknown. The sloping premaxilla leads to upper

incisor prognathism and increases the maxillary diastema (Figure 233, C and E). The palate is narrow and elongate, with an extensive maxillary sinus. In the postcranium (Figures 234 and 244), the long bones are similar to those of gibbons in being slender and showing little evidence of muscle marking, but they probably were not extremely long compared to trunk size. The humeral medial epicondyle is large and medially projecting, and the trochlea is smaller in size than the capitulum and bounded by two keels; the ulnar olecranon process is quite long (though broken) and the radial notch is shallow. The radius was slightly longer than the humerus; the astragalus and calcaneum are similar to those of cercopithecids in form, but the lower ankle joint is fully helical. Overall, the greatest similarities are probably to *Ateles* postcranially (Andrews, 1973 and personal communication; Andrews and Groves, 1975).

As a quite conservative early catarrhine, it is difficult to clearly distinguish *D. macinnesi* from various potential relatives. It was long grouped with *Dryopithecus (Limnopithecus) legetet,* mostly on the basis of size and rough similarity of lower molars, but can be distinguished from that species especially by the greater development of canine honing (seen on I^2–C^1 and $C_{\overline{1}}$–$P_{\overline{3}}$) and by the double mesial grove of C^1 and greater canine dimorphism, the narrower incisors, broader upper cheek teeth, relatively larger P^4, stronger lower molar crests, shallower notches(?), and weaker cingulum. The astragalus also differs, although that of *D. legetet* has not yet been described. Most of these features also distinguish *Dendropithecus* from other, larger species of *Dryopithecus,* some of which additionally have thicker molar enamel, elongate $M_{\overline{3}}$, shorter ulnar olecranon, and other distinguishing features. On the other hand, *Dendropithecus* and *Pliopithecus* are much more similar, although most of their shared character states are probably ancestral retentions in these two conservative forms. Distinctions from *Pliopithecus* and also from *Propliopithecus* are listed under those genera.

Le Gros Clark and Leakey (1950) first recognized the specific distinctness of the specimens here termed *Dendropithecus,* grouping them with the smaller *Limnopithecus legetet,* rather than the larger *Proconsul* species from the same sites. Only a few isolated specimens had previously (or since) been otherwise identified, if one accepts the allocations of Andrews (1973). The general superficial morphological and size

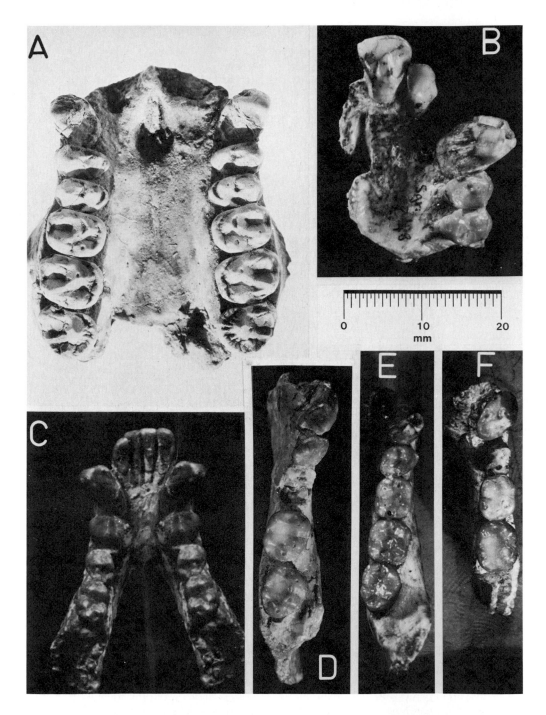

Figure 232. *Dendropithecus macinnesi.* Early Miocene, Africa. Palate with right and left C^1–M^3: A, occlusal view. Left premaxilla and part maxilla with I^1–P^4: B, occlusal view. Partial mandible with right $I_{\overline{1-2}}$ and left $I_{\overline{1}}$–$M_{\overline{1}}$, combined with mirror image of right $C_{\overline{1}}$–$M_{\overline{1}}$: C, occlusal view. Mandible with right $P_{\overline{3-4}}$ and $M_{\overline{2-3}}$: D, occlusal view. Right corpus with $P_{\overline{4}}$–$M_{\overline{3}}$: E, occlusal view. Right corpus with $P_{\overline{3}}$ and $M_{\overline{1-2}}$: F, occlusal view. Smallest scale divisions are 0.5 mm. [A–D courtesy P. Andrews.]

456

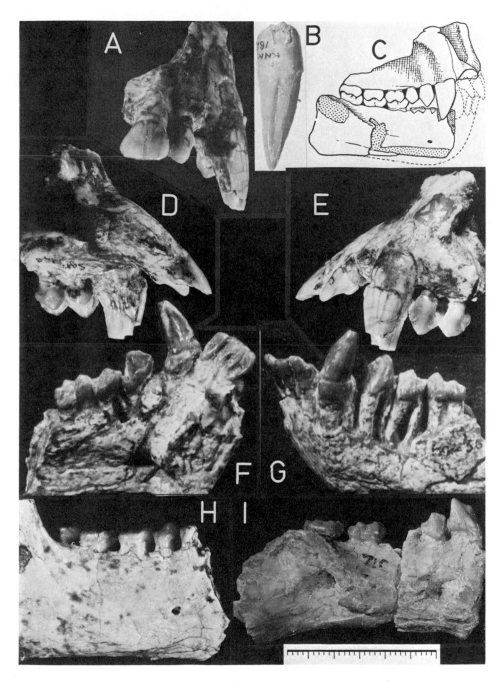

Figure 233. *Dendropithecus macinnesi.* Early Miocene, Africa. Left premaxilla and part maxilla with I^1–P^4: A, frontal view; D, lingual view; E, buccal view. Unworn erupting left C^1 from juvenile maxilla: B, mesial view (note secondary sulcus at right). Partly restored associated maxilla and mandibular corpus: C, right lateral view. Mandible with right $I_{\overline{1-2}}$ and left $I_{\overline{1}}$–$M_{\overline{1}}$: F, lingual view; G, buccal view. Right corpus with $P_{\overline{4}}$–$M_{\overline{3}}$ and broken $P_{\overline{3}}$: H, buccal view. Right corpus with $P_{\overline{3-4}}$ and $M_{\overline{2-3}}$: I, buccal view. Scale divisions are in millimeters; C is at reduced scale. [A, B, D–G courtesy of P. Andrews; C from Le Gros Clark and Thomas (1952) by permission of the Trustees of the British Museum (Natural History).]

457

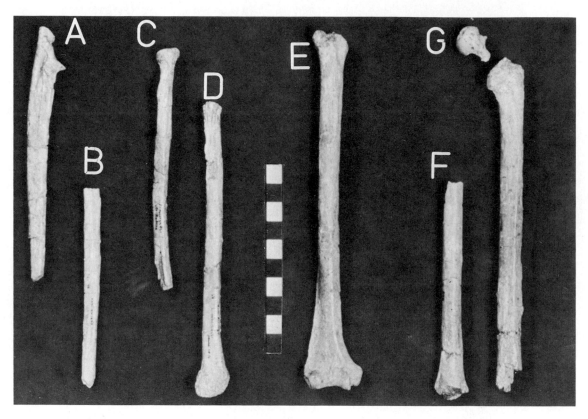

Figure 234. *Dendropithecus macinnesi.* Early Miocene, Africa. Partial forelimb of single individual: A, right ulna, lateral view; C, right radius, posterior view; E, right humerus, anterior view. Four partial femoral shafts: B and D, posterior view; F, anterior view of right femur; G, posterior view of right shaft and unassociated head fragment. Scale divisions are in centimeters. See also Figure 244. [Courtesy of and © R. L. Clochon.]

similarities of the teeth to gibbons led to the placement of *Limnopithecus* spp. among the Hylobatidae, as then interpreted. Limb bones associated with teeth of "*L.*" *macinnesi* were described by Le Gros Clark and Thomas (1951), who considered them even less "advanced" or modern than those of "*Proconsul*" species, but nonetheless suitable for an early pre-gibbon. Ferembach (1958) reinterpreted the dentition and skeleton of *Limnopithecus* species, considering that *L. legetet* was hardly separable from *D. (Proconsul)*, while "*L.*" *macinnesi* was a persistently primitive early catarrhine; much the same interpretation is accepted here, but Ferembach's views were long ignored, partly because she had only limited access to original material.

The major study of large amounts of *Dendropithecus*

fossil material (over 150 specimens, excluding postcrania) has been that of Andrews (1973), who accepted a close relationship, even one of ancestor and descendant, between *Dendropithecus* and *Hylobates*. This was mainly on the basis of gracile and unmarked limb bones, the same dental similarities used by previous authors, and the presence of more "pongid-like" features in contemporary *Dryopithecus* species, suggesting that gibbon ancestry had already become distinct. Groves (1972, 1974) at first denied such a relationship, but later Andrews and Groves (1975) modified their positions to suggest that, although *Dendropithecus* was anatomically suitable, it was not necessarily an actual gibbon ancestor. Simons and Fleagle (1973) also have accepted the strong possibility that *D. macinnesi* is in or near the ancestry of living gibbons, certainly closer to it than is *Pliopithecus*.

On the other hand, a few authors have refrained from this widespread view. Remane (1965) tentatively ranked "*Limnopithecus*" with *Pliopithecus* in a conservative family Pliopithecidae [which Zapfe (1961a) had used as a subfamily of Hylobatidae]; this would correspond to the cited views of Ferembach and Groves. Delson (1977 and in Delson and Andrews, 1975) went further in arguing that no derived features are shared between *Dendropithecus* and gibbons, the often-mentioned characters being either ancestral catarrhine ones or possibly convergent similarities based on specific locomotor adaptations.

The solution to this problem appears to lie in the limb bones, which have only been partially restudied since Le Gros Clark and Thomas's (1951) paper, despite the apparent presence of new material. Andrews and Groves (1975, pp. 171–172) have discussed the specimens from a comparative morphological point of view, indicating humeral shaft robusticity of 17.6%, most comparable to *Ateles* (15–18%), rather than to *Hylobates* (13–15%) or *D. africanus* (19.5%); low biepicondylar width, poorly developed brachialis flange; "trochlea bounded medially by a sharp keel and laterally by a low straight keel and smaller than capitulum" (ratio of widths 81 versus 104% in *D. africanus*), "distal articular surface nearly perpendicular to the line of the shaft; radial shaft rounded, not distally flattened, radial neck short and narrow, head probably had a pronounced slope." Portions of gracile femoral and tibial shafts are also known. Despite the several gibbon-like features they discussed, Andrews and Groves concluded that it had none of the diagnostic adaptations for brachiation, did not habitually brachiate, and probably had a locomotor repertoire closest to that of *Ateles*, "except presumably for lacking a prehensile tail." They then reversed themselves to some degree, suggesting that an early gibbon might well have had a locomotor morphology of this type, the view accepted by Le Gros Clark and Thomas (1951) and also by Tuttle (1972), among others. Preuschoft and Weinmann (1973) undertook a study of *Dendropithecus* limb bones from a stress–biomechanical viewpoint, but were frustrated by the damaged condition of the fossils; they did note that gracile limbs often denote robustly built animals, but could not interpret "*Limnopithecus*" *macinnesi* in this light.

A number of other recent studies have analyzed catarrhine fossil postcranial elements morphometrically, some including or commenting upon *Dendropithecus*. Morbeck (1975) compared both the distal humerus and the total elbow joint of *D. macinnesi*, *Dryopithecus africanus*, and *Pliopithecus* to a range of anthropoids, finding the two putative "pre-gibbons" most similar to *Presbytis* in the elbow and all three fossils linked to *Ateles* in the distal humerus; in both cases, "*Limnopithecus*" *macinnesi* was most distinct from its modern analogue. McHenry and Corruccini (1975) compared the distal humerus of the two African forms (using a more biologically interpretable method, but not including any platyrrhines) and found *D. macinnesi* closest to *Presbytis* and *Macaca*, with *Hylobates* next nearest. Corruccini *et al.* (1976) reviewed these and other studies, although their interpretation of the positions of *D. macinnesi* vis-à-vis *Hylobates* does not fully agree with the figure in McHenry and Corruccini. Finally, Ciochon and Corruccini (1977) have discussed this work again, noting that *Dendropithecus* appears to share no derived features with "hominoids," gibbons, or other taxa.

The majority (or even totality) of workers have thus concluded that *Dendropithecus* has gracile limb bones most similar to those of *Ateles* (or perhaps *Presbytis*) in articular morphology. Its locomotor behavior probably compared favorably with those features common to both living forms (thus excluding colobine leaping and ateline tail support). The same interpretation could be made for *Propliopithecus zeuxis* and *Pliopithecus* (q.v.). There is nothing in this to prevent a potential phyletic link to gibbon locomotion, but, more to the point, there is nothing to favor it, apart from conservative retentions from a common catarrhine anatomy.

The same could be said for the dentition, which also differs only in a few characters from that of *Propliopithecus* or *Pliopithecus*. The combination of these features serves to separate these species generically, as a matter of convenience, but links them together phenetically. Because the diagnostic facial and auditory regions are lacking in *Dendropithecus,* as is the hallucial metatarsal, it is not yet possible to determine if that genus shared any derived states with more "modern" ape-like catarrhines. In terms of dental adaptations and paleobiology, the general similarity to *Pliopithecus* is modified by less emphasis on molar furrowing and shorter tooth-row, and the placement of musculature and leverage is unknown. Probably,

Dendropithecus was less specialized for folivory, but its diet included a mixture of fruit and leaves. Posture and locomotion most likely were comparable to *Pliopithecus* and to atelines (except for the nonprehensile tail).

Family ?Pliopithecidae, *incertae sedis*

(= or including: "Kansupithecus" Bohlin, 1946.)

DISTRIBUTION
  ?Middle Miocene. China.
LOCALITIES: ?Yindirte (405); "Taben Buluk" (430).

DISCUSSION

Bohlin (1946) reported an edentulous fragment of a small mammalian symphysis and a chip of a molar tooth from two localities located 8 km apart in the Taben Buluk badlands of Kansu Province, China. He assigned them both to the genus "Kansupithecus," whose provisional nature he emphasized by not providing a species name, thus ensuring the invalidity of the taxon. Bohlin originally considered the age of the Yindirte local fauna (including the tooth chip) to be later Oligocene; the few scattered fossils associated with the symphysis suggested a younger age. Thenius (1959) placed Yindirte in what is here termed later early Miocene, and "Taben Buluk" even younger, on the basis of associated proboscideans, which did not exit Africa until this time. Most authors have ignored these fossils in the interim; Conroy and Bown (1976) discussed their age, following Thenius without citing him, but neglected to consider the morphology or meaning of the remains themselves.

The symphysis is about the size of *Pliopithecus antiquus*, with which Bohlin compared it briefly, finding that the European species had a slightly longer planum alveolare and perhaps a larger canine. In addition, it is interesting that there is no sign on the lateral face of the Chinese jaw of an extended mesiobuccal flange on $P_{\overline{3}}$, although the axis of the tooth is oblique to that of $P_{\overline{4}}$. The corpus is fairly deep and robust, with a mental foramen under $P_{\overline{4}}$ and some

indication of a median symphyseal canal in the illustrations. The incisor alveoli are relatively small, with the canine of about the same area as the premolars. Considering this and the $P_{\overline{3}}$ shape, the canine crown was probably not very tall, but whether the species was sexually dimorphic is obviously not detectable.

Bohlin indicated that he would not have identified the molar chip as primate were it not for the jaw fragment; he considered it to be from a right $M_{\overline{2}}$ and attempted to reconstruct the outline of a whole tooth. He based his comparisons on *Parapithecus fraasi*, especially because of his thoughts on the fossil's age, but there is no real morphological similarity. In fact, if the chip is indeed from a primate lower molar, it would more probably be of a left tooth, the identifications of the hypoconid and entoconid being reversed by Bohlin: The anthropoid hypoconulid is almost always closer to the hypoconid, thus buccal to the midline, if not on it; only *Oligopithecus* differs from this pattern. This tooth fragment, if primate, is hominoid rather than cercopithecid or parapithecid, and it would agree with the morphology seen in pliopithecids moderately well.

Taking the two fragments as indicative of a single taxon is questionable but parsimonious. There is no evidence of a cercopithecid in Asia before the later late Miocene but pliopithecids are present in Europe by the early middle Miocene, and other hominoids are known from Asia soon afterward. Both Kansu specimens are marginally acceptable as *Pliopithecus*-like in morphology, although no definitive characters, much less derived ones, link them to this genus or its relatives. For the moment, the fossils may be allocated tentatively to the Pliopithecidae, *incertae sedis*.

Family Hominidae
Gray, 1825

(= or including: Hominidae: Wilder, 1922; Delson and Andrews, 1975. Hominoidea: Simpson, 1931, restricted.)

DISTRIBUTION
  Early Miocene (Rusingan) to modern. Worldwide (fossil record essentially Old World).

INCLUDED TAXA

Subfamilies Homininae, Ponginae, and Hylobatinae.

DISCUSSION

The hominids as recognized here correspond essentially to the modern anthropomorphous primates and their closest extinct relatives ("dryopithecines," *sensu lato*). These animals may be characterized among catarrhines by relatively conservative dentition [e.g., lacking loph(id)s, premolar conules, or centroconids], a dental formula of $I\frac{2}{2}$, $C\frac{1}{1}$, $P\frac{3,4}{3,4}$, $M\frac{1,2,3}{1,2,3}$, quite variable cranial mosaic, relatively large brain, and, in most cases, derived shoulder–thorax complex and loss of external tail.

As discussed most recently by Andrews and Groves (1975), the forelimb–thoracic synapomorphies of hominids appear to be related to mobility and postural–locomotor use of the arm. They listed as important features: "the long clavicle; the orientation and dorsal positioning of the scapula; the orientation and shape of the head of the humerus; the free rotatory movements of the radioulnar joints; [and] the mobility of the wrist and hand, in particular the meniscus development of the wrist" (Andrews and Groves, 1975, p. 170). In particular, the scapula is axially elongated, with an oblique spine and cranially directed glenoid fossa; the clavicle shows a high degree of torsion; and the humerus has a large, globular head, deep bicipital groove, and relatively distal deltoid insertion. Moreover, Andrews and Groves (1975) noted that modern hominids share a pelvic complex involving long sacral and short lumbar region, expanded ilium, and reduction of the tail by transformation into a coccyx which may stabilize the pelvic floor; that thoracic broadening was in part related to an allometric trend (violated by *Hylobates*) which also explains the reorientation of the abdominal viscera; and that modern hominids also lack the vermiform appendix. Corruccini and Ciochon (1976) further analyzed the catarrhine shoulder, determining those features which most clearly distinguished hominids from cercopithecids and ceboids morphometrically: the shallow spinoglenoid notch, high glenoid and short acromion and coracoid lengths of the scapula, short clavicle, and wide humeral intertubercular sulcus and articular surface extent. The latter feature alone separated "apes" from "monkeys" completely. On the other hand, these features were not functionally analyzed, and it is surprising that hominids scored high on an axis to which clavicle length contributed negatively, implying a short clavicle for them, as the reverse is generally cited. As yet, none of the early fossil genera placed in the Hominidae here is known from the shoulder, while the wrist and elbow of *Dryopithecus africanus* do not show any derived similarities with later hominids, although a European ulna referred tentatively to *Sivapithecus darwini* does appear more "modern" in olecranon reduction at least (see below). The ancestral conditions for these derived hominid postcranial features would have been as seen in "monkeys," perhaps most like those of some atelids (especially as similar conditions are known in Pliopithecidae).

Dentally, hominids share a number of features with pliopithecids, but these are mainly conservative retentions from an ancestral catarrhine morphotype. Except for *Hylobates*, all hominids show some reduction of canine honing, but no other important derived characters unite all of even the non-hylobatine hominids. Relative brain size increase appears to be documented as a shared feature of the family not completely linked to body size increase, occurring in *Dryopithecus* and the small *Hylobates*. Skull morphology also is of little help in distinguishing hominids from other catarrhines, or in linking them to another family: The gibbons present the wide and short face and low choanae considered ancestral for the infraorder by Delson and Andrews (1975), but also have uniquely derived features; the face is elongated in other hominids (least in *Homo* and some *Australopithecus* and perhaps *Dryopithecus*), but rather broad usually, while choanal shape is narrow and tall irrespective of facial projection. Functional analyses of these regions are required before further interpretation is attempted. In terms of nonskeletal biology, hominids share delayed development of presumably ancestral catarrhine ischial callosities, with a morphocline in timing from Hylobatinae through Ponginae to *Homo*. Some *Hylobates* retain the ancestral diploid chromosome number of 44, but others have 50 or 52, while pongines have 48 and *Homo* 46. Finally, numerous biomolecular studies (see reviews in Goodman and Tashian, 1976) indicate at least phenetic similarity between *Homo* and *Pan*, with *Pongo* and then *Hylobates* more distinct, but all clearly separated from cercopithecids.

The phylogeny of Hominidae has recently been discussed by such authors as Simons (1972) and Walker (1976b), from a rather conservative perspective, and by Delson (1977b; Delson and Andrews,

1975; Delson *et al.*, 1977) with more divergent results, most of which are followed here. Orthodox views have seen *Hylobates* derived from a *Pliopithecus*-like ancestry or, more rarely, from later *Dryopithecus*, while other *Dryopithecus* were said to have given rise to modern great apes and "humans," in more recent studies via the "ground apes" or Sugrivapithecini of this classification. Such a placement of *Pliopithecus* and allies no longer seems tenable, however, and hylobatines must be considered an early offshoot from the hominid stock. *Dryopithecus* species would seem to have been closer to the later large apes, with one line leading to modern apes and also(?) to Sugrivapithecini; as discussed below, it seems most likely that Homininae is the sister-taxon of the latter. This phylogeny, seen in Figure 151, is not precisely reflected in the classification accepted here, for reasons detailed by Delson and Andrews (1975) and Delson (1977b). Instead, three subfamilies are recognized within the Hominidae, arbitrarily raising the *Homo* group to that rank, rather than leaving it as an "infrasubtribe" or less, a fragment of the sister-taxon of *Pan*. Moreover, the rank of the whole group under discussion here is, of course, lower than usually accepted, including great and lesser apes and their fossil relatives with men in a single family Hominidae, rather than as several families. The reasoning behind this move is again given by the two papers cited, essentially combining the relative diversity of this group, which Simpson (1945) argued was equivalent to other mammalian families, and the removal of *Pliopithecus* and other conservative early catarrhines to a separate family. The relationship of these two families is discussed above under Hominoidea and Pliopithecidae.

Given such a postulated phylogeny, it is possible to extrapolate somewhat the broad outlines of hominid adaptive history. The common hominid ancestor would probably have been much like pliopithecids, but with at least some modification of the pectoral girdle in common with modern forms. *Dryopithecus* species do not preserve this area, but if they were found to have a shoulder essentially identical with that of *Pliopithecus*, their position in the family would come under severe scrutiny. Fleagle (1976), as well as various other authors, has suggested that the use of the forelimb for support and climbing while feeding is one of the basal adaptations of Hominidae as construed here, which would agree with shoulder (and later elbow and wrist) modifications being of primary adaptive importance in the group's early history.

Other derived modifications of ancestral catarrhine anatomy to be expected in early hominids would include some relative brain size increase, beginning a long-lasting trend perhaps related to greater coordination; development of a tubular auditory meatus, possibly in parallel with cercopithecids (see under Catarrhini); perhaps the beginnings of lengthening of upper cheek teeth; and reduction or even loss of the external tail.

If *Dryopithecus* is correctly placed phyletically, the mosaic of derived wrist and ancestral elbow in known early Miocene forms suggests that the ancestral hylobatines had diverged by this time, with only the beginnings of a developmental canalization to guide them to near identity in these joints with modern large apes. Increased body size and/or changing use of the forelimb led to reduction of the ulnar olecranon and styloid, presumably by the end of the middle Miocene. By this time, there was an apparently rapid diversification into four major lineages: ancestors of *Pongo* and of *Pan*, Sugrivapithecini, and early Homininae, whose later deployment is discussed below. At the same time, early pongines underwent selection for some facial elongation and concomitant(?) choanal deepening, reduction of canine honing, and such soft anatomical changes as further delay in ischial callosity development and increase in chromosome number. Together, these changes suggest some increased use of the terrestrial environment and reduction of dental display paraphernalia, as well as, perhaps, the beginnings of nest building (cercopithecid monkeys with callosities do not require sleeping nests, while nest-building apes have less callosity development). No dietary change is postulated at this point, in part because Kay (1977c) has shown that early Miocene *Dryopithecus* was (conservatively) rather frugivorous.

SUBFAMILY HYLOBATINAE
Gray, 1870

(= or including: Hylobatina Gray, 1870. Hylobatinae Gill, 1872. Hylobatidae Blyth, 1875. Pongidae Elliott, 1913: numerous authors, in part.)

DISTRIBUTION

Early middle Pleistocene to modern. Fossil in southern China, Indonesia; modern from southern China through Burma and Malaysia to Indonesia (most islands).

INCLUDED TAXA
Hylobates.

DISCUSSION

Although two or more genera of "lesser apes" are often recognized today, we follow Groves (1972) in accepting only one, with three subgenera. *Hylobates* is so distinctive in its postcranial locomotor and positional adaptations, as well as its ethology, that its cladistic separation from other hominids must be ancient, and thus it is given subfamily rank in a monotypic higher taxon.

HYLOBATES Illiger, 1811

(= or including: *Pithecus* E. Geoffroy and G. Cuvier, 1795, suppressed: Latreille, 1801. *Satyrus* Oken, 1816, work rejected. *Brachiopithecus* "Blainville": Gray, 1870. *Methylobates* Ameghino, 1882. All without clear types; see also under subgenera.)

DISTRIBUTION
  See under subfamily.
INCLUDED SUBGENERA
  Hylobates (Hylobates), H. (Symphalangus), and *H. (Nomascus).*

HYLOBATES (HYLOBATES) Illiger, 1811

(= or including: *Homo* Linnaeus, 1758: Linnaeus, 1771, in part. *Simia* Linnaeus, 1758, suppressed: Schreber, 1774, in part. *Cheiron* Burnett, 1828. *Bunopithecus* Matthew and Granger, 1923. *Brachytanytes* Schultz, 1932.)

DISTRIBUTION
  See under subfamily.
KNOWN SPECIES
  1. *Hylobates (H.) lar* (Linnaeus, 1771), type species
LOCALITIES: ?Punung (981); Niah (1234).
  2. *Hylobates (H.) hoolock* (Harlan, 1834)
(= *Bunopithecus sericus* Matthew and Granger, 1923. *Hylobates* sp.: Colbert and Hooijer, 1953.)
LOCALITIES: Yenchingkou I (831); ?Bama (850); Tungtzu (976); Dexingzhen (980); ?Hang Hum lower (1022); ?Keo Leng (1027).
  3. *Hylobates (H.) pileatus* (Gray, 1861)
  4. *Hylobates (H.) klossi* (Miller, 1903)

HYLOBATES (SYMPHALANGUS) Gloger, 1841

(= or including: *Siamanga* Gray, 1843.)

DISTRIBUTION
  Middle Pleistocene to modern. Fossil on Java, "subfossil" and living on Sumatra and western Malayan peninsula.
KNOWN SPECIES
  5. *Hylobates (S.) syndactylus* (Raffles, 1821)
LOCALITIES: Javanese middle Pleistocene (842); Punung (981); Sumatran "Holocene" (1256).

HYLOBATES (NOMASCUS) Miller, 1933

DISTRIBUTION
  ?Later middle Pleistocene to modern. Southern China, Laos, Vietnam.
KNOWN SPECIES
  6. *Hylobates (N.) concolor* (Harlan, 1826)
LOCALITIES: (cf.) Tham Khuyen (922); (cf.) Tham Om (923).

DISCUSSION

Hylobates includes a group of small to medium-sized hominids, morphologically rather conservative above the neck but strongly derived in their limbs. Groves (1972) provided the most complete review of all aspects of lesser ape morphology and systematics, and his results are generally accepted here. Frisch (1965, 1973) has discussed the dentition in the most detail, Vogel (1966) has considered the cranium, and Schultz (e.g., 1973), Tuttle (1972), and Andrews and Groves (1975) have described and analyzed the skeleton and locomotor adaptations; Delson and Andrews (1975) summarized data from all these accounts briefly.

The dentition of *Hylobates* (Figure 235) is in many ways little changed from that of early catarrhines, which led to the long association of pliopithecids with gibbons. Frisch (1965, 1973) took that relationship as given in his studies, which renders them somewhat less useful, but he was nonetheless able to discuss "trends" in hylobatine dental evolution which might be reinterpreted as intrageneric morphoclines. The teeth of *H. (S.) syndactylus*, illustrated here, were considered relatively conservative by Frisch. The incisors of *Hylobates* are generally low crowned, the lowers narrow, I^2 conical, and I^1 spatulate. The canines are very high crowned, but only moderately compressed, and there is little if any clear sexual dimorphism in size or shape. The upper canine hones strongly on the long mesiobuccal flange of the low but greatly compressed $P_{\overline{3}}$, whose long axis is nearly in line with that of the molars. The $P_{\overline{4}}$ is elongate, with no cingulum. The upper cheek teeth are quite narrow, often with little or no cingulum lingually. The paracone projects strongly on $P^{\underline{3}}$, which is, as usual, larger than P^4. The upper molars are relatively large compared to incisors contrasted with Pongini especially, paraconules are small or absent, cingulum is reduced or absent lingually, and $M^{\underline{3}}$ (with a reduced hypocone)

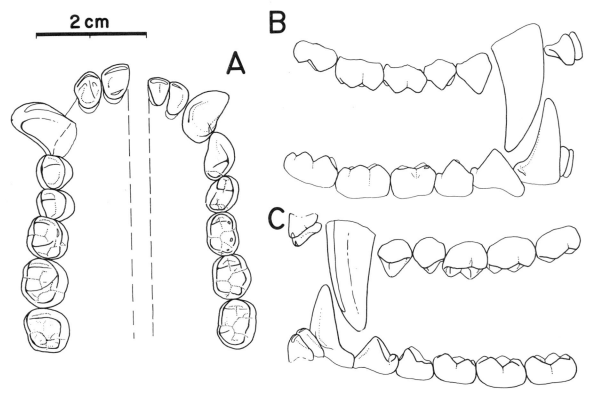

Figure 235. *Hylobates (Symphalangus) syndactylus.* Modern, Asia. Male dentition. A, right upper (to left) and lower tooth-rows, occlusal view; B, buccal view; C, lingual view. [By B. Akerbergs.]

is subequal in size to M^1. Upper molar breadth is moderate in *H. (Hylobates)*, but the teeth are elongated in *H. (Symphalangus)*, as otherwise found only in *Dryopithecus (Rangwapithecus)* among Hominidae. The lower molars are somewhat elongated teeth, with no cingulum [except in *H. (N) concolor*], and the cusps relatively high, but the ridges are not distinct or sharp. $M_{\overline{2}}$ is always the longest, but the relative lengths of $M_{\overline{1}}$ and $M_{\overline{3}}$ vary greatly among species and subspecies. The hypoconulid position on all three molars varies similarly, but this cusp is median at least as often as buccal, hardly ever lies in line with the other buccal cusps, and is often lacking, especially on $M_{\overline{3}}$ (again, see especially Frisch, 1973, 1965).

The mandibular symphysis and corpus are gracile, deepening mesially, with a relatively upright ramus; breadth across the canine region is relatively great, compared to that across the molars, among the Hominidae. The face is short and moderately wide,

the interorbital distance is great, and the nasals are short and wide, which are all states considered ancestral for catarrhines. The lacrimal fossa extends onto the maxilla, and there is never either a fronto-maxillary or an ethmoido-sphenoidal suture (the latter especially common in Pongini); the orbits are large with protruding, often thickened rims. The choanae are wide and low. The brain is larger than in monkeys, but may be rather conservative morphologically.

Postcranially, lesser apes share the basic distinguishing derived characters of modern pongines, as discussed under Hominidae. They have, however, adapted to a true brachiating mode of locomotion and its attendant positional behaviors, which have produced a number of uniquely derived character states of joint architecture (Figure 236A) and musculature (see Andrews and Groves, 1975, for a thorough review). The upper limb is not only long compared to the lower, but both are elongate compared to body

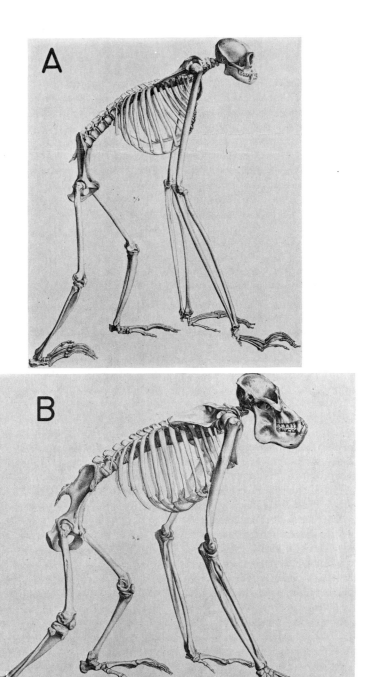

Figure 236. *Hylobates lar.* Modern, Asia. A, skeleton in right lateral view. *Pongo pygmaeus.* Modern, Asia. B, skeleton of male in right lateral view. [From de Blainville (1839).]

size, violating the allometric relationships between limb and trunk length generally found in catarrhines (Biegert and Maurer, 1972). Similarly, the hand is long, and the thumb, although not reduced, is short compared to palm length; moreover, thoracic breadth is much greater than would be expected from typical catarrhine allometry [compared to body size (Andrews and Groves, 1975)]. As discussed by Lewis (1972b), mobility of the wrist is especially high: There is a small meniscus between the reduced ulnar styloid and the carpals, but some direct articulation remains, with the addition of a lunula; in addition, the distal radius and ulnae are narrow, rather than expanded as in Pongini. The shoulder joint is also both mobile and muscularly stabilized, with long scapula and posteriorly facing humeral head. The long bones are gracile and not strongly muscle-marked, in part because of the small size of gibbons. Among soft anatomical characters of importance are the appearance of ischial callosities early in postnatal life [suggesting the presence of callosities early in catarrhine history, contrary to Groves (1972)] and a diploid chromosome number of 44 (ancestral for catarrhines?) in *H. (Hylobates)*, but higher in the other subgenera.

The fossil record of *Hylobates* is as sparse as that of most other living apes, with only scattered teeth known from China and Indonesia. Matthew and Granger's (1923) "genus" *Bunopithecus* is indistinguishable from *Hylobates*, and Groves (1972) has suggested that it might represent an extinct subspecies of *H. hoolock*, the closest in size and range. Specimens from other Chinese middle Pleistocene localities were reviewed by Delson (1977a), but without allocation to species—they might also be referable to *H. hoolock*. Hooijer (1960) reported numerous dental remains of *H. (S.) syndactylus* from Indonesia and rarer remains of *H. (Hylobates)*. Given this minimal record, no real patterns of distribution or morphological change in the genus can be suggested, although Groves (1972) has attempted some morphotype reconstructions (with which we are not in full agreement) based on character morphoclines. Tuttle (1972) also attempted to discern a pattern of locomotor evolution, especially of the extremities, in *Hylobates*, but was not fully successful. Both Delson and Andrews (1975) and, more clearly, Andrews and Groves (1975) have suggested the possibility that ancestral hylobatines were larger than modern forms, in large part because of their deviation from typical catarrhine allometry in limb length and

chest girth. The proportions of gibbons, once thus attained, might have been retained by the ancestors of *Hylobates* because of their functional advantage for brachiation, the development of which is clearly ancestral for the genus.

SUBFAMILY PONGINAE
Elliot, 1913

(= or including: Pithecidae Gray, 1821. Simiadae Fleming, 1822. Simiidae Bonaparte, 1850. Pongidae Elliot, 1913. Ponginae: Allen, 1925. Dryopithecinae Gregory and Hellman, 1939. Gigantopithecinae Gremyatskii, 1962. Gorillinae Hürzeler, 1968. Gorillidae: Verschuren, 1972. Paninae Delson, 1977b.)

DISTRIBUTION
    Early Miocene (Rusingan) to modern. Old World (eastern and central Africa, southern and central Europe, southern Asia).
INCLUDED TAXA
    Tribes Pongini, Dryopithecini, and Sugrivapithecini.

DISCUSSION

The Ponginae as recognized here is a paraphyletic subtaxon of the Hominidae, including all of its members except *Hylobates* and the closest relatives of *Homo* (*Australopithecus* and *Ramapithecus*). This approach is taken here in order to recognize the patristic "distinctiveness" of *Homo* and relatives at a moderate (subfamilial) rank. It is thus difficult to characterize the Ponginae, as it has been defined by the lack of the specializations of the extremities found in *Hylobates* or those of the Homininae (q.v.). All pongines do share relatively large canines whose honing function is less by comparison to hylobatines or primitive catarrhines, but even this feature is marginal in *Gigantopithecus*. The other main morphological complexes important in hominoid evolution (incisor size, cheek-tooth enamel thickness, interorbital and facial width, nasal length, brow ridge and sagittal crest development, mandibular proportions, ulnar olecranon reduction, and wrist and perhaps even shoulder morphology) are either strongly variable or not derived beyond the putative ancestral hominid conditions in this heterogeneous grouping of taxa, which are nonetheless clearly related.

In terms of evolutionary patterns, the Dryopithecini represent the most conservative subunit, probably little changed in fact from the ancestral Hominidae. They are ranked in this subfamily because they present no special relationships with the Hylobatinae, and, although there is no clear cladistic linkage, patristic ties are generally considered to be with the modern great apes (Andrews, 1973, 1976; Pilbeam, 1969). It is nonetheless entirely possible that the Hylobatinae are descended from a species comparable or identical to those now placed in *Dryopithecus*. The Pongini are in many features little changed from these ancestral conditions, at least in terms of their morphotype (Delson and Andrews, 1975; Delson *et al.*, 1977). The reduction in canine honing already present in *Dryopithecus* was carried further and size increased (probably independently) in *Pan* and *Pongo*. Because little is known of their fossil record, it is difficult to speculate on deployment (but see Kortlandt, 1972). The Sugrivapithecini are clearly derived in the direction of Homininae in terms of their increased molar enamel thickness, canine reduction, expansion of the $P_{\overline{3}}$ mesiobuccal corner, and increase of tooth size with respect to body size. Their overall patristic pattern is ape-like, however, and they are retained in this subfamily at present, although Pilbeam (in Pilbeam *et al.*, 1977) has suggested the possibility of grouping them taxonomically more closely with *Ramapithecus* and perhaps *Homo*. The fossil record suggests that *Dryopithecus* species departed Africa early in the middle Miocene, with *Sivapithecus* probably arising from isolated populations in Eurasian parkland habitats. The ancestors of *Pongo* (and perhaps even *Hylobates*) may also have migrated eastward at this time, while *Pan*'s forerunners remained in African forested environments (Andrews and Van Couvering, 1975; Andrews, 1976).

Tribe Pongini
Elliot, 1913

(= or including: Ponginae: Allen, 1925 and later authors.)

DISTRIBUTION
   Early Pleistocene to modern. Central Africa, southeastern Asia.
INCLUDED TAXA
   Pongo and *Pan*.

DISCUSSION

The Pongini includes all the living members of the Ponginae. These two genera have long been known as the closest living relatives of *Homo*, but the discovery of "intermediate" fossils has made their taxonomic placement subject to various interpretations. The results of diverse studies of genetic and other "molecular" characters in recent years have firmly established that *Pan* species are phenetically more similar and probably therefore more recently related to *Homo* than either is to *Pongo*, and thus the grouping of these two genera to the exclusion of "men" is paraphyletic, but such a step is taken here following Delson and Andrews (1975), Delson (1977b), and numerous other workers. On the other hand, *Pan* and *Pongo* do share a number of features which distinguish them from the more conservative *Dryopithecus* and *Hylobates*, and it may even be possible that the similarities between *Pan* and *Homo* do not reflect significantly closer cladistic (rather than patristic) affinity, given the phyletic position and zoogeographic implications of the Sugrivapithecini.

The Pongini may thus be defined by such derived features (see Andrews, 1973) as a general increase in the size of $I^{\underline{1}}$, with the lower incisor edges semicontinuous and all incisors somewhat procumbent; canines pointed and robust, not wearing through honing on $P_{\overline{3}}$–$C^{\underline{1}}$, but flatly at the tip or with a facet extending distally on $C^{\underline{1}}$; $P_{\overline{3}}$ slightly molarized, with a small lingual cuspule variably, oriented obliquely to the molar row, only slightly bilaterally compressed and not honing $C^{\underline{1}}$; the $P_{\overline{4}}$ slightly broad; upper cheek teeth relatively elongate, although width is generally still greater than length (see Mahler, 1973) and cingulum is reduced or absent; $P^{\underline{3}}$ larger than P^4 (as in other hominids) but $M^{\underline{1}}$ larger than $M^{\underline{3}}$ (both less than $M^{\underline{2}}$); on lower molars, cingulum reduced and occlusal ridges less distinct than in *Dryopithecus* (see Figure 237). The premaxilla in Pongini is elongated, the maxillary sinus is large, and the anterior palate is wide between the heavy canines; an inferior transverse mandibular torus ("simian shelf") is present but variable, and the mandible shallows posteriorly in general. The face is moderately high and long, with great depth in the maxilla and zygoma, the nasals are somewhat elongated, and the choanae are high and narrow (as in *Homo*). The brain is large, but a sagittal crest is present in larger males of both genera, with the main mass of temporalis placed rearward to give greatest leverage to the incisors. Postcranially, the pongins share the hominid features common to all genera except *Dryopithecus* in the shoulder, elbow, tail, and ankle; the wrist is derived, in adaptation to increased mobility, but different in the two genera (Lewis, 1972a,b); lumbar vertebrae are the fewest,

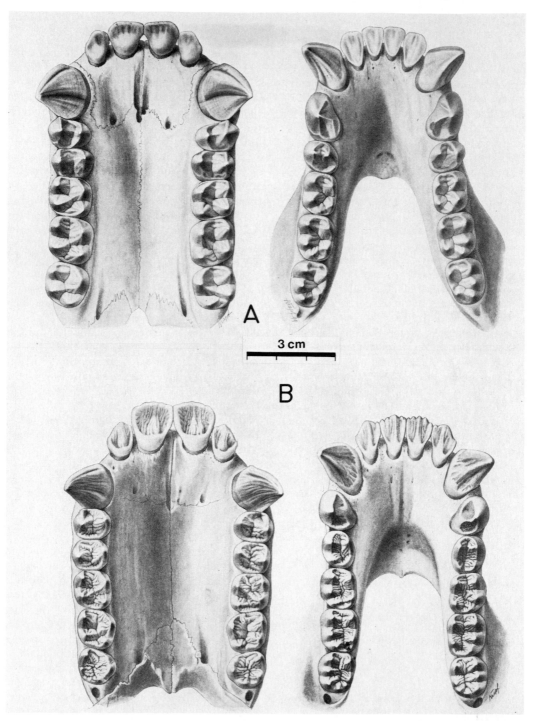

Figure 237. *Pan gorilla.* Modern, Africa. Male maxilla (to left) and mandible with complete dentition: A, occlusal view. *Pongo pygmaeus.* Modern, Asia. Male maxilla (to left) and mandible with complete dentition: B, occlusal view. [From Selenka (1899).]

sacrals the most numerous in the family (Schultz, 1968), the limbs long compared to body size but generally on the allometric trend for catarrhines [except for the elongated forelimb of *Pongo* (Figure 236B) (Biegert and Maurer, 1972)]. In terms of soft tissues, ischial callosities appear variably in later postnatal life in both genera, and the diploid chromosome number is 48,

which may have been ancestral for Ponginae (and Homininae), especially if *Pan* is phyletically closer to *Homo* than to *Pongo*.

As noted under the genera, little can be said about evolutionary history of the tribe because the fossil record of both genera is poor.

PONGO Lacépède, 1799

(= or including: *Simia* Linnaeus, 1758, in part; suppressed. *Papio:* Latreille, 1801, in part. *Pithecus* E. Geoffroy and G. Cuvier, 1795, suppressed: Cuvier, 1800. *Lophotus* Fischer, 1813. "Faunus" Oken, 1816, work rejected. *Brachiopithecus* Senechal, 1839. *Satyrus* Lesson, 1840: Mayer, 1856. ?"Metasimia" Ameghino, 1884, *nomen nudum*.)

DISTRIBUTION
  Early Pleistocene to modern. Fossil from South China to Borneo and Sumatra; living in Borneo and Java.
KNOWN SPECIES
  Pongo pygmaeus (Hoppius, 1763)
  (=*Pongo p. palaeosumatrensis* Hooijer, 1948. *P. p. weidenreichi* Hooijer, 1948.)
  LOCALITIES: Liucheng (784); Sangrian (834); Trinil (836); Bama (850); Tahsin (852); Hoshangtung (914); Hsingan E (918); Tham Khuyen (922); Tham Om (923); Tham Hai (924); Feishu (956); Liangfeng (964); Shaochun (966); Phnom Loang (967); Shuan (968); Tam Hang (970); Tam Pha Loi (972); Tungtzu (976); Punung (981); Hang Hum lower (1022); Hang Quit (1024); Houei Hoc (1026); Tung Lang (1028); ?Anyang (1071); Niah (1234); Sumatran "Holocene" (1256); Hang Hum upper (1260).

DISCUSSION

Pongo pygmaeus is a large pongin characterized by extreme occlusal wrinkling on the cheek teeth (see Figure 237B), large I¹, narrow interorbital distance, high orbits, nasal bones relatively long and narrow, weak supraorbital ridges, low and heavy zygoma,

rather flattened and vertical occiput, robust mandible, exceptional dimorphism in body size and cranial morphology, mobile wrist joint, and elongated forelimb. Compared to trunk length (Biegert and Maurer, 1972), the hindlimb is of the expected length following catarrhine allometric patterns, while the forelimb is rather longer, as a result of its extensive use in support and locomotion. *Pongo* is strongly frugivorous, as reflected in the low crown relief of its cheek teeth. These teeth are also extremely large by comparison to body size (Pilbeam and Gould, 1974), and the wrinkling may be an adaptation to further increase in functional area.

There is a relatively long but sparse fossil record, mostly consisting of isolated teeth, which documents the presence of *Pongo* in southern and central China from early Pleistocene to as late as 25,000 years ago, followed by a progressive restriction of its range to Indochina by 10,000 years ago and to Sumatra and Borneo today (Kahlke, 1972). Hooijer (1948) discussed large numbers of mostly isolated teeth from "Holocene" deposits in Indonesia, to which he gave subspecific recognition because of their large size, but Kahlke (1972) has considered that this distinction, as well as that of the large Chinese form, is unnecessary.

PAN Oken, 1816

(Synonymy under subgenera.)

DISTRIBUTION
  Modern. Central Africa.
INCLUDED SUBGENERA
  Pan (Pan) and *Pan (Gorilla)*.

PAN (PAN) Oken, 1816

(= or including: *Simia* Linnaeus, 1758, in part; suppressed. *Pithecus* E. Geoffroy and G. Cuvier, 1795, suppressed. *Troglodytes* E. Geoffroy, 1812, *nec* Vieillot, 1806. *Mimetes* Leach, 1820, *nec* Eschscholtz, 1818.

Theranthropus Brooks, 1828, not available? *Chimpansee* Voigt, 1831. *Anthropopithecus* de Blainville, 1839. *Hylanthropus* Gloger, 1841. *Pseudanthropus* Reichenbach, 1862; *Pseudoanthropus:* Schaufuss, 1875, lapsus. *Pongo* Haeckel, 1866, *nec* Lacépède, 1799. *Engeco* Haeckel, 1866. *Fsihego* De Pauw, 1905. *Boreopithecus* Friederichs, 1932. *Bonobo* Tratz and Heck, 1954.)

DISTRIBUTION
  Modern. Western central Africa, discontinuously from Guinea to Tanzania, concentrated around the Congo basin and the Guinea/Cameroon/Gabon regions.

KNOWN SPECIES
1. *Pan (P.) troglodytes* Gmelin, 1788, type species
2. *Pan (P.) paniscus* Schwarz, 1929

PAN (GORILLA) I. Geoffroy, 1852

[=or including: *Gorilla* I. Geoffroy, 1852. *Pseudogorilla* Elliot, 1913. *Pan (Gorilla):* Simonetta, 1957.]

DISTRIBUTION
Modern. Southern central Africa.
KNOWN SPECIES
3. *Pan (Gorilla) gorilla* (Savage and Wyman, 1847)
FOSSIL LOCALITIES: ?Kazinga (692).

DISCUSSION

Pan species are large to very large pongins which are more conservative than *Pongo pygmaeus.* The length of fore- and hindlimbs relative to trunk size is as predicted by the general catarrhine allometric trend, the apparent great length being due to large body size (Biegert and Maurer, 1972). Detailed morphological comparisons among the three species have not been seriously attempted recently, but there are studies of odontometrics. Numerous "biomolecular" studies have indicated closest phenetic relationship between *Pan* and *Homo*, with *Pongo* being the sister-taxon of that pair of living genera.

Pan (Gorilla) gorilla is the most folivorous species, as might be expected from its larger size; its teeth (Figure 237A) reflect this in higher crowns and greater development of occlusal ridges. It is also somewhat more conservative in its anterior dentition (conical I², rela-

tively smaller I¹). *Pan (P.) paniscus* is not well known in terms of dietary preference, but its dentition suggests frugivory, as seen in *P. troglodytes.* The fossil record of *Pan* is essentially nonexistent, although von Bartheld *et al.* (1970) have reported a partial incisor tentatively referred there. Kortlandt (1972, 1974) provided a discussion of possible evolutionary patterns in the genus, concentrating on ecology and zoogeography, but not morphology. Pilbeam and Gould (1974), among others, have shown that, as body size increases in *Pan* species, tooth area increases more rapidly than is predicted by allometric scaling (although simple ratios indicate the reverse). This may suggest that, as *Pan* increased in size from a presumably small ancestor, a greater dependence on folivory led to the very large teeth of gorillas, perhaps in part due to competition from Old World monkeys in the frugivorous niche. Studies in progress on *Pan paniscus* may reveal a series of morphoclines in *Pan* which could confirm or deny such a view.

Tribe Dryopithecini
Gregory and Hellman, 1939

(= or including: Dryopithecinae Gregory and Hellman, 1939, in part. Dryopithecini: Simonetta, 1957, in part. Sugrivapithecini Simonetta, 1957, in part. Dryopithecidae: Pilbeam, in Pilbeam *et al.,* 1977.)

DISTRIBUTION
Early to early late Miocene (Rusingan to Vallesian). Africa, Europe.
INCLUDED TAXA
Dryopithecus.

DRYOPITHECUS Lartet, 1856

(Synonymy under subgenera.)

DISTRIBUTION
Early to early late Miocene (Rusingan to Ternanian; Astaracian to Vallesian). Eastern Africa, central and western Europe.
INCLUDED SUBGENERA
Dryopithecus (Dryopithecus), D. (Proconsul), D. (Limnopithecus), and *D. (Rangwapithecus).*

DRYOPITHECUS (DRYOPITHECUS) Lartet, 1856

[= or including: *Hylobates* Illiger, 1811: Owen, in Kaup, 1861. *Semnopithecus* Desmarest, 1822: Kaup, 1861. *Paidopithex* Pohlig, 1895. *Pliohylobates* Dubois, 1895. *Anthropodus* Schlosser, 1901, *nec* Lapouge, 1894. *Neopithecus* Abel, 1902. *Hispanopithecus* Villalta and Crusafont, 1944. *Sivapithecus* Pilgrim, 1910: Villalta and Crusafont, 1944, in part. *Udabnopithecus* Burtschak-Abramovitsch and Gabachvili, 1950. *?Pliopithecus* Gervais, 1849: Hürzeler, 1954. *Rhenopithecus* von

Koenigswald, 1956. "Rahonapithecus" Crusafont and Hürzeler 1961, "possibly as subgenus": *nomen nudum. Dryopithecus (Hispanopithecus):* Crusafont and Hürzeler, 1961. *Dryopithecus (Dryopithecus):* Simons and Pilbeam, 1965.]

DISTRIBUTION
Late middle to early late Miocene (Astaracian to Vallesian). France, Spain, Germany, ?Austria, ?Czechoslovakia, ?Georgian S.S.R.
KNOWN SPECIES
1. *Dryopithecus (Dryopithecus) fontani* Lartet, 1856, type species
[=*Dryopithecus fontani* Lartet, 1856; Branco, 1897. *Hylobates fontani:* Owen in Kaup, 1861. *Paidopithex rhenanus* Pohlig, 1895. *Pliohylobates eppelsheimensis* Dubois, 1895. *Dryopithecus rhenanus:* Schlosser, 1901. *Dryopithecus "suevicus"* Koken, 1905, *nomen nudum.* "Dryopithecus germanicus" Abel, 1919. *Udabnopithecus garadziensis* Burtschak-Abramovitsch and Gabachvili, 1950. *Dryopithecus fontani carinthiacus* Mottl, 1957. *Dryopithecus "piveteaui"* Crusafont and Hürzeler, 1961,

nomen nudum. *Dryopithecus (Dryopithecus) fontani*: Simons and Pilbeam, 1965. *Dryopithecus (Dry.) fontani fontani carinthiacus*: Steininger, 1967, lapsus.]

LOCALITIES: La Grive (466); ?St. Stefan (470); St. Gaudens★ (486); ?Udabno (500); ?Eldar (502); Can Llobateres (510); ?Can Ponsic (512); Salmendingen (518); Trochtelfingen (520); Ebingen (524); ?Eppelsheim (526); Wissberg (536); Seu de Urgell (538).

2. *Dryopithecus (Dryopithecus) brancoi* (Schlosser, 1901)
[= *Semnopithecus* Kaup, 1861. *Dryopithecus fontani*: Schlosser, 1888, in part. *Dryopithecus fontani*: Branco, 1898, in part; Villalta and Crusafont, 1941, in part. *Anthropodus brancoi* Schlosser, 1901. *Neopithecus brancoi* Abel, 1902. *Dryopithecus rhenanus*: Remane, 1921, in part. *Dryopithecus brancoi*: Abel, 1931. *Semnopithecus eppelsheimensis* Haupt, 1935. *Hispanopithecus laietanus* Villalta and Crusafont, 1944; Crusafont, 1958; Crusafont and Golpe, 1973. *Sivapithecus occidentalis* Villalta and Crusafont, 1944. *?Pliopithecus eppelsheimensis*: Hürzeler, 1954. *?Pliopithecus brancoi*: Hürzeler, 1954. *Rhenopithecus eppelsheimensis* von Koenigswald, 1956. *Dryopithecus brancoi*: Simonetta, 1957. "*Rahonapithecus sabadellensis*" Crusafont and Hürzeler, 1961, *nomen nudum*. Dryopithecidos: Crusafont, 1965. *Dryopithecus (Dryopithecus) laietanus*: Simons and Pilbeam, 1965, in part. Anthropomorphe indet.: Zapfe, 1969.]

LOCALITIES: Can Mata I (468); Can Vila (478); Castel de Barbera (488); ?Mariatal (508); Can Llobateres (510); Can Ponsic (512); Salmendingen★ (518); ?Eppelsheim (526); Polinya 2 (534); Wissberg (536); La Tarumba I (548).

DRYOPITHECUS (PROCONSUL) Hopwood, 1933a

[= or including: *Dryopithecus*: Keith, 1932. *Proconsul* Hopwood, 1933a. *Xenopithecus* Hopwood, 1933a. *Limnopithecus* Hopwood, 1933a: Le Gros Clark and Leakey, 1951, Le Gros Clark, 1952, in part. *Sivapithecus* Pilgrim, 1910: Le Gros Clark and Leakey, 1951, in part. *Dryopithecus (Proconsul)*: Simons and Pilbeam, 1965. *Dryopithecus (Sivapithecus)*: Simons and Pilbeam, 1965, in part. *Kenyapithecus* L. Leakey, 1962: L. Leakey, 1967, 1968, in part. *Ramapithecus* Pilgrim, 1910: Pilbeam, 1969b, in part.]

DISTRIBUTION
Early and early middle Miocene (early Rusingan to early Ternanian). Kenya, Uganda.
KNOWN SPECIES
3. *Dryopithecus (Proconsul) africanus* (Hopwood, 1933a), subgeneric type
(= *Dryopithecus* sp.: Keith, 1932. *Proconsul africanus* Hopwood, 1933a. *Xenopithecus koruensis* Hopwood, 1933a; Hopwood, 1933b, in part. *Proconsul nyanzae* Le Gros Clark and Leakey, 1950: Le Gros Clark and Leakey, 1951, Le Gros Clark, 1952, in part. *Limnopithecus macinnesi* Le Gros Clark and Leakey, 1950: Le Gros Clark and Leakey, 1951, Le Gros Clark, 1952, in part. Cf. *Dryopithecus* cf. *africanus*: Andrews and Walker, 1976.)

LOCALITIES: Koru★ (394); Songhor (396); Rusinga (406); Mfwangano (408); ?Losidok (412); ?Moruarot (416); ?Maboko (440); ?Fort Ternan (462).

4. *Dryopithecus (Proconsul) nyanzae* (Le Gros Clark and Leakey, 1950)
[= *Proconsul africanus* Hopwood, 1933a: MacInnes, 1943, Le Gros Clark, 1952, in part. *Proconsul nyanzae* Le Gros Clark and Leakey, 1950. *Sivapithecus africanus* Le Gros Clark and Leakey, 1950, 1951, in part. *Dryopithecus (Proconsul) africanus* (Hopwood, 1933a): Simons and

Pilbeam, 1965. *Dryopithecus (Sivapithecus) sivalensis* (Lydekker, 1879): Simons and Pilbeam, 1965, in part. *Kenyapithecus africanus* (Le Gros Clark and Leakey, 1950); L. Leakey, 1967, 1968, in part. *Proconsul* sp.: L. Leakey, 1967. *Kenyapithecus wickeri* L. Leakey, 1962: L. Leakey, 1967, in part. *Ramapithecus punjabicus* (Pilgrim, 1910): Pilbeam, 1969b, in part. *Dryopithecus africanus*: Greenfield, 1972, 1973, in part. Cf. *Dryopithecus* cf. *nyanzae*: Andrews and Walker, 1976.]

LOCALITIES: Karungu (390); Rusinga★ (406); Mfwangano (408); Maboko (440); ?Fort Ternan (462).

5. *Dryopithecus (Proconsul) major* (Le Gros Clark and Leakey, 1950)
[= *Proconsul africanus* Hopwood, 1933a: Hopwood, 1933b, MacInnes, 1943, Le Gros Clark and Leakey, 1951, in part. *Proconsul major* Le Gros Clark and Leakey, 1950. *Proconsul nyanzae* Le Gros Clark and Leakey, 1950: Le Gros Clark and Leakey, 1951, Le Gros Clark, 1952, L. Leakey (in Bishop, 1958), in part. *Dryopithecus (Proconsul) major*: Simons and Pilbeam, 1965; Pilbeam, 1969b. *Dryopithecus (Proconsul) nyanzae*: Simons and Pilbeam, 1965, in part. *Kenyapithecus africanus* (Le Gros Clark and Leakey, 1950): L. Leakey, 1967, in part. *Dryopithecus nyanzae*: Madden, 1972.]

LOCALITIES: Koru (394); Songhor★ (396); Napak I, IV, V (402); Moroto II (404); Rusinga (406); Losidok (412); ?Moruarot (416); ?Maboko (440).

DRYOPITHECUS (LIMNOPITHECUS) Hopwood, 1933a, new rank

[= or including: *Limnopithecus* Hopwood, 1933a. *Pliopithecus* (Gervais, 1849) (*Propliopithecus*) Schlosser, 1910: Simonetta, 1957, in part. *Pliopithecus (Limnopithecus)*: Simons, 1965. *Victoriapithecus* von Koenigswald, 1969, in part.]

DISTRIBUTION
Early and early middle Miocene (early Rusingan to early Ternanian). Kenya and Uganda.
KNOWN SPECIES
6. *Dryopithecus (Limnopithecus) legetet* (Hopwood, 1933a), subgeneric type, new combination
[= *Limnopithecus legetet* Hopwood, 1933a. *Limnopithecus evansi* MacInnes, 1943. *Limnopithecus macinnesi* Le Gros Clark and Leakey, 1950: Le Gros Clark and Leakey, 1951, in part. *Pliopithecus (Propliopithecus) legetet*: Simonetta, 1957. *Victoriapithecus macinnesi* von Koenigswald, 1969, in part. Cf.: (cf. *Limnopithecus* sp.) Fleagle, 1975; Cf. *Limnopithecus legetet*: Andrews and Walker, 1976.]

LOCALITIES: Bukwa (388); Koru★ (394); Songhor (396); ?Napak IV (402); Rusinga (406); Loperot (410); Ombo (414); Maboko (440); ?Fort Ternan (462).

DRYOPITHECUS (RANGWAPITHECUS) Andrews, 1974

[= or including: *Xenopithecus* Hopwood, 1933a: MacInnes, 1943, in part. *Proconsul* Hopwood, 1933a: Le Gros Clark and Leakey, 1951, in part. *Limnopithecus* Hopwood, 1933a: Le Gros Clark and Leakey, 1951, in part. *Sivapithecus* Pilgrim, 1910: Le Gros Clark and Leakey, 1951, in part. *Kenyapithecus* L. Leakey, 1962: L. Leakey, 1967, in part. *Dryopithecus (Rangwapithecus)* Andrews, 1974. *Proconsul (Rangwapithecus)*: Andrews (1976) *Rangwapithecus*: Pilbeam *et al.*, 1977.]

DISTRIBUTION
Early and early middle Miocene. Kenya.
KNOWN SPECIES
7. *Dryopithecus (Rangwapithecus) gordoni* Andrews, 1974, subgeneric type
[= *Xenopithecus koruensis* Hopwood, 1933a: MacInnes, 1943, in part.

Proconsul africanus Hopwood, 1933a: Le Gros Clark and Leakey, 1951, Le Gros Clark, 1952, L. Leakey, 1967, in part. *Proconsul nyanzae* Le Gros Clark and Leakey, 1950: Le Gros Clark and Leakey, 1951, Le Gros Clark and Leakey, 1952, in part. *Limnopithecus macinnesi* Le Gros Clark and Leakey, 1950: Le Gros Clark and Leakey, 1951, Le Gros Clark, 1952, in part. *Sivapithecus africanus* Le Gros Clark and Leakey, 1950: Le Gros Clark and Leakey, 1951, in part. *Kenyapithecus africanus* (Le Gros Clark and Leakey, 1950): L. Leakey, 1967, in part. *Proconsul* sp.: Andrews, 1970.]
LOCALITIES: Songhor⋆ (396); Rusinga (406); Mfwangano (408).

8. *Dryopithecus (Rangwapithecus) vancouveringi* Andrews, 1974 (= or including: *Limnopithecus macinnesi* Le Gros Clark and Leakey, 1950: Le Gros Clark and Leakey, 1951, in part.)
LOCALITIES: Songhor (396); Rusinga⋆ (406); Mfwangano (408); Maboko (440).

DISCUSSION

Dropithecus (sensu lato) is one of the most widespread and widely discussed fossil primates, the subject of several revisions and innumerable short comments or descriptive notes. Much new material has only been partly described, and the recognition of the distinctions of *Sivapithecus* and allies has led to a major reorganization of the Miocene hominids. Here, eight species of *Dryopithecus* are arranged in four subgenera, a classification implying less diversity than other recent attempts. As thus envisioned, the genus *Dryopithecus* is difficult to diagnose on the basis of shared derived characters, but that will be attempted first, for the most part following Andrews (1973). Each subgenus and its included species can then be similarly diagnosed and briefly analyzed in turn, leading eventually to a discussion of generic distinctions, phylogeny, and paleobiology.

Dryopithecus species range in dental size from somewhat smaller than the small *Hylobates* to nearly as large as female *Pan gorilla*. The incisors are less stout, relatively higher crowned and more vertical than in *Pan* or *Pongo,* but relatively larger than in Sugrivapithecini; the canines also are less robust than in modern apes, but relatively more so than those of sugrivapithecins. Crown height, bilateral compression, and honing development of canines and $P_{\overline{3}}$ are variable, but generally intermediate again between the modern forms and *Sivapithecus* or *Gigantopithecus*; a diastema between C^1 and I^2 is present, but it is small, especially because of incisor verticality, while none is present between $C_{\overline{1}}$ and $P_{\overline{3}}$. The cheek teeth are more usually partly surrounded by cingulum than in other pongine genera, especially buccally on lowers and

lingually on uppers; the upper premolars are generally broad, the molars high-cusped and elongated, especially the lowers. In contrast to *Gigantopithecus*, the teeth are smaller, more elongated, and less crowded, and the cusps are somewhat higher in most forms. *Dryopithecus* is distinguished from *Sivapithecus* (and also from *Gigantopithecus*, *Ramapithecus*, and *Australopithecus*) especially by its thinner cheek-tooth enamel covering, leading to relatively rapid wear of circular dentine pockets and associated with low, flat crowns. In addition, the $P_{\overline{3}}$ is oval shaped, with no mesiobuccal expansion, and seldom if ever presents more than one cusp. As compared to *Ramapithecus* and later hominines, the canines of *Dryopithecus* are tall and robust, even if not fully honing.

The mandible is well known in the several species (e.g., Figure 243), with a moderately deep corpus of relatively constant depth, lacking a simian shelf (an inferior transverse torus is rare, the superior transverse torus well developed); the symphyseal region is generally narrow, the tooth-rows are somewhat more divergent than in modern apes, and the ramus is often subvertical. Only one cranium and a few facial fragments are known (Figure 238), rendering generalization difficult, but brow ridges were weak or absent, the face was moderately projecting, the maxillary sinus was less extensive than in Pongini, a frontal sinus was present where the site is preserved, the external auditory meatus was tubular, and the brain (Radinsky, 1974) was gibbon-like and of a size comparable to apes of similar mass. The postcranial elements are generally similar to those of larger platyrrhines, with no terrestrial specializations and few synapomorphies with those of *Pan* or *Pongo*. The ulnar olecranon is long to moderate, as is the styloid; the wrist, elbow, and ankle joints are basically similar to those of cercopithecids (especially arboreal forms), while the proximal femur is morphometrically like that of monkeys and *Hylobates* (reviewed by Corruccini *et al.,* 1976; also O'Connor, 1976). There may also be some superficial resemblance of the humeral and femoral shafts to those of chimpanzees, although the latter are more robust. A facet for the prehallux is present on the only known hallucial metatarsal, as in *Propliopithecus, Hylobates,* and some atelids, but not other catarrhines. The long bones are metrically comparable to those of living apes of similar dental size, which implies that cheek teeth are not enlarged by comparison to body size, as in Sugrivapithecini and early hominines.

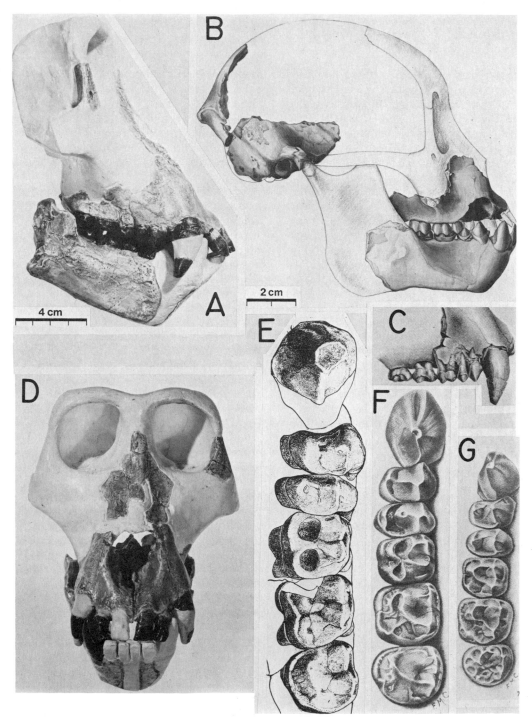

Figure 238. *Dryopithecus (Proconsul)* spp. Early Miocene, Africa. *D. major*. Reconstruction of male face and mandible (by D. Pilbeam): A, right lateral view; D, frontal view; E, left C¹–M³ of same individual (reversed from right), occlusal view. *D. africanus*. Reconstruction of subadult ?female cranium: B, right lateral view. Left ?male C¹ M³ of maxilla: G, occlusal view. *D. nyanzae*. Reconstruction of male maxilla with C¹–M³: C, right lateral view (reversed from left); F, left occlusal view. E–G to uniform scale. [A, D, E courtesy of and © D. Pilbeam: B from Davis and Napier (1963), courtesy of J. R. Napier; C, F, G from Le Gros Clark and Leakey (1951) by permission of the Trustees of the British Museum (Natural History).]

Dryopithecus is distinguished from the pliopithecids by its reduced canine–premolar honing complex, less-developed occlusal ridges, and/or more buccally placed hypoconulid, more chimp-like facial construction, somewhat longer upper cheek teeth, and tubular auditory meatus. At present, there is little to set it clearly apart postcranially (see Figure 244), except for the somewhat greater robusticity of its long bones and perhaps partial reduction of the olecranon process. From *Hylobates*, *Dryopithecus* differs in its wider, more cingulated upper cheek teeth, reduced canine honing, usually longer face, and lack of any postcranial specializations for brachiation.

As can be seen from the extensive synonymies, the study of *Dryopithecus* and related forms was long hampered by the tendency to assign new specific and generic names to each new specimen or small group of fossils showing slight differences from those which the describer chose for comparison. This situation was greatly clarified by Simons and Pilbeam (1965), who personally studied almost all of the then-known specimens and consolidated many species into three subgenera of *Dryopithecus: D. (Dryopithecus)* in Eurasia, *D. (Proconsul)* in Africa, and *D. (Sivapithecus)* in Asia and perhaps Africa. Some of this consolidation had been previously suggested by such authors as Lewis (1937) and Le Gros Clark and Leakey (1951), but it was formalized, documented, and, most important, presented in a generally acceptable fashion by Simons and Pilbeam. In the interim, various authors proposed new species (often with little documentation), Pilbeam (1969b) and Andrews (1973) reviewed the African forms, and Andrews (1974) formally proposed a new subgenus for two new species of East African *Dryopithecus*.

Recently, several authors have shown that a group of Eurasian species share a complex of derived dental features, especially thick cheek-tooth enamel, not found in *Dryopithecus* or Pongini. Some of these had been included previously in *Dryopithecus* but are treated here as the genus *Sivapithecus* (see that genus for details). In addition to that transfer, Andrews (1976) has suggested reelevating *Proconsul* to genus rank, with *P. (Rangwapithecus)* as a subgenus. He also recognized *Limnopithecus*, for a total of three dryopithecin genera. Most recently, Pilbeam *et al.* (1977) ranked *Rangwapithecus* as a genus. The known differences among the four genus–group taxa appear to be similar in degree, and the diversity is not sufficient

to recognize four full genera, so that we accept here only one genus, *Dryopithecus*, with four subgenera to receive eight species. When all known specimens have been published in detail, the number of taxa may change slightly, and it may be possible to link known forms differently, within a general framework of Neogene, non-gibbon "apes"; some problems are suggested below. Each recognized subgenus will now be briefly typified, its species, morphology, and adaptations discussed, and its differences from other forms indicated. As before, many of these data derive from Andrews (1973, 1976, and personal communications).

Dryopithecus (Limnopithecus) legetet (Figure 239) was originally considered a gibbon relative or ancestor (Le Gros Clark and Leakey, 1951), partly because of its small size and partly due to superficial similarities in the teeth. Andrews (1973) showed, however, that it was clearly different from *Hylobates* and linked to *Dryopithecus* (in which genus he tentatively placed it) by its reduced canine honing complex; Ferembach (1958) had made a similar suggestion from study of many fewer specimens. Among the major dental characteristics of this species are broad incisors of moderate height, the I^1 spatulate; canines moderately tall, without clear sexual dimorphism, the P_3 not sectorial and both $C_{\overline{1}}$ and $P_{\overline{3}}$ appearing to lean mesiad; $P_{\overline{4}}$ elongate, with a weak buccal cingulum; P^3 moderately wide with almost no cingulum, subequal cusps, and larger size than P^4; upper molars moderately broad, with strong lingual cingulum and a distinct paraconule, the main cusps placed near the crown margins; M^2 the largest tooth, with a large hypocone, M^3 slightly larger than M^1 and with a small hypocone (and metacone?) but a strong distolingual cingulum; lower molars not elongate, lacking clear talonid ridges, the talonid wider than the trigonid and the hypoconulid relatively medial (especially on $M_{\overline{1}}$, less distad); $M_{\overline{3}}$ somewhat longer than $M_{\overline{1}}$ ($M_{\overline{2}}$ widest but intermediate in length). The mandibular symphysis has a strong superior torus and lacks an inferior one; no ramus is known. Fleagle (1975) has described a palate and lower face of a small ape which probably is best considered *D. (L.)* cf. *legetet* (Figure 239, D and F), although no comparable anatomy is known from Kenya. Fleagle demonstrated that the specimen is the most similar to *Hylobates* of all known fossils, but the reconstruction offered may be biased by this view and the lack of upper facial remains. The Napak frontal identified as a cercopithecid by Pilbeam and Walker

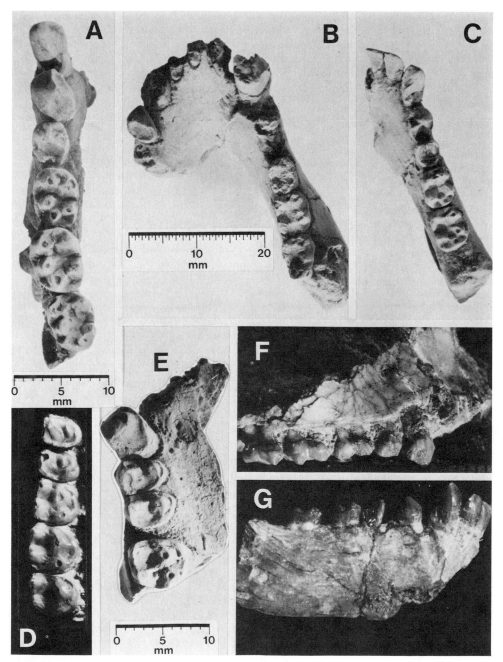

Figure 239. *Dryopithecus (Limnopithecus) legetet.* Early–middle Miocene, Africa. Right corpus with $C_{\overline{1}}$–$M_{\overline{3}}$, cf. *D. legetet:* A, occlusal view. Male mandible with left $P_{\overline{3}}$, right $C_{\overline{1}}$, and $M_{\overline{1-3}}$: B, occlusal view. Female right corpus with $I_{\overline{1}}$–$M_{\overline{2}}$: C, occlusal view; G, lateral view. Portion of palate with right $P^{\underline{3}}$–$M^{\underline{3}}$ visible, cf. *D. legetet:* D, occlusal view; F, lateral view. Right maxilla with $C^{\underline{1}}$–$M^{\underline{1}}$, ?male: E, occlusal view. The scale on B, smallest divisions being 0.5 mm, is for B–D, F, and G; the scales on A and E have 1-mm divisions. [A–C, E, G courtesy of P. Andrews.]

(1968) probably represents the same taxon. Further study is required to determine the allometric relationship between facial length and body size before phyletic links to gibbons are stressed. Nonetheless, facial distinctions apparently do separate *D. (Limnopithecus)* from *D. (Proconsul)* (see below). No limb bones attributed to *D. legetet* have been published, but Andrews (personal communication) indicated that the astragalus is similar to that of *D. africanus.*

The subgenus *D. (Proconsul)* is the best known of all *Dryopithecus,* among the best for all higher primates, being represented by hundreds of jaws and teeth, parts of three crania (one with an associated forelimb), and numerous other postcrania. Three species are recognized, of which the larger two are allopatric, differing mainly in size, and more closely related to one another than to the third, *D. africanus.* As a unit, all three share the following (Figures 238–242): Low crowned incisors, the I^1 spatulate; canines moderate to high crowned and not much bilaterally compressed; $P_{\overline{3}}$ low, not "sectorial"; upper premolars broad, with no lingual cingulum, $P^{\underline{3}}$ with relatively tall paracone, larger than P^4; upper molars much broader than long, with distinct occlusal ridges, usually distinct paraconule, strong lingual cingulum, and moderate occlusal crenulation; $M^{\underline{3}}$ slightly to much larger than $M^{\underline{1}}$, with some distal cingulum and often reduced distal cusps; lower molars with strong buccal cingulum, the $M_{\overline{1}}$ broad with nearly median hypoconulid, changing to $M_{\overline{3}}$ elongate, with enlarged buccal hypoconulid; mandibular body of moderate, constant depth, the ramus nearly vertical, the symphysis with massive superior transverse torus and inferiorly directed genial pit, but no inferior torus.

Dryopithecus africanus is known from distorted portions of two probably female crania, described by Le Gros Clark and Leakey (1951) (see Figure 240) and Napier and Davis (1959) and then reconstructed by Davis and Napier (1963) (see Figure 238B). The resulting skull is rather gracile and quite orthognathous, with no brow-ridge development, light zygomatic arch, slightly inclined ramus, pronounced inion, large, rectangular orbits and wide interorbital pillar, pneumatized mastoid, and distinct tubular external auditory meatus. A partial face of *D. major* from Uganda was described by Pilbeam (1969), who has kindly permitted the presentation here of previously unpublished reconstructions (Figure 238, A and D); although rather larger, this face also is relatively or-

thognathous, with slight brow ridges and wide orbits, and the specimen also preserves indications of a frontal sinus, otherwise known only in *Pan* species. Only part of a damaged lower face of *D. nyanzae* (the holotype, restored in Figure 238C) is known. Radinsky (1974) redescribed the endocast of *D. africanus,* considering it much like that of *Hylobates,* except for the lack of a frontal sulcus, but definitely not cercopithecid in form or grade.

Postcranial elements of *D. (Proconsul)* species are also mostly allocated to *D. africanus* and have been described by Le Gros Clark and Leakey (1951), Napier and Davis (1959), Walker and Rose (1968), Preuschoft (1973), and Andrews and Walker (1976) (Figure 244). Numerous authors have hotly contested the functional interpretation of locomotor adaptations of these remains, from comparative anatomical and morphometric points of view. The latter group have been summarized by Corruccini *et al.* (1976), who concluded that, in all studied joint systems and proportions, *D. (Proconsul)* is phenetically similar to platyrrhine (and some catarrhine) palmigrade, quadrupedal monkeys, rather than to anthropomorph brachiators or knuckle-walkers as others had asserted. Based on a study of casts, Lewis (1972a) suggested that *D. africanus* was a "brachiator" (in the loosest sense of the term), in that its wrist demonstrated ulnar styloid reduction and other features found in modern *Pan* and *Pongo* species.

Morbeck (1977, summarizing other anatomical studies) showed that the casts do not accurately preserve certain morphological details, and both she and O'Connor (1976) reaffirmed the original view of Napier and Davis (1959) that *D. africanus* was probably a quadruped similar in many aspects of locomotion to *Ateles* (but with a nonprehensile tail) or some arboreal cercopithecids. On the other hand, they have not apparently questioned Lewis's view that the distal ulna of *D. africanus* was more "ape-like" than that of *Hylobates,* while the distal humerus and proximal femur of *D. (Proconsul)* may also share some features with *Hylobates* (Corruccini *et al.,* 1976) or *Pan* species (Napier and Davis, 1959). In the proximal ulna, at least, there is much variation among early Miocene fossils (see also Preuschoft, 1973). Three figured specimens document the diversity: the damaged ulna of the *Dendropithecus* forelimb, with an apparently well-developed olecranon (Figure 244C); an isolated specimen, probably of *D. africanus* or *D. gordoni,* with

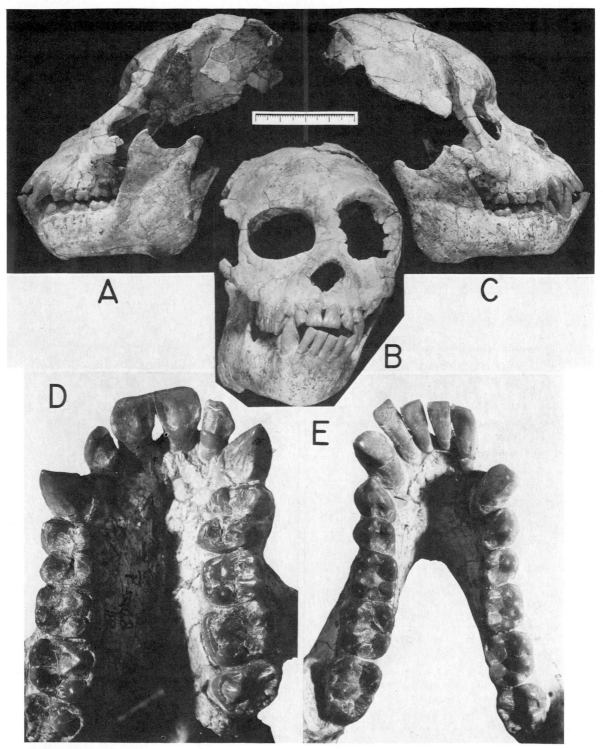

Figure 240. *Dryopithecus (Proconsul) africanus.* Early Miocene, Africa. Cranium and mandible of young male, deformed: A, left lateral view; B, right lateral view; C, frontal view; D, palate with complete dentition; E, mandible with complete dentition, except right C_T. Smallest scale divisions are in millimeters. [Courtesy of and © by the Trustees of the British Museum (Natural History).]

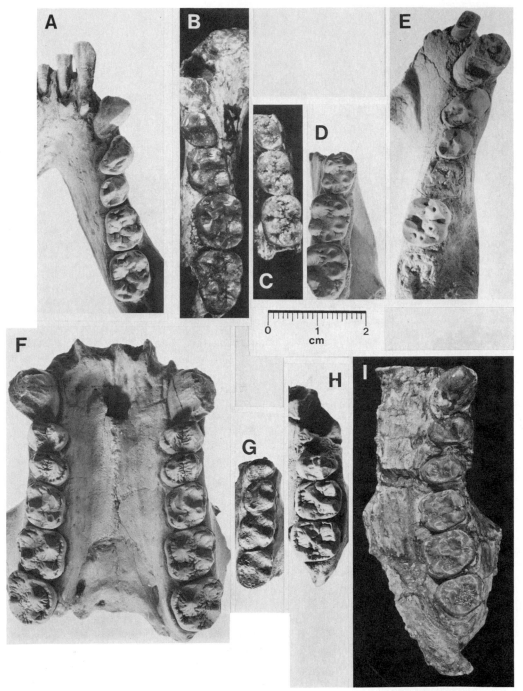

Figure 241. *Dryopithecus.* Early Miocene, Africa. Occlusal views of dentitions of medium-sized species. *D. (Proconsul) africanus:* A, subadult ?female mandible with right $I_{\overline{1}}$–$M_{\overline{2}}$; B, ?male left corpus with $P_{\overline{3}}$–$M_{\overline{3}}$; H, subadult ?female left maxilla with $P^{\underline{4}}$–$M^{\underline{2}}$; I, male maxilla with left $C^{\underline{1}}$–$M^{\underline{3}}$. *D. (Rangwapithecus) gordoni:* C, left $P_{\overline{4}}$–$M_{\overline{2}}$; D, right $M_{\overline{1-3}}$; E, male right corpus with $C_{\overline{1}}$–$P_{\overline{4}}$ and $M_{\overline{2-3}}$; F, male palate with right and left $C^{\underline{1}}$–$M^{\underline{3}}$. *D. (R.) vancouveringi:* G, left maxilla with $P^{\underline{4}}$–$M^{\underline{3}}$. Scale applies to all parts. [Courtesy of P. Andrews.]

478

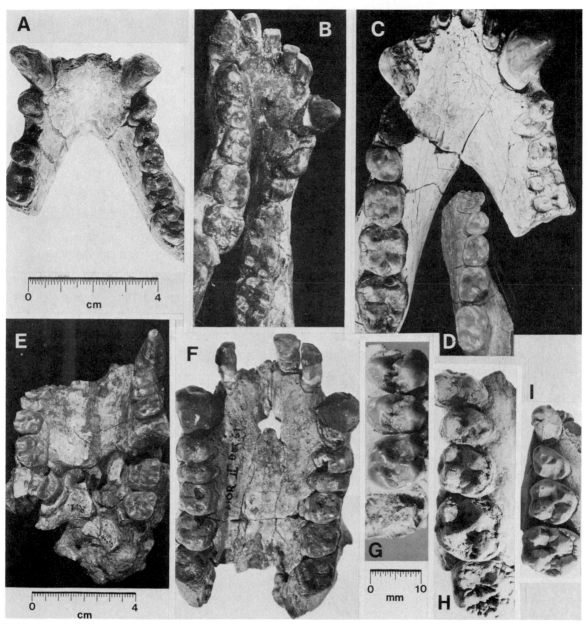

Figure 242. *Dryopithecus.* Early Miocene, Africa. Occlusal views of larger species. *D. nyanzae:* A, male mandible with left $C_{\overline{1}}$–$M_{\overline{2}}$ (part) and right $C_{\overline{1}}$–$M_{\overline{3}}$; B, distorted male mandible with complete dentition; E, crushed male palate with right P^3–M^3 and left C^1–M^3; G, left P^3–M^1 (*"Sivapithecus africanus"*); H, right P^3–M^3 (erupting). *D. major:* C, male mandible with right $C_{\overline{1}}$, left $P_{\overline{4}}$–$M_{\overline{3}}$, and most other roots; D, right corpus with $P_{\overline{4}}$–$M_{\overline{3}}$; F, male palate lacking only right I^1; I, juvenile right maxilla with dC^1–dP^4 and M^1. The scale on A is for A and B; the scale on E is for E and F; the scale on G is for C and G–I. [A–F, H, I, courtesy of P. Andrews.]

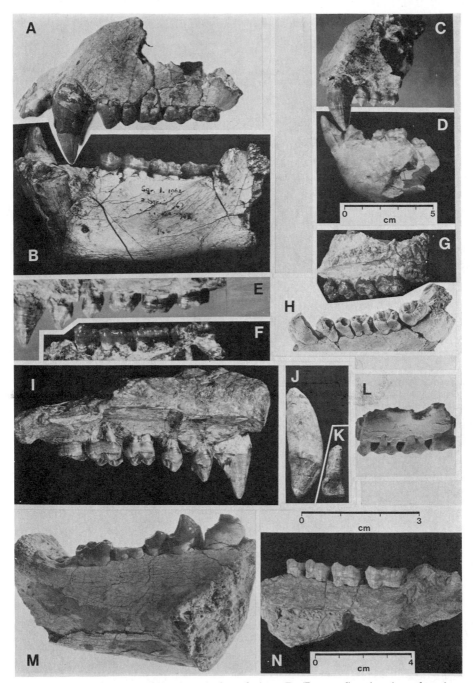

Figure 243. *Dryopithecus*, Early Miocene, Africa. Jaws in lateral view. *D. (Proconsul) major:* A, male palate with complete dentition, left buccal; B, mandible with left $P_{\overline{4}}$–$M_{\overline{3}}$ and right $C_{\overline{1}}$, left buccal; N, right corpus with $P_{\overline{4}}$–$M_{\overline{3}}$, lingual. *D. (Proconsul) nyanzae:* C, male palate with left C–$M^{\underline{1}}$, displaced $M^{\underline{2-3}}$, buccal; D, mandible with left $C_{\overline{1}}$, $P_{\overline{3}}$, and $M_{\overline{2}}$, buccal (some right teeth visible also); H, right $C_{\overline{1}}$–$M_{\overline{3}}$ from same mandible, oblique lingual; G, right $P^{\underline{3}}$–$M^{\underline{3}}$ (erupting), lingual; J, left $C^{\underline{1}}$ of same individual, lingual; K, left $I^{\underline{1}}$ of same individual, lingual. *D. (Proconsul) africanus:* E, left $C^{\underline{1}}$–$M^{\underline{3}}$ of male maxilla, buccal; I, same maxilla, lingual; F, left $P_{\overline{4}}$–$M_{\overline{3}}$, buccal. *D. (Rangwapithecus) vancouveringi:* L, left maxilla with $P^{\underline{4}}$–$M^{\underline{3}}$, buccal. *D. (Rangwapithecus) gordoni:* M, left corpus with $C_{\overline{1}}$–$P_{\overline{4}}$ and $M_{\overline{2}}$, lingual. The scale between L and N is for E–M; A, B, and N are at ¾ that scale, roughly. The scale on D is for C and D. [A, B, E, G–N, courtesy of P. Andrews.]

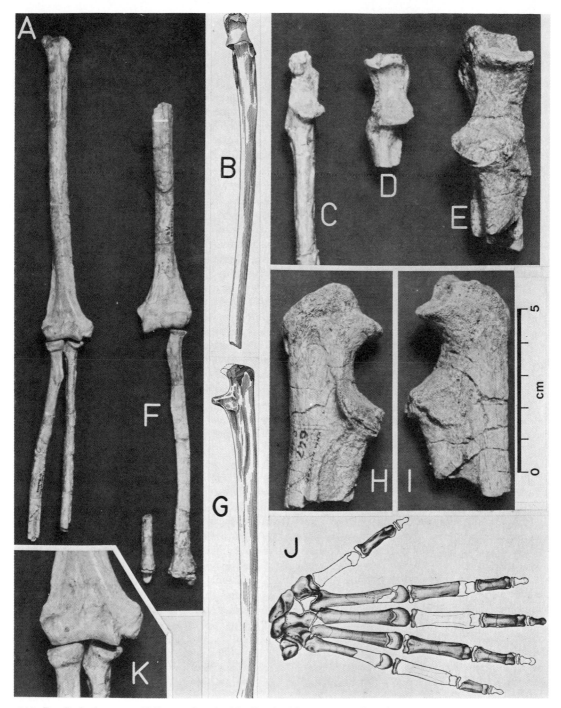

Figure 244. Forelimb elements of Miocene hominoids. *Dendropithecus macinnesi.* Early Miocene, Africa (see also Figure 234). Associated right humerus, ulna, and radius in anterior view: A, three bones in quasianatomical relationship; C, proximal ulna; K, close-up of elbow joint. ?*Sivapithecus darwini.* Middle Miocene, Europe. Partially restored left ulna: B, anterior view; G, lateral view. *Dryopithecus (Proconsul) africanus.* Early Miocene, Africa. Associated forelimb of subadult female: F, left humerus, distal ulna, and radius in quasianatomical position, anterior view; J, restored left hand, palmar view. Tentatively referred proximal end of right ulna (or possibly *D. gordoni?*): D, anterior view. ?*Dryopithecus (Proconsul)* cf. *nyanzae* (or *major?*). Early Miocene, Africa. Proximal end of left ulna: E, anterior view; H, medial view; I, lateral view. The scale is for C–E, H, I, and K; A, B, F, G, and J are ½ that scale. [A, C–F, H, I, K courtesy of and © R. L. Ciochon; B, G from Zapfe (1961a); J from Napier and Davis (1959) by permission of the Trustees of the British Museum (Natural History).]

a strongly reduced olecranon (Figure 244D); and a much larger specimen (Figure 244, E, H, and I) which could be cercopithecid, but no cercopithecids of this size are known, nor is any monkey tooth definitely from Rusinga. If the large ulna represents *D. major*, it had a very different locomotor repertoire than did *D. africanus*, to say the least. Finally, Lewis (1972b) showed that the *D. africanus* hallucial metatarsal retains a prehallux facet, as otherwise found only in some platyrrhines, *Hylobates*, and *Propliopithecus zeuxis* (Conroy, 1976b) among Anthropoidea. Further analysis is required to determine whether *D. (Proconsul)* species share any specifically derived character states with modern apes, but none has been identified to date.

The subgenus *D. (Rangwapithecus)* was formally named by Andrews (1974) to receive two new species of early Miocene ape, including a palate described by Andrews (1970). *Dryopithecus gordoni* and *D. vancouveringi* differ essentially in size, as do *D. major* and *D. nyanzae*, but the former pair are sympatric. *Dryopithecus gordoni* includes mandibles and maxillae (Figures 241 and 243), numerous teeth, and perhaps a few postcranial elements, and most of the subgeneric characters are drawn from this species, as *D. vancouveringi* is known by only ten specimens of upper teeth. Diagnostic features include the following: incisors high crowned and narrow, the I^1 spatulate but narrow; canines moderately bilaterally compressed and tall but quite long, so that relative crown height is low; P_3 strongly compressed and tall, possibly honing C^1; P_4 elongated, with slight buccal cingulum, but quite small compared to P_3 (Figure 243M); upper cheek teeth relatively elongate for *Dryopithecus* species, often longer than broad, low cusped and with much enamel wrinkling; P^3 molarized, smaller than P^4 and with less cingulum; molars increase in size distad, the M^1 always longer than broad, with larger, nearly central protocone, hypocone well distal to metacone and massive cingulum, M^{2-3} sometimes slightly broader than long, M^3 with well-developed, somewhat buccal hypocone; lower molars also elongate, with low cusps, the buccal ones separated by deep buccal grooves and notches, buccal cingulum slight, wrinkling common, size increasing distad. The mandibular body and symphysis are relatively deep and robust, with a strong superior transverse torus and no inferior torus; the root of the zygomatic process is low, laterally expanded, and placed above M^{1-2}, and the floor of the

maxillary sinus is greatly expanded. Both upper and lower molars present a marked wear gradient.

The type species of *Dryopithecus*, *D. (D.) fontani*, is one of the least well known, definitely including only several mandibles, a humerus, and a few isolated teeth from France and Spain (Figure 245). Several other groups of mostly isolated teeth from central and eastern Europe have been referred to *D. fontani*, for the most part correctly. Some of these teeth, however, especially the type series of *Dryopithecus darwini*, are large and have the thick enamel which typifies *Sivapithecus*, into which they are placed here even though their paleoenvironment was rather heavily forested (see Delson, 1975b) and not the open country considered characteristic for *Sivapithecus* (Andrews, 1976). A smaller European species, *D. (D.) laietanus* of Simons and Pilbeam (1965), is represented by numerous jaws and teeth from Spain, mostly unpublished in any detail (Figure 246), and also perhaps by fragmentary central European specimens. The isolated M_3 holotype of "*Anthropodus*" *brancoi* (Figure 246F) appears to be referable to the same species and bears the senior nomen, as also suggested by Simons (1972). Several jaws from the Siwaliks have been referred to this species. as well as to *Ramapithecus*, but they seem to share the diagnostic features of *Sivapithecus*. Andrews (1976) suggested this latter identification for the Spanish material also, but they show the *Dryopithecus* wear pattern of thin enamel. Postcranial elements allocated to *D. (Dryopithecus)* are limited to a juvenile humerus from the type locality (Pilbeam and Simons, 1971) and a femur from Germany (see Le Gros Clark and Leakey, 1951); the femur has recently been studied morphometrically by McHenry and Corruccini (1976), who found its proximal extremity, as well as other morphological features, most similar to those of *Hylobates*. A partial humerus and ulna often placed in *D. fontani* are here referred tentatively to *Sivapithecus darwini*.

Given the rarity, incomplete description, and uncertain allocation of many European specimens, the distinction of *D. (Dryopithecus)* is questionable, but the main characters indicated by Simons and Pilbeam (1965) and Andrews (1973) include incisors relatively broad and low; lower canines tall, with moderate bilateral compression; P_3 also moderately compressed and low, but with enamel extending well onto mesial root, probably partly honing C^1; P^4 broad, with no cingulum; upper premolars and molars relatively

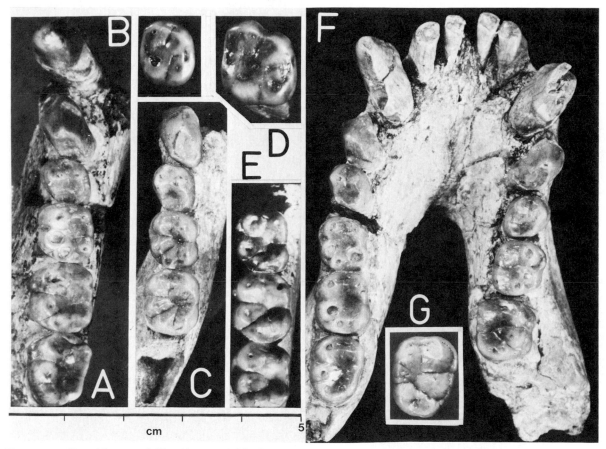

Figure 245. *Dryopithecus* and *Sivapithecus*. Middle–late Miocene, Europe. Occlusal views. *D. fontani*: A, left corpus with C$_{\overline{1}}$–M$_{\overline{3}}$; C, portion of left corpus of juvenile with P$_{\overline{3}}$–M$_{\overline{2}}$; E, left corpus with M$_{\overline{1-3}}$; F, distorted mandible lacking right M$_{\overline{3}}$. *Sivapithecus darwini*: B, left dP$^{\underline{4}}$; D, left M$^{\underline{2}}$; G, right M$_{\overline{3}}$.

long, no cingulum, P$^{\underline{4}}$ larger than P$^{\underline{3}}$, molars with well-separated main cusps, ridges not distinct; lower molars with variable buccal cingulum, hypoconulid slightly buccal on M$_{\overline{1}}$, increasingly so distad, size increase distad not great, M$_{\overline{3}}$ not elongate. The mandibular corpus is relatively robust, the symphysis has both superior and inferior transverse tori moderately (although variably) developed. The two recognized species differ mainly in size.

Relationships among *Dryopithecus* species and between these and various modern taxa have been proposed from the earliest days of their study; many such relationships are discussed by Simons and Pilbeam (1965, 1972), Pilbeam (1969b), and Andrews (1973,

1976). In brief, *D. africanus* has been thought to be ancestral to *Pan troglodytes*, *D. major* to *P. gorilla*, and "*D.*" *sivalensis* possibly to *Pongo*, while *D. nyanzae* and *D. fontani* (perhaps also "*D.*" *sivalensis*) were considered similar, as were *D. major* and "*D.*" *indicus*. Unfortunately, most of these relationships were based on similarities in size, ignoring the very characters which distinguished the taxa to which the species belonged.

If the subgenera of *Dryopithecus* are accepted as reasonably homogeneous units, the African three appear to be distinguished from *D. (Dryopithecus)*, which may be linked to other Eurasian taxa by such derived(?) features as cingulum reduction, symphysis with inferior torus, and relatively short lower molars.

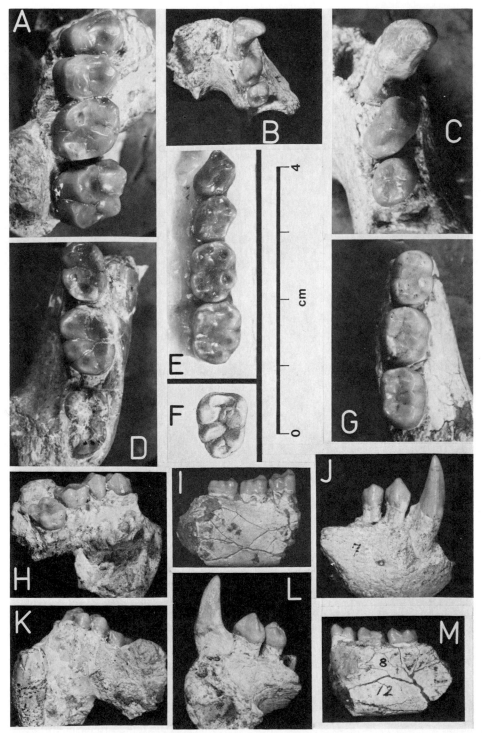

Figure 246. *Dryopithecus (Dryopithecus) brancoi.* Middle–late Miocene, Europe. ?Male left maxilla of juvenile with P³–M² and erupting C¹: A, occlusal view; H, oblique buccal view; K, oblique lingual view. ?Male right corpus and symphysis with right $C_{\overline{1}}$–$P_{\overline{4}}$: B, occlusal view; C, occlusal view of teeth only; J, lateral view; L, internal view. Left corpus with $M_{\overline{1-2}}$: D, occlusal view. Associated right $P_{\overline{3}}$–$M_{\overline{2}}$: E, occlusal view. Right $M_{\overline{3}}$: F, occlusal view. Right corpus with $M_{\overline{1-3}}$: G, occlusal view; I, lateral view; M, lingual view. The scale is for A and C–G; B and H–M are at ½ that scale. [F from Branco (1898).]

Of course *Sivapithecus* and allies are further distinguished by their thick molar enamel, so that *Dryopithecus* from western Europe is considered congeneric with the six African species. *Dryopithecus (Limnopithecus)* is perhaps only separated from *D. (Proconsul)* by allometric features of the face, while both of these are distinguished from *D. (Rangwapithecus)* by dental morphology and proportions. Some of these features in *D. (Rangwapithecus)* are suggestive of characters seen in *Sivapithecus* and *Ramapithecus*.

The ancestral morphology for the genus *Dryopithecus* probably included broad, low incisors; broad, cingulated upper cheek teeth and $P_{\overline{4}}$; "semisectorial," compressed $P_{\overline{3}}$ and canines; elongated, cingulated lower molars with nearly median hypoconulid on $M_{\overline{1-2}}$; mainly superior symphyseal torus; and well-developed ulnar olecranon (and styloid?). This pattern is retained most conservatively in *D. (Proconsul)* and *D. (Rangwapithecus)*, which differ strongly, however, in molar breadth and canine honing adaptations, so that neither is *the* ancestral subgenus by any interpretation. Moreover, some characters are shared by almost any imaginable combination of subgenera.

Andrews (1973) attempted to assess the dietary adaptations of some *Dryopithecus* species, determining that *D. (Rangwapithecus)* may have been more frugivorous than *D. (Proconsul)* because of narrower incisors and lower-cusped molars; he was certain that no species of *Dryopithecus* was adapted to folivory. Kay (1977c), however, has suggested that, of all early Miocene species, *D. (R.) gordoni* "alone had folivorous tendencies," while the molars of *D. (P.) major* approach partial lophodonty, as in the more folivorous *Pan gorilla*. Moreover, the African forms were clearly associated with forest faunas and floras, as may have also been true for some Eurasian populations, while most western European forms inhabited woodland (Andrews and Van Couvering, 1975; Andrews, 1976). In these forests, large size in *Dryopithecus* may have been preadaptive to folivory, even if the dental evidence suggests it was not facultative as yet.

It is possible that only one species of *Dryopithecus* exited Africa (in the late early Miocene?) to give rise to the Eurasian forms, but this is by no means certain; if so, the Eurasian forms may have to be linked more closely. On the other hand, the thick molar enamel in *Sivapithecus*, *Ramapithecus*, and *Gigantopithecus* is currently accepted as homologous among them, thus indicating their close relationship, to the exclusion of

Dryopithecus species. However, there is some suggestion by Andrews (1973) that molar enamel wore down faster in *Dendropithecus* than in African *Dryopithecus* species, which might imply the beginnings of enamel thickening at this stage, and thus merely its continuation and intensification in the Eurasian open country Sugrivapithecini (and Homininae).

No clear relationships exist with the living apes, except that at least *D. major* shares a frontal sinus with some *Pan*—it is most likely that its other similarities are due to size and ecological correlation. As now understood, ancestral *Dryopithecus* might well have been ancestral also to all modern anthropomorphs, but shared derived character states among them have not yet been delineated.

Tribe Sugrivapithecini
Simonetta, 1957, restricted

(= or including: Gigantopithecinae Gremyatskii, 1962. Sivapithecinae Pilbeam in Pilbeam *et al.*, 1977. Ramapithecinae Simonetta, 1957: Pilbeam in Pilbeam *et al.*, 1977, in part.)

DISTRIBUTION
Early middle Miocene (?late Rusingan, Astaracian) to middle Pleistocene. Southern Asia (China, India, Pakistan, Turkey), eastern Europe (Hungary, Greece, Czechoslovakia, ?Austria), and ?east Africa.
INCLUDED TAXA
Sivapithecus (including *Sugrivapithecus*) and *Gigantopithecus*.

DISCUSSION

A tribe Sugrivapithecini was named by Simonetta (1957) to include the "genera" *Sugrivapithecus* and *Hispanopithecus*, which he considered to be linked by numerous characters (what these were, other than small size, is difficult to determine!). More recently, Andrews (1976; Andrews and Tekkaya, 1976), Pilbeam (1976; Pilbeam *et al.*, 1977), and Simons (1976a,b) have discerned that *Sivapithecus* and *Gigantopithecus* (as well as *Ramapithecus*) can be distinguished from other advanced Miocene hominoids now placed in *Dryopithecus* by a character complex forming an adaptation to eating hard foods, probably in an open, terrestrial environment: thick cheek-tooth enamel, further reduced canine honing and perhaps expansion of the mesiobuccal portion (but not flange) of $P_{\overline{3}}$, probably somewhat reduced incisors, and apparently large cheek teeth compared to body size (limb length). Partial and tentatively allocated forelimb remains suggest some similarity of the elbow region to that of *Pan*, but no locomotor interpretations have yet been put forward. Not all these features are known in all species, and remains other than teeth and jaws are exceedingly rare, but the evidence to date supports the idea that these two genera shared a more recent common ancestor with the forerunner of Homininae than did any other taxon. In order to recognize the patristic "distinctness" of Homininae (including *Ramapithecus*), however, this group is placed with the pongines, as a separate, paraphyletic tribe. According to Pilbeam *et al.* (1977), *Ramapithecus* is cladistically closest to *Gigantopithecus*, but this view has not yet been substantiated morphologically. If it proves true, the merit of this admittedly nonholophyletic tribe might require reexamination. Simonetta's nomen is used in the belief that the type of "*Sugrivapithecus*" is a *Sivapithecus*, rather than a *Ramapithecus* as interpreted by Pilbeam (personal communication). If the latter view prevails, the name would revert to Sivapithecini, as essentially employed by Pilbeam *et al.* (1977).

It was long thought that the human lineage arose in Africa, with Eurasian Miocene representatives being merely outliers, but the above-cited authors have questioned this dogma. It is clear that African *Dryopithecus* are the most conservative species and probably close to the ancestral condition for that genus and the Sugrivapithecini, but *Sivapithecus* is essentially a Eurasian development, in adaptation to the growing plains habitats there. Parsimony would suggest that the European subgenus of *Dryopithecus* was closest to the origin of *Sivapithecus* and allies, but the latter are in fact known earlier in both Turkey and Czechoslovakia. Moreover, it has been suggested above that *D.* (*Rangwapithecus*) might show the beginnings of some *Sivapithecus*-like conditions, and the Rusinga "*S. africanus*" maxilla could also be pertinent. This would perhaps imply that there were two separate migrations of Miocene hominids out of Africa: one along the more forested northern shore of Tethys which flourished in Spain and southern France as *D.* (*Dryopithecus*) and a second group of ancestral sugrivapithecins which invaded more open environments. The latter form may already have been *Sivapithecus*-like when it entered Eurasia, or it may have evolved the basic adaptations in Eurasia, probably somewhere between Turkey and Pakistan, and then spread out to China and Hungary, as well as back to Africa, eventually to give rise to the hominine clade.

SIVAPITHECUS Pilgrim, 1910

(= or including: ?*Pithecus* E. Geoffroy and F. Cuvier, 1795: Falconer and Cautley, 1838, in part. *Palaeopithecus* Lydekker, 1879, *nec* Voigt, 1835. *Troglodytes* E. Geoffroy, 1812: Lydekker, 1886, in part. *Simia* Linnaeus, 1758: Lydekker, 1886, in part. *Anthropopithecus* Blainville, 1839: Trouessart, 1897, in part. *Griphopithecus** Abel, 1902. *Sivapithecus* Pilgrim, 1910. *Dryopithecus* Lartet, 1856: Pilgrim, 1915, in part. *Palaeosimia* Pilgrim, 1915. *Hylopithecus* Pilgrim, 1927. *Sugrivapithecus* Lewis, 1934. *Austriacopithecus* Ehrenberg, 1938. *Ramapithecus* Lewis, 1934, in part. *Indopithecus* von Koenigswald, 1949, in part. *Pongo* Lacépède, 1799: Hooijer, 1951, in part. *Mesopithecus* Wagner, 1839: Freyberg, 1951, in part. *Ankarapithecus* Ozansoy, 1957. *Graecopithecus* von Koenigswald, 1972. *Bodvapithecus* Kretzoi, 1975. *Ouranopithecus* de Bonis and Melentis, 1977.)

DISTRIBUTION

Early middle to middle late Miocene (?late Rusingan, Astaracian to early Turolian). ?Austria, Czechoslovakia, Hungary, Greece, Turkey, Pakistan, India, China, ?Kenya.

---

*This name has priority over *Sivapithecus*, but in view of its complete lack of usage, except as a synonym of *Dryopithecus*, we shall not resuscitate it here. The ICZN will be petitioned to suppress it formally for purposes of priority.

KNOWN SPECIES

1. *Sivapithecus indicus* Pilgrim, 1910, type species
[=?*Pithecus* cf. *satyrus* (Linnaeus, 1758): Falconer and Cautley, 1838. *Simia* sp. cf. *S. satyrus* (Linnaeus, 1758): Lydekker, 1886. *Simia satyrus fossilis* Trouessart, 1897. *Sivapithecus indicus* Pilgrim, 1910; Pilgrim, 1915, in part. *Dryopithecus*(?) *frickae* Brown, Gregory, and Hellman, 1924. *Sivapithecus himalayensis* Pilgrim, 1927. *Sivapithecus orientalis* Pilgrim, 1927. *Sivapithecus middlemissi* Pilgrim, 1927. *Dryopithecus* sp.: Pilgrim, 1927. *Dryopithecus chinjiensis* Pilgrim, 1915: Pilgrim, 1927, in part. *Sivapithecus giganteus* (Pilgrim, 1915): Lewis, 1937, in part. *Indopithecus giganteus* (Pilgrim, 1915): von Koenigswald, 1949, in part. *Pongo* cf. *pygmaeus* (Hoppius, 1763): Hooijer, 1951, in part. *Dryopithecus keiyuanensis* Woo, 1957: Woo, 1958, in part. *Sivapithecus aiyengari* Prasad, 1962. *Dryopithecus* (*Sivapithecus*) *indicus*: Simons and Pilbeam, 1965, in part. *Sivapithecus lewisi* Pandey and Sastri, 1968.]
Localities: "Kamlial" (456); Chinji★ (480); Hsiaolungtan (484); Ramnagar (492); Hasnot—middle (514); Bandal (532); Haritalyangar—lower (554); Sethi Nagri (571); Gandakas (576).

2. *Sivapithecus sivalensis* (Lydekker, 1879)
[=*Palaeopithecus sivalensis* Lydekker, 1879. *Troglodytes sivalensis*: Lydekker, 1886. *Anthropopithecus sivalensis*: Trouessart, 1897. *Simia sivalensis*: Trouessart, 1899. *Dryopithecus chinjiensis* Pilgrim, 1915. *Palaeosimia rugosidens* Pilgrim, 1915. *Dryopithecus pilgrimi* Brown, Gregory, and Hellman, 1924. *Dryopithecus cautleyi* Brown, Gregory, and

Hellman, 1924. *Hylopithecus hysudricus* Pilgrim, 1927. *Ramapithecus hariensis* Lewis, 1934. *Sugrivapithecus salmontanus* Lewis, 1934. *Sugrivapithecus gregoryi* Lewis, 1936. *Sivapithecus sivalensis:* Lewis, 1937. *Sivapithecus(?)* cf. *darwini* (Abel, 1902): Gregory, Hellman, and Lewis, 1938. *Sivapithecus(?)* sp.: Gregory, Hellman, and Lewis, 1938. *Ramapithecus* cf. *brevirostris* Lewis, 1934: Gregory, Hellman, and Lewis, 1938. *Sivapithecus cautleyi:* L. Leakey, 1953. *Pliopithecus (Pliopithecus) hysudricus:* Simonetta, 1957. *Dryopithecus (Sivapithecus) sivalensis:* Simons and Pilbeam, 1965, in part. *Ramapithecus punjabicus* (Pilgrim, 1910): Pilbeam, 1969a, in part.]
LOCALITIES: "Kamlial" (456); Chinji (480); Kanatti (482); Ramnagar (492); Kundal Nala (494); ?Domeli—lower (504); Hasnot—middle (514); Haritalyangar—lower (554); Jabi★ (574).

3. *Sivapithecus darwini* (Abel, 1902)
[=*Dryopithecus darwini* Abel, 1902. *Griphopithecus suessi* Abel, 1902. *Sivapithecus darwini:* Lewis, 1937; Andrews, 1976; Andrews and Tobien, 1977. *Austriacopithecus weinfurteri* Ehrenberg, 1938. *Austriacopithecus abeli* Ehrenberg, 1938. *Dryopithecus (Dryopithecus) fontani:* Simons and Pilbeam, 1965, in part. *Dryopithecus (Dryopithecus) fontani darwini:* Steininger, 1967. *Dryopithecus* cfr. *indicus:* Crusafont and Golpe, 1973. *Bodvapithecus altipalatus* Kretzoi, 1975 (1974, *nomen nudum*). *Sivapithecus indicus:* Andrews, 1976, in part.]
LOCALITIES: Paşalar (434); Neudorf-Sandberg★ (444); ?Klein Haders-

dorf (460); ?Rudabánya (506); ?Can Llobateres (510); ?Can Ponsic (512).

4. *Sivapithecus meteai* (Ozansoy, 1957)
[=*Mesopithecus pentelicus* Wagner, 1839: Freyberg, 1951. *Ankarapithecus meteai* Ozansoy, 1957. *Dryopithecus (Sivapithecus) indicus:* Simons and Pilbeam, 1965, in part. *Graecopithecus freybergi* von Koenigswald, 1972. *Dryopithecus macedoniensis* de Bonis, Bouvrain, Geraads, and Melentis, 1974; 1975. *Sivapithecus meteai:* Andrews, 1976. *Ramapithecus:* Simons, 1976a, in part. *Ouranopithecus macedoniensis* (de Bonis, Bouvrain, Geraads, and Melentis, 1974): de Bonis and Melentis, 1977.]
LOCALITIES: ?Ravin de la Pluie (528); Yassioren★ (540); ?Pyrgos (552).

DISCUSSION

The genus *Sivapithecus* was first proposed in the early part of this century, in the heyday of taxonomic profusion of new names. Simons and Pilbeam (1965) considered it a subgenus of *Dryopithecus*, a view which most subsequent authors have accepted; however, Pilbeam (1969b) and more strongly Andrews (1973;

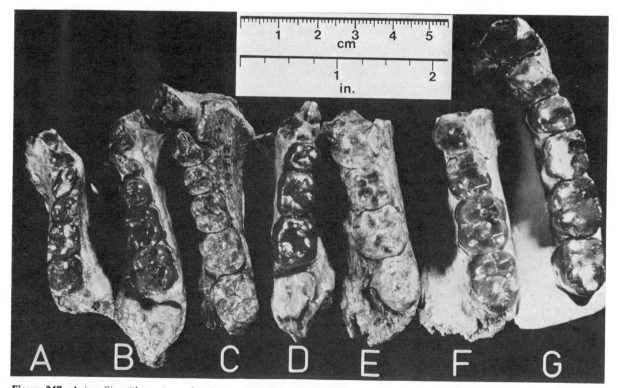

Figure 247. Asian *Sivapithecus* in occlusal view. Middle and late Miocene. A, cf. *S. sivalensis* ("*Ramapithecus* cf. *brevirostris*") cast; B, *S. sivalensis*; C, *S. sivalensis*; D–F, *S. indicus*; G, *S. meteai*, cast. Scale divisions are in centimeters and inches.

Delson and Andrews, 1975) have proposed that even that degree of distinction was too great. More recently, Andrews (e.g., 1976) and Pilbeam *et al.* (1977) have reelevated *Sivapithecus* to generic rank, while Simons (1976a) considered it at least subgenerically distinct. Here, we accord it full generic rank in a distinct tribe. Many new specimens referable to this taxon have been recovered recently in China, Pakistan, India, Turkey, Greece, and Hungary, and more detailed consideration of specific taxonomy must await their analysis and description (especially by Pilbeam and Andrews).

Clearly, the most important discovery of recent years is that these taxa have thick enamel on molar crown surfaces, in common with *Ramapithecus, Au-*

stralopithecus, and *Gigantopithecus,* suggesting either parallel adaptations to hard-object feeding or a shared ancestry separate from almost all other anthropomorphs. Other characters common to *Sivapithecus* species include the following (Figures 247–249): incisors broad, of moderate crown height, the I^1 spatulate; canines moderately tall, and compressed, as is $P_{\overline{3}}$, which probably engaged in little honing but is expanded mesiobuccally; $P_{\overline{4}}$ quite broad; upper premolars narrow, with no lingual cingulum, P^3 with a strongly projecting paracone, larger than P^4; upper molars moderately broad to only slightly broader than long, with no lingual cingulum, M^3 slightly larger than M^1, but smaller than M^2, lower molars relatively short

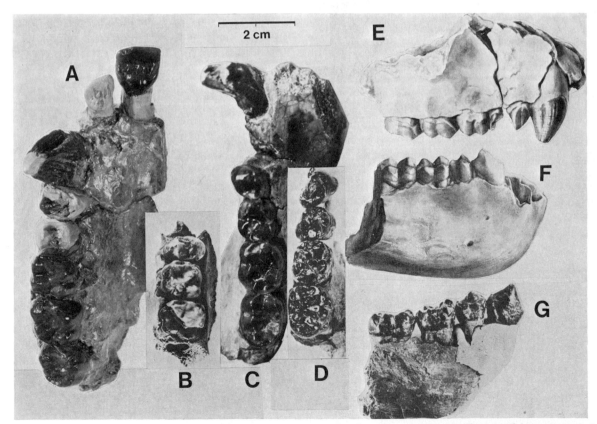

Figure 248. *Sivapithecus indicus.* Middle–late Miocene, Asia. Restored right male maxilla with all teeth, I^2 hypothetical: A, occlusal view; E, lateral view. Partly restored left male mandible with $C_{\overline{1}}$ and $P_{\overline{4}}$–$M_{\overline{3}}$: C, occlusal view. Male right mandibular corpus with $P_{\overline{3}}$–$M_{\overline{2}}$ (mirror image of left): F, buccal view. *Sivapithecus* cf. *darwini.* Middle Miocene, Europe. Right maxilla with damaged P^4–M^2: B, occlusal view. Portion of right corpus with $P_{\overline{3}}$–$M_{\overline{2}}$: D, occlusal view; G, buccal view. [A, C from E. L. Simons and D. Pilbeam, *Science, 173,* copyright 1971 by the American Association for the Advancement of Science; B, D, G courtesy of M. Kretzoi; E, F from Pilgrim (1927).]

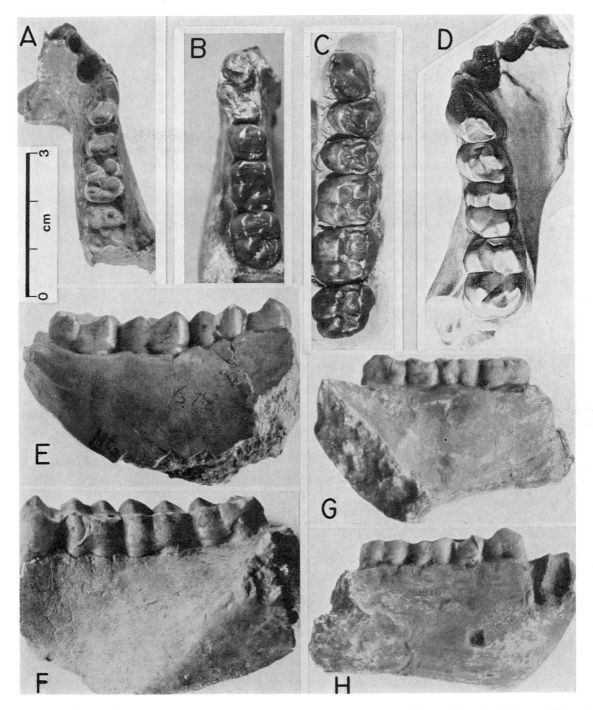

Figure 249. *Sivapithecus*. Middle–late Miocene, Asia. Cf. *Sivapithecus sivalensis* ("*Ramapithecus* cf. *brevirostris*"), cast of ?female right mandibular corpus with $P_{\overline{3}}$–$M_{\overline{2}}$ and alveoli of $I_{\overline{1}}$–$C_{\overline{1}}$: A, occlusal view; G, lingual view; H, buccal view. *Sivapithecus sivalensis*, ?female juvenile left mandibular corpus with $P_{\overline{4}}$–$M_{\overline{2}}$ and broken $C_{\overline{1}}$–$P_{\overline{3}}$ ($M_{\overline{3}}$ missing, erupting?): B, occlusal view. *Sivapithecus sivalensis*, ?associated female left $C^{\underline{1}}$–$M^{\underline{3}}$: C, occlusal view. *Sivapithecus indicus*. Left male mandibular corpus with $P_{\overline{3}}$–$M_{\overline{2}}$ and alveoli for $I_{\overline{1}}$–$C_{\overline{1}}$: D, occlusal view. Left mandibular corpus with $P_{\overline{4}}$–$M_{\overline{3}}$: E, lingual view; F, buccal view. [A, E–H from Gregory *et al.* (1938); D from Pilgrim (1927).]

and broad, most with little or no buccal cingulum, the $M_{\overline{3}}$ only slightly larger than $M_{\overline{1-2}}$. The maxillary sinus is small, and the mandible is robust, with a well-developed inferior torus. Kay (1977a) has discussed aspects of molar occlusion in *Sivapithecus*.

Because the status of *Sivapithecus* as a distinct taxon has only recently been recognized, and because many important specimens have been described only in a preliminary fashion, there is still disagreement as to the content and relationships of the included species. Here, four are recognized, basically following Andrews (1976). The two Siwalik forms differ mainly in size, although, as seen in Figure 247, there is a nearly continuous gradation from *S. sivalensis*, through *S. indicus* to the Turkish *S. meteai*. *Sivapithecus indicus* is much more common, especially after the recovery of new dentitions and referred fragmentary postcrania by Pilbeam *et al.* (1977), and may be further distinguished by relatively larger incisors. *Sivapithecus sivalensis* specimens remain difficult to diagnose compared to *Ramapithecus*, but anterior teeth are larger and mandibular corpora are deeper and more gracile— thus, the type of *Sugrivapithecus salmontanus* (Figure 249B) and the mandible described by Pilbeam (1969a) are questionably allocated here. Contemporary with these two sympatric species was a still larger form known from Turkey and Greece. Published specimens reveal a great range of variation in relative molar and incisor size, and the holotype of "*Ankarapithecus*" *meteai* (Figure 247G) is perhaps the most divergent, but all may be tentatively assigned to a single species. Simons (1976a) has argued that the "*Graecopithecus*" mandible is a *Ramapithecus*, but it more likely also belongs in *S. meteai*. The relationship between this species and *Gigantopithecus* mentioned by de Bonis and Melentis (1976) and by Andrews (1976) merits further analysis.

Sivapithecus darwini includes the earliest *Sivapithecus* (isolated teeth from Europe and Turkey) and perhaps some later European material. The Neudorf type sample of four teeth (Figure 245) was long considered to represent a variant of *Dryopithecus fontani*, but, as indicated by Andrews (1976; Andrews and Tobien, 1977), these molars are larger and appear to have thick enamel. The more numerous sample from Paşalar matches the Neudorf teeth, but differs from *S. indicus* (of similar size) in some crown features, while also retaining certain traits seen in *D. (Proconsul)* species (Andrews and Tobien, 1977). Tentatively referred to this species on geographic and minor metrical grounds are isolated teeth from Spain and the Rudabánya specimens termed "*Bodvapithecus*" (Figure 248, B, D, and G). The latter are often placed in *S. indicus,* although they appear to share relatively strong buccal cingulids with *S. darwini*. Moreover, the damaged humerus and ulna from Klein Hadersdorf ("*Austriacopithecus*," Figure 244, B and G), usually referred to *D. fontani*, is also included here. It is not only rather early and geographically close to the *S. darwini* type locality, but, in addition, the ulna shows clear reduction of the olecranon process as would be expected for a *Sivapithecus* elbow. Finally, it is worth noting that the maxilla from Rusinga described as *Sivapithecus africanus* but here included in *D. nyanzae* (Figure 242G) might yet prove referable to *Sivapithecus* or relevant to its origin.

As discussed by Simons (1976a), Campbell and Bernor (1976), Andrews (1976), and Pilbeam *et al.* (1977), *Sivapithecus* species (and also *Gigantopithecus* and *Ramapithecus*) are generally associated with assemblages of open-country or mixed habitat, rather than the forest faunas found with African and western European *Dryopithecus* species. This led Simons (1976a) to refer to this group as "ground apes," whose thick molar enamel was an adaptation to feeding on coarse or tough foodstuffs, often on the ground (see also under Homininae, below). *Sivapithecus* is the most conservative of the three genera, retaining many features seen in *Dryopithecus* species, especially in the early *S. darwini*, whose known habitats seem to have been the most forested. Detailed assessments of paleobiology await the more complete description of newer specimens.

GIGANTOPITHECUS von Koenigswald, 1935

(= or including: *Gigantanthropus* Weidenreich, 1946; *Giganthropus* Weinert, 1950; unjustified emendations. *Dryopithecus* Lartet, 1856: Pilgrim, 1915, in part. *Sivapithecus* Pilgrim, 1910: Lewis, 1937, in part. *Indopithecus* von Koenigswald, 1950, in part.)

DISTRIBUTION
  Late Miocene to early middle Pleistocene. Pakistan, north India, south China, ?Vietnam.

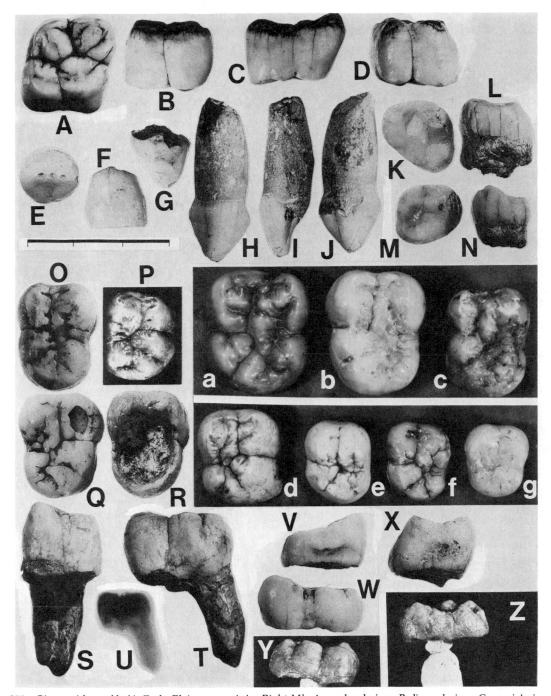

Figure 250. *Gigantopithecus blacki*. Early Pleistocene, Asia. Right M¹: A, occlusal view; B, lingual view; C, mesial view; D, buccal view. ?Left I¹: E, occlusal view; F, labial view; G, mesial view. Right C¹: H, labial view; I, mesial view; J, lingual view. Right P$_{\overline{4?}}$: K, occlusal view; L, mesial view. Left P$_{\overline{4}}$: M, occlusal view; N, lingual view. Right M$_{\overline{3}}$: Q, occlusal view; V, mesial view: W, lingual view. Right M$_{\overline{3}}$, heavily worn: R, occlusal view; X ,mesial view. Series of left M$_{\overline{3}}$ in occlusal view: O, a–g (d possibly M$_{\overline{2}}$); S, mesial view of O; T, buccal view of O; U, radiograph of T. *Gigantopithecus giganteus*. Late Miocene, Asia. Right M$_{\overline{3(2?)}}$; P, occlusal view; Y, buccal view; Z, lingual view. Scale divisions are in centimeters. [A–O, Q–X from von Koenigswald (1952).]

491

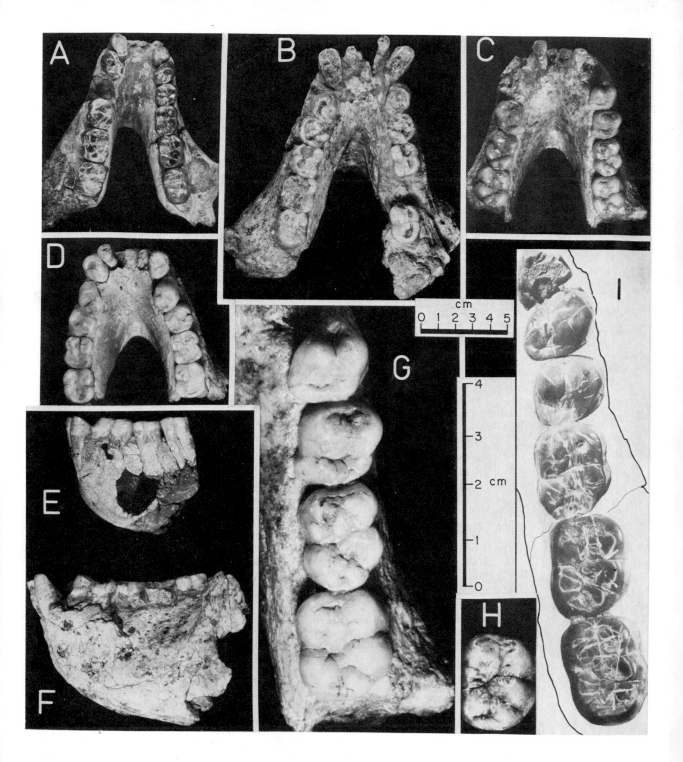

KNOWN SPECIES

1. *Gigantopithecus blacki* von Koenigswald, 1935, type species (= *Giganthropus blacki*: Weinert, 1950; unjustified emendation.)
LOCALITIES: Liucheng, Cave I and II (784), Chienshih (810), Bama (850), Tahsin (852), Wuming (854); ?Nghe-an, Vietnam; drugstore material presumably from Liucheng area⋆.

2. *Gigantopithecus giganteus* (Pilgrim, 1915), new combination [=*Dryopithecus giganteus* Pilgrim, 1915. *Sivapithecus giganteus*: Lewis, 1937. *Indopithecus giganteus* von Koenigswald, 1950. *Dryopithecus (Sivapithecus) indicus* Pilgrim, 1910: Simons and Pilbeam, 1965, in part. *Gigantopithecus bilaspurensis* Simons and Chopra, 1969. *Gigantopithecus* cf. *bilaspurensis*: Pilbeam *et al.*, 1977.]
LOCALITIES: Sethi Nagri (571); Alipur⋆ (588); Haritalyangar—upper (596).

DISCUSSION

Gigantopithecus species are extremely large advanced pongine hominids (sensu lato) characterized by the following features (Figure 250): small, low, crowded and vertically emplanted lower incisors, more robust, thicker uppers; canines robust, slightly low crowned, lacking honing facets, the uppers with rather long roots and lacking clear mesial grooving, sexual dimorphism apparently only in size, not shape, lowers especially worn down from the tip, indicating use as part of the cheek-tooth-rows; premolars strongly molarized, uppers with buccal cusp strongly to slightly larger and taller than lingual, the P^3 larger than P^4 (longer but slightly narrower, and longer buccally than mesially, rather than oval); P_3 bicuspid, the lingual cusp (very) small, with a large talonid, smaller trigonid, and small mesial flange; P_4 nearly square (slightly wider than long), with large trigonid taller than talonid; molars with thick enamel, high crowns, low cusp relief, and often accessory cuspules; lower molars long; uppers nearly square. The mandibular corpus (Figure 251) is extremely deep, shallowing mesially, with a long and strongly buttressed symphysis and probably a vertical ramus, all of which suggest powerful masticatory musculature and a deep and short face (or cranium as a whole).

For over 20 years, *G. blacki* was known only from rare isolated teeth purchased in Chinese drugstores, but in 1957–1958 specimens were recovered *in situ* (see White, 1975), and in 1962 Woo monographed the three mandibles and over 1000 teeth which had been recovered. More recently, small groups of specimens have been reported from localities in south China and possibly Vietnam (Chang *et al.*, 1973, 1975; Hsu *et al.*, 1974; Davidson, 1975). A much smaller group of specimens is known from significantly older deposits in northern India and Pakistan, including the mandible described as *G. bilaspurensis* and the isolated $M_{\overline{2}}$ (or $M_{\overline{3}}$) (Figure 251, A, H, and I) which Pilgrim (1915) named *D. giganteus*, and which was later placed in *Sivapithecus* and *Indopithecus*. These specimens, and remains newly recovered by Pilbeam *et al.* (1977) in Pakistan, would appear to be referable to a single species whose correct senior nomen is thus *Gigantopithecus giganteus*. In addition to being smaller than *G. blacki*, *G. giganteus* has fewer accessory cuspules on lower molars, which are also lower crowned, while the anterior teeth may be relatively even smaller (Simons and Chopra, 1969). The mandibular depth and symphyseal outline as given by Simons and Chopra are most comparable to the subadult male of *G. blacki*, rather than to the aged male with strongly worn teeth. The teeth of *G. blacki* show a great range in size for each element (Figure 250), which Woo (1962) interpreted as sexual dimorphism, but which might also represent variation over a long interval and/or the presence of more than one taxon. Only one postcranial element has yet been allocated to either species of *Gigantopithecus*, a fragment of distal humerus from Sethi Nagri said by Pilbeam *et al.* (1977) to be morphologically and metrically close to that of female gorillas. The lack of postcrania in the Liucheng deposit is taphonomically anomalous.

The thick enamel of *Gigantopithecus* species sets them apart from pliopithecids and most hominids, other than *Sivapithecus*, *Ramapithecus*, *Australopithecus*, and *Homo*. Reduced transformed incisors and canines are shared by all these except *Sivapithecus*, but the canine robusticity and apparent use in grinding rather than slicing (premolariform rather than incisiform

Figure 251. *Gigantopithecus giganteus.* Late Miocene, Asia. ?Female mandible with left $C_{\overline{1}}$–$P_{\overline{3}}$, $M_{\overline{1-3}}$, and right $C_{\overline{1}}$ (broken)–$M_{\overline{3}}$: A, occlusal view; I, close-up of right $C_{\overline{1}}$–$M_{\overline{3}}$, occlusal view. Right $M_{\overline{3(2?)}}$: H, occlusal view. *Gigantopithecus blacki.* Early Pleistocene, Asia. Male mandible lacking left $I_{\overline{1}}$, right $I_{\overline{1}}$, and $M_{\overline{2}}$: B, occlusal view; F, left lateral view. Male mandible with left $I_{\overline{2}}$, $P_{\overline{4}}$–$M_{\overline{2}}$, right $I_{\overline{2}}$, and $P_{\overline{3}}$–$M_{\overline{2}}$: C, occlusal view; G, close-up of right $P_{\overline{3}}$–$M_{\overline{2}}$, occlusal view. Female mandible with left $I_{\overline{2}}$–$M_{\overline{2}}$, right $I_{\overline{1}}$–$M_{\overline{2}}$: D, occlusal view; E, left lateral view. The horizontal scale is for A–F; the vertical scale is for G–I. [I from Simons and Chopra (1969), *Postilla* (Peabody Mus. Nat. Hist., Yale Univ.) No. 138, 1969, Fig. 3.]

canines) by *Gigantopithecus* are distinctive. Premolar molarization, elongation of $P_{\bar{4}}$–$M_{\bar{2}}$, and mandibular configuration are also characters distinguishing *Gigantopithecus* from all other hominids, with the closest approach in dental (and facial?) morphology possibly being to species of *Ramapithecus* or perhaps *Sivapithecus meteai*.

Various authors have commented on selected aspects of its morphology in assessing the relationships of *Gigantopithecus*. Pilbeam (1970) offered the most cogent analysis, much of which is followed above, but he had not yet realized (Pilbeam, 1976) that thick enamel and other features were actually shared with early hominines. In fact, nearly from the time of its first report by von Koenigswald (1935), *Gigantopithecus* has often been considered some sort of intermediate between men and apes (Weidenreich, 1946). Several authors even suggested altering the generic name to conform better to their idea of its placement in or near human ancestry. More recently, Eckhardt (1972, 1973, 1975) has suggested that *Gigantopithecus* species might have been ancestral to hominines (*Australopithecus* and *Homo*) because they were supposedly the only hominoids adapted to open country before the Pliocene. In retrospect, this view might be considered to have had some merit, but it clearly ignored morphology; moreover, in order to circumvent the size difference, Eckhardt argued that only a minimal percentage change in size each generation would be required to transform *Gigantopithecus* into early *Australopithecus*. This reasoning is patently absurd, its neglect of morphology and function implying that any phylogenetic sequence might be possible, such as a transformation of *Hyracotherium* into *Homo*, given the much longer span of time thus involved (see Delson *et al.*, 1977; also Corruccini, 1975b). Frayer (1973) gave slightly more consideration to morphology in trying to place *Gigantopithecus* as an ancestor of *Australopithecus*, and Robinson and Steudel (1973) reached a similar conclusion morphometrically, but Corruccini (1975a) reanalyzed their data with opposite results, arriving at some of the conclusions noted here.

In sum, *Gigantopithecus* would appear on present evidence to be one of the several late Miocene lineages of thick-enameled "ground apes" which included the origin of the hominine stock. This genus, however, increased greatly in size and specialized its canines (and incisors) quite differently from those of early hominines (Szalay, 1975e), adapting to a different, if not fully explained, feeding preference.

SUBFAMILY HOMININAE
Gray, 1825

(= or including: Hominidae Gray, 1825, and later authors, restricted. Hominina Gray, 1825. Primates, Bimana, Psychozoa of authors. Pithecanthropidae Dubois, 1894. "Homo-simiadae" Dart, 1925; not available. Australopithecinae Gregory and Hellman, 1939. Paranthropidae Arambourg, 1957. Ramapithecini Simonetta, 1957. Brahmapithecini Simonetta, 1957, lapsus. Ramapithecinae: Hill, 1968. Homininae: Delson and Andrews, 1975.)

DISTRIBUTION
?Middle Miocene (Ternanian) to modern. Worldwide (fossil record essentially Old World).
INCLUDED TAXA
Ramapithecus(?), *Australopithecus*, and *Homo*.

DISCUSSION

The hominines are an increasingly successful late radiation, originally probably adapted to open environments, but by early in the Pleistocene spreading into all available habitats. Although usually ranked as a family, they are here considered a subfamily as discussed under the Hominidae above. The basic adaptations of the group are shared by *Homo* and *Australopithecus*, while *Ramapithecus* appears to present several of these also and is thus tentatively included in the taxon.

By comparison to the ancestral hominids, the derived characters of hominines include a large brain weight to body weight ratio; relatively large cheek teeth with high square molar crowns, but with reduction of third molars and usually bicuspid $P_{\bar{3}}$; anterior dentition reduced in height, with subvertical incisors, low crowned canines closely appressed to the incisors and functioning in incisivation and with somewhat transversely aligned roots (in *Australopithecus* and *Homo*, there is no canine honing contact and the tooth-row is subparabolic, while *Ramapithecus* preserves ancestral conditions for these features); increased cranial base flexion and neurocranial height; anterior placement and horizontal orientation of the foramen magnum; lumbar lengthening and curvature; craniocaudally short but dorsoventrally broad illium, laterally facing acetabulum, short ischium; elongate femur with relatively large head and neck and "carrying angle," caused by prolongation of medial condyle with weight-bearing through lateral condyle; relative elongation of lower limb, especially by comparison to catarrhine allometric trends; and a complete remodeling of the foot for level-substrate locomotion, including pedal arching of metatarsals and loss of the ancestral helical astragalo-calcaneal articulation, reducing the possible range of movements in this joint.

This set of features would appear to be interpretable in terms of three main adaptive complexes: brain size and presumably "intelligence" affecting cerebral and cranial shape; dietary preferences affecting the dentition; and upright bipedal locomotion affecting the lower limb and pelvic girdle as well as cranial orientation. Of these, only the dentition is well represented throughout the fossil record of the subfamily and its near relatives, while the Plio-Pleistocene hominines appear with lower limb and craniocerebral patterns well defined. This has led some previous workers to suggest that dental–dietary alterations were the first element of the mosaic to occur, while others have argued that pre-human artifactual culture, or tool-using, was of prime importance in canalizing dental and/or locomotor adaptations and still others have awarded primacy to locomotion in the Plio-Pleistocene forms. It would seem more profitable to realize that, as in all evolving organisms, the mosaic pattern is subject to feedback modifications, with no one morphological complex "leading," except at a specific point in time. If each complex is briefly analyzed in terms of function and biological role, the known pattern may be interpreted more clearly.

Before embarking on such interpretations, however, it may be useful to recall the concentration on scenario building of most paleoanthropologists, as pointed out by Delson *et al.* (1977). A basic set of phylogenetic relationships must be developed first or at least concurrently to serve as a sound framework for erecting adaptive scenarios. Following Lewis (1934) and Simons (1961), Eldredge and Tattersall (1975; also Delson *et al.*, 1977) included *Ramapithecus* in the Homininae as it shares incisor and especially canine reduction with the later taxon; cranial and postcranial elements might remove the uncertainty. *Australopithecus* species share a locomotor pattern which may itself be uniquely derived, in addition to reflecting different pelvic adaptations to fetal head size, which is smaller than in *Homo* relative to body weight. Of the two *Australopithecus* species, *A. robustus* is clearly uniquely derived with regard to dental and craniofacial characteristics, as described below. The known morphology of *A. africanus*, however, consistently presents features which are interpretable as "intermediate" between ancestral hominines and *Homo*. In other words, it conforms completely to the ancestral morphotype for *Homo* and *Australopithecus*, except perhaps for the pelvofemoral features noted above. The three successive species of *Homo* may overlap only partly in time, if at all, and would appear to represent a single lineage. At present, the earliest fossils questionably referable to *Homo habilis* appear to be older than those of *Australopithecus* cf. *africanus*, but presumably members of the latter taxon were ancestral to the former. This phylogenetic scheme is shown in Figure 151.

Returning to the question of interpretations, hominine brain size is clearly central to all discussions, but, as Holloway (1977 and references) has repeatedly emphasized, it is especially neural reorganization which distinguished hominines from other hominids. This can be determined *in vivo* and *in vitro*, and by analogy in the earliest hominine endocasts accompanying the evidence for relative increase in brain size in *Australopithecus* and further in early *Homo*. Related to these changes would also be hormonally controlled alterations in relative growth rates, including the elongation of the dependency–learning period, as reflected by dental development, eruption, and perhaps graded wear. But the relation between brain size and such concepts as "intelligence" or "adaptability" is difficult to demonstrate (although we do not doubt such relationships) and thus cerebral changes are hard to interpret adaptively.

The dietary implications of early hominine dentitions have been discussed and interpreted differently by various recent workers, including Jolly (1970a), Szalay (1975e), and Wallace (1975). It is now clear that the Sugrivapithecini shared with *Ramapithecus* and *Australopithecus* some gnathic adaptations to a diet of tough food, as indicated by the large cheek teeth with thick enamel and high crowns, robust mandible and often maxillary alveolar processes, subvertical mandibular ramus, and convergently(?) reduced canine honing. Most of these extinct animals occupied a relatively open, dry environment as well. Wallace (1975, 1978) demonstrated that some of these adaptations were lost in early *Homo*, as molar enamel became thinner and a helicoidal chewing pattern developed, possibly correlated with the use of tools in food preparation. Jolly (1970a), concentrating on *Australopithecus* spp., argued that they were adapted to eating small, hard objects such as seeds, by analogy with the grass-eating *Theropithecus gelada* and its comparable distinctions from *Papio*. Szalay (1975e) noted the many dental differences between *Papio* and *Theropithecus*, on the one hand, and between pongines and hominines, on the other, and further emphasized the main distinctions between what are here termed Homininae and Sugrivapithecini in the dentition. While the Sugrivapithecini either have retained an ancestrally tall canine and moderately large incisors or have reduced incisors while retaining a robust low canine functionally incorporated into the cheek-tooth-row, the Homininae have modified the canine for incisivation, reducing its height and bulk and closing the diastemata between canines and incisors. In addition, sexual dimorphism, so characteristic of pongines, was reduced to only statistical significance.

While examining the morphological distinctions of early hominines from other hominids, Szalay (1975e), following some of Every's (1970) ideas, attempted to analyze the differences in terms of mechanical significance and subsequent biological roles. He argued that, in spite of its merits with respect to the general approach to the problem, the model of baboon-protogelada transition that Jolly proposed fails to explain the pongine–protohominine transition; the morphological, inferred functional, and inferred ethoecological changes in the protohominines do not parallel the origins of the gelada baboons from a more primitive stage represented today and in the fossil record by the various forms of *Papio* and *Parapapio*.

It appears that the most significant *morphological* and *mechanical-functional* contrast between the hominine morphotype and the relevant Miocene pongines lies in the nature of the anterior dentition. In order to understand the morphotype condition for the anterior dentition in known hominines, these and *Gigantopithecus* can be instructively compared. The most significant phylogenetic and, at its inception, adaptational contrast of these taxa lies in the fact that in *Gigantopithecus* the incisors are reduced independently from the canines, which are still relatively robust, whereas in both hominine lineages the size variations of the incisors and canines are apparently closely related to one another genetically. In *Gigantopithecus*, the robust canines functioned as part of the cheek-tooth-row (as indicated by their wear). Moreover, as far as it is possible to tell from the Chinese Pleistocene mandibles, a canine sexual dimorphism was present. The lack of reduction in the canines in

contrast to that in the incisors, the cheek-tooth function of the canines, and their retention of pongine sexual dimorphism are the combination of conditions found in *Gigantopithecus* that contrasts this genus to hominines. These unique trends, incidentally, appear to bar this taxon from significant close phyletic relationship with robust hominines in spite of statements in the literature to the contrary.

In the hominine anterior dentition, significant canine sexual dimorphism is all but absent in either gracile or robust specimens. This is in startling contrast to the cranial dimorphism of robust forms and a host of other dimorphic features in the extant gracile form. But the latter conditions, on the other hand, are usually accompanied in most catarrhine species by sexual dimorphism in canines. This unique occurrence of no sexual dimorphism in canines but its retention in cranial and somatic characters and in general size requires some special explanation. We are otherwise left with having to postulate that reduction of the canines and of sexual dimorphism in that area is due to lack of selection, while at the same time we must postulate causes *not affecting* the canines which maintained and added dimorphism to the rest of the body in hominines. If, however, there was positive selection (tied to feeding) for increasing the area of incisivation and accentuating the cutting ability of this region, this would result in the ontogenetic and genetic interdependence of the canine–incisor row. Thus, when future evolution of the hominine morphotype condition would require a further accentuation of the cheek dentition (P^3_3–P^4_4 hypertrophy) and relative neglect of the anterior one, we would expect the canines, along with the incisors, to diminish in size rather than expand with the premolars. This is how the reduced canine–incisor dentition of the robust Plio-Pleistocene hominines may be explained. The canines of the robust forms become reduced when the teeth distal to them are phyletically expanding only because their ancestral role has been intimately tied to incisivation, and genetic influences affecting the incisors are also influencing the canines. It therefore follows that the reduced anterior dentition of the robust forms should not be regarded as representative of the postulated hominine morphotype.

Adaptations of hominines have been assumed to be associated with "open-country" habitat. But "open country" can have quite different meanings in terms of availability of food resources. Morphological characters have no *direct* correlation with the openness or denseness of the habitat and vastly divergent morphological characters can have equally strong indirect correlations with this habitat. The mechanical explanation acceptable for the gelada morphology (i.e., increase in cutting edges) is unacceptable for hominine cheek teeth, in particular for their increase in the relative thickness of the enamel [beyond that seen in *Sivapithecus* and *Gigantopithecus* (D. Pilbeam, personal communication)] and their reduction of $M_{\bar{3}}$ relative to the other molars. Both the thickened enamel and the robustly constructed, thick jaws of early hominines are suggestive of great compressive stressing. Whether the flat crushing surface backed by thick enamel was a character that enabled the protohominines to withstand great compressive force on the tooth crowns or facilitated extensive and very frequent food preparation by the cheek teeth is a question difficult to determine from that aspect of the teeth alone. Consumption of grass (with seeds) or other leafy material is not a satisfactory explanation for it, as hominine teeth lack the characteristic extensive ridging of the cheek teeth of most grazers and browsers. Reduction of the relative size of the third molar also argues against large bulks of grasses or even pure seeds, as an increase rather than decrease in $M_{\bar{3}}$ surface area would be at a premium.

As the baboon–protogelada model does not account for the morphological and mechanical transition sequences from the pongine to the protohominines, it is equally clear that the biological roles performed by the divergent morphologies and mechanical functions were equally dissimilar. If one agrees that the canines became truly incisiform (inasmuch as they mesially closed rank with the incisors and reduced crown height to incisor levels), then the relative *area* of incisivation became enlarged phyletically. This is in contrast to consistently caniniform canines of all geladas, irrespective of the slightly reduced condition found in the giants of that group.

To postulate grass (and seed)-feeding specializations for the protohominines would suggest a similar ecological background for the pongine–hominine transition. But the functionally significant morphological changes (see Szalay, 1975e, for details) from pongines to protohominines as they relate to feeding adaptations do not parallel the protogelada–baboon transformation. Perhaps the protohominines and the thick-enameled apes (Pilbeam *et al.*, 1977) remained in

woodland–savannahs, an environment usually much closer to forest habitats than the relatively poor grasslands with which the living gelada is associated. The protohominine dentition may have evolved in such surroundings again in response to dietary behavior.

In the opinion of Szalay (1975e) and as Gregory (1916) first discussed for the Heidelberg jaw, strong vertically implanted incisors plus incisiform canines became tools to grasp and tear meat, tendon, and fascia. Selection for this role would have been intense as, without good tools, much meat could not be ripped off the carcasses left over by larger predators. Large, pongine-like canines would interfere with this role. Accentuation of other features of the face, bipedality, and subsequent dimorphism in height could produce a signaling apparatus as effective in threat as the canines, particularly when the food-getting needs of both males and females would tend to override selection for canine display. The cheek teeth of scavenging protohominines would not require the usual posteriorly increasing tooth-row of herbivorous species, therefore the reduction in the relative length of the molars. Crushing function, however, commonly performed by hyenas or other mammalian scavenger–carnivore species, would require a powerful mandible, but only with localized need for crushing. Thickened enamel, beyond that of the thick enameled apes, would be at a great selective premium for withstanding the point loading of cracking ribs, metapodials, and joints, and/or for increased longevity. However, before fully accepting any of the postulated biological roles of the protohominine dentition, we await further analysis of the mechanical function of thick enamel, wear patterns, and especially enamel prisms.

Finally, the many modifications in the homine lower body and trunk [but not of the skull (see Biegert, 1963)] are well known to be linked with bipedalism. But the selective value of this locomotor pattern is less clear in light of its energetic costs, unless it was concomitantly involved in freeing the forelimbs for nonlocomotor activity and raising the body for threat display (e.g., swinging clubs or bones or throwing bushes against predators at a kill) and perhaps for increased visibility. In this light, it is interesting that the hominine shoulder is basically identical to that of *Pan* and *Pongo*, but with some modifications for greater mobility.

Combining these lines of evidence, it would appear that the dentition and feeding pattern of hominines was the first to develop. From a *Sivapithecus*-like pattern, selection for a more carnivorous diet led to anterior dental remodeling, either via or in parallel with *Ramapithecus*. Opportunistic scavenging and hunting and perhaps tool-using to aid in meat removal would have slowly increased this selection, as well as that tending to increase eye–hand coordination and thus neural reorganization. As both A. L. Rosenberger (personal communication) and Darlington (1975) have suggested, in slightly different formulations, throwing of natural objects to chase other predator-scavengers from kills might have led to a feedback cycle in eye–hand improvement. Throwing accuracy appears to have a genetic basis in modern man (Kolakowski and Malina, 1974). As alluded to above, upright stance may have been also useful in intraspecific agonistic displays during times of high emotional tension, such as develop over kills or carrion among modern carnivores and scavengers. Moreover, in the late Miocene and early Pliocene, the dominant African vegetation was apparently a wooded grassland, whose height might also have required the more common use of upright posture to obtain sufficient visibility. In this way, bipedal locomotion might have developed in a hunting–scavenging creature with slightly higher relative brain size/neural organization than pongines, and its development would probably have caused further feedback for coordination. Early Pliocene hominines (*Australopithecus* cf. *africanus*) were probably opportunistic scavengers and part-time hunters of small game, perhaps employing thrown stones as missiles. One descendant lineage could have developed tool-making more intensively, leading to early *Homo* with still greater neural reorganization and brain increase and thence differing dental wear patterns. On the other hand, *Australopithecus robustus* would have entered the Plio-Pleistocene savannah and reemphasized the ancestral hominine dominance of the cheek teeth even more intensively, for as yet unclear biological roles, perhaps to escape competition with *Homo*.

In conclusion, it is our belief that the transformation of the protohominine species can be accounted for by the hunter–scavenger model outlined by Szalay (1975e). Admittedly this cannot be "proved." The mechanical results of the morphological transformation, however, do call for an explanation of the positive selection for both (*a*) an area of incisivation which captured the canine and reduced the dimorphism in the latter and (*b*) a cheek-tooth-row which curiously "shrank" in its relative dimensions when the molars are compared with one another, but one that had hypertrophied and had undergone selection for withstanding a specific kind of wear and great compressive forces beyond that seen in the closest relative of the hominines.

RAMAPITHECUS Lewis, 1934

(= or including: *Dryopithecus* Lartet, 1856: Branco, 1897, in part; Pilgrim, 1910, in part. *Palaeopithecus* Lydekker, 1879: Pilgrim, 1927, in part. *Bramapithecus* Lewis, 1934. *Sugrivapithecus* Lewis, 1934: Lewis, 1937, in part. *Sivapithecus* Pilgrim, 1910: Lewis, 1937, in part. *Kenyapithecus* L. Leakey, 1962a. *Rudapithecus* Kretzoi, 1969.)

DISTRIBUTION

Middle and late Miocene (Astaracian to Turolian, Ternanian). Turkey, Kenya, Hungary, ?Germany, India, Pakistan, China.

KNOWN SPECIES

1. *Ramapithecus punjabicus* (Pilgrim, 1910), type species
[=*Dryopithecus fontani* Lartet, 1856: Branco, 1897, in part. *Dryopithecus punjabicus* Pilgrim, 1910. *Dryopithecus indicus* Pilgrim, 1910: Pilgrim 1913, lapsus. *Dryopithecus* cf. *punjabicus*: Pilgrim, 1915. *?Palaeopithecus sylvaticus* Pilgrim, 1927. *Ramapithecus brevirostris* Lewis, 1934. *Bramapithecus thorpei* Lewis, 1934. *Dryopithecus sivalensis* Lewis, 1934. *?Bramapithecus sivalensis* (Lewis, 1934): Lewis, 1937, in part. *Sugrivapithecus salmontanus* Lewis, 1934: Lewis, 1937, in part. *Bramapithecus punjabicus*: Lewis, 1937. *Dryopithecus keiyuanensis* Woo, 1957. *Ramapithecus punjabicus*: Simons, 1964. *Dryopithecus sivalensis* (Lydekker, 1879): Simons and Pilbeam, 1965, in part; Greenfield, 1974, in part. Cf.: *Rudapithecus hungaricus* Kretzoi, 1969.]
LOCALITIES: Chinji⋆ (480); Kanatti (482); Hsiaolungtan (484); Ramnagar (492); (cf.) Rudabánya (506); ?Melchingen (522); Nagri (530); Haritalyangar—lower (554); Sethi Nagri (571); Gandakas (576).

2. *Ramapithecus wickeri* (L. Leakey, 1962a)
(=*Kenyapithecus wickeri* L. Leakey, 1962a. *Ramapithecus punjabicus*: Simons, 1964, in part. *Ramapithecus wickeri*: Andrews, 1971. *Sivapithecus alpani* Tekkaya, 1974.)
LOCALITIES: (Cf.) Paşalar (434); Maboko (438); Çandir (454); Fort Ternan⋆ (462).

DISCUSSION

Ramapithecus is a relatively small hominid whose patristic affinities lie with the Sugrivapithecini, but which appears to share certain derived characters only with Homininae, in which taxon it is tentatively placed. The genus is now recognized at a number of localities spanning a wide temporal and geographic range, but most of the published (and even unpublished) fossils are fragmentary gnathic elements, with no cranial vault or upper face portions and few if any postcranial remains. Diagnosed mainly on the basis of jaws and teeth, then, *Ramapithecus* shares with Sugrivapithecini and at least ancestral Homininae a complex of broad, thick-enameled, rather high crowned cheek teeth, low $P_{\overline{3}}$ on which the C^1 did not hone intensively (and lack of $C^1/C_{\overline{T}}$ honing also), and apparently large cheek teeth compared to limb length. In addition, *Ramapithecus* shares with other hominines and with *Gigantopithecus* a small metaconid on $P_{\overline{3}}$ and further reduction of canine crown height and general incisor size; it is distinguished from *Giganto-*

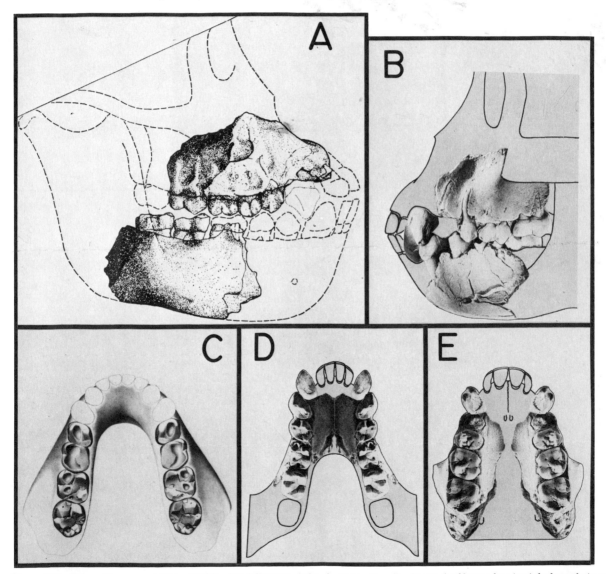

Figure 252. *Ramapithecus punjabicus*. Middle–late Miocene, Asia. A, restoration (by Simons) of lower face in right lateral view; C, restoration (by Simons) of mandibular dental arcade. *Ramapithecus wickeri*. Middle Miocene, Africa. Restoration (by Walker and Andrews) of lower face and dental arcades: B, left lateral view; D, mandible in occlusal view; E, maxilla in occlusal view. [A from Simons (1964); B, D, E from Walker and Andrews (1973), courtesy of P. Andrews; C courtesy of E. L. Simons.]

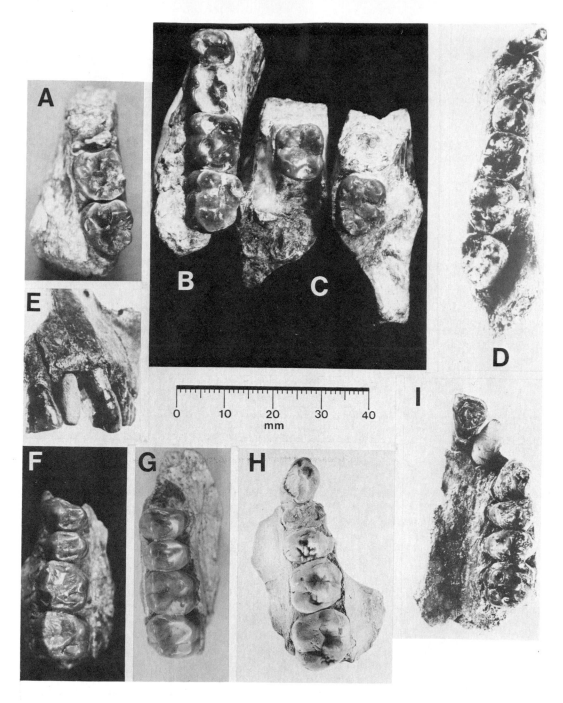

Figure 253. *Ramapithecus punjabicus.* Middle Miocene, Asia. Partial left corpus with M$_{\overline{2-3}}$: A, occlusal view. Partial left corpus with P$_{\overline{4}}$–M$_{\overline{3}}$: B, occlusal view. Partial left corpus with M$_{\overline{2}}$ and partial right corpus with M$_{\overline{3}}$: C, occlusal view. Right maxilla with P$^{\underline{3}}$–M$^{\underline{2}}$: F, occlusal view. Right maxilla with P$^{\underline{3}}$–M$^{\underline{2}}$ and anterior alveoli: G, occlusal view. *R.* cf. *punjabicus ("Rudapithecus")*. Middle Miocene, Europe. Right corpus with C$_{\overline{1}}$–M$_{\overline{3}}$: D, occlusal view. Left half palate with I$^{\underline{1}}$, I$^{\underline{2}}$ restored from another specimen, and C$^{\underline{1}}$–M$^{\underline{1}}$: E, anterior view; I, occlusal view. *R. wickeri.* Middle Miocene, Africa. Left maxilla with C$^{\underline{1}}$ and P$^{\underline{4}}$–M$^{\underline{2}}$: H, occlusal view. [D, E, I courtesy of M. Kretzoi; H courtesy of P. Andrews.]

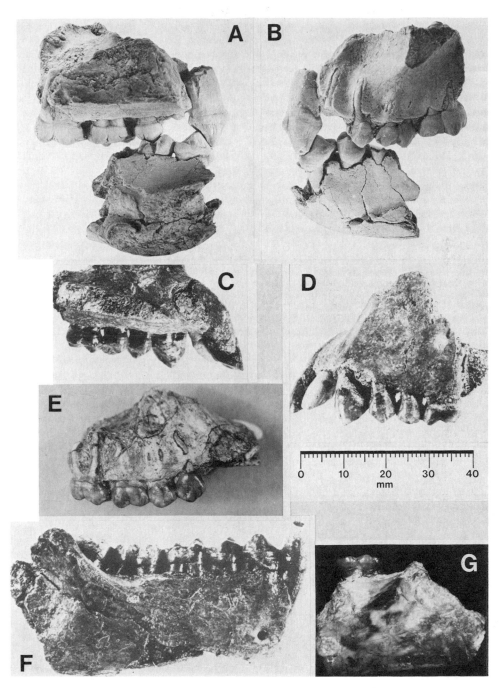

Figure 254. *Ramapithecus wickeri.* Middle Miocene, Africa. Left maxilla with C¹ and P⁴–M² and associated(?) left corpus with P₃₋₄: A, lingual view; B, buccal view. *Ramapithecus* cf. *punjabicus.* Middle Miocene, Europe. Left half palate with I¹ and C¹–M¹, I² restored from another specimen: C, lingual view; D, buccal view. Right corpus with C₁–M₃: F, lateral view. *Ramapithecus punjabicus.* Middle–late Miccene, Asia. Right maxilla with P³–M²: E, buccal view. Left corpus with M₃: G, lateral view. [A, B courtesy of P. Andrews; C, D, F courtesy of M. Kretzoi.]

pithecus and linked to hominines by the role of the canine, which is partly incorporated into the incisor row rather than becoming adapted to crushing occlusion with P$_{\overline{3}}$, especially. The mandible is robust, but not very deep, while the maxillary alveolar processes are deep and inflated, and the cheek teeth may have quite vertical sides and low relief, all shared somewhat with Homininae, rather than Sugrivapithecini. On the other hand, the extreme reduction of incisors and narrow palate with elongated tooth-rows seen at least in *R. wickeri* may be unique features, the presence of which is not certain in *R. punjabicus* as yet.

The long history of varied interpretations of *Ramapithecus* has been summarized by Simons (1976a; Simons and Pilbeam, 1965). It has recently been widely considered as a Miocene ancestor of hominines, but the evidence does not yet permit the ready acceptance of this view. Instead, it would appear that *Ramapithecus* shares a number of features only with later hominines and thus can be considered the sister-taxon of *Australopithecus* + *Homo,* of course among known taxa. Despite early reconstructions of the dental arcades indicating nearly parabolic, *Homo*-like shape (Simons, 1961) (Figure 252, A and C), later study of reconstructed arcades in *R. wickeri* (Walker and Andrews, 1973) (Figure 252, B, D, and E) indicated subparallel tooth-rows with elongated distal teeth. New specimens from Hungary (''*Rudapithecus*'' of Kretzoi, 1975) (Figures 253, D, E, and I, and 254, C, D, and F), Turkey (''*Sivapithecus alpani*'' of Tekkaya, 1974), and Pakistan (Pilbeam *et al.,* 1977) include partial mandibles and maxillae which support the Walker

and Andrews reconstruction. The Çandir mandible closely matches that from Fort Ternan, while one from Pakistan presents somewhat greater posterior divergence, perhaps with a narrower incisor region (Andrews, 1976). *Ramapithecus wickeri* would also appear to have had a more robust, shallower mandible than *R. punjabicus,* although tooth size is quite similar. The face in both species was quite short and flat, with little alveolar prognathism, a small premaxilla and broad middle region (Figure 252B), which is only slightly different from the original reconstruction attempted by Simons (1964).

Adaptively, *Ramapithecus* is somewhat analogous to robust australopiths. The Miocene form combines a robust mandible and strong inferior torus, deep maxillary alveolar region, short face, small incisor region, and large molars, all indicative of heavy chewing forces applied to crush and grind food objects. As reviewed by Simons (1976a) and Andrews (1976), *Ramapithecus* probably inhabited a mixed woodland–savannah environment (often alongside members of the Sugrivapithecini) which may have been responsible for selection for this gnathic complex. Fragmentary and insecurely allocated postcranial elements suggest large molars by comparison to *Dryopithecus* and modern pongins of similar body size, further supporting the postulated heavy use of the posterior dentition. It is unlikely on present evidence that *Ramapithecus* species from the middle and earlier late Miocene were either tool-makers or bipeds, despite previous preliminary suggestions of these attributes.

AUSTRALOPITHECUS Dart, 1925

(Synonymy under subgenera.)

DISTRIBUTION

?Mid-Pliocene to early Pleistocene (Rodolfian). Southern and eastern Africa.

INCLUDED SUBGENERA

Australopithecus (Australopithecus) and *A. (Paranthropus).*

AUSTRALOPITHECUS (AUSTRALOPITHECUS) Dart, 1925

[= or including: *Australopithecus* Dart, 1925. *Plesianthropus* Broom, 1938. *Homo* Linnaeus, 1758: Mayr, 1950, in part. *Australopithecus (Australopithecus):* L. Leakey, Tobias and Napier, 1964. *Paraustralopithecus* Arambourg and Coppens, 1967. Cf.: ?*Ramapithecus* Lewis, 1937: R. Leakey, 1976.]

DISTRIBUTION

Later Pliocene (mid-Rodolfian). Southern and eastern Africa.

KNOWN SPECIES

1. *Australopithecus (Australopithecus) africanus* Dart, 1925, type species

[= *Australopithecus africanus* Dart, 1925. *Australopithecus transvaalensis* Broom, 1936a. *Plesianthropus transvaalensis:* Broom, 1938. *Australopithecus prometheus* Dart, 1949, *Homo transvaalensis:* Mayr, 1950. *Australopithecus (Australopithecus) africanus:* Howell, 1965. *Homo africanus:* Brace and Montague, 1965, in part, *nec* Weidenreich, 1928. *Australopithecus robustus:* Howell, 1969, in part. *Australopithecus* aff. *africanus:* Howell and Coppens, 1976.]

LOCALITIES: Cf. Laetolil (666); Omo Usno (694), Shungura Mbs. B. (696), C (712), D (716), E (726), F (738), G (750); (cf.) Hadar (698);

Makapan (700); Sterkfontein (706); East Rudolf Koobi Fora Lower mb. (728); Taung⋆ (?730); ?Olduvai Bed I (760).

AUSTRALOPITHECUS (PARANTHROPUS) Broom, 1938

[= or including: *Paranthropus* Broom, 1938. *Homo:* Mayr, 1950, in part. *Australopithecus:* Washburn and Patterson, 1951, in part. *Zinjanthropus* L. Leakey, 1959. *Australopithecus (Paranthropus):* L. Leakey, Tobias and Napier, 1964. *Australopitheus (Zinjanthropus):* L. Leakey, Tobias. and Napier, 1964.]

DISTRIBUTION
  Late Pliocene to early Pleistocene (later Rodolfian). Southern and eastern Africa.
KNOWN SPECIES
  2. *Australopithecus (Paranthropus) robustus* (Broom, 1938)
[=*Paranthropus robustus* Broom, 1938. *Paranthropus crassidens* Broom, 1949. *Homo transvaalensis:* Mayr, 1950, in part. *Zinjanthropus boisei* L. Leakey, 1959. *Australopithecus (Zinjanthropus) boisei:* L. Leakey, Tobias, and Napier, 1964. *Homo africanus:* Brace and Montague, 1965, in part, *nec* Weidenreich, 1928. *Australopithecus (Paranthropus) robustus:* Howell, 1967a. *Australopithecus boisei:* Tobias, 1967. *Homo robustus:* Wolpoff, 1971. *Australopithecus africanus:* Campbell, 1972, in part. *Australopithecus crassidens:* Howell and Coppens, 1976.]
LOCALITIES: East Rudolf Koobi Fora Lower mb. (728), Upper mb. (796), Ileret mb. (798); Omo Shungura Mbs. E. (726), F (738), G (750); Olduvai Bed I (760), Lower Bed II (774), Upper Bed II (804); Swartkrans a (752); Peninj (772); Kromdraai B⋆ (782); Chesowanja (790).

DISCUSSION

The question of the degree of taxonomic distinction of *Australopithecus* is one which has been under constant discussion since 1925, when Dart first published the type specimen of *A. africanus*. As will be seen from the synonymy, the variety of formal expressions of this distinction has been immense, with several views still strongly supported in current literature. Here, we accept *Australopithecus* as a single, relatively conservative hominine genus distinguished from *Homo* by a suite of characters discussed below. Following Delson (1978) and references therein, two subgenera are recognized to reflect the infrageneric differences between the two major morphs, each of which is ranked only as a single species. There may be more internal variability in *A. robustus* than in *A. africanus*, on present evidence, and a superspecies complex, such as was suggested by Tobias (1973a), might be a reasonable way to reflect this variation.

Australopithecus basically shares the major morphological derived characters of the Homininae, including large brain to body weight ratio, large posterior and relatively small anterior dentition, with canines not honing but incisiform, parabolic dental arcades, flex-

ion of the cranial base and increasing cranial height, anterior placement of the foramen magnum, development of upright, bipedal posture as reflected in the pelvis, femur, and lumbar vertebrae, elongated lower limb compared to body size (allometrically), and compaction of the foot with loss of hallucial mobility. *Australopithecus* is distinguishable from *Ramapithecus* by usually larger $P_{\overline{3}}$ metaconid, lower crowned canines, and generally larger size, especially comparing the robust australopith variety to the morphologically similar *Ramapithecus*. Finally, from *Homo*, *Australopithecus* is differentiated by smaller estimated body size; relatively and absolutely smaller brain size (range, 400–600+ cm³); absolutely and relatively larger teeth, especially molars and premolars; face much larger as compared to neurocranium; relatively globular and thin-walled neurocranium with anteriorly placed sagittal crest in most robust individuals; maximum calvarial width about at mastoid level; mandibular fossa transversely elongated and especially laterally positioned; supraorbital tori prominent, but neither massive nor incorporated into steep frontal bone; nasal bones "V"-upward toward glabella; mandible more massive and with internal contour either "V"or "pointed U"-shaped, not an "open U," stronger internal tori and longer alveolar planum; corpus deepening somewhat mesially, rather than more constant in depth; apparently more pronounced sexual dimorphism, especially in canine and other dental dimensions; pelvis with relatively small sacroiliac articular surface and acetabulum, relatively large iliac fossa, and widely splayed iliac blades; femur with relatively small head, long neck, and low neck angle; and possibly a relatively long forelimb, at least in robust forms (see Walker, 1973, 1976a; McHenry, 1975; Wolpoff and Lovejoy, 1975).

Taken together, these common features of *Australopithecus* indicate two lineages which were adapted to bipedality of a nearly, if not completely, modern human type and to relatively strong mastication (crushing) of probably hard foodstuffs. The relatively small, although fully hominine, brain compared to modern humans has been suggested as a primary determinant of pelvic differences (Lovejoy *et al.*, 1973), with a smaller fetal head size permitting smaller femoral head/acetabular size while retaining low stresses at the joint. On the other hand, it is still not certain if this pattern is ancestral for the Homininae or if it is uniquely derived (as implied by Walker, 1976b), in which case it would be a strong character setting both varieties of *Australopithecus* apart from *Homo*; tentatively, this latter view is accepted here.

The question of distinctions between the varieties of this genus has also been subjected to much recent scrutiny, partly summarized by Delson (1978; Delson *et al.*, 1977) and by other authors in Jolly (1978). The overwhelming body of both morphological and distributional evidence now leaves little doubt that two main varieties of early hominines must be distinguished from each other as well as from *Homo*, although the levels of such distinctions are still argued, and individual specimens may continue to be the focus of disagreement. In brief, however, it would appear that the following characters may be used to separate *Australopithecus africanus* from *A. robustus* (sensu lato): smaller body size [about 3.5–4.5 ft (1–1.3 m) tall versus about 4.5–5+ ft (1.3–1.6 m); about 45–90 lb (20–40 kg) versus 80–120 lb (35–55 kg)], smaller cranial capacity (about 440 cm³ average, 425–490 range versus 520 average, 500–530 range); cranium in general more gracile, with more rounded neurocranium, apparently lacking strong sagittal crests even in large individuals (Figure 255); parieto-occipital plane not angulated; higher placement of neurocranium relative to face and greater separation of nasion and glabella; lower face more prognathous, nasal region not hollowed; supraorbital tori less pronounced; temporal fossa smaller and postorbital constriction less; mandibular ramus farther inclined posteriorly; anterior dentition larger both relatively and, in most cases, absolutely, and set in a more curving alveolar margin; cheek teeth smaller, although still large by comparison to body size (Figure 256). Postcranial distinctions discussed by Robinson (1972) and others are not substantiated by more complete material (Figure 257) thus far described (McHenry, 1975). On the other hand, the forelimb of *A. robustus* (Figure 257, C and F) is quite distinctive in its overall length, robusticity of the humerus and especially of its articular area and shoulder–abductor musculature, shortness of the ulnar olecranon, and curvature of its shaft, but there are no described remains of *A. africanus* for comparison, although the Hadar specimen (Figure 257A) will be of prime importance here.

The observed differences between the *Australopithecus* species would seem to reflect a combination of allometric (e.g., cranial and cerebral: Pilbeam and Gould, 1974) and developmental (e.g., dental and facial: Wallace, 1978) changes, resulting from strikingly divergent adaptations. As indicated by Eldredge and Tattersall (1975) and others, the *A. africanus* pattern is essentially identical with what might be predicted as an ancestral morphotype not only for *Australopithecus*, but also for *Homo*, at least craniodentally. In part, this may be due to its small size, but *A. robustus* presents several derived features of the gnathic complex which are not only size dependent: As Wallace (1978) has suggested, the end result of a greatly increased grinding component of chewing might have been attained by a combination of robusticity of teeth, skull, and temporal musculature with early fusion of the premaxillary suture leading to small, vertical incisors which wear flat, as well as a reduction of cusp height on all teeth. These features are seen to a varying degree in South and East African robust australopiths, thus clearly grouping these spatially separated populations taxonomically, despite some suggestions to the contrary. This morphological pattern also agrees with current estimates of sample ages, with the *A. africanus* specimens mostly between 3 and 2 MY old, while *A. robustus* fossils range between about 2.1+ and 1.3? MY. One group of hominine fossils older than this range has been tentatively allocated to *Homo habilis*, on the basis of the most preliminary descriptions, while other, more fragmentary remains are held aside as genus and species indeterminate (see pp. 511, 514, 515).

As to behavioral differences between the two australopiths, many of the earlier suppositions have not been supported (see Robinson, 1972). It was previously thought that the more "gracile" variety, *A. africanus*, was a more perfectly bipedal, omnivorous tool-user, while the robust form was more clumsy, facultatively vegetarian, and devoid of "culture." However, there is no significant difference in tooth wear patterns suggestive of dietary distinction (Wallace, 1978), the pelvofemoral differences have not been substantiated (McHenry, 1975), and the only reasonably clear cultural associations have been of the Oldowan complex with remains attributed to *Homo habilis*. Gnathic evidence suggests that robust australopiths were dependent on foodstuffs requiring more powerful mastication than the "graciles," which is compatible with their occurrence in a relatively dry landscape. Nonetheless, the large size of the postcanine dentition in *A. africanus* belies the implications

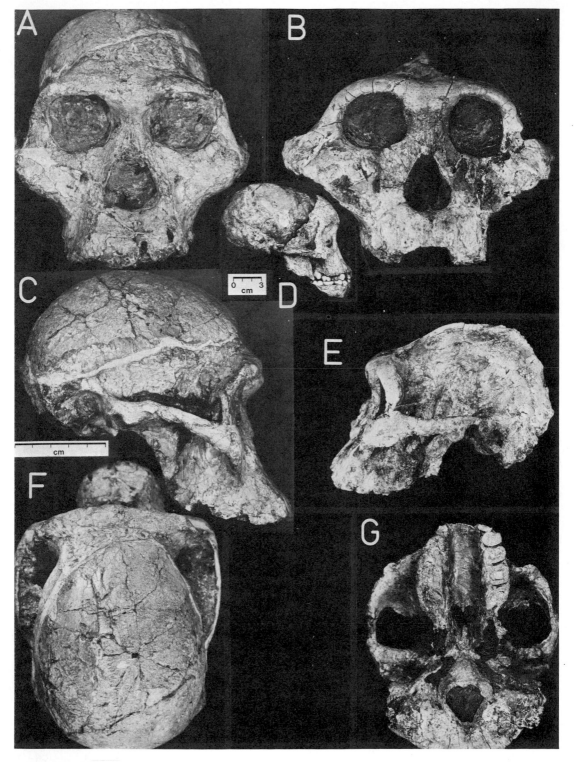

Figure 255. *Australopithecus (Australopithecus) africanus.* Pliocene, Africa. Female cranium: A, frontal view; C, right lateral view; F, dorsal view. Juvenile cranium: D, right lateral view. *Australopithecus (Paranthropus) robustus.* Late Pliocene, Africa. Male cranium: B, frontal view; E, left lateral view; G, basal view. The scale between C and F is for A, C, and F; B is slightly reduced; E and G are approximately 0.7 scale. Scale at D is for D only.

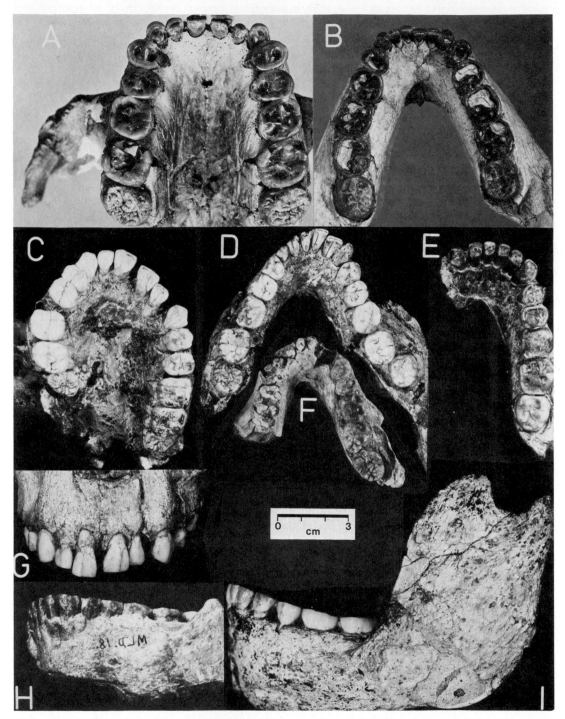

Figure 256. *Australopithecus (Paranthropus) robustus.* Late Pliocene, Africa. Palate with complete dentition, M³'s erupting: A, occlusal view. Mandible with complete dentition: B, occlusal view; I, left lateral view (different specimen). *Australopithecus (A.) africanus.* Pliocene, Africa. Warped palate with complete dentition, M³'s erupting: C, occlusal view; G, anterior view. Warped mandible of same individual, M$_{\overline{3}}$'s erupting: D, occlusal view. Slightly splayed partial mandible with left I$_{\overline{1-2}}$ and right I$_{\overline{1}}$–M$_{\overline{3}}$: E, occlusal view; H, left lateral view (photographically reversed). *A.* cf. *africanus.* Damaged female mandible (from skeleton of Figure 257A) with right P$_{\overline{3}}$–M$_{\overline{3}}$: F, occlusal view. [A, B courtesy of and © P. V. Tobias; F courtesy of and © D. C. Johanson.]

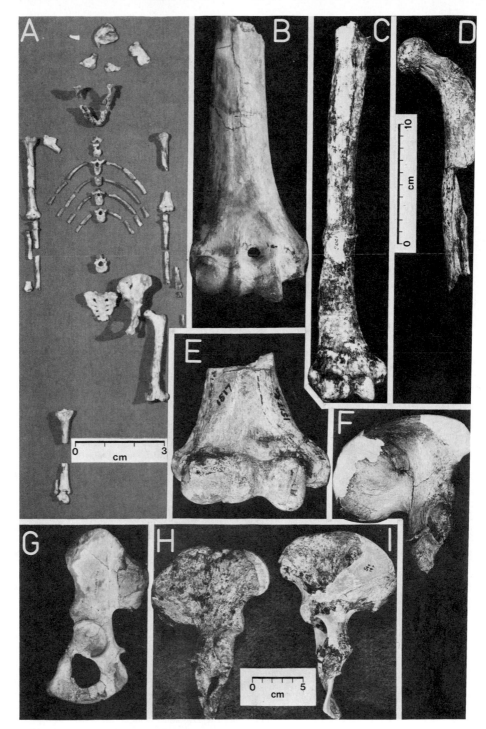

Figure 257. *Australopithecus (A.) africanus.* Pliocene, Africa. H, right, and I, left, female innominate, lateral view. *A.* cf. *africanus:* A, associated female partial skeleton; B, distal third of right humerus from skeleton, anterior view; G, left innominate from skeleton, anterolateral view. *Australopithecus (Paranthropus) robustus.* Late Pliocene, Africa: C, right humerus lacking proximal end, anterior view; D, damaged proximal half of left femur, anterior view; E, distal end of right humerus, anterior view; F, damaged and partly restored right innominate, lateral view. The scale between C and D is for both; the scale for E is to its left, B is at ca. 0.8 this scale, and A is at ca. ⅛ this scale; the lower scale is for F–I. [A courtesy of and © National Geographic Society; B, G courtesy of and © D. C. Johanson.]

of the term "gracile" and suggests that all members of the genus were adapted to a basically vegetarian diet, although the older and more "primitive" species might well have engaged in more regular but clearly opportunistic scavenging of animal protein than the robust, younger, more "specialized" form which was probably its descendant. As noted, both species were well adapted to a bipedal upright gait little different from that in modern humans, but recent studies of both taxa have also postulated that forelimb and shoulder morphology might have been adapted to climbing and thus continued use of an arboreal environment, for either sleeping or feeding (Robinson, 1972; McHenry et al., 1976; Ciochon and Corruccini, 1976). The last two sets of authors suggested that the observed morphology might have been only a "holdover" from an earlier, more arboreal ancestry, but it is perhaps more likely to have been important in the mode of life of Australopithecus species themselves.

HOMO Linnaeus, 1758

[= or including: Anthropopithecus Blainville, 1839: Dubois, 1892, in part. Pithecanthropus Dubois, 1893, 1894. Protanthropus Haeckel, 1895. Hylobates Illiger, 1811: Bumuller, 1899, in part. Proanthropus Wilser, 1900. Euranthropus Sergi, 1909. Heoanthropus Sergi, 1909. Notanthropus Sergi, 1909. Palaeanthropus Bonarelli, 1909a; Palaeoanthropus Reck and Kohl-Larsen, 1936, lapsus? Homo (Protanthropus) Bonarelli, 1909b. Pseudohomo Ameghino, 1909. Protanthropus Arldt, 1915. Anthropus Boyd-Dawkins, 1926. Sinanthropus Black and Zdansky, 1927, in Black, 1927. Cyphanthropus Pycraft, 1928. Hemianthropus Freudenberg, 1929. Homo (Javanthropus) Oppenoorth, 1932. Praehomo Eickstedt, 1932. "Metanthropus" Sollas, 1933. Homo (Africanthropus) Dreyer, 1935. Africanthropus Weinert, 1938, nec Dreyer, 1935. Maueranthropus Montandon, 1943. Homo (Homo): Kälin, 1945. Nipponanthropus Hasebe, 1948. "Präanthropus" Hennig. 1948. Telanthropus Broom and Robinson, 1949b. Meganthropus von Koenigswald, 1944, in Weidenreich, 1944: Weinert, 1950, in part. Europanthropus Wust, 1950. Atlanthropus Arambourg, 1954. Praeanthropus Seyürek, 1955. "Euranthropus" Arambourg, 1955. Homo (Pithecanthropus): Dolinar-Osole, 1956. "Homopithecus" Deraniyagala, 1960. "Tchadanthropus" Coppens, 1965. Pongo Lacépède, 1799: Krantz, 1975, in part.]

DISTRIBUTION
    Pliocene to modern. Worldwide.
KNOWN SPECIES
    1. Homo sapiens Linnaeus, 1758, type species.
        a. Homo s. sapiens Linnaeus, 1758
[=Horo spelaeus Lapouge, 1899. Homo niger var. primigenia Wilser, 1903, species nec Gmelin, 1788. Homo sapiens fossilis Gorjanovic-Kramberger, 1905. Homo grimaldii Lapouge, 1906; H. s. grimaldiensis: Gregory, 1921; H. grimaldicus Hilber, 1922, lapsi? Homo aurignacensis hauseri Klaatsch and Hauser, 1910. Homo breladensis Marett, 1911. Notanthropus eurafricanus recens Sergi, 1911. Notanthropus eurafricanus archaius Sergi, 1911. Homo mediterraneus fossilis Behm, 1915. Homo fossilis protoaethiopicus Giuffrida-Ruggieri, 1915. Homo capensis Broom, 1917. Homo predmostensis Absolon, 1920; Homo predmosti Matiegka, 1938, lapsus? Homo wadjakensis Dubois, 1921. Homo meridionalis protoaethiopicus Giuffrida-Ruggieri, 1921. Homo sapiens cromagnonensis Gregory, 1921. Homo sapiens wadjakensis: Kleinschmidt, 1922. Homo sapiens aurignacensis: Kleinschmidt, 1922. Homo gibraltarensis Battaglia, 1924. Homo larterti Pycraft, 1925. Homo australoideus africanus Drennan, 1929, subspecies nec Weidenreich, 1928. Hemianthropus osborni Freudenberg, 1929. Homo drennani Kleinschmidt, 1931. Homo (African-

thropus) helmei Dreyer, 1935. Homo florisbadensis Drennan, 1935. "Homopithecus sinhaleyus" Deraniyagala, 1960. Homo sapiens afer Linnaeus, 1758: Wells, 1969, and others.]
    LOCALITIES: ?Border Cave (1082); Velika Pecina (1232); Florisbad (1236); San Diego (1238); Combe-Capelle (1240); Cro-Magnon (1242); Lake Mungo (1246); Choukoutien Upper Cave (1248); Lagoa Santa (1298); and innumerable later fossil sites on all continents and living populations.
        b. Homo sapiens cf. sapiens
[=Palaeanthropus palestinus McCown and Keith, 1932 (1934) (in Weidenreich, 1932b); P. "palestinensis" Weidenreich, 1932b, lapsus. Homo "leakeyi" Paterson, 1940. Homo semiprimigenius palestinus Montandon, 1943. Homo sapiens palestinus: Campbell, 1972.]
    LOCALITIES: ?Omo Kibish Mb. I (1036); ?Kanjera man "site" (1078); Djebel Qafzeh (1120); Skhul (1233).
        c. Homo sapiens neanderthalensis King, 1864
[=Homo neanderthalensis King, 1864. "Protanthropus atavus" Haeckel, 1895. Homo europaeus primigenius Wilser, 1898. Homo neanderthalensis var. krapinensis Gorjanovic-Kramberger, 1902; Palaeanthropus krapiniensis Sergi, 1911, lapsus? Homo primigenius Schwalbe, 1903. Homo primigenius var. spyensis Gorjanovic-Kramberger, 1905. Homo antiquus Adloff, 1908. Homo transprimigenius mousteriensis Forrer, 1908. Homo (Protanthropus) neanderthalensis: Bonarelli, 1909b. Homo mousteriensis hauseri Klaatsch and Hauser, 1909. Homo priscus Krause, 1909. Palaeanthropus europaeus: Sergi, 1910. Homo chapellensis Buttel-Reepen, 1911. Homo calpicus Kieth, 1911. Homo acheulensis moustieri Wiegers, 1915. Homo lemousteriensis Wiegers, 1915. Archanthropus (neanderthalensis) Arldt, 1915. Homo naulettensis Baudouin, 1916. Archanthropus primigenius Abel, 1920. Homo sapiens neanderthalensis: Kleinschmidt, 1922. Anthropus neanderthalensis: Boyd-Dawkins, 1926. Homo heringsdorfensis Werthe, 1928. Homo "galilensis" Joleaud, 1931; Homo primigenius "galilaeensis": Hennig, 1932. "Metanthropus" Sollas, 1933. Homo neanderthalensis var. aniensis Sergi, 1935. Pithecanthropus neanderthalensis: Sklerj, 1937. Homo "ehringsdorfensis" Paterson, 1940. Homo kiikobiensis Bontsch-Osmolovskii, 1940. Protanthropus "tabunensis" Bonarelli, 1944. Homo (Protanthropus) neanderthalensis Blanc, 1961. Homo sapiens krapinensis: Campbell, 1962. Homo erectus "mapaensis" Kurth, 1965.]
    LOCALITIES: ?La Rafette (988); Temara (990); ?Asych (992); Lazaret (994); Grotte du Prince (996); Fontéchevade (998); Suard (1000); Kiikkoba (1006); Starosel'je (1008); Taubach (1010); Sedia del Diavolo (1012); Malarnaud (1014); Ganovce (1016); Cova Negra (1018); ?Hang Hum lower (1022); Ehringsdorf (1040); Bourgeois-Delaunay (1042);

Saccopastore (1044); Zuttiyeh (1046); Bañolas (1050); ?Quinzano (1052); Montmaurin upper (1054); Krapina (1056); Pofi (1058); ?Ushikawa (1060); ?Shuiyen (1062); ?Mapa (1064); ?Dingcun (1066); ?Sjara-osso-gol (1068); ?Chang-yang (1070); Spy (1086); Sipka (1088); Arcy-Renne (1090); Genay (1092); La Masque (1094); Monsempron (1096); Rigabe (1098); Soulabé (1100); Camerota (1102); Monte Circeo (1104); Uluzzo (1106); La Naulette (1108); St. Brelade (1110); Kulna (1112); Ochoz (1114); Sala (1116); Shanidar (1118); Angles sur l'Anglin (1124); Arcy-Loup (1126); Arcy-Hyène (1128); Caminero (1130); La Cave (1132); La Chapelle (1134); Chateauneuf (1136); Combe-Grenal (1138); La Crouzade (1140); La Croze del Dua (1142); La Ferrassie (1144); Hortus (1146); Marillac (1148); Montgaudier (1150); Le Moustier (1152); Pech de l'Azé (1154); Le Petit-Puymoyen (1156); Placard (1158); Putride (1160); Regourdou (1162); René Simard (1164); Roc du Marsal (1166); Vergisson (1168); Neandertal⋆ (1170); Neuessing (1172); Salzgitter-Lebenstedt (1174); Wildscheuer (1176); Devil's Tower (1178); Forbes Quarry (1180); Subalyuk (1182); Archi (1184); Bisceglie (1186); Ca'verde (1188); Cariguela (1190); Lezetxiki (1192); St. Brais (1194); Dzhruchula (1196); Rozhok (1198); Teshik-Tash (1200); Ohaba-Ponor (1202); Ksar-Akil (1204); Ras-el-Kelb (1206); Shukbah (1208); Shovakh (1210); ?Masloukh (1212); ?Geulah (1214); ?Kebarah (1216); ?Bisitun (1218); ?Tamtama (1220); ?Irhoud (1222); ?Haua Fteah (1224); Tabun (1226); La Quina (1228); Amud (1230).

d. *Homo sapiens heidelbergensis* Schoetensack, 1908
[=*Homo heidelbergensis* Schoetensack, 1908. *Palaeanthropus heidelbergensis*: Bonarelli, 1909a. *Pseudhomo heidelbergensis*: Ameghino, 1909. *Protanthropus heidelbergensis*: Arldt, 1915. *Homo sapiens heidelbergensis*: Kleinschmidt, 1922. *Praehomo europaeus* Eickstedt, 1934. *Homo steinheimensis* Berckhemer, 1936. *Homo murrensis* Weinert, 1936. *Anthropus heidelbergensis*: Weinert, 1937. *Homo neanderthalensis steinheimensis*: Peters, 1937. *Pithecanthropus erectus heidelbergensis*: Peters, 1937. *Homo "marstoni"* Paterson, 1940. *Homo "swanscombensis"* Kennard, 1942. *Homo sapiens protosapiens* Montandon, 1943. *Maueranthropus heidelbergensis*: Montandon, 1943. *Pithecanthropus heidelbergensis*: Kälin, 1945. *Homo (Protanthropus) neanderthalensis steinheimensis*: Kälin, 1945. *Europanthropus heidelbergensis*: Wust, 1950. *"Euranthropus"* Arambourg, 1955. *Homo erectus heidelbergensis*: Kurth, 1965. *Homo erectus mauritanicus* (Arambourg, 1954): Tobias, 1968, in part. *Homo erectus* seu *sapiens palaeohungaricus* Thoma, 1968. *Atlanthropus mauritanicus*: Ennouchi, 1970, in part. *Homo erectus heidelbergensis*: Campbell, 1972. *Homo palaeohungaricus*: Chaline, 1972. *Homo erectus*: Jaeger, 1975, in part.]
LOCALITIES: Mauer⋆ (860); Vértesszöllös (874); Petralona (882); ?Vergranne (886); Montmaurin-Niche (908); Littorina (910); Arago (932); Bilzingsleben (934); Thomas 1 (936); Thomas 3 (938); Salé (940); Swanscombe (942); ?Orgnac-3 (946); Steinheim (948); Rabat (982); ?Atapuerca (984); ?Kapthurin (987).

e. *Homo sapiens rhodesiensis* (Woodward, 1921)
[=*Homo rhodesiensis* Woodward, 1921. *Homo sapiens rhodesiensis*: Kleinschmidt, 1927. *Cyphanthropus rhodesiensis*: Pycraft, 1928. *Homo primigenius africanus* Weidenreich, 1928. *Homo kanamensis* L. Leakey, 1935. *Palaeoanthropus njarensis* Reck and Kohl-Larsen, 1936. *Homo neanderthalensis rhodesiensis*: Peters, 1937. *Africanthropus njarensis*: Weinert, 1938. *Pithecanthropus njarensis*: Kälin, 1945. *Homo (Protanthropus) neanderthalensis rhodesiensis*: Kälin, 1945. *Homo saldanensis* Drennan, 1955. *Homo erectus*: Coon, 1962, in part. *Homo sapiens neanderthalensis*: Brace, Nelson, and Korn, 1971, in part.]
LOCALITIES: Cave of Hearths (1002); ?Kanam hominid "site" (1004); Saldanha (1034); ?Omo Kibish Mb. I (1036); Broken Hill⋆ (1038); Bodo (1072); Eyasi (1076); ?Diré-Dawa (1080); ?Singa (1122).

f. *Homo ?sapiens soloensis* (Oppenoorth, 1932)
[= or including: *Homo (Javanthropus) soloensis* Oppenoorth, 1932. *Homo primigenius asiaticus* Weidenreich, 1932a, subspecies *nec* Linnaeus, 1758. *Homo neanderthalensis soloensis*: Peters, 1937. *Homo wadjakensis*: Dubois, 1940a, in part. *Homo sapiens soloensis*: Dubois. 1940b. *Homo (Protanthropus) neanderthalensis soloensis*: Kälin, 1945. *Homo erectus*: Coon, 1962, in part. *Homo sapiens neanderthalensis?*: Brace, Nelson, and Korn, 1971.]
LOCALITIES: Ngandong⋆ (986).

2. *Homo erectus* (Dubois, 1892)
[= *Anthropopithecus erectus* Dubois, 1892. *Pithecanthropus erectus*: Dubois (1893), 1894. *Homo javanensis primigenius* Houze, 1896. *Homo pithecanthropus* Manouvrier, 1896. *Hylobates giganteus* Bumuller, 1899. *Proanthropus erectus*: Wilser, 1900, *Pithecanthropus duboisii* Morselli, 1901. *Hylobates gigas* Kraus, 1909. *Homo trinilis* Alsberg, 1922. *Homo sapiens erectus*: Kleinschmidt, 1922. *Sinanthropus pekinensis* Black and Zdansky, 1927, in Black, 1927. *Pithecanthropus sinensis* Weinert, 1931. *Praehomo asiaticus sinensis* Eickstedt, 1932. *Praehomo asiaticus javanensis* Eickstedt, 1932. *Homo modjokertensis* von Koenigswald, 1936. *Pithecanthropus erectus erectus*: Peters, 1937. *Pithecanthropus erectus pekinensis*: Peters, 1937. *Homo erectus javanensis*: Weidenreich, 1940. *Homo erectus pekinensis*: Weidenreich, 1940. *Homo wadjakensis*: Dubois, 1940a, in part. *Homo soloensis*: Dubois, 1940a, in part. *Homo sapiens soloensis*: Dubois, 1940b, in part. *Pithecanthropus robustus* Weidenreich. 1944. *Nipponanthropus akashiensis* Hasebe, 1948. *Telanthropus capensis* Broom and Robinson, 1949b. *Sinanthropus officinalis* von Koenigswald, 1952. *Atlanthropus mauritanicus* Arambourg, 1954. *Homo (Pithecanthropus) mauritanicus*: Dolinar-Osole, 1956. *Homo (P.) "atlanticus"* Dolinar-Osole, 1956. *Homo (P.) "ternifinus"* Dolinar-Osole, 1956. *Pithecanthropus erectus mauritanicus*: Campbell, 1962. *Homo "leakeyi"* Heberer, 1963 (provisional). *Homo erectus erectus*: Campbell, 1963. *Sinanthropus lantianensis* Woo, 1964. *Homo habilis* Leakey, Tobias, and Napier, 1964, in part. *"Tchadanthropus uxoris"* Coppens, 1965, (provisional). *Australopithecus africanus*: Pilbeam and Simons, 1965, in part. *Homo erectus capensis*: Campbell, 1965. *Homo erectus mauritanicus*: Campbell, 1965. *Homo erectus "leakeyi"*: Campbell, 1965. *Homo* sp.: Fejfar, 1969. *Homo sapiens neanderthalensis*: Brace, Nelson, and Korn, 1971, in part. *Homo erectus yuanmouensis* Hu, 1973. *Homo ergaster* Groves and Mazak, 1975. *Pongo brevirostris* Krantz, 1975. in part.]
LOCALITIES: ?Omo Shungura Mb. H (776); Yuanmou (780); Modjokerto (786); Sangiran (Djetis) (788); Olduvai middle Bed II (792); East Rudolf Koobi Fora Upper mb. (796), Ileret mb. (798); ?Gomboré II (802); Olduvai upper Bed II (804); Omo Shungura Mb. K (806); Olduvai Bed III (820); ?Omo Shungura Mb. L (822); Sangiran (Trinil) (834); Trinil⋆ (836); Kedung Brubus (838); ?Sambungmachan (840); ?other Javanese mid-Pleistocene sites (842); Olduvai Bed IV (856); Ternifine (858); ?Yayo (862); ?Olduvai Masek (866); ?Lake Ndutu (872); Gongwangling (876); Choukoutien Loc 1 (898); Chenchiawo (902); Hong Kong drugstore ('*S. officinalis*'') (904); ?Nishiyagi (920); ?Tham Khuyen (922); ?Tham Hai (924); ?Olduvai lower Ndutu (928); ?Swartkrans b (930). Cf. ?Prezletice (848).

3. *Homo habilis* L. Leakey, Tobias, and Napier, 1964
(= or including: *"Präanthropus"* Hennig, 1948. *Meganthropus africanus* Weinert, 1950. *Telanthropus capensis*: Robinson, 1953, in part. *Praeanthropus africanus*: Senyürek, 1955. *Homo erectus*: Robinson, 1961, in part. *Australopithecus habilis*: Oakley, 1964. *Australopithecus africanus*: Robinson, 1967, in part. *?Australopithecus boisei*: Tobias, 1967, in part. *Homo* sp.: Clarke, Howell and Brain, 1970.)
LOCALITIES: Cf. Laetolil (666); cf. Hadar (698); East Rudolf Koobi Fora Lower mb. (728); ?Omo Shungura Mb. F (738), G (750); ?Swartkrans a

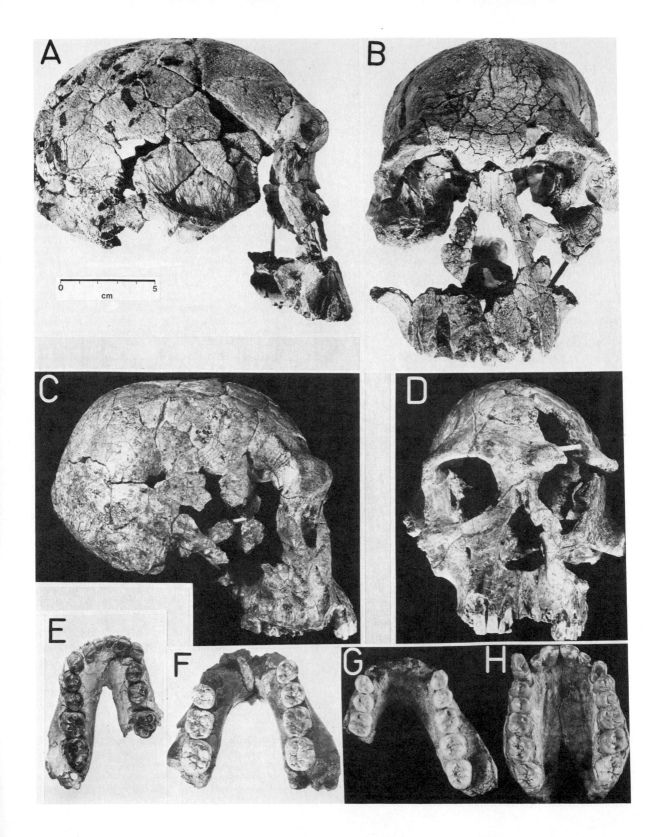

(752); Olduvai Bed I⋆ (760); ?Gombore I (761); Olduvai lower Bed II (774); Omo Shungura Mb. H (776); ?Sterkfontein Extension (778).

Discussion

Homo is one of the most derived of all primates (certainly the most so among Hominidae) both in "standard" morphological characters and in behavioral ones. It shares the basic hominine features with *Australopithecus*, but can be distinguished from that genus as indicated above. Diagnoses of *Homo* depend, to a greater extent than usual, on which specimens or taxa are included in the genus: Here, the diagnosis must be rather broad, as various early and somewhat conservative forms have been accepted as representing a distinct species, *Homo habilis*, along with the two more generally accepted, younger species. The major distinguishing characters of *Homo*, clearly, are the relatively large brain size (known minimum, 600–650 cm³), large neurocranium compared to smaller and less projecting face, relatively small cheek teeth with helicoidal wear and moderately thin enamel, often large anterior teeth set in a rounded arcade, the internal mandibular contour an open "U" shape, and "modern" pelvic girdle, that is, adapted to both bipedal striding and the birth of large-headed infants, such that the acetabulum and associated femoral head are large, as is the sacral articulation, while the iliac fossa is small, femoral neck short, and iliac blades not splayed.

The oldest recognized species of *Homo, H. habilis*, is still the topic of much controversy, with respect to both its distinction from other taxa and its contents. A quite broad view is taken here, with specimens from Laetolil and Hadar presenting U-shaped mandibles and other dental differences from contemporary *Australopithecus* tentatively included along with younger and more complete specimens. Most specimens from the two older sites are reasonably uniform morphologically, but further analysis of variability is needed to determine their precise taxonomic allocation. No complete and undistorted cranium of *H.*

habilis is known, the best preserved (ER 1470, Figure 258, A and B) showing distortion which causes the left side to be significantly more *Australopithecus*-like than the right, with little security as to the "correct" pattern (Walker, 1976a). In many ways similar to this skull is ER 1813 (Figure 258, C and D), often termed *Australopithecus* sp. due to its smaller cranial capacity, but which is here referred to this species tentatively, along with several specimens from Olduvai Bed I, Sterkfontein Extension, and Swartkrans a (specimen SK 847, which shows some features "transitional" to *Homo erectus*). The dentition of *Homo habilis* as known is hardly distinguishable from that of *Australopithecus africanus*, although many specimens have as yet been only partly described and not comparatively analyzed. Molar enamel is presumably as thick as in *A. africanus*. Mandibles appear to present a more open anterior contour than do those of *Australopithecus*, and some are similar to those of *Homo erectus*, as are certain maxillae (Figure 258, E–H). Femora (Figure 250E) allocated to *H. habilis* have large heads and short necks and indicate a functional pattern close to that of *H. sapiens* (McHenry, 1975). The value of accepting a definition based essentially on brain size is questionable, but appears supported by the mandibular and femoral evidence. No unique characters are yet known for this species which would remove it from the ancestry of later derived forms. Circumstantial evidence indicates an association with tools of the Oldowan complex in both eastern and southern Africa and further suggests a life-style involving active hunting of small animals, possible scavenging of larger prey, and gathering of plant foods. It is interesting, if not conclusive, that no clear change in artifactual remains occurs with either the advent of *Australopithecus robustus* or the last occurrences of *A. africanus*, but such a change is noticed with the presence of a new *Homo* species.

This form, *Homo erectus*, is apparently the first Plio-Pleistocene hominine to have exited from Africa, perhaps due to a partial reduction in forest barriers in the early Pleistocene. The species as recognized here is defined by increase in body(?) and brain size; rela-

---

Figure 258. *Homo habilis*. Late Pliocene, Africa. Reconstructed cranium (relationship of mid/lower face to neurocranium hypothetical): A, right lateral view; B, frontal view. Crushed juvenile mandible with left $I_{\overline{1}}$–$M_{\overline{2}}$ and right $I_{\overline{1}}$–$M_{\overline{1}}$: E, occlusal view. Juvenile mandible cracked in symphyseal region, with left $P_{\overline{4}}$–$M_{\overline{2}}$ and right $P_{\overline{3}}$–$M_{\overline{2}}$: F, occlusal view. Cf. *Homo habilis* (or cf. *Australopithecus africanus*). Mid–Late Pliocene, Africa. Cranium: C, right lateral view; D, frontal view. Mandible with left $P_{\overline{3}}$–$M_{\overline{1}}$ and right $P_{\overline{3}}$–$M_{\overline{3}}$: G, occlusal view. Palate with complete dentition (note right $C^{\underline{1}}$ slightly out of its alveolus): H, occlusal view. [A–F courtesy of M. G. Leakey and © Trustees National Museums of Kenya; G, H courtesy of and © D. C. Johanson.]

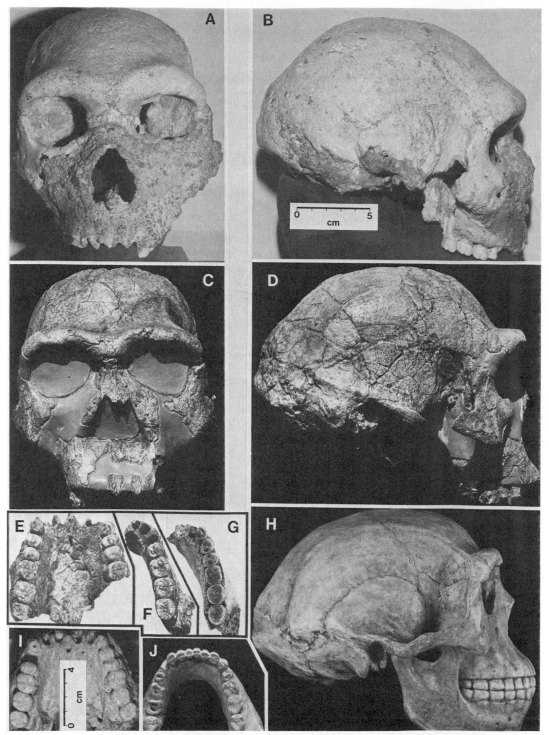

Figure 259. *Homo sapiens heidelbergensis.* Middle Pleistocene, Europe. Petralona cranium: A, frontal view; B, right lateral view; I, occlusal view, right P^4–M^3, left C^1–M^3. Mauer mandible: J, occlusal view, dentition only, crowns of left $P_{\overline{3}}$–$M_{\overline{2}}$ broken off, *Homo erectus.* Early Pleistocene, East Africa. Koobi Fora cranium: C, frontal view; D, right lateral view. Koobi Fora mandible: G, occlusal view right corpus with $C_{\overline{1}}$–$M_{\overline{3}}$. *Homo erectus.* Early–middle Pleistocene, Asia. Choukoutien reconstructed female cranium: H, right lateral view. Sangiran palate with right C^1–M^3 and left C^1–M^1: E, occlusal view. Sangiran right corpus with $P_{\overline{4}}$–$M_{\overline{3}}$: F, occlusal view. Scale divisions are in centimeters (that near B is for all). [A, B, I courtesy of and © F. C. Howell; C, D, G courtesy of M. G. Leakey and © Trustees National Museums of Kenya.]

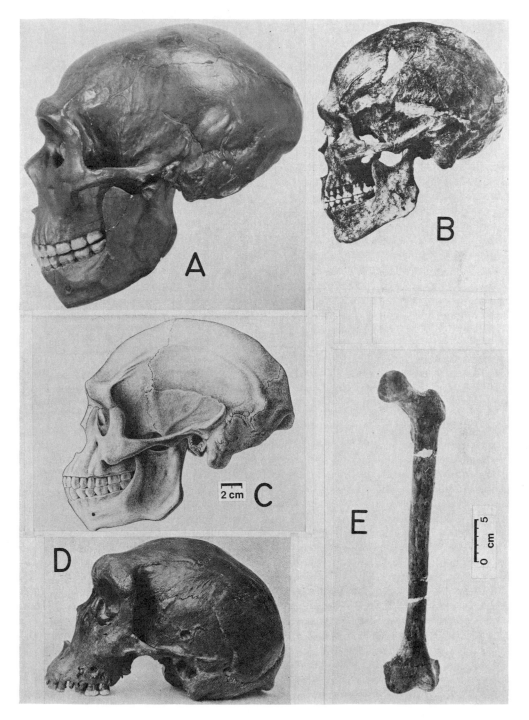

Figure 260. *Homo sapiens* subspecies. Late Pleistocene. Crania in left lateral view: A, *H. s. neanderthalensis*; B, *H. s. sapiens*; C, *H. ?s. soloensis*; D, *H. s. rhodesiensis*. Cf. *Homo habilis*. Late Pliocene, Africa. Left femur: E, anterior view. The scale at E is for E; that at C is for C and (approximately) D, while A is larger and B smaller. [C from Weidenreich (1951); E courtesy of M. G. Leakey and © Trustees National Museums of Kenya.]

tively larger anterior and smaller posterior teeth with thinner enamel; more robust face; extremely thick cranial vault bones and other unique features; and a set of distinctive femoral characters. As Delson *et al.* (1977) have noted, the first several of these are probably continuations of allometric trends which separate *Homo* from *Australopithecus* (Pilbeam and Gould, 1974); thus, they are not sufficient to further discriminate among *Homo* species. But the apparently unique cranial features (thick bone, sometimes mid-sagittal keeling, mound-shaped occipital torus and lack of external occipital protuberance, small mastoid process, undivided supraorbital torus with flaring "wings" and marked postorbital constriction) combined with a combination of femoral characters not seen in *Homo sapiens* [or in *H. habilis*: platymeria, low placement of minimum breadth, gluteal bulge, low linea aspera without pilaster, acute and longitudinally convex medial border (Day, 1976)] distinguish *H. erectus* from its congeners. The cranial and dental patterns are observable on specimens from Asia as well as more recently recovered fossils from eastern Africa (Figure 259). One of the latter has recently been made the holotype of a new species *H. ergaster* Groves and Mazak, 1975, but although the hypodigm was distinguished from *H. habilis* and *Australopithecus* spp., no comparison was made with *H. erectus*. The recovery of a nearly complete skull of the latter in the same horizon confirms allocation of this material to the known taxon. Various authors have discussed local samples of *Homo erectus* fossils as representing subspecies, but, while these may be useful as geographic terms, they are really not based on secure taxonomic differences, given the poor current understanding of inter and intra-site variability. Delson *et al.* (1977) have suggested that the presence of artifacts of the Acheulean complex with almost all known *Homo erectus* populations might be a significant taxonomic attribute, although not a morphological character. These tools and related archeological data also suggest that *Homo erectus* was an active big-game hunter as well as plant-food gatherer, and the widening of its ecological niche may well have led to indirect competition with *Australopithecus robustus* and to its eventual extinction. There is as yet no unequivocal evidence of temporal overlap between *H. habilis* and *H. erectus*, but some population of the former probably gave rise to the latter, which in turn spread and replaced its ancestor.

Homo sapiens, the only extant hominine, is even more difficult to diagnose with respect to *H. erectus*, as it also participated in the basic *Homo* cerebral, cranial, and dental trends. Delson *et al.* (1977) suggested that derived features of *H. sapiens* might relate to a different femoral complex (although no comparisons have been made which include extinct subspecies as well as *H. erectus*) and advanced tool-making techniques such as the use of prepared cores (although the relationship of these to the earliest *H. sapiens* fossils is still uncertain); cranial differences are open to even further question. Delson *et al.* (1977) further discussed a possible morphotype for ancestral *Homo sapiens* and the distinctions among the subspecies recognized here. There would appear to be some overlap between the youngest *Homo erectus* in Asia and the oldest specimens recognized as *H. s. heidelbergensis* (Figure 259), whose origin is postulated to be from a Mediterranean stock of *H. erectus* subjected to selection pressure by the increasingly harsh alternating glacial–interglacial climatic cycles of the middle Pleistocene. Isolation in this region led to speciation, followed in turn by spreading back into Africa and Asia, after which local populations differentiated to where several might be called subspecies [Neandertals, "Rhodesian," and perhaps "Solo" types (Figure 260) with Chinese fossils tentatively placed with the first of these on the basis of similarity between the Mapa cranium and European specimens]. The Rhodesian and Solo samples certainly do not represent Neandertal varieties—they share a number of ancestral characters with the latter and with early *H. sapiens*, but they lack Neandertal unique features and have their own; it is possible that Solo fossils should better be referred to *H. erectus*, but they require further comparative study in light of archaic *H. sapiens* remains recovered elsewhere. The origin of *Homo sapiens sapiens* is still uncertain, but a number of fossils are tentatively referred here, while the earliest more definite allocations are fossils from sub-Saharan Africa, not usually considered a source area for this taxon.

HOMO or AUSTRALOPITHECUS, sp(p). indeterminate

[= or including: *Meganthropus palaeojavanicus* von Koenigswald, 1944, in Weidenreich, 1944. *Pithecanthropus dubius* von Koenigswald, 1949.

Paranthropus palaeojavanicus: Robinson, 1954. *Hemianthropus* (*nec* Freudenberg, 1929) *peii* von Koenigswald, 1957a. *Hemianthropus peii*:

von Koenigswald, 1957b. *Australopithecus* sp. nov.: "Gao Jian," 1975. *Pongo brevirostris* Krantz, 1975, in part.]

HOMININAE, gen. et sp(p). indeterminate

[= or including: *?Australopithecus*: Patterson and Howells, 1967. Hominoidea indet.: L. Leakey, 1970 (in Bishop and Chapman, 1970). *Australopithecus* sp. cf. *A. africanus*: Patterson, Behrensmeyer, and Sill, 1970. *Australopithecus* aff. *africanus*: Tobias, 1973b. ?Hominidae: Andrews, 1975 (in Pickford, 1975).]
LOCALITIES: Ngorora B (516); Lukeino (606); Lothagam-1 (616); ?Kanapoi (646); ?Chemeron (688).

DISCUSSION

A small number of Asian fossils comprising isolated teeth or partial mandibles are not unambiguously referable to either known hominine genus, but probably belong in one of them. It is likely, but by no means definite, that the two or three jaws and other teeth from Java, all of which share large cheek teeth and robust corpora, represent a single species. This taxon has been compared or synonymized with *Australopithecus robustus*, *Homo habilis*, and *Homo erectus*, as otherwise recognized here, but diagnostic features are lacking. The even more fragmentary Chinese fossils could also represent a single species, possibly even the same one as that found in Java, but they have barely been adequately described, much less analyzed comparatively.

A similar situation holds for various fragmentary and early remains from eastern Africa. The Ngorora and Lukeino isolated molars are high crowned, rather large teeth which might pertain to *Ramapithecus* or conceivably to either of the younger hominine genera. The three younger specimens have been referred to various taxa, but, until *Homo* and *Australopithecus* can be readily distinguished from small fragments, even the Lothagam jaw, which may present a *Homo*-like helicoidal wear pattern (Wallace, 1978), must remain *incertae sedis*.

Infraorder Catarrhini, *incertae sedis*

PONDAUNGIA Pilgrim, 1927

DISTRIBUTION
  Late Eocene. Burma.
KNOWN SPECIES
  Pondaungia cotteri Pilgrim, 1927
LOCALITIES: Pondaung* (345).

DISCUSSION

This taxon is known from three jaw fragments, probably of a single individual (Figure 261). Since its original description, it has been seriously discussed by only two other students who troubled to examine the originals: von Koenigswald (1965) and Simons (e.g., 1972), whose interpretations varied widely. The teeth have been extensively weathered, apparently subjected to chemical erosion which produced surface pitting and destroyed details of the occlusal pattern. Nonetheless, enough remains to permit some description and interpretation.

The maxillary fragment contains the first two molars, whose occlusal pattern is quite similar. The crowns are wider than long, with four main cusps arranged in a square: The protocone is largest, the hypocone smallest, and the two buccal cusps subequal in size. The protocone is placed somewhat distal to the paracone, while the hypocone is nearly lingual to the metacone, thus rather close to the protocone; it is, however, a distinct cusp. Both Pilgrim (1927) and von Koenigswald (1965) indicated that the two lingual

cusps were linked, suggesting the idea of a "pseudo-hypocone," derived from a splitting of the protocone, but this does not seem to be the case here. However, there is a distinct and somewhat rugose lingual cingulum continuing past the distolingual corner, as in *Propliopithecus* (or *Notharctus*), rather than meeting the hypocone, as in adapine adapids. The fovea anterior is moderate in size, but there is no clear paraconule; there may be a small metaconule and/or a small mesocone between the two lingual cusps.

The third molar is preserved in both corpus fragments, but the right retains somewhat more detail, although it is quite pitted. There are only five clear cusps, the main four arranged in a square and the hypoconulid triangular; there is not a paraconid, despite Pilgrim's description of one. There appears to be a small buccal cingulum, visible as a groove between protoconid and hypoconid bases. The shape of $M_{\overline{3}}$ is most like that seen in *Propliopithecus haeckeli*, but *Pondaungia* is slightly larger, perhaps as *P. markgrafi* would have been (its $M_{\overline{3}}$ is unknown). The $M_{\overline{2}}$ is only present in the left corpus, and the enamel of the mesial half has been entirely chipped away; interestingly, this enamel may have been relatively thick for an early catarrhine. The crown was subsquare, with well-developed hypoconid and entoconid, but apparently no real hypoconulid. The median distal area of the tooth is quite featureless, although there seems to

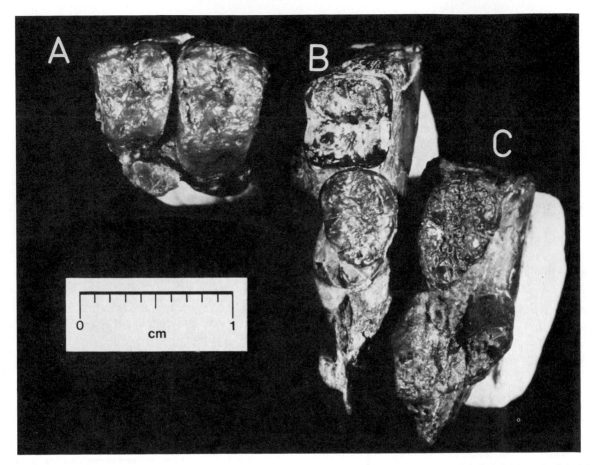

Figure 261. *Pondaungia cotteri.* Late Eocene, Asia. Occlusal view of dental fragments: A, left M^{1-2}; B, left M_{2-3}; C, right M_{3}.

have been a small distal fovea between the two distal cusps.

Overall, the closest phenetic similarity is to the pliopithecid *Propliopithecus,* which is also of similar age. Pilgrim (1927) originally considered *Pondaungia* more "primitive" than the known Fayum catarrhines, but his reasons rely on supposed links to more ancestral forms, such as the presence of a paraconid and a "pseudohypocone," neither of which is supported here. Simons (1972) also noted the similarity to what is here termed *Propliopithecus,* in the "enlargement of the lingual halves of the upper molars," but he was noncommittal about the relationships of *Pondaungia,* discussing it as a possible primitive catarrhine, along with fossil cercopithecids. On the other

hand, von Koenigswald (1965) took the supposed "pseudohypocone" and other doubtfully present features of upper molar morphology to deny relationship of *Pondaungia* to any primates, instead suggesting placement in Condylarthra. We reject this view, essentially accepting Pilgrim's original interpretation of *Pondaungia* as a conservative early catarrhine.

It is tempting to look for more precise relationships of the Burmese fossil, but they are elusive at present. There is no indication of any derived features shared with Parapithecidae, Oreopithecidae, or Hominidae. The lack of a hypoconulid on M_{2} is shared with Cercopithecidae, but may be convergent rather than homologous. It might be possible to refer the genus questionably to the Pliopithecidae of this classification, but, without more than the superficial evidence which suggests placement in the Catarrhini, that would be gratuitous. *Pondaungia* would appear to bear little in common with *Oligopithecus*, also ranked as Catarrhini incertae sedis; it is more likely to be related to later catarrhines than is the Fayum genus: It is noteworthy, however, that the Pondaung locality probably was on the northeastern side of the late Eocene Tethys seaway, suggesting strong zoogeographical separation from the apparent source area of later catarrhines. Von Koenigswald included zoogeography in his reasons to negate anthropoid relationships of both Pondaung genera, but, more recently,

Conroy and Bown (1976) noted that early anthracotheres (as well as early catarrhines) are found in both the Pondaung and Fayum areas. Perhaps an early anthropoid (protocatarrhine) migrated from western North America via the Bering route into Eurasia in the late middle Eocene, eventually reaching Africa in the Oligocene.

Interpretation of paleobiology is difficult, to say the least, in so little-known a fossil form as *Pondaungia*, but the apparent bunodonty and general similarity to pliopithecids suggest a frugivorous diet, doubtless in an arboreal milieu well documented in the Pondaung assemblage.

OLIGOPITHECUS Simons, 1962a

DISTRIBUTION
    Early Oligocene (early Fayumian). Fayum depression, Egypt.
KNOWN SPECIES
    Oligopithecus savagei Simons, 1962a
    Localities: Yale Fayum Quarry E⋆ (374).

Discussion

Oligopithecus, one of the oldest and most "primitive" known alleged catarrhines, is still known only from the single partial mandible described by Simons (1962a) (see Figures 262 and 263). It was one of the smallest catarrhines, roughly comparable to *Parapithecus fraasi* or the living platyrrhine *Pithecia monacha* in dental size, but smaller than any known Neogene catarrhine (except perhaps *Cercopithecus talapoin*). Simons (1962a, 1972) indicated corpus dimensions comparable to *Leontopithecus* and *Saimiri*. *Oligopithecus* is characterized by the mosaic of ($I\frac{2}{2}$); $C\frac{1}{1}$; $P\frac{3}{3}\cdot\frac{4}{4}$; $M\frac{1}{1}\cdot\frac{2}{2}\cdot\frac{3}{3}$ dental formula; large canines; honing ("sectorial") $P_{\overline{3}}$ with "prowlike" mesial prominence but no mesiobuccal flange; $P_{\overline{4}}$ with subequal protoconid and metaconid, small paraconid(?), and no cingulum; molars with moderate to high relief, paraconid on $M_{\overline{1}}$, but not $M_{\overline{2}}$, hypoconulid distolingual, other four cusps aligned and supporting low crests, no distal fovea (and no hypocone wear facets, thus probably low or no hypocone); and paracone wear facet distal rather than only distobuccal to trigonid. The last two features are conservative retentions; most of the others are shared with eucatarrhines, but the $P_{\overline{3}}$ "prow" (if not an artifact of breakage) and the close

hypoconulid–entoconid relationship are apparently unique features.

The holotype mandible consists of the left corpus between $C_{\overline{1}}$ and $M_{\overline{2}}$, with a small basal portion continuing under the site of the third molar, now lost but fully erupted during life as demonstrated by the presence of its anterior root (Simons, 1962a). The five teeth are well preserved with low to moderate wear, but slightly displaced, due to diagenetic processes. Several roots are broken away from crowns, the canines had rotated anteriorly away from $P_{\overline{3}}$ during recovery (Simons, 1971), and the mandibular corpus is extensively cracked and somewhat expanded. Interpretations of the relationships and even the morphology of *Oligopithecus* have varied greatly since its original description, but recent comments by Kay (1977a) have partly clarified the situation. A short summary of major morphological features is presented here; measurements are given by Simons (1962a).

The lower canine, as noted by Simons, is rather similar to that of *Propliopithecus haeckeli* (see Figure 225, D and E, p. 442) with a robust, long root and little or no increase in caliber of the crown above the cervix. The crown is worn down in both specimens but may have been of similar proportions originally, as that of *P. haeckeli* is more heavily abraded and lower, thus indicating an older individual. A strong lingual cingulum curves upward mesially on *Oligopithecus*, but does not continue labially; the same feature is present on *P. haeckeli*, but the crown is worn down to the cingular ledge. The labial face of $C_{\overline{1}}$ in *O. savagei* is smooth,

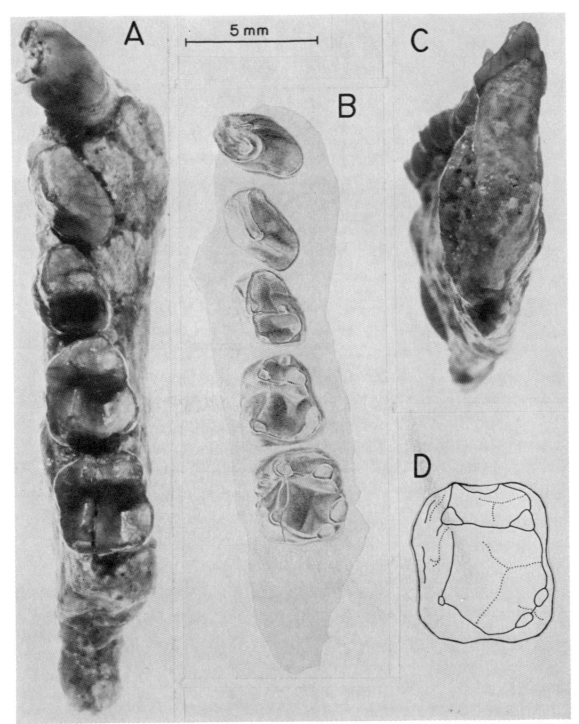

Figure 262. *Oligopithecus savagei.* ?Early Oligocene, Africa. Male mandible with left $C_{\overline{1}}$–$M_{\overline{2}}$: A and B, occlusal view; C, oblique inferior–mesial view; D, occlusal view of $M_{\overline{2}}$. The scale is for A. [A, C courtesy of and © E. L. Simons; B from Simons (1962), *Postilla* (Peabody Mus. Nat. Hist., Yale Univ.) No. 64, 1962, Fig. 4; D redrawn by M. Shepatin from Kay (1977a).]

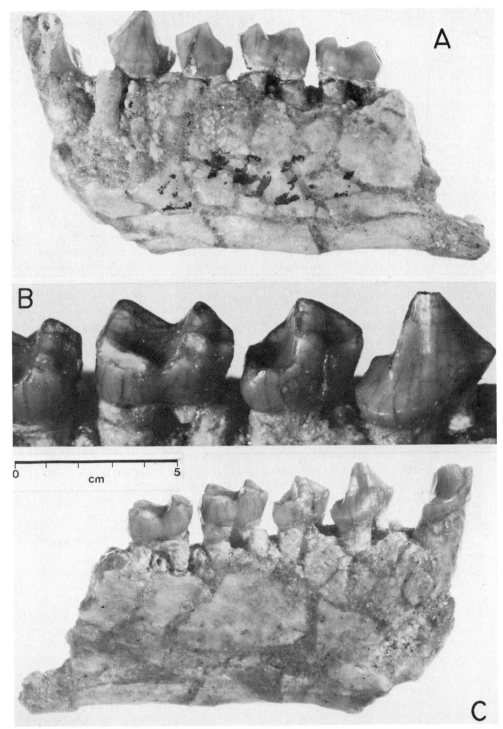

Figure 263. *Oligopithecus savagei.* ?Early Oligocene, Africa. Male mandible with left C$_{\overline{1}}$–M$_{\overline{2}}$: A, buccal view; B, enlarged lingual view of P$_{\overline{3}}$–M$_{\overline{1}}$; C, lingual view. The scale is for A and C. [Courtesy of and © E. L. Simons.]

except for a central patch where enamel has been removed, probably postmoitem, partly exposing the pulp cavity near the worn apex. The apparent procumbency of the crown is probably an artifact of collection (see above) so that, in life, it would not have protruded in front of the root. There is, however, a slight notch visible labially between the end of the cingular "ramp" and the worn central peak, a feature not seen in *P. haeckeli* or later catarrhines. The distolabial part of the crown corresponding to the base of the lingual cingulum is grooved through wear against the C^1, a feature less obvious on *P. haeckeli* but common on later catarrhines, especially males. The two premolars are strongly heteromorphic, with P_3 rather larger than P_4. The third premolar is a narrow unicuspid tooth whose long axis is slightly turned mesiobuccally to the axis of P_4–M_2. There is a weakly bulging lingual cingulum, the buccal face is nearly featureless, and a small "talonid" fossa forms the distal face. The most important feature of P_3 is the stripe of dentine indicating a contact surface for C^1 on the mesiobuccal edge, sloping down from the cusp apex to the most mesial point on the crown, which protrudes slightly mesially like a ship's prow. There is no extension of enamel onto the mesial root, but instead the cervix curves smoothly down from the "prow" to a level roughly in line with the P_4–M_2 cervixes; on the other hand, the mesial root of P_3 is broken away and displaced mesiad from the crown, and it is possible that a small flange may have been present but broken off, although no damage to this area is obvious [and E. L. Simons (personal communication) indicated that the root broke away during collection]. The enamel cover on P_3 is rather thin, as it has been completely worn through to dentine mesiobucally, where a thickening is usually found in catarrhines with honing P_3's. This suggested to Delson (1975c) that C^1–P_3 occlusion in *Oligopithecus* was a phylogenetically relatively recent and "unperfected" adaptation. The P_4 is a smaller, bicuspid tooth, only slightly longer than wide, with the metaconid somewhat lower than the protoconid; there may be a small paraconid at the end of the paracristid, well below the two main cusps. The talonid basin is wide but shallow, the trigonid is relatively long, crown relief is moderate, and cingulum is essentially absent.

The molars of *Oligopithecus* are its most conservative elements. They are of equal size and general configuration, but a paraconid is present only on M_1, the paracristid of M_2 being less developed as well. As

noted especially by Cachel (1975), the trigonid and talonid, although of roughly equal height, are not fully unified into a compact surface, as in later catarrhines. In part, this is due to the relatively high relief of the crown, with a deep median lingual notch and sloping cristid obliqua. The cusps are less bulbous than in other Fayum catarrhines, the main four arranged in transverse pairs, with the hypoconulid distolingual, close to the entoconid. Through a combination of original form and wear, a crest of sorts is formed around the distal margin of the tooth, from the hypoconid through the hypoconulid to the entoconid, partly parallel to the trigonid crest connecting the protoconid and metaconid. Simons (1962a) originally suggested that this might be relevant to cercopithecid origins but later withdrew the idea, and Kay (1977a) has now indicated what should have been clearly visible on the specimen: There is no distal fovea, neither between the hypoconulid and the entoconid, as in "apes," nor distal to the main cusps as in cercopithecids. Combined with the absence of hypocone wear facets in this region or on the anterior part of the metaconid, this suggests that *Oligopithecus* lacked a strong hypocone. Kay (1977a) also noted that the anterior paracone wear facet (his facet 1) continues from the hypoflexid behind the trigonid as in more primitive primates, while the anterior protocone facet (X) is not present. This is an ancestral retention, but possibly suggests that the protocone was less mesial than in later catarrhines. Additional conservative features are the apparent lack of a protoconule and the apparent presence of Kay's facet 10 on the broken M_2 trigonid, rather than hypocone facet 10n, as well as discontinuous mesial and buccal cingulum.

Given such a limited data base, interpretation of adaptation may be premature, but the overall impression is one of slight emphasis on crests, rather than bulbous cusps, and partial folivory and/or insectivory may be suggested, despite the small size of the animal. Considering the canine and P_3 together, especially by comparison to *P. haeckeli*, it appears that the holotype individual was male. As to phyletic relationships, the large canines, essentially bicuspid P_4 and small molar hypoconulids, are anthropoid-"grade" features, while C'–P_3 honing is shared only with eucatarrhines. There are also similarities in molar construction with the Chinese Eocene ?omomyid, *Hoanghonius* (q.v.). It is possible that *Oligopithecus* is a primitive eucatarrhine, but this would imply convergence between this group and the Parapithecidae in several features related to hypocone development (defined distal fovea, wear facet shifts). On the other hand, if *Oligopithecus* is considered the sister-taxon of all other catarrhines (Kay, 1977a; Delson, 1977c), honing would have been developed convergently at least twice, which also seems unlikely. Yet, at present, this is the only acceptable interpretation if the genus is to be retained as an anthropoid. *Oligopithecus* is thus ranked *incertae sedis* among the Catarrhini, and its $P_{\overline{3}}$ morphology is considered nonhomologous with that of eucatarrhines.

REFERENCES

Abel, O. (1902). Zwei neue Menschenaffen aus den Leith-akalkbildungen des Weiner Beckens. *S.-Ber. Akad. Wiss. Wien, Math.—Nat. Kl.* III. Abt. **1**, 1171–1207.

Abel, O. (1918–1919). Das Entwicklungszentrum der Hominiden. *Mitt. Anthrop. Ges. Wien* **49**, 25–29.

Abel, O. (1920). Lehrbuch der Paläozoologie. G. Fischer, Jena.

Abel, O. (1931). Die Stellung des Menschen im Rahmen der Wirbeltiere. G. Fischer, Jena.

Absolon, K. (1920). Die Funde von Predmost. *In* Der Werdegang der Menschheit und die Entstehung der Kultur (H. Klaatsch and A. Heilborn, eds.), pp. 357–373. Berlin.

Adam, K. D. (1959). Mittelpleistozäne Caniden aus dem Heppenloch bei Gutenberg (Württemberg). *Stuttgarter Beitr. Naturk* **27**, 1–46.

Adloff, P. (1908). Die Zähne des *Homo primigenius* von Krapina. *Anat. Anz.* **32**, 301–302.

Aguirre, E., and Soto, E. (1975). Nuevo fosil de Cercopithecido en el Pleistoceno inferior de Puebla de Valverde (Teruel). *Estud. Geol.* **30**, 213–217.

Allen, J. A. (1925). Primates collected by the American Museum Congo expedition. *Bull. Amer. Mus. Nat. Hist.* **27**, 283–499.

Alsberg, P. (1922). Das Menschheitsrätsel. Sinyllen, Dresden.

Alston, E. R. (1878). Indriidae (=Indrisidae). *Zool. Record Mammalia* (London) **13**, 1–24.

Ameghino, F. (1882). Zoología matemática. La Plata.

Ameghino, F. (1884). Filogenia. Buenos Aires.

Ameghino, F. (1891a). Sobre la distribución geografica de los Creodontes. *Rev. Argentina Hist. Nat.* **1**, 214–219.

Ameghino, F. (1891b). Nuevos restos de mamíferos fósiles descubiertos por Cárlos Ameghino en al Eoceno inferior de la Patagonia austral. *Rev. Argentina His. Nat.* **1**, 289–328.

Ameghino, F. (1893). New discoveries of fossil mammalia of southern Patagonia. *Amer. Naturalist* **27**, 439–449.

Ameghino, F. (1894). Enumération synoptique des espèces de mammifères fossiles des formations éocènes de Patagonie. *Bol. Acad. Nac. Córdoba* **13**, 259–445.

Ameghino, F. (1902). Première contribution à la connaissance de la faune mammalogique des couches à Colpodon. *Bol. Acad. Nac. Ciencias Cordoba* **17**, 71–140.

Ameghino, F. (1906). Les formations sedimentaires du Cretacé superieur et du Tertiaire de Patagonie, avec un parallèle entre leurs faunes mammalogiques et celles de l'ancien continent. *An. Mus. Nac. Hist. Nat. Buenos Aires* Ser. 3, **8**, 1–568.

Ameghino, F. (1907). Notas preliminares sobre el *Tetraprothomo argentinus:* un precursor del Hombre del Mioceno superior de Monte Hermoso. *An. Mus. Nac. Hist. Nat. Buenos Aires* Ser. 3, **9**, 107–242.

Ameghino, F. (1909). Le Diprothomo platensis, un précurseur de l'homme du pliocène de l'homme du pliocène inférieur de Buenos Aires. *An. Mus. Nac. Hist. Nat. Buenos Aires* **19**, 107–209.

Ameghino, F. (1911). *Montaneia anthropomorpha.* Un genero de monas hoy extinguido de la isla de Cuba. *An. Mus. Nac. Hist. Nat. Buenos Aires* **13**, 317–318.

Andrews, C. W. (1916). Note on a new baboon (*Simopithecus oswaldi*, gen. et. sp. n.) from the (?) Pliocene of British East Africa. *Ann. Mag. Nat. Hist.* **18**, 410–419.

Andrews, P. (1970). Two new fossil primates from the lower Miocene of Kenya. *Nature* (London) **228**, 537–540.

Andrews, P. (1971). *Ramapithecus wickeri* mandible from Fort Ternan, Kenya. *Nature* (London) **231**, 192–194.

Andrews, P. (1973). Miocene primates (Pongidae, Hylobatidae) of East Africa, Ph.D. thesis. Cambridge University, Cambridge, England.

Andrews, P. (1974). New species of *Dryopithecus* from Kenya. *Nature* (London) **249,** 188–190.

Andrews, P. (1976). Taxonomy and relationships of fossil apes. Abstract (and manuscript) from VI International Primatological Congress, Cambridge, 1976. *Abstracts,* p. 80.

Andrews, P., and Groves, C. (1975). Gibbons and brachiation. *Gibbon Siamang* **4,** 167–218.

Andrews, P., and Simons, E. (1977). A new African Miocene gibbon-like genus, *Dendropithecus* (Hominoidea, Primates) with distinctive postcranial adaptations: Its significance to origin of Hylobatidae. *Folia Primatol.* **28,** 161–170.

Andrews, P., and Tekkaya, I. (1976). *Ramapithecus* in Kenya and Turkey. *In* Les plus anciens hominides (P. V. Tobias and Y. Coppens, eds.), Colloque VI, IX Cong. Union Internat. Sci. Prehist. Protohist., Nice, 1976, preprint pp. 7–25.

Andrews, P., and Tobien, H. (1977). New Miocene locality in Turkey with evidence on the origin of *Ramapithecus* and *Sivapithecus. Nature* (London) **268,** 161–170.

Andrews, P., and Van Couvering, J. A. H. (1975). Palaeoenvironments in the East African Miocene. *In* Approaches to Primate Paleobiology. Volume 5: Contributions to Primatology (F. S. Szalay, ed.), pp. 62–103. Karger, Basel.

Ankel, F. (1965). Der Canalis Sacralis als Indikator für die Lange der Caudalregion der Primaten. *Folia Primatol.* **3,** 263–276.

Ankel, F. (1972). Vertebral morphology of fossil and extant primates. *In* The Functional and Evolutionary Biology of Primates (R. H. Tuttle, ed.), pp. 223–240. Aldine, Chicago.

Anthony, J. (1946a). Morphologie externe du cerveau des singes platyrrhiniens. *Ann. Sci. Nat. Zool.* **8**(11), 1–149.

Anthony, J. (1946b). Le trou malaire des Atelidae et son intérêt dans la classification des singes platyrrhiniens. *Mammalia* **10,** 69–77.

Antunes, M. T. (1962). Note sommaire sur quelques faunes de mammifères Quaternaires de l'Angola. *Actes C. N. R. S. Coll. Int.* **104,** 377–379.

Antunes, M. T. (1965). Sur la faune de vertebrès du Pleistocène de Leba, Humpata (Angola). *In* Actes V Congr. Panafricain de Prehistoire et de l'étude du Quaternaire, pp. 127–128.

Arambourg, C. (1947). Mission scientifique à l'Òmo. Vol. I: Geologie, Anthropologie, fasc. 3. Museum National d'Histoire Naturelle, Paris.

Arambourg, C. (1954). L'hominien fossile de Ternifine (Algérie). *C. R. Acad. Sci. (Paris)* **239,** 893–895.

Arambourg, C. (1956). Considérations sur l'état actuel du problème des origines de l'homme. *In* Problèmes actuels de paléontologie, Vol. 60, pp. 135–147. Colloques Internat. du C. N. R. S., Paris.

Arambourg, C. (1957). Les Pithecanthropiens. *In* Mélanges Pittard (pp. 33–41. Chastrusse, Praudel et Cie, Brive.

Arambourg, C. (1959). Vertébrès Continentaux du Miocène Supérieur de l'Afrique du Nord. Publications Service Carte Geol. Algérie (Nouvelle Série). *Paléontologie* **4,** 5–159.

Arambourg, C. (1969–1970). Les vertébrès du Pleistocène de l'Afrique du Nord. *Arch. Mus. Nat. Hist. Nat., Paris* Ser. 7, **10,** 1–126.

Arambourg, C., and Coppens, Y. (1967). Sur la découverte dans le Pleistocène inférieur de la vallée de l'Òmo (Éthiopie) d'une mandibule d'australpithecien. *C. R. Acad. Sci.* (Paris) **265D,** 589–590.

Arambourg, C., and Mouta, F. (1954). Les grottes et fentes à ossements du sud de l'Angola. *In* Actes 2nd Panafrican Congress on Prehistory (L. Balout, ed.), pp. 301–304. Algèrs.

Archibald, J. D. (1977). Ectotympanic bone and internal carotid circulation of eutherians in reference to anthropoid origins. *J. Human Evol.* **6,** 609–622.

Arldt, T. (1915). Die Stammesgeschichte der Primaten und die Entwicklung der menschenrassen. *Fortschr. Rassenkunde* **1,** 1–52.

Ashley-Montagu, M. F. (1933). The anthropological significance of the pterion in the primates. *Amer. J. Phys. Anthropol.* **18,** 159–336.

Athanasiu, S. (1912). Resturile de Mamifere Cuaternare dela Malusteni in Districtul Covurlui. *Anuar. Instit. Geol. al Reomanici* **6,** 397–430.

Azzaroli, A. (1946). La Scimmia Fossile della Sardegna. *Riv. Sci. Preist.* **1,** 168–176.

Baba, M. L., Goodman, M., Dene, H., and Moore, G. W. (1975). Origins of the Ceboidea viewed from an immunological perspective. *J. Human Evol.* **4,** 89–201.

Baker, W. E., and Durand, H. N. (1836). Sub-Himalayan fossil remains of the Dadoopoor collection. *J. Asiatic Soc.* **5,** 739–741.

Barnett, C. H., and Napier, J. R. (1953). The rotary mobility of the fibula in eutherian mammals. *J. Anat.* **87,** 11–21.

Bartheld, F. von, Erdbrink, D. P., and Krommenhoeek, W. (1970). A fossil incisor from Uganda and a method for its determination. *Proc. Koninkl. Nederlandse Akad. Wetensch.* **73,** 426–431.

Bartolomei, G. (1965). Primo rinvenimento di una Scimmia pleistocenica nell'Italia Settentrionale e considerazioni sul suo significato ecologico. *Rendiconti Accad. Naz. Lincei* Ser. 8, **39,** 533–535.

Battaglia, R. (1924). Osservazioni su l'uomo fossile di Broken Hill. *Bull. Soc. Adriatica Sci. Nat.* **28,** 305–322.

Bauchop, T., and Martucci, R. W. (1968). Ruminant-like digestion of the langur monkey. *Science* **161,** 698–699.

Baudouin, M. (1916). Sur l'anteriorité de la machoire trouvée à la Naulette. *C. R. Acad. Sci.* (Paris) **162,** 519–520.

Behm, H. W. (1915). Die Fossilmenschfunde von Oldoway und Oberkassel. *Prometheus* **26,** 161–164.

Bennett, E. T. (1831). Proceedings of the Comm. Sci. Zoological Society of London, Sept. 9.

Bennett, E. T. (1832). Proceedings of the Comm. Sci. Zoological Society of London, March 15.

Berckhemer, F. (1936). Der urmenschenschadel aus den zwischeneiszeitlichen Fluss-Schottern von Steinheim an der Murr. *Forsch. Fortschr.* **12,** 349–350.

Bergounioux, F.-M., and Crouzel, F. (1964). Les *Pliopithecus* de Sansan (Gers). *C. R. Acad. Sci.* (Paris) **258,** 3744–3746.

Bergounioux, F.-M., and Crouzel, F. (1965). Les Pliopithèques de France. *Ann. Paleontol. (Vertébrès)* **51,** 45–65.

Bernsen, J. J. A. (1930). On a fossil monkey found in the

Netherlands (*Macacus* cf. *florentina* Cocchi). *Proc. Royal Acad. Amsterdam* **33**, 771–778.

Berthold, A. A. (1827). *In* Latreille, P. A. Naturliche Familen des Thierreichs (A. A. Berthold, ed.). Landes-Industrie-Comptoirs, Weimar.

Beyrich, H. von. (1861). Über *Semnopithecus pentelicus. Phys. Abh. Kon. Akad. Wiss. Berlin* for 1860, 1–26.

Biedermann, W. G. A. (1863). Petrefacten aus der Umgegend von Winterthur, Vol. 2. Bleuler-Hausheer, Winterthur.

Biegert, J. (1963). The evaluation of characteristics of the skull, hands, and feet for Primate taxonomy. *In* Classification and Human Evolution (S. L. Washburn, ed.), pp. 116–143. Aldine, Chicago.

Bien, M. N., and Chia, Lan-Po. (1938). Cave and rock-shelter deposits in Yunnan. *Bull. Geol. Soc. China* **18**, 325–348.

Bigert, J., and Maurer, R. (1972). Rumpfskelettlänge, Allometrien und Korperproportionen bei catarrhinen Primaten. *Folia Primatol.* **17**, 142–156.

Bishop, W. W. (1958). Miocene Mammalia from the Napak volcanics, Karamoja, Uganda. *Nature* (London) **182**, 1480–1482.

Bishop, W. W., and Chapman, G. R. (1970). Early Pliocene sediments and fossils from the northern Kenya rift Valley. *Nature* (London) **226**, 914–918.

Black, D. (1927). On a lower molar hominid tooth from Chou-kou-tien deposit. *Palaeontol. Sin., D* **7**, 1–28.

Blainville, H. M. D. de. (1839). Ostéographie des Primates. *In* Ostéographie des Mammifères. I: Primates et Secundates. Baillière, Paris.

Blainville, H. M. D. de. (1839–1864). Ostéographie ou Description Iconographique Comparée du Squelette et du Système Dentaires de Mammifères. Livraison L. Des petits ours. Baillière, Paris.

Blanc, A. C. (1961). Leuca I, Il primo reperto fossile neandertaliano del Salento. *Quaternaria* **5**, 271–278.

Blanford, W. T. (1888). The fauna of British India, including Ceylon and Burma. Mammalia, Vol. 1. Taylor and Francis, Thancker, Spink and Co., London.

Bluntschli, H. (1931). *Homunculus patagonius* und die ihm zugereihten Fossilfunde aus den Santa-Cruz-Schichten Patagoniens. *Gegenbaurs Morpholohisches Jahrbuch* **67**, 811–982.

Blyth. E. (1875). Catalogue of mammals and birds of Burma. *J. Asiatic Soc. Bengal* **44**(Part 2, extra number), 1–167.

Bock, W. J. (1977a). Adaptation and the comparative method. *In* Major Patterns in Vertebrate Evolution (M. K. Hecht, P. C. Goody, and B. M. Hecht, eds.), pp. 57–82. Plenum Press, New York.

Bock, W. J. (1977b). Foundation and methods of evolutionary classification. *In* Major Patterns in Vertebrate Evolution (M. K. Hecht, P. C. Goody, and B. M. Hecht, eds.), pp. 851–896. Plenum Press, New York.

Bock, W. J. and G. von Wahlert. (1965). Adaptation and the form–function complex. *Evolution* **19**, 269–299.

Boddaert, P. (1768). Dierkundig Mengelwerk (6 vols., 1767–1770). Utrecht.

Boddaert, P. (1784). Elenchus Animalium, Quadrupedea. Rotterdam.

Bodini, R. (1972). Locomotion y musculature de los regiones glutea y femoral en los cebids de Venezula. *Bol. Soc. Venezolana Ciencias Nat.* **29**, 487–544.

Bohlin, B. (1946). The fossil mammals from the Tertiary deposit of Taben-Buluk, western Kansu. II. Simplicidentata, Carnivora, Artiodactyla, Perissodactyla and Primates. *Palaeontol. Sinica* N. S. C. (8b), 1–256.

Bolk, L. (1916). Problems of human dentition. *Amer. J. Anat.* **19**, 91–148.

Bolwig, N. (1961). *Mém. Inst. Scient. Madagascar* (A) **14**, 207.

Bonaparte, C. L. J. L. (1831). Saggio di una Distribuzione Metodica degli Animale Vertebrati. Antonio Boulzaler, Rome.

Bonaparte, C. L. J. L. (1838). Synopsis vertebratorum systematis. *Nuovi Ann. Sci. Nat. Bologna* **2**(anno 1), 105–133.

Bonaparte, C. L. J. L. (1850). Conspectus Systematis. Mastozoologie (edito altera reformata). E. F. Brill, Batavia.

Bonarelli, G. (1909a). *Palaeanthropus* (n.g.) *heidelbergensis* (Schoet.). *Riv. Ital. Paleontol.* **15**, 26–31.

Bonarelli, G. (1909b). Le razze umane e le loro probabile affinta. *Boll. Soc. Geogr. Ital.* Fasc. **8**, 827–851; **9**, 953–979.

Bonarelli, G. (1944). Sulloge Synonymica hominidarum fossilium hucusque cognitorum systematice ordinata. *Ultima Miscellanea* **1**, 1–67.

Bonifay, M.-F., and Bonifay, E. (1963). Un gisement à faune epi-villafranchienne à Saint-Esteve-Janson (Bouches-du-Rhone). *C. R. Adac. Sci.* (Paris) **260**, 1136–1138.

Bonifay, M.-F., and Bonifay, E. (1969). La Grotte de l'Escale, Complement No. 6, Guidebook to Excursion C 14, pp. 1–4. VIII Congress International Quaternary Research Association, Paris.

Bonis, L. de, Bouvrain, G., Geraads, D., and Melentis, J. (1974). Première découverte d'un Primate hominoide dans le Miocène supérieur de Macédoine (Grèce). *C. R. Acad. Sci.* (Paris) **278**, 3063–3066.

Bonis, L. de, Bouvrain, G., and Melentis, M. J. (1975). Nouveaux restes de Primates hominoides dans le Vallésien de Macédoine (Grèce). *C. R. Acad. Sci.* (Paris) **281**, 379–382.

Bonis, L. de, and Melentis, J. (1976). Les dryopithecines de Macédoine (Grèce): leur place dans l'évolution des primates hominoides du Miocène. *In* Les Plus Anciens Hominidés (P. V. Tobias and Y. Coppens, eds.), Coll. VI, preprint, pp. 26–38. IX Congress Union Internat. Sci. prehist. protohist., Nice.

Bonis, L. de, and Melentis, J. (1977). Un nouveau genre de primate hominoide dans le Vallésien (Miocène supérieur) de Macédoine. *C. R. Acad. Sci.* (Paris) **284**, 1393–1396.

Bontsch-Osmolovskii, G. A. (1941). [The hand of the fossil man from Kiik-Koba] (in Russian). Paleolit Kryma, Vol. 2, U.S.S.R. Academy of Science, Moscow.

Bown, T. M. (1974). Notes on some Early Eocene anaptomorphine primates. *Contrib. Geol. Univ. Wyoming* **13**, 19–26.

Bown, T. M. (1976). Affinities of *Teilhardina* (Primates, Omomyidae) with description of a new species from North America. *Folia Primatol.* **25**, 62–72.

Bown, T. M., and Gingerich, P. D. (1973). The Paleocene primate *Plesiolestes* and the origin of Microsyopidae. *Folia Primatol.* **19**, 1–8.

Bown, T. M., and Rose, K. D. (1976). New early Tertiary Primates and a reappraisal of some Plesiadapiformes. *Folia Primatol.* **26**, 109–138.

Boyd-Dawkins, W. (1926). The range of Anthropus Neanderthalensis on the Pleistocene continent. *Rept. Brit. Assoc.* **94,** 386.

Brace, C. L., and Montagu, M. F. A. (1965). Man's Evolution. An Introduction to Physical Anthropology. Macmillan, New York.

Brace, C. L., Nelson, H., and Korn, N. (1971). Atlas of Fossil Man. Holt, Rhinehart & Winston, New York.

Branco, W. (1897). Die menschenähnlichen Zähne aus dem Bohnerz der schwabischen Alb. *Jh. Ver. vaterl. Naturk. Wurttemburg* **54,** 1–144.

Brisson, M. J. (1762). Regnum animales in classes IX distributum sive synopsis methodica, edito altera auctior. Theodorum Haak, Leiden.

Brookes, J. (1828). A Catalogue of the Anatomical and Zoological Museum of Joshua Brookes, Esq. Privately printed. London.

Broom, R. (1917). Fossil man in South Africa. *Amer. Mus. J.* **17,** 141–142.

Broom, R. (1934). On the fossil remains associated with *Australopithecus africanus. S. Afr. J. Sci.* **31,** 471–480.

Broom, R. (1936a). A new fossil anthropoid skull from Sterkfontein, near Krugersdorp, South Africa. *Nature* (London) **138,** 486–488.

Broom, R. (1936b). A new fossil baboon from the Transvaal. *Ann. Transvaal Mus.* **18,** 393–396.

Broom, R. (1937). On some new Pleistocene Mammals from limestone caves of the Transvaal. *S. Afr. J. Sci.* **33,** 750–768.

Broom, R. (1938). The Pleistocene Anthropoid apes of South Africa. *Nature* (London) **142,** 377–379.

Broom, R. (1940). The South African Pleistocene Cercopithecid apes. *Ann. Transvaal Mus.* **20,** 89–100.

Broom, R. (1949). Another new type of fossil ape-man (*Paranthropus crassidens*). *Nature* (London) **163,** 57.

Broom, R., and Jensen, J. S. (1946). A new fossil baboon from the caves at Potgietersrust. *Ann. Transvaal Mus.* **20,** 337–340.

Broom, R., and Hughes, A. R. (1949). Notes on the fossil baboons of the Makapan caves. *Afr. Sci.* **2,** 194–196.

Broom, R., and Robinson, J. T. (1949a). A new type of Fossil Baboon, *Gorgopithecus major. Zool. Soc. London* **119,** 374–383.

Broom, R., and Robinson, J. T. (1949b). New type of fossil man. *Nature* (London) **164,** 322–323.

Broom, R., and Robinson, J. T. (1950). A new sub-fossil baboon from Kromdraai (Transvaal). *Ann. Transvaal Mus.* **21,** 242–245.

Brown, B., Gregory, W. K., and Hellman, M. (1924). On three incomplete anthropoid jaws from the Siwaliks, India. *Amer. Mus. Nov.* **130,** 1–9.

Brünnich, M. T. (1772). Zoologicae Fundamenta. Apud Frider, Christ, Pelt: Litteris Godichianis, Hafniae et Lipsiae.

Buettner-Janusch, J. (1966). A problem in evolutionary systematics: Nomenclature and classification of baboons, genus *Papio. Folia Primatol.* **4,** 288–308.

Bugge, J. (1967). The arterial supply of the middle ear of the rabbit with special reference to the contribution of the stapedial artery to the development of the superior tympanic artery and the petrosal branch. *Acta. Anat.* **67,** 208–220.

Bugge, J. (1971). The cephalic arterial system in New and Old World hystricomorphs, and in bathyergoids, with special reference to the systematic classification of rodents. *Acta Anat.* **80,** 516–536.

Bugge, J. (1972). The cephalic arterial system in the insectivores and the primates with special reference to the Macroscelidoidea and Tupaioidea and the insectivore-primate boundary. *Z. Anat. Entwickl. –Gesch.* **135,** 279–300.

Bugge, J. (1974). The cephalic arterial system in insectivores, primates, rodents and lagomorphs, with special reference to the systematic classification. *Acta Anat.* **87** (Suppl. 62), 1–160.

Bumuller, J. (1899). Das menschliche Femur nebst Beitragen zur Kentniss der Affenfemora. 12, Das Femur des *Pithecanthropus erectus,* pp. 124–138. Ausberg.

Burmeister, C. H. C. (1854). Systematische Uebersicht der Thiere Brasiliens, welch während einer Reise die Provinzen von Rio de Janiero und Minas Gerais gesammelt oder beobachtet wurden, Vol. 1. Georg Reimer, Berlin.

Burnett, G. T. (1828). Illustrations of the Manupeda or apes and their allies: Being the arrangement of the Quadrumana or Anthropomorphous beasts indicated in the outline. *Q. J. Sci. Lit. Art.* **26,** 300–307.

Burtschak-Abramovitsch, N. O., and Gabachvili, E. G. (1950). [Discovery of a fossil anthropoid in Georgia] (in Russian). *Prìroda,* Moscow **9,** 70–72.

Butler, P. M. (1956). Skull of *Ictops* and the classification of the Insectivora. *Proc. Zool. Soc. London* **126,** 453–481.

Butler, P. M., and Mills, J. R. E. (1959). A contribution to the odontology of *Oreopithecus. Bull. Brit. Mus. (Nat. Hist.), Geol.* **4,** 1–30.

Buttel-Reepen, H. von. (1911). Der Urmensch vor und wahrend der Eiszeit in Europa. Ein Sammelreferat. *Naturw. Wochenschr.* **26,** 177–189, 193–204, 209–219, 225–231.

Cabrera, A. (1900). Estudios sobre una colleción de monos americanos. *Anal. Soc. Española Hist. Nat., Madrid* **9**(2), 65–93.

Cabrera, A. (1956). Sobre la identificacion de *Simia leonia* Humboldt (Mammalia, Primates). *Neotropica* **2,** 49–53.

Cachel, S. (1975). The beginnings of the Catarrhini. *In* Primate Functional Morphology and Evolution (R. Tuttle, ed.), pp. 23–36. Mouton, The Hague.

Campbell, B. (1962). The systematics of man. *Nature* (London) **194,** 225–232.

Campbell, B. G. (1965). The nomenclature of the Hominidae. *Occas. Pap. Roy. Anthropol. Inst.* **22,** 1–34.

Campbell, B. G. (1972). Conceptual progress in physical anthropology: Fossil man. *Annu. Rev. Anthropol.* **1,** 27–54.

Campbell, B. G., and Bernor, R. L. (1976). The origin of the Hominidae: Africa or Asia? *J. Human Evol.* **5,** 441–454.

Cartmill, M. (1972). Arboreal adaptations and the origin of the order Primates. *In* The Functional and Evolutionary Biology of Primates (R. Tuttle, ed.), pp. 97–122. Aldine–Atherton, Chicago.

Cartmill, M. (1974a). Pads and claws in arboreal locomotion. *In* Primate Locomotion (F. Jenkins, ed.), pp. 45–84. Academic Press, New York.

Cartmill, M. (1974b). Rethinking primate origins. *Science* **184,** 436–443.

Cartmill, M. (1974c). *Daubentonia, Dactylopsila,* woodpeckers and klinorhynchy. *In* Prosimian Biology (R. D. Martin, G. A. Doyle, and A. C. Walker, eds.), pp. 655–670. Duckworth, London.

Cartmill, M. (1975). Strepsirhine basicranial structure and the affinities of the Cheirogaleidae. *In* Phylogeny of the Primates: A Multidisciplinary Approach (W. P. Luckett and F. S. Szalay, eds.), pp. 313–354. Plenum Press, New York.

Cartmill, M. and R. F. Kay (1978). Craniodental morphology, *Tarsier* affinities, and primate sub-orders. *In* Recent Advances in Primatology. vol. 3, Evolution (D. J. Chivers and K. A. Joysey, eds.), pp. 205–214. Academic Press, London.

Cartmill, M., and Milton, K. (1977). The lorisiform wrist joint and the evolution of "brachiating" adaptations in the Hominoidea. *Amer. J. Phys. Anthropol., n.s.* **47,** 249–272.

Cautley, P., and Falconer, H. (1837). Notice on the remains of a fossil monkey from the Tertitary strata of the Siwalik Hills in the North of Hindostan. *Trans. Geol. Soc. London* **5,** 499–504.

Chaline, J. (1972). Le Quaternaire. Doin, Paris.

Chang, Y., Wang, L.-h., Dong, X.-r., and Chen, W-c. (1975). Discovery of a *Gigantopithecus* tooth from Bama district in Kwangsi. *Vert. Palasiatica* **13,** 148–154.

Chang, Y.-y., Wu, M.-l., and Liu, C.-j. (1973). New discovery of *Gigantopithecus* teeth from Wuming, Kwangsi. *Kexue Tongebao (Sci. Bull.)* **18,** 130–133.

Chantre, E., and Gaillard, C. (1897). Sur la faune du gisement sidérolithique éocène de Lissieu (Rhone). *C. R. Acad. Sci.* (Paris) **125,** 986–987.

Charles-Dominique, P. (1977). Ecology and Behavior of Nocturnal Primates. Columbia University Press, New York.

Charlesworth, E. (1854). Report of the British Association for the Advancement of Science for 1854, p. 80. British Association for the Advancement of Science, Liverpool.

Chow, M.-c. (1958). Mammalian faunas and correlation of Tertiary and early Pleistocene of South China. *J. Paleontol. Soc. India* **3,** 123–130.

Chow, M.-c. (1961). A new Tarsioid primate from the Lushi Eocene, Honan. *Vert. Palasiatica* **5,** 1–5.

Chow, M-c. (1964). A lemuroid primate from the Eocene of Lantian, Shensi. *Vert. Palasiatica* **8,** 260–262.

Christol, M. de. (1849). Note (sur *Pithecus maritimus*). *Bull. Soc. Geol. France* Ser. 2, **6,** 1848–1849.

Ciochon, R. L., and Corruccini, R. S. (1975). Morphometric analysis of platyrrhine femora with taxonomic implications and notes on two fossil forms. *J. Human Evol.* **4,** 193–217.

Ciochon, R. L., and Corruccini, R. S. (1976). Shoulder joint of Sterkfontein *Australopithecus. S. Afr. J. Sci.* **72,** 80–82.

Ciochon, R. L., and Corruccini, R. S. (1977). The phenetic position of *Pliopithecus* and its phylogenetic relationship to the Hominoidea. *Syst. Zool.* **26,** 290–299.

Clark, J. (1941). An anaptomorphid primate from the Oligocene of Montana. *J. Paleontol.* **15,** 562–563.

Clarke, R., Howell, F. C., and Brain, C. K. (1970). More evidence of an advanced hominid at Swartkrans. *Nature* (London) **225,** 1219–1222.

Clemens, W. A. (1974). *Purgatorius,* an early paromomyid primate (Mammalia). *Science* **184,** 903–906.

Cocchi, I. (1872). Su di due Scimmie fossili italiane. *Boll. Comitata Geol. d'Italia* **3,** 59–71.

Colbert, E. H. (1937). A new primate from the upper Eocene Pondaung Formation of Burma. *Amer. Mus. Nov.* **951.**

Colbert, E. H. (1938). Fossil mammals from Burma in the American Museum of Natural History. *Bull. Amer. Mus. Nat. Hist.* **74,** 255–436.

Colbert, E. H., and Hooijer, D. A. (1953). Pleistocene mammals from the limestone fissures of Szechuan, China. *Bull. Amer. Mus. Nat. Hist.* **102,** 1–134.

Comaschi Caria, I. (1968). Fossili marini e continentali del Quarternario della Sardegna, Atti X Congr. internat. studi Sardi, pp. 141–228. Fossataro, Cagliari.

Conroy, G. C. (1976a). Primate postcranial remains from the Oligocene of Egypt. *Contrib. Primatol.* **8,** 1–134.

Conroy, G. C. (1976b). Hallucial tarsometatarsal joint in an Oligocene anthropoid *Aegyptopithecus zeuxis. Nature* (London) **262,** 684–686.

Conroy, G. C. and Bown, T. M. (1976). Anthropoid origins and differentiation: The Asian question. *Yb. Phys. Anthropol.* **18**(1974), 1–6.

Cooke, H. B. S. (1963). Pleistocene mammal faunas of Africa, with particular reference to southern Africa. *In* African Ecology and Human Evolution (F. Howell and F. Bourlière, eds.), pp. 65–116. Aldine, Chicago.

Cooke, H. B. S., and Coryndon, S. C. (1970). Pleistocene mammals from the Kaiso Formation and other related deposits in Uganda. *Foss. Vert. Afr.* **2,** 109–224.

Coon, C. (1962). The Origin of Races. Knopf, New York.

Cooper, C. F. (1932). On some mammalian remains from the Lower Eocene of the London clay. *Ann. Mag. Nat. Hist.* Ser. 10, **9,** 458–467.

Cope, E. D. (1872). Second account of new Vertebrata from the Bridger Eocene. *Paleontol. Bull.* **2,** 1–3.

Cope, E. D. (1872). Third account of new Vertebrata from the Bridger Eocene of Wyoming Territory. *Proc. Amer. Philos. Soc.* **12,** 469–472.

Cope, E. D. (1872). On a new vertebrate genus from the northern part of the Tertiary basin of Green River. *Proc. Amer. Philos. Soc.* **12,** 554.

Cope, E. D. (1874). Report upon vertebrate fossils discovered in New Mexico, with descriptions of new species," Append. FF3 in Ann. Rep. Chief Engineers, pp. 588–606. U.S. Government Printing Office, Washington, D.C.

Cope, E. D. (1875). Systematic catalogue of Vertebrata of the Eocene of New Mexico, collected in 1874. *In* Geog. Exp. and Surv. West of 100th Meridian (Wheeler, ed.), pp. 5–37.

Cope, E. D. (1876). On some supposed lemurine forms of the Eocene period. *Proc. Acad. Nat. Sci.* (Philadelphia) **28,** 88–89.

Cope, E. D. (1877). Report upon the extinct Vertebrata obtained in New Mexico by parties of the expedition of 1874. *In* Report of the geographical and geological explorations and surveys west of the 100th meridian (Wheeler, ed.), Vol. 4, Pt. 2, pp. 1–370.

Cope, E. D. (1881). On the Vertebrata of the Wind River Eocene beds of Wyoming. *Bull. U.S. Geol. Geog. Surv. Terr.* (Hayden) **6**(1), 183–202.

Cope, E. D. (1882). Contributions to the history of the verte-brata of the lower Eocene of Wyoming and New Mexico, made during 1881. I. The fauna of the Wasatch beds of the basin of the Big Horn River. II. The fauna of the *Catathlacus* beds, or lower Eocene, New Mexico. *Proc. Amer. Philos. Soc.* **10**, 139–197.

Cope, E. D. (1883). On the mutual relations of the bunothe-rian Mammalia. *Proc. Acad. Nat. Sci.* (Philadelphia) **35**, 77–83.

Coppens, Y. (1965). L'hominien du Tchad. *C. R. Acad. Sci.* (Paris) **260D**, 2869–2871.

Corruccini, R. S. (1975a). Multivariate analysis of *Gigantopithecus* mandibles. *Amer. J. Phys. Anthropol.* **42**, 167–170.

Corruccini, R. S. (1975b). *Gigantopithecus* and hominids. *Anthropol. Anz.* **35**, 55–57.

Corruccini, R. S., and Ciochon, R. L. (1976). Morphometric affinities of the human shoulder. *Amer. J. Phys. Anthropol.* **45**, 19–38.

Corruccini, R. S., Ciochon, R. L., and McHenry, H. M. (1976). The postcranium of Miocene hominoids: Were dryopithecines merely "dental apes"? *Primates* **17**, 205–223.

Crompton, A. W. and Z. Kielan-Jaworska. (1978). Molar structure and occlusion in Cretaceous therian mammals. *In* Development, Function and Evolution of Teeth (P. M. Butler and K. A. Joysey, eds.), pp. 249–287. Academic Press, London.

Cronin, J. E., and Sarich, V. M. (1975). Molecular systematics of the New World monkeys. *J. Human Evol.* **4**, 357–375.

Cronin, J. E., and Sarich, V. M. (1976). Molecular evidence for dual origin of mangabeys among Old World monkeys. *Nature* (London) **260**, 700–702.

Crook, J. H. (1966). Gelada baboon herd structure and movement, a comparative report. *Symp. Zool. Soc. London* **18**, 237–258.

Crusafont-Pairo, M. (1958). Nuevo hallazgo del pongido vallesiense *Hispanopithecus*. *Boll. Informativo Activ. Europeas Paleontol. Verteb.* No. 13–14, pp. 37–43.

Crusafont-Pairo, M. (1965). El dessarrollo de los Caninos en algunos Driopithecidos del Vallesiense en Cataluña. *Inst. Geol. Min. España* **80**, 179–192.

Crusafont-Pairo, M. (1967). Sur quelques prosimiens de l'Eocène de la zone préaxiale pyrénaique et un essai provisoire de reclassification. *Coll. Inter. Centre Nat. Rech. Sci., Problemes Actuels de Paleontol.* **163**, 611–632.

Crusafont-Pairo, M. (1976). El gibon fosil *(Pliopithecus)* del Vindoboniense terminal del Valles. *Boletin Informativo, Diputacion Provincial de Barcelona, Inst. Prov. Paleontol. de Sabadell* **7**, 36–39.

Crusafont-Pairo, M., and Golpe Posse, J. M. (1969). Los primeros cercopitecidos fosiles de Espana (Nota prelimi-nar). *Public. Dept. Paleontol., Univ. Barcelona* **15**, 1–2.

Crusafont-Pairo, M., and Golpe-Posse, J. M. (1973a). Yaci-mientos del Eoceno prepirenaico (nuevas localidades del Cuisiense). *Acta Geol. Hispanica* **8**(5), 145–147.

Crusafont-Pairo, M., and Golpe-Posse, J. M. (1973b). New Pongids from the Miocene of Valles Penedes Basin (Catalonia, Spain). *J. Human Evol.* **2**, 17–23.

Crusafont-Pairo, M., and Golpe-Posse, J. M. (1975). Les Prosimiens de l'Eocène de la Région Préaxiale Pyrénaïque. II. Adapidae. *In* Coll. Int. C. N. R. S., Vol. 218, Problèmes Actuels de Paléontol. (Evolution des Vertébrés), pp. 851–859. C. N. R. S., Paris.

Crusafont-Pairo, M., and Hürzeler, J. (1961). Les Pongidés fossiles d'Espagne. *C. R. Acad. Sci.* (Paris) **254**, 585–584.

Cuvier, F. (1807). Description d'un Papion qui pourrait se rapporter à l'une des espèces décrites par Pennant, *Simia leucophaea. Ann. Mus. Hist. Nat., Paris* **9**, 477–482.

Cuvier, F. (1824). Table générale et methodique. *In* Geoffroy Saint-Hilaire. E., and F. Cuvier (1818–1842). Hist. nat. mamm. III, Paris.

Cuvier, G. (1800). Leçons d'Anatomie Comparée. Baudouin, Paris.

Cuvier, G. (1821). Discours sur la Theorie de la Terre, Servant d'Introduction aux recherches sur les Ossements Fos-siles. Paris.

Cuvier, G. (1834). Recherches sur les Ossemens fossiles. Nouvelle edition, 3.

Dagosto, M. and F. S. Szalay. (1979). The elbow joint of early primates (abstr.). *Amer. J. Phys. Anthrop.* **50**,131.

Dahlbohm, A. G. (1856). Zoologiska studier, afhandlande Djurrijets naturliga familjer, Studia zoologica, familias Regni Animalis naturales tractantia. Lund.

Darlington, P. J., Jr. (1975). Group selection, altruism, rein-forcement and throwing in human evolution. *Proc. Natl. Acad. Sci. U.S.A.* **72**, 3748–3752.

Dart, R. (1925). *Australopithecus africanus;* the man-ape of South Africa. *Nature* (London) **115**, 195–199.

Dart, R. (1948). The Makapansgat protohuman *Australopith-ecus prometheus. Amer. J. Phys. Anthropol., n. s.* **6**, 259–283.

Dart, R. (1949). The predatory implemental technique of *Australopithecus. Amer. J. Phys. Anthropol., n. s.* **7**, 1–38.

Dashzeveg, D. T., and McKenna, M. C. (1977). Tarsioid primate from the early Tertiary of the Mongolian People's Republic. *Acta Palaeontol. Polonica* **22**(2), 119–137.

Davidson, J. H. C. S. (1975). Recent archaeological activity in Viet-Nam. *J. Hong Kong Arch. Soc.* **6**, 80–99.

Davis, P. R., and Napier, J. (1963). A reconstruction of the skull of *Proconsul africanus. Folia Primatol.* **1**, 20–28.

Darwin, C. (1871). The Descent of Man. Murray, London.

Day, M. (1976). Hominid postcranial remains from the East Rudolf succession: A review. *In* Earliest Man and Envi-ronments in the Lake Rudolf Basin (Y. Coppens, F. C. Howell, G. L. Isaac, and R. E. F. Leakey, eds.), pp. 507–520. University of Chicago Press, Chicago.

Decker, R. L., and Szalay, F. S. (1974). Origins and function of the pes in the Eocene Adapidae (Lemuriforms, Pri-mates). *In* Primate Locomotion (F. A. Jenkins, Jr., ed.), pp. 261–291. Academic Press, New York.

Dehaut, E.-G. (1911). Animaux Fossiles du Cap Figari. Matériaux pour servir à l'Histoire Zoologique et Paléon-tologique des Iles de Corse et de Sardaigne. G. Steinheil, Paris. [Fasc. **3**, 53–56.]

Dehaut, E.-G. (1914). Nouvelles Recherches sur les Mammi-fères Pléistocènes et Recemment Eteints de la Sardaigne. Materiaux pour servir à l'Histoire Zoologique et Paleontologique des Iles de Corse et de Sordaigne. G. Steinheil, Paris. [Fasc. **5**, 71–84.]

Delfortrie, E. (1873). Un singe de la famille des Lémuriens. *Act. Soc. Linn. Bordeaux* **24**, 87–95.

Delson, E. (1971a). Estudio preliminar de unos restos de simios pliocenicos procedentes de "Cova Bonica" (Gava) (Prov. Barcelona). *Acta Geol. Hispanica* **6**, 57.

Delson, E. (1971b). Fossil mammals of the early Wasatchian Powder River local Fauna, Eocene of Northeast Wyoming. *Bull. Amer. Mus. Nat. Hist.* **146**, 305–364.

Delson, E. (1973). Fossil colobine monkeys of the circum-Mediterranean region and the evolutionary history of the Cercopithecidae (Primates, Mammalia), Ph.D. thesis. Columbia University, New York.

Delson, E. (1974a). CA* comments on Butzer and Tuttle articles. *Current Anthropol.* **15**, 403–404.

Delson, E. (1974b). Preliminary review of cercopithecid distribution in the circum-Mediterranean region. *Mem. Bull. Rech. Geol. Min.* (France) **78**, 131–135.

Delson, E. (1975a). Evolutionary history of the Cercopithecidae. *In* Approaches to Primate Paleobiology. Volume 5: Contributions to Primatology (F. S. Szalay, ed.), pp. 167–217. Karger, Basel.

Delson, E. (1975b). Paleoecology and zoogeography of the Old World monkeys. *In* Primate Functional Morphology and Evolution (R. Tuttle, ed.), pp. 37–64. Mouton, The Hague.

Delson, E. (1975c). Toward the origin of the Old World monkeys. Evolution des vertébrés—Problèmes Actuels de Paléontologie. Actes C. N. R. S. Coll. Int. Vol. 218, pp. 839–850. Centre national recherche scientifique, Paris.

Delson, E. (1976). The family–group name of the leaf-eating monkeys (Mammalia, Primates): A proposal to validate Colobidae Blyth, 1875 with precedence over Semnopithecidae Owen, 1843 and Presbytina Gray, 1821. *Bull. Zool. Nomenclature* **33**, 85–89.

Delson, E. (1977a). Vertebrate paleontology, especially of non-human primates in China. *In* Paleoanthropology in the People's Republic of China (W. W. Howells and P. J. Tsuchitani, eds.), pp. 40–65. National Academy of Sciences, Washington, D.C.

Delson, E. (1977b). Catarrhine phylogeny and classification: Principles, methods and comments. *J. Human Evol.* **6**, 433–459.

Delson, E. (1978). Models of early hominid phylogeny. *In* Early Hominids of Africa (C. J. Jolly, ed.), pp. 517–541. Duckworth, London.

Delson, E. (in press a). Fossil macaques, phyletic relationships and a scenario of deployment. *In* The Macaques: Studies in Behavior, Ecology and Evolution (D. G. Lindburg, ed.), pp. 10–30. Van Nostrand-Reinhold, New York.

Delson, E. (in press b). *Prohylobates* (Primates) from the Early Miocene of Libya: A new species and its implications for cercopithecid origins. *Geobios* (Lyon).

Delson, E., and Andrews, P. (1975). Evolution and interrelationships of the Catarrhine primates. *In* Phylogeny of the Primates: A Multidisciplinary Approach (W. P. Luckett and F. S. Szalay, eds.), pp. 405–446. Plenum, New York.

Delson, E., Eldredge, N., and Tattersall, I. (1977). Recon-struction of hominid phylogeny: A testable framework based on cladistic analysis. *J. Human Evol.* **6**, 263–278.

Delson, E., and Napier, P. H. (1976). Request for determination of the generic names of the baboon and the mandrill (Cercopithecidae, Primates, Mammalia). *Bull. Zool. Nomenclature* **33**, 46–60.

Delson, E., and Plopsor, D. (1975). *Paradolichopithecus*, a large terrestrial monkey (Cercopithecidae, Primates) from the Plio-Pleistocene of Southern Europe and its importance for mammalian biochronology. *Proc. Sixth Session, Reg. Comm. Mediterranean Neogene Stratigraphy, Bratislava*, pp. 91–96.

De Pauw, L. (1905). Notes sur la Solidification et le Montage des Grands Mammifères. Saint Nichols, Belgium.

Dépéret, C. (1886). Sur l'importance et la durée de la periode pliocène, d'après l'étude du bassin du Roussillon; nouveaux documents pour la faune de mammifères pliocenès de ce bassin. *C. R. Acad. Sci.* (Paris) **103**, 158–160.

Dépéret, C. (1887). Communication sur la presence d'un macaque fossile dans le terrain pliocène moyen de Perpignan. *Bull. Soc. d'Anth. Lyon* **6**, 40–42.

Dépéret, C. (1889). Sur le *Dolichopithecus ruscinensis* nouveau singe fossile du Pliocene du Roussillon. *C. R. Acad. Sci.* (Paris) **109**, 982–983.

Dépéret, C. (1890). Les animaux pliocènes du Roussillon. *Mem. Soc. Geol. France, Paléontol.* **3**, 1–126.

Dépéret, C. (1929). *Dolichopithecus arvernensis* Dépéret: Nouveau singe du pliocène supérieur de Senèze (Haute-Loire). *Trayaux Lab. Geol., Lyon* **15**, 5–12.

Deraniyagala, P. E. P. (1960). Some mammals of the extinct Ratnapura fauna of Ceylon, part 4. *Spolia Zeylanica* **29**, 3–7.

Desmarest, A. G. (1804). Nouv. Dict. Hist. Natl., 24, Tab. Méth. Mamm., 8.

Desmarest, A. G. (1820). Mammalogie, ou description des especes de mammifères. *In* Encyclopedie Methodique. Agasse, Paris and Liège.

Desmarest, A. G. (1822). Mammalogie, ou Description des Espèces de Mammifères, Part 2. Agasse, Paris.

Dietrich, W. O. (1942). Altestquartäre Säugetiere aus der Sudlichen Serengti, Deutsch-Ostafrika. *Palaeontographica* **94**, 44–75.

Dolinar-Osole, Z. (1956). Nova Pitekantropoidna oblika hominida iz severne Afrike. *Arheoloski Vestnik* **7**, 173–180.

Dollman, G. (1912). A new snub-nosed monkey. *Proc. Zool. Soc. London* **1912**, 503–504.

Dorr, J. A. (1952). Early Cenozoic stratigraphy and vertebrate paleontology of the Hoback basin, Wyoming. *Bull. Geol. Soc. Amer.* **63**, 59–94.

Douglass, E. (1908). Vertebrate fossils from the Fort Union beds. *Ann. Carnegie Mus.* **5**, 11–26.

Drennan, M. R. (1929). An australoid skull from the Cape Flats. *J. Roy. Anthropol. Inst.* **59**, 417–427.

Drennan, M. R. (1935). The Florisbad skull. *S. Afr. J. Sci.* **32**, 601–602.

Drennan, M. R. (1955). The special features and status of the Saldanha skull. *Amer. J. Phys. Anthropol.*, n.s. **13**, 625–634.

Dreyer, T. F. (1935). A human skull from Florisbad, Orange Free State, with a note on the endocranial cast (by C. V. Ariens-Kappers). *Proc. Kon. Nederlasse Akad. Sci.* **38**, 119–128.

Dubois, E. (1892). Bivoegsel tot de Javasche Conrant. *Verslag Mijnwesen* (Batavia), 3rd quarter, pp. 10–14.

[Dubois, E.] (1893). Palaeontologische Onderzoekingen op Java. *Verslag Mijnwesen* (Batavia), 4th quarter.

Dubois, E. (1894). *Pithecanthropus erectus*. Eine menschenahnliche Ubergangsform aus Java. Landersdruckerei, Batavia.

Dubois, E. (1895). *Pithecanthropus erectus* du Pliocène de Java. *Proc. Verbaux Bull. Soc. Belge Geol.* **9**, 151–160.

Dubois, E. (1921). The proto-Australian fossil man of Wadjak Java. *Proc. Kon. Nederlandse Akad. Wet.*, **23**, 1013–1051.

Dubois, E. (1940a). The fossil human remains discovered in Java by Dr. G. H. R. von Koenigswald and attributed by him to *Pithecanthropus erectus*, in reality remains of *Homo wadjakensis* (syn. *Homo soloensis*). *Proc. Kon. Nederlandse Akad. Wet.* **43**, 494–496.

Dubois, E. (1940b). The fossil human remains discovered in Java by Dr. G. H. R. von Koenigswald and attributed by him to *Pithecanthropus erectus*, in reality remains of *Homo sapiens soloensis* (Cont.). *Proc. Kon. Nederlandse Akad. Wet.* **43**, 842–851.

Dubois, E. (1940c). The fossil human remains discovered in Java by Dr. G. H. R. von Koenigswald and attributed by him to *Pithecanthropus erectus*, in reality remains of *Homo sapiens soloensis* (Conclusion). *Proc. Kon. Nederlandse Akad. Wet.* **43**, 1268–1275.

Dufresne, C. L. (1797). Sur une nouvelle espèce de singe (*Simia entellus*). *Bull. Soc. philomatique Paris* **1**, 49.

Eck, G. G. (1976). Cercopithecoidea from the Omo Group deposits. *In* Earliest Man and Environments in the Lake Rudolf Basin (Y. Coppens, F. C. Howell, G. L. Isaac, and R. E. F. Leakey, eds.), pp. 332–344. University of Chicago Press, Chicago.

Eck, G. G. (1977). Diversity and frequency distribution of Omo Group Cercopithecoidea. *J. Human Evol.* **6**, 55–63.

Eck, G. G., and Howell, F. C. (1972). New fossil *Cercopithecus* material from the lower Omo Basin, Ethiopia. *Folia Primatol.* **18**, 325–355.

Eckhardt, R. B. (1972). Population genetics and human origins. *Sci. Amer.* **226**(1), 94–103.

Eckhardt, R. B. (1973). *Gigantopithecus* as a hominid ancestor. *Anthropol. Anz.* **34**, 1–8.

Eckhardt, R. B. (1975). *Gigantopithecus* as a hominid. *In* Paleoanthropology, Morphology and Paleoecology (R. L. Tuttle, ed.), pp. 105–127. Mouton, The Hague.

Edinger, T. (1938). Mitteilungen uber Wirbeltierreste aus dem Mittelpliocän des Natrontales (Agypten). 9. Das Gehirn des *Libypithecus*. *Z. Mineral.*, *B* pp. 122–128.

Ehrenberg, K. (1938). *Austriacopithecus*, ein neuer menschenaffenartiger primate aus dem Miozän von Klein-Haderdorf bei Poysdorf in Niederösterreich (Nieder-Donau). *S. Ber. Akad. Wiss. Wien, math.–nat. Kl. Abstr. 1,* **147**, 71–110.

Eickstedt, E. von (1932). Hominiden und Simioiden. Uber den derzeitigen Stand der Abstammungsfrage. *Z. artzl. Fortbild.* **29**, 608–613.

Eickstedt, E. von (1934). Rassenkunde und Rassengeschichte der Menschheit, 1st ed. Enke Verlag, Stuttgart.

Eisenhart, W. L. (1974). The fossil cercopithecoids of Makapansgat and Sterkfontein, unpublished A. B. thesis. Harvard College, Cambridge, Mass.

Eisenhart, W. L. (1975). A review of the fossil cercopithecoids from Makapansgat and Sterkfontein, South Africa (abstract). *Amer. J. Phys. Anthropol., n.s.* **42**, 299.

Eldredge, N., and Gould, S. J. (1972). Speciation and punctuated equilibria; an alternative to phyletic gradualism. *In* Models in Paleobiology (T. Schopf, ed.), pp. 82–115. Freeman, San Francisco.

Eldredge, N. and Tattersall, I. (1975). Evolutionary models, phylogenetic reconstruction and another look at hominid phylogeny. *In* Approaches to Primate Paleobiology. Volume 5: Contributions to Primatology (F. S. Szalay, ed.), pp. 218–242.

Ellerman, J. R., Morrison-Scott, T. C. S., and Hayman, R. W. (1953). Southern African Mammals 1758 to 1951: A Reclassification. British Museum (Natural History), London.

Elliot, D. G. (1904). The land and sea mammals of Middle America and the West Indies. *Publ. Field Columbian Mus., Zool. Ser.* **4**, i–xiii, 441–850.

Elliot, D. G. (1913). A Review of the Primates. Monograph No. 1, Vols. 1, 2, and 3. American Museum of Natural History, New York.

Elliot-Smith, G. (1924). The Evolution of Man. Oxford University Press, London.

Ennouchi, E. (1970). Un nouvel archanthropien au Maroc. *Ann. Paléont. (Vertébrès)* **56**, 95–107.

Erickson, G. E. (1963). Brachiation in New World monkeys and in anthropoid apes. *Symp. Zool. Soc. London* **10**, 135–164.

Erxleben, J. C. P. (1777). Systema regni animalis... Classis 1, Mammalia. Weygand, Lipsiae.

Eschscholtz, J. F. (1818). Decades tres Eleutheratorum novorum. *Mem. Acad. Imper. Sci. St. Petersbourg* **6**, 451–496.

Eschscholtz, J. F. von (1821). *In* Entedeckungs-Reise in die Süd-See und nach den Berings Strasse zur Erforschung einer nordöstlichen Dürchfahrt Unternommen in der Jahren 1815–1818 (O. von Kotzebue, ed.). Gebruder Hoffman, Weimar.

Every, R. G. (1970). Sharpness of teeth in man and other primates. *Postilla* **143**, 1–30.

Every, R. G. (1972). A New Terminology for Mammalian Teeth. Christchurch, New Zealand.

Falconer, H., and Cautley, P. T. (1838). On additional fossil species of the order quadrumana from the Siwalik Hills. *J. Asiatic Soc.* **6**, 354–361.

Falk, D. D. (1976). External Neuroanatomy of the Cercopithecoidea, Ph.D. thesis. University of Michigan, Ann Arbor.

Fejfar, O. (1964). The lower Villafranchian vertebrates from Hajnacka near Filakovo in southern Slovakia. *Rozpravy, Ustredniho ustavu Geol.* **30**, 1–115.

Fejfar, O. (1969). Human remains from the early Pleistocene in Czechoslovakia. *Curr. Anthropol.* **10**, 170–173.

Ferembach, D. (1958). Les limnopithèques du Kenya. *Ann. Paléontol.* **44**, 149–249.

Filhol, H. (1873). Sur un nouveau genre de Lémurien fossile récemment découvert dans les gisements de phosphate de chaux du Quercy. *C. R. Acad. Sci.* (Paris) **77**, 1111–1112.

Filhol, H. (1874). Nouvelles observations sur les mammifères des gisements de phosphates de chaux, Lémuriens et Pachylémuriens. Bibliothèque de l'école des hautes études. Sci. Nat. 9.

Filhol, H. (1880). Note sur des mammifères fossiles nouveaux provenant des phosphorites du Quercy. *Bull. Soc. Philom.* **7**(4).

Filhol, H. (1883). Observations relatives au memoire de M. Cope intitulé: Relation des horizons renfermant des debris d'animaux vertébrès fossiles en Europe et en Amerique. *Ann. Sci. Geol., Paris* **14**, 1–51.

Filhol, H. (1888). Description d'une nouvelle espèce d'*Adapis. Bull. Soc. philom. Paris* **7**, 10–12.

Filhol, H. (1889–1890). Description d'une nouvelle espèce de Lémurien fossile (*Necrolemur parvulus*). *Bull. Soc. philom. Paris* **8**(2), 39–40.

Filhol, H. (1895). Observations concernant les Mammifères contemporains des *Aepyornis* à Madagascar. *Bull. Mus. Hist. Nat. Paris* **1**, 12–14.

Fischer, J. B. (1829). Synopsis Mammalium. J. G. Catta, Stuttgart.

Fischer von Waldheim, G. (1806). *Mémoires de la Société Imperiale des Naturalistes de Moscou* **1**.

Fischer von Waldheim, G. (1813). Zoognosia tabulis synopticis illustrata, 2 vols. Nicolai Sergeidis Vsevolozsky, Moscow.

Fleagle, J. G. (1975). A small gibbon-like hominoid from the Miocene of Uganda. *Folia Primatol.* **24**, 1–15.

Fleagle, J. G. (1976). Locomotion and posture of the Malayan siamang and implications for hominoid evolution. *Folia Primatol.* **26**, 245–269.

Fleagle, J. G., Simons, E. L., and Conroy, G. C. (1975). Ape limb bone from the Oligocene of Egypt. *Science* **189**, 135–137.

Fleming, J. (1822). The Philosophy of Zoology: or a General View of the Structure, Functions, and Classifications of Animals. A. Constable, Edinburgh.

Flower, W. H., and Lydekker, R. (1891). An Introduction to the Study of Mammals Living and Extinct. Adam and Charles Black, London.

Fogden, M. (1974). A preliminary field study of the western tarsier, *Tarsius bancanus* Horsfield. *In* Prosimian Biology (R. D. Martin, G. A. Doyle, and A. C. Walker, eds.), pp. 151–165. G. Duckworth, London.

Fooden, J. (1969). Taxonomy and evolution of the monkeys of Celebes (Primates: Cercopithecidae). *Biblioth. Primatol.* **10**, 1–148.

Fooden, J. (1975). Taxonomy and evolution of liontail and pigtail macaques (Primates: Cercopithecidae). *Fieldiana, Zool.* **67**, 1–169.

Fooden, J. (1976). Provisional classification and key to living species of macaques (Primates: *Macaca*). *Folia Primatol.* **25**, 225–236.

Forbes, H. O. (1897). A Handbook to the Primates, Vols. I and II. Edward Arnold, London.

Fourtau, R. (1918). Contribution à l'étude des vertébrès miocènes de l'Egypte. Survey Department, Ministry of Finance, Cairo.

Forrer, R. (1908). Urgeschichte des Europäers. W. Spemann, Stuttgart.

Frayer, D. W. (1973). *Gigantopithecus* and its relationship to *Australopithecus. Amer. J. Phys. Anthropol.* **39**, 413–426.

Franzen, J. L. (1973). Ein Primate aus den altpleistozänen Schneckenmergelen von Hohensülzen (Rheinhessen). *Senckenbergiana lethaea* **54**, 345–358.

Freedman, L. (1957). The fossil Cercopithecoidea of South Africa. *Ann. Transvaal Mus.* **23**, 121–262.

Freedman, L. (1961a). New Cercopithecoid fossils, including a new species from Taung, Cape Province, South Africa. *Ann. S. Afr. Mus.* **46**, 1–14.

Freedman, L. (1961b). Some new fossil Cercopithecoid specimens from Makapansgat, South Africa. *Palaeontol. Afr.* **7**, 7–43.

Freedman, L. (1965). Fossil and subfossil primates from the limestone deposits at Taung, Bolt's Farm and Witkrans, South Africa. *Palaeontol. Afr.* **9**, 19–48.

Freedman, L. (1976). South African fossil Cercopithecoidea: A reassessment including a description of new material from Makapansgat, Sterkfontein and Taung. *J. Human Evol.* **5**, 297–315.

Freedman, L., and Brain, C. K. (1972). Fossil cercopithecoid remains from the Kromdraai Australopithecine site (Mammalia: Primates). *Ann. Transvaal Mus.* **28**, 1–16.

Freedman, L., and Stenhouse, N. S. (1972). The *Parapapio* species of Sterkfontein, Transvaal, South Africa. *Palaeontol. Afr.* **14**, 93–111.

Freudenberg, W. von. (1929). Vorlage von Schädelfragmenten und Scapularest des *Hemianthropus osborni* gen. et sp. nov. nebst anderes Primaten-resten aus Bammenthal a.d. elsenz. *Verh. Anat. Ges. Jena* **38**, 240–245.

Freudenberg, W. (1932). Die Heppenlochfauna und ein weiterer Beleg des *Inuus suevicus* Hedinger. *Palaeontol. Z.* **14**, 126–132.

Freyberg, B. von. (1951). Die Pikermi-Fauna von Tour La Reine (Attika). *Ann. Geol. des Pays Helleniques* Ser. 1, **3**, 7–10.

Friederichs, H. F. (1932). Schädel und Unterkiefer von Piltdown ("Eoanthropus dawsoni Woodward") in neuer Untersuchung. *Z. Anat. Entwick. Gesch.* **98**, 199–262.

Frisch, J. E. (1965). Trends in the evolution of the hominoid dentition. *Bibl. Primatol.* **3**, 1–130.

Frisch, J. E. (1973). The hylobatid dentition. *Gibbon Siamang* **2**, 55–95.

Flamand, M. G.-B.-M. (1902). Sur l'utilisation, comme instruments Néolithiques de coquilles fossiles à taille intentionnelle (Littoral du Nord-Africain). *C. R. Assoc. Francais l'Advancement Sci.* 30th session, pp. 729–734.

"Gao Jian" (1975). Australopithecine teeth associated with *Gigantopithecus. Vertebrata Palasiatica* **13**, 81–88.

Gaudry, A. (1862). Animaux Fossiles et Geologie de l'Attique. F. Savy, Paris.

Gawne, C. E. (1968). The genus *Proterix* (Insectivora, Erinaceidae) of the upper Oligocene of North America. *Amer. Mus. Nov.* **2315**, 1–26.

Gazin, C. L. (1942). Fossil mammalia from the Almy formation in western Wyoming. *J. Wash. Acad. Sci.* **32**(7), 217–220.

Gazin, C. L. (1952). The lower Eocene Knight formation of western Wyoming and its mammalian faunas. *Smithsonian Misc. Coll.* **111**(18), 1–82.

Gazin, C. L. (1956a). Paleocene mammalian faunas of the Bison Basin in south central Wyoming. *Smithsonian Misc. Coll.* **131**(6), 1–57.

Gazin, C. L. (1956b). The occurrence of Paleocene mammalian remains in the Fossil Basin of southwestern Wyoming. *J. Paleontol.* **30**, 707–711.

Gazin, C. L. (1956c). The upper Paleocene mammalia from the Almy formation in western Wyoming. *Smithsonian Misc. Coll.* **131**(7), 1–18.

Gazin, C. L. (1958). A review of the middle and upper Eocene primates of North America. *Smithsonian Misc. Coll.* **136**(1), 1–112.

Gazin, C. L. (1962a). A further study of the lower Eocene mammalian faunas of southwestern Wyoming. *Smithsonian Misc. Coll.* **144**(1), pp. 1–98 and Figs. 1 and 2, Plates 1–14.

Gazin, C. L. (1962b). Main body of the Wasatch Formation near La Barge, Wyoming. *Bull. Amer. Assoc. Petrol. Geol.* **46**, 2161–2173.

Gazin, C. L. (1968). A new Primate from the Torrejon middle Paleocene of the San Juan Basin, New Mexico. *Proc. Biol. Soc. Wash.* **81**, 629–634.

Gazin, C. L. (1971). Paleocene primates from the Shotgun Member of the Fort Union Formation in the Wind River Basin, Wyoming. *Proc. Biol. Soc. Wash.* **84**, 13–38.

Gear, J. H. S. (1926). A preliminary account of the baboon remains from Taungs. *S. Afr. J. Sci.* **23**, 731–747.

Gear, J. H. S. (1958). The fossil baboons from Taungs. *S. Afr. J. Sci.* **23**, 205–223.

Geoffroy Saint-Hilaire, E. (1795). Décad. phil. et litt., 28.

Geoffroy Saint-Hilaire, E. (1796). Mag. Encyclop., 2me Année, I.

Geoffroy Saint-Hilaire, E. (1806). Mémoire sur les Singes à main imparfaite ou les Atèles. *Ann. Mus. Hist. Nat. Paris* **7**, 260–273.

Geoffroy Saint-Hilaire, E. (1812). Tableau des quadrumanes, 1. Ord. Quadrumanes. *Ann. Mus. Hist. Nat. Paris* **19**, 85–122.

Geoffroy Saint-Hilaire, E. (1828). Cours de l'Histoire naturelle des Mammifères... partie comprenant quelques vues préliminaires de philosophie naturelle et l'Histoire des Singes, des Makis, des Chauve-Souris et de la Taupe; pouvant servir de complement à l'Histoire Naturelle des Quadrupèdes de Buffon. Paris.

Geoffroy Saint-Hilaire, E., and Cuvier, G. (1795). Mémoire sur une Nouvelle Division des Mammifères, et sur les Principes qui Doivent Servir de Base dans cette Sorte de Travail. Magasin Encyclopédique, 1ʳᵉ Année, t. II, pp. 164–190. Millin, Noel et Warens, Paris.

Geoffroy Saint-Hilare, I. (1829). Remarques sur les caractères generaux des singes americains, et description d'un genre nouveau, sous le nom d'Eriode. *Mem. Mus. Hist. Nat. Paris* **17**, 121–165.

Geoffroy Saint-Hilaire, I. (1831). Mammifères. *In* Voyage aux Indes-Orientales, Zoologie (M. C. Bélanger, ed.), pp. 1–160. Bertrand, Paris.

Geoffroy Saint-Hilaire, I. (1836). *In* Résumé des Leçons de Mammalogie ou Histoire Naturelle des Mammifères Professées au Muséum de Paris, pendant l'année 1835, par Geoffroy Saint-Hilare (P. Gervais, ed.). Mus. Hist. Nat., Paris.

Geoffroy Saint-Hilaire, I. (1842). Sur les singes de l'ancien monde, spécialement sur les genres Gibbon et Semnopithèque. *C. R. Acad. Sci. (Paris)* **15**(7), 6–720.

Geoffroy Saint-Hilaire, I. (1843). Description des mammifères nouveaux ou imparfaitement connus... Famille des Singes. *Arch. Mus. Hist. Nat. Paris* **2**, 486–592.

Geoffroy Saint-Hilaire, I. (1847). Note sur un singe américain appartenent au genre Brachyure. *C. R. Acad. Sci. (Paris)* **24**, 576–577.

Geoffroy Saint-Hilaire, I. (1850). *C. R. Acad. Sci. (Paris)* **31**, 876.

Geoffroy Saint-Hilaire, I. (1851). Catalogue Methodique de la Collection des Mammifères. Mus. d'Hist. Nat., Paris.

Geoffroy Saint-Hilaire, I. (1852). Sur le gorille. *C. R. Acad. Sci. (Paris)* **34**, 81–84.

Gervais, P. (1836). Mammalogie ou Mastologie. *In* Dictionaire Pittoresque d'Histoire Naturelle (F. E. Guérin-Menéville, ed.), Vol. 7, pp. 614–640. Bureau de souscription, Paris.

Gervais, P. (1839). Pithèque. *In* Dictionnaire Pittoresque d'Histoire Naturelle (F. E. Guérin-Menéville, ed.), Vol. 8, pp. 90–91. Bureau de Souscription, Paris.

Gervais, P. (1845). Zoologie de la France. Dubochet, Paris.

Gervais, P. (1848). Sur quelques mammifères fossiles du terrain tertiare éocène des environs d'Alais. *C. R. Acad. Sci. (Paris)* **26**, 49–50.

Gervais, P. (1849). Zoologie et Paléontologie françaises, ed. I. Bertrand, Paris.

Gervais, P. (1859). Zoologie et Paléontologie françaises, ed. II, 2 vols. Bertrand, Paris.

Gervais, P. (1867). Zoologie et Paléontologie générale. Bertrand, Paris.

Gervais, P. (1872). Sur un singe fossile, d'un espèce non encore décrite, qui a été découverte au monte Bamboli. *C. R. Acad. Sci. (Paris)* **74**, 1217.

Gervais, P. (1876). Zoologie et Paléontologie générale, ed. 2. Bertrand, Paris.

Gervais, P. (1877). Énumération de quelques ossements d'animaux vertébrés recueillis aux environs de Reims par M. Lemoine. *J. Zool.* **6**.

Gidley, J. W. (1923). Paleocene Primates of the Fort Union, with discussion of relationships of Eocene primates. *Proc. U.S. Nat. Mus.* **63**, 1–38.

Gill, T. (1872). Arrangement of the families of mammals with analytical tables. *Smithsonian Misc. Coll.* **11**, 1–98.

Gingerich, P. D. (1968). Pollen stratigraphy of the Polecat

Bench Formation, Park County, Wyoming, unpublished A. B. thesis. Princeton University, Princeton.

Gingerich, P. D. (1973a). First record of the Paleocene primate *Chiromyoides* from North America. *Nature* (London) **244**, 517–518.

Gingerich, P. D. (1973b). Anatomy of the temporal bone in the Oligocene anthropoid *Apidium* and the origin of the Anthropoidea. *Folia Primatol.* **19**, 329–337.

Gingerich, P. D. (1974). Cranial anatomy and evolution of early Tertiary Plesiadapidae (Mammalia, Primates), Ph.D. thesis. Yale University, New Haven.

Gingerich, P. D. (1975a). Systematic position of *Plesiadapis*. *Nature* (London) **253**, 111–131.

Gingerich, P. D. (1975b). New North American Plesiadapidae (Mammalia, Primates) and a biostratigraphic zonation of the middle and upper Paleocene. *Contrib. Mus. Paleontol. Univ. Mich.* **24**, 135–148.

Gingerich, P. D. (1975c). A new genus of Adapidae (Mammalia, Primates) from the late Eocene of southern France, and its significance for the origin of higher primates. *Contrib. Mus. Paleontol. Univ. Mich.* **24**, 163–170.

Gingerich, P. D. (1975d). Dentition of *Adapis parisiensis* and the origin of lemuriform primates. *In* Lemur Biology (I. Tattersall and R. Sussman, eds.), pp. 65–80. Plenum, New York.

Gingerich, P. D. (1976a). Cranial anatomy and evolution of early Tertiary Plesiadapidae (Mammalia, Primates). *Mus. Paleontol. Univ. Mich., Papers on Paleontol.* **15**.

Gingerich, P. D. (1976b). Systematic position of the alleged Primate *Lantianius xiehuensis* Chow, 1964, from the Eocene of China. *J. Mammal.* **57**, 194–198.

Gingerich, P. D. (1976c). Paleontology and phylogeny: Patterns of evolution at the species level in early Tertiary mammals. *Amer. J. Sci.* **276**, 1–28.

Gingerich, P. D. (1977a). New species of Eocene Primates and the phylogeny of European Adapidae. *Folia Primatol.* **28**, 60–80.

Gingerich, P. D. (1977b). Radiation of Eocene Adapidae in Europe. *Géobios, Mém. special* **1**, 165–182.

Gingerich, P. D. and K. D. Rose. (1977). Preliminary report on the American Clark Fork Mammal Fauna, and its correlation with similar faunas in Europe and Asia. *Geobios Mem.* **1**, 39–45.

Gingerich, P. D., and Simons, E. L. (1977). Systematics, phylogeny, and evolution of early Eocene Adapidae (Mammalia, Primates) in North America. *Contrib. Mus. Paleontol. Univ. Mich.* **24**, 245–279.

Ginsburg, L. (1974). Les faunes de mammifères burdigaliens et vindoboniens des Bassins de la Loire et de la Garonne. *Mém. bur. rech. géol. min. France* **78**, 153–168.

Ginsburg, L. (1975). Le Pliopithèque des Faluns Helvetiens de la Touraine et de l'Anjou. *C. N. R. S. Coll. Internatl.* **218**, 877–886.

Gistel, J. (1848). Naturgeschichte des Thierreichs. Hoffman, Stuttgart.

Giuffrida-Ruggieri, V. (1915). Quatro crani prehistorici dell' Italia meridonale. *Arch. Anthropol. Etnol.* **45**, 292–315.

Giuffrida-Ruggieri, V. (1921). Su L'Origine dell'Uomo. Nuove Teorie e Documenti. N. Zanichelli, Bologna.

Glaessner, M. F. (1931). Neue Zähne von Menschenaffen aus dem Miozän des Wiener Beckens. *Ann. Nat. Hist. Mus., Wien* **46**, 15–27.

Gloger, C. W. L. (1841). Gemeinnutziges Hand-und Hilfsbuch der Naturgeschichte, Vol. 1. Aug Schultz, Breslav.

Gmelin, J. F. (Ed.) (1788). *In* Systema Naturae (C. Linnaeus), 13th ed., Vol. 1. G. E. Beer, Leipzig.

Goeldi, E. A. (1907). On some new and insufficiently known species of marmoset monkeys from the Amazonian region. *Proc. Zool. Soc. London* 88–8).

Goldfuss, G. A. (1820). Handbuch der Zoologie, 2 vols. J. L. Schrag, Nuremberg.

Goodman, M. (1975). Protein sequence and immunological specificity: Their role in phylogenetic studies of primates. *In* Phylogeny of the Primates: A Multidisciplinary Approach (W. P. Luckett and F. S. Szalay, eds.), pp. 219–248. Plenum, New York.

Goodman, M., and Tashian, R. E. (eds.) (1976). Molecular Anthropology. Plenum, New York.

Gorjanovic-Kramberger, D. (1902). Der palaeolithische Mensch und seine Zeitgenossen aus dem Diluvium von Krapina in Kroatien. *Mitt. Anthropol. Gesell. Wien* **32**, 184–216.

Gorjanovic-Kramberger, D. (1905). Der paläolithische Mensch und seine Zeitgenossen aus dem Diluvium von Krapina in Kroatien, dritter Nachtrag. *Mitt. Anthropol. Gesell. Wien* **35**, 197–229.

Grand, T. I., and Lorenz, R. (1968). Functional analysis of the hip joint in *Tarsius bancanus* (Horsfield, 1821) and *Tarsius syrichta* (Linnaeus, 1758). *Folia Primatol.* **9**, 161–181.

Grandidier, A. (1866). *Rev. Mag. Zool.* **1**, 19.

Grandidier, A. (1867). *Rev. Mag. Zool.* **2**, 84.

Grandidier, G. (1899). Description des ossements de lémuriens disparus. *Bull. Mus. Hist. Nat. Paris* **5**, 272–276, 344–348.

Grandidier, G. (1904). Un nouveau Lemurien fossile de France, le *Pronycticebus gaudryi*. *Bull. Mus. Hist. Nat. Paris* **10**, 9–13.

Granger, W. (1910). Tertiary faunal horizons in the Wind River Basin, Wyoming, with descriptions of new Eocene mammals. *Bull. Amer. Mus. Nat. Hist.* **28**, 235–251.

Granger, W., and Gregory, W. K. (1917). A revision of the Eocene Primates of the genus *Notharctus*. *Bull. Amer. Mus. Nat. Hist.* **37**, 841–859.

Gravenhorst, J. L. C. (1843). Vergleichende Zoologie. Grass, Barth und Co., Breslau.

Gray, J. E. (1821). On the natural arrangement of vertebrose animals. *London Med. Repository Record* **15**, 296–310.

Gray, J. E. (1825). Outline of an attempt at the disposition of the Mammalia into tribes and families with a list of the genera apparently appertaining to each tribe. *Ann. Philos., n.s.* **10**, 337–344.

Gray, J. E. (1843). List of the specimens of mammalia in the collection of the British Museum. British Museum, London.

Gray, J. E. (1845). On the howling monkeys (*Mycetes*, Illiger). *Ann. Mag. Nat. Hist.* **16**, 217–221.

Gray, J. E. (1849). On some new or little-known species of monkeys. *Proc. Zool. Soc. London, 1849*, pp. 7–10.

Gray, J. E. (1850). Description of a new species of monkey,

recently living in the Society's Menagerie. *Proc. Zool. Soc. London, 1850*, pp. 77–78.

Gray, J. E. (1861). On the habits of the Gorilla and other tailless longarmed apes. *Proc. Zool. Soc. London, 1861*, pp. 212–213.

Gray, J. E. (1863). Revision of the species of lemuroid animals, with the description of some new species. *Proc. Zool. Soc. London, 1863*, pp. 129–152.

Gray, J. E. (1866a). Synopsis of the genera of Vespertilionidae and Noctilionidae. *Ann. Mag. Nat. Hist.*, Ser. 3, **17**, 89–93.

Gray, J. E. (1866b). Notice of an ape *(Macacus inornatus)* and a bushbuck *(Cephalophus breviceps)* in the gardens of the Society. *Proc. Zool. Soc. London, 1866*, pp. 202–203.

Gray, J. E. (1870). Catalogue of monkeys, lemurs, and fruit-eating bats in the collection of the British Museum. British Museum of Natural History, London.

Gray, J. E. (1872). Notes on *Propithecus, Indris,* and other lemurs (Lemurina) in the British Museum. *Proc. Zool. Soc. London, 1872*, pp. 846–860.

Greenfield, L. O. (1972). Sexual dimorphism in *Dryopithecus africanus*. *Primates* **13**, 395–410.

Greenfield, L. O. (1973). Note on the placement of the most complete *Kenyapithecus africanus* mandible. *Folia Primatol.* **20**, 274–279.

Greenfield, L. O. (1974). Taxonomic reassessment of two *Ramapithecus* specimens. *Folia Primatol.* **22**, 97–115.

Gregory, W. K. (1910). The orders of mammals. *Bull. Amer. Mus. Nat. Hist.* **27**, 3–524.

Gregory, W. K. (1915a). On the relationship of the Eocene lemur *Notharctus* to the Adapidae and to other primates. *Bull. Geol. Soc. Amer.* **26**, 419–425.

Gregory, W. K. (1915b). On the classification and phylogeny of the Lemuroidea. *Bull. Geol. Soc. Amer.* **26**, 426–446.

Gregory, W. K. (1917). Genetics vs. Paleontology. *Amer. Natural.* **51**, 631.

Gregory, W. K. (1920). On the structure and relations of *Notharctus*, an American Eocene primate. *Mem. Amer. Mus. Nat. Hist.*, n.s. **3**, 51–243.

Gregory, W. K. (1921). Origin and evolution of the human dentition. Part V. *J. Dental Res.* **3**, 88–228.

Gregory, W. K. (1922). The Origin and Evolution of the Human Dentition. Williams & Wilkins, Baltimore.

Gregory, W. K. (1951). Evolution Emerging: A Survey of Changing Patterns from Primeval Life to Man. Macmillan, New York.

Gregory, W. K., and Hellman, M. (1926). The dentition of *Dryopithecus* and the origin of man. *Amer. Mus. Anthropol. Papers* **28**, 1–123.

Gregory, W. K., Hellman, M., and Lewis, G. E. (1938). Fossil anthropoids of the Yale–Cambridge India expedition of 1935. *Carnegie Inst. Wash. Publ.* **495**, 1–27.

Gregory, W. K., and Hellman, M. (1939). The dentition of the extinct South African man–ape *Australopithecus (Plesianthropus) transvaalensis* Broom. A comparative and phylogenetic study. *Ann. Transvaal. Mus.* **19**, 339–373.

Gremyatskii, M. A. (1957). [Fossil monkeys on the territory of the Soviet Union.] *Sovetskaya Antropol.* **1**, 35–46 (in Russian).

Gremyatskii, M. A. (1960). [New finds of fossil primates on the territory of the U.S.S.R.] *Tezesi Doklady VI Vsesoyuznovo Tseda Anatomov, Gistologov, Embriologov*, Kharkov, 1958. (Papers presented to VIth All-Union Congr. of Anat., Histol., and Embryol.; Kharkov, 1958; in Russian, not seen.)

Gremyatskii, M. A. (1961). [The main line of higher primate evolution in the Neogene.] *Voprosy Antropol.* **7**, 3–8 (in Russian).

Gremyatskii, M. A. (1962). Order Primates. In Principles of Paleontology. Volume 11: Mammals (V. Gromova, ed.), pp. 90–107. [Transl., 1968, Tel Aviv, Israel Translation Project, pp. 118–141.]

Groves, C. P. (1970). The forgotten leaf-eaters and the phylogeny of the Colobinae. In Old World Monkeys (J. R. Napier and P. H. Napier, eds.), pp. 555–586. Academic Press, New York.

Groves, C. P. (1972). Systematics and phylogeny of gibbons. *Gibbon Siamang* **1**, 1–80.

Groves, C. P. (1974). New evidence on the evolution of the apes and man. *Vestnik Ustredniko ustavu geol.* **49**, 53–56.

Groves, C. P., and Mazak, U. (1975). An approach to the taxonomy of the Hominidae: Gracile Villafranchian hominids of Africa. *Casopis pro Mineral Geol.* **20**, 225–247.

Gunther, A. (1875). Notes on some Mammals from Madagascar. *Proc. Zool. Soc. London, 1875*, pp. 78–80.

Gunther, A. (1876). On some new mammals from Tropical America. *Proc. Zool. Soc. London, 1876*, pp. 743–751.

Guthrie, D. A. (1963). The carotid circulation in the Rodentia. *Bull. Mus. Comp. Zool.* **128**, 455–481.

Guthrie, D. A. (1967). The mammalian fauna of the Lysite member, Wind River Formation (early Eocene) of Wyoming. *Mem. So. Calif., Acad. Sci.* **5**, 1–53.

Guthrie, D. A. (1971). The mammalian fauna of the Lost Cabin member, Wind River Formation (lower Eocene) of Wyoming. *Ann. Carnegie Mus.* **43**, 47–113.

Haas, G. (1966). On the vertebrate fauna of the lower Pleistocene site 'Ubeidiya. Jerusalem, Israel Acad. Sci. Hum.

Haeckel, E. (1866). Generelle Morphologie der Organismen. Georg Reimer, Berlin.

Haeckel, E. (1895). Systematische Phylogenie der Wirbelthiere (Vertebrata) Dritter Theil. Georg Reimer, Berlin.

Hall-Craggs, E. C. B. (1964). The jump of the bushbaby—a photographic analysis. *Med. Biol. Ill*, **14**, 170–174.

Hall-Craggs, E. C. B. (1965). An analysis of the Lesser Galago *(Galago senegalensis)*. *J. Zool.* **147**, 20–29.

Harlan, R. (1826). Description of a Hermaphrodite Orang Outang. *J. Acad. Nat. Sci.*, Philadelphia **5**, 229–236.

Harlan, R. (1834). Description of a species of Orang from the northeastern province of British East India, lately the Kingdom of Assam. *Trans. Amer. Philo. Soc.*, n.s. **4**, 52–59.

Harlé, E. (1892). Une mandibule de singe du repaire des hyènes de Montsaunès (Haute-Garonne). *Bull. Soc. Hist. Nat. Toulouse* **26**, IX–XI.

Hasebe, K. (1948). A human coxal bone from lower Pleistocene deposits of Nishiyagi. *Zinruigaku Zassi* **60**, 32–36.

Haughton, S. H. (1925). Demonstration (of Taung fossils). *Trans. Roy Soc. S. Afr.* **12**, lxviii.

Haupt, O. (1935). Andere Wirbeltiere des Neozoikums. *In* Oberrheinischer Fossilkatalog (W. Salomon-Calvi, ed.), Vol. 4, No. 9, pp. 1–103. Gebruder Borntraeger, Berlin.

Hay, R. L. (1976). Geology of the Olduvai Gorge. University of California Press, Berkeley.

Heberer, G. (1963). Über einen neuer archanthropinen Typus aus der Oldoway-Schlucht. *Z. Morphol. Anthropol.* **53**, 171–177.

Hedinger, A. (1891). Ueber den pliocänen Affen des Heppenlochs. *N. Jb. Min., Geol., Paläontol.* **1**, 169–177.

Heller, F. (1930). Die Säugetierfauna der mitteleozänen Braunkohle des Geiseltales bei Halle a. S. *Jb. Halleschen Verbandes* **9**, 13–14.

Heller, F. (1936). Eine oberpliocäne Wirbeltierfauna aus Rheinhessen. *N. Jb. Min., Geol., Paläontol., Beilage* Abstr. B, **76**, 99–160.

Hemprich, W. (1820). Grundriss der Naturgeschichte für höhere Lehranstalten Entworfen von Dr. W. Hemprich. August Rucker, Berlin.

Hennig, E. (1932). Fortschritte der Altsteinzeit-Forschung in der Alten Welt. *Petermann's Mittl.* **78**, 134–137.

Hennig, E. (1948). Quartärfaunen und Urgeschichte Ostafrikas. *Naturwiss. Rundschau* **1**, 5.

Hennig, W. (1966). Phylogenetic Systematics. University of Illinois Press, Chicago.

Hershkovitz, P. (1969). The evolution of mammals on southern continents. VI. The recent mammals of the neotropical region; a zoogeographic and ecological review. *Q. Rev. Biol.* **44**(1), 1–70.

Hershkovitz, P. (1970a). Notes on Tertiary platyrrhine monkeys and description of a new genus from the late Miocene of Columbia. *Folia Primatol.* **12**, 1–37.

Hershkovitz, P. (1970b). Cerebral fissural patterns in Platyrrhine monkeys. *Folia Primatol.* **13**, 213–240.

Hershkovitz, P. (1972). Notes on New World monkeys. *Intl. Zoo Yrbk.* **12**, 1–12.

Hershkovitz, P. (1974a). A new genus of late Oligocene monkey (Cebidae, Platyrrhini) with notes on postorbital closure and Platyrrhine evolution. *Folia Primatol.* **21**, 1–35.

Hershkovitz, P. (1974b). The ectotympanic bone and origin of higher Primates. *Folia Primatol.* **22**, 237–242.

Hershkovitz, P. (1977). New World Monkeys (Platyrrhini), Vol. 1. University of Chicago Press, Chicago.

Heuglin, M. T. von. (1863). Beiträge zur Zoologie Afrika's ueber einige Säugethiere des Bäschlo-Gebietes. *Nova acta acad. Caesaria Leopoldino-Carolina* **30**, abh. 2, suppl., 10–24.

Hiiemae, K. M. (1978). Mammalian mastication: A review of the activity of the jaw muscles and the movements they produce in chewing. *In* Development, Function and Evolution of Teeth (P. M. Butler and K. A. Joysey, eds), pp. 361–398. Academic Press, London.

Hiiemae, K. M. and A. W. Crompton (1971). A Cinefluorographic study of feeding in the American Opposum, *Didelphis marsupialis. In* Dental Morphology and Evolution (A. A. Dahlberg, ed.), pp. 299–334. University of Chicago Press, Chicago.

Hiiemae, K. M. and R. F. Kay. (1973). Evolutionary trends in the dynamics of primate mastication. *In* Symp. IVth Internat. Congr. Primatol. Vol. 3. Craniofacial Biology of Primates, pp. 28–64. Karger, Basel.

Hilber, V. (1922). Urgeschichte Steiermarks. *Mitt. Nat. Var. Steiermark* **58**(B), 1–11.

Hill, J. P. (1919). The affinities of *Tarsius* from the embryological aspect. *Proc. Zool. Soc. London*, pp. 476–491.

Hill, W. C. O. (1953). Primates: Comparative Anatomy and Taxonomy. Volume I: Strepsirhini. The University Press, Edinburgh.

Hill, W. C. O. (1955). Primates: Comparative Anatomy and Taxonomy. Volume II: Haplorhini: Tarsioidea. The University Press, Edinburgh.

Hill, W. C. O. (1957). Primates: Comparative Anatomy and Taxonomy. Volume III: Hapalidae. The University Press, Edinburgh.

Hill, W. C. O. (1959). The anatomy of *Callimico geoldii* (Thomas), a primitive American primate. *Trans. Amer. Phil. Soc.* **49**, 1–116.

Hill, W. C. O. (1960). Primates: Comparative Anatomy and Taxonomy. Volume IV: Cebidae, Part A. The University Press, Edinburgh.

Hill, W. C. O. (1962). Primates: Comparative Anatomy and Taxonomy. Volume V: Cebidae, Part B. The University Press, Edinburgh.

Hill, W. C. O. (1966). Primates: Comparative Anatomy and Taxonomy. Volume VI: Cercopithecinae. The University Press, Edinburgh.

Hill, W. C. O. (1970). Primates: Comparative Anatomy and Taxonomy. Volume VIII: Cynopithecinae: *Papio, Mandrillus, Theropithecus.* The University Press, Edinburgh.

Hill, W. C. O. (1972). Evolutionary Biology of the Primates. Academic Press, New York.

Hill, W. C. O. (1974). Primates: Comparative Anatomy and Taxonomy. Volume VII: Cynopithecinae. The University Press, Edinburgh.

Hinton, M. A. C. (1908). Note on the discovery of a bone of a monkey in the Norfolk Forest Bed. *Geol. Mag., Ser. V* **5**, 440–444.

Hladik, C. M., Charles-Dominique, P., Valdebeuze, P., Delort-Laval, J., and Flanzyy, J. (1971). La coecotrophie chez un Primate phyllophage du genre *Lepilemur* et les correlations avec les particularités de son appareil digestif. *C. R. Acad. Sci.* (Paris) **272**, 3191–3194.

Hodgson, B. H. (1841). Three new species of monkey: With remarks on the genera *Semnopithecus* and *Macacus. J. Asiatic Soc. Bengal* **9**, 1211–1213.

Hofer, H. O. (1976). Preliminary study of the comparative anatomy of the external nose of South American monkeys. *Folia Primatol.* **25**, 193–214.

Hoffmannsegg, J. C. von. (1807). Beschreibung vier affenartiger Thiere aus Brasilien. *Mag. Ges. naturf. fr. Berlin*, pp. 83–104.

Hoffstetter, M. R. (1969). Un Primate de l'Oligocène inférieur sudAméricain: *Branisella boliviana* gen. et sp. nov. *C. R. Acad. Sci. (Paris)* **269**, 434–437.

Hoffstetter, R. (1972). Relationships, origins, and history of the ceboid monkeys and caviomorph rodents: A modern reinterpretation. *In* Evolutionary Biology (T. Dobzhansky, M. K. Hecht, and W. C. Steere, eds.), pp. 323–347. Appleton-Century-Crofts, New York.

Hoffstetter, R. (1974a). *Apidium* et l'origine des Simiiformes (=Anthropoidea). *C. R. Acad. Sci. (Paris)* **278**, 1715–1717.

Hoffstetter, R. (1974b). Phylogeny and geographical deployment of the Primates. *J. Human Evol.* **3**, 327–350.

Holloway, R. L. (1976). Paleoneurological evidence for language origins. *Ann. N.Y. Acad. Sci.* **280**, 330–348.

Hooijer, D. A. (1948). Prehistoric teeth of man and the orangutan from central Sumatra with notes on the fossil orangutan from Java and southern China. *Zool. Meded. Rijks Mus. Nat. Hist.* **29**, 175–301.

Hooijer, D. A. (1951). Questions relating to a new large anthropoid ape from the Mio-Pliocene of the Siwaliks. *Amer. J. Phys. Anthropol.* **9**, 79–95.

Hooijer, D. A. (1960). Quaternary gibbons from the Malay Archipelago. *Zool. Verh. Mus. Leiden* **46**, 1–42.

Hooijer, D. A. (1962). Quaternary langurs and macaques from the Malay Archipelago. *Zool. Verhandl. Mus. Leiden* **55**, 3–64.

Hooijer, D. A. (1963). Miocene Mammalia of Congo. *Ann. Mus. Roy. Afr. Cent., Ser. 8, Sci. Geol.* **46**, 1–71.

Hooijer, D. A. (1970). Miocene Mammalia of Congo, correction. *Ann. Mus. Roy. Afr. Cent., Ser. 8, Sci. Geol.* **67**, 163–167.

Hoppius, C. E. (1763). Anthropomorpha . . . proposuit C. E. Hoppius. *Amoenitates Academicae* **6**.

Hopwood, A. T. (1933a). Miocene primates from British East Africa. *Ann. Mag. Nat. Hist., Ser. 10* **11**, 96–98.

Hopwood, A. T. (1933b). Miocene primates from Kenya. *J. Linn. Soc. London, Zool.* **38**, 437–464.

Hopwood, A. T. (1934). New fossil mammals from Olduvai, Tanganyika territory. *Ann. Mag. Nat. Hist., Ser. 10* **14**, 546–547.

Hopwood, A. T. (1936). New and little-known fossil mammals from the Pleistocene of Kenya colony and Tanganyika territory. *Ann. Mag. Nat. Hist., Ser. 10* **17**, 636–638.

Hopwood, A. T., and Hollyfield, J. P. (1954). An annotated bibliography of the fossil mammals of Africa. *In* Fossil Mammals of Africa, Vol. 8, pp. 1–194. British Museum (Natural Hist), London.

Hornbeck, P. V., and Swindler, D. R. (1967). Morphology of the lower fourth premolar of certain Cercopithecidae. *J. Dent. Res. Suppl.* **46**, 979–983.

Horsfield, T. (1821). Zoological Researches in Java, 2.

Houzé, E. (1896). Le *Pithecanthropus erectus. Rev. Univ. Bruxelles* **1**, 401–438.

Howell, F. C. (1965). Comments to the article by P. V. Tobias. *Curr. Anthropol.* **6**, 399–401.

Howell, F. C. (1967a). Review of *Man-Apes or Ape-Men? Amer. J. Phys. Anthropol., n.s.* **27**, 95–101.

Howell, F. C. (1967b). Recent advances in human evolutionary studies. *Q. Rev. Biol.* **42**, 471–513.

Howell, F. C. (1969). Remains of Hominidae from Pliocene/Pleistocene formations in the lower Omo basin, Ethiopia. *Nature* (London) **223**, 1234–1239.

Howell, F. C., and Coppens, Y. (1976). An overview of Hominidae from the Omo succession Ethiopia. *In* Earliest Man and Environments in the Lake Rudolf Basin (Y.

Coppens, F. C. Howell, G. L. Isaac, and R. E. F. Leakey, eds.), pp. 522–532. University of Chicago Press, Chicago.

Hsu, C.-h., Han, K.-x., and Wang, L.-h. (1974). Discovery of *Gigantopithecus* teeth and associated fauna in western Hopei. *Vert. Palas.* **12**, 293–309.

Hsu, K. J., Montadert, L., Bernoulli, D., Cita, M. B., Erickson, A., Garrison, R. E., Kidd, R. E., Melieres, F., Müller, C. and Wright, R. (1977). History of the Mediterranean salintity crisis. *Nature* (London) **267**, 399–403.

Hu, C. C. (1973). Ape-man teeth from Yuanmou, Yunnan. *Acta Geol. Sinica* **1**, 65–71.

Hübner, J. (1806). Sammlung exotische Schmetterlinge, Vol. 1. C. Geyer, Augsburg.

Humboldt, (1912). Recueil d'Observations de Zoologie et d'Anatomie Comparée, Farites dans l'Océan Atlantique, dans l'Intérieur du Nouveau Continent et dans la Mer du Sud Pendant les Années 1799, 1800, 1801, 1802 et 1803, Vol. 1. F. Schoell and Dufour, Paris.

Hürzeler, J. (1946). Zur charakteristik, systematischen Stellung, Phylogenese und Verbreitung der Necrolemuriden aus demeuropäischen Eocaen. *Schweiz Palaeontol. Gesell.* **10**, 352–354.

Hürzeler, J. (1948). Zur Stammesgeschichte der Necrolemuriden. *Schweiz. Palaeontol. Abh.* **66**(1), 1–46.

Hürzeler, J. (1949). Neubeschreibung von *Oreopithecus bambolii* Gervais. *Schweiz. Palaeontol. Abh.* **66**(5), 1–20.

Hürzeler, J. (1952). Contribution à l'étude de la dentition de lait d'*Oreopithecus bambolii* Gervais. *Eclog. Geol. Helv.* **44**, 404–411.

Hürzeler, J. (1954). Contribution à l'odontologie et à la phylogenèse du genre *Pliopithecus* Gervais. *Ann. Paléontol.* **40**, 5–63.

Hürzeler, J. (1958). *Oreopithecus bambolii* Gervais, a preliminary report. *Verh. Naturf. Ges. Basel.* **69**, 1–47.

Hürzeler, J. (1960). The significance of *Oreopithecus* in the genealogy of man. *Triangle* **4**, 164–175.

Hürzeler, J. (1967). Nouvelles découvertes de mammifères dans les sediments fluviolacustres de Villafranca d'Asti. Problèmes actuels de paléontologie. Évolution des vertébrés. *Coll. Internat. Cent. Nat. Rech. Sci., Paris* **163**, 633–636.

Hürzeler, J. (1968). Questions et reflexions sur l'histoire des anthropomorphes. *Ann. Paleontol. (Vertébrés)* **54**, 195–233.

Huxley, T. (1871). A Manual of the Anatomy of Vertebrated Animals. Churchill, London.

Hylander, W. (1975). Incisor size and diet in anthropoids with special reference to Cercopithecidae. *Science* **189**, 1095–1098.

Illiger, C. (1811). Prodromus systematis mammalium et avium additis terminis zoographics utriudque classis. C. Salfeld, Berlin.

Iwamoto, M. (1975). On a skull of a fossil Macaque from the Shikimizu limestone quarry in the Shikoku district, Japan. *Primates* **16**, 83–94.

Jaeger, J.-J. (1975a). The mammalian fauna and hominid fossils of the Middle Pleistocene of the Maghreb. *In* After the Australopithecines (K. W. Butzer and G. L. Isaac, eds.), pp. 399–418. Mouton, The Hague.

Jaeger, J.-J. (1975b). Découverte d'un crâne d'hominidé dans le Pléistocène moyen du Maroc. *In* Problèmes actuels de paléontologie—évolution des vertébrés. *Coll. Internat. Cent. Nat. Rech. Sci.* **218**, 897–903.

Jánossy, D. (1969). Stratigraphische Auswertung der europaischen mittelpleistozänen Wirbeltierfaune. *Ber. Deutsche Ges. Geol. Wiss., A, Geol. Paläontol.* **14**, 367–438.

Jardine, W. B. (1866). Mammalia. Monkeys. *In* The Naturalist's Library, Vol. 27. London.

Jenkins, F. A. Jr. (1973). The functional anatomy and evolution of the mammalian humero-ulnar articulation. *Amer. Jour. Anat.* **137**, 281–298.

Jenkins, F. A. Jr. (1974). Tree shrew locomotion and the origins of primate arborealism. *In* Primate Locomotion (F. A. Jenkins, Jr., ed.), pp. 85–115. Academic Press, New York.

Jepsen. G. L. (1930a). New vertebrate fossils from the lower Eocene of the Bighorn basin, Wyoming. *Proc. Amer. Phil. Soc.* **69**(4), 117–131.

Jepsen, G. L. (1930b). Stratigraphy and paleontology of northeastern Park County, Wyoming. *Proc. Amer. Phil. Soc.* **69**(7), 463–528.

Jepsen, G. L. (1934). A revision of the American Apatemyidae and the description of a new genus *Sinclairella* from the White River Oligocene of South Dakota. *Proc. Amer. Phil. Soc.* **74**, 287–305.

Jepsen, G. L. (1963). Eocene vertebrates, coprolites and plants in the Golden Valley Formation of western North Dakota. *Bull. Geol. Soc. Amer.* **74**, 673–684.

Jerison, H. J. (1973). Evolution of the Brain and Intelligence. Academic Press, New York.

Jiménez de la Espada, D. M. (1870). Algunos datos neuvos o curiosos acerca de la fauna del alto Amazonas (mamíferos). *Bol. Rev. Univ. Madrid,* pp. 1–27.

Joleaud, L. (1931). L'expansion géographique des hommes de Néanderthal au quarternaire moyen dans les regions méditerranéennes. *Rev. Scientif.* **69**, 466–469.

Jolly, C. J. (1965). The origins and specializations of the Long-Faced Cercopithecoidea, Ph.D. thesis. University of London.

Jolly, C. J. (1966). Introduction to the Cercopithecoidea, with notes on their use as laboratory animals. *Symp. Zool. Soc. London* **17**, 427–457.

Jolly, C. J. (1967). The evolution of the baboons. *In* The Baboon in Medical Research (H. Vagtborg, ed.), Vol. 2, pp. 427–457. University of Texas Press, Austin.

Jolly, C. J. (1970a). The seedeaters: A new model of hominid differentiation based on a baboon analogy. *Man, n.s.* **5**, 5–26.

Jolly, C. J. (1970b). The large African monkeys as an adaptive array. *In* Old World Monkeys (J. R. Napier and P. H. Napier, eds.), pp. 141–174. Academic Press, New York.

Jolly, C. J. (1970c). *Hadropithecus,* a lemuroid small-object feeder. *Man, n.s.* **5**, 525–529.

Jolly, C. J. (1972). The classification and natural history of *Theropithecus (Simopithecus)* (Andrews, 1916), baboons of the African Plio-Pleistocene. *Bull. Brit. Mus. (Nat. Hist.), Geol.* **22**, 1–122.

Jolly, C. J., and Brett, F. L. (1973). Genetic markers and baboon biology. *J. Med. Primatol.* **2**, 85–99.

Jones, F. W. (1929). Man's Place among the Mammals. Arnold, London.

Jones, T. R. (1937). A new fossil primate from Sterkfontein, Krugersdorp, Transvaal. *S. Afr. J. Sci.* **33**, 709–728.

Jouffroy, F. K. (1959). Un crâne subfossile de Macaque du Pléistocène du Viet Nam. *Bull. Mus. Hist. Nat., Paris, Ser.* 2 **31**, 209–216.

Jourdan (1834). *L'Institut,* 2 (62).

Kahlke, H.-D. (1961). Revision der Säugetierfaunen der Klassischen deutschen Pleistozän-Fundstellen von Süssenborn, Mosbach und Tobach. *Geologie* **10**, 493–518.

Kahlke, H.-D. (1973). A review of the Pleistocene history of the Orang-Utan (*Pongo* Lacépède, 1799). *Asian Perspectives* **15**, 5–14.

Kälin, J. (1945). Zur systematik und Nomenklatur der fossilen Hominiden. *Bull. Schweiz. Gesell. Anthropol. Ethnol.* **21**, 1–25.

Kälin, J. (1961). Sur les primates de l'Oligocène inférieur d'Egypte. *Ann. Paleontol.* **47**, 1–48.

Kälin, J. (1962). Über *Moeripithecus markgrafi* Schlosser und die phyletischen Vorstufen der Bilophodontie der Cercopithecoidea. *Biblio. Primatol.* **1**, 32–42.

Kallen, F. C. and C. Gans (1972). Mastication in the little brown bat. *Myotis lucifugus. J. Morphology* **136**, 385–420.

Kampen, P. N. von. (1905). Die tympanalgegend des Säugetierschädels. *Morphol. Jb.* **34**(3–4), 322–722.

Kaup, I. J. (1835). Das Thierreich in seinen Hauptformen systematisch beschrieben. Diehl, Darmstadt.

Kaup, I. J. (1861). Beiträge zur naheren Kenntnis der urweltlichen Säugetiere. **5**, 1–32.

Kay, R. F. (1977a). The evolution of molar occlusion in the Cercopithecidae and early Catarrhines. *Amer. J. Phys. Anthropol. n.s.* **46**, 327–352.

Kay, R. F. (1977b). Post-Oligocene evolution of catarrhine diets. *Amer. J. Phys. Anthropol.* **47**, 141–142 (abstr.).

Kay, R. F. (1977c). Diets of early Miocene African hominoids. *Nature* (London) **268**, 628–630.

Kay, R. F. (1978). Molar structure and diet in extant Cercopithecidae. *In* Studies in the Development, Function, and Evolution of Teeth (P. M. Butler and K. Joysey, eds.), pp. 309–339. Academic Press, London.

Kay, R. F., and Cartmill, M. (1974). Skull of *Palaechthon nacimienti. Nature* (London) **252**, 37–38.

Kay, R. F., and Cartmill, M. (1977). Cranial morphology and adaptation of *Palaechthon nacimienti* and other Paromomyidae (Plesiadapoidea, ?Primates), with a description of a new genus and species. *J. Human Evol.* **6**, 19–53.

Kay, R. F. and K. M. Hiiemae (1974) Jaw movement and tooth use in recent and fossil primates. *Amer. J. Phys. Anthrop.* **40**, 227–256.

Keith, A. (1911). The early history of the Gibraltar cranium. *Nature* (London) **87**, 313–314.

Keith, A. (1932). Human palaeontology. Africa. *Man* **32**, 208.

Kelley, D. R., and Wood, A. E. (1954). The Eocene mammals from the Lysite member, Wind River Formation of Wyoming. *J. Paleontol.* **28**(3), 337–366.

Kennard, A. S. (1942). Faunas of the high terrace at Swanscombe. *Proc. Geol. Assoc.* **53**, 105.

Kerr, R. (1792). The Animal Kingdom, a Zoological System of

the Celebrated Sir Charles Linnaeus. Class 1: Mammalia. J. Murray and R. Faulder, London.

Khajuria, H. (1953). Taxonomic studies of the Celebes ashy-black monkey—A remarkable case of convergence. *Rec. Indian Mus.* **50**, 301–305.

King, W. B. R. (1864). The reputed fossil man of the Neanderthal. *Q. J. Sci.* **1**, 88–97.

Kinzey, W. G. (1974). Ceboid models for the evolution of hominoid dentition. *J. Human Evol.* **3**, 193–203.

Kinzey, W. G., Rosenberger, A. L., Heisler, P. S., Prowse, D. L., and Trilling, J. S. (1977). A preliminary field investigation of the yellow-handed titi monkey, *Callicebus torquatus torquatus*, in northern Peru. *Primates* **18**(1), 159–181.

Kinzey, W. G., Rosenberger, A. L., and Ramirez, M. (1975). Vertical clinging and leaping in a neotropical anthropoid. *Nature* (London) **255**, 327–328.

Kitching, J. W. (1952). A new type of fossil baboon: *Brachygnathopithecus peppercorni*, gen. et sp. nov. *S. Afr. J. Sci.* **49**, 15–17.

Kitching, J. W. (1953). A new species of fossil baboon from Potgietersrust. *S. Afr. J. Sci.* **50**, 66–69.

Kitching, J., Wells, L. H., and Westphal, E. (1948). Fossil Cercopithecid primates from the limeworks quarry, Makapansgat, Potgietersrust. *S. Afr. J. Sci.* **1**, 171–172.

Klaatsch, H., and Hauser, O. (1909). *Homo mousteriensis Hauseri*, ein altdiluvialer Skelettfund im Department Dordogne und sein Zugehorigkeit zum Neandertaltypus. *Arch. Anthropol.* **35**(N. F. 7), 287–297.

Klaatsch, H., and Hauser, O. (1910). *Homo aurignacensis Hauseri*, ein palaeolithischen skelettfund aus dem unteren Aurignacien der Station Combecapelle bei Montferrand (Perigord). *Prähist. Z.* **1**, 273–338.

Klaauw, C. J. van der. (1929). On the development of the tympanic region of the skull in the Macroscelididae. *Proc. Zool. Soc. London* **37**, 491–560.

Klaauw, C. J. van der. (1931). The auditory bulla in some fossil mammals. *Bull. Amer. Mus. Nat. Hist.* **62**, 1–352.

Kleinschmidt, O. (1922). Realgattung *Homo sapiens* (L.). *Berajah, zoographia infinita*, Vol. 27, pp. 1–30. Gebauer-Schwetschke, Halle.

Kleinschmidt, O. (1927). Realgattung *Homo sapiens*, Continuation. *Berajah, zoographia infinita*, Vol. 27, pp. 31–38. Gebauer-Schwetschke, Halle.

Kleinschmidt, O. (1931). Der Urmensch. Quelle und Meyer, Leipzig.

Koenigswald, G. H. R. von. (1935). Eine fossile Säugetierfauna mit *Simia*, aus Südchina. *Proc. Kon Nederlandse Akad. Wet.* **38**, 872–879.

Koenigswald, G. H. R. von. (1936). Erste mitteilungen über einen fossilen Hominiden aus dem Altpleistocän Ostjavas. *Proc. Kon. Nederlandse Akad. Wet.* **39**, 1000–1009.

Koenigswald, G. H. R. von. (1949). The fossil hominids of Java. *In* The Geology of Indonesia (R. W. Bemmelen, ed.), Vol. 1, pp. 106–111. Mouton, The Hague.

Koenigswald, G. H. R. von. (1950). Bemerkungen zu *Dryopithecus giganteus* Pilgrim. *Eclogae Geol. Helv.* **42**, 515–519.

Koenigswald, G. H. R. von. (1952). *Gigantopithecus blacki* von Koenigswald, a giant fossil hominoid from the Pleistocene of southern China. *Anthropol. Pap. Amer. Mus. Nat. Hist.* **43**, 291–326.

Koenigswald, G. H. R. von. (1956). Gebissreste von Menschenaffen aus dem Unterpliozän Rheinhessens. *Proc. Kon. Nederlandse Akad. Wet., Ser. B* **59**, 318–334.

Koenigswald, G. H. R. von. (1957a). Remarks on *Gigantopithecus* and other hominoid remains from southern China. *Proc. Kon. Nederlandse Akad. Wet., Ser. B* **60**, 153–159.

Koenigswald, G. H. R. von. (1957b). *Hemanthropus* n.g. not *Hemianthropus*. *Proc. Kon. Nederlandse Akad. Wet., Ser. B* **60**, 416.

Koenigswald, G. H. R. von. (1965). Critical observations upon the so-called higher primates from the Upper Eocene of Burma. *Proc. Kon. Nederlandse Akad. Wetensch., Ser. B* **68**, 165–167.

Koenigswald, G. H. R. von. (1969). Miocene Cercopithecoidea and Oreopithecoidea from the Miocene of East Africa. *Foss. Verts. Afr.* **1**, 39–51.

Koenigswald, G. H. R. von. (1972). Ein unterkiefer eines fossilen hominoiden aus dem Unterpliozän Greichenlands. *Proc. Kon. Nederlandse Akad. Wet., Ser. B* **75**, 386–394.

Kolakowski, D., and Malina, R. M. (1974). Spatial ability, throwing accuracy and man's hunting ability. *Nature* (London) **251**, 410–412.

Koken, W. (1905). Führer durch die Sammlungen des Geologisch-Mineralogischen Instituts in Tübingen, pp. 1–110. Stuttgart.

Kormós, T. (1914). Die phylogenetische und zoogeographische Bedeutung praeglazialer Faunen. *Verh. K-K Zool.-Bot. Gesell. Wien* **64**, 218–238.

Kormós, T. (1937). Zur frage der abstammung und Herkunft der quartären Säugetierfauna Europas. *In* Festschrift für Embrik Strand, Vol. 3, pp. 287–340. "Latvia", Riga.

Kortlandt, A. (1972). New Perspectives on Ape and Human Evolution. Stichting voor Psychobiologie, Amsterdam.

Kortlandt, A. (1975). Ecology and paleoecology of ape locomotion. *In* Symposia of the Fifth Congress of the International Primatological Society, pp. 361–364. Science Press, Tokyo.

Kowalski, K. and Zapfe, H. (1974). *Pliopithecus antiquus* (Blainville, 1839) (Primates, Mammalia) from the Miocene of Przeworno in Silesia (Poland). *Acta Zool. Cracoviensia* **19**, 19–30.

Kraglievich, J. L. (1951). Contribuciones al concimiento de los primates fosiles de la Patagonia. I. Diagnosis previa de un nuevo primate fosil del Oligoceno superior (Colhueuapiano) de Gaiman, Chubut. *Commun. Inst. Nac. Invest. Cien. Nat. Cien. Zool.* **2**, 57–82.

Krantz, G. (1975). An explanation for the diastema of Javan *erectus* skull IV. *In* Paleoanthropology. Morphology and Paleoecology (R. Tuttle, ed.), pp. 361–372. Mouton, The Hague.

Krause, W. (1909). Anatomie der Menschenrassen. *In* Handbuch der Anatomie des Menschen (K. von Bardeleben, ed.), Vol. 1, No. 3. G. Fischer, Jena.

Kretzoi, M. (1954). Bericht über die Calabrische (Villafranchische) fauna von Kieslang, Kom. Fejer. *Földtani Intézet Évi Jelentése* (for 1953), pp. 239–264.

Kretzoi, M. (1962). Fauna und Faunenhorizont von Csarnóta. *Földtani Intézet Évi Jelentése* (*Ann. Rept. Hungarian Geol. Soc.*, for 1959), pp. 344–385.

Kretzoi, M. (1974). Az emberréválás utján. *Anthropol. Közlemények* **18**, 121–128.

Kretzoi, M. (1975). New Ramapithecines and *Pliopithecus* from the lower pliocene of Rudabánya in north-eastern Hungary. *Nature* (London) **257**, 578–581.

Krishtalka, L., Black, C. C. and Reidel, D. W. (1975). Paleontology and geology of the Badwater Creek area, Central Wyoming. Part 10: A late Plaeocene mammal fauna from the Shotgun Member of the Fort Union Formation. *Ann. Carnegie Mus.* **45**, 179–212.

Kuhl, H. (1820). Beiträg zur Zoologie und vergleichenden Anatomie. Hermannschen Buchhandlung, Frankfurt am Main.

Kuhn, H. J. (1964). Zur Kentniss von Bau und Funktion des Magens der Schlankaffen (Colobinae). *Folia Primatol.* **2**, 193–221.

Kuhn, H. J. (1967). Zur systematik der Cercopithecidae. *In* Neue Ergesbnisse der Primatologie [First Congress of the International Primatology Society] (D. Starck, R. Schneider, and H. J. Kuhn, eds.), pp. 25–46. Gustav Fischer, Stuttgart.

Kurtén, B. (1968). Pleistocene Mammals of Europe. Aldine, Chicago.

Kurtén, B. (1972). Not from the Apes. Random House, New York.

Kurth, G. (1965). Die (Eu)Homininen. *In* Menschliche Abstammungslehre (G. Heberer, ed.), pp. 357–425. G. Fischer, Stuttgart.

Lacépède, B. G. E. (1799). Tableau des divisions sousdivisions, ordres et genres des mammifères. *In* Histoire Naturelle (G. L. F. de Buffon, ed.), Vol. 14, pp. 144–195. P. Didot L'Aine et Firmin Dido, Paris.

Lamberton, C. (1934). Contribution à la connaissance de la Faune subfossile de Madagascar. Lémuriens et Ratites. *Mém. l'Acad. Malgache* **17**, 1–168.

Lamberton, C. (1936a). [Verbal report on excavations carried out in the south of Madagascar, presented to the Académie Malgache on Feb. 20, 1936.] *Bull. Acad. Malgache, n.s.* **19**, XVIII–XXII.

Lamberton, C. (1936b). Nouveaux lémuriens fossiles du groupe des Propithèques et l'intéret de leur découverte. *Bull. Mus. Hist. Nat. Paris* **2**(8), 370–373.

Lamberton, C. (1936c). Fouilles faites en 1936. *Bull. Acad. Malgache, n.s.* **19**, 1–19.

Lamberton, C. (1938). Contribution à la connaissance de la faune subfossile de Madagascar. Note 3: Les Hadropithèques. *Bull. l'Acad. Malgache, n.s.* **20**, 1–44.

Lamberton, C. (1939). Contribution à la connaissance de la faune subfossile de Madagascar. Notes IV à VIII Lémuriens et Cryptoproctes. *Mem. l'Acad. Malgache* **27**, 5–197.

Lamberton, C. (1941). Contribution à la connaissance de la faune subfossile de Madagascar. Note IX: Oreille osseuse des Lémuriens. *Mem. l'Acad. Malgache* **35**, 1–132.

Lamberton, C. (1945). Contribution à la connaissance de la faune subfossile de Madagascar. Note XVI: Bradytherium ou Palaeopropithèque? *Bull. l'Acad. Malgache* **26**, 1–52.

Lamberton, C. (1948). Madagascar, il y a quelques millénaires. *Mém. Acad. Malgache*, pp. 95–106.

Lamberton, C. (1956). Examen de quelques hypothèses de Sera concernant les lémuriens fossiles et actuels. *Bull. Acad. Malgache, n.s.* **29**, 26–42.

Lampel, G. (1963). Variationsstatistische und morphologische untersuchungen am Gebiss der Cercopithecinen. *Acta Anat.* **3**(45), 1–122.

Lang, H. (1923). A new genus of African monkey, *Allenopithecus. Amer. Mus. Nov.* **87**, 1–5.

Lapouge, G. de (1894). Note sur un nouveau singe pliocène (*Anthropodus rouvillei*). *Bull. Soc. Sci. Med. Quest*, pp. 202–208.

Lapouge, G. de (1899). L'Aryen: Son Role Sociale. Paris.

Lapouge, G. de (1906). Die Rassengeschichte der französichen Nation. *Polit. –Anthropol. Rev.* **4**, 16–24.

Lartet, E. (1851). Notice sur la Colline de Sansan. J.-A. Portes, Paris.

Lartet, E. (1856). Note sur un grand singe fossile qui de rattache au groupe des singes supérieures. *C. R. Acad. Sci.* (Paris) **43**, 219–223.

Latreille, P. A. (1801). Histoire naturelle des singes. *In* Histoire Naturelle Genérale et Particulière par Leclerc de Buffon (C. S. Sonini, ed.), Vol. 36. Dufart, Paris.

Launay, L. (1908). La fourrure d'un ecureuil tertiaire. *La Nature* **36**, 393–395.

Leach, W. E. (1820). Historical sketch of improvements in physical science during the year 1819. II. Comparative anatomy and zoology. *Ann. Phil.* **16**, 102–111.

Leakey, L. S. B. (1935). The Stone Age Races of Kenya. Cambridge University Press, London.

Leakey, L. S. B. (1953). Adam's Ancestors, 4th ed. London.

Leakey, L. S. B. (1959). A new fossil skull from Olduvai. *Nature* (London) **184**, 491–493.

Leakey, L. S. B. (1962). A new lower Pliocene fossil primate from Kenya. *Ann. Mag. Nat. Hist., Ser. 13* **4**, 689–696.

Leakey, L. S. B. (1962). Mioeuoticus bishopi. *In* The Mammalian Fauna and Geomorphological Relations of the Napak Volcanics, Karamoja (W. W. Bishop, ed.), Rec. Geol. Surv. Uganda, Entebbe, for 1957–1958, pp. 1–18.

Leakey, L. S. B. (1965). Olduvai Gorge, 1951–1961: Fauna and Background. Cambridge University Press, Cambridge.

Leakey, L. S. B. (1967). An early Miocene member of Hominidae. *Nature* (London) **213**, 155–163.

Leakey, L. S. B. (1968). Lower dentition of *Kenyapithecus africanus. Nature* (London) **217**, 827–830.

Leakey, L. S. B. (1968). Upper Miocene Primates from Kenya. *Nature* (London) **218**, 527–530.

Leakey, L. S. B., Tobias, P. V., and Napier, J. R. (1964). A new species of genus *Homo* from Olduvai Gorge. *Nature* (London) **202**, 7–9.

Leakey, L. S. B., and Whitworth, T. (1958). Notes on the genus *Simopithecus* with a description of a new species from Olduvai. *Coryndon Mem. Mus. Occas. Papers* **6**, 3–14.

Leakey, M. G. (1976). Cercopithecoidea of the East Rudolf succession. *In* Earliest Man and Environments in the Lake Rudolf Basin (Y. Coppens, F. C. Howell, G. L.

Isaac, and R. E. F. Leakey, eds.), pp. 345–350. University of Chicago Press, Chicago.

Leakey, M. G., and Leakey, R. E. F. (1973a). Further evidence of *Simopithecus* (Mammalia, Primates) from Olduvai and Olorgesailie. *Foss. Verts. Afr.* **3**, 101–120.

Leakey, M. G., and Leakey, R. E. F. (1973b). New large Pleistocene Colobinae (Mammalia, Primates) from East Africa. *Foss. Verts. Afr.* **3**, 121–138.

Leakey, M. G., and Leakey, R. E. F. (1976). Further Cercopithecinae (Mammalia, Primates) from the Plio-Pleistocene of East Africa. *Foss. Verts. Afr.* **4**, 121–146.

Leakey, R. E. F. (1969). New Cercopithecidae from the Chemeron beds of Lake Baringo, Kenya. *Foss. Verts. Afr.* **1**, 53–69.

Leakey, R. E. F. (1976). Hominids in Africa. *Amer. Sci.* **64**, 174–178.

Le Conte (1857). *Proc. Acad. Nat. Sci. Philadelphia, 1857*, p. 10.

Le Gros Clark, W. E. (1934). Early Fore-Runners of Man. Baillière, London.

Le Gros Clark, W. E. (1936). The problem of the claw in primates. *Proc. Zool. Soc. London*, pp. 1–25.

Le Gros Clark, W. E. (1952). Report on fossil hominoid material collected by the British Kenya Miocene Expedition, 1949–1951. *Proc. Zool. Soc. London* **122**, 273–286.

Le Gros Clark, W. E. (1956). A Miocene Lemuroid skull from East Africa. Fossil Mammals of Africa, No. 9. pp. 1–6. British Museum (Natural History), London.

Le Gros Clark, W. E. (1959). The Antecedents of Man. University Press, Edinburgh.

Le Gros Clark, W. E. (1971). The Antecedents of Man, 3rd ed. University Press, Edinburgh.

Le Gros Clark, W. E., and Leakey, L. S. B. (1950). Diagnoses of East African Miocene Hominoidea. *Q. J. Geol. Soc. London* **105**, 260–262.

Le Gros Clark, W. E., and Leakey, L. S. B. (1951). The Miocene Hominoidea of East Africa. Fossil Mammals of Africa. No.1. pp. 1–117. British Museum (Natural History), London.

Le Gros Clark, W. E., and Thomas, D. P. (1951). Associated jaws and limb bones of *Limnopithecus macinnesi*. Fossil Mammals of Africa. No. 3. pp. 1–27. British Museum (Natural History), London.

Le Gros Clark, W. E., and Thomas, D. P. (1952). The Miocene Lemuroids of East Africa. Fossil Mammals of Africa. No. 5. pp. 1–20. British Museum (Natural History), London.

Leidy, J. (1869). Notice of some extinct vertebrates from Wyoming and Dakota. *Proc. Acad. Nat. Sci. Philadelphia* **21**, 63–67.

Leidy, J. (1870). Descriptions of *Palaeosyops paludosus, Microsus cuspidatus* and *Notharctus tenebrosus. Proc. Acad. Nat. Sci. Philadelphia* **22**, 113–114.

Leidy, J. (1872a). Remarks on some extinct mammals. *Proc. Acad. Nat. Sci. Philadelphia* **24**, 37–38.

Leidy, J. (1872b). Remarks on fossils from Wyoming. *Proc. Acad. Nat. Sci. Philadelphia* **24**, 12–21.

Leidy, J. (1872c). On the fossil vertebrates of the early Tertiary formation of Wyoming. *In* Preliminary Report of the U.S. Geological Survey of Montana and Portions of Adjacent Terrain (Hayden), pp. 353–372.

Leidy, J. (1873). Contribution to the extinct vertebrate fauna of the western territories. *Rep. U.S. Geol. Surv. Terr.* Part 1.

Lemoine, V. (1878). Communication sur les ossements fossiles des terrains tertiaires inférieures des environs de Reims. *Soc. Hist. Nat. Reims*, pp. 1–24.

Lemoine, V. (1880). Communication sur les ossements fossiles des terrains tertiaires inférieurs des environs de Reims. *In* Association Francaise pour l'Avancement des Sciences, Cong. de Montpellier, pp. 1–17. Matot-Braine, Reims.

Lemoine, V. (1887). Sur le genre *Plesiadapis*, mammifère fossile de l'éocène inférieur des environs de Reims. *C. R. Acad. Sci.* (Paris), 190–193.

Lesson, R.-P. (1827). Manuel de Mammalogie. Roret, Paris.

Lesson, R.-P. (1830). Compléments des Oeuvres de Buffon, Vol. 4. P. Frères and Roret, Paris.

Lesson, R.-P. (1840). Species de Mammifères: Bimanes et Quadrumanes; suivi d'un Mémoire sur les Oryctéropes. J.-B. Baillière, Paris.

Leutenegger, W. (1970). Das Becken der rezenten Primaten. *Morphol. Jb.* **115**(1), 1–101.

Leutenegger, W. (1976). Metric variability in the anterior dentition of African colobines. *Amer. J. Phys. Anthropol., n.s.* **45**, 45–52.

Lewis, G. E. (1933). Preliminary notice of a new genus of lemuroid from the Siwaliks. *Amer. J. Sci. Ser. 5* **26**, 134–138.

Lewis, G. E. (1934). Preliminary notice of new man-like apes from India. *Amer. J. Sci., Ser. 5* **27**, 161–179.

Lewis, G. E. (1936). A new species of *Sugrivapithecus. Amer. J. Sci., Ser. 5* **31**, 450–452.

Lewis, G. E. (1937). Taxonomic syllabus of Siwalik fossil anthropoids. *Amer. J. Sci., Ser. 5* **34**, 139–147.

Lewis, O. J. (1971). Brachiation and the early evolution of the Hominoidea. *Nature* (London) **230**, 577–579.

Lewis, O. J. (1972a). Osteological features characterizing the wrists of monkeys and apes, with a reconsideration of the region in *Dryopithecus (Proconsul) africanus. Amer. J. Phys. Anthropol.* **36**(1), 45–58.

Lewis, O. J. (1972b). Evolution of the hominoid wrist. *In* Functional and Evolutionary Biology of Primates (R. Tuttle, ed.), pp. 207–222. Aldine, Chicago.

Link, H. F. (1795). Beytrage zur Naturgeschichte, Vol. 1, No. 2, p. 63. K. C. Stiller, Rostock and Leipzig.

Link, H. F. (1806). Beschreib. Nat. Samm. Univers. Rostock, I, pp. 7, 8.

Linnaeus, C. (1758). Systema naturae per regna tria naturae, secundum classes, ordines genera, species cum characteribus, differentris, synonymis, locis. Editis decima, reformata. Laurentii Salvii, Stockholm.

Linnaeus, C. (1766). Systema naturae per regna tria naturae, secundum classes, ordines genera, species cum characteribus, differentris, synonymis, locis, 12th ed. Laurentii Salvii, Stockholm.

Linnaeus, C. (1771). Matissa Plantarum. Laurentii Salvii, Stockholm.

Lönnberg, E. (1919). Contributions to the knowledge about the monkeys of the Belgian Congo. *Rev. Zool. Africaine* **7**, 107–154.

Loomis, F. B. (1906). Wasatch and Wind River Primates. *Amer. J. Sci., Ser. 4* **21**, 277–285.

Lorenz, H. G. (1968). Stratigraphische und mikropalaontologische untersuchungen des braunkohlengebeites von Baccinello. *Riv. Italiana Paleontol.* **74**, 147–270.

Lorenz von Liburnau, L. R. (1899). Einen fossilen Anthropoiden von Madagascar. *Anz. K. Akad. Wiss. Wien* **19**, 255–257.

Lorenz von Liburnau, L. R. (1900). Über einige reste ausgestorbener Primaten von Madagscar. *Denkschr. K. Akad. Wiss. Wien, Math.-Nat. kl.* **70**, 243–254.

Louis, P., and Sudre, J. (1975). Nouvelles données sur les primates de l'Éocène Supérieur Européen. Problèmes actuels de paléontologie (evolution des vertébres). *Coll. Int. C. N. R. S.* **218**, 805–828.

Love, J. D. (1973). Harebell Formation (Upper Cretaceous) and Pinyon Conglomerate (uppermost Cretaceous and Paleocene), northwestern Wyoming. *U.S. Geol. Surv. Prof. Paper* 734A, pp. 1–54.

Lovejoy, C. O. Heiple, K. G. and Burstein, A. H. (1973). The gait of *Australopithecus. Amer. J. Phys. Anthropol., n.s.* **38**, 757–780.

Luckett, W. P. (1974a). Comparative development and evolution of the placenta in Primates. *In* Contributions to Primatology. Volume 3: Reproductive Biology of the Primates, (W. P. Luckett, ed.), pp. 142–234.

Luckett, W. P. (1974b). The phylogenetic relationships of the prosimian primates: Evidence from the morphogenesis of the placenta and foetal membranes. *In* Prosimian Biology (R. D. Martin, G. A. Doyle, and A. C. Walker, eds.), pp. 475–488. Duckworth, London.

Luckett, W. P. (1975). Ontogeny of the fetal membranes and placenta: Their bearing on Primate phylogeny. *In* Phylogeny of the Primates: A Multidisciplinary Approach (W. P. Luckett and F. S. Szalay, eds.), pp. 157–182. Plenum Press, New York.

Luckett, W. P. (1976). Cladistic relationships among Primate higher categories: Evidence of the fetal membranes and placenta. *Folia Primatol.* **25**, 245–276.

Ludwig (1883). Synopsis der Thierkunde. Hanover.

Lumley, H. de, *et al.* (1963). La Grotte du Vallonet. *Bull. Mus. Prehist. Monaco* **13**, 25–50.

Lund, P. W. (1841). Blik paa Brasiliens dyreverden for sidste Jordomsaelting. *K. Danske Vidensk. Selskskabs natur. Math. Afhandl.* **8**, 29–144.

Lydekker, R. (1878). Notices of Siwalik mammals. *Rec. Geol. Surv. India* **11**, 64–85.

Lydekker, R. (1879). Further notices of Siwalik mammalia. *Red. Geol. Surv. India* **12**, 33–52.

Lydekker, R. (1884). Rodents and new ruminants from the Siwaliks, and synopsis of Mammalia. *Mem. Geol. Surv. India, Palaeont. Ind., Ser. X* **3**, 105–134.

Lydekker, R. (1885a). Primates, Chiroptera, Insectivora, Carnivora and Rodentia. *In* Catalogue of the Fossil Mammalia in the British Museum (Natural History), Part 1. British Museum Natural History, London.

Lydekker, R. (1885b). Mammalia. Catalogue of the remains of the Siwalik Vertebrata contained in the Geology Department of the Indian Museum, Calcutta, Part 1.

Lydekker, R. (1886). Siwalik Mammalia, supp. 1. *Palaeontol. Indica* **10**(1), 1–18.

Lydekker, R. (1887). Catalogue of the Fossil Mammalia in the British Museum. Part V: Containing the Group Tillodontia, the Orders Sirenia, Cetacea, Edentata, Marsupialia, Monotremata and Supplement. British Museum (Natural History), London.

Lydekker, R. (1889). *In* A Manual of Paleontology (H. A. Nicholson and R. Lydekker, eds.). Blackwood, London.

Macdonald, J. R. (1963). The Miocene faunas from the Wounded Knee area of western South Dakota. *Bull. Amer. Mus. Nat. Hist.* **125**, 139–238.

MacInnes, D. G. (1943). Notes on the East African Miocene primates. *J. E. Afr. Uganda Nat. Hist. Soc.* **17**, 141–181.

MacIntyre, G. T. (1972). The trisulcate petrosal pattern of mammals. *In* Evolutionary Biology (T. Dobzhansky, M. K. Hecht, and W. C. Steere, eds.), Vol. 6. Appleton-Century-Crofts, New York.

MacPhee, R. D. E. (1977). Ontogeny of the ectotympanic-petrosal plate relationship in strepsirhine Prosimians. *Folia Primatol.* **27**, 245–283.

Madden, C. T. (1972). Miocene mammals, stratigraphy and environment of Moruarot Hill, Kenya. *PaleoBios* **14**, 1–12.

Maglio, V. J. (1973). Origin and evolution of the Elephantidae. *Trans. Amer. Phil. Soc., n.s.* **63**(3), 1–149.

Mahler, P. (1973). Metric variation in the Pongid dentition, Ph.D. thesis. University of Michigan, Ann Arbor.

Maier, W. (1970). Neue Ergebnisse der systematik und der Stammesgeschichte der Cercopithecoidea. *Z. Saugetierkunde* **35**, 193–214.

Maier, W. (1971a). New fossil Cercopithecoidea from the Lower Pleistocene cave deposits of the Makapansgat Limeworks, South Africa. *Palaeontol. Afr.* **13**, 69–108.

Maier, W. (1971b). Two new skulls of *Parapapio antiquus* from Taung and a suggested phylogenetic arrangement of the genus *Parapapio. Ann. S. Afr. Mus.* **59**, 1–16.

Maier, W. (1972a). Anpassungstyp und systematische Stellung von *Theropithecus gelada* Ruppell, 1835. *Z. Morphol. Anthropol.* **63**, 370–384.

Maier, W. (1972b). The first complete skull of *Simopithecus darti* from Makapansgat, South Africa, and its systematic position. *J. Human Evol.* **1**, 395–405.

Major, C. J. F. (1872). Note sur des singes fossiles trouves en Italie, précédée d'un apercu sur les quadrumanes fossiles en general. *Acts. Soc. Italiana Sci. Nat.* **15**, 1–17.

Major, C. J. F. (1875). Consliderazioni sulla Fauna dei Mammiferi pliocenici e postpliocenici della Toscana. *Atti Soc. Toscana Sci. Nat. Pisa* **2**, 223–242.

Major, C. J. F. (1893). On *Megaladapis madagascarensis*, an extinct gigantic lemuroid from Madagascar. *Phil. Trans. Roy. Soc. London* **185**, 15–38.

Major, C. J. F. (1894). Uber die Malayassischen Lemuriden Gattungen *Microcebus, Opolemur*, und *Chirogale. Nov. Zoologicae.*

Major, C. J. F. (1896). Preliminary notice on fossil monkeys from Madagascar. *Geol. Mag., n.s.* **3**, 433, 436.

Major, C. J. F. (1914). Observations sur la Faune des Mammifères quaternaires de la Corse et de la Sardaigne. IXe Congr. Internatl. Zool., Sec. IV, p. 594.

Malez, M. (1967). Donjopleistocenska fauna kostane brece kod sela Dubei u Dalmacyu. *Jugosl. Akad. Znanosti* **345**, (Zagreb) (not seen).

Manouvrier, L. (1896). Résponse aux objections contre le *Pithecanthropus. Bull. Soc. Anthropol. Paris* **7**, 396–460.

Macarovici, N. (1975). Sur la faune de vertébrés pléistocènes de la Roumaine. *In* Studies on Cenozoic Paleontology and Stratigraphy, pp. 89–95. University of Michigan Museum of Paleontology, Ann Arbor.

Marett, R. (1911). Pleistocene man in Jersey. *Archaeologia* **62**, 449–480.

Marsh, O. C. (1871). Notice of some fossil mammals from the Tertiary formation. *Amer. J. Sci.* **2**, 35–44, 120–127.

Marsh, O. C. (1872a). Preliminary description of new Tertiary mammals. Parts I–IV. *Amer. J. Sci.* **4**, 22–28, 202–224.

Marsh, O. C. (1872b). Notice of some remarkable fossil mammals. *Amer. J. Sci.* **4**, 343–344.

Marsh, O. C. (1872c). Communication on the discovery of new Rocky Mountain fossils. *Proc. Amer. Phil. Soc.* **12**, 578–579.

Marsh, O. C. (1872d). Discovery of fossil Quadrumana in the Eocene of Wyoming. *Amer. J. Sci.* **4**, 405–406.

Marsh, O. C. (1872e). Note on a new genus of carnivores from the Tertiary of Wyoming. *Amer. J. Sci.* **4**, 406.

Martin, R. D. (1972). Adaptive radiation and behavior of the Malagasy lemurs. *Phil. Trans. Roy. Soc. London, Ser. B, Biol. Sci.* **264**, 295–352.

Martin, W. C. L. (1841). A General Introduction to the Natural History of Mammiferous Animals. Wright, London.

Maser, R., and Maser, C. (1973). Notes on a captive long-tailed climbing mouse, *Vandeleuria oleracea* (Bennet, 1832) (Rodentia, Muridae). *Saugetierkundliche Mitteil.*, pp. 336–340.

Maslin, T. P. (1952). Morphological criteria of phyletic relationships. *System. Zool.* **1**, 49–70.

Mason, W. A. (1966). Social organization of the South American monkey *Callicebus moloch*: A preliminary report. *Tulane Stud. Zool.* **13**, 23–28.

Mason, W. A. (1968). Use of space by *Callicebus* groups. *In* Primates: Studies in Adaptation and Variability (P. C. Jay, ed.), pp. 200–216. Holt, Rhinehart, & Winston, New York.

Matiegka, J. (1938). *Homo Predmostensis fosilni* clovek z Predmosti na morave. II; Ostatni casti kostrove. Nakledem Ceské Akad, Prague.

Matschie, P. (1901). Die Säugetiere der von W. Kükernthal auf Halmahera, Batjan und Nordcelebes gemachten Ausbeute. *Abhandl. Senckenbergischen Naturf. Gesell.* **25**, 247–296.

Matschie, P. (1914). Neue Affen aus Mittelafrika. *Sitzungsb. Ges. naturf. Freunde Berlin* 1914, 323–341.

Matthew, W. C. (1909). The Carnivora and Insectivora of the Bridger Basin, Middle Eocene. *Mem. Amer. Mus. Nat. Hist.* **9**(6), 289–567.

Matthew, W. D. (1915). A revision of the lower Eocene Wasatch and Wind River faunas. Part IV. Entelonychia, Primates, Insectivora (part). *Bull. Amer. Mus. Nat. Hist.* **34**, 429–483.

Matthew, W. D. (1917a). A Paleocene Bat. *Bull. Amer. Mus. Nat. Hist.* **37**, 569–571.

Matthew, W. D. (1917b). The dentition of *Nothodectes*. *Bull. Amer. Mus. Nat. Hist.* **37**, 831–839.

Matthew, W. D. (1929). Critical observations upon Siwalik mammals. *Bull. Amer. Mus. Nat. Hist.* **56**, 437–560.

Matthew, W. D., and Granger, W. (1921). New genera of Paleocene mammals. *Amer. Mus. Novit.* **13**, 1–7.

Matthew, W. D., and Granger, W. (1923). New fossil mammals from the Pliocene of Szechuan, China. *Bull. Amer. Mus. Nat. Hist.* **48**, 563–598.

Mayer, (Prof.). (1856). Zur Anatomie des Orang-Utang und des Chimpanse. *Arch. Naturgesch.* **22**, 281–304.

Mayer, A. B. (1899). Säugethiere von Celebes—und Phillipinen-Archipel, pt. 2. Celebes—Sammlungen der Herren Sarasin. *Abh. ber. K. zool. Anthrop. Ethnol. Mus., Dresden* **7**, 1–55.

Mayet, L., and Lecointre, P. (1909). Étude Sommaire des Mammifères Fossiles des Faluns de la Touraine. J.-B. Bailliere, Paris.

Mayr, E. (1950). Taxonomic categories in fossil hominids. *Cold Spring Harbor Symp. Quant. Biol.* **15**, 109–117.

Mayr, E. (1969). Principles of Systematic Zoology. Mc-Graw Hill, New York.

Mayr, E. (1974). Cladistic analysis or cladistic classification? *Z. Zool. Syst. Evolutionsforschung* **22**, 344–359.

McClelland (1840). *In* Communications to the society of Mr. McClelland's list of Mammalia and birds collected in Assam (T. Horsefield, ed.), *Proceedings of the Zoological Society of London*, 1839, pp. 146–167.

McCown, T. D., and Keith, A. (1934). *Palaeanthropus palestinus*. *In* Proceedings of the First International Congress of the Prehistoric and Protohistoric Society (London, 1932). London.

McDowell, S. B., Jr. (1958). The Greater Antillean insectivores. *Bull. Amer. Mus. Nat. Hist.* **115**, 113–214.

McHenry, H. M. (1975). Fossils and the mosaic nature of human evolution. *Science* **190**, 425–431.

McHenry, H. M., and Corruccini, R. S. (1975). Distal humerus in hominoid evolution. *Folia Primatol.* **23L**, 227–244.

McHenry, H. M., Corruccini, R. S., and Howell, F. C. (1976). Analysis of an early hominid ulna from the Omo Basin, Ethiopia. *Amer. J. Phys. Anthropol.*, n.s. **44**, 295–304.

McKenna, M. C. (1960). Fossil Mammalia from the early Wasatchian Four Mile fauna, Eocene of Northwest Colorado. *Univ. Calif. Publ. Geol. Sci.* **37**(1), 1–130.

McKenna, M. C. (1963). The early Tertiary primates and their ancestors. *Proc. XVI Intl. Cong. Zool., Wash., D.C.*, pp. 69–74.

McKenna, M. C. (1966). Paleontology and the origin of the Primates. *Folia Primatol.* **4**, 1–25.

McKenna, M. C. (1967). Classification, range and deployment of the prosimian primates. Problèmes actuels de Paleontologie—Evolution des Vertebrès. *Coll. Int. Cent. Nat. Rech. Sci.* **163**, 603–610.

McKenna, M. C. (1975). Toward a phylogenetic classification of the Mammalia. *In* Phylogeny of the Primates: A Multidisciplinary Approach (W. P. Luckett and F. S. Szalay, eds.), pp. 21–46. Plenum Press, New York.

Mein, P. (1975). Resultats du groupe de travail des vertébrés. *In* Report on Activity of the R.C.M.N.S. Working Groups (J. Senes, ed.), pp. 78–81. Regional Committee on Mediterranean Neogene Stratigraphy, Bratislava.

Meyer, H. von. (1848). *In* Index Palaeontologicus (H. G. Bronn, ed.), Abl. I, 2nd half, N–Z. Schweitzerbart, Stuttgart.

Meyer, H. von. (1849). *In* Index Palaeontologicus (H. G. Bronn, ed.), Part 1, Nomenclator palaeontologicus, 2nd half, N–Z. Schweitzerbart, Stuttgart.

Michaux, J. (1966). Sur deux faunules de Micromammi-fères trouvées dans des assises terminales du Pliocène en Languedoc. *C. R. Soc. Geol. France* **9**, 343–344.

Michaux, J. (1969). Le remplissage karstique de Balaruc. *8th Cong. Int. Quarternary Assoc.* Excursion C-14, Suppl. 1, pp. 1–4 (mimeographed).

Mikan, J. C. (1823). Delectus Florae et Faunae Brasiliensis. Anthony Strauss, Vienna.

Miller, G. S. (1903). Seventy new Malayan mammals. *Smithsonian Misc. Coll.* **45**, 1–73.

Miller, G. S., Jr. (1924). List of North American recent mammals. *Bull. U.S. Nat. Mus.* **128**, 1–673.

Miller, G. S., Jr. (1929). Mammals eaten by Indians, owls and Spaniards in the coast region of the Dominican Republic. *Smithsonian Misc. Coll.* **66**, 1–3.

Miller, G. S. (1933). The classification of the gibbons. *J. Mammal.* **14**, 158–159.

Miller, J. F. (1777). Icon. Anim., pl. 13.

Miller, L. E. (1916). Field notes. *In* Allen, J. A., Mammals collected on the Roosevelt Brazilian expedition, with field notes by Leo E. Miller. *Bull. Amer. Mus. Nat. Hist.* **35**, 559–610.

Milne-Edwards, A. (1870). Note sur quelques Mammifères du Thibet oriental. *C. R. Acad. Sci.* (Paris) **70**, 341–342.

Milne-Edwards, A. (1872). Memoire sur la Faune mammalogique du Tibet Oriental et principalement de la principauté de Moupin. *In* Recherches pour Servir à l'Histoire Naturelle des Mammifères (E. Milne-Edwards and A. Milne-Edwards, eds.), pp. 231–379. Masson, Paris.

Minkoff, E. C. (1972). A fossil baboon from Angola, with a note on *Australopithecus*. *J. Paleontol.* **46**, 836–844.

Mivart, St. G. (1864). Notes on the crania and dentition of the Lemuridae. *Proc. Zool. Soc. London, 1864*, pp. 611–648.

Mivart, St. G. (1865). Contributions towards a more complete knowledge of the axial skeleton in the primates. *Proc. Zool. Soc. London, 1865*, pp. 545–592.

Mollett, O. D. Vds. (1947). Fossil mammals from the Makapan Valley, Potgeitersrust. I. Primates. *S. Afr. J. Sci.* **43**, 295–303.

Montandon, G. (1929). Un singe d'apparence anthropoide en Amérique du Sud. *C. R. Acad. Sci.* (Paris) **188**, 815–817.

Montandon, G. (1943). L'Homme Préhistorique et les Pré-humains. Payot, Paris.

Morbeck, M. E. (1975). *Dryopithecus africanus* forelimb. *J. Human Evol.* **4**, 39–46.

Morris, W. J. (1954). An Eocene fauna from the Cathedral Bluffs tongue of the Washakie Basin, Wyoming. *J. Paleontol.* **28**, 195–203.

Morselli, E. (1901). Il Precursore dell'uomo, pp. 1–19. Nota riassuntiva, Genoa.

Mottl, M. (1939). Die Mittelpliozäne Säugetierfauna von Gödöllö bei Budapest. *Ann. Inst. Regii Hungaricus Geol.* **32**, 255–350.

Mottl, M. (1957). Bericht uber die neuen Menschenaffunde aus Osterreich, von Sankt Steven im Lavanttal, Karnten.

Carinthia 2. *Nat.-wiss. Beitr. 2, Heimatkunde Karntens. Mitt. Nat. Wiss. Ver. Kärnten* **67**, 39–84.

Moynihan, M. (1976). The New World Primates: Adaptive Radiation and the Evolution of Social Behavior, Languages, and Intelligence. Princeton University Press, Princeton.

Muirhead (1819). *In* Brewster, Edinb. Encyclopedia, 13(2).

Müller, P. L. S. (1773). Des Ritters Carl von Linné koniglich Schwedischen Leibartes, vollstandiges Natursystem nach der zwölften Luteinischen Ausgabe und nach Anleitung de Hollandischen Houttuynishen Werks mit einer ausfuhrlichen Erklärung, Vol. 1. G. N. Raspe, Nürnberg.

Murray, P. (1975). The role of cheek pouches in cercopithecine monkey adaptive strategy. *In* Primate Functional Morphology and Evolution (R. L. Tuttle, ed.), pp. 151–194. Mouton, The Hague.

Nagel, U. (1973). A comparison of anubis baboons, hamadryas baboons and their hybrids at a species border in Ethiopia. *Folia Primatol.* **19**, 104–165.

Napier, J. R. (1970). Paleoecology and catarrhine evolution. *In* Old World Monkeys (J. R. Napier and P. H. Napier, eds.), pp. 55–95. Academic Press, London.

Napier, J. R., and Davis, P. R. (1959). The forelimb skeleton and associated remains of *Proconsul africanus*. Fossil Mammals of Africa, No. 16, pp. 1–69. British Museum (Natural History), London.

Napier, J. R., and Napier, P. H. (1967). A Handbook of Living Primates. Academic Press, New York.

Napier, P. H. (1976). Catalogue of Primates in the British Museum (Natural History). Part I: Families Callitrichidae and Cebidae. British Museum (Natural History), London.

Necrasov, O., Samson, P., and Radulesco, C. (1961). Sur un nouveau singe catarrhinen fossile, decouvert dans un nid fossilifère d'Oltenie (R. P. R.). *Ann. Stiintifice Univ. Al. I. Cuza, Iasi; Sec. II, stiinte naturale* **7**, 401–416.

Nicholson, H. A. (1870). A Manual of Zoology, Vols. 1 and 2. Blackwood, London.

Noble, H. W. (1969). Dental disease in animals (abstr.). *Proc. Roy. Soc. Med.* **62**, 1295–1297.

Oakley, K. P. (1964). Frameworks for Dating Fossil Man. Aldine, Chicago.

Ockerse, T. (1959). The anatomy of the teeth of the vervet monkey. *J. Dental Assoc. S. Afr.* **14**, 209–226.

O'Connor, B. L. (1976). *Dryopithecus (Proconsul) africanus*: Quadruped or non-quadruped? *J. Human Evol.* **5**, 279–283.

Ogilby, W. (1841). Characterization of a new species of monkey. *Proc. Zool. Soc. London, 1840*, p. 56.

Oken, L. (1816). Lehrbuch der Naturgeschichte. Theil 3: Zoologie, Abth 2. Fleischthiere, Leipzig.

Oppenoorth, W. F. F. (1932). *Homo (Javanthropus) soloensis.* Ein plistocene mensch van Java. *Wet. Meded, Dienst. Mijnb. Nederlandse-Ind.* **20**, 49–75.

d'Orbigny, A. D. (1836). Atlas Zoologique. Volume 9: Voyage dans l'Amerique méridionale. Bertrand, Paris.

Oriel, S. S. (1962). Main body of the Wasatch Formation near La Barge, Wyoming. *Bull. Amer. Assoc. Petrol. Geol.* **46**, 2161–2173.

Osborn, H. F. (1895). Fossil mammals of the Uinta Basin, Expedition of 1894. *Bull. Amer. Mus. Nat. Hist.* **7**, 71–105.

Osborn, H. F. (1902). The American Eocene Primates and the supposed rodent family Mixodectidae. *Bull. Amer. Mus. Nat. Hist.* **16**(17), 169–214.

Osborn, H. F. (1908). New fossil mammals from the Fayum Oligocene, Egypt. *Bull. Amer. Mus. Nat. Hist.* **24**, 265–272.

Osborn, J. W. (1973). The evolution of dentitions. *Amer. Scient.* **61**, 548–559.

Oudemans, A. C. (1890). Uber zwei seltene und eine neue Art Affen des Zoologischen Gartens im Haag. *Zool. Garten* **31**, 266–269.

Owen, R. (1843). Report on the British fossil Mammalia. Part I: Unguiculata and Cetacea. *In* Report on the 12th Meeting of the British Association for the Advancement of Science for 1842, pp. 54–74.

Owen, R. (1845). Notice sur la découverte, faite en Angleterre, de restes fossiles d'un quadrumane du genre Macaque, dans une formation d'eau douce appartenant au nouveau pliocène. *C. R. Acad. Sci.* (Paris) **21**, 573–575.

Owen, R. (1846). A History of British Fossil Mammals and Birds. John Van Voorst, London.

Owen, R. (1865). On a new genus (*Miolophus*) of mammal from the London Clay. *Geol. Mag.* **2**, 339–341.

Ozansoy, F. (1957). Faunes des mammifères du Tertiare de Turquie et leurs revisions stratigraphiques. *Bull. Min. Res. Exp. Inst. Turkey* **49**, 29–48.

Ozansoy, F. (1965). Étude des gisements continentaux et des mammifères du cénozoique de Turquie. *Mem. Soc. Geol. France* **102**, 1–92.

Palmer, T. S. (1903). Some new generic names of mammals. *Science* **17**, 873.

Pandey, J., and Sastri, V. V. (1968). On a new species of *Sivapithecus* from the Siwalik rocks of India. *J. Geol. Soc. India* **9**, 206–211.

Paterson, T. T. (1940). Geology and early man. *Nature* (London) **146**, 12–15, 49–52.

Patterson, B. (1968). The extinct baboon, *Parapapio jonesi*, in the early Pleistocene of northwestern Kenya. *Breviora, Mus. Comp. Zool. Harvard* **282**, 1–4.

Patterson, B., Behrensmeyer, A. K., and Sill, W. D. (1970). Geology and fauna of a new Pliocene locality in northwestern Kenya. *Nature* (London) **226**, 918–921.

Patterson, B., and Howells, W. W. (1967). Hominid humeral fragment from early Pleistocene of northwestern Kenya. *Science* **156**, 64–66.

Pei, W.-c. (1935). Fossil mammals from the Kwangsi caves. *Bull. Geol. Soc. China* **14**, 413–435.

Pei, W.-c. (1936). On the mammalian remains from Locality 3 at Choukoutien. *Paleontol. Sinica, C* **7**(5), 1–120.

Peters, H. B. (1937). Die wissenschaftlichen Namen der menschlichen Körperformgruppen. *Z. Rassenkunde* **6**, 211–241.

Peters, W. K. H. (1853). Naturwissenschaftliche Reise nach Mossambique, 1842 bis 1848, Säugethiere, Part 1. G. Reimar, Berlin.

Peters, W. K. H. (1874). Monatsb. K. Preuss. Akad. Wiss. Berlin. p. 690.

Peters, W. K. H. (1879). Uber die von G. A. Fischer auf einer im Jahr 1878 in Ostafrika von Mombas bis in das Pokômo-Land und das südliche Galla-Land, unternammenen Reise ein gesammelten Säugethiere. *Monatsb. K. Akad. Wissensch. Berlin, 1879,* pp. 829–831.

Petho, J. (1884). Uber die fossilen Säugethiereste von Baltavár. *Jb. Kon. Ungarische Geol. Anst.*

Petter, J.-J., and Petter-Rousseaux, A. (1967). The aye-aye of Madagascar. *In* Social Communication among Primates (S. Altmann, ed.), pp. 195–205. University of Chicago Press, Chicago.

Petter, J.-J., Schilling, A., and Pariente, G. (1971). Observations éco-éthologiques sur deux lémuriens malgaches nocturnes: *Phaner furcifer* et *Microcebus coquereli*. *Terre et la Vie* **3**, 287–327.

Petter-Rousseaux, A., and Petter, J.-J. (1967). Contribution à la systematique des Cheirogaleinae (Lemuriens, Malgaches). *Allocebus* gen. nov. pour *Cheirogaleus trichotis* Gunter, 1875. *Mammalia* **31**, 575–582.

Pickford, M. (1975). Late Miocene sediments and fossils from the Northern Kenya Rift Valley. *Nature* (London) **256**, 279–284.

Pictet, F. J., and Humbert, A. (1869). Mémoire sur les Animaux Vertébres trouvés dans terrain sidérolithique du canton de Vaud et appartenant à la Faune Éocène. *Materiaux pour la Paleontol. Suisse* **5**(2).

Pilbeam, D. (1969a). Newly recognized mandible of *Ramapithecus*. *Nature* (London) **222**, 1093–1094.

Pillbeam, D. (1969b). Tertiary Pongidae of East Africa: Evolutionary relationships and taxonomy. *Yale Peabody Mus. Bull.* **31**, 1–185.

Pilbeam, D. (1970). *Gigantopithecus* and the origins of Hominidae. *Nature* (London) **225**, 516–519.

Pilbeam, D. (1976). Neogene hominids of South Asia and the origins of Hominidae. *In* Les Plus Anciens Hominidés (P. V. Tobias and Y. Coppens, eds.), pp. 39–59. Coll. VI, IX Cong. Union Internat. Sci. Prehist. Protohist. Nice, 1976, preprint.

Pilbeam, D., and Gould, S. J. (1974). Size and scaling in human evolution. *Science* **186**, 892–901.

Pilbeam, D., Meyer, G. E., Badgley, C., Rose, M. D., Pickford, M. H. L., Behrensmeyer, A. K., and Ibrahim Shah, S. M. (1977). New hominoid primates from the Siwaliks of Pakistan and their bearing on hominoid evolution. *Nature* (London) **270**, 689–695.

Pilbeam, D., and Simons, E. L. (1965). Some problems of hominid classification. *Amer. Sci.* **53**, 237–259.

Pilbeam, D., and Simons, E. L. (1971). Humerus of *Dryopithecus* from Saint-Gaudens, France. *Nature* (London) **229**, 408–409.

Pilbeam, D., and Walker, A. (1968). Fossil monkeys from the Miocene of Napak, northeast Uganda. *Nature* (London) **220**, 657–660.

Pilgrim, G. E. (1910). Notices of new mammalian genera and species from the tertiaries of India. *Rec. Geol. Surv. India* **50**, 63–71.

Pilgrim, G. E. (1913). The correlation of the Siwaliks with mammal horizons of Europe. *Rec. Geol. Surv. India* **43**, 264–326.

Pilgrim, G. E. (1915). New Siwalik primates and their bearing on the question of the evolution of man and the anthropoidea. *Rec. Geol. Surv. India* **45**, 1–74.

Pilgrim, G. E. (1927). A *Sivapithecus* palate and other primate fossils from India. *Mem. Geol. Surv. India (Paleontol. Indica), n.s.* **14**, 1–26.

Pilgrim, G. E. (1932). The fossil Carnivora of India. *Palaeontol. Indica, n.s.* **18**, 1–232.

Piton, L.-E. (1940). Paléontologie du Gisement Éocène de Menat (Puy-de-Dome). Clermont-Ferrand, Vallier.

Piveteau, J. (1957). Traité de Paléontologie 7, Primates, Paléontologie Humaine. Masson, Paris.

Pocock, R. I. (1907). A monographic revision of the monkeys of the genus *Cercopithecus*. *Proc. Zool. Soc. London, 1907*, pp. 677–746.

Pocock, R. I. (1917). The external characters of the Hapalidae. *Ann. Mag. Nat. Hist.* **20**, 247–258.

Pocock, R. I. (1918). On the external characters of the lemurs and of *Tarsius*. *Proc. Zool. Soc. London, 1918*, pp. 19–53.

Pocock, R. I. (1920). On the external characters of the South American monkeys. *Proc. Zool. Soc. London, 1920*, pp. 91–113.

Pocock, R. I. (1924). A new genus of monkeys. *Proc. Zool. Soc. London, 1924*, pp. 330–331.

Pocock, R. I. (1925a). Additional notes on the external characters of some platyrrhine monkeys. *Proc. Zool. Soc. London, 1925*, pp. 27–47.

Pocock, R. I. (1925b). The external characters of the catarrhine monkeys and apes. *Proc. Zool. Soc. London, 1925*, pp. 1479–1579.

Pocock, R. I. (1934). The monkeys of the genera *Pithecus* (or *Presbytis*) and *Pygathrix* found to the East of the Bay of Bengal. *Proc. Zool. Soc. London*, pp. 895–961.

Pohlig, H. (1895). *Paidopithex rhenanus* n. g., n. sp., le singe anthropomorphe du Pliocène rhénan. *Procès Verbaux Bull. Soc. Belge Géol.* **9**, 149–151.

Pomel, A. (1892). Sur un macaque fossile des phosphorites quaternaires de l'Algérie. *C. R. Acad. Sci.* (Paris) **115**, 157–160.

Pomel, A. (1896). Singe et Homme. *Publ. Serv. Carte Geol. Algérie, Paléontol.* Monogr. no. 11, pp. 1–32.

Popper, K. R. (1965). The Logic of Scientific Discovery. Harper Torchbooks, New York.

Portis, A. (1917). I Primi Avanzi di Quadrumani del Suolo di Roma. *Boll. Soc. Geol. Italiana* **35**, 239–278.

Pousargues, E. de. (1895). Sur une collection de mammifères provenant du voyage de M. Max Maskowitz au pays de Kong. *Bull. Mus. d'Hist. Nat., Paris* **1**, 98–101.

Prasad, K. N. (1962). Fossil primates from the Siwalik beds near Haritalyangar, Himachal Pradesh, India. *J. Geol. Soc. India* **3**, 86–96.

Preuschoft, H. (1970). Functional anatomy of the lower extremities. *In* The Chimpanzee (G. H. Bourne, ed.), Vol. 3, pp. 221–294. Karger, Basel.

Preuschoft, H. (1973). Body posture and locomotion in some East African Miocene Dryopithecinae. *In* Human Evolution (M. Day, ed.), Symposium of the Society for the Study of Human Biology, Vol. 11, pp. 13–46.

Preuschoft, H. (1975). Body posture and mode of locomotion in fossil primates—method and example: *Aegyptopithecus zeuxis. In* Proceedings of the Fifth Symposium of the Congress of the International Primatology Society, pp. 346–359. Japan Science Press, Tokyo.

Preuschoft, H., and Weinmann, W. (1973). Biomechanical investigations of *Limnopithecus* with special reference to the influence exerted by body weight on bone thickness. *Amer. J. Phys. Anthropol., n.s.* **38**, 241–250.

Pucheran, J. (1845). Description de quelques mammifères Americains. *Rev. Zool.* **8**, 335–337.

Pucheran, J. (1857). Notices Mammalogiques. II. Primates. *Rev. Mag. Zool.* **2**, 193–203, 241–252, 289–303, 337–355.

Pycraft, W. P. (1925). Diagnoses of four species and one subspecies of the genus *Homo*. *Man* **25**, 162–164.

Pycraft, W. P. (1928). Description of human remains. *In* Rhodesian Man and Associated Remains, pp. 1–5. British Museum (Natural History), London.

Quenstedt, F. A. (1867). Handbuch der Petrefaktenkunde. Volume 2: Aufl. Tubingen, Laupp.

Quinet, G. E. (1964). Morphologie dentaire des mammifères éocènes de Dormaal. *Bull. Group. Eur. Rech. Sci. Stomat.* **7**, 272–294.

Quinet, G. E. (1966). *Teilhardina belgica*, ancêtre des Anthropoidea de l'ancien Monde. *Bull. Inst. R. Sc. Nat. Belg.* **42**, 1–14.

Radinsky, L. (1973). *Aegyptopithecus* endocasts: Oldest record of a pongid brain. *Amer. J. Phys. Anthropol.* **39**, 239–248.

Radinsky, L. (1974). The fossil evidence of anthropoid brain evolution. *Amer. J. Phys. Anthropol., n.s.* **41**, 15–27.

Radinsky, L. (1977). Early primate brains: Facts and fiction. *J. Human Evol.* **6**, 79–86.

Raffles, T. S. (1822). Second part of the descriptive catalogue of a zoological collection made in the island of Sumatra and its vicinity. *Trans. Linnaean Soc. London* **13**, 277–340.

Rafinesque, C. S. (1815). Analyse de la Nature ou Tableau de l'Univers et des Organises. Palerme.

Rahm, U. H. (1970). Ecology, zoogeography and systematics of some African forest monkeys. *In* Old World Monkeys (J. R. Napier and P. H. Napier, eds.), pp. 589–626. Academic Press, London.

Reck, H., and Kohl-Larsen, L. (1936). Erster Überblick über die jungdiluvialen Tier- und Menschenfunde Dr. Kohl-Larsen's im nordöstlichen Teil des Njarasa-Grabens (Ostafrika). *Geol. Rundschau* **27**, 401–441.

Reichenbach, H. G. L. (1862). Die vollständigste Naturgeschichte der Affen. *In* Die vollständigste Naturgeschichte In- und Auslandes. Parts 2–4, 14–16, 20–21. Central-Atlas für Zool. Garten, Dresden.

Reinhardt, J. (1873). Et Bidrag til Kundskab om Aberne i Mexiko og Central-amerika. *Vidensk. Meddr dansk. naturh. Foren (1872)* **6–9**, 150–158.

Remane, A. (1921). Zur Beurteilung der fossilen anthropoiden. *Zbl. Min. Geol. Paleontol.* **11**, 335–339.

Remane, A. (1924). Einige bemerkungen uber *Prohylobates tandyi* R. Fourtau und *Dryopithecus mogharensis* R. Fourtau. *Cbl. Min. Geol. Paläontol.* **14**, 220–224.

Remane, A. (1925). Der fossile pavian (*Papio* sp.) von Oldoway. *In* Wissenschaftliche Ergebnisss der Oldoway—Expedition 1913 (H. Reck, ed.), Neue Folge, Vol. 2, pp. 83–90. Leipzig.

Remane, A. (1965). Die Geschichte der Menschenaffen. *In* Menschliche Abstammungslehre (G. Heberer, ed.), pp. 249–309. Gustav Fischer Verlag, Göttingen.

Rensch, B. (1936). Die Geschichte des Sundabogens. Borntraeger, Berlin.

Ribiero, A. de Miranda. (1912). Dos Novos Simios da Nossa Fauna. Brasilianische Rundschau, Rio de Janiero.

Rich, T. H. V., and Rich, P. V. (1971). *Brachyerix*, a Miocene hedgehog from western North America, with a description of the tympanic regions of *Paraechinus* and *Podogymnura*. *Amer. Mus. Nov.* **2477**, 1–58.

Riesenfeld, A. (1975). Volumetric determinations of metatarsal robusticity in a few living primates and in the foot of *Oreopithecus*. *Primates* **16**, 9–15.

Rímoli, R. (1977). Una Nueva Especie de Monos (Cebidae: Saimirinae: *Saimiri*) de la Hispaniola. *Cuadernos del Cendia, Univ. Autonoma de Santo Domingo* **242**, 1–14.

Risso, A. (1826). Histoire Naturelle des Principales Productions de l'Europe Meridionale. Levrault, Paris.

Ristori, G. (1890). Le Scimmie fossili italiani. *Boll. R. Com. Geol. Italiana* **21**, 178–196.

Ritgen, F. F. A. (1824). Naturlichen Entheilung der Säugethiere.

Robinson, J. T. (1952). The australopithecine-bearing deposits of the Sterkfontein area. *Ann. Transvaal Mus.* **22**, 1–19.

Robinson, J. T. (1953). *Telanthropus* and its phylogenetic significance. *Amer. J. Phys. Anthropol.*, n.s. **11**, 445–501.

Robinson, J. T. (1954). The genera and species of the Australopithecinae. *Amer. J. Phys. Anthropol.*, n.s. **12**, 181–200.

Robinson, J. T. (1956). Ths dentition of the Australopithecinae. *Transvaal Museum Memoirs* **9**, 1–179.

Robinson, J. H. (1961). Ths australopithecines and their bearing on the origin of man and of stone tool-making. *S. Afr. J. Sci.* **57**, 1–13.

Robinson, J. H. (1967). Variation and the taxonomy of the early hominids. *In* Evolutionary Biology, Vol. 1, pp. 69–100. Appleton-Century-Crofts, New York.

Robinson, J. T. (1972). Early Hominid Posture and Locomotion. University of Chicago Press, Chicago.

Robinson, J. T., and Steudel, K. (1973). Multivariate discriminant analysis of dental data bearing on early hominid affinities. *J. Human Evol.* **2**, 509–528.

Robinson, P. (1957). The species of *Notharctus* from the middle Eocene. *Postilla* **28**, 1–27.

Robinson, P. (1966). Fossil Mammalia of the Huerfano Formation, Eocene, of Colorado. *Peabody Mus. Nat. Hist., Yale Univ. Bull.* **21**, 1–95.

Robinson, P. (1967). The mandibular dentition of *?Tetonoides* (Primates, Anaptomorphidae). *Ann. Carnegie Mus.* **39**, 187–190.

Robinson, P. (1968). The paleontology and geology of the Badwater Creek area, central Wyoming. Part 4: Late Eocene primates from Badwater, Wyoming, with a discussion of material from Utah. *Ann. Carnegie Mus.* **39**, 307–326.

Rochebrune, A. T. de. (1887). Faune de la Sénégambie. Supplement, Vol. 1: Mammifères. Octave Doin, Paris.

Romer, A. S. (1928). Pleistocene mammals of Algeria. *Bull. Logan Mus., Beloit* **1**, 80–163.

Romer, A. S. (1966). Vertebrate Paleontology, 3rd ed. University of Chicago Press, Chicago.

Rose, K. D. (1975). The Carpolestidae, Early Tertiary primates from North America. *Mus. Comp. Zool. Harvard Bull.* **147**, 1–74.

Rose, K. D. (1977). Evolution of Carpolestid Primates and Chronology of the North American Middle and Late Paleocene. *J. Paleontol.* **51**, 536–542.

Rose, K. D., and Gingerich, P. D. (1976). Partial skull of the Plesiadapiform Primate *Ignacius* from the Early Eocene of Wyoming. *Contrib. Mus. Paleontol. Univ. Mich.* **24**, 181–189.

Rose, K. D., and Simons, E. L. (1977). Dental function in the Plagiomenidae: Origin and relationships of the mammalian order Dermoptera. *Contrib. Mus. Paleontol. Univ. Mich.* **24**, 221–236.

Rosenberger, A. L. (1977). *Xenothrix* and Ceboid Phylogeny. *J. Human Evol.* **6**, 561–581.

Rosenberger, A. L. (1978). Loss of incisor enamel in marmosets. *J. Mammalogy* **59**, 207–208.

Rosenberger, A. L. (1979). Cranial anatomy and implications of *Dolichocebus*, a late Oligocene ceboid primate. *Nature* (London). **279**, 416–418.

Rosenberger, A. L., and Kinzey, W. G. (1976). Functional patterns of molar occlusion in platyrrhine primates. *Amer. J. Phys. Anthropol.*, n.s. **45**, 281–298.

Roth, J., and Wagner, A. (1854). Die fossilen Knochenüberreste von Pikermi in Griechenland. *Abh. k. Bayerische Akad Wiss. 2 Cl. (Math-phys.)* **7**, 371–388.

Rüppel, E. (1835). Neue Wirbeltiere zu der Fauna von Abyssinien gehorig, Vol. 1, Säugetiere. Schmerber, Frankfurt.

Rusconi, C. (1933). Nuevos restos de monos fosiles del terciario antiguo de la Patagonia. *Ann. Soc. Cient. Argentina* **116**, 286–289.

Rusconi, C. (1935a). Sobre morfogenesis basicraneana de algunos primates actuales y fosiles. *Rev. Argentina Paleontol. Antropol. Ameghinia* **1**, 3–23.

Rusconi, C. (1935b). Los especies de primates del oligoceno de Patagonia (gen. *Homunculus*). *Rev. Argentina Paleontol. Antropol. Ameghinia* **1**, 39–126.

Russell, D. E. (1964). Les mammifères Paléocènes d'Europe. *Mem. Mus. Nat. Hist. Nat. n.s., Ser. C* **13**, 1–324.

Russell, D. E. (1967). Le paléocène continental d'Amerique du Nord. *Mem. Mus. Nat. Hist. Nat. n.s., Ser. C* **16**, 37–99.

Russell, D. E., Louis, P., and Savage, D. E. (1967). Primates of the French early Eocene. *Univ. California Publ. Geol. Sci.* **73**, 1–46.

Rütimeyer, L. (1862). Eocaene Säugethiere aus dem Gebiet des schweizerischen Jura. *Allg. Schweizerische Gesell., neue Denkschrifte*, **19**, 1–98.

Rütimeyer, L. (1867). Herkunft unserer Thierwelt. Eine zoogeographische Skizze. H. Georg Verlagsbuchhandlung, Basel.

Rütimeyer, L. (1888). Ueber einige Beziehungen zwischen den Säugetierstammen Alter und Neuer Welt, Erster Nachtrag. *Abh. Schweiz. Pal. Ges.* **15**, 1–151.

Rütimeyer, L. (1890). Ubersicht der eocanen Fauna von Eger-kingen nebst einer Erwiderung an Prof. E. D. Cope. *Abh. Schweiz. Pal. Ges.* **17,** 1–24.

Rütimeyer, L. (1891). Die eocaene Säugethier-Welt von Eger-kingen. *Abh. Schweiz. Pal. Ges.* **18,** 1–151.

Saban, R. (1956). L'os temporal et ses rapports chez les Lémuriens subfossiles de Madagascar. *Mem. Inst. Sci. Madagascar A* **10,** 251–297.

Saban, R. (1963). Contribution à l'étude de l'os temporal des Primates. *Mem. Mus. Nat. Hist. Nat., n.s., Ser. A* **29,** 1–378.

Saban, R. (1975). Structure of the ear region in living and subfossil lemurs. *In* Lemur Biology (I. Tattersall and R. W. Sussman, eds.), pp. 83–109. Plenum Press, New York.

Savage, D. E., and Curtis, G. H. (1970). The Villafranchian stage-age and its radiometric dating. *Geol. Soc. Amer. Spec. Pap.* **124,** 207–231.

Savage, D. E., D. E. Russell, and B. T. Waters. (1977). Critique of certain Eocene primate taxa. *Geobios Mém.* **1,** 159–164.

Savage, T. S., and Wyman, J. (1847). Notice of the external characters and habits of *Troglodytes gorilla* . . . from the Gaboon River. *Boston J. Nat. Hist.* **5,** 417–442.

Schaeffer, B., Hecht, M., and Eldredge, N. (1972). Phylogeny and paleontology. *Evol. Biol.* **6,** 31–46.

Schaub, S. (1943). Die oberpliocaene Säugetierfauna von Senèze (Haute-Loire) und ihre verbreitungsgeschichtliche Stellung. *Eclogae Geol. Helvetica* **36,** 270–284.

Schaufuss, L. W. (1875). *Pseudanthropos fuliginosus* Schauf., eine neue Chimpanze-Varietät. *Nunquam otiosus, Zoologische Mittheilungen,* Vol. 2, pp. 345–357. T. O. Weigel, Leipzig.

Scheibout, J. A. (1974). Vertebrate paleontology and paleoecology of Paleocene Black Peaks Formation, Big Bend National Park, Texas. *Bull. Texas Mem. Mus.* **24,** 1–88.

Schinz, H. R. (1825). Das Thierreich. J. C. Cottaschen Buchhandlung, Stuttgart.

Schlegel, H. (1876). Revue Methodique et Critique des Collections Déposées dans cet Establissment, Vol. 7, Monogr. 40: Simiae. Mus. d'Hist. Nat. Pays-Bas. E. J. Brill, Leide.

Schlosser, M. (1885). Ueber das geologische alter der Faunen von Eppelsheim und Ronzon und die Berichtigung einiger von Lydekker angefochtenen Nagerspecies aus dem europaischen Tertiar. *Neues Jb. Min. Geol. Paläontol.* **2,** 136–144.

Schlosser, M. (1887). Die Affen Lemuren Chiropteren usw. des europaischen Tertiärs. *Beitr. Paläontol. Oesterreich-Ungarns Orients,* **6,** 1–162.

Schlosser, M. (1901). Die menschenahnlichen Zähne aus dem Bohnerz der Schwabischen Alb. *Zool. Anz.* **24,** 261–271.

Schlosser, M. (1910). Über einige fossile Säugetiere aus dem Oligocän von Ägypten. *Zool. Anz.* **34,** 500–508.

Schlosser, M. (1911). Beiträge zur kenntnis dër Oligozänen Landsäugetiere aus dem Fayum: Agypten. *Beitr. Paläontol. Oesterreich-Ungarns Orients* **6,** 1–227.

Schlosser, M. (1921). Beiträge zur Kenntnis der Säugetier-reste aus dem untersten Eocaen von Reims. *Palaeontographica* **63,** 97–144.

Schlosser, M. (1924). Fossil primates from China. *Palaeontol. Sinica* **1**(2), 1–16.

Schmidt-Kittler, N. (1971). Eine unteroligozäne Primaten fauna von Ehrenstein bei Ulm. *Mitt. Bayerlische Staatssamml. Paläontol. Hist. Geol.* **11,** 171–204.

Schoetensack, O. (1908). Der Unterkiefer des *Homo heidelbergensis* aus den Sanden von Mauer bei Heidelberg. W. Engelmann, Leipzig.

Schreber, J. C. D. von. (1774). Die Säugethiere in Abbildungen nach der Natur mit Beschreibungen, Vol. 1. Erlangen, Walther.

Schreuder, A. (1945). The Tegelen fauna, with a description of new remains of its rare components (*Leptobos, Archidiskodon meridionalis, Macaca, Sus strozzi*). *Arch. Neerlandaise Zool.* **7,** 153–204.

Schultz, A. H. (1932). The generic position of *Symphalangus klossi. J. Mammal* **13,** 368–369.

Schultz, A. H. (1968). The recent hominoid primates. *In* Perspectives on Human Evolution (S. Washburn and P. C. Jay, eds.), Vol. 1, pp. 122–195. Holt, Rhinehart & Winston, New York.

Schultz, A. H. (1973). The skeleton of the Hylobatidae and other observations on their morphology. *Gibbon Siamang* **2,** 1–54.

Schuman, E. L., and Brace, C. L. (1954). Metric and morphologic variations in the dentitions of the Liberian chimpanzee; comparisons with anthropoid and human dentitions. *Human Biol.* **26,** 239–268.

Schwalbe, G. (1903). Die Vorgeschichte des Menschen. Friedrick Vieweg und Sohn, Braunschweig.

Schwalbe, G. (1916). Über der fossilen affen *Oreopithecus bamboli. Z. Morphol. Anthropol.* **19,** 149–254.

Schwartz, J. H. (1975). Development and eruption of the premolar region of prosimians and its bearing on their evolution. *In* Lemur Biology (I. Tattersall and R. W. Sussman, eds.), pp. 41–63. Plenum Press, New York.

Schwarz, E. (1929). Das Vorkommen des Schimpansen auf den linken Kongo-Ufer. *Rev. Zool. Afr.* **16,** 425–526.

Schwarz, E. (1951). A new marmoset monkey from Brazil. *Amer. Mus. Nov.* **1508,** 1–3.

Schwartz, J. H. (1975). Re-evaluation of the morphocline of molar appearance in the primates. *Folia primatol.* **23,** 290–307.

Schwartz, J. H. (1978). If *Tarsius* is not a prosimian is it a haplorhine? *In* Recent Advances in Primatology, Vol. 3. Evolution. (D. J. Chivers and K. A. Joysey, eds.), pp. 195–202. Academic Press, London.

Schwartz, J. H. and L. Krishtalka. (1977). Revision of Picrodontidae (Primates, Plesiadapiformes) dental homologies and relationships. *Ann. Carnegie Mus.* **46,** 55–78.

Selenka, E. (1899). Menschenaffen. Studien über Entwickelung und Schädelbau Liefg. 2. Kapitel 2. Schädel des Gorilla und Schimpanse, pp. 93–160. Kreidel, Wiesbaden.

Seligsohn, D. (1977). Analysis of species-specific molar adaptations in strepsirhine Primates. *Contrib. Primatol.* **11**, 1–116.

Seligsohn, D., and Szalay, F. S. (1974). Dental occlusion and the masticatory apparatus in *Lemur* and *Varecia*: Their bearing on the systematics of living and fossil primates. *In* Prosimian Biology (R. D. Martin, G. A. Doyle, and A. C. Walker, eds.), pp. 543–561. Duckworth, London.

Seligsohn, D., and Szalay, F. S. (1978). Relationship between natural selection and dental morphology: Tooth function and diet in *Lepilemur* and *Hapalemur*. *In* Studies in the Development, Function and Evolution of Teeth (P. M. Butler and K. A. Joysey, eds.), pp. 289–307. Academic Press, London.

Senyürek, M. S. (1955). A note on the teeth of *Meganthropus africanus* Weinert from Taganyika Territory. *Belleten* **19**, 1–55.

Sera, G. l. (1917). La testimianza dei fossili di antropomorfi per la questione dell'origine dell'uomo. *Atti Soc. Italiana Sci. Nat.* **56**, 1–156.

Sergi, G. (1909). Di una nuova sistemazione di Hominidae e loro distribuzione geografica. *Atti. Soc. Italiana Progresso Sci.* **2**, 426–428.

Sergi, G. (1910). Paléontologie sud-americaine. *Scientia* **8**, 465–475.

Sergi, G. (1911). L'uomo secondo le origine l'antichita, le variazione e la distribuzione geographica. Turin.

Sergi, S. (1935). Die Entdeckurg eines weiteren Schädels des *Homo neandertalensis* var. *aniensis*, in der Grube von Saccopastore (Rom). *Anthrop. Anz.* **12**, 281–284.

Seton, H. (1940). Two new primates from the lower Eocene of Wyoming. *Proc. New Engl. Zool. Club* **18**, 39–42.

Simionescu, I. (1922). Uber eine pliocäne Wirbeltierfauna aus Rumanien. *Centralbl. Min. Geol., Paleontol.*, pp. 185–186.

Simionescu, I. (1930). Vertebratele Pliocene dela Malusteni (Covurlui). *Acad. Romana* **9**, 83–136.

Simonetta, A. (1957). Catalogo e sinonimia annotata degli ominoidi fossili ed attuali (1758–1955). *Atti Mem. Soc. Toscana Sci. Nat., Ser. Ae, B* **63–64**, 53–112.

Simons, E. L. (1959). An anthropoid frontal bone from the Fayum Oligocene of Egypt: The oldest skull fragment of a higher primate. *Amer. Mus. Nov.* **1976**, 1–16.

Simons, E. L. (1960). *Apidium* and *Oreopithecus*. *Nature* (London) **186**, 824–826.

Simons, E. L. (1961a). Notes on Eocene tarsioids and a revision of some Necrolemurinae. *Bull. Brit. Mus. (Nat. Hist.), Geol.* **5**, 43–49.

Simons, E. L. (1961b). The dentition of *Ourayia*: Its bearing on relationships of omomyid prosimians. *Postilla* **54**, 1–20.

Simons, E. L. (1961c). The phyletic position of *Ramapithecus*. *Postilla* **57**, 1–9.

Simons, E. L. (1962a). Two new primate species from the African Oligocene. *Postilla* **64**, 1–12.

Simons, E. L. (1962b). A new Eocene primate genus, *Cantius*, and a revision of some allied European lemuroids. *Bull. Brit. Mus. (Nat. Hist.), Geol.* **7**, 1–30.

Simons, E. L. (1963a). A critical reappraisal of Tertiary Primates. *In* Evolutionary and Genetic Biology of Primates (J. Buettner-Janusch, ed.), pp. 65–129. Academic Press, New York.

Simons, E. L. (1963b). Some fallacies in the study of hominid phylogeny. *Science* **141**, 879–889.

Simons, E. L. (1964). On the mandible of *Ramapithecus*. *Proc. Natl. Acad. Sci. U.S.A.* **51**, 528–535.

Simons, E. L. (1965). New fossil apes from Egypt and the initial differentiation of Hominoidea. *Nature* (London) **205**, 135–139.

Simons, E. L. (1967a). A fossil *Colobus* skull from the Sudan (Primates, Cercopithecidae). *Postilla* **111**, 1–12.

Simons, E. L. (1967b). The significance of primate paleontology for anthropological studies. *Amer. J. Phys. Anthropol., n.s.* **27**, 307–325.

Simons, E. L. (1967c). Review of the phyletic interrelationships of Oligocene and Miocene Old World Anthropoidea. *In* Evolution des Vertébrés. Problèmes actuels de paléontologie. Coll. Internat. du CNRS, Vol. 163, pp. 597–602.

Simons, E. L. (1968). Early Cenozoic Mammalian faunas Fayum Province, Egypt, Introduction. *Peabody Mus. Nat. Hist. Bull.* **28**, 1–21.

Simons. E. L. (1969a). Miocene monkey *(Prohylobates)* from northern Egypt. *Nature* (London) **223**, 687–689.

Simons, E. L. (1969b). The origin and radiation of the Primates. *Ann. N.Y. Acad. Sci.* **167**, 319–331.

Simons, E. L. (1970). The deployment and history of Old World monkeys (Cercopithecidae, Primates). *In* Old World Monkeys (J. R. Napier and P. H. Napier, eds.), pp. 97–137. Academic Press, New York.

Simons, E. L. (1971). Relationships of *Amphipithecus* and *Oligopithecus*. *Nature* (London **232**, 489–491.

Simons, E. L. (1972). Primate Evolution: An Introduction to Man's Place in Nature. Macmillan, New York.

Simons, E. L. (1974a). The relationships of *Aegyptopithecus* to other primates. *Ann. Geol. Surv. Egypt* **4**, 149–156.

Simons, E. L. (1974b). *Parapithecus grangeri* (Parapithecidae, Old World higher primates): New species from the Oligocene of Egypt and the initial differentiation of Cercopithecoidea. *Postilla* **166**, 1–12.

Simons, E. L. (1976a). The nature of the transition in the dental mechanism from pongids to hominids. *J. Human Evol.* **5**, 500–528.

Simons, E. L. (1976b). Relationships between *Dryopithecus*, *Sivapithecus* and *Ramapithecus* and their bearing on hominid origins. *In* Les Plus Anciens Hominidés (P. V. Tobias and Y. Coppens, eds.), Coll. VI, IX Cong. Union Internat. Sci. Préhist Protohist, Nice, 1976, preprint, pp. 60–69.

Simons, E. L. (1976c). The fossil record of Primate phylogeny. *In* Molecular Anthropology (M. Goodman, R. E. Tashian, and J. H. Tashian, eds.), pp. 35–62. Plenum Press, New York.

Simons, E. L., and Chopra, S. R. K. (1969). *Gigantopithecus* (Pongidae, Hominoidea)—A new species from north India. *Postilla* **138**, 1–18.

Simons, E. L., and Delson, E. (1978). Cercopithecidae and Parapithecidae. *In* Mammalian Evolution in Africa (H. B. S. Cooke and V. J. Maglio, eds.), pp. 100–119. Harvard University Press, Cambridge.

Simons, E. L., and Fleagle, J. (1973). The history of extinct gibbon-like primates. *Gibbon Siamang* **2**, 121–148.

Simons, E. L., and Pilbeam, D. R. (1965). Preliminary revision of the Dryopithecinae (Pongidae, Anthropoidea). *Folia Primatol.* **3**, 81–152.

Simons, E. L., and Pilbeam, D. R. (1971). A gorilla-sized ape from the Miocene of India. *Science* **173**, 23–27.

Simons, E. L., and Pilbeam, D. R. (1972). Hominoid paleoprimatology. *In* The Functional and Evolutionary Biology of Primates (R. Tuttle, ed.), pp. 36–62. Aldine–Atherton, Chicago.

Simons, E. L., and Russell, D. E. (1960). Notes on the cranial anatomy of *Necrolemur*. *Breviora* **127**.

Simpson, G. G. (1927). Mammalian fauna and correlation of the Paskapoo Formation of Alberta. *Amer. Mus. Nov.* **268**, 1–10.

Simpson, G. G. (1928). A new mammalian fauna from the Fort Union of southern Montana. *Amer. Mus. Nov.* **297**, 1–15.

Simpson, G. G. (1929). A collection of Paleocene mammals from Bear Creek Montana. *Ann. Carnegie Mus.* **19**, 115–122.

Simpson, G. G. (1931). A new classification of mammals. *Bull. Amer. Mus. Nat. Hist.* **59**, 259–293.

Simpson, G. G. (1933). The "Plagiaulacoid" type of mammalian dentition. *J. Mammal.* **14**, 97–107.

Simpson, G. G. 1935a. The Tiffany fauna, upper Paleocene. 2. Structure and relationships of *Plesiadapis*. *Amer. Mus. Nov.* **816**, 1–30.

Simpson, G. G. (1935b). The Tiffany fauna, upper Paleocene. 3. Primates, Carnivora, Condylarthra and Amblypoda. *Amer. Mus. Nov.* **817**, 1–28.

Simpson, G. G. (1936). A new fauna from the Fort Union of Montana. *Amer. Mus. Nov.* **873**, 1–27.

Simpson, G. G. (1937). The Fort Union of the Crazy Mountain field, Montana, and its mammalian faunas. *U.S. Nat. Mus. Bull.* **169**, 1–287.

Simpson, G. G. (1940). Studies on the earliest primates. *Bull. Amer. Mus. Nat. Hist.* **77**, 185–212.

Simpson, G. G. (1945). The principles of classification and a classification of mammals. *Bull. Amer. Mus. Nat. Hist.* **85**, 1–350.

Simpson, G. G. (1953). The Major Features of Evolution. Columbia University Press, New York.

Simpson, G. G. (1955). The Phenacolemuridae, new family of early Primates. *Bull. Amer. Mus. Nat. Hist.* **105**, 415–441.

Simpson, G. G. (1959). Primates [*In* The Geology and Paleontology of the Elk Mountain and Tabernacle Butte Area of Wyoming]. *Bull. Amer. Mus. Nat. Hist.* **117**, 152–157.

Simpson, G. G. (1961). Principles of Animal Taxonomy. Columbia University Press, New York.

Simpson, G. G. (1963). The meaning of taxonomic statements. *In* Classification and Human Evolution (S. L. Washburn, ed.), pp. 1–31. Aldine, Chicago.

Simpson, G. G. (1967). The Tertiary lorisiform primates of Africa. *Bull. Mus. Comp. Zool.* **136**, 39–62.

Simpson, G. G. (1969). South American mammals. *In* Biogeography and Ecology (E. J. Fittkau, J. Illies, H. Klinge, G. H. Schwabe, and H. Siolo, eds.), pp. 879–909. Mouton, The Hague.

Simpson, G. G. (1975). Recent advances in methods of phylogenetic inference. *In* Phylogeny of the Primates: A Multidisciplinary Approach (W. P. Luckett and F. S. Szalay, eds.), pp. 3–19. Plenum Press, New York.

Singer, R. (1962). *Simopithecus* from Hopefield, South Africa. *Biblio. Primatol.* **1**, 43–70.

Sloan, R. E. (1969). Cretaceous and Paleocene terrestrial communities of western North America. *Proc. N. Amer. Paleontol. Conv., Sept. 1969* Part E, pp. 427–453.

Smith, A. (1833). *S. Afr. Q. J.*, 2nd ser. **II**(1).

Smith, G. E. (1919). Discussion on the zoological position and affinities of *Tarsius*. *Proc. Zool. Soc. London, 1919*, pp. 465–475.

Smith, J. A. (1860). *Proc. Roy. Phys. Soc. Edinburgh* **2**.

Sollas, W. J. (1933). The sagittal section of the human skull. *J. Roy. Anthropol. Inst.* **63**, 389–431.

Sonek, A., Jr. (1969). Functional anatomy of the weight bearing and prehensile hand of a quadrupedal primate (*Saguinus oedipus*). Ph.D. thesis. Ann Arbor: University Microfilms.

Spix, J. de (1823). Simiarum et vespertiliarum brasiliensis species novae; ou, Histoire naturelle des espèces nouvelles de singes et de chauve-souris observées et recueillies pendant le voyage dans l'intérieur du Bresil. Monaco.

Standing, H. F. (1903). Rapport sur des ossements subfossiles provenant d'Ampasambazimba. *Bull. Acad. Malgache* **2**, 227–235.

Standing, H. F. (1904). Rapport sur des ossements subfossiles provenant d'Ampasambazimba. *Bull. Acad. Malgache* **3**, 305–310.

Standing, H. F. (1905). Rapport sur des ossements subfossiles provenant d'Ampasambazimba. *Bull. Acad. Malgache* **4**, 95–100.

Standing, H. F. (1908). On recently discovered subfossil primates from Madagascar. *Trans. Zool. Soc. London* **18**, 59–217.

Standing, H. F. (1910). Note sur les ossements subfossiles provenant des fouilles d'Ampasambazimba. *Bull. Acad. Malgache, n.s.* **7**, 61–64.

Stehlin, H. G. (1912). Die Säugetiere des schweizerischen Eocäens. Critischer Catalog der Materialen. part 7, first half *Ash. Schweiz. Pal. Ges.* **38**, 1165–1298.

Stehlin, H. G. (1916). Die Säugetiere des schweizerischen Eocäens. Critischer Catalog der Materialen. part 7, second half. *Abh. schweiz. Pal. Ges.* 41, 1299–1552.

Stehlin, H. G. (1925). Catalogue des ossements de mammifères tertiares de la collection Bourgeois à l'école de Pont-Levoy (Loir-et-Cher). *Bull. Soc. Hist. Nat. Anthrop. Loir-et-Cher* **18**, 1–200.

Steininger, F. (1967). Ein weiterer zahn von *Dryopithecus (Dry.) fontani darwini* Abel (1902) (Mammalia, Pongidae) aus dem Miozän des Wiener Beckens. *Folia Primatol.* **7**, 243–275.

Stirton, R. A. (1951). Ceboid monkeys from the Miocene of Colombia. *Bull. Dept. Geol. Sci.* **28**, 315–356.

Stirton, R. A., and Savage, D. E. (1951). A new monkey from

the La Venta Miocene of Columbia. *Compilacion de los Estudios Geol. Oficiales en Colombia, Serv. Geol. Nac. Bogota* **7**, 345–356.

Stock, C. (1933). An Eocene primate from California. *Proc. Natl. Acad. Sci. U.S.A.* **19**, 954–959.

Stock, C. (1934). A second Eocene primate from California. *Proc. Natl. Acad. Sci. U.S.A.* **20**, 150–154.

Stock, C. (1938). A tarsiid primate and a mixodectid from the Poway Eocene, California. *Proc. Natl. Acad. Sci. U.S.A.* **24**, 288–293.

Stoll, N. R., Dollfus, R. Ph., Forest, F., Riley, N. D., Sabrosky, C. W., Wright, C. W., and Melville, R. (eds.) (1961). International Code of Zoological Nomenclature. International Trust Zoological Nomenclature, London.

Storr, G. C. C. (1780). Prodromus method. Mammalium... inaugural disputationen propositus. Frid. Wolffer, Tubingen.

Straus, W. L., Jr. (1961). Primate taxonomy and *Oreopithecus. Science* **133**, 760–761.

Straus, W. L., Jr. (1963). The classification of *Oreopithecus. In* Classification and Human Evolution (S. L. Washburn, ed.), pp. 146–177. Aldine, Chicago.

Straus, W. L., Jr., and Schön, M. (1960). Cranial capacity of *Oreopithecus bambolii. Science* **132**, 670–672.

Stromer, E. (1913). Mitteilungen über die Wirbeltierreste aus dem Mittelpliocän des Natrontales (Ägypten). 1. Affen. *Z. Deutschen Geol. Gesell. Abh.* **65**, 349–361.

Stromer, E. (1920). Mitteilungen über Wirbeltierreste aus dem Mittelpliocän des Natrontales (Ägypten). 5. Nachtrag zu l. Affen. *Sitz.-ber. Bayerischen Akad. Wissen. Math.-phys. Kl.*, 1920, pp. 345–370.

Struhsaker, T. T. (1975). The Red Colobus Monkey. University of Chicago Press, Chicago.

Sudre, J. (1975). Un Prosimien du Paléogène ancien du Sahara nord-occidental: *Azibius trerki* n. g. n. sp. *C. R. Acad. Sci.* (Paris) **280**, 1539–1542.

Swainson, W. (1835). On the Natural History and Classification of Quadrupeds. Longman, London.

Swindler, D. R., and Orlosky, F. J. (1974). Metric and morphological variability in the dentition of colobine monkeys. *J. Human Evol.* **3**, 135–160.

Swinhoe, R. (1863). On the mammals of the Island of Formosa (China). *Proc. Zool. Soc. London, 1862*, pp. 347–365.

Szalay, F. S. (1968a). The beginnings of primates. *Evolution* **22**, 19–36.

Szalay, F. S. (1968b). The Picrodontidae, a family of early primates. *Amer. Mus. Nov.* **2329**, 1–55.

Szalay, F. S. (1969a). Mixodectidae, Microsyopidae and the insectivore–primate transition. *Bull. Amer. Mus. Nat. Hist.* **140**, 193–330.

Szalay, F. S. (1969b). Uintasoricinae, a new subfamily of early Tertiary mammals (?Primates). *Amer. Mus. Nov.* **2363**, 1–36.

Szalay, F. S. (1970). *Amphipithecus* and the origin of catarrhine primates. *Nature* (London) **227**, 355–357.

Szalay, F. S. (1971). The adapid primates *Agerina* and *Pronycticebus. Amer. Mus. Nov.* **2466**, 1–19.

Szalay, F. S. (1972a). Cranial morphology of the early Tertiary *Phenacolemur* and its bearing on primate phylogeny. *Amer. J. Phys. Anthropol. n.s.* **36**, 59–76.

Szalay, F. S. (1972b). Paleobiology of the earliest primates. *In* The Functional and Evolutionary Biology of Primates (R. Tuttle, ed.), pp. 3–35. Aldine–Atherton, Chicago.

Szalay, F. S. (1972c). *Amphipithecus* revisited. *Nature* (London) **236**, 179.

Szalay, F. S. (1973). New Paleocene primates and a diagnosis of the new suborder Paromomyiformes. *Folia Primatol.* **19**, 73–87.

Szalay, F. S. (1974a). New genera of European Eocene Adapid primates. *Folia Primatol.* **22**, 116–133.

Szalay, F. S. (1974b). A new species and genus of early Eocene primate from North America. *Folia Primatol.* **22**, 243–250.

Szalay, F. S. (ed.) (1975a). Approaches to Primate Paleobiology. Contributions to Primatology, Vol. 5. Karger, Basel.

Szalay, F. S. (1975b). Early primates as a source for the taxon Dermoptera (abstr.). *Amer. J. Phys. Anthropol., n.s.* **42**, 332–333.

Szalay, F. S. (1975c). Where to draw the nonprimate–primate taxonomic boundary. *Folia Primatol.* **23**, 158–163.

Szalay, F. S. (1975d). Haplorhine relationships and the status of the Anthropoidea. *In* Primate Functional Morphology and Evolution (R. Tuttle, ed.), pp. 3–22. Mouton, The Hague.

Szalay, F. S. (1975e). Hunting-scavenging protohominids: A model for hominid origins. *Man, n.s.* **10**, 420–429.

Szalay, F. S. (1975f). Phylogeny of primate higher taxa: The basicranial evidence. *In* Phylogeny of the Primates: A Multidisciplinary Approach (W. P. Luckett and F. S. Szalay, eds.), pp. 91–125. Plenum Press, New York.

Szalay, F. S. (1975g). Phylogeny. adaptations and dispersal of the tarsiiform primates. *In* Phylogeny of the Primates: A Multidisciplinary Approach (W. P. Luckett and F. S. Szalay, eds.), pp. 357–404. Plenum Press, New York.

Szalay, F. S. (1976). Systematics of the Omomyidae (Tarsiiformes, Primates): taxonomy, phylogeny and adaptations. *Bull. Amer. Mus. Nat. Hist.* **156**, 157–450.

Szalay, F. S. (1977a). Constructing primate phylogenies: A search for testable hypotheses with maximum empirical content. *J. Human Evol.* **6**, 3–18.

Szalay, F. S. (1977b). Ancestors, descendants, sister-groups, and testing of phylogenetic hypotheses. *Syst. Zool.* **26**, 12–18.

Szalay, F. S. (1977c). Phylogenetic relationships and a classification of the eutherian Mammalia. *In* Major Patterns of Vertebrate Evolution (M. K. Hecht, *et al.*, eds.), pp. 315–374. Plenum Press, New York.

Szalay, F. S. and M. Dagosto. (MS) Locomotor adaptations as reflected in the humerus of Paleogene primates.

Szalay, F. S., and Decker, R. L. (1974). Origins, evolution and function of the tarsus in late Cretaceous eutherians and Paleocene primates. *In* Primate Locomotion (F. A. Jenkins, Jr., ed.), pp. 223–259. Academic Press, New York.

Szalay, F. S. and J. Drawhorn. (in press). Evolution and diversification of the Archonta in an arboreal milieu. *In* Tree Shrews. (W. P. Luckett, ed.). Plenum Press, New York.

Szalay, F. S., and Katz, C. (1973). Phylogeny of lemurs, galagos and lorises. *Folia Primatol.* **19**, 88–103.

Szalay, F. S., and Seligsohn, D. (1977). Why did the strepsirhine tooth comb evolve? *Folia Primatol.* **27**, 75–82.

Szalay, F. S., Tattersall, I., and Decker, R. L. (1975). Phylogenetic relationships of *Plesiadapis*—postcranial evidence. *In* Contributions to Primatology. Volume 5: Approaches to Primate Paleobiology (F. S. Szalay, ed.), pp. 136–166. Karger, Basel.

Szalay, F. S., and Wilson, J. A. (1976). Basicranial morphology of the early Tertiary tarsiiform *Rooneyia* from Texas. *Folia Primatol.* **25**, 288–293.

Takai, F. (1970). Fossil mammals from the Amud cave. *In* The Amud Man and His Cave Site (H. Suzuki. ed.), pp. 53–76. Academic Press of Japan, Tokyo.

Tattersall, I. (1968). A mandible of *Indraloris* (Primates, Lorisidae) from the Miocene of India. *Postilla* **123**, 1–10.

Tattersall, I. (1971). Revision of the subfossil Indriinae. *Folia Primatol.* **16**, 257–269.

Tattersall, I. (1973). Cranial anatomy of the Archaeolemurinae (Lemuroidea, Primates). *Anthropol. Papers Amer. Mus. Nat. Hist.* **52**, 1–110.

Tattersall, I. (1975). Notes on the cranial anatomy of the subfossil Malagasy Lemurs. *In* Lemur Biology (I. Tattersall and R. W. Sussman, eds.), pp. 111–124. Plenum Press, New York.

Tattersall, I., and Schwartz, J. H. (1974). Craniodental morphology and the systematics of the Malagasy Lemurs (Primates, Prosimii). *Anthropol. Papers Amer. Mus. Nat. Hist.* **52**, 137–192.

Tattersall, I., and Schwartz, J. H. (1975). Relationships among the Malagasy Lemurs, the Craniodental Evidence. *In* Phylogeny of the Primates: A Multidisciplinary Approach (W. P. Luckett and F. S. Szalay, eds.), pp. 299–312. Plenum Press, New York.

Teilhard de Chardin, P. (1916–1921). Sur Quelques Primates des Phosphorites du Quercy. *Ann. Paléontol.* **10**, 1–20.

Teilhard de Chardin, P. (9121–1922). Les mammifères de l'Éocène inferieur Francais et leurs gisements. *Ann. Paléontol.* **10**, 171–176.

Teilhard de Chardin, P. (1927). Les mammifères de l'Éocène inferieur de la Belgique. *Mem. Mus. Roy. Hist. Nat. Belgique* **36**, 1–33.

Teilhard de Chardin, P. (1938). The fossils from locality 12 of Choukoutien. *Paleontol. Sinica, n. s.,* **114**, 2–46.

Tekkaya, I. (1974). A new species of Tortonian anthropoid (Primates, Mammalia) from Anatolia. *Bull. Min. Res. Explor. Inst. Turkey* **83**, 148–165.

Temminck, C. J. (1849). Coup d'Oeil General sur les Possessions Neerlandaises dans l'Inde Archipelagique. Arnz, Leiden.

Temminck, C. J. (1853). Esquisses Zoologiques sur la Cote de Guine. Part I: Les Mammifères. E. J. Brill, Leiden.

Theis, O. (1926). Beiträge zur Kenntnis der Heppenlochfauna und der Fauna der Frankenbacher Sand. *Jb. Preussischen Geol. Landesamt* **46**, 576–615.

Thenius, E. (1959). Tertiär. 2, Wirbeltierfaunen. F. Enke, Stuttgart.

Thenius, E. (1965). Ein primaten-rest aus dem Altpleistozän von Voigtstedt in Thuringen. *Paläontol. Abh.* **2**, 683–689.

Thomas, O. (1903a). Notes on South American monkeys, bats, carnivores, and rodents, with descriptions of new species. *Ann. Mag. Nat. Hist., Ser. 7* **14**, 455–464.

Thomas, O. (1903b). On a new monkey. *Proc. Zool. Soc. London* 1903, 224–225.

Thomas, O. (1904). New *Callithrix, Midas, Felis, Rhipidomys* and *Proechimys* from Brazil and Ecuador. *Ann. Mag. Nat. Hist.* **7**(14), 188–196.

Thomas, O. (1913a). On some rare Amazonian mammals from the collection of the Para Museum. *Ann. Mag. Nat. Hist., Ser. 8* **11**, 130–136.

Thomas, O. (1913b). New mammals from South America. *Ann. Mag. Nat. Hist., Ser. 8* **12**, 567–574.

Thomas, O. (1927). A remarkable new monkey from Peru. *Ann. Mag. Nat. Hist., Ser. 9* **19**, 156–157.

Thomas, P. (1884). Quelques formations d'eau douce de l'Algérie. *Mem. Soc. Géol. France* **3**,(2), 1–53.

Thorington, R. W., and Groves, C. P. (1970). An annotated classification of the Cercopithecoidea. *In* Old World Monkeys (J. R. Napier and P. H. Napier, eds.), pp. 631–647. Academic Press, New York.

Thorndike, E. E. (1968). A microscopic study of the marmoset claw and nail. *Amer. J. Phys. Anthropol., n. s.* **28**, 247–253.

Tobias, P. V. (1967). Olduvai Gorge. Volume 2: The Cranium of *Australopithecus (Zinjanthropus) boisei.* Cambridge University Press, Cambridge.

Tobias, P. V. (1968). Middle and early upper Pleistocene members of the genus *Homo* in Africa. *In* Evolution und Hominisation (G. Kurth, ed.), 2nd ed., pp. 176–194. Fischer, Stuttgart.

Tobias, P. V. (1973a). Darwin's prediction and the African emergence of the genus *Homo. In* L'Origine dell'Uomo, pp. 63–85. *Accad. Naz. Lincei,* Roma, Quaderno **182**.

Tobias, P. V. (1973b). New developments in hominid paleontology in South and East Africa. *Annu. Rev. Anthropol.* **2**, 311–334.

Tobien, H. (1952). Die oberpliozäne Säugerfauna von Wölfersheim-Wetterau. *Z. Geol. Ges.* **104**, 191.

Tozzi, C. (1969). Segnalazione di una grotta con fauna fossile a Borgio (Savona). *Atti. Soc. Sci. Nat. Mem.* **76**, 195–208.

Tratz, E., and Heck, H. (1954). Der afrikanische Anthropoide "Bonobo," eine neue Menschenaffen gattung. *Säugetierkundliche Mitt.* **2**, 97–101.

Trevor Jones, J. R. (1972). The ethmoid, the vomer and the palatine bones from the baboon skull. *S. Afr. J. Sci.* pp. 156–161.

Trofimov, B. A., and Reshetov, V. Yu. (1975). [Asia as the center of mammalian development.] *Priroda* **8**, 32–43 (in Russian).

Trouessart, E. L. (1878). Catalogue des mammifères vivants et fossiles. *Rev. Mag. Zool.* **6**, 108–140.

Trouessart, E. L. (1879). Catalogue des mammifères vivants et fossiles. *Rev. Mag. Zool.* **7**, 223–230.

Trouessart. E. L. (1897). Catalogus Mammalium tam Viventium quam Fossilium, Vol. 1, R. Friedlander und Sohn, Berlin.

Trouessart, E. L. (1899). Catalogus Mammalium tam Viventium quam fossilium, Vol. 2. R. Friedlander und Sohn, Berlin.

Trouessart, E. L. (1904). Catalogus Mammalium. Quinquennale supplementum. R. Friedlander und Sohn, Berlin.

Tuttle, R. (1972). Functional and evolutionary biology of hylobatid hands and feet. *Gibbon Siamang* **1**, 136–206.

Vanbeneden, P.-J. (1838). Notice sur une nouvelle espèce de singe d'Afrique. *Bull. Acad. Roy. Sci. Belles-Lettres Bruxelles* **5**, 344–349.

Van Houten, F. B. (1945). Review of latest Paleocene and early Eocene mammalian faunas. *J. Paleontol.* **19**, 421–461.

Van Valen, L. (1965). Treeshrews, primates and fossils. *Evolution* **19**, 137–151.

Van Valen, L. (1966). Deltatheridia, a new order of mammals. *Bull. Amer. Mus. Nat. Hist.* **132**, 1–126.

Van Valen, L. (1967). New Paleocene insectivores and insectivore classification. *Bull. Amer. Mus. Nat. Hist.* **135**, 217–284.

Van Valen, L. (1969). A classification of the Primates. *Amer. J. Phys. Anthropol.*, n. s. **30**, 295–296.

Van Valen, L., and Sloan, R. E. (1965). The earliest primates. *Science* **150**, 743–745.

Vereschagin, N. K. (1959). The mammals of the Caucasus: A history of the evolution of the Fauna. Zool. Inst. Acad. Sci. U.S.S.R. Moscow (in Russian). [English transl: Jerusalem, Israel Program for Scientific Translations, 1967.]

Verheyen, W. N. (1962). Contribution à la craniologie comparèe des primates. *Mus. Roy. Afr. Cent., Tervuren, Belgique, Ser. 8, Sci. Zool.* **105**, 1–247.

Verma, B. C. (1969). *Procynocephalus pinjorii*, sp. nov. A new fossil primate from Pinjor beds (lower Pleistocene), east of Chandigarh. *J. Paleontol. Soc. India* **13**, 53–57.

Verschuren, J. (1972). Contribution à l'écologie des Primates, Pholidota, Carnivora, Tubulidentata et Hyracoidea (Mammifères). *In* Exploration du Parc National des Virunga. Mission F. Bourlière et J. Verschuren. Fasc. **3**, pp. 1–61. Brussels, Fondation pour favoriser les recherches scientifiques en Afrique.

Vieillot, L. J. P. (1807). Histoire naturelle des oiseaux de l'Amerique septentrionale, Vol. 2. Paris.

Villalta, J. F.. and Crusafont-Pairo, M. (1944). Dos nuevos antropomorfos del Mioceno espanol y su situacion dentro de la moderna sistematica de los simidos. *Notas Comun. Ins. Geol. Min.* **3**, 9–139.

Virey, J. J. (1819). Singes. *In* Nouveau Dictionnaire d'Histoire Naturelle, Nouv. Ed., Volume 31, pp. 257–299. Déterville, Paris.

Vlcek, E. (1961). [Finds of old Pleistocene apes on the territory of Czechoslovakia.] *Acta Facultatis Rerum Nat. Univ. Comenianae, Anthropol.* **5**, 137–154 (in Czech).

Vogel, C. (1966). Morphologische studien am gesichtschädel Cattarrhiner primaten. *Biblio. Primatol.* **4**, 1–226.

Vogel, C. (1968). The phylogenetical evaluations of some characters and some morphological trends in the evolution of the skull in catarrhine primates. *In* Taxonomy and Phylogeny of Old World Primates with Reference to the Origin of Man (B. Chiarelli, ed.), pp. 21–55. Rosenberg and Sellier, Turin.

Voigt, F. S. (ed.) (1831). Cuvier's Das Theirreich. Brodhaus, Leipzig.

Voigt, F. S. (1835). Thierfahrten im Hildburghauser Sand-

steine (*Palaeopithecus*). *N. Jb. Min. Geol. Paläont.* 1835, 322–326.

Vram, U. G. (1922). Sul genere *Theropythecus*. *Arch. Zool. Ital.* **10**, 169–214.

Vrba, E. S. (1975). Some evidence of chronology and palaeoecology of Sterkfontein Swartkrans and Kromdraai from the fossil Bovidae. *Nature* (London) **254**, 3-1–304.

Wagner, A. (1839). Fossile ueberreste von einem affenschadel und andern Säugethieren aus Griechenland. *Gelehrte Anzeigen Bayerisches Akad. Wiss.* Munich **38**, 301–312.

Wagner, A. (1840). Fossile Ueberreste von einem Affen und einigen anderen Säugethieren aus Griechenland. *Abh. Kon. Bayerisches Akad. Wiss. Math-Nat. (II) Kl.* **3**, 153–190.

Wagner, A. (1847a) Urweltliche Säugthier-Ueberreste aus Griechenland. *Abh. Kon. Bayerische Akad. Wiss. Math.-Physik. (II) Kl.* **5**, 333–378.

Wagner, A. (1847b). Beiträge zur Kentniss der Säugethieres Amerika's. Pt. 3. *Abh. Kon. Bayerisches Akad. Wiss. Math-Nat. (II)-K1.* **5**, 405–480.

Wagner, A. (1855). Die Affen, Zahnlucker, Beutelthiere, Hufthiere, Insektenfresser und Handflugler, pt. 5. Palm, Erlangen.

Wagner, A. (1857). Neue beiträge zur Kenntniss der fossilen Säugthier Ueberreste von Pikermi. *Abh. K. Bayerische Akad. Wissen., II Cl.* **8**, 111–130.

Wahlert, J. H. (1973). *Protoptychus*, a hystricomorphous rodent from the late Eocene of North America. *Breviora* **419**, 1–14.

Walker, A. (1967a). Locomotor adaptations in recent and fossil Madagascan lemurs, Ph.D. thesis, pp. 1–535. University of London, London.

Walker, A. (1967b). Patterns of extinction among the subfossil Madagascan lemuroids. *In* Pleistocene Extinctions: The Search for a Cause (P. S. Martin and H. E. Wright, Jr., eds.), pp. 425–532. Yale University Press, New Haven.

Walker, A. (1970). Post-cranial remains of the Miocene Lorisidae of east Africa. *Amer. J. Phys. Anthropol.* **33**, 249–262.

Walker, A. (1972). The dissemination and segregation of early primates in relation to continental configuration. *In* Calibration of Hominid Evolution (W. W. Bishop and J. A. Miller, eds.), pp. 195–218. Scottish Academic Press, Edinburgh.

Walker, A. (1973). New *Australopithecus* femora from E. Rudolf, Kenya. *J. Human Evol.* **2**, 545–555.

Walker, A. (1974a). Locomotor adaptations in past and present prosimians. *In* Primate Locomotion (F. A. Jenkins, Jr., ed.), pp. 349–381. Academic Press, New York.

Walker, A. (1974b). A review of the Miocene Lorisidae of East Africa. *In* Prosimian Biology (R. D. Martin, G. A. Doyle, and A. C. Walker, eds.), pp. 435–447. Duckworth, London.

Walker, A. (1976a). Remains attributable to *Australopithecus* in the East Rudolf succession. *In* Earliest Man and Environments in the Lake Rudolf Basin (Y. Coppens, F. C. Howell, G. L. Isaac, and R. E. F. Leakey, eds.), pp. 484–489. University of Chicago Press. Chicago.

Walker. A. (1976b). Splitting times among hominoids deduced from the fossil record. *In* Molecular Anthropology (M. Goodman and R. E. Tashian, eds.), pp. 63–77. Plenum Press, New York.

Walker, A., and Andrews, P. (1973). Reconstruction of the dental arcades of *Ramapithecus wickeri*. *Nature* (London) **244**, 313–314.

Walker, A., and Rose. M. D. (1968). Fossil hominoid vertebra from the Miocene of Uganda. *Nature* (London) **217**, 980–981.

Walker, E. P. (1964). Mammals of the World. Johns Hopkins University Press, Baltimore.

Wallace, A. R. (1876). The Geographic Distribution of Animals, Vols. 1 and 2. MacMillan, London.

Wallace, J. (1975). Dietary adaptations of *Australopithecus* and early *Homo*. *In* Paleoanthropology. Morphology and Paleoecology (R. Tuttle, ed.), pp. 203–223. Mouton, The Hague.

Wallace, J. (1978). Evolutionary trends in the early hominid dentition: A study in paleoanatomy. *In* Early African Hominids (C. J. Jolly, ed.), pp. 285–310. Duckworth, London.

Warburton, F. E. (1967). The purpose of classification. *Syst. Zool.* **16**, 241–245.

Washburn, S. L., and Patterson, B. (1951). Evolutionary importance of the South African "man-apes." *Nature* (London) **167**, 650–651.

Waterhouse, G. R. (1838). *Proc. Zool. Soc. London*, 5(57), 87.

Weber. M. (1904). Die Säugetiere. G. Fischer, Jena.

Weber, M. (1928). Die Säugetiere; Systematischer Teil. G. Fischer, Jena.

Weber, M., and Abel, O. (1928). Die Säugetiere, Band II. G. Fischer, Jena.

Weidenreich, F. (1928). Entwicklungs-und Rassetypen des *Homo primigenius*. *Natur Mus.* **58**, 1–13, 51–62.

Weidenreich, F. (1932a). Eine neuentdeckte übergangsform und heutigen Menschen. *Natur Mus.* **62**, 384–389.

Weidenreich, F. (1932b). Uber pithekoide merkmale bei *Sinanthropus pekinensis* und seine stammesgeschichtliche Beurteilung. *Z. Anat. Entwicklungsges.* **99**, 212–253.

Weidenreich, F. (1940). Some problems dealing with ancient man. *Amer. Anthropol.* **42**, 375–383.

Weidenreich, F. (1943). The skull of *Sinanthropus pekinensis*; a comparative study on a primitive hominid skull. *Paleontol. Sinica* n.s. D, No. 10, pp. 1–484.

Weidenreich, F. (1944). Giant early man from Java and South China. *Science* **99**, 479–482.

Weidenreich, F. (1946). Apes, Giants and Man. University of Chicago Press, Chicago.

Weigelt, J. (1933). Neue Primaten aus der mitteleozänen (oberlutetischen) Braunkohle des Geiseltals. *Nova Acta Leopoldina* **1**, 97–156.

Weigelt, J. (1939). Die Aufdeckung der bisher ältesten tertiaren Säugetierfauna Deutschlands. *Nova Acta Leopoldina* **7**, 515–528.

Weinert, H. (1931). Der Sinanthropus pekinensis als Bestatigung des *Pithecanthropus erectus*. *Z. Morphol. Anthropol.* **28**, 159–187.

Weinert, H. (1936). Der Urmenschenschädel von Steinheim. *Z. Morphol. Anthropol.* **35**, 463–518.

Weinert, H. (1937). Der Unterkiefer von Mauer zur 30-jahrigen Wiederkehr seiner Entdeckung. *Z. Morphol. Anthropol.* **37**, 102–113.

Weinert, H. (1938). Der erste afrikanische Affenmensch, *Africanthropus njarensis*. *Der Biol.* **7**, 125.

Weinert, H. (1950). Uber die neuen Vor- und Fruhmenschenfunde aus Afrika, Java, China und Frankreich. *Z. Morphol. Anthropol.* **42**, 113–148.

Wells, L. H. (1969). *Homo sapiens afer* Linn.–Content and earliest representatives. *S. Afr. Arch. Bull.* **24**, 127–173.

Wells, L. H. (1971). Africa and the ancestry of man. *S. Afr. J. Sci.* **67**, 276–283.

Werthe, E. (1928). Der fossile mensch. Grundzuge einer Paläanthropologie. G. Borntraeger, Berlin.

West, R. M. (1973). Geology and Mammalian Paleontology of the New Fork–Big Sandy Area, Sublette County, Wyoming. *Fieldiana* (Geol.) **29**, 1–193.

White, T. D. (1975). Geomorphology to paleoecology: *Gigantopithecus* reappraised. *J. Human Evol.* **4**, 219–233.

Wiegers, F. (1915). Die geologische Alter des *Homo mousteriensis*. *Z. Ethnol.* **47**, 68–72.

Wilder, H. H. (1926). The Pedigree of the Human Race. Henry Holt, New York.

Williams, E. E., and Koopman, K. E. (1952). West Indian fossil monkeys. *Amer. Mus. Nov.* **1546**, 1–16.

Wilser, L. (1898). Menschenrassen und Weltgeschichte. *Naturw. Wochenschr.* **13**, 1–8.

Wilser, L. (1900). Der %*Pithecanthropus erectus* und die Abstammung des Menschen. *Verh. naturw. ver. Karlsruhe* **13**, 551–576.

Wilser, L. (1903). Die Namen der Menschenrassen. *Globus* **84**, 303–307.

Wilson, J. A. (1966). A new primate from the earliest Oligocene, West Texas, preliminary report. *Folia Primatol.* **4**, 227–240.

Wilson, J. A., and Szalay, F. S. (1976). New adapid primate of European affinities from Texas. *Folia Primatol.* **25**, 294–312.

Wilson, J. A., and Szalay, F. S. (1977). *Mahgarita*, new name for *Margarita* Wilson and Szalay, 1976, Non Leach 1814 (1819; Lea, 1836, 1838; Lister, 1894). *J. Paleontol.* **51**, 643.

Wilson, R. W., and Szalay, F. S. (1972). New Paromomyid Primate from Middle Paleocene Beds, Kutz Canyon Area, San Juan Basin, New Mexico. *Amer. Mus. Nov.* **2499**, 1–18.

Winge, H. (1895). Jordfundne og nulevende aber (primates) fra Lagôa Santa, Minas Gerais, Brasilien. *E. Mus. Lundii (Copenhagen)* **2**, 1–45.

Wolpoff, M. H., and Lovejoy, C. O. (1975). A rediagnosis of the genus *Australopithecus*. *J. Human Evol.* **4**, 275–276.

Woo, J. K. (1957). *Dryopithecus* teeth from Keiyuan, Yunnan province. *Vert. Palas.* **1**, 25–32.

Woo, J. K. (1958). New materials of *Dryopithecus* from Keiyuan, Yunnan. *Vert. Palas.* **2**, 31–43.

Woo, J. K. (1962). The mandibles and dentition of *Gigantopithecus*. *Palaeontol. Sinica* **11**, 1–94.

Woo, J. K. (1964). Mandible of the *Sinanthropus*-type discovered at Lantian, Shensi. *Vert. Palas.* **8**, 1–17.

Woo, J. K., and Chow, M. (1957). New materials of the

earliest primate known in China—*Hoanghonius stehlini*. *Vert. Palas.* **1**, 267–272.

Wood, A. E. (1962). The early Tertiary rodents of the family Paramyidae. *Trans. Amer. Phil. Soc.* **52**, 1–261.

Wood, A. E. (1968). Early Cenozoic Mammalian faunas Fayum Province, Egypt. *Bull. Peabody Mus. Nat. Hist. Yale Univ.* **28**, 23–105.

Wood, S. (1844). Record of the discovery of an alligator with several new mammalia in the freshwater strata at Hordwell. *Ann. Mag. Nat. Hist. London* **14**, 349–351.

Wood, S. (1846). On the discovery of an alligator and of several new Mammalia in the Hordwell Cliff, with observations on the geological phenomena of that locality. *Geol. J. London* **1**, 1–7.

Woodward, A. S. (1921). A new cave man from Rhodesia, South Africa. *Nature* (London) **108**, 371–372.

Wortman, J. L. (1903–1904). Studies of Eocene Mammalia in the Marsh Collections, Peabody Museum. Part 2. Primates. *Amer. J. Sci., Ser.* 4 (**15**): 163–176, 399–414, 419–436; (**16**) 345–368; (**17**) 23–33, 133–140, 203–214.

Wurmbach, F. van (1787). De Kahau, een lang-startige aap. *Verhandelingen van het Bataaviaansch Genootschap van Kunsten en Wetenschappen, Leiden* **2**, 345–354.

Wüst, K. (1950). Über den Unterkiefer von Mauer. *Z. Morphol. Anthropol.* **42**, 1–112.

Young, C. C. (1932). On some fossil mammals from Yunnan. *Bull. Geol. Soc. China* **9**, 383–393.

Young, C. C. (1934). On the Insectivora, Chiroptera, Rodentia and Primates other than *Sinanthropus* from locality 1 at Choukoutien. *Palaeontol. Sinica* **8**, 122–128.

Young, C. C., and Pei, W. C. (1933). On the fissure deposits of Chinghsinghsien with remarks on the Cenozoic geology of the same area. *Bull. Geol. Soc. China* **13**, 63–71.

Young, C. C., and Liu, P. T. (1950). On the mammalian fauna at Koloshan, near Chunking, Szechuan. *Bull. Geol. Soc. China* **30**, 43–90.

Zapfe, H. (1949). Eine mittelmiozäne Säugetierfauna aus einer Spaltenfullung bei Neudorf a. d. March (CSR). *Anz. Österreichischen Akad. Wiss., Math.-Nat. Kl., 1949* pp. 173–181.

Zapfe, H. (1952). Die *Pliopithecus*-Funde aus der Spaltenfüllung von Neudorf a. d. March (CSR). *Verhandel. Geol. Bundesanst., Sonderheft C*, pp. 126–130.

Zapfe, H. (1958). The skeleton of *Pliopithecus (Epipliopithecus) vindobonensis* Zapfe and Hürzeler. *Amer. J. Phys. Anthropol., n. s.,* **16**, 441–455.

Zapfe, H. (1961a). Die Primatenfunde aus der miozänen spaltenfüllung von Neudorf an der March (Devinska Nova Ves), Tschechoslowakei. *Mem. Suisses Paleontol.* **78**, 5–293.

Zapfe, H. (1961b). Ein Primatenfund aus der Miozänen Molasse von Oberösterreich. *Z. Morphol. Anthropol.* **51**, 247–267.

Zapfe, H. (1961c). Ergebnisse einer Untersuchung der *Austriacopithecus*-Reste aus dem Mittelmiozän von Klein-Hadersdorf, N.-Ö., und eines neuen Primatenfunds aus der Molasse von Trimmelkam, O.-Ö. *Sitz-Ber. Österreichischer Akad. Wiss. Wien, Math.-Nat. Kl.* **170**, 139–148.

Zapfe, H. (1969). Primates. *In* Catalogus Fossilium Austriae (O. Kuhn, ed.), pp. 1–16. Springer-Verlag, Wien.

Zapfe, H., and Hürzeler, J. (1957). Die fauna der Miozänen Spaltenfullung von Neudorf an der March (CSR), Primates. *Sitz-Ber. Österreichischer Akad. Wiss. Wien., Math.-Nat. Kl.* **166**, 114–123.

Zdansky, O. (1930). Die alttertiären Säugetiere Chinas nebst stratigraphischen Bemerkungen. *Palaeontol. Sinica* **6**, 1–87.

Zetterstedt, J. W. (1840). Insecta Lapponica. Voss, Leipzig.

Zimmerman, J. L. (1780). Geographische geschichte des menschen und der vierfussigen thiere. Weygandsche Buchhandlung, Leipzig.

Zittel, K. A. von. (1892). Handbuch der Palaeontologie. Volumes 3 and 4: Vertebrata. Munich and Leipzig.

GLOSSARY

A

acetabulum   the hip socket.

Adapisoricidae an archaic family of the Erinaceomorpha (hedgehogs, shrews, and moles, and the shrew-derived *Solenodon*), a member of which is probably ancestral to the hedgehogs.

adaptation an adaptation is an aspect of an organism, a feature, that has at least one biological role interacting with a selection force. Not all attributes of an organism can be labeled adaptations, nor can all differences between features be considered adaptive differences. Similarly, not all evolutionary changes of individual characters may be adaptive evolution (see W. Bock, 1977).

advanced character   *see* derived character.

afoveate lacking a small depression in the retina, the fovea centralis, where vision is most acute.

allometry (allometric) the relative growth relationships between two parts of an organism. This can be ascertained from either a growth series of the same species (developmental allometry) or a comparison of different-sized individuals of the same species. Often comparisons are made between different-sized individuals of closely related species, and the resulting patterns are evaluated to determine whether different morphological patterns are the results of size dif-

ferences only, based on a common developmental program.

allopatric inhabiting different regions (opposite of sympatric).

alpha taxonomy taxonomic work concerned with the recognition and diagnosis of species as distinct from others.

alveolus (pl., alveoli) the cavity or socket in the bone for the root of a tooth.

anagenesis (anagenetic) evolutionary change through time in a lineage, in contrast to cladogenesis, which is splitting of a lineage. Anagenesis can occur without speciation but cladogenesis axiomatically incorporates anagenetic change. Phyletic evolution and anagenesis may be interchangeably used.

ancestral character same as primitive or plesiomorphic. The term "generalized," although employed in the sense of ancestral, is not widely used and it is potentially confusing. Ancestral characters are the conditions in an ancestor that either were retained unmodified or were transformed into the derived condition(s). An ancestral character for a group of descendants can be a derived character of the ancestor. *See also* derived character.

ankylosed fused, as, for example, in the case of the mandibular symphysis of some taxa.

Anthropoidea   a grouping that unites the Platyrrhini and Catarrhini (see text discussion under Haplorhini, p. 189).

anthropomorph   an ape-like animal, hominoid. Used here in order to avoid the taxonomic bias inherent in the terms hominoid or hominid.

Apatemyidae   a Paleogene family of insectivorans adapted to a gnawing habitus, possibly similar (convergently) to those of the aye-aye and the marsupial striped phalangers.

apical wear   wear of any sort on the top (apex) of a tooth.

apomorphic character   *see* derived character.

appendicular skeleton   composed of the bones of the limbs.

arboreal   living in or being adapted to living in trees.

Archonta   a cohort of mammals which includes the Scandentia (the living tree shrews and fossil relatives), Primates, Dermoptera (the living colugos or "flying lemurs" and their fossil relatives), and Chiroptera (bats).

archontan   member of the cohort Archonta.

Arctocyonia   an order of ancient, primarily Paleogene ungulates which contains taxa ancestral or closely related to modern ungulates, whales, and possibly primates.

asterion   the point on the surface of the skull where the lambdoid, parietomastoid, and occipitomastoid sutures meet.

astragalus   the talus, the ankle bone.

autapomorphy   a uniquely derived condition of a taxon.

axial skeleton   composed of the bones of the head and trunk.

B

basion   the point at the forward tip of the foramen magnum on the sagittal line.

Bassarycyon   the cuataquil, an arboreal member of the Procyonidae, the family in which racoons are classified.

beta thegosed   a condition of dental wear in which the facet is parallel to the enamel prisms.

bipedalism   mode of locomotion, utilizing the hindlegs for support exclusively.

bilophodont   having two transverse crests on a tooth as in cercopithecids, some marsupial phalangers, tapirs, and several other groups of mammals.

biocenose   sampling of living fauna. In paleontology, implies an assemblage whose composition reflects the actual frequencies of species in a once-living local fauna. Often the result of a natural catastrophe.

biological role   the manner in which an organism uses a form–function complex (an adaptation) during the course of its life in its environment. The biological role of a character therefore is environmentally predicated. *See also* form; function.

biostratigraphy   the science of age and environment determination of rock formations by the study of both the rocks and fossils found in them.

boreal   pertaining to the northerly latitudes on land (e.g., boreal forests).

brachial index   radius length × 100 divided by humerus length.

brachiating   progression in trees by swinging with the arms from underneath one branch to under another.

bregma   the point at or near the top of the skull where the frontal and parietal bones meet.

buccal   pertaining to the outer side of the teeth facing the inside of the (lips and) cheek; same as labial.

buccal phase   during mastication when the lower teeth on the active side make extreme lateral (buccal) contact with the upper ones and proceed to centric occlusion.

buccolingual   pertaining to the transverse diameter of teeth or to direction.

bunodont   having teeth with low rounded cusps, usually capable of performing a variety of biological roles.

bulla   bone surrounding the middle ear ventrally.

C

calcaneus (calcaneum)   the heel bone.

calvarium   the braincase without the face.

calotte   the braincase without the face or base.

caniniform   caninelike, in reference to teeth that are attenuated with a sharp point.

Carabelli's cusp   a cusp on hominid teeth in the same position as the pericone; see Figure 6, p. 20.

carnivore (carnivorous) flesh-eating animals. Usually in reference to species that hunt at least as much as they scavenge. The term has behavioral but not taxonomic meaning.

carnivoran member of the order Carnivora.

catamenial monthly, menstrual.

caudal pertaining or closer to the tail end of the body.

category a group of taxa having the same rank in a Linnean hierarchy of classification; e.g., species, genus, or family categories. *See also* rank; taxon.

cementum the layer of bony tissue covering the root of a tooth, extending onto the crown in some nonprimates.

centric occlusion occlusion of teeth at rest when the protocone of the upper molars rests in the talonid basin of lower molars.

cervix pertaining to teeth it denotes the necklike constriction between root and crown, or often the enamel–dentine or enamel–cementum junction on the basal periphery of the crown.

character a particular aspect of an organism. Used interchangeably with feature. It is a part of the organism which the investigator chooses to delineate and treat as an entity in a study. Not all characters or features are necessarily adaptations.

cheiridia the rays, i.e., the metacarpals or metatarsals and phalanges of either the hand or foot.

cingulum a ledgelike rim, either partially or completely surrounding the base of the crown of a tooth, always above (apical to) the enamel-dentine junction.

clade a phyletic lineage.

cladogenesis evolution by speciation (i.e., branching or splitting).

claw climbing locomotion on and within trees by the use of sharp claws (falculae). It is considered to be the ancestral locomotor mode of primates. At its beginning, claw climbing may or may not have involved grasping by the pollex and hallux, but plesiadapiform foot bones suggest that grasping was already evolved within the first radiation of the order. Grasp leaping probably evolved from the claw climbing stage.

cline gradual change of a feature in a species or a lineage from one region to another, or from one time level to another.

Coleoptera an order of insects, including the beetles and weevils.

condyle a rounded eminence with a smooth surface which is received into a cavity of the bone with which it articulates.

conservative retaining many ancestral conditions, little changed from its ancestor.

conspecific of the same species.

contralateral the side opposite to the actively chewing side of the dentition.

convergence evolutionary development of similarities in two or more species from less similar conditions in their respective ancestries (essentially equivalent to parallelism). Such similarities are analogous.

corpus, mandibular the body of the mandible, as opposed to the ramus or vertical portion. The terms "horizontal ramus" (corpus) and "ascending ramus" are also used.

cranial pertaining or closer to the head end of the body.

crest a sharp and narrow ridge of bone; often also used as descriptive of ridges on tooth crowns.

crepuscular organisms which are active during twilight hours.

cristodont crown of tooth with distinct crest(s).

crural index tibia length × 100 divided by the length of the femur.

crus part of the leg between the knee and the tarsals. Usually used as a collective name for the tibia and fibula.

cursorial pertaining to habitually running or an adaptation to running.

curve of Spee the arc exhibited by the occlusal surfaces of the mandibular dentition on either side.

cuspidate having distinct, pointed cusps.

D

Dactylonax, Dactylopsila the two marsupial striped phalangers with ecological niches similar to the aye-aye (*Daubentonia*).

deciduous shed; refers to the elements of the first or "milk" dentition. The incisors, canines, and premolars are usually shed and are replaced in most placental mammals.

derived character same as advanced or apomorphic. The term "specialized," although employed sometimes in the sense of advanced, is not a preferred usage. Derived characters are the conditions in one or more species which transformed from a state designated as ancestral (or primitive, or plesiomorphic). The designation has only contextual significance in a given phylogenetic hypothesis. A derived character in one group may be an ancestral feature in a taxon descended from it. *See also* ancestral character.

Dermoptera   order of mammals that includes the living colugos ("flying lemurs") and fossil relatives.

dichobunid artiodactyls   early members of the order Artiodactyla ·which had bunodont rather than selenodont (crescent-ridged) teeth.

diaphysis   the shaft of a long bone.

diastema   the gap between two adjacent teeth.

dimorphism   marked bimodal differentiation in size and shape of certain features, for example, between the sexes.

distal   farther from the origin of a structure, opposite of proximal. When employed in relation to teeth, it is in reference to that surface of the tooth which is followed by the next tooth in the series, thus, the opposite of mesial; see the legend to Figure 6, p. 20. In terms of the appendicular skeleton, it refers to the ends toward the tips of long bones and digits.

distobuccal   distal and buccal on a tooth crown. *See also* buccal; distal.

distolingual   distal and lingual.

diurnal   active during the daytime.

dorsal   closer to the back.

E

epiphysis   the ossification at the end of a mammalian long bone.

epoch   a subdivision of a period of geological time, e.g., Paleocene, Pleistocene.

Erinaceidae   living and fossil hedgehogs.

Erinaceomorpha   a suborder of the Insectivora, consisting of hedgehogs and ancient relatives. *See also* Adapisoricidae.

eucatarrhine   the nonparapithecid catarrhines, families Cercopithecidae, Hominidae, Pliopithecidae, and Oreopithecidae. As recognized by Delson (1977b), a formal or informal taxon reflecting the major phyletic division between parapithecids (paracatarrhines) and all other catarrhines.

euprimate   a vernacular coined for the "modern" primates. Strepsirhines and haplorhines are jointly referred to by this term, in contrast to the more archaic plesiadapiforms.

Eutheria   the taxon which includes all placental mammals.

eversion   in anatomy, usually in reference to the foot as its sole is turned outward; opposite of inversion.

exodaenodont   pertaining to a tooth crown on which the enamel forms a broad and rounded rim well beyond the circumference of the width of the tooth at the cervix or at the base of the crown where the roots join; as in picrodontids and some nectarivorous and frugivorous bats.

extant   still existing, not extinct.

F

facet   a small smooth articular surface on a bone; also applies to contact surfaces of tooth crowns.

facial angle   the angle measuring projection or elongation of the face or snout, lower in long-faced taxa. Defined by the nasion–prosthion chord and the alveolar plane.

facultative   adapted to a certain habitus or role, but not restricted to it, as opposed to obligate.

falcula   compressed, curved claw with a sharp point.

fauna   the animal species of a geographical area at a stated age.

faunal level   biostratigraphical designation of the age within a particular rock unit.

Ferungulata   a cohort employed in the past to unite the Carnivora and the ungulate orders.

folivore (folivorous)   an animal with a diet consisting mainly of leaves.

foramen   an aperture or hole.

form   the properties of material composition and arrangement of a feature are its form. *See also* biological role; function.

fossa   any depression on a bone, or on the crown of a tooth.

frugivore (frugivorous)   an animal with a diet consisting of fruits primarily.

function (mechanical)   those physical–chemical properties which arise from the form of a feature or character. A form–function complex may have several biological roles. *See also* biological role; form.

G

gastropods groups of the Mollusca having either shells (e.g., snails or limpets, etc.) or no shells (e.g., slugs, etc.).

generitype *see* type species.

genotype the sum total of the hereditary factors of an organism.

genus (pl., genera) category of classification above the species level. A taxon in this category may include one or many species having a (unique) common ancestor and relatively similar adaptations.

glabella the central and most prominent point on the brow ridges.

glabrous hairless, smooth.

gnathal (gnathic) pertaining to the jaws and teeth.

glacial an interval of cold climate during which continental ice caps are formed; also glaciation.

gonion in primates which lost the spurlike process of the mandible, the lower rear corner of the mandible where corpus and ramus meet; roughly equivalent to the angle in other mammals. The gonial angle measures the angulation between corpus and ramus.

gradualism sometimes referred to as phyletic gradualism, a view which sees all (most) evolutionary change as slow and gradual. This has been previously called bradytelic (slow) evolution. It is not to be confused with phyletic evolution, a concept independent of the rate at which evolutionary change takes place. *See also* phyletic evolution.

grasp climbing and clinging progression by firm grasping and slow climbing with the body in various positions either above or below the branches. Locomotor mode characteristic of the lorisines and perhaps some of the Malagasy subfossils.

grasp leaping locomotor category hypothesized to be the behavior responsible for the development of the superior grasping adaptations of the first euprimates, the ancestral strepsirhines. Jumping rapidly from branch to branch necessitated the ability to land accurately on a particular segment of branch and be subsequently securely anchored to that point.

ground walking progression on the ground on the soles of all four feet.

gumivore (gumivorous) animal with a diet consisting mainly of gum or other tree exudates. Exudativory is another term for this diet category.

H

habitus aspects of an organism which reflect the modification of its form–function complexes to its way of life, in contrast to those aspects of its features which indicate habits and conditions preceding it. *See also* heritage.

hallux big toe.

Haplorhini Tarsiiformes, Platyrrhini, and Catarrhini; see suborder Haplorhini in text, p. 189.

herbivore (herbivorous) animal with a diet consisting primarily of plants.

heritage aspects of an organism's features which indicate adaptations to a way of life preceding the one to which that organism is adapted. *See also* habitus.

holophyletic pertaining to a monophyletic taxonomic group which includes all of the descendants of any member of that group. For example, the Chiroptera, the bats, presumably include all species which ever evolved from a winged ancestral chiropteran. *See also* monophyletic; paraphyletic.

holotype *see* type (type specimen).

homologous (homology) two or more features (form–function complexes) are said to be homologous if they were derived from a common ancestor having such a feature. This is clearly a theoretical definition. In practice, operational criteria are based on similarity among species anywhere in the ontogeny of the features analyzed. Unique and special similarities which are judged unlikely to be convergent are hypothesized to be homologues of each other. *See also* convergence.

honing sharpening, usually in reference to teeth. *See also* sectorial; thegosis.

Hymenoptera a large group of insects with a biting or sucking mouth. They include the wasps, bees, and ants, etc.

Hyopsodontidae a family of Paleogene arctocyonians (condylarths, proto-ungulates) members of which have often been mistaken for primates.

hypodigm the sample of specimens on which the parameters and characteristics of a particular species are based.

I

ICZN the International Commission for Zoological Nomenclature, the body which rules on questions of validity and priority of taxonomic names in zoology.

incisiform pertaining usually to a canine or premolar which is similar to the incisor shape of the same animal.

inca bones supernumerary bones on the skull at lambda.

inferior below.

inion a projection in the sagittal line of the occipital bone usually at or below the most posterior point of that bone. It serves as a point of origin for some of the neck muscles.

Insectivora the order Insectivora, as accepted here, consists of the suborders Erinaceomorpha, Soricomorpha, and Zalambdodonta (q.v.).

insectivoran a member of the order Insectivora.

insectivore (insectivorous) animal with a diet consisting mainly of insects and small vertebrates. The term has behavioral but no taxonomic meaning.

interglacial an interval of warm climate between two glaciations.

intermembral index humerus plus radius length × 100 divided by femur plus tibia length.

interorbital pillar region between the medial edges of the orbits. Composed of the nasal bones, frontal process of the frontal bone, and parts of the maxillae, ethmoids, and/or lacrimals.

interstadial a warm interval between two maxima (stadials) of a single glacial.

inversion in anatomy usually in reference to the foot as its sole is turned inward.

ipsilateral the side which is actively engaged in chewing (e.g., the condyle on the ipsilateral side). *See also* contralateral.

K

knuckle walking quadrupedal locomotor mode, utilizing the second row of phalanges of the hand for support; used by gorillas and chimps.

kyphosis in anatomy pertaining to the bending of the skull downward behind the sella turcica (the depression for the pituitary gland), thus effectively increasing the angle between the posterior and anterior floors of the skull.

L

labial *see* buccal.

Lagomorpha (lagomorph) an order of mammals accepted here as consisting of four suborders, the Duplicidentata (rabbits, hares, pikas), Macroscelididae (elephant shrews), and the two fossil suborders, Anagalida and Mixodontia.

lambda the point where two parietal bones and the occipital bone meet.

lamina a thin plate of bone.

land-mammal age a specific interval of geological time characterized by an assemblage of mammal species, usually of a given continent.

lateral farther from the midline of the body.

leaping and claw climbing locomotor mode characteristic of *Euoticus* and marmosets. This category may have evolved from leaping and vertical grasp clinging (for *Euoticus*) and grasp leaping (for marmosets) by the secondary compression of the nails into falculae. In marmosets this specialized mode is related to movement on broad, not easily graspable branches and trunks.

leaping and vertical grasp clinging referred to originally as vertical clinging and leaping, but used here in a more restricted sense. It is a special case of grasp leaping, when the animal lands on a vertical substrate, grasps by feet and then by hands, and then either remains in a vertical resting position or pushes off again. It is considered to be the ancestral locomotor mode of the strepsirhines by some students. In this book, vertical clinging and leaping (referred to as leaping and vertical grasp clinging) is considered a derived modification from the more ancient grasp leaping. *See also* claw climbing, leaping and claw climbing, and grasp leaping.

linea a bony ridge that is not as thick as a torus or as sharp as a crest.

lineage *see* phyletic lineage.

lingual pertaining to the side of the teeth facing the tongue when the tongue is in between the right and left tooth rows.

lingual phase during mastication when the lower teeth on the active side move lingually after a centric occlusion.

lithostratigraphy rock stratigraphy.

loph a pair of cusps joined by a ridge or crest, on upper teeth; lophid on lowers.

M

machairodont saber-toothed "cat" of the genus *Machairodus* or a close relative.

macropodid member of the kangaroo family, Macropodidae.

Marsupicarnivora (marsupicarnivoran) an order of the Metatheria (marsupials) including the primitive American didelphoids (including borhyaenids) and the Australasian dasyurids and thylacinids.

mastication the act of chewing.

meatus a short canal.

mechanical function the physical and chemical properties of a feature which arise from its form, without reference to the environment in which the organism lives.

medial closer to the midline of the body.

median on the midline of the structure involved.

meniscus a plate of fibrous cartilage which divides a joint cavity between two bones into two parts, as in the jaw joint of mammals or between the ulna and certain carpal bones in the hominoid wrist.

mesial the surface of a tooth which faces the tooth preceding it in the series; see the legend to Figure 6, p. 20.

mesiobuccally mesial and buccal on a tooth crown. *See also* buccal; mesial.

mesiodistal usually referring to the dimension of a tooth which runs from a point on the mesial to one on the distal surface.

mesiolingual mesial and lingual on a tooth. *See also* lingual; mesial.

Metatheria the taxon that includes all marsupial mammals.

metopic suture the suture between the two frontal bones.

miacoids the archaic stem group of the Carnivora.

Microsyopidae enigmatic family of Eocene mammals with primitive skulls, enlarged incisors, and primatelike molar teeth; here considered not to be primates, but possibly Leptictimorphs or Scandentians.

milk teeth *see* deciduous.

molariform usually in reference to the posterior premolars when these are molar–like.

monophyletic a taxonomic group whose members are descended from a common ancestor included in that group. *See also* holophyletic; paraphyletic.

monotypic a supraspecific category consisting of a single species.

morphocline the sum total of morphological patterns exhibited by a homologous character in different samples or species; also termed transformation series. *See also* morphocline polarity.

morphocline polarity arrangement of the total morphological variation (the character states) of a homologous character into the sequence(s) of its transformation. This consists of the determination of the primitive and the one or more derived conditions of a series of character states. Character states may be equally derived or they may represent an increasingly derived transformation series from a primitive condition. Determination of morphocline polarities and recognition of homologous characters are the most difficult and important facets of phylogenetic research.

morphotype the list of known character states which are likely to have been diagnostic of the ancestor of one or more species.

myology the study of muscles.

N

nasion the point where the two nasal bones and the frontal bone meet.

nectarivorous (nectarivore) animal with a diet consisting mainly of flower nectar.

neocarnivoran pertaining to members of the modern groups of Carnivora.

neomorph a biological feature which is the result of independent development; a new feature (e.g., the entotympanic ossification of eutherian mammals).

neoteny the persistence of fetal or juvenile characteristics into the adult (i.e., sexually reproducing) stage of life.

nocturnal active during the night.

nomen (pl. nomina) formal term in taxonomy pertaining to scientific names.

nomenclature application of distinct names to a recognized grouping of organisms, according to internationally accepted rules and regulations.

nuchal pertaining to the neck.

O

occlusal pertaining to the surface of a tooth which is in contact with its upper or lower counterpart during mastication.

occlusion the relation of upper and lower teeth when these are in contact with one another anytime during mastication or at rest.

odontology the study of teeth.

omnivore an animal with a diet consisting of both animal and plant foods in approximately even proportions. Several coexisting species may be omnivorous but each is usually characterized by a specific dietary regime.

ontogeny the growth and development of an individual organism.

ophryonic groove the shallow, mainly transverse depression on the frontal bone behind the supraorbital torus of some catarrhines, e.g., colobines, *Theropithecus*. Located between the temporal lines and generally anterior to the postorbital constriction.

orthal pertaining to the movements of the lower jaw in a straight up-and-down direction.

P

pachyostosis thickening of bone.

paracatarrhine parapithecid. *See also* eucatarrhine.

paraphyletic a monophyletic taxonomic group which does not include all of the descendants of the common ancestor of that group. For example, although the superfamily Lemuroidea is a monophyletic group, some of its descendants gave rise to the Indrioidea and Lorisoidea. *See also* holophyletic; monophyletic.

parsimony a philosophical position which holds that the hypothesis that accounts for all of the known facts in the most straightforward and "simple" manner is to be preferred in contrast to the more complicated ones. What the most parsimonious hypothesis is for a given problem is dictated by known facts and their details rather than by any a priori notions of "simple" vs. "complex." In choosing phylogenetic hypotheses, for example, those which explain new features in the least number of transformations possible are preferred.

patristic referring to the combination of both primitive and derived homologous similarities.

pedomorphy sexual maturation in the juvenile stage of growth.

periglacial zone the region peripheral to Pleistocene ice sheets, which suffered rigorous climate, frost action, and similar effects.

phalangeroids (phalangers) metatherians of Australasia which are ecologically roughly similar to squirrels and primates.

phenon (pl., phena) one or more individuals representing a morphologically rather uniform sample of a population or a species.

phenotype all the observable, measurable, and in any way recordable aspects of an organism, in contrast to its genotype.

philtrum the groove at the median line of the upper lip.

phyletic evolution change in a phyletic lineage through time, the change being a result of genetically based phenotypic variation. *See also* phyletic lineage.

phyletic lineage the consequence of a species reproducing itself in time. As a species is defined as the cross section of a phyletic lineage at one time, different cross sections of the same lineage, between cladogenetic events, at different times are not the same species. Nevertheless, this theoretical point is often necessarily ignored when samples through time are not appreciably different and thus, pragmatically, are referred to as the same species.

phyllostomatid member of the bat family, Phyllostomatidae.

phylogenetic inference term often used to describe the procedure of constructing and testing phylogenetic hypotheses.

phylogeny the evolutionary history of one or more species. Phylogeny of a taxon involves a history of ancestor-descendant, as well as cladistic, relationships and genetically based adaptational changes through time.

phytophagous an animal with a diet consisting mainly of plant materials, essentially equivalent to herbivorous. The opposite of zoophagous.

plagiaulacoid pertaining to teeth which have a single tall and sharp longitudinal crest, as in the lower premolars of multituberculates or carpolestids.

plantar pertaining to the sole of the foot.

platymeria flattening of the femur in an anteroposterior sense.

plesiomorphic character *see* ancestral character.

plantar flexion flexion of the foot downward away from the crus.

polarity *see* morphocline polarity.

pollex   thumb.

polydolopid   member of the Paleogene South American marsupial family Polydolopidae.

polytypic   a taxon consisting of several diverse classes of individuals or of several distinctive types of taxa. The term is usually used for species.

porion   a point on the upper border of the acoustic meatus, the earhole.

posterolingual   *see* distolingual.

potassium–argon dating   geochemical dating based on the measuring of argon-40 trapped in a rock, usually of volcanic origin. Argon-40 is a decay product of the radioactive potassium-40, which has a half-life of some 1.3 billion years.

primitive character   *see* ancestral character.

process   a general term which applies to any kind of bony projection.

Procyonidae   a family of the Carnivora which includes the racoons, coatis, kinkajous, and relatives.

prognathism   protrusion of the jaws.

pronograde   progression on all four limbs.

propalinal   pertaining to the fore-and-aft movements of the mandible.

prosthion   the most anterior point in the sagittal plane, between the bases of the central incisors, often slightly projecting.

proximal   closer to the origin of a structure; opposite of distal. For bones of the appendicular skeleton, the proximal end is closer to the trunk.

Pterodactyla   Mesozoic winged "reptiles."

Ptilocercus   genus of tupaiid scandentians, the pen-tailed tree shrew (species *P. lowii*).

punctuated equilibrium   a view of evolution which surmises that evolutionary change usually takes place when certain populations, peripheral isolates of a species, are subjected to intense selection and subsequently become reproductively isolated. This view of evolution postulates almost all change to be the result of speciation, the punctuation following long periods of equilibrium, or no change.

R

rank   the (relative) position of a category in a Linnaean taxonomic hierarchy.

replacement tooth   a tooth that replaces a deciduous tooth.

retroflexed   bent backward.

rhinarium   the nose.

rhinion   the most anteroinferior point on the internasal suture, between the nasal bones; the top of the nasal aperture.

rhizomes   rootlike stems of plants under or along the ground.

rostral   toward the rostrum (beak) or the nose.

S

Scandentia (scandentian)   the order containing the Tupaiidae and the fossil family Mixodectidae. Originally described to include the elephant shrews as well.

scansorial   adapted to climbing.

Sciuridae   family of rodents including the tree and ground squirrels.

sectorial   pertaining to modifications for the shearing function of teeth.

sinus   a bone cavity which is lined with mucous membranes in living animals.

sister groups   taxa which share a more recent common ancestor with each other than with any other taxon; also termed sister taxa.

Soricomorpha   a suborder of the Insectivora, consisting of the Soricidae (shrews), Talpidae (moles), and Solenodontidae (solenodons).

speciation   splitting of a phyletic lineage into two or more lineages. Although phyletic evolution can occur without speciation, speciation requires phyletic evolution in at least one of the resulting lineages.

species   composed of potentially or actually interbreeding populations at a particular point in time. This is a concept which has no dimension other than an instant in geological time. *See also* phyletic lineage.

spine   a sharp and thin bony projection.

stadial   one of the maxima of a glaciation which had two or more peaks.

stage   unit of time defined by the concurrence of certain fossil taxa.

stratum (pl., strata)   bed(s) of a rock formation.

stratophenetic   a methodological approach to the study of phylogeny which uses the overall similarity of taxa and their stratigraphic superposition to determine phyletic relationships. This method is in opposition to the stratocladistic one, which employs weighted derived similarities and selected use of stratigraphic data when morphological analysis does not contradict it.

strepsirhines   the Adapiformes and Lemuriformes; see suborder Strepsirhini in the text, p. 99.

superior   above.

sympatric   pertaining to species which inhabit the same region. Sympatry (without interbreeding) is the only test of species distinction among living species. The same concept is also extended to paleontology, where closely similar yet distinct (not sexually dimorphic) samples can be considered separate species (i.e., not only segments of the same lineage) if they occur on the same stratigraphic level of the same area.

symphyseal fusion   ossification of a symphysis.

symplesiomorphy   (sympleisomorph)   sharing of primitive characters.

synapomorphy   (synapomorph)   sharing of derived characters.

synostose   to fuse together, as the ossification of a symphysis or a suture between two bones.

systematics   the science of the diversity and relationships of organisms. In general, it refers to the study of phylogeny, adaptation, and biogeography of taxa of all categories.

T

taphonomy   study of the processes of burial and fossilization.

tarsifulcrumating   a mode of jumping where the point of push-off is at the distal end of the tarsal bones rather than at the end of the metatarsals.

taxon   (pl., taxa)   a group of organisms which are classified together, at a specified rank in a Linnaean hierarchy, e.g., a particular species, a genus, a family, etc. A taxon is a group of real organisms. *See also* category.

taxonomy   the organized system by which organisms are classified. In this book, the species treated are classified according to their known phylogenetic relationships and their inferred adaptations. Neither of these two attributes is perfectly known, but the combination of the two sets of criteria permits an approximation of their genetic relationships. The categories (ranks) of the classification employed here are subspecies, species, subgenus, genus, subtribe, tribe, subfamily, family, superfamily, infraorder, suborder, order, cohort, class.

tegula   (plural tegulae)   the somewhat longitudinally curved and laterally compressed and attenuated nails and claws found in platyrrhine primates. The tegulae of marmosets secondarily take on the appearance of falculae (claws) as a result of extreme mediolateral compression. *See also* falcula; ungula.

temporal line   the roughened low ridge on the cranial vault, usually on the parietal bone, where the superior edge of the temporal muscle attaches to the skull roof. When the two temporal lines meet in the midline, a sagittal crest may result.

terrestrial   living on the ground.

thanatocenose   a death assemblage. In paleontology, implies an accumulation of fossils over a significant time interval, in which the frequencies of taxa represented do not necessarily reflect those typical of the living faunal assemblage.

thegosis   the process of sharpening the teeth by forcing a lower tooth against an upper one and thus removing the jagged enamel edges from the crests and cusps in contact.

Theria   subclass of the Mammalia which includes prototherian, metatherian, and eutherian mammals.

tooth comb   pertaining to the arrangement of the lower incisors and canines of the ancestral and many derivative species of the Lemuriformes of this book. The attenuated lower canines and four (or two) incisors are arranged in such a manner that five (or three) narrow interdental spaces, as in a comb, result.

torus   a thickened bony ridge.

tribosphenic   a stage in the evolution of therian molar teeth in which the teeth have acquired a protocone lingual to the paracone and metacone and the appropriate talonid below, against which the protocone sits.

trochanter   prominent tuberosity on the femur which provides leverage to the muscles which attach to it.

tubercle   a small tuberosity.

tuberosity   a large projection with a rough surface to which muscles, ligaments, or tendons are attached.

Tupaiidae   tree shrews; see Scandentia.

type   (type specimen)   the specimen in systematic biology to which the name of the species is attached. The concept of a given species, however, is based, when available, on additional specimens besides the type. *See also* hypodigm.

type species a single species on which the concept of a genus is based; generitype. Although many species may be included in a genus, a generic taxon is based on a single type species.

U

Unguiculata Simpson's (1945) supraordinal concept, a cohort, included eight then-recognized orders among which were the Insectivora, Dermoptera, Chiroptera, Primates, and Edentata. *See also* Archonta.

ungula the broad and flattened nail found in catarrhines, a thin nail in which the deep stratum is lost.

ungulate hoofed mammal, such as artiodactyls and perissodactyls.

V

vascularized rich with blood vesssls.

ventral closer to the belly side.

vertical clinging and leaping *see* leaping and vertical grasp clinging.

vibrissa (pl., vibrissae) long, specialized hair on the snout and sometimes on other parts of the body, with a sensory nerve ending at its base.

volar pertaining to the palm of the hand or sole of the foot, as in volar pads.

Z

Zalambdodonta a suborder of the Insectivora, consisting of the Tenrecidae (tenrecs, potomagales) and Chrysochloridae (golden moles).

zoophagous feeding on a diet of animals (can be further broken down into the categories of insectivory and carnivory).

SYSTEMATIC INDEX

This refers exclusively to names of taxa appearing in synonymies and section headings. The page number given is that on which the synonymy begins, not necessarily (in the case of long synonymies) that of the page on which the nomen appears. Valid nomina, that is, those we accept in the text, are referenced by a boldface page number corresponding to their section heading. If a valid name also appears in the synonymy of another taxon, only its valid usage will appear in boldface type; any other usages appear in regular type. Names of the genus and species groups (including subgenera) are referenced to the valid genus in whose synonymy they appear rather than referenced to the page on which the synonymy of individual species is found. Valid subgenera are not indicated in boldface, but must be located under their respective genera. Modern species and genera which are not treated separately in the text are referenced to the page of the family or subfamily with which they are discussed.